D0401117

Scandinavia

written and researched by

Phil Lee, Lone Mouritsen, Roger Edward Norum and James Proctor

ROUGH
GUIDES

AUG 2 5 2009

www.roughguides.com

Contents

Scandinavian style
colour section
following p.248

The great outdoors
colour section
following p.472

Introduction to

Scandinavia

Scandinavia – Denmark, Norway, Sweden and Finland – conjures up resonant images: wild, untamed lands, fjords, reindeer and the midnight sun; and wealthy, healthy, blue-eyed blondes enjoying life in a benevolent welfare state. The region holds some of Europe's most unspoilt – and least known – terrain and is an enthralling and rewarding place to explore. The larger part of the population clusters in the south, where there's all the culture, nightlife and action you'd expect, but with the exception of Denmark, these are large, often physically inhospitable countries. Rural traditions remain strong, not least in the great tracts of land inside the Arctic Circle, where Scandinavia's indigenous people, the Sámi, survive as they have done for thousands of years – by reindeer herding, hunting and fishing.

Historically the Scandinavian countries have been closely entwined, but nevertheless they remain strikingly individual. Easy to reach and the most European of the four countries, **Denmark** is the geographical and social bridge between the Continent and Scandinavia. The Danes are by far the most gregarious of the Nordic peoples, something manifest in the region's most relaxed and appealing capital, Copenhagen, and the decidedly more permissive attitude to alcohol.

With great mountains, a remote and bluff northern coast and the mighty western fjords, **Norway**'s raw, often inaccessible landscapes can demand long, hard travel. Even by Scandinavian standards the country is sparsely populated, and people live in small communities along a coastline which stretches from the lower reaches of the North Sea right up to the Russian border.

The most "Scandinavian" country in the world's eyes, **Sweden** is affluent and boasts a social welfare system and a tradition of consensus politics that are considered an enlightened model – though both have been shaken in recent years, as globalization has forced an economic and social rethink.

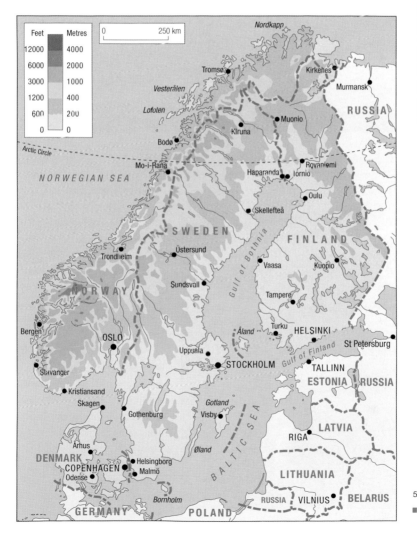

▼ Café culture, Copenhagen

Travelling around is simple enough, although Sweden has Scandinavia's least varied landscape – away from the southern cities and coastal regions, it offers an almost unbroken swathe of lakes, forests and hills, in which most Swedes own a second, peaceful, summer cottage.

▲ Two green cormorants, Norway

Perhaps the least known of the mainland Scandinavian countries, **Finland** was ruled for hundreds of years by the Swedes, and then the Russians – the country became independent only at the beginning of the twentieth century and has grown into a vibrant, confident nation. Its vast coniferous forests and great lake systems have led to a noticeably strong empathy between the Finns and the natural environment. Also, though Finland is undeniably Scandinavian and looks to the West for its lifestyle, its language is totally unrelated to the other Scandinavian tongues and is thought to originate from the East, most probably the Urals.

Travelling in Scandinavia is easy. Public transport is efficient and well coordinated; there are few, if any, border controls between the countries and excellent connections between all the main towns and cities: indeed, it's perfectly feasible to visit several, if not all, of the mainland countries on one trip. Overland from western Europe it's simplest to enter Denmark, from where you can continue northwards into Norway (by boat) or Sweden (by boat or train), the two countries separated by a long north–south border. From Sweden's east coast there are ferries across to Finland, as well as a land

The Finnish sauna

One of the few Finnish words understood worldwide, sauna originated in the countryside. After toiling in the fields, workers would cleanse themselves by sweating profusely in a wooden hut heated by the steam generated by water thrown on hot stones. Today, saunas are an integral part of national culture and Finns of all ages can't get enough of them. A Finnish sauna is usually single-sex, nudity is pretty much compulsory and bathers must sit on sheets of paper or a board provided at the door to prevent sweat soaking into the benches. The end to a perfect sauna is a dip in a nearby lake, or, in winter, a refreshing roll in the snow.

border between the two in the far north.

As for **costs**, the Scandinavian countries are relatively expensive by north European standards, but not excessively or uniformly so. Norway and Denmark are certainly more expensive than Sweden and Finland. This reputation for high prices is largely based on the cost of consumables – from books to meals and beer – rather than more substantial items, particularly accommodation, where first-rate budget opportunities are ubiquitous.

◄ Finnish glassware

When to go

D eciding **when to go** isn't easy since, except for Denmark, Scandinavia experiences intense seasonal changes. The short summers (roughly mid-June to mid-Aug) can be as hot as in any southern European resort, with high temperatures regularly recorded in Denmark, southern Norway and Sweden, and the Baltic islands. Even the northern areas of each country are temperate, and the whole of

► Stockholm sunset

◄ Maypole dancing, Dalarna, Sweden

the Norwegian west coast, for example, is warmed by the Gulf Stream. Rain, though, is regular and, in the far north of Norway especially – and to a lesser extent in Sweden and Finland – summer temperatures can plunge extremely low at night, so campers need decent equipment for extended spells of sleeping out. One bonus this far north, though not exactly a boon to sleep, is the almost constant daylight provided by the midnight sun.

The **summer** is celebrated everywhere with a host of outdoor events and festivities, and is the time when all facilities for travellers (tourist offices, hotel and transport discounts, summer timetables) are functioning. However, it's also the most crowded time to visit, as the Scandinavians are all on holiday too: go either side of summer (late May/early June or Sept), when the weather is still reasonable, and you'll benefit from more peace and space. Autumn, especially, is a beautiful time to travel, with the trees and hillsides turning golden brown in a matter of days.

◄ Gothenburg Opera House, Sweden

▼ Tuomiokirkko (Lutheran Cathedral), Helsinki

In **winter**, from November to around late May, only Denmark retains a semblance of western European weather, while the other countries suffer long, dark and extremely cold days. The cold may be severe, but it's crisp and sharp, never damp, and if you're well wrapped up nowhere need be off-limits; the far north is particularly appealing in winter when the northern lights illuminate the sky to stupendous effect. You'll find broad climatic details in the introductions to each country; for mean temperatures all year round, check the **temperature chart** opposite.

Sweden's fab four: ABBA

Having captured the world's attention by trouncing their Eurovision opponents with *Waterloo* in 1974, ABBA – lycra devotees Anni-Frid Lyngstad, Benny Andersson, Björn Ulvæus and Agnetha Fältskog – went on to become the big-gest-selling group in the world, second only to Volvo as Sweden's largest export earner and topping the charts for a decade with hits such as *Mamma Mia, Money Money Money* and *Dancing Queen* (the latter performed to celebrate the 1976 marriage of Sweden's King Carl Gustaf). Though the group split some 25 years ago following the divorces of the two band-member couples, ABBA's phenomenal kitsch appeal has endured, spawning a host of tribute bands and a successful musical and ensuring that record sales remain remarkably healthy.

What to take

I t's as well to give some thought as to **what to take** – and worth packing that bit more to stave off hardship later. Expect occasional rain throughout the summer, and take a waterproof jacket as well as a spare sweater; a small, foldaway umbrella is useful, too. If camping, a warm sleeping bag and good walking shoes are vital (and also useful in sprawling cities and the flat southern lands). Mosquitoes are a pest in summer, especially further north and in lake regions, and some form of repellent is essential. For winter travel, take as many layers as you can pack. Gloves, a hat or scarf that covers your face, thick socks and thermal underwear are all obligatory.

Average maximum temperatures

	Jan	Feb	Mar	Apr	May	Jun	Jul	Aug	Sep	Oct	Nov	Dec
Denmark												
Copenhagen												
°F	36	36	41	51	61	67	71	70	64	54	45	40
°C	2	2	5	10	16	19	22	21	18	12	7	4
Norway												
Oslo												
°F	28	30	39	50	61	68	72	70	60	48	38	32
°C	-2	-1	4	10	16	20	22	21	16	9	3	0
Bergen												
°F	38	38	43	49	58	61	66	65	59	52	46	41
°C	3	3	6	9	14	16	19	19	15	11	8	5
Sweden												
Stockholm												
°F	30	30	37	47	58	67	71	68	60	49	40	35
°C	-1	-1	3	8	14	19	22	20	15	9	5	2
Gothenburg												
°F	34	34	39	49	60	66	70	68	61	51	43	38
°C	1	1	4	9	16	19	21	20	16	11	6	4
Finland												
Helsinki												
°F	26	25	32	44	56	66	71	68	59	47	37	31
°C	-3	-4	0	6	14	19	22	20	15	8	3	-1
Ivalo												
°F	24	24	31	45	58	67	72	69	57	45	35	29
°C	-5	-4	0	7	14	19	22	20	14	7	2	-2

Note that these are *average maximum temperatures*. The Gulf Stream can produce some very temperate year-round weather and, in summer, southern Scandinavia can be blisteringly hot. In winter, on the other hand, temperatures of -40°F are not unknown in the far north.

things not to miss

It's not possible to see everything Scandinavia has to offer in one trip, and we don't suggest you try. What follows is a selective taste of the region's highlights, from magnificent scenery and imposing castles to absorbing galleries and pristine medieval towns. They're arranged in five colour-coded categories, which you can browse through to find the very best things to see and experience. All highlights have a page reference to take you straight to the Guide, where you can find out more.

01 **Århus old town, Denmark** Page **133** • Discover the laid-back old town charm of Århus, home to some of Denmark's best restaurants.

02 Vigelandsparken, Norway Page **198** • Whatever you do, don't miss this phantasmagorical open-air sculpture park.

03 Cycling in Copenhagen Page **67** • The perfect way to explore the narrow streets of the Danish capital is on two wheels.

04 Kalmar Slott, Sweden Page **443** • Beautifully remodelled into a Renaissance palace, this sensational twelfth-century stronghold lends a fairytale aspect to the Småland coast.

05 **Flåmsbana railway, Norway** Page **263** • Zigzagging down a mountainside and inching through hairpin tunnels, this precipitous ride is a thrilling experience.

06 **Vikingskipshuset, Norway** Page **197** • An excellent place to view Viking longships at close hand.

07 **Skåne, Sweden** Page **416** • The brilliantly hued southern countryside provides a wonderfully scenic backdrop for a gentle summertime drive.

08 **Aurora borealis, Norway, Sweden and Finland** See *The great outdoors* colour section • When conditions are right, these amazing technicolour displays are an unforgettable sight.

09 **Louisiana Museum of Modern Art, Denmark** Page **91** • An
outstanding collection housed in an equally arresting nineteenth-century villa overlooking
the Øresund.

11 **Santa Claus Village,
Finland** Page **622** • Log cabins,
reindeer and copious amounts of snow make
this *the* place to meet Mr Claus.

10 **Northeast Jutland** Page
150 • Denmark's sandy beaches rival
the best of the Mediterranean – but without
the crowds.

12 **Åland Islands, Finland** Page 569 • Enjoy solitude aplenty in this stunning archipelago off Finland's southwest coast

13 **Tivoli Gardens midnight fireworks, Denmark** Page 80 • These glorious pyrotechnics are the time-honoured way to wind up a day in Copenhagen.

14 **Inlandsbanan Railway, Sweden** Page **482** • A chance to experience the raw beauty of virgin forests and crystal-clear mountain streams close up.

15 **Herrings** Pages **57, 356** & **516** • The quintessential Scandinavian snack: fried herring – perfect at any time of day.

16 **Helsinki by night** Page **547** • Let your hair down on a Friday night in one of Helsinki's stylish bars or restaurants.

17 Stave churches, Norway
Page **235** • These elaborately carved churches are perhaps the most distinctive legacy of Norway's Viking era.

18 Danish pastry, Denmark
Page **57** • These ubiquitous buns are known as "Viennese bread" in their home territory – buy them fresh from bakeries in any town or city.

19 Sauna, Finland Page **520** & *The great outdoors* **colour section** • The traditional way to cleanse body and mind, saunas are best followed with an ice-cold dip in a lake or a roll in the snow.

20 Bergen Page **240** • Explore the fjords from Bergen – the prettiest town in Scandinavia.

21 Vasamuséet, Stockholm Page **379** • Discover Sweden's stirring maritime history at one of Scandinavia's finest museums.

22 **Grenen, Denmark** Page **155** • The meeting of the Skaggerak and Kattegat seas here makes suitably dramatic viewing.

23 **Whale-watching, Norway** Page **312** • Between late May and mid-September, tours from remote Andenes can pretty much guarantee sightings.

24 **Icehotel, Sweden** Page **501** • Experience a night in one of the most famous hotels in the world – at a chilly -5°C.

25 **Jotunheimen National Park, Norway** Page **232** • This craggy and severe mountain range is the most sumptuously beautiful example of Norway's wild mountain scenery.

26 **Århus nightlife, Denmark** Page **140** • With a host of excellent venues, Denmark's cultural capital is one of the best places in the country for a night out.

27 **Olavinlinna Castle, Finland** Page **593** • Perched atop an island, this is the best-preserved medieval castle in Scandinavia.

28 **Lofoten Islands, Norway** Page **315** • Huddled under a mighty and ravishingly beautiful mountain wall, the Lofotens' idyllic fishing villages are a highlight of any itinerary.

29 **Husky safari, Finland** Page **630** • Sledge through Lapland's silent snow-covered forests and across frozen lakes, and spend the night in a wilderness cabin.

30 **Gamla Stan, Stockholm** Page **370** • This maze of medieval lanes and alleys forms the heart of the Swedish capital.

Basics

Basics

Getting there

From the UK and Ireland, the most convenient way of getting to Scandinavia is by air – there's a good selection of flights and the cheapest fares are less expensive than the long and arduous journey by train or coach. Currently the only ferry service from Britain is to Denmark. It is pretty costly and only really worth considering if you're taking your car. From the US, a handful of airlines fly direct to the Scandinavian capitals, though it may be cheaper to route via London, picking up a budget flight onwards from there. There are no direct flights from Canada, Australia, New Zealand or South Africa.

Airfares depend on the **season**, with the highest from (roughly) early June to mid-September, when the weather is best; fares drop during the "shoulder" seasons – mid-September to early November and mid-April to early June – and you'll get the best prices during the low season, November through to April (excluding Christmas, New Year and Easter, when prices are hiked up and seats are at a premium). Bear in mind, though, that ticket prices from the UK are not subject to seasonal changes to the extent that they are in North America. Note also that flying on weekends is generally more expensive; price ranges quoted below assume midweek travel.

Flights from UK and Ireland

Until recently, there was an outstanding choice of direct flights **from London** to Copenhagen, Oslo, Stockholm and Helsinki. With the closure of Sterling Airways, the range has somewhat decreased, although there's still a scattering to the same four destinations from the UK's regional airports. Other cities and towns in Scandinavia are less well served, and although there are a handful of direct flights to the likes of Bergen and Stavanger, you'll probably end up flying to one of the four capital cities and catching a connecting flight from there, not necessarily for much more money. Scandinavian Airlines (SAS) is the main local carrier, but has recently come under intense pressure from several budget airlines, most notably Ryanair.

Routes

Routings from the UK at the time of writing include: SAS from London to Copenhagen, Stockholm (Arlanda), Gothenburg, Oslo (Gardermoen), Bergen, Stavanger, Ålesund, and Helsinki. It also has connections to Copenhagen from Birmingham, Manchester, Edinburgh, Glasgow and Aberdeen; to Stockholm (Arlanda) from Manchester and Edinburgh; to Oslo (Gardermoen) from Manchester and Bristol; and to Stavanger from Aberdeen. British Airways flies from London Heathrow to all the capitals and to Billund from Manchester, while Finnair serves Helsinki from Heathrow and Manchester.

Of the **budget airlines**, Ryanair now has the widest coverage, serving Århus from Stansted; Billund from Stansted, Birmingham

Air passes in Scandinavia

The SAS **Visit Scandinavia Air Pass** comes in the form of discount coupons for air travel between or within Norway, Sweden, Denmark and Finland. It can only be purchased in conjunction with an international flight on SAS in your home country. The coupons are valid for one year from arrival and cost £40–80 depending on the distance, route and availability. The main advantage of the pass is that you're guaranteed a low fare, although you may be able to get a cheaper flight once you're in Scandinavia.

Six steps to a better kind of travel

At Rough Guides we are passionately committed to travel. We feel strongly that only through travelling do we truly come to understand the world we live in and the people we share it with – plus tourism has brought a great deal of benefit to developing economies around the world over the last few decades. But the extraordinary growth in tourism has also damaged some places irreparably, and of course **climate change** is exacerbated by most forms of transport, especially flying. This means that now more than ever it's important to **travel thoughtfully** and responsibly, with respect for the cultures you're visiting – not only to derive the most **benefit** from your trip but also in order to preserve the best bits of the planet for everyone to enjoy. At Rough Guides we feel there are six main areas in which you can make a difference:

• Consider what you're contributing to the local economy, and indeed how much the services you use do the same, whether it's through employing local workers and guides or sourcing locally grown produce and local services.

• Consider the environment on holiday as well as at home. Water is scarce in many developing destinations, and the biodiversity of local flora and fauna can be adversely affected by tourism. Patronize businesses that take account of this rather than those that trash the local environment for short-term gain.

• Give thought to how often you fly and what you can do to redress any harm that your trips create. Reduce the amount you travel by air; avoid short hops by air and more harmful night flights.

• Consider alternatives to flying, travelling instead by bus, train, boat and even by bike or on foot where possible. Take time to enjoy the journey itself as well as your final destination.

• Think about making all the trips you take "climate neutral" via a reputable carbon offset scheme. All Rough Guide flights are offset, and every year we donate money to a variety of charities devoted to combating the effects of climate change.

• Travel with a purpose, not just to tick off experiences. Consider spending longer in a place, and really getting to know it and its people – you'll find it much more rewarding than dashing from place to place

and Edinburgh; Stockholm (Skavsta) from Stansted, Birmingham, Liverpool, Glasgow and Edinburgh; Stockholm (Vasteras) from Stansted; Gothenburg City from Stansted and Glasgow; Oslo (Torp) from Stansted, Birmingham, Liverpool and Glasgow; Haugesund from Stansted; and Tampere from Stansted. BMI currently connects Copenhagen with Heathrow, Leeds, Birmingham, Manchester, Glasgow and Edinburgh; Esbjerg with Aberdeen; Olso (Gardermoen) with London, Bristol and Manchester – although this might all change as they've just been taken over by Lufthansa. Smaller budget airline coverage includes: Easyjet from London to Copenhagen and Helsinki; Norwegian from London to Oslo (Gardermoen), Bergen, Stavanger, Tromsø and Tronheim, plus from Edinburgh to Oslo (Gardermoen) during summer; Cimber Air from Newcastle to Copenhagen; City Airline from Birmingham and Manchester to

Gothenburg; Eastern Airways from Aberdeen to Oslo (Gardermoen), and from Aberdeen and Newcastle to Stavanger; and Widerøe from Newcastle and Aberdeen to Stavanger.

Flights from the **Republic of Ireland** all depart from Dublin. They include: SAS to Copenhagen, Stockholm (Arlanda), and Oslo (Gardermoen); Ryanair to Billund, Stockholm (Skavsta), Gothenburg, Oslo (Torp), and Tampere; and Aer Lingus to Copenhagen and to Helsinki.

As for **tickets**, the prices vary enormously depending of which time of year you wish to travel, which airline and route you chose and how far in advance you buy your ticket. That said, there are no hard and fast rules. During promotional periods (read: low season), budget airlines such as Ryanair may sell tickets to most of their destinations for as little as £10 including taxes, while SAS charge around £140 for their cheapest return during the same period. In high season the difference between budget and regular fares lessens, with a Ryanair return from London Stansted to Oslo (Torp) costing around £160, while SAS charges around £210 for the same route.

Flight times are insignificant – it's just one hour from Aberdeen to Stavanger, about two hours fifteen minutes from London to Oslo. The only thing to watch is the **location of the airport** – Oslo (Torp), for example, is 110km from Oslo itself, and the same applies to Stockholm (Skavsta).

For air travel within Scandinavia, you might consider buying an **air pass**, usually sold only in conjunction with SAS tickets from Britain; for details, see the box on p.27.

Flights from the US and Canada

Scandinavia is served by a good spread of American and European airlines from the US, though the vast majority of flights involve **changing planes** in a European hub city such as London or Paris (for onward flights from the UK to Scandinavia, see p.27); and if you don't live in a US hub city you may well have to change planes more than once. **Direct flights** are obviously preferable, and if you can be fairly flexible with your departure dates you'll be able to take advantage of the special promotional fares offered regularly by the airlines concerned – Continental, United Airlines, Delta Airlines, US Airways, SAS and Finnair. However, the difference in price between nonstop and stopover flights is, in general terms at least, surprisingly small. The **flying time** on a direct, nonstop flight from the east coast of the US to Scandinavia is eight or nine hours. There are no direct flights from Canada to Scandinavia but good deals to be had with the nonstop Air Canada flight to London.

Fares from North America to Copenhagen, Helsinki, Oslo and Stockholm are fairly similar, whichever carrier you choose, but it's still worth shopping around for the fastest routings and the best deals. If you're visiting more than one country, an **air pass** (see box, p.27) might be another way of reducing costs. As sample summertime fares, an economy return on SAS's nonstop flight from New York to Stockholm will cost in the region of US$1400 while Continental's equivalent from New York to Oslo will cost between US$1300 and US$1600; a nonstop Finnair flight from New York to Helsinki anywhere between US$800 and US$1200; and a Delta stopover return from San Francisco to Copenhagen US$1600–1800. Special deals and flight agents (see p.31) can often halve these prices.

Flights from Australia, New Zealand and South Africa

There's no shortage of flights to Scandinavia **from Australia and New Zealand**, but all of them involve at least one stop. BA and Thai International offer two of the more direct routes out of Sydney (stopping in Heathrow and Bangkok respectively). Otherwise, airlines flying out of Australia and New Zealand often use SAS and Finnair for connecting services on to Scandinavia: SAS flies from Tokyo to Copenhagen, and Beijing and Bangkok to Copenhagen and Stockholm, Finnair from Beijing, Tokyo and Bangkok to Helsinki.

There are no direct flights from **South Africa** and the only option is to travel via a European hub such as Madrid, Paris, Amsterdam, Zurich or Frankfurt with Iberia, Air France, KLM, Swiss and Lufthansa or South African Airways respectively. One other option is to pick up a cheap ticket to London, and then continue your journey on to Scandinavia with one of the UK's no-frills budget airlines (see p.32). If you intend to take in a number of other European countries on your trip, it might be worth buying a Eurail or Eurail Scandinavia pass before you go (see p.31 & p.35); an SAS air pass (see box, p.27) is another money-saving option.

Fares from Australia and New Zealand to Europe range from A$2000/NZ$2300 in low season to A$3600/NZ$4300 in high season. From South Africa costs hover around the R8000 mark. Travel agents can offer better deals on fares, and have the latest information on special promotions, such as free stopovers en route and fly drive-accommodation packages. Flight Centre and STA generally offer the best discounts, especially for students and those under 26.

Taber Holidays

Your 'only' choice for Scandinavia...

The **'Nordic Only'** brochures for winter and summer feature a wide selection of exciting tours and excursions to Norway, Iceland, Sweden, Finland and Denmark.

For full details visit our website at:
www.taberhols.co.uk
Or call: 01274 875199
for your free **Nordic Only** brochure
E-mail: info@taberhols.co.uk
Fully bonded with over 30 years of experience.

RTW flights

For extended trips, visiting Scandinavia as part of a **round-the-world** (RTW) ticket can be good value. Fares are based either on the number of continents you visit, or the number of miles you travel, and tickets are usually cheapest through travel agents. The lowest-priced tickets usually involve three to four stopovers, with prices rising the further you travel or the more stops you add.

Trains

Taking a **train** can be a relaxing, if long-winded, way of getting from the UK to Scandinavia, though it is likely to work out much more expensive than flying, especially if you're over 26. A number of deals involving rail passes (see below) make it possible to cut costs, however, and there's the added advantage of being able to break your journey – travelling to Oslo from London, for instance, you could stop off at Brussels, Hamburg, Copenhagen and Gothenburg.

The largest UK company dealing with train travel within Europe is **Rail Europe** (see p.34). They sell all the rail passes available, and will through-ticket you from London Waterloo to Copenhagen on the fastest and most convenient routing, normally via Brussels (on Eurostar) and Cologne. To get the cheapest **fares** with Rail Europe, you'll need to book around fourteen days in advance, and include one Saturday night in your time away. With this type of ticket, the adult return fare from **London to Copenhagen** is currently around £300, more if you have a sleeper berth, and the journey takes around twenty hours. Getting to Norway, Sweden or Finland by train from Britain involves first travelling to Copenhagen, as described above, and then taking one of the daily services onward at the cost starting at another £50 or so return.

Rail passes

Rail passes can reduce the cost of train travel significantly, especially if you plan to travel extensively around Scandinavia or visit as part of a wider tour of Europe. There's a huge array of passes available, covering regions as well as individual countries. Some have to be bought before leaving home, while others can only be purchased in the country itself. **Rail Europe** is the umbrella company for all national and international rail tickets, and its comprehensive website (see p.34) is the most useful source of information on available passes; it also gives all current prices. For details of rail passes for use specifically within Scandinavia, such as Eurail Scandinavia, see "Getting around", p.35; for information on individual country passes see the "Getting around" section of the relevant country.

InterRail pass

If you have no clear itinerary, the so-called global **InterRail pass** (Ⓦ www.interrailnet .com) might be your best bet. These are only available to European residents, and you will be asked to provide proof of residency before being allowed to purchase one. They come in over-26 and (cheaper) under-26 versions, and cover all thirty European countries taking part. Global passes are available for five days' travel out of ten days' (£212), ten days' travel out of 22 days (£305), 22 days' continuous travel (£398) and one month's continuous travel (£508). Those aged 12 to 26 years get roughly a third off on the above prices. InterRail passes do not include travel between Britain and the continent, although holders are eligible for discounts on cross-Channel ferries and Eurostar trains. In addition to global passes, InterRail now also does excellent-value individual country passes. See the "Getting around" section of each country for more details.

Eurail pass

The **Eurail global pass** (only available to non-Europeans) is not likely to pay for itself if you're planning to stick to one Scandinavian country. The pass, which must be purchased before arrival in Europe, allows unlimited free first-class train travel in twenty European countries, including all four covered in this book, and is available in increments of fifteen days, 21 days, one month, two months and three months. If you're under 26, you can save money with a **Eurail global pass Youth**, which is valid for second-class travel; the same applies if you're travelling with between one and four companions on a joint **Eurail global pass Saver**, both of these are available in the same increments as the standard Eurail pass. You stand a better chance of getting your money's worth out of a **Eurail global pass Flexi**, which is good for ten or fifteen days' first-class travel within a two-month period. This, too, comes in under-26/second-class (**Eurail global pass Youth Flexi**) and group (**Eurail global pass Saver Flexi**) versions. A standard Eurail pass currently **costs** US$729 for fifteen days, US$946 for 21 days, US$1175 for one month, US$1659 for two months and US$2048 three months.

Details of prices for all these passes can be found on ⓦwww.raileurope.com; they can be purchased from the agents listed below.

Eurail also sells good-value country passes; see details in the individual "Getting around" sections of each country.

Buses

A **coach journey** to Scandinavia from Britain can be an endurance test, and with such low airfares it can actually prove more expensive than flying. It's only worth taking the bus if time is no object and price all-important, or if you specifically do not want to fly.

The major UK operator of international coach routes is **Eurolines** (UK ☏0870/514 3219), whose tickets are bookable online at ⓦwww.nationalexpress.com, though most major travel agents will oblige too. Eurolines runs six services weekly to **Copenhagen** either via Brussels (24hr) or Amsterdam (30hr). From Copenhagen there are connections on to **Gothenburg** and Oslo (2–4 times daily; 4hr 15min & 8hr 30min) and **Stockholm** (three weekly; 9hr 15min). There are no through-ticketed coach arrangements between Britain and Finland. **Fares** to Danish destinations start at £79 one-way and at £120 return with discounts for the over-60s and those under 26.

Another option is the **Eurolines Pass**, which offers unlimited coach travel throughout much of Europe, including Denmark, southern Norway and Sweden but excluding much of the rest of Norway and Finland. The pass is valid either for fifteen days (£139 Nov–Jan; £159 mid Sept to Oct & March to late June, £229 late June to mid-Sept), or thirty days (£209/219/299). Once again, seniors and the under-26s are entitled to discounts of around ten percent.

There are no through services from anywhere in Britain outside London, though **National Express** buses connect with Eurolines buses in London from all over the British Isles.

Ferries

There is currently only one **ferry route** linking the UK with Scandinavia: the overnight DFDS car ferry service between Harwich and Esbjerg in Denmark. Fares vary according to the season, number of passengers and type of compulsory cabin accommodation. Not surprisingly, fares are usually at their lowest during the winter months. Costs range from £98 per person, with four people sharing a basic cabin, for a low-season midweek return from Harwich to Esbjerg, plus £77 each way for a car; in summer prices are about 10–15 percent higher. The cheapest two-person cabin (the smallest there is) starts at £142 one-way during summer.

Once in Scandinavia a whole host of ferries connects the four countries. See the relevant "Getting around" section in each chapter.

Airlines, agents and tour operators

Online booking

ⓦ www.expedia.co.uk (in UK), ⓦ www.expedia
.com (in US), ⓦ www.expedia.ca (in Canada)
ⓦ www.lastminute.com (in UK)
ⓦ www.opodo.co.uk (in UK)
ⓦ www.orbitz.com (in US)
ⓦ www.travelocity.co.uk (in UK), ⓦ www
.travelocity.com (in US), ⓦ www.travelocity
.ca (in Canada)
ⓦ www.travelonline.co.za (in South Africa)
ⓦ www.zuji.com.au (in Australia), ⓦ www.zuji
.co.nz (in New Zealand)

Airlines

Aer Lingus US & Canada ☎ 1-800/IRISH-AIR, UK
☎ 0870/876 5000, Republic of Ireland ☎ 0818/365
000, South Africa ☎ 1-272/2168-32838, New
Zealand ☎ 1649/3083355; ⓦ www.aerlingus.com.
Air Canada ☎ 1-888/247-2262, UK ☎ 0871/220
1111, Republic of Ireland ☎ 01/679 3958, Australia
☎ 1300/655 767, New Zealand ☎ 0508/747 767;
ⓦ www.aircanada.com.
Air France US ☎ 1-800/237-2747, Canada
☎ 1-800/667-2747, UK ☎ 0870/142 4343,
Australia ☎ 1300/390 190, South Africa
☎ 0861/340 340; ⓦ www.airfrance.com.
Air New Zealand ☎ 0800/737000, Australia
☎ 0800/132 476, UK ☎ 0800/028 4149,
US ☎ 1800-262/1234, Canada ☎ 1800-663/5494;
ⓦ www.airnz.co.nz.
American Airlines ☎ 1-800/433-7300, UK
☎ 0845/7789 789, Republic of Ireland ☎ 01/602
0550, Australia ☎ 1800/673 486, New Zealand
☎ 0800/445 442; ⓦ www.aa.com.
bmi US ☎ 1-800/788-0555, UK ☎ 0870/607 0555
or 0870/607 0222, Republic of Ireland ☎ 01/407
3036; ⓦ www.flybmi.com.
bmibaby UK ☎ 0871/224 0224, Republic of Ireland
☎ 1890/340 122; ⓦ www.bmibaby.com.
British Airways US & Canada ☎ 1-800/AIRWAYS,
UK ☎ 0870/850 9850, Republic of Ireland
☎ 1890/626 747, Australia ☎ 1300/767 177,
New Zealand ☎ 09/966 9777, South Africa
☎ 114/418 600; ⓦ www.ba.com.
Cathay Pacific US ☎ 1-800/233-2742, Canada
☎ 1-800/2686-868, UK ☎ 020/8834 8888,
Australia ☎ 13 17 47, New Zealand ☎ 09/379
0861, South Africa ☎ 11/700 8900; ⓦ www
.cathaypacific.com.
City Airline UK ☎ 0870/220 6835, ⓦ www
.cityairline.com.

Cimber Air DK ☎ 70 10 12 18, ⓦ www
.cimber.dk.
Continental Airlines US & Canada ☎ 1-800/523-
3273, UK ☎ 0845/607 6760, Republic of Ireland
☎ 1890/925 252, Australia ☎ 02/9244 2242,
New Zealand ☎ 09/308 3350, International
☎ 1800/231 0856; ⓦ www.continental.com.
Delta US & Canada ☎ 1-800/221-1212, UK
☎ 0845/600 0950, Republic of Ireland ☎ 1850/882
031 or 01/407 3165, Australia ☎ 1300/302 849,
New Zealand ☎ 09/9772232; ⓦ www.delta.com.
Eastern Airways UK ☎ 0870/369 9100,
ⓦ www.easternairways.com.
easyJet UK ☎ 0905/821 0905, ⓦ www
.easyjet.com.
Finnair US ☎ 1-800/950-5000, UK ☎ 0870/241
4411, Republic of Ireland ☎ 01/844 6565, Australia
☎ 02/9244 2299, South Africa ☎ 11/339 4865/9;
ⓦ www.finnair.com.
Iberia US ☎ 1-800/772-4642, UK ☎ 0870/609
0500, Republic of Ireland ☎ 0818/462 000, South
Africa ☎ 011/884 5909; ⓦ www.iberia.com.
KLM (Royal Dutch Airlines) See also Northwest/
KLM. US & Canada ☎ 1-800/225-2525, UK
☎ 0870/507 4074, Republic of Ireland ☎ 1850/747
400, Australia ☎ 1300/392 192, New Zealand
☎ 09/921 6040, South Africa ☎ 11/961 6727;
ⓦ www.klm.com.
Lufthansa US ☎ 1-800/3995-838, Canada
☎ 1-800/563-5954, UK ☎ 0870/837 7747,
Republic of Ireland ☎ 01/844 5544, Australia
☎ 1300/655 727, New Zealand ☎ 0800-945 220,
South Africa ☎ 0861/842 538; ⓦ www
.lufthansa.com.
Norwegian NO ☎ 21 49 00 15, ⓦ www
.norwegian.no.
Qantas Airways US & Canada ☎ 1-800/227-
4500, UK ☎ 0845/774 7767, Republic of Ireland
☎ 01/407 3278, Australia ☎ 13 13 13, New Zealand
☎ 0800/808 767 or 09/357 8900, South Africa
☎ 11/441 8550; ⓦ www.qantas.com.
Ryanair UK ☎ 0871/246 0000, Republic of Ireland
☎ 0818/303 030; ⓦ www.ryanair.com.
SAS (Scandinavian Airlines) US & Canada
☎ 1-800/221-2350, UK ☎ 0870/6072 7727,
Republic of Ireland ☎ 01/844 5440, Australia
☎ 1300/727 707; ⓦ www.scandinavian.net.
South African Airways ☎ 11/978 1111, US &
Canada ☎ 1-800/722-9675, UK ☎ 0870/747 1111,
Australia ☎ 1800/221 699, New Zealand ☎ 09/977
2237; ⓦ www.flysaa.com.
Swiss US ☎ 1-877/3797-947, Canada ☎ 1-87755-
97947, UK ☎ 0845/601 0956, Republic of Ireland
☎ 1890/200 515, Australia ☎ 1300/724 666,
New Zealand ☎ 09/977 2238, South Africa
☎ 0860/040 506; ⓦ www.swiss.com.

Thai Airways US ☎1-212/949-8424, UK
☎0870/606 0911, Australia ☎1300/651 960,
New Zealand ☎09/377 3886, South Africa
☎11/455 1018; ⓦwww.thaiair.com.
United Airlines US ☎1-800/UNITED-1, UK
☎0845/844 4777, Australia ☎13 17 77;
ⓦwww.united.com.
US Airways US & Canada ☎1-800/428-4322, UK
☎0845/600 3300, Republic of Ireland ☎1890/925
065; ⓦwww.usair.com.
Widerøe NO ☎75 11 11 11, ⓦwww.wideroe.no.

Agents and operators

ebookers UK ☎0800/082 3000, Republic of
Ireland ☎01/488 3507; ⓦwww.ebookers.com,
ⓦwww.ebookers.ie. Low fares on an extensive
selection of scheduled flights and package deals.
North South Travel UK ☎01245/608 291,
ⓦwww.northsouthtravel.co.uk. Friendly,
competitive travel agency, offering discounted fares
worldwide. Profits are used to support projects in
the developing world, especially the promotion of
sustainable tourism.
STA Travel US ☎1-800/781-4040, UK
☎0871/2300 040, Australia ☎134 STA, New
Zealand ☎0800/474 400, SA ☎0861/781 781;
ⓦwww.statravel.com. Worldwide specialists in
independent travel; also student IDs, travel insurance,
car rental, rail passes, and more. Good discounts for
students and under-26s.
Trailfinders UK ☎0845/058 5858, Republic of
Ireland ☎01/677 7888, Australia ☎1300/780 212;
ⓦwww.trailfinders.com. One of the best-informed
and most efficient agents for independent travellers.

Packages and organized tours

Abercrombie and Kent US ☎1-800/554-7016,
ⓦwww.abercrombiekent.com. Upmarket company
offering tailor-made Scandinavian and Baltic coach
tours and cruises.
Adventure Center US ☎1-800/228 4747,
ⓦwww.adventurecenter.com. Good range of
treks and dogsledge safaris in Swedish and Finnish
Lapland, from four to fifteen days, mostly camping.
Adventurous stuff.
Adventures Abroad US/CA ☎1-800/665-3998,
UK ☎0144/247 3400, New Zealand ☎0800/800
434; ⓦwww.adventures-abroad.com. Specializing
in small-group tours, and offering a variety of
Scandinavian packages.
Anglers' World Holidays UK ☎01246/221 717,
ⓦwww.anglers-world.co.uk. Angling holidays in
Norway.
Backroads US ☎1-800/462-2848, ⓦwww
.backroads.com. Specializing in activity holidays,

Norway
Sweden
Finland
Denmark
Iceland
Latvia
Estonia
Lithuania
Greenland

Carefully Crafted Tours
SCANDINAVIA
High Quality Cultural Group
Tours for the
Discerning Traveller

• Informative,
knowledgeable tour
leaders
• Over 130 countries
worldwide
• All tours are fully
escorted

ADVENTURESABROAD

0114 247 3400
info@adventures-abroad.co.uk
www.smallgroup.travel   ABTA
ABTA No.W3508

including a six-day cycle tour of Denmark and a
seven-day hiking tour of the Norwegian mountains,
glaciers and fjords.
Bentours Australia ☎02/9241 1353, ⓦwww
.bentours.com.au. Rail passes and a host of scenic
tours throughout Scandinavia, including Lapland Ice
Safari and Norwegian Fjord Tour.
Borton Overseas US ☎1-800/843-0602,
ⓦwww.bortonoverseas.com. Adventure-vacation
specialists, with a large selection of biking, hiking,
rafting, birdwatching, dog-sledging and cross-country
skiing tours, plus farm and cabin stays and city
packages.
Brekke Tours – Spirit of Scandinavia US
☎1-800/437-5302, ⓦwww.brekketours.com.
A well-established company offering a host of
sightseeing and cultural tours in Scandinavia.
Crystal Holidays UK ☎0870/402 0291, ⓦwww
.crystalholidays.co.uk. Luxury tour of Finland's lakes
in the summer, and skiing holidays in winter. Also trips
to Sweden's Arctic Ice Hotel.
Discover the World UK ☎01737/218 800,
ⓦwww.discover-the-world.co.uk. Specialist
adventure tours including whale-watching in
Norway, wildlife in Spitsbergen and dog-sledging
in Lapland.
DFDS Seaways UK ☎0870 5333 000, ⓦwww
.dfdsseaways.co.uk. This ferry company offers mini
cruise breaks in Denmark, including two nights on

board ship and two or three nights at the destination; especially good deals out of season.

Emagine UK ☎01942/262 662, ✆www.emagine -travel.co.uk. Tailor-made Finnish holidays, Helsinki city breaks and cruises. Specialist in Lapland – and Santa Claus – trips.

Hurtigruten US ☎1-800/323-7436, ✆www .hurtigruten.us. A mixture of escorted and independent cruises along the Norwegian coastline, to Svalbard and on the Gota canal in Sweden.

Inntravel UK ☎01653/617 788, ✆www .inntravel.co.uk. Outdoor holidays in Norway including skiing, walking, dog-sledging, fjord cruises and whale- and reindeer-watching.

Insight UK ☎01475/741 203, ✆www.insighttours .com. Top-notch tours including a twenty-day "Grand tour of Scandinavia" and "Spectacular Scandinavia and its fjords" – a wonderful fifteen-day trip.

Nordic Saga Tours US ☎1-800/848 6449, ✆www.nordicsaga.com. A wide range of group and independent package tours as well as flights.

Passage Tours US ☎1-800/548-5960, ✆www .passagetours.com. Scandinavian specialist offering tours like "The Northern Lights" and dog-sledging, whale-watching, ski packages and fjord excursions.

Picasso Travel US ☎1-800/995-7997, ✆www .nordiquetours.com. Packages including "Scandinavian capitals", Lapland and the Norwegian fjords.

Scanam World Tours US ☎1-800/545-2204, ✆www.scanamtours.com. Scandinavian specialist offering group and individual tours and cruises, including a host of bike tours.

ScanMeridian UK ☎020/7431 5322, ✆www .scanmeridian.co.uk. Finland specialists offering winter breaks in Lapland.

Scantours UK ☎020/7839 2927, ✆www .scantoursuk.com; US ☎1-800/223-7226, ✆www .scantours.com. Huge range of packages and tailor-made holidays to every Scandinavian nook and cranny, offering vacation packages, hotel bookings and customized itineraries, including cruises and city sightseeing tours.

Specialised Tours UK ☎01342/712 785, ✆www .specialisedtours.com. Specialists in Scandinavia offering independent, tailor-made or group city breaks and holidays.

Taber Holidays UK ☎01274/594 656, ✆www .taberhols.co.uk. Scandinavian specialists with dozens of options, including self-catering holidays, fjord cruises, motoring tours, husky safaris and guided coach trips.

Rail contacts

CIT World Travel Australia ☎02/9267 1255 or 03/9650 5510, ✆www.cittravel.com.au.

European Rail UK ☎020/7387 0444, ✆www .europeanrail.com.

Europrail International Canada ☎1-888/667-9734, ✆www.europrail.net.

Rail Europe US ☎1-877/257-2887, Canada ☎1-800/361-RAIL, UK ☎0870/837 1371; ✆www.raileurope.com/us, ✆www.raileurope .co.uk.

STA Travel US ☎1-800/781-4040, UK ☎0871/2300 040, Australia ☎134 STA, New Zealand ☎0800/474 400, South Africa ☎0861/781 781; ✆www.statravel.com.

Bus contacts

Eurolines UK ☎0870/580 8080, ✆www .nationalexpress.com/eurolines.

STA Travel US ☎1-800/781-4040, UK ☎0871/2300 040, Australia ☎134 STA, New Zealand ☎0800/474 400, South Africa ☎0861/781 781; ✆www.statravel.com.

Trailfinders UK ☎0845/058 5858, Republic of Ireland ☎01/677 7888, Australia ☎1300/780 212; ✆www.trailfinders.com.

Ferry contacts

DFDS Seaways UK ☎0870/252 0524, ✆www .dfdsseaways.co.uk.

Getting around

Public transport systems are excellent throughout Scandinavia. Denmark, Norway, Sweden and Finland all have a reasonably comprehensive rail network which runs as far north as it dares before plentiful buses take over. Fjords and inordinate amounts of water – lakes, rivers and open sea – make ferries a major form of transport, too.

For more detailed transport information, see each country's individual "Getting around" section, and the "Travel details" at the end of every chapter.

By rail

Travel by train in Scandinavia isn't cheap, but a number of **passes** can ease the burden. If you're travelling to and around the region by train, the global InterRail and Eurail passes (see "Getting there", p.30) can cut costs. If you're planning to travel by train only within Scandinavia itself, and live outside Europe, it's well worth considering a Eurail Scandinavia pass. It covers all four countries and must be purchased before you leave home. The Eurail Scandinavia pass comes in increments of 4, 5, 6, 8 and 10 days' travel within a two-month period, costing US$335, US$375, US$425, US$475 and US$525 respectively. A youth pass (under 26) with the same increments costs roughly 25 percent less. Annoyingly, a similar pass doesn't exist for European residents, and the only option available, apart from the global InterRail pass, is the one-country pass which you can get for all four countries. See the "Getting around" sections under each country for full details.

By air

Internal **flights** can be a surprisingly good bargain in Scandinavia, particularly if you're heading for the far north. During July and the early part of August, the main carrier SAS often has cheap set-price tickets to anywhere in mainland Scandinavia plus other discounts for families and young people. Contact SAS offices in Denmark, Norway and Sweden for the latest deals – they're detailed under "Listings" in the accounts of the capital cities. Also, check out the **air passes** on offer before leaving home (see box, p.27).

By car

Car rental is pricey, although some tourist offices do arrange summer deals which can bring the cost down a little. On the whole, expect to pay upwards of £230/US$322 a week for a small car; see each country's "Getting around" section for specific prices and details of rules of the road and documentation.

You may well find it cheaper, especially if you're travelling from North America, to arrange car hire before you go; airlines sometimes have special deals with rental companies if you book your flight and car through them. For addresses of car rental firms in Scandinavia, see the "Listings" sections of major cities.

Car rental agencies

Alamo US ☎ 1-800/462-5266, ⓦ www.alamo.com.
Auto Europe US & Canada ☎ 1-888/223-5555, ⓦ www.autoeurope.com.
Avis US & Canada ☎ 1-800/331-1212, UK ☎ 0870/606 0100, Republic of Ireland ☎ 021/428 1111, Australia ☎ 13 63 33 or 02/9353 9000, New Zealand ☎ 09/526 2847 or 0800/655 111; ⓦ www.avis.com.
Budget US ☎ 1-800/527-0700, Canada ☎ 1-800/268-8900, UK ☎ 0870/156 5656, Australia ☎ 1300/362 848, New Zealand ☎ 0800/283 438; ⓦ www.budget.com.
Enterprise Rent-a-Car US ☎ 1-800/261-7331, ⓦ www.enterprise.com.
Europcar US & Canada ☎ 1-877/940 6900, UK ☎ 0870/607 5000, Republic of Ireland ☎ 01/614 2800, Australia ☎ 393/306 160; ⓦ www.europcar.com.

Europe by Car US ☎1-800/223-1516, ⊛www
.europebycar.com.

Hertz US & Canada ☎1-800/654-3131, UK
☎020/7026 0077, Republic of Ireland ☎01/870
5777, New Zealand ☎0800/654 321; ⊛www
.hertz.com.

Holiday Autos UK ☎0870/400 4461, Republic of
Ireland ☎01/872 9366, Australia ☎299/394 433,
US ☎866-392/9288, South Africa ☎11/2340 597,

⊛www.holidayautos.co.uk. Part of the LastMinute
.com group.

National US ☎1-800/CAR-RENT, UK ☎0870/400
4581, Australia ☎0870/600 6666, New Zealand
☎03/366 5574; ⊛www.nationalcar.com.

Thrifty US & Canada ☎1-800/847-4389, UK
☎01494/751 500, Republic of Ireland ☎01/844
1950, Australia ☎1300/367 227, New Zealand
☎09/256 1405; ⊛www.thrifty.com.

Accommodation

Accommodation is almost certainly going to be your major daily expense in Scandinavia. If you plan ahead, however, there are a number of ways to avoid paying over the (already high) odds. Youth hostels, campsites and cabins are the obvious budget options, and not just for tourists – they're popular with Scandinavians, too. There's also a series of discount passes available, for use in hotel chains all over Scandinavia.

Hotels

Scandinavian **hotels** are hardly ever inexpensive, but there again they often compare favourably with equivalent accommodation in, say, London or New York. Lots of Scandinavian hotels, usually dependent on business travellers, drop their prices drastically at weekends and during the summer holiday period, so it's always worth enquiring at the tourist office about special local deals. The major cities also feature cheap "packages", usually involving a night's hotel accommodation and a free city discount card. More details, and a guide to prices, are given under each country's "Accommodation" section, as well as under the specific town and city accounts.

Some Scandinavia-wide hotel chains operate a discount or **hotel cheque system** which you can organize before you leave. You either purchase cheques in advance, redeemable against a night's accommodation in any hotel belonging to the particular chain, or you buy a **hotel pass**, which entitles you to a hefty discount on normal room rates. There are a bewildering number of schemes available, but most only operate

from June to September and all offer basically the same deal: consult your travel agent or one of the national tourist boards for further details.

Hostels

Joining the **Hostelling International** (HI) association gives you access to what is sometimes the only budget accommodation available in a particular town or village. Non-members can use HI hostels but will pay slightly more – the difference may add up to a sizeable sum over a couple of weeks, considering the low cost of annual membership. You'll also need a **sheet sleeping bag (or a sheet and pillowcase)**. They can either be rented at the hostels or bought at camping shops.

You can join Hostelling International either at home (for addresses, see below) or in Scandinavia itself (the addresses of the relevant national hostelling organizations are given in each country's "Accommodation" section). For a complete listing of Scandinavian hostels, consult the annually produced Hostelling International Guide, available from hostel associations and online via their websites.

Youth hostel associations

UK and Ireland

Youth Hostel Association (YHA) England and
Wales ☎ 0870/770 8868, ⓦ www.yha.org.uk.
Scottish Youth Hostel Association
☎ 01786/891 400, ⓦ www.syha.org.uk.
Irish Youth Hostel Association Republic of
Ireland ☎ 01/830 4555, ⓦ www.irelandyha.org.
Hostelling International Northern Ireland
☎ 028/90324733, ⓦ www.hini.org.uk.

US and Canada

Hostelling International–American Youth
Hostels US ☎ 1-301/495-1240, ⓦ www
.hiayh.org.
Hostelling International Canada
☎ 1-800/663-5777, ⓦ www.hihostels.ca.

Australia and New Zealand

Australia Youth Hostels Association
☎ 02/9565 1699, ⓦ www.yha.com.au.

Youth Hostelling Association New Zealand
☎ 0800/278 299 or 03/379 9970, ⓦ www.yha
.co.nz.

Camping

Camping is hugely popular in Scandinavia. If
you're planning to use your tent a lot, a
Scandinavian camping card is, at just
£10/$14, a good and inexpensive invest-
ment. The card, which you can buy at the
first member site you visit, gives discounts at
member sites and serves as useful identification – indeed it is obligatory on some sites.
Many campsites will take it instead of making
you surrender your passport during your
stay, and it covers you for third-party
insurance when camping.

Further details on camping are given in each
country's "Accommodation" section, but one
general point to note is that most campsites
in Scandinavia have furnished **cabins**; if you
intend to use these, take a sleeping bag as
bedding is not usually provided.

Outdoor activities

Scandinavia is a wonderful place if you love the great outdoors, with marvellous
hiking, fishing, climbing and skiing to name but four of the most popular pursuits.
Even better, you won't find the countryside overcrowded – there's plenty of space
to get away from it all, almost everywhere, from one end of the region to the other.
As you might expect, any kind of hunting is forbidden without a permit, and freshwater fishing always requires a special licence as is often the case with sea
fishing too. Local tourist offices can fill you in on all the rules and regulations.

Hiking

Scandinavia offers the ultimate in **hiking**
experiences – a landscape of rugged
mountains, icy glaciers and deep green
fjords, much of it far from the nearest road.
Many of the best hiking areas have been set
aside as **national parks**, with information
centres, lodges and huts dotted along well-
marked trails. Huts are usually run by
national or local hiking organizations, and
you will have to become a member to be
able to use them or else pay premium rates;

joining is not expensive. Tourist offices in
hiking areas supply maps and leaflets
describing local routes, but serious hiking
requires proper maps – see p.42 for map
suppliers. Note also that in many areas, solo
hiking is strongly inadvisable; always take
local advice about local trail conditions,
camping rules and weather.

As far as **equipment** goes, for day walking
you'll need warm clothing and gloves,
waterproofs, and sun and mosquito protection; on all but the easiest and shortest

hikes, a compass is a good idea. For long-distance treks you'll also need a sleeping bag, medical kit and a torch, plus a pair of sturdy, comfortable boots. Note that Camping Gaz is only available from selected outlets in Scandinavia – details from national tourist boards – so take your own supply. For hiking campers, a plastic survival bag keeps you and your pack dry.

If you're planning to camp, you should be aware of some specific **ground rules**. The landscape is there for everyone's use and camping rough is legal much of the time – but the Scandinavians are concerned to protect the environment both from the damage caused by excessive tourism and the potential disasters that can result from ignorance or thoughtlessness.

Don't **light fires** anywhere other than at designated spots – and even these shouldn't be used in times of drought. **Tents** may only be placed on marked sites or, on some hikes, in other designated areas. When camping, do not break tree branches or leave **rubbish**; and try not to disturb nesting **birds**, especially in the spring.

In the northern reaches of Scandinavia, be wary of frightening **reindeer herds**, since if they scatter it can mean several extra days' work for the herder; also, avoid tramping over moss-covered stretches of moorland – the reindeer's staple diet. **Picking flowers, berries and mushrooms** is also usually prohibited in the north. If you are going to pick and eat anything, however, it's a wise idea, post-Chernobyl, to check on the latest advice from the authorities – tourist offices should know the score.

Finally, a word of warning about **glaciers**. They may seem slow-moving and innocuous, but they aren't. Never climb a glacier without a guide, never walk under one and always heed the instructions at the site. Guided crossings can be terrific; local tourist offices and hiking organizations have details – see the relevant accounts in the Guide.

Cycling, rafting and canoeing

Several package tour operators (see p.33) offer **cycling tours** within Scandinavia –

Denmark in particular is ideal for a cycling holiday, given its largely flat landscape and excellent network of cycle lanes covering more than 10,000km, all of them marked on the detailed cycling maps available from local bookshops and tourist offices.

Scandinavia's rivers and coastline afford ample opportunity for **canoeing**, **rafting** and **sea-kayaking**. Norway holds some of the wildest rivers on the continent, while Sweden, in particular, is criss-crossed with canoeing routes which have numerous places to stop and camp along the way, and all grades of difficulty from gentle paddling along winding rivers to white-water thrills. Scores of companies offer guided excursions in all these outdoor pursuits – see the Guide for further details.

Winter sports

Aside from the cities, which maintain their usual roster of activities and attractions, though sometimes with reduced opening hours, the big incentive for coming to Scandinavia in winter is the range of **winter sports** available: skiing, snowboarding, dog-sledging, tobogganing, ice-skating, ski-doo safaris and ice fishing, to name a few. All are easy to arrange after arrival – in the first instance, contact the local tourist office.

Skiing

Scandinavia is an excellent place to ski, though **skiing** packages here tend to be more expensive than other European destinations. Even if you can't afford a package it's always easy to arrange a few days' cross-country skiing wherever you are – there are even ski runs within the city boundaries of Oslo and Stockholm, and plenty of places to rent equipment. Norway is particularly well equipped for **cross-country skiing**, with a large network of special trails (many floodlit after dark) of varying lengths, which often have cabins along the route in which to overnight. Check out the tourist board websites for each country (see p.43) for more information and details on the various skiing associations, who will be able to recommend routes and destinations matched to your trip.

Travel essentials

Crime and personal safety

Scandinavia is one of the most **peaceful** corners of Europe. You will find that public places are generally well lit and secure, most people are genuinely friendly and helpful, and that street crime and hassle relatively rare.

It would be foolish, however, to assume that problems don't exist. Each of the capital cities has its share of **petty crime**, often committed by drug addicts after easy money. Keep tabs on your cash and passport (and don't leave anything visible in your car when you leave it) and you should have little reason to visit the **police**. If you do, you'll find them courteous, concerned and, perhaps most importantly, usually able to speak English. If you have something stolen, make sure you get a **police report** – essential if you are to make an insurance claim.

As for **offences** you might commit, being **drunk** on the streets can get you arrested, and **drinking and driving** is treated especially rigorously. **Drug** offences, too, meet with the same harsh attitude that prevails throughout most of Europe.

Electricity

The **current** all over Scandinavia is 220 volts AC, with standard European-style two-pin plugs. British equipment needs only a plug adaptor; American apparatus requires a transformer and an adaptor.

Entry requirements

EU, US, Canadian, Australian and New Zealand citizens need only a **valid passport** to enter Denmark, Norway, Sweden and Finland for up to three months. All other nationals should consult the relevant embassy about visa requirements.

For **longer stays**, EU nationals can apply for a residence permit while in the country, which, if it's granted, may be valid for up to five years. Non-EU nationals can only apply for residence permits before leaving home,

and must be able to prove they can support themselves without working. Contact the relevant embassy in your country of origin.

In spite of the lack of restrictions, **checks** are frequently made on travellers at the major points of entry. If you're young and are carrying a rucksack, be prepared to prove that you have enough money to support yourself during your stay. You may also be asked how long you intend to stay and why. **Border controls** between the Scandinavian countries are patchy – sometimes no one seems very bothered, while at other times you might have your car searched and have to answer endless questions.

Scandinavian embassies and consulates

Australia and New Zealand

Denmark Embassy in Canberra ☎ 02/6270 5333 ⓦ www.canberra.um.dk. Consulate in Sydney.
Finland Embassy in Canberra ☎ 02/6273 3800, ⓦ www.finland.org.au. There is also a consulate in Sydney.
Norway Embassy in Canberra ☎ 02/6273 3444, ⓦ norway.org.au.
Sweden Embassy in Canberra ☎ 02/6270 2700, ⓦ www.swedenabroad.com.

Canada

Denmark Embassy in Ottawa ☎ 613/562-1811, ⓦ www.ambottawa.um.dk.
Finland Embassy in Ottawa ☎ 613/288-2233, ⓦ www.finland.ca.
Norway Embassy in Ottawa ☎ 613/238-6571, ⓦ www.emb-norway.ca. All applications for tourist visas and work/residence permits handled by the Danish Embassy (see above).
Sweden Embassy in Ottawa ☎ 613/244-8200, ⓦ www.swedenabroad.com.

Republic of Ireland

Denmark Embassy in Dublin ☎ 01/475 6404, ⓦ www ambdublin.um.dk.
Finland Embassy in Dublin ☎ 01/478 1344, ⓦ www.finland.ie.
Norway Embassy in Dublin ☎ 01/662 1800, ⓦ www.norway.ie.

Sweden Embassy in Dublin ☏01/474 4400, Ⓦ www.swedenabroad.com.

South Africa

Denmark Embassy in Pretoria ☏12/430 9340 Ⓦ www.ambpretoria.um.dk. Consulates in Johannesburg, Cape Town and Durban.
Finland Embassy in Pretoria ☏12/343 0275, Ⓦ www.finland.org.za. There are also honorary consulates in Cape Town and Johannesburg.
Norway Embassy in Pretoria ☏12/342 6100, Ⓦ www.norway.org.za. There's also a branch In Cape Town.
Sweden Embassy in Pretoria ☏12/426 6400, Ⓦ www.swedenabroad.com.

UK

Denmark Embassy in London ☏020/7333 0200, Ⓦ www.amblondon.um.dk/en.
Finland Embassy in London ☏020/7838 6200, Ⓦ www.finemb.org.uk.
Norway Embassy in London ☏020/7591 5500, Ⓦ www.norway.org.uk.
Sweden Embassy in London ☏020/7917 6400, Ⓦ www.swedenabroad.com.

US

Denmark Embassy in Washington, DC ☏1-202/234-4300, Ⓦ www.ambwashington .um.dk/en. Consulates in Chicago and New York ☏1-212/223-4545, Ⓦ www.gknewyork.um.dk.
Finland Embassy in Washington, DC ☏202/298-5800, Ⓦ www.finland.org. There are also consulates in Los Angeles and New York.
Norway Embassy in Washington, DC ☏202/333-6000, Ⓦ www.norway.org. Consulates in New York, Houston and San Francisco.
Sweden Embassy in Washington, DC ☏202/467-2600, Ⓦ www.swedenabroad.com. There are also consulates in Los Angeles, New York and San Francisco.

Gay and lesbian travellers

For both **gays** and **lesbians**, Scandinavia comprises one of the most liberated and tolerant regions in Europe. Gays are rarely discriminated against in law, and the age of consent is almost uniformly the same as for heterosexuals – 15 in Denmark and Sweden, 16 in Finland and Norway. Nevertheless – and perhaps as a result of this very tolerance – there is not much of a scene outside the four capitals; the websites of the national associations are all a useful starting point for further information and listings.

Gay and lesbian organizations in Scandinavia

Denmark

The Danish Association for Gays and Lesbians (*Landsforeningen for Bøsser og Lebiske*) has its headquarters in Copenhagen at Nygade 2, 2nd floor. Their website (Ⓦ www.lbl.dk), which is in Danish and English, provides general information, but for details of the scene you'll need to go to an affiliated website, Ⓦ www.gayguide.dk.

Finland

In English, Swedish and Finnish, the website of **SETA** (Ⓦ www.seta.fi), the Organization for Sexual Equality in Finland, at Hietalahdenkatu 2 B 16, FI-001800 Helsinki, provides general background information and signposts other Finnish websites that focus on the scene.

Norway

Norway's a strong and politically effective gay and lesbian organization, the **LLH** (*Landsforeningen for lesbisk og homofil frigjøring*), has a national HQ in Oslo at Kongensgate 12 (☏23 10 39 39). Their website, Ⓦ www.llh.no has links to other affiliated sites giving details of gay and lesbian events.

Sweden

Riksförbundet för sexuelt likaberattigande, Sweden's national gay and lesbian organization, operate a useful website (Ⓦ www.rfsl.se), with links to Gay Pride and so on. They can be contacted at Sveavägen 57–59, 10126 Stockholm (☏08/457 13 00).

Health

Under **reciprocal health arrangements** involving members of the European Union (EU), nationals of all EU countries are entitled to free or discounted medical treatment within the respective public healthcare systems of Finland, Denmark and Sweden. Norway is not in the EU, but it is in the EEA (European Economic Area), under the terms of which nationals of all EU countries are entitled to discounted medical treatment.

Non-EU nationals have to pay for medical attention in full and should take out their own medical insurance to travel to Scandinavia. EU/EEA citizens may want to consider private health insurance too, as it will cover the cost of items not within the EU's scheme, such as dental treatment and repatriation on medical grounds. That said, most private insurance policies don't cover prescription charges – their "excesses" are usually greater than the cost of the medicines. The more worthwhile policies promise to sort matters out before you pay (rather than after) in the case of major expense; if you do have to pay upfront, get and keep the receipts. For more on insurance, see below.

Seeking medical treatment

Across Scandinavia, your local pharmacy, tourist office or hotel should be able to provide the address of an **English-speaking doctor** or **dentist**. If you're seeking treatment under EU/EEA **reciprocal public** health agreements, double-check that the doctor/dentist is working within (and seeing you as) a patient of the relevant public healthcare system. This being the case, you'll receive free or reduced-cost/ government-subsidized treatment just as the locals do; any fees must be paid upfront, or at least at the end of your treatment, and are non-refundable – a good reason to have a private insurance policy. Sometimes you will be asked to produce documentation to prove you are eligible for EU/EEA health-care, sometimes no-one bothers, but technically at least you should have your passport and your **European Health Insurance Card (EHIC)** to hand. If, on the other hand, you have a travel insurance policy covering medical expenses, you can seek treatment in either the public or private health sectors, the main issue being whether – at least in major cases – you have to pay the costs upfront and then wait for reimbursement or not.

At almost all of Scandinavia's hospitals and clinics, there will be someone who speaks English. For **medical emergencies**, call ☎112.

Insurance

Most people will want to take out some kind of **travel insurance**. A typical policy usually provides cover for loss of baggage, tickets and – up to a certain limit – cash or cheques, as well as cancellation or curtailment of your journey.

Internet

Internet access is pretty much omnipresent in Scandinavia. There are internet cafés in all large cities, and a plethora of wireless hubs throughout. Many hotels and hostels now have wireless access (some places even offer this service for free) and the vast majority have some form of internet access available to guests. Even campsites have succumbed and have either wireless access throughout the site or a dedicated room with computers with internet access. Nearly all libraries also provide free access, too, albeit time-limited.

Mail

Post office opening hours and more specific information on how to use the mail and telephone systems in each country is given under the respective "Mail" and "Phones" sections.

You can have letters sent **poste restante** to any post office in Scandinavia by addressing them "Poste Restante", followed by the name of the town and country. When picking mail up you'll need to take your passport; make sure to check under middle names and initials, as letters can get misfiled.

Rough Guides travel insurance

Rough Guides has teamed up with Columbus Direct to offer you tailor-made **travel insurance**. Products include a low-cost **backpacker** option for long stays; a **short break** option for city getaways; a typical **holiday package** option; and others. There are also annual **multi-trip** policies for those who travel regularly. Different sports and activities (trekking, skiing, etc) can usually be included.

See our website (🌐www.roughguides.com/website/shop) or call UK ☎0870/033 9988, Australia ☎1300/669 999, New Zealand ☎0800/559 911 or worldwide ☎+44 870/890 2843.

Maps

The **maps** in this book should be adequate for most purposes, but drivers, cyclists and hikers will require something more precise. Tourist offices often give out reasonably useful local road maps and town plans, but anything more detailed will require a trip to a bookshop. For **Scandinavia** as a whole, Cappelen (🅦www.cappelen.no) produces a good-quality road map on a scale of 1:800,000, though this can be hard to get hold of outside the region, in which case plump for the more readily available Freytag & Berndt version (🅦www.freytagberndt.com). For really detailed plans of the **capital cities**, it's Cappelen again – their 1:10,000 city map series is outstanding, as are their maps of all four Scandinavian countries: **Denmark** (1:300,000); **Norway** (1:325,000); **Sweden** (1:700,000); and **Finland** (1:800,000).

If you're **hiking**, you'll need something even more detailed – a scale of 1:50,000 is the minimum requirement, 1:25,000 even better.

Money

Of the three Scandinavian countries in the European Union (EU) – Denmark, Finland and Sweden – only Finland has joined the single **European currency** and converted to the euro. As a result you'll need a mixture of currencies if you're visiting more than one of the Scandinavian countries.

Finland changed over to the **euro** (€) in 2002, but Denmark and Norway use **kroner**, Sweden **kronor** – abbreviated respectively as Dkr, Nkr and Skr, or as DKK, NOK and SEK. In this guide, we've abbreviated each as "kr", except where it's not clear as to which country's money we're referring, in which case we've prefixed it with an "S" (Swedish), "D" (Danish) or "N" (Norwegian). Though they share a broadly similar **exchange rate**, the currencies are not interchangeable. See the "Costs" and "Money" sections of the individual country "Basics" for exchange rates, further details of the denominations of each currency and average daily costs.

ATMS, debit and credit cards

Scandinavia heaves with **ATMs,** most of which give instructions in a variety of languages, and accept a host of **debit cards**.

You'll rarely be charged a transaction fee as the banks make their profits from applying different exchange rates. **Credit cards** can be used in ATMs too, but in this case transactions are treated as loans, with interest accruing daily from the date of withdrawal. All major credit cards, including American Express, Visa and MasterCard, are widely accepted across Scandinavia.

All well-known brands of **traveller's cheque** in all major currencies are accepted throughout in Scandinavia, with euro and US dollar cheques being the most common. When you **cash your cheques**, you'll find that almost all banks make a percentage charge per transaction on top of a basic minimum charge. **Exchanging money** is easy but usually expensive. Banks have standard exchange rates, but commissions can vary enormously and it's always worth shopping around. Post offices often provide good exchange rates, too. **Banking hours** vary from country to country – check each country's "Basics" section under "Costs, money and banks". Outside those times, and especially in more remote areas, you'll often find that you can change money at hostels, hotels, campsites, tourist offices, airports and ferry terminals – though usually at worse rates than at the bank.

Phones

Most of Scandinavia is on the **mobile phone network**, which means hikers, skiers, climbers and other outdoors enthusiasts can contact someone by phone almost no matter where they are – invaluable if things go wrong. The region's mobile network is on the **GSM** band common to the rest of Europe, Australia and New Zealand. This means that the vast majority of mobile phones from these countries will work here though, if you haven't used your mobile abroad before, you should check with your phone company: some mobiles are, for example, barred from international use. It's also a good idea to check **call charges** as costs can be excruciating – particularly irritating is the supplementary charge that you pay on incoming calls. However, purchasing a **local SIM card** in any of the Scandinavian countries will reduce call charges dramatically; for more on this, see the "Phones" sections of the individual country's "Basics".

Useful telephone numbers and codes

International calls

Note that the initial zero is omitted from the area code when dialing the UK, Ireland, Australia, New Zealand, Finland and Sweden from abroad.

Phoning abroad from Scandinavia

UK international access code +44.

Republic of Ireland international access code +353.

US and Canada international access code +1.

Australia international access code +61.

New Zealand international access code +64.

South Africa international access code +27.

Phoning Scandinavia from abroad

Denmark international access code +45.

Finland international access code +358.

Norway international access code +47.

Sweden international access code +46.

Things are more complicated (and expensive) for Canadians and Americans. The **North American mobile network** is not compatible with the GSM system, so you'll need a **tri-band phone** which is able to switch from one band to the other.

Finally, international **texting** (SMS) via the GSM band is – or can be – dead easy. Depending on the mobile, there's often no need to tap in international codes, you just send the message as you would back home. Again, your phone company will, if necessary, offer advice and details of charges.

Time

Denmark, Sweden and Norway are one hour ahead of the UK and six to nine hours ahead of the continental USA; Finland is two hours ahead of the UK and seven to ten hours ahead of the continental USA.

Tourist information

Before you leave, it may be worth checking out the national **tourist information** websites (see details below) for accommodation listings and bookings, and timetables. You'll also be able to order free brochures online. Alternatively contact your local national tourist boards, if one such exists (details below) for free maps, timetables, accommodation listings and brochures.

Almost every Scandinavian town (and even some villages) has a **tourist office**, where you can pick up free town plans and information, brochures and other bumph. Many book private rooms (sometimes youth-hostel beds), rent bikes, sell local discount cards and change money. During summer, they're open daily until late evening; out of high season, shop hours are more usual, and in winter they're sometimes closed at weekends. You'll find full details of individual offices throughout the Guide.

National tourist board offices

ⓦ www.visitdenmark.com
ⓦ www.visitfinland.com
ⓦ www.visitnorway.com
ⓦ www.visitsweden.com

Britain

Denmark 55 Sloane St, London SW1X 9SY ☎ 020/7259 5959.
Finland 177–179 Hammersmith Rd, London W6 8BS ☎ 020/8600 7261.
Norway Charles House, 5 Regent St, London SW1Y 4LR ☎ 020/7389 8800.
Sweden ☎ 020/7108 6168. No walk-in service.

Canada

For all four countries, use the websites listed above, or contact the relevant tourist boards in New York (see p.44).

Ireland

No tourist board offices for Denmark, Finland and Norway in Ireland, contact the ones in London instead (see p.43), or the relevant websites. Sweden ☎01/247 5440. No walk-in service.

US

Denmark Danish Tourist Board, PO Box 4649, Grand Central Station, New York, NY10163–4649 ☎1-212/885-9700.
Finland Finnish Tourist Board, 655 Third Ave, New York, NY 10017 ☎1-800-FIN-INFO.
Norway Innovation Norway, 18th floor 655 Third Ave, New York, NY 10017 ☎1-212/885-9700.
Sweden PO Box 4649, Grand Central Station, New York, NY10163–4649 ☎1-212/885-9700.

Travellers with disabilities

As you might expect, the Scandinavians have adopted a progressive and thoughtful approach to the issues surrounding **disability** and, as a result, there are decent facilities for travellers with disabilities across the whole region. An increasing number of hotels, hostels and campsites are equipped for disabled visitors, and are credited as such in the tourist literature by means of the standard wheelchair-in-a-box icon. Furthermore, on most main routes the trains have special carriages with wheelchair space, hydraulic lifts and toilets for the disabled; domestic flights either cater for or provide assistance to disabled customers; and new ships on all ferry routes have lifts and cabins designed for disabled people.

In the cities and larger towns, many **restaurants** and most **museums** and public places are wheelchair-accessible, and although facilities are not so advanced in the countryside, things are improving rapidly. Drivers will find that most motorway **service stations** are wheelchair-accessible and that, if you have a UK-registered vehicle, the disabled **car parking badge** is honoured. Note also that several of the larger car rental companies have modified vehicles available. On a less positive note, city pavements can

be uneven and difficult to negotiate and, inevitably, winter snow and ice can make things much, much worse.

Getting to Scandinavia should be relatively straightforward too. Most airlines offer assistance to disabled travellers, while DFDS Scandinavian Seaways ferries have specially adapted cabins.

Contacts for travellers with disabilities

In Denmark

Disabled Peoples Organisations Denmark (*Danske Handicaporganisationer*) Kløverprisvej 10B, Hvidovre ☎3675 1777, ⓦwww.handicap .dk. National umbrella organization for a coalition of disability groups with offices all over Denmark – check the website for local contact details; the local offices act as referral agencies.
ⓦwww.visitdenmark.com The thorough and extensive "Disabled travel in Denmark" section within the Danish tourist board website has features on everything from transportation to services and organizations. Supporting brochures too can be ordered online.

In Finland

The Finnish Association of People with Physical Disabilities (*Invalidiliitto*) Mannerheimintie 107, 00280 Helsinki ☎09/613 191, ⓦwww.invalidiliitto.fi. A useful starting point for travellers with mobility concerns.

In Norway

Norwegian Association of Disabled (Norges Handikapforbund) Schweigaardsgt 12, Oslo ☎24 10 24 00, ⓦwww.nhf.no; postal address Postboks 9217, Grønland, 0134 Oslo. This organization produces a wide range of useful information, from general guidance on accessibility across the whole of the country through to comments about the major hotel chains and transport.

In Sweden

The Federation of Disabled Persons (*De Handikappades Riksförbund*; DHR) Katrinebergsvägen 6, Stockholm ☎86 85 80 00, ⓦwww.dhr.se. Postal address Box 47305, 100 74 Stockholm. An excellent source of information and advice; the website is currently only in Swedish.

Guide

Guide

Denmark

Denmark highlights

✳ Smørrebrød Rye bread loaded with Danish delicacies, these traditional open sandwiches are out of this world. See p.57

✳ Christiania Declared a "free city" in 1971, quirky and irreverent Christiania is a fascinating place for a wander. See p.79

✳ Ny Carlsberg Glyptotek Copenhagen's gallery of Greek, Roman and Egyptian art and artefacts boasts one of the biggest (and best) collections of Etruscan art outside Italy. See p.81

✳ Louisiana Museum of Modern Art This marvellous collection is set in an unusual building overlooking a sculpture park and the waters of the Øresund See p.91

✳ Christiansø, Bornholm One of the tiniest islands in the Baltic, the ramparts and fields of this ex-military outpost allow for days gazing out at the sea and nights up at the stars. See p.107

✳ Århus nightlife With an array of excellent, late-opening nightspots (and one of the best jazz festivals in Europe), western Denmark's cultural capital is a super place to paint the town red. See p.140

✳ Djursland beaches The white-sand beaches around Ebeltoft, Grenå and Fjellerup are some of Denmark's finest, and great for learning windsurfing. See p.143

▲ Beach life, Funen

Introduction and Basics

Denmark frequently tops surveys of the world's happiest places to live, a fact which doesn't surprise many Danes. But for foreigners, Denmark, delicately balanced between mainland Europe and the rest of Scandinavia, can remain a difficult country to pin down. In many ways it shares the characteristics of both regions: it's an EU member, and has prices and drinking laws that are broadly in line with the rest of Europe. But Danish social policies and style of government are distinctly Scandinavian: social benefits and the standard of living are high, and its politics are very much that of consensus.

It may seem hard to believe, but it wasn't so long ago that tiny Denmark ruled a good chunk of northern Europe. Since imperialist times, however, the country's energies have been turned inwards, towards the development of a well-organized but rarely over-bureaucratic society that does much to foster a pride in Danish arts and culture and uphold the freedoms of the individual. Indeed, once here, it becomes easy to share the Danes' puzzlement as to why other small, formerly empire-owning nations haven't followed their example.

Where to go

While Denmark is the easiest Scandinavian country in which to travel – both in terms of cost and distance – the landscape itself is the region's least dramatic: largely green, flat, farmland punctuated by innumerable fairytale half-timbered villages, with surprisingly few urban settlements. Apart from a scattering of small islands, the country is made up of three main landmasses – the islands of Zealand and Funen and the peninsula of Jutland, which extends northwards from Germany.

The vast majority of visitors make for **Zealand** (Sjælland) and, more specifically, **Copenhagen**, the country's one truly large city and an atmospheric and exciting focal point. The compact capital has everything: a beautiful old centre, a good array of museums – both national collections and smaller oddball establishments – and a boisterous nightlife. But Copenhagen has little in common with the rest of Zealand, which is largely quiet and rural. Zealand's smaller neighbour, **Funen** (Fyn), has an urban draw in **Odense** (and a quaint one at that), but is otherwise sedate, renowned for the cuteness of its villages, the sandy beaches of its southern

Denmark on the web

Ⓦ **www.visitdenmark.com** Official Danish Tourist Board website, with links to all regional sites.

Ⓦ **www.woco.dk** The stylish site of the Wonderful Copenhagen office, packed with the latest in restaurants, bars, nightlife and events.

Ⓦ **www.aok.dk** Extensive English-language site with the latest listings for Copenhagen.

Ⓦ **www.rejseplanen.dk** Door-to-door public transport journey planner, in English as well as Danish.

Ⓦ **www.net-bb.dk** Nationwide farm holiday and private accommodation booking.

Ⓦ **www.dmol.dk** Museum website with virtual tours of the best places.

Ⓦ **www.cphpost.dk** English-language online newspaper which covers stories from all around the country. It also has an excellent listings section for the Copenhagen area.

Ⓦ **www.lego.com** Lots of games, virtual plastic bricks and information about the original Legoland at Billund, Denmark.

Ⓦ **www.strandguide.dk** Guide to Danish nudist beaches with maps and details of facilities.

coast – a major holiday destination – and numerous explorable small islands.

Only **Jutland** (Jylland) is far enough away from Copenhagen to enjoy a truly individual flavour, as well as Denmark's most varied scenery, ranging from soft green hills to desolate heathlands and windswept coastline. In **Århus**, Jutland also has the most lively and enjoyable city outside the capital.

When to go

Copenhagen attracts visitors all year round, but the intake peaks during July and August – which means **May**, **early June** and **September** are probably the most pleasant times to be there, although there's plenty happening in the city throughout the year. Anywhere else is enjoyably crowd-free all year round except for **July**, the Danish vacation month, when the population heads en masse for the countryside and the coastal strips – though, even then, only the most popular areas are uncomfortably crowded. Many **outdoor events** – from big music festivals to the staging of Viking plays – take place between mid-June and mid-August, when all tourist facilities and transport services (including the more minor ferry links) are operating in full. In more isolated areas things begin to slacken off in September.

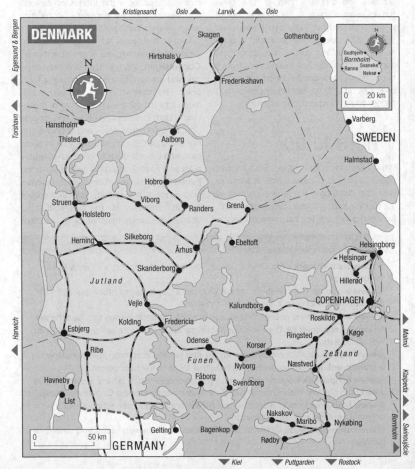

Denmark has the least extreme **climate** of the Scandinavian countries, but due to the proximity of the sea the weather can fluctuate rapidly. A wet day will as likely be followed by a sunny one and vice versa, and stiff breezes are common, especially along Jutland's west coast, where they can be particularly strong. **Summer** is on the whole sunny and clear: throughout July the temperature averages 20°C (68°F), often reaching 26°C (78°F). **Winter** conditions are cold but not severe: there's usually a snow covering from December to early February, and the temperature can at times drop as low as minus 15°C (5°F), but generally it hovers around or just below freezing point.

Getting there from the rest of Scandinavia

One look at a map will show you there'll be few problems **getting to Denmark** from the other Scandinavian countries. Links by **rail**, **sea** and **air** are fast and frequent all year round and, generally speaking, the journey to Denmark can be a rewarding part of your trip rather than a chore.

By train

Copenhagen is a major junction for **trains** between Europe and the rest of Scandinavia, with the **Øresunds Link** – a part-tunnel, part-bridge connection between Copenhagen and Malmö in Sweden – providing excellent, efficient access to the rest of Scandinavia. Trains depart every twenty minutes and the journey from Malmö takes only 35 minutes. There are also several daily services to Copenhagen from the major Scandinavian cities – Stockholm, Gothenburg, Oslo, Bergen, Turku and Helsinki – and less frequent links (usually one a day in summer) with remoter spots in the far north, such as Narvik (in Norway) and Kiruna (in Sweden). InterRail, ScanRail and Eurail **passes** are valid on all the international routes into Denmark (see p.30).

By bus

There are several direct **bus** links between the major Danish cities and the rest of

Scandinavia, using either the Øresunds Link or the ferry routes outlined below. From Sweden to Copenhagen, there are usually three buses a day from Stockholm: one with Eurolines (🌐www.eurolines.dk) and two others with Swebus Express (🌐www.swebusexpress.se). From Gothenburg there are dozen daily departures via Helsingborg and Malmö with either Swebus Express or Säfflebussen (🌐www.safflebussen.se). The Gråhundsbus line (🌐www.graahundbus.dk) connects Copenhagen with Malmö airport as well as Malmö city. Eurolines, Säfflebus and Swebus Express all run daily departures from Oslo (Norway), all of which run via Malmö and Gothenburg. **Fares** can vary enormously depending on the season and how far in advance tickets are booked. All companies have student/youth discounts.

By ferry

Since timetables and prices fluctuate constantly, ferry companies' websites or latest brochures are the best way to check precise details of the numerous **ferries** into Zealand and Jutland from Norway and Sweden; you can also contact any tourist office. There are sometimes reductions for railcard holders (see p.30), and **fares** are usually a lot cheaper outside the peak period, roughly from the end of June to early August – though bear in mind that services are likely to be less frequent out of season, and possibly non-existent in winter. Even if you're heading for Copenhagen, don't disregard the possibility of a quicker, and cheaper, crossing into north Jutland – an interesting part of Denmark, with easy rail and bus links to the capital; or, from Sweden, reaching Denmark by way of the pretty island of Bornholm.

By plane

SAS (🌐www.scandinavian.net) operates around nearly two dozen direct **flights** daily into Copenhagen **from Oslo and Stockholm**, and a dozen daily from **Helsinki**; Finnair (🌐www.finnair.com) flies several times daily to Copenhagen from Helsinki. A number of discount airlines operate flights to Copenhagen from smaller airports and, increasingly, from larger cities, with varying degrees of affiliation with SAS. The Finnish

SAS group airline **Blue 1** (@www.blue1 .com) offers five daily direct flights from Helsinki. **Widerøe Flyveselskab** (@www .wideroe.no) is the Norwegian equivalent, with daily services from Trondheim, Haugesund and Sandefjord. The independent budget airline **Norwegian** (@www.norwegian.no) offer six daily flights from Oslo, while the small Swedish **Skyways** (@www.skyways .se) offer connections to Copenhagen from Karlstad (1–3 daily). Check the websites for excellent deals, or contact a tourist office or travel agent to find out about special reduced-fare deals between the Scandinavian capitals – there are usually several each summer.

Copenhagen is very much the Danish hub of the SAS network (Århus is a poor second) and international arrivals often dovetail with domestic flights to other Danish cities, which cost little extra on top of the international fare; see p.54 for more details.

British Airways (@ www.britishairways .com) runs three daily flights from Oslo, Stockholm and Gothenburg to Århus, and one daily flight from Gothenburg and Helsinki to Billund. Cimber Air has two daily connections from Stockholm and Oslo to Billund, while Danish Air Transport (@www.dat.dk) connects Stavanger with Billund and Esbjerg up to twice daily.

Fares for the services listed above vary enormously; one-way fares with budget airlines start at under 100Dkr, while tickets with the larger national carriers are upwards of 1500Dkr. Under-26s can enjoy substantial discounts with the larger carriers, sometimes paying as little as 500Dkr. Again, check with a travel agent or visit the websites.

From Sweden

The cheapest route is the HH Ferries crossing **from Helsingborg** to Helsingør (@www.hhferries.se; 20min; one-way tickets 24Skr for foot passengers, 300Skr for cars), which runs around the clock and takes thirty minutes; you can walk, cycle or drive straight on board.

Stena Line (@www.stenaline.se) has luxury boats sailing several times a day in summer **from Gothenburg** to Frederikshavn in Jutland (3hr 15min; one-way fares from 155Skr for foot passengers, or from 495Skr for cars including up to five passengers; thirty percent discount for Eurail, ScanRail and InterRail pass holders). There's also a twice-daily Stena Line ferry (4hr 15min) **from Varberg** to Grenå (for Århus) for a basic passenger fare that starts at 155Skr one-way (cars from 595Skr). All Stena Line car fares include five passengers. Cheapest departures are always the overnight journeys.

With time to spare, you could reach Denmark proper by way of **Bornholm**, a sizeable Danish island in the Baltic that's actually nearer to Sweden's south coast. Bornholm Ferries (@www.bornholmferries .dk) runs a twice-daily service between Ystad in Sweden and Rønne on Bornholm (express 1hr 15min, regular ferry 2hr 45min; from 168Skr). From Rønne, you can take the Bornholm Ferries service to Køge, south of Copenhagen on the S-train network (1–2 daily), but it's quicker to take either the train (@www.dsb.dk) or the bus route run by Bornholmerbussen (@www.graahundbus .dk; 3hr; 245kr one-way) via Ystad.

From Norway

The only direct connection from Norway to Copenhagen is on the DFDS (@www .dfdsseaways.dk) crossing **from Oslo** (one-way fares from 480Nkr for foot passengers, 1460Nkr for car plus two passengers), though you'll save a lot of money by taking one of the numerous routes to either Hanstholm, Frederikshavn or Hirtshals in Jutland. From Oslo to Frederikshavn, there are four to seven crossings a week with Stena (@www .stenaline.no; 12hr; from 140Nkr one-way). There are also connections **from Bergen via Haugesund and Egersund** to Hanstholm with Fjord Line (@www.fjordline.com; one-way fares from Bergen 19hr, 270–515Nkr; from Haugesund 14hr, 215–310Nkr; from Egersund: 8hr, 194–494Nkr). Color Line also has services **from Larvik** (3hr 45min; 200Nkr one-way) and **Kristiansand** (3hr 45min; same fare) to Hirtshals.

Getting around

Despite being made up largely of islands, Denmark is a swift and easy country in which to travel. All types of **public transport** – trains, buses and the essential ferries – are punctual and efficient, and where you need to switch from one type to another, you'll find the timetables impressively well integrated.

And with Denmark being such a small country, you can get from one end to the other in half a day; even if, as is more likely, you're planning to see it all at leisure, you'll rarely need to do more than an hour's daily travelling. Besides being small, Denmark is also very flat, with scores of villages linked by country roads – ideal for effortless cycling.

By rail

Trains are easily the most efficient and convenient way to get about. Danske Statsbaner (DSB) – Danish State Railways (@www.dsb.dk) – runs an exhaustive and reliable network. InterRail, Eurail and ScanRail **passes** are valid on all routes except the few private lines that operate in some rural areas. There are just a few out-of-the-way regions that trains fail to penetrate, though these can be easily crossed by buses, which often run in conjunction with local train connections. Some of these buses are operated privately, but on those run by DSB, train passes are valid (for more on buses, see below).

Trains range from **inter-city expresses** (**IC Lyn**), with a buffet service, to smaller **local trains** (*regionaltog*). Departure times are listed both on station concourses and the platforms (departures in yellow, arrivals in white), and announced over the loudspeaker. Watch out for *stillekupé* – special quiet compartments where children, pets and mobile phones are prohibited.

Tickets should be bought in advance from train stations, either from ticket booths or automated machines, which take all major credit cards but no cash. Trains don't require advance seat reservations (20kr), but then there's no guarantee that you'll get a seat. There's an extra charge of 40kr if you buy tickets on board. All trains have an inspector who checks tickets: he/she is almost certain to speak English. **Fares** are calculated on a zonal system. Copenhagen–Odense, for example, costs 224kr one-way, Copenhagen–Århus, 311kr and Copenhagen–Bornholm 250kr (including ferry connection). All these fares include the cost of a seat reservation, and your train ticket will also get you around on the local buses (and S-trains in Copenhagen) in the departure and arrival town of your journey on the day the ticket is valid. If you're between 16 and 25 and plan to do lots of train travel, it may be worthwhile buying a DSB Wildcard (200kr), which gives you a 25 percent discount on normal tickets and 50 percent **discount** if you avoid travelling on Friday or Sunday from 4am until 4am the next day. There are no student discounts, but people over 65 qualify for the same discounts as Wildcard holders. Travelling in a group of eight or more also entitles you to a 25–30 percent discount – get details from any Danish tourist office.

As for **timings**, DSB's Køreplan (30kr from any newsagent) details all DSB train, bus and ferry services inside (and long-distance routes outside) the country, including the local Copenhagen S-train system and all private services, a sound investment If you're planning to do a lot of travelling within the country. Smaller **timetables** detailing specific routes can be picked up free at tourist offices and station ticket offices.

By bus

There are only a handful of **long-distance bus** services in Denmark. Abildskou Rutebiler (@70 21 08 88, @www.abildskou.dk) runs a swift service from **Copenhagen** to **Århus**, some via **Ebeltoft** (5–7 daily); to **Aalborg** (2–5 daily); **Thisted** via **Viborg** and **Nykøbing Mors** (generally 2 daily); and **Silkeborg** (2 daily). One-way tickets to Ebeltoft, Århus and Silkeborg cost 270kr (students pay 130kr Mon–Thurs). To Aalborg, Viborg, Nykøbing, Mors and Thisted, one-way tickets cost 310kr (students 150kr for travel at specified times).

Abildskou (details above) run a service between **Fjerritslev and Copenhagen** (1 daily), with stops in Løgstør, Hobro, Holbæk and Roskilde; one-way tickets cost 310kr (students 150kr Mon–Thurs). Gråhundbus (@44 68 44 00, @www.graahundbus.dk) runs a service (3–5 daily; 220kr one-way) between Copenhagen and Bornholm, via the Øresunds Link and Ystad in Sweden. Bus fares represent quite a saving over full train fares but, while just as efficient, long-distance buses are much less comfortable than trains. However, buses really come into their own in the few areas where trains are scarce or connections complicated – much of Funen and north-east Jutland, for example – and if you're travelling from Esbjerg to Frederikshavn or Aalborg you save several hours, and a lot of timetable reading, by taking the bus. Around Jutland, the excellent government-run **X-busser** (☎ 98 90 09 00, ⊛ www .xbus.dk) are especially worth checking out.

By ferry

Ferries connect all the Danish islands, and vary in size and speed from the state-of-the-art catamaran linking Zealand and Jutland to raft-like affairs serving tiny, isolated settlements a few minutes off the (so-called) mainland. Where applicable, train and bus fares include the cost of ferry crossings (although you can also pay at the terminal and walk on), while the smaller ferries charge 30–95kr for foot passengers. Contact the nearest tourist office for full details.

Flying

Domestic flights are hardly essential in somewhere of Denmark's size, but can be handy if you're in a rush: from Copenhagen it's less than an hour's flying time to anywhere in the country. Two **airlines** operate domestic flights: SAS (☎ 60 72 77 27, ⊛ www .scandinavian.net) and Cimber Air (☎ 70 10 12 18, ⊛ www.cimber.dk). **Fares** vary only slightly between them, and weekend tickets are generally cheaper than weekdays; get details from an SAS desk, tourist office or airline website.

By car

Given the excellent public transport system, the size of the country and the comparatively high price of petrol, **driving** isn't really economical unless you're in a group. **Car rental** is expensive, though it's worth checking the cut-price deals offered by some airlines. You'll need an international driving licence and must be aged at least 20, although many firms won't rent vehicles to anyone under 25 – and some require you to be over 28. Costs start at around 3000kr a week for a small hatchback with unlimited mileage. Rent a Wreck (Lej et Lig;

☎ 70 25 45 25, ⊛ www.lejetlig.dk) offers the best deal for limited mileage (100km per day) at 1575kr for a week, the cars aren't really wrecks, they're just not new. Danes drive on the right, and there's a speed limit in towns of 50kph, 80kph in open country and 110kph or 130kph on motorways. As in Sweden and Finland, headlights need to be used at all times. There are random breath tests for suspected drunken drivers, and the penalties are severe. When parked in a town, not on a meter, a parking-time disc must be displayed; get one from a tourist office, police station or bank. The national motoring organization, Forenede Danske Motorejere, operates a 24-hour **breakdown service** (☎ 45 88 00 25) for AA members; if you're not an AA member, Dansk Autohjælp (☎ 70 10 80 90, ⊛ www.dah.dk) and Falck (☎ 70 10 20 30, ⊛ www.falck.dk) can be summoned from call boxes by the road. A standard call-out fee will be charged – Dansk Autohjælp is the cheapest at 700kr per hour.

Cycling

Cycling is the ideal way to appreciate Denmark's pastoral (and mostly flat) landscape, as well as being a good method of getting around. Traffic is sparse on most country roads and all large towns have cycle tracks – though watch out for sometimes less-than-careful drivers on main roads. Bikes can be **rented** at nearly all youth hostels and tourist offices, at most bike shops and at some train stations for around 75–100kr per day or 300kr per week; there's often a 300–500kr refundable deposit, too. For long-distance cycling, take the frequent westerly winds into account when **planning your route** – pedalling is easier facing east than west. The Danish cycling organization Dansk Cyklistforbund (☎ 33 32 31 21, ⊛ www.dcf .dk) offers cycling advice.

You can take your bike on all types of public transport except city buses. On trains, you'll have to pay according to the zonal system used to calculate passenger tickets – for example, 50kr to take your bike from Copenhagen to Århus, with 20kr on top if you want to reserve a place in advance. You must make a 'seat' reservation ahead of time if you are travelling between May and

August. The brochure *Cyckle i Tog* (free from train stations) lists rates and rules in full. For a similar fee, long-distance buses have limited cycle space, while ferries let bikes on free or for a few kroner. Domestic flights charge around 200kr for airlifting your bike.

Accommodation

While less costly in Denmark than in other Nordic countries, **accommodation** is still going to be your major daily expense, and you should plan it carefully. **Hotels** are by no means off-limits if you seek out the better offers, and **youth hostels**, **sleep-ins** and **campsites** are plentiful – and of a uniformly high standard.

Hotels

Most Danish hotel rooms include phone, TV and bathroom, for which you'll pay from around 750kr for a double (singles from around 500kr); going without the luxuries can result in big savings, and in most towns you'll find hotels offering rooms with access to a shared bathroom for as little as 500kr for a double (350kr a single). You'll find that rates may vary according to the season or day of the week, especially in the so-called "conference towns" where hotels are packed with business travellers during the week (Mon–Thurs) outside the summer season (roughly mid-June to mid-Aug). In these towns, rates are reduced significantly during summer and on weekends, and we've given two rates where this is the case (see box below). In the rest of the country, room rates tend to go up during the summer season and holidays.

Some **inns** (called *kro*) in country areas match basic hotel-room prices – sometimes for rooms with full facilities. Other advantages of staying in a hotel or inn are the lack of a curfew (common in hostels in big cities) and the inclusion of an all-you-can-eat breakfast – so large you won't need to buy lunch.

Danish tourist offices overseas (see p.43) can provide a free list of hotels throughout the country, though much more accurate and extensive information can be found at local tourist offices and on tourist office websites. It's a good idea to **book in advance**, especially in peak season, which is most easily done via the tourist office or hotel website (listed in relevant places throughout the Guide chapters); booking directly on the net yourself can result in discounts of up to 50 percent.

Tourist offices can also supply details of **private rooms** in someone's home, vaguely akin to British-style bed and breakfasts (generally without the breakfast). These vary greatly, but reckon on paying upwards of 500kr for a double. Throughout the country, you'll come across places that call themselves **B&Bs**, though in reality no different to private rooms. There's a formal network of these B&Bs on Funen, and a useful annual catalogue details over one hundred rooms on the island. It's available from tourist offices and can also be accessed online at ⓦwww.bb-syddanmark.dk. The countrywide B&B site ⓦwww.net-bb.dk has listings for similar places to stay all over the country. Note that despite the name, breakfast isn't included in any B&B rates, and is only sometimes offered for an additional cost; there's often access to a kitchen, however.

Alternatively, staying on **farms** (*Bonde-gårdsferie*) is becoming increasingly popular in Denmark; as well as your room, there's the opportunity to watch a farm at

Accommodation price codes

The hotels and guesthouses listed in the Denmark chapters of this Guide have been graded according to the following price bands, based on the cost of the **least expensive double room in high season** (mid-June to mid-Aug). Where hotels have an off-peak or weekend rate we've given two grades, covering both the special and the regular rates. (ie ❷/❸).

❶ 400kr and under	❹ 801–1000kr
❷ 401–600kr	❺ 1001–1250kr
❸ 601–800kr	❻ 1251kr and over

work. Information and catalogues can be obtained from Ferie på Landet, Ceresvej 2, 8410 Rønde (☎86 37 39 00, ⓦwww .bondegaardsferie.dk).

Hostels and sleep-ins

Youth hostels (*vandrerhjem*) are Denmark's cheapest option under a roof. Every town has one, they're much less pricey than hotels, and they have a high standard of comfort. Most offer a choice of various sizes of private room (we've given price codes for these in the Guide chapters), often with toilets and showers, and all have dormitory accommodation; nearly all have cooking facilities, too. **Rates** are around 130kr for a dormitory bed to 400–500kr for a private room. Other than those in major towns or ferry ports, it's rare for hostels to be full, but during the summer it's always wise to phone ahead to make a reservation, and to check on location – some hostels are several kilometres outside the town centre.

As with all Scandinavian hostels, sleeping bags are not allowed, so you need to bring either a sheet sleeping bag or rent hostel linen (50–60kr) – which can become expensive over a long stay. It's a good idea, too, to get an **HI card**, since without one you'll be hit with the cost of either an overnight card (35kr) or a year-long Danish membership card (160kr). If you're planning on doing a lot of hostelling, it's worth contacting Danhostel Danmarks Vandrerhjem, Vesterbrogade 39, DK-1620, Copenhagen V (☎33 31 36 12, ⓦwww.danhostel.dk) to get a copy of their free guide to Danish hostels, *Danmarks Vandrerhjem*, which is published in several languages including English, and for their informative hostel/campsite map of Denmark.

Sleep-ins are a similarly cheap option if you're on a budget but don't want to camp. Originally run by the local authorities, sleep-ins are now just a more traveller-oriented version of a hostel – privately run and generally always packed with young backpackers. Some open between May and August only, but most now open year-round. For bed and (shared) shower facilities, expect to pay around 100kr; bear in mind that you'll need your own sleeping bag, that only one night's stay is permitted in a few cases, and that there may be an age restriction (typically 16- to 24-year-olds only, although this may not be strictly enforced).

Camping

If you don't already have an International Camping Card from a camping organization in your own country, you'll need a Camping Card Scandinavia which costs 90kr for both individuals and families, can be bought from any campsite and is valid on all official sites in Scandinavia until the end of the year in which it was bought. A Transit Pass can be used for a single overnight stay and costs 25kr per person. **Camping rough** without the landowner's permission is illegal and an on-the-spot fine may well be imposed. However, the Danish Forest and Nature Agency allows free low-impact camping in some two hundred designated woodland areas. The rules are strict: only one night at each site, only two tents per site, no open fires or camping stoves allowed and the site has to be left as you found it. Check ⓦwww .skovognatur.dk for information and a list of designated areas; local tourist offices should be able to advise if there are any nearby.

Campsites (*campingplads*) can be found virtually everywhere. All are open in June, July and August, many are open from April through to September, and a few operate all year round. There's a rigid **grading system**: one-star sites have toilets and at least one shower; two-stars also have basic cooking facilities and a food shop within 2km; three-stars include a laundry and a TV room; four-stars also have a shop; while five-stars include a cafeteria and other facilities such as a swimming pool. **Prices** vary only slightly from 50 to 70kr per person, though you may pay more at city sites or those in other particularly popular locations. Many campsites also have **cabin accommodation**, usually with cooking facilities, which at 3000–5000kr for a six-berth affair for a week (or 500–600kr a night) may represent a saving for several people sharing, although on busy sites cabins are often booked up throughout the summer. Any Danish tourist office can give you a free leaflet listing all the country's sites and the basic camping rules, or there's an official guide, *Camping Danmark*, available from kiosks, bookshops and tourist

①

offices (95kr). For further information, contact the Campingrådet, Hesseløgade 16, DK-2100 København Ø (☎39 27 88 44, ⓦwww.campingraadet.dk).

Food and drink

Although good **food** can get pretty pricey in Denmark, there are plenty of ways to eat affordably and healthily, and with plenty of variety, too. Much the same applies to **drink**: the only Scandinavian country free of social drinking taboos, Denmark is an imbiber's delight – both for its huge choice of tipples, and for the number of places where they can be sampled. Traditional **Danish food** is centred on meat and fish: beef, veal, chicken and pork are frequent menu items – though rarely bacon, which is mainly exported – along with various forms of salmon, herring, eel, plaice and cod (see p.700 for our Menu reader). Combinations of these are served with potatoes and another, usually boiled, vegetable. Ordinary **restaurant** meals can be expensive, especially in the evening, but there are other ways to eat Danish food that won't ruin your budget or your diet.

Breakfast

Breakfast (*morgenmad*) can be the tastiest and is certainly the healthiest (and most meat-free) Danish meal. Almost all hotels offer a sumptuous breakfast as a matter of course, as do youth hostels, though the latter don't include breakfast in their rates. You can often attack a buffet table laden with cereals, bread, cheese, boiled eggs, fruit juice, milk, coffee and tea for around 50kr. Breakfast elsewhere will be far less substantial: many cafés offer a very basic one for around 30kr, but you're well advised to go for **brunch** instead. Served until mid-afternoon, brunch is a filling option for late starters consisting of variations of international-style breakfasts (American, English etc) for 60–160kr depending on your craving.

Lunch and snacks

You can track down an excellent-value **lunch** (*frokost*) simply by walking around and reading the signs chalked up outside any café, restaurant or *bodega* (a bar that also sells no-frills food). On these notices, put out between 11.30am and 2.30pm, the word **tilbud** refers to the "special" priced dish, or **dagens ret**, meaning "dish of the day" – a plate of chilli con carne or lasagna for around 50kr, or a three-course set lunch for 80–120kr. Some restaurants offer a fixed-price (80–100kr) open buffet, where you can help yourself to as much as you like.

The traditional Danish lunch is a choice of **smørrebrød**, or open sandwiches: slices of rye bread heaped with meat (commonly either ham, beef or liver pâté), fish (salmon, eel, caviar, cod roe, shrimp or herring) or cheese, and generously piled with assorted trimmings (mushrooms, cucumber, pickles or slices of lemon). A selection of three or four of these costs about 75kr. You can buy *smørrebrød* to go for 15–35kr from the special shops you'll see in every fairly sizeable town; one of them usually opens late, too, until 10pm. At cafés you'll always be able to find a bulky sandwich (30–50kr) or a filling portion of salad (usually served with fresh bread) for 50–70kr. Otherwise, the American **burger** franchises are commonplace, as are **pizzerias**, which are dependable and affordable at any time of day, with many offering special deals such as all you can-eat salad with a basic pizza for about 50kr. **Shawarmas** (kebabs) and **China boxes** (your selection of Chinese dishes from a buffet served in a takeaway box) are also easy to find in most larger towns; both cost around 30kr. You can also get a very ordinary self-service meat, fish or omelette lunch in a **supermarket cafeteria** for 50–90kr.

Most Danes buy **snacks** from the very popular fast-food stands (*pølsevogn*) found on all main streets and at train stations. These serve various types of **sausage** (*pølser*) for 18–28kr: with trimmings such as roasted onion, remoulade and pickled cucumber, **toasted ham and cheese sandwich** (*parisertoast*) for 12–15kr – vegetarians can ask for the ham to be left out – and **chips** (*pommes frites*). Italian or French **coffee** is widely available, as is **tea** (usually a fairly exotic teabag brew); either will cost 12–35kr. You help it down with a **Danish pastry** (*wienerbrød*), tastier and much less sweet than the imitations sold abroad under the same name.

Dinner

Dinner (*aftensmad*) in Denmark presents as much choice as lunch, but the cost can be a lot higher. Pizzerias and similar places keep their prices unchanged from lunchtime, and many youth hostels serve simple but filling evening meals for 50–75kr, though you have to order in advance. The most cost-effective dinners (70–90kr), however, are usually found in **ethnic restaurants** (most commonly Chinese or Middle Eastern, with a smaller number of Indian, Indonesian and Thai), which, besides à la carte dishes, often have a buffet table – ideal for gluttonous over-indulgence – and you usually get soup and a dessert thrown in as well. The **Danish restaurants** that are promising for lunch often turn into expense-account affairs at night, offering an atmospheric, candle-lit setting for the slow devouring of immaculately prepared meat or fish; you'll be hard-pushed to spend less than 200kr per person.

Drinking

If you've arrived from near-teetotal Norway or Sweden, you're in for a shock. Not only is alcoholic **drink** entirely accepted in Denmark, it's quite common to see people strolling along the pedestrianized streets swigging from a bottle of beer, and although extreme drunkenness is frowned upon, alcohol is widely consumed throughout the day by most types of people.

Although you can buy booze more cheaply from supermarkets, the most sociable **places to drink** are pubs, bars and cafés, where the emphasis is on beer – although you can also get spirits and wine (or tea and coffee). There are also **bodegas** (see p.57), in which, as a very general rule, the mood tends to favour wines and spirits, and the customers are a bit older and more local than those found in cafés.

The cheapest type of beer is **bottled beer**, which costs 20–30kr for a third of a litre, and is less potent than so-called **gold beer** (*Guldøl* or *Elefantøl*). **Draught beer** (*fadøl*) is more expensive, with a quarter of a litre costing 18–40kr, half a litre as much as 80kr. It's a touch weaker than both types of bottled beer, but tastes fresher and is more popular. All Danish beer is lager-style, the most common brands being Carlsberg and Tuborg, and although a number of towns have their own locally brewed rivals, you'll need a finely tuned palate to spot much difference between them. One you will notice the taste of is Lys Pilsner, a very low-alcohol lager.

Most international **wines and spirits** are widely available, a shot of the hard stuff costing 20–40kr in a bar, a glass of wine upwards of 30kr. While in the country, you should investigate the many varieties of the schnapps-like **Akvavit**, which Danes consume as eagerly as beer, especially with meals; more than two or three turn most non-Danes pale. A tasty relative is the gloriously spicy and strong Gammel Dansk Bitter Dram – Akvavit-based but made with bitters, which tends to be drunk at breakfast time or as a pick-me-up during the day. Note that in January 2007, smoking was banned in many larger cafés, bars and restaurants, though some are allowed to set up special sections for smoking patrons.

The media

For a country of its size, Denmark has an impressive number of newspapers and freesheets. Denmark's 35 national newspapers tend to offer predominantly serious and in-depth coverage of worthy issues, and can't help but seem a little anachronistic when compared to the tabloid dominance elsewhere in Europe. Danish TV is dominated by subtitled imports, but the country's radio stations do offer the chance to take in plenty of Danish music.

The **English-language** *Copenhagen Post* (ⓦwww.copenhagenpost.dk), covers domestic issues and has an in-depth listings section covering events of interest to non-Danish speakers; it comes out every Friday and costs 15kr.

If you can read Danish, your choices among the main daily **newspapers** (each costing 15–22kr) are *Politiken*, a reasonably impartial broadsheet with strong arts features; the conservative/centrist *Berlingske Tidende*; *Kristeligt Dagblad*, a Christian paper; *Jyllands-Posten*, a well-respected Jutland-based right-wing paper; and *Information*, left-wing and intellectual.

The weekly *Weekendavisen*, published on Thursdays, has excellent background features. You'll find excellent **entertainment listings** in both *Jyllands-Posten* and *Politiken*, and every Thursday *Information* has a section devoted to listings, too. The free Danish **rock music** paper, the monthly *Gaffa*, lists most of the bigger shows, and innumerable similar regional papers do the same for their areas – find them in cafés, record shops and the like. In Copenhagen, overseas newspapers are sold at the Magasin du Nord department store, Illum department store, the stall on the eastern side of Rådhuspladsen, and newsagents along Strøget and in newsagents in the central station, which also stock foreign magazines. Most UK and US weekday titles cost 25–40kr and are available the day after publication. The **major foreign newspapers** are sold in all main towns.

If you're not a Danish speaker, the only thing you'll be able to understand is a very short "News In English" programme weekdays at 10.30am, 5.05pm and 10pm on Radio Denmark International (1062MHz). With television, though, you might have a bit more luck. Aside from the four national channels – DR1, DR2, TV2 and TV2 Zulu – cable channels in Denmark are all commercial and prolific in American sitcoms and soaps (usually with Danish subtitles). If you're staying in a hotel, or a youth hostel with a TV room, you may also have the option of German and Swedish channels – plus several dozen cable and satellite stations.

Travel essentials

Costs

Costs for virtually everything – eating, sleeping, travelling and entertainment – are **lower** in Denmark than in any other Scandinavian country.

If you stay in youth hostels or campsites and don't eat out, it's possible to get by on £25/US$35/€28 per day. Otherwise, staying in inexpensive hotels, moving around the country visiting museums, eating in a restaurant each day and buying a few snacks and going for a drink in the evening, you can expect to spend a minimum of £40–50/US$55–70/€45–55 per day. Going up a notch, staying in a mid-range hotel, eating lunch and dinner at restaurants, doing a couple of museums and maybe catching a club will set you back substantially more – often a minimum of £80–100/US$110–140/€90–115 per day.

Internet

Internet access in Denmark is ubiquitous, and free at most libraries (though you may have to book a one-hour slot in advance), while **internet cafés** can be found in almost all towns, and charge 20–30kr per hour. Larger airports such as Copenhagen and Billund, train stations and shopping malls also have self-service internet cafés. Most tourist-oriented hotels, hostels and campsites have dedicated rooms with several broadband-connected computers, while business-class hotels and many cafés and restaurants – such as the countrywide Baresso Coffee – have free wi-fi.

Mail

Denmark's national **post** is fast and efficient – domestically, anything you post is almost certain to arrive within two days. Stamps are sold at newsagents and post offices, most of which are open Monday to Friday 9.30am to 5pm, Saturday 9.30am to 1pm, with reduced hours in smaller communities. Mail under 50g costs 7.50kr to other parts of Europe, and 8.50kr to the rest of the world. **Poste restante** is available at any post office, and many hotels, youth hostels and campsites will hold mail ahead of your arrival.

Money

Danish currency is the **krone** (plural kroner), made up of 100 øre, and comes in notes of 1000kr, 500kr, 200kr, 100kr and 50kr, and coins of 20kr, 10kr, 5kr, 2kr, 1kr, 50øre and 25øre.

At the time of writing, the **exchange rate** was 8.30kr to one pound sterling; 5.95kr to one US dollar; 4.60kr to one Canadian dollar; 3.79kr to one Australian dollar; 2.94kr to one New Zealand dollar and 7.45kr to one euro.

Banks are plentiful, and the easiest place to change traveller's cheques and foreign cash; there's a uniform commission of 30kr per transaction, so change as much as is feasible in one go. Most international airports, train stations and ferry ports have late-opening exchange facilities. The cheapest means of withdrawing cash is at an **ATM**, which offers cash advances on credit and debit cards in local currency (check with your home bank for associated charges).

Opening hours and public holidays

Opening hours are Mon–Thurs 10am–5.30pm, Fri 10am–6pm or 7pm, Sat 9am–1pm or 2pm, Sun closed. Supermarkets in larger towns open a bit later. On the first Saturday of the month shops stay open until 5pm.

On the following days, all shops and banks are closed, while public transport and many museums run to Sunday schedules: January 1, Maundy Thursday, Good Friday, Easter Monday, Common Prayers Day (fourth Friday after Easter), Ascension Day (fortieth day after Easter), Whit Monday (seventh Monday after Easter), Labour Day (the afternoon of May 1 – unofficial, but observed by most work places), Constitution Day (June 5), Christmas Eve (afternoon only), Christmas Day and Boxing Day.

Phones

Danish **public telephones** come in two forms. Coin-operated ones are white and require a minimum of 3kr for a local call (the machines irritatingly swallow one of the coins if the number is engaged), and 5kr to go international; cards for the blue cardphones come in denominations of 30kr, 50kr and 100kr and work out a little cheaper – they're sold in newsagents and post offices. Most hotel rooms have a phone but it's much cheaper to make calls from the public phone at reception. Youth hostels and campsites generally have public phones; if not, the warden will probably let you use the house one for a payphone fee. Otherwise, you should be able to use your mobile phone in Denmark if you've notified your carrier that you'll be travelling abroad (North American

users will need a tri-band phone). Given the high roaming charges though, it often pays to invest in a Danish SIM card for use in your phone; 99kr gets you a Danish number plus about forty minutes of domestic calling time, and top-up cards can be bought in supermarkets, kiosks and phone shops.

Calling Denmark from abroad, the **international code** is ☏45; codes for international calls from Denmark are given on p.43. To make a **collect international call**, dial ☏80 30 40 00 for the operator and ask to be connected to the operator in your own country, who will then put through the collect call – full instructions for this "Country Direct" system are displayed in phone booths, and you can dial ☏80 60 40 50 for free assistance. Be warned that **directory enquiries** (international ☏113, domestic ☏118) start at an exorbitant 8kr per minute, so try to use a phone book (found in public phone booths) or the online (Danish-language) yellow pages, ⓦwww .degulesider.dk.

Shops and markets

An especially tight budget may well leave you dependent on **shopping for food**. Brugsen, Føtex and Irma are the most commonly found **supermarkets** (usually open Mon–Fri 9am–5.30pm, later on Thurs & Fri, Sat 9am–5pm), and there's little difference in price between them. You'll also come across Aldi, Netto and Fakta, which are cheaper but more chaotic and with less choice. Smaller supermarkets may be open shorter hours, especially on Saturdays, when they tend to close at 1 or 2pm except on the first Saturday of the month. Late-night shopping is generally impossible, although in bigger towns, the DSB supermarket at the train station is likely to be open until midnight. The best spots for fresh fruit and veg are the Saturday and (sometimes) Wednesday **markets** held in most towns. A tax of 25 percent is added to almost everything you'll buy – but it's always included in the marked price.

Tipping

Unless you need porters to help carry your luggage, you'll never be expected to tip – restaurant bills include a fifteen percent service charge.

> In an **emergency**, dial ☏**112** from any phone box for a fast free connection to the emergency services.

1.1

Zealand

As the largest of Denmark's islands and the home of its capital, Zealand (Sjælland) is the country's most important – and most visited – region. Though not an especially big city, Copenhagen dominates much of the island; the nearby towns, while far from being drab suburbia, tend inevitably to be dormitory territory. Only much further away, towards the west and south, does the pace become more provincial.

It would be perverse to come to Zealand and not visit **Copenhagen**, easily the most extroverted and cosmopolitan place in the country. A 2008 issue of *Monocle* magazine didn't name Copenhagen the best city in the world to live in for nothing, and it's as lively by night as it is by day, with jazz clubs, wine bars and artsy lounges that are quickly becoming known as some of the hippest spots in Europe. That being said, once you've spent some time in the capital it's well worth making at least a brief journey into the country to see how varied the rest of Zealand can be. Woods and expansive parklands appear almost as soon as you leave the city, and once you've had your nature fix the swiftness of the metropolitan transport network, which covers almost half the island, means that you can easily be back in the capital in time for an evening cocktail.

North of Copenhagen, the coastal road passes the outstanding modern art museum of **Louisiana** and the absorbing Karen Blixen museum at **Rungsted** before reaching **Helsingør**, site of the renowned **Kronborg Slot**, better known as Elsinore Castle. Though undeniably impressive, it nevertheless quite unfairly steals the spotlight from **Frederiksborg Slot**, an even more eye-catching royal castle in nearby **Hillerød**. West of Copenhagen on the main route to Funen is **Roskilde**, a former capital with an extravagant cathedral that's still the last resting place for Danish monarchs. With a choice location on the Roskilde fjord, it's home to one of Europe's best summertime rock festivals. South of Copenhagen, at the end of the urban S-train system, is **Køge**, which – beyond the industrial sites that flank it – has a well-preserved medieval centre and long, sandy beaches lining its bay.

Further out from the expanse of Copenhagen, central Zealand's towns are appreciably smaller, more scattered and far less full of either commuters or day-trippers. **Ringsted**, plumb in the heart of the island, is another one-time capital, a fact recalled by the twelfth- and thirteenth-century royal tombs in its church. Further south, **Næstved**, surrounded by lush countryside, is the jumping-off point for three smaller islands just off the coast: **Lolland**, **Falster** and **Møn**. Each of these is busy during the summer, but outside high season you'll find them green and peaceful, with Lolland offering a leisurely backdoor route, via Langeland, to Funen.

Not part of Zealand, but conveniently reached via the Øresunds Link from Copenhagen, is the island of **Bornholm**. A sunny slab of granite in the Baltic, it's home to a few small fishing communities, some fine beaches and an unusual history. If you're looking to engage in that beloved Danish pasttime of leisurely cycling, or if you're heading for Sweden – the island is nearer Sweden than Denmark, with regular ferry connections to both countries – Bornholm is the perfect detour.

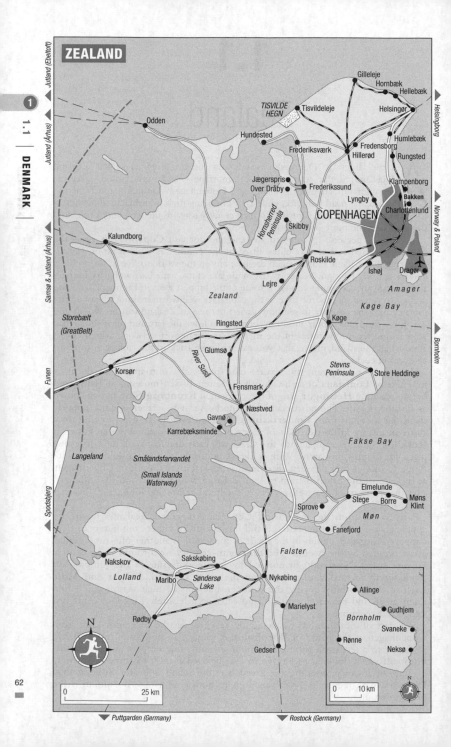

Copenhagen

As any Dane will tell you, **COPENHAGEN** is no introduction to Denmark; indeed, a greater contrast with the sleepy pastoralism of the rest of the country would be hard to find. Despite this, the city completely dominates Denmark: it's the seat of all the nation's institutions – political, financial and artistic – and provides the driving force for social reforms. Copenhagen is also Scandinavia's most affordable capital, and one of Europe's most user-friendly cities: small and welcoming, it's a place where people rather than cars set the pace, as evidenced by the multitude of pavement cafés and the number of thoroughfares that have been given over to pedestrians. During the white nights of summer, when it barely gets dark, the capital is filled with cosmopolitan street entertainment, with bands playing world-class jazz on temporary outdoor stages throughought the city. At other times of the year, cosy restaurants, stylish bars and intimate clubs give Copenhagen arguably the most cutting-edge nightlife in Scandinavia. The history museums and galleries of Danish and international art, as well as a worthy batch of smaller collections, shouldn't be overlooked, either. If you're heading north into Scandinavia's less populated (and pricier) reaches, you'd certainly be wise to spend a few days living it up in Copenhagen first.

Copenhagen has been Denmark's capital since 1443, but there was no more than a tiny fishing settlement here until the twelfth century, when Bishop Absalon oversaw the building of a castle on the site of the present Christiansborg. The settlement's prosperity grew after Erik of Pomerania granted it special privileges and imposed the Sound Toll on vessels passing through the Øresund strait, and the city eventually became the Baltic's principal harbour, earning the name København ("merchant's port"). A century later, Christian IV began the building programme that was the basis of the modern city: up went Rosenborg Slot, Børsen, Rundetårnet and the districts of Nyboder and Christianshavn, while in 1669 Frederik III graced the city with its first royal palace, Amalienborg, built for his queen, Sophie Amalie. These structures remain the highest points in what is a refreshingly low skyline. The beautiful golden-age city that evolved around them is largely from the early nineteenth century, rebuilt after three devastating and all-consuming fires.

This is an easy city to get around: you probably won't need to need to venture far from the central section, still largely hemmed in by the medieval ramparts (now a series of parks), which is where you're likely to spend most of your time.

Arrival, information and city transport

Whatever means you use to get to Copenhagen, you'll be within easy reach of the centre when you arrive. **Trains** pull into the central station (Hovedbanegården), near Vesterbrogade, while **long-distance buses** from abroad stop at DGI-byen on Ingerslevsgade behind the central station. The frequent Malmø bus also stops at various other points throughout the city including Kongens Nytorv, Nørreport and Rådhuspladsen. Buses from other parts of Denmark – Århus, Aalborg, Silkeborg, Thisted and Fjerritslev – stop at Valby station, a short S-train ride from the centre. Buses from Bornholm stop at the central station. **Ferries** from Bornholm dock at Køge Harbour, an S-train ride (line A and E) from the centre. Those from Norway and Poland dock at Dampfærgevej to the north of town; take bus #26 into the centre.

Modern **Kastrup airport**, 8km southeast of the city on the eastern edge of the island of Amager, is the air hub of Scandinavia and your most likely point of entry. Getting into Copenhagen from here couldn't be easier with two of the fastest airport-to-city train links in Europe: directly to the central station (13min) six times an hour, reduced to one an hour (16min before the hour) from midnight to 5am; and a new Metro link to Nørreport Station (15min) every five minutes, running every fifteen minutes at night. Both cost 30kr during the day and 60kr between 1 and 5am.

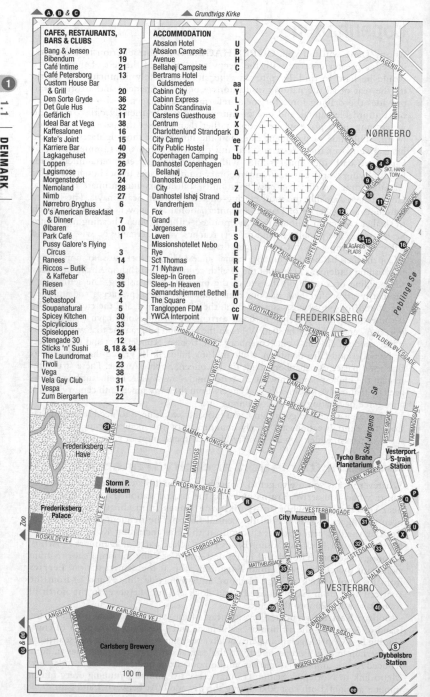

CAFES, RESTAURANTS, BARS & CLUBS

Bang & Jensen	37
Bibendum	19
Café Intime	21
Café Petersborg	13
Custom House Bar & Grill	20
Den Sorte Gryde	36
Det Gule Hus	32
Gefärlich	11
Ideal Bar at Vega	38
Kaffesalonen	16
Kate's Joint	15
Karriere Bar	40
Lagkagehuset	29
Loppen	26
Løgismose	27
Morgenstedet	24
Nemoland	28
Nimb	27
Nørrebro Bryghus	6
O's American Breakfast & Dinner	7
Ølbaren	10
Park Café	1
Pussy Galore's Flying Circus	3
Ranees	14
Riccos – Butik & Kaffebar	39
Riesen	35
Rust	2
Sebastopol	4
Soupanatural	5
Spicey Kitchen	30
Spicylicious	33
Spiseloppen	25
Stengade 30	12
Sticks 'n' Sushi	8, 18 & 34
The Laundromat	9
Tivoli	23
Vega	38
Vela Gay Club	31
Vespa	17
Zum Biergarten	22

ACCOMMODATION

Absalon Hotel	U
Absalon Campsite	B
Avenue	H
Bellahøj Campsite	C
Bertrams Hotel Guldsmeden	aa
Cabinn City	Y
Cabinn Express	L
Cabinn Scandinavia	J
Carstens Guesthouse	V
Centrum	X
Charlottenlund Strandpark	D
City Camp	ee
City Public Hostel	T
Copenhagen Camping	bb
Danhostel Copenhagen Bellahøj	A
Danhostel Copenhagen City	Z
Danhostel Ishøj Strand Vandrerhjem	dd
Fox	N
Grand	P
Jørgensens	I
Løven	S
Missionshotellet Nebo	Q
Rye	E
Sct Thomas	R
71 Nyhavn	K
Sleep-In Green	F
Sleep-In Heaven	G
Sømandshjemmet Bethel	M
The Square	O
Tangloppen FDM	cc
YWCA Interpoint	W

Grundtvigs Kirke

A, B & C

NØRREBRO

SKT. HANS TORV

FREDERIKSBERG

Frederiksberg Have

Storm P. Museum

Frederiksberg Palace

Zoo

ROSKILDEVEJ

Carlsberg Brewery

NY CARLSBERG VEJ

LANGGADE

Tycho Brahe Planetarium

Vesterport S-train Station

City Museum

VESTERBROGADE

VESTERBRO

Dybbølsbro Station

0   100 m

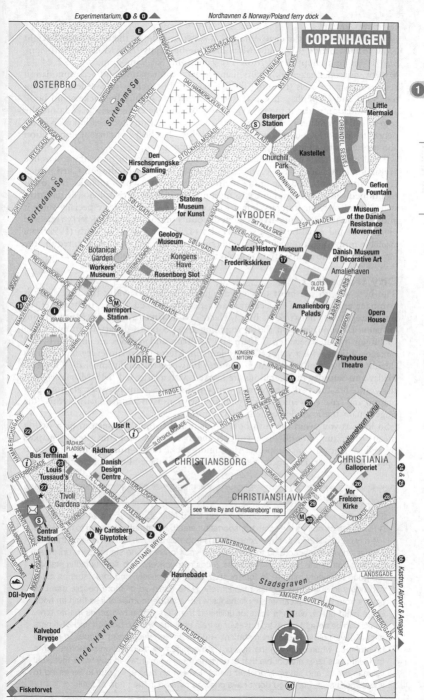

COPENHAGEN

ØSTERBRO

Sortedams Sø

Little Mermaid

Østerport Station

Kastellet

Churchill Park

Gefion Fountain

Den Hirschsprungske Samling

Statens Museum for Kunst

NYBODER

Museum of the Danish Resistance Movement

Geology Museum

Medical History Museum

Danish Museum of Decorative Art

Kongens Have

Amaliehaven

Botanical Garden

Frederikskirken

Workers' Museum

Rosenborg Slot

Amalienborg Palads

Opera House

Nørreport Station

INDRE BY

ISRAELSPLADS

KØBMAGERGADE

Playhouse Theatre

STRØGET

KONGENS NYTORV

NYHAVN

Use It

HOLMENS

CHRISTIANSHAVN KANAL

CHRISTIANIA

Galloperiet

Bus Terminal

Rådhus

Danish Design Centre

CHRISTIANSBORG

CHRISTIANSHAVN

Louis Tussaud's

Vor Frelsers Kirke

Tivoli Gardens

see 'Indre By and Christiansborg' map

Central Station

Ny Carlsberg Glyptotek

LANGEBROGADE

DGI-byen

Haunebådet

Stadsgraven

AMAGER BOULEVARD

LANDSGADE

Kalvebod Brygge

Inder Havnen

N

Fisketorvet

65

Information

Across the road from the central station at Vesterbrogade 4a, the Copenhagen Right Now **tourist office** (May–June Mon–Sat 9am–6pm; July–Aug Mon–Sat 9am–8pm, Sun 10am–6pm; Sept–April Mon–Fri 9am–4pm, Sat 9am–2pm; ☎70 22 24 42, ⊛www.visitcopenhagen.dk) offers maps, general information and accommodation reservations for hotels (booking fee 100kr) plus bus tickets to Sweden (booking fee 30kr) and Copenhagen Cards (see below). You can buy bus tickets and book accommodation without the fee via the row of available computers locked onto the tourist office website. Next to these, so-called Ispot computers are linked permanently to ⊛ispot.wonderfulcopenhagen.dk which has heaps of current information about restaurants, nightlife, sightseeing and shopping.

If you plan to visit many museums, either in Copenhagen or in nearby towns like Helsingør, Roskilde and Køge, you might want to buy a **Copenhagen Card**, which is valid for transport on the entire metropolitan system (which includes the towns mentioned above) and gives entry to most museums in the area. Obviously its worth will depend on your itinerary, but it can certainly save money – especially since it also gets you ten to twenty-five percent discounts on some car rental, ferry rides and guided bus and canal boat tours. Three-day (429kr) and 24-hour cards (199kr) are available from tourist offices, hotels and travel agents in the metropolitan region, the airport, and at most larger train stations throughout the country.

City transport

The best way to see most of Copenhagen is simply to **walk**: the inner city is compact and much of the central area pedestrianized. There is, however, an integrated zonal network of buses, electric **S-trains** (*S-tog*) and **Metro** trains covering Copenhagen and the surrounding areas. S-trains depart about every five to fifteen minutes between 5.30am and 12.30am and stations are marked by red hexagonal signs with a yellow "S" inside them. Metro trains run every few minutes during the day and every fifteen minutes between midnight and 5am Thursday, Friday and Saturday night; stations are marked with a large red "M". Most useful for the centre are the two Metro lines – they cross the S-train network at Nørreport Station and have convenient stops such as Christianshavn and Kongens Nytorv (the huge square/traffic circle beside Nyhavn canal).

So long as you avoid the rush hour (7–9am and 5–6pm), **buses** can be a swifter means of getting around once you get the hang of finding the stops – marked by yellow placards on signposts. After midnight a **night-bus** system comes into operation with services once or twice an hour; numbers always end with "N" and

---

Transport tickets

The best ticket option after a **Copenhagen Card** (see above) or the **24-timer ticket** (115kr) – which covers the same transportation area but without admission to museums – is a two-zone (125kr) or three-zone (165kr) **klippekort**, which has ten stamps that you cancel individually according to the length of your journey; one stamp gives unlimited transfers within one hour in two or three zones respectively. Two simultaneous stamps are good for ninety minutes in four or six zones respectively, and three stamps allow two hours in six or nine zones respectively. Note that two or more people can use tickets from the same carnet simultaneously. For a single journey of less than an hour, use a **billet** (20kr), which is valid for unlimited transfers within two zones in that time. *Billets* can be bought on board buses or at train stations, while *klippekort* and 24-timers are only available at bus or train stations and Movia Kortsalg kiosks; *klippekort* should be stamped when boarding the bus or via machines on train station platforms. Note that night-bus fares are double that of daytime rates (you'll have to buy twice the usual value in *billets*, and stamp *klippekort* twice). Except on buses, it's rare to be asked to show your ticket, but if you don't have one you face an instant **fine** of 500kr.

Guided tours

Aside from the usual selection of guided bus tours of the city – a full list and booking is available through tourist information (see p.66) – the two most noteworthy alternatives are City Safari (℡33 23 94 90, ⓦwww.citysafari.dk) with three-hour **guided bike tours** of the city, "Historic Copenhagen" at 1.30pm and "Copenhagen by Night" at 8pm, both for 250kr (including bike); and the enjoyable guided **kayak tours** with Kajak Ole (℡40 50 40 06, ⓦwww.kajakole.dk) departing from behind the Opera House (1.5hr 245kr; 2hr 295kr; 3hr 345kr). Booking is essential for both.

Boat tours leave frequently from Gammel Strand and Nyhavn and sail around the canals and harbour. Cheapest is Netto-Bådene (℡32 54 41 02, ⓦwww.havnerundfart.dk), which offers one-hour tours for 30kr that pass both Nyhavn and Christianshavn. DFDS Canal Tours (℡32 96 30 00, ⓦwww.canal-tours.dk) has two one-hour options in comfortable covered boats which go to either Nyhavn or Christianshavn; however, at 60kr, you'll get more for your money with Netto-Bådene. DFDS also run three **waterbuses**, one going east to the Trekroner fort and island, one going west to the new Fisketorvet shopping complex and one going to Christianshavn and the Opera House; they stop 12–15 times on the way. An unlimited-use day ticket costs 50kr, and a single trip 35kr.

are marked on the yellow bus stop placards. They charge double the daytime rates. To get across Inner Havnen to Christianshavn, or travel along the harbourfront, you can use the yellow **harbour bus** boats which have five stops between Nordre Toldbod (near the Little Mermaid) and the Royal Library, and several in Christianshavn including the Opera House.

The basic **taxi** fare within Copenhagen is generally a flat starting fare of 24kr (37kr if you book it in advance) plus 11.50kr per kilometre travelled (12.50kr after 4pm and at weekends) – only usually worthwhile if several people are sharing. There's a taxi rank outside the central station, or phone Taxamotor (℡38 10 10 10 for a cab, ℡35 39 35 35 for a minibus). Otherwise, just hail a cab in the street that's showing a green Fri sign on top. A fun alternative are the **cycle taxis** which you can hail just like regular taxis, or pick up at key transport points. Carrying a maximum of two people, these rickshaw-type bikes charge an initial fare of 40kr, then 4kr for each additional minute.

Getting around under your own steam **by bike** is perhaps the best way of exploring the city. A good-value place to rent bikes is at Københavns Cyklebørs, Gothersgade 157 (℡33 14 07 17, ⓦwww.cykelboersen.dk) where rates start at 60kr per day or 270kr per week, and there's a refundable deposit of 200kr. Otherwise Københavns Cykler, by the back (Istedgade) entrance to the central station at Reventlowsgade 11 (℡33 33 86 13, ⓦwww.copenhagen-bikes.dk) rents bikes from 75kr per day or 350kr per week, plus a 500kr deposit. Also bear in mind the free **City Bike scheme** (mid-April to early Nov; ⓦwww.bycyklen.dk), whereby over two thousand free bikes are scattered about the city at train stations and other busy locations; a refundable 20kr deposit unlocks one. The rules are simple: leave the bike in a rack when you've finished with it (you get your coin back automatically as you re-lock the bike), or just leave it out somewhere and someone else will happily return it and pocket the coin. Don't secure one with your own lock and don't take one outside the city limits (the old rampart lakes mark the border) or you risk a fine of up to 1000kr. If you want to cycle after dark, it's a good idea to get yourself some lights as you'll be fined if you're caught without.

Accommodation

Whether it's a hostel bed or a luxury hotel suite, **accommodation** isn't always easy to come by in Copenhagen, especially if you're arriving late in the day, or during

▲ Cycling in Copenhagen

July and August (the busiest time of year) when it's essential to book in advance. If you arrive without a reservation or are trying to get a bed in the busy summer season, the Copenhagen Right Now tourist information (see p.66) will find you a **hotel** room or a **private room** in someone's home, although queues for this service can be lengthy during high season, and it sets you back 100kr. Private rooms cost between 425kr and 700kr and you may be able to pay extra to your hosts for breakfast. You can also book hotel and private rooms in advance for free using the tourist office website (ⓦwww.bookcopenhagen.dk) or phone line (☎70 22 24 42).

Note that we list a couple of gay- and lesbian-friendly accommodation options on p.89, and that all the places listed below are in the city centre unless otherwise stated, and are marked on the Copenhagen map (pp.64–65).

Hotels

You'll seldom find a grotty **hotel** in Copenhagen, though the cheaper ones often forgo the pleasures of private bathroom and TV. Prices almost always include **breakfast** (unless otherwise stated, it's included in the rates for all places listed below).

A couple of the places below offer discounts at the weekend; where this is the case, we've given two price codes, separated by a forward slash.

Absalon Helgolandsgade 15, Vesterbro ☎33 24 22 11, ⓦwww.absalon-hotel.dk. Very large, quiet and relaxing family-run hotel two blocks from the central station with exceptionally helpful staff and rooms that run the gamut from rock-bottom-priced singles with shared facilities to plush suites with extra amenities such as free movies and mini bars. ❸/❺

Avenue Åboulevard 29, Frederiksberg ☎35 37 31 11, ⓦwww.avenuehotel.dk. Comfortable yet stylish place, on a main suburban boulevard a short Metro ride from the centre, with spacious rooms offering free wireless internet and free parking. During summer a scrumptious breakfast buffet is served outdoors on a lovely patio. Take the Metro to Forum or bus #12, #68 or #69 from the central station. ❺

Bertrams Hotel Guldsmeden Vesterbrogade 107, Vesterbro ☎33 25 04 05 ⓦwww.hotelguldsmeden.dk. Smart, excellently designed rooms at this central Vesterbro standby are done up with colonial-style furnishings –

four-poster cherry beds, deep oak desks, ornate curtains – with flat-screen TVs that give a modern finish. The same group operates two similarly appointed properties nearby at Vesterbrogade 66 and Helgolandsgade 11. ❻

Cabinn City Mitchellsgade 14, Indre By ☎ 33 46 16 16; **Cabinn Express** Danasvej 32, Frederiksberg ☎ 33 21 04 00; and **Cabinn Scandinavia** Vodroffsvej 57, Frederiksberg ☎ 35 36 11 11; ⓦ www.cabinn.com. Inspired by cabins on the Oslo ferry, the small rooms, flip-up tables and tiny showers here may make you feel like a passenger on an overnight boat, but they're clean and safe, with free internet, pleasant staff and unbeatable prices. Breakfast (50kr) is not included. The two Frederiksberg branches are reached by bus #29 from Rådhuspladsen, and are within walking distance of Forum Metro Station. *Cabinn City* is a 5min walk from the central station. ❸

Centrum Helgolandsgade 14, Vesterbro ☎ 33 31 31 11, ⓦ www.dgi-byen.com. Set within the modern DGI-byen complex, this trendy option is ideally placed for party-goers and late-nighters in Vesterbro. There are black sofas in the lobby, while the functional rooms are all whites, creams and wooden fittings. Guests get free access to the DGI-byen centre, which has pools and saunas. ❺

City Peder Skramsgade 24, Indre By ☎ 33 13 06 66, ⓦ www.hotelcity.dk. Environmentally friendly Best Western hotel serving lush organic breakfasts and offering free wireless internet throughout. Set in the central Nyhavn area, though you pay for the location. Bus #550S from the central station or a short walk from Kongens Nytorv Metro. ❹/❻

🏃 **Fox** Jarmer Plads 3 ☎ 33 95 07 70 55, ⓦ www.foxhotel.dk. A few minutes by bus #6A from the central station, this outstandingly funky so-called lifestyle hotel has 61 rooms individually decorated by street artists and young designers from all over the world and almost guaranteed to surprise. Breakfast (125kr) is not included. ❹

Grand Vesterbrogade 9A, Vesterbro ☎ 33 27 69 00, ⓦ www.grandhotel.dk. Very popular with British and American package travellers and European businessmen, this classically styled hotel is close to Tivoli Gardens and the central station. Gets very busy in the summer, but you can usually find a room last minute. ❹

Løven Vesterbrogade 30, Vesterbro ☎ 33 79 67 20, ⓦ www.loeven.dk. Ignore the anonymous, unkempt entrance and press on to settle down in one of central Copenhagen's real bargains, with no-frills accommodation in plain-ish but pleasantly decorated rooms (mostly en suite) sleeping up to five. Breakfast isn't included, but there's a large

and well-equipped communal kitchen. Ask for a room facing the courtyard. ❷

Missionshotellet Nebo Istedgade 6, Vesterbro ☎ 33 21 12 17, ⓦ www.nebo.dk. Small, clean and friendly, this former Christian mission is less of a deal than it used to be, but still good in a pinch. Rooms are done up with predictable oak furnishings and folksy art on the walls. The cheapest rooms have shared facilities. Parking 50kr per day. ❸

🏃 **Rye** Ryesgade 115, Østerbro ☎ 35 26 52 10, ⓦ www.hotelrye.dk. Small cosy hotel set in a former nursing home near Fælledparken and the lakes. It's a homely place spread over two floors with rooms sharing bathroom facilities (they all come equipped with slippers and house-coat). Bus #6A from Rådhuspladsen or the central station. ❸

🏃 **Sct Thomas** Frederiksberg Allé 7, Frederiksberg ☎ 33 21 64 64, ⓦ www.hotelsctthomas.dk. A brand-spanking-new renovation in the city's leafy old theatre district. The decor here has gone boutique, while the prices have stayed the same great value. Rooms vary in size and style – some share toilets, others all bathroom facilities – and there's a swanky breakfast space, free wi-fi and very welcoming staff. Bike hire for 100kr a day. Bus #6A from the central station and Rådhuspladsen.

71 Nyhavn Nyhavn 71, Indre By ☎ 33 43 62 00, ⓦ www.71nyhavnhotel.com. Nineteenth-century warehouse hotel at the inner harbour end of the famous Nyhavn canal which is lined with good restaurants and lively throughout the summer. Also only a stone's throw from the new Play House. The 84 smallish rooms are quaint, with wooden beams and loads of character, though they come at a price and breakfast is not included. Bus #29 from Vesterport station or a 5min walk from Kongens Nytorv Metro station. ❻

Sømandshjemmet Bethel Nyhavn 22, Indre By ☎ 33 13 03 70, ⓦ www.hotel-bethel.dk. Still aimed at professional sailors (visiting mariners get a 10 percent discount), this central hotel is perfectly located for a night on the town. The bare and basic rooms are nothing to write home about, but you're paying for the location – the views from the rooms are fantastic – and there's wireless internet. Bus #19 or Kongens Nytorv Metro station. ❸

The Square Rådhuspladsen 14 ☎ 33 38 12 00, ⓦ www.thesquare.dk. On the main city square, this stylish design hotel could hardly be more central (hence no parking). The sleek, minimalistic rooms are not huge but they have all the essentials, including a well-stocked mini bar and free high-speed internet. ❻

Hostels and sleep-ins

Copenhagen has an extensive selection of central and good-quality **hostels** and **sleep-ins**, which are ideal for those on a budget – a dormitory bed costs 95–215kr, and doubles around 600kr. Space is only likely to be a problem in the peak summer months (June–Aug), when you should call ahead or turn up as early as possible on the day you want to stay.

City Public Hostel Absalonsgade 8, Vesterbro ☎33 31 20 70, ⊛www.citypublichostel.dk. Conveniently situated a 10min walk from the central station next to the City Museum. There are several dorm rooms (beds 110–150kr depending on room size), breakfast for 30kr, free wi-fi, no curfew, a kitchen with a charcoal grill and an easygoing vibe. Buses #6A and #26 stop close by. Open May to mid-Aug.

Danhostel Copenhagen Bellahøj Herbergvejen 8, Brønshøj ☎38 28 97 15, ⊛www.copenhagen hostel.dk. In a peaceful lakeside setting in a distant residential part of the city, this HI hostel is more homely than its rivals, offering cheap beds (140kr) in large dorms (4- 6- and 14-beds). Reception is open 24hr and there's no curfew, although there's a dormitory lockout from 10am–1pm. In addition there's free safe parking, and the breakfast buffet is 55kr. Simple to reach, too: a 15min ride from the city centre on bus #2A (nightbus #82N). Open Feb to Dec.

Danhostel Copenhagen City H.C. Andersens Boulevard 50, Indre By ☎33 11 85 85, ⊛www.danhostel.dk. Hardly what you'd expect from an HI hostel, with sleek GUBI designer furniture, and views of the harbour and the green copper spires of the city; this place exceeds all expectations. With 1020 beds (145kr) in 4- to 8-bed rooms, it prides itself on being the largest city hostel in Europe. Breakfast buffet 65kr and free wireless internet. A short walk from the central station or bus #5A. No curfew and open all year.

Danhostel Copenhagen Downtown Vandkunsten 5 ☎32 52 29 08, ⊛www.copenhagendowntown .com. Excellent new HI hostel in the heart of the old city near a host of popular music venues and bars. The tidy rooms come in 2-, 3-, 4-, 8- and 10-bed versions, some with en-suite bathrooms, some sharing. Dorm beds cost 185kr during the week and 215kr at weekends. At ❷ to ❸, doubles cost 100kr less if you're sharing a bathroom. There's free wireless internet throughout and the reception is open 24hr. Open all year.

Danhostel Ishøj Strand Vandrerhjem Ishøj Strandvej 13, Ishøj ☎43 53 50 15,

⊛www.ishojhostel.dk. Family friendly HI hostel next to beautiful Køge beach and the Arken modern art gallery, with a few doubles (❷) as well as dorm beds July to mid-Sept (175kr). Thirty minutes from the centre on A, A+ or E line S-trains, then bus #300S. Breakfast buffet 59kr and check-in 2–6pm. Open all year.

Jørgensens Rømersgade 11, Indre By ☎33 13 81 86, ⊛www.hoteljoergensen.dk. A stone's throw from Nørreport station on Israels Plads, this was the city's first gay hotel in the 1980s and is now popular with both gay and straight travellers (though there's an upper age limit of 35). Predominantly dormitory accommodation (6-, 9- and 12-bed rooms; beds 150kr), plus a few basic doubles (❸), most with shared bathrooms. Breakfast included. Open all year.

Sleep-In Green Ravnsborggade 18, Nørrebro ☎35 37 77 77, ⊛www.sleep-in-green.dk. Eco-conscious hostel in hip Nørrebro overlooking a pretty interior courtyard. Also a training school for organic production; the all-student staff run the hostel as part of their course during the summer break. 8-, 20- and 38- bed bright rooms (120kr) with extra charges for bedding (30kr), and free wireless internet. There's a noon–4pm lockout. Bus #5A, #81N or #84N. 100kr. Open mid-May to Oct.

Sleep-In Heaven 7th floor, Struenseegade 7, Nørrebro ☎35 35 46 48, ⊛www.sleepinheaven .com. Popular hostel outside the city centre with 4-, 8 -and 14-bed dorms (130kr) and a 16–35 age limit. Special features include pool table, free lockers, free wireless internet, a hostel bar and a beer garden; breakfast is 40kr. Buses #12, #69 or #92N. Open all year, no curfew.

YWCA Interpoint Valdemarsgade 15, Vesterbro ☎33 31 15 74, ⊛www.ymca-interpoint.dk. Thirty-six ridiculously cheap dorm beds (95kr) in 4-, 6- and 10-bed rooms with courtyard views and free wi-fi. There are a few downsides: 12.30am curfew, no breakfast and a 15min walk from the central station (or bus #6A). Reception open daily 8–11.30am, 3.30–6pm and 8pm–12.30am. Reservations must be taken before 9pm. Early July to mid-Aug only.

Campsites

Only one of Copenhagen's various **campsites** is close to the city centre, but the others are reached fairly easily by public transport. There's little difference in price among them (60–75kr per person per night, plus up to 40kr per tent per night), nor in facilities: all have laundries, kitchen areas with cookers, television rooms, playgrounds and the like.

If you arrive by campervan, *City Camp* (℡21 42 53 84, Ⓦwww.citycamp.dk) on Vasbygade near the Fisketorvet shopping complex, offers safe parking and basic amenities such as showers and toilet-emptying facilities for 75kr per vehicle per day and 75kr per person. Open June–Aug only.

Absalon Korsdalsvej 132, Rødovre ℡36 41 06 00, Ⓦwww.camping-absalon.dk. Occupying a large field next to a motorway junction and the Brøndby sportsgrounds (2km from Brøndby football stadium), and about 9km to the southwest of the city. Offering facilities for campervans and a few fully kitted (except bedding) cabins sleeping five (275kr). Take S-train B to Brøndbyøster station followed by a signposted 10min walk (nightbus #93N and a 5min walk). Open all year.

Bellahøj Hvidkildevej Brønshøj ℡38 10 11 50, Ⓦwww.bellahoj-camping.dk. Near the Bellahøj youth hostel and next to the city's first high-rise buildings, this is Copenhagen's most central but least comfortable option, with long queues for the showers and cooking facilities. Bus #2A to Bellahøjvej (nightbus #82N). Open June–Aug.

Charlottenlund Strandpark Strandvejen 144B, Charlottenlund ℡39 62 36 88, Ⓦwww.camping copenhagen.dk. Beautifully situated at Charlottenlund Fort and beach, 6km north of the city centre; take bus #14 (nightbus #85N). Open May to mid-Sept.

Copenhagen Camping Bachersmindevej 13, Dragør ℡45 32 94 20 017, Ⓦwww.copenhagen camping.dk. New campsite near the village of Dragør, 12km south of the city centre on the Island of Amager. With Dragør beach on one side and a bird reservation on the other, the setting couldn't be more peaceful. The site includes a range of luxurious cabins sleeping two (515kr) or six (575kr plus 70kr per person). Take bus #350S (nightbus #81N) from Nørreport station or Tårnby Station and it's a 10min walk. Open all year.

Tangloppen FDM Ishøj Havn ℡43 54 07 67, Ⓦwww.fdmcamping.dk/en-GB/campsites /tangloppen. Some 18km south of the city centre, but next to 7km of excellent sandy beaches offering watersports such as windsurfing and sailing. Also offers a range of cabins, some right on the water's edge, others basic without running water, sleeping up to eight and costing from 515kr plus 77kr per person. Take S-train to Ishøj, then a 2min walk or bus #128. Open May to mid-Sept.

The City

Exploring Copenhagen is supremely easy. Most of what you're likely to want to see can be found in the city's relatively small – and effortlessly walkable – centre, between the long inlet of the inner harbour (Inder Havnen) on the east and a semicircular series of lakes on the west. Within this area the divisions are well defined. **Indre By** forms the city's inner core, an intricate maze of streets, squares and alleys whose pleasure lies as much in its general daily bustle as in specific sights. The area **northeast of Indre By**, beyond the major thoroughfare of Gothersgade, is quite different, a boldly proportioned grid-pattern of streets and avenues built to accommodate the dwellings of the Danish nobility in the seventeenth century and reaching a pinnacle of affluence with the palaces of Amalienborg and Rosenborg. The far end of this stretch is protected now, as three hundred years ago, by the Kastellet, which lies within the fetching open spaces of Churchill Park.

Separated by a moat from Indre By, **Christiansborg** is the administrative centre of the whole country, housing the national parliament and government offices, as well as a number of museums and the ruins of Bishop Absalon's original castle. **Christianshavn**, facing Christiansborg across the inner harbour, provides further contrast, with its tightly proportioned and traditionally working-class streets and a pretty waterfront lined by Dutch-style dwellings. A few blocks to the east lies **Christiania**, the "free city" colonized by the young and homeless in the early 1970s, whose alternative society remains an enduring controversy in Danish life – and still merits at least a quick look. **West of the city centre**, Vesterbrogade is the prime thoroughfare, beginning at the carefree delights of the Tivoli Gardens and running to the city fringes at Frederiksberg Have.

Indre By

The natural place from which to begin exploring Indre By (though not actually in it) is the buzzing open space of **Rådhuspladsen**. Here, the **Rådhus**, or City Hall (Mon–Fri 8am–5pm; guided tours in English Mon–Fri 3pm, Sat 10am; 30kr), has a spacious and elegant main hall that retains many of its original early twentieth-century features, not least the sculpted banisters. There's also a lift up to the **belltower** (tours June–Sept Mon–Fri 10am, noon & 2pm, Sat noon; Oct–May Mon–Sat noon; 20kr), but the view over the city from this point isn't particularly impressive. More interesting is **Jens Olsens Verdensur** (Jens Olsen's World Clock: Mon–Fri 8.30am–4.30pm, Sat 10am–1pm; 10kr), in a side room close to the entrance. What looks like a mass of inscrutable dials is in fact an astronomical timepiece which took 27 years to perfect and contains a 570,000-year calendar plotting eclipses of the moon and sun, solar time, local time and various planetary orbits – all with incredible accuracy. Note that the tower, but not the World Clock, is included in the Rådhus tour.

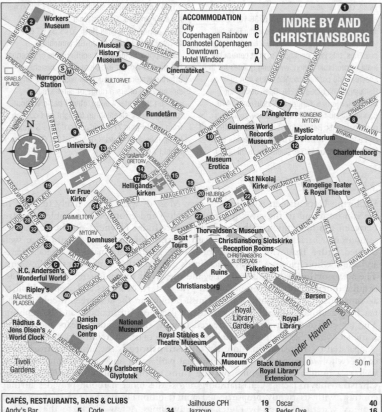

INDRE BY AND CHRISTIANSBORG

ACCOMMODATION
City	B
Copenhagen Rainbow	C
Danhostel Copenhagen	
Downtown	D
Hotel Windsor	A

0   50 m

Joint tickets

The four attractions Ripley's Believe It Or Not!, H.C. Andersen Eventyrhuset, Guinness World Records (see below), and The Mystic Exploratorie (see below) run a **joint ticketing system**. Entry into all four attractions costs 228kr, entry to three between 175kr and 190kr, and two between 114kr and 145kr. Prices vary depending on which three, or two, you choose. Joint tickets can be bought at all four attractions.

At no. 57 Rådhuspladsen, and with an appeal of an entirely different kind, **Ripley's Believe It Or Not!** (mid-June to Aug daily 10am–10pm; Sept to mid-May Mon–Thurs & Sun 10am–6pm, Fri & Sat 10am–8pm; 85kr, see box above about joint ticket prices; ⓦwww.topattractions.dk) is a collection of oddities based on the cartoons of American Robert L. Ripley – a life-size model of the world's tallest man and a bicycle made from matchsticks are just two of hundreds of exhibits. Next door, also at no. 57 but to the right, **H.C. Andersen Eventyrhuset** (Hans Christian Andersen's Wonderful World: same hours as Ripley's; 67kr, see box above about joint ticket prices; ⓦwww.topattractions.dk) opened in celebration of Hans Christian Andersen's two-hundredth anniversary in 2005. It brings his storytelling to life through large colourful tableaux that, when you press a button, play his fairy-tales out loud. However, it doesn't explore his own life with the same depth as the museum in Odense (see p.112), his place of birth.

Along Strøget

Indre By proper begins with **Strøget** (literally "level measure"), also variously named Frederiksberggade, Nygade, Vimmelskaftet, Amagertorv and Østergade, which runs east–west across the district, lined by pricey stores and graceless fast-food dives. Very much the public face of Copenhagen, the strip is perfect for ambling amongst the crowds of locals, tourists and street entertainers. The most active part is usually around **Gammeltorv** and **Nytorv**, two adjacent squares ("old" and "new") flanking Strøget, where there's a hotdog stand and a couple of cafés, as well as stalls selling handmade jewellery and bric-a-brac. It was between these squares that the fifteenth-century Rådhus stood before it was destroyed by fire in 1795. A new Rådhus was erected on Nytorv a century later, and this is now the city's **Domhuset**, or Law Courts, marked by a suitably forbidding row of Neoclassical columns.

A few blocks east of here is the **Helligåndskirken** (Mon–Fri noon–4pm), one of the oldest churches in the city, founded in the fourteenth century though largely rebuilt from 1728 onwards with vaulted ceiling and slender granite columns. While it's still in use as a place of worship, there are often art shows and other free exhibitions inside. Just beyond, the vast open **Højbro Plads** square, home to the Storkfountain, has for centuries been one of the most popular meeting points in the city. Encircled by outdoor cafés and some of the city's finest lunchtime restaurants, this is a good place to take a break. A path leads south off Højbro Plads and on to the grandiose (and now deconsecrated) **Skt Nikolaj Kirke** (Tues–Sun noon–5pm, Thurs until 9pm; 20kr, free on Wed; ⓦwww.kunsthallennikolaj.dk); the building's upper floors are employed as one of Copenhagen's prime exhibition spaces for contemporary artists, while at ground level there's another fine lunchtime restaurant.

The final section of Strøget is Østergade, where you'll find a further international tourist pull, the **Guinness World Records** (mid-June to Aug daily 10am–10pm; Sept to mid-May Mon–Thurs & Sun 10am–6pm, Fri & Sat 10am–8pm; 85kr, see box above about joint ticket prices; ⓦwww.topattractions.dk). It's much as you'd expect, with family-oriented exhibits on the world's tallest, fastest and smallest, and more. Next door, along the same theme, **The Mystic Exploratorie** (mid-June to Aug daily 10am–10pm; Sept to mid-May Mon–Thurs & Sun 10am–6pm, Fri & Sat 10am–8pm; 67kr, see box above about joint ticket prices) offers a surprisingly engaging chance to explore odd natural phenomena, such as how the weather can be manipulated (at least on a small scale). Beyond, Østergade flows past the swish and chic Hotel d'Angleterre into the biggest of the city squares, **Kongens Nytorv**. Built on what was the edge of the city in medieval times, the square has an equestrian statue of its creator, Christian V, at its centre and a couple of grandly ageing structures around two of its shallow angles. One of these, the **Kongelige Teater** or Royal Theatre, dates from 1874; the other, **Charlottenborg**, next door, was finished in 1683, at the same time as the square itself, for a son of Frederik III. It was later sold to Queen Charlotte Amalie, but since 1754 has been the home of the Royal Academy of Art, which uses some of the elegant, spacious rooms for eclectic art exhibitions (Tues–Sun noon–5pm; 60kr; ⓦ www.charlottenborg-art.dk).

The Latin Quarter and around

There's more of interest among the tangle of buildings and streets **north of Strøget**. Crossing Gammeltorv and following Nørregade leads to the old university area, sometimes called the **Latin Quarter** – parts of it retain an academic function, hence the number of book-carrying students milling around. The old university building is overlooked by Copenhagen's cathedral, **Vor Frue Kirke** (Mon–Thurs & Sat 8.30am–5pm, Fri 8.30–10.30am, Sun noon–3pm; free). Built on the site of a twelfth-century church, the present structure dates from 1829, when it was erected in the wake of the devastation caused by the British bombardment in 1807. The weighty figure of Christ behind the altar and the solemn statues of the apostles, some crafted by Bertel Thorvaldsen (see p.78), others by his pupils, merit a look. From the cathedral, dodge across Skindergade into **Gråbrødretorv**, a charming cobbled square filled with restaurants and often crowded with buskers. The square dates back to 1238, when the city's first monastery was built here; today, it's a popular place in good weather to dine or just enjoy a cool beer. Just northeast of here is **Rundetårn** (mid-May to mid-Sept daily 10am–8pm; mid-Sept to mid-May daily 10am–5pm; 25kr; ⓦ www.rundetaarn.dk), a round tower with a gradually ascending spiral ramp winding to its summit. It was built by Christian IV as an **observatory** – and perhaps also to provide a vantage point from which his subjects could admire his additions to the city. Today the best views are of the city's beautiful copper roofs and the more immediate maze of tightly packed medieval streets. Legend has it that Tsar Peter the Great sped to the top on horseback in 1715, pursued by the tsarina in a six-horse carriage – a smoother technique than descending the cobbles on a skateboard, a short-lived fad of more recent times. If you're not quite up to trying that, look in on the contemporary **art gallery** part of the way up instead, which stages temporary exhibitions.

After leaving the Rundetårn, you could easily spend half an hour browsing the bookshops of Købmagergade, or visit the **Museum Erotica** (May–Sept daily 10am–11pm; Oct–April Sun–Thurs 11am–8pm, Fri & Sat 10am–10pm; 109kr; ⓦ www.museumerotica.dk), which lurks along here at no. 24, a shrine to the erotic (and the just plain pornographic) through the ages. For something more traditional, head north along Købmagergade to the **Musikhistorisk Museum** just off Kultorvet at Åbenrå 30 (Musical History Museum: May–Sept Tues–Sun 1–3.50pm; Oct–April Tues, Wed, Sat & Sun 1–3.50pm; free; ⓦ www.natmus.dk /sw25193.asp). The museum holds an impressive quantity of musical instruments and sound-producing devices spanning the globe and the last thousand years, along with recordings. Naturally the bulk come from Denmark and there are some subtle insights into the social fabric of the nation to be gleaned from the yellowing photos of country dances and other get-togethers hung alongside the instruments.

Less musical sounds are provided by the cars hurtling along Nørre Voldgade, at the top of Kultorvet, which, with Nørreport station, marks the edge of the pedestrianized streets of the old city. There are two reasons to queue up at the traffic lights and cross over: the first is the fruit-and-vegetable **market** – and Saturday flea market – on Israel Plads; the second is the **Arbejdermuseet** (Workers' Museum) at

Rømersgade 22 (daily 10am–4pm; 50kr; ⓦwww.arbejdermuseet.dk), an engrossing and thoughtful guide to working-class life in Copenhagen from the 1930s to the 1990s. Mock-up house interiors contain family photos, newspapers and TVs showing newsreels from different periods, while a shop window hawks consumer durables of the 1950s. An original printing works, subsidized by the Marshall Plan, leads into a coffee shop, which sells an old-fashioned coffee-and-chicory blend by the cup and there's a lunchtime restaurant in the basement serving tasty traditional Danish fare from the period.

Gothersgade, the road marking the northern perimeter of Indre By, is home to the Danish Film Institut's **Cinemateket** (Aug–June Tues–Fri 9.30am–10pm, Sat & Sun noon to 10pm; ⓦwww.cinemateket.dk), which has a three-screen art-house cinema (tickets cost 65kr) and a videotek section where free films are shown.

North of Gothersgade

There's a profound change of mood **north of Gothersgade**. The congenial medieval alleyways of the old city give way to long, broad streets and a number of proud, aristocratic buildings. A whole group of these dominate the **harbour area** near Nyhavn, although perhaps the most remarkable of all is **Rosenborg Slot**, a short way to the west away from the harbour and close to several major **museums**.

From Nyhavn to Esplanaden

Running from Kongens Nytorv to the waterfront, its two sides following a slender canal, the picturesque cobbled street of **Nyhavn** is a former sailors' haunt that's now in the advanced stages of gentrification. One or two of the old tattoo parlours remain, now looking decidedly out of place and increasingly outnumbered by the restaurants and cafés crammed into the regenerated, brightly painted eighteenth-century townhouses lining the street, three of which (nos. 18, 20 & 67) were lived in at various times by Hans Christian Andersen. Nyhavn is one of the city's most beguiling spots, with attractive fishing vessels, wooden pleasure craft and the city's canal tour boats filling the water with activity, while well-off locals and tourists watch from the tranquil atmosphere of the outdoor cafés and restaurants. At the northern end of Nyhavn is the Royal Theatre's glimmering state-of-the-art **Skuespilhus** (Play House: Mon–Sat 8am–11.30pm, Sun 8am 3pm; ⓦwww .skuespilhus.dk) accessed via a wooden promenade along Inner Havnen. Take a peek inside to see the fabulous tubular lighting or the unusual bricks that give the building a sort of cave-like feel. It cost 780 million kroner to build, partly due to the seventy thousand-cubic-metre sandbank that had to be created to protect the precious new structure from drunken sea captains taking their ships through Inner Havnen. The Skuespilhus sits happily with the Opera House, situated across the Inner Havnen on Holmen, a view to enjoy while sipping a coffee or nibbling on snacks in the relaxing seafront terrace café.

From Skt Annæ Plads, Larsens Plads leads along the harbourfront to the lavish modern gardens of **Amaliehaven**, giving more views over to the grand Opera House building on the opposite bank. From the gardens, you pass under a colonnade into the cobbled **Slots Plads** with the statue of Frederik V in its centre. The statue reputedly cost more than all four of the identical Rococo palaces, **Amalienborg**, that flank it – thanks to French sculptor Jacques Saly, who spent thirty years in Copenhagen creating it at the court's expense. Dating from the mid-eighteenth century, this quartet of imposing palaces provides a sudden burst of welcome symmetry into the city's generally haphazard layout. Two of the palaces now serve as royal residences and there's a changing of the guard each day at noon when Queen Margarethe II is at home – generally attended by school kids and gangs of camera-toting observers.

In a straight line from Amalienborg, Amaliehaven and the Opera House, the great dome of **Frederikskirken** looms on Bredgade. Also known as the "Marmorkirken", or "Marble Church" (Mon, Tues, Thurs & Sat 10am–5pm; Wed 10am–6.30pm, Fri &

Sun noon–5pm), it is modelled on – and intended to rival – St Peter's in Rome. The church was begun in 1749, but because of its enormous cost lay unfinished until a century and a half later. If you can time your visit to coincide with the **guided tour of the tower** (mid-June to Aug daily 1pm & 3pm; rest of the year Sat & Sun 1pm & 3pm; 25kr), the reward is the chance to climb first to the whispering gallery and then out onto the rim of the dome itself. From here there's a stunning, and usually blustery, view over the sharp geometry of Amalienborg, Amaliehaven and the Opera House, and further afield to the factories of Malmö in Sweden.

Over the road at Bredgade 62, the former Danish Surgical Academy now holds the **Medicinsk Museion** (Medical History Museum: guided tours only; in English July–Aug Wed–Fri & Sun 2.30pm; rest of the year in Danish only Wed–Fri & Sun 1.30pm, 2.30pm & 3.30pm; 50kr; ⓦwww.museion.ku.dk) – not a place for the faint-hearted, since the enthusiastically presented hour-long tour features aborted foetuses, straitjackets, syphilis treatments, amputated feet, eyeballs and a dissected head. Further along Bredgade at no. 68, the former Royal Frederiks Hospital now houses the **Kunstindustrimuseet** (Danish Museum of Decorative Art: Tues–Sun 11am–5pm; 50kr, Wed free; ⓦwww.kunstindustrimuseet.dk), a definite must if you have any interest in design. The exhibits trace the development of European – and particularly Danish – design, and examine the influence of Eastern styles on Western design. There's also an excellent café.

The Kastellet and around

A little way beyond the Museum of Decorative Art, Bredgade concludes at Esplanaden, facing the green space of **Churchill Park**. To the right, the German armoured car that was commandeered by Danes and used to bring news of the Nazi surrender marks the entrance to the **Frihedsmuseet** (Museum of the Danish Resistance Movement: May–Sept Tues–Sun 10am–5pm; Oct–April Tues–Sun 10am–3pm; free; ⓦwww.frihedsmuseet.dk). Initially, the Danes put up little resistance to the German invasion, but later the Nazis were given a systematically wretched time. The museum records the growth of the organized response and has a special section on the youths from Aalborg who formed themselves into the "Churchill Club". Feeling the adults weren't doing enough, this gang of 15-year-olds set about destroying German telegraph cables, blowing up cars and trains and stealing weapons. There's also a small but moving collection of artworks and handicrafts made by concentration camp inmates.

The road behind the museum crosses into the grounds of the **Kastellet** (daily 6am–sunset; free), a fortress built by Christian IV and expanded by his successors through the seventeenth century, after the loss of Danish possessions in Skåne had put the city within range of Swedish cannonballs. Perched on some rocks just off the harbour bank **Den Lille Havfrue** (The Little Mermaid) exerts an inexplicable magnetism on tourists. Since its unveiling in 1913, this bronze statue of a Hans Christian Andersen character, sculpted by Edvard Erichsen and paid for by the boss of the Carlsberg brewery, has become the best-known emblem of the city – a fact which has led to it being the victim of several subversive pranks. The original head disappeared in 1964, a cow's head was forced over the replacement in 1986, and more recently one of its arms was stolen. A hundred metres away is the far more spectacular **Gefion Fountain**, created by Anders Bundgaard and showing the goddess Gefion with her four sons, whom she's turned into oxen, having been promised in return as much land as she can plough in a single night. The legend goes that she ploughed a chunk of Sweden, then picked it up (creating Lake Vänern) and tossed it into the sea – where it became Zealand.

West from the harbour: Rosenborg Slot and the museums

Just southwest of the Kastellet lies **Nyboder**, a curious area of short, straight and narrow streets lined with rows of compact yellow dwellings. Although some of these are recently erected apartment blocks, the original houses, on which the newer constructions are modelled, were built by Christian IV to encourage his sailors to live in the city. The area at one time declined into a slum, but recent vigorous revamping has made it an increasingly sought-after district. The oldest (and prettiest) houses can be found along Skt Pauls Gade.

Across Sølvgade from Nyboder is the main entrance to **Rosenborg Slot** (June–Aug daily 10am–5pm; May & Sept–Oct daily 10am–4pm; Nov–April Tues–Sun 11am–2pm; 70kr; ⓦwww.rosenborgslot.dk), a Dutch Renaissance palace and one of the most elegant buildings bequeathed by Christian IV to the city. Though intended as a country residence, Rosenborg served as the main domicile of Christian IV (he died here in 1648) and, until the early eighteenth century, the monarchs who succeeded him. It became a museum as early as 1838 and in the main building you can still see the rooms and furnishings used by the regal occupants. The highlights, though, are in the treasury downstairs, which displays the rich accessories worn by Christian IV (and his horse), the crown of absolute monarchs and the present crown jewels. Outside, the splendidly neat garden can be reached by leaving the palace itself and using the park's main entrance on the corner of Øster Voldgade and Sølvgade. On the west side of the Slot is **Kongens Have**, the city's oldest public park and a popular place for picnics, and, across Øster Voldgade, the Botanisk Have (Botanical Garden: May–Sept daily 8.30am–6pm; Oct–April Tues–Sun 8.30am–4pm; free; ⓦwww.botanik.snm.ku.dk), with its beautiful old Palm House.

Opposite Rosenborg Have is the **Statens Museum for Kunst** at Sølvgade 48–50 (National Art Museum: Tues & Thurs–Sun 10am–5pm, Wed 10am–8pm; free to see permanent collection; ⓦwww.smk.dk), a mammoth collection that's too large to take in on a single short visit. While there are some minor Picassos and major works by Matisse and Braque, Modigliani, Dürer and El Greco, it's the creations of Emil Nolde, with their bloated ravens, hunched figures and manic children, that best capture the mood of the place. In an effort to keep up with the times, the museum recently doubled in size, adding a new building for modern art (including contemporary Danish and other European work), which also houses a restaurant and children's room, and affords good views of Kongens Have.

Art fans will find further rich pickings across the park behind the museum, in the fine **Den Hirschsprungske Samling** (The Hirschsprung Collection: Mon & Wed–Sun 11am–4pm; 50kr, free Wed; ⓦwww.hirschsprung.dk) on Stockholmsgade. Heinrich Hirschsprung was a late-nineteenth-century tobacco baron who sunk some of his profits into the patronage of emerging Danish artists, including the Skagen artists (see p.155). It was Hirschsprung's wish that on his death the collection – which also features Eckersburg, Købke and lesser names from the Danish mid-nineteenth-century Golden Age – would be given to the nation, but the government of the day vetoed his plan so Hirschsprung set up his own gallery.

Christiansborg

Connected to Indre By by several short bridges, **Christiansborg** sits on the island of Slotsholmen. It's an authoritative part of the city, administratively and historically key to the country's governance, but it is also home to a few delightful attractions. It was here, in the twelfth century, that Bishop Absalon built the castle that was the origin of the city, and the drab royal palace (completed in 1916) that occupies the site is nowadays given over primarily to government offices and the state parliament or **Folketinget** (guided tours in English July–Sept daily 2pm; rest of the year Sun 2pm; free). Close to the bus stop on Christiansborg Slotsplads is the entrance to Christiansborg's main courtyard; in this passageway, you'll find the **Ruinerne under Christiansborg** (Ruins under Christiansborg: May–Sept daily 10am–4pm; Oct–April Tues–Sun 10am–4pm; 40kr), where a staircase leads down to the remains of Bishop Absalon's original castle. The first fortress suffered repeated mutilations by the Hanseatic League, and Erik of Pomerania had a replacement erected in 1390, into which he moved the royal court. This in turn was pulled down by Christian VI and another castle built between 1731 and 1745. The stone and brick walls that comprise the ruins, and the articles from the castles stored in an adjoining room, are surprisingly absorbing, the mood enhanced by the semi-darkness and lack of external noise. Turn left into the palace courtyard as you exit the ruins and you'll find the entrance to **De Kongelige Repræsentationslokaler** (Royal Reception Rooms: guided tours in English May–Sept daily 11am, 1 & 3pm; Oct–April Tues–Sun 3pm; 65kr) on the right. They're used by the royal family to entertain important visitors and the richly ornamented rooms, in particular the throne room with delicate silk from Lyon covering the walls, and the Great Hall covered in modern tapestries (made for the queen's fiftieth birthday) depicting Denmark's colourful past, should not be missed.

There are a number of other less captivating museums in and around Christiansborg Slotsplads, to which the ticket office for the ruins can provide directions – the confusing array of buildings makes it easy to get lost. That said, you could probably sniff your way to the **Kongelige Stalde og Kareter** (Royal Stables and Coaches: May–Sept Fri–Sun 2–4pm; Oct–April Sat & Sun 2–4pm; 20kr), dating from 1740 and one of the few remaining parts of the original Baroque Christiansborg, lavishly decorated with pillars, vaulted ceilings and walls of Tuscan marble. Apparently not even the king's own chambers were this extravagant. Nearby, the **Teatermuseet i Hofteatret** (Theatre Museum: Tues & Thurs 11am–3pm, Wed 11am–5pm, Sat & Sun 1–4pm; 30kr; ⓦwww.teatermuseet.dk) is housed in what was the eighteenth-century Court Theatre and displays original costumes, set-models and the old dressing rooms and boxes. Housed in the former Royal Boat House, the city's newest museum, the **Dansk Jødiske Museum** (Danish Jewish Museum: June–Aug Tues–Sun 10am–5pm; Sept–May Tues–Fri 1–4pm, Sat & Sun noon to 5pm; 40kr; ⓦwww.jewmus.dk) had its quirky inside space designed by world-renowned architect Daniel Libeskind. No floors are level, no angles straight, giving the dizzying impression of being onboard a ship rolling in the waves – a way of commemorating the Jewish exodus to Sweden on Danish fishing vessels during World War II. Libeskind expresses his heartfelt thoughts about this event in a short film played near the entrance. This is followed by an introduction to the Jewish history in Denmark. Continuing on to the waterfront at Christians Brygge, the beautiful **Black Diamond** royal library extension (Mon–Sat 8am–11pm) sparkles in the reflected light from the waves. It includes spaces for temporary exhibits, a concert hall, conference rooms and restaurants. Finally, adjacent to Christiansborg Slotsplads sits the long, low form of the seventeenth-century **Børsen**, or Stock Exchange. With its spire of four entwined dragons' tails, it's one of the most distinctive buildings in the city and worth seeking out.

Around Christiansborg

On the far north side of Slotsholmen island is the palace chapel, **Christiansborg Slotskirke** (Sun noon–4pm, July daily noon–4pm; free), designed by prominent Golden Age architect C.F. Hansen and a beautiful example of Neoclassical architecture, with a magnificent frieze by Bertel Thorvaldsen encircling the dome. In stark contrast to the elegant, light church, the bombastic and colourful **Thorvaldsens Museum** next door (Tues–Sun 10am–5pm; 20kr, free Wed; ⓦwww.thorvaldsensmuseum.dk) is home to an enormous collection of work and memorabilia of Denmark's most famous sculptor, and also houses the remains of the man himself. Despite negligible schooling, **Bertel Thorvaldsen** (1770–1844) drew his way into the Danish Academy of Fine Arts before moving onto Rome, where he perfected the heroic, classical figures for which he became famous. Nowadays he's not widely known outside Denmark, although in his lifetime he enjoyed international renown and won commissions all over Europe. A prolific and gifted sculptor, Thorvaldsen was something of a wit, too. Asked by the Swedish artist J.T. Sergel how he managed to make such beautiful figures, he held up the scraper with which he was working and replied, "With this."

There's another major collection a short walk west over the Slotsholmen moat: the **National Museum** (Tues–Sun 10am–5pm; free; ⓦwww.natmus .dk) is strongest (as you'd expect) on Danish history, and if you've any interest in the subject, you could easily spend a couple of hours – if not days – here. A lot of the early stuff, ranging from prehistory to the Viking days, comes from Jutland – jewellery, bones and even bodies, all remarkably well preserved; much of it was only discovered after wartime fuel shortages led to large-scale digging of the Danish peat bogs. Informative explanatory texts help clarify the **Viking section**, whose best exhibits – apart from the familiar horned helmets – are the sacrificial gifts, among them the Sun Chariot, a model horse carrying a sun disc with adornments of gold and bronze. Other floors store a massive collection of almost anything and everything that featured in Christian-era Denmark up to the nineteenth century – finely engraved wooden altarpieces, furniture, clothing and more – as well as a good section on peasant life.

Christianshavn

From Christiansborg, the Knippels Bro bridge crosses the Inder Havnen to the island of Amager and into **Christianshavn**, built as an autonomous new town by Christian IV in the early sixteenth century to provide housing for workers in the shipbuilding industry. It was given features more common to Dutch port towns of the time, even down to the small canals, and in parts the area is more redolent of Amsterdam than Copenhagen. Although its present inhabitants are fairly well-off – as evidenced by some immaculately preserved houses along Overgaden oven Vandet – Christianshavn still has the mood of a working-class quarter, with a cluster of secondhand shops along the district's main street, Torvegade.

Poking skywards through the trees near Torvegade is the blue-and-gold spire of **Vor Frelsers Kirke** (Church of Our Saviour: April–Aug Mon–Sat 11am–4.30pm, Sun noon–4.30pm; Sept–March Mon–Sat 11am–3.30pm, Sun noon–3.30pm; free; access to spire April–Oct only, 20kr), on the corner of Prinsessegade and Skt Annæ Gade. The **spire**, with its helter-skelter outside staircase, was added to the otherwise plain church in the mid-eighteenth century, instantly becoming one of the more recognizable features on the city's horizon. Climbing the spire (which you can do between April and Oct only) is fun, but not entirely without risk – though the rumour that its architect fell off it and died is, while plausible, untrue. To get to the spire, go through the church and up to a trap door which opens onto the platform where the external steps begin: there are four hundred of them, slanted and slippery (especially after rain) and gradually becoming smaller. The reward for reaching the top is a stunning vista of Copenhagen and beyond.

Christiania

A few streets northeast of Vor Frelsers Kirke, **Christiania** occupies an area that was for centuries used as a barracks, before the soldiers moved out and it was colonized by young, idealistic people. It was declared a **"free city"** on September 24, 1971, with the aim of operating autonomously from Copenhagen, and its continued existence has fuelled one of the longest-running debates in Danish (and Scandinavian) society. One by-product of its idealism and the freedoms assumed by its residents (and, despite recent lapses, generally tolerated by successive governments and the police) was to make Christiania a refuge for petty criminals and shady individuals from all over the city. But the problems have inevitably been overplayed by Christiania's critics, and a surprising number of Danes – of all ages and from all walks of life – do support the place, not least because Christiania has performed usefully, and altruistically, when established bodies have been found wanting; residents have stepped in to provide free shelter and food for the homeless at Christmas when the city administration declined to do so.

▲ Christiania gates

The population of around 650 is swelled in summer by thousands of curious and sympathetic visitors, many heading straight for Pusherstreet, where the selling of cannabis is unofficially tolerated by the government although raids do occur now and again. The craft shops and restaurants are fairly cheap, and nearly all are good, as are a couple of innovative music and performance art venues (see p.88). These, and the many imaginative dwellings, including some built on stilts in a small lake, make a visit well worthwhile. Additionally, there are a number of alternative political and arts groups based in Christiania; for **information** on these – and on the district generally – call in at **Galopperiet** (Tues–Sun 2–7pm; Ⓦwww.christiania .org), to the right of the area's main entrance on Prinsessegade. Christiania can be quite confusing to navigate, so it's a good idea to go on one of the ninety-minute **guided tours** of the area, which are conducted by local residents (July–Aug daily 3pm; Sept–June Sat & Sun 3pm; 30kr; Ⓣ32 57 96 70, Ⓦwww.christiania.org); if you're in a group of four people or more, try to book at least one day in advance; otherwise, you can just turn up. At the time of writing the government was again looking to "normalize" things – developers all agree that Christiania occupies prime real estate – so residents, once again, were finding ways of biding their time until a more amenable (read: left-wing) government comes into power. It's important to note that residents ask people not to camp at Christiania, and tourists not to point cameras on or near Pusherstreet.

Christiania is also the gateway to **Holmen**, once a forgotten naval station but now home to a complex of four art schools – the National School of Architecture, the National School of Theatre, the National Film School and the Rhythmical Music Conservatory – and destined to expand further in coming years. Check the area for current developments – change is in the air and it's quickly becoming Europe's latest industrial zone to be taken over by artists and other creative types.

Along Vesterbrogade

Hectic **Vesterbrogade** begins on the far side of Rådhuspladsen from Strøget, and its first attraction is Copenhagen's most famous after the Little Mermaid: the **Tivoli Gardens** (mid-June to mid-Aug Sun–Thurs 11am–midnight, Fri & Sat 11am– 12.30am; other times of the year Sun–Thurs 11am–11pm, Fri 11am–12.30am, Sat 11am–midnight; 85kr; Ⓦwww.tivoli.dk). This excellent classic theme park – a national treasure for Denmark and the capital's most popular tourist attraction – first flung open its gates in 1843, modelled on the Vauxhall Gardens in London, and in turn became the model for the Festival Gardens in London's Battersea Park. The name is now synonymous with Copenhagen at its most innocently pleasurable, and the opening of the gardens each April is taken to mark the beginning of summer. There are fountains, over 25 fairground rides (20–60kr each, paid with 20kr tickets bought in books from two ticket outlets; they also sell 200kr passes which cover all the rides) and fireworks displays on Wednesdays and Saturdays just before midnight, as well as nightly entertainment in the central arena, encompassing everything from acrobats and jugglers to top-rated international performers (look out for Friday Rock live music performances at 10pm). Naturally, it's overrated and overpriced, but it's still worth spending an evening wandering among the revellers of all ages indulging in the mass consumption of ice cream.

Behind the Tivoli, across Tietgensgade towards the harbour, is the dazzling **Ny Carlsberg Glyptotek**, Dantes Plads 7 (Tues–Sun 10am–4pm; 50kr, free Sun; ⓦwww .glyptoteket.dk), opened in 1897 by brewer Carl Jacobsen as a venue for ordinary people to see classical art exhibited in classical style. Its centrepiece is the conservatory: "Being Danes," said Jacobsen, "we know more about flowers than art, and during the winter this greenery will make people pay a visit; and then, looking at the palms, they might find a moment for the statues." It's an idea that succeeded, and even now the gallery is well used – and not just by art lovers. There's a programme of classical music concerts every Sunday and some Wednesdays (call ☏33 41 81 41 for details), as well as a seasonal roster of other events, some free; pick up a schedule at the entrance.

The contents – an impressive 10,000 individual art works and artefacts – make this by far Copenhagen's finest gallery, and it's been overhauled recently to better organize the exhibits. There is a stirring array of Greek, Roman and Egyptian goodies, as well as what is reckoned to be the biggest (and best) collection of Etruscan art outside Italy. There are excellent examples of nineteenth-century Danish, French and other European art too, including a complete collection of Degas casts made from the fragile working sculptures he left at his death, Manet's *Absinthe Drinker* and two small cases containing tiny caricatured heads by Honoré Daumier. Easily missed, but actually the most startling room in the place, is an antechamber with just a few pieces – early works by Man Ray, some Chagall sketches and a Picasso pottery plate. There's also a French wing containing Impressionist art and work from Danish painting's so-called "Golden Age" (1800–50), plus a French-themed café on a balcony overlooking greenhouses of palm trees.

Finally, if you're interested in Denmark's world-class tradition of design, don't leave this area without at least looking in on the **Danish Design Centre**, 27–29 Hans Christian Andersens Boulevard (Mon–Fri 10am–5pm, Wed 10am–9pm, Sat & Sun 11am–4pm; 50kr; ⓦwww.ddc.dk). The building, designed by Danish architect Henning Larsen, serves as an exhibition hall, research facility and showcase for all sorts of industrial design, from Bang & Olufsen stereo equipment to Børge Mogensen furniture.

Beyond the Tivoli Gardens

Just west of the train station, the streets between Vesterbrogade and **Istedgade** used to be Copenhagen's token red-light area, and the only part of the city where you might have felt unsafe. Over the years, though, the low rents attracted students and a large number of immigrant families, who are now, in turn, gradually being replaced by young middle-class artists, media types and families as the area succumbs to the unstoppable process of gentrification. While this part of Vesterbro is under immense change at the moment, you can still walk along Istedgade and be likely to find rastas and Turks sipping tea from tulip glasses, plus a number of diverse (but well-priced) ethnic eateries.

At Vesterbrogade 59 is the **Københavns Bymuseum** (City Museum: daily except Tues 10am–4pm, Wed 10am–9pm; 20kr, free on Fri; ⓦwww.bymuseum.dk), which has reconstructed ramshackle house exteriors and tradesmen's signs from early Copenhagen. Looking at these, the impact of Christian IV becomes resoundingly apparent, and a large room details the form and cohesion that this monarch and amateur architect gave the city, and even includes a few of his own drawings. The rest of the city's history is told by paintings – far too many, in fact. Head upstairs for the room devoted to **Søren Kierkegaard**, much the most interesting part of the museum. It's filled with bits and bobs – furniture from his home, paintings of his girlfriend Regine Olsen, jewellery, books and manuscripts – that form an intriguing footnote to the life of this nineteenth-century Danish writer and philosopher (see p.94).

A few minutes to the north of Vesterbrogade, on the corner with Vester Søgade at Gammel Kongevej 10, is the **Tycho Brahe Planetarium** (daily 10.30am–9pm; 75kr; ⓦwww.tycho.dk); the biggest in Scandinavia, it's named after the world-famous Danish astronomer who invented instruments to accurately plot the sun, planets and stars for the first time. Apart from an astronomical- and space-related section, the in-house Omnimax Theatre, with a thousand-square-metre dome screen, is the best part of the Planetarium. Films (in 3D) are shown every hour on the hour, and cost a steep 90kr (includes entrance ticket to Planetarium).

West to the Carlsberg Brewery and Frederiksberg Have

Way out west along Vesterbrogade (save your legs by taking bus #6A to Valby Langgade and crossing the street), down Gamle Carlsberg Vej, you'll find the **Carlsberg Brewery**'s Visitor Centre at no. 11 (Tues–Sun 10am–4pm; ⓦwww.visitcarlsberg .dk; 50kr). Once you've made your way through the completely renovated centre, which depicts the history of Danish beer-brewing and includes the new **Jacobsen Brewhouse** microbrewery, you get two free beer tastings at the upstairs bar (Jacobsen, Carlberg and Tuborg products) overlooking the copper brewing kettles.

Vesterbrogade finishes up opposite the **Frederiksberg Have**, which contains the Frederiksberg Palace, now used as a military academy and closed to the public. Throughout the eighteenth century, the city's top brass came here to mess about in boats along the network of canals that dissect the copious lime-tree groves, and its pleasant surrounds are now a popular weekend picnic spot for locals.

Beyond the Frederiksberg Palace, at Roskildevej 32 (buses #4A, #6A, #18 and #26), is Copenhagen's **Zoo** (April–May & Sept Mon–Fri 9am–5pm, Sat & Sun 9am–6pm; June daily 9am–6pm; July, Aug & Oct daily 9am–9pm; Nov–March daily 9am–4pm; 130kr; ⓦwww.zoo.dk), which has the usual array of caged lions, elephants and monkeys, plus a special children's section.

South of Copenhagen

If the weather's good, take a trip south to the **Amager Strand beaches**, about ten minutes away by Metro (get off at Amager Strand, from where it's a 10min walk). An exciting new development with an artificial island and bunker-like structures with showers and snackbars, this is a showcase in beach development. Always less pretentious than the beaches in the more affluent areas to the north of the capital, Amager Strand has heaps of activities going on throughout the year (check ⓦwww .amager-strand.dk for programme) such as beach volley competitions and kayak races, and the shallow waters are ideal for kids to paddle in.

Further out from the city centre, back on mainland Zealand, on the road to Køge, the southern suburb of **Ishøj** is home to many ethnic communities, and an excellent museum, **Arken** (Tues & Thurs–Sun 10am–5pm, Wed 10am–9pm; 85kr; ⓦwww.arken.dk) which has a delightful collection of international modern art from 1990 onwards. One piece to look out for is Damien Hirst's sickly pink *Birthday Card*. The sleek building, looking very much like a ship rising from Ishøj beach, is a work of art in itself. It houses, in addition to its permanent collection, excellent temporary exhibitions, plus a glassed-in restaurant overlooking the bay. From central Copenhagen take the S-train line A or E to Ishøj station and then bus #128, a thirty-minute journey altogether.

North of Copenhagen

Just outside the city limits, reached by S-train line C or bus #14 or #166, **CHARLOTTENLUND** has a lovely beach, good for sunbathing – as long as you can ignore the smoke-belching chimneys in the background. Its main attraction is the **Danish Aquarium** (daily: May to mid-Sept 10am–6pm; Sept–Oct & Feb–April 10am–5pm; Nov–Jan 10am–4pm; 90kr; ⓦwww.danmarksakvarium .dk), with its impressive collection of tropical fish, sharks, crocodiles and turtles. For a cheaper and less showy version of Tivoli, venture out to **Bakken** (daily: July to mid-Aug noon–midnight; mid-March to June & mid- to end Aug varying hours between noon and midnight, call ☎39 63 35 44; free, tour passes to all 34 rides 199kr; ⓦwww.bakken.dk), close to the Klampenborg stop at the end of line C on the S-train network. Set in a corner of Kongens Dyrehave (the royal deer park), it's possibly more fun than its city counterpart – and certainly more down-to-earth – and besides the usual swings and roller-coasters offers easy walks through oak and beech woods. Strolling back towards Klampenborg along Christiansholmsvej, a left turn at the restaurant *Peter Lieps Hus* gives superb views over the Øresund.

Eating

Whether you want a quick coffee and pastry, or to sit down to a five-course gourmet dinner, you'll find more choice – and lower prices – in Copenhagen than in any other Scandinavian capital. Many of the city's innumerable **cafés** offer fabulous, filling brunches, sandwiches and snacks, and double up in the evening as bars. **Restaurant** prices tend to be higher in the evenings, but there are generally good-value deals at lunchtime. Places in Indre By and Christiansborg are marked on the map on p.72; all others appear on the main Copenhagen map (pp.64–65).

If you're stocking up for a **picnic** take advantage of the numerous outlets selling smørrebrød (open sandwiches); Domhusets Smørrebrød, on Kattesundet 14, and Centrum Smørrebrød, Vesterbrogade 6C, are two of the most central, or use one of the **supermarkets**: ISO at Vesterbrogade 23, Irma at in Rådhusarkaden Vesterbrogade 1 and Superbrugsen by Nørreport station are all top-range. Netto and Fakta are by far the cheapest and more chaotic; you'll find Netto branches at Nørre Voldgade 94, Fiolstræde 9 and Landemærket 11; and Fakta on Vesterbrogade 66 and on Borgergade 27.

Brunch, snacks and light meals

Bang & Jensen Istedgade 130, Vesterbro. This Vesterbro standby at the quieter end of Istedgade will probably never go out of style. They serve a renowned daily brunch (8am–4pm) from 75kr, as well as a breakfast buffet (8–11am) at 50kr and sandwiches and light meals all day. The scene is painfully hip, with screenwriters, social entrepreneurs and a large number of well-known Danish musicians and artists often nursing a pint of Tuborg here. Turns into a bar at night, especially busy when there's music on at nearby *Vega* (see p.88).

Café Europa Amagertorv 1, Indre By. In a great spot, overlooking bustling Højbro Plads, this large glass-fronted place is a welcome stop along Strøget for a good cup of coffee and slice of delicious cake or a sandwich. The popular brunch, served from 8am onwards (9am on Sun), is somewhat pricey at either 159kr or 189kr. That said, it is guaranteed to set you up for the day.

Dalle Valle Fiolstræde 5, Indre By. In the corner of a former department store which now also houses the pretentious five-star St Petri Hotel, this stylish place is surprisingly relaxed. Serves delicious breakfast from 9am and filling brunch (120kr) from 10am as well as an 11am buffet brunch (169kr) on Sun. The large interior space opens out to Fiolstræde and is a fabulous place to sit back and watch the world go by. The 132kr burgers aren't bad either.

Den Grønne Kælder Pilestræde 48, Indre By ☎33 93 01 40. A simple tiled-floor vegetarian place offering very filling gourmet meals and organic wines. Lunch starts at 65kr for a main course, and the scrumptious evening à la carte menu won't break the bank. Closed Sun.

Den Sorte Gryde Istedgade 108, Vesterbro. Legendarily huge burgers and steaks are served in this carnivore's dream restaurant that also cooks up ribs, stews, steaks and chicken, all with a decidedly Danish slant. Try the *flæskesteg*, fat slices of pork with crackling, served in a sandwich or with potatoes. Primarily take-away.

Det Gule Hus Istedgade 46, Vesterbro. This unmissable yellow villa offering great breakfasts and brunches (one veggie, one decidedly carnivorous and one continental; all 85kr) is a popular meeting point for pushchair-wheeling parents. They serve a standard continental-type breakfast with fresh bread, and while it's really a morning and afternoon spot, dinner (burgers, nachos and the like) is served too.

La Galette Larsbjørnsstræde 9, Indre By. A bit difficult to find (you have to cross a courtyard to get to no. 9) but worth it for the authentic Breton pancakes (30–75kr), made with organic buckwheat and a whole array of fillings from spinach and goat's cheese to chocolate and chestnut mousse. Dinner only on Sun.

Lagkagehuset Christianshavns Torv, Christianshavn. Danish pastry at its best. From 6am onwards the warm freshly made flaky treats are best enjoyed with a cup of coffee at the long counter by the window. Also good organic bread and fruity muffins.

La Glace Skoubogade 29, Indre By. The place to go if you feel like spoiling yourself with something sweet – try the beautifully sculpted cream-heavy cakes (39kr) and pots of real hot chocolate, or just a Danish and coffee. The cakes and traditions haven't changed much since this place opened in 1870, and for good reason.

O's American Breakfast & Dinner Gothersgade 15, Indre By. American-style Southern cooking, with big greasy breakfasts until late afternoon (from 3am during weekends), then switches to Southern soul food and barbecue meals for dinner. There's another branch at Øster Farimagsgade, Nyboder.

Riccos – Butik & Kaffebar Istedgade 119, Vesterbro. Easily the best coffee in town is served in this minuscule shop with a pair of small tables out front. The owner is a self-confessed coffee nerd and if he's not working behind the counter, he's somewhere out in the world on the hunt for aromatic beans. Apart from coffee in various forms – hot and cold – there's also cakes and Italian ice cream. Lattes from 20kr.

Sebastopol Sankt Hans Torv 32, Nørrebro. Proper French style café on trendy Sankt Hans Torv square serving delicious and affordable breakfast (42kr) and brunch (68–92kr) from 8am onwards (from 9am during weekends). The outdoor seating in summer can hardly be bettered, with the gentle trickling of the square's fountain in the background while you catch the early morning rays. Also a popular spot for evening drinks.

Soupanatural Guldbergsgade 9, Nørrebro. A small, unusual place specializing in hot organic porridge (a different mix of grain each day – from millet and sorghum to barley and oats) from 7.30am, and lovely freshly made organic soup, including a veggie option, from 11am. Thurs–Sat evenings it transforms into a cocktail bar.

Sporvejen Gråbrødretorv 17, Indre By. Housed in the last of the city's old trams – the rest are now in Egypt – this place serves up some excellent-value burgers and omelettes, especially considering its location on trendy Gråbrødre torv. Very popular with students. Smoking allowed.

The Laundromat Elmegade 15, Nørrebro. Funky laid-back place which – as the name implies – doubles as a laundry. Open from 8am onwards with breakfast and brunch at reasonable prices, and serving good-quality burgers and light meals throughout the days. Also a wi-fi hotspot.

The Royal Café Amagertorv 6, Indre By. Tucked in next to the Royal Copenhagen porcelain and silverware shop, this showpiece of Danish design is home to a new concept in Danish cuisine, so-called smushi. Delicious finger-food-sized smørrebrød made with unusual toppings that go surprisingly well together (such as wasabi on gravad lax). Also the place to go for fantastic coffee and fabulous cakes.

Restaurants

Many of the city's **Danish restaurants** knock out good-value (around 80kr) and high-quality **lunches**, either from a set menu or from an open buffet. **Dinner** will always be more expensive, although Copenhagen's growing band of **ethnic restaurants** are making it increasingly affordable – many have adopted the Scandinavian open-table idea, offering all-you-can-eat meals from around 60kr, but don't plan a night's dancing after wading through one.

Danes tend to eat early so most restaurants start dinner service at around 6pm and stay open until 11pm or midnight. Roughly half the city's restaurants don't open at all on Sunday, and those that do keep shorter hours, usually opening for dinner only; we've specified closing days in the reviews below. Finally, it's still a good idea to phone ahead to **reserve a table**, especially at the city's more popular spots. We've given telephone numbers for places where reservations are advisable.

Restaurants

Atlas Bar Larsbjørnsstræde 18, Indre By ☏ 33 15 03 52. Small, eco-conscious café-restaurant serving primarily vegetarian Asian and South American dishes. The portions are enormous, with main courses starting at 95kr at lunchtime and 120kr in the evening. Closed Sun.

Café Petersborg Bredgade 76, Nyboder ☏ 33 12 50 16. Housed in an appealing eighteenth-century building, *Petersborg* offers traditional dishes such as meatballs with red cabbage for 98kr, or old fashioned egg-cake (a type of scrambled eggs with bacon and chives served on rye bread) for 95kr, as well as lots of smørrebrød choices at lunchtime including a platter for 125kr. Open Mon–Sat.

Café & Ølhalle 1892 Rømersgade 22, Nørreport ☏ 33 93 25 75. In the basement of the Workers' Museum (see p.74), this is the place to come for old-style Danish food that you won't find anywhere else. Try the *bidesild* (strong pickled herring) or *æbleflæsk* (stewed apple and pork), prepared just as they were a hundred years ago. Lunchtime only, closed Mon.

Caféen i Nikolaj Nikolaj Plads 12, Indre By ☏ 33 11 63 13. Through the side entrance of the deconsecrated Nikolaj church, this place has an extensive lunchtime menu. Everything is prepared from scratch and the produce is largely organic. If you can't decide what to go for, a good bet is the lunch platter (148kr) which is composed of a bit of the best of everything. Otherwise the filling herring smørrebrød will set you back 70kr.

Custom House Bar & Grill Havnegade 44, Indre By. Housed in the old hydrofoil terminal to Sweden alongside two more exclusive restaurants, this place has possibly the city's best view of Inner Havnen. Dining here is fine, too. The lunch dish of the day – from fried mackerel to gravad lax – costs 95kr, while the dinner menu is a tad pricier. Mains start at 175kr for fried duck with spring cabbage and apple-turnip purée.

Gold Prag Gothersgade 39, Indre By ☏ 33 91 47 12. Authentic Czech restaurant for the decidedly non-vegetarian. The huge portions of goulash with rosti and salad (85kr), washed down with mugs of Czech beer – of which there 10 different sorts on offer – are heavenly. Open for dinner only, closed Sun.

House of Souls Vestergade 3, Indre By ☏ 33 91 11 81. Cajun/American restaurant in light, bright rooms with lots of New Orleans atmosphere. Try the seafood gumbo (92kr) or the jambalaya (165kr), a rice dish made with sausage, ham, shellfish and okra. Expect things to be spicy. Dinner only, closed Sun in July.

Huset med det grønne træ Gammeltorv 20, Indre By ☏ 33 12 87 86. Frequented largely by lawyers and solicitors from the law courts next door, the "House with the Green Tree" offers some of the finer Danish lunches in the downtown area, including delectable and consistently good smørrebrød and fourteen different types of *snaps*. Lunch only. Closed Sun, and Sat April–Aug.

Kaffesalonen Peblinge Dossering 6, Nørrebro. Super-hip former workers' caff with outdoor tables looking out onto a lake, and a popular waterside terrace on a floating dock in the summer, when it's perfect for dishes such as lightly grilled tuna washed down with a cold beer.

Kate's Joint Blågårdsgade 12, Nørrebro ☏ 35 37 44 96. Although unimpressive from the outside, this is a small, funky place serving quality dishes from around the globe. A few regulars include Jamaican jerk chicken and chicken tikka for 85kr, and there's always at least one vegetarian option.

L'Education Nationale Larsbjørnsstræde 12, Indre By ☏ 33 91 53 60. Authentic French cuisine – all ingredients, including the wine, are imported from France. Lunchtime favourites include *moules-frites* from 115kr, while for dinner try the rabbit stew with prunes in filo pastry at 195kr. Sun dinner only.

Løgismose Bernstorffsgade 5, Vesterbro. The organic, gourmet hot dogs at this new, already one-of-a-kind grill bar are hand-made by a butcher in southern Jutland. The accompanying onions are fried in duck fat and rosemary, the remoulade prepared from a marinade of mushrooms and pickled vegetables. Quite possibly the best hot dogs in Denmark.

Morgenstedet Langgade, Christiania. Despite the name, "Morning Place" is not open until noon. Tasty and mostly organic vegan and vegetarian salads, snacks and main meals at very affordable prices (meal of the day is 55kr). Alcohol not allowed on the premises. Closed Mon.

Nimb Bernstorffsgade 5, Vesterbro ☏ 88 70 00 00. With a facade of Moorish towers and minarets, Copenhagen's newest boutique hotel includes this superb Danish-fusion restaurant oozing Scandinavian style. A three-course meal runs to 395kr, while you can pick up smaller lunch plates for around 100kr. There is an attached chocolate factory, deli and wine shop. Booking strongly recommended.

Nyhavns Færgekro Nyhavn 5, Indre By ☏ 33 15 15 88. Deservedly pricey traditional food – the scrumptious, fish-laden lunchtime buffet (119kr) is sublime. You can also try the upstairs *à la carte* restaurant with main courses such as entrecôte or salmon steak from 185kr. Outdoor seating in summer.

Pasta Basta Valkendorfsgade 22, Indre By
☎33 11 21 31. A cold buffet of nine different organic pasta salads for 89kr to which you can add hot dishes such as steak or wild mushroom stew from the menu. Open Fri & Sat until 5am, and until 3am during the rest of the week, this is a favourite final stop for night owls and is wildly popular with locals anytime.

Peder Oxe Gråbrødretorv 11, Indre By ☎33 11 00 77. Very popular steakhouse on a small square off Strøget. At lunchtime you can choose three pieces of heaped smørrebrød from a long, mouthwatering list of toppings (138kr) or freshly caught fried plaice, also 138kr. Served in the evenings, their organic burgers (129kr) are superb, and the cellar holds some fine wines.

Ranees Blågårds Plads 10, Nørrebro ☎35 36 85 05. Popular Thai restaurant serving authentic dishes from the Mekong delta, which is where Ranee, the proprietor/chef comes from. Try the pat gai – fried chicken breast with ginger, soya bean paste and jasmine rice (145kr). Dinner only and closed Mon.

🏃 **Ricemarket** Kultorvet 38, Indre By.
☎35 35 75 30 New Thai bistro-type place with outdoor seating on one of the city's main squares, serving a limited range of simple but beautifully prepared, and presented Thai dishes such as teriyaki noodles with avocado, king prawns and bean sprouts for 110kr. Things are a little crammed inside, perhaps in order to make space for the three private dining double beds which can make for either a very romantic or a very uncomfortable meal. Also a takeaway.

RizRaz Kompagnistræde 20, Indre By. Excellent-value Mediterranean food, with a vegetarian lunchtime buffet at 69kr, and an evening buffet at 79kr. Meat dishes have to be ordered separately. Popular with backpackers and open until midnight. Also a branch at Store Kanikkestræde 19.

Slotskælderen – hos Gitte Kik Fortunstræde 4, Indre By ☎33 11 15 37. It may not look much from the outside but this is one of the best places in the country to sample smørrebrød; you simply pick your toppings from the heaped plates. A favourite politicians' hangout (parliament is

across the canal). Lunchtime only. Closed Sun & Mon, and all of July.

Spicey Kitchen Torvegade 56, Christianshavn ☎32 95 28 29. Despite the name, this popular little restaurant serves lightly spiced Indian and Pakistani dishes (with eight veggie options) for under 70kr per main course. Takeaway also available.

Spicylicious Istedgade 27, Vesterbro ☎33 22 85 33. Chic, swish Thai restaurant with fairly priced and very spicy mains starting around 100kr. The food is excellent, though the portions occasionally rather small.

Spiseloppen Christiania ☎32 57 95 58. Since winning many culinary awards, *Spiseloppen* has hiked up its prices considerably (meals cost 140–200kr). That said, it's still excellent, and so are the portions; try roast New Zealand lamb or steamed cod in mustard sauce. Evenings only, closed Mon.

Sticks 'n' Sushi Nansensgade 59, Nørreport ☎33 11 14 07. Copenhagen's first sushi restaurant, and still its best: the menu is extensive, with every ingredient explained, and the food of extremely high quality, while the decor is suitably minimalist. There's a takeaway further down the road at no. 47, and other branches at Øster Farimagsgade 16 and Istedgade 62 which do both eat-in and takeaway. Closed Sun.

Thorvaldsens Hus Gammel Strand 34, Indre By ☎33 32 04 00. Across the canal from the colourful Thorvaldsens Museum, and with outdoor seating in the summer, *Thorvaldsens* has a great selection of delectable sandwiches and salads on the lunchtime menu, and continues into the evening with mouth-watering gourmet cuisine such as grilled fresh Atlantic salmon with caviar and truffle sauce, for a mere 195kr. Closed Mon.

🏃 **Vespa** Store Kongensgade 90, Frederiks-staden ☎33 11 37 00. Fabulous new place serving a set Danish/Mediterranean five-course menu at exactly 6pm, and Wed–Sat also at 9pm. House wine is served in carafes and costs 100kr for half a litre. The set menu changes every day and costs 275kr Mon–Thurs, and 300kr Fri & Sat. Very rustic and utterly delicious. Closed Sun.

Drinking, nightlife and entertainment

Copenhagen is covered by an almost unchartable network of **cafés** and bars that is constantly in flux, with hot new places popping up regularly and becoming the latest flavour of the month, though the appeal of the old-fashioned Danish pub remains undiminished. Many places seem to never sleep; you can get a **drink** – and usually a snack, too – at almost any time of the day or night. Almost all of the most exciting and popular cafés and bars are in – or close to – either Indre By, Vesterbro or the Nørrebro districts, and it's no hardship to sample several on the same night.

Most places open until midnight during the week and 2am at weekends; we've included opening hours for those that open later or close earlier.

Discos, as most Danes call nightclubs, are much like those in any major city, although they're generally more concerned with having a good time than defining the cutting edge of fashion. You'll be dancing alone if you turn up much before midnight; after that time, especially on Fridays and Saturdays, discos fill rapidly – and stay open until 5am. Drink prices are seldom hiked up and admission is fairly cheap at 30–80kr. For full **listings** of events and all kinds of entertainment, check out the free monthly tourist magazine *Copenhagen This Week* (available from the tourist office), and keep an eye out for notices at cafés.

It's with **live music** that Copenhagen really stands out. Minor gigs in cafés and bars are often free, though later in the week there may be a modest cover charge. Throughout the summer, there are many **free concerts** in the city's parks, some featuring leading Danish bands. The annual **Copenhagen Jazz Festival** (usually nine days in ealy July) hosts a bewildering number of big-name (and next-big-thing) bebop, fusion, swing, avant-garde and big-band jazz music, and there are live gigs at almost every street corner. *Gaffa*, free from music and record shops is a good source of info, as is ⓦwww.billetnet.dk, which has general entertainment **information** and sells advanced tickets to most gigs and events.

New **film** releases, often in English with Danish subtitles, are shown all over the city; more esoteric fare is screened at Cinemateket on Gothersgade, Indre By (☎33 74 34 12, ⓦwww.dfi.dk), Husets Biograf in the Huset building at Magstræde 14, Indre By (☎33 32 40 77), or Vester Vov Vov, Absalonsgade 5, Vesterbro (☎33 24 42 00, ⓦwww.vestervovvov.dk). Note that all the places in Indre By appear on the Indre By map (p.72); all the others are marked on the main Copenhagen map (pp.64–65).

Bars and cafés

Andy's Bar Gothersgade 33B, Indre By. Packed late-night traditional Danish bar (daily 11pm–6am) with a very jovial vibe – you'll end up leaving with lots of new friends, if only you could remember their names.

Bibendum Nansensgade 45, Indre By. Small, crowded wine bar in a cellar on trendy Nansensgade, with a huge selection of wines, most served by the glass. Tasty tapas, too. Closed Sun.

Bloomsday Bar Niels Hemmingsensgade 32, Indre By. Irish bar especially popular with Copenhagen's large Irish population, with a good selection of ales, lagers and cider, and a large-screen TV showing football. Live Irish music on Sun afternoons.

Charlie's Bar Pilestræde 33, Indre By. Award-winning Real Ale pub with an impressive array of draught beers and lagers, and even a Somerset cider. Generally packed with beer enthusiasts. Smoking allowed.

Hviids Vinstue Kongens Nytorv 19, Indre By. Old-fashioned bar whose crowded rooms are patrolled by uniformed waiters. Outdoor seating in the summer.

Ideal Bar at Vega Engahavevej 40, Vesterbro. Part of the Vega music complex (see p.88) and known for its excellent cocktail bar and relaxed post-gig atmosphere, when the large leather sofas come in handy. After midnight, everyone takes to the very crowded dancefloor. Open Wed–Sat from 7pm.

Nemoland Christiania. Despite the government crackdown on Christiania, this is still one of the city's most popular open-air bars. In winter, the punters move indoors to the pool tables and backgammon boards.

Nørrebro Bryghus Ryesgade 3, Nørrebro. Immensely popular brewery pub with a range of home brews that sell out quicker than they can be bottled. Also home to a pricey restaurant.

Ølbaren Elmegade 2, Nørrebro. The name means "Beer Bar", and there's an incredible range from around the world, and a bartender that knows them all and can advise accordingly. Always packed. Open Mon–Sat until 1pm.

Pussy Galore's Flying Circus Sankt Hans Torv 30, Nørrebro. Hugely popular café with outdoor seating on the sunny side of trendy Sankt Hans square serving an extensive selection of cocktails and long drinks, as well as beer and wine. Also good coffee.

Riesen Oehlenschlægersgade 36, Vesterbro. Small, crowded and often smoky neighbourhood bar featuring affordable draught and bottled import beers as well as gritty rock music playing on the jukebox. Artistically minded Copenhageners come here towards the end of the night; it really gets going after 1am.

Zum Biergarten Axeltorv 12, Indre By. Bavarian *bierstubbe* housed in the old waterworks building offering Oktoberfest atmosphere with long rickety tables and litre mugs of German micro-brewery beer. When the weather allows there's outdoor service, including food prepared on an open grill. Open Fri & Sat until 5am, closed Sun.

Live music venues and clubs

Drop Inn Kompagnistræde 34, Indre By. Easygoing, unpretentious place near Huset with live blues or rock almost every night. Cheap beer (especially before 7pm) and stays open until 5am.

Gefärlich Fælledvej 7, Nørrebro ⓦ www.gefahrlich .dk. Popular new place that's heaving every night when the ever-changing DJs get going in the downstairs club, playing pretty much anything they feel like. Also a café/restaurant upstairs. Open Fri & Sat until 4.30am. Closed Sun & Mon.

Huset i Magstræde Rådhusstræde 13, Indre By ⓣ 33 69 32 00, ⓦ www.husetmagstraede.dk. Copenhagen's culture house in a new incarnation with several stages featuring up-and-coming Danish jazz and rock bands most nights of the week. The centre also houses a theatre, a cinema and a café. Closed Sun, music starts from 5pm onwards.

Jazzcup Gothersgade 107, Indre By ⓣ 33 15 02 02. CD shop and café, with live jazz every Fri & Sat at 3.30pm and 2.30pm respectively. Some of the best local as well as international musicians from the world circuit play here.

JazzHouse Niels Hemmingsensgade 10, Indre By ⓣ 33 15 26 00, ⓦ www.jazzhouse.dk. Near Amagertorv, this is the country's premier jazz venue, with regular performances from international names as well as Denmark's finest. Jazz here is defined in its broadest sense from world music to fusion, followed by a funky late-night DJ-dancefloor Fri & Sat. Closed Sun & Mon.

🏃 **Karriere Bar** Flæsketorvet 57–67 ⓦ www .karrierebar.com. Heralded as an experimental café-bar-restaurant-club-art space, this is where *everyone* in Copenhagen is going these days. Located in the reclaimed Kødbyen (meat-packing district), it's packed to the gills most nights of the week with hipsters, the beautiful people and their acolytes. Great place for celeb spotting, and an even better place to dance until the sun comes up. Not to be missed. Officially open til 3am, though the party often lasts long after that.

Loppen Bådsmandsstræde 43, Christiania ⓣ 32 57 84 22, ⓦ www.loppen.dk. By the main entrance to Christiania in a suitably cool warehouse setting for both established and experimental

Danish rock, jazz and performance artists, and quite a few British and American ones, too. There's a DJ after the live act on Fri & Sat until 5am.

Mojo Løngangstræde 21, Indre By ⓣ 33 11 64 53, ⓦ www.mojo.dk. Cosy, low-key place that's renowned for its jazz and blues evenings. Live music every night followed by a DJ Thurs–Sat. Happy hour daily 8–10pm, and open till 5am every night.

Park Café Østerbrogade 79, Østerbro ⓣ 35 42 62 48, ⓦ www.park.dk. Plush high-ceilinged café/bar in grand surroundings with a nightclub upstairs (Thurs–Sat until 5am) in *Saturday Night Fever* style. Usually draws a fun, mixed crowd who spill out onto the rooftop terrace to cool off during summer. Fri over 20s, Sat over 22s.

Rust Guldbergsgade 8, Nørrebro ⓣ 35 24 52 00, ⓦ www.rust.dk. Huge complex catering for all tastes: live indie-rock and -pop, hip-hop and electronica acts on its main stage, and three dancefloors offering everything from breakbeat to Latin jazz. Open Wed–Sat 9pm–5am.

Stengade 30 Stengade 18, Nørrebro ⓣ 35 36 09 38, ⓦ www.stengade30.dk. Dark, small underground-type place with a mixed bag of live music and club nights including regular hardcore metal, punk and indie sessions. Also infamous for its RubA'Dub Sun which feature non-stop reggae. Closed Mon, open till 5am Thurs–Sun.

Tivoli Vesterbrogade 3, Vesterbro ⓦ www.tivoli .dk. Surprisingly good *fredagsrock* (Friday Rock) concerts with big names playing at this outdoor stage on Fri nights at 10pm from April–Sept. Pop and rock regulars include groups such as Flaming Lips, Alphabeat, Michael McDonald and the Danish electronica band Kashmir. Entry is free with general Tivoli admittance.

Vega Enghavevej 40, Vesterbro ⓣ 33 25 70 11, ⓦ www.vega.dk. Set in a former union hall, this top-billing venue subtly shows off its late 50s decor while showcasing plenty of great music. The Store Vega stage hosts renowned international acts, while Lille Vega is for more underground bands. Also has a nightclub hosting great DJs and the ever-trendy *Ideal Bar.* Invariably an excellent night out.

Woodstock Vestergade 12, Indre By ⓣ 33 11 20 71. Pulls a large, fun-loving crowd eager to dance to anything with a beat – though the music is predominantly 1960s. Close to the Rådhus. Open till 5am Thurs–Sat.

Gay and lesbian Copenhagen

As you'd expect from the capital of a country with a very liberal attitude to homosexuality (the age of consent is 15, and gay marriages are legal as long as one of the partners is Danish), Copenhagen has a lively **gay scene**, which includes a good sprinkling of bars and clubs (one with a sauna), a bookshop and a few exclusively gay **accommodation options**, the latter all in Indre By: *Copenhagen Rainbow*, Frederiksberggade 25C (☎33 14 10 20, ⓦwww.copenhagen-rainbow.dk; ❹), *Hotel Windsor*, Frederiksborggade 30 (☎33 11 08 30, ⓦwww.hotelwindsor.dk; ❸) and *Carstens Guesthouse*, Christians Brygge 28, 5th floor (☎40 50 91 07, ⓦwww.carstensguesthouse.dk; ❹; see main Copenhagen map).

For **information** the National Organization for Gay Men and Women, *Landsforeningen for Bøsser og Lesbiske* (☎33 13 19 48, ⓦwww.lbl.dk) provides a well-run advice service and is an excellent place to pick up news of any gay or lesbian events in the city. Alternatively check out their useful gay guide website ⓦwww.gayguide.dk or www.copenhagen-gay-life.dk which also has information about what's happening on the gay front in the city. Copenhagen Gay Life also produces a free English-language map of gay Copenhagen which you should be able to pick up at most gay bars.

Unless otherwise stated, the places in Indre By appear on the map on p.72, and all the others on the main Copenhagen map on pp.64–65.

Bars and clubs

Amigo Bar Schønbergsgade 4, Frederiksberg. Fun gay bar popular with gay and straight folk alike, not least since the karaoke was relaunched. Open daily until 6am.

Café Intime Allégade 25, Frederiksberg. Small, cosy piano bar frequented by those with a penchant for musicals, gay and straight.

Can Can Mikkel Bryggersgade 11, Indre By. A favourite late-night drinking spot for gay men, one block northwest of the Rådhus. Open until 5am Fri & Sat.

Centralhjørnet Kattesundet 12, Indre By. Copenhagen's oldest gay bar which has a slightly "greyer" clientele. Usually most busy on Sun.

Chaca Studiestræde 39, Indre By. Predominantly lesbian bar spread over two floors with lots of different events on the programme; games nights, speed-dating and karaoke nights the most renowned. Smoking allowed. Open Wed–Sat, Fri & Sat until 5am.

Code Rådhusstræde 1, Indre By. Newest addition on the gay scene attracting a good gay and lesbian mix. A café during daylight hours and a lounge bar at night with a DJ hitting the decks every Fri & Sat until 5am. Closed Sun–Tues.

Cosy Bar Studiestræde 24, Indre By. This popular, all-ages cruising venue gets busy late, and stays open right through until 8am Fri & Sat, 6am the rest of the week.

Jailhouse CPH Studiestræde 12, Indre By. Popular gay basement bar, designed as a jail with drinking "cells", handcuffs lying around and waiters dressed up in uniform. Upstairs there's a restaurant serving good-value traditional Danish food. Open until 6am Fri & Sat.

Masken Studiestræde 33, Indre By. Great club-bar on two floors, often featuring drag shows and popular with a student crowd due to its affordable booze. Things don't pick up until 11pm and Fri in particular are quite cruisey.

Oscar Rådhuspladsen 77, Indre By. One of Copenhagen's coolest gay café-bars, with an excellent information point that's well stocked with maps and guides. In the evening, the clientele are mostly young and trendy. Also a good restaurant. Daily noon–2am.

Vela Gay Club Victoriagade 2–4, Vesterbro. Funky oriental-style nightclub and popular lesbian hang-out, featuring dim lighting. As well as cocktails, the bar also serves up 'pussy-tails'. Open Wed–Sat until 5am.

Listings

Airlines British Airways, Rådhuspladsen 16 ☎70 12 80 22; easyjet ☎70 12 43 21; Finnair, Nyropsgade 47 ☎33 36 45 45; SAS, Hammerichsgade 1–5 ☎70 10 30 00 (domestic reservations), ☎70 10 20 00 (overseas reservations).

Banks and exchange There's a Den Danske Bank at Kastrup airport (daily 6am–8.30pm); Forex and X-Change at the central station (daily 7/8am–9pm) and Kontanten ATMs everywhere.

Bookshops Many of the city's bookshops are in the area around Fiolstræde and Købmagergade; all stock guidebooks and maps. The Book Trader, Skindergade 23 (ⓦwww.booktrader.dk), has a varied selection of old and new books in English. For new books try GAD, at Vimmelskaftet 32 (on Strøget) and inside the central station; Nordisk Korthandel, Studiestræde 26–30 (ⓦwww.scanmaps.dk); Arnold Busck, Købmagergade 49; and Boghallen, Rådhuspladsen 37.

Onward travel to Sweden and Norway – the Øresunds Link

Opened in July 2000, the **Øresunds Link** (see p.430) offers a quick tunnel and bridge connection between the Copenhagen central station and Kastrup airport, to Malmö and – via fast train – Stockholm, Gothenburg and Oslo. Using this link, the ride across the Øresund takes roughly thirty minutes and costs 73kr.

Car parks Usually pay-and-display, with different rates depending on zone colour: in descending level of expense, zones are coloured red (26kr per hour), green (16kr) and blue (9kr). Downtown car parks are thin on the ground, but there's one at the Statoil petrol station in Israel Plads near Nørreport (20kr per hr) and Saga P-hus on Vesterbrogade 23 (same rates).

Car rental Avis, Kampmannsgade 1 ☎70 24 77 07; Hertz, Ved Vesterport 3 ☎33 17 90 20; Europcar/InterRent, Gammel Kongevej 13 ☎33 55 99 00; Budget, Vester Farimagsgade 7 ☎33 55 05 00; Lej et Lig (Rent a Wreck), Strandvænget 30 ☎70 25 45 25.

Dentist Emergency Dentist Clinic, Hostrup Have 80, Frederiksberg ☎29 82 44 71, daily except Wed. Outside hours contact Tandlægevagten, Oslo Plads 14 ☎35 38 02 51. Open for emergencies only, daily 8–9.30pm, Sat & Sun also 10am–noon. Turn up and be prepared to pay at least 200kr in cash on the spot.

Doctors Call ☎70 13 00 41 and you'll be given the name of a doctor in your area, or, in emergency, a doctor will come and see you. There's a consultation fee of 400–600kr, which must be paid in cash.

Embassies Australia, Dampfærgevej 26 ☎70 26 36 76; Canada, Kristen Bernikowsgade 1 ☎33 48 32 00; Ireland, Østbanegade 21 ☎35 42 32 33; Netherlands, Toldbogade 33 ☎33 70 72 00; South Africa, Gammel Vartov Vej 8, Hellerup ☎39 18 01 55; UK Kastelsvej 40 ☎35 26 63 75; US, Dag Hammarskjölds Allé 24 ☎33 41 71 00. Note that New Zealand uses the UK office.

Emergencies ☎112 for police or ambulance.

Hospitals There are emergency departments at Bispebjerg Hospital, Bispebjerg Bakke 23 (☎35 31 35 31) and Frederiksberg Hospital, Nordre Fasanvej 57 (☎38 16 38 16); EU and Scandinavian nationals get free treatment, though in reality others are unlikely to have to pay either.

Internet access Free access is available at the city's libraries (but not the Royal Library), with general opening hours Mon–Thurs 10am–7pm, Fri noon–5pm, Sat 10am–2pm. Most central are Hovedbiblioteket, Krystalgade 15–17; Blågårds Bilbliotek, Blågårds Plads 5; Christianshavns Bibliotek, Dronningensgade 53; and Østerbro Bibliotek, Dag Hammarskölds Allé 19. Internet cafés include Boomtown, Axeltorv 1–3 (daily 24hr; 30kr per hr) the largest in the city, with 100 terminals.

Left luggage The DSB Garderobe office (Mon–Sat 5.30–1am, Sun 6–1am) downstairs in the central station stores luggage for 30–40kr per day per item, and there are also small and large lockers for 25–35kr per day.

Markets There's a good flea market at Israel Plads on Sat (mid-April to mid-Oct 9am–3pm; S-train or Metro to Nørreport Station or bus #5A), and a popular antique market at Gammel Strand (May–Sept Fri 8am–5pm, Sat 9am–5pm). Try also the various summertime markets that pop up around Christiania, and the Saturday-morning markets behind Frederiksberg Rådhus (mid-April to mid-Oct 8am–2pm; bus #14 or #15), on Kongens Nytorv square (June to mid-Sept Sat 10am–5pm) and along Assistens Kirkegårdens wall on Nørrebrogade (same hours; bus #5A).

Pharmacy Steno Apotek, Vesterbrogade 6C and Sønderbro Apotek, Amagerbrogade 158, are both open 24hr.

Post offices Main office at Fisketorvet (Mon–Fri 11am–6pm, Sat 10am–1pm); there's another at the central station (Mon–Fri 8am–9pm, Sat & Sun 10am–4pm). Poste restante is available at all post offices.

Travel agents Kilroy Travels, Skindergade 28 (☎33 11 00 44, ⓦwww.kilroytravels.com), can give advice on travelling around Denmark, the rest of Scandinavia and Europe. STA Travel, Fiolstræde 18 (☎33 14 15 01, ⓦwww.sta.com) offers youth and student tickets.

Around Zealand

It's easy to see more of Zealand by making day-trips out from the capital, although, depending on where you're heading next, it's often a better idea to pack your bags and leave Copenhagen altogether. Transport links are excellent throughout the region, making much of northern and central Zealand commuter territory. You'll pass through dozens of tiny villages and large forests on the way to historic centres such as **Helsingør**, **Køge** and – an essential call if you're interested in Denmark's past – **Roskilde**. The north coast of Zealand holds a number of prepossessing wind-swept beachfronts, memorable vistas of the sea and a string of great places to dine, while true nature lovers often head straight for the explorable smaller **islands** off southern Zealand and **Bornholm** to the east. Urbanites won't find much diversion though, and if you're 'craving' some city life, you'd do well to push on (which is easily done) to the bigger cities in Funen and Jutland.

North Zealand

The **coast north of Copenhagen**, as far as Helsingør, rejoices under the tag of the "Danish Riviera", a label which neatly describes its line of tiny one-time fishing hamlets, now inhabited almost exclusively by the super-wealthy. The lovely views of beckoning beaches are best seen on the hour-long bus journey (#388) north to Helsingør from Klampenborg, itself the last stop on line B, C or F of the S-train system. There's also a frequent 45-minute train service between Copenhagen and Helsingør; it's quicker than the bus, but views are obscured by trees almost the entire way. The north coast and the stretch of beaches between Helsingør and Gilleleje are served by a network of private trains, on which the Copenhagen Card is valid, although InterRail, Eurail and ScanRail passes are not.

The Karen Blixen Museum, Humlebæk and Louisiana

There are two good reasons to get off the bus before Helsingør. First is the **Karen Blixen Museum** (May–Sept Tues–Sun 10am–5pm; Oct–April Wed–Fri 1–4pm, Sat & Sun 11am–4pm; 45kr; ⓦ www.karen-blixen.dk), a fifteen-minute walk from Rungsted Kyst train station, on the *regionaltog* train line going north towards Helsingør; bus #388 stops just outside (and also at the station). The museum is housed in the family home of the writer who, while long a household name in Denmark for her short stories (often written under the pen name of Isak Dinesen) and outspoken opinions, enjoyed a resurgence of international popularity during the mid-1980s when *Out of Africa* was released. The film was based on her 1937 autobiographical account of running a coffee plantation in Kenya – after returning, Blixen lived here until her death in 1962, and much of the house is maintained as it was during her final years. The living quarters feature a short biographical film, surrounding texts on the walls describe Blixen's eventful life (her father committed suicide and she married the twin brother of the man she loved, among other things), and exhibits include a collection of first editions and the tiny typewriter she used in Africa. Even if you've never read a word of Blixen, it's hard not to be impressed by accounts of her spirit and strength, which shine through the museum. After seeing the house, make for the flower garden, where the author's simple grave lies beneath a protective beech tree.

In **HUMLEBÆK**, the next community of any size, you'll find **Louisiana** (Tues–Fri 11am–10pm, Sat & Sun 11am–6pm; 90kr; ⓦ www.louisiana.dk), a modern-art museum on the northern edge of the village at Gammel Strandvej 13, a short walk from the train station; bus #388 stops just outside. Even if you go nowhere else outside Copenhagen, it would be a shame to miss this: the setting alone is worth the journey, harmoniously combining art, architecture and landscape. It seems churlish to only mention individual items, but the museum's American section, in the south corridor, includes some devastating pieces by Edward Kienholz, Malcolm Morley's scintillatingly gross Pacific Telephone Los Angeles Yellow Pages, in which the telephone directory cover expands to monstrous proportions and coffee stains rib the city skyline like a weird metallic grid, and (in the reading room) Jim Dines' powerful series The Desire. You'll also find some of Giacometti's gangly figures haunting a room of their own off the north corridor, an equally affecting handful of sculptures by Max Ernst squatting outside the windows and leering inwards, and sundry works by Warhol, Lichtenstein and Anselm Kiefer. Except for some pieces by Per Kirkeby and paintings by various Danish luminaries of the CoBrA group, home-grown artists have a rather low profile, although their work is often featured in temporary exhibitions.

Helsingør

First impressions of **HELSINGØR** are none too enticing. The bus stops outside the noisy train station, opposite which Havnepladsen is usually full of transit passengers loitering around fast-food stalls before making for the active ferry terminal, 100m distant. Away from the hustle, though, Helsingør is a quiet and extremely likeable town. Strategically positioned on the four-kilometre strip of water linking the North Sea and the Baltic, the town's wealth was founded on the Sound Toll of 1429, which was levied on passing ships right up until the nineteenth century. Shipbuilding restored some of Helsingør's fortunes after the toll was abolished, but today it's once again the sliver of water between Denmark and Sweden, and the ferries across it to Helsingborg, which account for most of the town's livelihood. The **tourist office** (mid-June to mid-Aug Mon–Thurs 9am–5pm, Fri 9am–6pm, Sat 10am–3pm; rest of the year Mon–Fri 10am–5pm, Sat 10am–2pm; ☎49 21 13 33, ⓦwww.visithelsingor.dk), is across from the train station at Havnepladsen 3.

Accommodation

Due to the high numbers of visiting tourists, the closest thing to a cheap **hotel** here is the *Skandia*, Bramstræde 1 (☎49 21 09 02, ⓦwww.hotelskandia.dk; ❷), which is decent and clean; some rooms have a shared bath. If you can afford it, treat yourself to the "Hamlet" or "Ophelia" suites at the *Hotel Hamlet*, Bramstræde 5 (☎49 21 05 91; ⓦwww.hotelhamlet.dk; ❺), a handsome, if slightly dated, three-star with a fish and steak restaurant. There's also a **youth hostel** (☎49 21 16 40, ⓦwww.helsingorhostel.dk; Feb–Nov; dorm beds 150kr) literally on the beach; it's

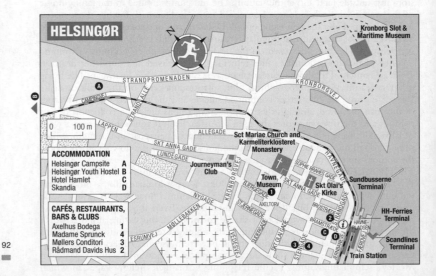

a twenty-minute walk to the north from the centre along the coastal road (Nordre Strandvej), or take bus #340 from the station and get off just after the sports stadium. The *Helsingør Camping* **campsite**, at Strandalleen 1 at the end of Skt Annagade (℡49 21 58 56, ⓦwww.helsingorcamping.dk; cabins 250kr per weekday plus 60kr per person, 3600kr per week in July for five people, 5900kr for six), is somewhat closer to town and also just alongside a beach.

The Town

Helsingør's main draw, on a sandy curl of land extending seawards like a raised fist, is **Kronborg Slot** (April & Oct Tues–Sun 11am–4pm; May–Sept daily 10.30am–5pm; Nov–March Tues–Sun 11am–3pm 50–85kr depending on areas visited; ⓦwww .kronborg.dk), famous principally as the setting – under the name of Elsinore Castle – for Shakespeare's *Hamlet*. Actually, the playwright never visited Helsingør, and his hero was based on one Amleth (or Amled), a tenth-century character lost in the mists of Danish mythology who certainly pre-dated the castle – none of which has affected Kronborg's thriving trade in Hamlet souvenirs, nor the hundreds of requests asking for the whereabouts of "Hamlet's bedroom". The castle was awarded UNESCO World Heritage Site status in 2000 and, consequently, it has become markedly more visitor-friendly. **Guided tours** of the royal chambers take place daily at 12.30pm and 2pm in English and well-informed attendants also hover in every room ready to answer questions.

Construction of the present castle, built on the site of Erik of Pomerania's fortress, was instigated during the sixteenth century by Frederik II. He commissioned the Dutch architects Van Opbergen and Van Paaske, who took their ideas from the buildings of Antwerp. Various bits have been destroyed and rebuilt since, but it remains a grand affair, enhanced immeasurably by its setting, and with an interior (particularly the royal chapel) that is spectacularly ornate – appreciation, though, is hampered by the steady flow of tourists. Crowds are less of a problem in the labyrinthine **cellars** – the casemates – which can be seen on an English-language guided tour (daily noon and 2pm), which departs from the cellar entrance. The body of Holger Danske, a mythical hero from the legends of Charlemagne, is said to lie beneath the castle, ready to wake again when Denmark needs him, although the tacky Viking-style statue depicting the legend detracts somewhat from the cellars' authentic aura of decay. The castle also houses the captivating national **Maritime Museum** (same hours; 50kr, joint ticket with the castle 85kr; ⓦwww.maritime-museum.dk) which, apart from a motley collection of model ships and nautical knick-knacks, contains relics from Denmark's colonial past in Greenland, India, the West Indies and West Africa, as well as, from 1852, the world's oldest surviving ship's biscuit.

Away from Kronborg and the harbour area, Helsingør has a well-preserved **medieval quarter**. Stengade is the main pedestrianized street, linked by Bjergegade to **Axeltorv**, the town's small market square and a good spot to linger over a beer. Alternatively, stroll into nearby **Brostræde**, a narrow alleyway that's famous for Brostræde Is, which sells immense ice creams made with traditional ingredients. Near the corner of Stengade and Skt Anna Gade the **Skt Olai's Kirke** (Mon–Fri: May–Aug 10am–4pm; Sept–April 10am–2pm) contains a small but interesting exhibit on the building's history. Just beyond is the fifteenth-century **Sct Mariæ Church** (Mon–Sat 9am–noon, Thurs also 4–6pm) and, within the same walls, the fourteenth-century **Karmeliterklosteret Monastery** (daily 10am–2pm; mid-May to mid-Sept guided tours of both Mon–Fri at 2pm; 20kr) which originally served as a hospital, when it prided itself on its brain operations. The unnerving tools of this profession are still on show next door at the **Town Museum** (Tues–Fri & Sun noon–4pm, Sat 10am–2pm; 20kr), together with diagrams of the corrective insertions made into patients' heads.

Eating, drinking and nightlife

Helsingør's best collection of restaurants and cafés – and, if you're in a hurry, fast-food joints – are splayed out on and around Stengade. Worth seeking out is *Møllers*

Ferries to Sweden

Two ferry companies operate regular boats between Helsingør and Helsingborg in Sweden. The trip takes approximately twenty minutes and as tickets are rarely sold out, it's easiest just to buy at the terminal when you want to travel. HH Ferries (☎49 26 01 55, ⊛www.hhferries.dk) has half-hourly return trips running virtually round the clock and costing 38kr, with open return car prices starting at 500kr (or 305kr for a family day return) and including up to nine passengers. The ships operated by Scandlines (☎33 15 15 15, ⊛www.scandlines.dk) run slightly more frequently, and cost 40kr return, or 550kr for a car plus up to nine passengers. Both advertise frequent special day-return deals (*dagsbillet*) on their websites.

Conditori, Stengade 39, Denmark's oldest bakery, which has sizeable sandwiches and Danish pastries to follow. *Rådmand Davids Hus* which dates from 1694 does fine Danish lunches, and is close to the train station at Standgade 70. Tasty pastas, burgers and salads are served at *Madame Sprunck*, Stengade 48. Given the proximity of the capital, nightlife of note is a rare commodity, but for an evening drink, stroll the streets on either side of Stengade, where there are several decent bars including *Axelhus Bodega*, Sudergade 27, with cheap beer and lively locals. Rowdier boozing goes on at the top end of Axeltorv, popular with Swedes taking advantage of Denmark's more liberal licensing laws.

Onwards from Helsingør: the North Zealand coast

Some of the best beaches in Zealand and several attractive fishing villages are within easy reach of Helsingør, either by bike, local bus or private train. No one particular place has the power to hold you for long, but the region as a whole is hard to beat for a few days' relaxation and indulgence.

Gilleleje and Tisvildeleje

Up around the small beach towns of Hellebæk and Hornbæk, trains continue fifteen minutes further along the coast to **GILLELEJE**, a lovely fishing village that does a roaring tourist trade in the peak of the summer. It's a good place for a short stopover, though unfortunately **accommodation** tends to be booked up far in advance; the best option is the grand *Gilleleje Badehotel* (☎48 30 13 47, ⊛www .gillelejebadehotel.dk; ❺), seconded by the prefab Swiss-chalet-style *Strand*, Vesterbrogade 4B (☎48 30 05 12, ⊛www.hotel-strand.dk; ❹). Alternatively the **tourist office** at Gilleleje Hovedgade 6F (May to mid-June Mon–Fri 19am–5pm,

Søren Kierkegaard

Søren Kierkegaard (1813–55) is inextricably linked with Copenhagen, yet his championing of individual will over social conventions and his rejection of materialism did little to endear him to his fellow Danes. Kierkegaard believed himself set on an "evil destiny" – partly the fault of his father, who is best remembered for having cursed God on a Jutland heath. Kierkegaard's first book, **Either/Or**, was a philosophical investigation into the conflicting emotions involved in his love affair with one **Regine Olsen**; she failed to understand it, however, and married someone else. Few other people understood *Either/Or*, in fact, and Kierkegaard, though devastated by the broken romance, came to revel in the enigma he had created, becoming a "walking mystery in the streets of Copenhagen" (he lived in a house on Nytorv). He was a prolific author, sometimes publishing two books on the same day and often writing under pseudonyms. His greatest philosophical works were written by 1846 and are often claimed to have laid the foundations of **existentialism**.

Sat 9am–1pm; mid-June to Aug Mon–Sat 9am–5pm; rest of the year Mon–Fri 9am–4pm, Sat 9am–noon; ☎48 30 01 74, ⓦwww.visitgribskov.dk) has a list of affordable **private rooms** from 350kr upwards, plus a 25kr booking fee. Another budget option is the year-round **campsite**, 3km outside the village at Bregnerødvej 21 (☎49 71 97 55). If none of these appeals, the final option is to head west to the youth hostel in Tisvildeleje (see below).

While in Gilleleje, negotiate at least some of the footpath that runs along the top of the dunes, where, in 1835, **Søren Kierkegaard** took lengthy contemplative walks, later recalling: "I often stood there and reflected over my past life. The force of the sea and the struggle of the elements made me realize how unimportant I was." Ironically, so important would Kierkegaard become that a monument to him now stands on the path bearing his maxim: "Truth in life is to live for an idea." The tourist office has maps of the different routes he used to walk.

From Gilleleje, bus #363 largely follows the coast to the wilder **TISVILDELEJE** (a hour-long journey), where there are yet more beaches and Tisvilde Hegn (locally called simply "Hegn"), a forest of wind-tormented trees planted here during the eighteenth century to prevent sand drifts. The **youth hostel** at Bygmarken 30 (☎48 70 98 50, ⓦwww.helene.dk) is part of a holiday complex, the Sankt Helene Centeret, and has forty-odd family rooms with dorm beds (185kr) and some doubles (❷). Of the town's several fetching food options, the best are the rustic French-styled *Bio & Bistro*, Hovedgaden 38 and *Tisvildeleje Caféen*, just down the road at no. 55, which offers a pricey but scrumptious outdoor grilled buffet.

Inland from the coast: Hillerød and Frederiksborg Slot

It's hard to continue along the coast without first detouring **inland**, and in any case the effort is barely worthwhile. Trains from both Tisvildeleje and Gilleleje run to **HILLERØD**, in the heart of North Zealand, which – thanks to its magnificent castle – is the place to make for. Hillerød is forty minutes by S-train from Helsingør, and a similar distance from Copenhagen (last stop on line A and E). The town's main claim to fame is **Frederiksborg Slot** (daily: mid-March to Oct 10am–5pm; Nov to mid-March 11am–3pm; 60kr; ⓦwww.frederiksborgmuseet.dk), a castle which easily pushes the more famous Kronborg into second place and lies decorously across three small islands within an artificial lake. Buses #701 and #702 run from the train station to the castle, or it's a twenty-minute walk, following the signs (*Slottet*) through the town centre.

Frederiksborg Slot was the home of Frederik II and birthplace of his son Christian IV. At the turn of the seventeenth century, under the auspices of Christian, rebuilding began in an unorthodox Dutch Renaissance style. It's the unusual and prolific use of towers and spires, Gothic arches and flowery window ornamentation that still stands out, despite the changes wrought by fire and restoration.

You can see the exterior of the castle for free simply by walking through the main gates, across the seventeenth-century S-shaped bridge, and into the central courtyard. Since 1878, the interior has functioned as a **Museum of National History**, largely funded by the Carlsberg brewery magnate Carl Jacobsen in an attempt to create a Danish Versailles, and to heighten the nation's sense of history and cultural development. The audio guides (20kr) are well worth it even though most of the sixty-odd rooms have detailed descriptions in English pasted on the walls. Many rooms are surprisingly free of furniture and household objects, and attention is drawn to the historical paintings and portraits – one of the finest collections in the country, a motley crew of flat-faced kings and thin consorts who between them ruled and misruled Denmark for centuries, giving way in later rooms to politicians, scientists and writers.

Away from the often crowded interior, the astonishingly intricate **Baroque gardens**, on the far side of the lake have some photogenic views of the castle from their stepped terraces and are a good spot for a rest. The quickest way to them is through the narrow Mint Gate to the left of the main castle building, which adjoins a roofed-in bridge leading to the King's Wing. In summer you can also do a half-hour trip on the lake aboard the M/F Frederiksborg ferry, which leaves every thirty minutes from outside the castle (mid-May to mid-Sept Mon–Sat 11am–5pm, Sun 1–5pm; 20kr).

If you do want to stay, the hostel section of the *Nordiske Lejerskole og Kursuscenter*, Lejerskolevej 4 (☎48 26 19 86, ✆www.nordlejr.dk), has inexpensive private rooms (➊) with shared bathrooms as well as dorms (160kr). The **tourist office**, Møllestræde 9 (Mon–Wed 10.30am–5.30pm, Tues & Fri 10.30am–4.30pm, Sun 10.30–2pm; ☎48 24 26 26, ✆www.hillerodturist.dk) can arrange **private rooms** for around 150kr per person (25kr booking fee). For **food**, the ✠ *Spisestedet Leonora*, in one of the castle's gatehouses, serves fantastic smørrebrød starting at 59kr a piece, as well as a scrumptious Sunday brunch (128kr). Otherwise, *Engelhardt's Café* in the Slotsarkaderne shopping arcade serves good-value sandwiches and light snacks.

Fredensborg Slot

Before leaving Hillerød altogether, it's worth a detour to the picturesque **Fredensborg Slot** (July daily 1–4.30pm; regular guided tours 50kr, joint ticket with the Reserved Garden 75kr). Take the train (on the line towards Helsingør) to Fredensborg, from where it's a short walk. A residence of Danish royalty, built by Frederik IV to commemorate the 1720 Peace Treaty with Sweden, the castle is only open in July when the Queen is staying at her other summer residence, Marselisborg in Århus (see p.138). During this period there are also guided tours of the so-called **Reserved Garden** next to the castle, where you'll find the Queen's veggie patch and herb garden, and a grand orangery (same hours as the castle; 50kr, joint ticket with the castle 75kr). The rest of the garden is open for the remainder of the year (daily dawn–dusk; free); stretching down to an expansive lake, its grand statue-lined alleyways are distinctly appealing for a wander.

Roskilde and around

Heading west out of Copenhagen towards the coast of West Zealand, there isn't too much to occupy your time save for the reconstructed Iron Age settlement at the Lejre Historical-Archeological Centre and the ancient former Danish capital of **ROSKILDE**. There's been a community here since prehistoric times, and later the Roskilde fjord provided a route to the open sea that was used by the Vikings. But it was the arrival of Bishop Absalon in the twelfth century that made the place the base of the Danish Church – and, as a consequence, the national capital for a while. In high season, especially, it can be crammed with day-trippers seeking the dual blasts from the past supplied by its royal tombs and Viking boats, while the first week of each July sees a massive influx of visitors when it hosts the **Roskilde Festival** – northern Europe's biggest open-air rock event. Yet at any other time the ancient centre makes Roskilde one of Denmark's most appealing towns, and the surrounding countryside is quiet and unspoilt.

Arrival, information and accomodation

Copenhagen is barely half an hour's **drive** northeast of Roskilde, but if you're heading west towards Funen or further south in Zealand it's easiest to **stay** here for the night. For general information or to arrange a private room, call in at Roskilde's **tourist office** at Stændertorvet 1 (April–June Mon–Fri 10am–5pm, Sat 10am–1pm; July–Aug Mon–Fri 10am–5pm, Sat 10am–2pm; Sept–March Mon–Thurs 10am–5pm, Fri 10am–4pm, Sat 10am–1pm; ☎46 31 65 65, ✆www.visitroskilde.com).

The best place to stay is the sleek wooden **youth hostel**, ✠ *Roskilde Vandrerhjem*, perfectly placed next to the Viking museum at Vindeboder 7 (☎46 35 21 84, ✆www .rova.dk), offering dorms (120kr), double rooms (➋), a communal kitchen and a view of the water. If that's full, there's a **campsite** (☎46 75 79 96, ✆www.roskildecamping .dk; mid-March to mid-Sept) on the wooded edge of the fjord about 4km north of

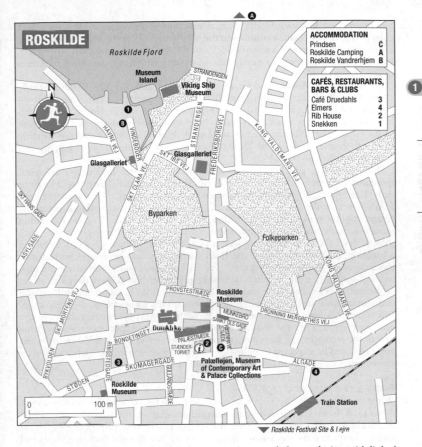

ROSKILDE

Roskilde Fjord

ACCOMMODATION
Prindsen   C
Roskilde Camping   A
Roskilde Vandrerhjem B

CAFÉS, RESTAURANTS, BARS & CLUBS
Café Druedahls 3
Elmers   4
Rib House   2
Snekken   1

Museum Island

Viking Ship Museum

STRANDENGEN

Glasgalleriet

Glasgalleriet

Byparken

Folkeparken

PROVSTESTRÆDE

Roskilde Museum

MUNKEBRO

DRONNING MERGRETHES VEJ

Domkirke

PALÆSTRÆDE

BONDETINGET

STÆNDER-TORVET

SKOMAGERGADE

ALGADE

Roskilde Museum

STØDEN

Palæfløjen, Museum of Contemporary Art & Palace Collections

Train Station

0   100 m

Roskilde Festival Site & Lejre

town – an appealing setting that means it gets very crowded at peak times; it's linked to the town centre by bus #603 towards Veddelev. Otherwise, there's the very pricey *Prindsen* hotel at Algade 13 (☎46 30 91 00, ⓦwww.prindsen.dk; ⓺).

The Town

The major pointer to the town's former status is the fabulous **Domkirke** (April–Sept Mon–Sat 9am–5pm, Sun 12.30–5pm; Oct–March Tues–Sat 10am–4pm, Sun 12.30–4pm; ⓦwww.roskildedomkirke.dk; 25kr), founded by Bishop Absalon in 1170 on the site of a tenth-century church erected by Harald Bluetooth, and completed during the fourteenth century – although portions have been added right up to the twentieth. The result is a mishmash of architectural styles, though it all hangs together with surprising neatness. Every square inch seems adorned by some curious mark or etching, but it's the claustrophobic collection of coffins containing the regal remains of 21 kings and eighteen queens in four large **royal chapels** that really catches the eye. Try to get to the Domkirke just before the hour strikes to see and hear the animated medieval **clock** above the main entrance.

From one end of the cathedral, a roofed passageway, the **Arch of Absalon** (not open to the public), feeds into the maize-yellow **Bishop's Palace**. The incumbent bishop nowadays confines himself to one wing; the others have been turned into showplaces for (predominantly) Danish art. The main building houses the **Museet for Samtidskunst** (Museum of Contemporary Art: Tues–Fri 11am–5pm, Sat &

Sun noon–4pm; @www.mfsk.dk; 30kr), whose diverse temporary exhibitions reflect current trends. The theme continues in the west wing, where the **Palæfløjen** gallery (Tues–Sun noon–4pm; @www.roskildekunst.dk; free), run by the local arts society, extends outdoors, turning up a collection of striking sculpture beneath the fruit trees of the bishop's garden.

The **Roskilde Museum**, close to the cathedral at Sankt Ols Gade 18 (daily 11am–4pm; @www.roskildemuseum.dk; 25kr), has strong sections on medieval pottery and toys. Look out for the strange photos that satirist Gustav Wied (who lived in Roskilde for many years and whose rooms are reconstructed here) took of his family. The museum extends to Ringstedgade 6, a shop kitted out in early twentieth-century style, where locals stop in to buy traditional salted herring and sugar loaves.

More absorbing, and better known – one of the most famous archeological museums in Europe, in fact – is the **Vikingeskibs Museet** (Viking Ship Museum: daily 10am–5pm; @www.vikingeskibsmuseet.dk; May–Sept 95kr; rest of the year 55kr), is set in the green surrounds of Strandengen on the banks of the fjord, fifteen minutes' walk north of the centre. This is one of Denmark's most interesting museums, with five excellent specimens of Viking shipbuilding given the space they deserve: there's a deep-sea trader, a merchant ship, a man-of-war, a ferry and a longship, each retrieved from the fjord where they had been sunk in order to block invading forces. Together, they give an impressive indication of the Vikings' nautical versatility, their skills in boat building and their far-ranging travels to places as various as Paris, Hamburg and North America. Boat building and sail making demonstrations also take place outdoors all year, on the museum island – the Vikings' sails were spun from a special wool produced from wild Norwegian sheep. In the summer months, when the weather allows it, you can also experience the seaworthiness of the reconstructed ships moored on the fjord – you'll be handed an oar when you board and be expected to pull your weight as a crew member (July to late Aug several times daily; 50min; 60kr on top of the museum ticket).

Eating, drinking and nightlife

While you'll be spoiled for choice of places to eat in Roskilde, make an effort to get down to ⚓ *Snekken*, a capacious café-lounge restaurant on the waterfront and across the docks from the museum at Vindeboder 16, where you'll find tasty, expensive mains, cheaper salads and sandwiches and a very economical sprawling weekend brunch (125kr). In town, restaurants, cafés and pubs line Skomagergade and Algade, just south of the Domkirke, and the maze of streets branching off them; *Café Druedahls*, Skomagergade 40, and the carnivore's haven *Rib House*, Djalma Lunds Gård 8, are two good bets.

Evening **entertainment** in Roskilde amounts to visiting the sprinkling of bars around the town centre (*Elmers*, opposite the train station at Hestetorvet 1, serves

---

The Roskilde Festival

Held over four days and nights at the end of June, the Roskilde Festival (@www .roskilde-festival.dk) is the largest outdoor music event in Europe, regularly attracting crowds of 100,000 strong. Close to 180 rock, electronica, hip-hop and world music bands perform on six stages; recent guests have included Pink Floyd, Neil Young, Sígur Ros, The Strokes and the Chemical Brothers. Most festival-goers pitch their tents in the free camping grounds conveniently located nearby the stages, where the festivities continue long after the bands stop playing at 2am, and it's all remarkably peaceful – if rather inebriated – with even soft drugs little abused, due in part to the extensive security measures taken by the festival organizers. Ticket prices are high – upwards of 2000kr for a four-day pass – but nearly always sell out several weeks in advance, so contact the tourist office or buy online early if you want to be assured entry.

▲ Roskilde Festival

over 60 beers), taking in the occasional free event in the town park, or a pleasant walk along the banks of the fjord. If you're looking for more, head for Copenhagen.

Lejre Historical-Archeological Centre

Some 8km west of Roskilde, Iron Age Denmark is kept alive and well at the **Lejre Historical-Archeological Centre**, by volunteer families who spend the summer living in a reconstructed Iron Age settlement, farming and carrying out domestic chores using implements – and wearing clothes – copied from those of the period. Visitors are welcome (May to late June & mid-Aug to Sept Tues–Fri 10am–4pm; late June to mid-Aug daily 10am–5pm; Sat & Sun 11am–5pm; 90kr/110kr depending on time of year; Ⓦwww.lejrecenter.dk), and can try their hand at grinding corn or paddling a dugout canoe. The serious scientific purpose is to gain an understanding of family life in Denmark 2500 years ago, but the centre can be a lot of fun as a day-trip. To get here, take a local train from Roskilde to the village of Lejre; from Lejre station, bus #233 covers the 4km to the historical centre's entrance.

Beyond Roskilde: western Zealand

Beyond Roskilde, western Zealand is flat and bland. You might find yourself traversing it on the way to **Kalundborg**, from where ferries depart for Århus and the island of Samsø, or to **Korsør**, the other main town on the west coast, where a bridge connects Zealand with Funen. Apart from these, the area's only real interest lies in the **Hornsherred Peninsula**, which divides the Roskilde fjord and Isefjord. There are long, quiet beaches along the peninsula's western coast, though the lack of a railway and the paucity of local buses mean that the region is best toured by bike – the Roskilde tourist office (see p.96) has maps of suggested routes. Make for the medieval frescoes in the eleventh-century churches at **Skibby** or **Over Dråby**, or keep on northward for **Jægerspris** and its **castle** (50min guided tours only: mid-March to late Oct Tues–Sun several times daily; ℡47 53 10 04 Ⓦwww.kongfrederik.dk 50kr), built during the fifteenth century as a royal hunting seat and last used by the eccentric Frederik VII, who lived here during the mid-1800s with his third wife, Grevinde Danner. She inherited the castle after the king's death and turned it into an institution for "poor and unfortunate girls". If you're looking to stay in the area, head just southeast of Jægerpris to Frederikssund, where you'll find seven lovely rooms at the perfectly quaint *Villa Bakkely*, Roskildevej 109 (☎30 63 45 10, ⓦwww.villabakkely.dk; ❶).

South from Copenhagen: Køge and around

Once best known for witch-burning, **KØGE** is on the map these days for its evocatively preserved medieval centre and quiet, sandy beaches. Placed at the far end of the S-train network, it's within reach easy reach of the capital.

The town and beaches

Saturday is the best day to visit Køge: a variety of free entertainment sweeps through the main streets in the morning and from noon onwards the harbourside bars are at their liveliest. Walk from the **train station** along Jernbanegade and turn left into Nørregade for Torvet, which is the hub of the action. On a corner of the square is the **tourist office** (Mon–Fri 9am–5pm, Sat 10am–1pm, also June–Aug Sat 9am–2pm; ☎56 67 60 01, ⓦwww.visitkoege.com), while nearby, at Nørregade 4, the **Køge Museum** (June–Aug Tues–Sun 11am–5pm; Sept–May Tues–Fri 1–5pm, Sat 11am–3pm, Sun 1–5pm; 30kr joint ticket with the Kunstmuseet Køge Skitsesamling) contains remnants from Køge's bloody past, not least the local executioner's sword, which was wielded frequently at Torvet – a spot which is said to harbour various ghostly presences, including that of the Devil, who has allegedly appeared here as a clergyman, a frog, a dog and a pig.

Once its market stalls are cleared away, a suitably spooky stillness falls over Torvet and the narrow cobbled streets that run off it. One of these streets, Kirkestræde, is lined with sixteenth-century half-timbered houses and leads to **Skt Nikolai Kirke** (July to early Aug Mon–Fri 10am–4pm, Sun noon–4pm; early Aug to late June Mon–Fri 10am–noon), where pirates captured in Køge Bay were hanged from the **tower** – it's opened up every half an hour from July to early August Monday to Friday between 10am and 1.30pm (10kr). Along the nave, look for the somewhat defaced countenances of angels carved into the pew-ends; their noses were sliced off by drunken Swedish soldiers during the seventeenth century. On a more aesthetic level, the intriguing **Kunstmuseet** at Køge Skitsesamling, Nørregade 29 (Køge Art Museum of Sketches:Tues–Sun 10am–5pm; 50kr joint ticket with Køge Museum, free guided tour every Sun at 2pm; ⓦwww.skitsesamlingen.dk), focuses on the creative process from idea to finished work. Its collection includes drawings, sculptures and models made by important Danish artists of the twentieth century, plus temporary exhibitions of works in progress by both local and international artists.The *pièce de résistance*, on the third floor, is Bjørn Nørregård's colourful preparatory work for the queen's tapestries on show at the Royal Reception Rooms in Copenhagen (see p.78).

The town's **beaches**, which draw many a Copenhagener on weekends, stretch along the bay to the north and south of town and are easily reached from the centre. Søndre Strand is a few minutes' walk from the train station (head south on Østre Banevej), while the more expansive Solrød and Greve are larger and have watersports outlets, and are just a few minutes' ride north on the S-train. To take full advantage of the local beaches, stay at one of the two campsites beside Søndre Strand: *Køge Sydstrand* (☎56 65 07 69, ⓦwww.publiccamp.dk/koge) is virtually on the sand, while Vallø (☎56 65 28 51, ⓦwww.valloecamping.dk) is across Strandvejen, close to a pine wood. Both are open late March to Sept. Further away, 3km from the town centre alongVamdrupvej, is Køge's **youth hostel** (☎56 65 14 74, ⓦwww.danhostelkoege.dk; April to mid-Dec) with bunks (200kr) and some double rooms (❶). Take bus #210 from the train station and get off when the bus turns into Agerskovvej, from where it's a ten-minute walk.There are a few cheap-ish places in town, but for some real pampering, try *Hvide Hus* (☎56 65 36 90, ⓦwww.hotelhvidehus.dk; ❻), Strandvejen 111, a luxury design hotel just 100m from the beach. For food, the best option in town is ⚔ *Slagter Stig & Co*,

Carlsenvej 8, a great rustic chic spot that serves buffet meals (11.30am–11pm; lunch 59kr, dinner 85kr), as well as tasty plates of charcuterie from 23kr.

Central Zealand: Ringsted and around

Though now little more than a small farming town, **RINGSTED**'s central location made it one of the most important settlements in Zealand from the end of the Viking era until the Reformation. It was the burial place of medieval Danish monarchs as well as being the site of a regional *ting*, the open-air court where prominent merchants and nobles made the administrative decisions for the province.

The three *ting* stones around which the nobles gathered remain in Ringsted's market square, but they're often concealed by the market itself, or the backsides of weary shoppers. It's the sturdy **Sct Bendts Kirke** (Mon–Wed & Fri 9am–noon, Thurs 4–7pm; ⓦwww.sctbendts.kirke.dk) that dominates the square, as it has done for over eight hundred years. Erected in 1170 under the direction of Valdemar I, the church was the final resting place for all Danish monarchs until 1341. Four thousand people are said to have been present for the church's consecration, and although these days it receives a mere trickle of visitors compared to those flocking to the royal tombs at Roskilde, it nevertheless represents a substantial chunk of Danish history. During the seventeenth century a number of the coffins were exhumed to create room for future coffins; the finds are collected in the **Museum Chapel** within the church. Besides the lead slab found inside Valdemar I's coffin, there is a decorative silk brocade from that of his son, plaster casts of the skulls of Queen Bengård and Queen Sofia and a replica of the Dagmar Cross, discovered when Queen Dagmar's tomb was opened in 1697 – the original is in the National Museum in Copenhagen.

Practicalities

For accommodation, Ringsted's year-round **youth hostel** (☏57 61 15 26, ⓦwww.danhostel.dk/ringsted) is handily situated across the road from the church – with no campsites nearby, this is the only budget option and has doubles (❷) as well as dorms (125kr). Ringsted does have inexpensive B&Bs and some pricey hotels, and the **tourist office** (mid-June to Aug Mon–Fri 10am–5pm, Sat 9am–2pm; Sept to mid-June Mon–Fri 10am–5pm, Sat 10am–1pm; ☏57 62 66 00, ⓦwww.visitringsted.dk), a few doors along from the hostel toward Torvet, can advise on these as well as arranging private rooms (from 125kr per person). One decent hotel choice is the *Scandic* at Nørretorv 57 (☏57 61 93 00, ⓦwww .scandichotels.dk/ringsted; ❻), which has comfortable rooms, a sauna, restaurant and children's playground. If you're hungry or thirsty, walk a few blocks east of the Torvet to ⅍ *Vallentin's Café & Bar*, Pileborggade 11, where Ringsteders congregate for their simple meals and drinks – especially during the summer, when beer tastings and barbecue dinners are held on the leafy terrace out back.

Around Ringsted

Beyond Ringsted, the road and rail network out of Copenhagen splits into two: one line heads further south to the islands of Falster, Lolland and Møn (see p.103 & p.102) via Næstved, while the other heads westwards towards the multimillion-kroner combined **bridge and tunnel** that has carried road and rail traffic across the 18km-wide Store Bælt since it opened in 1998. There was a regular ferry between **KORSØR** on Zealand and Nyborg on Funen for more than two centuries, and archeological research on the mid-channel island of Sprogø suggests that Danes have been boating back and forth for many thousands of years. If you have any interest in grand engineering feats, a stop at the **Storebælt Udstillingscenter** (Great Belt Bridge Centre: Wed–Sun 11am–4pm; free) is a must. Here you'll learn everything you could possibly want to know about the engineering of the Storebælt – Europe's second longest road-and-rail bridge after the Øresund – but were afraid to ask. Of particular note is a scale replica of the boring machine used to drill out the 8km-long railway tunnels that run 75m below the water's surface. The centre is located several hundred metres past the train station; if arriving from the bridge by car, take exit 43 at the toll station.

Southern Zealand and the islands

Southern Zealand is seriously rural, consisting almost solely of rich, rolling farmland and villages. South from Ringsted, most routes lead to **NÆSTVED**, by far the largest town in the region. Aside from a smartly restored medieval centre and a minor museum, however, Næstved has little to offer except its proximity to unspoilt countryside and the **River Suså**, whose lack of rapids and negligible current makes it a good base for novice **canoe trips** – although busy at weekends, it's free of crowds at other times. Canoes can be rented at Suså Kanoudlejning, Næsbyholm Allé 6, in nearby Glumsø (☎55 64 61 44, ⓦwww.kanoudlejning.dk), for 370kr a day. Off the river, time is best spent strolling amid the town's half-timbered buildings and visiting the Helligåndshuset outpost of the **Næstved Museum** at Ringstedgade 4 (Tues–Sat 10am–4pm, Sun 1–4pm; 20kr; ⓦwww.naestved-museum.dk), where there's a jumble of medieval artefacts squirreled away from the region's many churches – altarpieces, crucifixes and statues of saints.

The local **tourist office** (June & Aug Mon–Fri 9am–5pm, Sat 9am–2pm; July Mon–Fri 9am–6pm, Sat 9am–2pm; Sept–May Mon–Fri 9am–4pm, Sat 9am–noon; ☎55 72 11 22, ⓦwww.visitnaestved.com) in the yellow house known as Det Gule Pakhus, Havnen 1, can fill you in on practical details and offer suggestions for **staying over** in Næstved. Alternatively, there are dainty rooms at *Vinhuset* (☎55 72 08 07, ⓦwww.hotel-vinhuset.dk; ⑥), centrally located on the church square, Skt Peders Kirkeplads; the hotel's restaurant is one of Næstved's best dining spots. Nearby is ⅔ *Hotel Kirstine* (Købmagergade 20, ☎55 77 47 00, ⓦwww.hotelkirstine .dk), a gorgeous 250-year-old former mayoral home with classically furnished rooms. The only really cheap spot in town is the **youth hostel** at Præstøvej 65 (☎55 72 20 91, ⓦwww.danhostelnaestved.dk), which has dorm beds (150kr) and doubles (❶); from the train station (which is about 1km from the centre on Jernbanegade), turn left into Farimagsvej and left again along Præstøvej. The closest **campsite**, *De Hvide Svaner Camping* (☎55 44 24 29, ⓦwww.dehvidesvaner.dk; mid-June to mid-Oct), is on the coast by Karrebæksminde, 3km from a popular beach.

Møn, Falster and Lolland

Off the south coast of Zealand lie three sizeable islands – **Møn**, **Falster** and **Lolland**. All three are connected to the mainland by road, and Falster and Lolland have rail links too, making them relatively easy to reach, but once there you'll need your own transport to do any serious exploration outside the larger communities, since local buses are rare; bikes can be rented from virtually all tourist offices and campsites.

Møn

Since it's not connected by train, **Møn** is the most difficult of the three islands to get to from Zealand, but it's well worth the effort: take bus #62 or #64 from Vordingborg (a stop on the rail line from Copenhagen to Nykøbing). Møn is best known for its white chalk cliffs that are great for walking, sandy beaches and its unique whitewashed churches, many of which feature fourteenth-century frescoes depicting rural life – the work, apparently, of one peasant painter. The main town, **STEGE**, is, at least for those without their own transport, the most feasible base, since it's the hub of the island's minimal bus service and has a great selection of restaurants – the best of which is also a butcher-cum-delicatessen *Støberiet*, Storegade 59. There is an inexpensive **campsite** near town on Falckvej 5 (☎55 81 84 04; May to mid-Sept), though more appealing is *Camping Møns Klint*, Klintvej 544 out on the eastern part of the island at **Møns Klint** (April–Oct ☎55 81 20 25, ⓦwww.camping moensklint.dk; cabins sleep six, 550kr per day plus 75kr per person, 5900kr per week in July), with a pool and forested environs. If you'd rather sleep in a bed, check out current options with the helpful Stege **tourist office**, by the bus station at Storegade 2 (mid-June to Aug Mon–Fri 9am–4pm, Sat 9am–6pm; Sept to mid-June Mon–Fri 10am–4pm, Sat 9am–noon; ☎55 86 04 10, ⓦwww.visitvordingborg.dk).

Møn is best known for its many well-preserved medieval churches, notable for their vibrant frescoes painted by an anonymous fifteenth-century artist in a simple, unprepossessing style for rural peasants. The foremost frescoes, which depict the objects of everyday medieval life in sometimes humorous scenes, can be admired at **Keldby** and **Elemunde**, connected to Stege by bus #52, and **Fanefjord** (all daily: April–Sept 7am–4pm; free), reachable via bus #62 (get off at Store Damme, then walk); the latter also has a Neolithic barrow in its churchyard. As for the **cliffs** (*Møn Klint*), they're at the eastern end of the island and stretch for about eight kilometres. For a great introduction to the geology of the island and information on the best coastal walks, visit the GeoCenter **Møns Klint** at Stengårdsvej 8, (Sept–March 10am–5pm, July–Aug 10am–6pm; 100kr; ⓦwww.moensklint.dk) which has a series of exhibits on the cliffs. Bus #52 runs between the cliffs and Stege four to five times a day depending on the season. Fifteen minutes' walk from the cliffs, at Lange-bjergvej 1, is a basic **youth hostel** (☎55 81 20 30, ⓦwww.danhostel.dk/moen; mid-April to Aug), which has dorms (105kr) and some private double rooms (❶).

Falster

Falster has some pleasant woods on the eastern side and some good, but very crowded, beaches, particularly around the major resort of **MARIELYST** on the Baltic (eastern) coast. There's not much to do in Marielyst except enjoy the beach and the bustling **nightlife**: bars, clubs and cafés are plentiful. The newest place to stay is the modern but charming *Oldfruen B&B*, Marielyst Strandvej 25A (☎54 13 13 80, ⓦwww.oldfruen.dk; ❸). Much larger is *Hotel Nørrevang* (☎54 13 62 62, ⓦwww.norrevang.dk; ❹), close to the centre. You can also ask at the **tourist office** at Marielyst Strandpark 3, just off Skovby Ringvej as you enter Marielyst from Nykøbing (Mon–Sat 9am–4pm, Sun 10am–2pm; ☎54 13 62 98, ⓦwww.marielyst .org), for a list of private rooms. Of the five **campsites** in the area, the best is *Marielyst Camping* (☎54 13 53 07, ⓦwww.marielyst-camping.dk; April to early Sept), Marielyst Strandvej 36, offering pitches 400m from the beach.

Lolland

Larger and less crowded than Falster, **Lolland** is otherwise much the same: wooded, with excellent beaches and lots of quiet, explorable corners, though it certainly feels the least overrun of the southern islands. A private railway (InterRail, ScanRail and Eurail passes not valid) runs to Lolland from Nykøbing on Falster, taking in Sakskøbing, Maribo and finally Nakskov, at the western extremity of the island, near to where ferries cross to Langeland (alternatively, bus #800 goes straight from Nykøbing station onto the ferry, and continues on to Svenborg and Odense on Funen); there's also a DSB train from Nykøbing to Rødby on the south coast. Each town has a tourist office, youth hostel and campsite, but **MARIBO**, delectably positioned on the Søndersø lake, is the most scenic setting for a short stay. Located at the train station are the town's **Storstrøms Kunstmuseum** (Art Museum: Tues–Thurs 10am–4pm, Fri–Sun 11am–5pm; 65kr joint ticket with Stiftsmuseum; ⓦwww.storstroems-kunstmuseum.dk), with paintings, sketches and sculptures repre-senting artistic trends from Denmark's Golden Age through to the present day, and upstairs in the same building, the **Lolland-Falsters Stiftsmuseum** (Loland-Falster Provincial Museum: Tues–Sat 10am–4pm; same ticket; ⓦwww.aabne-samlinger .dk/maribo), displaying local archeological finds, costumes and rooms covering the experience of Polish immigrants who settled here in the late eighteenth century to work in the fields and the sugar-processing plants. There's a **youth hostel** with dorms (130kr) and doubles (❶) at Sdr Boulevard 82B (☎54 78 33 14, ⓦwww.danhostel-maribo.dk); a **campsite** at Bangshavevej 25 (☎54 78 00 71, www.maribo-camping.dk; Easter to mid-Oct), and a choice hotel, the lakefront ★ *Hotel Maribo Søpark* (☎54 78 10 11, ⓦwww.maribo-soepark.dk; ❹), Vestergade 29, whose spacious rooms (some with balconies) look out onto the lake. It also offers an outdoor swimming pool and a very good restaurant. The **tourist office** is easy to find in the old town hall on Torvet (Mon–Fri 10am–5pm, Sat 10am–1pm; ☎54 78 04 96, ⓦwww.turistlolland.dk).

Bornholm

Surrounded by the Baltic Sea and closer to Sweden than it is to Denmark – splayed some 200km away across the water – **Bornholm** is said to have been formed when God cobbled together the most beautiful parts of Scandinavia and flung them into the middle of the ocean. Known to Danes as *solskinsøen*, or "island of shining sun" – it has more hours of sunlight than anywhere else in Denmark – the island fell under Swedish rule for many years, and was only finally returned to Denmark in 1522 after a long and bloody revolt in which, according to legend, the infamous Swedish governor was killed by a single silver bullet in the heart. Today, with a string of gorgeous beaches in the south, a rugged and romantic coastline in

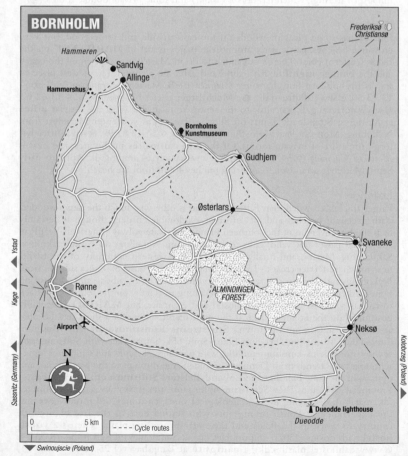

Getting to Bornholm

The cheapest and fastest way to get to Bornholm from Copenhagen is by taking the InterCity Bornholm train-boat link, which travels by train to Ystad in Sweden and then to Rønne by ferry, costing 245kr each way. There are five departures daily in the spring, summer and autumn, though as few as two daily in the winter. Buses also leave up to four times a day from Copenhagen, following the same route, but for a total journey time of two hours thirty minutes (visit ⓦwww.graahundbus.dk for timetables and online bookings). Another option is the six-hour thirty-minute direct ferry from Køge south of Copenhagen (see p.100) to Rønne, which costs 250kr. Bornholm is also quite feasible as a stopover if you're heading to Germany or Poland on one of several ferry crossings (see "Travel details", p.107).

the north, and an unspoilt interior criss-crossed by several hundred kilometres of well-marked cycling and hiking trails, Bornholm is an absolute haven for lovers of the great outdoors.

To get the most out of Bornholm, you really need to travel around the whole coast – not difficult, since the island is only about 30km across from east to west – and spend at least three or four days doing it. **Getting around** is easy and best done by **bike**: the island is covered with over 235km of coastal roads, bark-covered paths, gravelled forest roads and cycle tracks, of which a third follow the course of the old rail line. Bikes can be rented in the island's main town, Rønne, at Bornholms Cykeludlejning, Nordre Kystvej 5 (☎56 95 13 59, ⓦwww.bornholms -cykeludlejning.dk), as well as numerous other places around the island (ask at tourist offices; for maps, route suggestions and general inspiration visit ⓦwww .cykel.bornholm.info. If this seems too energetic, you can make use of the reliable **bus** services (all buses are equipped to carry bikes; information on ☎56 95 21 21, ⓦwww.bat.dk), but it's a good idea to check the timetable beforehand as some services are quite infrequent. **Accommodation** is straightforward, too: there is a range of hotels all around the island, a youth hostel in each of the main settlements, and campsites sprinkled fairly liberally around the coast; tourist offices can also help with private rooms. The peak of the summer is very busy, and you should phone ahead to check there's space. But at any other time of year there should be little difficulty. The **nightlife** on the island can also be surprisingly lively – in season, at least – although often limited to one spot in each town.

The island

Ferries from Copenhagen arrive in **RØNNE**, where the **tourist office** is right on the harbour at Ndr. Kystvej 3 (April–May & Sept–Oct Mon–Fri 9am–4pm, Sat 9am–noon; early to mid-June & mid-Aug to late Aug Mon–Sat 9am–4pm; mid-June to mid-Aug daily 9am–5pm; Nov–March Mon–Fri 9am–4pm; ☎56 95 95 00, ⓦwww.bornholminfo.dk). Staff can fill you in on accommodation and transport details, and sell you a good selection of booklets and maps. If you've arrived on an overnight or early boat, the only place open for breakfast is the café at the ferry terminal. Otherwise, there are plenty of places to **eat** and stock up around the main town square, Store Torv.

The triangle between Store Torv and Lille Torv (literally, "large" and "small" squares) and the ferry terminal has the most charm, its streets lined with traditional wood-beamed townhouses painted in bright colours. Before you set off to explore the island it's worth taking in some detail on its turbulent history at the **Bornholms Museum**, Sct Mortensgade 29 (mid-May to June & Sept to late Oct Mon–Sat 10am–5pm; July–Aug daily 10am–5pm; late Oct to mid-May Mon–Sat 1–4pm; 50kr; ⓦwww .bornholmsmuseum.dk); look out for the large golden clothes pin found in a field early in 2002, which is one of Denmark's largest-ever archeological gold finds.

If you do need to **stay over**, there are plenty of options: a youth hostel at Arsenalvej 12 (☎56 95 13 40, ⓦwww.danhostel-roenne.dk; June–Sept), which has some doubles (❷) as well as dorms (150kr); a campsite, *Galløkken Camping*, 1km from the ferry harbour at Strandvejen 4 (☎56 95 23 20, ⓦwww.gallokken.dk; mid-May to Aug; cabins 550kr per day in low season, 725kr in high season); or the small *Sverres Hotel* at Skt Snellemark 2 (☎56 95 03 03, ⓦwww.sverres-hotel.dk; ❸) with a range of different rooms.

If you're eager to get to the beach, head south to **DUEODDE**, where there's nothing but sand and a string of campsites. In summer Dueodde lighthouse is open to the public (May–Oct dawn–dusk; 10kr), offering superb views. At the other corner of the eastern coast, surrounded by spectacular scenery of steep cliffs and affording great views, **SVANEKE** is a quiet place which until a few years ago was favoured by Danish retirees, but more recently experienced a massive influx of **craftsmen** – mostly potters and glass-blowers – whose workshops and fantastic exhibits have come to dominate the town scene. Pernille Bülow glassworks (June–Aug Mon–Fri 9am–9pm, Sat & Sun 9am–6pm; Sept–May Mon–Fri 9am–6.30pm, Sat 9am–5pm, Sun 9am–4pm; ⓦwww.pernillebulow.dk), Brænderiegænget 8, is one such place to watch the craftsmen at work, and buy their wares. If you want to **stay**, first choice is the excellent ⅍ *Siemsens Gaard*, Havnebryggen 9 (☎56 49 61 49, ⓦwww.siemsens.dk; ❺), a former merchant's home that retains a lot of original character and boasts front rooms with views to the water. Otherwise, the youth hostel at Reberbanevej 9 (☎56 49 62 42, ⓦwww.danhostel-svanek.dk; June–Sept), near the Christiansø ferry landing, has doubles (❷) and dorms (160kr). *Svaneke Familie-camping*, Møllebakken 8, (☎56 49 64 62, ⓦwww.svaneke-camping.dk; mid-May to mid-Sept) is one of the area's best bets if you want to stay under canvas. In terms of **eating and drinking**, the cosy bar and restaurant inside the Bryghuset Brewery, Torvet 5 (ⓦwww.bryghuset-svaneke.dk), is a solid choice, both for its draught beers – best are the hoppy, golden ale and fresh-tasting, unfiltered pilsner – and for mains like local oven-baked salmon with hollandaise sauce (155kr) and marinated spare-ribs (145kr). The **tourist office** at Havnebryggen 2D (Mon–Fri 10am–4pm; ☎56 49 70 79) should be able to help with any queries.

Halfway along the north coast, **GUDHJEM** is pretty too, its tiny streets wending their way around the foot of a hill. The town lends its name to a traditional open sandwich combination called *Sol over Gudhjem* ("sunrise over Gudhjem") – a slice of rye bread layered with smoked herring, raw egg yolk, chopped onion and capers, sold nationally in smørrebrød shops. If you want to taste it at source, head for the white-chimneyed *Røgeri* (smokehouse) down at the harbour.

Accommodation in Gudhjem is plentiful. Most romantic is ⅍ *Jantzen's Hotel* (☎56 48 50 17, ⓦwww.jantzenshotel.dk; ❺) halfway down the hill at Brøddegade 33, whose rooms have cast-iron balconies and rates include a superb, dainty breakfast. Buses run the 5km or so north to the **Bornholms Kunstmuseum** (April–May & Sept–Oct Tues–Sun 10am–5pm; June–Aug daily 10am–5pm; Nov–March Tues & Thurs 1–5pm, Sun 10am–5pm; 70kr; ⓦwww.bornholms-kunstmuseum.dk), an excellent art gallery displaying evocative landscape and portraiture works from the Bornholm School that thrived here in the first half of the twentieth century. Further inland, right in the centre of the island, is Bornholm's largest (and Denmark's third largest) forest, **Almindingen**, traversed by cycle paths, and boasting a lookout tower in the centre which offers fabulous views of the entire island. The twin towns of **ALLINGE** and **SANDVIG**, on the island's northwest corner (12km from Gudhjem and reachable by bus #1 or #2 from Rønne and #7 or #9 from Gudhjem), mark the point of departure for another worthwhile walk, along **Hammeren**, the massive granite headland that juts out towards Sweden. Just south of Sandvig are the remains of the thirteenth-century **Hammershus castle**, not much in themselves but still worth a trundle over the moat's bridge and among the medieval foundation's bricks for the views from the tall crag which the castle occupied. Built in 1260, the stronghold has served as a citadel, barracks, prison and convent, and is noteworthy as northern Europe's largest castle ruin.

Since you've made it this far, there's no reason not to continue on to **Christiansø**, a tiny pebble of an island some 18km northwest of Bornholm itself. The island – actually a collection of about seven small rocky outposts – served as a naval base during the seventeenth century, and later as a prison; these days, the minuscule population of about a hundred prides itself on its spiced herring. There are usually two boats a day out to the island from Gudhjem, Allinge and Svaneke (ⓦwww.christiansoefarten.dk or any tourist office for the latest details), and a lovely day-trip is to be had walking the abandoned battlements and having a meal at the lone, lovely inn, the open-year-round ⚔ *Christiansø Gæstgiveriet* (☎56 46 20 15, ⓦwww.christiansoekro.dk; ❹). A camping space (☎24 42 12 22; ⓦwww.sitecenter .dk/christiansoeteltplads; March–Oct) is set a few hundred metres from here out towards the water and has a single dirt-cheap cabin to rent (150kr per person).

Travel details

Trains

Copenhagen to: Århus (every 30min; 3hr); Esbjerg (hourly; 3hr–3hr 20min); Helsingør (every 20min; 45min); Næstved (2–3 hourly; 1hr); Nykøbing F (hourly; 1hr 30min); Odense (every 30min; 1hr 30min); Ringsted (3–4 hourly; 40min); Roskilde (every 5–10min; 25min); Rønne (3–5 daily via ferry from Ystad; 3hr).
Helsingør to: Gilleleje (2–3 hourly; 25min); Hillerød (1–2 hourly, 30min).
Køge to: Fakse (1–2 hourly; 35min); Store Heddinge (1–2 hourly; 30min).
Nykøbing F to: Maribo (1–2 hourly; 25min); Nakskov (1–2 hourly; 45min); Rødby (10 daily; 26min).
Roskilde to: Kalundborg (hourly, connects with ferry to Jutland; 1hr 10min).

Buses

Copenhagen to: Aalborg (3–5 daily; 4hr 30min); Århus (4–7 daily; 3hr direct); Ebeltoft (2–3 daily; 3hr); Fjerritslev via Grenå, Randers, Hobro and Løgstør (4–6 daily; 5hr 55min); Rønne via Ystad (3–5 daily; 3hr).
Nykøbing to: Odense via Svendborg (hourly; 3hr 30min).

Ferries

Allinge to: Christiansø (May–Sept Mon–Fri 1 daily; 1hr 10min).
Gudhjem to: Christiansø (May–June & Sept 1 daily; July & Aug 2 daily; Oct–April Mon–Fri 1 daily; 55min).

Sjællands Odde to: Ebeltoft (7 daily; 50min); Århus (6–9 daily; 65min).
Svaneke to: Christiansø (May–Sept Mon–Fri 1 daily; 1hr 25min).
Tårs (Langeland) to: Spodsbjerg (6–7 daily; 50min).

International trains

Copenhagen to: Bergen (3 daily, change in Gothenburg and Oslo; 18–21hr 30min); Gothenburg (10 daily; 3hr 39min); Hamburg (4 daily; 5hr–6hr 30min); Helsinki (1–2 daily, change to ferry in Stockholm; 19hr 30min–22hr); Kiruna (2–3 daily, change in Stockholm; 22hr 40min–26hr); Malmö (every 20min; 35min); Narvik (1–2 daily, change in Stockholm; 25hr 15min–30hr 10min); Oslo (3–4 daily, change in Gothenburg or Malmö; 8hr 10min–9hr 50min); Stockholm (hourly, some change in Malmö; 5hr 20min); Turku (2–3 daily, change to ferry in Stockholm; 17hr 30min–21hr 15min).

International ferries and catamarans

Copenhagen to: Oslo, Norway (1 daily; 19hr 30min); Swinoujscie, Poland (4 weekly; 10hr 30min); Klaipeda, Lithuania (2 weekly; 21hr).
Gedser to: Rostock, Germany (6–7 daily; 1hr).
Helsingør to: Helsingborg, Sweden (HH Ferries several hourly; 20min).
Rødby to: Puttgarden, Germany (every half-hour; 45min).
Rønne to: Sassnitz, Germany (1 daily in summer, rest of year 3 weekly; 3hr 30min); Świnoujście, Poland (1 daily; 8hr); Ystad, Sweden (catamaran 2–5 daily; 1hr 20min; ferry 1–3 daily; 2hr 30min).

1.2

Funen

Known as "the garden of Denmark" for the lawn-like neatness of its fields and for the immense amount of fruit and vegetables that come from them, **Funen** (*Fyn*) is the smaller of the two main Danish islands, and one which most visitors pass quickly through on their way between Zealand and Jutland. The island's bucolic outlook and coastline draw many, but its attractions are relatively low-profile: grand castles and manor houses, the collections of the Funen painters and the birthplaces of writer Hans Christian Andersen and composer Carl Nielsen, who eulogized the distinctive sing-song Funen accent and claimed it inspired his music. Given its diminutive size, Funen is best explored by bicycle; otherwise, you'll be getting around on buses more often than trains, since the latter are relatively scarce.

Arriving from Zealand brings you through **Nyborg**, a town with a heavily restored thirteenth-century castle, though there's little reason to linger long on the east coast and it's preferable to stay on the cross-country railway that continues to **Odense**, Denmark's third-largest city and an obvious base if you want to explore villages by day but would like some urban zip by night. Close by, the former fishing town of **Kerteminde** retains some faded charm, and is a good base for visiting both the Ladby Boat, an important Viking relic, and the isolated **Hindsholm Peninsula**. To the south, Funen's coastal life centres on maritime **Svendborg**, possibly the top scenic draw on Funen with its good beaches and fragmented archipelago of pretty **islands**. This is vacation territory for the most part, well served by ferries and connected by train with Odense via the island's only branch rail line.

East Funen

Travelling from Zealand to Funen takes you over the **Store Bælt** ("Great Belt"), the eighteen-kilometre road and rail link which connects the two islands, before bringing you to **Nyborg**, Funen's easternmost town.

Unless you're in a rush to reach Odense, spare a few hours for Nyborg's strollable old streets and thirteenth-century **castle**, for two hundred years the seat of Danish political power. Otherwise, apart from countless lookalike villages, there's not much in east Funen to detain you.

Nyborg

NYBORG is small and easily navigated and you'll have no trouble finding your way to **Nyborg Slot** (April–May 10am–3pm; June–Aug Tues–Sun 10am–4pm; Sept to late Oct 10am–3pm; 30kr, for joint ticket with Mads Lerches Gård 45kr; Ⓦ www.museer-nyborg.dk), built around 1200 by Valdemar the Great as part of a chain of coastal fortresses to guard against Wend piracy. For more than two hundred years, the Danehof – a summertime national assembly involving king, clergy and nobility – met here (and in 1282 drew up the first Danish constitution), which effectively made Nyborg the Danish capital until 1443, when power moved to Copenhagen. The castle bears little evidence of those years, however. Most striking is the **Danehof Hall**, where the assembly met and debated the constitution. For more local history, head down Slotsgade 11

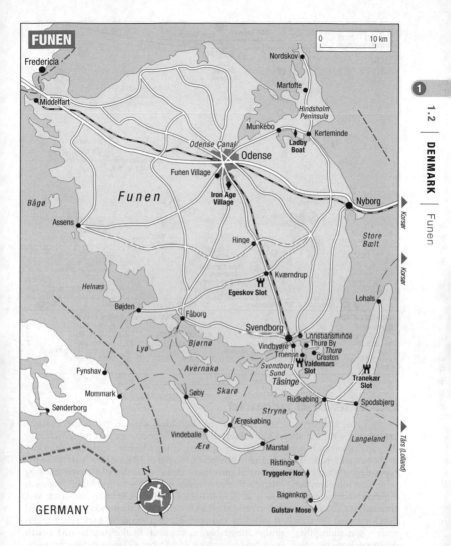

to **Mads Lerches Gård** (same hours; 25kr, joint ticket with Nyborg Slot 45kr), a half-timbered merchant's house from the sixteenth century now housing the quaint town museum.

With the bright lights of Odense just 25km away to the west, there's little temptation to spend a night in Nyborg, but a good option if you decide to do so is the *Villa Gulle*, Østervoldgade 44 (☏65 30 11 88, ⊛www.villa-gulle.dk; ❸), a B&B that is the best bargain in town. There's a beachside **campsite** (☏65 31 02 56, ⊛www.strandcamping.dk; mid-April to late Sept) at Hjejlevej 99. For further information, drop in at the **tourist office** at Torvet 9 (July–Aug Mon–Fri 9am–5pm, Sat 9am–2pm; rest of the year Mon–Fri 9am–4pm, Sat 9.30am–12.30pm; ☏65 31 02 80, ⊛www.visitnyborg.dk).

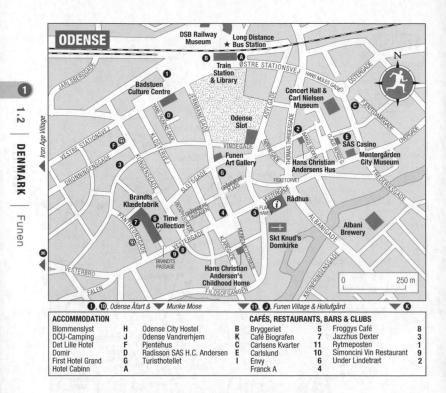

ACCOMMODATION				CAFÉS, RESTAURANTS, BARS & CLUBS	
Blommenslyst	H	Odense City Hostel	B	Bryggeriet	5	Froggys Café	8
DCU-Camping	J	Odense Vandrerhjem	K	Café Biografen	7	Jazzhus Dexter	3
Det Lille Hotel	F	Pjentehus	C	Carlsens Kvarter	11	Rytmeposten	1
Domir	D	Radisson SAS H.C. Andersen	E	Carlslund	10	Simoncini Vin Restaurant	9
First Hotel Grand	G	Turisthotellet	I	Envy	6	Under Lindetræt	2
Hotel Cabinn	A			Franck A	4		

Odense and around

Funen's sole industrial centre and one of the oldest settlements in the country, **ODENSE** – named after Odin, chief of the Norse gods – gained prominence in the early nineteenth century when the opening of the Odense canal linked the city to the sea and made it the major transit point for the produce of the island's farms. Nowadays it's a pleasant provincial university town, with the **old town** housing some fine museums and – thanks to the resident students – a surprisingly vigorous nightlife. Odense is also known as the birthplace of Hans Christian Andersen and, although it's all done quite discreetly, the fact is celebrated with souvenir shops and hotels catering for travellers lured by the prospect of a romantic Andersen experience – something they (almost inevitably) won't find. To the **north and south of town**, however, there are a few attractions of a rather different nature, from the reconstructed nineteenth-century buildings of Funen Village to the novel treatment of the prehistoric era at the Iron Age Village.

Arrival, information and city transport

Long-distance **buses** terminate at the efficient **train station**, a ten-minute walk north of the city centre. You'll find the **tourist office** (July–Aug Mon–Fri 9.30am–6pm, Sat 10am–3pm, Sun 11am–2pm; rest of year Mon–Fri 9.30am–4.30pm, Sat 10am–1pm; ☎66 12 75 20, ⓦ www.visitodense.com) in the centre, within the nineteenth-century Rådhus on Vestergade.

On Odense's **bus** system you pay 20kr as you enter to travel within the city limits: if you have to use more than one bus, ask the driver for a "change ticket" (*omstigning*) to use on the next bus. If you can't face the buses, you can **rent a bike** at City Cykler, Vesterbro 27 (☎66 13 97 83, ⊛www.citycykler.dk; from 100kr per day).

Accommodation

Thanks to Hans Christian Andersen, Odense has a plethora of pricey places to stay, although there are several less expensive alternatives, including a number of central and affordable **B&Bs** quite close to the Andersen museums. There are also a couple of **hostels**, as well as a campsite in the city and another on the outskirts.

Hotels and B&Bs

Det Lille Hotel Dronningensgade 5 ☎66 12 28 21, ⊛www.lillehotel.dk. Small hotel run by a friendly proprietor who has done plenty of travelling himself. Rooms are adequate with shared bathrooms. ❷

Domir Hans Tausens Gade 19 ☎66 12 14 27, ⊛www.domir.dk. Bright, welcoming recent renovation with great, designer-like rooms, all with en-suite baths. Also has a sleek lobby bar. Similar rooms are available at their sister hotel Ydes just down the street. ❸

First Hotel Grand Jernbanegade 18 ☎66 11 71 71, ⊛www.firsthotels.dk. Just emerging from a sparkling renovation, this 1897-era hotel has become one of Odense's swankiest places to stay. Every single room has been updated with plush linens, large beds and every mod con. Reception area can get quite busy, as it's now one of the city's most popular places to stay. ❹

Hotel Cabinn Østre Stationsvej 7–9 ☎63 14 57 00, ⊛www.cabinn.com. The smallest rooms at Odense's newest hotel resemble the cramped accommodations on an overnight ferry, while three other classes of rooms offer slightly more comfortable and spacious stays. Set just next to the train station, this is the cheapest and most central hotel for two people. Breakfast 50kr. ❷

Pjentehus Pjentedamsgade 14 ☎66 12 15 55, ⊛www.pjentehus.dk. Gorgeous, atmospheric old house set right in the heart of Andersen's Odense. Rooms are smallish, but there is a garden that guests can use. Breakfast costs 40kr extra. ❷

🏃 **Radisson SAS H.C. Andersen** Claus Bergs Gade 7 ☎66 14 78 00, ⊛www .radissonsas.dk. It might be a chain hotel, but it has the best location in the city – on the cobblestones just east of the city centre, 100m from the H.C. Andersen museum. Spacious, comfy rooms are filled with all the expected amenities, and service is first-rate. There's a sauna in the basement and the buffet breakfasts are memorably lavish. ❺/❻

Turisthotellet Gerthasminde 64 ☎66 11 26 92, ⊛www.turist-hotellet.dk. Cosy, Gothic-looking hotel with smallish rooms that aren't very spacious – one is set in the small castle-like tower – but rather reasonable rates. ❹

Hostels

Odense City Hostel Østre Stationsvej 31 ☎63 11 04 25, ⊛www.cityhostel.dk. Just next door to the train station, this is an efficient and brightly decorated hostel with somewhat antiseptic dorms (200kr) and doubles (❺) spread out over several floors.

Odense Vandrerhjem Kragsbjergvej ☎121 66 13 04 25, ⊛www.odense-danhostel.dk. Quieter, off-the-beaten-path kind of place that offers more dorms (200kr) and doubles (❹/❻) than its urban counterpart. The bland interiors are offset by the great building – a timbered farmhouse encircled by a cobbled and grassy courtyard, some 2km southeast of the town centre; take bus #61 or #62 from the train station or cathedral south towards Tornbjerg or Fraugde and get out along Munkebjergvej at the junction with Vissenbjergvej. Open March–Dec.

Campsites

Blommenslyst Middelfartvej 494 ☎65 96 76 41, ⊛www.blommenslyst-camping.dk. Facilities are pretty basic here, but the location, just next to a picturesque lake, is perfectly lovely. Extremely small cabins (370kr) sleep four and have basic kitchenettes. The site is about 10km from Odense; half-hourly buses #830, #831, #832 or #833 from the train station make the journey in 20min.

DCU-Camping Odensevej 102 ☎66 11 47 02, ⊛www.camping-odense.dk. Near Funen Village, this is the only campsite actually in Odense. It's fully equipped, with excellent cooking facilities and a few cabins (450kr; 3100kr per week, sleeps four). Take bus #21, #22 or #23 from the Rådhus or train station towards Højby, or take the Odense Åfart boat; it's a kilometre from the Funen Village stop.

The Town

Save for three outlying museums which are a bus ride away, Odense is easily explored on foot. There's a lot to be said for simply wandering around the compact **centre** with no particular destination in mind, but you shouldn't pass up the chance to visit the **Hans Christian Andersen** museums or to take in at least one of several absorbing **art collections**. Two other **museums** provide more offbeat fare: one celebrates composer Carl Nielsen and the other eulogizes Danish railways. Visit ⓦwww.odmus.dk for information on all Odense museums.

The Hans Christian Andersen museums and around

Odense's showpiece is the **Hans Christian Andersens Hus** (July–Aug daily 9am–6pm; Sept–June Tues–Sun 10am–4pm; 60kr), at Bangs Boder 29, the house where the writer was born and which he described in *The Fairy Tale of My Life*. Oddly enough, Andersen was only really accepted in his own country towards the end of his life; his real admirers were abroad, which was perhaps why he travelled widely and left Odense at the first opportunity. Since his death it's his **fairy tales** that have gained most renown, partly autobiographical stories (not least *The Ugly Duckling*) that were influenced by *The Arabian Nights*, German folk stories and the traditional Danish folk tales passed on by inmates of the Odense workhouse where his grandmother looked after the garden.

Few of the less-than-fairy-tale aspects of Andersen's life are touched upon in the museum, which was founded on the centenary of Andersen's birth when Odense first began to cash in on its famous ex-citizen. The son of a hard-up cobbler, Andersen's first home was a single room that doubled as a workshop in what was then one of Odense's slum quarters. It was a rough upbringing: Hans's ill-tempered mother was fifteen years older than his father, whom she married when seven months pregnant with Hans (she also had an illegitimate daughter by another man); his grandfather was insane; and descriptions of his grandmother, often given charge of the young Hans, range from "mildly eccentric" to "a pathological liar".

As Andersen was a first-rate hoarder it's stuffed with intriguing items: bits of school reports, his certificate from Copenhagen University, early notes and manuscripts of his books, chunks of furniture, his umbrella and paraphernalia from his travels, including the piece of rope he carried to facilitate escape from hotel rooms in the event of fire. A separate gallery contains a library of Andersen's works in seventy languages, and headphones for listening to some of his best-known tales as read by the likes of Sir Laurence Olivier. Nearby is a very mixed collection of illustrations and other art inspired by his writing.

For more local history, head to the **Møntergården City Museum** (Tues–Sun 10am–4pm; 25kr), a few streets away at Overgade 48–50, where there's an engrossing assemblage of important archeological pieces found on Funen, plus an immense coin collection – from as long ago and as far afield as England under Danelaw and Danish rule in Estonia.

There's more, but not much more, about Andersen at Munkemøllestræde 3–5, in the tiny **HC Andersens Barndomshjem** (Hans Christian Andersen's Childhood Home: July–Aug daily 10am–4pm; Sept–June Tues–Sun 11am–3pm; 25kr), the house where Andersen lived from 1807 to 1819 before moving to Copenhagen, where he spent the rest of his life. More interesting, though, is the nearby **Skt Knud's Domkirke** (April–Oct daily 10am–5pm; rest of the year until 4pm; ⓦwww.odense-domkirke.dk), whose crypt holds one of the most unusual and ancient finds Denmark has to offer: the **skeleton of Knud II**. Knud (aka Canute) was slain in 1086 – by Jutish farmers, angry at the taxes he'd imposed on them – in the original Skt Albani Kirke, the barest remains of which were found some years ago in the city park and then relocated here after his canonization as Knud the Holy.

Odense's art museums

The **Fyns Kunstmuseum** (Funen Art Museum: Tues–Sun 10am–4pm; 40kr), a few minutes' walk from the cathedral at Jernbanegade 13, gives an idea of the region's importance to Danish art during the late nineteenth century, when a number of Funen-based painters gave up creating portraits of the rich in favour of impressionistic landscapes and studies of the lives of the peasantry. The collection also contains some stirring works by many Nordic greats, among them Vilhelm Hammershøi, P.S. Krøyer, and Michael and Anne Ancher, but most striking of all is H.A. Brendekilde's enormously emotive *Udslidt* ("Worn Out"). The modern era isn't forgotten, with selections from Asger Jorn, Richard Mortensen and Egill Jacobsen, among many others, drawn from the museum's large collection.

For more modern art, walk along Vestergade and turn down Brandts Passage to reach **Brandts Klædefabrik** (®www.brandts.dk), a large former textile factory that's now given over to a number of cultural endeavours: three museums, a gallery, an art school, a music library and a cinema, along with cafés and restaurants. The **Kunsthallen** here (Art Exhibition Hall: Tues–Wed & Fri–Sun 10am–5pm, Thu noon–9pm; 40kr, combined ticket with the Photographic Art Museum and Danmarks Mediemuseum, the Danish Museum of Media, 70kr) is an increasingly prestigious spot for displays of work by high-flying new talent in art and design; close by are the varied displays of the **Museum of Photographic Art** (Museet for Fotokunst: same hours; 35kr), taken from the cream of modern (and some not so modern) art photography and almost always worth a look.

The Carl Nielsen museum

The **Carl Nielsen Museum**, inside the concert hall at Claus Bergs Gade 11 (June–Aug Fri–Sun noon–4pm; rest of the year Mon & Wed 2–5pm; free), celebrates the life and work of Odense's second most famous son. Born in a village just outside Odense in 1865, Nielsen displayed prodigious musical gifts from an early age and gained worldwide acclaim as a composer for his symphonies in particular. In the museum you can listen to some of his work on headphones, including excerpts from his major pieces and the polka he wrote when still a child. The actual **exhibits**, detailing Nielsen's life and achievements, are further enlivened by the accomplished sculptures made by his wife, Anne Marie, many of them early studies for her equestrian statue of Christian IX that now stands outside the Royal Stables in Copenhagen.

Eating and drinking

Recent years have brought a number of excellent dining establishments to Odense, with most of the city's **restaurants** and **snack bars** squeezed into the central part of town, making for a lot of competition and – in theory – some good bargains during the day. To be sure, those on a tight budget should find no shortage of kebab and pizza joints about the city. Many of the places listed below are also good for a **drink** in the evenings. If the weather is right for outdoor eating, pick up a freshly made sandwich or pastry from the in-house bakery at ※ *Bakers Café*, across the road from the tourist office on Fisketorvet. For details on Odense's **gay and lesbian** scene, head for the Lambda organization's café at Vindegade 100 (Wed 8pm–midnight, Fri & Sat 10pm–2am; ☎40 89 62 49, ®www.lambda.dk).

Restaurants

Bryggeriet Flakhaven 2 ®www.bryggeriet.dk
☎66 12 02 22. This brewery-cum-restaurant is a great place to ponder your day over a home-brewed pilsner, lager, ale or wheat beer, while meals range from light sandwiches – try the herring smørrebrød platter for 78kr – or pasta and meat dishes such as spareribs from 129kr. The shiny copper fermenting casks make the chartreuse green walls a little easier to handle, though there are also tables out front.

※ **Carlslund** Fruens Bøge Skov 7 ☎65 91 11 25, ®www.restaurant-carlslund.dk.

Typical Danish restaurant which does delicious smørrebrød and is famous for its *æggekage*, a scrumptious, eggy omelet (110kr). There's live jazz on summer Sat, and reservations recommended. You can get here on the Odense Åfart (see opposite), but if you're here past 4pm or so, you'll need to either walk the 3km back to town or take the train from Fruens Bøge.

Franck A Jernbanegade 4. Just renovated, very modern café serving decent food and a good brunch (daily 10am–4pm; 89kr), though it's best known for its after-dinner boozing, when the DJs get out their top-40 Euro hits and the dancefloor rumbles with the heels of the over-30 crowd. Cocktails start at 65kr.

Froggys Café Vestergade 68. A pleasant spot for a quick daytime bite, or for more substantial evening meals such as butterfish in white wine sauce or hazelnut chicken; the Sunday brunch buffet

(10.30am–3pm; 89kr) is popular with those nursing hangovers, and there's either a DJ or live music on weekend evenings until 5am. Decor is classic-meets-modern, with 1950s Hollywood posters, chandeliers and trendy leather benches.

Simoncini Vin Restaurant Vestergade 70 ☎66 17 92 95 ⓦwww.simoncini.dk. A new and superb gourmet restaurant with a range of excellently prepared dishes that may well redefine what you think about Italian food. The waiters can tell you exactly which wine goes best with which main dish.

Under Lindetræt Ramsherred 2 ☎66 12 92 86, ⓦwww.underlindetraet.dk. Set in a picture-perfect restored inn dating back to 1771, this is easily the most atmospheric and lavish Danish restaurant in town, but its superb setting and the excellent gourmet food make the prices – in excess of 400kr for a dinner – worth it.

Bars, music venues and nightclubs

Odense's nightlife centres around a gaggle of **late-opening cafés** that have usurped nightclubs as evening hangouts.

Café Biografen Brandts Passage 39–41 ☎66 13 16 16, ⓦwww.cafebio.dk. Enduringly fashionable Odense institution, decorated with a dazzling display of classic film posters. While the restaurant – serving sandwiches, salads and great weekend brunches – is quite popular, it's the bar that really gets going at night, mostly for a late-twenties to early-forties semi-professional crowd.

Carlsens Kvarter Hunderupvej 19 ⓦwww .carlsens.dk. Inexpensive, unpretentious pub serving fruity Belgian beers, English ales and a couple of Funen microbrews. Danish folk music occasionally accompanies. Mon–Sat 11am–1am, Sun 1–7pm.

Envy Brandts Passage 31 ⓦwww.envy-lounge .com. With tweed-covered seats, modern art and mood lighting on the terrace, this is one of

the city's trendiest nightspots, where the media hopefuls and tragically hip come to soak up the glam amidst Brazilian lounge and drum 'n' bass music. The expensive cocktails make the clientele here a bit more select than other places. Brunch (daily 10am–4pm, Sun from 11am; 95kr) is very popular.

Jazzhus Dexter Vindegade 65 ☎63 11 27 28, ⓦwww.dexter.dk. This expansive bar is a great place to hear some of the finest jazz in Denmark, from swing to fusion, four or five times a week until early morning. There is a cover (usually 50kr) all nights except Mon, when students show off their licks at the open-mike jam sessions.

Rytmeposten Østre Stationsvej 35 ☎66 13 60 20, ⓦwww.rytmeposten.dk. Funen's prime live music venue, this converted post office hosts a lot of heavy rock bands. Tickets generally start at 100kr.

Around Odense

A couple of kilometres south of the city centre on Sejerskovvej, the open-air **Funen Village** museum (April–June & mid-Aug to late Oct Tues–Sun 10am–5pm; late Oct to March Sun only 11am–3pm; 40–60kr) comprises a reconstructed nineteenth-century country village which is lent an air of authenticity by its period gardens and wandering geese. From the farmhouse to the poorhouse, all the buildings are originals from other parts of Funen, their exteriors painstakingly reassembled and interiors carefully refurbished. In summer, the old trades are revived in the former workshops and crafthouses, and there are free shows at the open-air theatre. Though often crowded, the village is well worth a visit – look out, too, for the village-brewed beer, handed out free on special occasions. Bus #42 runs to the village from the city centre (get out at the Den Fynske Landsby sign), or do what the locals do and get on the *Odense Åfart* boat (Ⓦwww.aafart.dk; 40kr one-way, 60kr return), which runs along the canal from Munke Mose park in the city centre and terminates at Fruens Bøge, from where it's a short canalside walk to Funen Village. From May to mid-September, it sails daily on the hour from 10am to 5pm.

Also easily reached from the town centre (bus #91 towards Allesø), the **Iron Age Village**, some 5km southeast at Store Klaus 40 (July to mid-Aug Mon–Fri & Sun 10am–4pm; mid-Aug to June Mon–Thurs 8.30am–3.30pm, Fri 8.30am–2pm; 40kr; Ⓦwww.jernalderlandsbyen.dk), is one of many prehistoric collections in Denmark, but one that at least makes an effort to be different. There's a simulated TV news broadcast covering events in Bronze Age Denmark, alongside displays describing how ancient symbols are used in modern times.

Kerteminde and around

A half-hour bus ride on bus #885 (40min with bus #890) northeast from Odense, past the huge cranes and construction platforms at Munkebo – until recently a tiny fishing hamlet but now the home of Denmark's biggest shipyard – lies **KERTEMINDE**, itself a place with firm maritime links, originally in fishing and now increasingly in tourism. The town is a centre for sailing and holidaymaking, and can get oppressively busy during the peak weeks of the summer. At any other time of year, though, it makes for a well-spent day, split between the town itself, the Viking-era **Ladby Boat** just outside and the verdant **Hindsholm Peninsula** just to the north.

The heart of Kerteminde, around the fifteenth-century Skt Laurentius Kirke and along Langegade and Strandgade, is a neat and prettily preserved nucleus of shops and houses. By the harbour, across the road from the bus station on Margrethes Plads 1, **Fjord&Bælt** (mid-Feb to June & Sept–Nov Mon–Fri 10am–4pm, Sat & Sun 10am–5pm; July–Aug daily 10am–6pm; 95kr; Ⓦwww.fjord-baelt.dk), is a state-of-the-art aquarium with a fifty-metre-long underwater tunnel from where you can observe seals and porpoises in their natural sea environment. On Strandgade itself, the **Farvergården** (town museum: March–Oct Tues–Sun 10am–4pm; 25kr) has several reconstructed craft workshops and a collection of local fishing equipment. On a grander note, a ten-minute stroll north around the waterfront brings you to the one-time house of the "birdman of Funen", the painter Johannes Larsen, on Møllebakken 14, which has been opened up as the **Johannes Larsen Museum** (March–May, Sept & Oct Tues–Sun 10am–4pm; June–Aug daily 10am–5pm; Nov–Feb Tues–Sun 11am–4pm; Ⓦwww.kertemindemuseer.dk; 60kr). During the late nineteenth century, Larsen produced etchings of rural landscapes and birdlife, going against the grain of prevailing art-world trends in much the same way as the Skagen artists (see p.155). The house is kept as it was when Larsen lived there, with his furnishings and knick-knacks, many of his canvases and, in the dining room, his astonishing wall paintings. Out back, a large modern building showcases hundreds of Larsen's sketches – most notably his breathtaking studies of birds mid-flight – as well as works by some fifty other Funen artists, including several haunting portraits by Fritz Syberg of his in-laws.

Practicalities

Kerteminde's **tourist office**, at Hans Schacksvej 5 (mid-June to Aug Mon–Fri 9am–5pm, Sat 10am–4pm; Sept to mid-June Mon–Fri 9am–4pm, Sat 9.30am–noon; ☎65 32 11 21, Ⓦwww.visitkerteminde.dk) has details of local **accommodation** bargains, which include a dozen odd private rooms and B&Bs. There's a hotel in town, the *Tornøes* (☎65 32 16 05, Ⓦwww.tornoeshotel.dk; ❹), and a much lower-cost option at the youth hostel, Skovvej 46 (☎65 32 39 29, Ⓦwww.danhostel.dk/kerteminde; dorms 150kr, doubles ❶), a ten-minute walk from the centre (cross the Kerteminde fjord by the road bridge, take the first major road left and then turn almost immediately right to reach it). There's also a **campsite**, *Kerteminde Camping* (☎65 32 19 71,

@www.kertemindecamping.dk; May–Dec), with a number of modern cabins (550kr, sleeps four, shared facilities) not far from the Larsen museum at Hindsholmvej 80, the main road running along the seafront – a twenty-minute walk from the centre.

Southern Funen and the islands

Southern Funen is noted above all for its many miles of sandy beaches, which are packed with tourists during the peak season. In July and August, the **islands** of the southern archipelago are more enticing: connected by an efficient network of ferries, they range from larger chunks of land such as Tåsinge, Langeland and Ærø – the latter two certainly worth a few nights' stay – to minute and sparsely populated places like Lyø or Avernakø, which are a pleasure to explore, if only for a few hours. From Odense, the simplest plan is to take a train to Svendborg, the main centre on the south coast, although you might also find the smaller Fåborg a good base; it's an hour's bus ride from Odense (#960, #961 or #962).

Svendborg

A favourite of the Danish yachting fraternity, with marinas clogging the southern coastline all the way to Fåborg, 24km to the west, **SVENDBORG** exudes a certain gritty charm, with colourful houses lining cobbled lanes dipping down to the water. Svendborg is a pleasant place to plot your travels around the archipelago, and boasts some of the best nightlife in an otherwise very quiet region. While you're there, spend an hour or two meandering around the narrow backstreets, spattered with beautiful bronzes by one of Denmark's best-known sculptors, the locally born Kai Nielsen, and head down to the harbourfront to take in the bustling shipyard, packed with beautiful old wooden boats from all over Scandinavia and the Baltic.

Before heading off to the islands might occupy a couple of historical collections a bit of your time. The town's museums (@www.svendborgmuseum.dk) include the **Social Welfare Museum**; May–Sept Tues–Sun 10am–4pm; Oct–April Tues–Sun

---

The Helge steamer

Between early May and mid-September, the *Helge* steamer (built in 1924) leaves Svendborg three to five times daily for the island of **Tåsinge**, calling at Vindebyøre, Svendborg's extension just across the Svendborg Sund; zigzagging back to Christiansminde, a beach resort next to Svendborg's exclusive marina; then on to the thatched village of Troense, criss-crossed by quiet streets of carefully preserved houses; Grasten, on the small island of Thurø and a few minutes' walk from a beach campsite; and the seventeenth-century castle Valdemar's Slot. The return sailing time is two hours, and **tickets** (100kr round-trip from the harbour; information from the Svendborg tourist bureau), good for one stop-off along the way, are purchased on board.

The *Helge's* last stop is the best: **Valdemar's Slot** (May–June & Aug daily 10am–5pm; July daily 10am–6pm; Sept Tues–Sun 10am–5pm; Oct & April Sat & Sun 10am–5pm; 70kr; @www.valdemarsslot.dk), an imposing pile with Baroque interiors begun by Christian IV and filled with three centuries of furniture, paintings and hunting trophies and paraphernalia. Other museums (joint ticket for all 110kr) include exhibits on **yachting and toys.** You might stay for a full-on meal at the exclusive *Restaurant Valdemars Slot* in the castle cellars, where they have great lunches (and a delicious, sprawling Sunday lunch buffet for 148kr). Should you want to stay over on Tåsinge, there are four **campsites** on the island; most convenient for the steamer and with access to a beautiful beach is *Vindebyøre Camping* (℡62 22 54 25, @www.vindebyoere.dk; mid-March to late Sept). The large *Troense* (℡62 22 54 12, @www.hoteltroense.dk; ❹), Strandgade 5 in Troense, has plain rooms with excellent water views.

1–4pm; 40kr), Grubbemøllevej 13, a captivating place housed in a former poorhouse with displays detailing how the Danish state has cared for (or ignored) its citizens over the years, and the half-timbered **Anne Hvides Gård** (early June to late Oct daily 11am–3pm; free), Fruestræde 3, which displays local archeological artefacts from the city and a series of rotating exhibits on Danish culture throughout the ages.

Lastly, **Naturama**, Dronningemaen 30 (late June to mid-Aug daily 10am–5pm, rest of the year closed Mon; 100kr; Ⓦwww.naturama.dk), offers a novel insight into the natural world, with three floors – representing the themes of water, land and air – that make sophisticated use of lighting, sound, film and photography to follow the habitats of northern European wildlife through a 24-hour day, with scenes that often make the animals look rather eerily life-like.

Practicalities

The Lange company's former foundry at Vestergade 45 is now the town's **youth hostel** (Ⓣ62 21 66 99, Ⓦwww.danhostel-svendborg.dk), which has dorms (200kr) and doubles (❷). Otherwise, there's the excellent *Ærø*, Brogade 1 (Ⓣ62 21 07 60, Ⓦwww.hotel-aeroe.dk; ❹), with classy, antique-ish rooms, or, via a ten-minute bus ride along the coast (#202), the reasonably priced *Stella Maris Missionhotel* (Ⓣ62 21 38 91, Ⓦwww.stellamaris.dk; ❹), a grand white building overlooking the Svendborg sound with a range of different rooms. The **tourist office** (July to mid-Aug Mon–Fri 9.30am–6pm, Sat 9.30am–2pm; mid-Aug to June Mon–Fri 9.30am–5pm, Sat 9.30am–12.30pm; Ⓣ62 21 09 80, Ⓦwww.visitsydfyn.dk), across the square from *Hotel Svendborg* at Centrumpladsen 4, deals with the entire southern Funen area and can provide details of accommodation, including numerous local **campsites**. It also stocks the latest ferry timetables.

For food, head straight for the scrumptious salads and burgers at ⚑ *Jettes Diner* on Kullinggade 1, and the snacks and drinks at *Børsen*, Gerritsgade 31. Come evening time, *Café Under Uret*, Gerritsgade 50, is the best bet for music and all-night dancing most days of the week.

Fåborg

An alternative base for the south coast, **FÅBORG** is a likeably small and sedate place, rarely as overwhelmed by holidaymakers as Svendborg and with equally good connections to the archipelago (ferries sail to Søby on Ærø, and to Bjørnø, Lyø and Avernakø). If you've an interest in Danish art, the town's other big attraction is the **Fåborg Museum** at Grønnegade 75 (April–Oct daily 10am–4pm; Nov–March Tues–Sun 11am–3pm; 50kr; Ⓦwww.faaborgmuseum.dk). Opened in 1910, it showcases the major works of the **Funen artists**, whose richly coloured landscapes put Funen on the map in the early twentieth-century art world. Together, the works demonstrate how little the Funen countryside has changed since they were painted over a century ago.

Almost next door to the museum, at Grønnegade 71–73, is one of the country's quaintest **youth hostels** (Ⓣ62 61 12 03, Ⓦwww.danhostel.dk/faaborg; April–Oct), with dorm beds (150kr) and eighteen inexpensive double rooms (❶). There's a **campsite** at Odensevej 140 (Ⓣ62 61 77 94, Ⓦwww.svanningecamping.dk), half a mile north of town, and a number of other camping areas on the beach as well. The bare-bones *Hotel Fåborg*, Torvet 13–15 (Ⓣ62 61 02 45, Ⓦwww.hotelfaaborg.dk; ❹), has rooms with a good deal of fin-de-siècle class. The **tourist office**, Banegård-spladsen 2A (June–Aug Mon–Sat 9am–5pm; Sept–May Mon–Fri 9am–4pm, Sat 10am–3pm; Ⓣ62 61 07 07, Ⓦwww.visitfaaborg-midtfyn.dk) can help with local travel information; they also sell DSB bus and train tickets.

Be sure to visit the traditional Danish ⚑ *Restaurant Tre Kroner*, Strandgade 1, with a gregarious owner, musically themed interior and great **food**. Otherwise, Fåborg has a few simpler places to eat, and you can stock up on provisions at the Super Brugsen or Føtex markets, which are next to each other on Mellemgade, near the bus station.

Around Fåborg: Egeskov Castle

In Kværndrup, just twenty minutes from Fåborg by bus #920 (ten minutes by train from Svendborg, then short walk or ride on bus #920), is the Renaissance castle **Egeskov Slot** (daily: late April to May & Sept 10am–5pm; June 10am–6pm; July to mid-Aug 10am–8pm; mid-Aug to late Aug 10am–6pm; 175kr; ⓦwww.egeskov .dk), which holds an array of rooms featuring a frightening armoury of daggers and swords, heads and hides and gorgeous Louis XVI furniture. Other museums here include one with displays on agriculture, horse-drawn vehicles and motorbikes and another holding several hundred antique cars. The stunningly lush castle **gardens** (120kr without castle entrance) include an intricate bamboo maze designed by Danish designer/philosopher/poet Peit Hein. It's easy to spend an entire day lounging around here, but bear in mind that the grounds are packed with visitors during high season. There's a free campsite (no facilities) next to the car park.

Langeland

The largest of the southern islands, long, thin and fertile **Langeland** is just off the southeast coast of Funen, to which it's connected by road bridge (hence you don't need to catch a ferry to reach it). Frequent buses (#910) make the half-hour journey from Svendborg to **RUDKØBING**, the main town, from where there are ferry links to Marstal on Ærø; there's also a ferry to Tårs on Lolland (see p.103), leaving from Spodsbjerg, about 6km to the east. Rudkøbing itself doesn't have a lot to offer except for a laid-back atmosphere, a pleasant fishing harbour and the historical collection in the **Langelands Museum** at Jens Winthersvej 12 (Mon–Thurs 10am–4pm, Fri 10am–1pm; 25kr; ⓦwww.langelandsmuseum.dk). The town's **tourist office**, at Torvet 5 (mid-June to Aug Mon–Fri 9am–5pm, Sat 9am–3pm; Sept to mid-June Mon–Fri 9.30am–4.30pm, Sat 9.30am–12.30pm; ℡62 51 35 05, ⓦwww.langeland.dk), can provide advice on **accommodation** and has a long list of **private rooms** across the island starting at 105kr per person.

Alternatively, head for the stocky yellow **youth hostel** at Engdraget 11 (℡62 51 18 30, ⓦwww.danhostel.dk/rudkobing), which has dorms (140kr) and doubles (❶). One of the island's best campsites, *Færgegårdens Camping*, Spodsbjergvej 335 (℡62 50 11 36, ⓦwww.spodsbjerg.dk), is 9km east of town and a few metres from the beach in Spodsbjerg, and has inexpensive cabins (sleep four, 325kr; only

▲ Egeskov Slot

available per week in July). Of the town's hotels, best is the super-central *Skandinavien*, Brogade 13 (☎62 51 14 95, ⓦwww.skanhotel.dk; ❸), whose agreeable rooms look onto the Gåsetorvet. If you plan on visiting on the last weekend in July, book accommodation early, as this is when the annual **Langelands Festival** takes place (ⓦwww.langelandsfestival.dk). Known as Denmark's largest garden party, this smallish music festival hosts mostly Scandinavian bands alongside a few international acts – groups such as Simple Minds and Runrig have played in the past.

North of Rudkøbing, Langeland consists mostly of farmland, sandy beaches and the occasional village, with just one sight to head for: the fairy-tale thirteenth-century **Tranekær Slot**, approximately 7km north of Rudkøbing and surrounded by the beautiful TICKON Park (year-round dusk till dawn; 25kr), dotted with sculptures made by international artists from natural materials. To find the island's best **beaches**, head 15km southwest of Rudkøbing to **Ristinge**, one of the loveliest in the country, or make for the southern coast, where there are also a couple of **bird sanctuaries**, Gulstav Mose and Tryggelev Nor. Local buses serve all the main sites on the island.

Ærø

For a more varied few days, take the ferry from Svendborg or Rudkøbing to **Ærø**, a pretty island just north of the German coast. Although getting here can require the better part of a day, it's worth the effort for the island's ancient burial sites, abundant stretches of sandy beach, traditional farms and, in the principal settlement of **Ærøskøbing**, a peach of a medieval merchants' town.

Ærøskøbing

When passing shipping brought prosperity to Ærø in the nineteenth century, the island historically split into three divisions: fisherfolk resided on the windy western tip at Søby, the wealthy shipping magnates and captains resided in Marstal, to the east, while the local middle classes collected in the town of **ÆRØSKØBING**. This is all beautifully described at the **Ærø Museum** (mid-March to late Oct Mon–Fri 10am–4pm, Sat & Sun 11am–3pm; late Oct to mid-March Mon–Fri 10am–1pm; 20kr, joint ticket for all museums 60kr; ⓦwww.arremus.dk), Brogade 3–5.

Ærøskøbing was awarded the European Nostra prize in 2003 as the best-preserved eighteenth-century Danish town, and its narrow streets, lined with tidy houses, are made for wandering – look out for the oldest building, dating from 1645, at Søndergade 36. If it's raining, you could drop in to see the eye-catching **Bottle Ship Collection** at Smedegade 22, (April to late June & late Aug to late Oct daily 10am–4pm; late June to mid-Aug daily 10am–5pm; late Oct to March Tues–Fri 1–3pm, Sat & Sun 10am–noon; ⓦwww.bottle-peter.dk; 25kr) or **Hammerichs House** at Gyden 22 (mid-June to Aug daily noon–4pm; 20kr), a riot of woodcarvings, furnishings and timepieces from bygone days.

Ærøskøbing's **tourist office** (Mon–Fri 9am–7pm, Sat 10am–7pm, Sun 10am–6pm; ☎62 52 13 00, ⓦwww.arre.dk), on Vestergade 1, can give information on the island's burial places and other secluded spots. A local bus serves the island's main roads, but the best way to get around is by **bike**, though you'll need to pedal hard to get up some of the hills; the tourist office supplies free bike maps to help plan your route, and three-speed bikes can be rented for 55kr a day at Pilebækkens Cykler (☎62 52 11 10), at Pillebækken 11, a BP gas station about 200m west of the main marketplace.

As for **accommodation**, the best spot in town is the British-run *Pension Vestergade 44*, Vestergade 44 (☎62 52 22 98, ⓦwww.vestergade44.com; ❹), where the prim, quaint rooms share facilities. There's also a terrific youth hostel (☎62 52 10 44, ⓦwww.aeroeskoebingvandrerhjem.dk; mid-April to mid-Oct) with ocean views, friendly management and some doubles (❶) as well as dorms (175kr); it's at Smedevejen 15, about 2km west of the ferry dock on the road to Marstal. Finally, *Ærøskøbing Camping* campsite, Sygehusvej 40B (☎62 52 18 54, ⓦwww.arrecamping.dk; May–Sept), is appealingly sited next to the beach and has a few sizeable, fully outfitted cabins (125kr per night plus 68kr per person per day, sleep four). **Eating** options include good Danish food at *Det Lille Hotel*, Smedegade 33, and the popular *Landbogården*, Vestergade 54, which has tasty and affordable *dagens ret* dinner menus like fried fish, shellfish pasta and smoked salmon (around 200kr) and also makes a good stop for an early evening or late-night **beer**. When getting on or off the Svendborg ferry, be sure to look in on the outstanding smoked-fish place, *Ærøskøbing Røgeri*, facing the water at Havnen 15.

Travel details

Trains

Odense to: Århus (2–3 hourly; 1hr 38min); Copenhagen (every 30min; 1hr 30min); Esbjerg (8 daily; 1hr 23min–2hr 30min); Nyborg (every 30min; 13min); Svendborg (every 20min; 41min).

Buses

Kerteminde to: Nyborg (1–2 hourly; 35min).
Odense to: Fåborg (1–2 hourly; 50min–1hr 18min); Kerteminde (every 15min; 33min); Nyborg (every 30min; 54min); Svendborg (2–3 hourly; 1hr 20min).
Rudkøbing to: Lohals (hourly; 36min); Spodsbjerg (8–10 daily; 10min); Svendborg (1–6 hourly; 25min).
Svendborg to: Fåborg (2–3 hourly; 40min); Rudkøbing (1–5 hourly; 25min); Nyborg (every 30min; 46min).

South coast ferries

Ferry connections are plentiful around the south coast archipelago and it's best to check the fine details locally. Some sailings continue all year; others only operate during the summer. Frequencies given below are for weekdays; sailings are often reduced on weekends and public holidays.
Bøjden to: Fynshav (6–7 daily; 50min).
Søby to: Mommark (2–5 daily; 1hr).
Fåborg to: Bjørnø (3–6 daily; 30min); Lyø (2–4 daily via Avernakø; 1hr 10min); Søby (2–5 daily; 1hr).
Marstal to: Rudkøbing (3–6 daily; 1hr).
Spodsbjerg to: Tårs (hourly; 45min).
Svendborg to: Ærøskøbing (4–6 daily; 1hr 15min); Drejø (4–5 daily via Skarø; 1hr 15min).

International trains

Odense to: Hamburg, changing in Fredericia or Kolding (1 daily; 4hr 20min).

1.3

Jutland

The people of Jutland (*Jylland*), the Jutes – pronounced "yutes" – like to see themselves as different from the folk of Zealand and Funen, and historically this was certainly the case. The Jutes were, in pre-Viking times, a quite separate tribe to the more warlike Danes who occupied the eastern islands and who gradually moved across to control Jutland, too. As you arrive in Jutland today it won't take long before you sense the distinction. The overriding impression of Jutland is of a friendly place of unhurried lifestyles and rural calm, even in the couple of very likeable cities populated by locals who seem to relish their position outside the national spotlight. There's much to enjoy in the unspoilt towns and villages, and Jutland's comparatively large size and distance from Copenhagen make it perhaps the most distinctive and interesting area in the country.

There are also more regional variations in Jutland than elsewhere in Denmark. **South Jutland**, a territory long battled over by Denmark and Germany, is home to the immaculately restored town of **Ribe** and the country's first national park, Vadehavet. Further north, **Esbjerg** gives easy access to the windswept beaches of the western coast. The picturesque green fjords of eastern Jutland, and some of the peninsula's better-known sights – from the old military stronghold of **Fredericia** and the ancient runic stones at **Jelling** to the modern bricks of **Legoland**, are easily reached from the country's second largest airport at **Billund**.

Århus, halfway up the eastern coast, is Jutland's lively main urban centre and Denmark's second city where, besides a wealth of history and cultural pursuits, you'll find plenty of excellent nightlife. Just to the east, **Djursland** – the peninsula known as Denmark's nose due to its distinctive shape – attracts thousands of visitors every year to its rolling hills and sandy beaches, the result of moraine formations after the last Ice Age. Århus is handy, too, for the optimistically titled **Lake District**, a small but appealing area tucked in between Skanderborg, Randers and Viborg. Further inland, the retreat of the ice sheets during the Ice Age left another terrain of sharp contrasts: stark heather-clad moors break suddenly into dense forests with swooping gorges and wide rivers – epitomized by the wild moorland at **Kongenshus** and the grassy vistas of **Hald Ege**. Ancient **Viborg** is a better base for seeing all this than dour **Randers**, and from here you can head north, either to the blustery fjord beaches of **Limfjordslandet** or to old and vibrant **Aalborg**, which sits on the southern bank of the Limfjorden, a massive fjord that separates the area from mainland Jutland.

North of the Limfjorden, you'll get a taste of Jutland at its most dramatic: a sandy semi-wilderness stretching north to **Skagen**, a quaint town at the very tip of the peninsula that boasts some of the country's best seafood. **Frederikshavn**, on the way, is the port for boats to Norway and Sweden, and is usually full of Swedes and Norwegians stocking up with (what is for them) cheap liquor.

South Jutland

Best known as an entry and exit point (to the UK by sea and air, to Germany overland), more people pass through **south Jutland** than probably any other part of the country. Though many head straight for Copenhagen or the holiday areas of the west coast, it's becoming increasingly popular to linger a little. The engaging

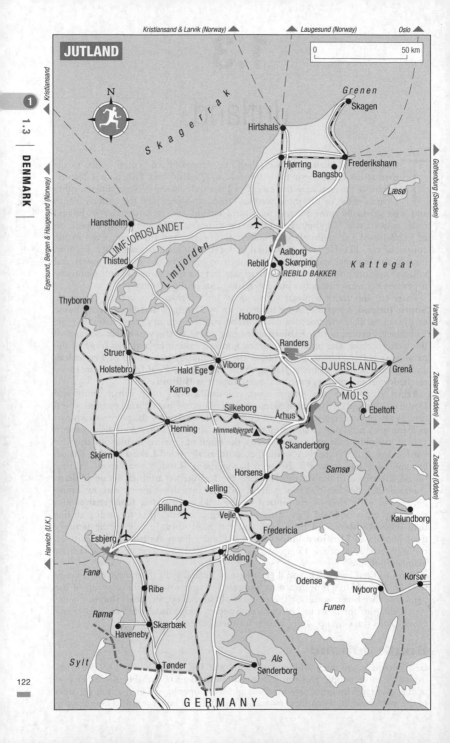

JUTLAND

0   50 km

Kristiansand & Larvik (Norway) ▲   ▲ Laugesund (Norway)   Oslo ▲

◄ Kristiansand

◄ Egersund, Bergen & Haugesund (Norway)

◄ Harwich (U.K.)

Gothenburg (Sweden) ►

Varberg ►

Zealand (Odden) ►

Zealand (Odden) ►

N

Grenen
Skagen

S k a g e r r a k

Hirtshals

Hjørring   Frederikshavn
Bangsbo

Læsø

Hanstholm

LIMFJORDSLANDET

Thisted

Limfjorden

Aalborg
Rebild   Skørping
REBILD BAKKER

K a t t e g a t

Thyborøn

Hobro

Struer

Randers

Holstebro   Hald Ege   Viborg

DJURSLAND   Grenå

Karup

MOLS

Silkeborg
Århus   Ebeltoft

Herning   Himmelbjerget

Skanderborg

Skjern

Horsens   Samsø

Jelling

Billund   Vejle

Kalundborg

Esbjerg   Fredericia

Fanø   Kolding

Odense
Ribe   Nyborg   Korsør

Rømø   Funen

Skærbæk
Haveneby

Als
Sylt   Tønder
Sønderborg

G E R M A N Y

and well-preserved medieval town of **Ribe** is well worth a day's wander, while the beautiful coastline of sandy beaches and windswept dunes, some great seafood restaurants and a wonderful array of summer cottages attract German tourists in their thousands.

Esbjerg and around

South Jutland's only city is **ESBJERG** – and if this is your first view of the country, bear in mind it's an entirely untypical one. Esbjerg is a new town by Danish standards: purpose-built as a deep-water harbour during the nineteenth century, it went on to become one of the world's biggest fishing ports. Nowadays, it's used as a supply point for the North Sea oil industry, though it does maintain an air of its original charm, and handsome townhouses abound. Since both DFDS Seaways ferries and regular BMI flights from the UK arrive here, you may find yourself staying for a day or so. If you do, there are a few places worth a nose, most notably the **Esbjerg Performing Arts Centre** and the **Fisheries Museum**. The city also makes a great base from which to explore the surrounding area, particularly the superb beaches on the island of Fanø, a short ferry ride away.

Arrival and information

The Esbjerg **tourist office**, at Skolegade 33 (mid-June to Aug Mon–Fri 9am–5pm, Sat 9.30am–2.30pm; Sept to mid-June Mon–Fri 10am–5pm, Sat 10am–1pm; ℡75 12 55 99, ⓦwww.visitesbjerg.dk), on a corner of the main square, Torvet, can give you all the practical information you might need, as well as leaflets describing a short self-guided walking tour of the city's early twentieth-century buildings, as well as three longer round-trip cycling routes around the area. The **passenger harbour** is a well-signposted fifteen-minute walk from the centre (or take bus #5), and trains depart to and from Copenhagen, Århus and Ribe from the **train station** on Skolegade. Esbjerg **airport** (ⓦwww.esbjerg-lufthavn.dk) is 9km south of the city centre and reached by bus #8 from the train station. **Internet** access is available at all of the hotels listed below plus at the tourist office and at the public library next to Esbjerg Museum (see p.124).

Accommodation

The tourist office can help in finding bed-and-breakfast-type **accommodation**.

Ådalens Camping Gudenåvej 20 ℡75 15 88 22, ⓦwww.adal.dk. Well equipped with cabins sleeping five (225kr plus 71kr per person), 6km north of Esbjerg along the Sædding Strandvej coast road, and reached by bus #1 from the train station.
Ansgar Skolegade 36 ℡75 12 82 44, ⓦwww.hotelansgar.dk. Central mid-range hotel with 52 comfortable rooms – each one slightly different from the next – and a homely atmosphere. ❸/❹
Britannia Torvet ℡75 13 01 11, ⓦwww.britannia.dk. Plush, modern place on the central square, with furniture created by Danish design legend

Arne Jacobsen – stylish Swan chairs and sofas – as well as free parking. ❹/❺
Cabinn Skolegade 14 ℡75 18 16 00, ⓦwww.cabinn.com. Twin-towered hotel, with a mixture of simple, inexpensive cabin-style rooms and more pricy traditional hotel accommodation. ❸
Danhostel Esbjerg Gammel Vardevej 80 ℡75 12 42 58, ⓦwww.esbjerg-danhostel.dk. The town's former Maritime School and now a comfy hostel, 25min walk north of the centre (or take bus #4 from the train station) with dorms (160kr) and some doubles ❷. Closed mid-Dec to mid-Jan.

The City

The best place to get your bearings – and appreciate the vastness of Esbjerg's harbour area is from the top of the **Vandtårn**, at Havnegade 22 (Water Tower: April–May & mid-Sept to Oct Sat & Sun 10am–4pm; June to mid-Sept daily 10am–4pm; 15kr; ⓦwww.esbjergmuseum.dk), a short walk towards the centre from the harbour. There are sweeping views of the sea and marshes, and on a good day

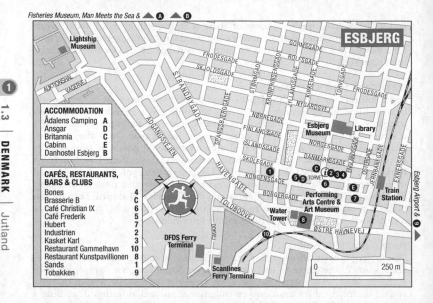

ESBJERG

Lightship Museum

ACCOMMODATION

Ådalens Camping	**A**
Ansgar	**D**
Britannia	**C**
Cabinn	**E**
Danhostel Esbjerg	**B**

CAFÉS, RESTAURANTS, BARS & CLUBS

Bones	**4**
Brasserie B	**C**
Café Christian IX	**6**
Café Frederik	**5**
Hubert	**7**
Industrien	**2**
Kasket Karl	**3**
Restaurant Gammelhavn	**10**
Restaurant Kunstpavillionen	**8**
Sands	**1**
Tobakken	**9**

Esbjerg Museum
Library
Performing Arts Centre & Art Museum
Water Tower
Train Station
DFDS Ferry Terminal
Scanlines Ferry Terminal
Esbjerg Airport & ⑨

0   250 m

1.3 | DENMARK | Jutland

you can see as far as Fanø. A small exhibit inside details the tower's history. Next door, at Havnegade 18–20, **Musikhuset Esbjerg** (Esbjerg Performing Arts Centre: ☏76 10 90 00) houses various concert halls and exhibition areas, including the **Esbjerg Kunstmusem** (Esbjerg Art Museum: daily 10am–4pm; 40kr), a modest collection of contemporary pieces, the highlight of which are the huge steel plates splattered in the blood of their creator, Danish *enfant terrible* Christian Lemmerz. The centre as a whole is one of Denmark's more groundbreaking cultural institutes and in recent times has exhibited – to much hand-wringing – a forum on sex and pornography and Lemmerz's gory collection of dead pigs. The building itself is a fascinating piece of modern architecture, resembling a giant concrete tomb surrounded by massive white flowers designed under the direction of Jørn Utzon, the architect responsible for the Sydney Opera House. The **Esbjerg Museum** at Torvegade 45 (June–Aug daily 10am–4pm; Sept–May Tues–Sun 10am–4pm; 30kr, free Wed; ⓦwww.esbjergmuseum.dk), displays replicas of the urban environment preceding the so-called "American period" of the 1890s during which Esbjerg's rapid growth matched that of the US gold rush.

If the Arts Centre has left you in the mood for more aesthetic appreciation, take a bus (#3 or #8 from the train station) out along the coastal road until you arrive at the four nine-metre-high imposing figures known as **Man Meets the Sea**. Installed in 1995 by artist Sven Wiig Hansen, this bizarre piece of public art reflects on Esbjerg's relationship with the sea and provides an excellent photo opportunity. Just around the corner is the wonderful **Fiskeri- og Søfartsmuseet Saltvandsakvariet** on Tarphagevej (Fisheries and Maritime Museum and Sealarium: daily: July–Aug 10am–6pm; Sept–May 10am–5pm; July & Aug 100kr, Sept–June 85kr; ⓦwww.fimus.dk), where you can cast an eye over the old boats and other vestiges of the early Esbjerg fishing fleet. This is an excellent place to take the kids, not least because of the adjoining Sealarium, part of a seal research centre (feeding times 11am and 2.30pm).

Eating, drinking and nightlife

Esbjerg's **eating** options are fairly limited if you're on a tight budget, though the usual run of hot-dog grills and bakeries is scattered throughout the city. **Nightlife**-wise, the city is geared to the thousands of sailors who pass through this busy port.

There are a run of strip bars on Skolegade, but these can get quite rowdy and aren't recommended for the fainthearted.

Eating

Bones Skolegade 17. On the opposite corner to *Cabinn*, this dependable chain offers decent-value meals, such as mouthwatering barbecue ribs for 129kr, burgers for 119kr and steak with all the trimmings from 139kr.

Brasserie B *Hotel Britannia*, Torvegade 14. A good range of excellent seafood dishes starting at 195kr – the 99kr herring lunch platter is also worth sticking around for.

Café Christian IX Torvet 17. Popular place on Esbjerg's main square, serving filling brunches from 10.30am, sandwiches and salads throughout the day and the choice between steak or fish dishes (all 198kr) for dinner. There's sometimes live music at weekends.

Café Frederik Skolegade 46. Small, French style café which starts with brunch from 11am (10.30am at weekends) and continues with well-prepared omelettes, soups, sandwiches and salads (from 79kr) throughout the day, culminating in an evening steak menu (from 179kr). Also the venue for regular, and hugely popular, drag shows costing 249kr including dinner.

Restaurant Gammelhavn Britanniavej 5, ☎76 11 90 00. Set in the old dock area, this outstanding restaurant leaves little left to be desired when it comes to their five-course gourmet menu (575kr) featuring unusual combinations such as braised sweetbreads served with smoked potatoes and mocha sauce.

There's also a more run-of-the-mill à la carte menu at lunch.

Restaurant Kunstpavillionen Performing Arts Centre, Havnegade 20. Excellent lunchtime menu including a mixed platter of fish, beef and cheese for 138kr. In the evening, a French-style three-course dinner menu for 275kr draws in a well-heeled crowd, as does the overwhelming lunchtime Sunday buffet for 138kr.

Sands Skolegade 60 ☎ www.sands .dk. Excellent for traditional Danish food and service – try the daily special for 79kr, or the lunch-time platter for 159kr which includes traditional delicacies such as marinated herring, fish meatballs with remoulade, baked beef inner loin, and some very mature *Gamle Ole* cheese. Closed Sun.

Drinking and nightlife

Hubert Kongensgade 10. Bar with more than seventy different types of beer on offer plus a couple of stages hosting blues and jazz bands.

Industrien Skolegade 27. Popular café-cum-bar-cum-nightclub with DJs and live music, and open till 5am from Thurs–Sun.

Kasket Karl Skolegade 29. English-style pub and a great place to make a gentle transition to Danish culture (and prices) while sipping a beer or two.

Tobakken Gasværksvej 2 ☎75 18 00 00, ☎www .tobakken.dk. The city's excellent concert venue hosting big Danish names and a few less known international names.

Around Esbjerg: Fanø

From Esbjerg it's a straightforward ferry trip to **Fanø**, the northernmost of the new Wadden Sea National Park islands (see box, p.128). A long, flat island, its superb west coast beaches draw German holidaymakers in droves during the summer. Fanø Trafikken ferries (☎70 23 15 15, ☎www.fanotrafikken.dk; 12min; 35kr return) run frequently between Esbjerg and the island's main village, **Nordby**, where the **tourist office** at the harbour (July–Aug Mon–Fri 9am–5pm, Sat & Sun 10am–4pm; Sept–June Mon–Fri 10am–5pm, Sat 10am–1pm; ☎70 26 42 00, ☎www .visitfanoe.dk) can provide information on accommodation, a few cultural sights (a couple of fairly ordinary local museums and a windmill) and the rich birdlife of the east coast marshes. There are seven **campsites**, of which the best is *Feldberg Strand Camping* (☎75 16 33 33, ☎www.feldbergcamping.dk), almost on the beach.

Ribe

Just over half an hour by train south from Esbjerg lies the exquisitely preserved town of **RIBE**. In 856 Ansgar built one of the first Danish churches here as a base for his missionaries arriving from Germany; a hundred years later the town was a major staging post for pilgrims making their way south to Rome. Ribe's proximity to the sea allowed it to evolve into a significant trading port, but continued expansion was thwarted by the dual blows of the Reformation and the silting-up of the harbour.

Since then, not much appears to have changed. The surrounding marshlands, which have prevented the development of any large-scale industry, and a long-standing conservation programme have enabled Ribe to keep roughly the appearance and size of medieval times, and its old town is a delight to meander around.

Arrival, information and accommodation

Ribe's **train** and **bus stations** are on the east side of Ribe Å river. From there, Dagmarsgade cuts a straight path to the central square, Torvet, where you'll find the **tourist office** (June & Sept Mon–Fri 9am–5pm, Sat 10am–1pm; July–Aug Mon–Fri 9am–6pm, Sat 10am–5pm, Sun 10am–2pm; Oct–May Mon–Fri 10am–4.30pm, Sat 10am–1pm; ☎75 42 15 00, ⓦwww.visitribe.dk), across the road to the rear of the grand cathedral. They have a computer for free **internet** access and can help with private **accommodation** (from 360kr per person per night) which may be useful as interesting and affordable options get packed during summer and advance booking is essential. Some 2km distant along Farupvej (take bus #771) is a pleasant campsite (☎75 41 07 77, ⓦwww.ribecamping.dk) with a range of different cabins (from 175kr plus 67kr per person for a basic mini-cabin sleeping four) as well as pitches; open April to November.

Hotels

Dagmar Torvet ☎75 42 00 33, ⓦwww .hoteldagmar.dk. If you can afford it, splash out on this beautifully restored place opposite the Domkirke, which dates from 1581 and claims to be the oldest hotel in Denmark. Its gorgeous doubles come with period furniture and loads of character, plus there's free wireless internet. ⑤

Den Gamle Arrest Torvet 11 ☎75 42 37 00, ⓦwww.dengamlearrest.dk. An intriguing option, having served both as a girls' school and as the town's jail, some of the quirky double rooms here are in the former cells, which these days lock from the inside. ③, en-suite ④

🎿 **Ribe Danhostel** Skt Pedersgade 16 ☎75 42 06 20, ⓦwww.danhostel-ribe.dk.

One of the country's best hostels, an easy walk over the river from the town centre and with views straight out onto the marshes of the Wadden Sea National Park (see box, p.128). Apart from some good-value, pleasant en-suite doubles (①), dorm beds (150kr) are also available from July to mid-Aug in the two to six-bed rooms. Other facilities include bike hire (70kr per day) and free wireless internet.

Weis Stue Torvet 2 ☎75 42 07 00, ⓦwww .weis-stue.dk. With creaking floorboards and wood-panelled walls, this wonderfully atmospheric place is where the Nightwatchman starts his tour (see box below). Eight rooms, filled with antique decorative china and furniture and all with shared toilet and bath. Advance booking is essential year-round. ③

The Nightwatchman of Ribe

At 10pm every evening between May and mid-September – and also at 8pm from June to August – the **Nightwatchman of Ribe** emerges from the bar of the *Weis Stue* inn, Torvet 2 (see above), and makes his rounds. Before the advent of gas lighting, a nightwatchman would patrol every town in Denmark to help keep the sleeping populace safe from fire and flood. The last real nightwatchman of Ribe made his final tour in 1902, but thanks to the early development of tourism in the town, the custom had been reintroduced by 1932.

Dressed in a replica of the original uniform and carrying an original morning-star pike and lantern (the sharp tip doubling as a weapon), the watchman – a role filled for the last thirty years by octogenarian Aage Gran – walks the narrow alleys of Ribe singing songs written by Thomas Kingo (a local priest who lived in Ribe in the mid-eighteenth century), and talking about the town's history while stopping at points of interest. One song tells people to go to bed and to be careful with lighting fires – sensible advice when most of the town's dwellings are built from wood. It's obviously laid on for the tourists, but the tour is free and good fun.

▲ Ribe Domkirke

The Town

Ribe's main attraction is without a doubt the **Domkirke** on Torvet (April & Oct Mon–Sat 11am–4pm, Sun noon–4pm; May–June & mid-Aug to Sept Mon–Sat 10am–5pm, Sun noon–5pm; July to mid-Aug Mon–Sat 10am–5.30pm, Sun noon–5.30pm; Nov–March Mon–Sat 11am–3pm, Sun noon–3pm; free, Citizens' Tower 10kr), which looms above the town and dominates the marshes for miles around. A successor to Ansgar's original church, the cathedral was begun around 1150 using tufa – a suitably light material for the marshy base – brought, along with some of the Rhineland's architectural styles, by river from southern Germany.

Originally raised on a slight hill, the Domkirke is now a couple of metres below the surrounding streets, their level having risen due to the many centuries' worth of debris accumulated beneath them. The **interior** is not as spectacular as the cathedral's size and long history might suggest, having been stripped of much of its decoration by Hans Tausen, Bishop of Ribe, during the mid-sixteenth century. The thirteenth-century "Cat's Head Door" outside, on the south side, a good example of the imported Romanesque design, is one of the few early decorative remains. More recent additions that catch the eye are the butcher's-slab altar and the colourful frescoes, mosaics and stained-glass windows by Carl-Henning Pedersen (a member of the CoBrA movement of mid-twentieth-century artists from Copenhagen, Brussels and Amsterdam), added in the mid-1980s. After looking around, climb the 248 steps to peer out from the top of the red-brick **Citizens' Tower**, so named since it doesn't belong to the church but to the people whose taxes pay for its upkeep. The original tower toppled into the nave on Christmas morning, 1283.

Ribe also has a couple of museums celebrating the town's Viking era. The **Museet Ribes Vikinger** (Museum of Ribe's Vikings: April–June, Sept–Oct daily 10am–4pm;

July–Aug daily 10am–6pm, Wed until 9pm; Nov–March Tues–Sun 10am–4pm; 60kr; ⓦwww.ribesvikinger.dk), opposite the train station, displays locally excavated remains, along with a full-size reconstructed Viking ship. If you've not had your fill, head for the **Ribe Vikinge Center** (May–June & Sept Mon–Fri 10am–3.30pm; July–Aug daily 11am–5pm; 75kr; ⓦwww.ribevikingecenter.dk), 3km south of the centre on Lystrupvej, which attempts to recreate the Viking lifestyle with costumed attendants demonstrating traditional Viking crafts.

Eating, drinking and nightlife

Backhaus Grydergade 12. Good-value smørrebrød and other traditional Danish dishes for lunch. Dinner is more a meat (or fish) and two veg affair (from 99kr).

Kolvig Ved Skibroen. In the centre of town, with a picturesque and relaxed riverside setting, you'll find excellent and reasonably priced salads and sandwiches on offer here. In the evening there's a set menu (2–4 course) as well as à la carte. The menu is made up of delightfully combined, locally sourced seasonal produce. Closed Sun.

Pepper's Torvet 9. Raucous café-bar which converts into a nightclub at midnight. Also featuring a pool table and the occasional live rock band. An in-house photographer snoops around every night and takes incriminating photos that are published on the website (ⓦwww.peppers.dk) the next day. Open Thurs–Sat from 8pm till late.

Stenbohus Stenbogade 1. Popular bar-disco across the road from Pepper's with live blues, folk or rock acts at least once a week. Open Thurs–Sat; live music starts at midnight.

Strygejernet Dagmarsgade 1. Atmospheric, tiny but distinctive pub, which serves light meals and snacks during the day and delightful draught ales at night.

Valdemar Skt Nicolaj Gade 6. Next to the art gallery, the relaxing garden setting here is a perfect spot for coffee or a cool draught beer during summer. In the evening, there's occasional live music inside. Closed Sun.

Vøgterkœlderen Torvet, in the basement of the *Dagmar* hotel. A reputable spot to eat, serving two- (259kr) and three-course (298kr) dinners, mostly fishy or meaty Danish specialities. At night, it's a lively bar.

Around Ribe: Vadehavscentret and Mandø

Half an hour by bus #711 from Ribe, **Vadehavscentret** (Wadden Sea Centre: April–Sept daily 10am–5pm; July & Aug Thurs to 9pm; Oct & March daily 10am–4pm; 60kr; ⓦwww.vadehavscentret.dk) is a great place to go for an in-depth introduction to the new Wadden Sea National Park's unique geography, history and ecology. Furthermore it's the starting point for the regular tractor-bus connection to the small Wadden Sea island of **Mandø** (daily May–Sept only; 40min; 50kr one-way, 60kr same-day return; ☎75 44 51 07, ⓦwww.mandoebussen.dk). Crossing over the muddy tidal flats you'll see numerous birds feeding and, if you're lucky, seals basking

The Wadden Sea National Park

In 2009 a new national park was designated along the west coast of southern Jutland. Vadehavet Nationalpark is a 1459-square-kilometre strip that encompasses a significant portion of one of the world's most important tidal areas stretching 500km from Den Helder in Holland to Blåvandshuk (north of Esbjerg) in Denmark. These marshy **tidal flats** give respite and protection to millions of migratory and breeding waterfowl each year, including wild geese and eider duck, and are regularly visited by vulnerable **bird species** such as red-breasted geese, Kentish plovers and barred warblers. Vadehavet Nationalpark includes three islands: from north to south Fanø (see p.125), Mandø (see above), and Rømø (see p.129). To get the best impression of this unique corner of Denmark, Mandø is probably your best bet. Its only link with mainland Jutland is via a tidal road, which has left the island relatively pristine and largely untouched by holidaymakers and developers. If you're looking to combine beach life and birdlife, Rømø and Fanø have more to offer.

in the sun just before you reach the island. With little human habitation, the main attraction on the island itself is the ten-kilometre circular route around its perimeter, easily done on foot or by bike before the tractor bus heads back again four hours later. Bikes can be hired for 30kr at the Mandø Centre (May–Sept daily 10am–5pm; free; ☎75 44 53 54), which also has a small exhibition describing the island's cultural and natural history. Alternatively, the Vadehavscentret organizes guided tours to the island which include treks out into the Wadden Sea mudflats to explore the sea bottom at low tide. Check their website for details.

Rømø and Tønder

From Skærbæk, a few kilometres south of Ribe by train, bus #29 heads across 12km of tidal flats to the Wadden Sea National Park island of **Rømø**. The eroding power of sea and wind have given the island a wild and unkempt appearance, as well as creating a broad beach along the eastern side and allowing wildlife to flourish all over. There's a good chance of seeing seals basking in the spring, while at the end of the summer many migratory wading birds can be found, dodging the island's plentiful sheep.

Information about the island's wildlife is available at the excellent Tønnisgård Nature Centre exhibition centre (March–Nov 10am–4pm; Dec–Feb 10am–3pm; 15kr; ⓦwww.tonnisgaard.dk) which also runs birdwatching trips and guided tours around the island. It's in the hamlet of Tvismark, just south of the causeway as you arrive. Next door, Rømø's **tourist office** (July & Aug daily 9am–6pm; rest of the year 9am–5pm; ☎74 75 51 30, ⓦwww.romo.dk) can provide details about the island's few cultural sights, and private **accommodation** on the island. The best **hotel** is the pricey *Kommandørgården* (☎74 75 51 22, ⓦwww.kommandoergaarden .dk; ❹) at Havnebyvej 21, just south of Tvismark on the road to the island's main town of **Havneby**. It also runs a **campsite** with four-person cabins. Of the two other camping options, best by far is *Lakolk Camping* (☎74 75 52 28, ⓦwww .lakolkcamping.dk; April to mid-Oct), on the island's windswept west coast at Kongsmark and reachable via bus #29. There's a **youth hostel** in Havneby itself at Lyngvejen 7 (☎74 75 51 88, ⓦwww.romo-vandrerhjem.dk; mid-March to mid-Nov), a beautiful old thatched building which has some doubles (❶) as well as dorms (150kr).

Besides enjoying nature and the sands, and the fact that Rømø is a noted **nude bathing** spot, you can also **cross the border to Germany** from here without returning to the Danish mainland by using the ferry that sails from Havneby to List, on the German island of Sylt (information on ☎73 75 53 03, ⓦwww.romo -sylt.dk; 40min).

Tønder

Back on the mainland, heading south from Skærbæk brings you to **TØNDER**, the chief settlement on the Danish side of the border with Germany. Founded in the thirteenth century, the town's cobbled streets still boast many ancient gabled buildings, and Tønder makes an attractive and low-key base for a day or two, especially if you're here around the end of August, when there's a terrific annual **jazz and folk festival**. In 2008, performers included Oysterband, Tom Paxton, Mary Black and a host of other international acts, and there are always many free outdoor events, too. Contact the Tønder Festival office (☎74 72 46 10, ⓦwww .tf.dk) for more details. Otherwise, the main sights in town are the cultural artefacts on display at the **Kulturhistorie Tønder** (Tønder Cultural History Museum: June–Aug daily 10am–5pm; Sept–May Tues–Sun 10am–5pm; 40kr, includes entry to the Art Museum) in the gatehouse of the sixteenth-century castle, featuring, in particular, lots of the famous Tønder lace. The adjoining **Sønderjyllands Kunst-museum** (South Jutland Art Museum: same hours; 40kr, includes entry to the Tønder Cultural History Museum), has changing exhibitions of twentieth-century North European works.

First call for local information should be the **tourist office** on Torvet (July to mid-Aug Mon–Fri 10am–5pm, Sat 10am–2pm; mid-Aug to June Mon–Fri 9am–4pm, Sat 9am–noon; ⊕74 72 12 20, ⓦwww.visittonder.dk). There's an excellent **youth hostel** 1km from the train station at Sønderport 4 (⊕74 72 35 00, ⓦwww.sydvest.dk; closed Christmas & Jan) with dorms (150kr) June–Aug and doubles (❶); a **campsite** at Holmevej 2a (⊕74 72 18 49, ⓦwww.sydvest; mid-March to Oct); the comfortable *Hotel Tønderhus* at Jomfrustien 1, opposite the museum building (⊕74 72 22 22, ⓦwww.hoteltoenderhus.dk; ❹), and the somewhat cheaper; *Hostrup Hotel*, Søndergade 30 (⊕74 72 21 29, ⓦwww.hostrupshotel.dk; ❷), overlooking Vidå Lake.

Sønderborg

Despite lush green landscapes subsiding gently into a peaceful coastline, southern Jutland's eastern section holds comparatively few spots of interest and is best seen as part of a southerly route to Funen or Ærø. A lively provincial town in an area laden with campsites, **SØNDERBORG** straddles the once strategically important **Alssund**, a deep but narrow channel dividing the island of Als from the Jutland mainland.

Arrival and information

Trains go no further than the mainland section of the town, though long-distance **buses** continue across the Alssund, via a graceful modern road bridge, to Als and the bus station on Jernbanegade. Just downhill from the bus station, you'll find the **tourist office**, on Rådhustorvet 7 (July to mid-Aug Mon–Fri 10am–5.30pm, Sat 10am–1pm; mid-Aug to June Mon–Fri 10am–5pm, Sat 10am–1pm; ⊕74 42 35 55, ⓦwww.visitsonderborg.com).

Accommodation

The tourist office (see above) can provide a list of private accommodation in the Sønderborg area. There's a centrally placed waterfront campsite at Rainggade 7 (⊕74 42 41 89, ⓦwww.sonderborgcamping.dk.), whose facilities include access to a child-friendly beach, an on-site shop and a well-equipped children's playground (April–Sept).

Arnkilhus Arnkilgade 13 ⊕74 42 23 36 ⓦwww .arnkilhus.dk. The best small hotel in town, with fourteen comfortable rooms, some self-contained, a large terrace and free parking out front. A 5min walk from the centre. ❸

Comwell Rosengade 2 ⊕74 42 19 00, ⓦwww .comwell.com. The most luxurious option, next door to Sønderborg Slot and a stone's throw from the beach, housing an indoor swimming pool, fitness centre and sauna. All the rooms come with internet access and the obligatory pricey minibar. ❹/❻

Sønderborg Kongevej 96 ⊕74 42 34 33 ⓦwww .hotelsoenderborg.dk. A good middle-ground choice, close to the centre yet near both beautiful woodlands and the beaches. This quirky three-star place, reminiscent of the Adams family's house from the outside, has eighteen self-contained rooms that come in different shapes and sizes. ❹

Sønderborg Hostel Vandrerhjem Kærvej 70 ⊕74 42 31 12, ⓦwww.sonderborgdanhostel.dk. Shiny, modern hostel with has dorms (June–Aug; 205kr including breakfast) and some doubles (❷). It's a 20min walk north of the centre (bus #6).

The Town

The main shopping street, **Perlegade**, runs past the tourist office on Rådhustorvet square towards the harbour, changing its name twice, first to Store Rådhusgade, then to Christian den Andens Gade. From Torvet onwards it takes on a Mediterranean air on warm evenings as smartly dressed Danes mill from bar to bar or **dine** outside at one of streets' many eateries.

The campsites are evidence of the appeal of the region's sandy coastline, while a line of preserved nineteenth-century defensive entrenchments on the mainland side of town is testament to Sønderborg's crucial place in Danish history, when northern Schleswig was lost to Germany. Beside them, and reachable by bus #1 from Sønderborg station, the **Historiecenter Dybbøl Banke** (Dybbøl Banke Battlefield Centre: mid-April to Sept daily 10am–5pm; 55kr; July to mid-Aug 80kr; Ⓦwww.1864.dk) is dedicated to the battle that took place here on April 18, 1864, when the Danes were defeated by the Prussians and medieval Sønderborg was all but destroyed. From then until 1918, when a plebiscite returned it to Denmark, northern Schleswig (in which Sønderborg stands) became part of Germany. The centre is built up around one of the reconstructed entrenchments and is largely run by volunteers who are passionate about enacting the circumstances leading up to the defeat. A short film at the start provides a good and objective (seeing that so many Germans visit the centre, too) introduction to this period of European history. A few hundred metres away, towards Sønderborg on the main road, **Dybbøl Mølle** (Dybbøl Mill: mid-April to Oct daily 10am–5pm; 25kr), where some of the most intense fighting took place, has been a national symbol for both Danes and Germans since 1864, and the story is recounted inside.

The bulk of the town lies across the Alssund, where the focus is **Sønderborg Slot** (April Tues–Sun 10am–4pm; May–Sept daily 10am–5pm; Oct–March Tues–Sun 1–4pm; 40kr; Ⓦwww.mussdj.dk), which may not be Denmark's grandest but is certainly one of its oldest castles, thought to have been begun by Valdemar I in 1170 as a defence against the Wends. Inside, it focuses on the complicated history of Schleswig and the devastating wars of 1848–50 and 1864 with military mementoes galore. A more interesting section tells of the industrial and architectural developments in Sønderborg while it was part of Germany – such as the construction of a host of stunning Art Nouveau buildings (the tourist office can give you details of where to find these). Look out also for the unusual strip of graffiti along a dark staircase made by bored choir boys between 1590 and 1650.

Eating, drinking and nightlife

Colosseum Sønder Havnegade 24. A family-run waterfront restaurant that serves traditional Danish homecooked food at its best. Try the *Stegt Flæsk* special (fried pork served with new potatoes with creamy white parsley sauce) for 83kr.

Ib Rehne Cairo Rådhustorvet 4. A French-style café named after one of Denmark's most famous foreign journalists, on the town's main square, serving brunch, sandwiches and the best coffee for miles around.

Maybe Not Bob Rådhustorvet 5. A slightly noisy pub-nightclub that's hugely popular with young locals as well as foreign students. Closed Sun; open till 5am Thurs–Sat.

OX EN Brogade 2. With outdoor seating overlooking the harbour, this place specializes in sublime Argentinean steaks with all the trimmings from 159kr onwards. It's lunchtime herring smørrebrød is not bad, either.

Penny Lane Rådhusgade 12. A good nightlife option with beers from all over the world and the occasional live jazz. Closed Sun; open till 5am Fri & Sat.

Torvet Rådhustorvet 5. Next door to the tourist information, this is an excellent spot for outstanding lunchtime smørrebrød and fabulous fresh fish for dinner (195kr).

Vejle and around

There's little that's unique about **east Jutland**, though its thick forests are a welcome change if you're coming directly from the windswept western side of the peninsula. As the main route between Funen and the big Jutland cities, it's a busy region with good transport links. **Vejle** is the region's most appealing town, though it hardly justifies a lengthy stay.

Vejle

VEJLE is a compact harbour town on the mouth of the Vejle fjord. With its good range of hotels and restaurants it's a convenient base for exploring the contrasting pleasures of the Viking burial mounds at Jelling and – rather more famously – the Legoland complex at Billund, both within easy reach by bus or train.

The chief attraction in Vejle itself is **Skt Nicolai Kirke** (Mon–Fri 9am–5pm, Sat 9am–noon) on Kirke Torvet, in which a glass-topped coffin holds the peat-preserved body of a woman found in the Haraldskær bog in 1853. Originally the body was thought to be that of a Viking queen, Gunhilde of Norway, but the claim was disputed and tests carried out in 1977 dated the body to around 490 BC – too old to be a Viking, but nonetheless still the best-preserved "bog body" in the country. It's hidden away behind bars in the north transept, but if you want to have a look up close, the verger will let you in. A macabre, hidden feature of the church are the 23 skulls hidden in sealed holes in the northern transept. Legend has it that they are the heads of thieves executed in 1630.

The **Vejle Kunstmuseum** at Flegborg 16-18 (Vejle Museum of Art: Tues–Fri 11am–4pm, Sat & Sun 10am–5pm; 40kr; Ⓦwww.vejlekunstmuseum.dk) with a stunning new entrance portal designed by Kim Utzon, specializes in graphics and drawings (look out for the remarkable self-portrait by Rembrandt from 1563). There's also a collection of twentieth-century painting and sculpture, and the museum often hosts innovative temporary exhibitions. Vejle Museum is due to reopen in a new location in 2009; check at the tourist office for an update. Also operated by the museum, and a fabulous destination on a sunny day, is **Vejle Vindmølle** (Vejle Windmill: May–Oct Tues–Sun 11am–4pm; free), a disused windmill which still has all its ropes, shafts and pinions and displays a through-the-ages account of milling, from Neolithic blocks to modern roller mills. From the windmill, reached by climbing Kiddesvej (which leads off Søndergade), there are stupendous views across Vejle and its fjord. Wind power is dealt with in another way at **Økolariet** interactive knowledge and exhibition centre (Feb–Nov Mon–Thurs & Sat–Sun 11am–4pm; free; Ⓦwww.okolariet.dk), next to the train station at Dæmningen 11. With imaginative displays it illustrates the detrimental effect human consumerism has had on the environment, focusing specifically on drinking water, waste, energy and home consumption. A fun little section depicting the history of the toilet is especially intriguing.

Practicalities

Across from the train station, at Banegårdspladsen 6, the **tourist office** (May–June & Aug–Oct Mon–Fri 10am–5pm, Sat 10am–1pm; July Mon–Sat 9.30am–6pm Sat 9.30am–2pm; Nov–April Mon–Fri 10am–4pm, Sat 10am–noon; ☎76 81 19 25, Ⓦwww.visitvejle.com) has a list of **accommodation** in private rooms. Otherwise, try for a room at the small cosy *Park*, Orla Lehmannsgade 5 (☎75 82 24 66, Ⓦwww .park-hotel.dk; ❸/❹), or the sleek, modern – and pricier – *Torvehallerne*, Kirketorvet 10–16 (☎79 42 79 10, Ⓦwww.torvehallerne.com; ❻), which also houses a popular greenery-filled restaurant, a theatre and Vejle's main concert venue. Much less convenient, but with some doubles (❷) as well as dorms (July–Aug 200kr), is the **youth hostel** on Vardevej 485 (☎75 82 51 88, Ⓦwww.vejle-danhostel.dk), a thirty-minute journey on bus #2. There's also a **campsite** at Helligkildevej 5 (☎75 82 33 35, Ⓦwww.dk-camp.dk/vejlecamp; mid-April to mid-Sept), a few kilometres east and a fifteen-minute journey on bus #4.

Central Vejle has plenty of fine **places to eat**. In the Smitskegård courtyard, at Søndergade 14, *Conrad Café* serves excellent salads, sandwiches and burgers from mid-morning, and drinks until midnight (sometimes with live music). Around the corner, the glass-walled *Brasseriet* at *Hotel Torvehallerne* has delicious, filling meals (two courses for 199kr) starting with brunch at 10am. Of a number of English-style **pubs** in town, most popular is the *Tartan* at Dæmningen 40.

Jelling and Legoland

A short hop northwest of Vejle, the village of **JELLING** is known to have been the site of pagan festivals and celebrations, and it has two **burial mounds** thought to have contained King Gorm, Jutland's tenth-century ruler, and his queen, Thyra. The graves were found in the early twentieth century and, although only one coffin was actually recovered, there is evidence to suggest that the body of Gorm was removed by his son, Harald Bluetooth, and placed in the adjacent church – which Bluetooth himself built around 960 after his conversion to Christianity. In the grounds of the present church are two big **runic stones**, one erected by Gorm to the memory of Thyra, the other raised by Harald Bluetooth in honour of Gorm. Hewn into granite, these particular runes date from the transition period between a Pagan and a Christian Denmark. Across the road from the stones, at Gormsgade 23, the hugely informative and elegant **Kongernes Jelling Exhibition Centre** (May to mid-June & Sept Tues–Sun 10am–4pm; mid-June to Aug daily 10am–5pm; Oct–April Tues–Sun 1–4pm; 40kr; ⓦwww.kongernesjelling.dk) provides a full breakdown of their history. It's a branch of the National Museum in Copenhagen and the wonderful state-of-the-art displays are among the best in the country.

Train services from Vejle to Struer or Herning stop at Jelling: both run about once an hour on weekdays and less frequently at weekends; **bus** #211 runs hourly from Vejle bus station. There's also a **vintage train** between Vejle and Jelling, running at 10.50am and 1.50pm every Sunday in July and on the first three Sundays in August (ⓦwww.klk.dk). By **bike**, it's a scenic ride through the hamlet of Uhre and along the shores of Fårup Sø lake; you can rent a bike in Vejle from Buhl Jensen, Gormsgade 14–16 (☎75 82 15 09; 85kr per day) or at Vejle Vandrerhjem (see p.132). If you want **to stay**, the small *Jelling Kro*, Gormsgade 16 (☎75 87 10 06, ⓦwww.jellingkro .dk; ❸), is pleasant and serves traditional Danish meals, or head for Jelling's **campsite** (☎75 87 16 53, ⓦwww.jellingcamping.dk; April to Aug), about 1km west of the church on Mølvangsvej.

Legoland Park

Twenty kilometres west of Vejle – to which it's linked by bus #244 – the village of **Billund** has been transformed into a major tourist centre, complete with international airport and rows of pricey hotels. It's all thanks to **Legoland Park** (April & Sept–Oct Mon–Tues & Fri 10am–6pm, Sat & Sun 10am–8pm; May, June & mid-to end Aug Mon–Fri 10am–6pm, Sat & Sun 10am–8pm; July to mid-Aug daily 10am–9pm; 259kr; ⓦwww.legoland.dk), a theme park celebrating the tiny plastic bricks that have filled many a Christmas stocking since a Danish carpenter, Ole Kirk Christiansen, started making wooden toys collectively named "Lego", from the Danish phrase *Leg Godt*, or "play well" (which also, by a happy coincidence, means "I study" and "I assemble" in Latin). In 1947, the Lego company began to manufacture its bricks in plastic, becoming the first company in Denmark to use the new plastic moulding-injection techniques – the Lego pieces (or "Automatic Binding Bricks", to be perfectly precise) we know today were first created in 1958. With some fifty-odd rides (included in the price) the park itself, featuring a cornucopia of elaborate model buildings, animals, planes and many other weird and wonderful things (such as Titania's Palace – home for the queen of the fairies), is aimed chiefly at kids, but anybody whose efforts at Lego construction have resulted in tears of frustration over missing corner bricks might like to discover what can be achieved when someone has 45 million pieces to play with.

If you want to stay, try the pricey *Hotel Legoland* (☎75 33 12 44, ⓦwww .hotellegoland.dk; ❻) within the perimetre of the theme park itself or the modern **youth hostel**, *Legoland Village*, 500 metres from its entrance at Ellehammers Allé (☎75 33 27 77, ⓦwww.legoland-village.dk). It has no dorms, but there are double rooms (❹) and other family options.

Århus

Geographically at the heart of the country, and often regarded as Denmark's cultural capital, **ÅRHUS** typifies all that's good about Danish cities. It's small enough to get to know in a few hours, yet big and lively enough to have plenty to fill both days and nights, and the combination of laid-back atmosphere and a surprising

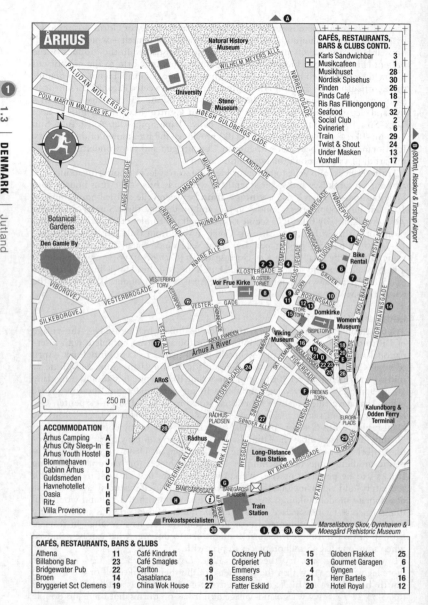

ÅRHUS

CAFÉS, RESTAURANTS, BARS & CLUBS CONTD.

Karls Sandwichbar	3
Musikcafeen	1
Musikhuset	28
Nordisk Spisehus	30
Pinden	26
Pinds Café	18
Ris Ras Filliongongong	7
Seafood	32
Social Club	2
Svineriet	6
Train	29
Twist & Shout	24
Under Masken	13
Voxhall	17

ACCOMMODATION

Århus Camping	A
Århus City Sleep-In	E
Århus Youth Hostel	B
Blommehaven	J
Cabinn Århus	D
Guldsmeden	C
Havnehotellet	I
Oasia	H
Ritz	G
Villa Provence	F

CAFÉS, RESTAURANTS, BARS & CLUBS

Athena	11	Café Kindrødt	5	Cockney Pub	15	Globen Flakket	25
Billabong Bar	23	Café Smagløs	8	Crêperiet	31	Gourmet Garagen	6
Bridgewater Pub	22	Carlton	9	Emmerys	4	Gyngen	1
Broen	14	Casablanca	10	Essens	21	Herr Bartels	16
Bryggeriet Sct Clemens	19	China Wok House	27	Fatter Eskild	20	Hotel Royal	12

number of sights might keep you around longer than you had planned. Århus is also
something of an architectural showcase, with several notable structures spanning a
century of Danish and international design. A number of these buildings form the
campus of Århus' university, whose students help to create a nightlife that's on a par
with that of Copenhagen.

Despite Viking-era origins, the city's present prosperity is due to its long, sheltered
bay (on which a harbour was first constructed during the fifteenth century) and the

more recent advent of railways, which made Århus a nationally important trade and transport centre. It's easily reached by train from all the country's bigger towns, is linked by sea with Zealand (a fast catamaran service links Århus with Odden, and a slower ferry links it with Kalundborg) and also has a small international airport.

Arrival, information and city transport

Whichever form of public transport brings you to Århus, you'll be deposited within easy reach of the hotels and main points of interest. **Trains** and **buses** stop at their respective stations on Banegårdspladsen and Nybanegårdsgade, both on the southern edge of the city centre, from where it's a short walk to the **tourist office** at Banegårdspladsen 20 (July–Aug Mon 10am–6pm, Tues–Fri 10am–5pm, Sat 10am–3pm; Sept–June Mon 10am–6pm, Tues–Thurs 10am–5pm, Fri 10am–4pm; ☎87 31 50 10, ⓦwww.visitaarhus.com) on the corner of Banegårdsgade. **Ferries** from Zealand dock just west of the centre at the end of Nørreport, a short distance from the heart of Old Århus. Buses from **Tirstrup airport**, some 45km northeast of the city, arrive at (and leave from) the train station; the one-way fare for the fifty-minute journey is 90kr.

Getting around is best done on foot: the city centre is compact and you'll need to use **buses** only if you're venturing out to Moesgård Museum, the beaches or the woods on the city's outskirts.

Cycling is another viable way to get around – as part of the very useful **citybike** scheme, there are 450 bikes distributed around the city between May and October, which you can use for free within the city limits by dropping a 20kr deposit into the slot on the bikes. If you're heading out of the city to Moesgård, for instance, the most central place to rent a bicycle is Bikes4rent, Vestergade 41 (☎87 99 10 20, ⓦwww .bikes4rent.dk), which charges 75kr for a day, and 245kr for a week.

Accommodation

Århus has some fairly reasonably priced hotel and hostel options, and the tourist office can help you find affordable **private rooms** (from 400kr a night).

Hotels and guesthouses

Cabinn Århus Kannikegade 14 ☎86 75 70 00, ⓦwww.cabinn.com. Next to Århus Å River, the functional cabin-like rooms here (everything folds up and packs away) are very good value. Breakfast is 50kr. ❸

Guldsmeden Guldsmedegade 40 ☎86 13 45 56, ⓦwww.hotelguldsmeden.dk. A small, homely hotel in the centre, 10min walk from the station. Rooms are delicately decorated in French colonial style, and no two are the same; some have shared bath. Scrummy organic breakfast buffet

Transport tickets

Note that the transport system divides into four zones: one and two cover the whole central area; three and four reach into the countryside. The **basic ticket** is the so-called "cash ticket", which costs 18kr from the machine at the rear of the bus and is valid for any number of journeys for up to two hours from the time stamped on it. If you're around for several days and doing a lot of bus hopping (or using local trains, on which these tickets are also valid), you have three good options. An **Århus Pass** costs 139kr for 24 hours and 169kr for 48 hours, and covers unlimited travel and entrance to most museums, including ARoS Art Museum, as well as sightseeing tours (though you must book these at the tourist office first). There's also a **multi-ride ticket** (Klippekort: 115kr), which is valid for ten trips within the immediate city area and can be used by more than one person at once. These tickets can be bought at news-stands, campsites and shops displaying the "midttrafik" sign. The driver won't check your ticket but a roving inspector might, and there's an instant fine of 500kr if you're caught travelling without one. You can get bus information at the long-distance bus station at Fredensgade 45 (daily 7am–10pm) or on ⓦwww.businfo.dk.

included in the rates. Bus #1, #6, #9 or #11 ④, en-suite ⑤

Havnehotellet Marselisborg Havnevej 20 ⓦwww .havnehotellet.dk. Stunningly located unmanned hotel – hence no phone number – on the Århus marina quay. The en-suite rooms are bright and breezy and there are a handful of good restaurants nearby. Checking in is done via a computer in the foyer and booking only possible online. Bus #6 or #19. ❸

🏃 **Oasia** Kriegersvej 7 ☎87 32 37 15, ⓦwww.hoteloasia.dk. New design hotel – the only one in Århus – a short walk from the station down a quiet cobbled street. The fabulous rooms, featuring Thorsen furniture and the famous Hästens beds, come at a price. They're worth every penny – if you can afford it. ❻

Ritz Banegårdspladsen 12 ☎86 13 44 44, ⓦwww.hotelritz.dk. As the name implies, this place, just next to the train station, is both pricey (though with discounts at weekends) and posh. Very elegant rooms with ornately carved furniture and plush bathrooms. ❻

🏃 **Villa Provence** Fredens Torv 12 ☎86 18 24 00, ⓦwww.villaprovence .dk. Classy small hotel a stone's throw from the bus station. The range of rooms are all beautifully decorated in Provencal style, featuring old French-Belgian film posters. ❺

Sleep-ins and youth hostels
Århus City Sleep-In Havnegade 20 ☎86 19 20 55, ⓦwww.citysleep-in.dk. Near both the city centre and harbour, offering dorm beds (130kr) and doubles (❷). Guests without their own sleeping bags have to rent sheets and blankets (50kr); other facilities include a games room, café and internet access (20kr per hr). Bus #3 from the station, but you might as well walk. Open 24/7.

Århus Youth Hostel Marienlundsvej 10 ☎86 16 72 98, ⓦwww.aarhus-danhostel.dk. Much more peaceful than the central *Sleep-In*, this is 4km northeast of town in the middle of Risskov wood, close to the popular Den Permanente beach. As well as dorms (150kr), it has a hotel-style wing with double rooms (❷), too. Bus #1, #6 #8, #9, #16, #56 or #58.

Campsites
Århus Camping Randersvej 400, Lisbjerg ☎86 23 11 33, ⓦwww.aarhuscamping.dk. Some 8km north of the city centre and convenient for the E45 motorway (take exit 46), this not nearly as well situated as *Blommehaven* but it's open all year. Bus #3, #117 or #118.

Blommehaven Ørneredevej 35, Højbjerg ☎86 27 02 07, ⓦwww.blommehaven.dk. Overlooking the bay, with access to a beautiful beach, and about 4km south of the city centre. Bus #6 or #19. Open April–Aug.

The City
For reasons of simple chronology, Århus divides into two clearly defined parts: even combined, these fill a small and easily walkable area. The **old section**, close to the Domkirke, is a tight cluster of medieval streets with several interesting churches and a couple of museums, as well as the bulk of the city's nightlife. The (relatively) **new sections** of Århus form a collar around the old centre, inevitably with less character, but they nonetheless hold plenty that's worth seeing, not least the city's major architectural works.

Old Århus
Søndergade is Århus's main street, a pedestrianized strip lined with shops and overpriced snack bars that leads from the train station (where it's initially called Ryesgade), through Skt Clemens Torv and across Århus Å River into the main town square, Bispetorvet. From here, the streets of the old centre form a web around the **Domkirke** (May–Sept Mon–Sat 9.30am–4pm, Tues until 3pm; Oct–April Mon–Sat 10am–3pm). Take the trouble to push open the cathedral's sturdy doors, not just to appreciate the soccer-pitch length – this is easily the longest church in Denmark – but to take in a couple of features that spruce up the plain Gothic interior, a mostly fifteenth-century rebuild after the original twelfth-century structure was destroyed by fire. At the eastern end is one of few pre-Reformation survivors, a grand tripartite altarpiece by the noted Bernt Notke. Look also at the painted – as opposed to stained – glass window behind the altar, the work of Norwegian Emmanuel Vigeland (brother of Gustav); it's most effective when the sunlight falls directly on it.

From the time of the first settlement here, in the tenth century, the area around the cathedral has been at the core of Århus life. A number of Viking remains have been excavated on Skt Clemens Torv, across the road from the cathedral, and some of them are now imaginatively displayed in the basement of the Nordea Bank at Skt Clemens Torv 6 (entrance inside the bank on the left) as part of the **Vikinge-museet** (Viking Museum: Mon–Fri 10am–4pm, Thurs until 5.30pm; free), which uses red light markers on the floor to show sections of the original ramparts and the location of huts and homesteads. There's also a section with Viking tools alongside informative accounts of early Århus – press the buttons on the displays to get the full story. Also close to the cathedral, in a former police station on Bispetorvet, the **Kvindemuseet** (Women's Museum: June–Aug daily 10am–5pm, Wed until 8pm; Sept–May Tues–Sun 10am–4pm, Wed until 8pm; 40kr; ⓦ www.kvindemuseet.dk) is one of Denmark's most innovative, staging exhibitions on all aspects of women's lives past and present from birth to education, jobs and power, or lack thereof. After visiting the museums, venture into the narrow and enjoyable surrounding streets, lined by innumerable old and well-preserved buildings, many of which now house browsable antique shops or chic boutiques. The area is also home to some of the city's most enjoyable drinking spots (see p.140).

West along Vestergade from the Domkirke, the thirteenth-century **Vor Frue Kirke** (May–Aug Mon–Fri 10am–4pm, Sat 10am–2pm; Sept–April Mon–Fri 10am–2pm, Sat 10am–noon) is actually the site of three churches, the most notable of which is the eleventh-century **crypt church** (go in through the main church entrance and walk straight ahead), which was discovered, buried beneath several centuries' worth of rubbish, during restoration work on the main church in the 1950s. There's not exactly a lot to see, but the tiny, rough-stone building – resembling a hollowed-out cave – is strong on atmosphere, especially during the candle-lit Sunday services.

Modern Århus

A short walk from the train station down Park Allé you'll come across what for years was one of the modern city's major sights: the functional **Rådhus** on Rådhuspladsen, completed in 1941 and as capable of inciting high passions – for and against – today as it was when it opened. From the outside, it's easy to see why opinions should be so polarized: the coating of grey Norwegian marble lends a sickly pallor to the building. But on the inside (enter from Rådhuspladsen), the finer points of architects Arne Jacobsen and Erik Møller's vision make themselves apparent, amid the harmonious open-plan corridors and the extravagant quantities of glass. You're free to walk in and look for yourself (Mon–Fri 9am–4pm). Above the entrance hangs Hagedorn Olsen's huge mural, *A Human Society*, symbolically depicting the city emerging from the last war to face the future with optimism. You can also tour the belltower Tuesdays and Thursdays at 2pm (Jun–Aug; 35kr), advance tickets sold at the tourist office.

More recent examples of Århus's municipal architecture include the glass-fronted **Musikhuset** (Concert Hall: daily 11am–9pm; ⓦ www.musikhusetaarhus.dk), a short walk from the Rådhus along Vester Allé, which has been the city's main venue for opera and classical music since it opened in 1982. It's worth dropping into, if only for the small café where you might be entertained for free by a string quartet or a lone fiddler. A monthly list of forthcoming concerts and events is available from the box office or the tourist office.

Next door, the imposing art museum, **ARoS** (Tues–Sun 10am–5pm, Wed till 10pm; 90kr; ⓦ www.aros.dk), is a remarkable building designed by the same architects as the Black Diamond extension to the Royal Library in Copenhagen (see p.78). Spread over seven floors, the collection gives a good overview of the main national trends, from late eighteenth-century formal portraits and landscapes by Jens Juel and finely etched scenes of domestic tension by Jørgen Sonne, through to more internationally renowned names, particularly Vilhelm Hammershøi, represented here by some of his moody interiors. There are lots of worthwhile modern pieces, too. Besides the radiant canvases of Asger Jorn and Richard Mortensen, don't miss Bjørn Nørgård's sculpted version of Christian IV's tomb: the original, in Roskilde Cathedral, is stacked with riches; this one features a coffee cup, an egg and a ballpoint pen. Other highlights include the spookily lifelike five-metre-high sculpture, *Boy*, by Ron Mueck.

It's just a few minutes' walk from the Concert Hall and ARoS to Viborgvej and the city's best-known attraction, **Den Gamle By** (The Old Town: Jan daily 11am–3pm; Feb to mid-March daily 10am–4pm; mid-March to June daily 10am–5pm; July–Aug daily 9am–6pm; Sept–Nov Mon–Fri 9am–5pm, Sat & Sun 10am–5pm, Dec Mon & Tues 9am–5pm, Wed–Fri 9am–7pm, Sat & Sun 10am–7pm; 100kr; ⑩www .dengamleby.dk). An open-air museum of traditional Danish life, it consists of around 75 half-timbered townhouses (including a popular Mayor's House of 1597) from all over the country which have been moved here since the museum's inception in 1914. With many of the buildings used for their original purpose, the overall aim of the place is to give an impression of an old Danish market town, complete with bakers, craftsmen and the like. This is done very effectively, although sunny summer days bring big crowds, and the period flavour is strongest outside high season, when visitors are fewer.

A fifteen-minute walk from Den Gamle By, the **university campus** is a prime example of modern Danish architectural style. Sprawled across a hillside overlooking the city, the distinctive red-brick buildings, mostly designed by C.F. Møller and completed just after World War II, feature white-framed rectangular windows, and no decorative touches whatsoever. While you're on campus, there are two museums that might appeal: the **Naturhistorisk Musem** (Natural History Museum: Mon–Thurs 10am–4pm, Fri 10am–2pm; 50kr; ⑩www.naturhistoriskmuseum.dk) has a large collection of stuffed birds and animals alongside some exhibits on Danish ecology, while the **Steno Museum** (Tues–Fri 9am–4pm, Sat & Sun 11am–4pm; 45kr; ⑩www.stenomuseet.dk) focuses on cartography, astrology and medical matters and also includes a small planetarium and a herb garden. To get to the campus from the centre, take bus #2, #3, #11, #14, #54, #56 or #58.

Out from the centre

On Sundays, post-brunch Århus resembles a ghost town, with most locals spending the day in the parks, woodlands or beaches on the city's outskirts. If you're around on a Sunday – or, for that matter, any sunny day in the week – you could do much worse than join them. The closest beaches and woods are just **north of the city** at Risskov, near the youth hostel, easily reached on buses #6 or #16, or on any local trains headed for Grenå or Hornslets, some of which halt at the tiny Den Permanente train platform by the beach (but check before boarding, as not all trains stop here). Risskov's beach is narrow but scenic, with an old-fashioned public bathhouse, and is clean enough for swimming, while the thick forest behind is criss-crossed with walking and cycling trails. There are a few ice cream and hot dog stalls on the beach, but you might be better off taking your own picnic.

For a more varied day, head **south** through the thick Marselisborg Skov forest and on to the prehistoric museum at Moesgård. This is also ideal territory for cycling or hiking – see p.135 for details of bicycle rental. Contact the tourist office for suggestions about routes and maps.

Marselisborg Skov and Dyrehaven

The **Marselisborg Skov**, 4km south of the city centre, is a large park that contains the city's sports stadium and race course and sees a regular procession of people exercising their dogs. It also holds the diminutive **Marselisborg Slot**, summer home of the Danish royals, whose landscaped grounds can be visited during daylight hours (free) when they're not in residence (usually at all times outside Easter, Christmas and late June to early Aug); if guards are posted by the gate, they're in, and there's a changing of guards at noon. Further south, across Carl Nielsen Vej, the park turns into a dense forest, with a maze of footpaths and easy to get lost in.

A simpler route to navigate, and one with better views, is along Strandvejen, which runs between the eastern side of the forest and the shore. Unbroken footpaths run along this part of the coast and there are many opportunities to scamper down to rarely crowded (though largely pebbly) beaches. Also on this route, near the junction of Ørneredevej and Thorsmøllevej, is the **Dyrehaven**, or Deer Park – a protected section of the wood that's home to many deer. The animals can be seen (if you're lucky – they're not the most gregarious of creatures) from the marked paths running through the park from the gate on the main road.

Moesgård Prehistoric Museum

Occupying the buildings and grounds of an old manor house 10km south of Århus city centre, **Moesgård Prehistoric Museum** (April–Sept daily 10am–5pm; Oct–March Tues–Sun 10am–4pm; 60kr; ⊚ www.moesmus.dk) traces the story of Danish civilizations from the Stone Age onwards with copious finds and easy-to-follow illustrations. It's the Iron Age which is most comprehensively covered and produces the most dramatic single exhibit: the **Grauballe Man**, the remains of a body, dated to 80 BC, which was discovered in a peat bog west of Århus in a state of such excellent preservation that it was even possible to discover what the deceased had eaten for breakfast (burnt porridge made from rye and barley) on the day of his death. Also remarkable is the extensive **Illerup Ådal** collection of weapons and military paraphernalia, dating from around 200 BC and recovered, in relatively good condition, from the Ådal bog. Only a roomful of imposing runic stones further on comes close to capturing the imagination as powerfully. Bus #6 runs here direct from the city, while bus #19 takes a more scenic route along the edge of Århus Bay, leaving you with at least a 2km walk through woods to the museum.

Eating

Central Århus is loaded with **eating** possibilities and, while nothing is particularly cheap, a good and affordable bite can still be found in the right places. In general, it's wise to follow locals and students away from the heavily touristed Domkirke and Store Torv to streets such as Mejlgade, Nørre Allé, Vestergade or Skolegade. You'll find the best **lunch** for around 65kr, simply by cruising the cafés and restaurants of the old city and reading the notices chalked up outside them. If you're prepared to pay a bit more, Åboulevarden – the northern bank of the Århus Å River – offers a string of trendy eating and drinking venues, and is a good place to head for **dinner**.

If money is tight, or you just want to stock up for a **picnic**, try Frokostspecialisten at Frederiks Allé 105, which also does mouthwatering smørrebrød to go. For more general food shopping, there's a branch of Brugsen on Søndergade and a late-opening DSB **supermarket** (8am–midnight) at the train station. There are several other downtown supermarkets of varying quality – try the decent Super Brugsen at Nørre Allé, or the slightly less good Aldi across the way; at the former, local merchants peddle berries and beans fresh from the fields when in season.

Athena Store Torv 18. Good-value Greek restaurant – try the moussaka for 149kr – on the first floor, overlooking the hustle and bustle of Store and Lille Torv below. Dinner only.

Bryggeriet Sct Clemens Kannikegade 10–12. A popular brewery-cum-restaurant which does mouthwatering spareribs for 171kr, best washed down with freshly tapped unfiltered beer; the Wagyu steaks aren't bad, either. Lunch ranges from 65kr for the seasonal soup to a filling smørrebrød platter for 115kr. Closed Sun.

China Wok House Sønder Allé 9. As well as standard Chinese fare, this place also does an all-you-can-eat buffet (58kr at lunchtime, 109kr in the evening). Takeaway China boxes are sold from the front window.

Crêperiet Marselisborg Havnevej 24. Overlooking the harbour with outdoor seating in summer; try a crêpe with one of 24 different savoury and sweet fillings (41–123kr), the fish soups or onion consommé. Take bus #6 from the station.

Emmerys Guldsmedegade 24–26. The city's oldest patisserie has now expanded its repertoire from wonderful freshly ground coffee and cakes to sandwiches and simple meals packed with flavour. Fine wines and good beer as well. Open daily from 7am.

Globen Flakket Åboulevarden 18. This large riverside café is one of the most popular places for brunch (9am–1pm, 2.30pm during weekends) as well as their lunch and dinner buffets for 88kr and 128kr respectively.

Gourmet Garagen Mejlgade 35 ☎86 12 30 24. Downstairs in the back building you'll find beautiful rustic Italian country cuisine with an ever-changing daily menu – three courses will set you back 245kr. Closed Sun & Mon.

Gyngen Mejlgade 53. Good-value, highly rated vegetarian meals and fabulous sandwiches served up within the Fronthuset culture centre; local bands sometimes play after dinner. Closed Sun & Mon.

Karls Sandwichbar Klostergade 32. Undisputedly the best burgers in town. Huge and homemade, served with large portions of fries. Can't beat it. Thurs–Sat open until 6am.

Nordisk Spisehus M.P. Bruuns Gade 31. Refreshingly unpretentious gourmet place serving high quality Nordic dishes such as a pork T-bone steak for 255kr and a platter of selected Nordic cheeses for 135kr. The giant lunchtime prawn sandwich with caviar (255kr) is out of this world.

🎿 **Pinden** Skolegade 29. Serving traditional Danish dishes, the speciality here is *Stegt*

flæsk med persille sovs (slices of fried pork with potatoes and parsley sauce). Six pieces of *flæsk* with potatoes go for 92kr, all-you-can-eat is 125kr. Also excellent smørrebrød. Closed Sun.

Pinds Café Skolegade 11. Although it often looks deceptively shut, *Pinds* nonetheless opens long hours and does excellent smørrebrød, as well as inexpensive set lunches (75kr). Closed Sun.

Seafood Marselisborg Havnevej 44. A great choice if you're prepared to splash out, with fantastic views of the Århus Bay area and a delectable range of seafood, from Brittany oysters to hake steamed in white wine.

🎿 **Svineriet** Mejlgade 35 ☎86 12 30 00. Climb upstairs to the first floor of the back building and you'll find one of the city's best gourmet restaurants. Using predominantly fresh, locally sourced produce, food here is best described as traditional Danish with a southern European twist. You can choose either from an à la carte menu or go for *Hele Svineriet* – literally "the whole hog" a five-course menu, including wine – a different one for each course – for 950kr.

Drinking and nightlife

Århus is the only place in Denmark with **nightlife** to match that of Copenhagen, offering a diverse assortment of ways to be entertained, enlightened or just inebriated, almost every night of the week. And while things sparkle socially all year round, if you visit during the **Århus Festival** (*Århus Festuge*), an orgy of arts events held annually over the first week in September (check what's on with the tourist office or visit ⓦwww.aarhusfestuge.dk), you'll find even more to occupy your time.

The city has a wonderful endowment of **cafés**, with many situated in the medieval streets close to the cathedral. There's little to choose between them – each pulls a lively, cosmopolitan crowd and the best plan is simply to wander around and try a few – but we've listed the most enduring options below. Between Thursday and Saturday, most cafés stay open until midnight (and some as late as 2am); we've specified these within our reviews.

Home to a music school that's produced some of the country's most successful performers, Århus boasts a music scene that's well known throughout Denmark – so if you're looking for **live music**, you won't have to go far. Basic details of all events are available from the tourist office where you can pick up flyers and free local magazines. Århus's **clubbing** scene is equally lively, with both *Voxhall* and *Train* (see opposite) staging club nights when they aren't hosting live bands, and plenty of more mainstream venues providing a less achingly cool place to dance. Early in the week, admission to any club is likely to be free; on Thursday, Friday or Saturday, you'll pay 40–60kr.

Cafés and bars

Billabong Bar Skolegade 26. The city's only Aussie bar, full of hardy outback types and serving local and foreign ales. Open daily till 3am.

Bridgewater Pub Åboulevarden 22. On the banks of Arhus Å River, this English pub – with stouts, ales and cider on tap, and three large screens – is

the place to go for your football fix. Open until 5am Fri & Sat.

Café Jorden Badstuegade 3. Popular café in the medieval cathedral area, which serves quality breakfast platters (25kr) and brunch until mid-afternoon, and gets very lively at night when the drinkers arrive. Open until 2am daily.

Café Kindrødt Studsgade 8. Near the old quarter's better shopping streets and a great place to rest your feet or sample some of the good food during the day. Livens up in the evenings. Open until 2am Thurs–Sat.

Café Smagløs Klostertorv 7. An old-timer of the café scene. Busy with lunchers during the day, and crowded with some of Århus's sizeable student population at night. Open until 3am Fri & Sat.

Carlton Rosengade 23. In the centre of this quaint, café-heavy medieval quarter, and always buzzing at night. The food is slightly pricey, so most people only come to drink.

Casablanca Rosengade 12. A good place to start the evening, this is Århus's oldest café, with movie-themed decorations and live jazz on Wed evenings. Open until 2am Mon–Sat.

Cockney Pub Maren Smeds Gyde 8. Popular real ale pub featuring haggis nights and whisky-tasting sessions – and they pride themselves on making a proper cup of tea. Open until 2am Thurs–Sat.

🏃 Essens Åboulevarden 30. Hugely trendy café on the Århus Å river-serving colourful cocktails accompanied by chilled lounge music. This is *the* place to be seen in Århus. Open Thurs–Sat until 3am

Ris Ras Filliongongong Mejlgade 24. Named after a well-known Danish children's rhyme, this is another popular student hangout. *Ris Ras* excels in good beer and still allows smoking. There's an art gallery in the basement that's well worth checking out. Open until 2am daily.

🏃 Under Masken Bispegade 3. Cosy yet quirky bar, with masks from around the globe decorating the walls and a wide selection of foreign beers on sale. Smoking permitted. Open until 2am daily.

Clubs

Broen Nordhavnsgade 20 ☎ 86 13 14 29. This club on a boat moored in the harbour is divided into five separate sections with different decor and styles of music, from mainstream hip-hop to Frank Sinatra. Fri & Sat only.

Herr Bartels Åboulevarden 46. Hugely popular bar/nightclub (over 23s only) with a long list of cocktails

includign a tasty selection of iced teas. With a packed dancefloor this isn't the place to go if you need personal space. Open Thurs–Sat until 3am.

Hotel Royal Store Torv 4 ☎ 86 12 00 11. Glitzy hotel basement housing a combined casino/nightclub that's liveliest early in the week. Smart dress code applies. Open daily until 4am.

🏃 Social Club Klostergade 34 ☎ 86 19 42 50, ⓦ www.socialclub.dk. The city's coolest club, playing the newest, hottest dance tunes. Massive discounts for students. Over 20s only. Fri & Sat 11pm–5am.

Twist & Shout Frederiksgade 29 ☎ 86 18 08 55. Three storeys of different music styles: most of it's pretty mainstream, so no real surprises. A short walk from the town hall and tourist office. Closed Sun.

Live music venues

Fatter Eskil Skolegade 25 ☎ 86 19 44 11, ⓦ www.fattereskil.dk. Piano bar hosting jazz jam sessions every Fri at 3.30pm and live jazz and R&B acts most days. Open until 5am Fri & Sat, closed Sun & Mon.

Musikcafeen Mejlgade 53 ☎ 86 76 03 44, ⓦ www.musikcafeen.dk. On the first floor of the Fronthuset cultural centre, this is Århus's main venue for up-and-coming Danish and international bands, as well as live jazz, rock and the odd techno act. Entrance fee ranges between 60kr and 150kr. Closed Sun.

Musikhuset Thomas Jensens Allé ☎ 86 40 90 50, ⓦ www.musikhusetaarhus.dk. City-centre concert hall which plays host to classical music, opera and, occasionally, mainstream pop bands.

Train Toldbodgade 6 ☎ 86 13 47 22, ⓦ www.train .dk. Attracting an older crowd and slightly more well-established bands than its rival *Voxhall* (see below). Gigs take place three or four nights a week; admission runs from 100kr to 600kr, with doors opening at 9pm and the main band starting a couple of hours later.

Voxhall Vester Allé 15 ☎ 87 30 97 97, ⓦ www .voxhall.dk. Århus's premier venue, hosting the cream of Danish and international independent acts from hip-hop to world music. Tickets cost 100–400kr.

Listings

Airlines SAS (domestic and international) ☎ 70 10 20 00, ⓦ www.sas.dk; British Airways ☎ 86 36 30 60, ⓦ www.ba.com.

Airport Tirstrup airport (☎ 87 75 70 00, ⓦ www .aar.dk) is 45km northeast of the city. Buses for the airport leave from outside the train station; the fare is 90kr and the journey takes 50min.

Bookshops English Books and Secondhand Things, Frederiks Allé 53 (☎ 86 19 54 55; Mon–Fri 11.30am–5.30pm, Sat 11am–2pm), fully lives up to its name.

Bus enquiries Local buses ☎ 86 12 86 22, ⓦ www .midttrafik.dk; Abildskou's Århus–Copenhagen coach reservations ☎ 70 21 08 88, ⓦ www.abildskou.dk.

Car rental Avis, Spanien 63 ☏ 86 19 23 99, Jens Baggesens Vej 27 ☏ 86 16 10 99 and Tirstrup airport ☏ 86363699, ⓦ www.avis.dk; Europcar, Sønder Allé 35 ☏ 89 33 11 11 and Tirstrup airport ☏ 86363744, ⓦ www.europcar.dk.

Doctor Between 4pm and 8pm, call ☏ 70 11 31 31. Outside these hours, contact the Universitethospital (see Hospitals, below).

Ferries and catamarans Mols Linien to either Odden or Kalundborg on Zealand ☏ 70 10 14 18, ⓦ www.mols-linien.dk.

Hospitals There is a 24hr emergency department at Århus Universitetshospital, Nørrebrogade 44 ☏ 89 49 44 44.

Internet There is free internet access at the tourist information and at the library, Møllegade 1. Internet cafés include Boomtown at Åboulevarden 21 and Gate 58, Vestergade 58.

Market There's a fruit, veg and flower market every Wed and Sat on Bispetorvet, beside the cathedral (early morning till noon), though the one on Sat mornings (until 2pm) along Ingerslevs Boulevard, south of the centre, is livelier.

Pharmacy Løve Apoteket, Store Torv 5 ☏ 86 12 00 22, is open 24hr.

Police Århus Politisation, Ridderstræde 1 ☏ 87 31 14 48.

Post office Banegårdspladsen, by the train station (Mon–Fri 9.30am–6pm, Sat 10am–1pm).

Train enquiries ⓦ www.dsb.dk has details of all services: ☏ 70 13 14 15 for domestic services; and ☏ 70 13 14 16 for international trains.

Randers and Djursland

From rolling hills and lush valleys to sandy beaches, **Djursland**, the nose-shaped peninsula east of Århus, boasts some of the prettiest landscapes in Denmark – sufficient ingredients for a couple of days' pleasurable exploration. The southern coastal stretch, known as **Mols**, is especially delightful, its hills affording some superb views. Base yourself in the countryside close to Randers, and see the area by bike (see p.143 for details of rental outlets) or local buses.

Randers

A trading and manufacturing base since the thirteenth century, **RANDERS** has grown significantly over the years, leaving a tiny medieval centre miserably corralled by a bleak new industrial zone. The town's main historical sight is the house at **Storegade 13**, said to be the place where Danish nobleman Niels Ebbesen killed the German count, Gerd of Holstein, in 1340; a shutter on the upper storey is always left open to allow the count's ghost to escape lest the malevolent spirit should cause the building to burn down. However, Randers' biggest tourist attraction these days – one of the most popular in Jutland – is the **Randers Regnskov** (Randers Rainforest: mid-June to mid-Aug daily 10am–6pm; mid-Aug to mid-June Mon–Fri 10am–4pm, Sat & Sun 10am–5pm; 140kr; ⓦ www.regnskoven.dk), a recreation of tropical rainforests – African, Asian and South American – alongside the River Gudenå. Visitors wander through the dense, damp foliage, enclosed within three giant domes watching out for the birds, animals and amphibians, which include a number of rare turtles and a flying fox, that for the most part are left to run about freely. One of the best bits is the new Asian snake temple built up around Cambodian ruin fragments, where a formidable assortment of vipers, boas and pythons lounge about. Also fascinating are the busy leaf-cutter ants whose trails you can follow through glass tubing to and from their glass-fronted nest.

There are also a couple of museums that are worth a visit, both in the Cultural Centre near the bus station on Stenmannsgade 2. The first floor holds the imaginatively presented **Kulturhistorisk Museum Randers** (Randers Cultural History Museum: Tues, Thurs & Sat 1–5pm; free; ⓦ www.khm.dk) while the second floor houses the **Randers Kunstmuseum** (Randers Museum of Art: Tues–Sun 11am–5pm; free; ⓦ www.randers-kunstmuseum.dk). You could easily kill a couple of hours here, if only for the wacky glass and mirror installation *Cosmic Space*, by the Faroese artist Trondur Patursson. A bit further down the road, at Stenmannsgade 9C, the **Elvis Unlimited Museum** (Mon–Fri 10am–5.30pm, Sat 10am–2pm; 30kr; ⓦ www.elvispresley.dk) prides itself on being the only Elvis museum outside the US – only for die-hard fans of the King. A worthwhile detour, 25km north of Randers, is to the thousand-year-old **Fyrkat** (daily: April–May & Sept–Oct 10am–4pm; June–Aug 10am–5pm; 55kr; ⓦwww.fyrkat.dk), a fortress said to have been built by the Viking king Harald Bluetooth, today found in the outskirts of the **HOBRO** which has a **hostel** at Amerikavej 24 (ⓣ98 52 18 47, ⓦwww.danhostelnord .dk/hobro; closed mid-Dec to mid-Jan) with dorm beds (mid-March to mid-Oct; 200kr) and doubles (②). Fyrkat is a good place to get an impression of life during Bluetooth's era: houses and farms have been reconstructed, and in summer there are demonstrations of traditional Viking activities like bronze casting.

Practicalities

The **bus station** is right in the centre at Dytmærsken 12, while the **train station** is ten minutes' walk out of town at Jernbanegade 29. The **tourist office**, on the ring road leading to Randers Regnskov at Tørvebryggen 12 (mid-June to mid-Aug Mon–Fri 9.30am–5pm, Sat 10am–1pm; mid-Aug to Oct & April to mid-June Mon–Fri 9.30am–4pm, Sat 9am–1pm; Nov–March Mon–Fri 9.30am–4pm; ⓣ86 42 44 77, ⓦwww.visitranders.com), has a list of **private rooms** which rent from 150kr per person per night – but be aware that some of them are a long way outside town. The two best **hotels** in town are the classic old Art Deco *Hotel Randers*, in the centre on Torvegade 11 (ⓣ86 42 34 22, ⓦwww.hotel-randers.dk; ④/⑤), and the slightly cheaper *Stephansen* (ⓣ86 44 27 77, ⓦwww.stephansenhotel.dk; ④), a beautifully refurbished old woodbeamed town house next door to the court-house on Møllestræde 4. Randers' **youth hostel**, with dorms (July to mid-Sept; 270kr) and private rooms (②), is only five minutes from the centre at Gethersvej 1 (ⓣ86 42 50 44, ⓦwww.danhostelranders.dk). The nearest **campsite**, with cabins sleeping four and six (from 175kr plus 67kr per person) and a swimming pool, is at Fladbro, 5km west of the town (ⓣ86 42 93 61, ⓦwww.fladbrocamping.dk); take bus #10 to the golf course, from where it's a ten-minute walk. Note that some #10 buses do go all the way to the campsite stop, so ask the driver.

Good **restaurants** in Randers include ♨ *Niels Ebbesens Spisehus* in the historic setting of Storegade 13 (see p.142), with the town's best smørrebrød costing 35kr per slice, a luncheon platter for 129kr, and tasty pork tenderloin with all the trimmings for 139kr on the dinner menu. Downstairs in *Hotel Randers* there's also the stylish *Café Mathisen* (closed Sun) which has a good range of salads and sandwiches on offer as well as the popular Mathisen burger (118kr). As for **nightlife**, try the popular *Tante Olga*, Søndergade 6 (ⓦwww.tanteolga.dk), which has something going on every weekend (Thurs–Sat) – live blues and rock, or the laid-back *Maren Knudsen Øl & Vinkælder* in the basement of no. 5. In early August the town celebrates **Randers Ugen**, a week packed with all sorts of cultural events; the rest of the year, major rock concerts and theatre performances are put on regularly at *Værket*, a converted power station on Mariagervej (ⓦwww.vaerket.dk).

The best way to see the countryside around Randers is by **bike**. You can rent bikes at Schmidt Cykler, Kirkegade 7 (ⓣ86 41 29 03) and at Fladbro camping (see above). For free access to the **internet**, head for Randers Library at the Culture Centre.

Djursland

East of Randers stretches the **Djursland peninsula**. With its hilly, wooded landscape, edged by some fine beaches, the southern area of **Mols** attracts huge numbers of tourists every year. **EBELTOFT** is the most popular destination, easily reached by regular bus from Århus, or by frequent ferry services from Odden in Zealand. A thriving market centre in medieval times, it was sacked by the invading Swedes in 1659 and has only emerged from economic decline thanks to tourism; try to arrive in early summer, before the cobbled streets are overrun by (mostly German) tourists shopping for souvenirs. The main sight in town is the **Fregatten Jylland** (daily: July–Aug 10am–7pm; Sept–Oct & April–June 10am–5pm; Nov–March 10am–4pm; 95kr; ⓦwww.fregatten-jylland.dk), moored just behind the tourist office. This beautifully restored nineteenth-century wooden frigate has lots of miniature famous sea battle scenarios on display downstairs in the galley. Nearby at Strandvejen 8, the **Glass Museum** (daily: April–June & Sept–Oct 10am–5pm; July–Aug 10am–6pm; Nov–March Tues–Sun 10am–4pm; 60kr; ⓦwww.glasmuseet .dk) has an outstanding collecting of glass art on display, plus it gives you the chance to see local artisans demonstrating the highly skilled art of glass-blowing. Should you fancy staying in town, the luxurious *Hotel Ebeltoft Strand*, is right on the beachfront at Nordre Strandvej 3 (ⓣ86 34 33 00, ⓦwww.ebeltoftstrand.dk; ❺). The management has recently taken on the less expensive *Hotel Hvidehus* (same details; ❹; registration and keys at *Ebeltoft Strand*) at Strandgårdhøj 1, overlooking the bay. There's also a central **youth hostel** at Søndergade 43 (ⓣ86 34 20 53, ⓦwww .danhostel.dk/ebeltoft) with bunks (150kr) and doubles (❶). There are several **campsites** along the bay, the best being *Ebeltoft Strand Camping* (ⓣ86 34 12 14, ⓦwww.ebeltoftstrandcamping.dk), right on the beach a little way north of town at Nordre Strandvej 23.

Jutland's easternmost point, **GRENÅ** grew up around its harbour in the nineteenth century and ran a regular ferry connection to Zealand. When the Storebælt Bridge connecting Funen with Zealand opened in 1997 the ferry became obsolete and – to add insult to injury – most of the harbour-driven industry died down. However, there's still a frequent ferry service to Varberg in Sweden and the harbour is now also home to the popular **Kattegatcentret** (Kattegat Centre: Feb–June & mid-Aug to Oct Mon–Fri 10am–4pm Sat & Sun 10am–5pm; July to mid-Aug 9.30am–6pm; Nov to mid-Dec Tues–Fri 10am–4pm, Sat & Sun 10am–5pm; 130kr; ⓦwww .kattegatcentret.dk), named after the body of water between Denmark and Sweden. The centre has a giant aquarium which has sharks kept in an enormous 550-thousand-litre tropical seawater tank. You can view the magnificent creatures from a glass tunnel that runs through the tank, an especially gruesome sight at 2pm when they're fed. Though the town centre – about 5km from the harbour – is pleasant

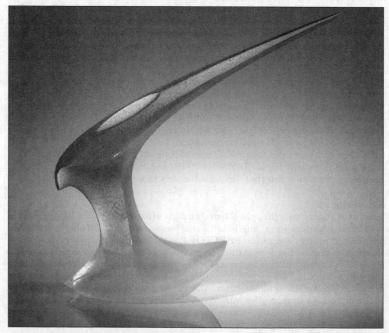

▲ Glass sculpture, Ebeltoft Glass Museum

enough, Grenå's other main draw is the stunning wide and sandy beaches to the south. If you need **to stay** overnight, try for a room at the yellow *Hotel Grenaa Strand*, close to the harbour at Havneplads 1 (T86 32 68 14, Wwww.grenaastrand .dk; ❸); alternatively, there's a **youth hostel**, with bunks (200kr) and doubles (❷), set in a large pine plantation west of the beach at Ydesvej 4 (T86 32 66 22, Wwww .danhostelgrenaa.dk). The best of the local **campsites** is *Grenå Strand Camping*, south of the harbour and a stone's throw from one of the country's best beaches at Fulgsangvej 58 (T86 32 17 18, Wwww.grenaastrandcamping.dk; April–Sept). Grenå is reachable by train from Århus (1hr 25min), while bus #214 runs hourly through the day from Randers bus station; the journey takes about ninety minutes.

The Lake District: Silkeborg, Viborg and around

Boundaried by a loose triangle formed by Skanderborg, Århus and Viborg, the grandly titled **Lake District** comprises several small lakes amid green, rolling woodlands which hold one of Denmark's highest points – the 147m Himmelbjerget, a mountain in Danish terms but really only a hill. If you've only seen Denmark's larger towns, this is a region well worth a couple of days' rural exploration – preferably by canoe, stopping overnight at one of the area's innumerable waterside campsites. The north–south rail route passes first through missable Skanderborg, but it's the Lake District's other main town, **Silkeborg**, spreading handsomely across several inlets, which serves as the area's lively nerve centre. The region is easily accessed by train, although if coming from Århus you'll need to change at Langå to get straight into the lush green countryside around historic **Viborg**.

Silkeborg

With its picturesque lakeside setting, **SILKEBORG** is a magnet for the country's many canoeists and today most of its visitors come here to set off into the countryside by paddle power. However, its history is also of interest – it was still a small village in 1845 when the Gudenå River was harnessed to power a paper mill that brought a measure of growth and prosperity, something you can learn more about at the **Paper Museum Bikuben**, Papirfabrikken 78 (May & Sept Sat & Sun noon–5pm; June–Aug daily noon–5pm; 20kr; Wwww.papirmuseet.dk) housed in the old paper mill. In 1938, the discovery of a well-preserved body of an Iron Age woman 15km west of Silkeborg added greatly to the appeal of the **Silkeborg Museum**, Hovedgårdsvej 7 (May to mid-Oct daily 10am–5pm; mid-Oct to April Sat & Sun noon–4pm; 45kr; Wwww.silkeborgmuseum.dk). As preserved bodies go, however, the so-called **Elling Girl** has been overshadowed since the 1950 discovery of the **Tollund Man**, a corpse of similar vintage also on display at the museum. Gruesome as it may sound, the man's head is in particularly good condition, with stubble still visible on the chin.

An equally worthwhile call is to see the excellent collection of abstract works by Asger Jorn and others in the **Museum of Art**, Gudenå 7 (April–Oct Tues–Sun 10am–5pm; Nov–March Tues–Fri noon–4pm, Sat & Sun 10am–5pm; 60kr; Wwww .silkeborgkunstmuseum.dk). It was to Silkeborg that Jorn, Denmark's leading modern painter and founder member of the influential CoBrA (Copenhagen-Brussels-Amsterdam) group, came to recuperate from tuberculosis. From the 1950s until his death in 1973, Jorn donated an enormous amount of his own and other artists' work to the town, which displays them proudly in this purpose-built museum.

For something less cultural, the **Aqua** freshwater aquarium (July to mid-Aug daily 10am–6pm; mid-Aug to June Mon–Fri 10am–4pm, Sat & Sun 10am–5pm; 105kr; Wwww.aqua-ferskvandsakvarium.dk), at Vejlsøvej 55 next door to the beautiful old tuberculosis sanatorium on the southern edge of town, has a variety of freshwater fish alongside numerous waterbirds and mammals, including some cute otters. You can get here by taking the *Hjejlen* steamer (4–6 trips daily; 70kr return), the world's oldest coal-burning paddle steamer, from the Silkeborg Museum. After the aquarium, the steamer carries on along the Gudenåen River to the foot of **Himmelbjerget** ("Sky Mountain"), one of Denmark's tallest hills; from here the trek to the top takes about thirty minutes, and your reward is magnificent views of the surrounding area.

Practicalities

The helpful **tourist office**, by the harbour at Åhavevej 2A (April to mid-June & Sept–Oct Mon–Fri 9am–4pm, Sat 10am–1pm; mid-June to Aug Mon–Fri 9am–5pm, Sat & Sun 10am–2pm; Nov–March Mon–Fri 10am–3pm; ☎86 82 19 11, Ⓦwww.silkeborg.com), has a lengthy list of affordable private **accommodation** in what's a surprisingly expensive town. Hotel options include the old and atmospheric *Dania*, on Torvet (☎86 82 01 11, Ⓦwww.hoteldania.dk; ⑥), a central hotel with en-suite rooms, offering reduced rates at weekends. Less expensive but a short bus journey (bus #8) from the centre is the recently renovated *Impala* (☎86 82 03 00, Ⓦwww.Impala.dk; ④) at Vestre Ringvej 53. Budget accommodation is limited to the **youth hostel**, Åhavevej 55 (☎86 82 36 42, Ⓦwww.danhostel-silkeborg.dk), which has dorms (July to mid-Sept; 200kr) and affordable four- and six-bed rooms, though no doubles. There are two **campsites** in town: *Gudenåens Camping* (☎86 82 22 01, Ⓦwww.gudenaaenscamping.dk), to the south on Vejlsøvej, and *Silkeborg Sø Camping* (☎86 82 28 24, Ⓦwww.seacamp.dk), on the Århus road. To get to the former, walk about 2km from the main square down Christian VIII Vej and turn left onto Marienlundsvej; for the latter, begin at the square and head down Østergade, through two traffic lights and across the Gudenå River to Århusbakken (also known as Århusvej). Outside of town, along the Gudenå River, there are many more campsites that cater to the thousands of canoeists that come here every year. They also organize **canoe package trips** starting at 1300kr per canoe for three days, which include canoe and tent rental as well as campsite fees along the way. If you want to go it alone, many of the campsites rent out canoes, or try Slusekioskens Kanoudlejning (☎86 80 08 93, Ⓦwww.kano4you.dk; 300kr per day, 1650kr per week) at the harbour.

Nearby, in the grounds of the old papermill, you'll also find a couple of good places to **eat**. In the old mill itself, there's the *Café 1 Række*, Papirfabrikken 80, which serves a splendid array of hot and cold dishes including excellent cod meatballs grilled on a skewer for 65kr, and the Sunday coffee and cake spread, also for 65kr. Around the corner, at no 10, the *Café Evald* brasserie rightly prides itself of its delicious range of tapas as well as an outstanding fish lasagna (149kr).

Viborg

For many years **VIBORG** was one of the most important communities in the country, at the junction of all the major roads across Jutland. From Knud in 1027 to Christian V in 1655, every Danish king was crowned here; Hans Tausen's Lutheran preaching began in Viborg in 1528, eight years before Denmark's official conversion from Catholicism; and until the early nineteenth century the town was the seat of a provincial assembly. As the national administrative axis shifted towards Zealand, however, Viborg's importance waned, and although it's still home to the high court of West Denmark, it's now primarily a market town.

Viborg is cut in half by a lake, which is spanned by the Randersvej bridge. Its centre is concentrated in a small area, though, and most parts of the old town are within a few minutes' walk of each other. The twin towers of the **Domkirke** (April–Sept Mon–Sat 11am–4pm, Sun noon–4pm; Oct–March Mon–Sat 11am–3pm, Sun noon–3pm) are the town's most visible feature and the most compelling reminder of its former glories. Begun by Bishop Eskil in 1130, the original cathedral was destroyed by fire in 1726 and rebuilt in the Baroque style by one Claus Stallknecht, though so badly that it had to be closed for two years and the work begun again. The interior is now dominated by the brilliant frescoes of Joakim Skovgaard, an artist commemorated by the **Skovgaard Museum** (June–Aug Tues–Sun 10am–5pm; Sept–May 11am–4pm; 35kr; Ⓦwww.skovgaardmuseet.dk) housed inside the former

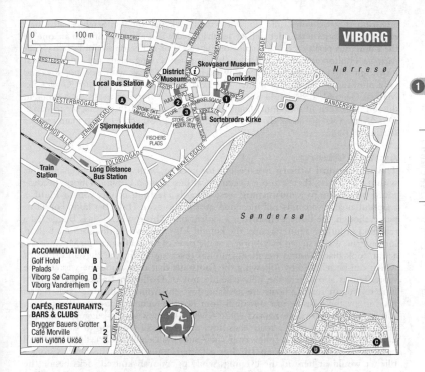

VIBORG

Nørresø

Skovgaard Museum
District Museum
Local Bus Station
Domkirke
Stjerneskuddet
Sortebrødre Kirke
Train Station
Long Distance Bus Station

Søndersø

ACCOMMODATION
Golf Hotel   B
Palads   A
Viborg Sø Camping   D
Viborg Vandrerhjem C

CAFÉS, RESTAURANTS, BARS & CLUBS
Brygger Bauers Grotter 1
Café Morville   2
Den Gyldne Okse   3

Rådhus across Gammel Torv from the cathedral – a neat building with which Claus Stallknecht made amends for his botched job of the cathedral. There's a good selection of Skovgaard's paintings on display – although they're a little anticlimactic after his splendid work in the cathedral – plus some works by other members of his family.

For a broader perspective on Viborg's past, keep an hour spare for exploring the **Viborg Stiftsmuseum** (District Museum: mid-June to Aug Tues–Sun 11am–5pm; Sept to mid-June Tues–Fri 1–4pm, Sat & Sun 11am–5pm; 25kr; Ⓦwww .viborgstiftsmuseum.dk), on the northern side of Hjultorvet between Vestergade and Skt Hans Gade. The three well-stocked floors hold everything from prehistoric and archeological artefacts to clothes, furniture and household appliances.

Practicalities

Trains and **long-distance buses** arrive at their respective stations on Viborg's western side, roughly 1km from the centre. The **tourist office** close to the cathedral, at Nytorv 9 (June–Aug Mon–Fri 9am–5pm, Sat 9am–2pm; Sept–May Mon–Fri 9am–4pm, Sat 10am–1pm; ☎87 87 88 88, Ⓦwww.visitviborg.dk) has a list of private rooms in and around Viborg, which start at about 175kr per person. All Viborg's **hotels** are fairly pricey – best bets are the handsome *Palads*, Skt Mathias Gade 5 (☎86 62 37 00, Ⓦwww.hotelpalads.dk; ④), or if a lake view appeals, the more expensive *Golf Hotel*, Randersvej 2 (☎86 61 02 22, Ⓦwww.golfhotelviborg .dk; ⑤), has serious discounts during summer and weekends. Also close to the lake, but on the opposite side to the town centre (a 2km walk or local bus #707), is the *Viborg Vandrerhjem* **youth hostel**, Vinkelvej 36 (☎86 67 17 81, Ⓦwww.danhostel.dk /viborg) which has dorms (135kr) and some doubles (②) and the *Viborg Sø* **campsite** (☎86 67 13 11, Ⓦwww.camping-viborg.dk). The tourist office hires out **bikes** for 50kr per hour and 100kr per day.

During the day, you could do worse than pick up some smørrebrød (the best outlet is the Stjerneskuddet deli at Jernbanegade 14), and **eat** alfresco in one of the numerous parks or on the banks of the lake. For coffee or a cool beer try *Café Morville*, Hjultorvet 2, a fancy French/Italian place serving salads and sandwiches at lunchtime and and things like mouthwatering pepper steak with new potatoes and wild mushrooms (185kr) for dinner. The cellar restaurant *Brygger Bauers Grotter*, Skt Mathias Gade 61 (☎86 61 44 88, closed Sun), is an atmospheric spot for a candlelit dinner, and excels in traditional Danish dishes. For super-quality steak, try the small *Den Gyldne Okse* (☎86 62 27 44) on Store Skt Peder Stræde 11, with main courses starting at 189kr.

Around Viborg

The area **around Viborg** is excellent for cycling, with plenty of pleasant spots within easy reach; there's also a decent local bus service. Leaving Viborg, heading south on Koldingvej and turning west towards Herning brings you to **Hald**, a beautiful area of soft hills and meadows on the shores of **Hald Sø lake**. For all its peace, though, the district's history is a violent one. This is where Niels Bugge led a rebellion of Jutland squires against the king in 1351, and where the Catholic bishop, Jorgen Friis, was besieged by Viborgers at the time of the Reformation. Much of the action took place around the manor houses that stood here, the sites and ruins of which can be reached by following the **footpath** that runs along the western lake shore. This is also where the hilly lakeside area of **Dollerup Bakker** starts. From June to August rowing boats are available for rent from the historic *Niels Bugges Kro* inn, by the lakeside just downhill from Hald, which also does excellent meals and has four comfortable **rooms** (☎86 63 80 11, ⓦwww.niels-bugges-kro.dk; ③). Just to the south of here, a road leads from the village of Dollerup to **LYSGÅRD**, home to **E. Bindstouw** (June–Aug Tues–Sun 10am–5pm; 20kr), the old school house where **Steen Steensen Blicher** gathered inspiration for his famous stories. Blicher would sit here in the evenings while poor locals knitted socks beside the stove and told folk tales, which Blicher noted down for posterity. The small building still contains the fixtures and fittings of Blicher's time, including his writing board, stove and even a few socks. To get here from Viborg by bus, take the irregular #54 from the bus station.

West of Viborg

The **Jutland Stone** marks the precise geographical centre of Jutland and can be found about 9km west of Viborg, beside the A16 between Mønsted and Raunstrup. There's not much to see, just a big inscribed rock and lots of cigarette ends. A few kilometres further, and markedly more interesting, are the **Mønsted Limestone Mines** (mid-March to Oct daily 10am–5pm; 60kr; ⓦwww.monsted-kalkgruber .dk), which wind underground for 60km. The mines stay at a constant temperature, regardless of external weather, and wandering around their cool, damp innards can be magically atmospheric, although a century ago conditions for the workers here were so horrific that when Frederik IV visited the place he was sufficiently appalled to bring about reforms – the mines were subsequently known as "Frederik's Quarries" or, more venomously, "The King's Graves". The site closes in winter, when the mines are taken over by an enormous colony of hibernating bats. Bus #28 from Viborg runs here.

A few kilometres further west near Daugbjerg (and also served

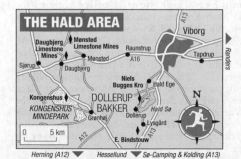

THE HALD AREA

Daugbjerg Limestone Mines · Mønsted Limestone Mines · Raunstrup · Viborg · Tapdrup · Randers · Sjørup · Mønsted · A16 · Daugbjerg · Niels Bugges Kro · Hald Ege · Kongenshus · DOLLERUP BAKKER · Hald Sø · N · KONGENSHUS MINDEPARK · Grønhøj · Dollerup · Lysgård · E. Bindstouw · A13 · A12 · 0 · 5 km

Herning (A12) ▼   Hesselund ▼ Sø-Camping & Kolding (A13)

by bus #28) is another set of **limestone mines** (daily: June 10am–4pm; July to mid-Aug 10am–6pm; mid-Aug to Oct & end March to May 11am–4pm; 50kr; ⓦwww.daugbjerg-kalkgruber.dk), unlit and much narrower than those at Mønsted, and therefore quite spooky. The entrance was found by chance fifty years ago and no one has yet charted the full extent of the passages; it's said that work began here at the time of Gorm, the tenth-century king of Jutland, and that the tunnels were used as hideouts by bandits.

Kongenshus Mindepark (parking 30kr for cars, 15kr per person between May and mid-Sept, rest of the year free) comprises an impressive three thousand acres of protected moorland, just south of Daugbjerg, on which there have been attempts at agriculture since the mid-eighteenth century, when an officer from Mecklenburg began keeping sheep here. In the centre of the park is a memorial to the early pioneers; standing here, as the wind howls in your ears and you look around the stark and inhospitable heath, you can only marvel at their determination. Kongenshus is now a **hotel** (☎97 54 81 25; ⓦwww.kongenshushotel.dk; ③) and the delightful restaurant does fine Danish food such as a smørrebrød lunch platter for 155kr. There are several **campsites** nearby: *Hessellund Sø-Camping* (☎97 10 16 04, ⓦwww.hessellund-camping.dk; mid-March to Sept) to the south near Karup is best.

Northwest Jutland: Limfjordslandet and around

Limfjordslandet is the name given to the area around the western portion of the **Limfjorden**, the body of water that separates northern Jutland from the rest of the peninsula. In the northwestern half, both the North Sea coast and the shore of the Limfjorden itself – which here resembles a large inland lake – has some fine beaches and plenty of opportunities to mess about in boats – and to catch them to Norway and beyond. There are also a number of small, neat old towns with a smattering of mildly diverting museums. But the weather here is unpredictable, with sharp winds blustering in off the North Sea, and getting around is difficult: trains only reach to the fringes, so you'll need to rely on buses if you're without your own transport.

For a quick taste of the area, take the train from Viborg and change at Struer for the short journey south to **HOLSTEBRO**, the largest town in the region, with an easygoing atmosphere and a small, walkable centre. There's a commendable **Art Museum** (July–Aug Tues–Sun 11am–5pm; Sept–June Tues–Fri noon–4pm, Sat & Sun 11am–5pm; 40kr, includes entry to Holstebro Museum; ⓦwww.holstebrokunst museum.dk) in the town park, with a strong contemporary Danish collection and some quality international pieces, including works by Matisse and Picasso. In the same building, the **Holstebro Museum** (same hours; 40kr, includes entry to the Art Museum; ⓦwww.holstebro-museum.dk) has a small but interesting local history collection. The **tourist office** at Slotsgade 2 (Mon–Fri 9.30am–5pm, Sat 10am–noon; ☎97 42 57 00; ⓦwww.holstebro-tourist.dk) can supply information on travelling deeper into Limfjordslandet. For staying overnight, there's the modern new *Hotel Royal* (☎97 40 23 33, ⓦwww.hotel-royal.dk; ⑤) in the centre at Den Røde Plads 10, with serious reductions at weekends. The nearest **campsite,** equipped with cabins sleeping four (375kr plus 60kr per person) and canoes for hire, is *Mejdal Camping* at Birkevej 25 (☎97 42 20 68, ⓦwww.camping-mejdal.dk; April–Sept).

Also reachable from Struer, **THISTED**, the main town in the newly designated Thy National Park and at the end of the local rail line, has access to good beaches and stunning countryside. There's a youth hostel (☎97 92 50 42, ⓦwww.danhostelnord .dk/thisted) with dorms (150kr) and doubles (①) at Kongemøllevej 8, as well as a campsite at Iversensvej 3 (☎97 92 16 35, ⓦwww.thisted camping.dk; April–Sept) on the bank of the Limfjord. Thisted is linked by bus #23 (40min) to **HANSTHOLM**, from where ferries leave for Egersund and Bergen in Norway. While waiting for the bus, head over to the quaint *Basses Kro*, in the centre at Vestergade 28A, a perfect place for a Danish meal or a glass of the fine Thy Pilsner, brewed in Thisted and one of the country's best lagers.

Northeast Jutland

Much easier to get to and travel around than Limfjordslandet, **northeastern Jutland** is nonetheless another portion of Denmark often ignored by foreign visitors. This is a shame, as the region has a highly convivial major city in **Aalborg**, as well as ferries to Sweden and Norway departing from **Frederikshavn**. What's more, once you cross the Limfjorden, the northeast boasts a landscape wilder than anywhere else on the peninsula: lush green pastures giving way to strangely compelling views of bleak moorland and windswept dunes. The highlight here is **Skagen**, a uniquely atmospheric place whose unusual natural light has long attracted artists.

Aalborg

Hugging the south bank of the Limfjorden, **AALBORG** is the obvious place to spend a night or two before venturing into the wilder countryside further on. The country's fourth largest city and the main transport terminus for northern Jutland, it boasts a notable modern art museum, a well-preserved old section and the brightest nightlife for miles around.

The profits from the seventeenth-century herring boom briefly made Aalborg the biggest and wealthiest Danish town outside Copenhagen, and much of what remains of **old Aalborg** – chiefly the area within Østerågade (commonly abbreviated to Østerå), Bispensgade, Gravensgade and Algade – dates from that era, standing in stark contrast to the new roads that slice through it to accommodate the traffic using the Limfjorden bridge.

Information and accommodation

The **tourist office** is centrally placed at Østerågade 8 (mid-June–Aug Mon–Fri 9am–5.30pm, Sat 10am–1pm; Sept to mid-June Mon–Fri 9am–4.30pm, Sat 10am–1pm; ☎99 31 75 00, ⊛www.visitaalborg.com).

If you want **to stay** in Aalborg, be aware that bargain-priced hotels are hard to find. The tourist office has a list of private rooms in the Aalborg area that all go for a fixed rate of 325kr per night (plus a 25kr fee if you want the tourist office to make the booking). For a little more adventure, catch the half-hourly **ferry** (☎98 11 78 23; 6.30am–11.15pm; 16kr) from near the campsite (bus #13 from the centre) to Egholm, an island in Limfjord, where there's free camping under open-sided shelters.

Accommodation

Aalborg Sømandshjem Østerbro 27 ☎98 12 19 00, ⊛www.hotel-aalborg.com. This family-oriented former seaman's home is now among the city's cheapest year-round options. It's rather plain-looking, but the rooms are fully modernized and clean. 600m east of the centre, or take bus #11, #14 or #17. **❹**

Aalborg Vandrerhjem Skydebanevej 50 ☎98 11 60 44, ⊛www.bbbb.dk. Large youth hostel and campsite to the west of the town, beside the marina on the bank of the Limfjorden, which has dorms (mid-June to Aug 270kr), doubles (**❷**) and rustic cabins sleeping up to seven (875kr for seven). Take bus #13 from the centre.

Helnan Phønix Hotel Vesterbro 77 ☎98 12 00 11, ⊛www.helnan.info. Appealing hotel on a busy thoroughfare leading onto the bridge crossing Limfjorden, and within easy reach of bus and train station. In an eighteenth-century building, the self-contained rooms ooze classic charm. **❺**

Krogen Skibstedsvej 4 ☎98 12 17 05, ⊛www.krogen.dk. Homely place, some 2km west of the city centre, with a large leafy garden; some rooms have shared facilities. Buses #15 and #38 run closest to the hotel; get off at Constancevej and continue along it for 5min. **❸**, en-suite **❹**

🏃 **Prinsen** Prinsensgade 14–16 ☎98 13 37 33, ⊛www.prinsen-hotel.dk. Inexpensive and comfortable hotel across from the train station, with a range of rooms of different shapes and size, a cosy in-house bar and free parking. It also offers reduced rates for the fitness centre across the street. **❸**

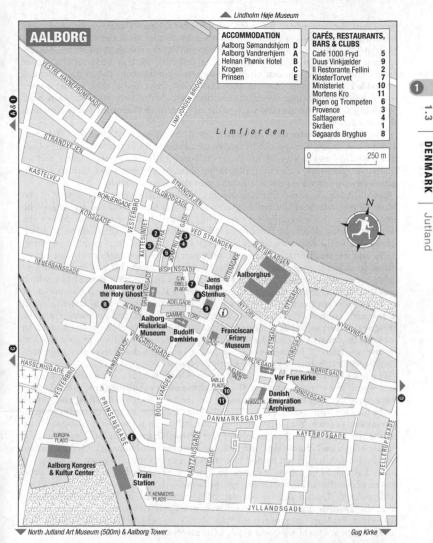

AALBORG

ACCOMMODATION

Aalborg Sømandshjem	D
Aalborg Vandrerhjem	A
Helnan Phønix Hotel	B
Krogen	C
Prinsen	E

CAFÉS, RESTAURANTS, BARS & CLUBS

Café 1000 Fryd	5
Duus Vinkjælder	9
Il Restorante Fellini	2
KlosterTorvet	7
Ministeriet	10
Mortens Kro	11
Pigen og Trompeten	6
Provence	3
Saltlageret	4
Skråen	1
Søgaards Bryghus	8

Limfjorden

0   250 m

N

The Old Town

The tourist office on Østerågade is as good a place as any to start exploring, with one of the town's major seventeenth-century structures standing directly opposite. The **Jens Bangs Stenhus** is a grandiose five storeys of Dutch Renaissance style and, incredibly, has functioned as a pharmacy ever since it was built. Jens Bang himself was Aalborg's wealthiest merchant but was not popular with the governing elite, who conspired to keep him off the local council. The host of goblin-like figures carved on the walls allegedly represent the councillors of the time, while another figure, said to be Bang himself, pokes out his tongue towards the former Rådhus, next door, the predecessor to the present eighteenth-century building further down Østerågade.

The commercial roots of the city are further in evidence within **Budolfi Domkirke** (June–Aug Mon–Fri 9am–4pm, Sat 9am–2pm; Sept–May Mon–Fri

9am–3pm, Sat 9am–noon), just a few steps behind the Jens Bangs Stenhus and easily located by its bulbous spire. Inside, there's a list (rather than the more customary portraits of nobles) of the town's merchants during the 1660s. A small but elegant specimen of sixteenth-century Gothic, the cathedral itself is built on the site of an eleventh-century wooden church; only a few tombs from the original remain, embedded in the walls close to the altar. Apart from these, there's little to see inside, but plenty to hear when the electronically driven bells ring out each hour – sending a cacophonous racket across the old square of **Gammel Torv**, on which the cathedral stands.

The **Aalborg Historiske Museum**, across the square at Algade 48 (Tues–Sun 10am–5pm; 20kr; ⓦwww.nordjyllandshistoriskemuseum.dk) houses local collections which provide a good record of Aalborg's early prosperity. There's also an impressive glasswork collection, illustrating different designs from various Danish glass-working centres – look out for the armadillo-shaped bottle.

Just off Adelgade is the fifteenth-century **Helligåndskloster** (Monastery of the Holy Ghost). Much of the building now serves as a senior citizens' home, and the remainder can be seen only on one of the guided tours which run during the summer (check details at the tourist office, as timings change frequently; 40kr). These take in the refectory, largely unchanged since the monks were thrown out in 1536, and the small Friar's Room, the only part of the monastery into which nuns (from the adjoining convent) were permitted entry. Indeed, this was one of the few monasteries where monks and nuns were allowed any contact at all, a fact which accounts for the reported hauntings of the Friar's Room – reputedly by the ghost of a nun who got too friendly with a monk, and as punishment was buried alive in a basement column (the monk was beheaded). Most interesting, however, are the **frescoes** of various biblical figures that cover the entire ceiling of the chapel. In more recent times, the corridor outside the chapel was used for shooting practice by the so-called "Churchill Gang", a group of local schoolboys who organized Denmark's first resistance group against the Nazis.

The rest of old Aalborg lies to the east across Østerågade, and is a mainly residential area – with just a few exceptions. The sixteenth-century **Aalborghus** (grounds daily 8am–9pm; free) is mainly worth visiting for the severely gloomy **dungeon** (May–Oct Mon–Fri 8am–3pm; free), to the right from the gateway, and the **underground passageways** (daily 8am–9pm; free) that run off it. From the castle, Slotsgade leads to the maze of narrow streets around **Vor Frue Kirke** (Mon–Fri 9am–2pm, Sat 9am–noon) a dull church that's surrounded by some meticulously preserved houses, many of which have been turned into upmarket craft shops. The best are along the oddly L-shaped Hjelmerstald: notice no. 2, whose ungainly bulge around its midriff has earned it the nickname "the pregnant house".

If you're of Danish descent, or particularly interested in Danish social history, visit the **Danish Emigration Archives**, nearby at Arkivstræde 1 (Mon–Thurs 9am–4pm, Fri 9am–2pm, plus until 8pm Mon May–Sept; ⓦwww.emiarch.dk) with its immense stacks of files and books. Given enough background facts, details of individual migrants can be traced.

Also east of Østerågade, just past the Budolfi Domkirke, at Algade 19, is the **Gråbrødrekloster Museet** (Franciscan Friary Museum: Tues–Sun 10am–5pm; ⓦwww.nordjyllandshistoriskemuseum.dk). Set below ground, it's entered by way of an elevator; insert 20kr into the machine for each descent. The remains of the friary were discovered during archeological excavations in the 1990s, and the foundations and walls that were unearthed, alongside skeletons from nearby graveyards, form the bulk of the display. Models, placards and information panels give an excellent introduction to Aalborg in the Viking and Middle ages.

Outside the old centre

The old centre sets the pleasant tone of the city, but just outside it are a couple of other notable targets. One is the **Nordjyllands Kunstmuseum** (Art Museum:

Tues–Sun 10am–5pm; 40kr, Dec free; ⓦwww.nordjyllandskunstmuseum.dk), south from the centre on Kong Christians Allé, close to the junction with Vesterbro (bus #15 or a fifteen-minute walk from the centre). Housed in a building designed by the Finnish architect Alvar Aalto, this is one of the country's better modern art collections, strikingly contemporary in both form and content. Alongside numerous Danish contributions, it features works by Max Ernst, Andy Warhol, Le Corbusier and, imposingly stationed next to the entrance, Claes Oldenburg's wonderful *Fagends in a Colossal Ashtray*. After leaving the museum, you can get a Danish pastry and coffee plus a grand view over the city and the Limfjorden by ascending the **Aalborgtårn tower** (April–June, Aug–Sept daily 11am–5pm; July daily 10am–7pm; 25kr ⓦwww.aalborgtaarnet.com), on the hill just behind.

Eating, drinking and nightlife

In pursuit of **food**, **drink** and most especially **nightlife**, almost everybody heads for Jomfru Ane Gade, a small street close to the harbour between Bispensgade and Borgergade. Jomfru Ane (literally "young maiden Anne") was a noblewoman and reputed witch who, because of her social standing, was beheaded rather than burnt at the stake – though the street nowadays, at least by night, is more synonymous with getting legless than headless. Aalborg Kongres & Kultur Center, Europa Plads 4 (☏99 35 55 65, ⓦwww.akkc.dk), is the city's theatre and concert venue. At the opposite end of the scale, several of the Jomfru Ane Gade bars host more lowbrow live acts; just walk along, listen, and decide which appeals.

Restaurants and cafés

Il Restorante Fellini Vesterå 13. Genuine Italian restaurant with good-value pizzas and pastas; the novel Italian brunch (Mon–Sat 11.30am–3pm; 99kr) is a delightful alternative – a platter of Italian cheeses and ham, served with fresh bread, fruit, cake and outstanding coffee.

KlosterTorvet C.W. Obels Plads 4. Great place for well-prepared salads and enormous sandwiches, with outdoor seating on the square during summer. Also brunch Sat & Sun 11am–3pm.

Ministeriet Mølleplads 19. Hugely popular café, on the corner of a quiet square, serving fabulous food throughout the day, starting with brunch at 10am.

Mortens Kro Møllå Arkaden, Mølleå 4–6 ☏98 12 48 60. Top gourmet restaurant set in a temple to modern Scandinavian design. It isn't cheap – prices start at 248kr for roasted veal tenderloin served with sautéed sour squash, glazed carrots and a purée of baked pepper – but it's worth every øre. Dinner only, closed Sun. Booking recommended.

Provence Ved Stranden 11 ☏98 13 51 33. Around the corner from Jomfru Ane Gade, the tightly packed tables at this romantic French restaurant overlook the Limfjorden. Delicious food from Provence. Book ahead.

Saltlageret Jomfru Ane Gade 16. Of the many bar-restaurants along Jomfru Ane Gade, this is the most reliable place food-wise, with great big juicy steaks starting at 159kr. Also a popular nightclub Thurs–Sat when it stays open until 6am, with live music on Fri.

Søgaards Bryghus C.W. Obels Plads 1A. Excellent combination of microbrewery, restaurant and butcher's shop, which does steaks (from 225kr) and home-made beer; you can also stock up on cold cuts for the picnic basket. Closed Sun.

Bars and nightlife

Café 1000 Fryd Kattesundet 10 ☏98 13 22 21, ⓦwww.1000fryd.dk. Hardcore music venue hosting alternative-type international acts.

Duus Vinkjælder Østerågade 9. This atmospheric wine bar in the cellar of the Jens Bangs Stenhus is the perfect place for a quiet evening drink. Closed Sun.

Pigen og Trompeten Jomfru Ane Gade 13. Bar-cum-nightclub with live music on Thurs and Fri, and DJs spinning the discs the rest of the week; also an excellent cocktail menu.

Skråen Strandvejen 19 ☏98 12 21 89, ⓦwww.skraaen.dk. A short walk from the centre, and a good place to catch gigs by better-known Danish rock acts; there's also a decent café.

Around Aalborg: Lindholm Høje and Rebild Bakker

A few kilometres north from Aalborg across the Limfjorden, **Lindholm Høje** was a major Viking and Iron Age burial ground, and is a captivating place, especially at dawn or dusk. There are a number of very rare Viking "ship monuments" here – burial places with stones arranged in the outline of a ship – as well as more than six hundred Iron Age cremation graves. Numerous burial sites and dwellings are reconstructed in the dedicated **Lindholm Høje Museum** (April–Oct daily 10am–5pm; Nov–March Tues 10am–4pm & Sun 11am–4pm; 30kr; ⓦwww.nordjyllandshistoriskemuseum.dk), which also gives an insight into life during the Viking era. From Aalborg you can get to the site by bus #2 (every 30min for most of the day), or walk there in under an hour: go over the Limfjorden bridge, along Vesterbrogade into Thistedvej, right into Viaduktvej, and straight on until Vikingvej appears to the left.

About 30km south of Aalborg is the **Rebild Bakker** area, rolling hills close to some scattered beech woods and the dense conifers that make up Rold Skov. The area is prime hiking territory, and has been a **national park** since a group of expatriate Danes in America purchased the land and presented it to the Danish government in 1912. It's also the site of the largest American Independence Day celebration outside the US, staged every July 4, and is home to the somewhat tacky **Blockhus Museet** (Lincoln's Log Cabin: daily: June 11.30am–4.30pm; July–Aug 11am–5pm; rest of the year open only on demand; ☎98 39 14 40, ⓦwww.rebildfesten.dk; 15kr, free on July 4), a re-creation of Abraham Lincoln's log cabin, filled with mundane articles from 49 American states alongside facts about Danish migration to the US. For an insight into the cultural history of the region and its isolation from the rest of Denmark head for the **Spillemands- Jagt- og Skovbrugs-Museet** (Fiddlers, Hunting and Forestry Museum: May–Aug daily 10am–5pm; Sept daily 11am–4pm; Oct–April Sun 1–5pm; 25kr). To get here from Aalborg, take a train to Skørping, and then bus #104 to **Rebild**, where the cosy **youth hostel** at Rebildvej 23 (☎98 39 13 40, ⓦwww.rebild-vandrerhjem.dk; March–Dec) has dorm beds (July to mid-Sept; 200kr) and doubles (❷); the adjacent **campsite** (☎98 39 11 10, ⓦwww.dk-camp .dk/safari) has four- and six-person cabins (450kr) and is open year-round.

Frederikshavn

FREDERIKSHAVN, on north Jutland's east coast, is neither pretty nor particularly interesting, but if you're heading north it's virtually unavoidable. As a major ferry port it's usually full of Swedes and Norwegians taking advantage of Denmark's liberal drinking laws. From the small train station there are regular services to Skagen – if you've an international sailing connection to meet at Hirtshals, change for the private train at Hjørring (holders of InterRail, Eurail and Scanrail passes get half-price fares).

If you have time on your hands, take the fifteen-minute ride on bus #3 to Mølle-huset at the edge of the Bangsbo estate and walk on through the beautifully groomed botanic garden to the **Bangsbo-Museet** (Tues–Sun 10am–5pm; 40kr; ⓦwww .bangsbo-museum.dk), set in the manor building. Here, comprehensive displays chart the development of Frederikshavn from the 1600s, alongside a slightly grotesque, but very engrossing, collection of pictures, bracelets, rings and necklaces all made of human hair. The barns and outbuildings store the twelfth-century *Ellingåskibet*, a ship found north of Frederikshavn, plus a worthwhile exhibition covering the occupation and the rise of the resistance movement during World War II.

Practicalities

Buses and **trains** both terminate at the train station; crossing Skippergade and walking along Denmarksgade brings you to the town centre in a few minutes. Arriving **ferries** dock near Havnepladsen, also near the centre, and close to the **tourist office** at Skandiatorv 1, on the corner of Rådhus Allé and Havnepladsen (July to mid-Aug Mon–Sat 9am–6pm, Sun 9am–2pm; mid-Aug to June Mon–Fri 9am–4pm, Sat 11am–2pm; ☎98 42 32 66, ⓦwww.frederikshavn-tourist.dk). The **bicycles** parked outside the tourist office are available to use for free and can be picked up during tourist office opening hours. If you need to **stay** *Turisthotellet* is a stone's throw from the harbour at Magrethevej 5 (☎98 42 90 55,

head straight for *Kaffelagret*, Søndergade 15, for delicious coffee, sandwiches,
salads burgers and burritos throughout the day.

Skagen and around

Forty kilometres north of Frederikshavn, **SKAGEN** perches at the very top of
Jutland amid a desolate landscape of heather-topped sand dunes, its houses painted
a distinctive bright yellow. Its tranquil, remote setting makes it a popular holiday
destination in the summer, when hotels and restaurants are packed to the limits and
pre-booking accommodation is essential. Visiting outside the peak period gives you
a much better chance of experiencing the area's uniqueness. Skagen can be reached
by a privately operated train (Scanrail, Eurail and InterRail passholders get half-price
fares), which leaves from Frederikshavn train station roughly once an hour.

The Town

Sunlight seems to gain extra brightness as it bounces off the two seas that collide off
Skagen's coast, something that attracted the **Skagen artists** in the late nineteenth
century. Painters Michael Ancher and Peder Severin (P.S.) Krøyer and writer
Holger Drachmann arrived in the small fishing community during 1873 and 1874,
and were later joined by Lauritz Tuxen, Carl Locher, Viggo Johansen, Christian
Krogh and Oscar Björck. The painters often met in the bar of *Brøndum's Hotel*, off
Brøndumsvej, and the owner's stepsister, Anna, herself a skilful painter, married
Michael Ancher. The grounds of the hotel now house the **Skagens Museum**
(Feb–April & Sept–Nov Tues–Sun 10am–5pm; May–Aug daily 10am–5pm, Wed
until 9pm; 80kr; @www.skagensmuseum.dk), which contains the most comprehensive collection of these artists' work anywhere in the world. The majority of the
canvases depict local scenes, capturing subtleties of colour using the area's strong
natural light. Many of the works are outstanding; but it's the work of Anna Ancher,
though perhaps the least technically accomplished of those on display, which often
comes closest to achieving the naturalism these artists sought.

A few strides away at Markvej 2–4, the **Michael & Anna Anchers Hus** (Feb–
March & Nov Sat 11am–3pm; April & Oct Mon–Thurs, Sat & Sun 11am–3pm;
May–Sept daily 10am–5pm; 60kr; @www.anchershus.dk) has been restored with the
intention of evoking the atmosphere of their time through an assortment of squeezed
tubes of paint, sketches, paintings, books, ornaments and piles of canvases. The arrival
and subsequent success of these artists inadvertently made Skagen fashionable, and
the town continues to be a popular holiday destination. But it still bears many marks
of its past as a fishing community, a history that is well documented in the **Skagens
By og Egnsmuseum** at P.K. Nielsensvej 8–10 (Skagen Town and Region Museum:
March–April & Oct Mon–Fri 10am–4pm; May–June & Aug–Sept Mon–Fri
10am–4pm, Sat & Sun 11am–4pm; July Mon–Fri 10am–5pm, Sat & Sun 11am–4pm;
Nov–Feb Mon–Fri 11am–3pm; 35kr; @www.skagen-bymus.dk), a fifteen-minute
walk south along Skt Laurentii Vej (or the much nicer Vesterbyvej) from the town
centre. Built on the tall dune where townswomen would watch for their husbands
returning from sea during storms, the museum examines local fishing techniques
in its main displays, reinforced by photos showing millions of fish strewn along the
quay before being auctioned. Among the auxiliary buildings are reconstructions of
rich and poor fishermen's houses: the rich house includes a macabre guest room kept
cool to facilitate the storage of bodies washed ashore from wrecks, while the poor
man's dwelling makes plain the contrast in lifestyles: it possesses just two rooms to
accommodate the fisherman, his wife and fourteen children.

Around Skagen: Grenen and the Buried Church

Some four kilometres north of Skagen (reachable via hourly Skagen Bybus bus
during summer) the mesmerizing **Grenen** is the northernmost tip of Denmark
and the actual meeting point of two seas – the **Kattegat** and **Skagerrak**. From

the bus stop and car park at the end of Fyrvej, the Sandormen tractor-drawn bus (April–Oct; 15kr return) runs along the beach to the tip, though it's nicer to walk the half-kilometre. The spectacle of their clashing waves (the seas flow in opposing directions) is a powerful draw, although only truly dramatic when the winds are strong. On the way back, spare a thought for Holger Drachmann, a man so enchanted by the thrashing seas that he chose to be buried in a dune close to them. His tomb is signposted from the car park. Overlooking the car park atop a large sand dune, the **Grenen Kunstmuseum** (Grenen Aut Museum: May–Aug daily 11am–4pm; Sept–Oct Sat 11am–4pm; 50kr; ⓦwww.grenenkunstmuseum.dk) is devoted to more recent Skagen artists such as Axel and Eva Lind, with Carl Milles' elegant bronze sculpture – a preliminary work for the UN building in New York – by the main entrance.

Returning towards Skagen, the forces of nature can be further appreciated at the architecturally serene **Skagen Odde Naturcenter** (daily: May–June & mid-Aug to mid-Oct 10am–4pm; July to mid-Aug 10am–5pm; 65kr; ⓦwww.skagen-natur .dk) at Batterivej 51. Five daily Skagen Bybus buses run from the station and Grenen during summer, or it's a half-hour walk. Designed by Danish architect Jørn Utzon – best-known for the Sydney Opera House – this exploration of natural forces is beautifully centred around the themes of sand, water, wind and light, and how these different forces interact with each other – something very evident just outside.

Amid the dunes to the south of town, about twenty minutes' walk along Skt Laurentii Vej, Damstedvej and Gammel Kirkestræde, then onto a signposted footpath, is **Den Tilsandede Kirke**, "the Buried Church" (June–Aug daily 11am–5pm; 10kr). The name is slightly misleading, however, since all that's here is the tower of a fourteenth-century church, built in what was then a minor agricultural area. From the beginning of the sixteenth century the church was assaulted by vicious sandstorms; by 1775 the congregation could only reach the building with the aid of shovels. In 1810 the nave and most of the fittings were sold, leaving just the tower as a marker to shipping – while not especially tall, its white walls and red roof are easily visible from the sea. Still under the sands are the original church floor and cemetery. Although part of the tower is open to the public, the great fascination is simply looking at the thing from outside, and appreciating the incredible severity of the storms which covered it.

Arrival and information

Buses stop at Skagen's **train station** on Skt Laurentii Vej, which has a convenient **bicycle** rental business next door at Skagen Cykeludlegning (☎98 44 10 70, ⓦwww.skagencykeludlejning.dk) for 75kr a day. The **tourist office** (April to mid-June & mid-Aug to Oct Mon–Fri 9am–4pm, Sat 10am–2pm; July to mid-Aug Mon–Sat 9am–6pm, Sun 10am–4pm; Nov–March Mon–Fri 10am–4pm, Sat 10am–1pm; ⓦwww.skagen-tourist.dk; ☎98 44 13 77) is located in the former harbourmaster's residence at Vesterstrandvej 10.

Accommodation

Staying overnight in Skagen is infinitely preferable to going back to Frederikshavn, and there are a number of options. **Private accommodation** (from 325kr upwards) can be arranged through the tourist office for a steep 75kr booking fee. All rooms are within a 3km radius of the centre and come without breakfast. The **youth hostel** at Rolighedsvej 2 (☎98 44 22 00; ⓦwww.skagenvandrerhjem.dk; closed Dec to mid-Feb) has dorms (150kr) and doubles (❸), and is only a couple of minutes west of the town centre. Of the many **campsites**, most accessible are *Grenen*, on the way to Grenen along Fyrvej (☎98 44 25 46, ⓦwww.grenencamping .dk; May to mid-Sept), and *Poul Eeg's* (☎98 44 14 70, ⓦwww.pouleegcamping.dk; May to mid-Sept), on Batterivej (the road to Skagen Odde Naturcenter).

Badepension Marienlund Fabriciusvej 8 ☏ 98 44 13 20, ⊕ www.marienlund.dk. A rustic, romantic thatched cottage a short walk from the centre with a small range of different rooms. Also bike hire. ❹
Brøndum's Hotel Anchervej 3 ☏ 98 44 15 55, ⊕ www.broendums-hotel.dk. Known for its artistic associations, this is by far the most atmospheric spot around; the fact that few of the rooms have their own bathrooms and all are far from luxurious keeps the price of doubles down, but book well ahead in summer. ❹, en suite ❺
Foldens Hotel Skt Laurentii Vej 41 ☏ 98 44 11 66, ⊕ www.foldenshotel.dk. Very comfortable en-suite rooms a stone's throw from the train

station and tourist office. Also a good place to go for a drink, with live music every evening during summer ❻
Hotel Lille Nord Vestre Strandvej 28 ☏ 98 44 67 16, ⊕ www.lille-nord.dk. Luxury accommodation in the old ships' smithy near the harbour, with bright, spacious rooms and a relaxing courtyard which doubles as a bar during summer. ❻
Skagen Sømandshjem Østre Strandvej 2 ☏ 98 44 25 88, ⊕ www.skagenhjem.dk. Next to the harbour, this former seaman's home has a range of basic rooms, some with shared bathrooms. The downstairs cafeteria serves up bargain meals. ❺, en suite ❻

Eating

There are plenty of **eating** options in Skagen – all of the hotels have restaurants, though most of them are expensive. Of the independent places, it's worth splashing out for a meal at the places listed below.

Pakhuset Rødspættevej 6. Set in the architecturally stunning former frozen-fish warehouse, *Pakhuset* serves fabulous fish dishes in its upstairs restaurant, while there's a more informal – and cheaper – café downstairs. Closed Jan.
Restaurant De 2 Have Fyrvej 42. At the tip of Grenen, with a wonderful vista of the two seas, this place provides fine dining in a dramatic setting. Try the superb Skagen shrimp lunchtime smørrebrød for 135kr, or the fried lobster tail with wild mushrooms and lobster bisque for 130kr at dinner.

Skagen Bryghus Kirkevej 10. Microbrewery pub near the town centre, selling a wide range of award winning homebrewed beer. Worth a thorough sampling.
🎣 Skagen Fiskerestaurant Fiskehuskaj 13. In a red wooden shack by the harbour you'll find superb fish dishes on the menu upstairs, and equally delicious fishy snacks in the less formal quayside setting downstairs. Open daily during summer when there's also live music. Oct–March open Thurs–Sat. Cafeteria serves up bargain meals.

Travel details

Silkeborg to: Copenhagen (2 daily; 4hr); Århus (1–2 hourly; 1hr); Viborg (1–2 hourly; 1hr).
Sønderborg to: Fynshav (8 daily; 30min).
Thisted to: Aalborg (8 daily; 1hr 45min); Hanstholm (15 daily; 45min).
Viborg to: Silkeborg (1–2 hourly; 1hr).

Ferries

Århus to: Kalundborg (1–6 daily; 2hr 40min); Odden (6–10 daily; 1hr 5min).
Ebeltoft to: Odden (5–11 daily; 45min).
Esbjerg to: Nordby - Fanø (1–3 hourly; 12min).
Fynshav to: Bøjden (5–9 daily; 50min).

International trains

Århus to: Flensburg (8–9 daily; 3hr); Vejle and Fredericia.

International ferries

Esbjerg to: Harwich (3–4 weekly in summer; 19hr).
Frederikshavn to: Gothenburg (up to 5 daily in summer; 2hr–3hr 15min); Oslo (up to 1 daily in summer; 8hr 30min–12hr).
Grenå to: Varberg (1–3 daily; 4hr).
Hanstholm to: Bergen (3 weekly; 16–18hr) via Egersund (7hr–11hr 30min) and Haugesund (11–13hr); Kristiansand (winter 2 weekly, summer 3 daily; 2–4hr).
Havneby to: List (4–6 daily; 40min).
Hirtshals to: Kristiansand (1–3 daily; 3hr 15min–5hr 30min); Larvik (1–2 daily; 3hr 45min–11hr); Laugesund (1 daily; 6hr 30min).

Norway

Norway highlights

* **Oslo's Viking Ships Museum**
See Viking longships at close hand in this excellent museum. See p.197

* **Oslo's Vigelandsparken**
Whatever you do, don't miss this phantasmagorical open-air sculpture park. See p.198

* **Oslo's Munch Museum**
A huge collection of works from Norway's finest artist. See p.199

* **Jotunheimen National Park** Craggy and severe, this mountain range is the most sumptuously beautiful example of Norway's wild mountain scenery. See p.232

* **Edvard Grieg's Troldhaugen** Norway's most celebrated composer, Grieg lived just outside Bergen and his old house makes for a delightful visit. See p.251

* **Urnes stave church** Viking carvings are seen to exquisite advantage at this country church. See p.270

* **Trondheim** This easygoing, laid-back city with its stirring medieval cathedral provides a taste of urban life before the wilds of the north. See p.287

* **Å** Tiny village at the tip of the Lofoten that's hard to beat, both for its setting and its assortment of eminently nautical nineteenth-century buildings. See p.323

▲ Cross-country skiing in the Jotunheimen National Park

Introduction and Basics

In many ways **Norway** is still a land of unknowns. Quiet for a thousand years since the Vikings stamped their distinctive mark on Europe, the country often seems more than just geographically distant even today. Beyond Oslo and the famous fjords, the rest of Norway might as well be blank for all many visitors know – and, in a manner of speaking, large parts of it are: vast stretches in the north are sparsely populated and starkly vegetated, and it is, at times, possible to travel for hours without seeing a soul.

Despite this isolation, Norway has had a pervasive influence on the world outside. Traditionally its inhabitants were explorers, from the Vikings – the first Europeans to reach Greenland and North America – to more recent figures like Amundsen, Nansen and Heyerdahl. And Norse traditions are common to many other isolated fishing communities, not least northwest Scotland and the Shetlands. At home, too, the Norwegian people have striven to escape the charge of national provincialism, touting the disproportionate number of acclaimed artists, writers and musicians (most notably Munch, Ibsen and Grieg) who have made their mark on the wider European scene. It's also a pleasing discovery that the great outdoors – great though it is – also harbours some lively historic towns.

Where to go

Beyond **Oslo**, one of the world's most prettily positioned capitals, the major cities of interest, in roughly descending order, are: medieval **Trondheim**; **Bergen** on the edge of the western fjords; hilly, southern **Stavanger**; and northern **Tromsø**. All are likeable cities, worth spending time in both for themselves and for the startlingly handsome countryside in which they're set. The perennial draw, though, is the **western fjords** – a must, and every bit as scenically stunning as they're cracked up to be. Dip into the region from Bergen or Åndalsnes, both accessible by direct train from Oslo, or take more time and appreciate the subtleties of the innumerable fjordside towns and villages. Elsewhere, the **south** of Norway has a clutch of pretty old sea ports and the remoter parts of central Norway are great for hiking and camping.

To the **north**, Norway grows increasingly barren. The vast lands of **Troms** and **Finnmark** boast wild and untamed tracts of breathtaking proportions. Here you'll find the Sámi people and their herds of reindeer, which you'll see on the thin, exposed road up to the North Cape, or **Nordkapp** – (nearly) the northernmost point of mainland Europe. The Cape is the natural end to the long trek north, although there are still several hundred kilometres to be explored further east, right the way to Kirkenes and the Russian border.

Norway on the web

ⓦ **www.goscandinavia.com** The official website of the Scandinavian Tourist Board in North America, offering a general introduction to Scandinavia, latest travel deals and links to the Norwegian Tourist Board website.

ⓦ **www.kulturnett.no** Comprehensive information on the country's museums and current exhibitions.

ⓦ **www.regjeringen.no** Government site of ODIN (Official Documentation and Information from Norway); despite the plain presentation, this has everything you ever wanted to know about contemporary Norway and then some. Especially good on political issues.

ⓦ **www.visitnorway.com** The official site of the Norwegian Tourist Board, with links to all things Norwegian and good sections on outdoor activities and events.

When to go

Norway is widely regarded as a remote, cold country – spectacular enough but climatically inhospitable. There is some truth in this of course – and winters are certainly cold – but **when to go** is not as clear-cut a choice as one might imagine. There are advantages to travelling during the long, dark **winters** with their reduced everything: daylight, opening times and transport services. If you are equipped and hardy enough to reach the far north, seeing the phenomenal **northern lights** (aurora borealis) is a distinct possibility; later, once the days begin to get lighter, **skiing** is excellent; while **Easter** is the time of the colourful Sámi festivals. But – especially in the north – it is cold, often bitterly so, and this guide has been deliberately weighted towards the **summer** season, when most people travel and when it is possible to camp and hitch to keep costs down. This is the time of the **midnight sun**: the further north you go, the longer the day becomes, until at Nordkapp the sun is continually visible from mid-May to the end of July. Something worth noting is that the **summer season** in Norway is relatively short, stretching roughly from the beginning of June to mid-August. Come much later than 16 to 20 August and you'll find that tourist offices, museums and other sights cut back their hours, while buses, ferries and trains often switch to reduced schedules.

As regards **temperatures**, January and February are generally the coldest months, July and August the warmest; the Gulf Stream makes the coastal north surprisingly temperate during summer.

The midnight sun

The midnight sun is visible as follows:

Alta: May 16–July 26
Bodø: May 30–July 12
Hammerfest: May 13–July 29
Nordkapp: May 11–July 31
Tromsø: May 18–July 26

Getting there from the rest of Scandinavia

By train

You can reach **Oslo** from both Stockholm (2–3 daily; 6hr) and Copenhagen (3–4 daily; 8–16hr). There are also regular services from Stockholm to **Trondheim** (2 daily; 12–16hr) and **Narvik** (2 daily; 19hr).

By bus

Three main **bus** companies provide services into Norway from other parts of Scandinavia. Eurolines buses from London to Oslo pass through several Danish and Swedish towns, including **Copenhagen**, **Malmo** and **Gothenburg**; Safflebussen has a fast and frequent service from Stockholm to Oslo and also operates buses to Oslo from Copenhagen, Malmo and Gothenburg; and Swebuss runs the same routes as Safflebussen. Note that there are no direct long-distance express buses to Norway from Finland, not even in the far north where the two countries share a common border.

By ferry

A number of car ferries shuttle across the Skagerrak **from Denmark** to Norway. There are sailings to Oslo from Copenhagen with DFDS Seaways (16hr); and from Frederikshavn with Stena Line (8hr 30min–12hr). Color Line links Hirtshals with both Kristiansand (3hr 15min) and Larvik (4hr); and Fjordline sails from Hirtshals to Stavanger and Bergen (12/20hr). There's also a Color Line ferry service to Norway **from Sweden**, linking Strömstad, north of Gothenburg, with Sandefjord, 120km or so from Oslo (2hr 30min).

By plane

Oslo Gardermoen **airport** is the hub of Norway's domestic and international flight network. Scandinavian Airlines, the main carrier (⍟ www.scandinavian.net), has frequent flights to Oslo Gardermoen from Stockholm and Copenhagen. SAS also offers flights from Copenhagen to Ålesund, Bergen, Kristiansand and Stavanger as well as from Stockholm to Stavanger, Bergen and Trondheim. The SAS subsidiary Blue 1 (⍟ www.blue1.com) has flights to Oslo Gardermoen from Helsinki, while a second SAS subsidiary, Wideroe (⍟ www.wideroe .no), has flights from Copenhagen to Sandefjord and Trondheim. SAS's main competitor is the Norwegian Air Shuttle (⍟ www.norwegian.no), which has direct flights from Copenhagen and Stockholm to Oslo Gardermoen. Flying times are insignificant – Copenhagen to Oslo takes 1hr 20min, one hour from Stockholm. To give an idea of fares: Copenhagen to Oslo Gardermoen costs around €50–80, and about the same from Stockholm, both with the Norwegian Air Shuttle.

Getting around

Norway's **public transport system** – a huge mesh of trains, buses, car ferries and passenger express ferries – is comprehensive and reliable. In the winter (especially in the north) services can be cut back severely, but no part of the country is unreachable for long. Bear in mind, however, that Norwegian villages and towns usually spread over a large distance, so don't be surprised if you end up walking a kilometre or two from the bus stop, ferry terminal or train station to get where you want to go. It's this sprawling nature of the country's towns and, more especially, the remoteness of many of the sights, that encourages visitors to **rent a car**. This is an expensive business, but costs can be reduced if you hire locally for a day or two rather than for the whole trip, though in high season spare vehicles can get very thin on the ground.

Timetables for most of the principal train, bus and ferry services are detailed in the *NRI Guide to Transport and Accommodation*, a free and easy-to-use booklet available in your home country from the Norwegian Tourist Board. In Norway itself, almost every tourist office carries a comprehensive range of free local and regional public transport timetables. In addition, all major train stations carry the *NSB Regiontog i Norge*, a brochure detailing Norway's principal train timetables, while long-distance bus routes operated by the national carrier, Nor-Way Bussekspress, are listed in the free *Rutehefte* (timetable), available at principal bus stations. Norwegian public transport timetables are also widely available on the internet, but although the major carriers are easy enough to track down, other companies are more elusive in English, less so if you can read Norwegian; we have provided public transport websites throughout the Guide.

By rail

With the exception of the Narvik line into Sweden, operated by SJ (Sweden: ☏0046/771 75 75 75 ⓦwww.sj.se), all Norwegian **train** services are run by Norges Statsbaner (NSB; dial ☏815 00 888, ⓦwww .nsb.no). Apart from a sprinkling of branch lines, NSB services operate on three main domestic routes, linking Oslo to Stavanger in the southwest, to Bergen in the west and to Trondheim and on to Bodø in the north. In places, the rail system is extended by a *TogBuss* (literally train-bus) service, with connecting coaches continuing on from train terminals. The nature of the country has made several of the routes engineering feats of some magnitude, worth the trip in their own right – the tiny **Flåm line** and the sweeping **Rauma line** from Dombås to Åndalsnes are exciting examples.

Fully flexible, **standard-fare prices** are bearable with the popular Oslo–Bergen run, for example, costing around 740kr one-way, Oslo–Trondheim 820kr – twice that for a return. Both journeys take around six and a half to seven hours; costs can be reduced by purchasing a rail pass in advance (see below). Inside Norway, NSB offers a variety of discount fares. The main discount ticket scheme is the **Minipris** (mini-price), under which you can cut up to fifty percent off the price of long-distance journeys. In general, the further you travel, the more economic they become. The drawback is that Minipris tickets must be purchased at least one day in advance, are not available at peak periods and on certain trains, and stopovers are not permitted. In addition, NSB offers a variety of special deals and discounts – inquire locally (and ahead of time) for details on any specific route.

In terms of **concessionary fares**, there are group and family reductions; children under 4 travel free; 4 to 15 year olds pay half-fare, and so do senior citizens (67+) and the disabled. It's worth noting that on many intercity trains and on all overnight and international services, an **advance seat reservation** is compulsory whether you have a rail pass or not. In high season it's wise to reserve a seat on main routes anyway, as trains can be packed. **Sleepers** (*sove*) are reasonably priced at 750kr if you consider you'll save a night's hotel accommodation.

NSB have two main sorts of train – local (*Lokaltog*) and regional (Regiontog). There is one standard **class** on both, but certain regional trains have a "*Komfort*" (read more luxurious, spacious) carriage, for which you pay a supplement of 75kr. General NSB **timetables** are available free at every train station and there are individual route timetables too. In the case of the more scenic routes, there are also leaflets describing the sights as you go.

The **Norway Rail Pass**, for non-European residents only, allows unlimited travel on all NSB services (except the Oslo Airport Express) on a specified number of days within a specific period. Three days in one month cost 1830kr, four days 1980kr, six days 2490kr and eight days 2770kr. This pass should be purchased before you arrive in Europe – most readily from Rail Europe (see p.34). Children under 4 travel free and there are substantial discounts for the under-26s and the over-60s. All rail-pass holders have to shell out a small additional surcharge on certain trains on certain routes, and also have to pay the compulsory **seat reservation fee** on many intercity trains and all overnight and international services. On the plus side, rail passes are good for travel on connecting

Togbuss services and two of them (Eurail, and Inter-Rail) give a fifty-percent discount on specified intercity bus and boat routes.

By bus

Both supplementing – and on occasion duplicating – the train network, **buses** reach almost every corner of the country. Costs are passable – especially as all tolls and ferry costs are included in the price of a ticket – and bus travel is almost invariably less expensive than the train, but prices are still fairly high. For instance, the ten-hour bus ride between Ålesund and Bergen, costs 600kr, the seven-hour trip from Oslo to Haugesund 560kr. Most long-distance buses are operated by the leading national carrier, **Nor-Way Bussekspress** (☎815 44 444, ⍟www .nor way.no). Supplementing these services is a dense network of **local buses**, whose timetables are available at most tourist offices and bus stations as well as on the internet. In the more mountainous regions, many local buses only run in June, July and August. **Tickets** are usually bought on board, but bus stations do sell advance tickets on some of the more popular long-distance routes.

In terms of **concessionary fares**, there are group and family reductions; children under 4 travel free; and youngsters (under 16) plus seniors (over 67) pay half-fare. Nor-Way Bussekspress also offers Inter-Rail pass holders a fifty-percent reduction on certain services and some local bus companies have comparable deals. Indeed, rail-pass and student-card holders should always ask about discounts when purchasing a ticket.

By ferry

Using a **ferry** is one of the highlights of any visit to Norway – indeed, among the western fjords and around the Lofoten Islands they are all but impossible to avoid. The majority are roll-on, roll-off **car ferries**. These represent an economical means of transport, with **prices** fixed on a nationwide sliding scale: short journeys (10–20min) cost foot passengers 20–30kr, whereas car and driver will pay 50–100kr. Ferry procedures are straightforward: foot passengers walk on and pay the conductor, car drivers usually wait in line with their vehicles on the jetty till the conductor comes to the car window to collect the money – although some busier routes have a drive-by ticket office. One or two of the longer car ferries – in particular Bodø–Moskenes – take **advance reservations**, but the rest operate on a first-come, first-served basis. In the off season, there's no real need to arrive more than twenty minutes before departure – with the possible exception of the Lofoten Islands ferries – but in the summer allow two hours, or two and a half hours to be really safe.

Hurtigbåt passenger express boats

Norway's **Hurtigbåt passenger express boats** are catamarans that make up in speed what they lack for in enjoyment: unlike in ordinary ferries, you're cooped up and have to view the passing landscape through a window, and in choppy seas the ride can be disconcertingly bumpy. Nonetheless, they're a convenient time-saving option: it takes just four hours on the Hurtigbåt service from Bergen to Balestrand, for instance, the same from Narvik to Svolvær, and a mere two and a half hours from Harstad to Tromsø. Hurtigbåt services are concentrated on the west coast around Bergen and the neighbouring fjords; the majority operate all year. There's no fixed tariff table, so **fares** vary considerably, though Hurtigbåt boats are significantly more expensive per kilometre than car ferries; Bergen–Flåm, for instance, costs 625kr for the five-and-a-half-hour journey, 720kr for the four-hour trip from Bergen to Stavanger. There are **concessionary fares** on all routes, with infants up to the age of 3 travelling free, and children (4–15) and senior citizens (over 67) getting a fifty-percent discount. In addition, rail-pass holders and students are often eligible for a fifty-percent reduction on the full adult rate and on some routes you get a similar discount for reservations on the internet.

The Hurtigrute

Norway's most celebrated ferry journey is the long and beautiful haul up the coast from Bergen to Kirkenes on the **Hurtigrute** (literally "rapid route"; ⍟www.hurtigruten.com) **coastal boat** – or "coastal steamer". In honour of its past rather than present means of locomotion. To many, the Hurtigrute remains the quintessential Norwegian experience, and it's certainly the best way to observe the drama of the country's extraordinary coastline. Twelve ships combine to provide one daily service in each direction, and the boats stop off at over thirty ports on the way.

The whole round-trip lasts thirteen days (and twelve nights), and in peak season (June & July) the one-way **fare** from Bergen to end-of-the-line Kirkenes is 13,000kr per person in a twin-bed cabin, forty percent less in the depths of winter, including all meals. There are, however, all sorts of special deals for early reservations and so forth – see the website for details. Making a Hurtigrute booking within Norway is easy too, either on the website, by phone (☏810 30 000), or via most west-coast tourist offices.

A **short or medium-sized hop** along the coast on a portion of the Hurtigrute route is also well worth considering. **Port-to-port fares** are not particularly cheap, especially in comparison with the bus, but they are affordable providing you are not sleeping on board, in which case you are required to have a cabin. The standard, mid-season (spring or autumn), one-way passenger fare from Harstad to Tromsø (6hr 30min), for example, costs 453kr without a cabin or meals, 849kr in high season; breakfast cost an extra 105kr, lunch 225kr and dinner 320kr. This compares very favourably with the cost of the 24-hour yomp from Trondheim to Bodø, which costs 2526kr per person in high season, including a berth in a cabin and breakfast – but not dinner or lunch. Last-minute bargains, however, can bring the rates down to amazingly low levels and there are often substantial, one-off discounts in winter too. All the tourist offices in the Hurtigrute ports have the latest details and should be willing to telephone the captain of the nearest ship to make a reservation on your behalf.

As for specifics, sleeping in the lounges is no longer allowed and bikes travel free. There are luggage racks and laundry as well as a restaurant and a 24-hour cafeteria supplying coffee and snacks on all Hurtigrute boats; the restaurant is very popular, so reserve a table as soon as you board.

Planes

Domestic flights can prove a surprisingly inexpensive way of hopping about Norway,

and are especially useful if you're short on time and want to reach, say, the far north: Tromsø to Kirkenes takes the best part of two days by bus, but it's just an hour by plane. Domestic air routes are serviced by several companies, but the major carrier is **SAS** (ⓦ www.sas.no), a conglomerate with many (airline) subsidiaries. A standard one-way fare with SAS from Oslo to Trondheim costs in the region of 620kr, while an air fare from Oslo to Tromsø is around 770kr. SAS also offer all sorts of deals and discounts, especially on return fares, which often cost just ten percent more than one-way tickets, but these bargains usually come with restrictions, regarding, for example, advance booking. In terms of **concessionary fares**, SAS permits infants under 2 to travel free, while children under the age of 16 receive a 25 percent discount on most flights, providing they are travelling in a group that includes at least one full-fare-paying adult. The details of these various discounts vary from year to year, so it's always worth checking them out.

You might also want to check out the special deals offered by Widerøe (ⓦ www.wideroe.no), a subsidiary of SAS, which specializes in internal flights. It flies to 35 Norwegian airports, mostly in the north, and, amongst its several offerings, it does an 'ODD' one-way ticket on all of their domestic flights for just 350kr. Another good bet is the budget airline **Norwegian Airlines** (ⓦ www.norwegian.no), which operates flights between twelve domestic airports at what can be staggeringly low prices – Bergen to Oslo, for example, for just 400kr.

Driving

Norway's **main roads** are excellent, especially when you consider the rigours of the climate, and nowadays, with most of the more hazardous sections either ironed out or tunnelled through, driving is comparatively straightforward. Nonetheless, you still have to be careful on some of the higher sections and in the longer, fume-filled **tunnels**. Once you leave the main roads for the narrow **mountain byroads**, however, you'll be in for some nail-biting experiences – and that's in the summertime. In winter the Norwegians close many roads and concentrate their efforts on keeping the main highways open, but obviously blizzards and ice can make driving difficult to dangerous anywhere, even with winter tyres, studs and chains. At any time of the year, the more adventurous the drive, the better equipped you need to be: on remote drives you should pack provisions, have proper hiking gear, check the car thoroughly before departure, carry a spare can of petrol and take a mobile phone.

Norway's main highways have an E prefix – E6, E18, etc; all the country's other significant roads (*riksvei*, or rv) are assigned a number and, as a general rule, the lower the number, the busier the road. In our guide, we've used the E prefix, but designated other roads as Highways, or "Hwy" (followed by the number). The E-roads are the nearest thing Norway has to motorways, but only rarely are they dual carriageways and they are often interrupted by roundabouts and even traffic lights. **Tolls** are imposed on certain roads to pay for construction projects such as bridges, tunnels and motorway improvements. Once the costs are covered the toll is normally removed. The older projects levy a fee of around 15–30kr, but the toll for some of the newer works runs to well over 100kr per vehicle. There's also a modest toll on entering the country's larger cities (15–20kr), but whether this is an environmental measure or a means of boosting city coffers is a moot point.

Paying on a toll road

On most **toll roads**, you simply pay at the toll booth, but at others drivers are presented with three lanes and choices: the *abonnement* lanes (with blue signs) are for passholders only and are always on the left; the *mynt/coin* lanes (with yellow signs) are for exact cash payments only and usually have a bucket-shaped receptacle where you throw your money; and the *manuell* lanes (grey) are also used for cash payments, but provide change. The busiest toll roads, like those into Oslo and Bergen, are now automatic – and are signed *automatisk bomstasjon*. At these, all number plates are read electronically and an invoice is sent to either the car hire company concerned or the registered owner of the vehicle wherever they may be.

To avoid getting flustered at toll booths, Norwegians tend to carry a supply of coins ready to hand. Finally, there's often a modest toll of 10–20kr on privately maintained country roads; drivers are expected to deposit their money in a roadside **honesty box**, and these are easy to spot.

Fuel, documentation and rules of the road

Fuel is readily available, even in the north of Norway, though here the settlements are so widely separated that you'll need to keep your tank pretty full; if you're using the byroads extensively, remember to carry an extra can. Current fuel prices are 12–15kr a litre, and there are four main grades, all unleaded (*blyfri*): 95 octane; 98 octane; super 98 octane; and diesel. It's worth remembering that some petrol stations don't accept credit cards, so be sure to double-check before filling up.

Opening dates of major mountain passes

Obviously enough, there's no preordained date for the opening of **mountain roads** in the springtime – it depends on the weather, and the threat of avalanches is often much more of a limitation than actual snowfalls. The dates below should therefore be treated with caution; if in doubt, seek advice from a local tourist office. If you do head along a mountain road that's closed, sooner or later you'll come to a barrier and have to turn round.

E6: Dovrefjell (Oslo–Trondheim). Usually open all year.

E69: Skarsvåg–Nordkapp. Closed late October to April.

E134: Haukelifjell (Oslo–Bergen/Stavanger). Usually open all year.

Hwy 7: Hardangervidda (Oslo–Bergen). Usually open all year.

Hwy 51: Valdresflya. Closed December to early May.

Hwy 55: Sognefjellet. Closed November to early May.

Hwy 63: Grotli–Geiranger–Åndalsnes (Trollstigen). Closed mid-October to May.

All EU/EEA **driving licences** are honoured in Norway, but other nationals will need – or are recommended to have – an **International Driver's Licence** (available at minimal cost from your home motoring organization). No form of provisional licence is accepted. If you're **bringing your own car**, you must have vehicle registration papers, adequate insurance, a first-aid kit, a warning triangle and a green card (available from your insurers or motoring organization). Extra insurance coverage for unforeseen legal costs is also well worth having, as is an appropriate **breakdown policy** from a motoring organization. In Britain, for example, the AA charges members and non-members about £100 for a month's Europe-wide breakdown cover, with all the appropriate documentation, including green card, provided.

Norway has strict **rules of the road**: you drive on the right, with dipped headlights required at all times; seat belts are compulsory for drivers and front-seat passengers, and for back-seat passengers too, if fitted. There's a speed limit of 30kph in residential areas, 50kph in built-up areas, 80kph on open roads and 80kph, 90kph or sometimes 100kph on E-roads. In parts of the country, but not the western fjords, **speed cameras** monitor hundreds of kilometres of road – watch out for the *Automatisk Trafikkontroll* warning signs – and they are far from popular with the locals: there are all sorts of folkloric (and largely apocryphal) tales of men in masks appearing at night with chainsaws to chop them down. Speeding fines are so heavy that local drivers stick religiously within the speed limit. If you're filmed breaking the limit in a hire car, expect your credit card to be stung by the car hire company to the tune of at least 600kr and a maximum of 7800kr (yes, that's right). If you're stopped for speeding, large spot fines are payable within the same price range and, if you are way over the limit (say 60kph in a 30kph zone) you could well end up in jail; rarely is any leniency shown to unwitting foreigners. **Drunken driving** is also severely frowned upon. You can be asked to take a breath test on a routine traffic-check; if you're over the limit, you will have your licence confiscated and may face a stretch in prison. It is also an offence to drive while using a hand-held mobile/cell phone. On-street parking restrictions are rigorously enforced and clearly signed with a white 'P' on a blue background; below the 'P' are the hours where parking restrictions apply – Monday to Friday first and Saturday in brackets afterwards; below this are any particular limits – most commonly denoting the maximum (*maks*) number of hours (*timer*) – and then there's *mot avgift*, which means there's a fee to pay at the meter.

If you **break down** in a hire car, you'll get roadside assistance from the particular repair company the car hire firm has contracted. This is a free service, though some car hire companies charge you if you need help changing a tyre in the expectation that you should be able to do it yourself. The same principles work with your own vehicle's breakdown policy. Two major **breakdown companies** in Norway are Norges Automobil-Forbund and Viking Redningstjeneste, who combine to operate a 24-hour emergency assistance line on ☏810 00 505. There are emergency telephones along some E-roads, and NAF trucks patrol all mountain passes between mid-June and mid-August.

Car rental

All the major international **car rental** companies are represented in Norway. To rent a car, you'll need to be 21 or over (and have been driving for at least a year), and you'll need a credit card. Rental **charges** are fairly high, beginning at around 3500kr per week for unlimited mileage in the smallest vehicle, but include collision damage waiver and vehicle (but not personal) insurance. To cut costs, watch for special local deals – a Friday to Monday weekend rental might, for example, cost you as little as 800kr. Bear in mind, too, that one-way car rental **drop-off charges** are almost always wallet-searing: if you pick up a car in Oslo and drop it in Bodø, it will cost you 6000kr – nearer 8000kr in Tromsø.

Cycling

Cycling is a great way to enjoy Norway's scenery – just be sure to wrap up warm and dry, and don't be overambitious in the distances you expect to cover. Cycle tracks as such are few and far between, and are mainly confined to the larger towns, but there's precious little traffic on most of the minor roads, and cycling along them is a popular pastime. Furthermore, whenever a road is improved or rerouted, the old highway is usually redesigned as a cycle route. At almost every place you're likely to stay in, you can anticipate that someone will **rent bikes** – either the tourist office, a sports shop, youth hostel or campsite. Costs are pretty uniform: reckon on paying between 120kr and 200kr a day for a seven-speed bike, plus a refundable deposit of up to 1000kr; mountain bikes are about thirty percent more.

A few tourist offices have maps of recommended **cycling routes**, but this is a rarity. It is, however, important to check your itinerary thoroughly, especially in the more mountainous areas. Cyclists aren't allowed through the longer tunnels for their own protection (the fumes can be life-threatening), so discuss your plans with whoever you hire the bike from. With regard to bike carriage, bikes mostly go free on car ferries and attract a nominal charge on passenger express boats, but buses vary. National carrier Nor-Way Bussekspress (W www.norway .no) accepts bikes only when there is space and charges a child fare, while local rural buses sometimes take them free, sometimes charge and sometimes do not take them at all. Taking a bike on an NSB train (W www .nsb.no) costs ten percent of the price of your ticket with a minimum price of 57kr; on some services, you have to make an advance reservation.

The **Norwegian Cyclist Association**, Syklistenes Landsforening, Storgata 23D, Oslo (T 22 47 30 42, W www.slf.no) has an excellent range of specific cycling **books** and **maps**, some of which are in English. Finally, the website Sykkelturisme i Norge (W www .bike-norway.com) has ideas for a dozen routes around the country from 100km to 400km, plus useful practical information about road conditions, repair facilities and places of interest en route.

Accommodation

Inevitably, **accommodation** is one of the major expenses you will incur on a trip to Norway – indeed, if you're after a degree of comfort, it's going to be the costliest item by far. There are, however, **budget alternatives**, principally guesthouses (*pensjonater*), rooms in private houses (broadly this is bed and breakfast arranged via the local tourist office), campsites and cabins, and last but certainly not least, an abundance of HI-registered hostels. Also bear in mind that many hotels offer special deals as well as substantial weekend discounts of 25–40 percent.

Almost everywhere, you can **reserve ahead** easily enough by calling or emailing the establishment direct; English is almost always spoken. Most tourist offices also operate an on-the-spot service for same-night accommodation either free or at minimal charge.

Hotels

Almost universally, Norwegian **hotels** are of a high standard: neat, clean and efficient. Special bargains and impromptu weekend deals also make many of them, by European standards at least, comparatively economical. Another plus is that the price of a hotel room always includes a buffet breakfast – in mid- to top-range hotels especially, these can be sumptuous banquets. The only negatives are the sizes of rooms, which tend to be small – singles especially – and their sameness: Norway abounds in mundanely modern, concrete and glass sky-rise chain hotels.

Prices are very sensitive to demand – a double room that costs 1000kr when a hotel is slack, soon hits the 2000kr mark if there's a rush on. Generally speaking, however, 1200kr should cover the cost of two people in a double room at most hotels most of the time, nearer to 1000kr at the weekend, slightly more in Oslo. Typically, the stated price includes breakfast.

Hotel and guesthouse passes

One way to cut costs is to join one of Norway's **hotel discount and pass schemes**, though this will put paid to any idea you might have of a flexible itinerary as advance reservation is a pre-requisite. Most Norwegian hotels are members of one discount/pass scheme or another, and you can usually join the scheme at any one of them or in advance on the internet. There

Accommodation price codes

All the accommodation listed in the Norway chapters of this Guide has been graded according to the following price bands, based on the cost of the **least expensive double room during the high season** (usually June to mid-Aug). However, almost every hotel offers seasonal and/or weekend discounts, which can reduce the rate by one or even two grades. Wherever hotels have an **official off-peak** or **weekend rate** we've given two bands, covering both the lower, special rate and the regular rate (ie ④/⑤). Single rooms, where available, usually cost between 60 and 80 percent of a double. At hostels, we have also given the price of a dormitory bed.

① 600kr and under	④ 1001–1200kr	⑦ 1601–1800kr
② 601–800kr	⑤ 1201–1400kr	⑧ 1801–2000kr
③ 801–1000kr	⑥ 1401–1600kr	⑨ 2001kr and over

are half a dozen major schemes to choose from and, although the majority are tied to a particular hotel chain, this is not the case with the **Fjord Pass** (☎815 68 222, ⓦwww .fjord-pass.com), which offers discounts of around 20 percent at 170 hotels, guesthouses, cottages and apartments all over Norway with a particular concentration in the western fjords. The Fjord Pass card costs just 120kr and is valid for two adults and children under the age of 15 for the whole year in which it is purchased. Under the scheme, you can either book online with the place you want to stay at or leave it to the booking service of the company who run the scheme, the exemplary Fjord Tours (ⓦwww .fjordtours.com). The discount card itself can be bought direct from Fjord Tours, at participating hotels, or at the sales outlets detailed on the website.

Pensions, guesthouses and inns

For something a little less anonymous than the average hotel, **pensions** (*pensjonater*) are your best bet – small, sometimes intimate guesthouses, which can usually be found in the larger cities and more touristy towns. Rooms go for 650–750kr single, 700–800kr double, and breakfast is generally extra. Broadly comparable in price and character is a *gjestgiveri* or *gjestehus*, a **guesthouse** or **inn**, though some of these offer superb lodgings in historic premises with prices to match. Facilities in all of these establishments are usually adequate and homely without being overwhelmingly comfortable; at the least expensive places you'll share a

bathroom with others. Some pensions and guesthouses also have kitchens available for the use of guests, which means you're very likely to meet other residents – a real boon (perhaps) if you're travelling alone.

Hostels

For many budget travellers, as well as hikers, climbers and skiers, the country's **HI hostels** (*vandrerhjem*; ⓦwww.vandrerhjem.no) are the accommodation mainstay. There are around seventy in total, with handy concentrations in the western fjords, the central hiking and skiing regions and in Oslo. The Norwegian hostelling association, **Norske Vandrerhjem**, has its headquarters in Oslo (☎23 12 45 10). It maintains an excellent website – where you can make bookings at any hostel – and publishes a free booklet, *Norske Vandrerhjem*, which details locations, opening dates, prices and telephone numbers; the booklet is available at most hostels. The hostels themselves are almost invariably excellent – the only quibble, at the risk of being churlish, is that those occupying schools tend to be rather drab and institutional.

Prices for a single bed per night range from 170kr to 220kr with the more expensive hostels nearly always including a grand breakfast. Where breakfast isn't included, it will cost you around 90kr extra; many hostels also offer a hot evening meal at around 110–140kr. Bear in mind also that almost all hostels have at least a few regular double and family rooms: at 450–700kr a double, these are among the least expensive rooms you'll find in Norway. If you're not an HI member you can still use the hostels, though there's a surcharge of 15 percent. If you don't have your own sheet sleeping bag, you'll mostly have to rent bedsheets for around 40–50kr a time.

It cannot be stressed too strongly that **reserving** a hostel bed will save you lots of unnecessary legwork. Many hostels are only open from mid-June to mid-August and many close between 11am and 4pm. There's sometimes an 11pm or midnight curfew, though this isn't a huge drawback in a country where carousing is so expensive. Where breakfast is included – as it usually is – ask for a breakfast packet if you have to leave early to catch transport; otherwise note that hostel **meals** are nearly always excellent value, though of variable quality, ranging from the bland and filling to the delicious. Most, though not all, hostels have small **kitchens**, but often no pots, pans, cutlery or crockery, so self-caterers should take their own.

Rooms in private houses

Tourist offices in the larger towns and the more touristy settlements can often fix you up with a **private room** in someone's house, possibly including kitchen facilities. Prices are competitive – from 300–350kr per single, 400–500kr per double – though there's usually a reservation fee (30–35kr) on top, and the rooms themselves are frequently some way out of the centre. Nonetheless, they're often the best bargain available and, in certain instances, an improvement on the local hostel. Where this is the case, we've said so in the Guide. If you don't have a sleeping bag, check the room comes with bedding – not all of them do; and if you're cooking for yourself, a few basic utensils may not go amiss.

Camping

Camping is a popular pastime in Norway, and there are literally hundreds of sites to choose from – anything from a field with a few tent pitches to extensive complexes with all mod cons. The Norwegian tourist authorities detail several hundred campsites in their free *Norway Camping* brochure (also online at ⓦ www.camping.no), classifying them on a one- to five-star grading depending on the facilities offered (and not on the aesthetics and/or the location). Most sites are situated with the motorist (rather than the cyclist or

walker) in mind, and a good few occupy key locations beside the main roads, though in summer these prime sites can be inundated by seasonal workers. The vast majority of campsites have at least a few cabins or chalets, called *hytter* – see below.

The majority of campsites are two- and three-star establishments, where prices are usually per tent, plus a small charge per person and then for vehicles; on average expect to pay around 200–250kr for two people using a tent and with a car, though four- and five-star sites average around twenty percent more. During peak season it can be a good idea to **reserve ahead** if you have a car and a large tent or trailer; contact details are listed online, in the free camping booklet and, in some cases, in this Guide. The Scandinavia **Camping Card** brings faster registration at many campsites across Scandinavia and occasionally entitles the bearer to special camping rates. It is valid for one year, costs 120kr and can be purchased from participating campsites or online at ⓦ www.camping.no.

Camping rough in Norway is a tradition enshrined in law. You can camp anywhere in open areas as long as you are at least 150m away from any houses or cabins. As a courtesy, ask farmers for permission to use their land – it is rarely refused. Fires are not permitted in woodland areas or in fields between April 15 and September 15, and camper vans are not allowed (ever) to overnight in lay-bys. A good sleeping bag is essential, since even in summer it can get very cold, and, in the north at least, mosquito repellent is absolutely vital.

Cabins

The Norwegian countryside is dotted with thousands of timber **cabins/chalets** (called *hytter*), ranging from simple wooden huts through to comfortable lodges. They are usually two- or four-bedded affairs, with full kitchen facilities and sometimes a bathroom, even TV, but not necessarily **bed linen**. Some hostels have them on their grounds, there are nearly always at least a handful at every campsite, and in the Lofoten Islands they are the most popular form of accommodation, many occupying refurbished fishermen's huts called *rorbuer*. **Costs** vary enormously, depending on location, size and amenities, and there are significant seasonal variations, too. However, a four-bed *hytter* will rarely cost more than 800kr per night – a more usual average would be about 600kr. If you're travelling in a group, they are easily the cheapest way to see the countryside – and in some comfort. Hundreds of *hytter* are also rented out as holiday cottages by the week.

Mountain huts

One further option for hikers is the **mountain huts** (again called *hytter*), which are strategically positioned on every major hiking route. Some are privately run, but the majority are operated by **Den Norske Turistforening** (DNT), and although you don't have to be a member of DNT to use their huts, you'll soon recoup your outlay (membership costs 480kr a year per adult) through reduced hut charges for members. For members staying in staffed huts, a bunk in a dormitory costs 120kr, a family or double room 220kr per person; meals start at 90kr for breakfast, 210kr for a three-course dinner. At unstaffed huts, where you leave the money for your stay in a box provided, an overnight stay costs 170kr.

Lighthouses

The **Norsk Fyrhistorisk Forening** (Norwegian Lighthouse Association; Ⓦ www.light houses.no) has taken the lead in preserving and conserving the country's **lighthouses**. Norway's coastal waters are notoriously treacherous and in the second half of the nineteenth century scores of lighthouses were built from one end of the country to the other. Initially, they were manned, but from the 1950s onwards they were mechanized and the old lighthousemen's quarters risked falling into decay. The Norsk Fyrhistorisk Forening is keen for new uses to be found for these quarters and already around forty are open to the public for overnight stays or day-trips – and more will follow. Some of these forty lighthouses can be reached by road, but others can only be reached by boat and, with one or two lavish exceptions, the **accommodation** on offer – where it is on offer – is fairly frugal and inexpensive with **doubles** averaging around 600kr. The

reward is the scenery – almost by definition these lighthouses occupy some of the wildest locations imaginable. A few of the forty are mentioned in our Guide, including Ryvingen Fyr (see p.215) and Lindesnes Fyr (see p.216).

Food and drink

At its best, **Norwegian food** can be excellent: fish is plentiful, and carnivores can have a field day trying meats like reindeer and elk or even, conscience permitting, seal and whale. Admittedly it's not inexpensive, and those on a tight budget may have problems varying their diet, but by exercising a little prudence in the face of the average menu (which is almost always in Norwegian and English), you can keep costs down to reasonable levels. Vegetarians, however, will have slim pickings (except in Oslo), and drinkers will have to dig very deep into their pockets to maintain much of an intake. Indeed, most drinkers end up visiting the supermarkets and state off-licences (Vinmonopolet) so that they can sup away at home (in true Norwegian style) before setting out for the evening.

Food

Many travellers to Norway exist almost entirely on a mixture of picnic food and by cooking their own meals, with the odd café meal thrown in to boost morale. Frankly, this isn't really necessary (except on the tightest of budgets), as there are a number of ways to eat out inexpensively. To begin with, a good self-service buffet breakfast, served in almost every hostel and hotel, goes some way to solving the problem, while special lunch deals will get you a tasty hot meal for 100–150kr. Finally, alongside the regular restaurants – which are expensive – there's the usual array of budget pizzerias, cafeterias and café-bars in most towns.

Breakfast, picnics and snacks

More often than not, **breakfast** (*frokost*) in Norway is a substantial self-service affair of bread, crackers, cheese, eggs, preserves, cold meat and fresh and pickled fish, washed down with tea and ground coffee.

It's usually first-rate at youth hostels, and often memorable in hotels, filling you up for the day for 100–130kr when and wherever it's not thrown in with the price of your room as it mostly is. If you're buying your own **picnic food**, bread, cheese, yoghurt and local fruit are all relatively good value, but other staple foodstuffs – rice, pasta, meat, cereals and vegetables – can be way above the European average. Anything tinned is particularly dear (with the exception of fish), but coffee and tea are quite reasonably priced. **Supermarkets** are ten-a-penny.

As ever, **fast food** offers the best chance of a hot, bargain-basement takeaway snack. The indigenous Norwegian stuff, served up from street kiosks or stalls – **gatekjøkken** – in every town, consists mainly of rubbery hot dogs (*varm pølse*), while pizza slices and chicken pieces and chips are much in evidence too. American burger bars are also creeping in – both at motorway service stations and in the towns and cities. A better choice, if rather more expensive, is simply to get a sandwich, normally a huge open affair called a **smørbrød** (pronounced "smurrbrur"), heaped with a variety of garnishes. You'll see them groaning with meat or shrimps, salad and mayonnaise in the windows of bakeries and cafés, or in the newer, trendier sandwich bars in the cities.

Good **coffee** is available everywhere, rich and strong, and served black or with cream. **Tea**, too, is ubiquitous, but the local preference is for lemon tea or a variety of flavoured infusions; if you want milk, ask for it. All the familiar **soft drinks** are also available.

Lunch and dinner

For the best deals, you're going to have to eat your main meal of the day at lunch or possibly tea time, when **kafeterias** (often self-service restaurants) lay on daily specials, the *dagens rett*. This is a fish or meat dish served with potatoes and a vegetable or salad, often including a drink, sometimes bread, and occasionally coffee, too; it should go for 100–150kr. Dipping into the menu is more expensive, but not cripplingly so if you stick to omelettes and suchlike. You'll find *kafeterias* hidden above shops and offices and adjoining hotels in larger towns, where they might be called *kaffistovas*. Most close

at around 6pm, and many don't open at all on Sunday. As a general rule, the food these places serve is plain-verging-on-the-ordinary (though there are exceptions), but the same cannot be said of the continental-style **café-bars** which abound in Oslo and, increasingly, in all of Norway's larger towns and cities. These eminently affordable establishments offer much tastier and much more adventurous meals like pasta dishes, salads and vegetarian options with main courses in the region of 160–200kr. Slightly different again are the **coffee houses** which have sprung up in all of Norway's cities and towns; the big deal here is the coffee and although many also offer light bites, few do it especially well.

In all of the cities, there are first-class **restaurants**, serving dinner (*middag*) in quite formal – and/or smart and chic – surroundings. Apart from exotica such as reindeer and elk, the one real speciality is the seafood, simply prepared and wonderfully fresh – whatever you do, don't go home without treating yourself at least once. In the smaller towns and villages, gourmets will be harder pressed – many of the restaurants are pretty mundane, though the general standard is improving rapidly. Main courses begin at around 220kr, starters and desserts at around 110kr. If in doubt, smoked salmon comes highly recommended, as does catfish and monkfish. Again, the best deals are at lunchtime, though some restaurants don't open till the evening. In the western fjords, look out also for the help-yourself, **all-you-can-eat buffets** available in many of the larger hotels from around 6pm; go early to get the best choice and expect to pay around 300–350kr to be confronted by mounds of pickled herring, salmon (*laks*), cold cuts of meat, a feast of breads and crackers, and usually a few hot dishes too – meatballs, soup and scrambled eggs.

In the towns, and especially in Oslo, there is also a sprinkling of **non-Scandinavian restaurants**, mostly Italian with a good helping of Chinese and Indian places. Other cuisines pop up here and there, too – Japanese, Moroccan and Persian to name but three.

Most restaurants have **bilingual menus** (in Norwegian and English), but we have provided a **menu reader** (see p.705).

Vegetarians

Vegetarians are in for a hard time. Apart from a handful of specialist restaurants in the big cities, there's little option other than to make do with salads, look out for egg dishes in *kafeterias* and supplement your diet from supermarkets. If you are a **vegan** the problem is greater: when the Norwegians are not eating meat and fish, they are attacking a fantastic selection of milks, cheeses and yoghurts. At least you'll know what's in every dish you eat, since everyone speaks English. If you're self-catering, look for **health food shops** (*helsekost*), found in some of the larger towns and cities.

Drink

One of the less savoury sights in Norway – and especially common in the north – is the fall-over drunk: you can spot one at any time of the day or night zigzagging along the street, a strangely disconcerting counter to the usual stereotype of the Norwegian as a healthy, hearty figure in a wholesome woolly jumper. For reasons that remain obscure – or at least culturally complex – many Norwegians can't just have a drink or two, but have to get absolutely wasted. The majority of their compatriots deplore such behaviour and have consequently imposed what amounts to alcoholic rationing: thus, although booze is readily available in the bars and restaurants, it's taxed up to the eyeballs and the distribution of wines and spirits is strictly controlled by a state-run monopoly, **Vinmonopolet**. Whether this paternalistic type of control makes matters better or worse is a moot point, but the majority of Norwegians support it.

What to drink

If you decide to splash out on a few drinks, you'll find Norwegian **beer** is lager-like and characteristically uninspiring; major brands include Hansa and Ringsnes. There's no domestically produced **wine** to speak of and most **spirits** are imported, too, but one local brew worth experimenting with at least once is **aquavit** (*akevitt*), a bitter concoction served ice-cold in little glasses and, at forty percent proof or more, real headache material – though it's more palatable with

beer chasers: Linie aquavit, made in Norway from potatoes, is one of the more popular brands.

Where to buy alcohol

Beer is sold in supermarkets and shops all over Norway, though some local communities, particularly in the west, have their own rules and restrictions; at around 25kr per third of a litre, the supermarket price is about seventy percent of the price you'd pay in a bar. The strongest beers, along with **wines and spirits**, can only be purchased from the state-run **Vinmonopolet** (Ⓦ www.vinmono polet.no) shops. There's generally one branch in each medium-size town and many more in each of Norway's cities. Specific opening hours are given in the Guide, but characteristically they are Monday to Friday 10am to 4/6pm and Saturday 10am–1/3pm; they all close on public holidays. At Vinmonopolet stores, wine is quite a bargain, from 70kr a bottle, and there's generally a wide choice.

Where to drink

Wherever you **go for a drink**, a third of a litre of beer should cost between 35kr and 45kr, and a glass of wine from 30kr. You can get a drink at most outdoor cafés, in restaurants and at bars, pubs and cocktail bars, but only in the towns and cities is there any kind of "European" bar life: in Oslo, Bergen, Stavanger, Trondheim and Tromsø you will be able to keep drinking in bars until at least 1am, 3.30am in some places.

The media

You can buy British and some American daily newspapers, plus the occasional periodical, in any major Norwegia n city, but elsewhere things are very patchy. The most likely outlets are the Narvesen kiosks at train stations and airports. Most hotels have cable or satellite TV access.

The press

British newspapers – from tabloid through to broadsheet – as well as the more popular **English-language magazines** are widely available either on the day of publication or the day after in all major Norwegian cities, along with internationally distributed **American newspapers** – principally the *Wall Street Journal*, *USA Today* and the *International Herald Tribune*.

As for the **Norwegian press**, state advertising, loans and subsidized production costs sustain a wealth of smaller papers that would bite the dust elsewhere. Most are closely linked with political parties, although the bigger city-based titles tend to be independent. The most popular newspapers in Oslo are the independent *Verdens Gang* and the independent-conservative *Aftenposten*; in Bergen it's the liberal *Bergens Tidende*. *Aftenposten* runs a very competent English-language summary of Norwegian news on the web (Ⓦ www.aftenposten.no/english).

Norway's **television network** has expanded over the last few years in line with the rest of Europe. Alongside the state channels, NRK1, NRK2 and TV2, there are satellite channels like TV Norge, while TV3 is a channel common to Norway, Denmark and Sweden; you can also pick up Swedish TV in many parts of the country. Many of the programmes are English-language imports with Norwegian subtitles, so there's invariably something on that you'll understand, though much of it is pretty unadventurous stuff. The big global cable and satellite channels like MTV and CNN are commonly accessible in hotel rooms.

Local tourist **radio**, giving details of events and festivals, is broadcast during the summer months; watch for signposts by the roadside and tune in. Shortwave frequencies and schedules for the BBC World Service (Ⓦ www.bbc.co.uk/worldservice), Radio Canada (Ⓦ www.rcinet.ca) and Voice of America (Ⓦ www.voanews.com) are listed on their respective websites.

Sports and outdoor activities

Most Norwegians have a deep and abiding love of the great outdoors. They enjoy many kinds of sports – from dog-sledging and downhill skiing in winter, through to mountaineering, angling and white-water rafting in the summer – but the two most popular activities are hiking and cross-country skiing.

Hiking

Norway boasts some of the most beautiful mountain landscapes in the world and substantial portions of these mountain ranges have been protected by the creation of a string of **national parks**. These parks attract thousands of hikers, who take full advantage of the excellent network of hiking trails and several hundred mountain cabins, which provide the most congenial of accommodation. Several possible hiking areas are described in the text as are a number of mountain lodges, which are owned and operated by local affiliates of the **Norwegian Mountain Touring Association** (DNT) – Ⓦ www.turistforeningen.no.

Skiing

Downhill skiing, cross-country skiing and **snowboarding** conditions in Norway are usually excellent from mid-November through to late April, though daylight hours are at a premium around the winter solstice. Norway scores well in comparison with the better-known skiing regions of southern Europe: temperatures tend to be a good bit colder and the country has, in general terms at least, a more consistent snowfall; Norway's resorts tend to be less crowded, have smaller class sizes and shorter lift queues, and are at a lower altitude. Three main centres for downhill skiing are Voss (see p.260), Oppdal and Geilo. Approximately half the population are active in the sport, and many Norwegians still use skis to get to work or school.

In recent years, **summer skiing** on Norway's mountains and glaciers – both alpine and cross-country – has become very popular. Lots of places offer this, but one of the largest and most convenient spots is the **Folgefonn Sommar Skisenter** (late May to late Sept daily 10am–4pm; ☏ 53 66 80 28, Ⓦ www .folgefonn.no), not far from Bergen, which has ski rental, a ski school, a café and a ski lift to the slopes.

Fishing

Norway's myriad rivers and lakes offer some of Europe's finest **freshwater fishing** with common species including trout, char, pike and perch, not to mention the salmon that once brought English aristocrats here by the buggy load. In the south of the country, the fishing is at its best from June to September, July and August in the north. **Seawater fishing** is more the preserve of professionals, but (amateur) sea angling off the Lofoten Islands is a popular pastime. Fresh- and seawater fishing are both tightly controlled. To do the first, you need a local licence, which costs anything from 50–400kr per day, and a national licence if you're after salmon, sea trout and char, while, that is, these fish are in fresh water. **Seawater fishing** does not require a national licence, but is subject to local restrictions. National licences are available at any post office and online (Ⓦ www.inatur.no) for 210kr and local licences (*fiskekort*) are sold at sports shops, a few tourist offices, some hotels and many campsites; the cost varies enormously from 50–350kr per day. If you take your own fishing tackle, you must have it disinfected before use.

Travel essentials

Costs

Norway has a reputation as one of the most **expensive** of European holiday destinations, and in some ways (but only some) this is entirely justified. Most of what you're likely to need – from a cup of coffee to a bottle of beer – is very costly, but on the other hand certain major items are reasonably priced, most notably **accommodation** which, compared with other north European countries, can be remarkably inexpensive: Norway's (usually) first-rate youth hostels, almost all of which have family, double and dormitory rooms, are particularly good value. **Getting around** is reasonably good news too, as the relatively high cost of normal bus, boat and train tickets can be offset by a number of passes and there are myriad discounts and deals. Furthermore, **concessions** are almost universally available at attractions and on public transport, with infants (under 4) going everywhere free, plus children and seniors (over 67, sometimes 60) paying – on average at least – half the standard rate. **Food** is, however, a different matter. With few exceptions – such as tinned fish – it's expensive, while the cost of **alcohol** is enough to make even a heavy drinker contemplate abstinence.

Travelling by bicycle, eating picnics bought from supermarkets and cooking your own food at campsites, it's possible to keep **average costs** down to 350kr a day per person. Moving up a notch, if you picnic at lunch, stick to less expensive cafés and restaurants, and stay in cheap hotels or hostels, you could get by on around 850kr a day. Staying in three-star hotels and eating out in medium-range restaurants, you should reckon on about 1300kr a day, the main variable being the cost of your room. On 1800kr a day and upwards, you'll be limited only by time, though if you're planning to stay in a five-star hotel and have a big night out, this still won't be enough. As always, if you're travelling alone you'll spend much more on accommodation than you would in a group of two or more: most hotels do have single rooms, but they're usually around sixty to eighty percent of the price of a double. For further information on accommodation costs, see p.170. See also 'Tax-free shopping', p.178.

Customs

There is (usually) little formality at either the Norway–Sweden or Norway–Finland borders, but the northern border with Russia is a different story. Despite the break-up of the Soviet Union, border patrols (on either side) won't be overjoyed at the prospect of you nosing around. If you have a genuine wish to visit Russia from Norway, it's best to sort out the paperwork – visas and so forth – before you leave home.

Internet

Norway is well geared up for internet access. There are internet cafés in all the big cities, and most hotels and hostels provide internet access for their guests either free or at minimal charge. Nearly all libraries provide free, albeit time-limited, internet access too.

Mail

Norway has a very efficient postal system. Post offices are plentiful and mostly open 8am/9am to 4/5pm and Saturday 9am to 1/3pm. **Postage** costs are currently 7kr for either a postcard or a letter under 20g sent within Norway, 9kr to the EU and 11kr to everywhere else. Mail to the US takes a week, two to three days within Europe.

Money

Norway has its own currency, the **kroner**, one of which, a krone (literally "crown"; abbreviated **kr** or **NOK**), is divided into 100 **øre**. Coins in circulation are 50 øre, 1kr, 5kr and 10kr; notes are for 50kr, 100kr, 200kr, 500kr and 1000kr. At time of writing the rate of exchange for 1kr is £0.10, €0.10, US$0.14, CDN$0.18, AUS$0.22, NZ$0.28, SAR1.44. For the most up-to-date rates, check the currency converter website ⓦ www.oanda.com.

ATMs are liberally dotted around every city, town and large village in Norway – and they accept a host of debit cards without charging a transaction fee. Credit cards can be used in ATMs too, but in this case transactions are treated as loans, with interest accruing daily from the date of withdrawal. All major credit cards, including American Express, Visa and Mastercard, are widely accepted. Typically, ATMs give instructions in a variety of languages.

All well-known brands of traveller's cheque in all major currencies are widely accepted in Norway, and you can change them as well as foreign currency into kroner at most banks, which are ubiquitous; banking hours are usually Monday to Friday 9am to 3.30pm, sometimes till 5/6pm on Thursdays. All major

post offices change foreign currency and traveller's cheques too, and they generally have longer opening hours, characteristically Monday to Friday 8/9am to 4/5pm and Saturday 9am to 2/3pm. Outside banking and post office hours, most major hotels, many travel agents and some hostels and campsites will change money at less generous rates and with variable commissions.

Opening hours and public holidays

Business hours (ie office hours) normally run from Monday to Friday 9.30/10am to 4.30/5pm. Normal **shopping hours** are Monday through Friday 10am to 5pm, with late opening on Thursdays till 6pm, 7pm or 8pm, plus Saturdays 10am to 1pm, 2pm or 3pm. Most supermarkets stay open much longer – from 9am until 8pm in the week and from 9am to 6pm on Saturdays, but close on Sundays. In addition, the majority of kiosks-cum-newsstands stay open till 9pm or 10pm every night of the week (including Sun), but much more so in the cities and towns than in the villages. Many fuel stations sell a basic range of groceries and stay open till 11pm daily. Vinmonopolet, the state-run liquor chain, has outlets in almost every town and large village, but they operate limited opening hours; each store fixes its own schedule, but generally they're open Monday to Friday 10am to 4/6pm and Saturday 10am to 1/3pm.

Norway's public holidays

New Year's Day January 1
Palm Sunday week before Easter
Maundy Thursday Thursday before Easter
Good Friday March/April variable
Easter Sunday March/April variable
Easter Monday first Monday following Easter
Labour Day May 1
Ascension Day early to mid-May
National (or Constitution) Day May 17
Whit Sunday the seventh Sunday after Easter
Whit Monday the seventh Monday after Easter
Christmas Day December 25
Boxing Day day after Christmas Day

Note that when a public holiday falls on a Sunday, then the next day becomes a holiday as well.

Norway has literally hundreds of **museums**. The more important open all year, but many close for winter from October or November to April, May or even mid-June. Opening hours are usually 9.30/10am to 5pm every day, including Saturday and Sunday, but some limit their hours on the weekend and many more close on Mondays.

There are thirteen national **public holidays** per year, most of which are keenly observed and, although much of the tourist industry carries on regardless, almost every museum and gallery in the land is closed. The result is that Easter, when four of these public holidays fall, is not a good time for museum-lovers to visit. Otherwise most businesses and shops close, and the public transport system operates a skeleton or Sunday service. Some of these public holidays are also **official flag-flying days**, but there are additional flag days as well – for example on Queen Sonja's birthday (July 4).

Phones

Given the sheer size of the country, it's no wonder that **mobile phone** (cell phone) coverage is partial, but the Norwegians are spreading the network at a rate of knots. Norway is on the mobile phone (cell phone) network at GSM900/1800, the band common to the rest of Europe, Australia and New Zealand. Mobile/cell phones bought in North America need to be of the triband variety to access this GSM band. If you intend to use your mobile/cell phone in Norway, note that call charges can be excruciating – particularly irritating is the supplementary charge that you often have to pay on incoming calls – so check with your supplier before you depart. You might also consider buying a Norwegian SIM card. The basic card costs 200kr, including 100kr worth of calls, and they are on sale at some 7-Eleven and Narvesen kiosks; note, however, that not all mobiles/cell phones take foreign SIM cards – check with your supplier. Text messages, on the other hand, are usually charged at ordinary rates – and with your existing SIM card in place.

Domestic and international phone cards for use in **public phones** can be bought at many outlets, including post offices, some supermarkets and most Narvesen kiosks. The most

Emergency numbers

Ambulance ℡113.
Fire ℡110.
Police ℡112.

common card is Telenor's Telekort, which comes in several specified denominations, beginning at 40kr. To make a reverse-charge or collect call, phone the international operator (they always all speak English). Remember also that although virtually all hotel rooms have phones, there is almost always an exorbitant surcharge for their use.

There are no area codes in Norway and the vast majority of Norwegian telephone numbers have eight digits; where this isn't the case, it's probably a premium-rated line, except those numbers beginning ℡800, which are toll-free.

Tax-free shopping

Taking advantage of their decision not to join the EU, the Norwegians run a **tax-free shopping scheme** for tourists. If you spend more than 315kr at any of the three thousand outlets in the tax-free shopping scheme, you'll get a voucher for the amount of VAT you paid. On departure at an airport, ferry terminal or frontier crossing, present the goods, the voucher and your passport and – provided you haven't used the item – you'll get an 12–19 percent refund, depending on the price of the item. There isn't a reclaim point at every exit from the country, however – pick up a leaflet at any participating shop to find out where they are – and note that many of the smaller reclaim points keep normal shop hours, closing for the weekend at 2/3pm on Saturday. The downside is the shops themselves: the bulk are dedicated to selling souvenir goods you can well manage without.

Tipping

Cafés and restaurants often add a service charge to their bills and this is – or at least should be – clearly indicated. Otherwise, few people **tip** at cafés or bars, but restaurant waiters and taxi drivers will be disappointed not to get a tip of between 10 and 15 percent. Rounding your bill up by a few kroner to make a round number is considered polite.

2.1

Oslo and the Oslofjord

With a population of about half a million, **OSLO** is the only major metropolis in a country brimming with small towns and villages – its nearest rival, Bergen, being less than half its size. This gives Oslo a powerful – some say overweening – voice in the political, cultural and economic life of the nation and has pulled in all of Norway's big companies, as a rash of concrete and glass tower blocks testifies. Fortunately, these monoliths rarely interrupt the stately Neoclassical lines of the late nineteenth-century **city centre**, Oslo's most beguiling district, which boasts a lively restaurant and bar scene as well as a clutch of excellent museums. Indeed, Oslo's biggest single draw is its **museums**, which cover a hugely varied and stimulating range of topics: the fabulous Viking Ships Museum, the Munch Museum showcasing a good chunk of the painter's work, the sculpture park devoted to the stirring bronze and granite works of Gustav Vigeland, and the moving historical documents of the Resistance Museum, are, to name just four, enough to keep even the most museum-averse visitor busy for days. There's also a first-rate **outdoor life** with Oslo rustling up a good range of parks, pavement cafés, street entertainers and festivals, especially in summer when virtually the whole population seems to live outdoors – and visiting is a real delight. Winter is also a good time to be here, when Oslo's location amid hills and forests makes it a thriving, convenient and affordable ski centre.

▲ Oslo Jazz Festival

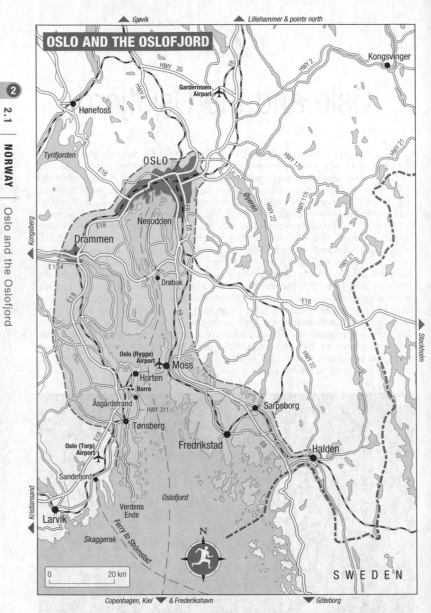

OSLO AND THE OSLOFJORD

▲ Gjøvik   ▲ Lillehammer & points north

Kongsvinger

HWY 35

HWY 4

E6

HWY 2

Gardermoen
Airport

Hønefoss

Tyrifjorden

OSLO

E16

HWY 170

HWY 21

Øyeren

Nesodden

HWY 22

HWY 115

Drammen

E18

E6

E134

Drøbak

E18

HWY 21

Oslo (Rygge)
Airport

Moss

HWY 22

Horten

Borre

Åsgårdstrand   HWY 311

Sarpsborg

Tønsberg

Fredrikstad

Halden

E6

Oslo (Torp)
Airport

E18

Sandefjord

Oslofjord

Larvik

Verdens
Ende

N

Skagerrak

Ferry to Strömstad

S W E D E N

0   20 km

◄ Kongsberg   ◄ Kristiansand   Stockholm ►

Copenhagen, Kiel ▼ & Frederikshavn   ▼ Göteborg

Although Oslo's centre is itself compact, the **outer districts** spread over a vast 453 square kilometres, encompassing huge chunks of forest, beach and water. Almost universally, the city's inhabitants have a deep and abiding affinity for these wide-open spaces and, as a result, the waters of the Oslofjord to the south and the forested hills of the Nordmarka to the north are tremendously popular for everything from boating and swimming to hiking and skiing. On all but the shortest of stays, there's ample opportunity to join in – the open forest and **cross-country ski** routes of the

Nordmarka and the **island beaches** just offshore in the Oslofjord, notably on the islet of Hovedøya, are both easily reached by metro or ferry.

Oslo

With its grand late nineteenth- and early twentieth-century buildings, most of **downtown Oslo** is easy and pleasant to walk around, a humming, good-natured place whose breezy streets and squares combine these appealing remnants of the city's early days with a clutch of good museums – in particular the National Gallery (Nasjonalgalleriet) and the Resistance Museum (Hjemmefrontmuseum) – plus dozens of lively bars, cafés and restaurants.

The city's showpiece museums – most memorably the remarkable **Viking-skipshuset** (Viking Ships Museum) – are on the **Bygdøy peninsula**, which is easily reached by ferry from the jetty behind the **Rådhus** (City Hall); other ferries head south from the Vippetangen quay behind the Akershus to the string of rusticated **islands** that necklace the inner waters of the Oslofjord, with wooded Hovedøya being the cream of the scenic crop. Back on the mainland, **east Oslo** is the least prepossessing part of town, a gritty sprawl housing the poorest of the city's inhabitants, though the recently revived district of **Grünerløkka** is now home to a slew of fashionable bars and clubs. The main sight on the east side of town is the **Munch-museet** (Munch Museum), which boasts a superb collection of the artist's work. **Northwest Oslo** is far more prosperous, with big old houses lining the avenues immediately to the west of the Slottsparken. Beyond is the **Frognerparken**, a chunk of parkland where the wondrous open-air sculptures of Gustav Vigeland are displayed in the **Vigelandsparken**.

The city's enormous reach becomes apparent only to the north of the centre in the **Nordmarka**, a massive forested wilderness, stretching far inland and patterned by hiking trails and cross-country ski routes. Two T-bane (Tunnelbanen) lines provide ready access, weaving their way up into the rocky hills that herald the region. The more easterly T-bane is the more appealing, ending up near **Sognsvannet**, a pretty little lake set amidst the woods and an ideal place for an easy stroll and/or a picnic.

Arrival

Downtown Oslo is at the heart of a superb public-transport system, which makes arriving and departing convenient and straightforward. The principal arrival hub is **Oslo Sentralstasjon** (usually shortened to **Oslo S**), a large complex that includes the main train and bus stations, city tram, metro and bus stops, a tourist office and exchange facilities; it is at the eastern end of the main thoroughfare, **Karl Johans gate**. The other transport hub is **Nationaltheatret**, at the west end of Karl Johans gate, which is handier for most city-centre sights and Oslo's main harbour. There's a **tourist information** office at Oslo S and another close to Nationaltheatret, on Fridtjof Nansens plass.

By air: Gardermoen airport

Oslo Gardermoen airport is 45km north of the city centre, just off the E6. There are three ways to get from the airport to the centre of Oslo by **public transport** – express train, local train and airport bus. The fastest and most expensive option is the **FlyToget** (Express train; daily 5.30am–12.30pm every 10–20 min; 170kr one-way, 340kr return; ⓦwww.flytoget.no), which takes twenty minutes to reach Oslo S, a couple more to Nationaltheatret. Alternatively, several NSB (Norwegian Railway) regional trains – including the hourly Lillehammer to Skien service – stop at the airport before proceeding on to Oslo S and usually Nationaltheatret. These trains take between thirty and forty minutes to make the journey and the one-way fare costs 86kr, 172kr return. Note also that there are express trains north

▲ Oslo harbour

from Gardermoen to a number of destinations, including Røros and Trondheim; long-distance services often require a reservation – details and reservations at the train ticket office in Arrivals.

By bus, **SAS Flybussen** (daily 5.20am–1am, every 20–30min; 140kr one-way, 240kr return; ⓦwww.flybussen.no/oslo) depart from outside the Arrivals concourse for the main downtown bus station, Oslo Bussterminalen, part of the Oslo S complex; the journey takes about 45 minutes, traffic depending. These buses then continue on to St Olavs plass and the *Radisson SAS Scandinavia Hotel* on Holbergs gate. For **Gardermoen departures**, the Flybussen follows the same route in the opposite direction. In addition, **Flybussekspressen** (ⓣ177 from within Oslo, ⓣ815 00 176 from without; ⓦwww.flybussekspressen.no) operates a variety of bus services from the airport direct to the small towns surrounding Oslo at regular intervals and at reasonable rates.

The **taxi fare** from Gardermoen to the city centre is 650kr. Finally, note that if you're heading into Oslo from Gardermoen by **car**, there is a 20kr toll on all approach roads into the city; it's an automatic toll, so you don't actually do anything: your number plate is read electronically and the bill is either sent to your car rental company or to the address of the owner of your vehicle.

By air: Oslo (Torp) and Oslo (Rygge) airports

Oslo has two other airports. The larger one, **Oslo (Torp)**, is just outside the town of Sandefjord, about 110km southwest of Oslo. The **Torp-Ekspressen bus** (ⓣ177 from within Oslo, ⓣ815 00 176 from without; ⓦwww.torpekspressen.no) links this airport with the main downtown bus station, Oslo Bussterminalen, part of the Oslo S complex, about six times daily; the bus schedule, both to and from Torp, links with flight arrivals and departures. The bus journey takes a little under two hours and costs 180kr one-way, 300kr return; you buy tickets from the driver. The third airport, Oslo (Rygge), is 8km west of Moss, a small town about 60km south of Oslo. From here, the **Rygge-Ekspressen bus** (ⓣ177 from within Oslo, ⓣ815 00 176 from without; ⓦwww.rygge-ekspressen.no) runs to the main bus terminal at Oslo S. Again, the bus schedule links with flight arrivals and departures and you buy tickets from the driver. A one-way fare is 120kr, return 210kr, and the journey time is about 45 minutes.

By train

International and domestic **trains** use **Oslo Sentralstasjon**, known as Oslo S (train information and reservations ☎815 00 888, ⓦwww.nsb.no), which is beside Jernbanetorget, the square at the eastern end of the main drag, Karl Johans gate. There are money-exchange facilities and a post office here, and just outside is a tourist office. Many domestic trains also pass through the Nationaltheatret station, at the west end of Karl Johans gate, which is slightly more convenient for the city centre. Note that reservations are compulsory on most long-distance trains heading out of Oslo (see p.206).

By bus

The central **Bussterminalen** (bus terminal) is part of the Oslo S complex; it is a short, signposted walk northeast from the train station on Schweigårdsgate. International and domestic long-distance buses arrive at and depart from here, as do the SAS Flybussen (from Oslo Gardermoen airport), the Torp-Ekspressen (from Oslo Torp airport), and the Rygge-Ekspressen (from Oslo Rygge airport).

There are two **bus information desks**. One is for the largest domestic carrier, Nor-Way Bussekspress (☎23 00 24 00 for services to and from Oslo, ☎815 44 444 for all other services; ⓦwww.nor-way.no), which also handles information on the airport buses; the second deals with a number of other companies, including Säfflebussen (☎815 66 010, ⓦwww.safflebussen.se), which operates frequent services to Copenhagen and Stockholm.

By car ferry

DFDS Seaways **car ferries** from Copenhagen, as well as Stena car ferries from Fredrikshavn in Denmark, arrive at the **Vippetangen quays**, a fifteen-minute walk (800m) south from Oslo S: take Akershusstranda/Skippergata to Karl Johans gate and turn right. Alternatively, catch bus #60 marked "Jernbanetorget" (Mon–Fri 6.30am–11.30pm, Sat from 8.30am, Sun from 9am, every 20–30min; 5min). On Color Line services from Kiel, you'll arrive at the **Hjortneskaia**, some 3km west of the city centre. From here, bus #33 runs to the Nationaltheatret, bang in the centre of the city (Mon–Fri 7am–8pm & Sat 10am–5pm every 30min) – but not to Oslo S. Failing that, a taxi to Oslo S will cost about 170kr.

Driving into the city – and parking

Arriving in Oslo **by car**, you'll have to drive through one of the automatic **toll points** that encircle the city; the toll for ordinary cars is 20kr. All number plates are read electronically and an invoice is sent to either the car rental company concerned or the registered owner of the vehicle. Oslo's ring roads encircle and tunnel under the city; if you follow the signs for "Ring 1" you'll be delivered right into the centre and emerge (eventually) at the Sentrum P-hus, a multistorey car park a short distance from Karl Johans gate.

You won't need your car to sightsee in Oslo, so you'd do best to use a designated **car park**. There are half a dozen **multistorey car parks** in the centre, though some of them operate restricted hours: both the Sentrum P-hus at CJ Hambros plass 1, two blocks north of Karl Johans gate, and Aker Brygge P-hus, Sjøgata 4, are open 24 hours. Costs begin at 25kr for 30 minutes during the day (Mon–Sat 7am–7pm), up to a maximum of 240kr for 24 hours; Sunday, evening (after 7pm) and overnight rates are heavily discounted.

Alternatively, you can park in **pay-and-display car parks** and at **on-street metered spaces** around the city. Identified by blue "P" signs, these metered spaces are owned and operated by the municipality, and are usually free of charge from Monday to Friday between 6pm and 8am and over the weekend after 3pm on Saturday. There

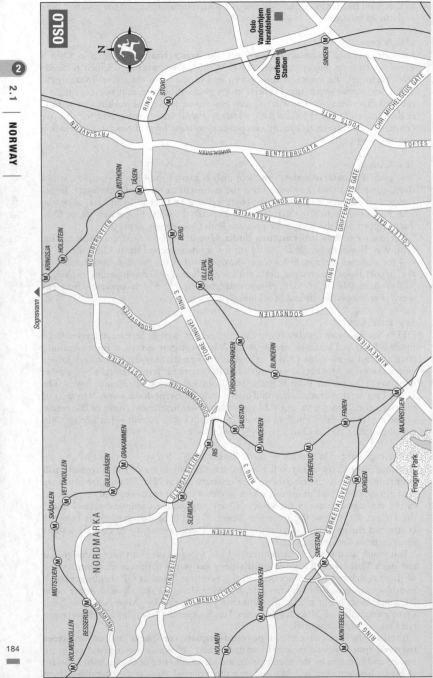

OSLO

Oslo
Vandrerhjem
Haraldsheim

Greifsen
Station

SINSEN

CHR. MICHELSENS GATE

VOGTS GATE

TOFTES

FRYSJAVEIEN

RING 3

STORO

MARIDALSVEIEN

BENTSEBRUGATA

GRIFFENFELDTS GATE

COLLETS GATE

ØSTHORN

TASEN

UELANDS GATE

TASENVEIEN

NORDBERGVEIEN

BERG

ULLEVÅL
STADION

RING 2

SOGNSVEIEN

KIRKEVEIEN

KRINGSJÅ

HOLSTEIN

SOGNSVEIEN

RING 3

STORE RINGVEI

FORSKNINGSPARKEN

GAUSTADVEIEN

SOGNSVANNSVEIEN

BLINDERN

SOGNSVEIEN

MAJORSTUEN

GRAKAMMEN

SLEMDALSVEIEN

RIS

GAUSTAD

VINDEREN

STEINERUD

FRØEN

NORDMARKA

GULLERÅSEN

SLEMDAL

RING 3

SØRKEDALSVEIEN

BORGEN

Frogner Park

VETTAKOLLEN

SKÅDALEN

DALSVEIEN

SMESTAD

MIDTSTUEN

STASJONSVEIEN

HOLMENKOLLVEIEN

MAKRELLBEKKEN

SØRKEDALSVEIEN

BESSERUD

AKERVEIEN

HOLMEN

RING 3

MONTEBELLO

HOLMENKOLLEN

Sognsvann ◄

Frognerseteren & Voksenkollen ▼

184

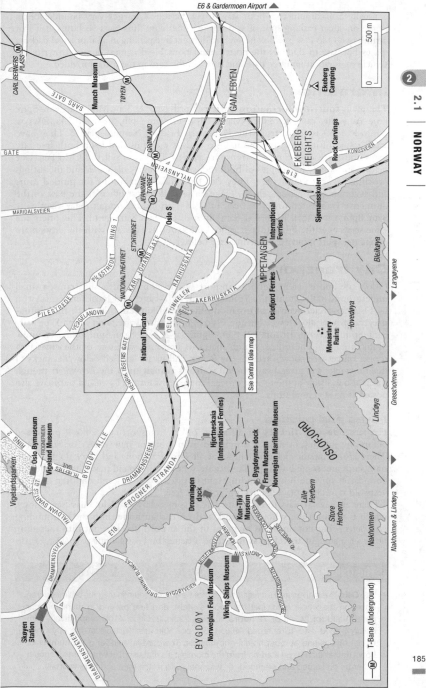

E6 & Gardermoen Airport ▲

0 ————— 500 m

Carl Berners Plass

Munch Museum

Tøyen

Sars Gate

Gate

Maridalsveien

Grønland

Jernbane-Torget

Nylandsveien

Oslo S

Gamlebyen

Schweigaards Gate

E18

Ekeberg Camping

Ekeberg Heights

Rock Carvings

Kongsveien

Sjømannskolen

Vippetangen

International Ferries

Osjofjord Ferries

Blekøya

Ring 1

Pilestredet

Stortinget

Karl Johans Gate

National Theatret

Nationaltheatret

Rådhusgata

Oslo Tunnelen

Akershuskaia

See Central Oslo map

Monastery Ruins

Hovedøya

Langøyene ▼

Pilestredet

Vigelandsvn

Henrik Ibsens Gate

National Theatre

Hjortneskaia (International Ferries)

Oslofjord

Gressholmen ▼

Lindøya

Oslo Bymuseum

Vigeland Museum

Frognerveien

Th Heftyes Gate

Bygdøy Alle

Drammensveien

Frogner Stranda

Dronningen dock

Kon-Tiki Museum

Bygdøynes dock

Fram Museum

Norwegian Maritime Museum

Lille Herbern

Store Herbern

Nakholmen ▼

Nakholmen & Lindøya ▼

Vigelandsparken

Haldan Svarts Gt

Ring 2

Frognerseteren

Drammensveien

E18

Dronning Blancas V

Bygdøyveien

Museumsveien

Langviksveien

Fredriksborgveien

Skøyen Station

Bygdøy

Norwegian Folk Museum

Viking Ships Museum

Langviksveien

Drammensveien

Ⓜ T-Bane (Underground)

Ⓜ — T-Bane (Underground)

is usually a maximum two-hour stay in pay periods. **Charges** vary considerably: a prime on-street parking spot (if you can get one) costs 70kr for two hours, half that further out. Oslo Pass (see box below) holders get free parking in all municipal parking spaces, but have to abide by the posted regulations. Holders must be sure to write the vehicle registration number, date and time on the card in the space provided.

Information

The main **tourist information office** (April–May & Sept Mon–Sat 9am–5pm; June–Aug daily 9am–7pm; Oct–March Mon–Fri 9am–4pm; ☎815 30 555, ⊛www .visitoslo.com) is across from the Rådhus at Fridtjof Nansens plass 5. They have a full range of information about Oslo and its environs, and issue both free city maps and maps of the public transport system. They also sell the Oslo Pass (see below) and supply free copies of both the very thorough *Oslo Guide* and the listings brochure *What's On in Oslo*. They can also make reservations for guided tours and accommodation (see below). There's a second tourist office at the base of the distinctive Trafikanten tower in front of Oslo S on Jernbanetorget (May–Sept daily 8am–8pm; Oct–April Mon–Fri 8am–8pm & Sat–Sun 8am–6pm). This offers the same services as the other tourist office and shares its premises with the city's main public transport information centre (see below).

City transport

Oslo's safe and efficient public-transport system consists of buses, trams, a small underground rail system (the Tunnelbanen, or T-bane) and local ferries. It's run by Oslo Sporveier, whose information office, **Trafikanten**, is beneath the distinctive, transparent clocktower outside Oslo S, on the Jernbanetorget (May–Sept daily 8am–8pm; Oct–April Mon–Fri 8am–8pm, Sat & Sun 8am–6pm; ☎177, ⊛www .trafikanten.no). The office, which shares its premises with one of the city's two tourist offices (see above), sells all the tickets and passes detailed below, has racks of free timetables and gives away a useful **visitor's transit map**, the *Besøkskart*, though this is also available at the tourist office. Route plans for the buses and trams are also posted at most central stops.

Fares and passes

Flat-fare **one-way tickets** for all forms of city transport cost 24kr if purchased before the journey, or 34kr if purchased from a bus or tram driver or on a ferry. There are automatic ticket machines at all T-bane stations and ferry docks, many tram stops and some bus stops. Tickets are valid for unlimited travel within the city boundaries for one hour including transfers; seniors (67+) and children 4 to 16 years old travel half-price, babies and toddlers free.

There are several ways to cut costs. The best is to buy an **Oslo Pass** (see below), which is valid on the whole network and on certain routes into the surrounding *kommunes* – but not on trains or buses to the airport. If you're not into museums, however, a straight **travel pass** might be a better buy. A 24-hour pass (*Dagskort*) is

---

The Oslo Pass

The **Oslo Pass** gives free admission to almost every museum in the city, unlimited free travel on the whole municipal transport system, and free parking in municipal car parks. **Valid for 24, 48 or 72 hours**, it costs 220kr, 320kr or 410kr respectively, with children aged 4 to 15 charged 95kr, 115kr or 150kr. It's available at the city's two tourist offices and at most hotels and hostels. The card is valid for a set number of hours (rather than days) starting from the moment it's first used, at which time it should either be presented and stamped, or you should fill in the date and time yourself.

valid for unlimited travel within the city limits and costs 60kr, while a seven-day pass costs 200kr. Alternatively, the Flexikort is valid for eight city trips and costs 160kr. All these passes and tickets can be bought at the automatic machines mentioned above, as well as from the Trafikanten office.

Buses

Many city **bus** services originate at – or pass through – Jernbanetorget, the square in front of Oslo S, while most suburban services depart from the Bussterminalen nearby. A second common port-of-call is Nationaltheatret further to the west near the harbour. Most buses stop running at around midnight, though on Friday and Saturday nights **night buses** (*nattbussen*) take over on certain major routes (flat-rate fare 50kr; Oslo Pass and other passes not valid).

Trams

The city's **trams** run on six routes through the city, crisscrossing the centre from east to west, and sometimes duplicating the bus routes. They are a bit slower than the buses, but are a rather more enjoyable and relaxing way of getting about. Major stops include Jernbanetorget, Nationaltheatret and Storgata. Most operate regularly – every ten or twenty minutes, from 6am to midnight.

Tunnelbanen

The Tunnelbanen – **T-bane** – has six lines which converge to share a common slice of track crossing the city centre from Majorstua in the west to Tøyen in the east, with Nationaltheatret, Stortinget, Jernbanetorget/Oslo S and Grønland stations in between. From this central section, lines run west (*Vest*) and east (*Øst*) out into the suburbs. The system mainly serves commuters, but you may find it useful for hopping around the centre and for trips out into the forested hills of the Nordmarka. Apart from the central section, trains travel above ground. The system runs from around 6am until 12.30am.

Ferries

Numerous **ferries** shuttle across the northern reaches of the Oslofjord to connect the city centre with the outlying district. As far as visitors are concerned, the most popular are the summertime ferries (mid-March to mid-Oct) that leave from Pier #3, immediately behind the Rådhus, bound for the museums of the Bygdøy peninsula. There are also all-year ferry services to a number of Oslofjord islets, including Hovedøya, and a June to August service to Langøyene, but these depart from the Vippetangen quay, 1300m south of Oslo S. To get to the Vippetangen quay by public transport, take bus #60 from Jernbanetorget.

Bicycles

Oslo has a **municipal bike rental scheme** (Easter–Nov) in which bikes are released like supermarket trolleys from racks all over the city. Visitors can join the scheme at the tourist office by paying 70kr for a 24-hour cycling pass plus a refundable deposit of 500kr. Bikes can be used for up to three hours before they have to be dropped off (or swapped) at one of the bike racks to avoid a penalty.

Accommodation

Oslo has the range of **hotels** you would expect of a capital city, as well as **B&Bs**, a smattering of **guesthouses** (*pensjonater*) and a trio of **youth hostels**. To appreciate the full flavour of the city, you're best off staying on or near the western reaches of Karl Johans gate – between the Stortinget and the **Nationaltheatret** (National Theatre) – though the well-heeled area to the north and west of Det Kongelige Slott (the Royal Palace) is enjoyable too. Many of the less expensive lodgings are, however, to be found in the vicinity of Oslo S, a rather grimy district which – along

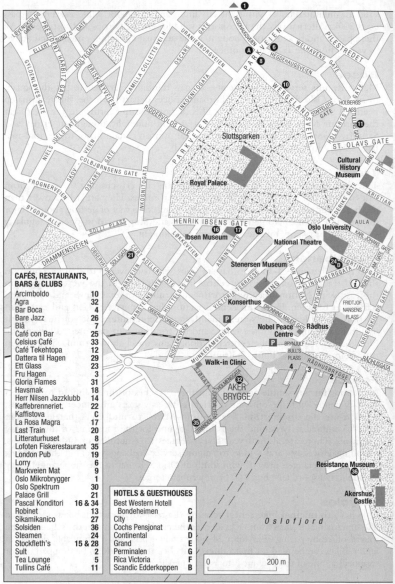

CAFÉS, RESTAURANTS, BARS & CLUBS

Arcimboldo	10
Agra	32
Bar Boca	4
Bare Jazz	26
Blå	7
Café con Bar	25
Celsius Café	33
Café Tekehtopa	12
Dattera til Hagen	29
Ett Glass	23
Fru Hagen	3
Gloria Flames	31
Havsmak	18
Herr Nilsen Jazzklubb	14
Kaffebrenneriet.	22
Kaffistova	C
La Rosa Magra	17
Last Train	20
Litteraturhuset	8
Lofoten Fiskerestaurant	35
London Pub	19
Lorry	6
Markveien Mat	9
Oslo Mikrobrygger	1
Oslo Spektrum	30
Palace Grill	21
Pascal Konditori	16 & 34
Robinet	13
Sikamikanico	27
Solsiden	36
Steamen	24
Stockfleth's	15 & 28
Sult	2
Tea Lounge	5
Tullins Café	11

HOTELS & GUESTHOUSES

Best Western Hotell Bondeheimen	C
City	H
Cochs Pensjonat	A
Continental	D
Grand	E
Perminalen	G
Rica Victoria	F
Scandic Edderkoppen	B

Drøbak & Nesodden ▼ ▼ Bygdøy

with the grey suburbs to the north and east of the station – hardly sets the pulse racing. That said, if money is tight and you're here any time between June and August, your choice of location may well be very limited as the scramble for **budget beds** – sometimes any bed at all – becomes acute, or at least tight enough to make it well worth phoning ahead to check on space. For peace of mind, it is advisable to make an advance reservation, particularly for your first night, either direct or via the tourist office's website (Ⓦ www.visitoslo.com).

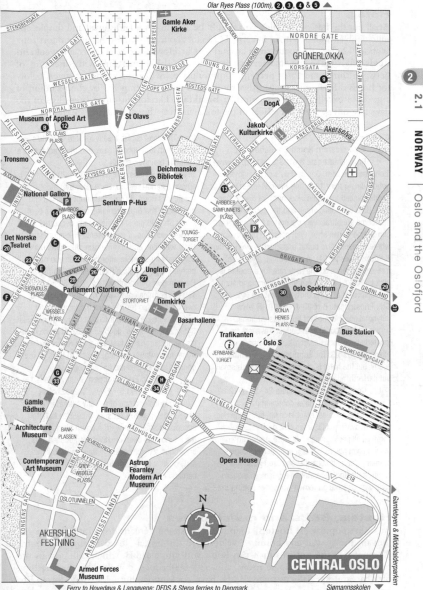

Olar Ryes Plass (100m), ❷,❸,❹ & ❺ ▲

CENTRAL OSLO

▼ Ferry to Hovedøya & Langøyene; DFDS & Stena ferries to Denmark   Sjømannsskolen ▼

Gamleby & Middelalderparken

If you don't want to reserve ahead, one way to cut the hassle after you arrive is to use the same-day and in-person **accommodation service** provided by the tourist office at both of their branches – one outside Oslo S train station (see p.186), the other near the Rådhus (see p.186). Each office has full accommodation lists and will make a reservation on your behalf for a minimal fee, altogether a real bargain when you consider that they often get discounted rates.

Hotels

At all but the busiest of times, you should be able to get a fairly small and simple, en-suite double room in a hotel in central Oslo for about 1000kr. You hit the comfort zone at about 1200kr, and luxury from around 1500kr. However, special offers and **weekend deals** often make the smarter hotels more affordable than this, with discounts of between thirty and forty percent commonplace (two price bands are given below for hotels offering discounts). Also, most room rates are tempered by the inclusion of a good-to-excellent self-service buffet **breakfast**. The tourist office keeps lists of the day's best offers, or try the places in the following list – but always ring ahead first.

Central

Best Western Hotell Bondeheimen Rosenkrantz gate 8 ☎ 23 21 41 00, ⓦ www .bondeheimen.com. One of Oslo's most enjoyable hotels, dating from 1913, the *Bondeheimen* is handily placed just 2min walk north of Karl Johans gate. Both the public areas and the comfortable bedrooms are attractively decorated in a modern, pan-Scandinavian style, with polished pine every-where. The inclusive buffet breakfast, served in the *Kaffistova* (see p.201), is substantial, and there's free internet access. The rack rate for a double is about 1300kr, but look out for weekend and summer discounts of up to thirty percent. ④/⑤

City Prinsensgate 6 ☎ 22 41 36 10, ⓦ www .cityhotel.no. This modest but pleasant hotel, a long-time favourite with budget travellers, is located above shops in a typical Oslo apartment block near Oslo S. The surroundings are a little seedy, but the hotel is cheerful enough, with small but perfectly adequate rooms. ③

Continental Stortingsgata 24–26 ☎ 22 82 40 40, ⓦ www.hotel-continental.no. Arguably the classiest hotel in town, family-owned and with swish public areas that ooze an easy comfort, all pastel shades, flowers, and even some Munch paintings (or at least near-perfect copies of them). The bedrooms beyond are extremely comfortable and decorated in a fetching, modern style with delicate patterned wallpaper setting the tone. The hotel is also ideally located, a stone's throw from Karl Johans gate, and the breakfast is a veritable banquet. ⑥/⑨

Grand Karl Johans gate 31 ☎ 23 21 20 00, ⓦ www.grand-hotel.no. Once Norway's most prestigious hotel, its café the haunt of Ibsen and his chums, the *Grand* remains one of Oslo's best hotels, its 300 guest rooms mostly decorated in a modern rendition of early twentieth-century style. Hefty weekend and summertime discounts make the *Grand* much more affordable than you might perhaps expect. Now a Rica hotel. ⑥/⑨

Perminalen Øvre Slottsgate 2 ☎ 23 09 30 81, ⓦ www.perminalen.no. This hostel-like hotel has two things going for it – a central location and budget prices: a bed in a four-berth room costs just 345kr, singles 595kr, doubles 795kr. At these rates, it's hardly surprising that the guest rooms are frugal to positively spartan, though at least all the doubles and singles are en suite. ②

Scandic Edderkoppen St Olavs plass 1 ☎ 23 15 56 00, ⓦ www.scandichotels .com. Overlooking one of the city's pleasanter, semi-pedestrianized squares, this *Scandic* hotel occupies a straightforward modern block, but the interior has been creatively remodelled in a bright and stylish modern manner, all spotlights, distinctive curved furniture and patterned carpets. ③/⑥

Hostels, B&Bs and guesthouses

At Oslo's popular HI **hostels**, members get fifteen percent discount, and you can join on the spot at any hostel – we've listed the hostel closest to the city centre. Alternatively, the tourist office can book you into a **B&B**, which will cost in the region of 330kr for a single room, and 530–600kr for a double. This is something of a bargain especially as many B&Bs have cooking facilities, but they do tend to be out of the city centre, and there is often a minimum two-night stay; note also that the tourist office will only arrange them when you turn up at either of their offices (see p.186) in person. Another option is a **guesthouse**, or *pensjonater*, and these start at around 440kr for a single room, 650kr for a double. They offer basic but generally adequate accommodation, either with or without en-suite facilities, but breakfast is not included, and at some places you may need to supply your own sleeping bag. Unfortunately, there are very few guesthouses in Oslo, and only two near the city centre.

Cochs Pensjonat Parkveien 25 ☎ 23 33 24 00, ⓦ www.cochspensjonat.no. Friendly and engaging guesthouse occupying the upper floors of an old apartment block, in a handy location behind the Slottsparken. There are 88 rooms, each decorated in a frugal modern style – wood laminate floors and so on – and of three different types: those with shared facilities cost 620kr for a double (440kr single), en suite 720kr (540kr) and those with a kitchen unit 780kr (590kr). Breakfasts are served just along the street at *KafeCaffé*, Parkveien 21. ❷

 Oslo Vandrerhjem Haraldsheim Haraldsheimveien 4, Grefsen ☎ 22 22 29 65, ⓦ www.haraldsheim.no. The pick of Oslo's HI youth hostels, 4km northeast of the centre, and open all year except Christmas week. The public areas

are comfortable and attractively furnished in brisk, modern style and the bedrooms are frugal but clean. There are 270 beds in seventy rooms, most of which are four-bedded, and a good number have their own showers and WC. There are self-catering facilities, a restaurant, internet access and washing machines. The only downside can be parties of noisy schoolchildren. It's a very popular spot, so advance reservation is essential throughout summer. To get there, take tram #17 from Storgata, near the cathedral, northeast to the Sinsenkrysset stop, from where it's a five-minute (signposted) walk. By road, the hostel is close to – and signed from – Ring 3. The basic dorm bed price is 235kr, 260kr en suite; singles cost 395kr (450kr), doubles 520kr. Breakfast is included. ❶

Central Oslo

Despite the mammoth proportions of the Oslo conurbation, the **city centre** has remained surprisingly compact, and is easy to navigate by remembering a few simple landmarks. From the Oslo S train station, at the eastern end of the centre, the main thoroughfare, **Karl Johans gate**, heads directly up the hill, passing the **Domkirke** (Cathedral) and cutting a pedestrianized course until it reaches the **Stortinget** (Parliament building). From here it sweeps down past the **University** to **Det Kongelige Slott**, or Royal Palace, situated in parkland – the **Slottsparken** – at the western end of the centre. South of the palace, on the waterfront, sits the harbourside **Aker Brygge** shopping complex, across from which lies the distinctive twin-towered **Rådhus** (City Hall). South of the Rådhus, on the lumpy peninsula overlooking the harbour, rises the severe-looking castle, **Akershus Slott**.

Along Karl Johans gate to the Cathedral

Heading west and uphill from Oslo S train station, **Karl Johans gate** begins unpromisingly with a clutter of tacky shops and hang-about junkies. But things soon pick up at the **Domkirke** (Cathedral: daily 10am–4pm; free), which dates from the late seventeenth century, though its heavyweight tower was remodelled in 1850. From the outside the cathedral appears plain and dour, but the elegantly restored interior is a delightful surprise, its homely, low-ceilinged nave and transepts awash with maroon, green and gold paintwork.

Outside the cathedral, **Stortorvet** was once the main city square, but it's no longer of much account, its nineteenth-century **statue** of a portly Christian IV merely the somewhat forlorn guardian of a modest flower market.

To the Parliament building

Returning to Karl Johans gate, it's a brief stroll up to the **Stortinget** (Parliament building), an imposing chunk of neo-Romanesque architecture, whose stolid, sandy-coloured brickwork, dating from the 1860s, exudes bourgeois certainty. The Stortinget is open for guided tours (late June to late Aug 3 daily; Sept to late June Sat 3 daily; free; ⓦ www.stortinget.no), but the interior is notably unexciting. In front of the Parliament, a narrow **park-piazza** runs west to the **Nationaltheatret** (National Theatre), filling in the gap between Karl Johans gate and Stortingsgata. In summer, the park brims with promenading city folk, who dodge between the jewellery hawkers, ice-cream kiosks and street performers; in winter the magnet is the dinky little open-air and floodlit ice-skating rinks – where skates can be rented at minimal cost.

The Royal Palace and the Slottsparken

Standing on the hill at the west end of Karl Johans gate, the **Kongelige Slott** (Royal Palace) is a monument to Norwegian openness. Built between 1825 and 1848, when the monarchs of other European nations were nervously counting their friends, it now stands without railings and walls, its grounds – the **Slottsparken** – freely open to the public. A snappy changing of the guard takes place daily outside the palace at 1.30pm, and hour-long guided tours take in certain sections of the interior (late June to mid-Aug), though tickets (95kr) can be hard to come by – ask at the tourist office. Directly in front of the palace is an equestrian statue of king **Karl XIV Johan** (1763–1844), formerly the Napoleonic Marshal **Jean-Baptiste Bernadotte**.

The Ibsen Museum

The grand, nineteenth-century mansions bordering the southern perimeter of the Slottsparken once housed Oslo's social elite. It was here, in a fourth-floor apartment at Arbins gate 1, on the corner of what is now Henrik Ibsens gate, that Norway's most celebrated playwright, Henrik Ibsen spent the last ten years of his life, strolling down to the *Grand Café* every day to hold court. Admirers did their best to hobnob with the great man as he took his daily walk, but Ibsen was unenthusiastic about being a tourist attraction in his own lifetime and mostly ignored all comers – no one could ever accuse him of being overly sociable. Ibsen's old apartment is now incorporated within the **Ibsen Museet**, whose entrance is just along the street at Henrik Ibsens gate 26 (Ibsen Museum: Tues–Sun: mid-May to mid-Sept 11am–6pm; mid-Sept to mid-May noon–3pm; 85kr; ⓦwww.ibsenmuseet .no). The museum kicks off with a well-considered introduction to Ibsen and his

Ibsen

Henrik Johan Ibsen (1828–1906), Norway's most famous and influential playwright, is generally regarded as one of the greatest dramatists of all time, and certainly his central themes have powerful modern resonances. In essence, these concern the alienation of the individual from an ethically bankrupt society, loss of religious faith and the yearning of women to transcend the confines of their roles as wives and mothers. Ibsen's central characters often speak evasively, mirroring the repression of their society and their own sense of confusion and guilt with venomous exchanges – a major characteristic of the playwright's dialogue – appearing whenever the underlying tensions break through. Ibsen's protagonists do things which are less than heroic, often incompetent, even malicious. Nevertheless, they aspire to *dåd*, the act of the hero/heroine, arguably a throwback to the old Norse sagas. These themes run right through Ibsen's plays, the first of which, *Catalina* (1850), was written while he was employed as an apothecary's assistant at Grimstad on the south coast.

It was *A Doll's House* (1879) that really put Ibsen on the literary map, its controversial protagonist, Nora, making unwise financial decisions before walking out not only on her patronising husband, Torvald, but also on her loving children – all in her desire to control her own destiny. *Ghosts* followed two years later, and its exploration of moral contamination through the metaphor of syphilis created an even greater furore, which Ibsen rebutted in his next work, *An Enemy of the People* (1882). Afterwards, Ibsen changed tack (if not theme), first with *The Wild Duck* (1884), a mournful tale of the effects of compulsive truth-telling, and then *Hedda Gabler* (1890), where the heroine is denied the ability to make or influence decisions, and so becomes perverse, manipulative and ultimately self-destructive.

Ibsen returned to Oslo after a self-imposed exile in 1891. He was treated as a hero, and ironically – considering the length of his exile and his comments on his compatriots – as a symbol of Norwegian virtuosity. Ibsen was incapacitated by a heart attack in 1901 and died from the effects of another one five years later.

plays, exploring, over two small floors, the themes that underpinned his work and his uneasy relationship with his home country. Beyond, Ibsen's apartment has been restored to its appearance in 1895, including many of the original furnishings, but it can only be visited on a guided tour (hourly; no extra charge). Both Ibsen and his wife died here: Ibsen breathed his last as he lay paralysed in bed, but his wife, unwilling to expire in an undignified pose, dressed herself to die sitting upright in a chair in the library. Ibsen was argumentative to the end – famously, his final words were "To the contrary".

For more on Ibsen, see box opposite.

The National Gallery

From the Ibsen Museum, it's a five- to ten-minute walk back down the hill to Norway's largest and most prestigious art gallery, the **Nasjonalgalleriet**, at Universitetsgata 13 (National Gallery: Tues, Wed & Fri 10am–6pm, Thurs 10am–7pm, Sat & Sun 10am–5pm; free; ⓦwww.nationalmuseum.no). Housed in a whopping nineteenth-century building, the collection may be short on internationally famous painters – apart from a fine body of work by Edvard Munch – but there's compensation in the oodles of Norwegian art, including work by all the leading figures up until the end of World War II. The only irritation is the way the museum is organized: the kernel of the collection is displayed on the **first floor**, which is convenient enough, but paintings of individual artists tend to be displayed in several different rooms, which can be very frustrating. The **free plan** available at reception helps illuminate matters; the text below mentions room numbers where it's helpful, but note that locations are sometimes rotated.

The National Gallery's star turn is its **Munch** collection. Representative works from the 1880s up to 1916 are gathered together in Room 24. His early work is very much in the Naturalist tradition of his mentor Christian Krohg, though by 1885 Munch was already pushing back the boundaries in *The Sick Child*, a heart-wrenching evocation of his sister Sophie's death from tuberculosis. Other works displaying this same sense of pain include *The Dance of Life*, *Madonna* and *The Scream*, a seminal canvas of 1893 whose swirling lines and rhythmic colours were to inspire the Expressionists. Munch painted several versions of *The Scream*, but this is the original, so it is hard to exaggerate the embarrassment felt by the museum when, in 1994, someone climbed in through the window and stole it. The painting was eventually recovered, but the thief was never caught.

The gallery's sample of Munch's work serves as a good introduction to the artist, but for a more detailed appraisal – and a more comprehensive selection of his work – check out the Munch Museum (see p.199).

To the water: the Rådhus

From the Parliament building (see p.191), it's just a couple of minutes' walk south to the **Rådhus** (City Hall: daily 9am–6pm; guided tours Mon–Fri 3 daily; free, except May–Aug 40kr), which rears high above the waterfront. Nearly twenty years in the making, Oslo's City Hall finally opened in 1950 to celebrate the city's nine-hundredth anniversary. Designed by Arnstein Arneberg and Manus Poulsson, this firmly Modernist, twin-towered building of dark brown brick was intended to be a grandiose statement of civic pride. At first, few locals had a good word for what they saw as an ugly and strikingly un-Norwegian addition to the city, but with the passing of time the obloquy has fallen on more recent additions to the skyline – such as Oslo S – and the Rådhus has become one of the city's more popular buildings.

Inside, the principal hall – the **Rådhushallen** – is decorated with vast, stylized and very secular murals. On the north wall, Per Krohg's *From the Fishing Nets in the West to the Forests of the East* invokes the figures of polar explorer Fridtjof Nansen (on the left) and dramatist Bjørnstjerne Bjørnson (on the right) to symbolize, respectively, the nation's spirit of adventure and its intellectual development. On the south wall is the equally vivid *Work, Administration and Celebration*, which took Henrik Sørensen a decade to complete. The self-congratulatory nationalism of these two murals is hardly attractive, although the effect is partly offset by the forceful fresco in honour of the Norwegian Resistance of World War II, which runs along the east wall.

Outside, at the back of the Rådhus, a line of six muscular **bronzes** represents the trades – builders, bricklayers and so on – who worked on the building. Behind them stand four massive, granite female sculptures surrounding a fountain, and beyond is the busy central **harbour**, with the bumpy Akershus peninsula on the left and the islands of the Oslofjord filling out the backdrop. This is a delightful spot, one of the city's happiest moments, and a stone's throw away is the Nobels Fredssenter.

Nobel Peace Centre and Aker Brygge

The **Nobels Fredssenter** (Nobel Peace Centre: Jan–May Tues–Fri 10am–4pm, Sat & Sun 11am–5pm; June–Aug daily 10am–6pm; Sept–Dec Tues–Sun 10am–6pm; 80kr; ⓦ www.nobelpeacecenter.org) was founded to celebrate and publicize the Nobel Peace Prize. Born in Sweden, **Alfred Nobel** (1833–96) invented dynamite in his 30s and went on to become extraordinarily rich with factories in over twenty countries. In his will, Nobel established a fund to reward good works in five categories – physics, chemistry, medicine, literature and peace. The awards were to be made annually, based on the recommendations of several Swedish institutions, with the exception of the Peace Prize, the recipient of which was to be selected by a committee of five, itself appointed by the Norwegian parliament.

Inside, the Peace Centre's ground floor features a series of temporary displays designed to get visitors into thinking about conflict and peace, poverty and wealth. Upstairs, there's a small display on the Nobel family; "wall papers" (broadly, information sheets) on all things to do with peace; and the so-called "Nobel Field", where each of the past holders of the Peace Prize is represented by a light bulb on a wispy stalk. With the overhead lights dimmed down, the stalks make a sort of miniature electrical forest, which really looks both effective and very engaging.

Behind the Peace Centre, the old Aker shipyard has been turned into the swish **Aker Brygge** shopping-cum-office complex, a gleaming concoction of walkways, circular staircases and glass lifts, all decked out with neon and plastic; the bars and restaurants here are some of the most popular in town.

East to Bankplassen

Running east from the Rådhus, **Rådhusgata** cuts off the spur of land dominated by the Akershus Castle (see p.196) with **Bankplassen**, arguably the city's most attractive square, lying one block to the south between Kongens gate and Kirkegata. Framed by Gothic Revival and Second Empire buildings, the square, with its trees and water fountain, is a perfect illustration of the grandiose tastes of the Dano-Norwegian elite who ran the country at the start of the twentieth century. The square's proudest building is the former Norges Bank headquarters of 1907, a redoubtable Art Nouveau-meets-Romanesque edifice that has been refurbished to house the **Museet for Samtidskunst** (Contemporary Art Museum).

The Contemporary Art Museum

The enterprising **Museet for Samtidskunst** (Contemporary Art Museum: Tues, Wed & Fri 11am–5pm, Thurs 11am–7pm, Sat & Sun noon–5pm; free; ⓦ www .nationalmuseum.no) owns work by every major post–World War II Norwegian artist and many leading foreign figures too, and for the most part the **displays** take the form of a series of temporary, thematic exhibitions spread over three floors. The works, some of which are massive, are each allowed a generous amount of space, so – given that the museum also hosts prestigious international exhibitions of contemporary art – only a fraction of the permanent collection can be shown at any one time.

The museum's exhibits hang from every wall and offset every corner and stairwell, but it's still difficult not to be just as impressed by the building itself, its polished, echoing halls resplendent with gilt and marble, ornamental columns and banisters. The museum also does a good line in t-shirts – a recent offering was inscribed "Welcome foreigners – don't leave us alone with the Danes".

The Architecture Museum

The, **Arkitekturmuseet** at Bankplassen 3 (Architecture Museum: Tues–Fri 11am–5pm, Thurs 11am–7pm, Sat & Sun noon–5pm; free; ⓦ www.nationalmuseum .no), is a new and lavish development in which keynote architectural displays are laid out in a handsome modern pavilion at the back of an older structure, dating from 1830. Opened in 2008, the whole development cost millions of kroner and although the initial exhibitions have focused on Norwegian architects – and Norwegian design – international figures are destined to follow.

The Akershus complex

Though very much part of central Oslo by location, the thumb of land that holds the sprawling fortifications of the **Akershus complex** (outdoor areas daily 6am–9pm; free) is quite separate from the city centre in feel. Built on a rocky knoll overlooking the harbour in around 1300, the original **castle** (slott) was already the battered veteran of several unsuccessful sieges when Christian IV (1596–1648) took matters in hand, transforming the medieval Akershus castle into a Renaissance residence. Around the castle he also constructed a new fortress – the **Akershus Festning** – whose thick earth-and-stone walls and protruding bastions were designed to resist artillery bombardment. Refashioned and enlarged on several later occasions, and now bisected by Kongens gate, parts of the fortress have remained in military use until the present day.

The Akershus complex has several **entrances**, the most appealing being at the west end of **Myntgata**, from where a footpath leads up to a side gate in the perimeter wall. Just beyond the gate is a dull museum-cum-information centre, which makes a strange attempt to tie in the history of the castle with modern environmental concerns. You're much better off keeping going along the signed **footpath** that twists its way up to the castle and the Resistance Museum, offering the possibility of heady views over the harbour on the way.

▲ Akershus Castle

The Resistance Museum

The **Hjemmefrontmuseum** (Resistance Museum: June–Aug Mon–Sat 10am–5pm, Sun 11am–5pm; Sept–May Mon–Fri 10am–4pm, Sat & Sun 11am–4pm; 30kr; ⓦwww.mil.no/felles/nhm) occupies a separate building just outside the castle entrance, an apt location given that the Gestapo tortured and sometimes executed captured Resistance fighters in the castle. Labelled in English and Norwegian, the displays detail the history of the war in Norway, from defeat and occupation through resistance to final victory. There are tales of extraordinary heroism here – notably the determined resistance of hundreds of the country's teachers to Nazi instructions and the sabotaging of German attempts to produce heavy water for an atomic bomb deep in southern Norway, at Rjukan. There's also an impressively honest account of Norwegian collaboration: fascism struck a chord with the country's petit bourgeois, and hundreds of volunteers joined the Wehrmacht. The most notorious collaborator was **Vidkun Quisling**, who was executed by firing squad for his treachery in 1945.

Akershus Castle

Next door to the Resistance Museum, the severe stone walls and twin spires of the medieval **Akershus Slott** (Akershus Castle: May–Aug Mon–Sat 10am–4pm, Sun 12.30–4pm; 65kr, including frequent guided tour; out of season one guided tour in English weekly – call ☎22 41 25 21 for details) perch on a rocky ridge high above the zigzag fortifications added by Christian IV. The castle is approached through two narrow tunnel-gateways, which lead to a cobbled courtyard at the heart of the castle. So far so good, but thereafter the interior is a bit of a disappointment, mostly comprising a string of sparsely furnished rooms linked by bare-brick passageways. Nevertheless, there are one or two items of interest, primarily the royal crypt, holding the sarcophagi of Norway's current dynasty – not that there have been many of them, just two in fact, Håkon VII (1872–1957) and Olav V (1903–91) – and the royal chapel.

The Opera House

From the castle, it's a short walk back to Tollbugata, where you turn right to reach one of the elevated walkways that leads over to the waterside **Operahuset** (Opera House: ⓦwww.operaen.no), one of the city's proudest buildings. Home to Den Norske Opera and Ballet, this is a glassy, Cubist structure, whose exterior ramps look like extended ski slopes, all to a loquacious design by the Norwegian company, Snøhetta. It is meant to impress, with no expense spared with the interior, and since its opening in 2008 Norwegians have visited in their thousands (Mon–Fri 10am–11pm, Sat 11am–11pm, Sun noon–10pm; free).

Southwest of the centre: the Bygdøy peninsula

Other than the city centre, the place where you're most likely to spend any time in Oslo is the **Bygdøy peninsula**, across the bay to the southwest of the main harbour, where there are no fewer than **five museums**, of which two, the Viking Ships Museum and the Fram Museum, are essential viewing. The most enjoyable way to reach Bygdøy is by **ferry #91**. This leaves from the Rådhusbrygge (pier 3) behind the Rådhus every twenty to thirty minutes (mid-May to Aug daily 8.45am–8.45pm; mid-March to mid-May & Sept to mid-Oct daily 8.45am–6pm; 34kr), returning to a similar schedule. All ferries to the peninsula perform a loop, calling first at the **Dronningen** dock (10min from Rådhusbrygge) and then the **Bygdøynes** dock (15min) before returning to the Rådhusbrygge; note that the ferries only go **one way** – so there is no service from Bygdøynes to Dronningen. The Viking Ships Museum is within easy walking distance of the Dronningen dock; the Fram Museum is a stone's throw from Bygdøynes. If you decide to walk between the two, allow about fifteen minutes: the route is well signposted but dull. The alternative to the ferry is **bus #30** (every 15–30min; 20min), which runs all year from Jernbanetorget and the National Theatre to the Viking Ships Museum.

The Viking Ships Museum

From the Dronningen dock, it's a ten-minute walk to the **Vikingskipshuset** (Viking Ships Museum: daily: May–Sept 9am–6pm; Oct–April 11am–4pm; 50kr; @www .khm.uio.no), which occupies a large, cross-shaped hall specially constructed to house a trio of ninth-century Viking ships, with viewing platforms to enable you to see inside the hulls. The three oak vessels were retrieved from ritual burial mounds in southern Norway around the turn of the twentieth century, each embalmed in a subsoil of clay, which accounts for their excellent state of preservation.

The museum's star exhibits are the Oseberg and Gokstad ships, named after the places on the west side of the Oslofjord where they were discovered in 1904 and 1880 respectively. The first ship you see as you enter the museum, the **Oseberg ship** is, at 22m long and 5m wide, representative of the type of vessel the Vikings used to navigate fjords and coastal waters. The ship has an ornately carved prow and stern, both of which rise high above the hull, where thirty oar-holes indicate the size of the crew. It is thought to be the burial ship of a Viking chieftain's wife and much of the treasure buried with it was retrieved and is now displayed just behind it. The grave goods reveal an attention to detail and a level of domestic sophistication not traditionally associated with the Vikings. There are marvellous decorative items like the fierce-looking animal-head posts and exuberantly carved ceremonial items, including a sledge and a cart, plus a host of smaller, more mundane household items such as shoes, rattles, agricultural tools and cooking pots.

Here also are finds from the **Gokstad ship**, most memorably an ornate bridle and two dragonhead bedposts, though the Gokstad burial chamber was ransacked by grave robbers long ago and precious little has survived. The Gokstad ship itself is slightly longer and wider than the Oseberg vessel and is quite a bit sturdier too. Its seaworthiness was demonstrated in 1893 when a replica sailed across the Atlantic to the US. The third vessel, the **Tune ship**, is the smallest of the nautical trio and only fragments survive; these are displayed unrestored, much as they were discovered in 1867 on the eastern side of the Oslofjord.

The Fram Museum

Just up from the Bygdøynes dock stands the **Gjøa**, the one-time sealing ship in which **Roald Amundsen** (1872–1928) made the first complete sailing of the Northwest Passage in 1906. By any measure, this was a remarkable achievement and the fulfilment of a nautical mission that had preoccupied sailors for several centuries. It took three years, with Amundsen and his crew surviving two ice-bound winters deep in the Arctic, but this epic journey was soon eclipsed when, in 1912, the Norwegian dashed to the South Pole famously just ahead of the ill-starred Captain Scott. The ship that carried Amundsen to within striking distance of the South Pole, the *Fram*, is displayed inside the mammoth triangular display hall that is the **Frammuseet** (Fram Museum: daily: March, April & Oct 10am–4pm; May & Sept 10am–5pm; June–Aug 9am–6pm; Nov–Feb 10am–3pm; 50kr; @www.fram.museum.no). Designed by Colin Archer, a Norwegian shipbuilder of Scots ancestry, and launched in 1892, the *Fram*'s design was unique, its sides made smooth to prevent ice from getting a firm grip on the hull, while inside a veritable maze of beams, braces and stanchions held it all together. Living quarters inside the ship were necessarily cramped, but – in true Edwardian style – the Norwegians found space for a piano.

Northwest of the centre: Frogner Park

The green expanse of **Frognerparken** (Frogner Park), to the northwest of the city centre, incorporates one of Oslo's most celebrated and popular cultural targets, the open-air **Vigelandsparken** which, along with the nearby museum, commemorates a modern Norwegian sculptor of world renown, **Gustav Vigeland** (1869–1943). Between them, the park and the museum display a good proportion of his work, including over two hundred figures in bronze, granite and cast-iron, all presented to the city in return for favours received by way of a studio and apartment during the years 1921–30.

Frogner Park is readily reached from the centre on **tram #12**; one of the places it stops is Aker Brygge; get off at Vigelandsparken, the stop after Frogner plass.

The Vigeland Sculpture Park

A country boy, **Gustav Vigeland** began his career as a woodcarver but later, when studying in Paris, he fell under the influence of Rodin, and switched to stone, iron and bronze. He started work on the **Vigelandsparken** (daylight hours; free) in 1924, and was still working on it when he died almost twenty years later. It's a literally fantastic concoction, medieval in spirit and complexity, and it was here that Vigeland had the chance to let his imagination run riot. Indeed, when the place was unveiled, many city folk were simply overwhelmed – and no wonder. From the monumental wrought-iron gates on Kirkeveien, the central path takes you to the footbridge over the river and a world of frowning, fighting and posturing bronze figures – the local favourite is *Sinnataggen* (The Angry Child), who has been rubbed smooth by a thousand hands. Beyond, the **central fountain** is an enormous bowl representing the burden of life, supported by straining, sinewy bronze Goliaths, and with a cascade of water tumbling down into a pool flanked by figures engaged in play or talk, or simply resting or standing.

Yet it's the twenty-metre-high **obelisk** up on the stepped embankment just beyond that really takes the breath away. It's a deeply humanistic work, a writhing mass of sculpture which depicts the cycle of life as Vigeland saw it: a vision of humanity playing, fighting, teaching, loving, eating and sleeping – and clambering on and over each other to reach the top. The granite sculptures grouped around the obelisk are exquisite too, especially the toddlers, little pot-bellied figures who tumble over muscled adults, providing the perfect foil to the real Oslo children who splash around in the fountain down below.

The Vigeland Museum

From the obelisk, it's a five- to ten-minute walk south (head to the right) across the lawns of the Frognerparken – and over the river by a second footbridge – to the **Vigeland-museet** (Vigeland Museum: June–Aug Tues–Sun 10am–5pm; Sept–May Tues–Sun noon–4pm; 50kr, but free Oct–March; ⓦwww.vigeland.museum.no), on the far side of Halvdan Svartes gate. This was the artist's studio and home during the 1920s, built for him by the city, who let him live here rent free on condition that the building – and its contents – passed back to public ownership on his death. It's still stuffed with all sorts of items related to the sculpture park, including photographs of the workforce, discarded or unused sculptures, woodcuts, preparatory drawings and scores of plaster casts. Vigeland was obsessed with his creations during his last decades, and you get the feeling that given half a chance he would have had himself cast and exhibited. As it is, his ashes were placed in the museum tower.

North of the centre: the Nordmarka

Crisscrossed by **hiking trails** and **cross-country ski routes**, the forested hills and lakes that comprise the **Nordmarka** occupy a tract of land that extends deep inland from central Oslo – but is still within the city limits for some 30km. A network of byroads provides dozens of access points to this wilderness, which is extremely popular with the capital's outdoor-minded citizens. **Den Norske Turistforening** (DNT), the Norwegian hiking organization, maintains a handful of staffed and unstaffed huts here. Its Oslo branch, in the city centre at **Storgata 3** (Mon–Fri

10am–5pm, Thurs 10am–6pm, Sat 10am–3pm; ☎22 82 28 22; ⓦwww.dntoslo.no), has detailed **maps** and can sell a year's DNT membership for 480kr, which confers a substantial discount at its huts.

Sognsvannet

It takes fifteen minutes for T-bane #3 to reach its northerly **Sognsvann terminus** from central Oslo. From the terminus, it's just five minutes' walk straight ahead down the slope to **Sognsvannet**, an attractive loch flanked by forested hills and encircled by an easy four-kilometre hiking trail. The lake is iced over until the end of March or early April, but thereafter it's a perfect spot for swimming, though Norwegian assurances about the warmth of the water should be treated with caution.

Northeast of the centre: the Munch Museum

Nearly everyone who visits Oslo makes time for the **Munch-museet** (Munch Museum: June–Aug daily 10am–6pm; Sept–May Tues–Fri 10am–4pm, Sat & Sun 11am–5pm; 75kr; ⓦwww.munch.museum.no) – and with good reason. In his will, Munch donated all the works in his possession to Oslo city council, a mighty bequest of several thousand paintings, prints, drawings, engravings and photographs, which took nearly twenty years to catalogue and organize before being displayed in this purpose-built gallery. The museum has, however, had its problems: in August 2004, two armed **robbers** marched into the museum and, in full view of dozens of bemused visitors, lifted two Munch paintings – the *Madonna* and *The Scream*, his most famous work, though fortunately Munch painted several versions (the earliest is in the National Gallery, see p.193). The two works of art were finally recovered two years later and, in a classic case of closing the stable door after the horse has bolted, the gallery has beefed up its security, though plans are afoot to close it down and move the collection to central Oslo.

The museum is located to the northeast of the city centre in the workaday suburb of Tøyen, at Tøyengata 53. Getting there by public transport couldn't be easier: take the T-bane to Tøyen station and it's a signposted, five-minute walk.

The collection

The Munch Museum's **permanent collection** is huge, and only a small – but always significant – part can be shown at any one time. Consequently, the paintings are frequently rotated and the museum also sources a lively programme of temporary exhibitions concentrating on various aspects of Munch's work. Naturally, all this means that you can't be certain what will be displayed and when, but the key paintings mentioned below are almost bound to be on view. At the start of the museum, an illustrated, potted biography of Munch and a short film on his life and times sets the scene. The finest paintings date from the **1890s**, and it's these that form the core of the collection. Among many, there are searing representations of *Despair* and *Anxiety*; the chilling *Red Virginia Creeper*, a house being consumed by the plant; and, of course, *The Scream* – of which the museum holds several versions.

Munch's style was never static, however. **Later paintings** such as *Workers On Their Way Home* (1913), produced after he had recovered from his breakdown and had withdrawn to the tranquillity of the Oslofjord, reflect his renewed interest in nature and physical work. His technique also changed: in works like the *Death of Marat II* (1907) he began to use streaks of colour to represent points of light. Later still, paintings such as *Winter in Kragerø* and *Model by the Wicker Chair*, with skin tones of pink, green and blue, begin to reveal a happier, if rather idealized, attitude to his surroundings, though this is most evident in works like *Spring Ploughing*, painted in 1919.

South of the centre: the islands and beaches of the inner Oslofjord

The compact archipelago of low-lying, lightly forested **islands** to the south of the city centre in the **inner Oslofjord** is the capital's summer playground, and makes going to the **beach** a viable option, especially on warm summer evenings when the less populated islands become favourite party venues for the city's youth. **Ferries** to the islands leave from the Vippetangen quay, at the foot of Akershusstranda – a twenty-minute walk or a five-minute ride on bus #60 from Jernbanetorget. Ferry tickets cost 34kr each way, though the Oslo Pass and all other transport passes are valid and there's also a ferry day-pass (Øybilletten) allowing unlimited inter-island travel for 40kr. There's an automatic ticket machine at the Vippetangen quay.

Hovedøya

Conveniently, **Hovedøya** (ferry #92; daily: mid-March to late May & Sept to mid-Oct 7.30am–6.30pm, every hour to ninety minutes; late May to Aug 7.30am–11pm hourly; Oct to mid-March 4–5 daily; 5min), the nearest island, is also the most interesting. Its rocky, rolling hills comprise both pastureland and deciduous woods as well as the substantial ruins of a **Cistercian monastery** built by English monks in the twelfth century. There are also incidental remains from the days when the island was garrisoned and armed to protect Oslo's harbour. A map of the island at the jetty helps with orientation, but on an islet of this size – it's just ten minutes' walk from one end to the other – getting lost is pretty much impossible. There are plenty of footpaths to wander, you can swim at the shingle beaches on the south shore, and there's a seasonal café opposite the monastery ruins. Camping, however, is not permitted as Hovedøya is a protected area, which is also why there are no summer homes.

Langøyene

The pick of the other islands is **Langøyene**, a pint-sized, H-shaped islet, just ten minutes' walk or so from one side to the other, where a central meadow is flanked on either side by low, lightly forested rocky hills. There are no houses on the island and no roads to speak of, but there is a long and narrow sandy(ish) beach, plus a rudimentary café, though most visitors bring their own supplies, especially those who camp here – there's no campsite as such but wilderness camping is permitted and quite a few visitors do just that. To get to Langøyene, take ferry #94 (late May to Aug hourly 9am–7/8pm; 15min) from the Vippetangen quay.

Eating and drinking

At the top end of the market, Oslo possesses dozens of fine **restaurants**, the pick of which feature Norwegian ingredients, especially fresh North Atlantic fish, but also more exotic dishes of elk, caribou and salted-and-dried cod – for centuries Norway's staple food. Many of these restaurants have also assimilated the tastes and **styles** of other cuisines and there is a reasonable selection of less expensive foreign restaurants too, everything from Italian to Vietnamese.

Even more affordable – and more casual – are the city's **cafés and café-bars**. These run the gamut from homely family places, offering traditional Norwegian stand-bys, to student haunts and ultra-trendy joints. Nearly all serve inexpensive lunches, and many offer excellent, competitively priced evening meals as well, though some cafés close at around 5pm or 6pm as do the city's many **coffee houses**, where coffee is, as you might expect, the main deal alongside maybe a light snack. Downtown Oslo also boasts a vibrant **bar** scene, boisterous but generally good-natured and at its most frenetic at summer weekends, when the city is crowded with visitors from all over Norway.

Cafés, café-bars and coffee houses

For sit-down food, **cafés** often represent the best value in town. Traditional *kafeterias* (usually self-service) offer substantial portions of Norwegian food in pleasant surroundings, though they are becoming thin on the ground. Oslo also has a slew of **café-bars**, where the best deals are generally at lunchtime.

Downtown

Celsius Café Rådhusgata 19. Smashing café-bar occupying imaginatively refurbished old premises just off the cobbled square at the junction of Rådhusgata and Nedre Slottsgate. Especially attractive courtyard seating too – for either a drink or a light meal: the menu is strong on beef and seafood, with a home-made burger, for instance, costing 140kr. Daily 11am–midnight.

Kaffebrenneriet Grensen 45 at Akersgata. One of the most central branches of this popular Norwegian coffee-house chain. Serves particularly good espresso, as well as snacks and cakes. Bright, modern decor. Mon–Fri 7am–7pm, Sat 9am–5pm.

Kaffistova Rosenkrantz gate 8. Part of the *Hotell Bondeheimen* (see p.190), this spick-and-span self-service café serves quite tasty, traditional Norwegian cooking at very fair prices – reckon on 130kr for a main course. Meatballs, gravy and potatoes are the house speciality. There's usually a vegetarian option, too. Mon–Fri 10am–9pm, Sat & Sun 11am–7pm.

Pascal Konditori Tollbugata 11. Lovely little café-patisserie comprising two rooms – one pleasantly modern, the other in the original bakery, which is decorated with ceramic tiles of cherubs and fruit dating from the 1890s. Mouthwatering pastries, great coffee and delicious, freshly prepared lunches – the fish soup is, for example, first-rate and costs 120kr. Mon–Sat 10am–5pm. Also in smart, modern premises at Henrik Ibsens gate 36 (Mon–Sat 10am–5pm & Sun noon–5pm).

Stockfleth's Lille Grensen, off Karl Johans gate. With good reason, many locals swear by the coffee served at this small chain, which regularly wins awards for its brews. Also on CJ Hambros plass and at Prinsens gate 6. Lille Grensen hours: Mon–Fri 7am–7pm, Sat 10am–6pm & Sun noon–6pm.

Tullins Café Tullins gate 2. The building may be glum – it's a dull, modern high-rise – but this ground-floor café-bar is painted in exuberant modern style and furnished with an idiosyncratic mix of bygones. Pasta dishes are the mainstay here – reckon on 100kr per main course – and there's

inexpensive beer (at least inexpensive by Norwegian standards) as the place morphs into a late-night bar. Handy central location too. Mon–Thurs 10am–2am, Fri 10am–3.30am, Sat noon–3.30am & Sun noon–1am.

Westside

Arcimboldo Wergelandsveien 17. Fashionable but unpretentious café-bar on the ground floor and adjoining terrace of the Kunstnernes Hus, an artist-run gallery whose Art Deco facade faces the Slottsparken. Offers good-quality food with a Norwegian slant, with main courses 140–240kr. Tues–Thurs 11am–11.30pm, Fri 11am–2.30am, Sat noon–1.30am & Sun noon–6pm.

Litteraturhuset Wergelandsveien 29. Opposite the tail end of the Slottsparken, this most amenable café-bar-cum-bookshop spreads its net wide with poetry readings and book signings as well as a café and outside terrace. Light meals here – the salads are good – will rush you around 150kr. The café-bar is open Mon–Wed 10am–midnight, Thurs & Fri 10am–3.30am, Sun noon–8pm.

Eastside: Grønland and Grünerløkka

Dattera til Hagen Grønland 10. Extremely popular spin-off venture of *Fru Hagen* (see below), serving tasty snacks and light meals during the daytime (11am–4pm) and authentic tapas later on (4–10pm). Later still, the place turns into a happening bar with live DJs on the first floor (Mon–Sat). The outdoor area at the back is great on a hot summer's night. Mon–Thurs 11am–1am, Fri & Sat 11am–3am, Sun noon–1am.

Fru Hagen Thorvald Meyers gate 40, Grünerløkka. Long-standing, colourful joint; still trendy, and serving tasty snacks and meals from an inventive menu with a Mediterranean slant. Filling sandwiches, salads and wok-cooked dishes too. Main courses 100–150kr. The kitchen closes at 9.30pm, after which the drinking gets going in earnest, plus DJ guest spots Thurs–Sat. Very popular spot – so go early to be sure of a seat. Mon–Wed 11am–midnight, Thurs–Sat 11am–3am, Sun noon–midnight.

Restaurants

Oslo's better **restaurants** have creative menus marrying Norwegian culinary traditions with those of the Mediterranean – and a lousy meal is a rarity, though dining out can make a dent on your wallet.

Downtown

Agra Holmens gate, Aker Brygge ☏ 22 83 07 12. Smart, North Indian restaurant serving all the classics – chicken tikka and so forth – with main courses averaging 210–250kr. Decorated in traditional style, from the Moghul prints to the mini-chandeliers. The only problem is that it is a little difficult to find: take the first right – Grundigen – go up the right-hand side of the Aker Brygge complex, turn left through the old factory gates and you are there. Mon–Sat 4–11pm, Sun 4–10pm.

Havsmak Henrik Ibsens gate 4 ☏ 24 13 38 00. Smart, specialist seafood restaurant kitted out in cool modern style – and oodles of blue paint. First-rate range of fresh fish, albeit of minimalist portions, with main courses averaging 200kr. Set meals too – two courses for 300kr, 490kr with wine. Mon–Sat 11am–11pm & Sun noon–10pm.

La Rosa Magra Arbins gate 1 at Henrik Ibsens gate ☏ 22 56 14 00. Bright, modern and cheerful, this first-rate Italian restaurant has a short(ish) but well-chosen menu featuring fresh pastas (130–180kr) and a handful of meat and fish dishes (220–240kr). Exemplary service; delicious, unpretentious food; and no pizzas. Mon–Sat 3–11pm & Sun 3–10pm.

Lofoten Fiskerestaurant Stranden 75, Aker Brygge ☏ 22 83 08 08. This smart, modern restaurant offers an outstanding selection of fish and shellfish, all immaculately prepared and served. It's beside the harbour at the far end of the Aker Brygge jetty, which makes it popular with locals and tourists alike. Mains kick off at around 260kr, but some of the more unusual fish – including the wonderfully textured cat fish (*steinbit*) cost another 90kr or so. Mon–Sat 11am–1am & Sun noon–midnight.

Solsiden Søndre Akershus Kai 34 ☏ 22 33 36 30. Tucked in below the Akershus castle, right on the harbourside, this lively and relaxed restaurant specializes in seafood, which is generally reckoned to be as good as anywhere in Oslo – try the turbot in a mustard purée. The emphasis is on natural, organic ingredients and the place has its own lobster tank. A three-course set meal costs 450kr, à la carte mains from 270kr. Open May–Aug only, daily 5–10pm.

Eastside: Grønland and Grünerløkka

Markveien Mat & Vinhus Torvbakkgata 12, Grünerløkka ☏ 22 37 22 97. This popular, top-quality restaurant and wine bar serves up Mediterranean-inspired dishes as well as traditional Norwegian favourites. Main courses average 150–200kr in the restaurant, half that in the wine bar, and the service is excellent. Also boasts one of the best wine cellars in the city. The entrance is on Markveien. Restaurant: Mon–Sat 5pm–12.30am, but kitchen closes at 11pm; wine bar: Mon–Sat 4pm–1am.

Sult Thorvald Meyers gate 26, Grünerløkka ☏ 22 87 04 67. One of the city's most popular restaurants – its name means "Hunger", after the novel by Knut Hamsun – the informal, fashionable but very relaxed *Sult* features a short but inventive menu using only the freshest of (local) ingredients. Main courses cost 180–200kr and star such delights as Hardanger trout and chicken from Stange. As if that wasn't enough, the adjacent bar *Tørst* (Thirst) serves mouthwatering margaritas. *Sult* kitchen open Tues–Thurs 4–10pm, Fri 4–11pm, Sat 1–11pm & Sun 1–10pm.

Bars

The more mainstream (meat-market) **bars** are in the centre along and around Karl Johans gate, while the sharper, more alternative spots are concentrated to the east in the Grønland and Grünerløkka districts.

Central

Café Tekehtopa St Olavs plass 2. '*Tekehtopa*' is '*Apotheket*' (pharmacy) spelt backwards – an appropriate little verbal play as this busy bar, which attracts a student crew, occupies a former pharmacy, complete with the original wooden fittings. There's a wide range of beers on draft and in bottles – look out for the ales of the micro-brewery Nøgne Ø – plus inexpensive pizzas, salads, omelettes and so forth. Mon–Thurs 10am–1am, Fri 10am–3am, Sat noon–3am & Sun noon–1am; kitchen closes at 11pm.

Steamen Olavs gate 2. Owned by the *Hotel Continental* (see p.190), this bright and lively sidewalk bar, with its nautical paraphernalia, is popular with the young(ish) and well-heeled. Mon noon–midnight, Tues–Sat noon–2.30am, & Sun noon–midnight.

Westside

Lorry Parkveien 12. Popular and enjoyable bar with old-fashioned (verging on the eccentric) fixtures and fittings that attracts a mixed crowd. There's a wide choice of beers – well over a hundred – and outdoor seating in the summer. Also serves food. At the corner of Hegdehaugsveien. Mon–Sat 11am–3.30am, Sun noon–1.30am.

Oslo Mikrobryggeri Bogstadveien 6 – but entrance on Holtegata. Dark, almost gloomy bar with loud music and a dart board plus a tasty range of ales, the pick of which are brewed on the premises – the equipment is in full view. Mon–Sat noon–3.30am, Sun noon–1.30am.

Palace Grill Solligata 2. Popular New Age-meets-alternative café-bar with a roots, rock and jazz soundtrack. Good food too. Mon 5pm–12.30am, Tues–Sat 5pm–3am & Sun 5pm–12.30am. In summertime, there's an outside bar, *Skaugum*, in the yard behind and beside the *Palace* – and it heaves.

Eastside: Grønland and Grünerløkka

Bar Boca Thorvald Meyers gate 30, Grünerløkka. Tiny 1950s retro-style bar serving some of the best cocktails in town. The bartenders take their work very seriously, and you need to get there early to avoid the crush. Live jazz once or twice weekly. Daily noon–3am.

Café con Bar Brugata 11, Grønland. Hip-as-you-like with retro interior and a long bar that can make buying a drink hard work. Good atmosphere, loungy decor and unisex toilets for those surprise meetings. Mon–Thurs 11am–11pm, Fri & Sat 11am–3am, Sun noon–11pm.

Robinet Mariboes gate 7. Possibly the smallest bar in Oslo – 1950s retro kitsch combined with excellent drinks and an intellectual crowd. Daily noon–2am.

Tea Lounge Thorvald Meyers gate 33B. Lounge-type café-bar with velvety red couches and big windows. As you might guess from the name, tea is a big deal here – all sorts and served to a soft house backtrack. Cocktails also. Mon–Wed 11am–1am, Thurs–Sat 11am–3pm & Sun noon–2am.

Entertainment and nightlife

With the city's bars staying open till the wee hours, Oslo's **nightclubs** struggle to make themselves heard – indeed there's often little distinction between the two – though there is still a reasonably good and varied nightclub scene. **Live music** is not perhaps Oslo's forte, and the domestic **rock** scene is far from inspiring, but **jazz** fans are well served, with a couple of first-rate venues in the city centre, and **classical music** enthusiasts benefit from an ambitious concert programme. Most **theatre** productions are in Norwegian, but English-language theatre companies visit often, and at the **cinema** films are shown in the original language with Norwegian subtitles.

For **entertainment listings** it's worth checking out *What's On Oslo*, a monthly English-language freebie produced by the tourist office. One other useful free publication is *Streetwise*, which is produced annually by Use-It, the city's youth information shop at Møllergata 3 (☎24 14 98 20, ⓦwww.use-it.no); it carries descriptions of – among much else – the city's best bars and clubs.

For **tickets**, contact the venue direct or try Billettservice (☎815 33 133, ⓦwww .billettservice.no), who use thirty of the city's post offices as outlets – details are on the website.

Nightclubs and live music

Oslo's hippest bars and **nightclubs** are located on the east side of the city, away from the centre in or near the Grønland and Grünerløkka districts, but there are also several clubs in the centre and out west. Nothing gets going much before 11pm and closing times are generally around 3.30am. Many nightclubs also host a variety of **live music**, ranging from local home-grown talent to big-name bands. Generally speaking, entry will set you back about 100kr and at the smarter places there's an informal dress code – go scruffy and you will be turned away.

Blå Brenneriveien 9C ☎40 00 42 77, ⓦwww .blx.no. Creative, cultural nightspot in Grünerløkka, featuring everything from live jazz and cabaret through to poetry readings. Also features some of the best DJs in town, keeping the crowd moving until 3.30am at the weekend. In summer, there's a pleasant riverside terrace too.

Gloria Flames Grønland 18 ☎22 17 16 00, ⓦwww .gloriaflames.no. Not the easiest bar-cum-club to find – there's just a small sign on the door – but worth searching out if you're into rock and rockabilly. Regular live acts and a summer rooftop bar. Mon–Thurs 4pm–1.30am, Fri & Sat 3pm–3.30am.

Last Train Karl Johans gate 45 ☎22 41 52 93, ⓦwww.lasttrain.no. The best rock-pub/club in town. Good old-style rock played at volume to a leather and jeans clientele. Entrance downtown on Universitets-gata. Mon–Fri 3pm–3.30am, Sat 6pm–3.30am.

Oslo Spektrum Sonja Henies plass 2 ☎815 11 211, ⓦwww.oslospektrum.no. Major venue, close to Olso S, showcasing big international acts, as well as small-fry local bands.

Sikamikanico Møllergata 2 ☎22 41 44 09, ⓦwww.sikamikanico.no. Hip-hop, drum 'n' bass, jazz and house in heaving club near Oslo S. Great DJ nights too. Wed–Sun from 10pm.

Jazz venues

Oslo has a strong **jazz** tradition, and in early or mid-August its week-long **Jazz Festival** attracts internationally renowned artists as well as showcasing local talent. The Festival Office, at Tollbugata 28 (☎22 42 91 20, ⓦwww.oslojazz.no), has full programme details of all the gigs, including those where there's an admission charge as well as the many free outdoor performances. At other times of the year, try one of the following for regular jazz acts.

Bare Jazz Grensen 8 ☎22 33 20 80, ⓦwww .barejazz.no. Split-level joint with a superb selection of jazz CDs for sale on the ground floor and a jazz café up above with frequent live sounds, both home-grown and imported. Mon & Tues 10am–6pm, Wed–Sat 10am–midnight.

Herr Nilsen Jazzklubb CJ Hambros plass 5 ☎22 33 54 05, ⓦwww.herrnilsen.no. Small and intimate bar whose brick walls are decorated with jazz memorabilia. Live jazz – often traditional and bebop – most nights. With A/c; central location. Daily 2pm–2.30am.

Classical music and opera

Oslo's major orchestra, the **Oslo Filharmonien** (☎23 11 60 60, ⓦwww .oslofilharmonien.no), gives regular concerts in the city's Konserthus, at Munkedam-sveien 14. As you might expect, programmes often include works by Norwegian and other Scandinavian composers. Tickets for most performances cost around 400kr. In August and September, the orchestra traditionally gives a couple of free evening concerts in the Vigeland sculpture park, as part of the city's summer entertainment programme, which also sees classical performances at a variety of other venues; for details of the summer programme, contact the tourist office (see p.186).

Den Norske Opera, Norway's prolific opera company, offers a popular repertoire – Mozart, R. Strauss and the Italians – but also undertakes a number of contemporary works each year. Performances are held at the new, super-modern Operahuset (Opera House), on the waterfront near Oslo S at Kirsten Flagstads plass 1 (information ☎21 42 21 00, box office ☎815 44 488, ⓦwww.operaen.no).

Cinema

Cinema listings – including information on late-night screenings – appear daily in the local press, and the tourist office has details too. All the main commercial cinemas share the **same telephone number** and website (☎820 50 001; ⓦwww .oslokino.no), and the following is a selection of central screens. Prices are surprisingly reasonable, with tickets averaging 80–90kr.

Eldorado Torggata 9. Mainstream cinema showing the usual blockbusters. Near the cathedral.

Filmens Hus Dronningens gate 16 at Tollbugata. Art-house cinema with a varied and extremely enjoyable programme mixing mainstream and alternative/avant-garde films.

Klingenberg Olav V's gate 4. Mainstream cinema with four screens. Central location, metres from the National Theatre.

Saga Stortingsgata 28 at Olav V's gate. Main-stream cinema with six screens. Metres from the National Theatre.

Theatre

Nearly all of Oslo's theatre productions are in Norwegian, making them of limited interest to (most) tourists, though there are occasional English-language performances by touring theatre companies. The principal venue is the **Nationaltheatret**, Stortingsgata 15 (℡815 00 811, ⓦwww.nationaltheatret.no), which hosts the prestigious, annual Ibsen Festival. Touring companies may also appear at the more adventurous **Det Norske Teatret**, Kristian IV's gate 8 (℡22 42 43 44, ⓦwww .detnorsketeatret.no).

Listings

Airlines British Airways ℡815 33 142; Brussels Airlines ℡23 16 25 68; Finnair ℡810 01 100; KLM ℡22 64 37 52; Norwegian Air Shuttle ℡815 21 815; SAS/Braathens ℡05400; Widerøe's ℡810 01 200. For a comprehensive list, see under *Flyselskaper* in the *Yellow Pages*.

Car rental Bislet Bilutleie, Pilestredet 70 (℡22 60 00 00, ⓦwww.bislet.no); Europcar, several downtown locations and at Gardermoen airport (℡64 81 05 60, ⓦwww.europcar.no); Hertz, several Oslo locations including Holbergs gate 30 (℡22 21 00 00), and at the airport (℡64 81 05 50, ⓦwww .hertz.no); National, at the airport (℡64 82 06 40, ⓦwww.nationalcar.no). See also under *Bilutleie* in the *Yellow Pages*.

Cycling The Syklistenes Landsforening, in the Operapassasjen, at Storgata 23D (Norwegian Cyclist Association: Mon–Fri noon–3pm; ℡22 47 30 42, ⓦwww.slf.no), gives advice and information on route planning and sells cycling maps. For bike hire in Oslo, see p.187.

Dentist Municipal dental information on ℡22 67 30 00. Otherwise, see under *Tannleger* in the *Yellow Pages*.

Gay Oslo There's not much of a scene as such, primarily because Oslo's gays and lesbians are mostly content to share pubs and clubs with heteros. That said, gay men do congregate at the *London Pub*, CJ Hambros plass 5 (daily 3pm–3am; ⓦwww.londonpub.no), with a busy pub-bar on one floor and a disco on another; and at *Ett Glass*, a lively café-bar on Rosenkrantz gate, just up from Karl Johans gate (daily 11am–1am, 3am at the weekend; kitchen closes at 10pm). The main gay event is the *Skeive Dager* (Queer Days; ⓦwww .skeivedager.no) festival usually held over ten days in late June with parties, parades, political meetings, a film festival and incorporating Gay Pride. Norway's national gay and lesbian organization is LLH (Landsforeningen for lesbisk og homofil frigjøring; ⓦwww.llh.no); their Oslo office is at Kongens gate 12.

Hiking Den Norske Turistforening (DNT; ⓦwww .turistforeningen.no), the Norwegian hiking organization, has its Oslo branch in the city centre at

Storgata 3 (Mon–Fri 10am–5pm, Thurs 10am–6pm, Sat 10am–3pm; ℡22 82 28 22, ⓦwww.dntoslo .no). It offers a full range of Norwegian hiking maps, books and equipment plus DNT membership – a relative snip at 480kr per year. See the Hiking colour section for more on DNT and hiking in general.

Internet Almost all city hotels and hostels provide internet access for their guests either free or at (fairly) reasonable rates. Internet access is also available free at the main city library, the Deichmanske bibliotek, at Arne Garborgs plass 4 (June–Aug Mon–Fri 10am–6pm, Sat 11am–2pm; Sept–May Mon–Fri 10am–7pm, Sat 10am–4pm; ⓦwww.deichman.no), and, if you are under 26, at Oslo's youth information shop, Use-it, Møllergata 3 (July–Aug Mon & Wed–Fri 9am–6pm, Tues 11am–6pm; Sept–June Mon–Fri 11am–5pm; ℡24 14 98 20, ⓦwww.use-it.no). There's also an internet pit-stop, the Sidewalk Express, inside Oslo S (30kr for 90min).

Laundry Majorstua Myntvaskeri, Vibes gate 15 (℡22 69 43 17); Snarvask, Thorvald Meyers gate 18, Grünerløkka (℡22 37 57 70). See also under *Vaskerier* in the *Yellow Pages*.

Left luggage Coin-operated lockers (24hr) and luggage office at Oslo S.

Lost property (*hittegods*) Trams, buses and T-bane at the Nationaltheatret station (℡22 08 53 61). NSB railways, Oslo S (℡815 68 340); police, call ℡22 66 98 65.

Medical treatment For medical emergencies, call ℡113. For lesser problems, either head for the nearest pharmacy (see "Pharmacy" below) or the Walk-In Clinic, to the rear of the Aker Brygge complex at the corner of Munkedamsveien and Sjøgata (℡22 83 10 83, ⓦwww.walk-in-clinic.com). The clinic is fast, efficient, friendly – and expensive. For cheaper treatment, stick to the A&E department of the nearest hospital, at the north end of Storgata, beside the river.

Pharmacy Oslo has scores of pharmacies – see under *Apotek* in the *Yellow Pages* or call the 24hr infoline, ℡23 35 81 00. See also "Medical Treatment" above.

Police In an emergency, phone ☏112.
Post offices There are lots of post offices dotted across the city, including a branch in Oslo S. All post offices exchange currency and cash traveller's cheques at very reasonable rates. Normal opening hours are Mon–Fri 8am–5pm & Sat 9am–1pm.

Taxis There are taxi ranks dotted all over the city centre. You can also telephone Oslo Taxi on ☏02323 or Norgestaxi on ☏08000.
Trains NSB (Norwegian State Railways) has two stations in central Oslo – Oslo S and Nationaltheatret. Enquiries and bookings on ☏815 00 888, ⓦwww.nsb.no.

Travel details

Principal NSB trains (ⓦwww.nsb.no)

Oslo to: Åndalsnes (2–3 daily; 5hr 30min); Arendal (4–5 daily, change at Nelaug; 4hr 10min); Bergen (4 daily; 7hr 20min); Dombås (3–4 daily; 4hr); Geilo (3–4 daily; 3hr); Hamar (hourly; 1hr 30min); Hjerkinn (3–4 daily; 4hr 30min – request stop only); Kongsberg (4–5 daily; 1hr 10min); Kongsvoll (3–4 daily; 4hr 40min – request stop only); Kristiansand (4–5 daily; 4hr 30min); Lillehammer (hourly; 2hr); Myrdal (4 daily; 4hr 50min); Otta (6 daily; 3hr 30min); Røros (6 daily; 5hr); Sandefjord (every 1–2hr; 1hr 50min); Stavanger (4–5 daily; 8hr); Trondheim (3–4 daily; 6hr 40min); Tønsberg (every 1–2hr; 1hr 30min); Voss (4 daily; 6hr 40min).

Oslo Gardermoen airport to: Åndalsnes (2–3 daily; 5hr); Dombås (3–4 daily; 3hr 30min); Hamar (hourly; 1hr); Hjerkinn (3–4 daily; 4hr – request stop only); Kongsvoll (3–4 daily; 4hr 10min – request stop only); Kvam (1–2 daily; 3hr – request stop only); Lillehammer (hourly; 1hr 30min); Otta (6 daily; 3hr); Røros (6 daily; 4hr 30min); Trondheim (3–4 daily; 6hr 10min).

Principal Nor-Way Bussekspress buses (ⓦwww.nor-way.no)

Oslo to: Ålesund (2 daily; 10hr); Åndalsnes (2 daily; 8hr); Balestrand (3 daily; 8hr 30min); Bergen (3 daily; 10hr 30min); Dombås (2 daily; 6hr 15min); Haugesund (3 daily; 8hr 45min); Kongsberg (3 daily; 1hr 30min); Kristiansand (6 daily; 5hr); Lillehammer (4 daily; 3hr); Lom (4 daily; 6hr 40min); Måløy (3 daily; 11hr); Mundal, Fjaerland (3 daily; 7hr 50min); Odda (3 daily; 7hr); Otta (4 daily; 5hr 30min); Rjukan (3–4 daily; 3hr 30min); Sogndal (3 daily; 7hr); Stavanger (2–3 daily; 10hr); Stryn (3 daily; 8hr 40min); Trondheim (1–3 daily; 8hr).

2.2

South Norway

Arcing out into the Skagerrak between the Oslofjord and Stavanger, Norway's **south coast** may have little of the imposing grandeur of other, wilder parts of the country, but its eastern half, running down to Kristiansand, is undeniably lovely. Speckled with islands and backed by forests, fells and lakes, it's this part of the coast that attracts Norwegians in droves, equipped not so much with bucket and spade as with boat and navigational aids – for these waters, with their narrow inlets, islands and skerries, make for particularly enjoyable **sailing**. Hundreds of Norwegians have summer cottages along this stretch of the coast and camping on the offshore islands is very popular too, especially as there are precious few restrictions: you can't stay in one spot for more than 48 hours, nor light a fire either on bare rock or among vegetation, and you must steer clear of anyone's home, but other than that you're pretty much free to go and come as you please. Leaflets detailing further coastal rules and regulations are available at any local tourist office.

The south coast down to Kristiansand is within easy striking distance of Denmark and as such it has always been important for Norway's international trade. Many of the region's larger towns, Larvik and Porsgrunn for instance, started out as timber ports, but are now humdrum industrial centres in their own right, whereas several of their smaller neighbours – **Lillesand** is the prime example – have dodged (nearly) all the industry to become pretty, pocket-sized resorts, whose white-painted clapboard houses provide an appropriately nautical, almost jaunty, air. Larger Arendal does something to bridge the gap between the resorts and the industrial towns and does so very nicely. There's also **Sandefjord**, an amenable if somewhat uninspiring place that may well be first up on your itinerary as it has its own international airport – **Oslo** (**Torp**) (see p.182).

Anchoring the south coast is Norway's fifth largest city, **Kristiansand**, a bustling port and lively resort with enough sights, restaurants, bars and beaches to while away a night, maybe two. Beyond Kristiansand lies **Mandal**, an especially fetching holiday spot with a great beach, but thereafter the coast becomes harsher and less absorbing, heralding a lightly populated region with precious little to detain you before **Stavanger**, a burgeoning oil town and port with a clutch of historical sights and a full set of first-rate restaurants. Bergen (see pp.240–254) may lay claim to being the "Gateway to the Fjords", but actually Stavanger is closer, with the splendid Lysefjord leading the scenic charge

There are regular **trains** from Oslo to Kristiansand and Stavanger, but the rail line runs inland for most of its journey, only dipping down to the coast at the major resorts, which makes for a disappointing ride with the sea mostly shielded from view by the bony, forested hills. The same applies to the main **road and bus** route – the **E18/E39** – which also sticks stubbornly inland for most of the 330km from Oslo to Kristiansand (E18) and again for the 250km on to Stavanger (E39). Thanks to the E18/E39, even the tiniest of coastal villages is easy to reach, but you do need your own vehicle for most of the smaller places unless you are infinitely diligent with bus and rail timetables.

The E18 to Lillesand

The fretted shoreline that stretches the 200km southwest from Tønsberg to Lillesand is home to a series of small resorts that are particularly popular with weekenders

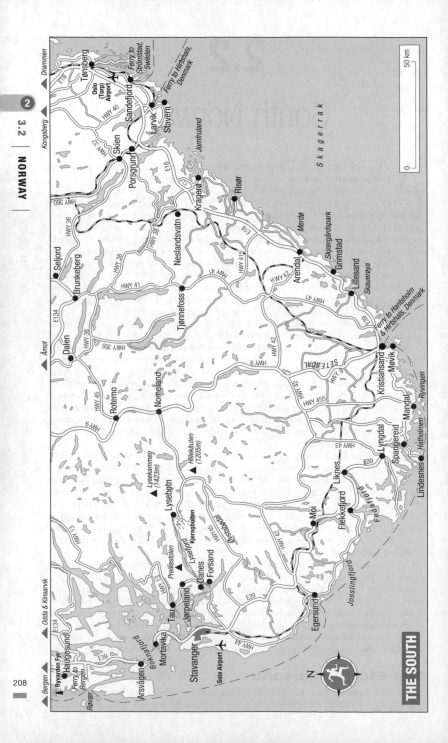

THE SOUTH

from Oslo. The liveliest is **Arendal**, and the prettiest is **Lillesand**; both have decent places to stay. Many of the resorts, including Lillesand and Arendal, offer **boat trips** out to the myriad islets that dot this coast, with trippers bent on a spot of swimming and beach – or at least rock – combing. The islands were once owned by local farmers, but many are now in public ownership, and zealously protected from any development. In addition, most of the resorts offer longer cruises along the coast during the summer, the most agreeable being the delightful three-hour trip from Lillesand to Kristiansand.

Fast and frequent express **buses** scuttle along the **E18** from Oslo to Kristiansand and these connect with local buses that run from the E-road to individual resorts – see "Travel details", p.223. A **train** line runs along the coast too, stopping at Arendal and near Sandefjord, but bypassing Lillesand. Kristiansand is also a major international port with **ferries** arriving from Denmark and from Newcastle in the UK.

Sandefjord

SANDEFJORD, some 120km south of Oslo, is best known as an international ferry port and as the site of **Oslo (Torp) airport**. It's an amiable, low-key kind of place, whose wide and open waterfront culminates in a spectacular water fountain – the **Hvalfangstmonumentet** (Whalers' Monument) in which, amidst the billowing spray, a slender rowing boat and its crew ride the tail fluke of a whale. This is perhaps as good as it gets, but the town does rustle up a couple of other minor attractions, beginning with the nearby Kurbadet, the former thermal baths housed in a distinctive wooden complex built in a Viking-inspired dragon style in 1899; the baths closed at the beginning of World War II and have come close to being demolished on several occasions, but they have managed to hang on and are now in use as a cultural centre. The complex is located a couple of minutes' walk from the fountain – to the right as you face inland.

Practicalities

Oslo (Torp) airport is about 11km north of Sandefjord. The airport has expanded dramatically in recent years and now picks up a slew of domestic and international flights, with Ryanair to the fore. The Torp-Ekspressen bus (see p.182) links the airport with Oslo and there are also airport buses to Sandefjord Torp train station, just one stop along the line from Sandefjord station (hourly; 3min; 33kr each way) – and a little under two hours from Oslo S (200kr each way).

From Sandefjord's **train** and neighbouring **bus station**, it's about 900m to the waterfront, straight down Jernbanealleen. The **tourist office** is just back from the waterfont, next to the Kurbadet at Thor Dahlsgate 7 (late June to late Aug Mon–Fri 9am 6pm, Sat 10am–4.30pm & Sun 12.30–4.30pm; rest of year Mon–Fri 9am–4pm; ⓣ33 46 05 90, ⓦwww.visitsandefjord.com). A few metres away is the Color Line quay (ⓦwww.colorline.com), where **car ferries** to and from Strömstad in Sweden arrive and depart (see "Travel details", p.223).

Of Sandefjord's several **hotels**, one of the more appealing is the large, plush *Rica Park Hotel Sandefjord*, in a big, modern tower block just back from the waterfront at Strandpromenaden 9 (ⓣ33 44 74 00, ⓦwww.rica.no; ❺/❽). Rather more distinctive – and a good bit more economical – is the *Hotel Kong Carl*, in an old timber building right in the centre of town at Torggata 9 (ⓣ33 46 31 17, ⓦwww .kongcarl.no; ❸). The 25 rooms are each kitted out with a potpourri of old furnishings – pleasant if hardly stunning. There are also a couple of attractive B&Bs in the old part of town, notably *Lisbet's Guesthouse*, where there is one room to rent in the annexe with bunk beds and a shower (ⓣ33 46 08 26, ⓔlisbe-ti@online.no; ❶).

For food, *Mathuset Solvold*, between the tourist office and the main square at Thor Dahlsgate 9, is a well-turned-out café-restaurant offering a wide-ranging menu – from pasta to mussels – with main courses 160–200kr.

Arendal

Heading south from Sandefjord, it's about 150km to the bustling town of **ARENDAL**, one of the most appealing places on the coast, its sheltered harbour curling right into the centre, which is further crimped by the forested hills pushing in from behind. The town's heyday was in the eighteenth century when its shipyards churned out dozens of the sleek wooden sailing ships that then dominated international trade. The shipyards faded away in the late nineteenth century, but there's an attractive reminder of the boom times in the striking medley of old timber buildings that make up the oldest part of town, **Tyholmen**, which rolls over the steep and bumpy promontory just to the southwest of the modern centre. The architectural highlight here is the **Gamle Rådhus** (Old Town Hall), Norway's tallest wooden house, a handsome, four-storey structure, whose classical symmetries overlook the Tyholmen waterfront.

Perched on a rocky knoll at the northern edge of Tyholmen, the massive and massively ugly red-brick **Trefoldighetskirken** (Church of the Trinity) was meant to celebrate the town's economic success as well as its spirituality. Instead, it almost ended up being a total fiasco: Arendal hit the financial skids in 1886 and, although the church had been finished, there was no money to equip the interior, and the altar was only installed twenty years later. The church overlooks the town centre, where the most conspicuous building is the glassy, modern Kulturhus (ⓦwww.arendalkulturhus.no), which hosts conferences, public meetings, and concerts to suit (almost) every musical taste. From here, it's a couple of minutes' walk north to Pollen, the short, rectangular inner harbour, which is flanked by pavement cafés and bars.

Merdø island

Among the scattering of islands lying just offshore from Arendal, the most diverting is **Merdø**, a fairly flat, lightly wooded islet, whose safe anchorages, orchards and fresh water made it a popular haven for sailing ships right up until the end of the nineteenth century. Footpaths network the island, there's a shingle beach and a café, and Merdø's one and only village is a pretty affair that spreads along the foreshore. It's here you'll find the **Merdøgaard Museum** (late June to mid-Aug daily noon–4pm; 20kr), a brightly painted eighteenth-century sea captain's house, complete with original fixtures and fittings.

The passenger ferry to **Merdø** departs from Pollen, right in the centre of Arendal (June to late Aug daily 10am–4pm every 30min to 1hr; 40kr; rest of year, sporadic service – details from the tourist office).

Practicalities

Arendal **train station** is on the north side of town, a five- to ten-minute walk from the main square, Torvet: go to the roundabout close to the station and then either proceed up and over the steep hill along Iuellsklev and then Bendiksklev, or (more easily) stroll through the tunnel (signed: P–Torget). Torvet is metres from the inner harbour, Pollen. The **bus station** is in the centre of town beside the Kulturhus on Vestre gate, just west of Torvet. The **tourist office** is in the Kulturhus (July Mon–Fri 9am–7pm, Sat & Sun 11am–6pm; Aug–June Mon–Fri 9am–7pm, Sat 11am–2pm; ☎37 00 55 44, ⓦwww.arendal.com).

There's one smashing hotel in Arendal, the ⚑ *Clarion Hotel Tyholmen*, Teaterplassen 2 (☎37 07 68 00, ⓦwww.choicehotels.no; ❹/❻), which occupies a matching pair of buildings in the style of two old warehouses on the Tyholmen quayside. Full marks here to the architects, who designed the second, newer block to blend in seamlessly with its older neighbour. The guest rooms are resolutely modern, with blues and whites throughout, and most have splendid sea views. A second, very much more modest option is the *Thon Hotel Arendal*, Friergangen 1 (☎37 05 21 50, ⓦwww.thonhotels.com/arendal; ❹/❺), a straightforward, modern hotel in the centre just off the west side of Pollen.

A string of **cafés and restaurants** line up along Pollen, with one of the best being *Restaurant 1711* (Mon–Sat 6–10.30pm; ☎37 00 17 11), a smart and intimate little place in an old wooden building on the south side of the harbour. The house speciality is seafood, and main courses cost 250–300kr. The grooviest place in town is *Café Det Lindvedske Hus* (Mon–Sat 11am–11pm, Sun noon–11pm), a laid-back, arty sort of place where they serve light meals – pastas, salads and so forth – upstairs in an old building just to the south of Pollen. Mains start at around 60kr and the kitchen closes at 9pm, whereupon it's over to the drinking. For a small town, Arendal has a lively drinking scene with a clutter of bars on and around Pollen keeping the punters going till the wee hours of the morning each and every weekend.

Lillesand

Bright and cheery **LILLESAND**, just 40km south of Arendal, is one of the most popular holiday spots on the coast, the white clapboard houses of its tiny centre draped prettily round the harbourfront. One or two of the buildings, notably the sturdy **Rådhus** of 1734, are especially fetching, but it's the general appearance of the place that appeals, best appreciated from the terrace of one of the town's waterfront café-bars: the *Sjøbua*, midway round the harbour, does very nicely.

To investigate Lillesand's architectural nooks and crannies, sign up at the tourist office (see below) for one of their hour-long **guided walks** (1 daily mid-June to Aug; 40kr) The tourist office also has information and sailing schedules for a wide variety of local **boat trips**, from fishing trips and cruises along the coast to the summertime *badeboot* (bathing boat), which shuttles across to Hestholm bay on the island of **Skauerøya**, where swimmers don't seem to notice just how cold the Skagerrak actually is. Perhaps better still is the three-hour cruise aboard **M/B Øya** (July to early Aug Mon–Sat 1 daily; 225kr each way; ☎95 93 58 55), a dinky little passenger ferry which wiggles south to Kristiansand (see p.212) in part along a narrow channel separating the mainland from the offshore islets. Sheltered from the full force of the ocean, this channel – the **Blindleia** – was once a major trade route, but today it's trafficked by every sort of pleasure craft imaginable, from replica three-mast sailing ships and vintage tugboats to the sleekest of yachts. Other, faster, boats make the trip too, but the M/B *Øya* is the most charming.

Practicalities

Lillesand is not on the train line and although some buses – principally those from Arendal and Grimstad – halt at the bus station in the town centre, most long-distance services pull into Lillesand Borkedalen, from where connecting local buses proceed to Lillesand, a five-minute journey. Lillesand bus station is at the southern end of the harbour, footsteps from the **tourist office** (mid-June to mid-Aug Mon–Fri 10am–6pm, Sat 10am–4pm & Sun noon–4pm; ☎93 01 17 81, ⓦwww.lillesand.com).

Lillesand has one central **hotel**, the first-rate ⚓ *Hotel Norge*, Strandgata 3 (☎37 27 01 44, ⓦwww.hotelnorge.no; ⑥/⑦), which occupies a grand old wooden building metres from the harbour. Refurbished in attractive period style, the interior holds some charming stained-glass windows and the rooms are named after some of the famous people who have stayed here – the novelist Knut Hamsun and the Spanish king Alfonso XIII for starters. Alternatively, try *Tingsaker Familiecamping* (☎37 27 04 21, ⓦwww.tingsakercamping.no), a well-equipped and very busy seaside campsite with self-catering facilities, canoe hire, a pool and cabins (850–1500kr), about 1km north of the centre on Øvre Tingsaker. To get there, take Storgata and keep going. The *Hotel Norge* has an excellent **restaurant**, but it's more expensive and formal than the harbourfront *Beddingen* (☎37 27 24 22), where you can sample excellent fish dishes for around 220kr.

Kristiansand

With 80,000 inhabitants, **KRISTIANSAND**, some 30km west along the E18 from Lillesand, is Norway's fifth-largest town and part-time holiday resort – altogether a genial, energetic place which thrives on its ferry connections with Denmark, its busy marinas, its passable sandy beaches and, last but not least, its offshore oil industry. In summer, the seafront and adjoining streets are a frenetic bustle of bars, fast-food joints and flirting holidaymakers, and even in winter Norwegians come here to live it up.

Like so many other Scandinavian towns, Kristiansand was founded by – and named after – **Christian IV**, who saw an opportunity to strengthen his coastal defences here. Building started in 1641, and the town has retained the spacious quadrant plan that characterized all Christian's projects. There are few specific sights as such, but the place is well worth a quick look around, especially when everyone else has gone to the beach and left the central pedestrianized streets relatively empty.

Arrival and information

Trains, **buses** and international **ferries** all arrive close to each other, beside Vestre Strandgate, on the edge of the town grid. The main regional **tourist office** is nearby, at Rådhusgaten 6 (mid-June to Aug Mon–Fri 8.30am–6pm, Sat 10am–6pm, Sun noon–6pm; Sept to mid-June Mon–Fri 8.30am–3.30pm; ☎38 12 13 14, ⓦ www.sorlandet.com). It issues free town maps and public transport timetables, will assist with accommodation and have information on local boat cruises, island bathing and beaches. The main car parks are along Vestre Strandgate and, although spaces can be hard to find at the height of the season, they remain your best bet as on-street parking in the rest of the town centre is strictly limited.

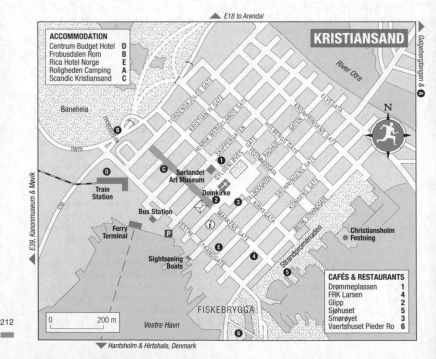

Accommodation

Kristiansand has a reasonably good choice of **accommodation** with a fair sprinkling of hotels, a guesthouse or two and a nearby campsite.

Centrum Budget Hotel Vestre Strandgate 49 ☎38 70 15 65, ⊛www.budgethotel.no. Hard by the train station, this hostel-like hotel provides frugal, modern and very clean lodgings at budget prices. Doubles are in the form of bunk beds, and all rooms are en suite. Breakfasts are served close by at the *Jernbanekafeen* café and cost just 60kr. **❶**

Frobusdalen Rom Frobusdalen 2 ☎91 12 99 06, ⊛www.gjestehus.no. Undoubtedly the best place in town, this delightful guesthouse is a family-run affair occupying a good-looking mansion built for a ship-owner in 1917. The interior has been sensitively restored, with individually decorated en-suite rooms and public areas sprinkled with period antiques. It's just a 5–10min walk from the train station, but is a little hard to find: on foot, head north up Vestre Strandgate; go straight on at the roundabout by the flyover (signed Evje), then take the path immediately to your right; Frobusdalen is 10m along on the left. Drivers should head north along Festningsgata; turn left on to Tordenskjolds gate; and then watch for the short right turn that leads to a narrow bridge spanning the E18, the far side of the bridge is a few metres from the

guesthouse. Breakfast is not provided, but there are self-catering facilities. **❸**

Rica Hotel Norge Dronningens gate 5 ☎38 17 40 00, ⊛www.rica.no. No prizes for architectural charm, but this large chain hotel is right in the centre of town and its 170 guest rooms are decorated in attractive modern style. Has its own spa too. **❹/❻**

Roligheden Camping Framnesveien ☎38 09 67 22, ⊛www.roligheden.no. Large and fairly formal campsite 3km east of the town centre behind a car park, which edges a yacht jetty. To get there, drive over the bridge at the end of Dronningens gate, turn right along Marviksveien, then right again near the end, following the signs. Unusually, there are no cabins here. Open June to Aug.

Scandic Kristiansand Markensgate 39 ☎21 61 42 00, ⊛www.scandic-hotels.com. The enterprising Scandic group, with its first-rate environmental policy, has about a dozen hotels in Norway and this one occupies a large modern block in the heart of downtown. The rooms are immaculate, all pastel shades and unfussy furnishings and fittings, and the breakfasts are top-notch. **❹/❼**

The Town

Neat and trim, the gridiron streets that make up Kristiansand's compact centre hold one architectural high point, the **Domkirke** (late June to mid-Aug Mon–Fri 10am–4pm & Sat 10am–3pm; free), an imposing neo-Gothic edifice dating from the 1880s, whose spire pokes high into the sky at the corner of Kirkegata and Rådhusgaten. Its only rival is the **Christiansholm Festning**, on Strandpromenaden (mid-May to mid-Sept daily 9am–9pm; free), a squat fortress whose sturdy circular tower and zigzagging earth-and-stone ramparts overlook the marina in the east harbour. Built in 1672, the tower's walls are 5m thick, a defensive precaution that proved unnecessary since it never saw action. These days it houses various arts and crafts displays. The pick of the town's several museums is the, Skippergaten 24 **Sørlandets Kunstmuseum** (Sørlandet Art Museum: June–Aug Tues–Fri 11am–4pm, Sat & Sun noon–4pm; Sept–May Tues–Fri noon–5pm, Sat & Sun noon–4pm; free, exhibitions 40kr), which is best known for its temporary exhibitions of contemporary art, though it also rustles up a reasonable selection of Norwegian paintings from 1800 onwards.

If you fancy a **swim**, one option is to head off to **Galgebergtangen** (Gallows' Point), an attractive rocky cove with a small sandy beach, 2km east of the town centre. To get there, go over the bridge at the end of Dronningens gate, take the first major right at the lights – Kuholmsveien – and follow the signs.

Eating and drinking

There are lots of **cafés and restaurants** in the centre of Kristiansand, with a particular concentration in the Fiskebrygga, a huddle of mostly modern timber houses set around a small harbour just off the eastern end of Vestre Strandgate. Standards are, however, very variable, so it pays to be selective – we've given a few of the choicer places. Kristiansand also has a fairly active nightlife based around a handful of downtown **bars**, which stay open until 2 or 3am.

Drømmeplassen corner of Skippergata and Kirkegata. Part clothes shop, part bakery, part café, this attractive little place sells an excellent range of bread as well as tasty coffee and the freshest of snacks. Mon–Fri 7am–7pm, Sat 9am–6pm & Sun 11am–4pm.

FRK Larsen Markensgate 5. It's something of a surprise to find that this resolutely alternative café-bar has survived for so long – but here it is in all its retro-New Age glory. Cocktails from 8pm and occasional live acts. Near the corner of Kongensgate. Daily 11am to midnight, 3am at the weekend.

Glipp Rådhusgaten 11. Popular, sometimes slick café-bar that does a good line in tapas (40–80kr), though its main pull is perhaps its outside terrace, which looks out over the spacious main square. Daily 11am–11pm.

🏃 Sjøhuset Østre Strandgate 12A ☎ 38 02 62 60. In an old converted warehouse by the harbour at the east end of Markensgate, this

excellent restaurant serves superb fish dishes from 250–300kr – less if you stick to the bar menu. Nautical fittings and wooden beams set the scene and there's an attractive outside terrace with sea views too. Daily 11am–11pm, restaurant 3–11pm.

Smørøyet Rådhusgaten 12. Arguably better as a bar than as a restaurant, this imaginatively decorated, modern spot occupies an older building overlooking the main square. Attractive outside terrace. Daily 11am–11.30pm.

🏃 Vaertshuset Pieder Ro Gravane 10 ☎ 38 10 07 88. Many locals swear this is the best seafood restaurant in town and has the liveliest atmosphere. It occupies an ersatz traditional timber building down in the Fiskebrygga complex. Reservations advisable at all times, and essential for the herring buffet on Sat. Main courses average 250kr, though note that prices are a little less at lunchtime than they are in the evening. Lunch Mon–Fri 11.30am–6pm; dinner daily 4–11pm.

West from Kristiansand to Stavanger

West of Kristiansand lies a sparsely inhabited region, where the rough uplands and long valleys of the interior bounce down to a shoreline that is pierced by a string of inlets and fjords. The highlight is undoubtedly **Mandal**, a fetching seaside resort with probably the best sandy beach in the whole of Norway, but thereafter it's a struggle to find much inspiration. The best you'll do is the old harbour town of **Flekkefjord**, though frankly there's not much reason to pause anywhere between Mandal and Stavanger.

The **E39** weaves its way west for 250km from Kristiansand to Stavanger, staying inland for the most part and offering only the odd sight of the coast. The **train line** follows pretty much the same route – though it does, unlike the E39, bypass Flekkefjord, only returning to the coast for the final 80km of its journey.

Mandal

Pocket-sized **MANDAL**, just 40km from Kristiansand along the E39, is Norway's southernmost town. This old timber port reached its heyday in the eighteenth century, when pines and oaks from the surrounding countryside were much sought after by the Dutch to support their canal houses and build their trading fleet. The timber boom dried up decades ago, but Mandal has preserved its quaint **old centre**, a narrow strip of white clapboard buildings spread along the north bank of the Mandalselva River just before it rolls into the sea. It's an attractive spot, well worth a stroll, and you can also drop by the municipal **museum** (late June to mid-Aug Mon–Fri 11am–5pm, Sat 11am–2pm & Sun noon–4pm; 20kr), whose rambling collection – from agricultural implements to seafaring tackle – occupies an antique merchant's house overlooking the river.

Moving on from Kristiansand

When it comes to **moving on from Kristiansand**, the obvious choice – the 250-kilometre trip west to Stavanger – is also the best. It's a journey that can be made by train as well as by bus or car along the E39, though both the train line and the highway only afford glimpses of the coast, travelling for the most part a few kilometres inland.

Staying in a lighthouse

Mandal tourist office has the details of a couple of remote, offshore lighthouses, which offer simple accommodation during the summertime – ⚓ Hatholmen Fyr (no contact details; ①) and ⚓ Ryvingen Fyr (Ⓦ www.ryvingenfyr.no; ①). Both lie out in the Skagerrak to the south of Mandal and in both cases you're responsible for your own food and bed linen. The biggest expense involved in staying at either is the return boat trip, which the tourist office will arrange on your behalf: it costs 750kr each way to Ryvingen, about half that to Hatholmen. It's also possible to stay at – and drive to – Lindesnes Fyr (see p.216).

Sjøsanden

It's not, however, its art that makes Mandal a popular holiday spot, but its fine beach, **Sjøsanden**. An 800-metre stretch of golden sand backed by pine trees and framed by rocky headlands, it's touted as Norway's best beach – and although this isn't saying a lot, it's a very enjoyable place to unwind for a few hours. The beach is about 1km from the town centre: walk along the harbour, past the tourist office to the end of the road and keep going through the woods on the signed footpath. You can also explore **Furulunden**, a tiny wooded peninsula directly to the west of the beach, where a network of paths winds through the trees and rocks to reveal hidden sand and shingle coves; pick up a leaflet at the tourist office.

Practicalities

There are no trains to Mandal, but buses from Kristiansand (2–4 daily; 50min) and Stavanger (2–4 daily; 3hr 10min) pull in at the **bus station** by the bridge on the north bank of the Mandalselva River. From here, it's a brief walk west along the riverbank to the old town centre and a couple of hundred metres more to the **tourist office**, facing the river at Bryggegata 10 (June–Aug Mon–Fri 9am–7pm, Sat & Sun 10am–4pm; Sept–May Mon–Fri 9am–4pm; ☎38 27 83 00, Ⓦ www.visitregionmandal.com).

There are a couple of good places to **stay in Mandal**, beginning with the handy and economical *Kjøbmandsgaarden Hotel*, which occupies an old timber house in a street of such buildings, across from the bus station at Store Elvegate 57 (☎38 26 12 76, Ⓦ www.kjobmandsgaarden.com; ④). All the dozen or so rooms here are spick-and-span and the decor is bright and cheerful albeit a little staid. You can also **camp** or rent a cabin (850–1120kr for six persons) very close to the western end of the **Sjøsanden** beach at the *Sjøsanden Feriesenter*, Sjøsandvei 1 (☎38 26 10 94, Ⓦ www.sjosanden-feriesenter.no); note that the access road to the camp detours round the back of the woods, which back on to the beach, but it's well signposted.

Among the cafés and restaurants in the town centre, nowhere really catches the eye, but *Jonas B Gundersen*, a popular pizzeria-restaurant across from the old water fountain at Store Elvegate 25 (Mon–Sat 11am–11pm, Sun 1–11pm), serves filling food at affordable prices with pizzas from 110kr. Alternatively, the café-restaurant of the *Kjøbmandsgaarden Hotel*, metres from the bus station at Store Elvegate 57 (Mon–Thurs 8am–9pm, Fri & Sat 8.30am–10pm & Sun 8.30am–6pm), takes a stab at more traditional Norwegian cuisine, offering a tasty range of dishes with mains averaging 220kr.

Lindesnes

Heading west from Mandal on the E39, it's about 12km to Highway 460, which snakes its way south to – and then along – **Lindesnes** (literally "where the land curves round") , a chubby, thirteen-kilometre-long promontory jutting out into the Skagerrak. Formidable seamen they may have been, but the Vikings feared the cape's treacherous waters to such an extent that they cut a canal across its base at Spangereid to avoid the vagaries of the open sea. In 2007, a replica canal was created, along with a new attraction, Vikingland (mid-June to late Aug daily 11am–5pm; 80kr; ⓦ www.vikinglandspangereid.no), a sort of Viking theme park with axe-throwing, archery and boat trips on two motorized mock-ups of Viking longships,

Pushing on from Spangereid, it's a short drive to Norway's most southerly point, where a sturdy red-and-white lighthouse – **Lindesnes Fyr** – perches on a knobbly, lichen-stained headland. There has been a lighthouse here since the seventeenth century, but today's structure dates from 1916. The history of the lighthouse and its keepers is explored in a modest museum, which has been cut into the rock of the headland (May, June and mid-Aug to Sept daily 11am–5pm; July to mid-Aug daily 9am–9pm; Oct–April Sat & Sun 11am–5pm; 50kr), and the tower is open to the public too. The most dramatic time to visit is during bad weather: the headland is exposed to extraordinarily ferocious storms, when the warm westerly currents of the Skagerrak meet cold easterly winds. You can also overnight here, in some of the old lighthouse-keepers' quarters, which have been modernized in a pleasant, modern manner (☎38 25 88 51, ⓦ www.lindesnesfyr.no; ❸); reservations are essential.

Heading on to Flekkefjord

Moving on from Mandal, the **E39** hurries west, running past the turning for the Lindesnes lighthouse (see above) before proceeding over the hills to **FLEKKE-FJORD**, 70km from Mandal. With a population of 6000, Flekkefjord is the big deal hereabouts, the old and picturesque timber houses of its tiny centre strung along the banks of a short (500m) channel that connects the Lafjord and the Grisefjord. Flekkefjord boomed in the sixteenth century on the back of its trade with the Dutch, who purchased the town's timber for their houses and its granite for their dykes and harbours. Later, in the 1750s, the herring industry was the main money-spinner, along with shipbuilding and tanning, but the Flekkefjord economy had pretty much collapsed by the end of the nineteenth century when sailing ships gave way to steam. The oldest and prettiest part of Flekkefjord – known as **Hollenderbyen** after the town's Dutch connections – is on the west side of the channel, and only takes a few minutes to explore, though you can extend this pleasantly enough by visiting the nearby nineteenth-century period rooms of the **Flekkefjord Museum** (mid-June to Aug Mon–Fri noon–5pm, Sat & Sun noon–3pm; 20kr).

Practicalities

Buses pull in on Løvikgata, about 200m east of the central waterway; the **tourist office** is on the waterway's west side at Elvegata 9 (mid-June to mid-Aug Mon–Fri 9am–5pm, Sat & Sun 10am–3pm; mid-Aug to mid-June Mon–Fri 9am–4pm; ☎38 32 69 95, ⓦ www.visitsydvest.no). There's no pressing reason to overnight here, but if you do want **to stay**, the unassuming, fifty-room *Maritim Fjordhotell* (☎38 32 58 00, ⓦ www.fjordhotellene.no; ❸/❺), overlooking the east side of the central waterway at Sundgata 9, is the best bet.

Stavanger and around

STAVANGER, 130km from Flekkefjord, is something of a survivor. While other Norwegian coastal towns have fallen foul of the precarious fortunes of fishing, Stavanger has diversified and is now the proud possessor of a dynamic economy, which has swelled the population to over 100,000. It was the herring fishery that first put money into the town, crowding its nineteenth-century wharves with coopers and smiths, net-makers and -menders. Then, when the fishing failed, the town moved into shipbuilding and now it's oil: nowadays Stavanger builds the rigs for Norway's offshore oilfields and refines the oil as well.

None of which sounds terribly enticing perhaps, but in fact Stavanger is an excellent place to start a visit to Norway: all the town's amenities are within easy

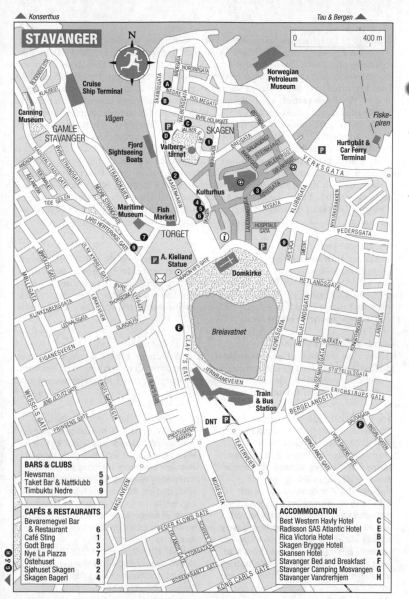

STAVANGER

Konserthus

Tau & Bergen

0   400 m

Cruise
Ship Terminal

Canning
Museum

GAMLE
STAVANGER

Vågen

Norwegian
Petroleum
Museum

Fiske-
piren

Fjord
Sightseeing
Boats

Valbergs-
tårnet

SKAGEN

Hurtigbåt &
Car Ferry
Terminal

Kulturhus

Maritime
Museum

Fish
Market

TORGET

A. Kielland
Statue

Domkirke

Breiavatnet

Train
& Bus
Station

DNT

BARS & CLUBS

Newsman	5
Taket Bar & Nattklubb	9
Timbuktu Nedre	9

CAFÉS & RESTAURANTS

Bevaremegvel Bar & Restaurant	6
Café Sting	1
Godt Brød	3
Nye La Piazza	7
Ostehuset	8
Sjøhuset Skagen	2
Skagen Bageri	4

ACCOMMODATION

Best Western Havly Hotel	C
Radisson SAS Atlantic Hotel	E
Rica Victoria Hotel	B
Skagen Brygge Hotell	D
Skansen Hotel	A
Stavanger Bed and Breakfast	F
Stavanger Camping Mosvangen	G
Stavanger Vandrerhjem	H

walking distance of each other; it has excellent train, bus and ferry connections; and it possesses an especially attractive harbour, a couple of enjoyable museums, a raft of excellent restaurants plus several lively bars. The town is also – and this comes as a surprise to many first-time visitors – nearer to the fjords than Bergen, the self-proclaimed "Gateway to the Fjords". Within easy reach of Stavanger are the **Lysefjord** and the dramatic rock formation of the **Preikestolen**.

Arrival

Stavanger's international **airport** is 14km southwest of the city centre at **Sola**. There's a Flybussen into Stavanger (Mon–Fri 8am–midnight, Sat 9am–10pm, Sun 10am–11pm; every 20–30min; 40min; 80kr each way) and this stops at major downtown hotels, the Fiskepiren ferry terminals and the bus and train stations. The **bus terminal** and the **train station** are adjacent to each other on the southern side of the **Breiavatnet**, a tiny lake that's the most obvious downtown landmark. Inside the bus station, Rogaland Kollektivtrafikk Kolumbus, an agency run collectively by several transport companies (Mon–Fri 7am–8pm, Sat 8am–3pm, Sun 11am–4pm; ☏177, ☻www.kolumbus.no), provides comprehensive details of buses, boats and trains in the city and surrounding area.

Most **domestic ferries**, including Hurtigbåt passenger express boats and car ferries from the islands and fjords around Stavanger, dock at the Fiskepiren terminal, a short walk to the northeast of the Breiavatnet – and about 800m from the train and bus stations. There are no longer international ferries to and from Stavanger. On-street **parking** is difficult, but not impossible; central car parks include those behind the bus station and on Skagenkaien, beside the main harbour.

Information

Stavanger **tourist office** is opposite the cathedral, right in the centre of town at Domkirkeplassen 3 (June–Aug daily 7am–8pm; Sept–May Mon–Fri 9am–4pm, Sat 9am–2pm; ☏51 85 92 00, ☻www.visitstavanger.com). It publishes a useful free guide to *Stavanger*, provides local bus and ferry timetables, issues free cycling maps and makes bookings on guided tours both on land and sea. The most popular excursion is to the **Preikestolen**.

Accommodation

There's no shortage of **accommodation** in Stavanger. Half a dozen **hotels** are dotted around the town's compact centre, each offering substantial weekend discounts. Alternatively, there are a couple of convenient, no-frills **guesthouses** and, further afield, an HI **hostel** and **campsite**.

Hotels and guesthouses

Best Western Havly Hotel Valberggata 1 ☏51 93 90 00, ☻www.havly-hotell.no. Unassuming, quiet hotel occupying a somewhat clumsy modern building squeezed into a narrow side-street off Skagenkaien. ❸/❺
Radisson SAS Atlantic Hotel Olav V's gate 3 ☏51 76 10 00, ☻www.atlantic.stavanger .radissonsas.com. There was a time when this was *the* place to stay in Stavanger, hosting every celebrity who ever set foot in the place from Paul Gascoigne to Fats Domino. The hotel looks a tad jaded now – and it certainly occupies a big bruiser of a modern block – but the rooms are large and spacious and most offer attractive views over the central lake. ❹/❽
Rica Victoria Hotel Skansegata 1 ☏51 86 70 00, ☻www.rica.no. This substantial hotel occupies a big old building, with a fancy portico, that peers out towards the east side of the main harbour. The interior has preserved a few period trimmings, but is mostly modern as are the bedrooms beyond. ❹/❼

Skagen Brygge Hotell Skagenkaien 30 ☏51 85 00 00, ☻www.skagenbryggehotell .no. A delightful quayside hotel, built in the style of an old warehouse but with lots of glass, and great views over the harbour. The rooms are modern and tastefully decorated, the buffet breakfast outstanding and delicious mid-afternoon nibbles are free. The only quibble concerns the noise from outside at summer weekends, when your best bet is probably to get a room at the back or on the top floor. ❹/❼
Skansen Hotel Skansegata 7 ☏51 93 85 00, ☻www.skansenhotel.no. In a revamped and remodelled old building down by the main harbour, this unassuming place has about thirty hotel rooms decorated in brisk modern style plus sixteen guesthouse rooms that are somewhat plainer but still perfectly adequate. All rooms are en suite. Guesthouse ❷/❹; hotel ❸/❺
Stavanger Bed and Breakfast Vikedalsgata 1A ☏51 56 25 00, ☻www.stavangerbedandbreakfast .no. This friendly, hostel-like B&B has 22 simple and straightforward modern rooms, most of which

have showers and sinks (but shared toilets). Every night at 9pm, guests gather in the dining room for the complimentary coffee and waffles – and a very sociable affair it is too. The B&B is in a residential area just 5min walk from the train station. A real snip at ❷.

Hostels and campsites

Stavanger Camping Mosvangen Tjensvollveien 1b ℡51 53 29 71, Ⓦwww.stavangercamping .no. On the south bank of lake Mosvatnet, a 3km walk from the centre and metres from the HI hostel (see below), this large campsite has cabins (750–1500kr) as well as areas for tents and caravans. To get there, take Kannikgata/Madlaveien west from near the station, continue along the north side of the lake and turn left just beyond it onto Tjensvollveien. Open mid-May to mid-Sept.

Stavanger Vandrerhjem Henrik Ibsens gate 19 ℡51 54 36 36, Ⓦwww.vandrerhjem.no. This no-frills HI hostel stands on the south side of lake Mosvatnet, a 3km walk from the centre – directions are as for *Stavanger Camping* (see above), with Henrik Ibsens gate being a continuation of Tjensvollveien. The hostel has self-catering and laundry facilities; advance reservations are advised. Open early June to late Aug. Dorm beds 280kr, doubles ❷

The City

Much of **central Stavanger** is strikingly modern, a flashy but surprisingly likeable ensemble of mini-tower blocks that spreads over the hilly ground which abuts the main harbour and surrounds the decorative central lake, **Breiavatnet**. The principal relic of the medieval city is the **Domkirke** (June–Aug daily 11am–7pm; Sept–May Tues–Thurs & Sat 11am–4pm; free), whose pointed-hat towers signal a Romanesque church dating from the early twelfth century, though it has been modified on several occasions. Inside, the squat pillars and rough stonework of the narrow, three-aisled nave are the Romanesque heart of the church, but the choir beyond, with its curling tracery and pointed windows, is Gothic, the work of English masons who were brought here in the 1270s.

Torget

From the Domkirke, it's a few metres to the top of **Torget**, the main square, from where there is a fine view of Stavanger's principal harbour, Vågen, a tapering finger of water that buzzes with cruise ships, yachts, ferry boats and catamarans. At the foot of Torget, beyond the flower and knick-knack vendors, is the covered fish market (Mon–Fri 9.30am–4pm & Sat 9am–3pm), where half a dozen stalls sell a wide range of seafood, including hot fish cakes and the west coast's traditional staple, *klippfisk*, dried-and-salted cod, sometimes – depending on how it is cured – known by its Spanish name, *bacalao*.

Old Stavanger

On the western side of the main harbour is the city's star turn, **Old Stavanger** (Gamle Stavanger). Though very different in appearance from the modern structures back in the centre, the buildings here were also the product of a boom. From 1810 until around 1870, herring turned up just offshore in their millions, and Stavanger took advantage of this slice of luck. The town flourished and expanded, with the number of merchants and ship-owners increasing dramatically. Huge profits were made from the exported fish, which were salted and later, as the technology improved, canned. Today, some of the wooden stores and warehouses flanking the western quayside hint at their nineteenth-century pedigree, but it's the succession of narrow, cobbled lanes behind them that shows Old Stavanger to best advantage. Formerly home to local seafarers, craftsmen and cannery workers, the area has been maintained as a residential quarter, mercifully free of tourist tat; the long rows of white-painted, clapboard houses are immaculately maintained, complete with gas lamps, picket fences and tiny terraced gardens.

In the heart of Old Stavanger, at Øvre Strandgate 88, the **Norsk Herme-tikkmuséet** (Canning Museum: mid-June to mid-Aug daily 11am–4pm; mid-Aug to mid-June Tues–Sun 11am–4pm; 60kr) occupies an old **sardine-canning factory** and gives a glimpse of the industry that saved Stavanger from collapse at the end of the nineteenth century. When the herring vanished from local waters in the 1870s, the canning factories switched to imported fish, thereby keeping the local economy afloat. They remained Stavanger's main source of employment until as late as 1960: in the 1920s there were seventy canneries in the town, and the last one only closed down in 1983.

You can watch the museum **smoking its own sardines** on the first Sunday of every month and every Tuesday and Thursday from mid-June to mid-August, and then munch away to your heart's content.

Skagen

Skagen, the bumpy promontory on the east side of the main harbour, is an oddly discordant district, a sometimes clumsy, sometimes charming mixture of the old and new, and it incorporates a busy shopping zone, whose mazy street plan is the only legacy of the original Viking settlement. The spiky **Valbergtårnet** (Valberg tower), sitting atop Skagen's highest point and guarded by three rusty cannons, is the one specific sight, a nineteenth-century firewatch offering sweeping views of the city and its industry.

Norwegian Petroleum Museum

The intricate workings of the offshore oil industry are explored in depth at the excellent **Norsk Oljemuseum** (Norwegian Petroleum Museum: June–Aug daily 10am–7pm; Sept–May Mon–Sat 10am–4pm & Sun 10am–6pm; 80kr; ℗ www .norskolje.museum.no), in a sleek modern building beside the waterfront on the far side of Skagen. The first tentative searches for oil beneath the North Sea began in the early 1960s and the first strike was made in 1969. Production started two years later and has continued ever since with Norway owning about half of western Europe's oil and gas reserves – enough to transform what had once been one of the poorer countries on the continent to one of the richest. The museum is not especially large, but it is a little confusing, so be sure to pick up a free plan at reception.

The most agreeable way to return to the centre is by walking northwest along the waterfront, which is lined with old ferries and schooners.

Eating and drinking

Although prices are marginally inflated by the oil industry, Stavanger is a great place to **eat**, with a gaggle of first-rate restaurants on the east side of the main harbour along and around Skagenkaien. Alternatively, if your wallet won't stretch that far, there are several inexpensive cafés in the vicinity of the Kulturhus, in the heart of the Skagen shopping area, and you can often buy fresh prawns from the fishing smacks that dock on the waterfront to the west of the Fiskepiren.

Stavanger is lively at night, particularly at weekends when a rum assortment of oil workers, sailors, fishermen, executives, tourists and office workers gathers in the **bars and clubs** on Skagen and Skagenkaien to live (or rather drink) it up. Most places stay open until 2am or later, with rowdy – but usually amiable – revellers lurching from one bar to the next.

Cafés and restaurants

Bevaremegvel Bar & Restaurant Skagen 12 ℗ 51 84 38 60. Bistro-style restaurant – with an adjoining bar – where the wide-ranging menu covers everything from burgers (155kr) to seafood (270kr). Better to go early in the evening before the place gets too packed (and the service slows down). Mon–Wed 11am–midnight, Thurs–Sat 11am–1am & Sun 4pm–midnight; kitchen closes at 11pm.

Café Sting Valberget 3 ℗ 51 89 38 78, ℗ www .cafe-sting.no. Right next to the Valbergtårnet this laid-back café-bar is the coolest spot in town in a young, arty sort of way. The food is filling and inexpensive and the place also doubles as an art gallery and live-music venue, hosting anything from indie to rock. Mon–Thurs noon–midnight, Fri & Sat noon–3am & Sun 3pm–midnight.

Godt Brød Sølvberggata. Inexpensive, modern café that sells a good range of freshly baked bread as well as inexpensive sandwiches. Opposite the Kulturhus. Mon–Sat 7am–6pm.

Nye La Piazza Rosenkildetorget 1. By the main harbour, just off Torget, this smart Italian restaurant serves delicious pizzas, pasta and more. Pizzas begin at 140kr, other main courses 250kr. Mon–Sat noon–midnight, Sun noon–10pm.

Ostehuset Klubbgata 3. Attractive modern café, where the speciality is pizza: the basic pizza costs 100kr and then you customize by selecting from a delicious range of extra toppings for 25–30kr each. There's also a daily menu featuring the freshest of local ingredients with mains from about 120kr plus sandwiches and baguettes. Tastiest coffee in town too. Mon–Fri 8am–9pm, Sat 8am–6pm.

Sjøhuset Skagen Skagenkaien 16 ☎51 89 51 80. Popular restaurant in an antique harbourside building, whose dark timber interior, with its several small storeys, resembles an old warehouse. The fish dishes are the tastiest items on the menu; main courses cost 260–290kr. Mon–Sat 11.30am–midnight & Sun 1–11pm.

Skagen Bageri Skagen 18. This pleasantly old-fashioned coffee house, with its dinky wooden furniture, occupies the prettiest of the old timber buildings on Skagen – note the finely carved antique door and lintel. Serves tasty pastries, cakes and snacks at reasonable prices. Mon–Fri 7am–3.30pm & Sat 8am–3.30pm.

Bars and clubs

Newsman Skagen 14. One block back from the east side of the harbour, this dark and boisterous English-style pub heaves at the weekend. Open Mon–Fri noon–1.30am, Sat 11am–1.30am & Sun 3pm–midnight.

Taket Bar & Nattklubb Nedre Strandgate 15 ☎51 84 37 00, Ⓦwww.herlige-restauranter.com. The best club in town, strong on house music with special DJ nights; don't be surprised if you have to queue; above *Timbuktu* (see below), just west of Torget, the main square. Open Tues–Thurs midnight–3am, Fri & Sat 10pm–3am & Sun midnight–3am.

Timbuktu Nedre Strandgate 15. Flashy café-bar noted for its imaginative modern decor and trendy atmosphere; beneath *Taket* (see above). Mon–Sat 6pm–12.30am.

Entertainment

The **Stavanger Konserthus** (Concert Hall: ☎51 53 70 00, Ⓦwww.stavanger -konserthus.no) is north of the centre beyond Gamle Stavanger in Bjergsted park. It features regular concerts by visiting artists and is home to the Stavanger Symphony Orchestra (Ⓦwww.sso.no). Among several central cinemas, the eight-screen Kino 1 is inside the Kulturhus, at Sølvberggata 2 (☎51 51 07 00, Ⓦwww.kino1.no).

Listings

Airlines Norwegian Air Shuttle (☎815 21 815); SAS/Braathens (☎05400); Widerøe (☎810 01 200).

Car rental Hertz, Olav V's gate 13 (☎51 52 00 00). For a comprehensive list, see under *Bilutleie* in the *Yellow Pages*.

Emergencies Fire ☎110; Police ☎112; Ambulance ☎113.

Ferries Domestic: Rogaland Kollektivtrafikk Kolumbus for regional bus, boat and train enquiries (☎177, Ⓦwww.kolumbus.no); Flaggruten (☎53 40 91 20, Ⓦwww.flaggruten.no) for Hurtigbåt passenger express boat services to Bergen.

Hiking The DNT-affiliated Stavanger Turistforening, in the underpass at the top of Olav V's gate (Mon–Wed & Fri 10am–5pm, Thurs 10am–6pm, Sat 10am–2pm; ☎51 84 02 00, Ⓦwww.stavanger-turistforening.no), will advise on local hiking routes and sells a comprehensive range of hiking maps. It maintains around 900km of hiking trails and runs more than thirty cabins in

the mountains east of Stavanger, as well as organizing ski schools at winter weekends. It also offers general advice about local conditions, weather etc, and you can obtain DNT membership here too.

Internet Internet access is free at the main library, inside the Kulturhus at Sølvberggata 2 (Mon–Wed & Fri 10am–5pm, Thurs 10am–7pm & Sat 10am–3pm). There's also an internet café, Café Com, close by at Sølvberggata 15 (Mon–Sat 11am–9pm, Sun noon–9pm; ☎51 55 41 20) which charges 20kr for the first 20min.

Laundry Renseriet, Kongsgata 40, by Breiavatnet. Coin-operated machines (☎51 89 56 53).

Pharmacy Vitusapotek, Olav V's gate 11 (daily 9am–11pm).

Post office The main post office is on Lars Hertevigs gate, just a few metres from Håkon VII's gate (Mon–Fri 9am–6pm & Sat 10am–3pm).

Taxis Norgestaxi (☎08000).

Around Stavanger: Preikestolen

Stavanger sits on a long promontory that pokes a knobbly head north towards the Boknafjord, whose wide waters form a deep indentation in the coast and lap against a confetti of islets and islands. To the east of Stavanger, longer, narrower fjords drill far inland, the most diverting being the blue-black **Lysefjord**, famous for its precipitous cliffs and an especially striking rock formation, the **Preikestolen**. This distinctive 25-metre-square table of rock, with its sheer 600-metre drop to the fjord down below on three of its sides, makes an outstanding day-trip by ferry, bus and foot.

To get to the rock, take the **ferry** east from Stavanger to **Tau** (every 30min to 1hr; 40min; passengers 39kr, car & driver 116kr) and then drive south along Highway 13 until, after about 14km, you reach the signed side road leading to Preikestolen. A local **bus** covers the Tau–Preikestolen road too (mid-May to mid-Sept 3–6 daily; 35min), but you'll need to check with the tourist office as to which of the ferries connects with the bus. From the car park at the end of the road, it's a four-hour **hike** there and back to Preikestolen along a clearly marked trail. The first half is steep in parts and paved with uneven stones, while the second half – over bedrock – is a good bit easier. The change in elevation is 350m and you should take food and water; the hike is not feasible in winter.

Back at the Preikestolen car park is a first-rate HI **hostel**, *Preikestolen Vandrerhjem* (T51 74 52 51, Wwww.vandrerhjem.no; dorm beds 250kr, doubles **②**; June–Aug), perched high on the hillside with great views over the surrounding mountains. Built on the site of an old mountain farm, the hostel comprises a small complex of turf-roofed lodges, each of which has a spick-and-span pine interior. There are self-catering facilities, a laundry and boat rental as well as a café serving breakfasts and simple evening meals; reservations are advised as the place is popular with school groups.

From Stavanger to Bergen

With great ingenuity, Norway's road builders have cobbled together the **E39** coastal road, the **Kystvegen** (Wwww.kystvegen.no), which traverses the west coast from Stavanger to Haugesund, Bergen and ultimately Trondheim with eight ferry trips breaking up the journey. The first part of the trek, the 190-kilometre haul up to Bergen, includes two ferry trips and sees the highway slipping across a string of islands, which provide a pleasant introduction to the scenic charms of western Norway – and hint at the sterner beauty of the fjords beyond.

By **car**, it takes between five and six hours to get from Stavanger to Bergen. En route, the first of the two E39 **ferries** shuttles across the Boknafjord from Mortavika to Arsvågen, about 30km out of Stavanger (24hr service, every 30min–1hr; 25min; car & passenger 143kr; Wwww.fjord1.no); the second, another 120km beyond, links Sandvikvåg with Halhjem 40km short of Bergen (daily 7am–11pm every 30min–1hr; 40min; car & driver 177kr; Wwww.fjord1.no). A fast and frequent **bus** service – the **Kystbussen** – plies the E39 too, taking a little under six hours to get from Stavanger to Bergen (Mon–Fri hourly, Sat & Sun every 1–2hr); it's slower, but more economical (450kr one-way) and offers much better views than the **Hurtigbåt** passenger express boat which plies the same route (720kr each way).

▲ Pulpit Rock (Preikestolen), Lysefjord

Travel details

Principal NSB trains (@www.nsb.no)

Kristiansand to: Oslo (4–5 daily; 4hr 30min); Stavanger (4–5 daily; 3hr).
Oslo to: Arendal (4–5 daily, change at Nelaug; 4hr 10min); Kristiansand (4–5 daily; 4hr 30min); Sandefjord (every 1–2hr; 1hr 50min); Stavanger (4–5 daily; 8hr).
Sandefjord to: Oslo (every 1–2hr; 1hr 50min).
Stavanger to: Kristiansand (4–5 daily; 3hr); Oslo (4–5 daily; 8hr).

Principal Nor-Way Bussekspress buses (@www.nor-way.no)

Arendal to: Kristiansand (7 daily, local bus to Harebakken bussterminalen, then change; 1hr 30min); Oslo (7 daily, local bus to Harebakken bussterminalen, then change; 4hr 10min).
Kristiansand to: Flekkefjord (3–4 daily; 2hr); Mandal (3–4 daily; 50min); Oslo (7 daily; 5hr 10min); Stavanger (3–4 daily; 4hr).
Lillesand to: Kristiansand (7 daily, local bus to Lillesand Borkedalen, then change; 30min); Oslo (7 daily, local bus to Lillesand Borkedalen, then change; 4hr 45min).
Mandal to: Kristiansand (3–4 daily; 50min); Stavanger (3–4 daily; 3hr 10min).
Oslo to: Arendal (7 daily, change at Harebakken bussterminalen for the last 10min of the journey by local bus; 4hr 10min); Kristiansand (7 daily; 5hr 10min); Lillesand (7 daily, change at Lillesand Borkedalen for the last 5min of the journey by local bus; 4hr 45min); Stavanger (2–3 daily; 10hr).

Stavanger to: Bergen (Mon–Fri hourly, Sat & Sun every 1–2hr; 5–6hr); Kristiansand (3–4 daily; 4hr); Mandal (3–4 daily; 3hr 10min).

Principal Nettbuss buses (@www .nettbuss.no)

Arendal to: Kristiansand (hourly; 1hr 30min); Lillesand (hourly; 50min).
Lillesand to: Arendal (hourly; 50min).

International car ferries

Hantsholm (Denmark) to: Egersund/ Haugesund/ Bergen (3 weekly; 8hr/14hr/19hr; @www.fjordline .com); Kristiansand (1 daily to 2 weekly; 2hr; @www.fjordline.com).
Hirtshals (Denmark) to: Kristiansand (1–2 daily; 3hr 30min; @www.colorline.com); Larvik (1–2 daily; 4hr; @www.colorline.com).
Strömstad (Sweden) to: Sandefjord (4–6 daily; 2hr 30min; @www.colorline.com).

Domestic car ferries (@www.fjord1.no)

Mortavika to: Arsvågen, about 30km north of Stavanger on the E39 (24hr service, every 30min–1hr; 25min).
Sandvikvåg to: Halhjem, about 150km north of Stavanger on the E39 (daily 7am–11pm every 30min–1hr; 40min).

Principal Flaggruten Hurtigbåt passenger express boats (@www.flaggruten.no)

Stavanger to: Bergen (1–2 daily; 4hr 30min); Haugesund (2–4 daily; 1hr 20min; .

2.3

Central Norway

Preoccupied by the fjords and the long road to Nordkapp, few tourists are tempted to explore **central Norway**. The Norwegians know better. Trapped between Sweden and the fjords, this great chunk of land boasts some of the country's finest scenery, with the forested dales that trail north and west from Oslo heralding the region's rearing peaks. It's here, within shouting distance of the country's principal train line and the E6 – long the main line of communication between Oslo, Trondheim and the north – that you'll find three of Norway's prime **hiking areas**. These comprise a trio of mountain ranges, each partly contained within a national park – from south to north, Jotunheimen, Rondane and the Dovrefjell. Of the three, **Jotunheimen** is the harshest and most stunning, with its string of icy, jagged peaks; the **Dovrefjell** is more varied with severe mountains in the west and open moors and rounded ridges in the east; while **Rondane**, a high alpine zone, has more accessible mountains and low vegetation. Each of the parks is equipped with well-maintained walking trails and DNT huts, and **Kongsvoll**, on both the E6 and the train line, makes a particularly good starting point for hiking expeditions into one of them, the Dovrefjell.

Despite these attractions, it's easy to think of the whole region as little more than a **transport corridor** whose four main highways rush from Oslo across the interior heading north and west. Of these, the **E6** is the most interesting, as it runs up the **Gudbrandsdal** valley past several historic sights on its way to the Jotunheimen and Dovrefjell national parks. The E6 is also the starting point for **Highway 15** and the **E136**, two wonderful roads that thread through the mountains to the fjords: the first goes to Lom (see p.271) and Geiranger (see p.277), the second to Åndalsnes (see p.280). To the west of Oslo, the **E16** is the fastest of the three main roads to the fjords, as it bangs across to Lærdal and through the series of tunnels that enable it to fast track to Bergen. It has much to recommend it west of Flåm (see p.263), but its dull eastern reaches are enlivened only by the handsome **Borgund stave church**. Further south, the easterly section of **Highway 7** to Flåm via Highway 50) or Eidfjord (see p.257) is also pretty routine, but further west, beyond Geilo, the road traverses the wonderfully wild Hardangervidda mountain plateau (see p.258), passing several useful trail-heads such as Halne (see p.259). Finally, there's the **E134** to Lofthus (see p.257), which has the advantage of passing through the attractive former silver-town of **Kongsberg**.

Nor-Way Bussekspress **buses** (🌐 www.nor-way.no) ply the E6, E16 and the E134, but once you get onto the minor roads, including Highway 7, the bus system thins out and travelling becomes much more difficult without your own vehicle. **Trains** are fast and fairly frequent too, shuttling along the two main railway lines that cross central Norway. The Oslo-to-Bergen line shadows Highway 7 until just after Geilo, while the Oslo–to–Trondheim line passes through Lillehammer and Dombås, the junction for the superbly scenic run down to the fjords at Åndalsnes on the Rauma branch line.

The E6 north to Kongsvoll

Hurrying from Oslo to Trondheim and points north, the **E6** remains the most important highway in Norway, and is consequently kept in excellent condition – often with the roadworks to prove it. Inevitably, the road is used by many of the region's long-distance **buses**, and for much of its length it's also shadowed by Norway's principal **train** line. To begin with, both the E6 and the railway thump northwards across the lowlands, clipping past the international airport at Gardermoen (see p.181) before following the east bank of Lake Mjøsa en route to **Lillehammer**, home to one of the best of Norway's many open-air folk museums. Thereafter, road and rail sweep on up the **Gudbrandsdal** river valley, within sight of a string of modest little towns and villages, with the first significant attraction being **Ringebu stave church**. The Gudbrandsdal witnessed some of the fiercest fighting of World War II when the Norwegians and their British allies tried to stem the northward German advance, a campaign remembered at the war museum in **Kvam**. Pushing on, it's just a few kilometres more to **Sjoa**, a centre for whitewater rafting, and a little further north, **Otta**, an undistinguished town but one that is within easy reach of two magnificent national parks, **Jotunheimen** and **Rondane**. Further north still is the rugged **Dovrefjell** national park, which is most pleasingly approached from tiny **Kongsvoll**. All three parks are networked by an extensive and well-planned system of **hiking trails**. From Kongsvoll, Trondheim is within comfortable striking distance.

Lillehammer

LILLEHAMMER (literally "Little Hammer"), 190km from Oslo, is Lake Mjøsa's most worthwhile destination. In **winter**, it's one of Norway's top ski centres, a young and vibrant place whose rural lakeside setting and extensive cross-country ski trails contributed to its selection as host of the 1994 Olympic Winter Games. In preparation for the games, the Norwegian government spent a massive two billion kroner on the town's **sporting facilities**, which are now among the best in the country. As you would expect, most Norwegians arriving here in winter come fully equipped, but it's possible to rent or buy equipment locally – the tourist office (see below) will advise.

Lillehammer is a popular **summer** holiday spot too. As soon as the weather picks up, hundreds of Norwegians hunker down in their second homes in the hills that flank the town, popping into the centre for a drink or a meal. Cycling, walking, fishing and canoeing are popular pastimes at this time of year, with all sorts of possibilities for guided tours. Yet, however appealing the area may be to Norwegians, the countryside hereabouts has little of the wonderful wildness of other parts of Norway, and unless you're someone's guest or bring your own family, you'll probably feel rather out on a limb. That said, Lillehammer is not a bad place to break your journey, and there are a couple of attractions to keep you busy for a day or two, most notably the **Maihaugen** open-air museum.

Arrival, information and orientation

The E6 runs along the lakeshore about 500m below the centre of Lillehammer, where the ultramodern **Skysstasjon**, on Jernbanetorget at the bottom of Jernbanegata, incorporates the **train station** and the **bus terminal**. The **tourist office** is also here (late June Mon–Sat 9am–6pm & Sun noon–5pm; July Mon–Sat 9am–8pm & Sun 11am–6pm; rest of year Mon–Fri 9am–4pm & Sat 10am–2pm; ☏61 28 98 00, ⓦ www.lillehammer.com). Staff have information on local events and activities, and will help with finding accommodation. **Orientation** couldn't be easier, with all activity focused on the pedestrianized part of Storgata, which runs north from Bankgata, across Jernbanegata to the tumbling Mesnaelva River; Anders Sandvigsgate and Kirkegata run parallel on either side to east and west respectively.

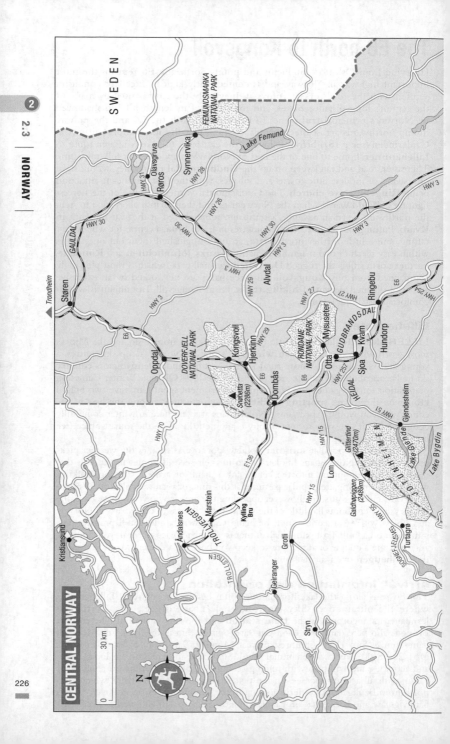

CENTRAL NORWAY

N

0   30 km

SWEDEN

FEMUNDSMARKA
NATIONAL PARK

Lake Femund

Olavsgruva
Røros   Synnervika
HWY 31
HWY 28
HWY 26
GAULDAL
HWY 30   HWY 30
HWY 3
HWY 30
Støren   Alvdal
HWY 3   HWY 3
▲ Trondheim
HWY 29
HWY 27
HWY 3
E6   Ringebu   E6
HWY 254
Oppdal   Kongsvoll   HWY 21
DOVREFJELL   Hjerkinn   Mysuseter   Kvam   Hundorp
NATIONAL PARK   HWY 29   RONDANE   Otta GUDBRANDSDAL
E6   NATIONAL PARK   Sjoa
▲ Snøhetta   Dombås   HEIDAL
(2286m)   E6   HWY 257
HWY 70   HWY 51   Gjendesheim
HWY 15   Lake Gjende   Øvre
Lom   Glittertind   ▲   Lake Bygdin
E136   (2470m) ▲ JOTUNHEIMEN
Marstein   HWY 15   Galdhøpiggen
Åndalsnes   (2469m)
TROLLVEGGEN   Kylling Bru   SOGNEFJELLSVEGEN   HWY 55
Grotli   Turtagrø
TROLLSTIGEN
Geiranger
Kristiansund   Stryn

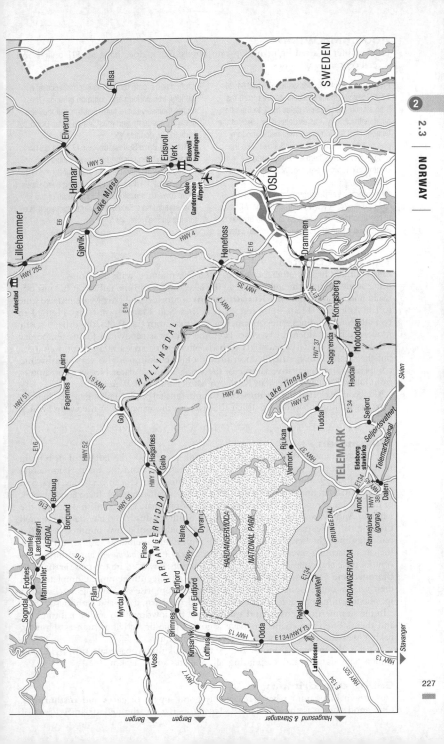

SWEDEN

Flisa

Elverum

HWY 3

Hamar

E6

Eidsvoll Verk

Eidsvoll-bygningen

Oslo Gardermoen Airport

Lillehammer

HWY 255

Auleestad

E6

Gjøvik

Lake Mjøsa

HWY 4

OSLO

Leira

Fagernes

HWY 51

E16

HWY 52

Gol

HWY 50

Borlaug

Borgund

E16

Sogndal

Fodnes

Gamle

Mannheller

Lærdalsøyri

LÆRDAL

E16

Flåm

Myrdal

Finse

HARDANGERVIDDA

HWY 7

Hagafoss

Geilo

HWY 7

Haugastøl

Dyranut

Halne

HWY 7

Øvre Eidfjord

Eidfjord

Brimnes

Kinsarvik

Lofthus

Voss

HWY 7

HARDANGERVIDDA NATIONAL PARK

Odda

HWY 13

E134/HWY 13

Latefossen

Røldal

Haukelifjell

E134

HARDANGER/IDDA

HWY 52

E134

HALLINGDAL

Hønefoss

E16

HWY 35

HWY 7

Drammen

E134

Kongsberg

HWY 37

Saggrenda

Notodden

HWY 37

Heddal

Lake Tinnsjø

HWY 40

HWY 37

Tuddal

Rjukan

Vemork

Seljord

Seljordsvatnet

E134

TELEMARK

Eidsborg stawkirke

Telemarkskanal

Åmot

HWY 38

E134

Dalen

Ravnejuvet (gorge)

GRUNGEDAL

E134

Skien

Stavanger

Bergen

Bergen

Haugesund & Stavanger

Accommodation

Lillehammer is a tad light on top-rate hotels, but it does have an HI hostel and several central guesthouses.

First Hotell Breiseth Jernbanegata 1 ☏61 24 77 77, ⓦwww.firsthotels.com. Metres from the train station, the *Breiseth* dates back to the late nineteenth century – as evidenced by parts of the facade – but the interior is minimalist-modern give or take the odd rhetorical flourish (like the wing-back chairs). There are ninety-odd comfortable rooms here, mostly in browns and creams. ④/⑤

Lillehammer Vandrerhjem Jernbanetorget 2 ☏61 26 00 24, ⓦwww.vandrerhjem.no. All-year HI hostel in the same block as the train station. Has a good range of facilities, from a self-catering kitchen and a café through to internet access, a laundry, free parking and common grounds. The rooms themselves are fairly spartan, but they are perfectly adequate and most are en suite. Dorm beds 325kr, doubles ③

Suttestad Gård Suttestådvegen 17 ☏61 25 04 44, ⓦwww.lillehammerturist.no/suttestad.htm. Large former farmhouse with eight modern guest rooms, most of which are en suite and have views down towards the lake. It's 1.5km south of the train station; take Kirkegata – Suttestådvegen is a turning on the right. ②

The town centre

Lillehammer's briskly efficient centre, just a few minutes' walk from one end to the other, is tucked into the hillside above the lake, the E6 and the railway. It has just one really notable attraction, the **Kunstmuseum** at Stortorget 2 (Art Museum: late June to late Aug daily 11am–5pm; rest of year Tues–Sun 11am–4pm; 60kr). Housed in two adjacent buildings, one a municipal structure from the 1960s, the other a flashy modern edifice added thirty years later, the gallery is renowned for its temporary exhibitions of contemporary art (which often carry an extra admission charge), but the small permanent collection (in the older building) is also very worthwhile, comprising a representative sample of the works of most major Norwegian painters, from Johan Dahl and Christian Krohg to Munch and Erik Werenskiold.

After you've visited the art museum, the obvious target is Maihaugen (see below), though you might wander up along the river on the west side of the centre, which is the prettiest part of town.

Maihaugen

The much-vaunted **Maihaugen** open-air folk museum – the largest of its type in northern Europe – is a twenty-minute walk southeast from the town centre along Anders Sandvigsgate (mid-May to Sept daily 10am–5pm; Oct to mid-May Tues–Sun 11am–4pm; 80kr, mid-May to Sept 100kr; ⓦwww.maihaugen.no). Incredibly, the bulk of the collection represents the lifetime's work of one man, a magpie-ish dentist by the name of Anders Sandvig (1862–1950). Since Sandvig's death, the city has augmented the original collection, and Maihaugen now holds around two hundred relocated buildings, brought here from all over the region and including several real rarities such as a charming seventeenth-century presbytery (*prestegårdshagen*) and a thirteenth-century stave church from Garmo. The key exhibits, however, are the two **farms** from Bjørnstad and Øygarden, dating from the late seventeenth century. Complete with their various outhouses and living areas, the two comprise 36 buildings, each with a specific function, such as food store, sheep-shed, hay barn, stable and bathhouse.

In the summertime, **costumed guides** give the lowdown on traditional rural life and there's often the chance to have a go at domestic activities such as spinning, baking, weaving and pottery – good, wholesome fun.

To get to the museum from the train station, walk up Jernbanegata, turn right onto Anders Sandvigsgate, and keep going; all in all, it's about 1.5km.

Eating and drinking

Downtown Lillehammer has a reasonably good supply of **cafés** and **restaurants**. One good choice is the *Blåmann Restaurant & Bar*, off the pedestrianized part of

Storgata at Lilletorvet 1, which has a leafy terrace suspended over the cascading river below and has a wide-ranging menu with the likes of *klippfisk*, Mexican dishes, crab and moussaka; main courses are around 230–250kr. There's also *Svare & Berg*, in old timber premises by the river on Elvegata, where they serve first-rate snacks and light meals – try the meatballs (120kr).

The town has an animated **nightlife**, with bars clustered around the western end of Storgata – try *Nikkers* at Elvegata 18 for lively low-key drinks, or *Brenneriet*, just over the road, a swanky nightclub and restaurant combo.

The Gudbrandsdal

Heading north from Lillehammer, the E6 and the railway leave the shores of Lake Mjøsa to run along the **Gudbrandsdal**, a 160-kilometre river valley, which was for centuries the main route between Oslo and Trondheim. Enclosed by mountain ranges, the valley has a comparatively dry and mild climate, and its fertile soils have nourished a string of farming villages since Viking times.

Ringebu stave church

The Gudbrandsdal begins pleasantly enough, the easy sweep of its forested hills interrupted by rocky outcrops and patches of farmland dotted with brightly coloured farmsteads. After about 60km, the E6 swings past the turning to **Ringebu stave church** (daily: late May to June & Aug 9am–5pm; July 8am–6pm; 40kr, 60kr including Weidemannsamlingen, see below), whose distinctive maroon spire stands on a hill 1km off the E6 – and a couple of kilometres south of Ringebu village. Dating from the thirteenth century, the original church was modified and enlarged in the 1630s, reflecting both an increase in the local population and the new religious practices introduced after the Reformation. The exterior is rather glum, but the western **entrance portal** sports some superb if badly weathered zoomorphic carvings from the original church.

The old vicarage behind the church was in ecclesiastical hands until the 1990s, but it now holds the **Weidemannsamlingen** (late May to Aug Tues–Sun 10am–5pm; 40kr, 60kr including church) featuring a selection of paintings by the prolific Jacob Weidemann (1923–2001), one of Norway's most talented modern artists. Many of Weidemann's works were inspired by the Norwegian landscape, but he eschewed realism for deeply coloured abstract canvases of great emotional intensity. His liking for strong colours is often tied to an accident that befell him during World War II.

Kvam

Pressing on from Ringebu, the E6 weaves its way north following the course of the river to reach, after about 30km, **KVAM**, a modest chipboard-producing town that witnessed some of the worst fighting of World War II. Once the Germans had occupied Norway's main towns in the spring of 1940, they set about extending their control of the main roads and railways, marching up the Gudbrandsdal in quick time. At Kvam, they were opposed by a scratch force of Norwegian and British soldiers, who delayed their progress despite being poorly equipped. The battle for the Gudbrandsdal lasted for two weeks (April 14–30, 1940) and is commemorated at the **Gudbrandsdal Krigsminnesamling** (War Museum: late June to July daily 10am–5pm; early Aug Wed–Sun 10am–4pm; 40kr; ⓦwww.krigsminne.no), in the centre of Kvam beside the E6. In the museum, a series of excellent multi-lingual displays runs through the campaign, supported by a substantial collection of military mementoes and lots of fascinating photographs. Across the main street from the museum, in the **church graveyard**, is a Cross of Sacrifice, honouring the 54 British soldiers who died here while trying to halt the German advance.

Buses travel through Kvam on the E6 and there's a request stop metres from the museum; Kvam train station, also a request stop, is about 200m south of the museum.

Sjoa

From Kvam, it's 9km further up the valley to **SJOA**, a scattered hamlet set beside
the junction of the E6 and Highway 257. The latter cuts west along the **Heidal**
valley, where the Sjoa River boasts some of the country's most exciting **white-
water rafting**. If you want to come to grips with the river's gorges and rapids,
contact the local specialists, Heidal Rafting (℡61 23 60 37, ⓦwww.heidalrafting
.no). An all-inclusive, one-day rafting excursion costs around 1000kr, 800kr for half
a day; a more strenuous two-day expedition inclusive of meals and lodgings will set
you back around 2000kr. The season lasts from May to October and reservations
are recommended, though there's a reasonably good chance of being able to sign
up at the last minute. Heidal Rafting is based at the HI **hostel**, *Sjoa Vandrerhjem*
(℡61 23 62 00, ⓦwww.vandrerhjem.no; dorm beds 270kr, chalets ❶/❷; mid-May
to Sept), which is itself worth a second look. Perched on a wooded hillside high
above the river, the main building is a charming log farmhouse dating from 1747,
and, although visitors sleep in more modern quarters, this is where you eat. Breakfasts are banquet-like, and dinners (by prior arrangement only) are reasonably priced
if rather less spectacular. The hostel offers two types of accommodation: there's a
no-frills dormitory block at the bottom of the slope and a handful of spacious and
comfortable chalets up above. Reservations are advisable for the chalets at weekends.
The hostel is just off Highway 257, about 1500m west of the E6. There's no train
station – the nearest is at Otta 10km to the north – but buses stop on the E6 near
the Highway 257 intersection.

Beyond the Heidal valley, Highway 257 continues west to meet Highway 51, the
main access road to the east side of the Jotunheimen national park at Gjendesheim
(see p.232).

Otta

OTTA, just 10km beyond Sjoa, is an unassuming and unexciting little town
at the confluence of the rivers Otta and Lågen. It may be dull, but Otta does
make a handy base for hiking in the nearby Rondane national park (see p.231),
especially if you're reliant on public transport – though staying in one of the
park's mountain lodges is much to be preferred. The town is also within easy
driving distance of the Jotunheimen (see p.232). In Otta itself, everything
you need is within easy reach: the E6 passes within 300m of the town centre,
sweeping along the east bank of the Lågen, while Highway 15 bisects the town
from east to west with the few gridiron streets that pass for the centre lying a few
metres to the south.

Practicalities

Clumped together in the Skysstasjon on the north side of Highway 15 are the
train station, **bus terminal** and **tourist office** (late June to mid-Aug daily
8.30am–4pm; mid-Aug to late June Mon–Fri 8.30am–4pm; ℡61 23 66 70, ⓦwww
.visitrondane.com). The latter can provide local bus timetables, book accommodation and reserve Lake Gjende boat tickets; it also sells fishing licences and local
hiking maps. **Accommodation** is thin on the ground, but the *Norlandia Otta
Hotell*, in the centre on Ola Dahls gate (℡61 21 08 00, ⓦwww.norlandia.no; ❹)
makes a reasonable hand of its uninspiring modern premises. The nearest **campsite**,
Otta Camping (℡61 23 03 09, ⓦwww.ottacamping.no; May to mid-Oct), lies about
1500m from the town centre on the wooded banks of the Otta River, with cabins
350–750kr for five persons, with facilities) and space for tents: to get there, cross the
bridge on the southwest side of the centre, turn right and keep going.

Otta's choice of **places to eat** is also constrained, but there is one recommendable spot, the *Pillarguri*, Storgata 7 (℡61 23 01 04), a café-restaurant, offering a good
range of traditional Norwegian dishes with mains about 150kr; it's normally open
daily from noon to 10pm.

Moving on from Otta to the western fjords

Running west from Otta, **Highway 15** sweeps along wide river valleys bound for **Lom** (see p.271), where there's a choice of wonderful routes on into the western fjords: you can either carry on along Highway 15 towards Stryn (see p.275) and Loen (see p.274), or branch off north on to the rattling **Ørnevegen** (Eagle's Highway: Highway 63) to Geiranger (see p.277). Alternatively, you can turn off Highway 15 at Lom, on to the **Sognefjellsveg** (Highway 55) which climbs steeply to the south, travelling along the western flank of the Jotunheimen National Park and offering breathtaking views of its jagged peaks before careering down to Sogndal (see p.269).

The Nor-Way Bussekspress (⊛www.nor-way.no) Oslo–Måløy **service** (3 daily) runs along Highway 15 from Otta to Lom, Langvatn and Stryn. The journey time from Otta to Lom is one hour, three hours to Stryn. From mid-June to August, a twice-daily local bus links Langvatn with Geiranger and ultimately Åndalsnes. From late June to August, there's also a twice-daily bus from Otta and Lom to Sogndal via the Sognefjellsveg, Highway 55.

Most fjordland bus and ferry services are provided by either Tide (⊛www.tide.no) or Fjord1 (⊛www.fjord1.no); both websites carry timetables.

From Otta to the Rondane and Jotunheimen national parks

From Otta, it's about 20km east to **Rondane National Park**: take the byroad to the sprawling chalet settlement of Mysuseter and keep going a further 5km to the Spranghaugen car park, right on the edge of the park itself and an easy ninety-minute walk from the *Rondvassbu* mountain lodge (see below). In the summer, a local bus plies this route, but it is a very limited service (late Aug only, Sat & Sun 1–2 daily; 1hr; ⊛www.fjord1.no); the alternative is to go by taxi – try Otta Taxi (☎61 23 05 01). There's currently no bus service from Otta to Gjendesheim (see p.232) in Jotunheimen National Park, but it only takes an hour or two to drive the 100km along Highway 15 and then 51.

Rondane National Park

Spreading north and east from Otta, **Rondane Nasjonal Park** (Rondane National Park) was established in 1962 as Norway's first national park and is now one of the country's most popular hiking areas. Its 527 square kilometres, one third of which is in the high alpine zone, appeal to walkers of all ages and abilities. The soil is poor, so vegetation is sparse, and lichens, especially reindeer moss, predominate, but the views across this bare landscape are serenely beautiful, and a handful of lakes and rivers plus patches of dwarf birch forest provide some variety. Wild mountain peaks divide the Rondane into three distinct areas to the west, north and east of **Rondvatnet**, a centrally located lake. The mountains, ten of which exceed the 2000-metre mark, are mostly accessible to any reasonably fit and eager walker, thanks to a dense network of trails and hiking huts/lodges.

From the **Spranghaugen car park**, where the bus from Otta terminates (see above), it's a ninety-minute level walk northeast along the service road to the southern tip of lake **Rondvatnet** with the bleak and bare peaks of the Rondane slowly revealing themselves – a dozen peaks in all, surrounding the lake's shadowy waters. At the southern tip of the lake is the DNT ⚐ **Rondvassbu lodge** (late June to early Oct; ☎61 23 18 66, ⊛www.rondvassbu.com; dorm beds for DNT members 180kr, 250kr for non-members, doubles ❶), the most accessible of the park's several huts and lodges. It's a typical staffed DNT lodge, with more than one hundred beds, filling meals and pleasant service. For all but the briefest of hikes, it's best to arrive at the lodge the day before to have a chance of starting first thing the next morning. If, however, visibility is poor or you don't fancy a climb, there is a delightful summer **boat service** (July–Aug 2–3 daily; 30min each way; 100kr return) to the far end of Rondvatnet, from where it takes about two and a half hours to walk back to *Rondvassbu* along the lake's steep western shore.

Jotunheimen National Park

Norway's most celebrated hiking area, **Jotunheimen** ("Home of the Giants") **National Park** lives up to its name: pointed summits and undulating glaciers dominate the skyline, soaring high above river valleys and lake-studded plateaux. Covering only 3900 square kilometres, the park offers an amazing concentration of high peaks, more than two hundred of which rise above 1900m, including Norway's (and northern Europe's) two highest mountains, Galdhøpiggen (2469m) and Glittertind (2464m). Here also is Norway's highest waterfall, **Vettisfossen**, boasting a 275-metre drop and located a short walk from the *Vetti* lodge on the west side of the park. A network of footpaths and mountain lodges lattices the **Jotunheimen**, but be warned that the weather is very unpredictable and the winds can be bitingly cold – take care and always come well equipped.

There are no public/asphalted roads into the park; visitors usually hike or ski into the interior from the Sognefjellsveg (Highway 55) in the west (see p.271) or make the slightly easier approach from the east, driving to **Gjendesheim**, 2km off Highway 51 and some 90km from Otta. The only half-reasonable bus service to Gjendesheim is provided by Nor-Way Bussekspress (Ⓦwww.nor-way.no): their Valdresekspressen bus (4–6 daily) links Oslo with Fagernes (see p.235), where you change for Beitostølen (2–4 daily), changing again for Gjendesheim (late June to early Sept 1–2 daily; 40min). Gjendesheim has long been a popular base for exploring the Jotunheimen – the first mountain hut was built here in the 1870s – but it is still no more than a ferry dock and a couple of buildings, one of which is the excellent, staffed DNT ⚒ *Gjendesheim* lodge (mid-Feb to March & mid-June to early Oct; ☎61 23 89 10, Ⓦwww.gjendesheim.no; dorm beds for DNT members 220kr, non-members 285kr, doubles ❶), at the eastern tip of long and slender **Lake Gjende**. Some 18km long and 146m deep, the lake is one of Norway's most beautiful, its glacially fed waters tinted green by myriad clay particles; it was also here that Ibsen had his Peer Gynt tumble into the water from the back of a reindeer. Boats (mid-June

▲ Kylling bru over Rauma River

The E136 and the Rauma branch line to Åndalsnes

Dombås is where the **E136** and the **Rauma train line** (2–3 daily; 1hr 45min) branch west for the thrilling 110-kilometre rattle down to Åndalsnes. The journey begins innocuously enough with road and rail slipping along a ridge high above a wide, grassy valley, but soon the landscape gets wilder as both nip into the hills. After 65km, they reach **Kylling bru**, an ambitious stone railway bridge, 56m high and 76m long, which spans the Rauma River. Pressing on, it's a further 20km to the shadowy hamlet of **Marstein** with the grey, cold mass of the Trollveggen ("Troll's Wall") rising straight ahead. At around 1100m, the **Trollveggen** incorporates the highest vertical overhanging mountain wall in Europe and as such is a favourite with experienced mountaineers, though it wasn't actually scaled until 1967. Somehow, the E136 and the railway manage to squeeze through the mountains and soon afterwards they slide down to the attractive little town of Åndalsnes (see p.280), the fjord glistening beyond.

to mid-Sept 1–3 daily; ☏61 23 85 09, ⓦwww.gjende.no) travel the length of the lake, connecting with mountain trails and dropping by two more lodges. These are the privately owned lodge at *Memurubu* (mid-June to mid-Sept; ☏61 23 89 99, ⓦwww.memurubu.no; ❷), halfway along the lake's north shore; and *Gjendebu*, a staffed DNT lodge (early to late March & late June to late Sept (☏61 23 89 44, ⓦwww.gjendebu.com; dorm beds for DNT members 220kr, non-members 285kr, doubles ❶), right at the lake's western end. A one-way fare from Gjendesheim to Memurubu costs 100kr, Gjendebu 130kr; returns are twice that unless you make the round-trip on the same day, in which case fares are 130kr and 160kr respectively. It takes the boat twenty minutes to reach Memurubu, forty-five for Gjendebu. Naturally, you get to see a slice of the Jotunheimen and avoid a hike by riding the boat and sleeping at the lodges – a prudent choice in bad weather.

North along the E6 to Kongsvoll

From Otta, the E6 and the railway lead 45km north to **DOMBÅS**, a mundane crossroads settlement, where the E6 and the main train line head north through the mountains towards Kongsvoll (see below) and ultimately Trondheim, while the E136 and the dramatic Rauma branch line lead west to the port of Åndalsnes (see box above).

Kongsvoll

Beyond Dombås, the E6 slices across barren uplands before descending into a narrow ravine, the **Drivdal**. Hidden away here, just 40km from Dombås, is **KONGSVOLL**, home to a tiny train station and the delightful ⚜ *Kongsvold Fjeldstue* (☏72 40 43 40, ⓦwww.kongsvold.no; shared facilities ❹, en suite ❺), which provides some of the most charming accommodation in the whole of Norway. An inn has stood here since medieval times and the present complex, a huddle of tastefully restored timber buildings with sun-bleached reindeer antlers tacked onto the outside walls, dates back to the eighteenth century. Once a farm as well as an inn, its agricultural days are recalled by several outbuildings: there are the little turf-roofed storehouses (*stabbur*), the lodgings for farmhands (*karstuggu*) and the barn (*låve*), atop which is a bell that was rung to summon the hands from the fields. The main building retains many of its original features and also holds an eclectic sample of antiques. The bedrooms, dotted round the compound, are of the same high standard – and the old vagabonds' hut (*fantstuggu*), built outside the white picket fence that once defined the physical limits of social respectability, contains the cosiest family rooms imaginable. Dinner is served in the excellent **restaurant**, with mains averaging 220kr, and the complex also includes a **café** and a small Dovrefjell National Park **information centre**.

The inn makes a lovely spot to break your journey and an ideal base for hiking into the park, which extends to the east and west. If you're arriving by **train**, note that only some services stop at Kongsvoll station, 500m down the valley from the inn – and then only by prior arrangement with the conductor.

From Kongsvoll, it's about 160km to Trondheim (see pp.287–296).

Dovrefjell National Park

Bisected by the railway and the E6, **Dovrefjell National Park** is one of the more accessible of Norway's national parks. A comparative minnow at just 265 square kilometres, it comprises two distinct zones: spreading east from the E6 are the marshes, open moors and rounded peaks that characterize much of eastern Norway, while to the west the mountains become increasingly steep and serrated as they approach the jagged spires backing onto Åndalsnes (see p.280).

Hiking trails and **huts** are scattered across the western part of the Dovrefjell. **Kongsvoll** (see p.233) makes an ideal starting point: it's possible to hike all the way from here to the coast, but this takes all of nine or ten days. A more feasible expedition for most visitors is the two-hour circular walk up to the mountain plateau, or a two-day, round-trip hike to one of the four ice-tipped peaks of mighty **Snøhetta**, at 2286m. There's accommodation five hours' walk west from Kongsvoll at the unstaffed **Reinheim hut** (all year). On the first part of any of these hikes, you're likely to spot **musk ox**, the descendants of animals imported from Greenland in the 1950s. Conventional wisdom is that these chunky beasts will ignore you if you ignore them and keep at a distance of at least 100m. They are, however, not afraid of humans and will charge if irritated – retreat as quickly and quietly as possible if one starts snorting and scraping. Further hiking details and maps are available at the park **information centre** in the *Kongsvold Fjeldstue* (see p.233).

From Oslo to the western fjords

The forested dales and uplands that fill out much of **central Norway** between Oslo and the western fjords rarely inspire: in almost any other European country, these elongated valleys would be attractions in their own right, but here in Norway they simply can't compare with the mountains and fjords of the north and west. Furthermore, almost everywhere the architecture is routinely modern and most of the old timber buildings, which once lined the valleys, are long gone – except in the ten-a-penny open-air museums that are a feature of nearly every town. Neither does it help that the towns and villages of the region almost invariably string along the roads in long, seemingly aimless ribbons.

Of the three major trunk roads crossing the region, the **E16** is the fastest and least scenic, a quick 350-kilometre gallop up from Oslo to both the fjord ferry near Sogndal (see p.269) and the colossal 24-kilometre tunnel leading to Flåm (see p.263). Otherwise, the E16's nearest rival, the slower and much prettier **Highway 7**, branches off the E16 at Hønefoss to weave its way up Hallingdal before slicing across the wild wastes of the Hardangervidda plateau en route to the fjords at Eidfjord near Hardangerfjord, a distance of 350km; Highway 7 also intersects with **Highway 50**, offering another possible route to Flåm. For most of its length, Highway 7 is shadowed by the **Oslo–Bergen train line**, though they part company when the train swings north for its spectacular traverse of the mountains. The third road, the **E134**, covers the 417km from Drammen near Oslo to Haugesund, passing near Odda on the Sørfjord after 310km. Again, it's a slower route, but it has the advantage of passing through the attractive town of **Kongsberg**. The E134 also inches its way over the southern reaches of the Hardangervidda plateau and crosses one of the country's highest mountain passes, the dramatic Haukelifjell.

Regular long-distance **buses** serve all three of the major roads, but the train is quicker albeit more limited in its range of destinations: Oslo to Bergen by train takes about seven hours with stops at Finse on the Hardangervidda (see p.258) and Voss, near the Hardangerfjord (see p.255); the bus takes about three hours more.

The E16 to Fagernes and Borgund stave church

Clipping along the **E16** from Oslo, it's about 190km up through a series of river valleys to ribbon-like **FAGERNES**, where you can break your journey in some comfort at the amenable *Quality Hotel Fagernes* (☎61 35 80 00, ⓦwww.choice .no; doubles ❹/❻), which occupies a large lakeside complex with every facility and some lushly traditional public rooms. Fagernes is also where Highway 51 branches north to run along the eastern edge of the Jotunheimen Nasjonalpark, passing near Gjendesheim and its lodge (see p.232) before finally joining Highway 15 west of Otta (see p.230). In summertime, Nor-Way Bussekspress buses (ⓦwww .nor-way.no) depart from Fagernes (2–4 daily) for Beitostølen, where you change for Gjendesheim (late June to early Sept 1–2 daily; 40min).

About 30km west of Fagernes along the E16, the scenery begins to improve as you approach the coast. The road dips and weaves from dale to dale, slipping between the hills until it reaches the **Lærdal valley**, whose wooded slopes shelter the stepped roofs and angular gables of the **Borgund stave church** (daily: May to mid-June & late Aug to Sept 10am–5pm; mid-June to late Aug 8am–8pm; 65kr). One of the best-preserved stave churches in Norway, this was built beside what was one of the major pack roads between east and west until bubonic plague wiped out most of the local population in the fourteenth century. Much of the church's medieval appearance has been preserved,

---

Stave churches

The majority of Norway's 29 surviving stave churches (ⓦwww.stavechurch.com) are inland in the south and centre of the country, but taken together they represent the nation's most distinctive architectural legacy. The key feature of their design is that their timbers are placed vertically into the ground – in contrast to the log-bonding technique used by the Norwegians for everything else. Thus, a stave wall consists of vertical planks slotted into sills above and below, with the sills connected to upright posts – or **staves**, hence the name – at each corner. The general design seems to have been worked out in the twelfth century and common features include external wooden galleries, shingles and finials. There are, however, variations: in some churches, nave and chancel form a single rectangle, in others the chancel is narrower than, and tacked onto, the nave. The most fetching stave churches are those where the central section of the nave has been raised above the aisles to create – from the outside – a distinctive, almost pagoda-like effect. In virtually all the stave churches, the **door frames** (where they survive) are decorated from top to bottom with surging, intricate carvings that clearly hark back to Viking design, most memorably fantastical long-limbed dragons entwined in vine tendrils.

The origins of stave churches have attracted an inordinate amount of academic debate. Some scholars argue that they were originally pagan temples, converted to Christian use by the addition of a chancel, while others are convinced that they were inspired by Russian churches. In the nineteenth century, they also acquired symbolic importance as reminders of the time when Norway was independent. Many had fallen into a dreadful state of repair and were clumsily renovated – or even remodelled – by enthusiastic medievalists with a nationalist agenda. Undoing this repair work has been a major operation, and one that continues today. For most visitors, seeing one or two will suffice – and two of the finest are those at Heddal (see p.238) and Borgund (see above).

its tiered exterior protected by shingles and decorated with finials in the shape of dragons and Christian crosses, the whole caboodle culminating in a slender ridge turret. Inside, the dark, pine-scented nave is framed by the upright wooden posts that define this style of church architecture, and the adjacent visitor centre fills in some of the historical and architectural background.

Beyond the church, the valley grows wilder as the E16 travels the 40km down to **Fodnes**, where a 24-hour car ferry zips over to **Mannheller** (every 20min, hourly midnight–6am; 10min; car & driver 103kr, including a road toll of 48kr), some 19km from Sogndal (see p.269). En route, you'll pass the entrance to the 24-kilometre tunnel that extends the E16 to Flåm (see p.263) – for the fastest route to Bergen.

Highway 7 to Geilo and the fjords

Highway 7 branches off the E16 about 70km from Oslo at **Hønefoss**, and then cuts an unexciting course along the **Hallingdal valley**, shadowed by the main Oslo–Bergen train line. Some 180km from Hønefoss, the road forks at Hagafoss, with Highway 50 descending the dales to reach, after 100km, the Aurlandsfjord just round the coast from Flåm (see p.263). Meanwhile, Highway 7 presses on west to the winter ski resort of **GEILO**, 250km from Oslo. Frankly, Geilo is a boring town out of the skiing season, but it does have several inexpensive places to stay, including an HI **hostel** (☎32 08 70 60, ⓦwww.vandrerhjem.no; all year; dorm beds 275kr, doubles ❷), housed in two large mountain-lodge-style buildings in the town centre just off the main drag. Details of other accommodation are available from the **tourist office** (June & late Aug Mon–Fri 8.30am–5pm, Sat 9am–3pm; July to mid-Aug Mon–Fri 8.30am–9pm, Sat 9am–5pm & Sun 11am–5pm; Sept–May Mon–Fri 8.30am–2pm & Sat 9am–2pm; ☎32 09 59 00, ⓦwww.geilo.no).

Just beyond Geilo, the rail line stops following the road, breaking off to barrel its way over the mountains to Finse, Myrdal (where you change for the scenic branch line down to Flåm; see p.263) and points to Bergen. Highway 7, meanwhile, continues west for a further 100km, slicing across the Hardangervidda mountain plateau (see p.258). It's a lonely, handsome road that passes several places – such as **Halne** (see p.259) and **Dyranut** (see p.259) where you can pick up the Hardangervidda's network of hiking trails. On the far side of the plateau, Highway 7 rushes down a steep valley, passing the Vøringsfossen waterfall (see p.258) en route to the fjords at Eidfjord (see p.257).

The E134 – west to Kongsberg

Stuck up in the hills some 80km from Oslo, **KONGSBERG** is one of the most interesting towns in the region and a key attraction along the **E134**, the third main road linking Oslo with the western fjords. A local story claims that the **silver** responsible for Kongsberg's existence was discovered by two goatherds, who stumbled across a vein of the metal laid bare by the scratchings of an ox. True or not, Christian IV (1577–1648), with his eye on the main chance, was quick to exploit the find, sponsoring the development of mining here – the town's name means "King's Mountain" – at the start of a silver rush that boosted his coffers no end. In the event, it turned out that Kongsberg was the only place in the world where silver could be found in its pure form, and there was enough of it to sustain the town for a couple of centuries. By the 1750s, it was the largest town in Norway, with half its eight thousand inhabitants employed in and around the three-hundred-odd mine shafts that dotted the area. The silver works closed in 1805, but by this time Kongsberg was also the site of a royal mint, which still employs people to this day.

Downtown Kongsberg

To appreciate the full economic and political clout of the mine-owners, it's necessary to visit the church they funded – **Kongsberg kirke** (mid-May to mid-Aug Mon–Fri 10am–4pm, Sat 10am–1pm & Sun 2–4pm; mid- to late Aug Mon–Fri

10am–noon; Sept to mid-May Tues–Thurs 10am–noon; 30kr), the largest and arguably most beautiful Baroque church in Norway. It dates from 1761, when the mines were at the peak of their prosperity, its ruddy-brown brickwork and copper-green spire shadowing a large square, whose other three sides are flanked by period wooden buildings. The interior is a grand affair too, with its enormous and showy mock-marble western wall incorporating the altar, pulpit and organ. This arrangement was dictated by political considerations: the pulpit is actually above the altar to ram home the point that the priest's stern injunctions to work harder were an expression of God's will.

As for the rest of Kongsberg, it's an amenable if quiet little town with plenty of green spaces. The **River Lågen** tumbles through the centre, and statues on the town bridge at the foot of Storgata, commemorate various local activities, including foolhardy attempts to locate new finds of silver – one of which involved the use of divining rods. Mining enthusiasts will enjoy the **Norsk Bergverksmuseum**, Hyttegata 3 (Mining Museum: daily: mid-May to Aug 10am–5pm; Sept to mid-May noon–4pm; 60kr), housed in the old smelting works near the river and sharing its premises with a tiny ski museum and coin collection, but merely wandering around the town is as enjoyable a way as any of spending an hour or two.

Kongsberg practicalities

Kongsberg **train and bus stations** are on the north side of town, a five-minute walk from the centre. The **tourist office** is inside the train station (May to late June & late Aug to Sept Mon–Fri 9am–4pm, Sat 10am–2pm; late June to late Aug Mon–Fri 9am–7pm, Sat & Sun 10am–2pm; Oct–April Mon–Fri 9am–4pm; ☎32 29 90 50, Ⓦwww.visitkongsberg.no) and can help with accommodation – not that there's much to choose from. The HI 🏠 **hostel**, *Kongsberg Vandrerhjem*, Vinjesgate 1 (☎32 73 20 24, Ⓦwww.vandrerhjem.no) is the place to stay if you've an eye on your expenses, with both dorm beds (270kr) and comfortable en-suite doubles (②) in an attractive timber lodge close to the town centre. Drivers need to follow the signs on the E134; train- and bus-users should walk south from the station along Storgata, cross the bridge, walk round the back of the church on the right-hand side, then head down the lane beside the bandstand and cross over the footbridge – it's about a fifteen-minute walk in all. As for central **hotels**, easily the most appealing option is the *Quality Hotel Grand*, in a modern block down near the river at Christian Augusts gate 2 (☎32 77 28 00, Ⓦwww.choicehotels.no ④/⑤). From the outside, the hotel is undistinguished, but the interior, which is decorated in crisp modern style, is extremely well maintained and the 175 guest rooms are large and extremely comfortable; the best, on the top floors, offer wide views over the churning, tumbling Lågen River. The only disappointment is breakfast, which is very average.

Circa, at Storgata 13, serves the best coffee in town as well as sandwiches, snacks and light lunches; in the evening, it morphs into a very pleasant, laid-back bar (Mon & Tues 10am–5pm, Wed & Thurs 10am–11.30pm, Fri & Sat 10am–3am, Sun noon–5pm). The pick of the town's several **restaurants is the** *Opsahlgården*, a smart and cosy little place near the church at Kirkegata 10 (Mon–Fri 3–10pm & Sat 5–10pm; ☎32 76 45 00). They do a particularly good line in seafood here with main courses averaging just 100kr.

The E134 west of Kongsberg – Heddal stave church

A few kilometres west of Kongsberg, the **E134** slips into **Telemark** (Ⓦwww .visittelemark.no), a county that covers a great forested chunk of southern Norway. In a country where the fjords are the apple of the tourist industry's eye, Telemark is often neglected, but it can be stunningly beautiful, its deep valleys, blue-black lochs and bulging forested hills intercepted by tiny villages in a manner that resembles the Swiss Alps. Heading into the county on the E134, things begin inauspiciously with **Notodden**, a workaday industrial town, but from here it's just 5km to the delightful

Heddal stave church (late May to late June & late Aug to mid-Sept Mon–Sat 10am–5pm, Sun 1–5pm; late June to late Aug Mon–Sat 9am–7pm, Sun 1–7pm; 50kr; ⓦ www.heddalstavkirke.no), which stands beside the road fronted by the neatest of cemeteries. The largest surviving stave church in Norway, it has a pretty tumble of shingle-clad roofs which was restored to something like its medieval appearance in 1955, rectifying a heavy-handed nineteenth-century remodelling. The crosses atop the church's gables alternate with dragon-head gargoyles, a mix of Christian and pagan symbolism typical of many stave churches (see box, p.235). Inside, the twenty masts of the nave are surmounted by masks, and there's some attractive seventeenth-century wall decoration in light blues, browns and whites. Across from the church, there's a **café** and a modest museum illustrating further aspects of the church's history.

To Seljord and Røldal

Pushing on west, the E134 rattles up the valley before making a dramatic passage over the mountains on its way to **SELJORD**, a small but straggly industrial town at the head of Seljordsvatnet lake, about 55km from Heddal. Modest it may be, but Seljord seems to have attracted more than its fair share of "Believe It or Not" stories: a monster is supposed to lurk in the depths of the lake; elves are alleged to gather here for some of their soirees; and the medieval stone church, with its whitewashed walls and dinky little spire, was, so the story goes, built by a goblin.

Beyond Seljord, it's a further 50km west along the E134 to the **Åmot cross-roads**, after which the road zigzags across hill and dale before beginning its long climb up to the bare and bleak wastes of the Hardangervidda plateau (see p.258) via Haukelifjell, one of Europe's highest mountain passes. The road cuts a nervous course across the plateau, diving into a series of tunnels before slipping down into the hamlet of **RØLDAL**, a remote little place nestled in the greenest of valleys. Røldal has its own **stave church** (mid-May to mid-Sept daily 10am–5pm; 30kr), a trim, rustic affair dating from the twelfth century but much amended.

On to Odda

After Røldal, the E134 makes another stirring climb to reach its junction with Highway 13, the road to Stavanger (see pp.216–221). The E134 – combined with the northerly extension of Highway 13 – then plunges across the Hardangervidda on its way to another crossroads, where you turn on to Highway 13 for Odda and Lofthus (see p.257). This Highway 13 drops down a severe, boulder-strewn river valley, passing, in 5km, the **Latefossen** waterfall, where two huge torrents empty into the river with a deafening roar. From the waterfall, it's a short drive north to **ODDA**, an unappetizing industrial town and an unfortunate introduction to the fjords: try to allow enough time to avoid the place altogether and carry on to the much more appealing hamlet of Lofthus (see p.257); Odda is 43km from Røldal – allow an hour, more in poor weather.

Travel details

Principal NSB trains (ⓦ www.nsb.no)

Åndalsnes to: Dombås (2–3 daily; 1hr 45min); Oslo (2–3 daily; 5hr 30min).

Dombås to: Åndalsnes (2–3 daily; 1hr 45min); Oslo (3–4 daily; 4hr).

Geilo to: Oslo (3–4 daily; 3hr).

Kongsberg to: Oslo (4–5 daily; 1hr 10min).

Lillehammer to: Oslo (hourly; 2hr); Trondheim (3–4 daily; 4hr 40min).

Oslo to: Åndalsnes (2–3 daily; 5hr 30min); Bergen (4 daily; 7hr 20min); Dombås (3–4 daily; 4hr); Geilo (3–4 daily; 3hr); Kongsberg (4–5 daily; 1hr 10min); Kongsvoll (3–4 daily; 4hr 40min – request stop only); Kvam (1–2 daily; 3hr 30min – request stop only); Lillehammer (hourly; 2hr); Myrdal (4 daily;

4hr 50min); Otta (6 daily; 3hr 30min); Trondheim (3–4 daily; 6hr 40min); Voss (4 daily; 6hr 40min).
Oslo Gardermoen airport to: Åndalsnes (2–3 daily; 5hr); Dombås (3–4 daily; 3hr 30min); Kongsvoll (3–4 daily; 4hr 10min – request stop only); Kvam (1–2 daily; 3hr – request stop only); Lillehammer (hourly; 1hr 30min); Otta (6 daily; 3hr); Trondheim (3–4 daily; 6hr 10min).
Otta to: Oslo (6 daily; 3hr 30min).

Principal Nor-Way Busseskspress buses (ⓦwww.nor-way.no)

Kongsberg to: Haugesund (3 daily; 7hr 30min); Oslo (3 daily; 1hr 30min).
Lillehammer to: Bergen (1 daily; 9hr); Flåm (1 daily; 5hr 30min); Lom (3 daily; 3hr 40min); Oslo (4 daily; 3hr); Otta (3 daily; 2hr 30min); Stryn (3 daily; 5hr 40min).
Oslo to: Ålesund (2 daily; 10hr); Åndalsnes (2 daily; 8hr); Beitostølen (3–4 daily; 4hr, change at Fagernes); Bergen (3 daily; 10hr 30min); Dombås (2 daily; 6hr 15min); Fagernes (6–8 daily; 3hr); Gjendesheim in the Jotunheimen (late June to early Sept 2 daily; 5hr, changing at Fagernes and then Beitostølen); Kongsberg (3 daily; 1hr 30min); Kongsvoll (1 daily; 7hr); Kvam (Mon–Fri 1 daily; 4hr 45min); Lillehammer (4 daily; 3hr); Lom (4 daily; 6hr 40min); Odda (3 daily; 7hr); Otta (4 daily; 5hr 30min); Sjoa (Mon–Fri 1 daily; 4hr 45min); Sogndal (3 daily; 7hr); Stryn (3 daily; 8hr 40min); Trondheim (1–3 daily; 8hr).

2.4

Bergen and the western fjords

I f there's one familiar and enticing image of Norway, it's the **fjords**: huge clefts in the landscape running from the coast deep into the interior. Wild, rugged and serene, these water-filled wedges are visually stunning; indeed, the entire fjord region elicits inordinate amounts of purple prose from tourist office handouts, and for once it's rarely overstated. The fjords are undeniably beautiful, especially around early May after the brief Norwegian spring has brought colour to the landscape.

The fjords run all the way up the coast to the Russian border, but are most easily – and impressively – seen on the west coast near **Bergen**, the self-proclaimed "Capital of the Fjords". Norway's second largest city, Bergen is a welcoming place with an atmospheric old warehouse quarter, a relic of the days when it was the northernmost port of the Hanseatic trading alliance. It's also a handy springboard for the nearby fjords, including the Flåmsdal valley to the east, where the inspiring **Flåmsbana** mountain train trundles down to the **Aurlandsfjord**, a small arm of the mighty **Sognefjord**. Lined with pretty village-resorts, the Sognefjord is the longest, deepest and most celebrated of the country's fjords, and is certainly one of the most beguiling. North of here lies the **Jostedalsbreen** glacier, mainland Europe's largest ice sheet, the relatively uninspiring **Nordfjord** and the narrow, S-shaped **Geirangerfjord**, perhaps the most scenically impressive of all the fjords – though here, for once, the tourist hordes can be off-putting. Further north, towards the **Romsdalsfjord**, the landscape becomes more extreme still, reaching pinnacles of isolation in the splendid **Trollstigen** mountain highway, a stunning prelude to the amiable little town of **Åndalsnes** and the ferry port of **Ålesund**, with its attractive Art Nouveau buildings.

Bergen

As it has been raining ever since she arrived in the city, a tourist stops a young boy and asks if it always rains here. "I don't know," he replies, "I'm only 13." The joke isn't brilliant, but it does contain a grain of truth. Of all the things to contend with in **BERGEN**, the weather is the most predictable: it rains on average 260 days a year, often relentlessly, even in summer, and its forested surroundings are frequently shrouded in mist. Yet, despite its dampness, Bergen is one of Norway's most enjoyable cities. Its setting – amidst seven hills and sheltered to the north, south and west by a series of straggling islands – is spectacular. There's plenty to see in town too, from sturdy old stone buildings and terraces of tiny wooden houses to a veritable raft of **museums**, and just outside the city limits is Edvard Grieg's home, **Troldhaugen**.

More than anything else, though, it's the general flavour of the place that appeals. Although Bergen has become a major port and something of an industrial centre in

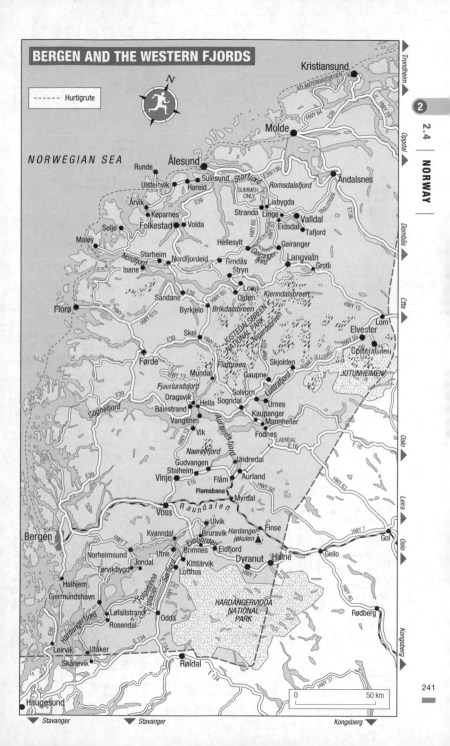

BERGEN AND THE WESTERN FJORDS

- - - - - Hurtigrute

NORWEGIAN SEA

Kristiansund

Molde

Ålesund

Runde
Ulsteinvik
Sulesund
Hareid
Storfjord
Andalsnes
Romsdalsfjord

Árvik
Køparnes
Folkestad
Volda
SUMMER
ONLY
Liabygda

Selje
Stranda
Linge
Valldal
Eidsdal
Tafjord

Maløy
Starheim
Nordfjordeid
Hellesylt
Geiranger
Langvatn

Isane
Nordfjord
Grodås
Stryn
Geiranger-
fjord
Grotli

Florø
Sandane
Byrkjelo
Loen
Olden
Kjenndalsbreen

Brikdalsbreen
Lom

Skei
Flatbreen
Nigardsbreen
Elvester

JOSTEDALSBREEN
NATIONAL PARK
Opperstulen

Førde
Mundal
Gaupne
Skjolden
JOTUNHEIMEN

Fjaerlandsjord
Solvorn
Lustrafjord

Dragsvik
Hella
Urnes
Balestrand
Sognefjord
Sogndal
Kaupanger
Vangsnes
Mannheller

Vik
Aurlandsfjord
Fodnes
LAERDAL
E 16

Naerøyfjord
Undredal

Gudvangen
Stalheim
Aurland
Vinje
Flåm

Flamsbana
Myrdal

Voss
Raundalen
Finse
Ulvik

Kvanndal
Bruravik
Hardanger-
jøkulen
Geilo
Gol

Norheimsund
Utne
Brimnes
Eidfjord
Dyranut
Halne

Jondal
Kinsarvik
Lofthus

Tørvikbygd

Halhjem
Bergen

Gjermundshavn
Folgefonna
glacier
Odda

Løfallstrand
Rosendal
HARDANGERVIDDA
NATIONAL PARK
Rødberg

Hardangerfjord
Leirvik
Utaker
Skånevik
Røldal

Haugesund

0   50 km

Stavanger   Stavanger   Kongsberg

Trondheim
Oppdal
Dombås
Otta
Lom
Oslo
Leira
Oslo
Kongsberg

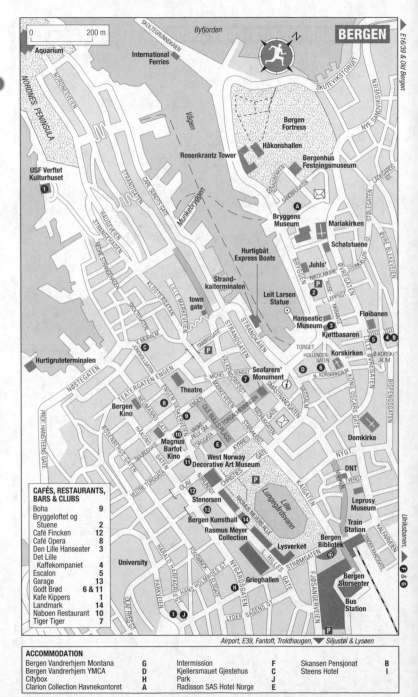

BERGEN

CAFÉS, RESTAURANTS, BARS & CLUBS

Boha	9
Bryggeloftet og Stuene	2
Café Fincken	12
Café Opera	8
Den Lille Hanseater	3
Det Lille Kaffekompaniet	4
Escalon	5
Garage	13
Godt Brød	6 & 11
Kafe Kippers	1
Landmark	14
Naboen Restaurant	10
Tiger Tiger	7

ACCOMMODATION

Bergen Vandrerhjem Montana	G	Intermission	F	Skansen Pensjonat	B
Bergen Vandrerhjem YMCA	D	Kjellersmauet Gjestehus	C	Steens Hotel	I
Citybox	H	Park	J		
Clarion Collection Havnekontoret	A	Radisson SAS Hotel Norge	E		

recent years, it remains a laid-back, easygoing town with a firmly nautical air. Fish and fishing may no longer be Bergen's economic lynchpins, but the bustling main harbour, **Vågen**, is still very much the focus of attention. If you stay more than a day or two – perhaps using Bergen as a base for viewing the nearer **fjords** – you'll soon discover that the city also has the region's best choice of **restaurants**, some impressive **art** galleries and a decent nightlife.

Arrival

Bergen's **train station** (local ☏55 96 69 00, national ☏815 00 888) is located on Strømgaten, just along from the entrance to the Bergen Storsenter shopping mall, within which is the **bus station**. From Strømgaten, it's a five- to ten-minute walk west to the most interesting part of the city, on and around Bergen's main harbour, **Vågen**. The **airport** is 20km south of the city at Flesland and it's connected to the centre by **Flybussen** (Mon–Fri & Sun 5am–9pm, Sat 5am–5pm, every 15–30min; 45min; 80kr one-way). These Flybussen pull in at the bus station, the *SAS Hotel Norge*, on Ole Bulls plass, and the tourist office before proceeding to the harbourfront *SAS Royal Hotel*, on the Bryggen. **Taxis** from the rank outside the airport arrivals hall charge around 350–400kr for the same trip.

By boat

Fjord Line (☏815 33 500, ⓦwww.fjordline.com) international car ferries from Egersund, Haugesund and Hantsholm in Denmark dock at the Skoltegrunnskaien, at the tip of the main harbour, Vågen. Bergen is also the home port of the **Hurtigrute coastal boat** (☏810 30 000, ⓦwww.hurtigruten.com), which docks at the Hurtigruteterminalen, on the south side of the city centre, off Nøstegaten, about 900m due south of the main harbour, Vågen. **Hurtigbåt passenger express boats** (ⓦwww.fjord1.no or ⓦwww.tide.no) from Haugesund, Stavanger and the Hardangerfjord, as well as those from Sognefjord and Nordfjord, line up on the south side of the Vågen at the Strandkaiterminalen. Some local **sightseeing boats** use this terminal too, though the majority dock on the north side of Vågen or at the back of Torget.

By car

If you're driving into Bergen, note that a **toll** (15kr) is charged on all vehicles entering the city centre, but you don't have to stop anywhere – it's levied electronically with cameras reading number plates. In an attempt to keep the city centre relatively free of traffic, there's a confusing and none-too-successful one-way system in operation, supplemented by rigorously enforced on-street parking restrictions. Outside peak periods, on-street **parking** is relatively easy and free, but during peak periods (Mon–Fri 8am–5pm, Sat 8am–10am) metered parking is available only, for a maximum of two hours at 15kr an hour. Your best bet, therefore, is to make straight for one of the four central car parks: the largest is the 24-hour Bygarasjen, a short walk from the city centre, behind the Storsenter shopping mall and bus station. Charges here are heavily discounted – it costs just 90kr for 24 hours, 30kr overnight. The 24-hour Rosenkrantz P-Hus, on Rosenkrantzgaten, is much handier for the harbourfront, but charges are higher: 24-hours costs 170kr. To get there, follow the international ferry signs until you pick up the car park signs.

Information

Bergen **tourist office** is handily located in a large, mural-decorated hall across the road from Torget at Vågsallmenningen 1 (May & Sept daily 9am–8pm; June–Aug daily 8.30am–10pm; Oct–April Mon–Sat 9am–4pm; ☏55 55 20 00, ⓦwww.visitbergen.com). It supplies free copies of the exhaustive *Bergen Guide*, sells the Bergen Card (see box, p.244), changes foreign currency, arranges car hire,

The Bergen Card

The **Bergen Card** is a 24-hour (190kr; children 3–15 years 75kr) or 48-hour (250kr; children 3–15 years 100kr) pass that provides free use of all the city's buses and free or substantially discounted admission to most of the city's sights, plus reductions on many sightseeing trips. It also gives free on-street parking within the posted limits – if you can find a space. The pass comes with a booklet listing all the various concessions. Obviously, the more diligent a sightseer you are, the better value the card becomes – doubly so if you're staying a bus ride from the centre. The card is sold at a wide range of outlets, including the tourist office and major hotels.

and sells train, city-tour and fjord-tour tickets. It also operates an accommodation service, booking hotel rooms and rooms in private houses (see below). In high season, expect long queues. Available here too, and in many other places across the city centre, is (the Bergen version of) *Natt & Dag*, a free monthly **magazine**, containing local news, entertainment listings and reviews. Naturally enough, it's in Norwegian, but the listings are still easy(ish) to use.

City transport

Most of Bergen's key attractions are located in the city centre, which is compact enough to be readily explored **on foot**. For outlying sights and accommodation, however, you may well need to take a city **bus**. These are operated by Tide (☎177, ⓦwww.tide.no), which provides a dense network of local services that reaches every corner of Bergen and its environs; the hub of the network is the **bus station**, in the Storsenter shopping mall on Strømgaten. Flat-fare tickets for travel within the city limits cost 23kr; they are available from the driver. Finally, two passenger **ferries** offer useful short cuts: one bobs across Vågen between Munkebryggen, on Carl Sundts gate, and a point near the Bryggens Museum on the Bryggen (Mon–Fri 7am–4pm; 15kr); the second links Torget with the Nordnes peninsula, docking not far from the Akvariet (late May to Aug daily 10am–6pm; 60kr return, 40kr one-way).

Accommodation

Finding budget **accommodation** in Bergen can be a bit of a problem at the height of the season, but is usually straightforward. There are three hostels and a choice of guesthouses, and some of the central hotels are surprisingly good value. Also among the better deals are the **rooms** in private houses – or "private rooms" – that can be reserved through the tourist office. The vast majority provide self-catering facilities and some are fairly central, though most are stuck out in the suburbs. Prices are at a fixed nightly rate – currently 430kr for a double room without en-suite facilities (300kr one-way), and 500kr for en suite (350kr one-way). They are very popular, so in summer you'll need to arrive at the tourist office early to secure one for the night. The tourist office makes a small supplementary charge (of 30kr, 50kr in advance) for making a booking, as it does for hotel and guesthouse reservations.

Hotels

Citybox Nygårdsgaten 31 ☎55 31 25 00, ⓦwww.citybox.no. Great emphasis here on economy prices in return for what you actually need – a brightly decorated, albeit rather spartan room – as distinct from what you can manage without, for instance a mini-bar and room service. Rooms are either en suite (an extra 100kr) or with shared facilities. Internet access. Central location. ❶

Clarion Collection Havnekontoret Slottsgaten 1 ☎55 60 11 00, ⓦwww.choicehotels.no. Prestige development in which Bergen's former harbour office has been tastefully converted into a deluxe hotel. The handsome public areas are capacious and although the emphasis is on the modern, the original 1920s stone archways and vaulted side-rooms, with their intricate murals, have been preserved. The best of the guest rooms, where browns and creams predominate, have harbour views. ❺/❼

🏃 **Park** Harald Hårfagres gate 35 ☎55 54 44 00, ⓦwww.parkhotel.no. This excellent, family-run hotel occupies two handsome late nineteenth-century town houses on the edge of the town centre near the university. The charming interior is painted in soft pastel colours and the public areas are dotted with antiques. The bedrooms are smart, neat and appealing. It's very popular, so reservations are advised. ❹/❺

Radisson SAS Royal Hotel Bryggen ☎55 54 30 00, ⓦwww.radissonsas.com. Full marks here to the architects, who have built an extremely smart, first-rate hotel behind a brick facade that mirrors the style of the old timber buildings that surround it. All facilities – pool, health club and so forth – plus attractively appointed rooms. ❻/❽

Steens Hotel Parkveien 22 ☎55 30 88 88, ⓦwww.steenshotel.no. In a good-looking, late nineteenth-century villa, this well-established hotel boasts all sorts of period detail, from the bygones in the foyer through to the neo-Baronial touches – and stained-glass windows – in the dining room. The guest rooms are well kept if a little spartan, and the hotel overlooks the miniature lake and parklet that form the western tip of the green and leafy Nygardsparken. Ten minutes' walk from Vågen. ❻/❼

Guesthouses

Kjellersmauet Gjestehus Kjellersmauet 22 ☎55 96 26 08, ⓦwww.gjestehuset.com.

Immaculately maintained 1880s timber house whose interior has been turned into three en-suite apartments of varying size but all with kitchenettes. On a narrow alley off a busy main street – Jonsvollsgaten – about 10min walk west from Ole Bulls plass. ❸

🏃 **Skansen Pensjonat** Vetrlidsallmenningen 29 ☎55 31 90 80, ⓦwww.skansen -pensjonat.no. This pleasant little guesthouse occupies a nineteenth-century stone house of elegant proportions just above – up the steps and hairpins from – the terminus of the Fløibanen funicular railway, near Torget: it's a great location, in one of the most beguiling parts of town. The pension has eleven guest rooms, most of which are en suite, and all are very homely. A real snip at ❷

Hostels

Bergen Vandrerhjem Montana Johan Blyttsveien 30, Landås ☎55 20 80 70, ⓦwww.montana .no. This large and comfortable HI hostel occupies lodge-like premises in the hills overlooking the city. Great views and great breakfasts, plus self-catering facilities, a café, a laundry and internet access. Has dorm accommodation, family rooms and doubles – almost all of which are en suite. The hostel is 6km east of the centre, 15min on bus #31 (stop Montana) from the train station. Popular with school parties, who are (usually) housed in a separate wing. Dorm beds 180–200kr, doubles ❷

Bergen Vandrerhjem YMCA Nedre Korskirkealmenning 4 ☎55 60 60 55, ⓦwww .vandrerhjem.no. No-frills HI hostel in the city

▲ The Bryggen, Bergen

centre, a short walk from Torget. Has room for 170 guests, but fills up fast in summer. Facilities include self-catering and a laundry. Open May–Sept. Breakfast 55kr. Dorm beds 155kr, doubles ❸ **Intermission** Kalfarveien 8 ☎ 55 30 04 00, Ⓦ www.intermissionhostel.no. Christian-run, private hostel in a two-storey, oldish wooden building, a 5min walk from the train station – just beyond one of the old city gates. Open mid-June to mid-Aug. Breakfast 25kr, dorm beds 150kr.

The City

Founded in 1070 by King Olav Kyrre ("the Peaceful"), a Norwegian survivor from the battle of Stamford Bridge in 1066, **Bergen** was the largest and most important town in medieval Norway and a regular residence of the country's kings and queens. In the fourteenth century Bergen also became an ecclesiastical centre, supporting no fewer than thirty churches and monasteries, and a member of the **Hanseatic League**, confirmation of its status as a prosperous port linked to other European cities by a vigorous trading life. The League was, however, controlled by German merchants and, after Hansa and local interests started to diverge, the Germans came to dominate the region's economy, reducing the locals to a state of dependency. Neither could the people of Bergen expect help from their kings and queens. Indeed it was the reverse: in return for easily collected taxes from the Hansa merchants, Norway's medieval monarchs compelled west-coast fishermen to sell their catch to the merchants – and at prices the merchants set themselves. As a result, the German trading station that flourished on the Bryggen, Bergen's main wharf, became wealthy and hated in equal measure, a self-regulating trading station with its own laws and an administration that was profoundly indifferent to local sentiment.

In the 1550s, with Hansa power finally evaporating, a local lord – one **Kristoffer Valkendorf** – reasserted Norwegian control, but not out of the goodness of his heart. Valkendorf and his cronies simply took over the monopolies that had enriched their German predecessors, and continued to operate this iniquitous system, which so pauperized the region's fishermen, right up to the late nineteenth century. In fact, it's only after World War II that local fishermen started to receive their financial dues, a prerequisite of the economic boom that has, since the 1960s, transformed Bergen from a fish-dependent backwater to the lively city of today.

Torget

In 1890, Lilian Leland, author of *Traveling Alone: A Woman's Journey Around the World*, complained of Bergen that "Everything is fishy. You eat fish and drink fish and smell fish and breathe fish." Those days are long gone, but now that Bergen is every inch a go-ahead, modern city, tourists in search of all things piscine flock to **Torget**'s open-air **fish market** (June–Aug daily 7am–5pm, Sept–May Mon–Sat 7am–4pm). It's not a patch on the days when scores of fishing vessels crowded the quayside to empty their bulging holds, but the stalls still display mounds of prawns and crab-claws, dried cod, buckets of herring and a hundred other varieties of marine life on slabs, in tanks, under the knife and in packets. Fruit, vegetables and flowers – as well as souvenirs – have a place in today's market too, and there's easily enough variety to assemble an excellent picnic lunch, so load up or eat up.

Bryggen

Spearing down the north side of Vågen, **Bryggen** is the obvious historical and cultural target after Torget. The site of the original settlement, Bryggen recalls its medieval provenance by a string of wooden and stone warehouses, whose distinctive gable ends face out to the waterfront. The whole area between the Bryggen and Øvregaten just to the rear was once known as Tyskebryggen, or "German Quay", after the Hanseatic merchants who operated their **trading station** here, but the name was unceremoniously dumped after World War II.

The Hanseatic Museum

The **medieval buildings** of the Bryggen were destroyed by fire in 1702, to be replaced by another set of wooden warehouses. In turn, many of these were later demolished to make way for brick and stone warehouses built in a style modelled on – and sympathetic to – that of the Hansa period. Nevertheless, a significant number of early eighteenth-century timber buildings have survived, though the first you'll come to, at the north end of Torget, has brick-and-stone neighbours. This is the **Hanseatisk Museum** (Hanseatic Museum: mid-May to mid-Sept daily 9am–5pm; mid-Sept to mid-May Tues–Sat 11am–2pm & Sun 11am–4pm; 50kr, includes Schøtstuene), a delightfully well-preserved, early eighteenth-century merchants' dwelling, kitted out in late Hansa style. As per standard Hansa format, it was a rabbit warren of a place in which the trading area occupied the ground floor and the junior staff the top, with the merchants in between.

The rest of the Bryggen

A few metres further on from the Hanseatic Museum is the main block of old **timber buildings**, now housing souvenir shops, restaurants and bars. Despite the crowds of tourists, it's well worth nosing around here, wandering down the passageways wherever you can. Interestingly, these eighteenth-century buildings carefully follow the original building line: the governing body of the Hansa trading station stipulated the exact depth and width of each merchant's building, and the width of the passage separating them – a regularity that's actually best observed from Øvregaten (see p.248).

The Bryggens Museum

Just off the Bryggen, beside the *SAS Royal Hotel*, stands the lumpily modern **Bryggens Museum** (mid-May to Aug daily 10am–5pm; Sept to mid-May Mon–Fri 11am–3pm, Sat noon–3pm & Sun noon–4pm; 50kr), where a visit begins in the basement, which exhibits all manner of things dug up in the archeological excavations of the Bryggen in the 1950s. A wide range of items was unearthed, from domestic implements like combs and pots through to shoes, buckles and trade goods plus several runic sticks. The museum displays these finds thematically both to illustrate the city's early history and provide the backcloth to a set of twelfth-century foundations at the back of the basement, left *in situ* where they were unearthed. The museum's two upper floors are given over to temporary exhibitions exploring other aspects of Bergen's past.

St Mary's Church

Behind the museum, the perky twin towers of the **Mariakirken** (St Mary's Church: late June to late Aug Mon–Fri 9–11am & 1–4pm; late Aug to late June Tues–Fri 11am–12.30pm; 20kr, free in winter) are the most distinctive feature of what is Bergen's oldest extant building, a Romanesque-Gothic church dating from the twelfth century. Still used as a place of worship, St Mary's is now firmly Norwegian, but from 1408 to 1706 it was the church of the Hanseatic League merchants, who purchased it lock, stock and barrel. The merchants installed the church's ostentatious Baroque pulpit and its gaudy north German altarpiece, a fifteenth-century triptych, whose exquisite framing is really rather wasted on the sentimental carvings of saints and apostles it surrounds.

Schøtstuene and Øvregaten

At the back of St Mary's Church, at Øvregaten 50, the **Schøtstuene** (mid-May to mid-Sept daily 10am–5pm; mid-Sept to mid-May Sun only 11am–2pm; 50kr, includes the Hanseatic Museum) comprises the old Hanseatic assembly rooms, where the merchants would meet to lay down the law or just relax – it was the only building in the whole trading post allowed heating and so it was here that they held their feasts, ceremonies and celebrations. As you explore the comfortable and commodious rooms, it's hard not to conclude that the merchants cared not a jot for their employees shivering away nearby – though, to be fair, their bunk beds weren't much fun either.

Saving the mildly interesting Bergenhus Festning for later (see below), stroll east from the Schøtstuene along **Øvregaten**, an attractive cobbled street which has marked the boundary of the Bryggen for the last 800 years. From Øvregaten, it's still possible to discern the **layout** of the old trading station, a warren of narrow passages separating warped and crooked buildings surmounted by their hat-like, high-pitched roofs. On the upper levels, the eighteenth-century loading bays, staircases and higgledy-piggledy living quarters are still much in evidence, while the overhanging eaves of the passageways were designed to shelter trade goods.

At the eastern end of Bryggen's timber houses, cobbled Nikolaikirkeallmenningen leaves Øvregaten to run down to the harbourfront, where you turn right for the Bergenhus; if you stay on Øvregaten, it's a couple of minutes to the lower terminus of the Fløibanen (see p.249).

Bergen Fortress

Overlooking the mouth of the harbour, the **Bergenhus Festning** (Bergen Fortress) is a large and roughly star-shaped fortification now used mostly as a park (daily 6.30am–11pm; free). The fort's thick stone-and-earth walls date from the nineteenth century, but they enclose the remnants of earlier strongholds – or rather their copies: the building was wrecked when a German ammunition ship exploded just below the walls in 1944. Of the two main medieval replicas, the more diverting is the forbidding **Rosenkrantztårnet** (Rosenkrantz Tower: mid-May to Aug daily 10am–4pm; Sept to mid-May Sun noon–3pm; 40kr), whose spiral staircases, medieval rooms and low rough corridors make an enjoyable gambol. It's also possible to walk out onto the rooftop battlements, from where there is a wide view over the harbour.

Metres from the tower is the entrance to a large cobbled courtyard, which is flanked by nineteenth-century officers' quarters and the **Håkonshallen** (mid-May to Aug daily 10am–4pm; Sept to mid-May daily noon–3pm, Thurs 3–6pm; 40kr), a careful reconstruction of the Gothic ceremonial hall built for King Håkon Håkonsson in the middle of the thirteenth century. After Norway lost its independence, the capacious hall became surplus to requirements and no one knew quite what to do with it for several centuries, but it was revamped in 1910 and rebuilt after the 1944 explosion and is now in use once again for public ceremonies.

Frequent **guided tours** of both the Rosenkrantz Tower and the Håkonshallen start at the Håkonshallen; there's no extra charge.

Bergen Fortress Museum

From the entrance to the Bergenhus Festning, it's a couple of minutes' walk to the **Bergenhus Festningsmuseum** (Bergenhus Fortress Museum: Tues–Sun 11am–5pm; free), on Øvre Dreggsallmenningen, where, on the first floor, several displays explore the effects of World War II on Bergen. There's a detailed account of the German naval attack on Bergen in 1940 and on the development of the Resistance thereafter. Bergen had long-standing seafaring links with Great Britain and had also suffered grievously from U-boat attacks on Norwegian shipping in World War I, and as a result the Resistance to the occupation was particularly strong here. Unfortunately, the Germans proved adept at tracking down their enemies, and time and again they broke the back of the main Resistance groups, though they were flummoxed by the explosion which levelled much of the Bergenhus on Hitler's birthday in 1944: they thought it was sabotage, but in fact it was an accident. The museum's second floor is far less interesting, being given over to a detailed exploration of the history of the Bergen Fortress; the ground floor is for temporary displays.

From the museum, it's a few minutes' walk back along Bryggen to Torget and the Fløibanen funicular railway.

Scandinavian style

Whatever your aesthetic sensibilities, Scandinavia's universally high standards of design are sure to strike a chord. Even the most humdrum of public spaces – airport terminals, museum restrooms, student cafeterias – command a few extra moments of appreciation, with simple and subtle touches that make bold statements without screaming for attention. Finer hotels and restaurants, meanwhile, are often homages to exemplary design, and Scandinavia's urban architecture provides a remarkable smorgasbord of styles – from the magnificent thirteenth-century passageways of Stockholm's Gamla Stan to the imposing Modernist structures by Alvar Aalto scattered all over Finland.

Series 7 chairs, Arne Jacobsen ▲

Finnish ceramics ▼

IKEA shopping trolleys ▼

Pure design

It was remarkably original pieces of furniture such as Dane **Arne Jacobsen's** cradle-like Egg Chair that first put Scandinavian design on the map, and from the early 1950s onwards, objects from the region's designers became synonymous with outstanding craftsmanship, quality and innovative style. Housewares and the applied arts – woodwork, glassmaking, metalwork and ceramics in particular – have since been widely imitated for their simplicity and purity of line. Alongside Jacobsen, revolutionary designers like **Alvar Aalto** (Finland) and **Carl Malmsten** (Sweden) envisioned smooth, sensual motifs that evoked nature itself, contrasting with many other, overly technical European creations. Looking to the landscapes that surrounded them, they employed beech or cherry woods and muted colours in uncomplicated, understated designs – decisions which made perfect sense in a place where standing out in a crowd has always been a social no-no. Today, classic works such as Aalto's Paimio Chair (1933), Hans Wegner's Round Chair (1949) and Jacob Jensen's plastic matt-red bowls (1954) are heralded in design museums worldwide and contemporary cutting-edge design can be picked up in shops across Scandinavia.

The most successful proponent of Scandinavian style is, of course, **IKEA**. Founded in 1943 by 17-year-old farmhand Ingvar Kamprad, the company began selling pens, watches and nylon stockings, later adding low-cost, **flat-pack furniture** to its range. Today an almost exclusively Scandinavian design team conceives the company's 12,000 products, many of which take their names from the region's lakes, rivers and towns.

Architecture

"The best standardization committee in the world is nature herself."

Alvar Aalto (1898–1976)

Perhaps the most striking thing about contemporary **Scandinavian architecture** is its simplicity. For hundreds of years, the region's landscape was defined by ornate stave churches and magnificently turreted castles. In the early twentieth century, however, modesty and understatement came to dominate: frill and showiness were out, restraint and clarity were in, and the rest of the world soon followed. While most European building design employed the Modernist standbys of glass, steel and concrete, Scandinavian architects embarked upon an inventive incorporation of traditional forms with modern techniques, and a return to organic materials like wood and brick. Long before **'eco-friendly'** became a buzzword, this regressive move established Scandinavian architecture as the most forward-looking in the world, setting a global standard for a modern architectural aesthetic.

Twentieth-century building design was profoundly influenced by Finnish architects **Eliel Saarinen** and **Alvar Aalto**, while more recent visionaries like Danes **Jørn Utzon** and **Henning Larsen** and the Swede **Erik Asplund** have wielded significant influence, both at home and abroad. Today, many Scandinavian towns and cities offer rich architectural pickings, and a stroll around most urban centres – from Copenhagen's Indre By district (see p.72) to the garden city of Tapiola (see p.552) just outside Helsinki – can provide endless hours of visual stimulation.

▲ Helsinki Central Railway Station

▼ Nordea Bank, Copenhagen, by Henning Larsen

Bryggen, Norway ▲

Øresunds Link ▼

The must-sees of Scandinavian style

▶▶ **Bryggen, Bergen**. This superbly preserved medieval old quarter features a string of gabled wooden warehouses that front the municipal wharf. See p.246.

▶▶ **Helsinki Central Railway Station**. Guarded by four towering granite giants, Eliel Saarinen's bold Neoclassical edifice of 1909 is the defining structure of the cityscape. See p.534.

▶▶ **Danish Design Centre, Copenhagen**. Scandinavia's most comprehensive design museum, where the newest industrial design objects are presented alongside timeless Modernist classics. See p.81.

▶▶ **Finlandia Hall, Helsinki**. Hidden behind an austere marble facade, the interior of Alvar Aalto's Cubist-meets-Modernist concert hall boasts grand, sweeping foyers and asymmetric curves. See p.537.

▶▶ **Øresunds Link**. Connecting Denmark to southern Sweden, the breathtaking steel swathes of this sixteen-kilometre-long road and rail bridge exemplify the confluence of form and function. See p.430.

▶▶ **Smålands Museum, Växjö**. This riveting exhibition explores five hundred years of Swedish glassblowing history, with some remarkable pieces by modern masters Wilke Adolfsson and Jan-Erik Ritzman. See p.449.

▶▶ **Stave churches, Norway**. With their characteristic vertical timbers, grooved sills and richly expressive carvings, several dozen of these tiered medieval churches still dot the landscape of central Norway. See p.235.

▶▶ **T-Bana stations, Stockholm**. The stations on the T-Bana's blue line are outstanding displays of innovation in design and sculpture, each the work of a different local designer. See p.366.

The Fløibanen funicular railway

At the east end of Øvregaten, back near Torget, stands the distinctly Ruritanian lower terminus of the **Fløibanen funicular railway** (May–Aug Mon–Sat 8am–midnight & Sun 9am–midnight; Sept–April same details, but only until 11pm; departures every 15–30min; return fare 70kr), which shuttles up to the top of **Mount Fløyen** – "The Vane" – at 320m above sea level. When the weather is fine, you get a bird's-eye view of Bergen and its surroundings from the plateau-summit, and here also is a large and popular café-restaurant. Afterwards, you can walk back down to the city in about 45 minutes, or push on into the woods along several well-marked, colour-coded footpaths.

Lille Øvregaten to the Leprosy Museum

Running east from the lower Fløibanen terminal, **Lille Øvregaten** is lined by an appealing mix of expansive nineteenth-century villas and dinky timber houses, all bright-white clapboard and angular gables. Lille Øvregaten curves round to the **Domkirke** (Cathedral: late June to late Aug Mon–Fri 11am–4pm; late Aug to late June Tues–Fri 11am–12.30pm; free), a heavy-duty edifice whose stern exterior has been restored and rebuilt several times since its original construction in the thirteenth century.

Rather more promising is the fascinating **Lepramuseet** (Leprosy Museum: mid-May to Aug daily 11am–4pm; 40kr), just up from the Domkirke at Kong Oscars gate 59. The museum is housed in the charming, eighteenth-century buildings of **St Jørgens Hospital** (St George's Hospital), whose assorted dwellings are ranged around a paved courtyard, and it tells the tale of the Norwegian fight against leprosy. The disease first appeared in Scandinavia in Viking times and became especially prevalent in the coastal districts of western Norway, with around three percent of the population classified as lepers in the early nineteenth century. The hospital specialized in the care of lepers, assuming a more proactive role from 1830, when a series of Norwegian medics tried to find a cure for the disease. The last lepers left St Jørgens in 1946 and the hospital has been left untouched, the small rooms off the central gallery revealing the patients' humble living quarters. Dating from 1702, the adjoining hospital **chapel** is delightfully homely, its rickety, creaking timbers holding a domineering pulpit topped off by half a dozen folksy cherubs and an altarpiece decorated with yet more cherubs and some dainty scrollwork.

Lille Lungegårdsvann: Bergen's art galleries

Bergen's attractively landscaped central lake, **Lille Lungegårdsvann**, is a focus for summertime festivals and parades, and its southern side is flanked by the city's five main art galleries, three of which comprise the **Bergen Kunstmuseum** (Bergen Art Museum: Ⓦwww.kunstmuseene.no). These three galleries have the same opening hours and a common admission fee (50kr covers all), but the other two – one devoted to decorative art, the other to temporary exhibitions of contemporary art – are separate.

Also on the southern side of the lake, behind the galleries on Nygårdsgaten, is the **Grieghallen** concert hall, a large modern edifice that serves as the main venue for the annual Bergen International Festival (see p.253).

Bergen Art Museum – Lysverket

The easternmost of the five lakeside galleries is **Lysverket**, Rasmus Meyers Allé 9 (mid-May to mid-Sept daily 11am–5pm; mid-Sept to mid-May Tues–Sun 11am–5pm), which occupies a distinctive Art Deco/Functionalist building, complete with its own mini-rotunda, that started out as offices for a power company. The gallery spreads over three floors with the ground floor divided between temporary exhibitions and modern art from the 1950s onwards.

The next floor up has a whole room devoted to Johan Christian Dahl (1788–1857; one of Norway's finest landscape painters, and several minor Munchs as well as a proselytizing canvas by Christian Krohg (1852–1925) entitled *Fight for Survival*, which rails against urban poverty. The third room on this floor holds the Kunstmuseum's modest selection of old masters, mostly Dutch and Italian paintings, plus an engaging miscellany of medieval Greek and Russian icons.

The top floor has one room devoted to twentieth-century Norwegian art and another features the paintings of Nikolai Astrup (1880–1929), generally regarded as the last of the Norwegian Romantics – or at least neo-Romantics: sometimes Astrup's paintings portray a benign rural idyll, at other times – as in *Kollen* – the Norwegian landscape appears dangerous and malevolent. A final room holds a small selection of twentieth-century international works, most notably from Picasso, Braque, Ernst, Rivera and the Bauhaus painter Paul Klee.

Bergen Art Museum – Rasmus Meyers Collection

The **Rasmus Meyers Samlinger** (Rasmus Meyers Collection: mid-May to mid-Sept daily 11am–5pm; mid-Sept to mid-May Tues–Sun 11am–5pm) is housed in a large and distinctive building with a pagoda-like roof at Rasmus Meyers Allé 7. It boasts a superb survey of Norwegian art from 1815 to 1915, gifted to the city by one of its old merchant families – the Meyers – and now displayed broadly chronologically on two easily absorbed and well-organized floors. The museum is best known for its large sample of the work of **Edvard Munch** (1863–1944) – if you missed out in Oslo (see p.193 & p.199), this is the place to make amends. There are examples from all Munch's major periods, with the disturbing – and disturbed – works of the 1890s inevitably stealing the spotlight, especially the searing and unsettling *Jealousy* and the fractured *Woman in Three Stages*.

Bergen Art Gallery and the Stenersen gallery

Just along the street from the Rasmus Meyer Collection is the **Bergen Kunsthall**, Rasmus Meyers Allé 5 (Bergen Art Gallery: Tues–Sun noon–5pm; 40kr; ⓦwww .kunsthall.no), which has developed into the city's most imaginative contemporary arts venue with up to three separate exhibitions at any one time. It's all very hit or miss – banal at worst, stunning at best – but no one could say the exhibitions were predictable.

Next door, in a glum concrete block, the **Stenersen gallery** (mid-May to mid-Sept daily 11am–5pm; mid-Sept to mid-May Tues–Sun 11am–5pm) specializes in temporary exhibitions of contemporary art, mostly international but with a strong Norwegian showing. The gallery occupies two smallish floors above the ground-floor shop and coffee bar.

The West Norway Decorative Art Museum

Across the road from the Stenersen, the, at the corner of Christies gate and Nordahl Bruns gate **Vestlandske Kunstindustrimuseum** (West Norway Decorative Art Museum: mid-May to mid-Sept daily 11am–5pm; mid-Sept to mid-May Tues–Sun noon–4pm; 50kr; ⓦwww.kunstmuseene.no), occupies the Permanenten building, a whopping neo-Gothic structure built as a cultural centre in the 1890s. A lively exhibition programme with the focus on contemporary craft and design brings in the crowds, and some of the displays are very good indeed – which is perhaps more than can be said for much of the permanent collection, a hotch-potch of everything from chests and cupboards to jewellery and porcelain.

Torgalmenningen and Ole Bulls plass

The broad sweep of pedestrianized **Torgalmenningen** is a suitably handsome setting for the commercial heart of modern Bergen, lined with arcaded shops and department stores and decorated at its Torget end by the vigorous large-scale granite and bronze **Sjøfartsmonumentet** (Seafarers' Monument), celebrating the city's seafaring traditions.

At the far end of Torgalmenningen is **Ole Bulls plass**, also pedestrianized and sporting a rock pool and fountain, above which stands a jaunty statue of local lad Ole Bull, the nineteenth-century virtuoso violinist and heart-throb. Ole Bulls plass stretches up to the municipal **theatre**, Den Nationale Scene, at the top of the hill, worth the short walk for a look at the fearsome, saucer-eyed statue of Henrik Ibsen that stands guard in front.

The Nordnes peninsula

Beyond the theatre, the hilly **Nordnes peninsula** juts out into the fjord, its western tip accommodating the large **Akvariet** (Aquarium: May–Aug daily 9am–7pm, 150kr; Sept–April daily 10am–6pm, 100kr; bus #11; ⓦwww.akvariet .no) and a pleasant park. It takes about fifteen minutes to walk there from Ole Bulls plass – via Klostergaten/Haugeveien – but the effort is perhaps better spent in choosing a different, more southerly, route along the peninsula. This takes you past the charming timber houses and nineteenth-century stone villas of Skottegaten and Nedre Strangehagen before it cuts through the bluff leading to the old, waterside United Sardine Factories, imaginatively converted into an arts complex, the **USF Verftet Kulturhuset** (ⓦwww.usf.no); this incorporates a groovy, harbourside café-bar, *Kafe Kippers* (see p.252). From here, it takes about ten minutes to get to the aquarium.

Out from the centre – Troldhaugen

The lochs, fjords and rocky wooded hills surrounding central Bergen have channelled the city's **suburbs** into long ribbons, which trail off in every direction. These urban outskirts are not in themselves especially appealing, but tucked away amongst them, about 8km south of downtown off the E39, is **Troldhaugen** (May–Sept daily 9am–6pm; Oct & Nov Mon–Fri 10am–2pm, Sat & Sun noon–4pm; mid-Jan to April Mon–Fri 10am–2pm, April Sat & Sun noon–4pm; 60kr; ⓦwww.kunstmuseene. no), or "Hill of the Trolls", the lakeside home of **Edvard Grieg** (1843–1907) for the last 22 years of his life – though "home" is something of an exaggeration, as he spent several months every year touring the concert halls of Europe. Norway's only composer of world renown, Grieg has a good share of commemorative monuments in Bergen – a statue in the city park and the Grieghallen concert hall to name but two – but it's here that you get a sense of the man, an immensely likeable and much-loved figure of leftish opinions and disarming modesty: "I make no pretensions of being in the class with Bach, Mozart and Beethoven," he once wrote, "Their works are eternal, while I wrote for my day and generation."

A visit begins at the **museum**, where Grieg's life and times are exhaustively chronicled, and a short film provides yet further insights. From here, it's a brief walk to the **house** (guided tours only), a pleasant and unassuming villa built in 1885, and still pretty much as Grieg left it, with a jumble of photos, manuscripts and period furniture. Grieg didn't, in fact, compose much in the house, but preferred to walk round to a tiny **hut** he had built just along the shore. The hut has survived, but today it stands beside a modern concert hall, the **Troldsalen**, where there are **recitals** of Grieg's works from mid-June through to October. Recital tickets (160–220kr) can be bought from Bergen tourist office; free buses for these concerts leave from near the tourist office one hour before the concert begins. The bodies of Grieg and his wife – the singer Nina Hagerup – are inside a curious **tomb** blasted into a rock face overlooking the lake, and sealed with twin memorial stones; it's only a couple of minutes' walk from the main footpath, but few people venture out to this beautiful, melancholic spot.

To get to Troldhaugen by public transport, take **bus #20 #21 #22 #23 or #24** from the city bus station (every 10–20min; 23kr each way) and ask the driver to drop you off; from the bus stop, it's a stiff and dull twenty-minute walk along Troldhaugensveien.

Eating, drinking and nightlife

Bergen has a first-rate supply of **restaurants**, the pick of which focus on seafood – the city's main gastronomic asset. The pricier tourist haunts are concentrated on the Bryggen, but these should not be dismissed out of hand – several are very good indeed. Other, marginally less expensive, restaurants dot the side-streets behind the Bryggen and there's another cluster on and around Engen, but many locals tend to eat more economically and informally at the city's many **café-bars** and these are dotted all over the city centre as are the city's coffee houses, where the big deal – as you might expect– is coffee in its many different guises. The busiest late-night **bars** are gathered in the vicinity of Ole Bulls plass, which is also the heart of Bergen's fairly limited club scene.

For **picnics**, the **fish market** on the Torget (June–Aug daily 7am–5pm, Sept–May Mon–Sat 7am–4pm) offers everything from dressed crab, prawn rolls and smoked-salmon sandwiches to pickled herring and canned caviar. There's also a covered market, the **Kjøttbasaren** (Mon–Fri 10am–5pm & Sat 9am–4pm), where half a dozen stalls sell all manner of fresh produce and freshly baked breads. The covered market is in the long and narrow, fancily gabled building at the Torget end of the Bryggen.

Cafés, coffee houses and café-bars

Café Opera Engen 24, near Ole Bulls plass. Inside a white wooden building with plant-filled windows, a fashionable crowd gathers to drink beer and good coffee. Tasty, filling snacks from as little as 60kr. DJ sounds – mostly house – at the weekend. Mon 11am–12.30am, Tues–Sat 11am–3am & Sun noon–12.30am.

Det Lille Kaffekompaniet Nedre Fjellsmug 2. Many locals swear by the coffee here, reckoning it to be the best north of the Alps. Great selection of teas too, plus delicious cakes and funky premises – just one medium-sized room in an old building, two flights of steps above the Fløibanen funicular terminal. Mon–Fri 10am–10pm, Sat noon–6pm, Sun noon–10pm.

Godt Brød Nedre Korskirkealmenning 12. Eco-bakery and café (in that order), with great bread and good pastries, plus coffee and made-to-order sandwiches too. Mon–Fri 7am–6pm, Sat 7am–4.30pm & Sun 10am–5pm. Also at Vestre Torggate 2 (Mon–Fri 7am–6pm, Sat 8am–5pm & Sun 10am–5pm), though here the order is reversed – it's a café first and then a bakery.

Kafe Kippers USF Verftet Kulturhuset, Georgernes Verft @www.usf.no. Part of the city's leading contemporary arts complex (see p.253) on the Nordnes peninsula, this laid-back café-bar serves inexpensive, canteen-style food, with mains about 100–120kr; occasionally rustles up great barbecues too. With its sea views and terrace, this is *the* place to come on a sunny evening when the crowds gather, especially when there's some live music or DJ sounds. Mon–Fri 11am–11.30pm, Sat & Sun noon–11pm.

Restaurants

Boha Vaskerelveien 6 ☎55 31 31 60. Smart and popular restaurant kitted out in attractive modern style and offering a small(ish) but well-chosen menu. Main courses – for example chicken in pancetta with paprika – hover around 240kr. Mon–Thurs 4–10pm, Fri 4–11pm & Sat 5–11pm.

Bryggeloftet og Stuene Bryggen 11 ☎55 30 20 70. A tourist favourite, this restaurant may be a little old-fashioned – the decor is too folksy for its own good – but they do serve a very good range of seafood here, delicious, plainly served meals usually with a good wallop of potatoes. Elk, reindeer and other Nordic beasts too. Main courses around 220kr, much less at lunchtime. Mon–Sat 11am–11pm, Sun 1–11.30pm.

Den Lille Hanseater Kjøttbasaren. The Kjøttbasaren, the covered market where the Torget meets the Bryggen, has a clutch of food stalls and this pleasant café-restaurant, where they serve tasty, straight-forward food at reasonable prices – try the meatballs at 150kr. Café: Mon–Fri 8am–5pm, Sat 9am–4pm & Sun 10am–4pm; restaurant: daily 4–10pm.

Escalon Vetrlidsallmenningen 21 ☎55 32 90 99. Cheery basement tapas bar-cum-restaurant, where they serve authentic Spanish food at competitive prices – tapas cost 60–100kr. Metres from the lower terminus of the Fløibanen. Daily 3–11.30pm.

Naboen Restaurant Sigurdsgate 4 ☎55 90 02 90. Easygoing, pleasantly presented restaurant featuring a lively, inventive menu – including Swedish specialities and, on occasion, the likes of kangaroo and ostrich.

Offers a good range of fish dishes, including unusual offerings such as sea bass with blood-orange sauce; the cod is especially good. When you've finished eating, you can venture down to the basement bar. Reckon on 200–220kr for a main course. Restaurant: Mon–Sat 4–11pm, Sun 4–10pm.

Late-night bars and clubs
Garage at the corner of Nygårdsgaten and Christies gate ☎55 32 19 80, ⓦwww.garage.no. Very busy place catering to a mixed crowd. Two bars on the ground floor, and a live music area in the basement – mostly rock and pop. Packed at the weekend.

Landmark Rasmus Meyers Allé 5. Club/pub with an arty atmosphere and a student scene; occasional live music and DJ sounds. In the same building as the Bergen Kunsthall gallery (see p.250). Open Tues–Thurs noon–1.30am, Fri & Sat noon–3.30am & Sun noon–6pm.

Tiger Tiger Christian Michelsensgate 4 ⓦwww.bergen.tigertiger.no. Immensely popular club with house the big deal and the city's best DJ roster. Occasional live bands too. Thurs to Sat from 10pm till the wee hours.

Festivals and the performing arts

Bergen takes justifiable pride in its **performing arts**, especially during the **Festspillene i Bergen** (Bergen International Festival: ☎55 21 06 30, ⓦwww.festspillene.no), held over twelve days at the end of May and the beginning of June and presenting an extensive programme of music, ballet, folklore and drama. The principal venue for the festival is the **Grieghallen**, on Lars Hilles gate (☎55 21 61 50, ⓦwww.grieghallen.no), where you can pick up programmes, tickets and information, as you can at the tourist office. The city's contemporary arts centre, the **USF Verftet Kulturhuset**, down on the Nordnes peninsula (☎55 30 74 10, ⓦwww.usf.no), contributes to the festival by hosting **Nattjazz** (☎55 30 72 50, ⓦwww.nattjazz.no), a prestigious and long-established international jazz festival held over the same period.

The Bergen International Festival is also the main player in the wide-ranging programme of cultural events that is coordinated by the tourist office in its **Sommer Bergen** programme (ⓦwww.visitbergen.com). Part of this summer programme is devoted to **folk music** and **folk events** – singing, dancing and costumed goings-on of all kinds. Catch folk dancing at either the Schøtstuene (June to mid-Aug; 100kr; ☎55 55 20 06) or at **Fana Folklore**'s "country festivals" (☎55 91 52 40, ⓦwww.folklore.no), a mix of Norwegian music, food and dancing held on a private estate outside the city. These take place at 7pm a couple of times a week from June to August and cost 300kr per person, including meal and transport; tickets for both from the tourist office. There are also **chamber music and organ recitals** at St Mary's Church in June, July and August, and **Grieg recitals** at Grieg's home, Troldhaugen, from mid-June to October.

Outside the summer season, the **USF Verftet Kulturhuset** (see p.252) puts on an ambitious programme of concerts, art-house films and contemporary plays; the **Bergen Philharmonic** performs regularly in the Grieghallen (tickets on ☎55 21 61 50, ⓦwww.harmonien.no); and Bergen's main **theatre**, Den Nationale Scene, on Engen (☎55 60 70 80, ⓦwww.dns.no), offers a wide range of performances on several stages. Most productions are, of course, in Norwegian, but there are occasional appearances by English-speaking troupes.

The **tourist office** (see p.243) has all the details of upcoming events and performances – and they are available on their website too.

Listings

Bookshop Norli (ⓦwww.norli.no), right in the city centre at Torgalmenningen 7, is easily the best bookshop in town, with a good range of English titles as well as a wide selection of Norwegian hiking and road maps. Very competitive prices also. Mon–Fri 9am–8pm, Sat 9am–4pm. There's also a smaller branch across the street at Torgalmenningen 4.
Bus enquiries Timetable information on ☎177, ⓦwww.tide.no.

Car rental All the major international car rental companies have offices in town and/or at the airport, including Hertz, Nygårdsgaten 59 (T 55 96 08 20); Avis at Lars Hilles gate 20 (T 55 55 39 55); and National, at the airport (T 55 22 81 66). For the full list see under *Bilutleie* in the Yellow Pages.

Cinema Bergen has two large city-centre cinemas and both are on Neumannsgate, a 5min walk southwest of Ole Bulls plass. They are Bergen Kino, Konsertpaleet with thirteen screens (T 82 05 00 05, W www.filmweb.no/bergenkino) and Magnus Barfot Kino with five screens (same details).

Dentist Emergency dental care is available at Vestre Strømkai 19 (Mon–Fri 6–8.30pm, Sat & Sun 3.30–8.30pm; T 55 56 87 17).

Emergencies Ambulance T 113; Fire T 110; Police T 112.

Gay scene Bergen's low-key gay scene is focused on its main gay café-bar, *Café Fincken*, Nygårdsgaten 2A (T 55 32 13 16, W www.fincken.no). It's open Wed–Fri & Sun 7pm–1.30am, Sat 8am–2.30am.

Hiking The DNT-affiliated Bergen Turlag, Tverrgaten 4–6 (Mon–Fri 10am–4pm, Thurs till 6pm, Sat 10am–2pm; T 55 33 58 10, W www.bergen-turlag .no), advises on hiking trails in the region, sells hiking maps and arranges guided walks.

Internet Many of Bergen's hotels and hostels now provide free internet access for their guests and there's also free access at the main city library, Bergen Bibliotek (Mon–Thurs 10am–8pm, Fri 10am–4.30pm & Sat 10am–4pm), on Strømgaten, immediately in front of the Bergen Storsenter shopping centre.

Laundry Coin-operated and service wash at Jarlens Vaskoteque, Lille Øvregate 17, near the funicular (T 55 32 55 04).

Pharmacy Vitusapotek, in Bergen Storsenter, by the bus station (Mon–Sat 8am–11pm, Sun 10am–11pm).

Post office Bergen's main post office is in the Xhibition shopping centre at the junction of Olav Kyrresgate and Småstrandgaten (Mon–Fri 9am–8pm & Sat 9am–6pm). Also a handy branch just off the Bryggen, opposite the Cathedral at Dreggsallmenningen 20 (Mon–Fri 8.30am–5pm & Sat 10am–2pm).

Taxi Bergen Taxi T 07000.

Trains National timetable information on T 81 50 08 88.

The western fjords

From Bergen, it's a hop, skip and jump over the mountains to the **western fjords**. The most popular initial target is the **Hardangerfjord**, a delightful and comparatively gentle introduction to the wilder terrain that lies beyond, but similarly popular is **Voss**, inland perhaps, but still an outdoor sports centre of some renown. Voss is also a halfway house on the way to the **Sognefjord** by train, bus or car. By **train**, it's a short journey from Voss east to **Myrdal**, at the start of a spectacularly dramatic train ride down the Flåmsdal valley to **Flåm**, sitting pretty against the severe shores of the **Aurlandsfjord**, one of the Sognefjord's many subsidiaries; by **road**, you can head north direct to Flåm along the E16 or stick to Highway 13 as it careers over the mountains bound for Vik and Vangsnes. Both of these little towns are on the Sognefjord and it's this fjord, perhaps above all others, that captivates visitors, its stirring beauty amplified by its sheer size, stretching inland from the coast for some 200km. Beyond, and running parallel, lies the **Nordfjord**, smaller at 120km long and less intrinsically enticing, though its surroundings are more varied, with hunks and chunks of the **Jostedalsbreen glacier** visible and visitable nearby. From here, it's another short journey to the splendid **Geirangerfjord** – narrow, sheer and rugged – bringing you close to the dramatic **Trollstigen**, zigzagging over the mountains bound for **Åndalsnes**, which boasts an exquisite setting with rearing peaks behind and the tentacular Romsdalsfjord in front. At the western end of the Romsdalsfjord is the region's prettiest town, **Ålesund**, whose centre is liberally sprinkled with charming Art Nouveau buildings, courtesy of Kaiser Wilhelm II.

This is not a landscape to be hurried – there's little point in dashing from fjord to fjord. Stay put for a while, go for at least one hike or cycle ride, and it's then that you'll really appreciate the western fjords in all their grandeur. The sheer size is breathtaking – but then the **geological movements** that shaped the fjords were

Fjord ferries

Throughout this chapter there are numerous mentions of fjord **car ferries** and **Hurtigbåt passenger express boats**. The details given in parenthesis concern the frequency of operation, the duration of the crossing and the price. Hurtigbåt services are usually fairly infrequent – three a day at most – whereas many car ferries shuttle back and forth every hour or two, if not more, from around 7am in the morning until 10pm at night every day of the week. **Hurtigbåt fares** are fixed individually with prices starting at around 100kr for every hour travelled: the four-hour trip from Bergen to Balestrand, for example, costs 455kr, 625kr to Flåm. Rail-pass holders are often entitled to discounts of up to fifty percent and on some routes there are special excursion deals – always ask. **Car ferry fares**, on the other hand, are priced according to a nationally agreed sliding scale, with ten-minute crossings running at around 24kr per person and 60kr per car and driver, 29kr and 80kr respectively for a 25-minute trip.

on a grand scale. During the Ice Age, around three million years ago, the whole of Scandinavia was covered in ice, the weight of which pushed the existing river valleys deeper and deeper to depths well below that of the ocean floor – the Sognefjord, for example, descends to 1250m, ten times deeper than most of the Norwegian Sea. Later, as the ice retreated, it left huge coastal basins that filled with seawater to become the fjords, which the warm Gulf Stream keeps ice-free.

Getting around the fjords

The convoluted topography of the western fjords has produced a dense and complex public transport system that is designed to reach all the larger villages and towns at least once every weekday, whether by train, bus, car ferry, Hurtigrute coastal boat or Hurtigbåt passenger express boat. By **train**, you can reach Bergen, Finse and Flåm in the south and Åndalsnes in the north. For everything in between – the Nordfjord, Jostedalsbreen glacier and Sognefjord – you're confined to **buses** and **ferries**, although (mercifully) virtually all services connect up with each other so at least you shouldn't get stranded anywhere. General travel details for this chapter are given on p.284, and in the chapter itself we've detailed local connections where they are especially useful; this information should be used in conjunction with the **timetables** that are widely available across the region and on the internet (see box above). Bear in mind also that although there may be a transport connection to the town or village you want to go to, many Norwegian settlements are scattered and you may be in for a long walk after you've arrived – a particularly dispiriting experience if it's raining.

The Hardangerfjord

To the east of Bergen, the most inviting target is the hundred-kilometre long **Hardangerfjord** (@www.hardangerfjord.com), whose wide waters are overlooked by a rough, craggy shoreline and a scattering of tiny settlements. At its eastern end the Hardangerfjord divides into several lesser fjords, and it's here you'll find the district's most appealing villages, **Lofthus** and **Ulvik**, both of which have an attractive fjordside setting and at least one an especially good place to stay. To the east of these tributary fjords rises the **Hardangervidda**, a mountain plateau of remarkable, lunar-like beauty and a favourite with Norwegian hikers. The plateau can be reached from almost any direction, but one popular starting point for the extremely fit is **Kinsarvik**, with this approach involving a stiff day-long climb up from the fjord.

Of the two principal **car ferries** negotiating the Hardangerfjord, one shuttles between Kvanndal, Utne and Kinsarvik, the other links Brimnes with Bruravik,

All the region's **public transport timetables** are available on the internet, but the problem is that there's no guarantee the companies running the routes one year will be the same the next: the whole network is subject to competitive tendering. At time of writing, most car ferries and Hurtigbåt passenger boats are operated by either **Fjord 1** (ⓦwww.fjord1.no) or **Tide** (ⓦwww.tide.no). Fjord 1 also operates a large number of bus routes around the Hardangerfjord, which is pretty much the preserve of Skyss (ⓦwww.skyss.no).

More secure are the positions of **Nor-way Bussekspress** (ⓦwww.nor-way.no), who handle all long-distance bus routes; NSB, which operates the trains (ⓦwww.nsb.no); and the Hurtigrute coastal boat (ⓦwww.hurtigruten.com). Any tourist office in the fjords can help with public transport timetables.

though this is scheduled to be replaced by a bridge in the near future. There are no trains in the Hardangerfjord area, but **buses** are fairly frequent, except possibly on Sundays when services are reduced. The buses are operated by Skyss (ⓦwww.skyss .no), the ferries by **Tide** (ⓦwww.tide.no).

Finally, if you're planning to travel south along Highway 13 from Kinsarvik bound for either Oslo or Stavanger – or the other way round – be sure your itinerary does not involve an overnight stay in the eminently missable industrial town of **Odda**, at the head of the Storfjord. Note also that if you going to, or coming from, Oslo along the E134, you'll climb onto, or come down from, the Hardangervidda plateau via Haukelifjell, one of the region's bleakest and windiest approaches.

East from Bergen to Norheimsund and the Kvanndal ferry

Heading east from Bergen en route to the Hardangerfjord by bus or car, the **E16** begins by travelling through a string of polluted tunnels, an unpleasant thirty-kilometre journey before you can fork off along **Highway 7**. By contrast, this is a rattlingly good trip, with the road twisting over the mountains and down the valleys, gliding past thundering waterfalls and around tight bends before racing down to **NORHEIMSUND** on the Hardangerfjord. From June to August, Norheimsund is useful as a minor transport hub with a once-daily **Hurtigbåt passenger express boat** service to Utne, Lofthus, Kinsarvik, Ulvik and Eidfjord, operated by Tide.

Leaving Norheimsund by road, Highway 7 sticks to the rugged shoreline as it travels east to the ferry dock at **Kvanndal**, another pleasant journey with every turning bringing fresh mountain and fjord views as the Hardangerfjord begins to split into its various subsidiaries. There's a choice of routes from Kvanndal: you can either press on down the northern shore of the Hardangerfjord towards Ulvik and Voss (see p.260 & p.259), or take the Tide **ferry** over from Kvanndal to Utne and/or Kinsarvik (1 or 2 hourly; 20min/50min). Kvanndal to Kinsarvik costs 36kr passengers, 107kr car and driver. There are **buses** from Bergen to Norheimsund every couple of hours and most continue to the Kvanndal ferry; the whole journey takes two hours and twenty minutes, ninety minutes to Norheimsund.

Kinsarvik

From Kvanndal, the Tide car ferry (every 1hr–1hr 30min; 25min; passengers 29kr, driver & car 80kr; ⓦwww.tide.no) bobs over the fjord to **KINSARVIK**, a tiny little place, which was once an important Viking marketplace. It was just the sort of place the Vikings liked. The foreshore was gentle, making it easy for them to beach their ships, and it was buried deep in the fjords, making it difficult for any enemy to approach unseen. Nothing now remains from that period, but the sturdy, whitewashed stone **church** (late May Tues–Fri 10am–3pm; June to mid-Aug daily

10am–7pm; free) lurking on the foreshore dates back as far as the middle of the twelfth century.

Kinsarvik lies at the mouth of the forested **Husedalen valley**, with its four crashing waterfalls. The valley makes an enjoyable hike, with most visitors choosing to drive up to the first cascade before proceeding on foot – the road beyond the first waterfall is really too difficult for ordinary vehicles. The valley is also used as an access route up to the Hardangervidda plateau. From Kinsarvik, it takes six hours to reach the nearest DNT hut, the self-service **Stavali** (at 1024m), but the route up to the plateau is very steep and in rainy conditions very slippery. Hiking maps can be purchased and hiking advice is dispensed at Kinsarvik **tourist office** near the ferry jetty (late June to late Aug daily 9am–7pm; late Aug Mon–Fri 9am–5pm; Sept to late June Mon–Fri 9am–4pm; ☎53 66 31 12, ⊛www.visitullensvang.no). For more on the Hardangervidda and its various access routes, see p.258.

As for a place **to stay**, the obvious choice is the *Best Western Kinsarvik Fjord Hotel* (☎53 66 74 00, ⊛www.kinsarvikfjordhotel.no; ❺/❻), in a well-kept and reasonably attractive modern block down by the fjord, metres from the ferry dock. Skyss **buses** link Kinsarvik with Eidfjord, Lofthus, Eidfjord and Odda (2–4 daily).

Lofthus

In a fine location, **LOFTHUS** strings along the Sørfjord, beginning about 10km to the south of Kinsarvik, with the Folgefonna glacier glinting in the distance. The first part of the village – around the *Hotel Ullensvang* – is somewhat routine, but the second is an idyllic place of narrow lanes and mellow stone walls, where a scattering of timber houses sits among the orchards, pinky-white with blossom in the springtime. It's the overall impression that counts, though the **Ullensvang church** (May Tues–Fri 10am–3pm; June–Aug daily 10am–7pm; free), which dates from 1250 and is named after the district not the village, is a good-looking stone structure with immensely thick walls; below it is a pebble beach and a miniature jetty, where the brave propel themselves into the waters of the fjord. A stream gushes through the village, tumbling down the steep escarpment behind Lofthus to bubble past the delightful *Ullensvang Gjesteheim* (☎53 66 12 36, ⊛www.ullensvang-gjesteheim.no; ❸), a huddle of antique wooden buildings with thirteen cosy and unassuming rooms. There are other places to stay too – the plush *Hotel Ullensvang* (☎53 67 00 00, ⊛www.hotel-ullensvang .no; ❻/❼), a sprawling affair plonked on the water's edge in a building that mixes modern and traditional Norwegian design in a (fairly) successful manner; and an HI hostel, *Hardanger Vandrerhjem* (☎53 67 14 00, ⊛www.vandrerhjem.no; June to early Aug), about 500 metres up the slope from the fjord in a residential rural high school, a *Folkehøgskule*. The hostel has a café, self-catering facilities and a laundry; dorm beds cost 235kr, double rooms ❶. Both the *Ullensvang Gjesteheim* and the *Hotel Ullensvang* serve evening meals.

As at Kinsarvik, a steep **hiking trail** leads up from Lofthus to the Hardangervidda plateau; part of the trail includes the **Munketreppene**, stone steps laid by the monks who farmed this remote spot in medieval times. It takes about four hours to reach the plateau at Nosi (959m), and about seven or eight hours to reach the Stavali self-service DNT hut. For more on access to the Hardangervidda, see p.258.

Skyss (⊛www.skyss.no) operates a **bus** service between Kinsarvik and Lofthus (2–4 daily), part of a longer route from Eidfjord to Odda.

Eidfjord and Øvre Eidfjord

Heading north from Kinsarvik, **Highway 13** fidgets its way along the coastline to reach, after 19km, Brimnes, from where a Tide **car ferry** (1–2 hourly; passengers 28kr, car & driver 75kr; 10min; ⊛www.tide.no) shuttles over the fjord to Bruravik, for Ulvik (see p.259) and Voss (see p.260), though plans are afoot to span the water with a bridge. Beyond Brimnes, Highway 13 becomes **Highway 7**, whose first significant port of call, after another 11km or so, is the large village of **EIDFJORD**, which straggles over a neck of land facing the fjord with a lake, the Eidfjordvatnet, just inland.

From Eidfjord, it's 7km southeast along Highway 7 to **ØVRE EIDFJORD**, where the **Hardangervidda Natursenter** (daily: April–May & Sept–Oct 10am–6pm; June–Aug 9am–8pm; 80kr) tells you all you ever wanted to know about the Hardangervidda, including its natural history and geology. Staff also dispense hiking advice and sell hiking maps.

Practicalities

Skyss buses (ⓦwww.skyss.no) from Odda and Kinsarvik (2–4 daily) pull in beside Highway 7 just to the east of the **tourist office** (May Mon–Fri 9am–6pm; early June & late Aug Mon–Sat 9am–6pm; mid-June to mid-Aug Mon–Fri 9am–7pm, Sat & Sun 10am–6pm; Sept–April Mon–Fri 9am–4pm; ⓉT53 67 34 00; ⓦwww .visiteidfjord.no). There are two recommendable **hotels** in Eidfjord, the grander of which is the fjordside *Quality Hotel & Resort Vøringfoss* (ⓉT53 67 41 00, ⓦwww .choicehotels.no; ❺), a large, modern complex built in a (relatively) pleasing version of traditional style with mini-towers and decorative gable ends. The second is the *Eidfjord Fjell og Fjord Hotel* (ⓉT53 66 52 64, ⓦwww.effh.no; ❺), a crisply designed, medium-sized modern place with attractively furnished rooms that perches on a knoll high above the fjord. The *Vøringfoss* has the better restaurant. If these hotels don't suit, the tourist office has the details of a handful of private rooms (❷/❸).

The Vøringfossen waterfalls

Heading southeast from Eidfjord, Highway 7 clips past the **Hardangervidda Natursenter** (see above) before starting its long climb up to the Hardangervidda plateau. After 20km, the road passes the mighty, 145m-high **Vøringfossen waterfalls**, which are best viewed from the hamlet/hotel of **FOSSLI**, perched on a clifftop, about 1km off Highway 7. Inevitably, the main pull here at the hotel (ⓉT53 66 57 77, ⓦwww.fossli-hotel.com; mid-May to mid-Sept; ❹) is the view of the waterfall, but the place also chips in with 21 plain but perfectly adequate bedrooms and a better-than-average restaurant.

Beyond the waterfalls, Highway 7 creeps its way up through the mountains to finally emerge on the Hardangervidda plateau.

The Hardangervidda plateau

The **Hardangervidda** is Europe's largest mountain plateau, occupying a one-hundred-kilometre-square slab of land east of the Hardangerfjord and broadly south of the Oslo–Bergen railway. The plateau is characterized by rolling fells and wide stretches of level ground, its rocky surfaces strewn with pools, ponds and rivers. The whole plateau is above the tree line, and in places has an almost lunar appearance, although even within this elemental landscape there are variations. To the north, in the vicinity of Finse, there are mountains and a glacier, the **Hardangerjøkulen**, while the west is wetter – and the flora somewhat richer – than the barer moorland to the east. The lichen that covers the rocks is savoured by herds of reindeer, who leave their winter grazing lands on the east side of the plateau in the spring, chewing their way west to their breeding grounds before returning east again after the autumn rutting season.

For centuries, the Hardangervidda was one of the main crossing points between east and west Norway, with horse traders, cattle drivers and Danish dignitaries all cutting across the plateau along cairned paths, many of which are still in use as part of a dense network of trails and tourist huts that has been developed by several DNT affiliates. Roughly one third of the plateau has been incorporated within the **Hardangervidda National Park**, but much of the rest is protected too, so hikers won't notice a great deal of difference between the park and its immediate surroundings. Many hikers and skiers are content with a day on the Hardangervidda, but some find the wide-skied, lichen-dappled scenery particularly enchanting and travel from one end of the plateau to the other, a seven- or eight-day expedition.

Approaches to the Hardangervidda

Access to the Hardangervidda can be gained from the **Oslo–Bergen train line** which calls at Finse (see p.261), from where hikers and skiers head off across the plateau in all directions. Finse is not, however, reachable by road, so motorists (and bus travellers) mostly use **Highway 7**, which runs across the plateau between Eidfjord (see p.257) and Geilo. There's precious little in the way of human habitation on this lonely hundred-kilometre stretch of road, but you can pick up the plateau's hiking trails easily enough at several points. **Dyranut** and **Halne** are two such places, respectively 39km and 47km from Eidfjord. Some hikers prefer to walk eastwards on to the Hardangervidda from Kinsarvik and Lofthus (see p.257), an arduous day-long trek up from the fjord, or from Rjukan, to the southeast of the plateau, where a cable car eases the uphill part of the trek. Local tourist offices all carry hiking maps and will advise about hiking routes as will the **Hardangervidda Natursenter** (see opposite). If all that sounds too arduous, there are also **boat trips** (late June to early Sept; 1–3 daily; 1hr) from Halne along the Halnefjord, which cuts across the Hardangervidda for around 15km. For times of departure, consult Eidfjord tourist office (see p.258).

Ulvik

Tucked away in a snug corner of the Hardangerfjord, the pocket-sized village of **ULVIK** strings prettily along the shoreline with orchards dusting the green, forested hills behind. This is one of the gentlest of fjord landscapes, with little of the harsh beauty of many of its neighbours, and although there's nothing specific to see, Ulvik does have one or two claims to fame: this the place where potatoes were first grown in Norway (in 1765) and it took a particularly heavy pummelling from the Germans during World War II.

Nowadays, Ulvik is an excellent place to unwind, and the favourite pastime is walking. **Hiking trails** lattice the rough uplands behind Ulvik and also explore the surrounding coastline. The tourist office (see below) produces a detailed guide to the *Heritage Trails of Ulvik* (15kr) and a series of excellent A4 (10kr) sheets describing particular mapped walks that can be done inside a day. One of the most enjoyable is the three-hour round-trip up into the hills to the east of Ulvik, which takes in a set of Iron Age burial mounds and the **Ljonakleiv crofter's farm**, an old farmstead from where there are splendid views over the fjord.

Practicalities

Ulvik is off the main bus routes, but there is a **Skyss bus** service here from Voss (2–6 daily; 1hr; ⓦwww.skyss.no); this is routed via Bruravik to pick up passengers who've arrived on the Brimnes–Bruravik ferry (see p.257). From May to September, there are also **Tide Hurtigbåt passenger express boat** services to Ulvik from Norheimsund via Utne, Lofthus and Kinsarvik (1 daily; 2hr 15min; ⓦwww.tide .no); the same service continues to Eidfjord. Buses pull into the centre of the village, metres from the jetty and the waterfront **tourist office** (mid-May to mid-Sept Mon–Sat 8.30am–5pm & Sun 1–5pm; Jan to mid-May Mon–Fri 8.30am–1.30pm; ⓣ56 52 63 60, ⓦwww.visitulvik.com). Staff here issue all the usual information, including bus and ferry timetables, sell detailed hiking maps and rent out bikes.

Among the **hotels**, the big deal hereabouts is the *Brakanes* (ⓣ56 52 61 05, ⓦwww .brakanes-hotel.no;➐), a large modern place hogging the waterfront in the centre of the village. The *Brakanes* has all the facilities you would expect of a big hotel, including a fitness centre, and is popular as a conference centre. Quite different is the fjordside ⌖ *Ulvik Fjord Hotel* (ⓣ56 52 61 70, ⓦwww.ulvikfjordpensjonat .no; late May to Sept; ➌), a well-maintained and very appealing **hotel** situated at the beginning of the village, an easy ten-minute walk west from the centre along the waterfront. It has nineteen guest rooms, some in the main house, an attractive wooden, two-storey building dating from the 1940s, and some in the modern annexe, where most of the rooms have their own outside area beside a babbling brook. It's not a luxury res – and makes no claim to be so – but it is very comfortable and the family who own and run the place are the friendliest of hosts. Breakfasts are first-rate and home-made evening meals, which come recommended by several of our readers, are available by prior arrangement; their three-course set menu dinner costs 250kr.

Voss

Travelling east from Bergen on the E16 or by train, you first have to clear some markedly polluted tunnels, but thereafter it's an enjoyable jaunt over the hills and round the mountains to **VOSS**, which, at 100km from Bergen, has an attractive lakeside setting and a splendid thirteenth-century church. Voss is, however, best known as an adventure sports and winter skiing centre, with everything from skiing and snowboarding through to summertime rafting, kayaking and horse riding. Consequently, unless you're here for a sweat, your best bet is to have a quick look round and then move on, though there is a caveat: Voss is the ideal base for a **day-trip by train** east up the Raundal valley, an especially scenic part of the Bergen–Oslo rail line. The most popular target on this stretch of the line is the Myrdal junction, where you change for the dramatic train ride down to Flåm (see box, p.263).

Arrival

Buses stop outside the **train station** at the western end of the town centre. From here, it's a five-minute walk to the **tourist office** (June–Aug Mon–Fri 8am–7pm, Sat 9am–7pm & Sun 2–7pm; Sept–May Mon–Fri 8.30am–3.30pm; ☎56 52 08 00, ⓦ www.visitvoss.no) on the main street, Uttrågata – veer right round the Vangskyrkja church and it's on the right. They have oodles of information on hiking, rafting, skiing and local touring, the bones of which are detailed in the free *Voss Guide*; they also operate an accommodation booking service.

Accommodation and restaurants

To cater for all the visiting sportsfolk, Voss has lots of inexpensive **accommodation**, from guesthouses to camping. The best budget bet is the excellent HI **hostel** (☎56 51 20 17, ⓦ www.vandrerhjem.no; Jan–Sept), which has both double rooms (❷) and dorm beds (260kr), and is in a modern lodge overlooking the water about 700m from the train station. To get there, turn right outside the station building and head along the lake away from the town centre – a ten-minute walk. The hostel serves good breakfasts and inexpensive evening meals – though these need to be pre-booked – and has self-catering facilities; it also has its own laundry and internet access, and rents out bikes and canoes. Reservation is strongly recommended. A second inexpensive option is the rudimentary *Voss Camping* (☎56 51 15 97, ⓦ www.vosscamping.no), a short walk south of the Vangskyrkja church: turn left from the train station, take the right fork at the church and then turn right again, along the Prestegardsalléen footpath. It's open all year and has a few cabins (500–700kr for five persons), an outside pool and washing machines. As for the town's **hotels**, one or two barely pass muster and the pick by a long chalk is *Fleischer's* (☎56 52 05 00, ⓦ www.fleischers.no; ❺/❻), next door to the train station. Dating from the 1880s, the hotel's high-gabled and towered facade overlooks the lake and consists of the original building and a modern wing built in the same style. Parts of the hotel – and many of the bedrooms – have the whiff of real luxury, but others are more mundane. The **restaurant** serves the best food in town and there's a terrace bar as well. Their all-inclusive food-and-lodging deals offer substantial savings on the normal rate.

Voss sports

Every **summer**, hundreds of Norwegians make a beeline for Voss on account of its **watersports**. The rivers near the town offer a wide range of conditions, suitable for everything from a quiet paddle to a finger-chewing white-water ride. There are several operators, but **Voss Rafting Senter** (☎56 51 05 25, ⊛www.vossrafting.no) sets the benchmark. Their four-hour white-water rafting trips venture out onto two rivers – the Stranda and Raun; the price, including a swimming test and a snack, is 820kr. Other options with the same operator and at about the same price include river-boarding (5hr), sports rafting, which is akin to canoeing (4hr), and white-water rappelling (4hr). In addition, Nordic Ventures (☎56 51 00 17, ⊛www.nordicventures .com) offers all sorts of **kayaking** excursions as well as **tandem paragliding and parasailing**; and Voss Fjellhest (☎56 51 91 66, ⊛www.vossfjellhest.no) specializes in mountain **horseback riding**.

In **winter**, **skiing** in Voss starts in mid-December and continues until mid-April – nothing fancy, but good for an enjoyable few days. From behind and above the train station, a **cable car** – the Hangursbanen – climbs 700m to give access to several short runs as well as the first of three chair lifts that take you up another 300m. In January and February some trails are floodlit. There's a choice of red, green and black downhill ski routes, and amongst the greens is a long and fairly gentle route through the hills above town; cross-country skiing here is limited to 20km of tracks. Full **equipment** for both downhill and cross-country skiing can be rented by the day from Voss Ski, at the upper Hangursbanen station (⊛www.vossresort.no). They also offer lessons in skiing and snowboarding techniques.

The Town

With the lake on one side and the River Vosso on the other, **Voss** has long been a trading centre of some importance, though you'd barely guess this from the modern appearance of the town centre. In 1023, King Olav visited to check that the population had all converted to Christianity, and stuck a big stone cross here to ram home his point. Two centuries later another king, Magnus Lagabøte, built a church in Voss to act as the religious focal point for the whole region. The church, the **Vangskyrkja** (June–Aug Mon–Sat 10am–4pm & Sun 1–4pm; 15kr), still stands, its eccentric octagonal spire rising above stone walls which are up to 2m thick. The interior is splendid, a surprisingly flamboyant and colourful affair with a Baroque reredos and a folksy rood screen showing a crucified Jesus attended by two cherubs. The ceiling is even more unusual, its timbers painted in 1696 with a cotton-wool cloudy sky inhabited by flying angels – and the nearer you approach the high altar, the more angels there are. That's pretty much it as far as specific sights go, though you could take a stroll along the leafy Prestegardsalléen footpath, which heads south along the shore of lake **Vangsvatnet** from opposite the church; or wander the central shops and cafés – if you've come from the hamlets and villages further north, the shopping might seem something of a treat.

East from Voss by train: Myrdal and Finse

Trains pulling east out of Voss head up the Raundal valley before climbing up to the bare but eerily beautiful wastes of the Hardangervidda plateau. All trains stop at **MYRDAL**, a remote railway junction where you change for the extraordinary train ride down to Flåm (see box, p.263), and proceed to **FINSE**, just half an hour by train from Myrdal and the highest point on the Bergen–Oslo train line. A solitary lakeside outpost on the northern peripheries of the plateau, Finse comprises nothing more than its station and a few isolated buildings, hunkered down against the howling winds that rip across the **Hardangervidda** in winter-time. There's snow here from the beginning of November until well into June, and

Moving on from Voss

When it comes to **moving on from Voss**, there are two obvious routes to choose from – one each by train and road. **By train**, Voss is on the main Bergen–Oslo train line and from here it's a short haul east up the Raundal valley (3–4 trains daily; ⓦwww .nsb.no) to the **Myrdal junction**, where you change for the world-famous train ride down to Flåm on the **Flåmsbana** (see box opposite). You can, however, choose instead to disembark two stops further down the line at **Finse** (see p.261), an isolated outpost on the Hardangervidda plateau, which offers a bevy of hiking and skiing routes amidst stirring scenery. Incidentally, drivers should note that Myrdal and Finse cannot be reached by car.

Alternatively, it's a quick and easy 65km north from Voss along the **E16** to the village of **Flåm**, a pleasant and much-visited little place amidst magnificent fjordland scenery. The E16 is the main road between Bergen and Oslo and there are **regular Nor-Way Bussekspress buses** (2–6 daily; ⓦwww.nor-way.no) linking Voss with Flåm and points east.

the **cross-country skiing** is particularly enthusiastic, with locals skiing off from the station in every direction. You can rent cross-country ski equipment at the *Finse 1222 Hotel* (see below), but you'll need to reserve. After the snow has melted, cycling (see below) and **hiking** take over, with one especially popular hike being the four-hour round-trip to the northeast edge of the **Hardangerjøkulen glacier**.

Cycling from Finse

Cycling from Finse is made possible by the **Rallarvegen** ("The Navvy Road"), which was originally built to allow men and materials to be brought up to the railway during its construction. Now surfaced with gravel and sometimes asphalt, the Rallarvegen begins in Haugastøl beside Highway 7, runs west to Finse and then continues to Myrdal, from where you can cycle or take the Flåmsbana down to Flåm. It's 27km by bicycle from Haugastøl to Finse, 37km from Finse to Myrdal and another 16km to Flåm. The Finse to Flåm section, which passes through fine upland scenery before descending the Flåmsdal, is the most popular part of the Rallarvegen. Most cyclists travel east to west as Finse is a good deal higher than Myrdal, and the whole journey from Finse to Flåm takes around nine hours; the return trip is usually made by train, with NSB railways transporting bikes for 100kr. Locals reckon that the best time to cycle the Rallarvegen is usually from mid-July to late September. However, snow is not cleared from the route and its highest section – between Finse and Myrdal – can be blocked by snow until very late in summer, so check conditions locally before you set out. **Mountain bike rental** is available from the *Finse 1222 Hotel* (see below), but advance reservations are required.

Finse practicalities

Finse has two **places to stay**: both are chalet complexes, geared up for hikers, cyclists and skiers. Of the two, the *Finse 1222 Hotel* (☎56 52 71 00, ⓦwww.finse1222.no; ❽ including meals; Jan to late May & mid-July to Oct) is the more comfortable, with pleasant rooms, a good restaurant and a sauna. The more frugal option is DNT's fully staffed *Finsehytta* (☎56 52 67 32, ⓦwww.finsehytta.no; mid-March to late May & July to mid-Sept; dorm beds 180–220kr, doubles ❶), which sleeps up to 150.

From Finse, the train takes an hour to reach Geilo (see p.236), three and a half hours more to Oslo.

North from Voss to Flåm

Heading north along the **E16** from Voss, it's a short, scenic hop to **Flåm**, one of the region's most visited villages and justifiably famous for its railway, the **Flåmsbana** (see box below). Flåm is also an excellent base for further explorations, whether it be the ferry trip up along the **Nærøyfjord** or a day-long hike in the surrounding mountains. Nearing Flåm you'll pass through two spirited pieces of tunnelling, with stretches of 11km and 5km bored through the mountainside at colossal expense. Yet, these are but pip-squeaks when compared with the 24-kilometre-long **tunnel** that links Aurlandsdal – from a point just east of Flåm – with Lærdal and, more importantly, completes the fast road, the E16, from Bergen to Oslo. Even better, there are no tolls (hurrah).

As for public transport, **Nor-way Bussekspress** (⊛www.nor-way.no) operates the **Sognebussen express bus** service, which begins in Bergen and passes through Voss bound for Flåm, the Fodnes-Mannheller and ultimately Sogndal (2–6 daily).

Flåm

Fringed by meadows and orchards, **FLÅM** village sits beside the Aurlandsfjord, a slender branch of the Sognefjord, with the mountains glowering behind. It's a splendid setting, but otherwise first impressions are poor: the fjordside complex adjoining the train station is crass and commercial – souvenir trolls and the like – and on summer days the place heaves with tourists, who pour off the train, have lunch and then promptly head out by bus and ferry. But a brief stroll is enough to leave the crowds behind at the harbourside, while out of season or in the evenings, when the day-trippers have all moved on, Flåm is a pleasant spot – and an eminently agreeable place to spend the night. If you're prepared to risk the weather, late September is perhaps the best time to visit: the peaks already have a covering of snow and the vegetation is just turning its autumnal golden brown.

Not only is Flåm the terminus for the Flåmsbana (see box below), but it's also the starting point for one of the most stupendous **ferry trips** in the fjords, the two-hour cruise up the Aurlandsfjord and down its narrow offshoot, the **Nærøyfjord** (1–5 daily; 2hr; 205kr one way, 325kr return; ⊛www.fjord1.no) to Gudvangen. With high and broody cliffs keeping out the sun throughout the winter, Nærøyfjord is the narrowest fjord in Europe, and its stern beauty makes for a magnificent excursion.

Practicalities

Flåm's harbourside complex may be ugly, but it is convenient, holding a supermarket, public-access computers, a train station and the **tourist office** (daily: May & Sept 8.30am–4pm; June–Aug 8.30am–8pm; ☎91 35 16 72, ⊛www.alr.no), where you can pick up a very useful free booklet on Aurland, Flåm and Lærdal that includes all sorts of local information. Staff also have details on local hiking routes, sell hiking maps and rent mountain bikes. You can also go **fjord kayaking** with Flåm-based Njord (☎97 19 45 11, ⊛www.njord.as/no), which offers an interesting

---

The Flåm railway – the Flåmsbana

Lonely **Myrdal**, just forty minutes by train from Voss, is the start of one of Europe's most celebrated branch rail lines, the **Flåmsbana** (⊛www.flaamsbana.no), a twenty-kilometre, 900-metre plummet down the Flåmsdal valley to **Flåm** – a fifty-minute train ride that should not be missed if at all possible; it is part of the "Norway in a Nutshell" route. The track, which took four years to lay in the 1920s, spirals down the mountainside, passing through hand-dug tunnels and, at one point, actually travelling through a hairpin tunnel to drop nearly 300m. The gradient of the line is one of the steepest anywhere in the world, and as the tiny train squeals its way down the mountain, past cascading waterfalls, it's reassuring to know that it has five separate sets of brakes, each capable of bringing it to a stop. The service runs all year round, a local lifeline during the deep winter months. There are ten departures daily from mid-June to late September, between four and eight the rest of the year; Myrdal–Flåm fares are 210kr one-way, 310kr return.

range of tours, the shortest and cheapest of which is their two-hour Aurlandsfjord paddle for 350kr per person.

If you decide to overnight here, there's inexpensive **accommodation** at *Flåm Camping og Vandrerhjem*, which has tent spaces and cabins (750–1000kr) and incorporates a small and well-kept HI **hostel** (May to mid-Sept; ☎57 63 21 21, Ⓦwww.vandrerhjem.no; dorm beds 170k, doubles ❶). It's about 300m from the train station towards the back of the village by the stream. Alternatively, the *Heimly Pensjonat* (☎57 63 23 00, Ⓦwww.heimly.no; ❹) provides simple but perfectly adequate lodgings in a modern block about 450m east of the train station along the shore; it's a friendly place and the views down the fjord are charming. A third choice, about 200m back from the station, is the *Fretheim Hotel* (☎57 63 63 00, Ⓦwww.fretheim-hotel.no; ❺/❼), a rambling structure whose attractive older part, with its high-pitched roofs and white-painted clapboard, is now joined to a flashy glass structure that is, in turn, attached to a matching, modern wing whose well-appointed rooms are furnished in brisk modern style. The hotel is the best place to **eat** in the village, with a banquet-like buffet every night; go early to get the pick of the buffet crop.

The Sognefjord

Profoundly beautiful, the **Sognefjord** (Ⓦwww.sognefjord.no) drills in from the coast for some 200km, its inner recesses splintering into half a dozen subsidiary fjords. Perhaps inevitably, none of the villages and small towns that dot the fjord quite lives up to the splendid setting, but **Balestrand** and **Mundal**, on the Fjærlandsfjord, come mighty close and are easily the best bases. Both are on the north side of the fjord which, given the lack of roads on the south side, is where you want (or pretty much have) to be – Flåm (see p.263) apart. Mundal is also near two southerly tentacles of the Jostedalsbreen glacier: **Flatbreen** and easy-to-reach **Bøyabreen**.

Highway 55 hugs the Sognefjord's north bank for much of its length, but at **Sogndal** it slices northeast to clip along the lustrous **Lustrafjord**, which boasts a top-notch attraction in **Urnes stave church**, reached via a quick ferry ride from **Solvorn**. Further north, a side road leaves Highway 55 to clamber up from the Lustrafjord to the east side of the Jostedalsbreen glacier at the **Nigardsbreen nodule**, arguably the glacier's finest vantage point. Thereafter Highway 55 – as the **Sognefjellsveg** – climbs steeply to run along the western side of the **Jotunheimen mountains**, an extraordinarily beautiful journey even by Norwegian standards and one which culminates with the road thumping down to **Lom** on the flatlands beside Highway 15.

Public transport to and around the Sognefjord is generally excellent, its assorted car ferries, buses and Hurtigbåt express passenger boats mostly run by Fjord 1

Moving on from Flåm

From May to September, daily **Hurtigbåt passenger express boats** (Ⓦwww.fjord1 .no) leave Flåm to travel up the Aurlandsfjord and along the Sognefjord to Balestrand and Bergen. The one-way trip to Bergen takes five and a half hours and costs 625kr; Balestrand is an hour and a half away and costs 215kr. By **train** (Ⓦwww.nsb.no), Myrdal, at the top of the Flåmsbana (see box, p.263), is on the main Oslo–Bergen line, while **Nor-way Bussekspress** (Ⓦwww.nor-way.no) operates the **Sognebussen express bus** service, which begins in Bergen and passes through Voss, Flåm and Fodnes en route to Sogndal (2–6 daily). Heading east by car, it's tempting to use the enormous, 24-kilometre-long – and free – tunnel through to Lærdal, but the 48-kilometre **mountain road** that the tunnel replaced – the **Aurlandsvegen** – has survived to provide splendid views and some hair-raising moments; it's open from the beginning of June to around the middle of October.

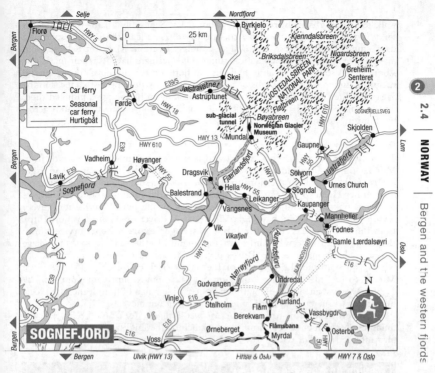

(Ⓦwww.fjord1.no). Operating about halfway along the fjord, perhaps the most useful of the **car ferries** plies between Vangsnes (see p.266), Hella and Dragsvik (for Balestrand), and in the east another useful link is the 24-hour ferry shuttle between Mannheller and Fodnes. Amongst a number of **Hurtigbåt passenger express boat** services, one handy route connects Bergen, Vik, Balestrand and Sogndal, another links Balestrand with Flåm (May–Sept only). These services are supplemented by Nor-Way Bussekspress **long-distance buses** (Ⓦwww.nor-way.no), which depart Bergen for Sogndal, arriving via Voss, Flåm and the Fodnes–Mannheller ferry; others arrive in Sogndal from Oslo and points east before proceeding to Balestrand. Sogndal is something of a transport hub with buses leaving here to travel northwest to Mundal and the Nordfjord (see p.272); and, in the summertime only, north to the Nigardsbreen glacier arm and Lom, which is reached along the stirring Sognefjellsveg (Highway 55).

Balestrand

BALESTRAND, an appealing first stop on the Sognefjord, has been a tourist destination since the middle of the nineteenth century, when it was discovered by European travellers in search of cool, clear air and picturesque mountain scenery. Kaiser Wilhelm II got in on the act too, becoming a frequent visitor and sharing his holiday spot with the tweeds and bustles of the British bourgeoisie. These days, the village is used as a touring base for the immediate area, as the battery of small hotels above the quay testifies, but it's all very small-scale, and among the thousand-strong population farming remains the principal livelihood.

An hour or so will suffice to take a peek at Balestrand's several low-profile attractions. Lining up along the harbour are the old post office, which features temporary displays on the town and its environs; a brace of art galleries; and an aquarium, the Sognefjord Akvarium. From the harbour, it's a couple of minutes' walk to the **English church of St Olav** (May–Sept daily 10am–10pm; free), a spiky brown-and-beige wooden structure of 1897, built in the general style of a stave church at the behest of a British émigrée, a certain Margaret Kvikne, who moved here after she married a local curate. The Germans have left their mark, too. About 300m south of the church along the fjord are two humpy **Viking burial mounds**, supposedly the tombs of King Bele and his wife, who both appear in the Sagas. On the larger of them is a statue of the king in heroic pose, plonked there by the Kaiser in 1913 to match the statue of Bele's son-in-law that stands across the fjord in Vangsnes.

Practicalities

The only **car ferry** direct to Balestrand is the summertime service south from Mundal, on the Fjærlandsfjord (see box below); otherwise, the nearest you'll get is **Dragsvik**, 9km along the fjord to the north of Balestrand, and reached by ferry from either **Hella** to the east (every 40min to hourly; 15min; passengers 25kr, car & driver 65kr; ⓦ www.fjord1.no) or **Vangsnes** on the fjord's south shore (every 40min to hourly; 30min; passengers 28kr, car & driver 76kr; ⓦ www.fjord1.no). Both the Mundal ferry and **Hurtigbåt passenger express boat** services (from Bergen and Vik to the west, and Flåm and Sogndal to the east) dock at the village quayside, plumb in the centre. **Buses** stop beside the quayside too and this is also where you will find the **tourist office** at the back of the shop (May & Sept Mon–Sat 10.30am–5pm; June–Aug Mon–Sat 8am–6pm & Sun 10am–5pm; ☎57 69 12 55, ⓦ www.sognefjord.no). Staff hand out a wide range of fjord leaflets, sell local hiking maps, issue bus and ferry timetables and rent out bicycles.

For **accommodation**, the all-year *Midtnes Pensjonat* (☎57 69 11 33, ⓦ www .midtnes.no; ❸), about 300m from the dock behind the English church, is a low-key, pleasantly sedate affair with a few workaday but spacious rooms in a modern wing

---

Moving on from Balestrand

When it comes to **moving on from Balestrand**, you're spoilt for choice. In the summertime, one especially tempting proposition is the **car ferry** (May–Sept 4 daily; 1hr 30min; passengers 195kr one-way, 290kr return; car & driver 350kr each way; ⓦ www.fjord1.no) north up along the stunningly beautiful Fjærlandsfjord to the eminently appealing hamlet of Mundal (see p.267). There is also a **Hurtigbåt passenger express boat** service linking Balestrand with Bergen and Vik in one direction, Sogndal in the other (1 daily), and another to Flåm (May–Sept 1–2 daily; 1hr 30min; ⓦ www.fjord1.no). **Driving** north from Balestrand, **Highway 13** cuts a scenic route over the mountains on its way to its junction with the E39 (near Førde), which itself proceeds north to the Nordfjord (see p.272), but **Highway 55** to Sogndal and the eastern reaches of the Sognefjord has much more to offer – not least the wondrous Sognefjellsveg mountain road (see p.271). To get to Sogndal from Balestrand, it's necessary to cross the mouth of the Fjærlandsfjord by ferry from Dragsvik, 9km up along the coast to the north of Balestrand. This **Dragsvik car ferry** operates a triangular service shuttling both east across the fjord to Hella on Highway 55 (15min) and south to Vangsnes (30min); see above for prices and sailing details. The other significant cost for drivers is the 175kr toll payable as you approach Mundal from the south on Highway 5.

As for **buses**, Nor-Way Bussekspress **express buses** travel west from Balestrand to Vadheim, where you change for services along the E39 (3 daily; 2hr; ⓦ www .nor-way.no). The same company also operates a service east from Balestrand to Sogndal and ultimately Oslo (3 daily). At Sogndal, passengers change for Mundal and Lom (see p.271). Note, however, that connecting services can be few and far between – mostly you'll have to hang around for an hour or two (at least) between buses.

adjoining the original clapboard house; make sure to get a room with a fjord view. Close by, the *Balestrand Hotell* (☎57 69 11 38, ⓦwww.balestrand.com; mid-May to mid-Sept; ❹) is comparable, with thirty unassuming rooms kitted out in modern, modest style. The big cheese hereabouts, though, is *Kvikne's Hotel* (☎57 69 42 00, ⓦwww.kviknes.no; ❻/❼; May–Sept), whose various buildings – some old, some new – dominate much of the waterfront. If you do decide to stay here, don't take a room without having a gander first: the best and most expensive overlook the fjord, but some are at the back in the modern annexe. Finally, the town **campsite**, *Sjøtun Camping* (☎57 69 12 23, ⓦwww.sjotun.com; June to mid-Sept), occupies a treeless field just beyond the burial mounds, 1km or so south of the dock; there are cabins (250kr for four persons) as well as tent and caravan pitches.

For **food**, the *Midtnes* serve tasty, excellent-value dinners (at 235kr) and there are competent snacks and light lunches at *Gekkens Café*, to the rear of the building that holds the tourist office. The cream of the gastronomic crop is the restaurant at *Kvikne's Hotel*, which serves up a banquet-sized, help-yourself buffet (440kr) every night – go early to get the pick and be sure to leave room for the ground-moving, earth-shattering mousse. The hotel also has a small and separate, à la carte restaurant – but stick to the buffet.

North to the Fjærlandsfjord and Mundal

To the north of Balestrand, the **Fjærlandsfjord** is a wild place, its flanks blanketed by a thick covering of trees that extends down to the water's edge, with a succession of thundering waterfalls tumbling down vast clefts in the rock up above. The village of **MUNDAL** – sometimes inaccurately referred to as Fjærland – matches its surroundings perfectly, a gentle ribbon of old wooden houses edging the fjord, with the mountains as a louring backcloth. Moreover, Mundal has eschewed the crasser forms of commercialism to become the self-styled "Norwegian Book Town" (Den Norske Bokbyen, ⓦwww.bokbyen.no), with a dozen rustic buildings accommodating antiquarian and second-hand **bookshops**. Naturally enough, most of the books are in Norwegian, but there's a liberal sprinkling of English titles too. The bookselling season runs from May to September and the bookshops are mostly open daily from 10am to 6pm.

Bookshops aside, the village has two good-looking buildings, the first of which is the **Hotel Mundal** (see p.268), whose cream-painted, nineteenth-century high-pitched roofs, turrets and verandas overlook the fjord from amongst the handful of buildings that amount to the village centre. Next door, the maroon **church** (June–Sept daily 10am–6pm; free), which dates from 1861, lacks ornamentation but is immaculately maintained and its graveyard hints at the hard but healthy life of the district's farmers – most of them seem to have lived to a ripe old age.

Many locals are still farmers, but in summer few herd their cattle up to the mountain pastures, as was the custom until the 1960s. The disused tracks to these summer farms (*støls*) now serve as **hiking trails** of varying length and difficulty – the tourist office (see p.268) will advise, but one of the easier routes is the two-hour (each way) jaunt west from the village up the country lane that follows **Mundalsdal** to **Fjellstølen**, at 350m.

Around Mundal: Flatbreen and Bøyabreen

Just 2.5km from Mundal, back on the main road, is the **Norsk Bremuseum** (Norwegian Glacier Museum: daily: April, May, Sept & Oct 10am–4pm; June–Aug 9am–7pm; information free but displays 110kr; ☎57 69 32 88, ⓦwww.bre.museum .no), which tells you more than you ever wanted to know about glaciers and then some. It features several lavish hands-on displays and screens films about glaciers; package tourists turn up in droves.

The museum is one of the **Jostedalsbreen National Park**'s three information centres (see p.274 for details of the others), and as such has the details of all the various **guided glacier walks** on offer across the park as outlined in their *Breturar*

▲ Mundal, Fjærlandsfjord

(glacier walks) leaflet; this same leaflet is also available at Mundal tourist office (see below). The usual target from Mundal is the **Supphellebreen**, the Jostedalsbreen's nearest hikeable arm, or, to be precise, that part of it called **Flatbreen**, though this is a challenging albeit beautiful part of the glacier; nor is it easy to get to. Flatbreen excursions take between seven and nine hours and the season runs from late June to early September. Advance reservations, at least a day beforehand, are essential – in the first instance contact Mundal tourist office. The cost is 650kr per person including special equipment and you get two to three hours on the ice.

At the other extreme, you can get close to the glacier without breaking sweat just 10km north of Mundal on Highway 5. Here, just before you enter the tunnel, look out for the signposted, dirt and gravel side road on the right that leads to the **Bøyabreen**, just 800m away. You can drive the first 600m, to the café and car park, and from here it's an easy stroll to the slender glacial lake that is fed by the sooty shank of the Bøyabreen glacier arm up above.

Mundal practicalities

Arriving **by car** from the south on Highway 5, there's a whopping 175kr toll to pay just before you reach the turning for Mundal. **Car ferries** from Balestrand (May–Sept 4 daily; 1hr 30min; passengers 195kr one-way, 290kr return; car & driver 350kr each way; ⓦwww.fjord1.no) dock a couple of minutes' walk from the centre of the village. Drivers should note that by using the ferry, they can avoid the toll providing, that is, they are continuing north from Mundal. The nearest you'll get to Mundal by **bus** is the Norsk Bremuseum on Highway 5, from where it's an easy 2.5-kilometre stroll south along the fjord to the village. Mundal **tourist office**, about 300m from the boat dock (May–Sept daily 10am–6pm; ☎57 69 32 33, ⓦwww.fjaerland.org), advises on local hiking routes, sells hiking maps and has bus and ferry timetables. **Cycle rental** is available from them too, at 140kr per day.

There are two fjordside **hotels** in Mundal. The obvious choice is the splendid ⚐ *Hotel Mundal* (☎57 69 31 01, ⓦwww.hotelmundal.no; May–Sept; ⑥), a quirky sort of place whose public rooms, which date back to 1891, display many original features, from the parquet floors and fancy wooden scrollwork through to the old-fashioned sliding doors of the expansive dining room. The rooms are perhaps a tad frugal, but somehow it doesn't matter much. As usual, the overnight rate includes breakfast, but given that Mundal hardly heaves with restaurants, you'll probably want dinner at the hotel too – the four-course set menu costs 500kr. A second choice, the *Fjærland Fjordstue Hotell* (☎57 69 32 00, ⓦwww.fjaerland.no; mid-May to mid-Sept; ④, ⑤ with fjord view) is very different – a well-tended family hotel

Bus routes on from Mundal

Moving on from Mundal, long-distance **Nor-Way Bussekspress buses** (ⓦwww
.nor-way.no) depart from the bus stop beside the Norsk Bremuseum. Services head
either south to Sogndal and ultimately Oslo (3 daily) and north to Skei and Førde
(3 daily). Change at Skei for onward services north to Loen and Stryn (see p.275).

with smart modern furnishings and a conservatory overlooking the fjord. They
offer dinners too, at a cost of 360kr. The third option is *Bøyum Camping* (☎57
69 32 52, ⓦwww.fjaerland.org/boyumcamping) near the Bremuseum, which has
huts (❸) as well as spaces for tents.

East to Sogndal
From Balestrand, it's 9km north along the fjord to **Dragsvik**, where ferries shuttle
over to the jetty at **Hella**, which is itself 40km from **SOGNDAL** – bigger and
livelier than Balestrand, but still hardly a major metropolis, with a population of just
six thousand. Neither is Sogndal as appealing: it has, admittedly, a pleasant fjord setting
in a broad valley, surrounded by low, green hills dotted with apple and pear trees, but
its centre is a rash of modern concrete and glass. Frankly, there are other much more
agreeable spots within a few kilometres' radius and your best option is to keep going.
   Buses drop passengers at the **bus station** on the west side of the town centre
near the end of Gravensteinsgata, the long main drag. From the bus station, it's about
600m east along Gravensteinsgata to the **tourist office** (May to mid-June & mid-
Aug to Sept Mon–Fri 10am–4pm; mid-June to mid-Aug Mon–Fri 9am–6pm &
Sat 10am–4pm; ☎97 60 04 43, ⓦwww.sognefjorden.no), housed in the town's large
and modern Kulturhus. Staff issue bus and ferry timetables, and have a list of local
accommodation, but pickings are fairly slim.

Northeast from Sogndal: Solvorn and Urnes stave church
Travelling northeast from Sogndal, it's about 13km up along Highway 55 to the
steep 3km-long side road that threads its way down to **SOLVORN**, an immaculate
hamlet of bright-white timber houses clustering the sheltered foreshore of the
Lustrafjord with the mountains louring behind. Solvorn is a lovely little place,
both a quick boat ride from one of the region's star attractions – Urnes stave
church (see p.270) – and the site of two really good places to stay. First up is the

Moving on from Sogndal

From Sogndal, there is a **Hurtigbåt passenger express boat** service **along the
Sognefjord** to Balestrand, Vik and Bergen (May–Sept 1–2 daily; ⓦwww.fjord1.no).
Sogndal is also on the route of the long-distance **Sogn og Fjordane ekspressen
bus** services west to Langvatn (3 daily; ⓦwww.nor-way.no), which – amongst several
permutations – links Oslo with Gol, the Fodnes–Mannheller ferry, Sogndal, Mundal
on the Fjærlandsfjord and Skei (for Stryn). **Local buses** from Sogndal include a
limited service north to Lom up along the Sognefjellsveg, the highest parts of which
are closed by snow throughout the winter (late June to Aug; 2 daily). There are also
local bus services to Solvorn (July & Aug 1–3 daily; rest of year 2–3 daily, but no Sat
service) and the Nigardsbreen glacier nodule (July & Aug 1 daily).
   Finally, **drivers** should remember that the road to Oslo, Bergen and Flåm is interrupted some 18km southeast of Sogndal by the round-the-clock Mannheller–Fodnes
car ferry (every 20min, hourly midnight to 6am; 10min; car and driver 103kr, including
a road toll of 48kr).

harbourside *Walaker Hotell* (☎57 68 20 80, ⓦwww.walaker.com; ❺), the prettiest part of which is the old house, a comely, pastel-painted, two-storey building whose porch is supported by a pair of columns, a Neoclassical extravagance that must have once amazed the locals. The hotel has a lovely garden and first-rate period bedrooms, although most of the guest rooms are in the modern annexe, a low-slung really rather successful building that also looks out at the fjord. The second option is the distinctive *Eplet Bed & Apple* (☎41 64 94 69, ⓦwww.eplet.net; May–Sept), a self-styled "Modern Guest House & Apple Juice Farm" in the village about 300m back up the road from dock – just watch for the sign. The host, a long-distance cyclist and traveller, seems to have been just about everywhere and he has created a laid-back, easygoing place with dormitory accommodation (140kr) and a few neat trim modern guest rooms (❹). You can camp in the grounds, mountain bike hire is free for guests, and there's internet access.

Urnes stave church

From Solvorn, a local **car ferry** (June–Aug daily 10am–4pm, hourly; Sept–May Mon–Fri 4–5 daily, no Sat & Sun service; 20min; passengers 28kr, car & driver 76kr; ☎91 79 42 11, ⓦwww.urnesferry.com) shuttles across the Lustrafjord to the hamlet of **Ornes**, from where it's a stiff, ten-minute hike up the hill to **Urnes stave church** (June–Aug daily 10.30am–5.30pm; 45kr; ⓦwww.stavechurch.com). Magnificently sited with the fjord and the snow-dusted mountains as its backdrop, this is the oldest and most celebrated stave church in Norway. Parts of the building date back to the twelfth century, and its most remarkable feature is its wonderful medieval **carvings**. On the outside, incorporated into the north wall, are two exquisite door panels, the remains of an earlier church dating from around 1070 and alive with a swirling filigree of strange beasts and delicate vegetation. These forceful, superbly crafted panels bear witness to the sophistication of Viking woodcarving – indeed, the church has given its name to this distinctively Nordic art form, found in many countries where Viking influence was felt and now generally known as the "Urnes" style. A small display in the neighbouring house-cum-ticket office fills in all the details and has photographic enlargements of carvings that are hard to decipher inside the (poorly lit) church.

If you're driving, there's a choice of routes on from the church. You can head north along the minor road that tracks along the east shore of the Lustrafjord to rejoin Highway 55 at Skjolden (see opposite), or retrace your steps back to Highway 55 via Solvorn. The latter is the route you'll need to take if you're heading to the Nigardsbreen arm of the Jostedalsbreen glacier.

North to the Nigardsbreen

North from the Solvorn turning, it's about 13km along Highway 55 to **Gaupne**, where **Highway 604** forks north for the delightful 34-kilometre trip up the wild, forested river valley that leads to the **Breheimsenteret Jostedalsbreen National Park information centre** (daily: May to late June & late Aug to Sept 10am–5pm; late June to late Aug 9am–7pm; displays 50kr; ☎57 68 32 50, ⓦwww.jostedal.com). This angular, ultramodern structure fits in well with the bare peaks that surround it and, as you sip a coffee on the terrace, you can admire the glistening glacier dead ahead – the **Nigardsbreen**, an eastern arm of the Jostedalsbreen. From the centre, it's an easy three-kilometre drive or walk along the toll road (25kr) to the shores of an icy green lake, where a tiny **boat** (mid-June to early Sept daily 10am–6pm; 30kr return) shuttles across to the bare rock slope beside the glacier, a great rumpled and seamed wall of ice that sweeps between high peaks. It's a magnificent spectacle and most visitors are satisfied with the short hike up from the jetty to the glacier's shaggy flanks, but others plump for a **guided glacier walk**. There is a plethora to choose from, beginning with a quick and easy one- to two-hour jaunt suitable for children over 6 (daily July to late Aug; 200kr, children 100kr), through to much tougher seven-hour excursions (July to late Aug 4 weekly; 675kr). Prices include equipment.

The guided glacier walk season lasts from mid-May to mid-September. Tickets for the family walks can be purchased direct from the guides at the glacier (cash only), but longer excursions need to be pre-booked and pre-paid with the Breheimsenteret at least one hour before departure. Advance reservations for overnight trips must be made at least four weeks beforehand. For more on the Jostedalsbreen glacier, see p.272; further information on glacier walks is given on p.274.

Along the Sognefjellsveg

Back at Gaupne, Highway 55 continues 26km northeast to **SKJOLDEN**, a dull little town that is both at the head of the Lustrafjord and the start of the hundred-kilometre **Sognefjellsveg** road over the mountains to Lom. Despite the difficulty of the terrain, the Sognefjellsveg – which is closed from late October to May depending on conditions – marks the course of one of the oldest trading routes in Norway, with locals transporting goods by mule or, amazingly enough, on their shoulders: salt and fish went northeast; hides, butter, tar and iron went southwest.

Beyond Skjolden, the Sognefjellsveg worms its way up the Bergsdal valley to a mountain plateau which it proceeds to traverse, providing absolutely stunning views of the jagged, ice-crusted Jotunheimen peaks to the east. En route are several roadside **lodges**, easily the best of which is the comfortable and very modern *Turtagrø Hotel* (☏57 68 08 00, ☒www.turtagro.no; dorm bunks 340kr, 470kr with breakfast, hotel rooms ❼; Easter–Oct), just 15km out from Skjolden. There's been a hotel here since 1888, but the present structure, a large and attractive red-timber building, was only constructed in 2001, after fire destroyed its predecessor. The interior is very Scandinavian, with spacious public rooms and even a library, and the food is first-rate, with a three-course midday meal costing 400kr. The hotel is a favourite haunt for **mountaineers**, but it also provides ready access to the **hiking trails** that network the Jotunheimen National Park (see p.232), though the terrain is unforgiving and the weather unpredictable – novice hikers beware.

On the far side of the plateau, the Sognefjellsveg clips down through forested **Leirdal**, from where it's a short hop over the hills to **Bøverdal**, which runs down into the crossroads settlement of **Lom**.

Lom

A long-time trading and transport centre, **LOM** benefits – in a modest sort of way – from the farms that dot the surrounding valleys. It also makes a comfortable living from the passing tourist trade, with motorists pausing here before the last thump down Highway 15 to the Geirangerfjord. Even so, with a population of just two thousand, it could hardly be described as a boom town. Lom's eighteenth-century heyday is recalled by its **stave church** (mid-June to mid-Aug daily 9am–8pm; 45kr), a strikingly attractive structure perched on a grassy knoll above the river. The original church was built here about 1200, but it was remodelled and enlarged after the Reformation, when the spire and transepts were added and the flashy altar and pulpit installed. Its most attractive features are the dinky, shingle-clad roofs, adorned by dragon finials, and the Baroque acanthus vine decoration inside.

Museum enthusiasts will also want to visit Lom's **Norsk Fjellmuseum** (Norwegian Mountain Museum: May to mid-June & mid-Aug to Sept Mon–Fri 9am–4pm, Sat & Sun 11am–5pm; mid-June to mid-Aug Mon–Fri 9am–7pm, Sat & Sun 10am–7pm; Oct–April Mon–Fri 10am–3pm; 50kr), a modern place that focuses on the Jotunheimen mountains. It's all here in admirable detail, from the fauna and the flora to the landscapes, farmers and past mountaineers, who scaled the peaks in tweeds and hobnail boots.

Practicalities

Buses to Lom pull in a few metres west of the main crossroads, and most of what you're likely to need is within easy walking distance of here. The church and the open-air museum are across the bridge on the other side of the river, as is the

Car and bus routes on from Lom

Heading west from Lom along **Highway 15**, you are within comfortable driving distance of either the Geirangerfjord (see p.276) or Stryn and the western flanks of the Jostedalsbreen glacier (see below). Lom is also at the northern end of the wondrous Sognefjellsveg (Highway 55), running over the Jotunheimen mountains before proceeding down to the Sognefjord (see p.264). In the opposite direction, also along Highway 15, it's another very manageable drive to Otta (see p.230) and the main E6 highway between Oslo and Trondheim.

By **bus** from Lom, there are fast and frequent **Nor-Way Bussekspress** (Ⓦwww .nor-way.no) services west to Langvatn, Stryn and ultimately Bergen, and east to Otta, Lillehammer and Oslo or Trondheim. From mid-June to the end of August, you can change onto a local bus at Langvatn for the Geirangerfjord – but check connections with Lom tourist office before you depart. There is also a local bus service south from Lom along the Sognefjellsveg (Highway 55) to Turtagrø, Solvorn and Sogndal (late June to Aug 1–2 daily).

mountain museum, which shares its premises – and opening times – with the **tourist office** (Ⓣ61 21 29 90, Ⓦwww.visitjotunheimen.com).

The choicest **accommodation** is the ♨ *Fossheim Turisthotell* (Ⓣ61 21 95 00, Ⓦwww.fossheimhotel.no; ❺), about 300m east of the crossroads along Highway 15. The main lodge here has been added to over the years and the guest rooms, which are at the back, have a real rural feel with their timber walls, floors and ceilings. It's all very cosy and so are the delightful little wooden cabins (1000–1200kr) that trail up the wooded hillside beside the main building; some of them are very old and all are en suite. The hotel **restaurant** is outstanding and wherever possible features local ingredients. They serve set meals with three courses costing 350kr, four courses 500kr – try the beef in a rosemary jus with broad beans. A second good place to stay is the *Fossberg Hotel* (Ⓣ61 21 22 50, Ⓦwww.fossberg.no; ❹), a chalet-like modern place made mostly of timber and a few metres from the town crossroads.

Nordfjord and the Jostedalsbreen glacier

The most direct way to get from the Sognefjord to the **Nordfjord**, the next great fjord system to the north, is to travel north from Mundal (see p.267) on Highway 5. The inner recesses of the Nordfjord are readily explored on Highway 60, which weaves a tortuous course through a string of unexciting little towns between the fjord and the glacier's west side. Amongst them, **Loen** is easily the best base for further explorations, including the glacier, though humdrum **Stryn** is larger and more important. Stryn is also where Highway 60 meets **Highway 15**. The former presses on north to Hellesylt on the Geirangerfjord (see p.276), while the latter runs east to Langvatn (for Geiranger).

High up in the mountains, dominating the whole of the inner Nordfjord region, lurks the **Jostedalsbreen glacier**, a five-hundred-kilometre-square ice plateau that creaks, grumbles and moans out towards the Sognefjord, the Nordfjord and the Jotunheim mountains. The glacier stretches northeast in a lumpy mass from Highway 5, its myriad arms – or "**nodules**" – nudging down into the nearby valleys, the clay particles of its meltwater giving the local rivers and lakes their distinctive light-green colouring.

For centuries, the glacier presented an impenetrable east–west barrier, crossed only at certain points by determined farmers and adventurers. It's no less daunting today, but access is much freer, a corollary of the creation of the **Jostedalsbreen National Park** in 1991. Since then, roads have been driven deep into the glacier's flanks, the comings (but mostly goings) of the ice have been closely monitored and there has been a proliferation of officially licensed **guided glacier walks** (*breturar*)

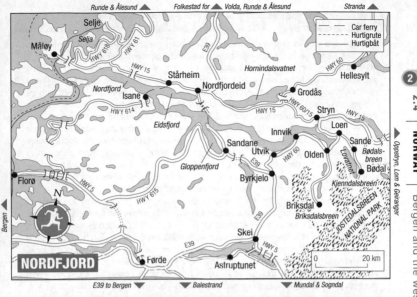

on its various arms (see box, p.274). If that sounds too energetic and all you're after is a **close look at the glacier**, then this is possible at several places, with the easiest approach being the five-minute stroll to the Bøyabreen on the south side of the glacier near Mundal (see p.267). By contrast, the east side's Nigardsbreen (see p.270) requires much more commitment – getting to the ice involves a boat ride and a short, stiff hike – as does the **Briksdalsbreen**, here on the west side of the glacier, off Highway 60. It takes about 45 minutes to walk from the end of the road to the Briksdalsbreen, but it's still the most visited approach by a long chalk, partly on account of its pony-and-trap rides up towards the ice. Much less crowded and far prettier is the easy twenty-minute walk to the **Kjenndalsbreen**, near Loen – a delightful way to spend a morning or afternoon.

Travelling around the Nordfjord region by **bus** presents few problems if you stick to the main highways, but services from Highway 60 to the glacier are limited. There are no buses at all to Kjenndalsbreen and an infrequent service (June–Aug 1 daily) from Stryn, Loen and Olden to Briksdal (for Briksdalsbreen). The good news is that the times of the Briksdal buses are coordinated so you get three hours at Briksdalsbreen between arrival and departure. The most useful long-distance bus service hereabouts is the Nor-way Bussekspress (ⓦ www.nor-way.no) **Nordfjordekspressen**, which links Stryn with Langvatn (for Geiranger), Lom, Otta and ultimately Oslo.

North from Mundal to Olden and the Briksdalsbreen

Heading north from Mundal on Highway 5, it's about 30km to **SKEI**, where you turn north for the twenty-kilometre yomp up the valley to the **Byrkjelo crossroads**. From here, it's a further 55km over the mountains and along the Nordfjord to Olden, where you turn off for the Briksdalsbreen (see below), and 7km more to Loen, at the start of the road to the Kjenndalsbreen (see p.274).

Hard by the Nordfjord, the hamlet of **OLDEN** doesn't have much going for it, but it is at the start of the 24-kilometre byroad south to **BRIKSDAL**, a scattering of mountain chalets that serves as the starting point for the easy 45-minute (2–3km) walk to the **Briksdalsbreen glacier arm**. The path skirts waterfalls and weaves up the river until you finally reach the glacier, surprisingly blue except for streaks

273

Guided glacier walks and national park information centres

Most **guided glacier walks** on the Jostedalsbreen are scheduled between late June and early September, though on some arms of the glacier the season extends from May until late September. The walks range from two-hour excursions to five-day expeditions. Day-trip prices start at 500–600kr per person for a two- to four-hour gambol, rising to 700kr for six to eight hours. A comprehensive leaflet detailing all the various walks is widely available across the region and at the national park's three **information centres**. These are the **Norsk Bremuseum**, on the south side of the glacier near Mundal (see p.267); the **Breheimsenteret Jostedal** on the east side at the Nigardsbreen (see p.270); and the **Jostedalsbreen Nasjonalparksenter** (Jostedalsbreen National Park Centre: daily: May & early Sept noon–4pm; June & Aug 10am–4pm; July 10am–6pm; exhibitions 70kr; ☎57 87 72 00, ⊛www.jostedalsbre .no) in Oppstryn, 20km east of Stryn on Highway 15. Each of the centres has displays on all things glacial and sells books, souvenirs and hiking maps.

Booking arrangements for the shorter glacier walks vary considerably. On some of the trips – for example those at the Nigardsbreen – it's sufficient to turn up at the infor-mation centre an hour or two beforehand, but in general it's a good idea to make a reservation at least a day ahead. Sometimes this is best done through the information centre, sometimes direct with the tour operator. In the case of the overnight trips, however, you must reserve generally at least four weeks beforehand. In all cases, basic **equipment** is provided, though you'll need to take good boots, waterproofs, warm clothes, gloves, hat, sunglasses – and sometimes your own **food** and **drink** too.

of dirt. It's a simple matter to get close to the ice as the only precaution is a flimsy rope barrier with a small warning sign – but do be careful. Alternatively, you can hop on a twee-looking **battery-driven golf car** at the café area for the twenty-minute drive up to the glacier. Several operators offer **guided glacier walks** on the Briksdalsbreen and the adjacent Brenndalsbreen: Olden Aktiv (☎57 87 38 88, ⊛www.oldenaktiv.no) is as good as any.

A local **bus** service connects Stryn, Loen and Olden with Briksdal (June–Aug 1 daily); schedules mean that passengers get three hours at Briksdal before the departure of the return service.

Loen and the Kjenndalsbreen

LOEN spreads ribbon-like along the Nordfjord's low-lying, grassy foreshore, with ice-capped mountains breathing down its neck. The village is home to one of Norway's most famous hotels, the outstanding, family-run ⚑ *Alexandra* (☎57 87 50 00, ⊛www.alexandra.no; ❽), whose exterior hardly does it justice. The hotel occupies a large and fairly undistinguished modern block overlooking the fjord, but inside the lodge-like public rooms are splendid – wide, open and extremely well appointed. There's every convenience, including a sauna and solarium, while the bedrooms are spacious, infinitely comfortable and furnished in bright modern style. Breakfasts are banquet-like, but the evening **buffets** (from 7pm; 470kr, 250kr for hotel guests) are even better, a wonderful selection that lays fair claim to being the best in the fjords. The *Alexandra* is, of course, fairly pricey, but across the road and right on the water's edge, the *Hotel Loenfjord* (☎57 87 57 00, ⊛www.loenfjord .no; ❺/❻) is an excellent and less expensive second choice. A happy cross between a motel and a lodge, the *Loenfjord* comprises a long and low modern building in a vernacular version of traditional Norwegian style. More of a bargain still is *Loen Pensjonat* (☎57 87 76 24, ⊛www.loen-pensjonat.com; ❶), in a chalet-like, modern house about 500m inland from the *Alexandra* – and across from the church in the old village.

Loen church

Both of Loen's hotels are located on land reclaimed from the fjord and the handful of dwellings that make up the old village are located about 500m inland. Here, perched on top of a gentle ridge, is **Loen kyrkje**, a tidy structure dating from 1837. Its interior is unremarkable, though the folksy furnishings and fittings are pretty enough, but the views from outside over the fjord are delightful. Its churchyard and precincts also hold a couple of items of interest, namely a stone Celtic cross that is at least a thousand years old, and a pair of **memorial plinths** to the villagers who were drowned in the disasters of 1905 and 1936. On both occasions, a great hunk of the Ramnefjell mountain fell into lake Lovatnet behind the village and the ensuing tidal wave swept dozens of local farmsteads away. The second disaster was particularly tragic as the government had only just persuaded many of the villagers to return home after the first trauma.

To the Kjenndalsbreen

From beside the *Hotel Alexandra*, a 21-kilometre byroad leads south to the **Kjenndalsbreen** arm of the Jostedalsbreen glacier. The road starts by slipping up the river valley past lush meadows, before threading along the northerly shore of **Lovatnet**, a long and thin lake of glacial blue. After about 7km, the road reaches the **café** (May–Sept) at the very end of the Lovatnet – and the spot where the boat docks. From here, it's 5km more to the car park and then an easy and very pleasant twenty-minute ramble through rocky terrain to the **ice**, whose fissured, blancmange-like blue-and-white folds tumble down the rock face, with a furious white-green river, fed by plummeting meltwater, flowing underneath. If the weather holds, it's a lovely spot for a picnic.

There are no **buses** from Loen to the Kjenndalsbreen.

Stryn

STRYN, merely 12km around the Nordfjord from Loen, is the biggest town hereabouts, though with a population of just 1600 that's hardly a major boast. For the most part, it's a humdrum modern sprawl straggling beside its long main street, but there is a pleasant pocket of antique **timber houses** huddled round the old bridge, down by the river near the tourist office and just to the south of the main drag; take a few moments to have a look.

Stryn **bus station** is beside the river to the west of the town centre on Highway 15/60 (the road to Nordfjordeid). From here, it's a 600-metre walk to the **tourist office**, in the centre just off the main street, Tonningsgata (early June & late Aug Mon–Fri 8.30am–6pm & Sat 9.30am–5pm; late June & early Aug Mon–Fri 8.30am–6pm, Sat & Sun 9.30am–5pm; July daily 8.30am–8pm; Sept–May Mon–Fri 8.30am–3.30pm; ☎57 87 40 40, ⓦ www.nordfjord.no). Staff issue free town maps, rent mountain bikes, have a wide range of local brochures and sell hiking maps.

By boat from Loen to the Kjenndalsbreen

From June to August, a small **passenger boat** (1 daily) weaves a leisurely course from one end of lake **Lovatnet** to the other, a delightful cruise through beguiling scenery. The departure point is the pint-sized **Sande jetty**, 4.4km down the Kjenndalsbreen road from the *Hotel Alexandra* in Loen, and the boat docks about 5km from the Kjenndalsbreen ice face. The excursion costs 180kr, including onward transportation by bus from the dock to the car park at the end of the Kjenndalsbreen road and the return journey – again by bus and boat – back to Sande; in total the round-trip takes four hours. The *Hotel Alexandra* (see opposite) issues tickets and takes bookings and will, at a pinch, give you a lift down to Sande if required.

Heading west out of Stryn, highways 15 and 60 share the same stretch of road for 16km before they separate: Highway 60 then spears north to reach, after another 35km, Hellesylt, on the Geirangerfjord (see below).

The Geirangerfjord

The **Geirangerfjord** is one of the region's smallest fjords, but also one of its most breathtaking. A convoluted branch of the Storfjord, the Geirangerfjord cuts deep inland and is marked by impressive waterfalls, with a village at either end of its snake-like profile – **Hellesylt** in the west and **Geiranger** in the east. Of the two, Geiranger has the smarter hotels as well as the tourist crowds, whereas Hellesylt is tiny and dull.

You can reach Geiranger in dramatic style from both ends along the rip-roaring, nerve-jangling Highway 63, the aptly named **Ørnevegen** ("Eagle's Highway"). The approach to Hellesylt along Highway 60 is comparatively demure, though taken as a whole this highway is an especially appealing route between the Nordfjord and Ålesund.

In summertime, **car ferries** link Hellesylt and Geiranger in what is one of the most celebrated trips in the entire region (May to mid-Oct 4–8 daily; 1hr; passengers 110kr one-way, 140kr return; car & driver 230kr each way; ⓦwww .fjord1.no). With rearing cliffs to either side, the ferry follows the S-shaped profile of the fjord, whose cold waters are about 300m deep and fed by a series of plunging waterfalls up to 250m in height.

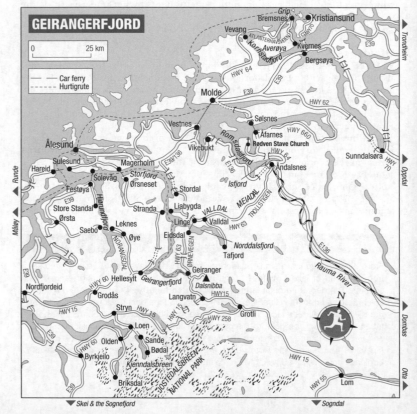

Long-distance **Nor-Way Bussekspress buses** travelling west along Highway 15 link Otta (see p.230) and Lom (see p.271) with Stryn (see p.275) via Langvatn, where you change for the **local bus** north to Geiranger, though note that this onward connecting service only operates from mid-June to August. This same local bus pushes on from Geiranger to Åndalsnes (see p.280). Hellesylt is on the main Bergen–Ålesund bus route operated by **Nor-Way Bussekspress**. This service connects, amongst many other places, Skei, Olden, Loen, Stryn and Hellesylt.

Hellesylt

A well-protected trading station in Viking times, tiny **HELLESYLT** is now little more than a stop-off on tourist itineraries, with most visitors staying just long enough to catch the ferry down the fjord to Geiranger (see below) or scuttle off along Highway 60. The **tourist office** (June–Aug daily 11am–7pm; Sept Sat & Sun 11am–7pm; ☎94 81 13 32, ⓦwww.hellesylt.no) is a five-minute walk from the jetty in a modern building that doubles as the Peer Gynt Galleriet (same times; 50kr). On display is a set of kitsch-meets-Baroque woodcarvings illustrating Ibsen's *Peer Gynt* by a certain Oddvin Parr from Ålesund. It's rather strange, but good(ish) fun all the same.

Geiranger

Any approach to **GEIRANGER** is spectacular. Arriving by ferry reveals the village tucked away in a hollow at the eastern end of the fjord, while approaching from the north by road involves thundering along a fearsome set of switchbacks on the **Ørnevegen** (Highway 63) for a first view of the village and the fjord glinting in the distance. Similarly, the road in from Highway 15 to the south squeezes through the mountains before squirming down the zigzags to arrive in Geiranger from behind; note, however, that both approaches are closed as soon as the snow comes.

Geiranger boasts a beautiful setting, one of the most magnificent in western Norway, the only fly in the ointment being the excessive number of tourists at the peak of the season. That said, the congestion is limited to the centre of the village and it's easy enough to slip away to appreciate the true character of the fjord, hemmed in by sheer rock walls interspersed with hairline waterfalls, with tiny-looking ferries and cruise ships bobbing about on its blue-green waters.

Arrival and information

Buses to Geiranger stop a stone's throw from the waterfront and the **ferry terminal**. The latter is used by both the ferry from Hellesylt (see opposite) and the **Hurtigrute coastal boat**, which detours from – and returns to – Ålesund on its northbound route between the middle of April and the middle of September only; it leaves Geiranger at 1.30pm. The **tourist office** is also on the waterfront, a couple of minutes' walk away, beside the sightseeing boat dock (mid-May to mid-June & mid-Aug to mid-Sept 9am–5pm; mid-June to mid-Aug daily 9am–7pm; ☎70 26 30 99, ⓦwww.visitgeiranger.no). Staff here issue bus and ferry timetables, sell hiking maps and supply free village maps, which usefully outline local hiking routes. They also promote expensive boat tours of the fjord, though the car ferry from Hellesylt is perfectly adequate.

From mid-June to August, local **buses** run north into Geiranger from Langvatn on Highway 15. There are two buses daily. One goes straight from Langvatn to Geiranger (45min), the other makes the detour to the **Dalsnibba viewpoint** (1hr 15min; see p.279). After Geiranger, both these local buses push to Åndalsnes (see p.280) via the Trollstigen (see p.280). The journey from Geiranger to Åndalsnes takes about three hours. Two buses daily complete the same route from north to south, again from mid-June to August. **Nor-Way Bussekspress** long-distance buses travelling along Highway 15 connect with these local services to and from Geiranger, but check connections before you set out.

Accommodation

Considering its popularity, Geiranger doesn't have many hotels, so vacant rooms are at a premium during the high season, when you should always reserve ahead. The village does better for campsites, the main one being *Geiranger Camping* (℡70 26 31 20; late May to early Sept), which sprawls along the fjordside fields a couple of hundred metres to the east of the tourist office. In summer it's jam-packed with caravans, cars and motorbikes – frankly not much fun at all. Rather more comfortable – and usually a good bit quieter – are the two fjordside campsites a couple of kilometres north of the village on the road to Eidsdal. These are the *Geirangerfjorden Feriesenter* (℡95 10 75 27, Ⓦwww.geirangerfjorden.net; May–Sept) and the *Grande Hytteutleige og Camping* (℡70 26 30 68, Ⓦwww.grande-hytteutleige .no; May to mid-Sept). Both have **cabins** (400–750kr and 600–1000kr respectively).

Grande Fjordhotell ℡70 26 94 90, Ⓦwww .grandefjordhotel.com. Ultramodern, timber-built hotel with few architectural surprises, but a pleasing fjordside location about 2km north of the centre on the Eidsdal road. The hotel is adjacent to the *Geirangerfjorden Feriesenter* (see above). ❹

🏃 **Hotel Union** ℡70 26 83 00, Ⓦwww .union-hotel.no. Cream of the Geiranger crop, this large and lavish hotel perches high on the hill-side about 500m up the road from the jetty. There's been an hotel here since 1891, and although the present building is firmly modern, it's an attractive structure and the public rooms are spacious and eminently comfortable. The bedrooms are pleasantly

furnished in modern style and the best have fjord-facing balconies; those on the fourth floor are the pick. Open March to mid-Dec. ❻/❽

Villa Utsikten ℡70 26 96 60, Ⓦwww .villautsikten.no. On the south side of Geiranger, high up on the hill beside the main approach road, the family-run *Utsikten* offers simply wonderful views across the fjord and its surrounding mountains. There's been an hotel here since the 1890s, but today's building is resolutely modern, the public areas a tad retro. The thirty-odd bedrooms are decorated in a simple, modern manner, but the pick look out over the fjord. Open May–Sept. ❺, with fjord view ❻

The village

Geiranger's principal man-made attraction is the **Norsk Fjordsenter** (daily: May to mid-June 9am–4pm; late June and early Aug 9am–6pm; July 9am–10pm; mid-Aug to mid-Sept 9am–4pm; 85kr; Ⓦwww.fjordsenter.info), just across from the *Hotel Union* (see above). The centre follows the usual pattern of purpose-built

▲ View over Geirangerfjord

museums, with separate sections exploring different aspects of the region's history from communications and transportation through to fjord farms and the evolution of tourism. Perhaps the most interesting display examines the problem of fjordland avalanches – whenever there's a major rock fall into a fjord, the resulting tidal wave threatens disaster.

Hiking trails and viewpoints

The Norsk Fjordsenter is, however, small beer when compared with the scenery. A network of **hiking trails** lattices the mountains that crimp and crowd Geiranger: some make their way to thundering waterfalls, while others visit abandoned mountain farmsteads or venture up to vantage points where the views over the fjord are exhilarating if not downright scary. One popular and very enjoyable excursion involves both a boat ride and a four-hour hike. It begins with a short cruise along the fjord on the MS *Geirangerfjord* (mid- to late May & early Sept 1 daily; June–Aug 4–6 daily; 135kr) to a small jetty, from where it's a stiff, one-hour walk up to the mountain farm of **Skageflå**, followed by a three-hour trek back to Geiranger; if that sounds too much like hard work, speak to the crew about picking you up again at the jetty.

There's also the short but precarious trail to the **Flydalsjuvet**, an overhanging rock high above the Geirangerfjord that features in a thousand leaflets. To get there, drive south from the Geiranger jetty on Highway 63 and watch for the sign after about 5km; the car park offers extravagant views, but the Flydalsjuvet is about 200m away, out at the end of a slippery and somewhat indistinct track. A second famous viewpoint, **Dalsnibba**, at 1476m, is another 12km or so to the south along Highway 63 and then up a clearly signed, five-kilometre mountain toll road. Remarkably enough, two of the four local buses that run into Geiranger from north and south make the detour (mid-June to Aug).

Eating

As for **food**, it's got to be the *Hotel Union* (see p.278), which does a magnificent, help-yourself buffet dinner for 435kr; check with the hotel to see when things get started as it's best to get there early before the munching starts in earnest. The restaurant also does an à la carte menu with mains costing around 250kr. The main competitor is the *Aida Restaurant* at *Villa Utsikten* (see p.278), where they focus on local, seasonal ingredients and traditional Norwegian cuisine; mains hover around 220kr.

North to Åndalsnes via the Trollstigen

Promoted as the "Golden Route", the ninety-kilometre journey **from Geiranger to Åndalsnes** along Highway 63 is famous for its mountain scenery – no wonder. Even by Norwegian standards, the route is of outstanding beauty, the road bobbing past a whole army of austere peaks whose cold severity is daunting. Yet, the most memorable section is undoubtedly the **Trollstigen**, a mountain road that cuts an improbable course between the Valldal valley and **Åndalsnes**, which is itself a useful base for further fjordland explorations and has a couple of pleasant places to stay. Åndalsnes is also the northern terminus of the dramatic **Rauma train line** (see p.233) from Dombås to the east.

Twice daily from mid-June to August, a **local bus** travels the length of the Golden Route, taking the sweat out of driving round its hairpins and hairy-scary corners; the trip takes three hours and includes one ferry ride. Drivers should note that the higher parts of the road are generally closed from early October to mid-May – earlier/later if the snows have been particularly heavy.

Over the Ørnevegen to Valldal

Heading north from Geiranger, the first part of the Golden Route is the 26-kilometre jaunt up and over the **Ørnevegen** (Highway 63) mountain road to **Eidsdal** on the Norddalsfjord. From here, a **car ferry** (every 20–45min; 10min; passengers 23kr, car & driver 55kr) shuttles over to the **Linge jetty**, from where it's just 4km east to **VALLDAL**, a shadowy, half-hearted village that straggles along the fjord at the foot of the **Valldal valley** at the start of the Trollstigen (see below).

Over the Trollstigen

The alarming heights of the **Trollstigen** ("Troll's Ladder"), a trans-mountain route between Valldal and Åndalsnes, are equally compelling in either direction. The road negotiates the mountains by means of eleven hairpins with a maximum gradient of 1:12, but it's still a pretty straightforward drive until, that is, you meet a tour bus coming the other way – followed by a bit of nervous backing up and repositioning. Drivers (and cyclists) should also be particularly careful in wet weather.

From Valldal, the southern end of the Trollstigen starts gently enough with the road rambling up the **Valldal valley**. Thereafter, the road swings north, building up a head of steam as it bowls up the **Meiadal valley** bound for the barren mountains beyond. It's here that the road starts to climb in earnest, clambering up towards the bleak and icy plateau-pass, the **Trollstigplatået**, which marks its high point. In recent years, the assorted cafés and souvenir shops on the Trollstigplatået had begun to look rather tired, so the Norwegians are in the process of bringing it all bang up to date with a brand-new complex due for completion in 2010. They have installed enhanced observation points and a new footbridge over the fast-flowing river that rushes off the plateau to barrel down the mountain below. From the main **Utsikten** (viewing point), there is now a magnificent panorama over the surrounding mountains and valleys. From here, the sheer audacity of the road becomes apparent, zigzagging across the face of the mountain and somehow managing to wriggle round the tumultuous, 180-metre **Stigfossen falls**.

Beyond the hairpins on the northern part of the Trollstigen, the road resumes its easy ramblings, scuttling along the **Isterdal** to meet the **E136** just 6km from Åndalsnes.

Åndalsnes

At the end of the splendid Rauma train line from Dombås (see p.233), **ÅNDALSNES** is for many travellers their first – and sometimes only – contact with the fjord country, a distinction it suits well enough. Damaged during World War II, the town centre may be modern and mundane, but it does possess a wonderful setting between lofty peaks and chill waters and, with a population of just 3500, it's small and restfully quiet. Åndalsnes is also an excellent place to start a visit to the fjordland: everything you're likely to need is near at hand, there's some economical accommodation, and the town is within easy reach by ferry, bus and/ or car of some wonderful scenery, from the stern peaks that bump and hump away inland through the fretted fjords that stretch towards the open sea.

Practicalities

Buses to Åndalsnes all stop outside the **train station**, where you'll also find the **tourist office** (mid-June to mid-Aug Mon–Fri 9am–6pm, Sat & Sun 11am–4pm; mid-Aug to mid-June Mon–Fri 9am–3.30pm; ☎71 22 16 22, ⊛www.visitandalsnes .com). Staff here provide bus and train timetables, rent mountain bikes at 180kr per day, issue regional guides and carry a wide range of local information geared to make you use Åndalsnes as a base. Their free *Dagsturer* (day-trips) booklet gives details of all sorts of motoring excursions in which most of their recommendations include a short hike. They also have details of local day-long hikes, fishing trips out on the fjord and guided climbs, not to mention fixed-rate sightseeing expeditions with Åndalsnes Taxisentral (☎71 22 15 55). Local **hiking maps** are sold at Romsdal Libris (Mon–Fri 9.30am–5pm & Sat 10am–3pm), a couple of minutes' walk northwest from the tourist office in the centre of town.

Accommodation

The tourist office has a small supply of en-suite **private rooms**, which go for 350–450kr per double per night, with self-catering facilities often provided, though most are a good walk from the town centre. Alternatively, Åndalsnes has a delightful ⚲ HI **hostel** (late May to Aug; ☎71 22 13 82, ⓦwww.vandrerhjem.no; dorm beds 260kr, doubles ❷, both including breakfast), a two-kilometre hike west out of town on the E136. To get there, head up the hill out of the centre to the roundabout, where you veer right (signed "E136 Dombås") under the flyover; keep going to the junction, where you keep straight, following the E136 in the direction of Ålesund – not Dombås; shortly afterwards, beyond the river, you'll see the sign on the right. The hostel has an attractive rural setting with open views down to the fjord and its simple rooms, set in a group of antique wooden buildings, are extremely popular, making reservations pretty much essential. The buffet-style **breakfast**, with its fresh fish, is one of the best hostellers are likely to get in the whole country, but note that the hostel doesn't do evening meals, though there are self-catering facilities. There are cycle storage, common rooms and a laundry; reception is closed from 11am to 4pm. There's one good hotel in the centre, the *Grand Hotel Bellevue* (☎71 22 75 00, ⓦwww.grandhotel.no; ❸/❺), which occupies a large whitewashed block with a distinctive, pagoda-like roof on a hillock just up from the train station. The hotel is now attached to the ultra modern Rauma Kulturhus, a combined library and theatre, which detracts from the atmosphere of the place, but the rooms are perfectly adequate in a plain sort of way and those on the top floors – four and five – have great fjord views. Among several local **campsites**, *Åndalsnes Camping og Motell* (☎71 22 16 29, ⓦwww.andalsnescamp.no) has a fine riverside setting about 3km from the town centre – follow the route to the youth hostel but turn first left immediately after the river. It's a well-equipped site with cabins (475–550kr for four persons) and it does bicycle and boat rental.

Eating

Åndalsnes is short of places to eat. The restaurant at the *Grand Hotel Bellevue* is really rather ordinary, offering standard Norwegian dishes – salad and poached salmon for example – for around 220kr per main course. Alternatively, you might try the *China House*, just up from the centre and below the *Grand*, where they serve all the Chinese classics from 130kr and up; it's open daily from noon to 10pm.

Ålesund

On the coast at the end of the E136, about 120km west of Åndalsnes, the fishing and ferry port of **ÅLESUND** is immediately – and distinctively – different from any other Norwegian town. Neither old clapboard houses nor functional concrete and glass is much in evidence, but instead the centre boasts a proud conglomeration of stone and brick, three-storey buildings, whose pastel-painted facades are lavishly decorated and topped off by a forest of towers and turrets. There are dragons and human faces, Neoclassical and mock-Gothic facades, decorative flowers and even a pharaoh or two, the whole ensemble ambling round the town's several harbours. These architectural eccentricities sprang from disaster: in 1904, a dreadful fire left

Moving on from Åndalsnes

Travelling on from Åndalsnes, there are regular **Nor-Way Bussekspress buses** west along the E136 to Ålesund (2 daily; 2hr 10min), which has good bus and ferry connections along the coast south to Bergen and north to Trondheim; Ålesund is also a port of call for the **Hurtigrute coastal boat** (see p.165). Heading southwest from Åndalsnes, a **local bus** (mid-June to Aug 2 daily; 3hr; ⓦwww.fjord1.no) negotiates the so-called "Golden Route" over the Trollstigen mountain road to Geiranger.

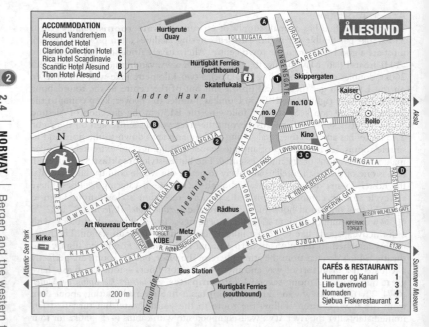

ten thousand people homeless and the town centre destroyed, but within three years a hectic reconstruction programme saw almost the entire area rebuilt in an idiosyncratic **Art Nouveau** style, which borrowed heavily from the German Jugendstil movement. Many of the Norwegian architects who undertook the work had been trained in Germany, so the Jugendstil influence is hardly surprising, but this was no simple act of plagiarism: the Norwegians added all sorts of whimsical, often folkloric flourishes to the Ålesund stew. The result was – and remains – an especially engaging stylistic hybrid, and Kaiser Wilhelm II, who footed the bill, was mightily pleased.

Arrival and information

From north to south, Ålesund's town centre is about 700m wide. The **bus station** is situated on the southern waterfront and from beside it **Hurtigbåt passenger express boats** depart for points south on the coast; northbound Hurtigbåt services leave from the Skateflukaia quay on the other side of the town centre, just metres from the quay for the **Hurtigrute coastal boat** (Ⓦwww.hurtigruten.com). Hurtigrute sailing times vary with the seasons. From mid-April to mid-September, the **northbound** Hurtigrute sails daily for Geiranger at 9.30am and for Trondheim at 6.45pm; from mid-September to mid-April, it does not call at Geiranger, but sails north to Trondheim at 3pm. **Southbound** services are, however, the same all year, with sailings to Bergen departing at 12.45am.

Ålesund's **tourist office** is also on the Skateflukaia (mid- to late June & mid- to late Aug Mon–Fri 8.30am–7pm, Sat & Sun 11am–4pm; July to mid-Aug Mon–Fri 8am–7pm, Sat & Sun 8am–6pm; Sept–May Mon–Fri 9am–4pm & Sat 10am–2pm; ☎70 15 76 00, Ⓦwww.visitalesund.com). They operate an accommodation booking service, supply free town brochures, issue a free if somewhat unrevealing leaflet describing Ålesund's architectural attractions and coordinate **guided walking tours** of the centre (mid-June to mid-Aug 1 daily; shoulder seasons 1 weekly; 1hr 30min; 75kr).

Accommodation

One of Ålesund's real pleasures is the quality of its downtown **hotels** and **guest-houses**. If your purse is showing signs of strain, however, there are other, less expensive options too, most economically an HI **hostel**.

Ålesund Vandrerhjem Parkgata 14 ☏70 11 58 30, ⓦ www.vandrerhjem.no. Small and central HI hostel in a pleasant 1920s building at the top of Rådstugata. Has a laundry, self-catering facilities and a café plus internet access. Dorm beds 245kr, doubles ❷

Brosundet Hotel Apotekergata 5 ☏70 11 45 00, ⓦ www.brosundet.no. An excellent hotel occupying an attractively converted, waterside warehouse right in the centre of town. ❹/❺

Clarion Collection Hotel Bryggen Apotekergata 1 ☏70 12 64 00, ⓦ www.choicehotels.no. Smart hotel in a carefully modernized old waterside warehouse, where the public areas are kitted out with all sorts of nautical knick-knacks. The guest rooms are set out around three internal galleries that overlook the public areas in the manner of a cruise ship – and it all works very well. ❹/❽

Rica Hotel Scandinavie Løvenvoldgata 8 ☏70 15 78 00, ⓦ www.rica.no. Exemplary chain hotel inhabiting a grand Art Nouveau edifice,

which has been sympathetically modernized, from the handsome wrought-iron work of the main doors through to the intricate friezes and medallion frescoes beyond. Has the real sniff of luxury, but unlike several of its rivals is not down by the water. ❹/❻

Scandic Hotel Ålesund Molovegen 6 ☏21 61 45 00, ⓦ www.scandichotels.com. It may be one of a chain and occupy a routine modern block, but there's something very appealing about this relaxed and friendly hotel, not least its sea and harbour views. The breakfasts are excellent – and the breakfast room overlooks the water – and the rooms are bright and cheerful, each comfortably furnished in contemporary style with the pick – once again – offering charming sea views. ❺/❻

Thon Hotel Ålesund Kongensgate 27 ☏70 12 29 38, ⓦ www.thonhotels.no. Suffers by comparison with its more atmospheric rivals, but this modern block is right in the centre and the rooms are perfectly adequate. ❹/❺

The town centre

To get better acquainted with Ålesund's architectural peccadilloes, you might begin by visiting the **Jugendstil Senteret** bang in the centre of town at Apotekergata 16 (Art Nouveau Centre: June–Aug daily 10am–5pm; Sept Mon–Fri 11am–5pm, Sat 11am–4pm & Sun noon–4pm; Oct–May Tues–Fri 11am–5pm, Sat 11am–4pm & Sun noon–4pm; 50kr, 70kr for joint ticket with KUBE, see below; ⓦ www.jugendstilsenteret.no). The Centre occupies one of the town's proudest Art Nouveau buildings, the old **apothek** (pharmacy), whose spiky tower and heavy-duty stonework lend it a decidedly neo-Baronial appearance. Inside, the ground floor is dominated by the ornate wooden display cabinets of the former pharmacy and here also is a rather gimmicky "Time Machine" in which visitors are "beamed back" to 1904 to watch a short film on the fire that ripped through Ålesund and the reconstruction that followed.

Approached via a handsome corkscrew staircase, the Centre's first floor holds a modest assortment of Art Nouveau pieces – vases, plates, furniture, jewellery and so forth – plus a magnificent, panelled dining room original to the house. Also on this floor are two more film shows, one on Art Nouveau as art, the other providing its international and socio-political context.

KUBE and Ålesund church

Adjoining the Art Nouveau Centre, in what was formerly a bank, is the town's top art gallery, **KUBE** (June–Aug daily 10am–5pm; Sept–May Tues–Fri 11am–5pm, Sat 11am–4pm & Sun noon–4pm; 50kr, 70kr joint ticket with the Jugendstil Senteret), whose temporary displays focus on contemporary art, architecture and design.

From KUBE, it's just a few metres to Kirkegata, probably Ålesund's most harmonious street, its long line of Art Nouveau houses decorated with playful turrets and towers reminiscent of a Ruritanian film set. Up along this street stands the town's finest building, its church (June–Aug Tues–Sun 10am–2pm; free), which was completed in 1909 to a decidedly Romanesque design, from the hooped windows through to the roughly dressed stone blocks and the clunky tower.

Kongensgate and around

From the church, it's a few minutes' walk across town to Ålesund's main drag, pedestrianized **Kongensgate**, which is flanked by a string of Art Nouveau buildings. It's the whole ensemble that impresses most, but one or two are of special note, particularly the whimsical medieval tower, hooped windows and geometrical friezes of the Skippergaten, at no. 18. There's more ersatz medievalism round the corner on Løvenvoldgata, where the Kino (cinema) is housed in a large and lugubrious stone tower topped by a cutesy cupola.

Architecture aside, the other obvious objectives in the town centre are the main harbour, with its assorted ferries and yachts coming and going, and the pretty little park at the top of Lihauggata, which runs up from Kongensgate. It's a surprise to find monkey puzzle and copper beech trees here, as well as a large statue of **Rollo**, a Viking chieftain born and raised in Ålesund, who seized Normandy and became its first duke in 911. Rollo was an ancestor of William the Conqueror, the epitome of the Norman baron and thus evidence of the speed with which the Vikings were absorbed into their host communities. From the park, several hundred steps lead to the top of the **Aksla hill**, where the view out along the coast and its islands is nothing short of fabulous.

Eating and drinking

For a town of just forty thousand, Ålesund does well for cafés and restaurants, with the pick all within a stone's throw of the main harbour. If it's hot, anyone and everyone heads down to the harbourside terrace of the *Metz* pub.

Hummer og Kanari Kongensgate 19 ⑦70 12 80 08. Relaxed and amenable café-restaurant, where they serve up a good line in seafood at around 220–280kr per main course. Also a good place to try a Norwegian favourite, *klippfisk* (salted-and-dried cod) cooked every which way and costing about 250kr. After the kitchen closes down – at about 9.30pm – the place turns into one of the grooviest bars in town. Mon–Fri 4pm till late, Sat & Sun from 2pm.

Lille Løvenvold Løvenvoldgata 2. Grooviest café in town, attracting a mixed but (nearly always) cool crew, who sip away at the best coffee in town. New Age-meets-lighter-shade-of-Goth decor in a rabbit warren of rooms. Mon–Sat 11am–11pm, sometimes later, Sun 2–11pm.

Nomaden Apotekergata 10. Tasty sandwiches, light meals, coffees and cakes in this cosy little café, where the decor is vaguely Edwardian – antique cupboards and so forth – with prints and paintings on the walls. Smooth, jazzy background music too. Great cheesecake. Mon–Sat 11am–4pm.

Sjøbua Fiskerestaurant Brunholmgata 1 ⑦70 12 71 00. Smart, fairly formal restaurant serving an outstanding range of seafood from its harbourside cellar premises. They even have their own lobster tank – something of a rarity in Norway. It's expensive, with main courses hovering around 300kr, but very popular, so reservations are advised. Mon–Fri 4–11pm.

Travel details

Principal Nor-Way Bussekspress buses (ⓦ www.nor-way.no)

Ålesund to: Åndalsnes (2 daily; 2hr 10min); Bergen (1–2 daily; 10hr 30min); Hellesylt (1–2 daily; 2hr 45min); Oslo (2 daily; 10hr); Stryn (2–3 daily; 3hr 20min); Trondheim (3 daily; 7hr).

Åndalsnes to: Ålesund (2 daily; 2hr 10min).

Balestrand to: Oslo (3 daily; 8hr 30min); Sogndal (3 daily; 1hr 30min).

Bergen to: Ålesund (1–2 daily; 10hr 30min); Flåm (4–5 daily; 3hr); Hellesylt (1–2 daily; 7hr 45min); Langvatn (2 daily; 8hr); Loen (3–4 daily; 6hr 30min); Lom (2 daily; 9hr); Norheimsund (1–3 daily; 1hr 30min); Odda (1–3 daily; 3hr 30min); Oslo (3 daily; 10hr 30min); Otta (3 daily; 10hr); Skei (3–5 daily; 5hr 15min); Sogndal (4–5 daily; 4hr 30min); Stavanger (every 1–2hr; 5hr, 5hr 45min via Haugesund); Stryn (3–4 daily; 7hr); Trondheim (1 daily; 14hr); Utne (1–3 daily; 2hr 50min); Voss (4–5 daily; 1hr 50min).

Kristiansund to: Oslo (1 daily; 11hr).

Mundal to: Oslo (3 daily; 7hr 50min); Sogndal (3 daily; 30min).

Sogndal to: Balestrand (3 daily; 1hr 15min); Bergen (4–5 daily; 4hr 30min); Mundal (3 daily; 30min); Oslo (3 daily; 7hr); Voss (4–5 daily; 2hr 40min).

Stryn to: Bergen (3–4 daily; 7hr); Hellesylt (1–2 daily; 1hr); Oslo (3 daily; 9hr); Trondheim (1 daily; 7hr 30min).

Voss to: Bergen (4–5 daily; 1hr 50min); Flåm (4–5 daily; 1hr); Sogndal (4–5 daily; 2hr 50min).

Principal local bus services

Åndalsnes to: Geiranger (mid-June to Aug 2 daily; 3hr).

Geiranger to: Åndalsnes (mid-June to Aug 2 daily; 3hr).

Lom to: Sogndal (late June to Aug 2 daily; 3hr 30min); Turtagrø (late June to Aug 2 daily; 1hr 45min).

Sogndal to: Lom (late June to Aug 2 daily; 3hr 30min); Nigardsbreen glacier nodule (July & Aug 1 daily; 2hr); Otta (late June to Aug 2 daily; 5hr); Solvorn (July & Aug 1–3 daily; rest of year 2–3 daily, but no Sat service; 30min); Turtagrø (late June to Aug 2 daily; 1hr 50min).

Car ferries

There are two main operators – Tide (ⓦ www .tide.no) and Fjord 1 (ⓦ www.fjord1.no). Principal services include:

Balestrand to: Mundal on the Fjærlandsfjord (May to Sept 4 daily; 1hr 30min).

Bruravik to: Brimnes (1–2 hourly; 10min).

Dragsvik to: Hella (every 40min to hourly; 15min); Vangsnes (every 40min to hourly; 30min).

Fodnes to: Mannheller (every 20min, hourly midnight to 6am; 10min).

Geiranger to: Hellesylt (May to mid-Oct 4–8 daily; 1hr).

Hella to: Dragsvik (every 40min to hourly; 15min); Vangsnes (every 40min to hourly; 30min).

Kvanndal to: Kinsarvik (1 or 2 hourly; 50min); Utne (1 or 2 hourly; 20min).

Hellesylt to: Geiranger (May to mid-Oct 4–8 daily; 1hr).

Utne to: Kinsarvik (1 or 2 hourly; 30min).

Principal Hurtigbåt passenger express boats

There are two main operators – Tide (ⓦ www .tide.no) and Fjord 1 (ⓦ www.fjord1.no). Principal services include:

Balestrand to: Bergen (1–3 daily; 4hr); Flåm (May–Sept 1–2 daily; 1hr 30min).

Bergen to: Ålesund (Mon–Fri 1 daily; 8hr 30min); Balestrand (1–3 daily; 4hr); Flåm (May–Sept 1–2 daily; 5hr 40min); Sogndal (1–3 daily; 5hr); Stavanger (1–2 daily; 5hr 30min).

Flåm to: Balestrand (May–Sept 1–2 daily; 1hr 30min).

Norheimsund to: Eldfjord (May–Sept 1 daily; 2hr 45min); Kinsarvik (May–Sept 1 daily; 1hr 30min); Lofthus (May–Sept 1 daily; 1hr 10min); Utne (May–Sept 1 daily; 50min).

Hurtigrute coastal boat

Summertime (mid-April to mid-Sept):

Northbound departures: daily from Bergen at 8pm; Ålesund at 9.30am for Geiranger & 6.45pm for Molde; Geiranger at 1.30pm; arrives Trondheim at 8.15am.

Southbound departures: daily from Trondheim at 10am; Ålesund at 12.45am; arrives Bergen, where the service terminates, at 2.30pm.

Wintertime (mid-Sept to mid-April):

Northbound departures: daily from Bergen at 10.30pm; Ålesund at 3pm; Molde at 6.30pm; arrives Trondheim at 6am.

Southbound departures: daily from Trondheim at 10am; Ålesund at 12.45am; arrives Bergen, where the service terminates, at 2.30pm.

Note: that it's only the northbound, summertime Hurtigrute service that detours to Geiranger.

2.5

Trondheim to the Lofoten Islands

arking the transition from the rural south to the blustery north is the 900-kilometre-long stretch of Norway that extends from **Trondheim** to the island-studded coast near Narvik. Easily the biggest town hereabouts is **Trondheim**, Norway's third city, a charming place of character and vitality, which has an imposing cathedral – the finest medieval building in the country. Trondheim is also the capital of the **Trøndelag** province, whose sweeping valleys are – by Norwegian standards at least – very fertile, and is readily accessible by train, plane and bus from Oslo. Push on north and you begin to feel far removed from the capital and the more intimate, forested south. Distances between places grow ever greater, travelling becomes more of a slog, and as Trøndelag gives way to the province of **Nordland** the scenery becomes ever wilder and more forbidding – "Arthurian", thought Evelyn Waugh. The **E6** and the train line thrash north from Trondheim over the hills and down the dales, but with the exception of the rugged landscape there's not much to detain you until you reach **Mo-i-Rana**, industrial perhaps but attractively sited beside the Ranafjord and partly rejigged to attract passing tourists. Just north of Mo-i-Rana on the E6, you cross the **Arctic Circle** – one of the principal targets for many travellers – at a point where the cruel and barren scenery seems strikingly appropriate. On the Arctic Circle, the midnight sun and 24-hour polar night occur once a year, at the summer and winter solstices respectively; the further north you go from here, the longer these two phenomena last (see box, p.328).

Beyond the Arctic Circle, the mountains of the interior lead down to a fretted, craggy coastline, and even the towns, the largest of which is the port of **Bodø**, have a feral quality about them. The iron-ore port of **Narvik**, in the far north of Nordland, has perhaps the wildest setting of them all, and was the scene of some of the fiercest fighting between the Allied and Axis forces in World War II. To the west lies the offshore archipelago that makes up the **Vesterålen** and **Lofoten Islands**. In the north of the Vesterålen, between **Harstad** and **Andenes**, the coastline of this island chain is mauled by massive fjords, whereas to the south, the Lofoten Islands are backboned by a mighty and ravishingly beautiful mountain wall – a highlight of any itinerary. Among a handful of idyllic fishing villages in the Lofoten the pick is the tersely named **Å**, though **Henningsvær** and **Stamsund** come a very close second.

Art in Nordland

Dotted across the province of Nordland are 33 open-air **sculptures** by some of the world's leading contemporary sculptors, including Dorothy Cross, Anish Kapoor, Antony Gormley and Inge Mahn. Together these sculptures comprise the **Skulpturlandskap** (Ⓦ www.skulpturlandskap.no) and although many of the sculptures are in remote, even obscure locations, others – like Gormley's *Havmannen* in Mo-i-Rana (see p.297) – are more likely to crop up on your route.

The **E6**, or "Arctic Highway", is the main road north from Trondheim: it's kept in excellent condition, though in summer motor homes and caravans can make the going frustratingly slow. **Public transport** is good, which is just as well given the isolated nature of much of the region. The **Hurtigrute** coastal boat stops at all the major settlements on its route up the Norwegian coast from Bergen to Kirkenes, while the islands are accessed by a variety of **car ferries** and **Hurtigbåt passenger express boats**. The **train** network reaches as far north as Fauske and nearby Bodø, from both of which **buses** connect with Narvik, itself the terminal of a separate rail line – the **Ofotbanen** – that runs the few kilometres to the border and then south through Sweden. The only real problem is likely to be **time**: it's a day or two's journey from Trondheim to Fauske, and another day from there to Narvik. In fact, unless you've several days to spare, you should think twice before venturing further north: the travelling can be arduous, and is really pretty pointless if done at a hectic pace.

Trondheim

An atmospheric city with much of its nineteenth-century centre still intact, **TRONDHEIM** was known until the 1500s as Nidaros ("mouth of the river Nid"), its importance as a military and economic power base underpinned by the excellence of its harbour and its position at the head of a wide and fertile valley. A fire destroyed almost all of medieval Trondheim in 1681 and the city was rebuilt on a grid plan, with broad avenues radiating from the centre to act as firebreaks. This layout has survived pretty much untouched, giving today's city centre an airy, open feel, though the buildings themselves mostly date from the commercial boom of the late nineteenth century. Amongst them are scores of doughty stone structures that were built to impress and a handsome set of old timber warehouses that line up along the river. Together, they provide a suitably expansive setting for the **cathedral**, one of Scandinavia's finest medieval structures.

With a population of around 160,000, Trondheim is now Norway's third city, but the pace of life here is slow and easy, and the main **sights** are best appreciated in leisurely fashion over a couple of days. Genial and eminently likeable, Trondheim is also a pleasant place to wave goodbye to city life before heading for the wilds of the north.

Arrival

Trondheim is on the E6 highway, a seven- or eight-hour drive (500km) from Oslo. In the city centre, on-street **parking** during restricted periods (Mon–Fri 8am–8pm, Sat 8am–3pm) is expensive (20kr per hour) and hard to find, but is otherwise free with spaces commonplace. During restricted periods, you're best off heading for a car park: try the handy Torget P-hus, in the centre at Erling Skakkes gate 16 (Mon–Fri 7am–9pm & Sat 7am–7pm); or the Bakke P-hus, east across the bridge from the centre at Nedre Bakklandet 60 (Mon–Fri 6.30am–11pm & Sat 6.30am–9pm). Car-park rates are 15kr per hour up to a maximum of 150kr in any 24-hour period.

The city's combined bus and train terminal, **Sentralstasjon**, is on the northern edge of the centre, a ten-minute walk from the main square, Torvet. Inside, an **information** kiosk (☏177) deals with all local transport enquiries. The year-round **Kystekspressen** (ⓦwww.kystekspressen.no) passenger express boat from Kristiansund docks at the Pirterminalen, from where it's a dull fifteen-minute walk south to Sentralstasjon. The quay for the **Hurtigrute coastal boat** (ⓦwww .hurtigruten.no) is near the Pirterminalen, another 300m or so away to the north. Local buses #2 and #46 run from the Pirabadet swimming pool, in between the two quays, to **Sentralstasjon**.

Trondheim **airport** is 35km northeast of the city centre at Værnes. From here, Flybussen (Mon–Fri 4am–8.30pm every 15min; Sat 4am–6pm every 30min; Sun 4am–9pm every 15–30min; 45min; 90kr) run to Sentralstasjon and various points in the city centre, including the *SAS Royal Garden Hotel*.

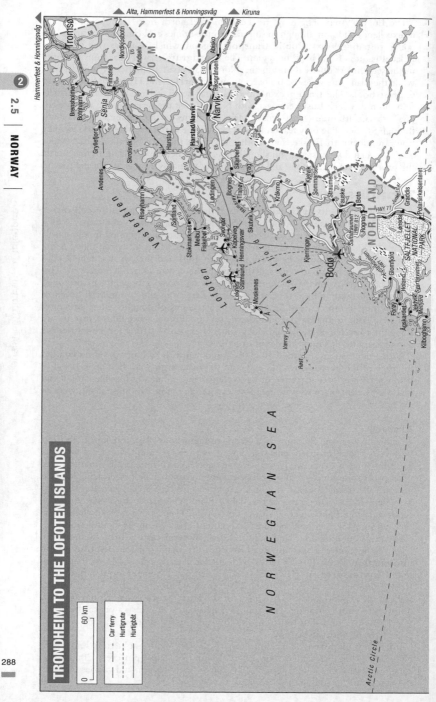

TRONDHEIM TO THE LOFOTEN ISLANDS

0   60 km

— · — Car ferry
— — — Hurtigrute
——— Hurtigbåt

Hammerfest & Honningsvåg

Alta, Hammerfest & Honningsvåg   Kiruna

Tromsø
E8
Nordkjosbotn
Brensholmen
Botnhamn
Finnsnes
Andselv
T R O M S
Senja
Gryllefjord
Skrolsvik
Harstad
Abisko
E6
Riksgränsen
Narvik
Ofotbanen (Railway)
Andenes
Risøyhamn
E10
Harstad/Narvik
E6
Sortland
Lødingen
Skårberget
Drag
V e s t e r å l e n
Melbu
Fiskebøl
Bognes
Tranøy
Krákmo
93
Kjelvik
Stokmarknes
E10
Svolvær
Skutvik
Sommarset
Straumen
Kåpelveg
Honningsvær
Storvik
Fauske
Botn
NORDLAND
Leknes
Stamsund
V e s t f j o r d
Kjerringøy
Saltstraumen RV 812
Rognan
RV 77
Graddis
Moskenes
Bodø
Holand
SALTFJELLET
NATIONAL
PARK
Lønsdal
Polarsirkelsenteret
Å
Føvy
Glomfjord
Værøy
Ørnes
Kilboghamn
Agskardet
Kvarnsvatnet
Mefjorda
Røst
L o f o t e n

N O R W E G I A N   S E A

Arctic Circle

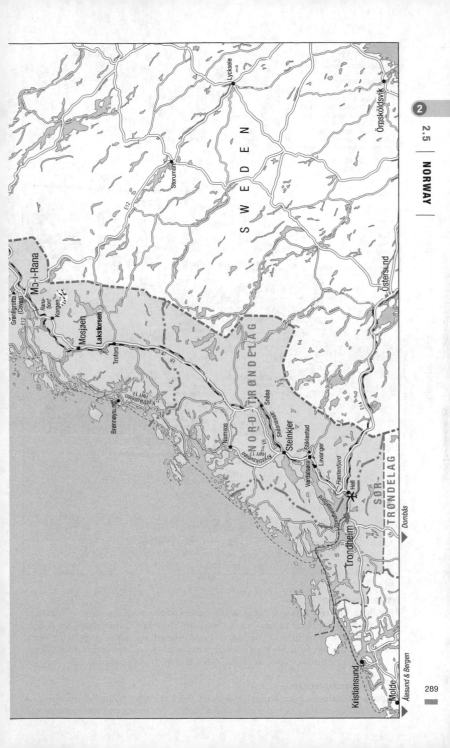

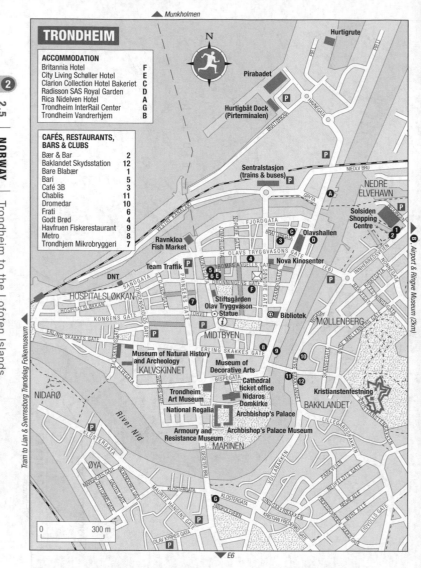

TRONDHEIM

ACCOMMODATION
Britannia Hotel	F
City Living Schøller Hotel	E
Clarion Collection Hotel Bakeriet	C
Radisson SAS Royal Garden	D
Rica Nidelven Hotel	A
Trondheim InterRail Center	G
Trondheim Vandrerhjem	B

CAFÉS, RESTAURANTS, BARS & CLUBS
Bær & Bar	2
Baklandet Skydsstation	12
Bare Blabær	1
Bari	5
Café 3B	3
Chablis	11
Dromedar	10
Frati	6
Godt Brød	4
Havfruen Fiskerestaurant	9
Metro	8
Trondhjem Mikrobryggeri	7

Information

Trondheim **tourist office** is bang in the centre of town on the edge of Torvet at Munkegata 19 (late May to late June & late Aug Mon–Fri 8.30am–6pm, Sat & Sun 10am–4pm; late June to mid-Aug Mon–Fri 8.30am–8pm, Sat & Sun 10am–6pm; early Aug Mon–Fri 8.30am–10pm, Sat & Sun 10am–8pm; Sept to late May Mon–Fri 9am–4pm, Sat 10am–2pm; ☎73 80 76 60, ⓦwww.trondheim.no).

Accommodation

Accommodation is plentiful in Trondheim, with a choice of private rooms, two hostels, and a selection of reasonably priced hotels. What's more, most of the more appealing places are dotted round the city centre, which is precisely where you want to be. The exception is the private rooms booked via the tourist office, which are usually out in the suburbs. These **private rooms** are good value at around 500–600kr per double per night (400–500kr single), plus a small booking fee.

Hotels

Britannia Hotel Dronningens gate 5 ☎73 80 08 00, ⓦwww.britannia.no. Right in the middle of town, this long-established hotel has a splendid, bright-white façade that dates back to the nineteenth century. Inside, a couple of the public rooms have splendid wood panelling and the breakfast room comes complete with a Moorish fountain, Egyptian-style murals and Corinthian columns. The well-appointed bedrooms manage to be both unfussy and cosy with browns and creams to the fore. ⑥/⑧

City Living Schøller Hotel Dronningens gate 26 ☎73 87 08 00, ⓦwww.cityliving.no. Economy chain hotel above shops in the centre of the city. The modern rooms are spick-and-span verging on the spartan, but the price is right. ②/③

Clarion Collection Hotel Bakeriet Brattørgata 2 ☎73 99 10 00, ⓦwww.choicehotels .no. Competent chain hotel in an intelligently revamped former bakery. The guest rooms, which were once occupied by the bakery workers, are kitted out in standard modern style. Central location. ④/⑥

Radisson SAS Royal Garden Kjøpmannsgata 73 ☎73 80 30 00, ⓦwww.radissonsas.com. Full marks to the architects here, who have designed this large, modern, riverside hotel in the style of the old timber warehouses that it replaced. Lots of glass – indeed the interior of the hotel looks a bit like a series of enormous greenhouses – but the rooms themselves can feel a bit frumpy. Banquet-like breakfasts. ④/⑥

🏃 **Rica Nidelven Hotel** Havnegata 1–3 ☎73 56 80 00, ⓦwww.rica.no. Large and flashy chain hotel nudging out into the river with lots of glass to maximize views. The public areas are bold and expansive – Modernism at its most decisive – but the guest rooms are not perhaps quite as distinctive as they could be. Every facility. ⑤/⑧

Guesthouses, hostels and camping

Trondheim InterRail Center Elgeseter gate 1 ☎73 89 95 38, ⓦwww.tirc.no. Bargain-basement lodgings in the unusual, big red round building – the Studentersamfundet (university student centre) – that stands just over the bridge at the south end of Prinsens gate, a 5min walk from the cathedral. Offers basic mixed-dorm accommodation at 150kr per person per night and breakfast is served in the downstairs café. No curfew. Internet access. Open early July to mid-Aug only.

Trondheim Vandrerhjem Weidemannsveien 41 ☎73 87 44 50, ⓦwww.trondheim-vandrerhjem .no. This large, well-equipped hostel is mostly parcelled up into four-bed dorm rooms, only a few of which are en suite. Looks more like a hospital than somewhere you'd want to stay from the outside, but the interior is pleasant enough – especially the comfortable, newer rooms. It has self-catering facilities, a laundry and a canteen. A 20min, 2km hike east from the centre: cross the Bakke bru (bridge) onto busy Innherredsveien (the E6) and walk uphill; turn right onto Wessels gate and hang a left at the fourth crossroads. To save your legs, take any bus up Innherredsveien and ask the driver to let you off as close as possible. Open all year. Dorm beds 230kr, doubles ②

The city centre

The historic **centre of Trondheim** sits on a small triangle of land bordered by a loop of the Nid River, with the sweep of the long and slender Trondheimsfjord beyond. **Torvet** is the main city square, a spacious open area anchored by a statue of Olav Tryggvason perched high on the top of his column. The broad avenues that radiate out from here were once flanked by long rows of wooden buildings, which served all the needs of a small town and administrative centre. Most of these older structures are long gone, replaced for the most part by uninspiring modern buildings, though one notable survivor is the **Stiftsgården**, a fine timber mansion erected in 1774. Nonetheless, this is small beer when compared with the **Nidaros Domkirke** (Cathedral), an imposing, largely medieval structure that is the city's architectural high point. The cathedral dominates the southern part of the centre and close by is the much-restored Erkebispegården (Archbishop's Palace) as well as the pick of Trondheim's several museums, the Nordenfjeldske Kunstindustrimuseum

(Museum of Decorative Arts) and the Trondheim Kunstmuseum (City Art Gallery). Near here too, on the far side of the **Gamle Bybro** – the old town bridge – is the clutter of old warehouses and timber dwellings that comprises the prettiest and most fashionable part of town, **Bakklandet**, home to some of its best bars and restaurants.

Nidaros Cathedral

The goal of Trondheim's pilgrims in times past was the rambling **Nidaros Domkirke**, whose copper-green spire and multiple roofs lord it over the south end of Munkegata (Cathedral: May to early June & mid-Aug to mid-Sept Mon–Fri 9am–3pm, Sat 9am–2pm & Sun 1–4pm; early June to mid-Aug Mon–Fri 9am–6pm, Sat 9am–2pm & Sun 1–4pm; mid-Sept to April Mon–Fri noon–2.30pm, Sat 11.30am–2pm & Sun 1–3pm; 50kr, combined ticket with Erkebispegården 100kr; Ⓦwww.nidarosdomen.no). Gloriously restored following several fires and the upheavals of the Reformation, the cathedral, which is dedicated to the Viking-turned-Christian St Olav, remains the focal point of any visit to the city and is best explored in the early morning, when it's reasonably free of tour groups. In the summer, there are free English-language **guided tours** (mid-June to mid-Aug 4 daily; 30min) and you can climb the cathedral tower for a panoramic view over the city and its surroundings (mid-June to mid-Aug Mon–Fri 10am–5pm, Sat 10am–12.30pm, Sun 1–3.30pm).

The crowning glory of this magnificent blue- and green-grey soapstone edifice is its west façade, a soaring cliff-face of finely worked stone sporting a magnificent rose window, rank after rank of pointed arches, biblical, religious and royal figures by the dozen and a fancy set of gargoyles. The west facade and the nave behind may look medieval, but date from the nineteenth century: the originals were erected in the early Gothic style of the early thirteenth century, but they were destroyed by fire in 1719 and what you see today is a painstakingly accurate reconstruction. The fire did not, however, raze the Romanesque transepts, whose heavy hooped windows and dog-tooth decoration were the work of English stonemasons in the twelfth century.

Inside, the gloomy half-light hides much of the lofty decorative work, but it is possible to examine the strikingly ascetic early twentieth-century **choir screen**, whose wooden figures are the work of Gustav Vigeland (see p.198). Vigeland was

▲ Trondheim Cathedral

also responsible for the adjacent soapstone **font**, a superb piece of medievalism sporting four biblical bas-reliefs. What you won't see now is the object of the medieval pilgrims' veneration: St Olav's silver casket-coffin was taken to Denmark and unceremoniously melted down for coinage in 1537.

Archbishop's Palace

Behind the cathedral stands the heavily restored **Erkebispegården** (Archbishop's Palace), a courtyard complex that was originally built in the twelfth century for the third archbishop, Øystein, though two stone-and-brick wings are all that survive of the medieval quadrangle – the other two wings were added later. After the archbishops were kicked out during the Reformation, the palace became the residence of the Danish governors. It was subsequently used as the city armoury, and many of the old weapons are now displayed in the west wing in the **Armoury and Resistance Museum**, though the museum's most interesting displays deal with the German occupation of World War II. Next door, also in the west wing, the Norwegian crown jewels are exhibited in the **National Regalia**, not that there's actually much to see, whilst the south wing chips in with the medieval sculptures of the **Archbishop's Palace Museum**.

Norway's crown jewels, the **Riksregaliene** (National Regalia: May to early June & early Aug to mid-Sept Mon–Sat 10am–3pm & Sun noon–4pm; early June to early Aug Mon–Fri 10am–5pm, Sat 10am–3pm & Sun noon–4pm; mid-Sept to April Tues–Sat 11am–3pm & Sun noon–4pm; 70kr, combined ticket for cathedral and Erkebispegården 100k), are displayed in the basement of the first part of the Erkebispegården's west wing. At the end of the Napoleonic Wars, Britain and her allies forced Denmark to cede Norway to Sweden (see p.654). The Swedish king was himself new to the throne and although he received Norway as a welcome bonus, he was deemed to be a ruler of two kingdoms rather than one. Sweden already had its own crown jewels, but Norway, which hadn't been independent for centuries, had nothing at all. As a consequence, Bernadotte, now Karl IV Johan, scuttled around Stockholm ordering a new set of crown jewels in preparation for his coronation in Trondheim. The results are on display here, principally a crown, a sceptre, an orb and a tiny anointing horn, all made in the 1810s. Another set of ceremonial gear was made for the queen, but it's still a very thin collection. The last Norwegian coronation took place here in Trondheim cathedral in 1906 on the accession of Håkon VII, but his successors – Olav V and Harald V – elected for benedictions instead, in 1958 and 1991 respectively.

The extensive **Rustkammeret med Hjemmefrontmuseet** (Armoury and Resistance Museum: June–Aug Mon–Fri 9am–3pm, Sat & Sun 11am–4pm; free) spreads over two main floors. The **first floor** gives the broad details of Norway's involvement in the interminable **Dano–Swedish wars** that racked Scandinavia from the fifteenth to the nineteenth century. Of more general interest, the **second floor** describes the German invasion and occupation of **World War II**, dealing honestly with the sensitive issue of collaboration. In particular, you can hear **Vidkun Quisling**'s broadcast announcing – in a disarmingly squeaky voice – his coup d'état of April 9, 1940. There are also some intriguing displays on the daring antics of the Norwegian Resistance, notably an extraordinary – perhaps hare-brained – attempt to sink the battleship *Tirpitz* as it lay moored in an inlet of the Trondheimsfjord in 1942.

The **south wing** of the old Archbishop's Palace holds the **Museet Erkebispegården** (Archbishop's Palace Museum: May to early June & early Aug to mid-Sept Mon–Sat 10am–3pm & Sun noon–4pm; early June to early Aug Mon–Fri 10am–5pm, Sat 10am–3pm & Sun noon–4pm; mid-Sept to April Tues–Sat 11am–3pm & Sun noon–4pm; 50kr, combined ticket for Cathedral and Archbishop's Palace 100k), which is largely devoted to a few dozen medieval statues retrieved and put away for safekeeping during the nineteenth-century reconstruction of the cathedral's nave and west facade. Many of the statues are too battered and bruised to be engaging, but they are well displayed and several are finely carved.

Trondheim Art Museum

Metres from the cathedral, at Bispegata 7B, the **Trondheim Kunstmuseum** (Trondheim Art museum: June to late Aug daily 10am–5pm; rest of year Tues–Sun 11am–4pm; 50kr; @www.tkm.museum.no) is perhaps best known for its temporary exhibitions of contemporary art. The downside is that these exhibitions often leave little space for the museum's permanent collection, which features a particularly enjoyable selection of Norwegian paintings from 1850 onwards. The museum also owns the first overtly political work by a Norwegian artist, *The Strike (Streik)*, painted in 1877 by the radical Theodor Kittelsen (1857–1914), who is better known for his illustrations of the folk tales collected by Jorgen Moe and Peder Asbjørnsen. Additionally, the museum possesses a substantial selection of Munch woodcuts, sketches and lithographs, including several of those disturbing, erotically charged personifications of emotions – *Lust, Fear* and *Jealousy* – that are so characteristic of his oeuvre. However, after the theft of the Munch paintings in Oslo (see p.199), the museum has become notably chary about displaying its Munch pieces, so you'll never see many at any one time.

The National Museum of Decorative Arts

The **Nordenfjeldske Kunstindustrimuseum** delightful is a couple of minutes' walk north from the cathedral at Munkegata 5 (National Museum of Decorative Arts: June to late Aug Mon–Sat 10am–5pm, Sun noon–5pm; late Aug to May Tues–Wed & Fri–Sat 10am–3pm, Thurs 10am–5pm, Sun noon–4pm; 60kr; @www.nkim.museum.no). The museum has a wide-ranging permanent collection, but it's too extensive to be shown in its entirety at any one time and so the exhibits are regularly rotated. Start in the **basement**, where the historical collection illustrates bourgeois life in Trøndelag from 1500 to 1900 by means of an eclectic assemblage of furniture, faïence, glassware and silver. The modern collection follows on, featuring a small but well-chosen international selection of Arts and Crafts and Art Nouveau pieces, from glass, ceramics and textiles through to furniture – there's even an immaculate William Morris chair. The domestic theme is developed on the **ground floor**, where one small room has been kitted out with early 1950s furnishings and fittings by the Danish designer Finn Juhl and a second room does the same with the work of the Belgian designer and architect **Henri van de Velde** (1863–1957).

On the **first floor**, fourteen wonderful tapestries by **Hannah Ryggen** occupy an entire room. Born in Malmø in 1894, Ryggen moved to the Trondheim area in the early 1920s and stayed until her death in 1970. Her tapestries are classically naive, the forceful colours and absence of perspective emphasizing the feeling behind them. This is committed art at its best, railing in the 1930s and 1940s against Hitler and Fascism, later moving on to more disparate targets such as the atom bomb and social conformism. But Ryggen still made time to celebrate the things she cherished: *Yes, we love this country* (tapestry no. 11) is as evocative a portrayal of her adopted land as you're likely to find.

Torvet

Metres from the National Museum of Decorative Arts, **Torvet** is the main city square, a spacious open area anchored by a statue of Olav Tryggvason (c.968–1000), Trondheim's founder, perched on a tall stone pillar like some medieval Nelson. Tryggvason is kitted out in a full set of chain mail with helmet and sword, and has one arm outstretched presenting an orb, the symbol of monarchical power. One of the foremost warriors of his time, Tryggvason cut his Viking spurs in a series of piratical raids before wresting control of most of Norway, though his brutal imposition of Christianity infuriated many of his subjects and after just five years as king, he was ambushed and killed. One of his feats was to found Trondheim in 997, but ironically – considering the statue that dominates Torvet – the Tronders were determined to hang onto their pagan gods and were especially hacked off by Olav's bloody attempts to force them to be Christians.

The Stiftsgården

One conspicuous remnant of old timber-town Trondheim survives in the city centre – the **Stiftsgården**, which stretches out along Munkegata just north of Torvet (guided tours every hour on the hour till 1hr before closing: June to late Aug Mon–Sat 10am–5pm, Sun noon–5pm; 60kr). Built in 1774–78, this good-looking yellow structure is claimed to be the largest wooden building in northern Europe. These days it serves as an official royal residence, a marked social improvement on its original function as the home of the provincial governor. Inside, a long string of period rooms illustrates the genteel tastes of the mansion's late eighteenth- to early nineteenth-century occupants with a wide range of styles, from Rococo to Biedermeierstil, but it's the fanciful Italianate wall paintings that steal the decorative show. The obligatory anecdotal guided tour brings a smile or two – but not perhaps 60kr wide.

North to the Ravnkloa

If the **Stiftsgården** has wetted your appetite for old wooden buildings, then you'll enjoy the tangle of narrow alleys and pastel-painted clapboard frontages that fills out the side streets just **north of Kongens gate** and west of Prinsens gate. There's nothing special to look at, but it's a pleasant area for a stroll, after which you can wander over to **Ravnkloa**, the jetty at the north end of Munkegata and the site of the fish market (Mon–Fri 10am–5pm & Sat 10am–4pm).

To Nedre Elvehavn, Bakklandet and the Kristianstenfestning fortress

From Ravnkloa, it's a few minutes' walk east to the slender footbridge that spans the river to link Havnegata with **Nedre Elvehavn**, where the former shipyard has been turned into a leisure and shopping complex that trundles along beside the old quays. This is one of the busiest parts of the city, thronged with revellers every summer weekend, and from here you can stroll along the east side of the river down to the next bridge along, Bakke bru. Beyond this second bridge is tiny **Bakklandet**, Trondheim's own "Left Bank", a one-time working-class district of brightly painted timber houses that now holds a battery of cafés and restaurants, including some of the best in town. Bakklandet abuts the **Old Town Bridge** (Gamle Bybro), a quaint wooden structure offering splendid views over **Kjøpmannsgata**'s eighteenth-century gabled and timbered warehouses, now mostly restaurants and offices. In the opposite direction from the bridge, Brubakken leads up the hill from Bakklandet to Kristianstensbakken and the **Kristianstenfestning** fortress (June–Aug daily 11am–4pm; free), dating from 1681 and providing wide views back over Trondheim. The earth and stone fortifications have survived in reasonably good condition here as have several of the old buildings. During the war, this was where the Germans tortured their prisoners, many of whom had been betrayed by Arthur Rinnan, a clever and sadistic Norwegian collaborator who was executed in 1947.

From the Gamle Bybro, it's a couple of minutes' walk back to the cathedral.

Eating and drinking

Trondheim has a good selection of first-rate **restaurants** serving a variety of cuisines, though the Norwegian places almost always have the gastronomic edge. In particular, there's a couple of especially fine restaurants in the **Bakklandet** district, by the eastern end of Gamle Bybro, and a third at the south end of neighbouring Kjøpmannsgata. Bars are found all over the city centre, but the weekend scene is at its liveliest on and around Brattørgata and in the **Nedre Elvehavn** district, where the former municipal shipyard has been turned into a large leisure complex of shops, bars and restaurants.

Cafés and café-bars

Dromedar Nedre Bakklandet 3A. Laid-back, cosy, cramped coffee bar in antique wooden premises a few metres north of the Gamle Bybro. Arguably the best coffee in town plus snacks and light meals – filled bagels, sandwiches etc – at bargain prices. One of a small chain. Mon–Fri 7am–7pm, Sat 10am–7pm & Sun 11am–7pm.

Godt Brød Thomas Angells gate 16. The aroma of baking bread, rolls and pastries, all organic, wafts around this cosy little café-cum-bakery, where the coffee is good and the breads and pastries even better. Sandwiches made to order too. Daily except Sun 6am–6pm.

Restaurants

Baklandet Skydsstation Øvre Bakklandet 33 ☎ 73 92 10 44. Friendly, intimate former coaching inn with a warren of homely dining rooms and a small courtyard. A reasonably priced menu with mains from as little as 200kr features home-cooked staples such as that old Norwegian favourite *bacalao* (dried-and salted-cod), and an earth-moving cheesecake. Daily noon–1am.

Bare Blabær Innherredsveien 16, Nedre Elvehavn. The excellent-value, stone-baked pizzas at this fast-moving café-restaurant make it very popular with a youthful clientele. Pizzas from 90kr. Daily 11am–1am.

Chablis Øvre Bakklandet 66 ☎ 73 87 42 50. Just metres from the Gamle Bybro, this polished restaurant, with its modish furnishings and fittings, features a creative menu in which traditional Norwegian ingredients – fish, pork and so forth – are served with the unexpected, like cod with a lentil and bacon ragout. In summertime, you can eat outside on a floating pontoon that's moored on the river. Main courses hover around 290kr. Open Mon–Sat 5–11pm.

Frati Munkegata 25 ☎ 73 52 57 33. Much favoured by locals, this traditional, family-run Italian restaurant serves all the classics in plentiful and authentic portions. Above a bar. Main courses from 140kr. Mon–Fri 3–11pm, Sat & Sun 2–11pm.

Havfruen Fiskerestaurant Kjøpmannsgata 7 ☎ 73 87 40 70. In an old and cleverly refashioned riverside warehouse, this smart and extremely popular seafood restaurant is one of the best in town with main courses – cod, coalfish, char and so forth – averaging around 290kr. Mon–Sat 6–11.30pm.

Bars and nightclubs

Bær & Bar Innherredsveien 16. Managing to straddle that fine line between trendy and pretentious, this is the pick of the bars along the Nedre Elvehavn dockside strip. The sister of the neighbouring *Bare Blabær* restaurant (see opposite), Bær & Bar has house and electro until 3am at the weekend, fresh fruit cocktails and outdoor seating. Daily from 11am.

Bari Munkegata 26. Smooth and polished bar-restaurant, all dark-stained wood and soft lighting. Attracts an older/smarter crew, who sip wine and cocktails (rather then downing litres of ale). Below the *Frati* restaurant (see above). Daily from 10.30am–1am, 2.30am at the weekend.

Café 3B Brattørgata 3B. Rock 'n' roll and indie club-cum-bar, where you can drink well into the wee hours. One of the grooviest places in town. Tues–Fri 8pm–2.30am, Sat 4pm–2.30pm & Sun 10pm–2.30am.

Metro Kjøpmannsgata 12 ⊛ www.gaytrondheim.com. Trondheim's principal gay and lesbian bar, tastefully decorated and with DJ sounds at the weekend. Wed 9pm–1am, Fri & Sat 10pm–2am.

Trondhjem Mikrobryggeri Prinsens gate 39. Mainstream bar serving up its own microbrewery brews. In a pleasant little courtyard just off Prinsens gate. Filling pub food too. Mon 5–10pm, Tues–Fri 3pm–2am & Sat noon–2am.

Listings

Car rental Avis, Kjøpmannsgata 34 (☎ 73 84 17 90) and at the airport (☎ 74 84 01 00); Europcar, at the airport (☎ 74 82 29 90); Hertz, Innherredsveien 103 (☎ 73 50 35 00), and at the airport (☎ 74 80 16 60).
Dentist Dental emergencies ☎ 73 50 55 00.
Internet There's free internet access at the library, Kongensgate (Mon–Thurs 9am–7pm, Fri 9am–4pm & Sat 10am–3pm; also Sept–April Sun noon–4pm).

Performing arts Olavshallen, Kjøpmannsgata 44 (☎ 73 99 40 50, ⊛ www.olavshallen.no) is the city's main concert hall, offering everything from opera to rock, comedy and musicals. It's also home to the city's symphony orchestra.
Post office Main office at Dronningens gate 10 (Mon–Fri 8am–5pm & Sat 9am–2pm, though hours are reduced somewhat in the summer).

North from Trondheim to Bodø

North of Trondheim, it's a long haul up the coast to the next major places of interest, Bodø, the main ferry port for the Lofoten, and the gritty but likeable port of Narvik – respectively 720km and 910km distant. The easiest way to make the bulk of the trip is by **train**, a rattling good journey on the **Nordlandsbanen** (Nordland Line) with the scenery becoming wilder and bleaker the further north you go, but be sure to sit on the left of the carriage going north as the views are much better. The train takes nine hours to reach **Fauske**, where the line reaches its northern limit and turns west for the final 65-kilometre dash to Bodø. There's precious little to detain you in Fauske, but there are **bus** connections north to Narvik, a five-hour drive away, and many travellers take an overnight break here, though in fact nearby Bodø makes a far more pleasant stopover and there are buses to Narvik from here too.

If you're **driving**, you'll find the main highway, the **E6**, which runs all the way from Trondheim to Narvik and points north, too slow to cover more than three or four hundred kilometres comfortably in a day. Fortunately, there are several pleasant places to stop, beginning with **Snåsa**, a relaxed – and relaxing – village beside the E6. Further north, in Nordland, the next province up, aim for **Mo-i-Rana**, a rejigged and revamped former industrial town that makes an amenable pit stop. Just beyond Mo-i-Rana is the **Saltfjellet National Park**, a wild and windswept mountain plateau that extends east towards the Swedish border. The E6 and the train line cut through the park, giving ready access, but although this is a popular destination for experienced hikers, it's too fierce an environment for the novice or the lightly equipped.

The E6 north to Snåsa

Heading north from Trondheim on the E6, it's about 200km to the sleepy, scattered hamlet of **SNÅSA**, a fine example of a Trøndelag rural community. It looks as if nothing much has happened here for decades, but there is one sight of note, a pretty little hilltop **church** of softly hued grey stone, dating from the Middle Ages and very much in the English style. On the west side of the village – and 6km from the E6 – is the *Snåsa Hotell* (T74 15 10 57, Wwww.snasahotell.no; ❸/❹), a modern place in a lovely setting overlooking the lake; the decor is somewhat dated, but the bedrooms are comfortable and it's a peaceful spot, ideal if you want to rest after a long drive. The hotel also operates a small **campsite** (same number; all year) with huts (❶) as well as spaces for tents and caravans. There's a restaurant here too, serving humdrum but filling Norwegian staples, but if you're likely to arrive after 7pm, you should telephone ahead to check it will still be open.

Mo-i-Rana

Hugging the head of the Ranfjord, **MO-I-RANA**, or more usually "**Mo**", was a minor port and market town until World War II, after which its fortunes, and appearance, were transformed by the construction of a steel plant. The plant dominated proceedings until the 1980s, when there was some economic diversification and the town began to clean itself up: the fjord shore was cleared of its industrial clutter and the E6 re-routed to create the pleasantly spacious, surprisingly leafy town centre of today. Most of Mo is resolutely modern, but look out for **Mo kirke**, a good-looking structure of 1832, with a high-pitched roof and onion dome, perched on a hill on the eastern edge of the centre. Also in Mo, standing in the shallows, is an Antony Gormley sculpture, **Man of the Sea** (*Havmannen*), a large and stern-looking figure, which gazes determinedly down the fjord.

Arrival, information and transport

Mo's **bus and train stations** are close together, down by the fjord on Ole Tobias Olsens gate. The compact town centre lies east of this street, with the foot of the main pedestrianized drag, Jernbanegata, opposite the bus station. The tourist office is about 300m to the south of the bus and train stations, also on Ole Tobias Olsens gate (mid-June to mid-Aug Mon–Fri 9am–8pm, Sat 9am–4pm & Sun 1–7pm; mid-Aug to mid-June Mon–Fri 9am–4pm; ☎75 13 92 00, ⒲www.arctic-circle.no). They have the usual local leaflets and will also make reservations for a wide range of guided excursions, from rafting, kayaking and fishing through to caving, climbing and trekking.

Accommodation

The pick of the town's several hotels is the excellently run and very comfortable 🎄 *Meyergården Hotell*, a short walk north of the train station, off Ole Tobias Olsens gate at Fridtjof Nansensgate 28 (☎75 13 40 00, ⒲www.meyergarden .no; ❹/❻). Most of the hotel is modern, but the original lodge has survived and is maintained in period style, with stuffed animal heads on the wall and elegant panelled doorways. A less expensive, but much plainer, alternative is the *Fjordgården Hotell Mo i Rana*, a tour-group favourite down by the waterfront at Søndregate 9 (☎75 15 28 00, ⒲www.fjordgarden.no; May to Aug; ❹). A third option is *Mo Gjestegård*, tucked into the backstreets near the church at Elias Blix gata 5 (☎75 15 22 11, ⒲www.mo-gjestegaard.no; ❷). This family-run guesthouse is a little heavy on the pine finishings, but it's quiet and peaceful and the rooms are pleasantly homely.

Cafés and restaurants

Mo's best **restaurant** is the *Søilen* (daily from 1–10pm; ☎75 13 40 80) at the *Meyergården Hotell*, where you can sample an excellent range of Norwegian dishes featuring local ingredients; main courses here average around 220kr. A second choice is the *Abelone mat & vinstue*, Ole Tobias Olsens gate 6 (daily 2–9pm; ☎75 15 38 88), which serves competent pizzas and steaks from around 170kr.

The Arctic Circle

Given its appeal as a travellers' totem, and considering the amount of effort it takes actually to get here, crossing the Arctic Circle, about 80km north of Mo, is a bit of a disappointment. Uninhabited for the most part, the landscape is undeniably bleak, but the gleaming **Polarsirkelsenteret** (Arctic Circle Centre: daily: May 10am–6pm; June to mid-July 9am–8pm; late July to late Aug 8am–10pm; late Aug 9am–8pm; early Sept 10am–6pm; ⒲www.polarsirkelsenteret.no) only serves to disfigure the scene – it's a giant lampshade of a building plonked by the roadside and stuffed with every sort of tourist bauble imaginable. You'll whizz by on the bus, the train toots its whistle, and drivers can, of course, shoot past too, though the temptation to brave the crowds is strong. Inside, you'll probably get snared by either the "Polarsirkelen" certificate, or the specially stamped postcards. Less tackily, there are poignant reminders of crueller times back outside, where a couple of simple stone memorials pay tribute to the Yugoslav and Soviet POWs who laboured under terrible conditions to build the Arctic train line – the Nordlandsbanen – to Narvik for the Germans in World War II.

The louring mountains in the vicinity of the Arctic Circle Centre are part of the **Saltfjellet**, a vast mountain plateau whose spindly pines, stern snow-tipped peaks and rippling moors extend west from the Swedish border to the Svartisen glacier. En route to Fauske (see below), the E6 and the railway cut across this range, part of which – to the immediate west of the E6 – has been protected as the **Saltfjellet National Park**.

Fauske

From the Arctic Circle Centre, it's about 100km up the E6 to **FAUSKE**, which, but for a brief stretch of line from Narvik into Sweden, marks the northernmost point of the Norwegian rail network and is, consequently, an important transport hub. Along with nearby Bodø, the town is a departure point of the twice-daily Nord-Norgeekspressen (@www.nor-way.no), the express **bus** service that carries passengers to Narvik, where you change for either the bus to Tromsø or the Nordkappekspressen bus, which covers the next leg of the journey up to Alta (for Honningsvåg and Nordkapp). It takes about five and a half hours to get from Fauske to Narvik, a gorgeous run with the E6 careering round the mountains and along a series of blue-black fjords, but if you are aiming for Alta, you'll have to overnight in Narvik – which is no hardship at all (see p.303). In Fauske, the Nord-Norgeekspressen leaves from beside the **train station** and tickets can be purchased from the driver or in advance at any bus station.

Fauske practicalities

From Fauske's train and long-distance bus station, it's a five- to ten-minute walk down the hill and left at the T-junction to the local bus station and a few metres more to the main drag, **Storgata**, which doubles as the E6. Storgata runs parallel to the fjord and holds the handful of shops that passes for the town centre. There's certainly no strong reason to linger here – nearby Bodø is a much more palatable place to stay, never mind Narvik – but Fauske can still be a handy if unexciting place to break your journey. Of the town's **hotels**, the pick is the *Fauske Hotell*, Storgata 82 (☎75 60 20 00, @www.fauskehotell.no; ④/⑥), a chunky square block whose interior is made slightly sickly by a surfeit of salmon-coloured streaky marble. The hotel rooms are – marble apart – comfortable enough and the breakfasts are large and tasty. Otherwise, the best bet is the *Lundhøgda* campsite (☎75 64 39 66, @www.lundhogdacamping.no; May–Sept). This occupies a splendid location about 3km west of the town centre, overlooking the mountains and the fjord: head out of town along the E80 (the Bodø road), and turn off down a signposted country lane, ablaze with wild flowers in the summertime and flanked by old timber buildings. The campsite takes caravans, has spaces for tents and also offers cabins from 490kr a night.

Bodø and around

BODØ, some 65km west of Fauske along the E80, is the terminus of the Trondheim train line and the starting point of the Nord-Norgeekspressen express bus to points north. Founded in 1816, the town struggled to survive in its early years, but was saved from insignificance by the herring boom of the 1860s, a time when the town's harbourfront was crowded with the net-menders, coopers, oilskin-makers and canneries that kept the fleet at sea. Later, it accrued several industrial plants and became an important regional centre, but was then heavily bombed during World War II and today there's precious little left of the proud, nineteenth-century buildings that once flanked the waterfront. Nonetheless, Bodø manages a cheerful modernity, a bright and breezy place whose harbour looks out onto a batch of rugged, treeless hills. Bodø is also within comfortable striking distance of the old trading post of **Kjerringøy**, one of Nordland's most delightful spots. It has long been a regular stop for the Hurtigrute coastal boat route, and, perhaps most important of all, is much the best place from which to hop over to the choicest parts of the Lofoten Islands (see pp.315–324).

Arrival and information

With regular connections to and from other cities on the mainland as well as the Lofoten, Bodø **airport** is just 2km south of the town centre. From the airport, there are hourly buses to the local bus station right in the heart of Bodø (10min; 30kr one-way). From the local bus station, it's metres to the **tourist office**, at Sjøgata 3 (June–Aug Mon–Fri 9am–8pm, Sat 10am–6pm & Sun noon–8pm; Sept–May Mon–Fri 9am–3.30pm; ☎75 54 80 00, @www.visitbodo.com). It gives out information on connections to the Lofoten Islands, rents out bikes and also issues a

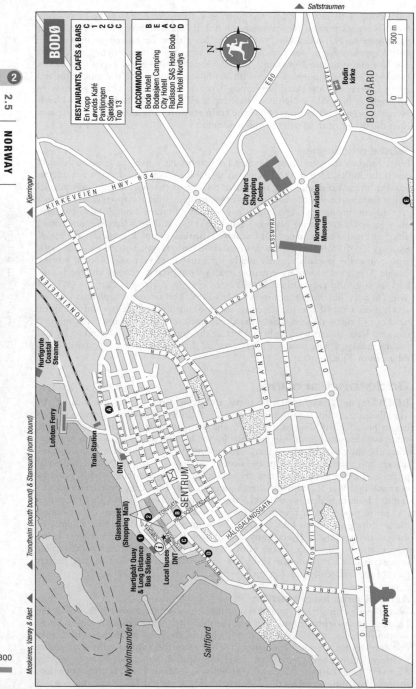

▲ Saltstraumen

BODØ

RESTAURANTS, CAFÉS & BARS
En Kopp   C
Løvolds Kafé   1
Paviljongen   2
Sjøsiden   C
Top 13   C

ACCOMMODATION
Bodø Hotel   B
Bodøsjøen Camping   E
City Hotell   A
Radisson SAS Hotel Bodø C
Thon Hotel Nordlys   D

N

0   500 m

BODØGÅRD

Bodin kirke

Norwegian Aviation Museum

City Nord Shopping Centre

E80

GAMLE RIKSVEI

PLASSMYRA

KIRKEVEIEN HWY. 834

RONVIKVEIEN

▲ Kjerringøy

Hurtigrute Coastal Steamer

Lofoten Ferry

Train Station

DNT

SENTRUM

Glasshuset (Shopping Mall)

Hurtigbåt Quay & Long Distance Bus Station

Local buses

DNT

Nyholmsundet

Saltfjord

Airport

HERNESVEIEN

OLAV V GATE

HÅKON VII GATE

PRINSENS GATE

HÅLOGALANDSGATA

TORVGATA

SJØGATA

SIVERTS GATE

BANKGATA

STORGATA

DRONNINGENS GATE

PRINSENS GATE

BØRTINDGATA

PARKVEIEN

RENSÅSGATA

detailed town and district guide. At the back of the tourist office is the long-distance bus station and the quay for local ferries, most usefully the **Hurtigbåt passenger express boat** to Svolvær (see p.318).

Bodø **train station** is at the other end of the town centre, 700m east of the tourist office, just off the long main street, Sjøgata. The southern **Lofoten ferry** (to and from Moskenes plus the islets of Værøy and Røst) and the **Hurtigrute** coastal boat use the docks 400m and 600m respectively northeast along the waterfront from the train station.

Accommodation

Bodø has a reasonable supply of accommodation, including half a dozen hotels, a campsite and a couple of guesthouses.

Bodø Hotell Professor Schyttes gate 5 ⑦ 75 54 77 00, ⑩ www.bodohotell.no. Well-kept rooms with all the usual mod cons in this mid-sized, mid-range hotel housed in a five-storey block right in the centre of town. ④/⑤

Bodøsjøen Camping Bodøsjøen ⑦ 75 56 36 80. Year-round lakeside campsite located about 3.5km to the southeast of the centre, not far from the Bodin kirke. Tent pitches, caravan hook-ups and cabins (from 55kr).

City Hotell Storgata 39 ⑦ 75 52 04 02, ⑩ johansst@online.no. Simple, unassuming rooms at this bargain-price hotel-cum-guesthouse near the train station. Twenty-three en-suite rooms; free internet access. ②

Radisson SAS Hotel Bodø Storgata 2 ⑦ 75 51 90 00, ⑩ www.bodo.radissonsas.com. The biggest hotel in town. Occupies an overly large, modern concrete and glass tower, but has commodious and well-appointed rooms – and those on the upper floors have great views out to sea. ④/⑦

Thon Hotel Nordlys Moloveien 14 ⑦ 75 53 19 00, ⑩ www.thonhotels.no. This smart, very modern chain hotel is right on the harbourfront, and most of the guest rooms have some kind of sea view. Nothing too special perhaps, but it's a very pleasant place to stay. Free internet access. ⑤/⑦

The Town

Bodø rambles over a low-lying peninsula that pokes out into the Saltfjord, its long and narrow centre concentrated along two parallel streets, Sjøgata and Storgata. The town is short of specific sights, but 2km southeast of the centre, on Olav V's gate, is its most popular attraction, the imaginative **Norsk Luftfartsmuseum** (Norwegian Aviation Museum: mid-June to mid-Aug daily 10am–6pm; & mid-Aug to mid-June Mon–Fri 10am–4pm, Sat & Sun 11am–5pm; ⑩ www.luftfart.museum.no; 90kr), which tracks through the general history of Norwegian aviation. Among the planes to look out for are a Spitfire, a reminder that two RAF squadrons were manned by Norwegians during World War II, and a rare Norwegian-made Hønningstad C-5 Polar seaplane. Bodø was used by the US air force throughout the Cold War, and you can also see one of their U2 spy planes.

From the museum, it's a short drive east along the ring road to the Gamle Riksvei roundabout, where you turn right for the one-kilometre detour to the onion-domed **Bodin kirke** (late June to mid-Aug Mon–Fri 10am–3pm; free), a pretty little stone church sitting snugly among clover meadows. Dating from the thirteenth century, the church was modified after the Reformation by the addition of a tower and the widening of its windows – the Protestants associated dark, gloomy churches with Catholic superstition. It is, however, the colourful seventeenth-century fixtures that catch the eye, plus the lovingly carved Baroque altarboard and pulpit.

Eating and drinking

Bodø is hardly a gourmet's paradise, but there are one or two competent cafés and restaurants, kicking off with the traditional and inexpensive Norwegian menu of the canteen-style *Løvolds Kafé* (Mon–Fri 9am–6pm & Sat 9am–3pm), down by the quay at Tollbugata 9; main courses here feature local ingredients and average around 120kr. More upmarket is the wood-panelled *Sjøsiden* restaurant (daily 5–11pm; ☎75 51 90 00) upstairs in the *Radisson SAS Hotel*; they do a good line in local fish here with mains averaging 250–300kr. Also in the Radisson SAS tower block is the ground-floor *En Kopp* coffee bar, which serves the best coffee in town, and the bar with the best view, the rooftop *Top 13*. There's also the congenial *Paviljongen* café-bar in the distinctive glass chalet at the east end of the Glasshuset shopping mall (Mon–Sat 10am–11.30pm & Sun 12.30–11.30pm). A nice way to fill up cheaply is to buy a big bag of prawns (40–50kr) from one of the fishing boats along the quayside and eat alfresco at the water's edge.

Out from Bodø: Kjerringøy and Saltstraumen

There are two obvious excursions from Bodø: one northeast to the old trading station at Kjerringøy, the other southeast to the tidal phenomenon known as the Saltstraumen. Both places can be reached by car or bike, Kjerringøy along Highway 834 and the other via Highway 17. As for **public transport**, Kjerringøy is reachable by bus and ferry, the Saltstraumen by bus.

Kjerringøy

The **KJERRINGØY trading post** (mid–May to Aug daily 11am–5pm; 60kr; ☎75 55 77 41, ⓦwww.kjerringoy.no), just 40km north along the coast from Bodø by road and ferry, has a superbly preserved collection of nineteenth-century timber buildings set beside a slender, islet-sheltered channel. This was once the domain of the **Zahl family**, merchants who supplied the fishermen of Lofoten with everything from manufactured goods and clothes to farmyard foodstuffs in return for fish. It was not, however, an equal relationship: the Zahls, who operated a local monopoly until the 1910s, could dictate the price they paid for the fish, and many of the islanders were permanently indebted to them. This social division is still very much in evidence at the trading post, where there's a marked distinction between the guest rooms of the main house and the fishermen's bunk beds in the boat- and cookhouses. Indeed, the **family house** is remarkably fastidious, with its Italianate busts and embroidered curtains – even the medicine cabinet is well stocked with formidable Victorian remedies like the bottle of "Sicilian Hair Renewer".

There are enjoyable, hour-long **guided tours** around the main house throughout the summer (daily, every hour on the hour; 40kr), and afterwards you can nose around the reconstructed general store, drop in at the café and stroll the fine sandy beach.

Practicalities

Getting here from Bodø **by car** is easy enough – a straightforward coastal drive north along Highway 834 with the added treat of a ferry ride from Festvåg to Misten (every 30min to 1hr 30min, less frequently on Sun; 10min; passengers 23kr, car & driver 55kr return; ☎177, ⓦwww.177nordland.com). Things are more complicated **by bus**, but a day-return trip beginning at Bodø bus station is possible on Saturday; pick up a combined bus-and-ferry timetable at Bodø tourist office. More generally, there are one or two buses daily from Bodø to Kjerringøy, where there's **accommodation** at both the new *Kjerringøy Brygge Hotell* at the trading post (☎75 52 54 00, ⑤) and the old parsonage, *Kjerringøy Prestegård*, about 700m north of the trading post along the main road (☎75 51 11 14, ⓦwww.kjerringoy.no). The latter has simple double rooms in the main building (②) and slightly pleasanter ones in the renovated cowshed next door (③).

Saltstraumen

Less interesting than Kjerringøy, but more widely publicized, is the maelstrom known as the **Saltstraumen**, 33km east of Bodø round the bay on Highway 17. Here, billions of gallons of water are forced through a narrow, 150m-wide channel four times daily, making a headlong dash between the inner and outer fjord. The whirling creamy water is at its most turbulent at high tide, and its most violent when the moon is new or full – and a timetable is available from Bodø tourist office. However, although scores of tourists troop here every high tide, you can't help but feel they wish they were somewhere else – the scenery is, in Norwegian terms at least, flat and dull, and the view from the bridge which spans the channel unexciting.

It takes about fifty minutes to **drive** from Bodø to the Saltstraumen, or you could take a local **bus** from the bus station (Mon–Sat 4–6 daily, Sun 1 daily; 1hr; ⓦwww .nbuss.no), though its times rarely coincide with high tide. In this case, you can kill a couple of hours very pleasantly at *Kafé Kjelen*, a little red house on the west side of the bridge, whose terrace offers views over the maelstrom.

North to Narvik

The 240-kilometre journey north from Fauske to Narvik is spectacular, with the **E6** rounding the fjords, twisting and tunnelling through the mountains and rushing over high, pine-dusted plateaus. This stretch of the highway presents two opportunities to catch a **car ferry** to Lofoten – one at Skutvik, the other at Bognes. The more southerly of the two is **Skutvik**, 35km to the west of the E6 along Highway 81, with ferries to Svolvær (1 daily; 2hr; passengers 76kr, car & driver 262kr; reservations advised: ☎177 in Nordland, otherwise ☎75 77 24 10). At **Bognes**, where the E6 is interrupted by the Tysfjord, there's a choice of ferries. One sails to Lødingen and the E10 on the Vesterålen (late June to mid-Aug 16 daily; mid-Aug to late June 13 daily; 1hr; passenger 51kr, car & driver 163kr), while a second hops across the Tysfjord to **Skarberget** to pick up the E6, just 80km south of Narvik (every 1hr to 1hr 30min; 25min; passengers 31kr, car & driver 87kr). All these ferries are operated by Hurtigruten (ⓦwww.hurtigruten.no), the same company that operates the Hurtigrute coastal boat, and work on a first-come, first-served basis, though reservations can be made – and are strongly advised on the once-daily **Skutvik** to Svolvær ferry. Long-distance **buses** link Bodø, Fauske and Narvik twice daily; the bus journey from Fauske to Narvik takes five and a half hours.

Narvik

A relatively modern town, **NARVIK** was established just a century ago as an ice-free port to handle the iron ore brought here by train from the mines in northern Sweden. Neither does it make any bones about what is still its main function: the **iron-ore docks** are immediately conspicuous, slap-bang in the centre of town, the rust-coloured machinery overwhelming much of the waterfront. Yet, for all the mess, the industrial complex is strangely impressive, its cat's cradle of walkways, conveyor belts, cranes and funnels oddly beguiling and giving the town a frontier, very Arctic, feel. Not content with its iron, Narvik has also had a fair old stab at reinventing itself as an **adventure sports** centre, becoming a popular destination for skiers, paraglidlers and scuba-divers – and developing a good range of guesthouses to match.

Arrival and information

Fifteen minutes' walk from one end to the other, Narvik's sloping centre straggles along the main street, **Kongens gate**, which doubles as the E6. The **train station** is at the north end of town and from here it's a five- to ten-minute walk along Kongens gate to the **tourist office**, at Kongens gate 57 (June to mid-Aug Mon–Fri 9am–7pm, Sat & Sun 10am–5pm; mid–Aug to Sept Mon–Fri 9am–5pm & Sat 10am–2pm; Oct–May Mon–Fri 9am–4pm; ☎76 96 56 00, ⓦwww.destinationnarvik .com). The **bus station** is a little further to the south in the basement of the Amfi shopping centre, on the west side of the main drag.

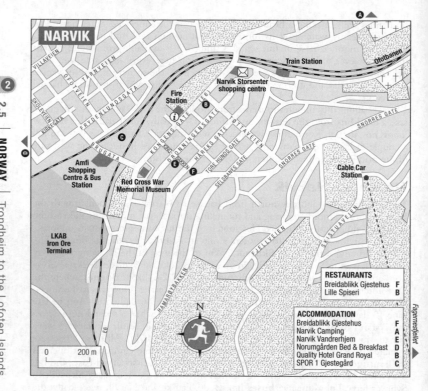

NARVIK

Train Station
Ofotbanen
Narvik Storsenter
shopping centre
Fire Station
Amfi Shopping Centre & Bus Station
Red Cross War Memorial Museum
Cable Car Station
LKAB Iron Ore Terminal
Fagernesfjellet

RESTAURANTS	
Breidablikk Gjestehus	F
Lille Spiseri	B

ACCOMMODATION	
Breidablikk Gjestehus	F
Narvik Camping	A
Narvik Vandrerhjem	E
Norumgården Bed & Breakfast	D
Quality Hotel Grand Royal	B
SPOR 1 Gjestegård	C

0   200 m

N

As regards adventure sports, a number of operators combine to offer everything from hang- and para-gliding through to **mountain climbing**, caving, canoeing and **glacier walking.** There's also **scuba diving** amidst the wreck-studded waters around Narvik with Divenarvik (☏99 51 22 05, ⓦwww.divenarvik.com). Most operators rent out the appropriate specialist tackle – but check when you reserve.

Accommodation

Narvik is a tad short of **hotels**, but it does have several very recommendable **guest-houses**, an HI **hostel** and a reasonably convenient **campsite**, *Narvik Camping*, about 2km north of the centre on the E6 at Rombaksveien 75 (☏76 94 58 10, ⓦwww.narvikcamping.com). It's open all year and has tent and caravan pitches, hook-ups and cabins (from 650kr).

Hotels and guesthouses

Breidablikk Gjestehus Tore Hunds gate 41 ☏76 94 14 18, ⓦwww.breidablikk.no. This pleasant, unassuming guesthouse is neat and trim, with homely en-suite rooms. Those on the upper floors have attractive views over town, and a good, hearty breakfast is included in the room rate. It's located at the top of the steps at the end of Kinobakken, a side road leading east off Kongens gate, just up from the main town square. ④
Narvik Vandrerhjem Dronningensgate 58 ☏76 96 22 00, ⓦwww.vandrerhjem.no. Part of a

larger hotel, the hostel rooms are plain and pretty frugal, but at least you're in the town centre. Free internet access, a laundry, a café and a self-catering kitchen. Some of our readers have complained about the noise from the neighbouring nightclub at the weekend. Dorm beds 270kr, doubles ②
Norumgården Bed & Breakfast Framnesveien 127 ☏76 94 48 57, ⓦwww .norumgaarden.narviknett.no. Lavish but good-value B&B in a 1920s timber villa. The Germans used the place as an officers' mess during the war and today, tastefully restored, it holds three

large guest rooms, two of which have kitchenettes. Antiques are liberally distributed across the house and breakfast is included. A snip at ❶
Quality Hotel Grand Royal Kongens gate 64 ☎76 97 70 00, ☯www.choicehotels.no. Some of Narvik's hotels have seen better days, but the Grand, just down from the train station, is well kept and well maintained; its public rooms are wood-panelled and appealing, while the bedrooms are perfectly adequate albeit in standard chain style. ❺/❼

SPOR 1 Gjestegård Brugata 2A ☎76 94 60 20, ☯www.spor1.no. This spick-and-span place is the pick of the budget/backpacker options with clean if spartan modern rooms. Doubles, quads and a larger dorm plus kitchen facilities, a sauna and a bar. Occupies a creatively recycled former railway building, a simple one-storey block just below the main town bridge. Dorm beds from 200kr, doubles ❶

The Town

Narvik's first settlers were the navvies who built the train line, the **Ofotbanen,** to the mines in Kiruna, over the border in Sweden at the end of the nineteenth century – a herculean task commemorated every March by a week of singing, dancing and drinking, when the locals dress up in period costume. The town grew steadily up until World War II, when it was demolished during ferocious fighting for control of the harbour and its iron-ore supply. Perhaps inevitably, the rebuilt town centre is rather lacking in appeal, with modern concrete buildings replacing the wooden houses that went before, but it still musters a breezy northern charm. It also possesses the fascinating **Nordland Røde Kors Krigsminnemuseum** (Red Cross War Memorial Museum: May to early June Mon–Sat 10am–4pm & Sun noon–4pm; early June to late Aug Mon–Sat 10am–9pm & Sun noon–6pm; late Aug to mid-Sept Mon–Sat 10am–4pm & Sun noon–4pm; rest of year Mon–Fri 11am–3pm; 50kr; ☯www.warmuseum.no), just down from the tourist office. Run by the Red Cross, the museum documents the wartime German saturation bombing of the town, and the bitter and bloody sea and air battles in which hundreds of foreign servicemen died alongside a swathe of the local population. The museum gives a thoroughly moving and thoughtfully presented account of the battle for Narvik and then tracks through the German occupation of Norway until liberation in 1945.

Narvik also offers **guided tours** of the LKAB mining company's ore-terminal complex (mid-June to mid-Aug 3pm daily; 50kr), interesting if only for the

Moving on from Narvik

There's a choice of routes on from Narvik. The **Nordkappekspressen bus** (1 daily except Sat; ☯www.nor-way.no) shoots north along the E6 to Alta (see p.334), a journey of ten hours, whilst the **Nord-Norgeekspressen bus** (1–3 daily; ☯www.nor-way .no) makes the four-hour hop north to Tromsø (see p.329). Both trips give sight of some wonderfully wild and diverse scenery, from craggy mountains and blue-black fjords to gentle, forested valleys. A third bus service, the **Lofoten Ekspressen** (1 daily; ☯www.nor-way.no) runs west from Narvik to Fiskebøl, Svolvær and Leknes in the Lofoten Islands (see pp.315–324). There are no buses direct to the Vesterålen.

One of the real treats of a visit to Narvik is the train ride into the mountains that rear up behind the town and spread east across the Swedish border. Called the Ofotbanen, this rail line passes through some wonderful scenery, slipping between hostile peaks before reaching the rocky, barren and loch-studded mountain plateaus beyond. Operated by a Swedish company, **SJ** (☯www.sj.se), trains leave **Narvik train station** two or three times daily and take fifty minutes to reach **RIKSGRÄNSEN,** a pleasant hiking and skiing centre just over the border in Sweden – so take your passport; the one-way fare is 33kr. Many train travellers nose around **Riksgränsen** for a few hours before returning to Narvik, but others push on east to Kiruna (see p.499) and Luleå (see p.476) in Sweden; the ride from Narvik to Luleå takes around six and a half hours.

opportunity to spend ninety minutes amid such giant, ore-stained contraptions. After its arrival by train, the ore is carried on the various conveyor belts to the quayside, from where some thirty million tons of it are shipped out each year. Sign up for the tours at the tourist office.

Eating

Narvik is short of recommendable **cafés** and **restaurants**. Easily the best of the bunch is the *Lille Spiseri*, a smart restaurant in the *Quality Hotel Grand Royal* (see p.305), where they specialize in local ingredients with main courses averaging around 200kr. Alternatively, guests can pre-book filling, home-made dinners at the *Breidablikk Gjestehus* (see p.305).

The Vesterålen Islands

A raggle-taggle archipelago nudging into the Norwegian Sea, the **Vesterålen Islands**, and their southerly neighbours the Lofoten, are like western Norway in miniature: the terrain is hard and unyielding, the sea boisterous and fretful, and the main – often the only – industry is fishing. The weather is temperate but wet, and the islanders' historic isolation has bred a distinctive culture based, in equal measure, on Protestantism, the extended family and respect for the ocean.

The archipelago was first settled by semi-nomadic hunter-agriculturalists some 6000 years ago, and it was they and their Iron Age successors who chopped down the birch and pine forests that once covered the coasts. It was boatbuilding, however, which brought prosperity: by the seventh century, the islanders were able to build ocean-going vessels, a skill that enabled the islanders to join in the Viking bonanza. In the early fourteenth century, the islanders **lost their independence** and were placed under the control of Bergen: by royal decree, all the fish the islanders caught had to be shipped to Bergen for export. This may have suited the economic interests of the Norwegian monarchy and the Danish governors who succeeded them, but it put the islanders at a terrible disadvantage. With their monopoly guaranteed, Bergen's merchants controlled both the price they paid for the fish and the prices of the goods they sold to the islanders – a **truck system** that was to survive, increasingly under the auspices of local merchants, until the early years of the twentieth century. Since World War II, improvements in fishing techniques and, more latterly, the growth in tourism and the extension of the road system have all combined to transform island life, and at last the hard times are over.

The Vesterålen Islands are the less rugged of the two island groups – greener, gentler and less mountainous than the Lofoten, with more of the land devoted to agriculture, though this gives way to vast tracts of peaty moorland in the far north. The villages are less immediately appealing too, often no more than narrow ribbons straggling along the coast and across any available stretch of fertile land. Consequently, many travellers simply pass by on their way to Lofoten, a mistake in so far as the fishing port of **Andenes**, tucked away at the far end of the island of Andøya, has a strange but enthralling back-of-beyond charm and is a centre for **whalewatching** expeditions. In summer, Andenes also has the advantage of being linked by ferry to Gryllefjord, on the island of Senja. Other Vesterålen highlights are the magnificent but extremely narrow **Trollfjord**, where cruise ships and the Hurtigrute coastal boat perform some nifty manoeuvres, and **Harstad**, a comparative giant with a population of 23,000 and the proud possessor of a splendid medieval church.

Transport to and around the Vesterålen Islands

Getting to the Vesterålen Islands from the mainland by **public transport** is easy enough, but getting around them can be more troublesome. The **E10** is the main island road, running the 240km or so west from the E6 just north of Narvik to Sortland, Stokmarknes and then **Melbu**; from here a **car ferry** (see below) shuttles over to Fiskebøl on the Lofoten Islands (see p.307).

If you have your own **vehicle** it's possible to drive from one end of the whole island chain to the other, catching the ferry from Gryllefjord on the mainland to Andenes and then driving south across the Vesterålen and the Lofoten Islands to return to the mainland by ferry from Moskenes (see p.317). Drivers intent on a less epic trip could investigate the **car rental** outlets at Harstad, which offer special short deals from around 600kr a day. Be aware, however, that finding a rental car on the spot is nearly impossible in summer and that advance reservation is strongly advised. **Andenes** has most to offer as a base, thanks to its whale- and birdwatching trips and choice of accommodation.

All Nordland **public transport** timetables – including those for much of Vesterålen – are online at ⓦwww.177nordland.com; you can also call ☏177 in Nordland, otherwise ☏75 77 24 10.

By car ferry
The principal **car ferry** from the mainland to the Vesterålen Islands departs from the jetty at Bognes, on the E6 between Fauske and Narvik, and sails to **Lødingen** (late June to mid-Aug 16 daily; mid-Aug to late June 13 daily; 1hr; passengers 51kr, car & driver 163kr; ⓦwww.hurtigruten.no). From Lødingen, it's just 4km to the E10 at a point midway between Harstad and Sortland. A second, but this time seasonal, car ferry runs from remote **Gryllefjord**, 110km west of the E6 well to the north of Narvik, to **Andenes** at the northern tip of the Vesterålen (late May to mid-June & early to late Aug 2 daily, mid-June to early Aug 3 daily; 2hr; passengers 145kr, car & driver 375kr). Reservations are strongly advised by email or phone with the ferry company concerned, Senjafergene (☏76 14 12 03, ⓦwww.senjafergene.no). A third car ferry links the Vesterålen Islands with Lofoten, running across the Hadselfjord between **Melbu** and **Fiskebøl**, both of which are on the E10 (daily 7am–11pm, every 80min; 30min; passengers 31kr, car & driver 85kr; ⓦwww.177nordland.com).

By boat: the Hurtigrute
Heading north from Bodø (departing daily at 3pm), the **Hurtigrute coastal boat** (ⓦwww.hurtigruten.no) threads a scenic route up through the Lofoten to the Vesterålen Islands, where it calls at four places: **Stokmarknes** and **Sortland** in the south, **Risøyhamn** in the north and **Harstad** in the east. None of these four destinations is especially appealing, but workaday Risøyhamn is well on the way to Andenes, while Harstad is a regional centre and transport hub with a fine old church (see p.311). Cruising southwards from Tromsø (departing daily at 1.30am), the Hurtigrute follows the same itinerary, but in reverse; the sailing time from Tromsø to Harstad is six and a half hours. The **passenger fare** from Bodø to Risøyhamn is 792kr in summer, 555kr in winter, 849/594kr to Harstad and 1226/858kr to Tromsø. The all-year fare for transporting a car from Bodø to Harstad is 453kr, 592kr to Tromsø. For vehicles, advance reservations are essential, and can be made either online (ⓦwww.hurtigruten.no) or by phoning the ship – ask down at the harbour or at the port's tourist office for assistance.

Scenically, the highlight of the Hurtigrute cruise through the Lofoten and Vesterålen Islands is the **Raftsundet**, a long and narrow sound between Svolvær and Stokmarknes, off which branches the magnificent **Trollfjord**. Unfortunately, the northbound Hurtigrute leaves Svolvær at 10pm and so the Raftsundset is only visible during the period of the midnight sun (late May to mid-July); in the opposite direction, however, boats leave Stokmarknes at a much more convenient 3.15pm. The Svolvær/Stokmarknes trip takes three hours and the passenger fare is 245kr in summer, 172kr in winter; cars cost an extra 353kr throughout the year.

By boat: Hurtigbåt passenger express boats
Hurtigbåt boats provide a speedy alternative to the car ferries and the Hurtigrute. The main **Hurtigbåt** service from the mainland to the **Vesterålen** runs from Tromsø to Harstad (2–4 daily; 2hr 45min; 380kr; ⓦwww.hurtigruten.no). There's

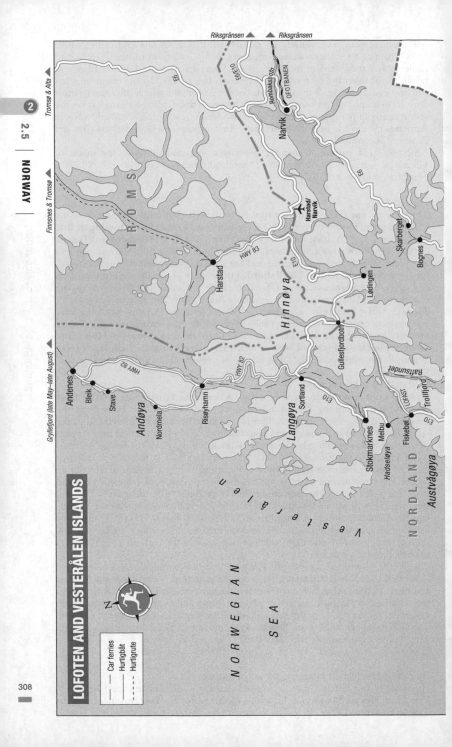

LOFOTEN AND VESTERÅLEN ISLANDS

Car ferries
Hurtigbåt
Hurtigrute

Riksgränsen ▲   ▲ Riksgränsen

Tromsø & Alta ▲

Finnsnes & Tromsø ▲

Gryllefjord (late May–late August) ▲

E6

E6/E10

Rombaksbotn
OFOTBANEN

Narvik

E6

T R O M S

Harstad/
Narvik

Skarberget

Bognes

E10

Løødingen

Harstad

Gullesfjordbotn

HWY 83

H i n n ø y a

Raftsundet

HWY 82

HWY 82

Risøyhamn

Andenes
Bleik
Stave
Nordmela

A n d ø y a

L a n g ø y a

Sortland

E10

Stokmarknes
Melbu

Hadseløya

Fiskebøl

Trollfjord

LOFAST

E10

N O R D L A N D

A u s t v å g ø y a

V e s t e r å l e n

N O R W E G I A N

S E A

N

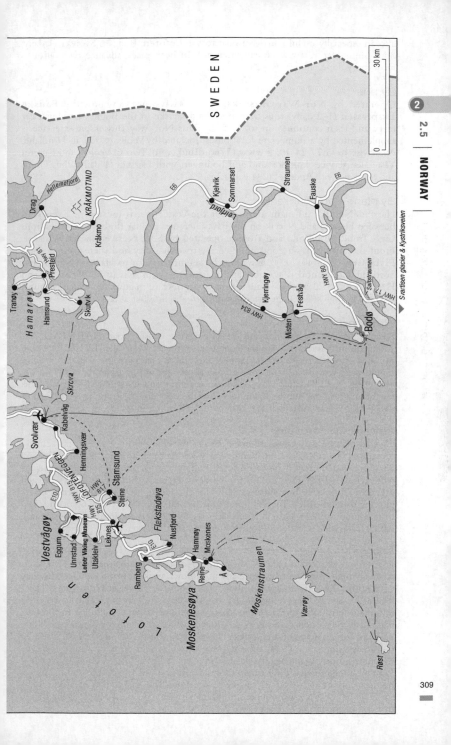

also an especially useful Hurtigbåt boat to the **Lofoten**: Bodø to Svolvær (1 daily; 3hr 30min; 297kr; ⓦ www.hurtigruten.no). In both cases, advance reservation – most easily done online – is a good idea.

By bus

Operated by **Nor-Way Bussekspress** (ⓦ www.nor-way.no), the **Fauske Ekspressen** (1–2 daily) runs from Bodø and Fauske to the Bognes-Lødingen car ferry and then continues on to Sortland. This Nor-Way Bussekspress service is supplemented by a number of local buses operated by Veolia (ⓣ 177 in Nordland, otherwise ⓣ 75 77 24 10, ⓦ www.177nordland.com). Two of Veolia's most useful Vesterålen services link Sortland and Lødingen with Harstad (1 daily; 2hr 30min) and Sortland with Andenes (2–4 daily; 2hr).

By plane – and car rental

Harstad/Narvik, the main **airport** for the Vesterålen, is located in Evenes, in between Harstad and Narvik on the E10. There are regular **flights** to Evenes from Oslo, Trondheim, Bodø and Tromsø, operated by SAS, Norwegian and Widerøe. From the airport, it's a good hour's drive to either city and there's also a good **Flybussen** (ⓣ 78 40 70 00; ⓦ www.flybussen.no) service to Harstad, Narvik and Sortland. **Car rental** is available at the airport – both Avis (ⓣ 76 98 21 33) and Hertz (ⓣ 41 58 22 28) have outlets here. If you reserve in advance (which is almost essential in high season), the price can drop to about 600kr a day.

Harstad

Readily reached by car, bus and the Hurtigrute coastal boat, **HARSTAD**, just 130km from Narvik, is easily the largest town on the Vesterålen Islands. It's home to much of northern Norway's engineering industry, its sprawling docks a tangle of supply ships, repair yards and cold-storage plants spread out along the gentle slopes of the Vågsfjord. This may not sound too enticing, and it's true that Harstad wins few beauty contests, but the town does have the odd attraction, and if you're tired of sleepy Norwegian villages, it at least provides a bustling interlude.

Arrival and information

Harstad may be easy to reach, but if you're travelling along the E10 it's actually something of a cul-de-sac, involving a thirty-kilometre detour north along Highway 83. Once you've arrived, however, you'll find almost everything you need conveniently clustered together around the harbour. Here, within a few metres of each other, you'll find the **bus station**, jetties for the Hurtigbåt and **Hurtigrute boats** plus the **tourist office**, Torvet 8 (mid-June to mid-Aug daily 10am–6pm; mid-Aug to mid-June Mon–Fri 8am–3.30pm; ⓣ 77 01 89 89, ⓦ www.destinationharstad.no), which has a wide selection of tourist literature on the Vesterålen.

Accommodation

For a town of limited charms, the number of large chain **hotels** in Harstad is relatively high, which is why, especially in summer, walk-in prices can be extremely competitive. The *Arcticus Hotel*, a short walk from the Torvet at Havnegata 3 (ⓣ 77 04 08 00, ⓦ www.choice.no; ❷/❹), has the best rates by far, offering recently revamped retro chic rooms. A breakfast and dinner buffet is included in the rate, making it very good value. A good alternative, also occupying a modern block near the Torvet, is the neat and trim *Grand Nordic Hotell*, Strandgata 9 (ⓣ 77 00 30 00, ⓦ www.nordic.no; ❷/❹) although the interior could do with a makeover. For something more up to date, try the *F2 Hotel* at Fjordgata 2 (ⓣ 77 00 32 00, ⓦ www .f2hotel.no; ❸) offering 88 smart rooms right in front of the bus station plus a modern indoor spa. Most expensive of the lot is the *Thon Hotel* at Sjøgaten 11 (ⓣ 77 00 08 00, ⓦ www.thonhotels.no; ❹/❺), stylishly decorated in a marine theme that complements the harbour view.

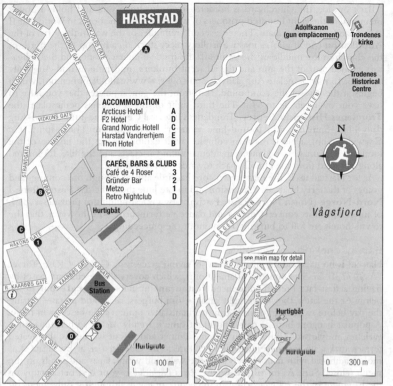

HARSTAD

Adolfkanon
(gun emplacement)

Trondenes
kirke

Trodenes
Historical
Centre

ACCOMMODATION

Arcticus Hotel   A
F2 Hotel   D
Grand Nordic Hotell   C
Harstad Vandrerhjem   E
Thon Hotel   B

CAFÉS, BARS & CLUBS

Café de 4 Roser   3
Gründer Bar   2
Metzo   1
Retro Nightclub   D

Hurtigbåt

Hurtigrute

Bus
Station

Vågsfjord

see main map for detail

Hurtigbåt

Hurtigrute

N

0   100 m

0   300 m

Further afield, the HI **hostel** *Harstad Vandrerhjem* (June to mid-Aug; ☎77 04 00 77, ⓦ www.vandrerhjem.no; dorm beds 295k, doubles ❶; reception closed 4–5pm) has the advantage of a pleasant fjordside location, near the Trondenes kirke. The hostel has self-catering facilities, washing machines and comfortable double rooms, the only problem being that the building is a school for most of the year and so has a rather cold, institutional feel. The hostel is easy to reach on the local "Trondenes" bus from the station (Mon–Sat 1 hourly; 10min).

The Town

Harstad's historical pride and joy is **Trondenes kirke** (opening times vary; free; guided tours mid-June to mid-Aug daily at 5pm; 40kr), which occupies a lovely leafy location beside the fjord 3km north of the town centre at the end of the slender Trondenes peninsula. To get there, take the local "Trondenes" bus (Mon–Sat 1 hourly; 10min), which leaves the bus station beside the tourist office and goes past the church – or take a taxi. By car, follow Highway 83 north from the centre and watch for the signposted turning on the right. The original wooden church was built at the beginning of the twelfth century and had the distinction of being the northernmost church in Christendom for several centuries. The stone church that replaced it – the one that survives today – was erected in the 1300s, its thick walls and the remains of its surrounding ramparts reflecting its dual function as a church and fortress, for these were troubled, violent times. After the exterior, stern of necessity, the warm and homely **interior** comes as a surprise. Here, the dainty arches of the rood screen lead into the choir, where a late medieval, bas-relief wooden triptych surmounts each of the three altars.

Back outside, the churchyard is bordered by a dry-stone wall and holds a Soviet memorial to the eight hundred prisoners of war who died hereabouts in World War II at the hands of the Germans. There's a second reminder of the war in the form of the **Adolfkanon** (Adolf gun), a massive artillery piece stuck on a hilltop to the north of the church in the middle of the peninsula. It's inside a military zone, and the obligatory guided tour of the gun and the adjacent **bunkers** (mid-June to mid-Aug daily at 11am, 1pm & 3pm; late Aug daily at 3pm; 60kr; Ⓦwww.adolfkanonen.no), which begins at the gate of the compound, 1km from the gun, stipulates that you have to have your own vehicle to visit. The third sight on the Trondenes peninsula is the **Trondenes Historiske Senter** (Trondenes Historical Centre: mid-June to mid-Aug daily 11am–5pm; mid-Aug to mid-June Mon–Fri 10am–2pm, Sun 11am–4pm; 70kr; Ⓦwww.tdm.no), a plush modern complex with exhibitions on the history of the locality – dioramas, mood music, incidental Viking artefacts and the like. It's located along the fjord from the church, back towards the town centre.

As for Harstad itself, the downtown core has little appeal, though the comings and goings of the ferry boats are a diversion and in late June the eight-day **Festspillene i Nord-Norge** (North Norway Arts Festival: Ⓦwww.festspillnn.no) provides a spark of interest with its concerts, drama and dance performances; note, however, that the town's hotels are full to bursting throughout the proceedings.

Eating, drinking and nightlife

Harstad is no gastronomic nirvana, but its saving grace is ✻ *Café de 4 Roser*, Torvet 7A (Ⓣ77 01 27 50; Mon–Sat 10am–10pm), which covers all the culinary bases by having a first-rate French-influenced **restaurant** upstairs and a **café-bar** down below. At the latter, they serve light meals – fish burgers, salads and pastas – during the day before switching to fresh-fruit cocktails after 6pm: it's the best bar in town. A popular hangout both at day- and night time is trendy *Metzo* with many coffee varieties, simple wok dishes for lunch and dinner and DJs at weekends; the heated terrace makes up for the Nordic temperatures. The *Gründer Bar*, at Fjordgata 2, is more traditional with nautical relics on the walls and wraps, tapas and salads on the menu (closed Sun). As for **nightlife**; the *Retro Nightclub* is your best bet, occupying the basement of the *F2 Hotel* right in the centre of town, although it only opens on Friday and Saturday nights.

On to Andenes

Back on the **E10** south of Harstad, it's 50km southwest along the fjord to the turning for the Lødingen ferry (see p.307) and 50km more to the bridge that spans the sound over to Sortland (see p.314). On the near side of this Sortland bridge, **Highway 82** begins its hundred-kilometre trek north, snaking along the craggy edge of Hinnøya island before crossing a second bridge over to humdrum **Risøyhamn**, the only Hurtigrute stop on **Andøya**, the most northerly of the Vesterålen Islands. Beyond **Risøyhamn**, the scenery is much less dramatic, as the mountains give way to hills in the west and a vast, peaty moor in the east. Highway 82 heads across this moorland and, despite offering panoramic views of the mountains back on the mainland, it's an uneventful journey on to Andenes.

At the old fishing port of **ANDENES**, lines of low-slung buildings lead up to the clutter of wooden warehouses and mini boat-repair yards that edge the harbour and its prominent breakwaters. "It is the fish, and that alone, that draws people to Andenes – the place itself has no other temptations," said the writer Poul Alm when he visited in 1944, and although this is too harsh a judgement today, the main emphasis does indeed remain firmly nautical. Among Scandinavians at least, Andenes is famous for its **whale safaris**, four- to five-hour cruises with a marine biologist on board to point out sperm, killer and minke whales as well as dolphins and porpoises; even better, the operators claim – with every justification – a ninety-five percent chance of a whale sighting: the edge of the continental shelf, which is closer to land here than anywhere else in Norway, boasts a large stock of sperm whales, who form the basis of the tours

Moving on from Harstad

From Harstad, the **Hurtigrute** (ⓦwww.hurtigruten.no) sails north for Tromsø at 8am and south for points in the Vesterålen and Lofoten Islands at 8.30am. Alternatively, there's a **Hurtigbåt** service to Tromsø (2–4 daily; 2hr 45min; 480kr; ⓦwww.hurtigruten.no) and frequent **buses** to Narvik, Sortland (for Andenes) and Lofoten (ⓦwww.177nordland .com). For **car rental**, several firms in Harstad offer short-term deals: try Europcar, Samagata 33 (ⓣ77 01 86 10), or Hertz, by the harbour (ⓣ77 06 13 46).

and dawdle in these waters all year. Safaris take place at least once daily between late May and mid-September but can be as frequent as five daily in high season, subject to demand. Taking an evening safari during the midnight sun period can be especially rewarding, as the calmer sea makes it easier to spot the surfacing sperm whales, and the light is simply enchanting. **Tickets** cost 795kr each (children 5–13 years, 500kr) and covers the guided tour of the Whale Centre (see below) that precedes the boat trip. The safari isn't recommended for children under 5 as the sea can get rough; warm clothing and sensible shoes are essential. **Reservation** (ⓣ76 11 56 00, ⓦwww.whalesafari.no) at least a day in advance is strongly advised as the trips are popular, and even with multiple departures in high season, they tend to fill up quickly.

The other recommended boat trip hereabouts is a **puffin safari** round the bird island of **Bleiksøya** (June to mid-Aug 1–2 daily; 1hr 30min; 350kr, children 150kr; reservation through the tourist office or direct ⓣ97 19 52 75, ⓦwww.puffinsafari .no), a pyramid-shaped hunk of rock populated by thousands of puffins, kittiwakes, razorbills and, sometimes, white-tailed eagles. Cruises leave from the jetty at **Bleik** (see p.314), an old and picturesque fishing hamlet around 7km southwest of Andenes that has a clear view of the islet; a local bus often makes the trip from Andenes to coincide with sailings.

Andenes' **Hvalsenter** (Whale Centre: late May to mid-June & mid-Aug to mid-Sept daily 8am–4pm; mid-June to mid-Aug daily 8am–7.30pm; 60kr; 140kr discount ticket for all of the town's sights on sale at the tourist office), metres from the harbour, may not be the most exciting way to start a safari, but it does give you a good explanation of what you're about to witness on the open ocean. That said, the centre's incidental displays on the life and times of the animal hardly fire the imagination, and neither does the massive – and deliberately dark and gloomy – display of a whale munching its way though a herd of squid. More diverting is the **Hisnakul natural history centre** (mid-June to Aug daily 10am–6pm; Sept to mid-June daily 10am–4pm; 50kr), which explores various facets of Andøya life from its premises in a refurbished timber warehouse near the Whale Centre. The centre is short on historical artefacts, plumping instead for imaginative displays such as the two hundred facial casts of local people made in 1994 and an assortment of giant replica bird beaks. The adjacent **Nordlyssenteret** (Northern Lights Centre: late June to late Aug daily 10am–6pm; 40kr) provides a comprehensive explanation of the northern lights (see box, p.328) – Andenes is a particularly good spot to see them – illustrated by first-class photographs and a slide show.

Close by, **Andenes fyr** (Andenes lighthouse: mid-June to Aug daily noon–4pm; 35kr) is a forty-metre-high maroon structure dating from the 1850s and offering wide views over the town from its top. From the lighthouse, it's a brief stroll south to the **Polarmuseet** (Polar Museum: late June to mid-Aug daily 10am–6pm; 30kr), inside a modest little building with a pretty wooden porch. Its main exhibit is the giant stuffed polar bear gazing at you from a frightening height; it was allegedly shot by accident on a recent expedition to Spitsbergen. The rest of the interior is mostly dedicated to the Arctic knick-knacks accumulated by a certain Hilmar Nøis, an Andøya man who wintered on Svalbard no fewer than 38 times. Unfortunately all the labelling is in Norwegian, but the helpful staff are willing to translate.

Practicalities

Bisecting the town, Andenes' long and straight main street, **Storgata**, ends abruptly at the seafront. The **bus station** is just a few metres to the east of Storgata, just back from the seafront, while the **tourist office** (mid-June to Aug daily 10am–6pm; Sept to mid-June daily 9am–4pm; ☎76 14 12 03, ⓦwww .andoyturist.no) is on the harbour, sharing the same premises as the **Northern Lights Centre**. The office has a comprehensive range of local information and can make reservations for bird-island boat trips, whale safaris and the car ferry to Gryllefjord (see p.307). It also has details of local **bicycle rental** and of **hiking trails** in the surrounding district.

Andenes has a fair sprinkling of inexpensive **accommodation** and several house-holds offer **private rooms** (②/③) – look out for the signs – but, considering how isolated a spot this is, you'd be well advised to make a reservation before you get here. One of the nicest places to stay is a guesthouse, the ⚒ *Fargeklatten Veita*, Sjøgata 38 (☎97 76 00 20, ⓦwww.fargeklatten.no; May–Sept; ②), a cluster of eighteenth- and nineteenth-century buildings that incorporates a small museum showing fishermen's odds and ends, an art gallery and a stylishly decorated guesthouse near the harbour. Nearby, on the seafront, is the green-timbered *Grønnbua* (☎76 14 14 99, ⓦwww .rorbucamping.no) comprising two *sjøhus* (for more about a *sjøhus*, see p.317), each of which has been parcelled up into **apartments**: one set is cosy and modern (from 865kr), the other older and slightly shabbier (from 540kr), though both have good views over the water. As an alternative to Andenes, you might also consider staying in tiny **BLEIK**, a pretty little place where a string of clapboard houses huddles between craggy hills and a long sandy beach. Bleik is just 7km southwest down along the coast from Andenes and it's home to the *Norlandia Bleik Apartments* (☎76 14 12 22, ⓦwww.norlandia.no/bleik), where there are modern double rooms (④) and apartments (from 700kr) in a handful of *sjøhus*. As regards **food**, nothing really stands out, but the timber terrace of the *Grønnbua II* is very pleasant and prices are reasonable with main courses – like whale steak (conscience permitting) – averaging 175kr. For daytime snacks, head for *Jul. Nilsens Bakeri* (Mon–Fri 8.30am–4.30pm, Sat 8.30am–2.30pm), close to the bus station at Kong Hansgate 1.

Sortland and points south to Melbu

Small-town **SORTLAND** is little more than an unappetizing modern sprawl that straggles along the coast beside the bridge linking the islands of Hinnøya and Langøya. By virtue of its location, Sortland is also something of a **transport hub**, and bus passengers sometimes have to change here for the onward journey south to Stokmarknes and Lofoten, and always to catch the local bus north to Andenes (see p.310), which originates here. The **tourist office** at Kjøpmannsgata 2 (mid-June to late Aug Mon–Fri 9am–6pm, Sat 10am–2pm, & Sun 10am–noon; Sept to mid-June Mon–Fri 8am–4pm; ☎76 11 14 80, ⓦwww.visitvesteralen.no) is in the centre of town, a couple of hundred metres from the Hurtigrute quay and a five- to ten-minute walk from the bus station.

Stokmarknes – and the Trollfjord

Travelling southwest from Sortland along the E10, it's about 30km to **STOKMARKNES**, an unremarkable little town whose mediocrity is partly relieved by its pleasant shoreline setting. Here also you can sample the delights of the **Hurtigrutemuseet** (mid-May to mid-June & mid-Aug to mid-Sept daily noon–4pm; mid-June to mid-Aug daily 10am–6pm; mid-Sept to mid-May Mon–Fri 2–4pm, Sat noon–4pm & Sun 2–4pm; 80kr; ⓦwww.hurtigrutemuseet .no), which is entirely devoted to the history of the Hurtigrute coastal boat, with a genuine 1950s ferry, the M/S *Finnmarken*, parked up outside on the quayside, looking very much its age.

Museum aside, the main reason to stop off in **Stokmarknes** is to catch the **Hurtigrute coastal boat** south to Svolvær via the Trollfjord. The boat leaves

Operated by **Veolia** (☎177 in Nordland, otherwise ☎75 77 24 10; ⊕www.177nordland .com), local **buses** run south from Andenes to Risøyhamn and Sortland for the E10 (2–4 daily; 1–2hr). Heading north, it's possible to weave your way up along the coast from Andenes to Tromsø (see p.329), beginning with the seasonal **Senjafergene car ferry** (☎76 14 12 03, ⊕www.senjafergene.no) linking Andenes with Gryllefjord on the mainland, but note that advance reservations are strongly advised (late May to mid-June & early to late Aug 2 daily; mid-June to early Aug 3 daily; 2hr; passengers 145kr, car & driver 375kr). From Gryllefjord, it's about 220km via Highway 86 to Finnsnes, then along the scenic Highway 861 to **Botnhamn**, where a second Senjafergene car ferry crosses over to **Brensholmen** (May to Aug 5–7 daily; 45min; passengers 60kr, cars 155kr); from **Brensholmen** it's 70km or so on to Tromsø.

daily at 3.15pm, sailing down the **Raftsundet**, the narrow sound separating the harsh, rocky shanks of Hinnøya and Austvågøya. Towards the southern end of the sound, the ship usually makes a short detour to the **Trollfjord**, a majestic tear in the landscape just 2km long. Slowing to a gentle chug, the vessels inch up the narrow gorge, smooth stone towering high above and blocking out the light. At the head of the Trollfjord, the boats effect a nautical three-point turn and then crawl back to rejoin the main waterway. It's very atmospheric, and the effect is perhaps even more extraordinary when the weather is up. One caution: the Hurtigrute will not enter the Trollfjord when there's the danger of a rock fall, but pauses at the fjord's mouth instead. Check locally before embarkation, though you're only likely to miss out, if at all, in spring. The Hurtigrute cruise from Sortland to Svolvær takes a little over three hours and costs 207kr per passenger in winter, 295kr in summer; cars cost 377kr all year. It's also possible to visit the Trollfjord on special boat trips from Svolvær – see p.320.

Stokmarknes practicalities

Buses to Stokmarknes pull in near the harbourfront tourist office (late May to mid-Aug Mon–Fri 10am–5pm, Sat & Sun 10am–3pm; ☎76 16 46 60), which has details of what little local **accommodation** there is both in and around town. The best choice is the *Turistsenteret* (☎76 15 29 99, ⊕www.hurtigrutenshus .com; ❸/❺), a brassy, modern hotel-cum-conference centre plonked on Børøya islet, about fifteen minutes' walk from the museum, at the far end of the first of two bridges back towards Sortland. The modern *rorbuer* that constitute the hotel all have magnificent views of the Hurtigrute as it makes its way into Stokmarknes harbour.

From Stokmarknes, it's 15km south along the E10 to **MELBU**, from where there is a **car ferry** over to Fiskebøl on Lofoten (daily 7am–11pm, every 90min; 25min; passengers 31kr, car & driver 85kr; ☎177, ⊕www.177nordland.com).

The Lofoten Islands

A skeletal curve of mountainous rock stretched out across the Norwegian Sea, the **Lofoten Islands** have been the focal point of northern Norway's winter fishing from time immemorial. At the turn of the year, cod migrate from the Barents Sea to spawn here, where the coldness of the water is tempered by the Gulf Stream. The season lasts only from February to April, but fishing impinges on all aspects of island life and is impossible to ignore at any time of the year. At almost every harbour stand the massed ranks of wooden racks used for drying the cod, burgeoning and odoriferous in winter, empty in summer like so many abandoned climbing frames.

Sharing the same history, but better known and more beautiful than their neighbours the Vesterålen, the Lofoten Islands have everything from sea-bird colonies in the south to beaches and fjords in the north. The traditional approach is by boat from Bodø and this brings visitors face to face with the islands' most striking feature, the towering peaks of the **Lofotenveggen** (Lofoten Wall), a 160-kilometre stretch of mountains, whose jagged teeth bite into the skyline, trapping a string of tiny fishing villages tight against the shore. The mountains are set so close together that on first inspection there seems to be no way through, but in fact the islands are riddled with straights, sounds and fjords.

The Lofoten have their own relaxed pace, and are perfect for a simple, uncluttered few days. For somewhere so far north, the weather can be exceptionally mild: summer days can be spent sunbathing on the rocks or hiking and biking around the superb coastline, and when it rains – as it frequently does – life focuses on the *rorbuer* (fishermen's huts), where freshly caught fish are cooked over wood-burning stoves, stories are told and time gently wasted. If that sounds rather contrived, in a sense it is – the way of life here is to some extent preserved like this for tourists – but it's rare to find anyone who isn't less than completely enthralled by it all.

The **E10** weaves a scenic route across Lofoten, running the 170km from **Fiskebøl** in the north to **Å** in the south, hopping from island to island by bridge and causeway and by occasionally tunnelling through the mountains and under the sea. The highway passes through or within a few kilometres of all the islands' main villages, amongst which **Henningsvær** and **Å** are breathtakingly beautiful, with **Stamsund** coming in close behind. All three make great bases for further explorations on foot or by boat. Indeed, there's an abundance of marine activity with everything on offer from island cruises, sea-rafting and fishing excursions through to birdwatching trips. Scores of places also rent out fishing boats and equipment, although, because of the strong currents, you should always seek advice about local conditions. Back on land, the islands may not have a well-developed network of huts and hiking trails, but the byroads, where you'll rarely see a car, provide mile after mile of excellent **walking** as they delve deep into the heart of the landscape.

As regards accommodation, the Lofoten Islands have a sprinkling of **hotels**, a few of which are first-rate, though some are blandly modern, as well as three HI **hostels**, numerous **campsites** and the local speciality, the **rorbuer** (see box opposite). There's

▲ Lofoten

Staying in a rorbu or sjøhus

Right across Lofoten, **rorbuer** (fishermen's shacks) are rented out to tourists for both overnight stays and longer periods. The name *rorbu* is derived from *ror*, "to row" and *bu*, literally "dwelling" – and some older islanders still ask "Will you row this winter?", meaning "Will you go fishing this winter?" Traditionally, *rorbuer* were built on the shore, often on poles sticking out of the sea, and usually coloured with a red paint based on cod-liver oil. They consisted of two sections, a sleeping and eating room and a smaller storage area.

At the peak of the fisheries in the 1930s, some 30,000 men were accommodated in *rorbuer*, but during the 1960s fishing boats became more comfortable and since then many fishermen have preferred to sleep aboard. Most of the original *rorbuer* disappeared years ago, and, although a few have survived, visitors today are much more likely to stay in a modern version, mostly prefabricated units churned out by the dozen with the tourist trade in mind. At their best, they are comfortable and cosy seashore cabins, sometimes a well-planned conversion of an original *rorbu* with bunk beds and wood-fired stoves; at their worst, they are little better than prefabricated hutches in the middle of nowhere. Most have space for between four and six guests and the charge for a hut averages around 1000kr per night – though some cost as little as 600kr, while others rise to about 2000kr. Similar rates are charged for the islands' **sjøhus** (literally sea-houses), originally the large quayside halls where the catch was processed and the workers slept. Most of the original *sjøhus* have been cleverly converted into attractive apartments with self-catering facilities, a few into dormitory-style accommodation – and again, as with the *rorbuer*, the quality varies enormously. A full list of *rorbuer* and *sjøhus* is given in the *Lofoten Info-Guide*, a free pamphlet that you can pick up at any local tourist office and on ⓦ www.lofoten.info.

comprehensive tourist information on ⓦ www.lofoten.info, though ⓦ www.lofoten -info.no covers two of the more southerly islands, Moskenesøya and Flakstadøya, in greater detail.

Transport to and around the Lofoten Islands

The opening of the **Lofast**, the new stretch of road between Gullesfjordbotn and Fiskebøl, has made it much easier to get to the Lofoten and it's now possible to **drive** from Evenes (Harstad/Narvik) airport to Svolvær in less than three hours. This new route is ferry free, but you can still reach the Lofoten by car **ferry**, Hurtigbåt passenger express boat and the Hurtigrute coastal boat. Once you've got to the Lofoten, you'll find **public transport** thin on the ground. What local bus services there are stick almost exclusively to the E10, the islands' only main road, and elsewhere you'll mostly have to **walk** – hardly an onerous task in such beautiful surroundings.

If you have your own **vehicle**, village-hopping is easy and quick, but it's only when you leave the car and head off into the landscape that the real character of Lofoten begins to reveal itself; allow time for at least one walk or sea trip. Conversely, if you don't have a vehicle and want to reach the islands' remoter spots, it's worth considering renting a car, an inexpensive option if a few people share the cost. There are local **car rental** outlets at Svolvær, Stamsund and Svolvær and Leknes airports, where special short-term deals can bring costs down to around 600kr a day.

All Nordland **public transport** timetables – including those for Lofoten – are online at ⓦ www.177nordland.com; you can also call ☏ 177 within Nordland, otherwise ☏ 75 77 24 10.

By car ferry

From the mainland, the traditional approach to the Lofoten is by **car ferry** from **Bodø**. There are three destinations to choose from, all on the southern

peripheries of the archipelago, but the most important is **Moskenes**, a tiny port
just a few kilometres from the end of the E10. The trip from Bodø to Moskenes
takes about four hours: be prepared for a rough crossing. The **fare** from Bodø to
Moskenes is 155kr for passengers, 561kr for a car and driver. These ferries are
operated by **Hurtigruten** (ⓦwww.hurtigruten.no) on a first-come, first-served
basis, so it's a good idea to turn up a couple of hours before departure. Note,
however, that in the summertime (June–Aug) advance reservations are permitted
– and are strongly recommended; Bodø tourist office will arrange things for
you or you can contact Hurtigruten direct, either online or on the company's
reservation line ☎810 30 000.

The shortest **car ferry** service to the Lofoten links **Skutvik**, 35km west of the E6
midway between Fauske and Narvik, with **Svolvær** (1 daily; 2hr; passengers 76kr,
car & driver 262kr). This is also operated by Hurtigruten (ⓦwww.hurtigruten.no)
and, given the infrequency of the service, advance reservations are strongly advised
– either with Hurtigruten direct (see above) or at Bodø tourist office.

Heading for the Lofoten from the **Vesterålen**, you can either use the Lofast
connection or take the **Melbu to Fiskebøl** car ferry (daily 7am–11pm, every
80min; 30min; passengers 31kr, car & driver 85kr; ☎177 in Nordland, otherwise
☎75 77 24 10, ⓦwww.177nordland.com).

By boat: the Hurtigrute

The northbound **Hurtigrute** leaves Bodø daily at 3pm calling at two ports in the
Lofoten islands – Stamsund and Svolvær – before nudging through the Raftsundet
en route to Stokmarknes, on the Vesterålen. The passenger fare for the four-and-
a-half-hour cruise from Bodø to Stamsund is 397kr in summer, 278kr winter,
and cars cost 353kr all year; the six-hour journey to Svolvær costs 425/297kr, cars
377kr. Advance reservations for cars are essential, and can be made online (ⓦwww
.hurtigruten.no) or by phoning the ship – ask down at the harbour or at the port's
tourist office for assistance.

By boat: Hurtigbåt passenger express boats

A **Hurtigbåt** passenger express boat service runs from **Bodø to Svolvær**
(1 daily; 3hr 30min; 297kr; ☎177 in Nordland, otherwise ☎75 77 24 10, ⓦwww
.hurtigruten.no). Advance reservation is advised.

By bus

The long-distance **Lofoten Ekspressen**, operated by **Nor-Way Bussekspress**
(ⓦwww.nor-way.no) in conjunction with a couple of smaller companies provides
the main bus service from the mainland to the Lofoten. It leaves Narvik twice
daily to run along the E6 and then the E10, calling at Evenes airport and Lødingen
before taking the Lofast highway to Fiskebøl in the Lofoten; it then proceeds on to
Svolvær, where one bus daily continues to Leknes, or you change for the once-daily
bus to Leknes and Å. As an example of **journey times**, Narvik to Leknes takes six
hours, just under eight hours to Å.

This long-distance bus service is supported by a number of somewhat intermit-
tent **local buses** operated by **Veolia** (☎177 in Nordland, otherwise ☎75 77 24
10, ⓦwww.177nordland.com). Two of Veolia's more useful offerings are Svolvær to
Henningsvær (Mon–Sat 4–7 daily) and Leknes to Stamsund (Mon–Sat 3–6 daily).

By plane – and car rental

Flights leave Bodø for the Lofoten airports – or rather airstrips – at Svolvær and
Leknes four to seven times a day. The operator is **Widerøe** (ⓦwww.wideroe.no), an
SAS subsidiary, and tickets can be purchased at any travel agent or SAS agent as well
as online; fares from Bodø to the islands vary enormously, but a standard summer
return ticket costs in the region of 900kr, half that one-way. Note also that whereas
Svolvær airport is merely 5km from town, Leknes airport is miles from anywhere

you might want to visit, and the onward taxi will cost an arm and a leg. There is **car rental** at both airports: Svolvær has, for instance, Avis (☎76 07 11 40) and Hertz (☎76 07 07 20) outlets, as does Leknes – Hertz (☎76 08 18 44) and Avis (☎76 08 01 04). Good-value short-term deals abound – from around 600kr per day.

Svolvær

SVOLVÆR strings over and around several headlands and bays on the southeast coast of **Austvågøya**, the largest of the Lofoten islands, but somehow contrives to be a somewhat disappointing introduction to the archipelago. The region's administrative and transport centre, it has all the bustle but little of the charm of the other island towns, though it does have more accommodation and better restaurants than its neighbours and – to be fair – its surroundings are suitably mountainous. The town also possess three attractions of some interest, beginning with the **Lofoten Krigsminnemuseum**, close to the Hurtigrute quay (War Memorial Museum; June–Sept Mon–Fri 10am–4pm, Sat 11am–3pm & Sun noon–3pm; by appointment out of season; 50kr; ⊛ www.lofotenkrigmus.no), which chronicles the British commando raids on Lofoten by means of photographs and original artefacts. There's also **Magic Ice** (mid-June to mid-Aug daily noon–11pm; mid-Aug to mid-June daily 6–10pm; 95kr; ⊛ www.magic-ice.no), a quayside gallery depicting Lofoten life in winter by means of giant ice sculptures. The temperature is permanently below zero, so warm jackets and boots are issued for free. Finally, the **Nordnorsk Kunstnersentrum**, across the bridge from the centre on the islet of Svinøya (Northern Norway Art Centre: mid-June to late Aug daily 10am–6pm; late Aug to mid-June Wed–Sun 11am–3pm; 30kr; ⊛ www.nnks.no), has some fine paintings by Gunnar Berg (1863–93), including the *Battle of the Trollfjord*, as well as work by contemporary Norwegian artists.

Arrival and information

Ferries to Svolvær dock about 1km west of the town centre, and the Hurtigrute docks in the centre, a brief walk from the **bus station** and the busy **tourist office**, just off the main town square near the harbour (late May to mid-June Mon–Fri 9am–4pm & Sat 10am–2pm; mid- to late June Mon–Fri 9am–8pm, Sat 10am–2pm & Sun 4–8pm; late June to early Aug Mon–Fri 9am–10pm, Sat 9am–8pm & Sun 10am–8pm; early Aug to late Aug Mon–Fri 9am–8pm, Sat 10am–2pm; Sept to mid-May Mon–Fri 9am–3.30pm; ☎76 06 98 07, ⊛ www .lofoten.info); it has maps, accommodation lists and public transport details. Svolvær is also a good place to **rent a car**: Europcar, for example, have an outlet at Sivert Nilsens Gate 43 (☎76 07 00 00).

Accommodation

Although Svolvær isn't short of **accommodation**, finding a room in high season can be a real pain. Consequently, advance reservation is highly recommended – especially if you want to avoid the town's clutch of mundane, mini-high-rise hotels.

Anker Brygge Lamholmen ☎76 06 64 80; ⊛ www.anker-brygge.no. The town's smartest accommodation, consisting of 22 spacious and tastefully decorated *rorbuer* in a prime location on a tiny islet – Lamholmen – at the end of a causeway in the middle of the harbour. ❺

Rica Hotel Svolvær Lamholmen ☎76 07 22 22, ⊛ www.rica.no. This well-above-average chain hotel has an attractive modern design, its acres of glass perched on top of timber piles. Has small but comfortable rooms, half with balcony.

On the islet of Lamholmen in the middle of the harbour. ❺

Svinøya Rorbuer Svinøya ☎76 06 99 30, ⊛ www.svinoya.no. At the northeast end of town, a causeway crosses over to the long and slender island of Svinøya, which is home to this set of *rorbuer*. They range from the plain and simple (❷) to the deluxe (❺/❻) and there's a low-budget, summertime hostel here too, with large and clean double rooms that are exceptionally good value at ❶

Svolvær Sjøhus Parkgata ☎76 07 03 36,
ⓦwww.svolver-sjohuscamp.no. Modest rooms
here at this long-established place by the seashore
at the foot of Parkgata. To get there from the
square, turn right up the hill along Vestfjordgata

and it's to the right, past the library. ❶
Thon Hotel Svolvær O.J. Kaalbøes gate 5
☎76 04 90 00, ⓦwww.thonhotels.no. Smart,
recently revamped chain hotel right in the centre of
town with thirty bedrooms. ❺

Around Svolvær

It doesn't take long to explore Svolvær, and afterwards you could do no better
than to venture out into its dramatic environs on one of several local **boat trips**.
Every day throughout the summer boats (return trip 3hr; 400kr; buy tickets on
board; ⓦwww.lofoten-charterboat.no) leave Svolvær for the **Trollfjord**, an impossibly narrow, two-kilometre-long stretch of water that's also on the Hurtigrute
itinerary (see p.318). The intrepid should also consider making the same excursion
by **speedboat** – heavy jackets and goggles are included (return trip 2hr; 500kr;
ⓦwww.lofoten-explorer.com).

Svolvær also boasts one of the archipelago's most famous **climbs**, the haul up to
the top of the **Svolværgeita** (the "Svolvær Goat"), a twin-pronged peak that rises
high above the E10 to the northeast of town. The lower slopes of the mountain are
hard enough, but the last 40m – up the horns of the "Goat" – require considerable expertise. Daring-daft mountaineers complete the thrill by jumping from one
pinnacle to the other.

Restaurants and bars

Svolvær has a reasonable selection of bars and restaurants, the best you'll find on
Lofoten, though they don't come cheap. The 🍴 *Café Bacalao*, down on the quay, is a
spacious café-restaurant with snappy service and a menu that mixes Mediterranean
and Norwegian cuisine with flair and imagination: lunches, and main courses in
the evening, hover around 175kr. It serves excellent coffee too, and at night turns
into the town's liveliest bar, jam-packed at the weekend. If you're considering
splashing out on dinner, *Du Verden*, in the centre at J.E. Paulsens gate 12 (☎76 07
70 99) is your best bet. The creative menu features the freshest of local ingredients
with main courses average around 250kr. At lunchtime the place is a snip – try the
mouthwatering fish soup. Alternatively, the restaurant at the *Svinøya Rorbuer* is highly
competent, with seafood its forte; mains from around 240kr.

Henningsvær

Heading west from Svolvær, it's 17km on the E10 to the 8km-long turning that
leads to **HENNINGSVÆR**, the most beguiling of headland villages, a cobweb
of cramped and twisting lanes lined with brightly painted wooden houses. These
frame a tiny inlet that literally cuts the place in half, forming a sheltered, picture-
postcard harbour. Almost inevitably, coach parties are wheeled in and out, despite
the narrowness of the two high-arched bridges into the village, but for all the hustle
and bustle Henningsvær richly deserves an **overnight stay**.

One of the town's main draws is the **Galleri Lofotens Hus**, on Hjellskjæret (late
May to mid-Sept daily 9am–7pm; 75kr; ⓦwww.galleri-lofoten.no), which exhibits
(and sells) the work of the contemporary Norwegian artist Karl Erik Harr. Also on
display is a competent selection of late nineteenth- and twentieth-century Lofoten
paintings by artists such as Einar Berge, Adelsteen Normann, Gunnar Berg and Otto
Sinding – you can't miss the latter's whopping *Funeral in Lofoten* of 1886 – plus historic
and contemporary photographs and slides mostly of the islands. Henningsvær's Arctic
light, plus the might of the mountains, have long attracted Norwegian painters, making
it something of an arts centre, and, indeed, there's more art for sale – plus ceramics
and glassware – at the nearby **Engelskmannsbrygga**, on the main square (late Feb to
early June & mid-Aug to Dec Tues–Fri 10am–4pm, Sat & Sun noon–4pm; mid-June
to early Aug daily 10am–8pm; free; ⓦwww.engelskmannsbrygga.no).

The intrepid should make a beeline for Lofoten's best mountaineering school, **Nord Norsk Klatreskole**, Misværveien 10 (☎90 57 42 08, ⊕www.nordnorsk klatreskole.no), which operates a range of all-inclusive **climbing holidays** in the mountains near Henningsvær, catering for various degrees of fitness and experience. Prices vary depending on the trip, but a three-day, one-climb-a-day package costs in the region of 4800kr per person, including equipment, food and accommodation. Much less strenuous are **fishing trips**, a morning or afternoon's excursion for around 450kr, which can be booked down at the harbour, or **sea-eagle safaris** (☎90 58 14 75; 370kr; ⊕www.lofoten-opplevelser.no), which depart daily at 2.30pm throughout the summer. Finally, Henningsvær's an especially windy little place – so come (or be) prepared.

Arrival, accommodation, eating and drinking

The Lofoten Ekspressen **bus** (see p.318) does not detour off the E10 to get to Henningsvær, but there is a local bus service from Svolvær (7 daily). The town has ample **accommodation**, the smartest hotel being the quayside *Henningsvær Brygge-hotell* (☎76 07 47 50, ⊕www.henningsvaer.no; ❺/❻), an attractive modern building in traditional style right on the waterfront. Another stylish option is the *Henningsvær Rorbuer* (☎76 06 60 00, ⊕www.henningsvar-rorbuer.no), offering 26 well-equipped *rorbuer* (930–2600kr) at the far end of the town. A far more economical choice is the frugal *Den Siste Viking*, Misværveien 10 (☎90 57 42 08, ⊕www.nordnorskklatreskole .no; ❶), which provides unadorned lodgings also right in the centre; the place doubles as the island's mountaineering school (see above). Perhaps the most cheerful hotel is the *Henningsvær Hotell* (☎76 07 07 00, ⊕www.nordnorskenytelser.no; ❸), where all the rooms are themed up in different colour schemes and there's a spacious restaurant downstairs (see below).

Henningsvær has a good supply of **cafés and restaurants**, beginning with the inviting *Klatrekafeen*, at *Den Siste Viking* (see above), which serves up a good range of Norwegian standbys from 100kr, plus soup and salads and some killer chocolate cupcakes, all washed down with first-rate coffee; climbing relics and candle light gives the place oodles of atmosphere. A good alternative is the *Baker-iteateret* with its stylish interior and tasty waffles and coffees; at night time, the place doubles as a bar. For something a little more unusual, consider having lunch in the *Lysstøperi* – the local candle shop at Gammelveien 2 – where they serve *kanelsnurr* and *skolebolle*, both sweet treats designed to test your dental fillings. The classiest restaurant is the waterside *Fiskekrogen*, Dreyersgate 19 (☎76 07 46 52), where the seafood in general, and the fish soup in particular, are simply superb; main courses like cod, monkfish and mussels from 225kr. A smashing second option is the spacious restaurant at the the *Henningsvær Hotell*, which specializes in halibut, cod and *bacalao*.

Vestvågøy: Stamsund

It's the next large island to the southwest of Austvågøya, Vestvågøy, that captivates many travellers to Lofoten. This is due in no small part to the laid-back charm of **STAMSUND**, whose older buildings string along the rocky, fretted seashore in an amiable jumble of crusty port buildings, wooden houses and *rorbuer*. There have been some recent additions to the Stamsund stew, but it's all pretty low-key; the modern art gallery, **Galleri 2** (June–Aug Tues–Sun noon–4pm & 6.30–9.30pm; 20kr; ⊕www .galleri2.no), about 100m from the Hurtigrute dock, is well worth a gander.

The main **bus** service to Stamsund (Mon–Sat 3–4 daily) is from Leknes, which is both the dull administrative centre of Vestvågøy and the site of the island's **airport**, just 15km away to the west; Leknes is reachable on the long-distance **Lofoten Ekspressen** (see p.318). Stamsund is also the first port at which the Hurtigrute **coastal boat** docks on its way north from Bodø. By **car**, the quickest way to Stamsund from Svolvær is to turn south off the E10 down Highway 815, a scenic forty-kilometre coastal drive.

The best place to **stay** in Stamsund is the ⚥ HI **hostel** (☎76 08 93 34, ⓦwww .vandrerhjem.no; March to mid-Oct; dorm beds 120kr, doubles ❶), about 1km down the road from the port. The hostel consists of several *rorbuer* and a *sjøhus* perched over a bonny, pin-sized bay, and has a washing machine, tumble dryer and self-catering facilities. You can rent **bikes** here at 100kr a day, and the warden is very knowledgeable on everything about Vestvågøy, from cycling through to hiking and fishing. The **fishing** is, in fact, first-class: you can borrow the hostel's rowing boats and lines to take out on the (usually still) water. Afterwards you can barbecue your catch and eat alfresco on the veranda overlooking the bay – it's this sort of easygoing activity that makes the place incredibly popular. For something a little more conventionally comfortable – or just conventional – head for the stylishly decorated and intelligently revamped old *rorbuer* at Skjærbrygga (☎76 05 46 00, ⓦwww.skjaerbrygga.no; ❹), right in the centre of Stamsund by the harbour. The old *Skjærbrygga sjøhus* has been attractively renovated too, and now contains a café and an excellent restaurant, which features the freshest of local ingredients; main courses at the restaurant go for around 250kr, much less at the café. Less pricey *rorbuer* can also be found 3km west along the coast from Stamsund in the minuscule hamlet of **STEINE**, where the cosy if rather spartan *Steine Rorbuer & Hytter* (☎76 08 92 83; from 650kr) snuggle tight against the seashore.

South to Ramberg

By any standard, the next two islands of the archipelago, **Flakstadøya** – known to the Vikings as "Vargfot", or wolf's paw, on account of its shape – and **Moskenesøya**, are extraordinarily beautiful. As the Lofoten taper towards their southerly conclusion, the rearing peaks of the Lofotenveggen crimp the sea-shredded coastline, providing a thunderously scenic backdrop to a necklace of tiny fishing villages. The E10 travels along almost all of this shoreline, leaving Leknes to tunnel west under the sound separating Vestvågøy from Flakstadøya. About 25km from Leknes, the road passes **Flakstad kirke**, a distinctive onion-domed, red timber church built in 1780. The church's ornate pulpit was painted by the itinerant German artist Gottfried Ezechiel (see also the Bodin kirke, p.301), as was the painting above the altar, whose main motif is the Last Supper. The church announces the beginning of **RAMBERG**, the island's administrative centre – if that's what you can call the smattering of services (garage, supermarket and suchlike) that strings along the sandy beach.

On to Hamnøy and Sakrisøya

Pressing on over the first of several narrow bridges, you're soon on **Moskenesøya**, where the road squirms across the mouth of the Reinefjord, hopping from islet to islet to link the fishing villages of **HAMNØY**, on the north side of the inlet, with Reine (see below) a little to the south. Both villages boast impossibly pictur-esque settings and Hamnøy also lays claim to an excellent **restaurant**, *Hamnøy Mat & Vinbu* (☎76 09 21 45; May–Sept), whose short menu provides traditional Norwegian cuisine at its best, with excellent seafood including cods' tongues – an island delicacy – and the rarely seen, but delicious, sago pudding. Hamnøy also possesses some very plain *rorbuer* – *Hamnøy Rorbuer* (☎76 09 23 20, ⓦwww .lofoten-info.no/hamnoy; 600–900kr), but far more appealing are those on the tiny islet of Sakrisøya, midway between Hamnøy and Reine, where the pretty original 1870 cabins of ⚥ *Sakrisøy Rorbuer* (☎76 09 21 43, ⓦwww.lofoten.ws; 500–1100kr) are both well kept and cosy with a wood stove adding to the atmosphere. The owners of the *rorbuer* also run the little fishmongers opposite, where they dish out delicious home-made fishburgers and sell freshly caught fish. A tiny dolls' museum and bric-a-brac store complete the scene.

Reine

On the far side of the inlet, **REINE** has a fabulous location, ambling along a tiny islet, which is connected to the rest of Moskenesøya by a narrow causeway branching off the E10. Right next to the boat dock, the **Eva Harr gallery** (late May to late Aug daily 10.30am–6pm; ⊛www.evaharr.no; 60kr) is devoted to Harr a contemporary artist, whose paintings of Lofoten are displayed alongside a selection of her graphic work. The best place to stay in the village is the *Reine Rorbuer* (☏76 09 22 22, ⊛www.reinerorbuer.no; 1100–2100kr for two persons), consisting of 22 recently renovated *rorbuer* and three apartments in what was once the police station. The restaurant (May–Aug) occupies the old general store and offers top-notch seafood risottos, local lamb and marinated salmon with a terrace overlooking the harbour; mains from 180kr.

Reine is a departure point for a variety of **boat trips**, including midnight sun cruises, coastal voyages, fishing expeditions and excursions to the Moskenstraumen (see below). For further information about these trips, ask around locally or contact the Moskenes tourist office (see below).

Moskenes

From Reine, it's about 5km to **MOSKENES**, the main island port for ferries to and from Bodø – not that there's much here beyond a handful of houses dotted round a horseshoe-shaped bay. There is, however, a helpful **tourist office** by the jetty (March–April & Sept Mon–Fri 10am–2pm; early to mid-June & mid- to late Aug daily 10am–5pm; late June to early Aug daily 9am–7pm; ☏98 01 75 64, ⊛www .lofoten-info.no), and a basic **campsite** (☏99 48 94 05; June–Aug), up a gravel track a five-minute walk away.

Å

Five kilometres south of Moskenes the road ends abruptly at tersely named **Å**, one of Lofoten's most delightful villages, its huddle of old buildings rambling along a foreshore that's wedged in tight between the grey-green mountains and the surging sea. Unusually, so much of the nineteenth-century village has survived that a good portion of Å has been incorporated into the **Norsk Fiskevaersmuseum** (Norwegian Fishing Village Museum: late June to late Aug daily 10am–5.30pm; late Aug to late June Mon–Fri 11am–3.30pm; 50kr; ⊛www.lofoten-info.no /nfmuseum), an engaging attempt to recreate life here at the end of the nineteenth century. There are about fifteen buildings to examine, including a boathouse, forge, cod-liver-oil-processing plant, *rorbuer* and the houses, both of the traders who dominated things hereabouts and the fishermen who did their bidding. The museum has a series of **displays** detailing every aspect of village life – and very well presented it is too. Afterwards, you can extend your knowledge of all things fishy by visiting the **Tørrfiskmuseum** (Stockfish Museum: early to late June Mon–Fri 11am–4pm; late June to late Aug daily 10am–5.30pm; 40kr) – stockfish being the air-dried fish that was the staple diet of most Norwegians well into the twentieth century.

Hiking and boat trips from Å – the Moskenstraumen

Å doesn't offer too much in the way of hiking trails, but there is an enjoyable route leading west from the village to the other side of the island. This begins by skirting the south shore of Lake Ågvatnet, before climbing over a steep ridge and then pushing on to the sea cliffs of the exposed west coast. The hike takes a whole day, and shouldn't be attempted in bad weather. Less energetic are the **boat trips** that leave from Å's jetty from May through to September, including day-long fishing expeditions (500kr per person), coastal cruises (3hr; 500kr) and, weather and tides permitting, cruises to the abandoned fishing village of Refsvik and the **Moskenstraumen** (5hr; 800kr), the dramatic maelstrom at the southern tip of Moskenesøya

Practicalities

Beginning in Narvik – and using the Lofast highway – the **Lofoten Ekspressen bus** (Ⓦwww.177nordland.com) runs the length of the E10 all the way down to Svolvær twice daily; from Svolvær, one bus daily continues to Leknes and Å. The journey time from Narvik to Å is about eight hours, a little under four hours from Svolvær. Times do not, however, usually coincide with ferry sailings to and from Moskenes. Consequently, if you're heading from the Moskenes ferry port to Å, you'll either have to walk – it's an easy 5km – or take a taxi.

Most of the **accommodation** in Å is run by one family, which owns the year-round HI **hostel** (singles 180kr, doubles ❶); an assortment of smart one- to eight-bedded *rorbuer* that surround the dock (850–1550kr per *rorbu*); and the adjacent *sjøhus*, which offers comfortable and equally smart hotel-standard rooms (❷). The same family also runs the cosy bar, with seagull-egg bar snacks, and the only restaurant, where the seafood is excellent. Bookings for all these can be made on ☎76 09 11 21, Ⓦwww .lofoten-rorbu.com. While you are here, you should also try the cinnamon buns made at the old bakery, which still uses the original, vintage oven.

Å is, to some extent at least, a victim of its own success and in summertime it can heave with tourists. Don't despair. From the village, it's a short (600m) walk back down the road to **TIND**, much less visited and with fifteen spacious but cosy *rorbuer* (☎92 89 36 74; Ⓦwww.tindlofoten.no; ❸); the spa and outdoor hot tubs here are a real treat.

Travel details

Principal NSB trains (Ⓦwww.nsb.no)

Trondheim to: Bodø (2 daily; 10hr); Fauske (2 daily; 9hr); Mo-i-Rana (3 daily; 6hr 30min); Oslo (4 daily via Dombås, Lillehammer and Oslo Gardermoen airport; 5hr, some services 7hr); Stockholm (2 daily; 12hr).

Ofotbanen SJ trains from Narvik (Ⓦwww.sj.se)

Narvik to: Kiruna, Sweden (2–3 daily; 3hr); Luleå, Sweden (2–3 daily; 6hr 30min); Riksgränsen, Sweden (2–3 daily; 50min).

Principal Nor-Way Bussekspress buses (Ⓦwww.nor-way.no)

Note that the Lofoten Ekspressen from Narvik to the Lofotens is operated by Nor-Way Bussekspress in conjunction with two other companies.
Bodø to: Fauske (2–3 daily; 1hr 10min); Lødingen (2 daily; 6hr); Narvik (2 daily; 6hr 30min); Sortland (2 daily; 7hr).
Fauske to: Bodø (2–3 daily; 1hr 10min); Lødingen (2 daily; 4hr); Narvik (2 daily; 5hr 30min); Sortland (2 daily; 5hr).
Narvik to: Å (1 daily; 7hr 50min); Alta (2 daily except Sat; 9hr 30min); Bodø (2 daily; 6hr 30min); Fauske (2 daily; 5hr 30min); Gullesfjordbotn

(2 daily; 3hr); Leknes (2 daily; 6hr); Lødingen (2 daily; 2hr 30min); Svolvær (2 daily; 4hr 20min); Tromsø (2–3 daily; 4hr).
Sortland to: Fauske (2 daily; 5hr).
Svolvær to: Leknes (2 daily; 1hr 30min); Narvik (2 daily; 4hr 20min).
Trondheim to: Ålesund (3–4 daily; 7hr); Bergen (1 daily; 14hr 30min); Loen (1 daily; 8hr); Lom (1 daily; 5hr 40min); Oslo (1–3 daily; 8hr); Otta (1 daily; 4hr 30min); Stryn (1 daily; 8hr).

Nor-Way Bussekspress's Nord-Norgeekspressen and Nordkapp ekspressen (Ⓦwww.nor-way.no)

The **Nord-Norgeekspressen** (North Norway Express Bus) complements the railway system. It runs north from Bodø and Fauske to Alta in three segments: Bodø to Narvik via Fauske (2 daily; 6hr 30min); Narvik to Tromsø (1–3 daily; 4hr); and Tromsø to Alta (1 daily; 6hr 30min). Alternatively, the **Nordkappekspressen** (North Cape Express Bus) runs direct from Narvik to Alta (2 daily except Sat; 9hr 30min), where passengers overnight before picking up the second leg of the Nordkappekspressen to Honningsvåg and Nordkapp (see p.346 for details).

The Lofoten Ekspressen

The long-distance **Lofoten Ekspressen**, operated by Nor-Way Bussekspress (Ⓦwww.nor-way.no) in conjunction with a couple of smaller companies provides the main bus service from the mainland to the Lofoten. It leaves Narvik twice daily to run along the E6 and then the E10, calling at Evenes airport and Lødingen before taking the Lofast highway to Fiskebøl in the Lofoten; it then goes on to Svolvær, from where one bus daily continues to Leknes, or you change for the once-daily bus to Leknes and Å. As an example of journey times, Narvik to Leknes takes six hours, just under eight hours to Å.

Selected local bus services (www.177nordland.com)

Å to: Harstad (1 daily; 7hr 15min); Leknes (2–3 daily; 1hr 40min); Reine (2–3 daily; 20min); Sortland (3 daily; 5hr 45min); Stokmarknes (3 daily; 5hr 15min); Svolvær (1–2 daily; 3hr 15min).
Andenes to: Sortland (2–4 daily; 2hr).
Harstad to: Å (1 daily; 7hr 15min); Lødingen (2 daily; 1hr 30min); Svolvær (2–4 daily; 3hr 45min).
Sortland to: Å (1–3 daily; 5hr 45min); Andenes (2–4 daily; 2hr); Svolvær (1–3 daily; 2hr 15min).
Svolvær to: Å (1–2 daily; 3hr 15min); Harstad (2–4 daily; 3hr 45min); Leknes (3–6 daily; 1hr 30min); Sortland (1–3 daily; 2hr 15min); Stokmarknes (1–4 daily; 1hr 45min).

Principal Hurtigruten car ferries (www.hurtigruten.no).

Bodø to: Moskenes (June–Aug 5–6 daily; Sept–May 1–2 daily except Sat; 3hr 45min); Røst (June–Aug 1–2 daily, Sept–May 4 weekly; 4hr 45min); Værøy (June–Aug 1–2 daily except Sun, Sept–May 4 weekly; 6hr 30min).

Bognes to: Lødingen (every 1hr to 2hr daily; 1hr); Skarberget (every 1hr or 1hr 30min; 25min).
Skutvik to: Svolvær (1 daily; 2hr).
Svolvær to: Skutvik (1 daily; 2hr).

Other car ferry services

Andenes to: Gryllefjord (late May to mid-June & early- to late Aug 2 daily, mid-June to early Aug 3 daily; 2hr) with Senjafergene (www.senjafergene.no).
Botnhamn to: Brensholmen (May to Aug 5–7 daily; 45min) with Senjafergene (www.senjafergene.no).
Fiskebøl to: Melbu (daily 7am–11pm, every 1hr 30min; 25min) with Veolia (www.177nordland.com).

Hurtigbåt passenger express boats

Bodø to: Svolvær (1 daily; 3hr 30min) with Hurtigruten car ferries (www.hurtigruten.no).
Harstad to: Tromsø (2–3 daily; 2hr 45min) with Hurtigruten car ferries (www.hurtigruten.no).

Hurtigrute coastal boat (www.hurtigruten.no)

Northbound departures: daily from Trondheim at noon; Bodø at 3pm; Stamsund at 7.30pm; Svolvær at 10pm; Stokmarknes at 1am; Sortland at 3am & Harstad at 6am.
Southbound departures: daily from Harstad at 8.30am; Sortland at 1pm; Stokmarknes at 3.15pm; Svolvær at 7.30pm; Stamsund at 9.30pm; Bodø at 4am & Trondheim at 10am.
Journey times: Trondheim to Harstad 43hr; Trondheim to Tromsø 51hr.

2.6

North Norway

B aedeker, writing a hundred years ago about Norway's remote **northern provinces** of Troms and Finnmark, observed that they "possess attractions for the scientific traveller and the sportsman, but can hardly be recommended for the ordinary tourist" – a comment that isn't too wide of the mark even today. These are enticing lands, no question; the natural environment they offer is stunning in its extremes, with the midnight sun and polar night emphasizing the strangeness of the terrain, but the travelling can be hard, the specific sights widely separated and, when you reach them, subtle in their appeal.

Troms's intricate, fretted coastline has shaped its history since the days when powerful Viking lords operated a trading empire from its islands. Indeed, over half the population still lives offshore in dozens of tiny fishing villages, but the place to aim for is **Tromsø**, the so-called "Capital of the North" and a lively university town. Beyond Tromsø, the long trek north begins in earnest as you enter **Finnmark**, a vast wilderness covering 48,000 square kilometres, but home to just two percent of the Norwegian population. Much of the land was laid waste during World War II, the combined effect of the Russian advance and the retreating German army's scorched-earth policy, and it's now possible to drive for hours without coming across a building more than sixty or so years old. The first obvious target in Finnmark is **Alta**, a sprawling settlement and important crossroads famous for its prehistoric rock carvings. From here, most visitors head straight for the steely cliffs of **Nordkapp** (the North Cape), supposedly but not actually Europe's northernmost point and leave it at that; but some doggedly press on to **Kirkenes**, the last town before the Russian border, where you feel as if you're about to drop off the end of the world. From Alta, the other main alternative is to travel inland across the eerily endless scrubland of the **Finnmarksvidda**, where winter temperatures plummet to -35°C. This high plateau is the last stronghold of the **Sámi**, northern Norway's indigenous people, some of whom still live a semi-nomadic life tied to the movement of their reindeer herds. You'll spot Sámi in their brightly coloured traditional gear all across the region, but especially in the remote towns of **Kautokeino** and **Karasjok**, strange, disconsolate places in the middle of the plain.

Transport practicalities

Public transport in the provinces of Troms and Finnmark is by **bus**, the **Hurtigrute** coastal boat and **plane** – there are no trains. For all but the most truncated of tours, the best idea is to pick and mix these different forms of transport – for example by flying from Tromsø to Kirkenes and then taking the Hurtigrute back, or vice versa. What you should try to avoid is endless doubling-back on the **E6**, though this is often difficult as it is the only road to run right across the region. To give an idea of the distances involved, from Tromsø it's 400km to Alta, 640km to Nordkapp and 970km to Kirkenes.

Norway's principal long-distance bus company, Nor-Way Bussekspress (ⓦwww .nor-way.no), provides two services in the region – the **Nord-Norgeekspressen**, which links Tromsø with Narvik and Alta once daily, and the **Nordkappekspressen**, linking Narvik and Alta twice daily except on Saturdays. At Alta, passengers overnight before proceeding on the next leg of the Nordkappekspressen journey north to Honningsvåg, where – from early June to late August – they can

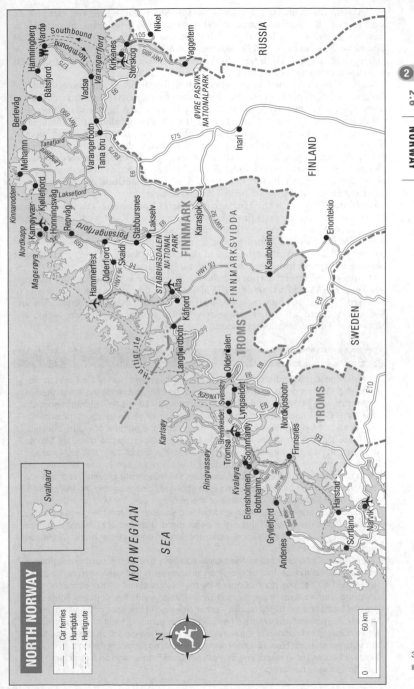

change onto the connecting bus to Nordkapp. Alta is also where you can pick up local buses to Kautokeino, Karasjok and Kirkenes. Bus **timetables** are available at most tourist offices and bus stations; they are also available online – Cominor for Tromsø and its environs (☎177, ⓦwww.cominor.no) and FFR for the whole of Finnmark (☎177, ⓦwww.ffr.no). On the longer rides, it's a good idea to buy **tickets** in advance, or turn up early, as buses fill up fast in the summer.

Northern Norway's main **highways** are all well maintained, but **drivers** will find the going a little slow as they have to negotiate some pretty tough terrain. You can cover 250–300km in a day without any problem, but much more and it all becomes rather wearisome. In **winter**, driving conditions can be appalling and, although the Norwegians make a spirited effort to keep the E6 open, they don't always succeed. If you're not used to driving in these sorts of conditions, don't start here – especially during the polar night. If you intend to use the region's minor, **unpaved roads**, be prepared for the worst and certainly take food and drink, warm clothes and a mobile phone. Keep an eye on the fuel indicator too, as **petrol stations** are confined to the larger settlements and they are often 100–200km apart.

Much more leisurely is the **Hurtigrute coastal boat**, which takes the best part of two days to cross the huge fjords between Tromsø and Kirkenes. En route, it calls at eleven ports, mostly remote fishing villages but also Honningsvåg, where northbound services pause for four hours so that special buses can cart passengers off to Nordkapp and back. At the other end of the nautical extreme, there's a **Hurtigbåt passenger express boat** service from Tromsø to Harstad.

The region has several **airports**, including those at Alta, Honningsvåg, Kirkenes and Tromsø. SAS and its subsidiary, Widerøe, have the widest range of flights to northern Norway, but Norwegian Airlines chips in too, flying to Tromsø, Alta and Kirkenes. Standard return fares are usually expensive, but discounts are legion and Norwegian Airlines are most economical.

Arctic phenomena

On and above the **Arctic Circle**, an imaginary line drawn round the earth at latitude 66.5 degrees north, there is a period around midsummer during which the sun never makes it below the horizon, even at midnight – hence the **midnight sun**. On the Arctic Circle itself, this only happens on one night of the year – at the summer solstice – but the further north you go, the greater the number of nights affected: in Bodø, it's from the first week of June to early July; in Tromsø from late May to late July, in Alta, from the third week in May to the end of July; and at Nordkapp early May to the end of July. Obviously, the midnight sun is best experienced on a clear night, but fog or cloud can turn the sun into a glowing, red ball – a spectacle that can be wonderful but also strangely disconcerting. All the region's tourist offices have the exact dates of the midnight sun, though note that these are calculated at sea level; climb up a hill and you can extend the dates by a day or two. The converse of all this is the **polar night**, a period of constant darkness either side of the winter solstice; again the further north of the Arctic Circle you are, the longer this lasts.

The Arctic Circle also marks the typical southern limit of the **northern lights**, or aurora borealis, though this extraordinary phenomenon has been seen as far south as latitude 40 degrees north. Caused by the bombardment of the atmosphere by electrons carried away from the sun by the solar wind, the northern lights take various forms and are highly mobile – either flickering in one spot or travelling across the sky. At relatively low latitudes hereabouts, the aurora is tilted at an angle and is often coloured red but nearer the North Pole, it hangs like gigantic luminous curtains, often tinted greenish blue. Naturally enough, there's no predicting when the northern lights will occur, but in wintertime they are not uncommon – and on a clear night they can be strangely humbling.

▲ At the Arctic Circle

As for **accommodation**, all the major settlements have at least a couple of hotels and the main roads are sprinkled with campsites. If you have a tent and a well-insulated sleeping bag, you can, in theory, bed down more or less where you like, but the hostility of the climate and the ferocity of the mosquitoes, especially in the marshy areas of the Finnmarksvidda, make most people think (at least) twice. There are HI **hostels** at Tromsø, Alta, Honningsvåg, Lakselv and Karasjok.

Tromsø

TROMSØ has been called, rather preposterously, the "Paris of the North", and though even the tourist office doesn't make any pretence to such grandiose titles today, the city is without question the effective capital of northern Norway. Easily the region's most populous town, Tromsø started out as a fishing port and trading station, and flourished in the middle of the nineteenth century when its seamen ventured north to reap rich rewards hunting arctic foxes, polar bears, reindeer, walruses and, most profitable of all, seals. Subsequently, Tromsø became famous as the jumping-off point for a string of Arctic expeditions, its celebrity status assured when the explorer Roald Amundsen flew from here to his death somewhere on the Arctic icecap in 1928. Since those heady days, Tromsø has grown into an urbane and likeable small city with a population of 63,000 employed in a wide range of industries and at the university. Give or take the odd museum, Tromsø is perhaps short on top-ranking **sights**, but its amiable atmosphere, fine mountain-and-fjord setting and clutch of lively restaurants and bars more than compensate.

Arrival

At the northern end of the E8, 73km from the E6 and 260km north of Narvik, Tromsø's compact centre slopes up from the waterfront on the eastern shores of the hilly island of Tromsøya. The island is connected to the mainland by bridge and tunnel. The **Hurtigrute coastal boat** docks in the town centre beside the Prostneset quay at the foot of Kirkegata, while **Hurtigbåt** services arrive at the jetty about 150m to the south. Long-distance **buses** pull in at the stops on Prostneset, metres from the Hurtigrute quay. The **airport** is 5km west of the centre on the other side of Tromsøya; from the airport, frequent Flybussen (Mon–Fri 5am–7pm every 30min to 1hr, Sat 5am–3pm hourly, Sun 9am–7.30pm hourly;

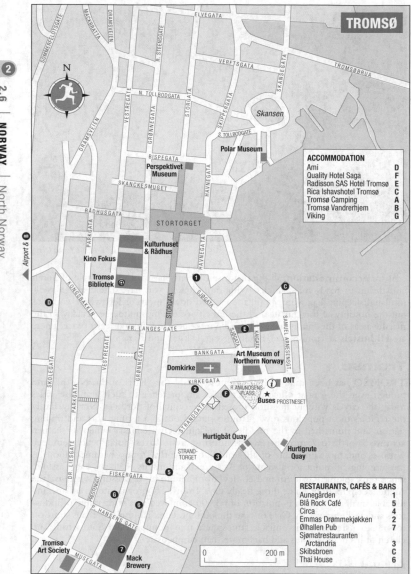

Polaria (100m) & Tromsø Museum (3km)

55kr) run into the city, stopping at the *Radisson SAS Hotel* on Sjøgata and at several other central hotels.

Information and city transport

Tromsø's **tourist office** is a few paces from the Prostneset quay at Kirkegata 2 (mid–May to Aug Mon–Fri 9am–7pm, Sat & Sun 10am–5pm; rest of year Mon–Fri 9am–4pm, Sat 10am–4pm; ☎77 61 00 00, ⓦwww.visittromso.no). It issues free town maps, offers a small supply of B&Bs (see below), and provides oodles of local information.

Local **buses** are operated by **Cominor** (T177, Wwww.cominor.no) with the standard, flat-rate fare for a local bus journey costing 25kr. You can also **rent a bike** from the tourist office.

Accommodation

Tromsø has a good supply of modern, central **hotels**, though the majority occupy chunky concrete high-rises. Less expensive – and sometimes more distinctive – are the town's **guesthouses** (*pensjonater*) and there's also a rudimentary HI **hostel**. In addition, the tourist office has a small list of **B&Bs** (❶/❷), but most are stuck out in the suburbs. Tromsø is a popular destination, so advance reservation is recommended, especially in the summer.

Hotels

Ami Skolegata 24 T77 62 10 00, Wwww
.amihotel.no. With seventeen simple rooms, this amiable guesthouse/hotel has wide views over the city from the hillside behind the town centre. Free internet access too. ❷

Quality Hotel Saga Richard Withsplass 2 T77 60 70 00, Wwww.choicehotels.no. Although there has been some Ikea-ization at this medium-sized, 1960s chain hotel, the public areas remain reassuringly old-fashioned with lots of pine (rather than chipboard). Right in the centre of town opposite the cathedral. ❸/❻

Radisson SAS Hotel Tromsø Sjøgata 7 T77 60 00 00, Wwww.tromso.radissonsas.com. The biggest hotel in town, occupying two large and clumpy tower blocks down by the harbour. The rooms are kitted out in standard-issue, chain-hotel style – unadventurous but perfectly adequate. Ultra-efficient service. ❻/❼

Rica Ishavshotel Tromsø Fr. Langes gate 2 T77 66 64 00, Wwww.rica.no. Perched on the harbourfront, this imaginatively designed hotel is partly built in the style of a ship, complete with a sort of crow's-nest bar. Lovely rooms

and unbeatable views over the harbour with the mountains glinting behind make it the best place in town. ❻/❼

Viking Grønnegata 18 T77 64 77 30, Wwww
.viking-hotell.no. Modern, bright and breezy hotel-cum-guesthouse with 24 fully functional guest rooms. Centrally located near the Mack brewery. Very competitive prices. ❸

Hostels and campsites

Tromsø Camping Elvestrandvegen T77 63 80 37, Wwww.tromsocamping.no. Reasonably handy site about 2km east of the Arctic cathedral (Ishavskatedralen), on the mainland side of the main bridge, with cabins (from 070kr) as well as tent pitches. Open all year.

Tromsø Vandrerhjem Åsgårdveien 9 T77 65 76 28, Wwww.vandrerhjem.no. Basic, barracks-like HI hostel located some 2km west of the centre. No food is available, but there's a store close by and self-catering facilities. Local bus #26 runs from the centre to about 300m from the hostel, or else it's a stiff 30min walk. Open mid-June to mid-Aug. Dorm beds 210kr, doubles ❶

The City

Completed in 1861, the Lutheran **Domkirke** (cathedral: June–Aug Tues–Sat noon–4pm, Sun 10am–4pm; Sept–May Tues–Sat noon–4pm, Sun 10am–2pm; free), bang in the centre on Kirkegata, bears witness to the prosperity of the town's nineteenth-century merchants, who became rich on the back of the barter trade with Russia. They part-funded the cathedral's construction, the result being the large and handsome structure of today, whose slender spire and dinky little tower poke high into the sky above the neo-Gothic pointed windows of the nave. In a large old building just along from the church is the **Nordnorsk Kunstmuseum** at Sjøgata 1 (Art Museum of Northern Norway: late June to late Aug daily noon–6pm; rest of year Tues–Fri 10am–5pm, Sat & Sun noon–5pm; Wwww.museumsnett
.no/nordnorsk-kunstmuseum; free). It's not a large ensemble, but the museum's permanent collection, which is enhanced – and sometimes disturbed – by an ambitious programme of temporary exhibitions, covers all of Norway's artistic bases, including a handful of minor works by Edvard Munch.

To Stortorget and the Polar Museum

Back in front of the cathedral, it's a gentle five-minute stroll north past the shops of Storgata to the main square, **Stortorget**, site of a daily open-air **market** selling flowers and knick-knacks. The square nudges down towards the waterfront, where fresh fish and prawns are sold direct from inshore fishing boats throughout the summer. From the square, it's a five-minute walk to the city's most enjoyable museum, the **Polarmuseet** (Polar Museum: daily: March to mid-June & mid-Aug to Sept 11am–5pm; mid-June to mid-Aug 10am–7pm, Oct–Feb 11am–4pm; ⓦwww.polarmuseum.no, 50kr), which has sections on all the most renowned polar hunters and explorers – notably **Roald Amundsen** (1872–1928) and **Fridtjof Nansen** (1861–1930) – and an outstanding section on the remote Arctic archipelago of Svalbard, including archeological finds retrieved in the 1980s from an eighteenth-century **Russian whaling station**.

Mack brewery, Tromsø Kunstforening and Polaria

Just to the south of the town centre, at the corner of Storgata and Musegata, the profitable **Mack brewery** proudly claims to be the world's northernmost brewery – and dreams up all sorts of bottle labels with ice and polar bears to hammer home the point. Nearby, just up Musegata, **Tromsø Kunstforening** (Tromsø Art Society: Tues–Sun noon–5pm; 30kr; ⓦwww.tromsokunstforening.no) occupies part of a large and attractive Neoclassical building dating from the 1890s. The art society puts on imaginative temporary exhibitions of Norwegian contemporary art with the emphasis on the work of Nordland artists.

Doubling back down Musegata, it's a couple of hundred metres south along Storgata to **Polaria** (daily: mid-May to mid-Aug 10am–7pm; mid-Aug to mid-May noon–5pm, ⓦwww.polaria.no; 100kr), a lavish waterfront complex which deals with all things Arctic. There's an aquarium filled with Arctic species, a 180-degree cinema showing a film on the far Arctic north and several exhibitions on polar research. Parked outside in a glass greenhouse is a 1940s sealing ship, **M/S Polstjerna**.

Eating, drinking and nightlife

With a clutch of first-rate **restaurants**, several enjoyable **cafés** and a good supply of late-night **bars**, Tromsø is as well served as any comparable Norwegian city. The best of the cafés and restaurants are concentrated in the vicinity of the Domkirke, and most of the livelier bars – many of which sell Mack, the local brew – are in the centre, too.

The **Kulturhuset**, beside Grønnegata (☎77 66 38 10, ⓦwww.kulturhuset.tr.no), is the principal venue for cultural events of all kinds, while the main **cinema**, Kino Fokus, is next door (☎90 88 99 00, ⓦwww.tromsokino.no).

Cafés and restaurants

Aunegården Sjøgata 29. Cosy and popular café-restaurant within the old – and listed – late nineteenth-century Aunegården building. All the standard Norwegian dishes are served, at moderate prices (mains 80–100kr), but these are as nothing when compared with the cakes – wonderful confections, which are made at their own bakery. Weep with pleasure as you nibble at the cheesecake. Mon–Sat 10.30am–11pm, Sun noon–6pm.

Emmas Drømmekjøkken Kirkegata 8 ☎77 63 77 30. Much praised in the national press as a gourmet treat, "Emma's dream kitchen" lives up to its name, with an imaginative and wide-ranging menu focused on Norwegian

produce. The grilled arctic char with chanterelle risotto is a treat and, giving reindeer a wide berth, a delicious venison dish with rowanberries is handled with finesse. Excellent service in smart premises. Main courses are 126kr and up. Mon–Sat from 6pm, closed Sun.

Sjømatrestauranten Arctandria Strandtorget 1 ☎77 60 07 20. Some of the best food in town. The upstairs restaurant serves a superb range of fish, with the emphasis on Arctic species, and there's also reindeer and seal; main courses start at around 260kr. Prices are about twenty percent less at the café-bar *Vertshuset Skarven*, downstairs, where there's a slightly less varied menu. Mon–Sat 4pm–midnight.

Thai House Storgata 22 ☎77 67 05 26. Decent Thai cooking with the welcome inclusion of some excellent fish and vegetable dishes; the Thai spicy salads are especially good, and prices are moderate (mains from around 160kr). Daily 3–11pm.

Bars

Blå Rock Café Strandgata 14 ☜www.blarock .no. Definitely the place to go for loud rock music – with and without the roll. Occasional live acts too, plus delicious burgers. Mon–Thurs 11.30am–2am, Fri & Sat 11.30am–3.30am, Sun 1pm–2am.
Circa Storgata 36. With DJs Thurs–Sat and intimate jazz concerts at least once a week, the sense of fun in this laid-back bar makes it one of the best in town. Mon–Thurs 11.30am–1.30am, Fri & Sat 11.30am–3.30am, Sun 1pm–1.30am.
Ølhallen Pub Storgata 4. Solid (some would say staid) basement pub adjoining the Mack brewery, whose various ales are its speciality. It's the first pub in town to start serving, and so pulls in the serious drinkers. Mon–Thurs 9am–5pm, Fri 9am–6pm & Sat 9am–3pm.
Skibsbroen Fr. Langes gate 2. Inside the *Rica Ishavshotel* (see p.331), this smart little bar overlooks the waterfront from on high – it occupies the top of a slender tower with wide windows and sea views. Relaxed atmosphere; lots of tourists. Mon–Thurs 6pm–1.30am, Fri & Sat 3pm–3am; closed Sun.

Listings

Airlines Norwegian ☎815 21 815; SAS ☎05400; Widerøe ☎810 01 200.
Car rental Europcar, Alkeveien 5 and at the airport (☎77 67 56 00); Hertz, Richard Withsplass 4 and at the airport (☎77 62 44 00).
DNT Troms Turlag, next door to the tourist office at Kirkegata 2 (Wed noon–4pm, Thurs noon–6pm & Fri noon–2pm; ☎77 68 51 75, ☜www .turistforeningen.no/troms). DNT affiliate with bags of information on local hiking trails and DNT huts.
Hiking See DNT (p.172) and Outdoor Pursuits.
Internet Free access at Tromsø Bibliotek, on Grønnegata near Stortorget (Mon–Thurs 9am–7pm, Fri 9am–5pm, Sat 11am–3pm & Sun noon–4pm).
Maps and books Bokhuset Libris, Storgata 86 (☎77 68 30 36).

Outdoor pursuits Amongst several wilderness-tour specialists, Tromsø Villmarkssenter (Tromsø Wilderness Centre; ☎77 69 60 02, ☜www .villmarkssenter.no) offers a wide range of activities from guided glacier walks, kayak paddling and mountain climbing in summer, to ski trips and dog-sledge rides in winter. Overnight trips staying in a *lavvo* (a Sámi tent) can also be arrranged. The Centre is located about 6km from downtown Tromsø, beyond the airport at Kvaløysletta, on the island of Kvaløya.
Pharmacy Vitus Apotek, opposite the *Radisson SAS Hotel* at Fr. Langes gate 9 (Mon–Fri 8.30am–4.30pm & Sat 10am–2pm).
Post office Main office at Strandgata 41 (Mon–Fri 8.30am–5pm, Sat 10am–2pm).
Taxi Tromsø Taxi ☎77 60 30 00 (24hr).

Into Finnmark: from Tromsø to Alta

Beyond Tromsø, the vast sweep of the northern landscape slowly unfolds, with silent fjords cutting deep into the coastline beneath ice-tipped peaks which themselves fade into the high plateau of the interior. This forbidding, elemental terrain is interrupted by the occasional valley, where those few souls hardy enough to make a living in these parts struggle on – often by dairy farming. In summer, cut grass dries everywhere, stretched over wooden poles that form long lines on the hillsides, like so much washing hung out to dry.

Slipping along the valleys and traversing the mountains in between, the **E8** and then the **E6** follow the coast pretty much all the way from Tromsø to Alta, some 410km – and about nine-hours' drive – to the north. Drivers can save around 100km (although not necessarily time and certainly not money) by turning off the E8 25km south of Tromsø onto **Highway 91** – a quieter, even more scenic route, offering extravagant fjord and mountain views. Highway 91 begins by cutting across the rocky peninsula that backs on to Tromsø to reach the **Breivikeidet–Svendsby car ferry** (see p.334) over to the glaciated Lyngen peninsula. From the Svendsby ferry dock, it's just 24km over the Lyngen to the **Lyngseidet–Olderdalen car ferry** (see p.334), by means of which you can rejoin the E6 at Olderdalen, some 220km

Running up from Narvik, Nor-Way Bussekspress's (Ⓦwww.nor-way.no) **Nord-Norgeekspressen bus** leaves Tromsø to push on north to Alta (1 daily; 6hr 30min); it's a fine journey that begins on the E8, but then detours off along Highway 91 to take in two car-ferry rides – **Breivikeidet to Svendsby** (every 1–2hr; Mon–Fri 6am–10pm, Sat 8am–8pm, Sun 10am–9pm; 25min; 76kr car and driver; ☏177, Ⓦwww.bjorklid .no) and Lyngseidet to Olderdalen, which is back on the E6 (every 1–2hr; Mon–Fri 7am–8pm, Sat 9am–7pm, Sun 10.30am–8pm; 40min; car & driver 107kr; ☏177, Ⓦwww.bjorklid.no). At Alta, passengers change – and overnight – to catch the same company's **Nordkappekspressen bus** on to Honningsvåg (1–2 daily; 4hr), where they change again to get to Nordkapp (early June to late Aug 2 daily; 45min). There are also FFR buses (Ⓦwww.ffr.no) from Alta to Karasjok (1–2 daily except Sat; 5hr), Kautokeino (1–2 daily except Sat; 2hr 15min) and Kirkenes (3 weekly; 10–13hr).

Northbound, the **Hurtigrute coastal boat** (Ⓦwww.hurtigruten.no) leaves Tromsø daily at 6.30pm; southbound it sails at 1.30am, arriving in Harstad six and a half hours later. The main **Hurtigbåt passenger express boat** service links Tromsø with **Harstad** (2–3 daily; 2hr 45min; Ⓦwww.hurtigruten.no); there are no boats between Tromsø and Alta.

For **drivers**, the quickest route from Tromsø to Alta is south along the E8 and then north on the E6, a total distance of about 410km. The shortest route – and also the prettiest – is, however, the one followed by the Nord-Norgeekspressen bus along Highway 91.

As you drive west from Tromsø past the airport, Highway 862 crosses the Sandnessundet straits to reach the mountainous island of **Kvaløya**, whose three distinct parts are joined by a couple of narrow isthmuses. On the far side of the straits, Highway 862 meanders south offering lovely fjord and mountain views en route to the **Brensholmen–Botnhamn** car ferry (May–Aug 5–7 daily; 45min; Ⓦwww.senjafergene .no), about 60km from Tromsø. From Botnhamn, it's a further 160km to **Gryllefjord**, where a second car ferry (late May to mid-June & early- to late Aug 2 daily, mid-June to early Aug 3 daily; 2hr; Ⓦwww.senjafergene.no; reservations advised) takes you across to Andenes on Vesterålen (see p.312).

south of Alta. This route is at its most spectacular between Svendsby and Lyngseidet, with the road nudging along a narrow channel flanked by the imposing peaks of the Lyngsalpene, or Lyngen Alps.

Beyond Olderdalen, the E6 eventually enters the province of **Finnmark** as it approaches the hamlet of **LANGFJORDBOTN**, at the head of the long and slender Langfjord. Thereafter, the road sticks tightly to the coast to reach, after another 60km, the tiny village of **KÅFJORD**, whose sympathetically restored nineteenth-century church was built by the English company who operated the area's copper mines until they were abandoned as uneconomic in the 1870s. The Kåfjord itself is a narrow and sheltered arm of the Altafjord, which was used as an Arctic hideaway by the *Tirpitz* and other German battleships during World War II. From here, it's just 20km further to Alta.

Alta

First impressions of **ALTA** are not encouraging. With a population of just 17,000, the town comprises a string of unenticing, modern settlements that spread along the E6 for several kilometres. The ugliest part is **Alta Sentrum**, now befuddled by a platoon of soulless concrete blocks. Alta was interesting once – for a couple of centuries not Norwegian at all but Finnish and Sámi, and host to an ancient and much-visited Sámi fair. World War II polished off the fair and destroyed all the old wooden buildings that once clustered together in Alta's oldest district, **Bossekop**, where Dutch whalers settled in the seventeenth century.

For all that, Alta does have one remarkable feature, the most extensive area of **prehistoric rock carvings** in northern Europe, the **Helleristningene i Hjemmeluft** (Rock Carvings in Hjemmeluft), which are impressive enough to have been designated a UNESCO World Heritage Site. The carvings are located beside the E6, some 2.5km before the Bossekop district as you approach Alta from the southwest, and they form part of the **Alta Museum** (May daily 9am–6pm; June to late Aug daily 8am–9pm; late Aug daily 8am–6pm; Sept daily 9am–6pm; Oct–April Mon–Fri 9am–3pm, Sat & Sun 11am–4pm; Ⓦwww.alta.museum.no; May–Sept 85kr, Oct–April 45kr). A visit begins in the museum building, where there's a wealth of background information on the carvings in particular and on prehistoric Finnmark in general. The **rock carvings** themselves extend down the hill from the museum to the fjordside. A clear and easy-to-follow footpath and boardwalk circumnavigate the site, taking in all the carvings in about an hour. On the trail, there are a dozen or so **vantage points** offering close-up views of the carvings, which provide an insight into a prehistoric culture that was essentially settled and largely reliant on the hunting of land animals, who were killed with flint and bone implements; sealing and fishing were of lesser importance. Many experts think it likely the carvings had spiritual significance because of the effort that was expended by the people who created them, but this is the stuff of conjecture.

Arrival and information

Long-distance buses pull into the **bus station** just off the E6 at Alta Sentrum. From the bus station, there's a limited local bus service – *bybussen* – south to Bossekop and the rock carvings, about 5km away (Mon–Sat every 30min to 1hr; 10min). To call a taxi, ring Alta Taxi on ☎78 43 53 53.

Alta **tourist office** is in the Parksenteret shopping centre in Alta Sentrum (Aug–June Mon–Fri 8.30am–4pm & Sat 10am–2pm; July Mon–Fri 8.30am–6pm & Sat 10am–2pm; ☎78 44 50 50, Ⓦwww.visitalta.no). In the summertime, there's also

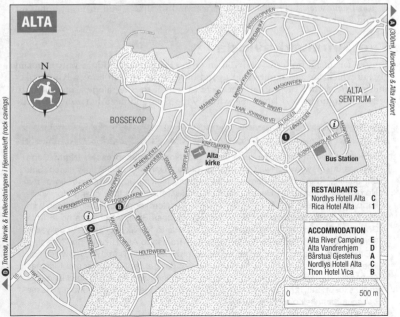

ALTA

N

BOSSEKOP

ALTA SENTRUM

Alta kirke

Bus Station

Ⓓ Tromsø, Narvik & Helleristningene i Hjemmeluft (rock carvings)

Ⓐ (300m), Nordkapp & Alta Airport

RESTAURANTS
Nordlys Hotell Alta   C
Rica Hotel Alta   1

ACCOMMODATION
Alta River Camping   E
Alta Vandrerhjem   D
Bårstua Gjestehus   A
Nordlys Hotell Alta   C
Thon Hotel Vica   B

0   500 m

Ⓔ, Alta Friluftspark & Kautokeino

a branch near the Coop supermarket in the Bossekop shopping centre (daily: June & Aug 10am–6pm, July 10am–8pm; same number). Both issue free town maps and help with finding accommodation. The latter is a particularly useful service if you're dependent on public transport – the town's hotels and motels are widely dispersed – or if you're here at the height of the season.

Accommodation, eating and drinking

Amongst Alta's several **hotels**, one of the more appealing is the *Thon Hotel Vica*, a couple of minutes' walk from the Bossekop tourist office at Fogdebakken 6 (℡78 48 22 22, ✆www.thonhotels.com; ❹/❼). It's a small, cosy place with smart, modern rooms, and occupies a wooden building that started out as a farmhouse; it has a suntrap of a terrace and free internet access. A second option, opposite the Bossekop tourist office, is *Nordlys Hotell Alta*, Bekkefaret 3 (℡78 45 72 00, ✆www.nordlyshotell .no; ❹/❺), a rather uninviting mishmash of styles, but with large, comfortable if somewhat spartan rooms nonetheless. Alta also possesses a handful of guesthouses, with one of the more appealing being ❖ *Bårstua Gjestehus*, just off the E6 on the north side of town at Kongleveien 2A (℡78 43 33 33, ✆www.baarstua.no; ❸). The eight rooms here are large and pleasantly appointed and all of them have kitchenettes.

The bargain-basement choice is the all-year, HI **hostel**, *Alta Vandrerhjem*, in a plain chalet in the countryside off the E6 about 6km southwest of Alta (℡48 24 11 69, ✆www.vandrerhjem.no; dorm beds 300–350kr, doubles ❷). The hostel has self-catering facilities, a café and a laundry. There's no public transport, but they will pick you up from Alta by prior arrangement. In the vicinity of Alta are several **campsites**. The best is the well-equipped, four-star *Alta River Camping* (℡78 43 43 53, ✆www .alta-river-camping.no), by the river about 5km out of town along Highway 93, which branches off the E6 in between Bossekop and the rock paintings. They have tent spaces here as well as hotel-style rooms (❷) and cabins (from 500kr per night for two).

Two of Alta's restaurants are members of the reliable Arctic Menu Scheme – one at *Nordlys Hotell Alta* (see above), the other at the (large and very smart) *Rica Hotel Alta*, in Alta Sentrum at Løkkeveien 61 (℡78 48 27 00). Both specialize in regional delicacies – cloudberries, reindeer and the like – and mains at both cost around 200kr.

The Finnmarksvidda

Venture far inland from Alta and you enter the **Finnmarksvidda**, a vast mountain plateau which spreads southeast up to and beyond the Finnish border. Rivers, lakes and marshes lattice the region, but there's barely a tree, let alone a mountain, to break the contours of a landscape whose wide skies and deep horizons are eerily

---

Moving on from Alta

Alta is something of a transport hub. The **Nordkappekspressen** (North Cape Express Bus; ✆www.nor-way.no) runs direct from Narvik to Alta (2 daily except Sat; 9hr 30min), where passengers overnight before picking up the second leg of the Nordkappekspressen to Honningsvåg (1–3 daily; 4hr); here they change for Nordkapp (early June to late Aug 2 daily; 45min). The Nordkappekspressen links in with the **Nord-Norgeekspressen** (North Norway Express Bus), which runs north from Bodø and Fauske to Alta in three segments: Bodø to Narvik via Fauske (2 daily; 6hr 30min); Narvik to Tromsø (1–3 daily; 4hr); and Tromsø to Alta (1 daily; 6hr 30min).

Other long-distance routings from Alta are provided by **FFR** (℡177, ✆www.ffr.no). They operate buses from Alta to Karasjok (1–2 daily except Sat; 5hr) and Kirkenes (3 weekly; 10–13hr) along the E6; and across the Finnmarksvidda to Kautokeino (1–2 daily except Sat; 2hr 15min). Note, however, that there are no currently buses between Kautokeino and Karasjok.

beautiful. Distances are hard to gauge – a dot of a storm can soon be upon you, breaking with alarming ferocity – and the air is crystal clear, giving a whiteish lustre to the sunshine. A couple of roads cross this expanse, but for the most part it remains the preserve of the few thousand semi-nomadic **Sámi** who make up the majority of the local population. Many still wear traditional dress, a brightly coloured affair of red bonnets and blue jerkins or dresses, all trimmed with red, white and yellow embroidery. You'll see permutations on this traditional costume all over Finnmark, but especially at roadside souvenir stalls and, on Sundays, outside Sámi churches.

Despite the slow encroachments of the tourist industry, lifestyles on the Finnmarksvidda have remained remarkably constant for centuries. The main occupation is **reindeer-herding**, supplemented by hunting and fishing, and the pattern of Sámi life is still mostly dictated by these animals. During the winter, the reindeer graze the flat plains and shallow valleys of the interior, migrating towards the coast in early May as the snow begins to melt, and temperatures inland begin to climb, even reaching 30°C on occasion. By October, both people and reindeer are journeying back from their temporary summer quarters. The long, dark winter is spent in preparation for the great **Easter festivals**, when weddings and baptisms are celebrated in the region's two principal settlements, **Karasjok** and – more especially – **Kautokeino**. As neither place is particularly appealing in itself, this is without question the best time to be here, when the inhabitants celebrate the end of the polar night and the arrival of spring. Details of the Easter festivals are available at any Finnmark tourist office. Summer visits, on the other hand, can be disappointing, since many families and their reindeer are at coastal pastures and there is precious little activity.

From **Alta**, the only direct route into the Finnmarksvidda is south along **Highway 93** to Kautokeino, a distance of 130km. Just short of Kautokeino, about 100km from Alta, Highway 93 connects with **Highway 92**, which travels the 100km or so northeast to Karasjok, where you can rejoin the E6 (but well beyond the turning to Nordkapp). Operated by FFR (℡177, ⊛www.ffr.no), **bus** services across the Finnmarksvidda are patchy: except on Saturdays, there are one or two buses a day from Alta to Kautokeino, a journey that takes two hours, but nothing between Kautokeino and Karasjok. There's also an FFR bus service from Alta to Karasjok along the E6 and this takes five hours and runs once or twice daily except on Saturdays when it doesn't run at all.

Kautokeino

It's a two-hour drive or bus ride from Alta across the Finnmarksvidda to **KAUTO-KEINO** (Guovdageaidnu in Sámi), the principal winter camp of the Norwegian Sámi and the site of a huge reindeer market in spring and autumn. The Sámi are not, however, easy town-dwellers and although Kautokeino is very useful to them as a supply base, it's still a desultory, desolate-looking place straggling along Highway 93 for a couple of kilometres, with the handful of buildings that pass for the town centre gathered at the point where the road crosses the Kautokeinoelva River. Nevertheless, the settlement has become something of a tourist draw on account of the **jewellers**, who set up their stalls here every summer, attracting Finnish day-trippers like flies. The jewellery bigwigs hereabouts are **Frank and Regine Juhls**, who braved all sorts of difficulties to set up their workshop here in 1959. The Juhls were much influenced by the Sámi style of self-adornment, repeating and developing it in their own work, and their business prospered – perhaps beyond their wildest dreams – and they now have shops in Oslo and Bergen. As further testimony to the Juhls' commercial success, the plain and simple workshop they first built has been replaced by **Juhls' Silver Gallery** (daily: June to early Aug 8.30am–9pm; early Aug to May 9am–6pm; ring in winter to confirm hours on ℡78 48 43 30, ⊛www.juhls.no), an extensive complex of low-lying showrooms and workshops, whose pagoda-like roofs are derived from the Sámi. Exquisitely beautiful, high-quality silverwork is made and sold here alongside a much broader range of classy craftwork. The complex's **interior** (regular, free guided tours; 30min) is intriguing in its own right, with some rooms

The Sámi

The northernmost reaches of Norway, Sweden and Finland, and the Kola peninsula of northwest Russia, are collectively known as **Lapland**. Traditionally, the indigenous people were called "Lapps", though in recent years this name has fallen out of favour and been replaced by the term **Sámi**, although the change is by no means universal. The new name comes from the Sámi word *sámpi*, meaning both the land and its people, of whom there are around seventy thousand spread across the whole of the region. Among the oldest peoples in Europe, the Sámi are probably descended from prehistoric clans who migrated here from the east by way of the Baltic. Their **language** is closely related to Finnish and Estonian, though it's somewhat misleading to speak of a "Sámi language" as there are, in fact, three distinct versions, and each of these breaks down into a number of markedly different regional dialects. All three share many common features, however, including a superabundance of words and phrases to express variations in snow and ice conditions.

Originally, the Sámi were a semi-nomadic people, living in small communities (*sii-das*), each of which had a degree of control over the surrounding hunting grounds. They mixed hunting, fishing and trapping, but it was the wild reindeer that supplied most of their needs. This changed in the sixteenth century when the Sámi switched over to **reindeer herding**, with communities following the seasonal movements of the animals. What little contact the early Sámi had with other Scandinavians was almost always to their disadvantage, but these early depredations were nothing compared with the **dislocation of Sámi culture** that followed the efforts of Sweden, Russia and Norway to control and colonize Sámi land from the seventeenth century onwards. Things got even worse for the Norwegian Sámi towards the end of the nineteenth century, when the government, influenced by the Social Darwinism of the day, embarked on an aggressive policy of **"Norwegianization"**. New laws banned the use of the Sámi languages in schools, and stopped Sámi from buying land unless they could speak Norwegian. This policy was only abandoned and slowly replaced by a more considerate and progressive approach in the 1950s.

Since the international anti-colonial struggles of the 1960s, the Norwegians have been obliged to re-evaluate their relationship with the Sámi. In 1988, the country's **constitution** was amended with an article that stated "It is the responsibility of the authorities of the state to create conditions enabling the Sámi people to preserve and develop its language, culture and way of life", and the following year the **Sameting** (Sámi Parliament) was opened in Karasjok. Certain deep-seated problems do remain and, in common with other aboriginal peoples marooned in industrialized countries, there have been heated debates about land and mineral rights and the future of the Sámi as a people, above and beyond one country's international borders. Neither is it clear quite how, in the long term, the Norwegian Sámi will adjust to having something akin to dual citizenship – but at least Oslo is asking the right questions.

decorated in crisp, modern pan-Scandinavian style, others done out in an elaborate version of Sámi design. The gallery is located on a ridge above the west bank of the Kautokeinoelva, 2.5km south of the town centre – follow the signs.

The rest of Kautokeino

Also south of the centre is the modern **Kautokeino kirke** (June to mid-Aug daily 9am–9pm; free), a delightful wooden building whose interior is decorated in bright, typically Sámi colours; it looks particularly appealing when the Sámi turn up here in their Sunday best. There are two more modest attractions on the north side of the river, beginning with the small **Kautokeino Bygdetun og Museum** or Guovdageaidnu Gilisillju (Kautokeino Parish Museum: mid-June to mid-Aug Mon–Sat 9am–7pm, Sun noon–7pm; mid-Aug to mid-June Mon–Fri 9am–3pm; 30kr), which features a history of the town inside and a number of draughty-looking Sámi dwellings outside. You'll spot the same little turf huts and skin tents (known as *lavvo*) all over Finnmark – often housing souvenir stalls. Not far away, and clearly signposted to the north, is the **Kautokeino Kulturhuset** or Guovdageaidnu Kulturviessu (Kautokeino Cultural Centre: ⊛www.beaivvas.no). Winner of various architectural awards, the building houses the only state-sponsored Sámi theatre in Norway.

Practicalities

Buses to Kautokeino stop beside Highway 93 in the town centre on the north side of the river – and about 300m to the north of the **tourist office** (daily: late June to early Aug 9am–4pm, July 9am–8pm; ☎78 48 65 00, ⊛www.kautokeino.nu). The latter provides town maps and has details of local events and activities, from fishing and hiking through to "**Sámi adventures**", which typically include a boat trip and a visit to a *lavvo* ("tent") where you can sample traditional Sámi food and listen to *joik* (rhythmic song poems) for around 350kr. One leading local tour operator is Cavzo Safari (☎78 48 75 88, ⊛www.cavzo.no).

Easily the largest **hotel** in Kautokeino is the *Thon Hotel Kautokeino*, in a fortress-like modern structure north of the river just off Highway 93 at Biedjovaggeluodda 2 (☎78 48 70 00, ☎www.thonhotels.no; June–Dec; ●). There are seventy guest rooms here and each is decorated in a bright and breezy style. Alternatives include the modest and modern *Kautokeino Villmarkssenter*, across the highway from the tourist office at Hannoluohka 2 (①78 48 76 02; ●), and the *Arctic Motell & Camping*, near the river on the southern edge of town at Suomaluodda 16 (☎78 48 54 00, ⊛www .kauto.no) with cabins (from 400kr) and a few frugal motel rooms (●).

Eating establishments are thin on the ground, but there's good coffee, cakes and sandwiches at *Kaffe Galleriet*, behind the tourist office, and a full-scale restaurant at the *Thon Hotel*, which specializes in local dishes; mains here average 250kr.

Karasjok

The only other settlement of any size on the Finnmarksvidda is **KARASJOK** (Kárášjohka in Sámi), Norway's Sámi capital, which straddles the E6 on the main route from Finland to Nordkapp – and consequently sees plenty of tourists. Spread across a wooded river valley, the town has none of the desolation of Kautokeino, yet it still conspires to be fairly mundane despite the presence of the Sámi parliament and the country's best Sámi museum. The busiest place in town is the **tourist office**, Karasjok Opplevelser (early June to mid-Aug daily 9am–7pm; rest of year Mon–Fri 9am–4pm; ☎78 46 88 00, ⊛www.karasjokinfo.no), located on the north side of the river beside the E6 and Highway 92 crossroads, which is, to all intents and purposes, the centre of town. Staff here issue free town maps, book overnight accommodation and organize authentic(ish) Sámi expeditions. The office is also incorporated within a miniature Sámi theme park, **Sámpi Park** (same times; 100kr), which offers a fancy multimedia introduction to the Sámi in the Stálubákti ("Magic Theatre"). Here also are examples of traditional Sámi dwellings, Sámi shops and a restaurant plus displays of various ancient Sámi skills with the obligatory reindeer brought along as decoration or to be roped and coralled.

From the tourist office, it's a 200-metre walk north along the Nordkapp road to Museumsgata, where you turn right for the **Samiske Samlinger** or Sámi vourká dávvirat (Sámi Museum: June–Aug Mon–Fri 9am–6pm, Sat & Sun 10am–6pm; Sept–May Tues–Fri 9am–3pm; 75kr; ☎www.rdm.no). This attempts an overview of Sámi culture and history, with the outdoor exhibits comprising an assortment of old dwellings that illustrate the frugality of Sámi life. Inside, a large and clearly presented collection of incidental bygones includes a colourful sample of folkloric Sámi costumes.

Hikes and tours into the Finnmarksvidda

However diverting Karasjok's sights may be, you'll only get a real feel for the Finnmarksvidda if you venture out of town. The tourist office has the details of a wide range of local **guided tours**: options include dog-sledging, a visit to a Sámi camp, a boat trip on the Karasjokka River, cross-country skiing and even gold-panning. The region's most popular long-distance **hike** is the five-day haul across the heart of the Finnmarksvidda, from Karasjok to Alta via a string of strategically located huts; ask at Alta's tourist office (see p.335) for details, but note that this is not for the faint-hearted or inexperienced.

Practicalities

There's a limited **bus** service from Alta to Karasjok along the E6 (1–2 daily except Sat; 5hr; ☎177, ⊛www.ffr.no), but there are currently no buses from Kautokeino. Schedules mean that it's often possible to spend a couple of hours here before moving on, which is quite enough to see the sights, but not nearly long enough to get the true flavour of the place. Buses pull into Karasjok **bus station**, on Storgata, from where it's a signposted five- to ten-minute walk west to the **tourist office** (see p.339).

The best **hotel** in town is the *Rica Hotel Karasjok* (☎78 46 88 60, ⊛www.rica .no; ❺/❼), a breezy modern establishment in a large chalet-like building a short stroll north of the tourist office along the E6. Much more distinctive, however, is ⚐ *Engholm's Husky Lodge* (☎78 46 71 66, ⊛www.engholm.no), a fantastic all-year HI **hostel and lodge**, which has a number of home-made **cabins** ranging from the large (23 dorm beds at 300kr per person) through to cosy four- to six-bed versions (800kr per night for 2 in a shared cabin, 600kr singles; full board 1800kr, 1000kr per person respectively). The hostel is open all year and offers self-catering facilities, a sauna and Arctic dinners, sitting on reindeer skins around an open fire. The owner, the illustrious Sven, is an expert dog-sledge racer and keeps about forty huskies; he uses them on a variety of winter guided tours – dog sledging and so forth – and in summer organizes everything from fishing trips and guided wilderness hikes to horseback riding. The hostel is 7km west out of town on the Kautokeino road (Highway 92), but that's no problem as Sven will pick up guests from Karasjok by prior arrangement for 100kr.

Sven hits all the gastronomic buttons, but the *Rica Hotel Karasjok* possesses the unusual *Storgammen* restaurant, a set of turf-covered huts where Sámi-style meals are served. It's all good fun, but the choices are pretty much limited to reindeer or salmon plus (delightful) cloudberries with sweetened cream. Reckon on 220kr for a main course.

From Karasjok, it's 130km west to Kautokeino; 270km north to Nordkapp; and 330km east to Kirkenes.

Magerøya and Nordkapp

At the northern tip of Norway, the treeless and windswept island of **Magerøya** is mainly of interest to travellers as the location of the **Nordkapp** (North Cape), generally regarded as Europe's northernmost point – though in fact it isn't: that distinction belongs to Kinnarodden, a remote headland about 80km further to the east on a different island altogether. Somehow, everyone seems to have conspired to ignore this simple latitudinal fact and now, while Nordkapp has become one of the most popular tourist destinations in the country, there isn't even a road to Kinnarodden, which can only be reached on a long and difficult 25-kilometre hike from the Hurtigrute port of Mehamn. Neither has the development of the Nordkapp as a tourist spot been without its critics, who argue that the large and lavish visitor centre – **Nordkapphallen** – is crass and grossly overpriced; their opponents simply point to the huge number of people who visit. Whichever side you're on, it's hard to imagine making the long trip to Magerøya without at least dropping by Nordkapp, and the island has other charms too, notably a bleak, rugged beauty that's readily seen from the **E69** as it threads across the mountainous interior from Honningsvåg, on the south coast, to Nordkapp, a distance of 34km.

The obvious base for a visit to Nordkapp is the island's main settlement, **Honningsvåg**, a middling fishing village with a clutch of chain hotels. More appealing, however, is the tiny hamlet of **Kamøyvaer**, nestling beside a narrow fjord just off the E69 between Honningsvåg and Nordkapp, and with a couple of family-run guesthouses. Bear in mind also that Nordkapp is within easy striking distance of other places back on the mainland – certainly the picturesque fishing-station-cum-hotel at **Repvåg**, and maybe even Alta (see p.334), 240km away.

Getting to Magerøya and Nordkapp

Arriving along the E6 and then the E69 from Alta, Nor-Way Bussekspress's **Nordkappekspressen bus** (1–3 daily; ☻www.nor-way.no) stops at Honningsvåg, where passengers change for the FFR service (☎177, ☻www.ffr.no) on to Nordkapp (early June to early Sept 2 daily; 45min). The schedule is such that if you take the first bus from Honningsvåg to Nordkapp, you can spend a couple of hours there before catching the first bus back. If you take the second bus, you'll arrive at Nordkapp at 10.15pm with the return bus departing two hours later at 12.15am, which means, of course, that you can view the midnight sun. Note also that, depending on timings, you can wait for as little as fifteen minutes and as much as two and a half hours between arriving at Honningsvåg on the Nordkappekspressen and leaving for Nordkapp with FFR. Finally, the Hurtigrute coastal boat arrives in Honningsvåg twice daily (once going north, once south), but on neither occasion does its arrival match FFR bus times; alternative transport to Nordkapp is provided for passengers, however – ask on board.

Buses apart, the best way of proceeding from Honningsvåg to Nordkapp is to rent a car or take a taxi. Honningsvåg tourist office has the details of local **car hire** companies offering special deals – reckon on 800kr for a five-hour rental. The **taxi fare** to Nordkapp, including an hour's waiting time after you get there, is about 900kr return, 500kr one-way; contact Nordkapp Taxisentral (☎78 47 22 34). Arriving **by car**, bear in mind that the last stretch of the Honningsvåg–Nordkapp road is closed by snow in winter, roughly from November to early April.

North from Skaidi to Repvåg and Magerøya island

Beyond the **Skaidi** crossroads, the **E6** veers east to clip across a bleak plateau that brings it, 23km later, to the turning for Nordkapp. This turning, the **E69**, scuttles north along the shore of the **Porsangerfjord**, a deep and wide inlet flanked by bare, low-lying hills whose stone has been fractured and made flaky by the biting cold of winter. After 48km, the E69 zips past the byroad to **REPVÅG**, an old timber fishing station on a promontory just 2km off the main highway. A rare and particularly picturesque survivor from prewar days, the station is painted red in the traditional manner and perches on stilts on the water's edge. The whole complex has been turned into the ⚓ *Repvåg Fjordhotell og Rorbusenter* (☎78 47 54 40, ☻www.repvag-fjordhotell .no; May to late Sept), with simple, unassuming rooms (❷/❸) in the main building, as well as a cluster of old fishermen's shacks – *rorbuer* (650–750kr for 2). It's a charming place to stay – solitary and scenic in equal proportions, the public areas of the hotel decked out with authentic nautical tackle and cosy furniture. Repvåg is an ideal base from which to reach Nordkapp, though once you're ensconced here, you may settle instead for one of the hotel's boat and fishing trips out on the Porsangerfjord. Almost inevitably, the hotel **restaurant** specializes in seafood – and very good it is too.

Back on the E69, it's about 25km to the ambitious series of tunnels and bridges (145kr toll) that spans the straits between the mainland and Honningsvåg, on the island of **Magerøya**, which you'll spy long before you get there, a hunk of brown rock looking like an inverted blancmange.

Honningsvåg

HONNINGSVÅG, 210km from Alta and just 2km off the E69, is largely composed of a jumble of well-worn modern buildings that reflect its role as a minor fishing- and sea-port. It straggles along the seashore, sheltered from the blizzards of winter by the surrounding crags – though, given the conditions, sheltered is a comparative term. Honningsvåg has accumulated several chain hotels, which make a steady living from the tourists that stream through bound for the Nordkapp, and is at its prettiest at the **head of the harbour**, where an assortment of timber warehouses, dating back to the days when the village was entirely reliant on fish, make an attractive ensemble.

Practicalities

Honningsvåg strings out along its main drag for about 1km. Buses from the mainland pull into the **bus station** at its southern end. **Hurtigrute** coastal boats dock at the adjacent jetty, with northbound boats arriving at 11.45am and departing 3.15pm; southbound, the boats don't overlay here, arriving and departing at 6.15am; the northbound service is met by special Nordkapp excursion buses – details on board. The **tourist office** is here too (mid-June to mid-Aug Mon–Fri 8.30am– 8pm, Sat & Sun noon–8pm; rest of year Mon–Fri 8.30am–4pm; ☎78 47 70 30, ⓦwww.nordkapp.no).

All of Honningsvåg's **hotels** are along or near the main street. Walking south from the bus station, it's a few metres to the first, the *Rica Hotel Honningsvåg* (☎78 47 72 20, ⓦwww.rica.no; mid-May to Aug; ❹), a routine modern block with nearly two hundred modern rooms. More appealing is the nearby *Honningsvåg Brygge Hotel* (☎78 47 64 64, ⓦwww.hvg-brygge.no; ❺), a tasteful and intelligent conversion of a set of wooden warehouses perched on one of the old jetties. The rooms are neat and cosy – and advance reservations are strongly advised. For lighter wallets, there's an HI **hostel**, *Nordkapp Vandrerhjem*, a twenty-minute walk north of Honningsvåg – and just 1km from the end of the tunnel from the mainland (☎91 82 41 56, ⓦwww .vandrerhjem.no; May–Dec; dorm beds 330kr, doubles ❷). There are self-catering facilities here, but no café or restaurant.

For **food**, the *Honningsvåg Brygge Hotel* boasts the best **restaurant** by far, the *Sjøhuset* (June to early Aug daily 2–11pm; limited hours the rest of year), where the seafood is delicious and main courses hover around 220kr; reservations are strongly advised as preference is given to hotel guests.

North from Honningsvåg

The E69 winds its way out of Honningsvåg, staying close to the shore for the first part of its journey north. After 9km, just beyond the conspicuous *Rica Hotel Nordkapp*, you'll spot the turning for **KAMØYVÆR**, a pretty little village tucked in tight between the sea and the hills, just 2km from the main road. Here, metres from the jetty, is the *Hotel Årran Nordkapp* (☎78 47 51 29, ⓦwww.arran.as; ❹; May to early Sept), a pleasant, family-run hotel, whose forty-odd guest rooms are distributed amongst several brightly painted and well-tended houses. They serve dinner here too, though it's best to book it ahead of time.

Beyond the Kamøyvær turning, the E69 twists a solitary course up through the hills to cross a high-tundra plateau, the mountains stretching away on either side. It's a fine run, with snow and ice lingering well into the summer and impressive views over the treeless and stripped Arctic terrain.

Nordkapp

When they finally reach **Nordkapp** (North Cape), many visitors feel desperately disappointed – it is, after all, only a cliff and, at 307m, it isn't even all that high. But for others there's something about this greyish-black hunk of slate, stuck at the end of a bare, wind-battered promontory, that exhilarates the senses – and some such feeling must have inspired the prehistoric Sámi to establish a sacrificial site here. It was the English explorer **Richard Chancellor** who gave the North Cape its name in 1553, as he drifted along the Norwegian coast in an attempt to find the Northeast Passage from the Atlantic to the Pacific. He failed, though the name stuck, and the visit of the Norwegian king

Oscar II in 1873 opened the tourist floodgates. Nowadays the lavish **Nordkapphallen** (North Cape Hall: daily: early May & Sept 11am–3pm; late May to Aug 11am–1am; 200kr for 48hrs, including parking; Ⓦwww .rica.no), cut into the rock of the Cape, entertains hundreds of visitors every day, who all pay handsomely for the pleasure of standing at mainland Europe's supposed northern extremity. Fronted by a statue of King Oscar II, the main building contains a restaurant, café, a post office where you get your letters specially stamped and a cinema showing – you guessed it – films about the Cape. There's a viewing area too, but there's not much to see except the sea – and, weather permitting, the midnight sun from May 12 to July 29. A **tunnel** runs from the main building to the cliff face and the cavernous *Grotten Bar*, which offers long views out to sea through the massive glass wall.

East to Kirkenes

East of Nordkapp the landscape is more of the same – a relentless expanse of barren plateaus, mountain and ocean. Occasionally a determined village relieves the monotony with commanding views over the fjords that slice deep into the mainland, but generally there is little for the eyes of a tourist. Nor is there much to do in what are predominantly fishing and industrial settlements, and there are few tangible attractions beyond the sheer impossibility of the chill wilderness.

The **E6** weaves a circuitous course across this vast territory, hugging the Finnish border for much of its length. The only obvious target is the Sámi centre of **Karasjok** (see p.339), 270km from Nordkapp and easily the region's most interesting town. Frankly, there's not much reason to push on further east unless you're intent on picking up the **Hurtigrute coastal boat** as it bobs along the remote and spectacular shores of the Barents Sea. Among the Hurtigrute's several ports of call, the most diverting is **Kirkenes**, the Hurtigrute's northern terminus, 320km to the east of Karasjok at the end of the E6 and near the Russian frontier. Taking the boat also means that you can avoid the long haul back the way you came – and by the time you reach Kirkenes you'll certainly be heartily sick of the E6. The other shortcut is to **fly**: Kirkenes has its own airport and from here there are regular Widerøe (Ⓦwww.wideroe.no) flights to a hatful of north Norwegian towns, including Alta and Tromsø; as a sample fare, a one-way ticket from Kirkenes to Alta can go for as little as 600kr, though 800kr is more usual. As regards **buses**, FFR (☎177, Ⓦwww.ffr.no) reaches most corners of Finnmark with reasonable regularity, but its principal long-distance service links Alta with Kirkenes along the E6, via Skaidi, Olderfjord, Karasjok and Tana Bru; the whole Alta–Kirkenes journey takes between ten and thirteen hours and there are three buses weekly.

Finally, **accommodation** is very thin on the ground, being confined to a handful of the larger communities. Reservations, therefore, are strongly advised. Campsites are more frequent and usually have cabins for rent, but they are mostly stuck in the middle of nowhere.

East from Nordkapp: by land

Beyond its junction with the E69 Nordkapp road, the **E6** bangs along the western shore of the **Porsangerfjord**, a wide inlet that slowly shelves up into the sticky marshes and mudflats at its head. After about 45km, the road reaches the hamlet of **STABBURSNES**, which is home to the small but enjoyable **Stabbursnes Naturhus og Museum** (Stabbursnes Nature House and Museum; early June daily 11am–6pm; mid-June to mid-Aug daily 9am–8pm; late Aug daily 9am–6pm; Sept–May Tues & Thurs noon–3pm, Wed noon–4pm; 50kr), which provides an overview of the region's flora and fauna.

From Stabbursnes, it's about 15km south on the E6 to **LAKSELV**, an inconsequential fishing village at the head of the Porsangerfjord, and another 75km to Karasjok (see p.339), the best place hereabouts to spend the night. Pushing on, the **E6** weaves its way northeast along the Finnish border, joining with the **E75** from Finland long before it reaches, 180km from Karasjok, **TANA BRU**, a Sámi settlement clustered around a suspension bridge over the Tana River, one of Europe's best salmon rivers. **Tana Tourist Information** (late June to late Aug Mon–Fri 9am–6pm, Sat & Sun 10am–5pm; rest of year Mon–Fri 8am–3.30pm; ℡78 92 53 00, Ⓦwww.tana.kommune.no), at the *Hotel Tana*, beside the main road as you near the bridge, has local information and details of fishing trips.

Beyond Tana Bru, the E6 tracks along the southern shores of the Varangerfjord, a bleak, weather-beaten run with all colour and vegetation being confined to the northern shore, with its scattered farms and painted fishing boats, but then the road loops inland, clipping across the tundra, before it regains the coast for its final spurt into Kirkenes (see below).

East from Nordkapp: by sea

Beyond Nordkapp, the Hurtigrute steers a fine route round the top of the country, nudging its way between tiny islets and craggy bluffs, and stopping at a series of solitary fishing villages and small-town **VARDØ**, Norway's most easterly town and a busy fishing port of 2700 souls. Like everywhere else in Finnmark, Vardø was savaged in World War II and the modern town that grew up in the 1950s could hardly be described as beautiful, though its geography is at least unusual: Vardø spreads out over two little islets that are connected by a narrow causeway, which in turn the apex of the town's harbour; a tunnel connects Vardø with the mainland, just a couple of kilometres away.

Vardø's main attraction is the **Vardøhus Festning** (Vardø Fortress; daily: mid-April to mid-Sept 10am–9pm; mid-Sept to mid-April 10am–6pm; 30kr), a tiny star-shaped fortress, located about 600m southwest of the Hurtigrute quay. The site was first fortified in 1300, but the present structure dates from the 1730s, built at the behest of King Christian VI. When this singularly unprepossessing monarch toured Finnmark he was greeted, according to one of his courtiers, with "expressions of abject flattery in atrocious verse" – and the king loved it. Christian had the fortress built to guard the northeastern approaches to his kingdom, but it has never seen active service – hence its excellent state of preservation. A small **museum** gives further details of the fort's history.

The northbound **Hurtigrute** reaches Vardø at 4am and leaves just fifteen minutes later; southbound it docks at 4pm and leaves an hour later – quite enough time to get to the fort and back.

Kirkenes

During World War II, the mining town and ice-free port of **KIRKENES** was bombed more heavily than any other place in Europe apart from Malta. The retreating German army torched what was left as they fled in the face of liberating Soviet soldiers, who found 3500 locals hiding in the nearby iron-ore mines. The mines finally closed in 1996, threatening the future of this four-thousand-strong community, which is now trying hard to kindle trade with Russia to keep itself afloat.

▲ Hurtigrute coastal boat

Kirkenes is almost entirely modern, with long rows of uniform houses spreading out along the Bøkfjord, a narrow arm of the Barents Sea. If that sounds dull, it's not to slight the town, which makes the most of its inhospitable surroundings with some pleasant public gardens, lakes and residential areas – it's just that it seems an awfully long way to come for not very much. That said, once you've finally got here it seems churlish to leave quickly, and it's certainly worth searching out the **Sør-Varanger museum** (early June to mid-Aug daily 10am–6pm; mid-Aug to early June daily 10am–3.30pm; 40kr; ☎ www.sor-varanger.museum.no), one of whose sections – the **Grenselandmuseet** (Frontier Museum) – focuses on the history of the region and its people, and includes a detailed account of the events of World War II. In the same building is a display of the work of **John Savio** (1902–38), a local Sámi artist whose woodcuts and paintings evoke the Sámi way of life and the overbearing power of nature. The museum is about 1.5km south of the main harbourfront at the end of Solheimsveien (the E6), beside one of the town's several little lakes.

Practicalities

Kirkenes is the northern terminus of the **Hurtigrute** coastal boat, which arrives here at 10am and departs for points south at 12.45pm. The Hurtigrute uses the quay just over 1km east of the town centre; a local bus shuttles between the two. Kirkenes **airport** is 15km west of town just off the E6; Flybussen (2–5 daily; 20min; 85kr one-way) connect the airport with the centre. The **bus station** is at the west end of the main harbourfront, and from here it's about 400m east along Kirkegata to the **tourist office**, at Presteveien 1 (June–Aug Mon–Fri 10am–6pm, Sat & Sun 10am–4pm; Sept–May Mon–Fri 9am–4pm; ☎78 99 25 44, ☎ www.kirkenesinfo.no).

The town's best **hotel** is the *Rica Arctic*, whose eighty well-appointed rooms occupy a smart modern block in the centre near the town square at Kongensgate 1 (☎78 99 59 00, ☎ www.rica.no; ❹/❻). The similarly modern *Rica Hotel Kirkenes* is in three-storey block about 800m south of the main square at Pasvikveien 63 (☎78 99 14 91, ☎ www.rica.no; ❹/❻).

As for **food**, the *Rica Arctic Hotel* has a very competent restaurant, though it's slightly bettered by *Vin og Vilt*, Kirkegata 5 (daily 6–11pm; ☎78 99 38 11), where they serve up an excellent range of Arctic specialities from reindeer to char and beyond. Main courses at both hover at around 260kr.

Travel details

Principal Nor-Way Bussekspress bus services (@www.nor-way.no)

Alta to: Honningsvåg (1–2 daily; 4hr); Narvik (2 daily except Sat; 9hr 30min); Tromsø (1 daily; 7hr).
Honningsvåg to: Alta (1–2 daily; 4hr); Nordkapp (early June to late Aug 2 daily; 45min).
Tromsø to: Alta (1 daily; 7hr); Narvik (2–3 daily; 4hr).

Principal FFR bus services (@www.ffr.no)

Alta to: Karasjok (1–2 daily except Sat; 5hr); Kautokeino (1–2 daily except Sat; 2hr 15min); Kirkenes (3 weekly; 10–13hr).
Note that all these services are routed through Skaidi, where you usually change for points north and south along the E6 – but check connecting times before you set out.
Karasjok: to: Alta (1–2 daily except Sat; 5hr); Kirkenes (2 weekly; 5–7hr).
Kautokeino to: Alta (1–2 daily except Sat; 2hr 15min).
Kirkenes to: Alta (3 weekly; 10–13hr); Karasjok (2 weekly; 5–7hr).

Nor-Way Bussekspress's Nord-Norgeekspressen and Nordkappekspressen (@www.nor-way.no)

The **Nord-Norgeekspressen** (North Norway Express Bus) complements the railway system. It runs north from Bodø and Fauske to Alta in three segments: Bodø to Narvik via Fauske (2 daily; 6hr 30min); Narvik to Tromsø (1–3 daily; 4hr); and Tromsø to Alta (1 daily; 6hr 30min). Alternatively, the **Nordkappekspressen** (North Cape Express

Bus) runs direct from Narvik to Alta (2 daily except Sat; 9hr 30min), where passengers overnight before picking up the second leg of the Nordkappekspressen to Honningsvåg (1–2 daily; 4hr), where they change again to reach Nordkapp (early June to late Aug 2 daily; 45min).

Principal car ferries

Breivikeidet to: Svendsby (every 1–2hr; Mon–Fri 6am–10pm, Sat 8am–8pm, Sun 10am–9pm; 25min) with Bjørklids (@www.bjorklid.no).
Brensholmen to: Botnhamn (May to Aug 5–7 daily; 45min) with Senjafergene (@www.senjafergene.no).
Gryllefjord to: Andenes (late May to mid-June & early to late Aug 2 daily, mid-June to early Aug 3 daily; 2hr) with Senjafergene (@www.senjafergene.no).
Lyngseidet to: Olderdalen (every 1–2hr; Mon–Fri 7am–8pm, Sat 9am–7pm, Sun 10.30am–8pm; 40min) with Bjørklids (@www.bjorklid.no).

Principal Hurtigbåt passenger express boat

Tromsø to: Harstad (2–3 daily; 2hr 45min) with Hurtigruten car ferries (@www.hurtigruten.no).

Hurtigrute coastal boat (year-round; daily; @www.hurtigruten.no)

Northbound from: Tromsø at 6.30pm; Honningsvåg at 3.15pm; Berlevåg at 10.45pm; Vardø at 4.15am; Vadsø at 8.15am; terminates at Kirkenes at 10am.
Southbound from: Kirkenes at 12.45pm; Vardø at 5pm; (no southbound stop at Vadsø); Berlevåg at 10.30pm; Honningsvåg at 6.15am; Tromsø at 1.30am.
The Tromsø–Kirkenes journey time is 40hrs.

Sweden

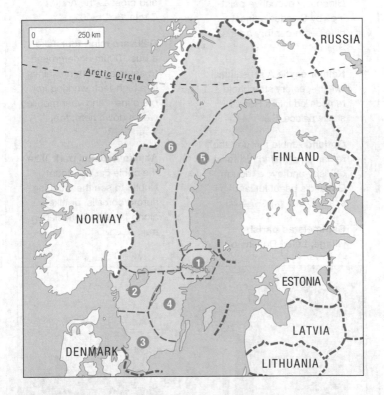

Sweden highlights

✳ **Gamla Stan, Stockholm**
Stroll through the beautiful
Baroque old town.
See p.370

✳ **Fürstenberg Galleries,
Gothenburg Art Museum**
Gloriously evocative paint-
ings by Sweden's finest
nineteenth-century artists.
See p.407

✳ **Kalmar castle** A sensational
twelfth-century stronghold
remodelled into a Renais-
sance palace. See p.445

✳ **Gotland** Amble through the
remarkable walled old town
of Visby and cycle though
Gotland's beautiful land-
scapes. See pp.457–465

✳ **Gammelstad parish
village, Luleå** Dozens of
superbly preserved wooden
cottages around a beautiful
church. See p.478

✳ **Inlandsbanan** This single-
track railway traverses
some dramatic landscapes
and crosses the Arctic
Circle. See p.482

✳ **Gällivare mine tour** Take
a bus 1000m underground
to see mammoth machines
in a high-tech working iron
ore mine – and your mobile
works down here, too.
See p.498

✳ **Abisko national park** Take
the cable car up Mount
Nuolja to see the stunning
aurora borealis, or hike
along the wild Kungsleden
trail. See p.503

▲ The wall around Visby

Introduction and basics

In geographical terms, Sweden is easily the biggest of the Scandinavian countries – a massive 450,000 square kilometres, larger than California and twice as big as Britain – although its population numbers barely nine million. Essentially one vast coniferous forest punctuated by some 100,000 crystal-clear lakes, Sweden reposes contentedly within an endless natural beauty. Remote, austere, cold – all these generalizations may be partly true, but Sweden is also friendly and efficient and, as it boasts no single concentration of sights (other than in Stockholm and Gothenburg), you're as likely to fetch up on a sunny Baltic beach as camp in the forest or hike through the national parks of Swedish Lapland.

One aspect of the country most likely to impinge on the cluttered eye of Europeans is the sense of space. Away from the relatively densely populated south, it's easy to travel for miles without seeing a soul, and taking in these vast, unpopulated stretches in a limited time can be exhausting and unrewarding. Better, on a short trip, to delve into one or two regions and experience the natural beauty that pervades and shapes the Swedes' attitude to life: once you've broken through the oft-quoted reserve of the people there's a definite emotive feel to the country. And initial contact is easy, as almost everyone speaks English.

Where to go

The **south and southwest** of the country are flat holiday lands. For so long territory disputed with Denmark (which the landscape closely resembles), the provinces now harbour a host of historic ports – including **Gothenburg**, **Helsingborg** and **Malmö** – and less frenetic beach towns, all old and mostly fortified. Off the **southeast** coast, the Baltic Islands of **Öland** and **Gotland** are the country's most hyped resorts – and with good reason, supporting a lazy beach-life to match that of the best southern European spots, but without the hotel blocks, crowds and tat.

Central and northern Sweden is the stuff of tourist brochures: great swathes of forest, inexhaustible lakes ideal for nude bathing and some of the best wilderness hiking in Europe. Two train routes link north with south. The eastern run, close to the **Bothnian coast**, passes old wood-built towns and is handy for the city of **Umeå**,

Sweden on the web

Ⓦ **www.visitsweden.com** The official site of the Swedish tourist board with links to tourism, transport and accommodation resources, and a useful search engine.

Ⓦ **www.eniro.se** This combination of the Yellow Pages, a search engine and an incredibly detailed interactive map allows you to find anything, anywhere.

Ⓦ **www.resplus.se** Excellent site for finding public transport links across the country, including all train and regional bus connections.

Ⓦ **www.sj.se** Home page of Sweden's main rail company, with timetables, pricing and advance online ticket sales.

Ⓦ **www.stfturist.se** Details of all of Sweden's youth hostels and mountain cabins, with opening times and prices.

Ⓦ **www.stockholmtown.com** Copious amounts of information on the Swedish capital from the city's tourist board.

Ⓦ **www.abbasite.com** Official shrine to Stockholm's fab four, with picture galleries, sound clips and assorted Eurovision trivia.

with its ferry connections to Vaasa in Finland. In the centre of the country, the trains of the **Inlandsbanan** (inland railway) strike off through some remarkably changing landscapes of lakelands to mountains, clearing reindeer off the track as they go. Both routes meet in Sweden's **far north**, home of the Sámi, the oldest indigenous Scandinavian people, and of the **midnight sun**, which in high summer never sets.

Of the cities, **Stockholm** is supreme. A bundle of islands housing regal and monumental architecture, fine museums and the country's most active culture and nightlife, it's a likely point of arrival and a vital stop-off. Two university towns, **Uppsala** and **Lund**, also demand a visit, while nearly all the other major cities – chiefly Östersund, Umeå, and Kiruna – can make some sort of cultural claim on your attention. Time is rarely wasted in humbler towns either, as the beauty of the

local surroundings adequately compensates for any lack of specific sights.

When to go

Summer in Sweden is short and hectic. Generally speaking, Swedes consider summer to run from mid-June to mid-August, and during this time accommodation is reduced in price (to fill rooms occupied by business people during the rest of the year) and most of the country's attractions are open for business. Conversely, though, summer also sees something of a shutdown: many bus timetables are at their most skeletal, and facilities such as swimming pools and cinemas in sparsely populated parts of the country close completely. Most Swedes take their holidays during the summer, with the result that popular destinations such as

Dalarna can be tediously overcrowded. From rowdy Midsummer's Night (June 21) onwards, accommodation is scarce and trains packed as Swedes head out into the country and to the beaches. Outside the peak month of **July**, however, things are noticeably quieter; by mid-August, most Swedes have returned to work and the feeling of summer has gone – by late August, some parts of northern Sweden see their first frost.

To avoid the rush, try visiting in September or late May – both are usually bright and relatively warm. The **midnight sun** extends the days in June and July, and north of the Arctic Circle it virtually never gets dark. Elsewhere it stays light until very late, up to midnight and beyond. Thanks to the Gulf Stream, temperatures in Sweden are surprisingly high – see the temperature chart on p.11 – and on the south coast it can be as hot as any southern European resort.

Winter, on the other hand, can be a miserable experience. It lasts a long time (Nov–April solid) and gets very cold indeed: temperatures of -15°C and below are not unusual even in Stockholm. Further north it's positively arctic. Days are short and dark (in the far north the sun barely rises at all) and biting winds cut through the most elaborate of padded coats. On the plus side, the snow stays crisp and white, the air is clean, the water everywhere frozen solid: a paradise for skaters and skiers. Stockholm, too, is particularly beautiful with its winter covering of snow and ice.

Getting there from the rest of Scandinavia

The cheapest **Scandinavian connection** with Sweden is from Denmark, by bus and ferry, and regular trains and ferries connect other mainland countries.

By train

There are several possible **train** routes into Sweden **from Denmark and Norway, though no rail links exist with Finland**. In the south trains run **from** Copenhagen and Kastrup airport to Malmö, Gothenburg and Stockholm using the Øresunds Link. Trains also operate from the Norwegian capital, Oslo, to both Gothenburg and Stockholm; further north, services run from Trondheim to Östersund, and, in the far north, from Narvik to Kiruna and points south. **Rail passes** (InterRail, Eurail and Eurail Scandinavia) are valid on all these routes.

By bus

There are several **bus** routes into Sweden from other Scandinavian cities, though the frequent services **from Denmark** are the only ones that will get you there quickly. The easiest – and cheapest – connection is on one of the several daily buses **from Copenhagen** to Stockholm (9hr) or Oslo (8hr), via the Øresunds Link and Malmö. **From Norway** there are several daily buses from Oslo to Gothenburg, the journey taking four hours, and frequent daily buses from Oslo to Stockholm, a seven-hour ride. **From Finland** most routes converge upon Helsinki or Turku and then use the ferry crossings to Stockholm.

By ferry

Ferry services to Sweden are plentiful, but can be confusing – not least because several operators run rival services on the same route. To make any sense of the routes, timetables and prices, which change from year to year, check the ferry company websites, or consult their brochures at any tourist office. You'll find other details – frequencies and journey times – in the "Travel details" at the end of each section. In addition, rail passes give **discounts and free travel** on some of the ferry routes.

From Denmark

The shortest and cheapest ferry crossing is **Helsingør–Helsingborg** (Ⓦwww.scandlines .dk; 20min; foot passengers 23Dkr); just walk on board and go. There are also year-round sailings to Gothenburg **from Frederikshavn** (Ⓦwww.stenaline.dk; 2hr; foot passengers from 160Dkr). Stena Line also sails daily to Varberg **from Grenå** (4hr; foot passengers from 160Dkr). The other approach from Denmark is to come via the Danish island of

Bornholm; ferries and catamarans (Ⓦwww
.bornholmstrafikken.dk; foot passengers
174Dkr) cross from Rønne to Ystad, on the
southern Swedish coast.

From Finland

Longer ferry journeys link Sweden with
Finland, the major crossing being the
Helsinki–Stockholm route, a sixteen-hour
trip with either Silja Line (Ⓦwww.tallinksilja
.com; foot passengers from €128 with
cabin accommodation) or Viking (Ⓦwww
.vikingline.fi; foot passengers from €36).
There are also regular crossings **from Turku**
and **from Mariehamn** in the Finnish Åland
Islands to Stockholm (both Silja and Viking;
4hr; foot passengers from €16). If you're
aiming for the north of Sweden, you might
be better off crossing **from Vaasa** (Ⓦwww
.rgline.com; foot passengers €60): there are
year-round four-hour services to Umeå.

From Norway

There's one year-round crossing from Norway
to Sweden, **from Sandefjord** to Strömstad,
north of Gothenburg (Ⓦwww.colorline.com;
2hr 30min; foot passengers 125Nkr, cars
132Nkr).

By plane

The cost of **flying** to Sweden from the other
Scandinavian countries has decreased
thanks to the competition offered to SAS
(Ⓦwww.scandinavian.net) by Norwegian
(Ⓦwww.norwegian.no) from Norway. The
SAS off-shoot, Blue1 (Ⓦwww.blue1.com),
offers reasonably priced flights from Finland.
If you shop around and book far in advance,
a flight within Scandinavia including taxes
can cost as little as €40.

SAS operates regular daily flights from
its **Copenhagen** hub to Gothenburg and
Stockholm. Norwegian has regular flights
from Oslo to Stockholm. **From Oslo**,
SAS also operates regular departures
to Stockholm. Of all the Scandinavian
countries, **Finland** has the greatest
number of regional flights to Sweden. Most
services are operated by Blue1, but are too
numerous to list here. Information on most
of Sweden's commercial airports including
airlines and timetables can be found at
Ⓦwww.lfv.se.

Getting around

Sweden's internal **transport** system is quick,
efficient and runs in all weathers. Services
are often reduced in summer (especially
on northern bus routes), but it's unlikely
you'll ever get stranded. In summer, when
everyone is on holiday, trains and, to a lesser
extent, buses are packed, making seat
reservations a good idea on long journeys.
All train, bus and ferry schedules can be
found at Ⓦwww.resplus.se.

Trains

Apart from flying, **trains** are the quickest way
to get around Sweden's vast expanses. The
service is excellent, especially on the main
routes, and prices not too expensive when
tickets are bought well in advance. Several
companies operate regional trains in Sweden
(see below).

SJ (*Statens Järnvägar* – Swedish State
Railways; Ⓦwww.sj.se) has an extensive
network of routes, running right across
the country. Their high-speed X2000 train
services can often shave a couple of hours
off the normal journey time, particularly on
the Stockholm–Gothenburg run. **Tågkompaniet** (Ⓦwww.tagkompaniet.se) runs
trains on several smaller lines in central
Sweden, including Sundsvall–Östersund and
Gävle–Falun–Borlänge–Mora. Tickets for
Tågkompaniet trains can be bought on the
train in question and rail passes are valid.

In Skåne in southern Sweden, Skånetrafiken operates local trains known as
Pågatågen (Ⓦwww.skanetrafiken.se)
between Helsingborg, Lund, Malmö and
Ystad. Finally, **Inlandsbanan** (Ⓦwww
.grandnordic.se) runs trains on the summer-
only (mid-June to mid-Aug) route between
Mora and Gällivare in Swedish Lapland, and
if you're in the country during the summer
months, then travelling at least a section of
the Inlandsbanan is a must. InterRail and
Eurail holders travel free. Individual tickets
cost 123kr per 100km and seat reservations
cost 50kr.

Tickets and reservations

Buying individual **train tickets** is easy and
is best done online. Alternatively, tickets are

also available from ticketing machines at most stations or, for a slightly higher fare, at the station counters. Tickets sales for SJ services open three months before departure and start at 99kr per direct journey. The closer to the departure, generally the higher the price will be. Buying tickets **in advance from abroad is easy**; select the ticket on the SJ website and pay for it by credit card, and you'll get a code that can later be punched into any SJ machine to print out your actual ticket.

On long **overnight** train journeys it's worth paying for a couchette (*bädd* or *liggplats*) or a sleeping car (*säng* or *sovplats*) in mixed or women-only compartments. There are several night-train connections within Sweden, as well as services from Malmö to Berlin. Prices are low: the cost of either a couchette in a six-berth cabin or a sleeping berth in a two-person cabin depends on the length of the journey and how far in advance you buy.

Rail passes

If you're planning to travel a lot by train, you're generally better off buying a **train pass**, such as InterRail, Eurail or Eurail Scandinavia pass, which needs to be purchased before you leave home (for details, see Basics, p.35). If you're planning to travel only in Sweden, then it might be worth buying a one-country Interrail pass for Sweden (from £149), though if you buy individual tickets well in advance you'll pay much less than the pass itself.

Buses

The main **long-distance bus** companies in the southern half of Sweden are Swebus Express (@www.swebusexpress.se) and Säfflebussen (@www.safflebussen.se). Routes change frequently but are shown on each company's website. The two companies charge similar fares; a one-way from Stockholm to Gothenburg, for example, costs from 299kr.

In the north, there are a number of smaller companies, including **Y-buss** (@www.ybuss.se), which operates services from Stockholm to Sundsvall, the High Coast and Umeå, as well as inland to Östersund. **Kustbussen** operates from Sundsvall to Härnösand, the

High Coast, Umeå, Skellefteå, Luleå and Haparanda at the Finnish border. Major routes are listed in the "Travel details" at the end of each section, and you can pick up comprehensive **timetables** at bus terminals or tourist offices, or view them online.

Ferries and cruises

Unlike Norway and Finland, there are few domestic long-distance **ferry** services in Sweden. The various archipelagos on the southeast coast are served by small ferries, the most comprehensive network being within the **Stockholm archipelago**, for which you can buy a boat pass (see p.389). The other major link is between the Baltic island of **Gotland** and the mainland at Nynäshamn and Oskarshamn, both very popular routes for which you should book ahead in summer; all routes are operated by Destination Gotland (@www.destination gotland.se); see p.459 for more details.

Planes

The **domestic flight** network is predominantly operated by SAS (@www.scandinavian.net) and Noxtjet (@www.nextjet.se), and flying can be a real steal, depending on when the ticket is booked. A one-way trip from Stockholm to Gothenburg, for example, costs from 450kr with SAS.

Other useful operators include City Airline (@www.cityairline.com), Gotlandsflyg (@www.gotlandsflyg.se) and Malmö Aviation (@www.malmoaviation.se). For the latest overview of who flies where, visit @www.whichbudget.com.

Driving

Driving presents few problems: roads are excellent, and the only real dangers are the reindeer and elk that can wander onto the tarmac. Keep to the speed limits and watch out around dawn and dusk particularly – if you hit one you'll know about it; every year, dozens of drivers are hospitalized or killed after hitting elk. As for **documentation**, you need a full licence and the vehicle registration document; an international driving licence and insurance "green card" are not essential. **Speed limits** are 110kph on motorways, 90kph and 70kph on other roads, 50kph in built-up areas; note that there are hundreds of speed cameras across Sweden, mainly in the south. It's compulsory to use **dipped headlights** during daylight hours (on rented cars they will probably come on automatically) and, if you are taking your own car from Britain, remember to get the beam of your headlights adjusted to suit **driving on the right**. If you're motoring into northern Sweden then it's recommended that you fit mud flaps to your wheels and stone guards on the front of caravans. Swedish **drink-driving laws** are among the toughest in Europe and random breath tests the norm. Even the smallest amount of alcohol can lead to lost licences (always), fines (often) and prison sentences (not infrequently).

If you **break down** or are in an **accident**, call either the police or the Larmtjänst (☎ 112), a 24-hour rescue organization run by Swedish insurance companies. If you're heading into a city for the first time, keep an eye out for the excellent **information points** along the motorways, usually a few kilometres before the turnoff; apart from listing tourist information, some now have machines that spit out free city or regional maps. Town centre tourist offices are usually well indicated, and those in larger towns and cities often have special spaces where you can park free of charge for 15–30 minutes.

Car rental and petrol

Car rental is uniformly expensive, though most companies have special weekend tourist rates – from around 750kr, Friday to Monday, for a small car. It's worth checking out local tourist offices in the summer, as they sometimes recommend or operate reasonable weekly deals; otherwise, expect to pay around 3500kr a week, unlimited mileage, for a VW Golf or similar-sized car. Both Avis (🕸 www.avis.se) and Hertz (🕸 www.hertz.se) are represented in all the large towns and cities. **Petrol** currently costs around 15kr per litre, diesel a few kronor less per litre; ethanol is also available. Most filling stations are self-service (*tanka själv*) and lots of them have automatic pumps (*sedel automat*), where you can fill up at any time using your credit card (international cards usually accepted) at a slightly lower price.

Cycling

A much better way to get around Sweden independently is to **cycle**. Some parts of the country were made for it, the southern provinces (and Gotland in particular) being ideal for a leisurely pedal. Many towns are best explored by bike, too – there are even public air pumps for soft tyres – and tourist offices, campsites and youth hostels often **rent** bicycles from around 150kr a day; you may have to pay a returnable deposit as well. If you're touring, be prepared for long-distance hauls in the north and for rain in summer. **Taking a bike on a train** is more trouble than it's worth as you need to book well ahead.

Accommodation

Finding somewhere cheap to sleep is not difficult provided you're prepared to do some advance planning. There's an excellent network of **youth hostels**, **pensions** and **campsites**, while **private rooms** and **bed-and-breakfast** places are common in the cities. Year-round discounts even make **hotels** affordable.

Hotels and pensions

Hotels and **pensions** (the latter usually family-run B&B-type places) come cheaper than you'd think in Sweden. Although there's little chance of a room under 450kr a night anywhere, you'll find that rates vary according to season and the day of the week. Outside the summer period (roughly mid-June to mid-Aug), rates are reduced at weekends (usually Fri & Sat), while a higher price is applied from Sunday to Thursday to take advantage of business travellers. During the summer, the winter weekend rates generally apply throughout the week. Bear in mind, though, that this is a general rule that varies from place to place.

In summer and at weekends outside of summer, expect to pay from 600kr for a single, and 750kr for a double room with a TV and private bathroom. From Sunday to Thursday outside of summer, prices average 900kr for a single and 1200kr for a double. Nearly all hotels include a self-service buffet breakfast in the price – which, given its size, can make for a useful saving.

Accommodation price codes

The hotels and guesthouses listed in the Sweden chapters of this Guide have been graded according to the following price bands, based on the cost of the **least expensive double room in high season** (usually Sun–Thurs outside summer, mid-June to mid-Aug). Many hotels offer summer and/or weekend discounts, and in these instances we've given two price bands, covering both the discounted and the regular rate(ie ❷/❸).

❶ 500kr and under
❷ 501–700kr
❸ 701–900kr

❹ 901–1200kr
❺ 1201–1500kr
❻ 1501kr and over

Youth hostels

One of the biggest choices of accommodation lies with the country's huge chain of youth hostels (*vandrarhem*), operated by the Swedish Tourist Association (STF; ⓦ www .stfturist.se). There are over three hundred hostels in the country, mainly in southern and central Sweden, but also at regular and handy intervals throughout the north. Forget any preconceptions about youth hostelling: in Sweden rooms are family-oriented, modern, clean and hotel-like, existing in the unlikeliest places – old castles, schoolrooms, country manors, and even in old prisons and on boats. Virtually all have well-equipped self-catering kitchens and serve a buffet breakfast, and many offer free use of a washing machine. Prices are low, at 100–280kr for a bed; depending on the hostel, the bed can be either in a room (generally shared with one to three others), or in a larger dorm. Most hostels will charge you about 50kr extra for the use of **sheets** (some expressly forbid the use of sleeping bags), so if you're planning to stay in more than one hostel it pays to bring your own. Most hostels have cheap private double rooms, and we've given price codes for these where they exist. Note that non-members of Hostelling International (see p.37) pay an extra 50kr per night, and that some hostels apply the same seasonal reductions to rates as hotels (see p.36).

Apart from the STF establishments, there are a number of independently run hostels, some of them united under the Swedish Youth Hostel Association, **SVIF** (ⓦ www .svif.se). These usually charge similar prices to STF hostels; local tourist offices will have

details, and we've included the best places in the Guide.

Bear in mind that hostels are used by Swedish families as cheap, hotel-standard accommodation and can fill quickly, so always **book ahead** in the summer; it's also worth noting that hostels are sometimes closed between 10am and 5pm, and some have curfews around 11pm/midnight.

Private rooms and B&Bs

A further option are **private rooms** in people's houses. Affordable and usually pleasant, these have access to showers and/or baths, sometimes a kitchen too, and hosts are rarely intrusive. Where rooms are available they are mentioned in the text, or look for the words *rum* or *logi* by the roadside.

Farms throughout Sweden offer B&B accommodation and self-catering facilities; rooms can be booked directly via the website of *Bo på Lantgård* (ⓦ www.bopalantgard .org), or from local tourist offices. Farm accommodation costs roughly 350–500kr per night per person, with discounts for children. If you want to book before you leave, the Swedish Tourist Board should be able to point you in the right direction.

Campsites

Practically every town or village has at least one **campsite**. These are generally of a high standard and will usually have a shower block, though you may have to pay for hot water. The larger campsites may have outdoor pools, too. Pitching a tent costs 100–200kr a night and there's often a charge of 15–30kr per person, too. Most sites are open from June to September; some (in winter-sports areas) throughout the year. Note that you'll need a **camping card** (125kr from your first stop) at most sites.

Thanks to a tradition known as *Allemansrätt* ("everyman's right"), it's perfectly possible to **camp rough** throughout the country. This gives you the right to pitch a tent anywhere for one night without asking permission, provided you stay a reasonable distance (100m) away from other dwellings. In practice (and especially if you're in the north) no one will object to discreet camping for longer periods, although it's as well, and polite, to ask first. The wide open spaces within most town and city borders make free camping a distinct possibility in built-up areas, too.

Cabins and mountain huts

Many campsites also boast **cabins** (look for the word *stugor*), usually decked out with bunk beds, kitchen and equipment, but not sheets. For groups or couples, these make an excellent alternative to camping; cabins start at around 500kr per night for a four-bed affair. Again, it's wise to ring ahead to secure one. Sweden also has a whole series of **chalet villages**, which – on the whole – offer high-standard accommodation at prices to match. If you're interested in a package along these lines, contact the Swedish Tourist Board for more details.

In the more out-of-the-way places, STF operate a system of **mountain huts** (*fjällstugor*), strung along hiking trails and in national parks. Usually staffed by a warden, and with cooking facilities, the huts cost around 260kr per person per night for youth hostel members, and 100kr more for non-members.

Food and drink

There's no escaping the fact that **eating** and **drinking** are going to take up a large slice of your daily budget in Sweden. However, if you choose to eat your main meal of the day at lunchtime, as the Swedes do, you'll save a small fortune.

At its best, **Swedish food** is excellent. It's largely meat-, fish- and potato-based, but

varied for all that, and generally tasty and filling. There are unusual northern delicacies to look out for as well – reindeer and elk meat, and wild berries – while herring comes in so many different guises that fish fiends will always be content.

Drinking is more uniform, the lager-type beer and imported wine providing no surprises, although the local spirit, *akvavit*, is worth trying at least once – it comes in dozens of different flavours. Note that **smoking** is banned in all restaurants, bars and clubs.

Food

Eating well and cheaply in Sweden are often mutually exclusive aims, at least as far as a sit-down restaurant meal is concerned. The best strategy is to fuel up on breakfast and lunch, both of which offer good-value options. There's also a large number of foreign restaurants – principally pizzerias and Chinese places – which are more likely to serve decently priced evening meals. In the Guide, we've included telephone numbers only for places where you need to **book a table**. Note that quite a few small restaurants close in July; we've stated where this is the case in the Guide.

Breakfast, snacks and self-catering

Breakfast (*frukost*) in most youth hostels and hotel restaurants is almost invariably a help-yourself buffet; it usually costs around 50kr in hostels, and is free in hotels. If you can eat vast amounts between 7am and 10am, it's nearly always good value. Juice, milk, cereals, bread, jam, boiled eggs, salami, tea and coffee appear on even the most limited tables. Swankier venues will also add herring, porridge, yoghurt, pâté and fruit. Something to watch out for is the jug of *filmjölk* next to the ordinary milk – it's thicker, sour milk for pouring on cereals. **Coffee** in Sweden is always freshly brewed and very good; often it's free after the first cup, or at least greatly reduced in price – look for the word *påtår*. **Tea** is less exciting – weak Lipton's as a rule – but costs around the same: 15kr a cup.

For **snacks** and lighter meals the choice expands, although availability is inversely related to health value. A *gatukök* (street kitchen) or *korvstånd* (hot-dog stall) will serve

356

a selection of hot dogs, burgers, pizza slices, chicken bits, chips, ice cream, Coke, crisps and ketchup – something and chips will cost around 60kr. These stalls and stands are on every street in every town and village. A hefty burger-and-chips meal in a **burger bar** goes for around 65kr.

It's often nicer to hit the **konditori**, a coffee shop with succulent pastries and cakes. They're not particularly cheap (coffee and cake cost 45–65kr) but are generally as good as they look, and the coffee is often free after you've paid for the first cup. This is also where you'll come across *smörgåsar*, open **sandwiches** piled high with an elaborate variety of toppings. Favourites include shrimps, smoked salmon, eggs, cheese, pâté and mixed salad – around 50–60kr a time. *Konditorier* often make delicious **ice cream**, too; if you see it, try the unique *lakrits* (salty liquorice) flavour.

Restaurants: lunch and dinner

Eating in a **restaurant** (*restaurang*) needn't be out of your price range, but remember that **lunch** is always around a third cheaper than dinner. Most restaurants offer something called the **dagens rätt** ("daily dish") at 60–75kr, an excellent way to sample real Swedish *husmanskost* – "home cooking". Served Monday to Friday between 11am and 2pm, *dagens rätt* is simply a choice of main meal (usually one meat and one fish dish) which comes with bread/crispbread and salad, sometimes a soft drink or light beer, and usually coffee. Some Swedish dishes, like *pytt i panna* and *köttbullar*, are standards. On the whole, though, more likely offerings in the big cities are pizzas, basic Chinese meals and meat or fish salads. If you're travelling **with kids**, look out for the word *barnmatsedel* (children's menu).

More expensive – but good for a blowout – are restaurants and hotels that put out the **smörgåsbord** at lunchtime. Following the breakfast theme, you help yourself to unlimited portions of herring, hot and cold meats, eggs, fried and boiled potatoes, salad, cheese, desserts and fruit for 200–250kr. To follow local custom you should start with *akvavit*, drink beer throughout and finish with coffee, although this will add to the bill unless it is a fancier all-inclusive spread (usually found on Sundays). If you don't eat the set lunch, meals in restaurants, especially at **dinner** (*middag*), can be expensive. Expect to pay at least 450kr per head for a three-course affair, to which you can add 40–50kr for a beer, and 150kr for the cheapest bottle of house wine. The food in Swedish restaurants is generally *husmanskost*, although another trend is for "crossover" cuisine: Swedish cooking with an international edge that's usually delicious.

Swedes eat early and lunch in most restaurants is served from around 11am, dinner from around 6pm. See our Menu reader on p.710.

Vegetarians

It's not too tough being **vegetarian** in Sweden, given the preponderance of buffet-type meals, most of which are heavy with salads, cheeses, eggs and soups. The cities, too, have salad bars and sandwich shops where you'll have no trouble feeding yourself, and if all else fails the local pizzeria will always deliver the meat-free goods. At lunchtime you'll find that the *dagens rätt* in many places has a vegetarian option.

Drinking

Drinking in Sweden is no longer the notoriously pricey pursuit it once was – in fact, a beer in Stockholm now costs roughly the same as in London. Nonetheless, it's still cheaper to forgo bars every once in a while and buy your booze from the state-licensed **Systembolaget** liquor stores – though doing so is, of course, not nearly as enjoyable. Swedes still perceive drinking to be an expensive activity: consequently, you won't find yourself stuck buying a round, and it's perfectly acceptable to nurse your drink as long as you like. It's worth noting, though, that some bars have happy hours, often known as After Work, when half a litre of beer goes for around half-price.

What to drink

If you drink anything alcoholic in Sweden, a good choice is **beer**, which, while expensive, at least costs the same almost everywhere, be it a café, bar or restaurant. For 45–55kr, you'll get a half-litre of good, lager-type brew – unless you specify, it will be *starköl*, the strongest Class III beer; cheaper will be *folköl*, Class II and weaker; whilst cheapest (around half the price of *folköl*) is *lättöl*, a Class I concoction notable only for its virtual absence of alcohol. Classes I and II are available in supermarkets, although the real stuff is only on sale in the *Systembolaget* liquor stores – see below – where it's around a third of the price you'll pay in a bar. **Wine** is good value when bought in the *Systembolaget* but can be expensive in restaurants and bars, where you'll pay around 50kr for a glass and upwards of 150kr for a bottle. **Spirits** are the most expensive alcoholic drinks; vodka, for example, costs around 55kr a shot. For experimental drinking, **akvavit** – clear and tasteless – is a good bet. Served ice cold in tiny shots, it's washed down with beer: hold onto your hat. There are various different "flavours" too, in which spices and herbs are added to the finished brew to produce some unusual headaches. Or try **glögg**: served at Christmas, it's a mulled red wine with cloves, cinnamon, sugar and more than a dash of *akvavit*.

Where to drink

You'll find **bars** in all towns and cities and most villages. In Stockholm and the larger cities the move is towards brasserie-type places – smart and flash – and fast-expanding chains of British-style pubs. Elsewhere, you still come across more down-to-earth drinking dens, but the drink's no cheaper and the clientele heavily male and drunk. Either way, the bar is not the centre of Swedish social activity – if you really want to meet people, you'd be better off heading for the campsite or the beach.

In the summer, **café-bars** spread out onto the pavement, better for kids and handy for just a coffee. In out-of-the-way places, when you want a drink and can't find a bar, head for a hotel. Things close down at 11pm or midnight except in Gothenburg and Stockholm where – as long as your wallet is bottomless – you can drink all night.

Systembolaget

Venturing into a **Systembolaget** (a state-run off-licence) used to be a move into a twilight world, with buying alcohol made as unattractive as possible. Things are changing though, and *Systembolaget* is making moves towards

becoming a service-oriented, responsible and knowledgeable retail enterprise before the EU – or loss of income because of Swedes shopping abroad – forces it to lose its monopoly. However, responsibility, rather than profit, is the pervading ethos. Many Swedes don't mind being mothered by the state, and are convinced that *Systembolaget's* purchasing policy gets them a better and cheaper selection of wine and liquor than in normal market circumstances. Buying from the *Systembolaget* is the only option for many budget travellers, although apart from strong beer (20kr or so for a half litre), the only bargain is the wine – from around 65kr a bottle for some surprisingly good European and New World imports. *Systembolaget* shops are open Monday to Saturday only (10am–6pm or 7pm, Sat until 2pm); minimum age for being served is 20, and you may need to show ID, although in bars and pubs the age limit is 18.

The media

Assuming that you don't read Swedish, you can keep abreast of world events by buying **foreign newspapers** in the major towns and cities, sometimes on the day of issue, more usually the day after. Of **Swedish newspapers**, *Dagens Nyheter* is the best source of non-biased Swedish-language news. Its main competitor, *Svenska Dagbladet*, is another serious source of news, albeit with a slight right-of-centre slant. *Aftonbladet* and *Expressen* are Sweden's two tabloids.

Swedish **television** is fairly unchallenging. On top of the two state channels, SVT1 and 2, there are two commercial stations, TV4 and TV5, while the dire cable station TV3 is shared with Denmark and Norway. On the **radio**, there's national (Swedish) news in English on **Radio Sweden** (Ⓦ www.sr.se/rs). Their English-language programming can be heard daily in Stockholm on 89.6FM.

Travel essentials

Costs

Sweden is not much more expensive than, say, France or Germany, and certainly much cheaper than neighbouring Norway. If you don't already have a rail pass, using budget airlines is a fast and affordable option in cutting travel **costs**, while city and regional discount travel passes ease what could otherwise be a burden. **Accommodation**, too, can be good value: a bed in one of Sweden's well-appointed STF youth hostels costs an average of 150kr (£11/$16) per night for members (plus another 50kr for non-members), while campsites are plentiful and cheap. Virtually every hotel in Sweden halves its prices in summer, bringing even the most palatial places within reach of most travellers, and the cost of eating is made bearable by the three-course daily *dagens rätt* lunch offers found throughout the country on weekdays – around £7/$10 for a main dish with a side salad, bread, coffee and a soft drink.

Put all this together and you'll find you can exist – camping, self-catering, hitching, no drinking – on around £15/$21 a day. Stay in hostels, eat lunch, get out and see the sights and this will rise to at least £25/$35. Add on £3/$4 for a drink in a bar, around £2/$3 for coffee and cake and £40/$57 minimum a night in a hotel (for a double room) and you're looking at a figure of more like £60–75/$85–107 a day. Remember, though, that the countryside (and much of your camping) is free, museums usually have low (or no) admission charges, and that everything everywhere is clean, bright and works.

Customs

Coming from another European Union country where tax has been paid, your customs allowance for your own use is 10 litres of spirits, 90 litres of wine and 110 litres of strong beer; under-20s are not allowed to import alcohol into Sweden.

Internet

Internet cafés are extremely thin on the ground. Instead, look out for the expanding number of Sidewalk Express coin-operated terminals (Ⓦ www.sidewalkexpress.se; 19kr/hr), which are currently found in airports, train stations and 7-Eleven shops.

Mail

Post offices no longer exist in Sweden; instead most newspaper kiosks, supermarkets, tobacconists and hotels sell **stamps** for letters and parcels.

Money

Swedish **currency** is the **krona** (plural kronor), made up of 100 öre. It comes in coins of 1kr, 2kr, 5kr and 10kr; and notes of 20kr, 50kr, 100kr, 500kr and 1000kr. The **exchange rates** at time of writing were: 13kr for £1; 9.2kr for $1 and 11.7kr for €1.

The easiest way to get local currency is to use your debit card in one of thousands of **ATMs** (for more on which, see Basics, p.42); it's also the cheapest method, as Swedish banks won't charge for ATM transactions. Alternatively, you can change money in **banks** all over Sweden, which open Monday to Friday from 9.30am until 3pm (plus late opening on Thurs until 5.30pm), or in **exchange offices** at airports and ferry terminals, where rates are generally a little better than at banks – though still not as good as the interbank rate used for ATMs.

Phones

Payphones are extremely rare in Sweden so it's much better to make international **telephone calls** from an internet terminal using Skype, for example. If you have a GSM mobile phone, it's easy to buy a Swedish **SIM card** with which you can call at local rates; ask for a *startpaket* costing around 100kr, after which you need to buy recharge cards to start making calls. SIM cards are best bought from a Phone House shop (Ⓦ www.phone house.se) or from Pressbyrån newsagents.

Public holidays

Banks, offices and shops are closed on the following days and may shut early on the preceding day: January 1, January 6

Emergencies

Dial ☎112 for police (*polis*), fire brigade (*brandkår*) or ambulance (*ambulans*), free of charge from any public phone.

(Epiphany), Good Friday, Easter Monday, May 1 (Labour Day), Ascension Day (fortieth day after Easter), Whit Monday (eighth Monday after Easter), Midsummer's Day, All Saints' Day, Christmas Day, Boxing Day.

Shops

Shop opening hours are Mon–Fri 9am–6pm, Sat 9am–4pm. Some department stores stay open until 8–10pm in cities, and may open on Sunday afternoons as well.

Tipping

Hotels and restaurants include their service charge in the bill, though a small 5–10 percent tip for good service is not unusual. You should tip cloakroom attendants in bars and discos around 10kr a time.

3.1

Stockholm and around

Stockholm is one of the most beautiful cities in Europe. Built on no fewer than fourteen islands, where the fresh water of Lake Mälaren meets the brackish Baltic Sea, it has clean air and open space in plentiful supply: one-third of the area inside the city limits is made up of water, another third of parks and woodland, and it's easy to find a quiet corner to enjoy what's one of Europe's saner and more civilized capitals. Broad boulevards lined with elegant buildings are reflected in the deep blue water of the Baltic, while the world's first urban national park offers a unique opportunity to swim and fish virtually in the city centre.

You can appreciate Stockholm's unique geography by taking one of a number of boat trips around the city and through the **Stockholm archipelago** – a staggering 24,000 islands, rocks and skerries, as the Swedish mainland slowly dissolves into the Baltic Sea. A boat trip inland along the serene waters of Lake Mälaren is another easy day-trip, with the target of seventeenth-century **Drottningholm**, the Swedish royal residence, right on the lakeside. Also within day-trip range is the ancient Swedish capital and medieval university town of **Uppsala**, easily reached from Stockholm by frequent trains, as well as the odd boat.

Stockholm

"It is not a city at all," he said with intensity. "It is ridiculous to think of itself as a city. It is simply a rather large village, set in the middle of some forest and some lakes. You wonder what it thinks it is doing there, looking so important."

Ingmar Bergman interviewed by James Baldwin

STOCKHOLM often feels like two cities. Its self-important status as Sweden's most forward-looking commercial centre can seem at odds with the almost pastoral feel of its open spaces and expanses of water. First impressions can be of a distant and unwelcoming place – provincial Swedes call it the Ice Queen – but stick around for the weekend, when the population really lets its hair down, and you'll see another side to Stockholm.

Gamla Stan (meaning Old Town) was the site of the original settlement of Stockholm. Today it's an atmospheric mixture of pomp and history, with ceremonial buildings surrounded by a lattice of medieval lanes and alleyways. Close by to the east is the tiny island of **Skeppsholmen**, with fantastic views of the curving waterfront, while to the north is the modern centre, **Norrmalm**, with its shopping malls, huge department stores and conspicuous wealth, plus the lively Kungsträdgården park and the transport hub of Central Station. East of Norrmalm is the grand residential area of **Östermalm**, southeast of which is the green park island of **Djurgården**, home to two of Stockholm's best-known attractions: the extraordinary seventeenth-century warship **Vasa**, and **Skansen**, Europe's oldest open-air museum. South of Gamla Stan, the island of **Södermalm** was traditionally Stockholm's working-class area; it's known today for its cool bars and restaurants and lively streetlife. To the west of the centre is **Kungsholmen** island, which is coming to rival its southern neighbour with its trendy eateries and drinking establishments.

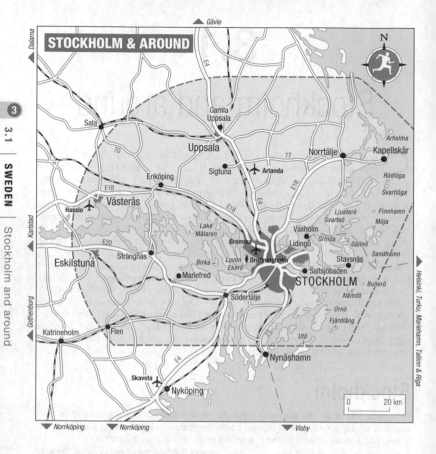

Arrival and information

Most planes – international and domestic – arrive at **Arlanda airport**, 45km north of Stockholm. A high-speed rail link, the **Arlanda Express**, connects the airport with the city every fifteen minutes (220kr one-way, 420kr return valid one month, 240kr one-way for two adults valid Sat & Sun all year and daily mid-June to Aug; Ⓦwww.arlandaexpress.com), and is the easiest way to get into Stockholm. A cheaper option is to take the **airport buses**, Flygbussarna (40min; 99kr one-way, 179kr return; Ⓦwww.flygbussarna.se), which run every ten minutes from the airport to Cityterminalen (Stockholm's central bus station; see opposite); buy your ticket in the airport arrivals hall or from the driver. **Taxis** into Stockholm should cost around 495kr, an affordable alternative for a group – choose the ones that have prices displayed in their back windows to avoid being ripped off.

Some flights arrive at the more central **Bromma airport**, 10km to the west of the city centre near Brommaplan T-bana station. Bromma is also connected to the Cityterminalen by Flygbussarna – buses run in connection with flight arrivals and departures (20min; 69kr one-way, 130kr return). Budget airlines arrive at **Skavsta airport**, 100km to the south of the capital close to the town of Nyköping, as well as at **Västerås**, 100km west of Stockholm (see p.391); Flygbussarna buses to and from Stockholm's Cityterminalen operate in conjunction with flights from both airports (both routes 1hr 20min; 150kr one-way, 249kr return).

By **train**, you'll arrive at and depart from **Central Station**, a cavernous structure on Vasagatan in the Norrmalm district. Inside there are **ATM**s and a Forex **money exchange** office. From the station, it's a ten-minute walk across a pedestrian bridge to Gamla Stan, and another ten minutes uphill along Götgatan to central Södermalm.

By **bus**, your arrival point will be the huge glass structure known as **Cityterminalen**, a bus terminal adjacent to Central Station and reached by a series of escalators and walkways from the northern end of the main hall. It handles all bus services: airport and ferry shuttle services, and domestic and international buses. There are ATMs, an exchange office and Sidewalk Express Internet terminals here.

There are two main **ferry** companies connecting Stockholm with Helsinki, Turku and Mariehamn in Finland. **Viking Line** (Ⓦwww.vikingline.fi) ferries dock at Vikingterminalen on the island of Södermalm, from where you can catch a bus or walk to Slussen or Gamla Stan for the T-bana. **Silja Line** ferries (Ⓦwww.tallinksilja .com) dock at Värtahamnen on the northeastern edge of the city; it's a short walk to the Gärdet T-bana station, or hop on bus #76, departing from beneath the pedestrian walkway, to Gamla Stan and Södermalm.

Information

You should be able to pick up a map of the city at most points of arrival, but it's still worth dropping into Sverigehuset or, Sweden House the city's **tourist office** at Hamngatan 27, on the corner of Kungsträdgården (Mon–Fri 9am–7pm, Sat 10am 5pm, Sun 10am–4pm; ☎08/508 285 08, Ⓦwww.stockholmtown.com). Fistfuls of free information are available, and you'll find good **maps** in some of the brochures and booklets. The tourist office also sells the Stockholm Card (see p.367). Look out also for *What's On*, the free listings and entertainment guide.

From the tourist office it's a short walk to the **Sweden Bookshop**, next to the royal palace at Slottsbacken 10 (Mon–Fri 10am–6pm, Sat 11am–4pm; ☎08/453 78 00, Ⓦwww.swedenbookshop.com), which has an unsurpassed stock of English-language books on Sweden as well as calendars, videos and souvenirs.

City transport

Stockholm winds its way across islands, over water and through parkland: the best way to get to grips with it is to equip yourself with a map and walk – it only takes about half an hour to cross central Stockholm on foot. Sooner or later, though, you'll have to use some form of **transport** and, while routes are easy enough to master, there's a bewildering array of passes available. One thing to try to avoid is paying as you go on the city's transport system – a very expensive business. It's much better to buy a **travelcard:** the **one-day travelcard** is valid for 24 hours (100kr). There are also **3-day** (200kr), 7-day (260kr) and 30-day options (690kr); these cover unlimited travel by bus and T-bana plus travel on ferries to Djurgården. Cards can be bought from Pressbyrån newsagents.

City bus, local train and T-bana **timetables** are easily obtained from the SL-Centers dotted around the city (see below); timetables for mainline trains operated by Swedish Railways (SJ) can be found at Central Station, or online at Ⓦwww.sj.se. For general public transport **information**, consult the English-language website Ⓦwww.resplus.se.

Storstockholms Lokaltrafik (SL; Ⓦwww.sl.se) operate a comprehensive system of buses and trains (underground and regional) that extends well out of the city centre. For information and timetables, the main **SL-Center** (Mon–Fri 7am–6.30pm, Sat & Sun 10am–5pm) is at Sergels Torg, just by the entrance to T-Centralen, and has timetables for the city's buses, metro, regional trains and archipelago boats.

The quickest and most useful form of transport both around the centre and out to the suburbs is Stockholm's metro system, the Tunnelbana or **T-bana**. There are three main lines (red, green and blue) and a smattering of branches; station

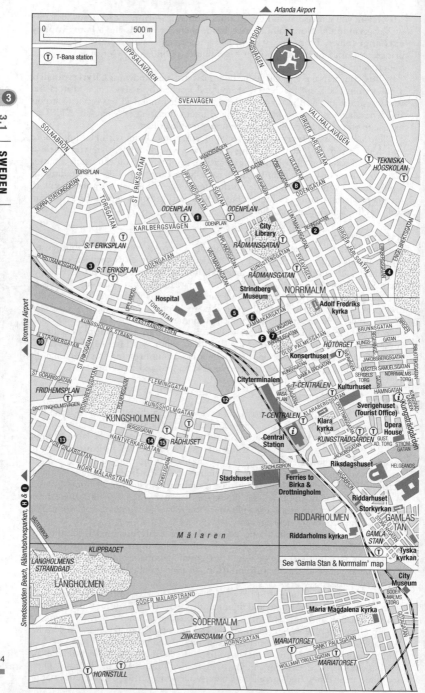

Arlanda Airport

0   500 m

(T) T-Bana station

N

ROSLAGSVÄGEN

UPPSALAVÄGEN

SOLNABRON

E4

TORSPLAN

NORRA STATIONSGATAN

TORSGATAN

S:T ERIKSGATAN

SVEAVÄGEN

BIRGER JARLSGATAN

VALLHALLAVÄGEN

VANADISVÄGEN

NORRTULLSGATAN

HAGAGATAN

FREJGATAN

TULEGATAN

ODENGATAN

BIRGER JARLSGATAN

TEKNISKA
HÖGSKOLAN

(T)

(T)

(T)

SVEAVÄGEN

8

ODENPLAN

(T)

ODENPLAN
1

ODENPLAN

ODENGATAN

UPPLANDSGATAN

VÄSTMANNAGATAN

ODENGATAN

LINTMAKARGATAN

HERKULESGATAN

City
Library

RÅDMANSGATAN

2

ENGELBREKTSGATAN

(T)
S:T ERIKSPLAN

KARLBERGSVÄGEN

S:T ERIKSPLAN
(T)

RÖRSTRANDSGATAN

3

S:T ERIKSPLAN

ODENGATAN

UPPLANDSGATAN

KUNGSTENSGATAN

SVEAVÄGEN

RÅDMANSGATAN

4

Strindberg
Museum
E

NORRMALM

Adolf Fredriks
kyrka

BRUNNSGATAN

BIRGER

Hospital

TORSGATAN

5

KAMMAKARGATAN

WALLINGATAN

F
7

BAHNHUSGATAN

OLOF PALMESGATAN

HÖTORGET
(T)

KUNGS-
GATAN

JAKOBSBERGSGATAN

ALSTRÖMERGATAN

10

KUNGSHOLMS STRAND

KLARASTRANDSLEDEN

Konserthuset

GAMLA BROGATAN

MÄSTER SAMUELSGATAN

SERGELS
TORG

NORRMALMS-
TORG

PÄRLBERGSGATAN

ST GÖRANSGATAN

FLEMINGGATAN

Cityterminalen

T-CENTRALEN
(T)

Kulturhuset

HAMNGATAN

FRIDHEMSPLAN
(T)

DROTTNINGHOLMSVÄGEN

KRONOBERGSGATAN

POLHEMSGATAN

KUNGSHOLMGATAN

BERGSGATAN

12

VASA-
PLAN

T-CENTRALEN
(T)

KLARABERGSGATAN

DROTTNINGGATAN

Sverigehuset
(Tourist Office)

KUNGSTRÄDGÅRDEN

Opera
House

KUNGSTRÄDGÅRDEN

KUNGSHOLMEN

HANTVERKARGATAN

14 15

RÅDHUSET
(T)

(i)

Klara
kyrka

KUNGSTRÄDGÅRDEN

GUST.
AD. TORG

STROM.

13

POL. ONLARGATAN

SCHELEGATAN

Central
Station

JAKOBSGATAN

NORR MÄLARSTRAND

STADHUSBRON

Stadshuset

Ferries to
Birka &
Drottningholm

Riksdagshuset

HELGEANDS

VASABRON

RIDDARHOLMEN

Riddarholms kyrkan

Riddarhuset

Storkyrkan

GAMLA
STAN

GAMLAS
TAN

Smedssudden Beach, Rålambshovsparken, & ①

Bromma Airport

KLIPPBADET

LANGHOLMENS
STRANDBAD

M ä l a r e n

GAMLA
STAN
(T)

Tyska
kyrka

City
Museum

LANGHOLMEN

SÖDER MÄLARSTRAND

SÖDER-
MALMS
TORG

SÖDERMALM

ZINKENSDAMM
(T)

HORNSGATAN

Maria Magdalena kyrka

SANKT PAULSGATAN

GÖTGATAN

MARIATORGET

MARIATORGET

(T)

(T)

WOLLMAR YXKULLSGATAN

HORNSTULL
(T)

See 'Gamla Stan & Norrmalm' map

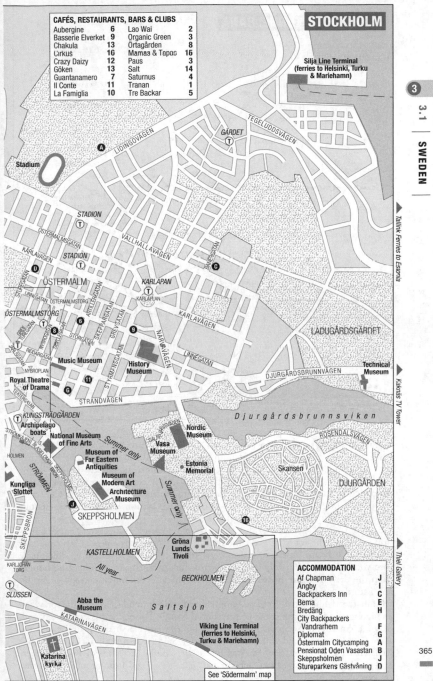

STOCKHOLM

CAFÉS, RESTAURANTS, BARS & CLUBS

Aubergine	6	Lao Wai	2
Basserie Elverket	9	Organic Green	3
Chakula	13	Örtagården	8
Cirkus	16	Mamas & Tapas	16
Crazy Daizy	12	Paus	3
Göken	13	Salt	14
Guantanamero	7	Saturnus	4
Il Conte	11	Tranan	1
La Famiglia	10	Tre Backar	5

Silja Line Terminal
(ferries to Helsinki, Turku
& Mariehamn)

Stadium

STADION Ⓣ

ÖSTERMALMSGATAN

KARLAVÄGEN

STADIÖN Ⓣ

VALLHALLAVÄGEN

GÄRDET Ⓣ

TEGELUDDSVÄGEN

LIDINGÖVÄGEN

Ⓐ

ÖSTERMALM

STUREGATAN

Linnégatan

ÖSTERMALMSTORG

KARLAPAN Ⓣ
KARLAPLAN

Ⓒ

LÅDUGÅRDSGÄRDET

ÖSTERMALMSTORG Ⓣ

Ⓓ

ARTILLERIGATAN

SKEPPARGATAN

GREVGATAN

Ⓑ

KARLAVÄGEN

Ⓖ STORGATAN

Ⓗ

NARVAVÄGEN

LINNEGATAN

Music Museum

History Museum

Technical Museum

DJURGÅRDSBRUNNSVÄGEN

Royal Theatre of Drama

STRANDVÄGEN

Ⓖ

KUNGSTRÄDGÅRDEN Ⓣ

Djurgårdsbrunnsviken

ROSENDALSVÄGEN

Archipelago boats

STRÖMKAJEN S/S

National Museum of Fine Arts

HOLMEN

Summer only

Nordic Museum

Vasa Museum

Estonia Memorial

Skansen

DJURGÅRDEN

STRÖMMEN

Museum of Far Eastern Antiquities

Museum of Modern Art

Architecture Museum

Ⓙ SKEPPSHOLMEN

Kungliga Slottet

SKEPPSBRON

Summer only

Ⓖ

KASTELLHOLMEN

Gröna Lunds Tivoli

BECKHOLMEN

KARL JOHAN TORG

All year

Ⓣ SLUSSEN

Abba the Museum

KATARINAVÄGEN

Saltsjön

Viking Line Terminal
(ferries to Helsinki,
Turku & Mariehamn)

Katarina kyrka

ACCOMMODATION

Af Chapman	J
Ängby	I
Backpackers Inn	C
Bema	E
Bredäng	H
City Backpackers Vandrarhem	F
Diplomat	G
Östermalm Citycamping	A
Pensionat Oden Vasastan	B
Skeppsholmen	J
Stureparkens Gästvåning	D

See 'Södermalm' map

▶ Tallink Ferries to Estonia

▶ Kaknäs TV Tower

▶ Thiel Gallery

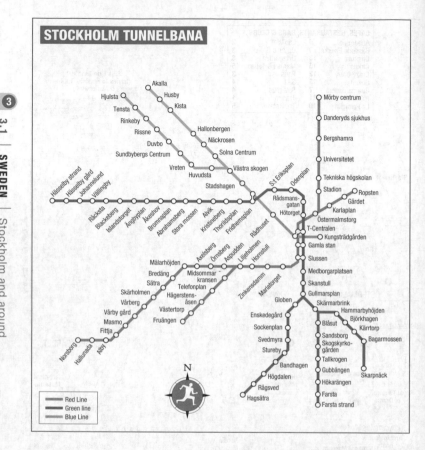

STOCKHOLM TUNNELBANA

Red Line
Green line
Blue Line

entrances are marked with a blue letter "T" on a white background. Trains run from early morning until around midnight (and all through the night on Fri & Sat). All branches of the T-bana meet at **T-Centralen**, the metro station below Central Station. The T-bana is something of an artistic venture, too, with all stations decorated in some way: the most impressive are on the blue line – the T-Centralen station is a huge blue cave, while Kungsträdgården station is littered with statues, spotlights and fountains.

Bus routes can be less direct due to Stockholm's islands and central pedestrianization – consult the route map on the back of the *Stockholms innerstad* bus timetable for help. You board buses at the front, get off at the back or in the middle; make sure you have a travelcard before you board since tickets can no longer be bought from the driver. **Night buses** replace the T-bana after midnight, except on Friday and Saturday nights.

From outside the *Grand Hotel* on Strömkajen, **ferries** provide access to the sprawling archipelago and also link some of the central islands: Djurgården is connected with Skeppsholmen and Nybroplan (summer only), the latter a small square behind the *Grand* in Norrmalm, and with Slussen in Gamla Stan (year-round). **Cruises** on Lake Mälaren leave from outside the Stadshus at the southeastern tip of Kungsholmen, and city boat tours leave from outside the *Grand Hotel* and from around the corner on Nybroplan.

Travel passes and tickets

If you're planning to do any sightseeing, the best pass to have is the **Stockholm Card** (*Stockholmskortet*), which gives unlimited travel on city buses, T-bana, regional trains and the Djurgården tram and ferry, as well as free sightseeing tours and museum entry. Cards are valid for 24, 48 or 72 hours (330, 460 and 580kr respectively). They're sold undated, and are valid from first use. You can buy the card from the tourist office or online at ⓦwww.stockholmtown.com. Note that now many museums have free admission, it may make sense to buy only a travelcard.

In terms of passes that cover transport only, the reduced-price SL **ticket coupons** (*rabattkuponger*) are a good idea for infrequent journeys. They're available at any T-bana station (sixteen coupons cost 180kr), and you have them stamped at the T-bana entrance or by the bus driver before each trip. However, travelcards (see p.363) represent much better value for money.

One-way tickets for the **ferries** to Djurgården cost a basic 30kr, and for longer trips into the **archipelago** up to 120kr. Tickets can be bought on board or in advance from the offices of the main ferry company, *Waxholmsbolaget*, on Strömkajen in Norrmalm, outside the *Grand Hotel*. If you intend to spend a week or so exploring the islands of the archipelago, it may be worth buying a special pass – see p.363 for details.

Bikes, taxis and parking

Bike rental is available from *Djurgårdsbrons Sjöcafé* at Galärvarvsvägen 2 (ⓣ08/660 57 57), just over the bridge that leads to Djurgården, or from Servicedepån-Cykelstallet at Scheelegatan 15 on Kungsholmen (ⓣ08/651 00 66, ⓦwww .cykelstallet.se). Reckon on paying 250kr per day.

To get a **taxi**, either try to hail one in the street or, more reliably, call one of the three main operators: Taxi Stockholm (ⓣ08/15 00 00, ⓦwww.taxistockholm .se), Taxi Kurir (ⓣ08/30 00 00, ⓦwww.taxikurir.se) or Taxi 020 (ⓣ020/20 20 20, ⓦwww.taxi020.se). A trip across the city centre should be in the region of 150–200kr.

If you're driving, be warned that **parking** in Stockholm is a hazardous business. First, it's forbidden to park within ten metres of a road junction, however small; nor can you park within the same distance of a pedestrian crossing; and on one particular night of the week (as specified on the rectangular yellow street signs) no parking is allowed, to permit street cleaning and, in winter, snow clearance. You should never stop in a bus lane or in a loading zone. Also, the closer to the city centre you park the more expensive it will be, though it's free at the clearly signed municipality-run lots for Stockholm Card users. For details on **car rental**, see p.387.

Accommodation

Stockholm has **accommodation** to suit all tastes and budgets, from elegant hotels with waterfront views to some unusual youth hostels. Demand is high, however, particularly from mid-June to mid-August, and it's always advisable to book at least your first night's accommodation in advance. Unless otherwise stated, for hotels and pensions in southern Stockholm see the map on p.381; for those in central Stockholm, see the map on p.371; all other places are on the main Stockholm city map on pp.364–365. All hostels are on the main Stockholm map.

Hotels and pensions

In summer, when business trade dwindles, it's a buyer's market in Stockholm. The cheapest **hotels** and **pensions** are generally found to the north of Cityterminalen in the streets to the west of Adolf Fredriks kyrka, but don't rule out the more expensive places either – there are some attractive weekend and summer prices that can make a spot of luxury a little more affordable. All the following places include breakfast in the price unless otherwise stated and, where applicable, we've given the lower summer and non-summer weekend rate followed by the higher weekday rate outside of summer (see p.335 for more details on price codes).

Bema Upplandsgatan 13, Norrmalm (see Stockholm map, pp.364–365) ℡08/23 26 75, ⓦwww.hotelbema.se. Small pension-style hotel 10min walk north of the station. Twelve en-suite rooms, with modern Swedish decor and beechwood furniture. Bus #47 or #69 from Central Station. ❸/❹

Central Vasagatan 38, Norrmalm ℡08/566 208 00, ⓦwww.profilhotels.se. Modern hotel that's one of the least expensive of those around the station. T-bana T-Centralen. ❺/❻

Columbus Tjärhovsgatan 11, Södermalm ℡08/503 112 00, ⓦwww.columbushotell.se. Simple rooms with shared bathrooms, set in a building that looks like a school. T-bana Medborgarplatsen. ❹/❻

Diplomat Strandvägen 7C ℡08/459 68 00, ⓦwww.diplomathotel.com. Art Nouveau hotel with top-of-the-range suites and views out over Stockholm's grandest boulevard and inner harbour. It's not cheap, though much better value than the cheaper rooms at the *Grand* (see below). T-bana Östermalmstorg. ❻

First Reisen Skeppsbron 12, Gamla Stan ℡08/22 32 60, ⓦwww.firsthotels.se. Traditional place with a heavy wood-panelled interior. All rooms have baths; some also have excellent views over the Stockholm waterfront. T-bana Gamla Stan. ❻

Grand Södra Blasieholmshamnen 8, Norrmalm ℡08/679 35 00, ⓦwww.grandhotel.se. Set in a late nineteenth-century harbourside building overlooking Gamla Stan, Stockholm's most refined hotel provides the last word in luxury at world-class prices. Only worth it if you're staying in the best rooms – otherwise, the *Diplomat* has suites with a view for the same price as rooms here. T-bana Kungsträdgården. ❻

Lydmar Sturegatan 10, Norrmalm ℡08/566 113 00, ⓦwww.lydmar.se. Well located for the nightlife options around Stureplan, with functional rooms overlooking the park, and one of the city's trendiest bars (see p.385). T-bana Östermalmstorg. ❻

🏃 **Mälardrottningen** Riddarholmen (see Gamla Stan map, p.371) ℡08/545 187 80, ⓦwww.malardrottningen.se. This elegant white ship moored by the side of the island of Riddarholmen was formerly American millionairess Barbara Hutton's gin palace. Its cabin-style rooms can be tiny, but still represent good value for such a central location. T-bana Gamla Stan. ❹/❺

Nordic Sea and Nordic Light Vasaplan, Norrmalm ℡08/50 56 30 00, ⓦwww.nordichotels.se. Right next to Citytermi-nalen, the *Light* has incredibly sleek if somewhat overdesigned interiors with fabulous lighting, while the slightly cheaper *Sea* has green-blue colours throughout, plus huge fish tanks and the novelty *Icebar* (see p.385) downstairs. ❻

Pensionat Oden Söder Hornsgatan 66B, Södermalm ℡08/796 96 00, ⓦwww.pensionat .nu. A good-value choice in the heart of Södermalm, with tastefully decorated rooms at excellent prices. T-bana Mariatorget. ❹

Pensionat Oden Vasastan Odengatan 38 ℡08/796 96 00, ⓦwww.pensionat.nu. A good central location and modern rooms. T-bana Rådmansgatan. ❸

Queen's Drottninggatan 71A, Norrmalm ℡08/24 94 60, ⓦwww.queenshotel.se. Mid-range pension-style hotel, with some en-suite rooms and a breakfast buffet. T-bana Hötorget. ❺/❻

Rica City Gamla Stan Lilla Nygatan 25, Gamla Stan ℡08/723 72 59, ⓦwww.rica.se. Wonderfully situated, elegant building with rooms to match; all 51 are individually decorated. T-bana Gamla Stan. ❻

🏃 **Rival** Mariatorget 3, Södermalm ℡08/545 789 00, ⓦwww.rival.se. A funky boutique hotel, owned by Benny of ABBA fame, with film- and music-themed designer rooms, a bar, café, bakery and cinema. T-bana Mariatorge. ❻

Scandic Continental Vasagatan/Klara Vattugrand 4, Norrmalm ℡08/51 73 42 00, ⓦwww.scandic .se. Right next to Central Station, this business-oriented eco-hotel has good deals in summer and at weekends; the cabin rooms are excellent value. ❺/❻

🏃 **Stureparkens Gästvåning** Sturegatan 58, Östermalm (see Stockholm map, pp.364–365) ℡08/662 72 30, ⓦwww .stureparkens.nu. Charming bed and breakfast with just nine rooms, shared bathrooms and a communal kitchen. T-bana Stadion. ❸

🏃 **Tre Små Rum** Högbergsgatan 81, Södermalm ℡08/641 23 71, ⓦwww .tresmarum.se. Seven small semi-basement rooms, all clean, modern and simple, with a help-yourself breakfast from the kitchen fridge. Very popular and often full. T-bana Mariatorget. ❸

Zinkensdamm Zinkens Väg 20, Södermalm ℡08/616 81 10, ⓦwww.zinkensdamm.com. Pleasant hotel rooms in a separate wing of the youth hostel (see opposite). T-bana Hornstull or Zinkensdamm. ❺/❻

Hostels and private rooms

Stockholm has a wide range of good, well-run **hostel** accommodation, costing from 150kr to 200kr a night per person. There are several STF youth hostels in the city, two of which – *Af Chapman* and *Långholmen* – are among the best in Sweden, and you'll have to plan ahead if you want to stay at most of the hostels listed below, particularly in summer.

Several agencies can help book a **private room**, though some close during the summer months when business travel dwindles. Try Hotelltjänst, Nybrogatan 44 (☏08/10 44 37, ⓦwww.hotelltjanst.com), which rents out centrally located double rooms and apartments with a fridge and cooking facilities from 700kr per night.

Af Chapman Flaggmansvägen 8, Skeppsholmen ☏08/463 22 66, ⓦwww .stfchapman.com. Newly refitted, beautiful rigged 1888 ship that offers (at least for the price) unsurpassed views over Gamla Stan from the deck and some dorms. Double rooms are also available (❷). Open all year; book well in advance. T-bana Kungsträdgården or bus #65 from Central Station.

Backpackers Inn Banérgatan 56, Östermalm ☏08/660 75 15, ⓦwww.backpackersinn.se. Reasonably central former school residence with three hundred beds in large dorms, plus laundry facilities. Open late June to mid-Aug. T-bana Karlaplan (Valhallavägen exit) or bus #4.

City Backpackers Vandrarhem Upplandsgatan 2A ☏08/20 69 20, ⓦwww .citybackpackers.se. Five minutes from central station, this is a friendly, conveniently located non-HI hostel with a hundred beds and some double rooms (❷). The owners and staff have travelled widely, and can provide lots of advice for backpackers, plus there's internet access, coffee, tea and sauna. Open all year. T-bana T-Centralen.

City Lodge Klara norra kyrkogata 15, Norrmalm ☏08/22 66 30, ⓦwww.citylodge.se. Some 200m east of Cityterminalen, this compact forty-bed hostel offers central lodging, and free internet access.

Långholmen Långholmsmuren 20, Långholmen ☏08/720 85 10, ⓦwww.langholmen.com. Stockholm's grandest STF hostel is set on the island of Långholmen inside a 1724 prison building, the cells converted into smart dorms and private rooms (❷) with their original small and high windows. It's not very central, but the beach and the whole of Södermalm are on the doorstep. T-bana Hornstull, then a 10min walk, crossing over the small bridge onto the island.

Skeppsholmen Flaggmansvägen 8, Skeppsholmen ☏08/463 22 66, ⓦwww.stfchapman.com. Located at the foot of the gangplank to *Af Chapman*, this is an immensely popular hostel housed in the former royal firewood storehouse – you're unlikely to get in without a reservation. Kitchen or laundry facilities are shared with *Af Chapman*, and there's no lockout. T-bana Kungsträdgården or bus #65.

Zinkensdamm Zinkens väg 20, Södermalm ☏08/616 81 00, ⓦwww.zinkensdamm.com. Huge hostel with 490 beds and kitchen and laundry facilities. It's in a good location for exploring Södermalm, though a 30min walk from the city centre. T-bana Zinkensdamm.

Camping

With only one summer option near the city centre, **camping** in Stockholm can prove a bit of a drag. The tourist offices provide free booklets detailing facilities at all Stockholm's campsites, and the sites below represent the best the city has to offer. With the exception of the site in Östermalm, they're all a 45-minute (or thereabouts) T-bana ride from the city centre. In July and August it costs from 155kr for two people to pitch a tent; half that the rest of year.

Ängby ☏08/37 04 20, ⓦwww.angbycamping .se. West of the city on the lakeshore, with cabins (600kr) and camping beneath the trees. Open all year, but book ahead between Sept and April. Five minutes' walk from T-bana Ängbyplan.

Bredäng ☏08/97 70 71, ⓦwww.camping.se/a04. Large campsite southwest of the city with views over Lake Mälaren. Open all year, but phone ahead to book between Nov and April. 5min walk from T-bana Bredäng.

Östermalm Citycamping Fiskartorpsvägen 2, Östermalm ☏08/10 29 03, ⓦwww.camping.se. The most centrally located of all Stockholm's campsites but only open from mid-June to mid-Aug. Walkable from the city centre in around 20min. T-bana Stadion or bus #55 from Slussen/Gamla Stan.

The City

Visitors have been responding to Stockholm's charms for 150 years, and today the combination of elegant Old Town architecture, wide tree-lined boulevards and great expanses of open water right in the centre all conspire to offer an unparalleled city panorama. Seeing the sights is straightforward: everything is easy to get to, opening hours are long, and the city is a relaxed and spacious place to wander. There's also a bewildering range of galleries and museums, many of which are now free to enter.

Old Stockholm: Gamla Stan and Riddarholmen

The islands of Riddarholmen, Staden and Helgeandsholmen make up the **oldest part of Stockholm**, a historic cluster of seventeenth- and eighteenth-century Baroque and Renaissance buildings backed by narrow alleys. Here, on these three adjoining polyps of land, Birger Jarl erected the first fortification in 1255, and for centuries this was the nucleus of the first city of Stockholm. Rumours abound about the derivation of the name Stockholm, but it's generally thought that it means "island cleared of trees" – trees on the island that is now home to Gamla Stan were probably felled to make way for settlers. Incidentally, today the words *holm* ("island") and *stock* ("log") are still in common use.

Strictly speaking, the **Gamla Stan** or Old Town area refers only to the streets of the largest island, **Staden**, although in practice the name is usually applied to all three islands. Nowadays Gamla Stan is primarily a tourist enclave, a rich tableau of cultural history embodied by the royal palace, parliament and cathedral. The central spider's web, especially if you approach it over the bridges of Norrbron or Riksbron, invokes potent images of the past, with sprawling, monumental buildings and airy churches forming a protective girdle around the narrow streets. The tall, dark houses in the centre were mostly those of wealthy merchants, still picked out today by intricate doorways and portals bearing coats of arms. Some of the alleys in between are the skinniest thoroughfares imaginable, steeply stepped between battered walls; others are covered passageways linking leaning buildings. It's easy to spend hours wandering around here, although the atmosphere these days is not so much medieval as mercenary: there's a dense concentration of antique shops, art showrooms and chichi cellar restaurants, though the frontages don't really intrude

▲ Stockholm's harbour

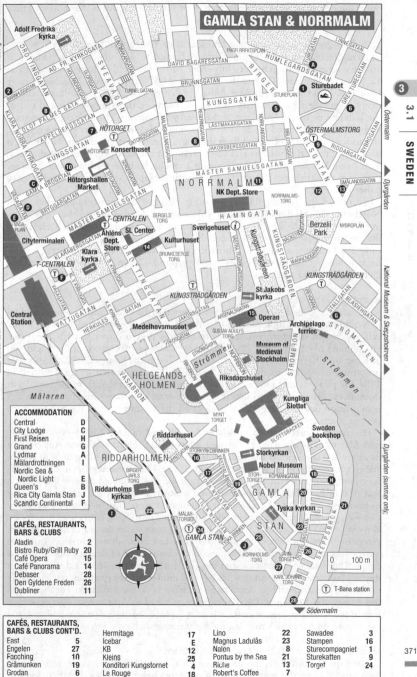

GAMLA STAN & NORRMALM

Östermalm ▶

Djurgården ▶

National Museum & Skeppsholmen ▶

Djurgården (summer only) ▶

◀ Strindberg Museum

◀ Stadshuset

Mälaren

◀ Södermalm ▼

ACCOMMODATION

Central	D
City Lodge	C
First Reisen	H
Grand	G
Lydmar	A
Mälardrottningen	I
Nordic Sea & Nordic Light	E
Queen's	B
Rica City Gamla Stan	J
Scandic Continental	F

CAFÉS, RESTAURANTS, BARS & CLUBS

Aladin	2
Bistro Ruby/Grill Ruby	20
Café Opera	15
Café Panorama	14
Debaser	28
Den Gyldene Freden	26
Dubliner	11

N

ⓣ T-Bana station

0   100 m

CAFÉS, RESTAURANTS, BARS & CLUBS CONT'D.

East	5	Hermitage	17	Lino	22	Sawadee	3
Engelen	27	Icebar	E	Magnus Ladulås	23	Stampen	16
Facching	10	KB	12	Nalen	8	Sturecompagniet	1
Gråmunken	19	Kleins	25	Pontus by the Sea	21	Sturekatten	9
Grodan	6	Konditori Kungstornet	4	Richie	13	Torget	24
		Le Rouge	18	Robert's Coffee	7		

upon the otherwise light-starved streets. Not surprisingly, this is the most exclusive part of Stockholm in which to live.

The Riksdagshuset and the Museum of Medieval Stockholm

Entering or leaving the Old Town, you're bound to pass the Swedish parliament building, the **Riksdagshuset** (July–Aug Mon–Fri guided tours in English at 12.30pm & 2pm; free). Despite the assassinations of former Swedish prime minister Olof Palme and foreign minister Anna Lindh (see box, p.377), politicians still go freely about their business here, and you'll often see them nipping in and out of the building or lunching in one of the nearby restaurants. The Riksdagshuset itself was completely restored in the 1970s (though only seventy years old even then), and today the grand columned front entrance, seen to best effect from Norrbron, is hardly ever used, the business end concentrated in the new glassy bulge at the back. This being Sweden, the building contains a crèche, and the seating in the chamber itself is in healthy, non-adversarial rows, with members grouped by constituency rather than party.

In front of the Riksdagshuset, accessible by a set of steps leading down from Norrbron, the **Medeltidsmuseum** (Museum of Medieval Stockholm: ⓦwww .medeltidsmuseet.stockholm.se) showcases the medieval ruins, tunnels and walls discovered during excavations under the parliament building. Due to reopen in early 2010 following extensive renovation (check the website for the latest details), there will be reconstructed houses to poke around, alongside a selection of models, pictures, boats and skeletons.

Kungliga Slottet

South across a second section of bridges is the most distinctive monumental building in Stockholm, **Kungliga Slottet** (the Royal Palace: ⓦwww.royalcourt.se), a low, yellowy-brown structure whose two front arms stretch down towards the water. Stockholm's old Tre Kronor (Three Crowns) castle burned down at the beginning of King Karl XII's reign, leaving his architect, Tessin the Younger, with a clean slate on which to design his simple but beautiful Renaissance structure. Finished in 1754, the palace is a striking achievement: uniform and sombre from the outside, its magnificent Baroque and rococo interior is a swirl of state rooms and museums. A combination ticket costing 120kr valid for all the various parts of the palace can be bought at any entrance.

The **Apartments** (Feb to mid-May & mid-Sept to Dec Tues–Sun noon–3pm; mid-May to mid-Sept daily 10am–4pm; 90kr) form a relentlessly linear collection of furniture and tapestries. It's all basically Rent-a-Palace stuff, too sumptuous to take in and inspirational only in terms of its colossal size. The **Treasury** (same times; 90kr) is certainly worthy of the name, with its ranks of jewel-studded crowns: the oldest is that of Karl X (1650); the most charming are intricately worked crowns belonging to princesses Sofia (1771) and Eugène (1860). Also worth catching is the **Armoury** (June–Aug daily 10am–5pm; Sept–May Tues–Sun 11am–5pm, Thurs until 8pm; 60kr; ⓦwww.livrustkammaren.se), which is less to do with weapons and more to do with ceremony, featuring suits of armour, costumes and horse-drawn carriages from the sixteenth century onwards. It certainly couldn't be accused of skipping over historical detail. King Gustav II Adolf died in the Battle of Lützen in 1632 and the museum displays his horse (stuffed) and the blood- and mud-spattered garments retrieved after the enemy had stripped him down to his underwear on the battlefield. For those with the energy, the **Museum Tre Kronor** (same times as Apartments; 90kr) contains part of the older Tre Kronor castle, whose ruins lie beneath the present building, and exhibitions on the castle's role as a medieval stronghold.

Into Gamla Stan: Stortorget and around

Beyond the Royal Palace, the streets get narrower and darker and you're in Gamla Stan proper. Here, the highest point of old Stockholm is crowned by **Storkyrkan**

(May–Sept daily 9am–6pm; Oct–April daily 9am–4pm; 25kr), the "Great Church", consecrated in 1306. Pedantically speaking, Stockholm has no cathedral, but this rectangular brick church fulfils the same role and is the place where the monarchs of Sweden are married and crowned. Storkyrkan gained its present shape at the end of the fifteenth century, with a Baroque remodelling in the 1730s. Inside, twentieth-century restoration has removed the white plaster from the red-brick columns, and although there's no evidence that this was intended in the original, it lends a warm colouring to the rest of the building. Much is made of the fifteenth-century sculpture of St George and the Dragon, though this is easily overshadowed by the golden, throne-like royal pews and the monumental black-and-silver altarpiece. Organ recitals take place here on winter Saturdays at 1pm.

Stretching south from the church is **Stortorget**, Gamla Stan's handsome and elegantly proportioned main square, fringed by eighteenth-century buildings and surrounded by narrow shopping streets. In 1520 Christian II used the square as an execution site during the "Stockholm Bloodbath", dispatching his opposition en masse with gory finality. Housed in the former stock exchange overlooking the square, the **Nobel Museum** (mid-May to mid-Sept daily 10am–5pm, Tues till 8pm; mid-Sept to mid-May Tues 11am–8pm, Wed–Sun 11am–5pm; 60kr; ⓦ www.nobelmuseum.se) is an innovative presentation of the history of Alfred Nobel and the six Nobel prizes, with fascinating short films about the laureates' creativity and their milieus.

Gamla Stan's busiest thoroughfares, **Västerlånggatan**, **Österlånggatan**, **Stora Nygatan** and **Lilla Nygatan** run the length of the Old Town, and today their time-worn buildings hold a succession of art and craft shops and restaurants. Happily, though, the consumerism is largely unobtrusive and in summer buskers and evening strollers clog the narrow alleyways, making it an entertaining area in which to wander and to eat and drink. There are few real targets, though at some stage you'll probably pass the copy of the St George and Dragon statue in the small **Köpmantorget** square (off Österlånggatan). Take every opportunity too to scuttle up side streets, where you'll find fading coats of arms, covered alleyways and worn cobbles at every turn.

Just off Västerlånggatan, on Tyska Brinken, the **Tyska kyrkan** (German Church: May–Aug daily noon–4pm; Sept–April Sat & Sun noon–4pm; free) was originally owned by Stockholm's medieval German merchants, when it served as the meeting place of the Guild of St Gertrude. A copper-topped red-brick building atop a rise, it abandoned its secular role in the seventeenth century when Baroque decorators got hold of it: the result, a richly fashioned interior with the pulpit dominating the nave, is outstanding. Sporting a curious royal gallery in one corner, designed by Tessin the Elder, it comes complete with mini palace roof, angels and the three crowns of Swedish kingship.

Riddarhuset and Riddarholmen

If Stockholm's history has gripped you, it's better to head west from Stortorget towards the handsome Baroque **Riddarhuset** (Mon–Fri 11.30am–12.30pm; 50kr; ⓦ www.riddarhuset.se), the seventeenth-century "House of Nobles". It was in the Great Hall here that the Swedish aristocracy met during the Parliament of the Four Estates (1668–1865) and their coats of arms – 2326 of them – are splattered across the walls. Some six hundred of the noble families survive; the last ennoblement was in 1974. Take a look downstairs, too, at the Chancery, which stores heraldic bone china by the shelf-load, and racks full of fancy signet rings – essential accessories for the eighteenth-century noble-about-town.

From Riddarhuset it takes only seconds to cross the bridge onto **Riddarholmen** (Island of the Knights), to visit the **Riddarholmskyrkan** (June–Aug daily 10am–5pm; Sept–May daily 10am–4pm; 30kr), the burial place for Swedish royalty ever since Magnus Ladulås was sealed up here in 1290. Amongst others, you'll find the tombs of Gustav II Adolf (in the green marble sarcophagus), Karl XII, Gustav III and Karl Johan XIV, plus other innumerable and unmemorable descendants. There's a daily English-language tour at 1pm. Walk around the back of the church for stunning views of Stadshuset, the City Hall and Lake Mälaren. Incidentally, the island to the left of Västerbron (the bridge in the distance) is Långholmen; in winter people skate and even take their dogs for walks on the ice along here, as the water freezes solid right up to the bridge and beyond.

Skeppsholmen

A ten-minute walk east from Stortorget lie the islands of **Skeppsholmen** and the microscopic **Kastellholmen**, connected by a bridge to the south. Originally settled by the Swedish navy – some of whose old barracks are still visible – in the nineteenth century, Skeppsholmen is now home to two of the city's youth hostels and an eclectic clutch of museums, the most impressive of them just by the Skeppsholmsbron, the bridge onto the island.

The National Museum of Fine Arts

As you approach the bridge it's impossible to miss the striking waterfront National-museum (National Art Museum; June–Aug Tues 11am–8pm, Wed–Sun 11am–5pm; Sept–May Wed & Fri–Sun 11am–5pm, Tues & Thurs 11am–8pm; 100kr; ⓦwww .nationalmuseum.se), looking right out over the Royal Palace. The impressive collection is contained on three floors: the **ground floor** is taken up by changing exhibitions of prints and drawings, and there's a shop and café here too, as well as luggage lockers. So much is packed into the museum that it can quickly become overwhelming – it's worth splashing out on the guidebook.

The **first floor** is devoted to applied art, and if it's curios you're after, this museum has the lot – beds slept in by kings, cabinets leaned on by queens, plates eaten off by nobles – mainly from the centuries when Sweden was a great power. There's modern work alongside the ageing tapestries and furniture, including Art Nouveau coffee pots and vases, and examples demonstrating the intelligent simplicity of Swedish chair design.

It's the **second floor**, however, that's most engaging, featuring a plethora of European and Mediterranean sculpture and some mesmerizing sixteenth- and seventeenth-century Russian icons. The paintings are equally wide-ranging and of a similarly high quality, including pieces by El Greco, Canaletto, Gainsborough and, most notably, Rembrandt's *Conspiracy of Claudius Civilis*, one of his largest monumental works, a bold depiction of well-armed Roman chieftains. There are also minor paintings by other later masters (most notably Renoir and Gauguin) and some fine sixteenth- to eighteenth-century works by Swedish artists.

Skeppsholmen's museums

One of the better collections in Europe, Stockholm's **Moderna Muséet** (Museum of Modern Art; Tues 10am–8pm, Wed–Sun 10am–6pm; 80kr; ⓦwww.moderna museet.se), is one of the city's must-see museums, with enthusiastic attendants and a comprehensive selection of works by some of the leading artists of the twentieth century. Highlights include Dali's monumental *Enigma of William Tell*, showing the artist at his most conventionally unconventional, and Matisse's striking *Apollo*. Look out also for Picasso's *Guitar Player*; a whole host of Warhol, Lichtenstein, Kandinsky, Miró and Magritte; and the provocative video-painting *In Orgia* by Lars Nillson. Sharing the same building, the Arkitekturmuseet (Architecture Museum; same times; 50kr) showcases Swedish architectural models and sketches through the centuries, focusing on the post-war social city planning projects that were meant to promote democracy and welfare through egalitarian building practices.

A steep climb up the northern tip of the island brings you to the **Östasia-tiska Muséet** (Museum of Far Eastern Antiquities; Tues 11am–8pm, Wed–Sun 11am–5pm; 60kr; ⓦwww.ostasiatiska.se), which holds an array of objects displaying incredible craftsmanship – fifth-century Chinese tomb figures, delicate jade amulets, an astounding assembly of sixth-century Buddhas, Indian watercolours and gleaming bronze Krishna figures – and that's just one room.

Norrmalm and Kungsholmen

Modern Stockholm lies immediately to the north and east of Gamla Stan, and is split into two distinct sections. **Norrmalm**, to the north, is the buzzing commercial heart of the city, packed with restaurants, bars, cinemas and shops, while to the east is the more sedate Östermalm, a well-to-do area of classy boulevards. The island of **Kungsholmen**, linked by bridge to the west of Norrmalm, is a mostly residential and administrative district, though with one positive draw in Stockholm's landmark City Hall.

Around Gustav Adolfs Torg

Down on the waterfront, at the foot of Norrbron, is **Gustav Adolfs Torg**, more a traffic island than a square these days, with the nineteenth-century **Opera** (Opera House) its proudest, most notable building. It was here in an earlier opera house on the same site, at a masked ball in 1792, that King Gustav III was shot by one Captain Ankarström, an admirer of Rousseau and member of the aristocratic opposition. The story is recorded in Verdi's opera *Un ballo in maschera*, and you can see Gustav's ball costume, as well as the assassin's pistols and mask, on display in the royal palace Armoury in Gamla Stan.

A statue of King Gustav II Adolf marks the centre of the square, between the Opera and the Foreign Office opposite. Look out hereabouts for fishermen pulling salmon out of **Strömmen**, the fast-flowing tributary that winds its way through the centre of the city. Stockholmers have had the right to fish this outlet from Lake Mälaren to the Baltic since the seventeenth century; it's not as difficult as it sounds and there's usually a group of hopefuls on one of the bridges around the square trying their luck.

Just off the square, at Fredsgatan 2 in the heart of Swedish government land, is the Medelhavsmuséet (Mediterranean Museum: Tues–Thurs noon–8pm, Fri–Sun noon–5pm; 80kr; ⓦwww.medelhavsmuseet.se), a sparkling collection devoted to ancient Mediterranean cultures, notably Egypt, Cyprus, Greece and Rome. Its enormous Egyptian section covers just about every aspect of life in Egypt up to the Christian era, with several whopping great mummies and some attractive bronze weapons, tools and domestic objects from the time before the pharaohs. The Cyprus collections are the largest outside Cyprus itself, spanning a period of over six thousand years, and there are also strong displays of Greek, Etruscan and Roman art. A couple of rooms examine Islamic culture through pottery, glass and metalwork, as well as decorative elements of architecture, Arabic calligraphy and Persian miniature painting.

Walk back towards the Opera and continue across the main junction onto Arsenalsgatan to reach the red **St Jakobs kyrka** (Tues, Wed & Sat 11am–4pm, Thurs & Fri 11am–6pm, Sun 10am–7pm), one of the many easily overlooked churches in Stockholm. It's the pulpit that draws the eye, a great, golden affair, while the date of the church's consecration – 1642 – is stamped high up on the ceiling in gold figures. Organ recitals are held here, generally on Fridays at 5pm (free).

Kungsträdgården

Just beyond St Jakobs kyrka and the Opera, Norrmalm's eastern boundary is marked by **Kungsträdgården**, the most fashionable and central of the city's numerous squares, reaching from the water northwards as far as Hamngatan. The name means "the king's gardens", though if you're expecting neatly trimmed flower beds and rose gardens you'll be sadly disappointed – it's actually a great expanse of concrete with a couple of lines of trees. The area may once have been a royal kitchen garden, but nowadays it serves as Stockholm's main meeting place, especially in summer when there's almost always something happening, with free evening gigs, theatre and other performances taking place on the central open-air stage. Look out too for the cafés on the square, packed out in spring with winter-weary Stockholmers soaking up the sun. In winter the square is equally busy, particularly at the Hamngatan end where there's an open-air ice rink, the **Isbanan** (early Nov to early March Mon, Wed & Fri 8.30am–6pm, Tues & Thurs 8.30am–8pm, Sat & Sun 10am–6pm; skate rental 40kr). The main tourist office is here, too, in the Sverigehuset at the corner of Hamngatan (see p.363). Hamngatan runs east to **Birger Jarlsgatan**, the main thoroughfare that divides Norrmalm from Östermalm, and now a mecca for eating and drinking.

Sergels Torg to Hötorget

At the western end of Hamngatan, beyond the enormous NK department store, lies **Sergels Torg**, the ugliest part of modern Stockholm. It's an unending free show centred on the five seething floors of **Kulturhuset** (June–Aug Tues–Fri 11am–6pm, Sat & Sun 11am–4pm; Sept–May Tues–Fri 11am–7pm, Sat & Sun 11am–5pm), a cultural centre whose windows look down upon the milling concrete square. Inside are temporary art and craft exhibitions together with workshops open to anyone willing to get their hands dirty. Admission to Kulturhuset is free, but you have to pay to get into specific exhibitions or performances; check the information desk as you come in for details of the programme of poetry readings, concerts and theatre performances. The *World News Café* on the first floor is stuffed with foreign newspapers, books, records and magazines, and you can also watch foreign TV news reports. Check out the *Panorama* café on the top floor for delicious apple pie with custard and views of central Stockholm, an area that saw massive demolition and construction from the 1930s to the 1970s, with all the usual results. From the café terrace you'll get a bird's-eye view of the tall glass column that dominates the square, and the surrounding spewing fountain. Down the steps, below Sergels Torg, is **Sergels Arkaden**, a set of grotty underground walkways home to buskers, brass bands and demented lottery ticket vendors; look out for the odd demonstration or ball game, too. There are also entrances down here into **T-Centralen**, the central T-bana station, and Stockholm's other main department store, Åhléns, not quite as posh as NK and easier to find your way around.

A short walk west from Kulturhuset along Klarabergsgatan will bring you to **Central Station** and **Cityterminalen**, hub of virtually all Stockholm's transport. The area around here is given over to unabashed consumerism, and as you explore the streets around the main drag, **Drottinggatan**, you'll find little to get excited about: run-of-the-mill clothing stores and twee gift shops punctuated by *McDonald's* and the odd sausage stand. In summer the occasional busker or jewellery stall livens up what is essentially a soulless grid of pedestrianized shopping streets. The only point of culture is the **Klara kyrka** (daily 10am–5pm), just to the right off Klarabergsgatan, opposite the station. Hemmed in on all sides, with only the spires visible from the surrounding streets, it's a particularly delicate building, with a light and flowery eighteenth-century painted interior and an impressive golden pulpit. Out in the churchyard, a memorial stone commemorates eighteenth-century Swedish poet Carl Michael Bellman, whose popular, lengthy ballads are said to have been composed extempore.

Three blocks further up Drottinggatan, the cobbled square of **Hötorget** holds a fruit and veg market on weekdays, as well as the wonderful indoor **Hötorgshallen** market, an orgy of Middle Eastern smells and sights and a good place to pick up ethnic snacks. Grab something to eat and plonk yourself on the steps of the **Konserthuset** (Concert House), one of the venues for the presentation of the Nobel Prizes, and a good place to hear classical music recitals (often free on Sunday afternoons). The tall building opposite, **PUB**, is the former department store where Greta Garbo once worked as a sales assistant in the hat department. Today, though, Hötorget is better known for its superb cinema complex, Filmstaden Sergel, the capital's biggest; to the east, canyon-like **Kungsgatan**, which runs down to Stureplan and Birger Jarlsgatan, holds more cinemas, interspersed with some agreeable cafés (see pp.383–384).

North to the Strindberg Museum

From Hötorget the two main streets of Drottninggatan and Sveavägen run parallel uphill and north as far as Odengatan and the cylindrical **Stadsbiblioteket** (City Library), in its own little park. Close by, set in secluded gardens between the two roads, sits the eighteenth-century **Adolf Fredriks kyrka**. Although it has a noteworthy past – the French philosopher Descartes was buried here in 1650 before his body was moved to France – the church would be insignificant today were it not the final resting place for the assassinated Swedish prime minister, **Olof Palme**: a simple headstone and flowers mark his grave. A plaque now marks the spot on Sveavägen, at the junction with Tunnelgatan, where the prime minister was gunned down; the assassin escaped up the nearby flight of steps (see box below).

Continue north along Drottninggatan and you'll come to the "Blue Tower" at no. 85, the last building in which the writer **August Strindberg** lived, now turned into the Strindbergsmuséet (Strindberg Museum: Tues–Sun noon–4pm, March–Oct Tues until 7pm; 40kr; ⓦ www.strindbergsmuseet.se). Strindberg lived here between 1908 and 1912, and his house has been preserved to the extent that you must put plastic bags on your feet to protect the floors and furnishings. The study remains as he left it on his death, a dark and gloomy place – he would work with both Venetian blinds and heavy curtains closed against the sunlight. Upstairs is his library, a musty room with all the books firmly behind glass, which is a shame because Strindberg wasn't a passive reader: he underlined heavily and made notes in the margins as he read, though these are rather less erudite than you'd expect: "Lies!", "Crap!", "Idiot!" and "Bloody hell!" seem to have been his favourite comments. Good explanatory notes in English are available.

Kungsholmen: Stadshuset

Take the T-bana back to T-Centralen and it takes only a matter of minutes to cross the Stadshusbron bridge to the island of **Kungsholmen** and Stockholm's **Stadshuset** (City Hall: June–Aug guided tours daily every hour 10am–4pm; Sept–May daily 10am & noon; 60kr; ⓦ www.stockholm.se/cityhall). Finished in 1923, the Stadshuset is a landmark of the modern city. Its simple exterior, comprising some eight million bricks, is no preparation for the intricate decor within. Visiting heads of state are escorted from their boats up the elegant waterside steps, but for lesser mortals, the only way to view the innards is on one of the guided tours, which reveal the kitschy Viking-style legislative chamber and impressively echoing Golden Hall. The quay just across the Stadshusbron bridge is the departure point for **boats** to destinations around Lake Mälaren: Birka and Drottningholm. Venture further into Kungsholmen and you'll discover a rash of excellent bars and restaurants that have sprung up here – see p.384 – and an excellent **beach** at Smedsudden (buses #4 to Västerbroplan,

---

The murders of Olof Palme and Anna Lindh

The assassination of **Prime Minister Olof Palme** in February 1986 sent shock-waves through a society unused to political extremism of any kind. As for most Nordic leaders, Palme's fame was his security, and he died unprotected, shot down in front of his wife on their way home from the cinema on Sveavägen. Sweden's biggest-ever **murder inquiry** was launched and as the years went by so the allegations of police cover-ups and bungling grew. **Christer Pettersson** was eventually jailed for the murder in July 1989 (see "History", p.670), but was released after five months for lack of evidence. Recent theories have suggested that the regime in South Africa was behind the killing – Palme was an outspoken critic of apartheid, leading calls for an economic blockade against Pretoria.

In September 2003, another brutal killing shook Sweden. The popular foreign minister **Anna Lindh** was stabbed whilst shopping in the NK department store, just four days before Sweden's referendum on joining the euro, for which she had been campaigning. The police had learnt from earlier mistakes, and this time there was no bungling, with the murderer – the 25-year-old psychiatric patient **Mijailo Mijailovic** – soon arrested and sentenced to life imprisonment. The motive for the killing remains unknown, and it seems Lindh was the random victim of a deranged man. Ironically, it was Lindh's party that earlier supported reforms of Sweden's psychiatric system that saw many patients reintegrated into society and others refused treatment.

then a short walk). Another attraction is the popular **Rålambshovsparken**, a large expanse of open grassland gently sloping down to the waters of Lake Mälaren, where you can take a swim with fantastic views of the City Hall and Old Town.

Östermalm

East of Birger Jarlsgatan, the streets become noticeably broader and grander as you enter the district of **Östermalm**, one of the last areas of central Stockholm to be developed. The first place to head for is the waterside square, **Nybroplan**, just east along Hamngatan from Sergels Torg, and dominated by the white, relief-studded Kungliga Dramatiska Teatern (Royal Theatre of Drama: ✆ www.dramaten .se), Stockholm's showpiece theatre. The curved harbour in front is the departure point for all kinds of archipelago **ferries** and tours (see p.366), and for the ferry service (late April to late May & late Aug to mid-Sept Sat & Sun 7.30am–7pm; every 15min; late May to late Aug daily 7am–10pm; every 15min; 35kr one-way, 60kr return) via the Nordic and Vasa museums and Skeppsholmen to Gröna Lunds Tivoli (see p.379); some ferries stop at the Royal Palace as well.

Behind the theatre and up the hill of Sibyllegatan, **Östermalmstorg** is an absolute find: the square is home to **Östermalms Saluhallen**, an indoor market hall not unlike Norrmalm's Hötorgshallen, but selling more refined delicatessen – reindeer hearts and the like – and attracting a clientele to match. Wander round at lunchtime and you'll spot any number of fur-coated Stockholmers, sipping Chardonnay and munching shrimp sandwiches.

History Museum

As you plod your way around Östermalm's affluent streets, you're bound to end up at the circular **Karlaplan** sooner or later, full of media types coming off shift from the Swedish Radio and Television buildings at the end of Karlavägen. From here it's a short walk down Narvavägen to the impressive **Historiska Muséet** (Museum of National Antiquities: May–Sept daily 10am–5pm; Oct–April daily 11am–5pm, Thurs until 8pm; 50kr; ✆ www.historiska.se); from Norrmalm, take bus #56 via Stureplan and Linnégatan. The most wide-ranging historical display in Stockholm, it's really two large collections: a museum of National Antiquities and the underground Gold Room, with its magnificent fifth-century gold collars and other fine jewellery. Ground-floor highlights include a Stone Age ideal home – flaxen-haired youth, stripped pine benches and rows of neatly labelled herbs – and a mass of Viking weapons, coins and boats. Upstairs there's a worthy collection of medieval church art and architecture, with odds and ends turned up from all over the country, evocatively housed in massive vaulted rooms. If you're heading to Gotland, be sure to look out for the reassembled bits of stave churches uncovered on the Baltic island – some of the few examples that survive in Sweden.

Djurgården

When you tire of pounding the streets, there's respite at hand in the form of Stockholm's so-called National City Park, and in particular the section just to the east of the centre, **Djurgården**. Originally royal hunting grounds from the sixteenth to eighteenth centuries, it is actually two distinct park areas separated by the water of **Djurgårdsbrunnsviken** – popular for swimming in summer and skating in winter, when the channel freezes over. Djurgården also holds some of Stockholm's finest **museums**: the massive open-air Skansen village museum, and the impressive *Vasa* warship at the Vasa museum.

You can walk to Djurgården through the city centre out along Strandvägen, but it's quite a hike; in summer, trams (30kr) trundle regularly between Norrmalmstorg in Norrmalm and Djurgården. Alternatively, take bus #44 from Karlaplan, or buses #47 and #69 from Norrmalm to the bridge, Djurgårdsbron, which crosses over onto the island. There are also ferries from Skeppsbron in Gamla Stan (all year) and Nybroplan in Östermalm (May–Aug only).

The Nordic Museum, Skansen and Gröna Lunds Tivoli

A full day is just about enough to see everything on Djurgården. Just over Djurgårds-bron from Strandvägen is the palatial **Nordiska Muséet** (Nordic Museum: June–Aug daily 10am–5pm; Sept–May Mon–Fri 10am–4pm, Wed until 8pm, Sat & Sun 11am–5pm; 60kr; ⍟www.nordiskamuseet.se). The displays attempt to represent five hundred years of Swedish cultural history in an accessible fashion – including 1950s furniture design and a collection of toys and doll's houses. On the ground floor of the cathedral-like interior is Carl Milles's phenomenal statue of Gustav Vasa, the sixteenth-century king who drove out the Danes and whose inspirational qualities summoned the best from the sculptor (for more on Milles, see p.388).

However, it's for **Skansen** (daily: May & Sept 10am–8pm; June–Sept 10am–10pm; Oct–April 10am–4pm; 40–100kr depending on time of year; ⍟www.skansen.se) that most people come here: a great open-air museum with 150 reconstructed buildings ranging from an entire town to windmills and farms. They're all laid out on a region-by-region basis, with each section boasting its own daily activities – traditional handicrafts, games and displays – that anyone can join in. The best of the buildings are the small Sámi dwellings, warm and functional, and the craftsmen's workshops in the old town quarter. You can also potter around a small **zoo** and a bizarre **aquarium**, where fish live cheek by jowl with crocodiles, monkeys and snakes. Partly because of the attention paid to accuracy, partly due to the admirable lack of commercialization, Skansen manages to avoid the tackiness associated with similar ventures in other countries. Even the snackbars dole out traditional foods and in winter serve up great bowls of warming soup.

Immediately opposite Skansen's main gates (and at the end of the tram and the #44 bus route; bus #47 also goes by), **Gröna Lunds Tivoli** (daily: late April to Sept noon–10pm; admission 70kr; an optional all-day *åkband* pass costs 280kr for unlimited rides or alternatively you can pay per ride; ⍟www.gronalund.com) is not a patch on its more famous namesake, Copenhagen's Tivoli Gardens. It's definitely more of a place to stroll through rather than indulge in the rides, which are generally rather tame. One notable exception is the Fritt Fall, a hair-raising vertical drop of 80m in just six seconds; do lunch later. At night, the emphasis shifts as the park becomes the stomping ground for Stockholm's youth, with raucous music, cafés and some enterprising chat-up lines to be heard.

Vasa Museum

In a new building close to the Nordic Museum, the Vasamuséet (Vasa Museum: daily: June–Aug 8.30am–6pm; Sept–May 10am–5pm, Wed until 8pm; 95kr; ⍟www.vasamuseet.se) is head and shoulders above anything else that Stockholm has to offer in the way of museums. Built on the orders of King Gustav II Adolf, the *Vasa* warship sank in Stockholm harbour on her maiden voyage in 1628 – built to a design that was both too tall and too narrow, it keeled over and sank as soon as it was put afloat. Preserved for over three hundred years by the Baltic's brackish waters – not salty enough for the taste of wood-boring worms – the ship was raised along with 12,000 objects in 1961, and now forms the centrepiece of a startling, purpose-built hall on the water's edge.

Though the building itself is impressive, nothing prepares you for the sheer size of the **ship** itself: 62m long, with a main mast which was originally 50m above the keel, it sits virtually complete in the hall. Surrounding walkways bring you nose to nose with cannon hatches and restored decorative relief, the gilded wooden sculptures on the soaring prow designed to intimidate the enemy and proclaim Swedish might. Faced with its frightening bulk, it's not difficult to understand the terror that such ships must have generated. Adjacent **exhibition halls** and presentations on several levels take care of all the retrieved bits and bobs. There are reconstructions of life on board, detailed models of the *Vasa*, displays relating to contemporary social and political life, an hourly English-language film about the history of the *Vasa*, excellent explanations and regular English-language **guided tours** (included in the entrance fee).

Thiel Gallery

At the far eastern end of Djurgården (take bus #69 from Norrmalm) is one of Stockholm's major treasures, the Thielska Galleriet (Thiel Gallery: Mon–Sat noon–4pm, Sun 1–4pm; 50kr; ⓦ www.thielska-galleriet.se), a fine example of Swedish architecture and art. The house was built by Fredinand Boberg at the beginning of the twentieth century for a banker, Ernet Thiel, who then sold it to the state in 1924, after which it entered its present incarnation. Thiel, who knew many contemporary Nordic artists, gathered an impressive collection of paintings over the years, including works by Carl Larsson, Anders Zorn, Edvard Munch, Bruno Liljefors and even August Strindberg. The views back towards the city alone are attractive enough to warrant a visit.

The Kaknäs TV Tower

Bus #69 from Norrmalm will take you directly to Stockholm's landmark TV tower, in the northern stretch of parkland known as **Ladugårdsgärdet** (or, more commonly, Gärdet); it's also possible to walk here from Djurgården proper – head northwards across the island on Manillavägen over Djurgårdsbrunnsviken. At 160m, the Kaknästornet (Kaknäs TV Tower: daily: Jan–March Mon–Wed 10am–6pm, Thurs–Sat 10am–9pm, Sun 10am–6pm; April & May Mon–Sat 10am–9pm, Sun 10am–6pm; June–Aug 9am–10pm; Sept–Nov 10am–9pm; Dec Mon–Sat 10am–11pm, Sun 10am–9pm; 30kr) is one of the highest buildings in Scandinavia, allowing fabulous views over the city and archipelago; there's a restaurant about 120m up, should you fancy a vertiginous cup of coffee or lunch.

Södermalm

Whatever you do in Stockholm, don't miss the delights of the city's southern island, **Södermalm**, whose craggy cliffs, turrets and towers rise high above the traffic interchange at Slussen. The perched buildings are vaguely forbidding, but venture beyond the main roads skirting the island and a lively and surprisingly green area unfolds, one that's emphatically working class at heart, though Swedish-style – there are no slums here. To get here, take bus #2 or #3 or ride the T-bana to Slussen or, to save an uphill trek, Medborgarplatsen or Mariatorget.

On foot, you reach the island over a double bridge from Gamla Stan into Södermalmstorg – the square around the entrance to the T-bana at Slussen. Just to the south of the square is the rewarding Stadsmuséet (City Museum: Tues–Sun 11am–5pm, Thurs until 8pm; free; ⓦ www.stadsmuseum.stockholm.se), hidden in a basement courtyard. The Baroque building, designed by Tessin the Elder and finished by his son in 1685, was once the town hall for this part of Stockholm; it now houses a set of collections relating to the city's history as a seaport and industrial centre.

Abba the Museum at Stora Tullhuset, Stadsgården (check ⓦ www.abbamusem .se for opening times; 245kr), ten minutes' walk from Slussen along Stadsgårdsleden, will be the first-ever museum dedicated to ABBA in Sweden when its opens its doors in June 2009. Featuring a whopping 6500 square metres of floor space, four floors of exhibitions, stages on the water in the harbour and quayside marquees, the museum will trace the story of ABBA by recreating, amongst other things, the stage at the Eurovision Song contest in Brighton, the helicopter used in Arrival and even the Polar recording studio where the group put down many of their music tracks. Visitors will be able to ogle the supergroup's stage costumes, strut their stuff in the Voulez-Vous disco and even sing the ABBA songs and record their own music videos.

An altogether more sobering experience, however, awaits just ten minutes' walk to the south, the Renaissance-style **Katarina kyrka** on Högbergsgatan stands on the site where the victims of the Stockholm Bloodbath – the betrayed nobility of Sweden who opposed King Christian II's Danish invasion – were buried in 1520. Their bodies were burned as heretics outside the city walls and it proved a vicious and effective coup, Christian disposing of the opposition in one fell swoop. The

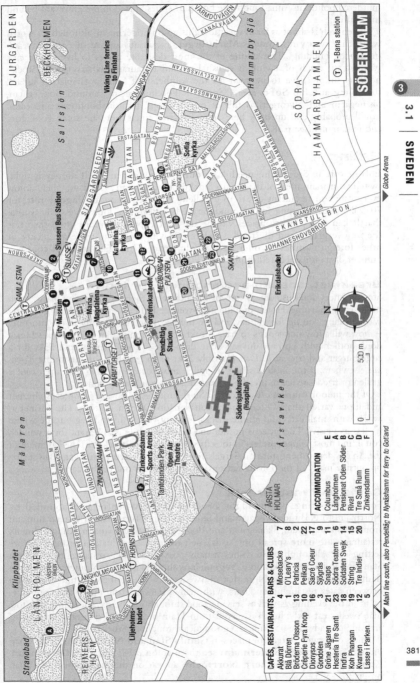

SÖDERMALM

3

▼ Globe Arena

▼ Main line south, also Pendeltåg to Nynäshamn for ferry to Gotland

Ⓣ T-Bana station

ACCOMMODATION

Columbus	E
Långholmen	A
Pensionat Oden Söder	B
Rival	C
Tre Små Rum	D
Zinkensdamm	F

CAFÉS, RESTAURANTS, BARS & CLUBS

Akkurat	4	Mosebacke	7
Blå Dörren	1	O'Leary's	8
Bröderna Olsson	13	Patricia	2
Créperie Fyra Knop	10	Pelikan	22
Dionysos	16	Sacré Coeur	17
Gondolen	3	Sjögräs	9
Gröne Jägaren	21	Snaps	11
Hosteria Tre Santi	23	Södra Teatern	6
Indira	18	Soldaten Svejk	14
Koh Phangan	15	String	19
Kvarnen	12	Tre Indier	20
Lasse i Parken	5		

murdered politician Anna Lindh (see box, p.377) lies buried in the graveyard behind the church.

The church is about as far as specific sights go on Södermalm, although it's worth wandering westwards towards **Mariatorget**, a spacious square of Art Nouveau-influenced buildings. This is one of the most desirable places to live in the city, within easy reach of a glut of stylish bars and restaurants where trendy Stockholmers simply have to be seen. To the southeast of Medborgarsplatsen square, the young and hip **SoFo** area ("South of Folkungagatan", around Bondegatan, Skånegatan and Nytorget) is full of trendy shops, fashion boutiques and cafés. You'll probably end up back here after dark too, since there are some good bars and restaurants (see p.383).

Eating

Eating out in Stockholm needn't be outrageously expensive. If money is tight, switch your main meal of the day to lunchtime, at least on weekdays, when almost every café and restaurant offers an excellent-value set menu, or **dagens rätt**, for 70–90kr. In the evening, look around for the best deals but don't necessarily assume that Italian and Chinese places will be the least expensive; more often than not they're overpriced and the food is tasteless. Having said that, there are plenty of other foreign cuisines on offer, particularly Japanese and Thai, plus, of course, a number of traditional Swedish places.

Breakfast, snacks and shopping for food

Stockholmers don't usually go out for **breakfast**, so there are very few places open in the early morning. Hotels provide help-yourself buffet breakfasts which go a long way to filling you up for the day, and are the best place to go early in the morning – most will allow non-guests to have breakfast for around 50kr. In terms of **snacks**, don't bother with burgers unless you're desperate – you'll pay around 55kr for a large burger and fries at *McDonald's*, only 20kr or so less than the lunchtime *dagens rätt* elsewhere. If the nibbles strike, it's much more economical to pick up a *korv*, a grilled or fried sausage in bread, for around 20kr from a street vendor.

Of the indoor **markets** (both closed Sun), Hötorgshallen in Hötorget is cheaper and more varied than Östermalms saluhallen on Östermalmstorg. The former is awash with small cafés and ethnic snacks, but buy your fruit and veg outside where it's less expensive. The latter is posher and pricey – while it's pleasant for a wander, you'll find most things cost less in the city's biggest **supermarket** in the basement of the Åhléns department store on Sergels Torg. In summer, **fruit and veg** stalls spring up outside many of the T-bana stations, especially those out of the centre.

Cafés and restaurants

For decent eating, day or night, head for the city-centre area bounded by Norrmalmstorg, Birger Jarlsgatan and Stureplan; Grev Turegatan in Östermalm; and around Folkungagatan, Skånegatan and Bondegatan on Södermalm. Kungsholmen's restaurants are more spread out, so it's best to have a destination in mind before setting out. Although main dishes usually cost 150–200kr, restaurants in Gamla Stan tend to be 50–100kr more. **Vegetarians** shouldn't have too much difficulty in finding something to eat. Note that in Sweden as a whole there's a fine distinction between cafés, restaurants and bars, with many places offering music and entertainment in the evening as well as serving food throughout the day. Bear in mind, too, that Swedes eat early: lunch is served from 11am to 2pm and dinner from 6pm to around 9pm; advance booking is a good idea throughout Stockholm.

Unless otherwise stated, for places in **Gamla Stan and Norrmalm**, see the map on p.371; for those in **Södermalm** see the map on p.381; those in **Östermalm**, **Kungsholmen** and **northern Norrmalm** appear on the main Stockholm map on pp.364–365.

Gamla Stan

Bistro Ruby/Grill Ruby Österlånggatan 14 ☎08/20 57 76. A French bistro, tastefully done out in Parisian style, but pricey. Main dishes go for 169–325kr. *Grill Ruby*, next door, serves up similarly priced American-style grills and weekend brunches.

Den Gyldene Freden Österlånggatan 51 ☎08/24 97 60. Stockholm's oldest restaurant, *The Golden Peace* was opened in 1772, and its vaulted cellars edged with elegant wall paintings remain marvellously atmospheric. Expect to pay around 350kr for a main course of Swedish fare, without drinks. The simpler home-cooking choices such as meatballs are better value.

Hermitage Stora Nygatan 11 ☎08/411 95 00. Vegetarian restaurant well worth checking out for its hearty, moderately priced food – look out for the spicy Middle Eastern dishes in particular. Closes at 8pm (Sun 7pm).

Le Rouge Österlånggatan 17 ☎08/505 244 60. Gamla Stan T-bana. A gloriously O.T.T. Moulin Rouge-style bistro, inspired by nineteenth-century Paris. The frequently changing *plat du jour* is 160kr, whilst other French classics start at 140kr.

Pontus by the Sea Skeppsbrokajen, Tullhus 2 ☎08/20 20 95. Gamla Stan T-bana. Housed in a former brewery, this waterfront brasserie specializes in seafood platters though it also serves French classics like minute steak, onion soup and lobster. Mains are in the region of 150–250kr per dish.

Norrmalm

Café Panorama Sergels Torg 3. T-Centralen T-bana. Top-floor café inside Kulturhuset with superb views over central Stockholm (try to get one of the window tables). Lunch is dependable and inexpensive, though it's the apple pie with vanilla sauce that's the real winner.

East Stureplan 13 ☎08/611 49 59. One of the city's finest restaurants. Trendy to a T, and serving some excellent food – lots of fish and Asian-style dishes. Dinner 106–217kr.

Grodan Grev Turegatan 16 ☎08/679 61 00. "The Frog" serves up great French cuisine (mains around 165kr) and transforms into a popular club with dancing later on in the night. The terrace is also good for people-watching in the summer.

KB Smålandsgatan 7 ☎08/679 60 32. Östermalmstorg T-bana. Excellent Swedish and Scandinavian food with plenty of seafood; posh 1930s surroundings with curious Alice in Wonderland-style drawings adorning the walls. Reckon on 160–260kr and upwards for a main course.

Konditori Kungstornet Kungsgatan 28. Popular 1950s-style coffee house with excellent cakes and sandwiches from 40kr.

Riche Birger Jarlsgatan 4 ☎08/545 035 60. Östermalmstorg T-bana. An inordinately popular French brasserie serving a range of Swedish and French dishes for 200–250kr.

Robert's Coffee Kungsgatan 44. Just inside the door of the Kungshallen food hall, and a popular place to meet for a good cup of coffee, muffins or a light lunch.

Sawadee Olofsgatan 6 ☎08/20 98 00. Next to Hötorget T-bana. Attractive Thai restaurant with mains for 150–200kr.

Sturekatten Riddargatan 4. With antique tables and chairs, this is one of Stockholm's best cafés, serving tremendous cakes and pastries as well as filling sandwiches.

Södermalm

Blå Dörren Södermalmstorg 6. Beer hall and restaurant serving excellent Swedish food for 120–200kr.

Bröderna Olsson Folkungagatan 84 ☎08/640 84 46. A fun restaurant with a black-and-white-tiled butcher-shop look, specializing in garlic-laced dishes, accompanied by shots of vodka.

Crêperie Fyra Knop Svartensgatan 4 ☎08/640 77 27. Excellent crêpes at affordable prices (around 110kr).

Dionysos Bondegatan 56 ☎08/641 91 13. Small Greek restaurant with accomplished fare: grilled *halloumi* for 70kr, *souvlaki* for 150kr. All mains are accompanied by potato wedges.

Gondolen Stadsgården 6 ☎08/641 70 90. Breathtaking views over Stockholm from this high-level place serving up local dishes right on the waterfront at the top of the Katarina lift. Choose the smaller of the two restaurants here and prices fall dramatically – around 185kr for a main course.

Hosteria Tre Santi Blekingegatan 32 ☎08/644 18 16. One of Södermalm's better Italian restaurants and excellent value for money – always busy. Pasta dishes from 135kr, meat mains around 200kr.

Indira Bondegatan 3B ☎08/641 40 46. The area's biggest Indian restaurant, with a good, inexpensive tandoori-based menu. Takeaway food, too.

Koh Phangan Skånegatan 57 ☎08/642 50 40. Swedes love Thailand, and this is a small chunk of paradise 11,070km from Bangkok – a crammed, heaving bar-restaurant with great food (mains around 165kr), lots of bamboo and imitation tropical storms.

Kvarnen Tjärhovsgatan 4. A wonderful beer hall serving Swedish food: lunch for around 50kr, meatballs for 115kr and *pytt i panna* mash for 98kr. Open till 3am, kitchen until 11pm.

Lasse i Parken Högalidsgatan 56. Daytime café (April–Sept only) housed in an eighteenth-century house with a pleasant garden. Very popular in summer; also handy for the beaches at Långholmen.

Pelikan Blekingegatan 40. Atmospheric, working-class beer hall with excellent traditional food, such as *pytt i panna* for 132kr.

Sacré Coeur Skånegatan 83–85 ☏ 08/694 88 15. With orange and green walls hung with artsy photos, this trendy place specializes in French classics such as garlic escargots (73kr) and wild duck (179kr).

Sjögräs Timmermansgatan 24 ☏ 08/84 12 00. A modern approach to Swedish cooking, influenced by world cuisines, and offering mains at 200–260kr. Always packed.

Snaps Götgatan 48 ☏ 08/640 28 68. Good, old-fashioned Swedish food served in a 300-year-old building with mains around the 200kr mark. Very popular.

Soldaten Svejk Östgötagatan 35. Lively Czech-run joint that draws in a lot of students, with a simple menu around 120kr. Large selection of Czech beers – a Pilsner Urquell goes for 48kr.

String Nytorgsgatan 38. Trendy daytime café, good for people-watching from the large windows, which churns out moderately priced cakes and snacks.

Tre Indier Åsögatan 92 ☏ 08/641 03 55. Lively, moderately priced Indian restaurant, slightly tucked away in a tiny street off Åsögatan, but well worth hunting out.

Östermalm

Aubergine Linnégatan 38 ☏ 08/660 02 04. Upmarket and expensive place, decked out with lots of wood and glass and located on one of Östermalm's busiest streets. Mostly serves Mediterranean cuisine; the separate bar menu brings prices within reach.

Brasserie Elverket Linnégatan 69 ☏ 08/661 25 62. Moderately priced Swedish "crossover" food (international dishes given a Swedish flavour with use of local produce and flavours), served up in a restaurant attached to a theatre. Spacious lounge for drinks before dinner or relaxation afterwards.

Il Conte Grevgatan 9 ☏ 08/661 26 28. One of the best Italian restaurants in town, doling out excellent pasta dishes for around 140–200kr.

Örtagården Nybrogatan 31 ☏ 08/662 17 28. Inexpensive, top-notch vegetarian restaurant, with food dished up under a huge chandelier in c.1900 surroundings. Dozens of different salads, warm dishes and soups.

Kungsholmen

Chakula Pontonjärgatan 28 ☏ 08/654 90 30. This African restaurant run by Swedes who've lived and worked in Africa has truly superb food from Kenya, Tanzania and South Africa. Mains from 145kr.

Göken Pontonjärgatan 28 ☏ 08/654 49 28. An excellent choice for modern Swedish food served up in a small neighbourhood restaurant. Mains around 150kr.

La Famiglia Alströmergatan 45 ☏ 08/ 650 63 10. One of Kungsholmen's better Italian places (Frank Sinatra once ate here), and a good one for a date. Mains 100–180kr. Mains from 135kr.

Mamas & Tapas Scheelegatan 3 ☏ 08/653 53 90. Time and again voted one of Stockholm's best eateries and *the* place to come for authentic and reasonably priced Spanish cuisine.

Salt Hantverkaregatan 34 ☏ 08/652 11 00. Inexpensive, traditional Swedish fare, including delicious elk burgers with chips. Reckon on 120–200kr per dish.

Northern Norrmalm

Lao Wai Luntmakargatan 74 ☏ 08/673 78 00. A vegetarian Szechuan restaurant serving main dishes at around 185kr; for cheaper fare, head next door for the snackbar/takeaway department.

Organic Green Rehnsgatan 24. A new-agey organic café serving vegan fare such as home-made bread, soups, a vegetable buffet and freshly pressed juices, for 60–80kr. Closed Sun.

Paus Rörstrandsgatan 18 ☏ 08/34 44 05. Bright and airy neighbourhood restaurant serving modern Swedish at its most accomplished – for example, Arctic char, veal fillet or duck breast from 245kr.

Saturnus Erikbergsgatan 6. Café food during the day, including good, reasonably priced pasta, huge cakes and massive sandwiches, with more substantial dishes on offer in the evening.

Drinking, nightlife and entertainment

You'll find plenty to keep you entertained in Stockholm, from pubs, gigs and clubs to the cinema and theatre. There's a particularly good **live-music** scene in the bars and pubs, but you'll generally have to pay a cover charge of around 100kr. Wear something other than jeans and trainers if you don't want to feel very scruffy – many places won't let you in dressed like that anyway – and be prepared to cough up around 20kr to leave your coat in the cloakroom, a requirement at many bars, discos and pubs, particularly in winter. As well as the weekend, Wednesday is a busy night in Stockholm – there's usually plenty going on and queues to get into the more popular places.

Bars, brasseries and pubs

The scourge of Swedish **nightlife** – high alcohol prices – is gradually being neutralized and beer prices have dropped considerably; these days, you'll pay roughly the same as in most Western European capitals. On Södermalm especially there are some very good deals. **Happy hours** (also known as After Work) can throw up some bargains – look out for signs outside bars and pubs. Like clubs, most bars and pubs have long queues and evil bouncers at the doors; dress up and arrive before 11pm for easy entry. Many Stockholmers do their drinking over a meal, or tank up before hitting the streets, and several of the places listed below are primarily cafés or restaurants.

Most places listed below are open until around 1am, and till 2am at weekends; we've indicated which stay open later. Unless otherwise stated, for places in **Gamla Stan** and **Norrmalm**, see the map on p.371; for those in **Södermalm** see the map on p.381; those in **Östermalm**, **Kungsholmen** and **northern Norrmalm** appear on the main Stockholm map, on pp.364–365.

Norrmalm and Östermalm

Café Opera Gustav Adolfs Torg, Norrmalm. If your Gucci gear isn't too crushed and you can stand just one more Martini, join the queue outside the Opera House. Daily till 3am.

Dubliner Smålandsgatan 8. One of the busiest Irish pubs in town, with live music most evenings.

Icebar *Nordic Sea* hotel, Vasaplan, Norrmalm. Icy, pricey but unique. Constructed from Jukkasjärvi river ice, this bar serves vodka cocktails and lingonberry juice in ice glasses. The hefty entrance fee includes a warm cape and a drink.

Lydmar *Lydmar* hotel, Sturegatan 10, Norrmalm. A very popular, very elegant bar with occasional jazz and soul music.

Sturecompagniet Sturegatan 4. Three floors of heaving bars, with something for everybody.

Tranan Karlbergsvägen 14, Östermalm (see Stockholm map, pp.364–365). Atmospheric old workers' beer hall.

Gamla Stan

Gråmunken Västerlånggatan 18. Cosy café-pub, usually busy and sometimes with live music to jolly things along.

Kleins Kornhamnstorg 51. One of the better bars in Gamla Stan, generally full with young professional

Stockholmers dying to practise their English.

Magnus Ladulås Österlånggatan 26. Rough brick walls and low ceilings make this bar-cum-restaurant an appealing place for a drink or two.

Torget Mälartorget 13. Gamla Stan T-bana. This elegant place is Stockholm's main gay bar, good for a drink at any time of the evening and always busy.

Södermalm

Akkurat Hornsgatan 18. This famous spot is known for its 280 different whiskies and extensive beer selection, including an impressive array of Belgian varieties. Often has live music at weekends.

Gröne Jägaren Götgatan 64. Some of the cheapest beer in Stockholm. Perhaps inevitably, the clientele tends to get raucously drunk.

Kvarnen Tjärhovsgatan 4. Busy beer hall with two bars.

O'Learys Götgatan 11–13. Södermalm's most popular Irish pub – great fun and within stumbling distance of the nearby T-bana at Slussen.

Pelikan Blekingegatan 40. A fantastic old beer hall full of character – and characters.

Sjögräs Timmermansgatan 24. Wonderful bar specializing in rum, and playing bebop, reggae and world music to chilled-out locals.

Clubs

The **club scene** in Stockholm is limited, with several places doubling as bars or restaurants (where you have to eat). Entrance charges aren't too high (around 100kr), but beers sometimes get more expensive as the night goes on.

Aladdin Barnhusgatan 12, Norrmalm. One of the city's most popular dance restaurants, often with live bands. Expensive.

Crazy Daizy Flemingatan 2–4, Norrmalm. Very popular club with 30- and 40-somethings: a mix of disco and live music.

Guantanamero Upplandsgatan 2, Norrmalm. A combination of Latin, Cuban, salsa and R'n'B really

draws the crowds – especially Stockholm's large Spanish-speaking community – to this unpretentious club on Sat nights.

Lino Riddarkällaren, Södra Riddarholmshamnen 19. Undoubtedly the best gay club in town with three dancefloors (one outside which is heated in winter) offering you picture-perfect views of Lake Mälaren as you groove the night away to a buzzing mix of house, trance and 1980s and 1990s. Sat only.

Mosebacke Mosebacke torg 3, Södermalm. One of the longest-established clubs in town; every night sees a different type of club or event taking place – everything from jazz to new bands, R&B to disco.

Patricia Stadsgårdskajen, Slussen. Formerly the royal yacht of Britain's Queen Mother, today a restaurant-disco-bar with good views of the city across the harbour. Swedish stand-up comedy nights and fantastic food. Arrive early. Wed–Sun.

Sturecompagniet Sturegatan 4, Norrmalm. Strut to house and techno and a fantastic light show or work your way through three floors of bars. Very popular.

Live music: rock and jazz

Apart from the cafés and bars already listed, there's no shortage of specific venues that put on **live music**. Most of the performers will be local bands, for which you'll pay 60–70kr entrance, but nearly all the big names make it to Stockholm, playing at a variety of seated halls and stadiums – naturally, tickets for these are much more expensive. The main venue is the Stockholm Globe Arena (T-bana Globen; ℡0771/31 00 00, ⎙www.globen.se), supposedly the largest spherical building in the world – ring for programme details or ask at the tourist offices.

Cirkus Djurgårdsslätten 43, Djurgården (see Stockholm map, pp.364–365) ℡08/587 987 00, ⎙www .cirkus.se. Occasional rock and R&B performances.

Debaser Karl Johans torg, Gamla Stan ℡08/30 56 20. Perhaps Stockholm's best rock club, with live performances on most days.

Engelen Kornhamnstorg 59, Gamla Stan ℡08/20 10 92, ⎙www.wallmans.com. Live jazz, rock or blues nightly until 3am, but arrive early to get in; the music starts at 8.30pm (9pm Sun).

Fasching Kungsgatan 63, Norrmalm ℡08/21 62 67, ⎙www.fasching.se. Local and foreign contemporary jazz; a good place to go dancing too. Closed Sun.

Nalen Regeringsgatan 74, Norrmalm ℡08/566 398 00, ⎙www.nalen.com. Once *the* place to hear music in the city (even the Beatles played here), now offering jazz, swing and big band.

Södra Teatern Mosebacke torg 3, Södermalm ℡08/556 972 30. This is one of the best places in the capital for world music, hip-hop, rock and pop – if it's happening anywhere, it's happening here. Weekends only.

Stampen Stora Nygatan 5, Gamla Stan ℡08/20 57 93. Long-established and rowdy jazz club, both trad and mainstream; occasional foreign names, too.

Tre Backar Tegnérgatan 12–14, Norrmalm (see Stockholm map, pp.364–365) ℡08/673 44 00. Good, cheap pub with a cellar for live music performances. Rock and blues nightly Mon–Sat until midnight.

Classical music, theatre and cinema

For up-to-date **information** about what's on where, check the special Saturday supplement of the *Dagens Nyheter* newspaper, "På stan". *What's On*, free from the tourist office, is also indispensable for **arts listings**, with day-by-day information about a whole range of events – gigs, theatre, festivals, dance – sponsored by the city, many of which are free and based around Stockholm's many parks. Popular venues in summer are Kungsträdgården and Skansen, where there's always something going on.

Classical music and opera

Classical music is always easy to find. There's generally something on at one of the following venues: Konserthuset, Hötorget, Norrmalm (℡08/786 02 00, ⎙www .konserthuset.se); Berwaldhallen, Strandvägen 69, Östermalm (℡08/784 18 00, ⎙www.berwaldhallen.se); and Musikaliska Akademien, Blasieholmstorg 8, near the National Art Museum (℡08/407 18 00, ⎙www.musakad.se). **Organ music** can be heard at Adolf Fredriks kyrka, Holländargatan 16, Norrmalm; St Jakobs kyrka in Kungsträdgården, Norrmalm; Gustav Vasa kyrka in Odenplan; and Storkyrkan in Gamla Stan.

Theatre and cinema

Stockholm has dozens of **theatres**, but naturally most productions are in Swedish. However, for **English-language performances** check out Sweden's oldest

English-language theatre company, Stockholm Players (@www.stockholmplayers .se), established in the 1920s. If you want tickets for anything else theatrical, it's often worth waiting for reduced-price standby tickets, available from the kiosk in Norrmalmstorg.

Cinema-going is an incredibly popular pastime in Stockholm, with screenings of new releases nearly always full. The largest venue in the city centre is Filmstaden Sergel in Hötorget (@08/562 600 00, @www.sf.se), but there's also a good number of cinemas along the entire length of Kungsgatan between Sveavägen and Birger Jarlsgatan, always very lively on Saturday night. Tickets cost around 85kr and films are never dubbed into Swedish.

Listings

Airlines British Airways @www.ba.com; Continental @www.continental.com; Delta Air Lines @www .delta.com; Icelandalr @www.icclandair.se; Ryanair @www.ryanair.com; SAS @www.sas.se; US Airways @www.usairways.com

Airport enquiries Arlanda @www.arlanda.se; Bromma @www.lfv.se/bromma; Skavsta @www.skavsta air.se; Västerås @www .vasterasflygplats.se.

Bookshops English-language books are available at Akademibokhandeln, corner of Regeringsgatan and Mäster Samuelsgatan; and Sweden Bookshop, Slottsbacken 10 in Gamla Stan.

Car rental Avis @www.avis.se; Europcar @www .europcar.se; Hertz @www.hertz.oo.

Health care CityAkuten, Apelbergsgatan 48 @08/412 29 60.

Embassies and consulates Australia, Sergels Torg 12 @08/613 29 00, @www.sweden .embassy.gov.au; Canada, Tegelbac ken 4 @08/453 30 00, @www.canadaemb.se; Ireland, Östermalmsgatan 97 @08/661 80 05, @swedenembassy@dfa.ie; New Zealand – use the Australian Embassy; UK, Skarpögatan 6–8 @08/671 30 00, @www.britishembassy.se; US, Dag Hammarskjöldsväg 31 @08/783 53 00, @http://stockholm.usembassy.gov.

Emergencies Ring @112 for police, ambulance or fire services.

Exchange Forex exchange offices at Central Station, Cityterminalen, Vasagatan 14, Sverigehuset tourist office, Terminal 2 & 5, Arlanda airport and Skavsta airport. More information at @www .forex.se.

Gay information RFSL (National Association for Sexual Equality), Sveavägen 57 @08/457 13 00, @www.rfsl.se. The free newspaper, QX (@www .qx.se), available at gay bars and clubs, is handy for listings. Gay beaches are at Freskati: turn left out of the Universitetet T-bana, then walk past Pressbyrån, under the bridge and towards the trees; and at Kärsön, Brommaplan T-bana then any bus towards Drottningholm palace. Get off at the stop over the bridge and walk to the right along the water's edge.

Internet access Sidewalk Express has dozens of internet points across Stockholm, for example, at Central Station, Cityterminalen and most 7-Eleven supermarkets. See @www.sidewalkexpress.se for complete listings. One hour costs 19kr.

Laundry Self-service laundry at Västmannagatan 61 (Mon–Fri 8.30am–6.30pm, Sat 9.30am–3pm, @www.tvattomaten.se).

Left luggage There are lockers at Central Station and the Cityterminalen bus station.

Lost property Klara Östra Kyrkogatan 6, @08/600 10 00.

Pharmacy 24-hour service at Klarabergsgatan 64, @08/454 81 30.

Police Kungsholmsgatan 37 @08/401 01 00.

Radio English-language programming from Radio Sweden as well as broadcasts from the BBC can be heard on 89.6 FM.

Travel information (SL) Bus and T-bana information on @08/600 10 00, @www.sl.se.

Around Stockholm

Such are Stockholm's attractions, it's easy to overlook the city's surroundings; yet only a few kilometres from the centre the countryside becomes noticeably leafier, the islands less congested and the water brighter. As further temptation, some of the country's most fascinating sights are within easy reach, like the spectacular **Milles-gården** sculpture museum at **Lidingö** and **Drottningholm**, Sweden's greatest royal palace. Other trips from Stockholm – out into the stunning **archipelago** or to the university town of **Uppsala** – really merit more time, although if you're pressed it's possible to travel to each and return the same day.

Lidingö and Millesgården

A residential island just northeast of the city centre, **Lidingö** is where the well-to-do of Stockholm live – you'll already have glimpsed it if you arrived from Finland or Estonia on the Silja or Tallink ferries, as they dock immediately opposite. It's worth visiting for the statues in the startling **Millesgården** at Carl Milles väg 2 (mid-May to Sept daily 11am–5pm; Oct to mid-May Tues–Sun noon–5pm; 80kr; Ⓦwww .millesgarden.se), the outdoor sculpture collection of **Carl Milles** (1875–1955), one of Sweden's greatest sculptors and collectors. To **get there**, take the T-bana to Ropsten, then the rickety Lidingöbanan train over the bridge to Torsvikstorg, and walk down Herserudsvägen.

The statues are placed on terraces carved from the island's steep cliffs, with many of Milles's animated, classical figures perching precariously on soaring pillars, overlooking the distant harbour. A huge *Poseidon* rears over the army of sculptures, the most remarkable of which, *God's Hand*, has a small boy delicately balanced on the outstretched finger of a monumental hand. If you've been elsewhere in Sweden much of the work may seem familiar – copies and casts of the originals adorn countless provincial towns. If this collection inspires, it's worth tracking down three other pieces by Milles in the capital: his statue of *Gustav Vasa* in the Nordic Museum on Djurgården, the *Orpheus Fountain* in Norrmalm's Hötorget and, at Nacka Strand (reached most enjoyably by Waxholmsbolaget boats from Strömkajen), the magnificent *Gud på Himmelsbågen*, a claw-shaped vertical piece of steel topped with the figure of a boy – a stunning marker at the entrance to Stockholm harbour.

Drottningholm and Birka

Even if your time in Stockholm is limited, it's worth saving a day for a visit to the harmonious UNESCO-listed royal palace of **Drottningholm** (May–Aug daily 10am–4.30pm; Sept daily noon–3.30pm; Oct–April Sat & Sun noon–3.30pm; 70kr; Ⓦwww.royalcourt.se), beautifully located on the shores of leafy Lovön island, 11km west of the city centre. The fifty-minute boat trip there is part of the experience, with hourly departures from Stadhusbron (May to early Sept daily 9.30am–6pm, hourly; early Sept to late Oct Sat & Sun 2 daily; 90kr one-way, 120kr return); alternatively, take the T-bana to Brommaplan and then any bus towards Drottningholm (the bus stop is marked as such) – a less thrilling ride, but one that's covered by the SL travelcards and the Stockholm Card.

Drottningholm is perhaps the greatest achievement of the architects **Tessin**, father and son. Work began in 1662 on the orders of King Karl X's widow, Eleonora, Tessin the Elder modelling the new palace in a thoroughly French style – leading to that tired and overused label of a Swedish Versailles. Apart from anything else it's considerably smaller than its French counterpart, utilizing false perspective and trompe l'oeil to boost the elegant, rather narrow interior. On Tessin the Elder's death in 1681, the palace was completed by his son, already at work on Stockholm's Royal Palace. Inside, good English notes are available to help you sort out each room's detail, a riot of Rococo decoration largely dating from the time when Drottningholm was bestowed as a wedding gift on Princess Louisa Ulrika (a sister of Frederick the Great of Prussia). Since 1981 the Swedish royal family has slummed it out at Drottningholm, using the palace as a permanent home, a move that has accelerated efforts to restore parts of the palace to their original appearance – so that the monumental **Grand Staircase** is now exactly as envisaged by Tessin the Elder.

Nearby in the palace grounds is the Slottsteater (Court Theatre: May–Sept, guided tours only, every 30min; 60kr), dating from 1766. Its heyday came a decade later when Gustav III imported French plays and acting troupes, making Drottningholm the centre of Swedish artistic life. Take a guided tour and you'll get a flowery though accurate account of the theatre's decoration: money to complete the building ran out in the eighteenth century, meaning that not everything is quite what it seems, with painted papier-mâché frontages masquerading as the real thing. The original backdrops and stage machinery are still in place, though, and the tour comes complete with a display of eighteenth-century special effects – wind and thunder machines, trapdoors and simulated lighting. With time to spare, the extensive palace grounds also yield the **Chinese Pavilion** (May–Aug daily 11am–4.30pm; Sept daily noon–3.30pm; 60kr), an eighteenth-century royal summer house.

Birka

Further into Lake Mälaren lies the island of **Björkö**, known for its rich flora and good swimming beaches. Its real draw, though, are the remnants of Sweden's oldest town, **BIRKA**, founded in around 750 AD, and now listed by UNESCO as a World Heritage Site. A Viking trading centre at its height during the tenth century, it has a few obvious remains scattered about, including the fragments of houses and a vast cemetery. Major excavations were carried out between 1990 and 1995 and a museum, **Birka the Viking Town**, now displays rare artefacts recovered during the excavations as well as scale models of the harbour and craftsmen's quarters. You can get there from Stadshusbron in Stockholm on a Strömma boat (May to early Sept daily 9.30am & 2.45pm; also July to mid-Aug daily 1.15pm; 1hr 45min; Ⓦwww .strommakanalbolaget.com). Tickets can be bought on board and cost 200kr one-way or 270kr return, which includes entry to the museum.

Stockholm archipelago

If you arrived in Stockholm by ferry from Finland or Estonia, you'll already have had a tantalizing glimpse of the **Stockholm archipelago**, a unique array of hundreds upon hundreds of pine-clad islands and islets. The archipelago can be split into three distinct sections: inner, centre and outer. In the inner section there's more land than sea; in the centre it's pretty much fifty-fifty; while in the outer archipelago distances between islands are much greater – out here, sea and sky merge into one and the nearest island is often no more than a dot on the horizon. It's worth knowing that if it's cloudy in Stockholm, chances are that the sun will be shining somewhere out on the islands. Even if your trip to the capital is short, don't miss the chance to come out here.

Practicalities

Getting to the islands is easy and cheap, with Waxholmsbolaget (Ⓣ08/679 58 30, Ⓦwww.waxholmsbolaget.se) operating the majority of sailings. Most boats leave from Strömkajen in front of the *Grand Hotel*; others leave from just round the corner at Nybrokajen, next to the Royal Theatre of Drama. Buy tickets either from the Waxholmsbolaget office on Strömkajen or on the boats themselves; you can also pick up free timetables from the office to help you plan your route – timetables are also posted on every jetty. **Departures** to the closest islands are more frequent (often around four daily) than those to the outer archipelago; if there's no direct service, connections can often be made at the island of Vaxholm. Ticket prices are reasonable, costing a maximum of 120kr depending on the length of the journey, though if you're planning to visit several islands it might be worth buying the **Interskerries Card** (*båtluffarkort*), which gives five days' unlimited travel on all Waxholmsbolaget lines for 340kr.

Though there are few hotels in the archipelago, **accommodation** is most easily available in a number of several well-equipped and comfortable **youth hostels** – the most useful are at **Finnhamn** (Ⓣ08/542 462 12, Ⓦwww.finnhamn.se; dorm beds 295kr, double rooms ❷); **Grinda** (Ⓣ08/542 490 72, Ⓦwww.grindawardshus. se; late April to late Oct; 250kr dorm beds; double rooms ❷); **Gällnö** (Ⓣ08/571 661 17, Ⓦwww.gallno.se; mid-May to Sept; dorm beds 230kr, double rooms ❶); and

▲ Stockholm archipelago

Utö (☎08/504 203 00, ⓦwww.uto-vardshus.se; May–Sept; dorm beds 270kr, double rooms ❷), which also has luxury year-round cabins and rooms (1000kr). It's also possible to rent **cottages** on the islands during summer, though you'll need to book way in advance – get hold of the Stockholm hotels brochure from the city tourist office. **Campsites** are surprisingly hard to find – you'll be much better off camping rough, as a few nights' stay in most places won't cause any problems. Remember, though, that open fires are prohibited throughout the archipelago.

Archipelago highlights
Of the vast number of islands, several are firm favourites with Stockholmers, **Vaxholm** in particular; others offer more secluded beaches and plenty of opportunity for lovely walks. The following are a few of the better islands to make for.

Inner and central archipelago
Lying just an hour's ferry ride northeast of Stockholm, **Vaxholm** is a popular weekend destination. The main settlement on the island, **Vaxholm town**, has an atmospheric wooden harbour with an imposing fortress which once guarded the waterways into the city, successfully staving off attacks from Danes and Russians in the seventeenth and eighteenth centuries; it's now an unremarkable museum of military bits and pieces. Also within easy reach is **Grinda**, two hours or so east, a thickly wooded island typical of the inner archipelago, whose magnificent sandy beaches are much favoured by families.

In the central archipelago, low-lying **Gällnö** is covered with dense pine forest. One of the most beautiful islands, it has been designated a nature reserve, with deer and eider duck the most likely wildlife you'll spot. Ferries take about two hours to get here from Stockholm.

Also two hours by boat from Stockholm, **Svartsö**, near the island of Möja (see p.391), lies in the most scenic part of the archipelago, where dozens of surrounding islands give the impression of giant stepping stones leading to the mainland. Known for its fields of grazing sheep, virgin forest and crystal-clear lakes, Svartsö has good roads, making the island ideal for cycling or walking.

Outer archipelago

If you're heading into the outer archipelago from Stockholm, you can sometimes cut the journey time by taking a bus or train to a further point on the mainland and picking the boat up there – where this is the case, we've given details below.

Three hours from Stockholm, the tiny island of **Finnhamn** lies in the outer reaches of the archipelago, where the islands start to become fewer and where the sea takes over. It's a good place for walking, through forests, meadows and along cliff tops.

Möja (pronounced roughly as "Murr-ya"), three and a half hours from the city, is one of the most popular islands, home to around three hundred people, who make their living from fishing and farming. There's a small craft museum in the main town, **Berg**, and even a cinema, though as there are no beaches (private houses line the entire shoreline), it's not the place to come if you want to go swimming.

Sandhamn has been a destination for seafarers since the 1700s and remains so today, its tiny harbour packed with sailing yachts of all shapes and sizes. The main village is a haven of narrow alleyways, winding streets and overgrown verandas. It takes three and a half hours to get here from Stockholm by boat, or you can save time by taking bus #434 from Slussen to Stavsnäs – the furthest point on the mainland – and picking up a boat for the hour-long sailing to Sandhamn.

Lying far out in the southern reaches of the archipelago, **Utö** is ideal for cycling, with the sandy beaches at Ålö storsand perfect for a picnic stop. You can also walk along Utö's cliffs at Rävstavik. The journey time from Stockholm is three hours.

Västerås

Around 100km inland from Stockholm, **VÄSTERÅS**, Sweden's sixth biggest city and capital of the county of Västmanland, is an immediately likeable mix of old and new. Today the lakeside city carefully balances its dependence on industrial technology giant ABB with a rich history dating back to Viking times – and it's also home to two very wacky hotels.

Arrival, information and accommodation

The **airport**, served by direct Ryanair flights from London Stansted, is 6km east of the centre and is connected to the centre by bus #941; Ryanair flights are met by the Flygbussarna bus which drives directly to Stockholm's Cityterminalen (see p.363). The airport has no ATM or exchange office. The **train** and **bus stations** are located together on Södra Ringvägen, opposite the **tourist office** at Kopparbergsvägen 1 (Mon–Fri 10am–6pm, Sat 10am–3pm, also July to mid-Aug Sun 10am–2pm; ℡021/39 10 00, ⓦwww.vasterasmalarstaden.se). The lakeside Lövudden **youth hostel** (℡021/18 52 30, ⓦwww.lovudden.nu; dorm beds 200kr, private rooms ❶) is 5km west of the city; take bus #25 from the bus station.

Hotels

Arkad Östermalmsgatan 25 ℡021/12 04 80, ⓦwww.hotellarkad.se. Individually designed rooms ranging from contemporary Swedish to nineteenth-century classic. Good value for money, especially in summer and at weekends. ❸/❺

Elite Stadshotellet Stora Torget ℡021/10 28 00, ⓦwww.vasteras.elite.se. A Västerås fixture: good-quality modern rooms right in the heart of the city. ❸/❺

First Plaza Karlsgatan 9A ℡021/10 10 10, ⓦwww.firsthotels.se. Known locally as the "skyscraper", this 25-storey glass-and-chrome structure is the last word in Scandinavian chic, and offers good value in summer. ❹/❻

Klipper Kungsgatan 4 ℡021/41 00 00. Charming rooms in the old town, close to the Svartån River. If you're prepared to "bädda själv" – put the sheets on the bed yourself – you can avail yourself of the lowest room rates in town (495kr). Breakfast is included, as is lunch on weekdays. ❸

Utter Inn & Hackspett Lake Mälaren & Vasaparken ℡021/39 10 00, ⓦwww.vasterasmalarstaden.se. Built by a local artist, the *Utter Inn* is a double room hanging three metres below a tiny hut floating on Lake Mälaren, with windows on all sides for observing the fish. The *Hackspett* ("woodpecker") consists of a one-bed tree hut perched in an oak tree in the middle of the city park. Open April to mid-Oct; book well in advance. ❻

From the tourist office, it's a short stroll up Köpmangatan to the twin cobbled squares of **Bondtorget** and **Stora Torget**. A narrow lane leads from the south-western corner of Bondtorget to the narrow **Svartån River**, which runs right through the centre of the city; the bridge across it affords great views of the old wooden cottages which nestle eave to eave along the riverside. Although it may not appear so significant, the Svartån was a decisive factor in making Västerås the headquarters of one of the world's largest engineering companies, **Asea-Brown-Boveri** (ABB), which needed a ready source of water for production. North of the two main squares is the thirteenth-century brick **Domkyrkan** (Mon–Fri 8am–5pm, Sat & Sun 9.30am–5pm), last resting place of Erik XIV, who died an unceremonious death in Örbyhus castle in 1577 after eating pea soup laced with arsenic. His tomb lies to the right of the altar; local rumour has it that his feet had to be cut off in order to fit his body into its coffin. Beyond the cathedral is the most charming district of Västerås, **Kyrkbacken**, a hilly area with steep cobblestone alleys winding between well-preserved old wooden houses where the craftsmen and the petit bourgeoisie lived in the 1700s.

A quick walk past the restaurants and shops of Vasagatan will bring you back to Stora Gatan and eventually to the modern **Stadshuset**, a far cry from the Dominican monastery which once stood on this spot. Although home to the city's administration, the building is best known for its 47 **bells**, the largest of which (known as "The Monk") can be heard across Västerås at noon. Across Fiskartorget square, the **castle** was under renovation at time of writing and it's uncertain if the **county museum** inside will reopen, but if it does, don't miss the Viking boat grave from nearby Tuna in Badelunda – the richest female burial yet discovered in Sweden.

Eating and drinking

Västerås has a good selection of **restaurants**, with numerous cuisines represented: from Thai to Greek, traditional Swedish to British-style pub food. The city also has a lively **drinking** scene, including one cocktail bar 24 floors up, from where there are unsurpassed views of the lake.

Atrium Smedjegatan 6 ☎021/12 38 48. Greek favourites from 109kr in an enjoyable restaurant complete with Olympic-style torches.

Bellman Stora Torget 6 ☎021/41 33 55. Elegant restaurant in a yellow wooden house overlooking the main square, with Swedish fare from 125kr.

Bill o Bob Stora Torget 5 ☎021/41 99 21. A bustling restaurant on the main square, with all the usual meat and fish dishes from 124kr.

Bishops Arms Stora Torget. British-style drinking hole with a large selection of beers, single-malt whisky and pub grub.

Kalle på Spången Kungsgatan 2. Great old-fashioned café with outdoor seating close to the river. *The* place for coffee, cakes, grilled baguettes and fresh orange juice.

Karlsson på taket Karlsgatan 9A. Chichi restaurant and café on the 24th floor of the Skrapan skyscraper, which also houses the *First Hotel Plaza*. Expensive, but fantastic views.

Piazza di Spagna Vasagatan 26 ☎021/12 42 10. The best pizzeria in town and a very popular place for lunch (69kr). Otherwise, pizzas and pasta are from around 79kr, and meat dishes start at 200kr.

Spicy Hot Sturegatan 20A ☎021/18 17 40. Understated interior with simple wooden tables and chairs, and inordinately popular: excellent Thai curries and stir fries for 89kr, as well as a range of vegetarian dishes. Takeaway prices 20kr less.

Varda Vasagatan 14 ☎021/14 81 50. Trendy, above-average restaurant with international dishes from 200kr. A great spot for lunch.

Around Västerås: the Anundshög burial mound

Six kilometres northeast of Västerås, **Anundshög** is the largest royal burial mound in Sweden. Dating from the sixth century, it's thought to be the resting place of King Bröt-Anund and the stash of gold with which he was buried. Several other smaller burial mounds are located close by, suggesting that the site was an important Viking meeting place for several centuries. Beside the main mound lie a large number of **standing stones** arranged end to end in the shape of two ships. Bus #12 leaves the centre of town two to four times an hour; the mound is a twenty-minute walk from its final stop, Bjurhovda. Alternatively, take the new daily "museum bus" which leaves from Fiskartorget square near the art museum (mid-June to mid-Aug, hourly noon–4pm; 50kr).

Uppsala

First impressions as the train pulls into **UPPSALA**, less than an hour north of Stockholm, are encouraging. The red-washed **castle** looms up behind the railway sidings, while the **cathedral** dominates the foreground. A sort of Swedish Oxford, Uppsala clings to the past through a succession of striking buildings connected with and scattered about its cathedral and **university**. Regarded as the historical and religious centre of the country, it serves as a tranquil daytime alternative to Stockholm – with an active student-oriented nightlife.

Arrival and information

Uppsala's new Resecentrum, combining the **train** and **bus stations**, is on Kungsgatan. If you're flying in or out of Sweden, you can bypass Stockholm entirely by taking the train from Arlanda C station to Uppsala (daily every 20min; 20min; 120kr), or bus #801 (daily every 15–30min; 40min; 100kr). A short walk from the Resecentrum, the **tourist office** is at Fyristorg 8 (Mon–Fri 10am–6pm, Sat 10am–3pm; end June to mid-Aug same hours plus Sun 11am–3pm; ☎018/727 48 00, ⓦwww.uppland.nu). You can pick up the free *What's On* guide, or buy the Uppsala Card (125kr; valid for three days), which allows free admission to most sights, as well as free parking and use of local buses.

Accommodation

Though Uppsala can easily be seen as a day-trip from Stockholm, you may want to stay around a little longer. As well as a fair range of hotels, there are two central

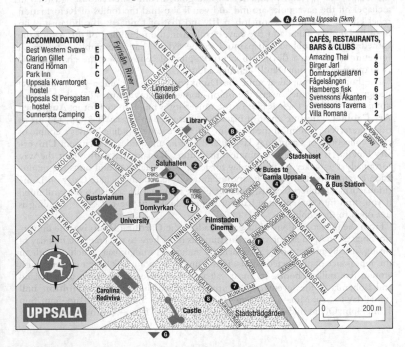

▲ Ⓐ & Gamla Uppsala (5km)

ACCOMMODATION	
Best Western Svava	E
Clarion Gillet	D
Grand Hörnan	F
Park Inn	C
Uppsala Kvarntorget hostel	A
Uppsala St Persgatan hostel	B
Sunnersta Camping	G

CAFÉS, RESTAURANTS, BARS & CLUBS	
Amazing Thai	4
Birger Jarl	8
Domtrappkällaren	5
Fågelsången	7
Hambergs fisk	6
Svenssons Åkanten	3
Svenssons Taverna	1
Villa Romana	2

UPPSALA

0   200 m

youth hostels: *Uppsala Kvarntorget Vandrarhem*, Kvarntorget 3 (☎018/24 20 08, ⓔkvarntorget@uppsalavandrarhem.se; dorm beds 220kr; double rooms ①), and *Uppsala St Persgatan Vandrarhem*, St Persgatan 16 (☎018/10 00 08, ⓔbokning @uppsalavandrarhem.se; dorm beds 220kr; double rooms ①).

For **camping**, head a few kilometres north to the open spaces of Gamla Uppsala (see p.395), or use the regular site, *Sunnersta Camping* (☎018/727 60 84), 7km from town by Lake Mälaren (bus #20).

Best Western Svava Bangårdsgatan 24 ☎018/13 00 30, ⓦwww.hotelsvava.com. Modern hotel with all mod cons, offering good summer discounts. ③/⑥

Clarion Gillet Dragarbrunnsgatan 23 ☎018/68 18 00, ⓦwww.clarionhotelgillet.se. This formerly dowdy pile has been transformed into a contemporary beauty with Scandinavian designer rooms and stylish bathroom; just a stone's throw from the cathedral. ④/⑥

Grand Hörnan Bangårdsgatan 1 ☎018/13 93 80, ⓦwww.grandhotellhornan.com. Wonderfully elegant place with large, old-fashioned rooms and a restaurant. ⑤/⑥

Park Inn Storgatan 30 ☎018/68 11 00, ⓦwww .uppsala.parkinn.se. This trendy hotel next to the new concert hall is perfectly located for the train station. Invitingly cosy designer rooms feature the latest Scandinavian chic. ④/⑥

The City

The centre of the medieval town is the great Gothic **Domkyrkan** (daily 8am–6pm; free; ⓦwww.uppsaladomkyrka.se), Scandinavia's largest cathedral. Built to show the people of Trondheim in Norway that even their mighty church could be overshadowed, it loses out to its competitor by reason of the building material – local brick rather than imported stone – and only the echoing interior remains impressive, particularly the French Gothic ambulatory, bordered by tiny chapels and bathed in a golden glow. One chapel contains a lively set of restored fourteenth-century wall paintings that recount the legend of St Erik, Sweden's patron saint: his coronation, crusade to Finland, eventual defeat and execution at the hands of the Danes. The relics of Erik, encased in a golden coffin, are zealously guarded in a chapel off the nave: poke around and you'll also find the tombs of Reformation rebel Gustav Vasa and his son Johan III, and that of Linnaeus, the botanist, who lived in Uppsala. Time and fire have resulted in the rebuilding of the rest of the cathedral, now scrubbed and painted to the extent that it resembles a historical museum more than a thirteenth-century spiritual centre; even the characteristic twin spires are late nineteenth-century additions.

The buildings grouped around the Domkyrkan can all claim a purer historical pedigree. Opposite the towers, the onion-domed **Gustavianum** (Tues–Sun 11am–4pm; 40kr), built in 1625 as part of the university, is much touted for its **Augsburg Art Cabinet**, a treasure chest of black oak presented to Gustav II Adolf, and for its tidily preserved anatomical theatre from 1663. The same building houses a couple of small collections of Egyptian, Classical and Nordic antiquities. The current **University** building is the imposing nineteenth-century Renaissance edifice over the way. Originally a seminary, it's used today for lectures and seminars and hosts the graduation ceremonies each May. The more famous of its alumni include Carl von Linné (Linnaeus) and Anders Celsius, inventor of the temperature scale. No one will mind if you stroll into the entrance hall for a quick look, but the rest of the building is not open to the public.

From the university, Övre Slottsgatan leads to the **Carolina Rediviva**, the university library. On April 30 each year the students meet here to celebrate the first day of spring (usually in the snow), all wearing a traditional student cap, which gives them the appearance of disaffected sailors. This is one of Scandinavia's largest libraries, with around five million books. Its most valuable treasures – some stolen from Poland and Bohemia in the seventeenth century – are on show in the **exhibition hall** (mid-May to Sept Mon–Thurs 9am–6.30pm, Fri until 5.30pm, Sat 10am–5pm, Sun 10am–4pm; Oct to mid-May Mon–Fri 9am–8pm, Sat 10am–5pm; mid-May to Sept

20kr, otherwise free). Look out for the beautiful sixth-century Silver Bible, Mozart's drafts for *The Magic Flute* and Ptolemy's 1477 map of the world. There's also a pretty café on the ground floor.

After this, the **Castle** (guided tours mid-June to Aug Tues–Sun 1pm & 3pm; 70kr) up on the hill is a disappointment. In 1702, a fire that destroyed three quarters of the city did away with much of the building, and only one side and two towers remain of what was once an opulent rectangular palace. Inside, admission also includes access to the castle's art museum but, quite frankly, it won't make your postcards home.

Seeing Uppsala's central sights will take up a good half-day. If the weather holds out, use the rest of your time to stroll from the lush Stadsträdgården park along the Fyrisån River through the centre of town. One beautiful spot worth lingering in is the **Linnaeus Garden** (May–Sept Tues–Sun 11am–8pm; 50kr includes the museum; ⓦ www.linnaeus.uu.se) over the river on Svartbäcksgatan. Sweden's oldest botanical gardens, established in 1655 by Olof Rudbeck the Elder, they were relaid by Linnaeus (Carl von Linné) in 1741, and some of the species he introduced and classified still survive. The adjoining **museum** (May–Sept Tues–Sun 11am–5pm; 50kr includes the garden) was once home to Linnaeus and his family, and it attempts to re-create his life through a partially restored library, writing room and a collection of natural history specimens.

Gamla Uppsala

Five kilometres to the north of the present city, and a pleasant walk or bike ride from the centre, three huge **barrows** – royal burial mounds dating back to the sixth century – mark the original site of Uppsala, **Gamla Uppsala** (ⓦ www.raa.se/olduppsala), a pagan settlement and a place of ancient sacrificial rites. Every ninth year the festival of Fröblot demanded the death of nine people, hanged from a nearby tree until their corpses rotted. The pagan temple where this bloody sacrifice took place is now marked by the Christian **Gamla Uppsala kyrka** (daily 9am–4pm), built over pagan remains when the Swedish kings were first baptized into the new faith. What survives is only a remnant of what was, originally, a cathedral – look inside for the faded wall paintings and the tomb of Celsius, of thermometer fame. An eleventh-century rune stone is set into the wall outside, and others can be found nearby.

Arriving by bus from Uppsala (#2 or #110 from Vaksalagatan), first cross the train tracks to see the worthwhile **Gamla Uppsala Historical Centre** (May–Aug daily 11am–5pm; Sept to mid-Dec & Jan–April Wed, Sat & Sun noon–3pm; 50kr). The exhibitions illustrate the origin of local myths from Roman times as well as Uppsala's era of greatness until the thirteenth century. There's little else to Gamla Uppsala, and perhaps that's why the site remains so mysterious and atmospheric. If the nibbles strike after an afternoon of pillaging and plundering, there's a **restaurant**, *Odinsborg*, near the museum, and snacks are served in the museum itself.

Eating, drinking and nightlife

Commensurate with its status as one of Sweden's largest cities and major university centres, Uppsala boasts an impressive range of sophisticated **restaurants** and **bars**. Almost all of them are located in the grid of streets bordered by the Fyrisån River, St Olofsgatan and Bangårdsgatan and, though many places get pretty busy in the summer, it's not necessary to book a table. For affordable snacks, visit the Saluhallen on St Eriks Torg, where there are sushi, kebab and sandwich bars. If you're travelling north from here into the Swedish provinces, it's a good idea to splurge and make the most of the city's eateries, while the bars, often packed with pub-crawling students, are usually pretty lively.

Cafés and restaurants

Amazing Thai Bredgränd 14 ☎018/15 30 10. This small and friendly place has even won awards from the Thai state for its tasty food, which is widely regarded as the best in town: stir fries from 99kr, curries from 109kr.

Birger Jarl Nedre Slottsgatan 3 ☎018/71 17 34. More than just a playground for students, this large, ramshackle wooden-built restaurant and bar is a must. There's a range of burgers for around 130kr, and wild partying later at night. Outdoor tables in summer.

Domtrappkällaren St Eriks Gränd 15 ☎018/13 09 55. One of the most chichi places in town, with an old vaulted roof and great atmosphere. The Swedish mains go for around 135–275kr, and lunch for only 85kr.

Fågelsången Munkgatan 3. Café and lunch place with cheap sandwiches and a pleasant terrace overlooking the park.

Hambergs fisk Fyristorg 8 ☎018/71 21 50. Very good fresh fish and seafood, though rather pricey with mains around 200kr.

Ofvandahls Sysslomansgatan 3–5. A lively café dating from 1878 furnished with shabby old wooden tables and sofas. Don't leave town without trying the home-made cakes.

Svenssons Åkanten St Eriks torg. Outdoor café right by the river; a delightful place to relax in summer.

Svenssons taverna Sysslomangatan 14. One of Uppsala's best eateries, with a large outdoor seating area under the shade of huge linden trees, specializing in deep pan pizzas, though with other international dishes, too.

Villa Romana St Persgatan 4 ☎018/12 50 90. Across the river from the tourist office, in an old stone building with outdoor seating in summer. Excellent Italian food for 150–250kr.

Nightlife

At night, most of Uppsala's action is generated by the **students** and since many stay around during the summer, the city is also busy outside term time. Otherwise, *Birger Jarl* (see above) is a sure bet for a party, as is *Katalin and all that jazz*, open late and with jazz nights – it's in the old goods shed just behind the train station.

Travel details

Trains

Stockholm to: Gällivare (2 daily; 15hr); Gävle (hourly; 1hr 20min); Gothenburg (hourly; 3hr by X2000, 5hr by InterCity); Karlstad (9 daily; 2hr 30min); Kiruna (2 daily; 16hr); Luleå (2 daily; 13hr); Malmö (hourly; 4hr 30min); Mora (2 daily; 4hr); Östersund (3 daily; 6hr); Sundsvall (9 daily; 3hr 20min); Umeå (1 daily; 11hr 30min); Uppsala (every 20min; 40min); Västerås (1 hourly; 1hr).
Uppsala to: Gällivare (2 daily; 14hr); Gävle (hourly; 40min); Kiruna (2 daily; 15hr); Luleå (2 daily; 12hr); Mora (2 daily; 3hr); Östersund (3 daily; 5hr); Stockholm (every 20min; 40min); Sundsvall (9 daily; 2hr 35 min); Umeå (1 daily; 11hr).
Västerås to: Gothenburg (6 daily; 4hr); Luleå (1 daily; 15hr); Stockholm (1 hourly; 1hr).

Buses

Stockholm to: Gothenburg (10 daily; 7hr); Gävle (2 daily; 4hr 30min); Helsingborg (2 daily;

8hr 30min); Kalmar (2 daily; 6hr); Malmö (2 daily; 10hr); Norrköping (hourly; 1hr 20min); Östersund (1 daily; 8hr 30min); Umeå (1 daily; 9hr 20min).

Ferries

For details of Stockholm city ferries, see p.366; for the services to the archipelago, see p.389; for Birka see p.389.

International trains

Stockholm to: Copenhagen (2 daily; 5hr); Narvik, Norway (1 daily; 19hr); Oslo (2 daily; 6hr).
Uppsala to: Narvik, Norway (1 daily; 18hr 30min).

International ferries

Stockholm to: Helsinki (2 daily; 15hr 30min); Mariehamn, Finland (5 daily; 4hr); Riga (1 daily; 17hr); Tallinn (1 daily; 17hr); Turku, Finland (4 daily; 11hr).

3.2

Gothenburg and around

Gothenburg is Sweden's second city and the largest seaport in Scandinavia – facts that have been enough to persuade many travellers arriving here by ferry to move quickly on to the surrounding countryside. But beyond the gargantuan shipyards, Gothenburg's Dutch-designed cityscape of broad avenues, elegant squares, trams and canals is one of the prettiest in Sweden, and with its well-established café society and rich cultural life, it's worth a lot more time than some visitors give it. The city's image has also suffered from the inevitable comparisons with the capital, and while there is a certain resentment on the west coast that Stockholm wins out in the national prestige stakes, many Swedes far prefer Gothenburg's more relaxed atmosphere and its closer proximity to western Europe, particularly since the Øresunds Link near Malmö has put it within three hours of Copenhagen.

The counties to the north and east of the city are prime targets for domestic tourists. The closest highlight to Gothenburg is the glorious fortress island of **Marstrand**, an easy and enjoyable day-trip away, while heading further towards Norway, the uninhabited islands, tiny fishing villages and clean beaches of the craggy **Bohuslän coastline** attract thousands of holidaymakers.

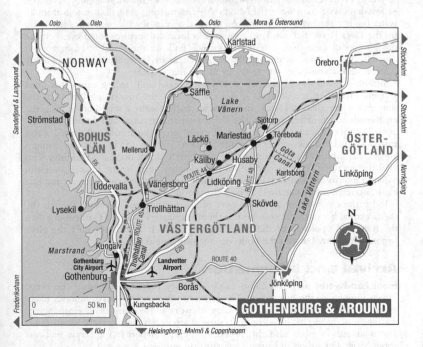

▲ The Paddan sightseeing boat, Gothenburg

Gothenburg

With its long history as a trading centre, **GOTHENBURG** (Göteborg in Swedish, pronounced "Yur-te-borry") is a truly cosmopolitan city. Founded on its present site in the seventeenth century by Gustav Adolf, it was the last in a long line of attempts to create a trade centre free from Danish influence – Denmark had enjoyed control of Sweden's west coast since the Middle Ages, extracting extortionate tolls from all water traffic travelling into Sweden. An original medieval settlement was sited 40km up the Göta River, but was later moved to a location north of the present city in order to avoid these tolls; a third attempt was built on the island of Hisingen, but this fell to the Danes during the Battle of Kalmar in 1611. Six years later, Gustav Adolf founded a new city on the site of today's main square.

Although Gothenburg's reputation as an industrial and trading centre has been severely eroded in recent years – as evidenced by the motionless cranes in the shipyards – the British, Dutch and German traders who settled here during the eighteenth and nineteenth centuries left a rich architectural and cultural inheritance. The city is graced with terraces of grand merchant houses, all carved stone, stucco and painted tiles, while the trade between Sweden and the Far East brought an oriental influence, still visible in the chinoiserie detail on many buildings. This vital trading route was monopolized for over eighty years by the hugely successful Swedish East India Company, whose auction house, selling exotic spices, tea and fine cloth, attracted merchants from all over the world.

Today, the city remains a regular port of call for business travellers, though the flashy central hotels that accommodate them say much less about Gothenburg than the restrained opulence of the older buildings, which reflect not only the city's bygone prosperity but also the understatement of its citizens.

Arrival and information

From **Landvetter airport**, 25km east of the city, Flygbussarna buses run every fifteen minutes to the bus station. The journey takes around thirty minutes (daily every 15–20min; 30min; 75kr). The **City airport** is 15km north of Gothenburg; the Flygbussarna airport bus (from City airport after each flight arrival; 30min; 60kr) to the bus station meets all flights. A taxi from either airport to the centre will cost about 350kr. For airline and airport information numbers, see p.411.

All **trains** arrive at Central Station, on Drottningtorget in the centre of the city. Just behind, the modern glass **bus** station handles all regional, national and international bus services. For regional bus tickets, visit the **Tidpunkten** office (Mon–Fri 7.30am–5.45pm, Sat 8am–2pm; there's another office located in Brunnsparken). Stena Line ferries from Frederikshavn in Denmark dock close to Masthuggstorget, twenty minutes' walk or a tram (#3, #9 or #11) ride west of the city centre, while those from Kiel in Germany dock 3km outside Gothenburg – take tram #3 or #9 into the centre.

Information

Gothenburg has two **tourist offices**. Handiest for new arrivals is the kiosk in the middle of the Nordstan shopping centre, linked to the train and bus stations by a pedestrian tunnel (Mon–Sat 10am–6pm, Sun noon–5pm). The busy **main tourist office** is on the canalfront at Kungsportsplatsen 2 (May Mon–Fri 9.30am–6pm, Sat & Sun 10am–2pm; June & mid- to late Aug daily 9.30am–6pm; July to mid-Aug daily 9.30am–8pm; Sept–April Mon–Fri 9.30am–5pm, Sat 10am–2pm; ☎031/61 25 00, ⓦwww.goteborg.com). From the train station, it's five minutes' walk across Drottningtorget and along the canal. Both offices can provide information and sell the Gothenburg Pass. You can also pick up a free copy of the trilingual, annually updated *Göteborgsguiden*, which details sights, events, music and nightlife, and contains city and transport maps.

City transport

Almost everywhere of interest in Gothenburg is within easy walking distance of the centre. The wide streets are pedestrian-friendly, and the canals and grid layout of the avenues make orientation simple. If you're staying further out, however, some sort of transport may be necessary; consult the maps in the *Göteborgsguiden*.

Public transport

The most convenient form of public transport are the **trams**, which clunk around the city and its outskirts on a colour-coded, eight-line system, passing all the central areas every few minutes – you can tell at a glance which line a tram is on as the route colour appears on the front. The main pick-up points are outside Central Station and in Kungsportsplatsen. Gothenburg also has a fairly extensive **bus** network, using much the same routes as the trams, although central pedestrianization can lead to some odd and lengthy detours. You shouldn't need to use them in the city centre; routes are detailed in the text where necessary.

If you have a Gothenburg Pass, all public transport within the city is free; otherwise, **tickets** are available from vending machines onboard the trams and direct from bus drivers, and allow you to travel for up to ninety minutes. Fares are a standard 25kr for adults, while 7- to 16-year-olds go for half price. If you are staying for a couple of days and travelling around the city quite a bit, it's better value to buy **carnets** from the Tidpunkten travel information offices at Brunnsparken, Drottningtorget and Nils Ericsonsplatsen, or from Pressbyrån newsagents or 7-Eleven supermarkets. A ten-trip carnet, known as *Maxirabatt 100*,

---

The Gothenburg Pass

Buying a **Gothenburg Pass** is an excellent money-saver if you're planning to do any sightseeing. Available from tourist offices or online at ⓦwww.goteborg.com, it gives unlimited bus and tram travel within the city (airport buses excluded), free entry to city museums, admission to the Liseberg amusement park (not including rides), free car parking, boat excursions and various other reductions. Passes are available for either 24hr (225kr) or 48hr (310kr).

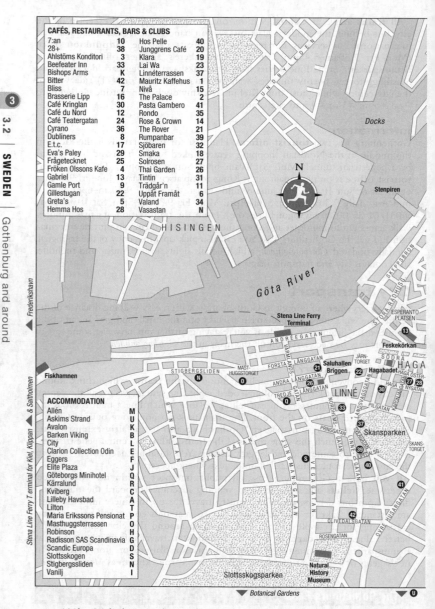

CAFÉS, RESTAURANTS, BARS & CLUBS

7:an	10	Hos Pelle	40
28+	38	Junggrens Café	20
Ahlstöms Konditori	3	Klara	19
Beefeater Inn	33	Lai Wa	23
Bishops Arms	K	Linnéterrassen	37
Bitter	42	Mauritz Kaffehus	1
Bliss	7	Nivå	15
Brasserie Lipp	16	The Palace	2
Café Kringlan	30	Pasta Gambero	41
Café du Nord	12	Rondo	35
Café Teatergatan	24	Rose & Crown	14
Cyrano	36	The Rover	21
Dubliners	8	Rumpanbar	39
E.t.c.	17	Sjöbaren	32
Eva's Paley	29	Smaka	18
Frågetecknet	25	Solrosen	27
Fröken Olssons Kafe	4	Thai Garden	26
Gabriel	13	Tintin	31
Gamle Port	9	Trädgår'n	11
Gillestugan	22	Uppåt Framåt	6
Greta's	5	Valand	34
Hemma Hos	28	Vasastan	N

ACCOMMODATION

Allén	M
Askims Strand	U
Avalon	K
Barken Viking	B
City	L
Clarion Collection Odin	E
Eggers	F
Elite Plaza	J
Göteborgs Minihotel	Q
Kärralund	R
Kviberg	C
Lilleby Havsbad	A
Lilton	T
Maria Erikssons Pensionat	P
Masthuggsterrassen	O
Robinson	H
Radisson SAS Scandinavia	G
Scandic Europa	D
Slottsskogen	S
Stigbergssliden	N
Vanilj	I

costs 100kr. Stick these in the machines on a tram or bus, and press twice for an adult, once for a child.

Taxis, bikes and cars

There are several **taxi** companies in Gothenburg: Kurir (☎031/27 27 27) and Göteborg (☎031/65 00 00) are the most reliable, with fixed prices to and from the airport.

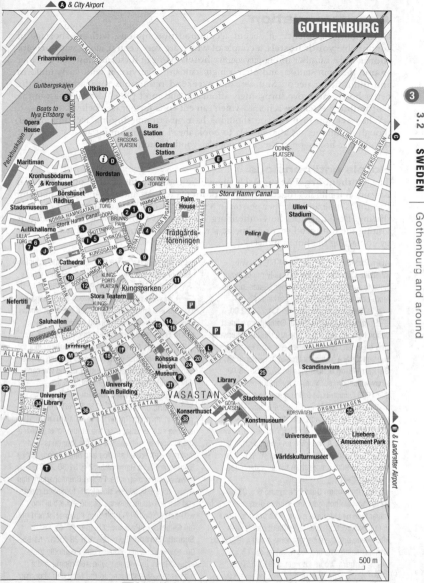

▲ **A** & City Airport

Frihamnspiren

Gullbergskajen

Utkiken

Boats to
Nya Elfsborg

Opera
House

Maritiman

Kronhusbodarna
& Kronhuset

Börshuset
Rådhus

Stadsmuseum

Antikhallarna

Nefertiti

Saluhallen

Rosenlunds Canal

ALLÉGATAN

GATAN

University
Library

University
Main Building

VASASTAN

Cathedral

Stora Teatern

Kungsparken

Nordstan

Bus
Station

Central
Station

Palm
House

Trädgårds-
föreningen

Police

Ullevi
Stadium

Stora Hamn Canal

Scandinavium

VALHALLAGATAN

Röhsska
Design
Museum

Library

Stadsteater

Konserthuset

Konstmuseum

Universeum

Världskulturmuséet

Liseberg
Amusement Park

Botanical Gardens ▼

0   500 m

▶ **G** & Landvetter Airport

Cycling is a popular and easy way to get around, since Gothenburg boasts a comprehensive series of cycle lanes and plenty of bike racks. You can rent bikes from Chalmersgatan 19 (☎031/18 43 00, ⓦwww.cykelkungen.se; 120kr per day) or, alternatively, the *Slottsskogens* and *Stigbergssliden* hostels (see p.403).

For information on **car rental**, see p.411.

Accommodation

Gothenburg has plenty of decent accommodation options, with no shortage of comfortable **youth hostels**, a couple of which are very central, along with **private rooms** and a number of big city-centre **hotels**. Most of these are clustered together around the train station, and offer a high standard of service, if with fairly uniform and uninspiring decor. Summer and weekend reductions mean that even the better hotels can prove surprisingly affordable, and most places also take part in the **Gothenburg Package** scheme, which can cut costs further (see below).

Whenever you turn up, you shouldn't have any trouble finding accommodation, though in summer it's a good idea to book ahead if you're aiming to stay in one of the cheaper hotels, or in the most popular youth hostels.

Hotels and pensions

The **Gothenburg Package** scheme, coordinated by the tourist office, is a real bargain, as it bundles together accommodation, breakfast and a 24-hour Gothenburg Pass for as little as 540kr per person in a twin bedroom, with discounts for children sharing. Bookings for the Gothenburg Package have to be made by phoning or visiting the tourist office, or online at ⓦwww.goteborg.com; you can't get this offer by contacting the hotels direct.

Allén Parkgatan 10 ☏31/10 14 50, ⓦwww
.hotelallen.se. Very central, sensibly priced hotel close to Avenyn and the Old Town. Rates include room-service breakfasts and parking. ❸/❺

Avalon Kungstorget 9 ☏031/751 02 00, ⓦwww.avalonhotel.se. Gothenburg's latest design hotel stuffed full of pop art, mosaic pillars and lime-green and orange drapes – there's even a pool and sun terrace on the roof (open April–Sept). ❺/❻

Barken Viking Gullbergskajen ☏31/63 58 00, ⓦwww.liseberg.se. Moored by the Opera House, this 1906 Danish-built training ship is a charismatic and comfortable choice, with dark, cosy rooms and good service. ❺/❻

City Lorensbergsgatan 6 ☏31/708 40 00, ⓦwww
.cityhotelgbg.se. A cheapish and popular hotel, excellently positioned close to Avenyn. En-suite rooms cost 300kr more than those with shared facilities. ❷/❸

Clarion Collection Odin Odinsgatan 6 ☏031/745 22 00, ⓦwww.hotelodin.se. Offering designer studios rather than regular hotel rooms, this place is unique in Gothenburg. Each mini-apartment has its own kitchenette and the superior rooms boast a fully fitted kitchen, dining area and work space. ❺/❻

Eggers Drottningtorget ☏31/80 60 70, ⓦwww.bestwestern.se. The original station hotel and now part of the Best Western chain, this very characterful establishment has individually furnished bedrooms and a wealth of grand original features. One of the best-value central hotels, especially if you stay here using the Gothenburg Package. ❹/❻

Elite Plaza Västra Hamngatan 3 ☏31/720 40 40, ⓦwww.elite.se. With its magnificently opulent facade, painted ceilings and mosaic floors, this is the perfect place if money is no concern: a stunning blend of contemporary and classical design. ❺/❻

Lilton Föreningsgatan 9 ☏31/82 88 08, ⓦwww.hotellilton.com. Close to the Haga district, this is a small, old, ivy-covered place set among trees with very friendly, informal service. ❹/❺

Maria Erikssons Pensionat Chalmersgatan 27A ☏31/20 70 30, ⓦwww.mariaspensionat.nu. Just ten rooms, but well positioned on a road running parallel with Avenyn. Breakfast isn't included, and you can't stay as part of the Gothenburg Package. ❹

Radisson SAS Scandinavia Södra Hamngatan 59–65 ☏31/80 60 00, ⓦwww
.radissonsas.com. Opposite the train station, and exuding all the usual glitz: the atrium foyer is like a shopping mall with glass lifts and fountains; bedrooms are all pastel shades and birch wood. ❺/❻

Robinson Södra Hamngatan 2 ☏31/80 25 21, ⓦwww.hotelrobinson.se. Facing Brunnsparken, this cheap central hotel has classically furnished rooms, and still boasts its original facade – the building was part of the old Fürstenberg Palace. Not part of the Gothenburg Package scheme. ❷/❸

Scandic Europa Köpmansgatan 38 ☏31/751 65 00, ⓦwww.scandic-hotels.com. Reputedly the biggest hotel in Sweden, with 460 rooms and a massive facade attached to the Nordstan shopping centre. Very plush – all rooms are en suite with bath tubs – and breakfasts are huge. ❹/❻

Vanilj Kyrkogatan 38 ☏031/711 62 20, ⓦwww
.hotelvanilj.se. Housed in a former snuff factory from the 1800s, all 32 rooms in this small and friendly hotel are a delight: contemporary and elegant but with a touch of old-fashioned charm. At this price, they get snapped up fast so book early. ❸/❹

Hostels and private rooms

Gothenburg's cheapest accommodation options are either a **private room** (from 250kr per person in a double, 300kr for a single), bookable through the tourist office, or a bed in one of the **youth hostels**. All the hostels listed below are run by the STF and are open all year unless otherwise stated. They all have private double rooms (**❶**), too. It's wise to book ahead in summer.

Göteborgs Minihotel Tredje Långgatan 31 ☎31/24 10 23, ⊛www.minihotel.se. Open all year, this uninspiring hostel is nevertheless well placed for the alternative scene around the Linné area.

Kärralund Olbergsgatan 1 ☎31/84 02 00, ⊛www.liseberg.se. Four kilometres from the centre, close to Liseberg amusement park – take tram #5 to Welandergatan, in the direction of Torp. Non-smoking rooms available, plus cabins and a campsite (see below).

Kviberg Kvibergsvägen 5 ☎31/43 50 55, ⊛www .vandrarhem.com. In Gamlestad, 10min by tram #6, #7 or #11 from Central Station. Cheap private rooms (sleeping 1–6) with bunk beds and shared facilities.

Masthuggsterrassen Masthuggsterrassen 8 ☎31/42 48 20, ⊛www.mastenvandrarhem.com.

Up the steps from Masthuggstorget and a couple of minutes' walk from the Stena Line ferry terminal from Denmark.

Slottsskogen Vegagatan 21 ☎31/42 65 20, ⊛www.sov.nu. Superbly appointed and well-designed family-run hostel, just 2min walk from Linnégatan and not far from Slottsskogsparken. Take tram #1 or #2 to Olivedalsgatan.

Stigbergssliden Stigbergssliden 10 ☎31/24 16 20, ⊛www.hostel-gothenburg.com. Excellent hostel, well placed for ferries to or from Denmark, being just west of the Linné area, down Första Långgatan. All rooms have basins, and there's disabled access, laundry facilities and a pleasant back courtyard.

Campsites and cabins

Two of the following campsites also provide **cabins**, which are worth considering, especially if there are more than two of you. Facilities are invariably squeaky clean and in good working order – there's usually a well-equipped kitchen, too – but you'll have to pay extra for bedding. Prices for cabins are given below; if you want to **camp**, you'll pay around 100kr for two people in July or August (50kr the rest of year).

Askims Strand ☎31/28 62 61, ⊛www.liseberg .se. Set beside sandy beaches 12km from the centre; bus #80 towards Snipen. Open late April to early Sept; two-bed cabins (1000kr).

Kärralund Olbergsgatan ☎31/84 02 00, ⊛www .liseberg.se. Four kilometres from the centre, close to Liseberg amusement park – take tram #5 to Welandergatan, in the direction of Torp. Set among

forest and lakes, it's open all year; two-bed cabins (1250kr). Massive discounts outside June–Aug.

Lilleby Havsbad ☎31/56 50 66, ℗56 16 05. About an hour from the city centre in Torslanda (bus #121 from Centralstation and change to #23 towards Silvik at Torslanda torg); the splendid seaside location is some compensation for the trek. May–Aug only.

The City

Everything of interest in Gothenburg lies south of the **Göta River**, and there's rarely any need to cross the water. This is a fairly compact city, and easy to get around, so you can cover most of the sights in just a day or two, although to get the most from your stay, allow a few more days and slow your pace down to a stroll – which will put you in step with the locals.

At the heart of the city is the historic **Old Town**, and while Gothenburg's attractions are by no means restricted to this area, its picturesque elegance makes it the best place to start. Tucked between the Göta River to the north and the zigzagging Rosenlunds Canal to the south, old Gothenburg's tight grid of streets is lined with impressive facades and boasts an interesting food market and a couple of worthwhile museums – the **City Museum** and, up by the harbour, the Maritime **maritime museum**.

Heading further south, **Avenyn** (officially Kungsportsavenyn) is Gothenburg's showcase boulevard, alive with showy restaurants and bars. However, it's the roads off Avenyn that hold the area's real interest, with trendy 24-hour café-bars and some of Gothenburg's best museums: in a small area called **Vasastan** to the southwest, you'll find the **Röhsska Design Museum** and, further south in **Götaplatsen**, the city **Konstmuseum**. For family entertainment day or night, the famous **Liseberg amusement park**, just to the southeast of Avenyn, has been pulling in the crowds (and throwing them about) since the 1920s.

Vasastan stretches west to **Haga**, the city's old working-class district, now thoroughly gentrified and fashionable. Haga Nygatan, the main thoroughfare, heads towards Linnégatan, the arterial road through the **Linné** district. The area is home to Gothenburg's most interesting evening haunts, with cafés, bars and restaurants dotted amongst long-established antique emporiums and sex shops. Further out, the rolling **Slottsskogsparken** holds the **Natural History Museum**, but is perhaps most appealing as a place to relax and enjoy the sun.

The Old Town and harbour

The **Old Town** is divided in two by the **Stora Hamn Canal**, to the north of which are most of the main sights and the harbour, where the decaying shipyards make for a dramatic backdrop. The streets south of the Stora Hamn, stretching down to the Rosenlunds Canal, are perfect for an afternoon's leisurely stroll, with some quirky cafés, food markets and junk shops to dip into. Overlooking the Stora Hamn is Gothenburg's main square, **Gustav Adolfs Torg**, the best place to start your explorations.

North of the Stora Hamn Canal

At the centre of stately **Gustav Adolfs Torg**, a copper statue of the city's founder, Gustav Adolf, points ostentatiously at the ground where he reputedly declared "Here I will build my city." The statue is a copy, however: the German-made original was kidnapped on its way to Sweden and the Gothenburgers commissioned a new one rather than pay the ransom.

To the west of the square stands the **Rådhus**. Beyond its rather dull classical colon-naded facade, the interior of its extension was designed by the innovative function-alist architect E.G. Asplund in 1936 and retains its original glass lifts, mussel-shaped drinking fountains and huge areas of laminated aspen. Facing the canal is the white, double-columned 1842 **Börshuset**, the former stock exchange.

Heading north from the square along the filled-in canal of Östra Hamngatan leads you to the **Nordstan shopping centre**, Sweden's biggest. Despite several attempts to jazz it up, it remains a depressingly bland design; the shopping is good, though, and you might also venture inside to visit the tourist kiosk or one of the ferry company offices. It's worth cutting through Nordstan to see the city's impressive **Central Station**. One of the oldest in the country, dating from 1856, it retains its original facade and boasts a grand and marvellously preserved interior. Look out for the wood beam-ends in the ticket hall, each one carved into the likeness of a city council member of the day.

At its far end, Östra Hamngatan runs into **Lilla Bommen** (until the completion of the large traffic tunnel that will divert the ring road under the city centre, it may be better to use the pedestrian bridge from the northern end of the Nordstan shopping centre). Here, Gothenburg's industrial decline comes together with its artistic regeneration to dramatic visual effect: to the west, the cranes of dormant shipyards loom across the sky, a backdrop to industrial-themed sculptures in bronze and pink granite dotted along the waterfront. The **Göteborgsoperan** (Opera House: daily noon–6pm; guided tours late June to mid-Aug daily 3pm; ☎031/10 80 00, ⓦwww.opera.se) to the left was designed with conscious industrial styling; phone ahead or contact the tourist office for information about tours. To the right, **Utkiken** (Lookout Point: June–Aug daily 11am–4pm; Sept–May Mon–Fri 11am–4pm; 30kr), designed by the Scottish architect Ralph Erskine in the late 1980s, is an 86-metre-high office block taking the form of a half-used red lipstick. Its top storey offers panoramic views of the city and harbour.

Boats leave Lilla Bommen harbour for the popular half-hour excursion to the island fortress of **Nya Elfsborg** early May to Aug daily every 90min 9/10am–4/5pm; 30min; 140kr). Built in the seventeenth century to defend the harbour and the city, the surviving buildings have been turned into a **museum** and café. There are tours in English (included in the price of the boat trip) given by guides in period dress around the square tower, chapel and prison cells.

Just west along the quay is **Maritiman** (March & Nov Fri–Sun 10am–4pm; April, May & Oct daily 10am–4pm; June–Sept daily 10am–6pm; 80kr; ⓦwww.maritiman .se), the self-proclaimed "biggest floating marine museum in the world". An interesting experience, even for non-enthusiasts, it comprises nineteen boats, including a 1915 lightship, a submarine and a fire float, giving a glimpse of how seamen lived and worked on board, plus exhibits on Gothenburg's long-gone shipbuilding era. There's a good café and restaurant here, too.

A couple of blocks further south, the **Stadsmuseum** (City Museum: Tues–Sun 10am–5pm, Wed 10am–8pm; 40kr; ⓦwww.stadsmuseum.goteborg.se) is Gothenburg's primary museum. Located at Norra Hamngatan 12, it's housed in Ostindiska Huset, the offices, store and auction house that were constructed in 1750 for the enormously influential **Swedish East India Company**. Granted sole Swedish rights to trade with China in 1731, the company monopolized Far East commerce for over eighty years, the only condition being that the spices, silk and porcelain it brought back were to be sold in Gothenburg. The museum itself is well worth a browse, not least for its rich interior, a mix of stone pillars, stained glass and frescoes. Head first to the third floor, where there are exhibitions on the East India Company, allowing a look at the renovated auction hall. The section devoted to industry here is also impressive, a well-designed exhibition relating Gothenburg's twentieth-century history, with displays on shipping and working conditions in the textile factories at the beginning of the century.

South of the Stora Hamn Canal

Across Stora Hamn just to the west of the Stadsmuseum lies **Lilla Torg**, with its statue of Jonas Alstromer, who introduced the potato to Sweden in the eighteenth century. Walk on to the quayside at **Stenpiren**, the spot where hundreds of emigrants said their last goodbyes before sailing off to the United States. The original granite **Delaware Monument** was carted off to America in the early twentieth century, and it wasn't until 1938 that celebrated sculptor Carl Mille cast a replacement in bronze, which stands here looking out to sea.

Back at Lilla Torg, walk down Västra Hamngatan, which leads off the southern side of the square, to the city's **Cathedral** (Mon–Fri 8am–6pm, Sat 9am–4pm, Sun 10am–3pm). Built in 1827 (the two previous cathedrals were destroyed by fires at a rate of one a century), four giant sandstone columns stand at the portico, and inside there's an opulent gilded altarpiece. The plain white walls concentrate your eyes on the unusual post-Resurrection cross, devoid of a Jesus, whose gilded grave clothes are strewn below. Another quirky feature are the twin glassed-in verandas that run down either side, designed for the bishop's "private conversations".

Continuing east past the cathedral and north, on Östra Hamngatan, towards Stora Hamn Canal, the leafy square known as **Brunnsparken** soon comes into view, with Gustav Adolfs Torg just across the canal. The sedate house facing the square (now the snazzy *Palace* restaurant and nightclub) was once home to Pontus and Gothilda Fürstenberg, the city's leading arts patrons in the late nineteenth century, who converted the top floor into an art gallery, the first in Gothenburg to be lit with electric light. They later donated their entire collection – the biggest batch of Nordic paintings in the country – to the city's Konstmuseum. As a tribute to the Fürstenbergs, the museum has made over the *Palace*'s top floor into an exact replica of the original gallery (see p.407) – you can wander upstairs and see the richly ornate plasterwork and gilding much as it was.

Marking the southern perimeter of old Gothenburg, the meandering Rosenlunds Canal follows the spiky contours of the former city walls, and its banks make for a fine twenty-minute stroll past pretty waterside views and a number of interesting diversions.

Just east of Brunnsparken, **Stora Nygatan** wends its way south along the canal's most scenic stretch, with classical buildings stuccoed in cinnamon and cream on one side, and the green expanse of Trädgårdsföreningen park on the other. Shortly, you pass **Kungsportsplatsen**, in the centre of which stands a useful landmark, a sculpture known as the *Copper Mare* – though whoever gave it its name obviously knew more about metallurgy than physiology. Also on the square is the main tourist office. A few minutes further on, and a block in from the canal at Kungstorget (the square adjacent to Kungsportsplatsen) is **Stora Saluhallen** (Mon–Fri 10am–6pm, Sat 10am–2pm), a pretty, barrel-roofed indoor market built in the 1880s. Busy and full of atmosphere, it's a great place to wander around; there's a flower market outside.

Five minutes from here is another food market, the neo-Gothic **Feskekôrkan**, or "Fish Church" (Tues–Thurs 9am–5pm, Fri 9am–6pm, Sat 9am–1.30pm). Despite its undeniably ecclesiastical appearance, the closest this 1874 building gets to religion is in the devotion shown by the fish lovers who come to buy and sell here. Inside, every kind of fish lies gaping in gleaming, pungent mounds of silver, pink and black flesh.

Avenyn and around

From the park, the wide cobbled length of Kungportsavenyn runs all the way southeast to Götaplatsen. Known more simply as **Avenyn**, this is the city's liveliest – if most blandly showy – thoroughfare, lined with nineteenth-century buildings, almost all of their ground floors converted into cafés, bars or restaurants. Gothenburg's young and beautiful strut up and down and sip overpriced drinks at tables that spill onto the street from mid-spring till September. It's enjoyable to sit here and watch life go by, but for all its glamour most of the tourist-oriented shops and brasseries are interchangeable and the grandeur of the city's industrial past is better evoked in the less spoiled mansions along roads such as Parkgatan, at right angles to Avenyn.

Vasastan, Götaplatsen and Liseberg

Once you've had your fill of Avenyn, take one of the roads off to the west and wander into the district of Vasastan, where the streets are lined with fine nineteenth-century and National Romantic architecture, and the cafés are cheaper and more laid-back. On Vasagatan, the main street through the area, is the excellent **Röhsska Design Museum** at 37–39, Sweden's only museum of applied arts (Tues noon–8pm, Wed–Fri noon–5pm, Sat & Sun 11am–5pm; 40kr; Ⓦwww.designmuseum.se). Built in 1916, it's an aesthete's Aladdin's cave, each floor concentrating on different areas of decorative and functional art, from early dynasty Chinese ceramics to European arts and crafts of the sixteenth century. The first floor holds an especially interesting section devoted to twentieth-century design. The exhibition ends with a brilliant film about consumerism and the need for anarchy in order to achieve true happiness.

At the top of Avenyn, **Götaplatsen** is modern Gothenburg's main square, its focal point Carl Milles' **Poseidon**, a giant bronze nude with the physique of a body-builder and a staggeringly ugly face; the size of the figure's penis caused outrage when the sculpture was unveiled in 1930 and it was subsequently dramatically reduced. From the front, Poseidon appears to be squeezing the daylights out of a large fanged fish – a symbol of local trade – but if you climb the steps of the **Konserthuset** (Concert House) to the right, it becomes clear that Milles won the battle over Poseidon's manhood to stupendous effect.

Behind *Poseidon* looms the impressive **Konstmuseum** (Art Museum: Tues & Thurs 11am–6pm, Wed 11am–9pm, Fri–Sun 11am–5pm; 40kr; Ⓦwww .konstmuseum.goteborg.se), whose massive, symmetrical facade is reminiscent of

1930s Fascist architecture. It is one of the city's finest museums, and it is easy to spend half a day absorbing the diverse and extensive collections. The **Hasselblad Centre** (Ⓦwww.hasselbladcenter.se) on the ground floor shows excellent changing photographic exhibitions, while upstairs there are postwar and contemporary Scandinavian paintings, a room full of French Impressionists, and a collection of Italian and Spanish paintings from the sixteenth to eighteenth centuries. Best of all, though, are the **Fürstenberg Galleries** on the sixth floor, which celebrate the work of some of Scandinavia's most prolific and revered artists from the early twentieth century. Well-known paintings by Anders Zorn and Carl Wilhelmson depict the seasons and landscapes of the Nordic countries and evoke a vivid picture of life a hundred years ago. Keep an eye out for Ernst Josephson's sensitive portraits and a couple of Hugo Birger paintings depicting the interior of the Fürstenberg Gallery. Also worth a look is the room of Carl Larsson's fantastical and bright wall-sized canvases.

Just a few minutes' walk southeast from Götaplatsen lies Sweden's largest amusement park, **Liseberg amusement park** (daily: late April to May & Sept 3pm–10pm; June 1pm–10pm; July & Aug 11am–midnight; 70kr, under-7s free; all-day ride pass 290kr, or buy tickets as you go – a coupon costs 20kr, each attraction requires 1–3 coupons; Ⓦwww.liseberg.se). Dating from 1923, it's a league away from today's neon and plastic entertainment complexes, with flowers, trees, fountains and clusters of lights – more Hansel and Gretel than Disneyland. Old and young dance to live bands, and while the young and raucous predominate at night, it's all good-humoured.

Near Liseberg, a glass, wood and concrete building draped against a hill holds the impressive **Universeum** nature and science discovery centre (daily: late June to late Aug 10am–7pm; late Aug to late June 10am–6pm; 145kr; Ⓦwww.universeum .se). Water is the main theme: starting with a glacier at the top of the building, 3km of paths follow its journey through a variety of Swedish landscapes to the Baltic Sea. There are detailed English texts about the flora and fauna of each environment. The tour ends in a tropical rainforest with free-flying birds and butterflies. Huge sharks glide around the walk-through oceanarium, while an open tank nearby allows you to stroke a friendly ray. There are good-value cafés on the roof or in the atrium.

Next door stands the brand new **Världkulturmuseet** (Museum of World Culture: Tues & Fri–Sun noon–5pm, Wed & Thurs noon–9pm; 40kr; Ⓦwww .varldskulturmuseet.se), a successful blend of public meeting place and museum. The changing exhibitions focus on current themes seen from an international perspective – recent displays have focused on sexuality in India, human trafficking around the world and the native people who live along the Orinoco. There's a good café, a theatre and a cinema, too; check the website for the programme.

Haga and Linné

West of Avenyn, and a ten-minute stroll up Vasagatan (or tram #2 or #13), lies the district of **Haga**, the city's oldest working-class area, now transformed into the Greenwich Village of Gothenburg. Centred on **Haga Nygatan**, Haga is one of the city's most picturesque quarters, its cobbled streets lined with pricey alternative-type cafés and antique clothes shops, frequented by right-on and well-off 20- and 30-somethings. Although there are a couple of good restaurants along Haga Nygatan, this is really somewhere to come during the day, when tables are put out on the street and the atmosphere is friendly and villagey, if a little self-consciously fashionable.

West of Haga is the cosmopolitan district of **Linné**, named after the botanist Carl von Linné (better known by the Latinized version of his name, Linnaeus), who originated the system of plant classification that's used the world over. Recent years have seen so many new cafés and restaurants spring up along **Linnégatan** – which runs along the western end of Haga Nygatan – that this street of tall, Dutch-style buildings has become a second Avenyn, but without the attitude.

Eating

Gothenburg has a multitude of **eating** places catering for every taste and budget. There's a whole host of pan-European eateries that draw on Swedish staples such as herring and salmon dishes, good breads and, in summer, glorious soft fruits. Naturally, there are great fish restaurants, including some of the most exclusive establishments in town, while for less costly eating you'll find a growing number of low-priced pasta places, alongside the staple pizza parlours and burger bars.

Café life has really come into its own in Gothenburg, with a profusion of places throughout the city joining the traditional *konditori*. Nowadays, it's easy to stroll from one café to another at any time of day or night, and tuck into enormous sandwiches and gorgeous cakes.

Markets and supermarkets

The bustling, historic **Saluhallen** at Kungstorget is a delightful sensory experience, with a huge range of meat, fish, fruit, vegetables and delectable breads; there are also a couple of cheap coffee and snack bars here. **Saluhall Briggen**, on the corner of Tredje Långgatan and Nordhemsgatan in the Linné area, is more continental and much smaller than Saluhallen, specializing in high-quality meats, fish, cheeses and mouthwatering deli delights. Also in Linné, at Övra Husargatan 12, Delitalia is a terrific Italian delicatessen selling anything you could want for a picnic. The Konsum supermarket at Avenyn 26 (Mon–Sat 9am–11pm, Sun 11am–11pm) has a wide range of the usual staples and a good deli counter.

Cafés and restaurants

If you want to avoid paying over the odds, it's generally a good idea to steer clear of Avenyn itself (where prices are much higher than in Haga or Linné), and to eat your main meal at **lunchtime**. It's usually necessary to **book** tables, so we've given phone numbers accordingly.

The Old Town

Ahlströms Konditori Korsgatan 2. Dating from 1901, this traditional-style café/bakery is very much of the old school, as are many of its patrons. While modernization has watered down the original features, it's still worth a visit for its good selection of cakes, plus lunches for 79kr.

Café du Nord Kungstorget 3. Serving the best meatballs in town: four meatballs with mashed potato and lingonberries costs just 65kr. Alternatively, buy them individually and add green salad, mash and lingonberries.

E.t.c. Vasaplatsen 4 ☎031/13 06 02. This cool, elegant, grey-painted basement is the best place in town for superb home-made pasta from 120kr. It also has good meat and fish dishes in the range 195–235kr.

Fröken Olssons Kafe Östra Larmgatan 14. Ecological coffee, lactose-free drinks, vegetarian and vegan meals are the specialities at this right-on café decked out in orange tiles and swirly wallpaper. Look out also for the truly enormous cheesecakes in silver cake trays.

Gabriel Feskekörkan fish market ☎31/13 90 51. Excellent fish restaurant overlooking the stalls below, with mains from around 300kr.

Greta's Drottninggatan 35 ☎031/13 69 49. Stylish, casual and popular bar-restaurant drawing a mixed gay and straight clientele. The wide-ranging menu has fish, meat and vegetarian options with mains in the range 150–200kr.

Mauritz Kaffehus Fredgatan 2. Small and unassuming café run by the great-grandson of its founder, who began importing coffee into Gothenburg in 1888. Come here for espressos and cappuccinos; there's hardly room to sit down, but the owner will tell you that standing makes the ambience more Italian.

Avenyn and around

28+ Götabergsgatan 28 ☎31/20 21 61. Very fine French-style gourmet restaurant, whose name refers to the fat percentage of its renowned cheese, sold in the shop near the entrance (9am–11pm). Service is excellent; mains starts at 325kr. Closed Sun.

Café Teatergatan Teatergatan 36. Somewhat artsy place where you can sit at one of the black-and-white swivel chairs and try sandwiches and salads.

Eva's Paley Avenyn 39. A popular sprawling café-bar with great cakes and muffins, reasonably priced food and Avenyn's largest and nicest terrace.

Frågetecknet Södravägen 20 ☏ 031/16 00
30. Very popular spot just a minute's walk from
Götaplatsen, with a name that translates as "the
question mark". Eat out in the conservatory, or
inside to watch the chefs at work, carefully
preparing Italian-influenced food.
Junggrens Café Avenyn 37. One of only a couple
of decently priced Avenyn cafés, with good snacks
and sandwiches. Atmospheric and convivial, it's
been run for decades by a charismatic old Polish
woman and her sulky staff.
Lai Wa Storgatan 11 ☏ 031/711 02 39. One of
Gothenburg's better Chinese restaurants, with a wide
variety of dishes (from 98kr) – try the Peking soup.
Smaka Vasaplatsen 3 ☏ 31/13 22 47. Traditional Swedish dishes (mains 140–180kr)
enjoyed by a lively, young crowd in a striking blue
interior.
Tintin Engelbrektsgatan 22. Very busy 24hr café
with mounds of food and cheap coffee, and a laid-
back student atmosphere.

Haga and Linné
Bitter Linnégatan 59 ☏ 031/24 91 20. Upmarket
Swedish home cooking at great-value prices: the
classic of the week is 126kr; otherwise mains are
150–200kr.
Café Kringlan Haga Nygatan 13. The best spot in
town for wonderful chocolate pies, bagels, strudels,
generous open sandwiches and people-watching.
Great breakfast and lunch deals.
Cyrano Prinsgatan 7 ☏ 31/14 31 10. This
superb, authentic Provençal bistro is a
must, specializing in wood-fired pizzas and French
cooking with three-course pizza (105kr) and meat
(240kr) menus. There's a smaller, more central
sister restaurant at Viktoriagatan 26.
Hemma Hos Haga Nygatan 12 ☏ 31/13 40 90.
Popular restaurant full of quaint old furniture,

serving upmarket Swedish food including fish
dishes (mains from 140kr) till midnight. Closed Sun.
Hos Pelle Djupedalsgatan 2 ☏ 31/12 10 31. This
sophisticated wine bar and restaurant off
Linnégatan offering modern Swedish fare has
three-course menus for 350kr where the starter
and dessert (each consisting of three small dishes)
is set, allowing you to choose the main.
Linnéterrassen Linnégatan 32 ☏ 031/24
08 90. Upmarket Swedish home cooking
served in a beautifully restored wooden house with
wooden wall panelling and chandeliers or on the
extensive open-air terrace. Exceptional value with
mains in the range 95–230kr, including a herring
platter with *akvavit*, meatballs, fish gratin and pan-
fried pork with onions and potatoes.
Pasta Gambero Övre Husargatan 5 ☏ 31/13 78
38. The best of a number of good, reasonably
priced Italian eateries on this long street just south
of Skansparken. The servings are generous and the
service very obliging.
Rumpanbar Linnégatan 38B ☏ 031/775 83 00.
Lovely Mediterranean-style café-restaurant on the
up-and-coming section of Linnégatan, with outdoor
seating and great-value meals (mains from 129kr,
pizza from 92kr).
Sjöbaren Haga Nygatan 27 ☏ 031/711 97 80.
Small fish and shellfish restaurant on the ground
floor of a traditional governor's house building.
Moderate prices around 140kr per main dish
Solrosen Kaponjargatan 4a ☏ 31/711 66 97. The
oldest vegetarian restaurant in Gothenburg, this is
the place to come for well-prepared veggie and
vegan delights; the *dagens* costs 75kr including the
salad buffet.
Thai Garden Andra Långgatan 18
☏ 031/12 76 60. Nothing special to look
at, but big portions and excellent service at good
prices – stuff yourself silly at the 70kr lunch buffet.

Drinking

There's an excellent choice of places to **drink** in Gothenburg, but aside from a small
number of British- and Irish-style pubs, even the hippest bars also serve food, and have
more of a restaurant atmosphere. Although there are a number of long-established bars
in the Old Town, the atmosphere in this area is generally a bit low-key at night.

The Old Town
Bishops Arms Västra Larmgatan 1 (and Avenyn
36). Attached to the glamorous *Elite Plaza*
hotel, this pub boasts a wide range of beers. It's
all faux "olde Englishe" inside, but very nicely
done.
Dubliners Östra Hamngatan 50B. For a while now,
Swedes have been overtaken with a nostalgia for

all things old and Irish – or at least a Swedish
interpretation of what's old and Irish. This is the
most popular exponent.
The Palace Brunnsparken. The rather splendid
former home of the Fürstenbergs and their art
galleries (see p.407) is a very lively spot, with
bands on Thurs.

Avenyn and around

7:an Södra Larmgatan 7. Pronounced *shoo-ann* and meaning simply "number seven", this is one of the city's better beer halls, located close to Stora Saluhallen. The interior is dark, intimate and old-fashioned in feel – a quintessential Gothenburg experience.

Brasserie Lipp Avenyn 8. No longer the hippest place on Avenyn, *Lipp* is expensive and so attracts a slightly older crowd – but a crowd it is, especially during summer.

Gamle Port Östra Larmgatan 18. The city's oldest watering hole, with cosy leather chairs in the downstairs pub and a loud and raucous disco upstairs playing 80s music and techno.

Nivå Avenyn 9. Stylish, popular bar with a modern interior heavy on black and white tiling and several dancefloors for a fun mix of 1980s classics, disco and R'n'B.

Haga and Linné

Beefeater Inn Plantagegatan 1. One of the bevvy of British-oriented neighbourhood pubs that are very in vogue with Swedes generally. This one really goes overboard, with a stylistic mishmash of red-telephone-box doors, tartan walls and staff in kilts.

Gillestugan Järntorget 6. Cosy and panelled without being over the top, this bar has plenty of outdoor seating and offers full meals such as beef fillet or seafood burgers at reasonable prices.

Rose & Crown Avenyn 6. Perfect location on Avenyn and consequently this pseudo British pub really draws the crowds, who love the live sports matches, karaoke and Saturday night fever 1970s disco.

The Rover Andra Långgatan 12. Run-of-the-mill Anglo-Irish pub selling Boddingtons, with other lagers, ales and cider on tap, plus a wide range of bottled beers. Lamb, steaks and trout dishes from 70kr.

Nightlife and entertainment

There are plenty of other things to do in Gothenburg at night besides drink. The city has a brisk **live music scene** – jazz, rock and classical – as well as the usual cinema and theatre opportunities. Pick up the Saturday edition of the *Göteborgs-Posten* newspaper, whose weekend supplement, *Två Dagar*, has the latest listings of bars, concerts and clubs.

Clubs

During the past few years, Gothenburg's old, mediocre **clubs** have been usurped in popularity by a cluster of smaller, laid-back joints around Viktoriagatan and Storgatan in Vasastan.

Bliss Magasingatan 3. Next door to *Uppåt Framåt*, this place is regularly filled to the gills with revellers over 28 and is currently one of the hottest clubs in town, with a mix of live music and DJs – be prepared to queue.

Klara Viktoriagatan 1A. A long-established and likeable bar with live music and a more varied mix of people and conversation – when the latter can be heard at all. Mon are 1980s nights, Tues has reggae and Wed sees jamming sessions with local DJs.

Rondo Liseberg amusement park. Reputedly has Sweden's biggest dancefloor, packed out with locals of all ages, and blends contemporary bands with foxtrot evenings, the latter usually

encouraging the whole place onto the dancefloor. Great fun.

Trädgår'n Nya Allén 11. One of the city's liveliest haunts, this hip club offers five bars, a casino, a disco playing house and party favourites and show bands.

Uppåt Framåt Magasingatan 3. A trendy club and bar that's really drawing the crowds from across town for its live music nights and resident DJs playing house music.

Valand Vasagatan 3. Perhaps the most popular place in town, with three bars and a club floor.

Vasastan Victoriagatan 2A. A very popular, suave club where confident 20- to 30-somethings bask in the mellow atmosphere.

Live music

Gothenburg's large student community means there are plenty of local **live bands** who tend to play in a cluster of bars in the city centre. The best nights to catch a live performance are Friday and Saturday. **Classical music** concerts are held regularly in the Konserthuset, Götaplatsen (☎031/726 53 90, ⓦwww.gso.se), and occasionally at Stadsteatern, Götaplatsen (☎031/708 71 00, ⓦwww.stadsteatern .goteborg.se; programme details from the tourist office). For opera, head to the renowned Göteborgsoperan at Christina Nilssons gata at the harbour (☏031/13 13 00, ⊛www.opera.se).

Jazzhuset Erik Dahlbergsgatan 3 ☏031/13 35 44. Puts on trad and Dixieland jazz plus swing, and is something of a pick-up joint for executives.
Nefertiti Hvitfeldtsplatsen 6 ☏031/711 15 33. The premier place for jazz in Gothenburg with modern jazz, big-band and folk music as well as reggae, blues and soul.

Sticky Fingers Kaserntorget 7 ☏031/701 07 17. A rock club supporting local talent, which hosts live bands several nights a week.
Storan Kungsparken 1 at the foot of Avenyn ☏031/60 45 00. Hosts frequent bands who're big on the club scene. Enter at the back of the theatre building.

Cinema

There are plenty of **cinemas** around the city, and English-language films (which make up the majority of what's shown) are always subtitled in Swedish, never dubbed. The most central complexes are Bio Palatset, Kungstorget 2 (☏031/774 22 90), and Bergakungen, at Skånegatan 16B (☏0771/11 12 13). For a great **art-house cinema**, check out Hagabio at Linnégatan 21 (☏031/42 88 10).

Listings

Airlines City Airline ⊛www.cityairline.com; Ryanair ⊛www.ryanair.com; SAS ⊛www.scandinavian.net.
Airports Gothenburg City airport ☏031/92 60 60, ⊛www.goteborgcityairport.se; Landvetter ☏031/94 10 00, ⊛www.lfv.se.
Buses City bus information from Västtrafik on ☏0771/11 43 00, ⊛www.vasttrafik.se. Long-distance buses: SwebusExpress ⊛www.swebus express.se; Säfflebussen ⊛www.safflebussen.se.
Car rental Avis ⊛www.avis.se; Europcar ⊛www.europcar.se; Hertz ⊛www.hertz.se.
Dentist Akuttandvården, Odinsgatan 10 ☏031/80 78 00.
Doctor Sahlgrenska Hospital at Per Dubbsgatan (☏031/342 10 00). City Akuten, a private clinic, has doctors on duty 8am–6pm at Drottninggatan 45 (☏031/10 10 10).
Emergency services Ambulance, police, and fire brigade are on ☏112.
Exchange Forex exchange offices Centralstation, Avenyn 22, Nordstan shopping centre and

Kungsportsplatsen. More information at ⊛www.forex.se.
Gay information RFSL Stora Badhusgatan 6 ☏031/13 83 00, ⊛www.rfsl.se.
Internet access Sidewalk Express have lots of internet points across Gothenburg, for example, at Centralstation and at most 7-Eleven supermarkets. See ⊛www.sidewalkexpress.se for complete listings. One hour costs 19kr.
Laundry At Nordstan Service Centre inside the Nordstan shopping centre.
Left luggage Lockers at Centralstation.
Pharmacy Apoteket Vasen, Götgatan 12, in Nordstan shopping centre ☏031/80 44 10. Daily 8am–10pm.
Police Spannmålsgatan 6 ☏031/739 20 00.
Swimming The biggest and best pool is Valhallabadet, Valhallagatan 3 (☏031/61 19 56), next to the Scandinavium sports complex.
Train information SJ trains ☏0771/75 75 75, ⊛www.sj.se.

Around Gothenburg

North of Gothenburg, the rugged and picturesque **Bohuslän coast** attracts countless Scandinavian and German tourists each summer. However, the crowds can't detract from the wealth of natural beauty and the many dinky fishing villages that make this stretch of country well worth a few days' exploration. The most popular destination is the island town of **Marstrand**, with its impressive fortress and richly ornamented ancient buildings.

The Bohuslän coast

A chain of **islands** linked by a thread of bridges and short ferry crossings make up the county of **Bohuslän** and, despite the summer crowds, it's still easy enough to find a private spot to swim or bathe. Sailing is a popular pastime among the Swedes, many of whom have summer cottages here, and you'll see yachts gliding through the water all the way along the coast. Another feature of the Bohuslän landscape you can't fail to miss is the large number of **churches** – for long stretches these are the only buildings of note. Dating from the 1840s to 1910, they are mostly simple white structures with little variation in design.

Travelling up the coast by **train** is feasible, and though **buses** also cover the coast, services are sketchy and infrequent. If you really want to explore Bohuslän's most dramatic scenery, you need a **car**. From Gothenburg, the E6 motorway is the quickest route north, with designated scenic routes leading off it every few kilometres.

Marstrand

About 50km northwest of Gothenburg, the island town of **MARSTRAND** buzzes with summer activity, as holidaymakers flock in to sail, bathe and take tours around the impressive castle. With ornate wooden buildings lining the bustling harbour, Marstrand is a delightful place and is easily visited on a day-trip from Gothenburg.

Founded under Norwegian rule in the thirteenth century, the town achieved remarkable prosperity through herring fishing in the following century; rich herring pickings, however, eventually led to greed and corruption, and Marstrand became known as the most immoral town in Scandinavia. The murder of a cleric in 1586 was seen as an omen: soon after, the whole town burned to the ground and the herring mysteriously disappeared. The fish – and Marstrand's prosperity – eventually returned in the 1770s, only to disappear again, for good, forty years later. By the 1820s, the old herring salting houses had been converted into bathhouses, and Marstrand had been reborn as a fashionable bathing resort.

▲ The Bohuslän coast

From the harbour, turn left, and it's a lovely walk up a cobbled lane, past the Renaissance-style *Grand Hotel*, to a small square surrounded by exquisite wooden houses painted in pastel shades. Across the square is the squat, white **St Maria kyrka**; beyond, the streets climb steeply to the castle, **Carlstens Fästning** (early to mid-June & mid- to late Aug daily 11am–4pm; mid-June to mid-Aug 11am–6pm; rest of year Sat & Sun 11am–4pm; 70kr including guided tour; for English-language tours, book ahead on ☎0303/602 65; ⓦwww.carlsten.se), an imposing sweep of stone walls solidly wedged into the rough rock. You could easily spend half a day clambering around the walls and down the weather-worn rocks to the sea, where there are always plenty of places to bathe in private. The most interesting tales spun by the **tour guides** are related down in the grim prison cells: Carlstens' most noted prisoner was **Lasse Maja**, a thief who got rich by dressing as a woman and seducing rich farmers. A sort of Swedish Robin Hood, Maja was known for giving his spoils to the poor. Once incarcerated here, he ingratiated himself with the officers via his impressive cooking skills, a talent that, after 26 years, won him a pardon from the king.

Some of the tours (depending on the guide; ask in advance) lead up through the castle's hundred-metre tower, built in 1658. The views from the top are stunning, but you'll have to be fit to get there, as the steep, spiral climb is quite exhausting. Once a year, at the end of July, the fortress hosts a huge **festival**, with an eighteenth-century-style procession and live theatrical performances. It's a colourful occasion and well worth catching.

Practicalities

Bus #312 leaves from Nils Ericson Terminalen in Gothenburg for Marstrand hourly (7.25am–6.40pm; 1hr). By **car**, take the E6 north out of Gothenburg, and then Route 168 west, leading right to the ferry stop; cars are not permitted on Marstrand, so you must park at the ferry quay on the island of Koön and travel across to Marstrand as a foot passenger (every 15min; 5min; 20kr). The **tourist office** at Hamngatan 33 (June Mon–Fri 9.30am–4.30pm, Sat & Sun noon–4pm, late June to early Aug Mon–Fri 9am–6pm, Sat & Sun 11am–5pm; mid-Aug to May Mon–Fri 10am–4pm; ☎0303/600 87, ⓦwww.marstrand.se) can book **private rooms** in old barracks for a minimum of two people from 370kr per room, and apartments at 600kr for two people.

The island's **youth hostel**, *Båtellet* (☎0303/600 10, Ⓔmarstrandsvarmbadhus @telia.com; dorm beds 225kr, double rooms ❷) is situated in an atmospheric old bath house overlooking the sea, and has a sauna, washing facilities, a swimming pool and a restaurant (see below). Of the several very pleasant **hotels** on the island, the finest is the 1892-built *Grand* at Rådhusgatan (☎0303/603 22, ⓦwww .grandmarstrand.se; ❻). *Nautic*, Långgatan 6 (☎0303/610 30, ⓦwww.hotelnautic .com; ❹), is rather simpler in style, but perfectly adequate.

Eating out is a major sport on Marstrand, but it comes at a price. About the most interesting place to eat on the island is the *American Bar*, opened in 1919, overlooking the harbour, which serves good but pricey meat and fish meals with mains costing 150–250kr. Another very popular choice is *Lasse-Maja Krog*, in a jolly, yellow-painted house on the harbourfront, whose wide-ranging meat and fish menu has mains from 150kr, as well as pizzas at around 100kr. Decent meals are also served in *Drott*, the rather fine restaurant attached to the youth hostel: pasta dishes cost around 100kr; meat and seafood 150–200kr. Or try the gourmet restaurant in the classic old *Societetshuset* (☎0303/606 00), close to the youth hostel. The cheapest place to eat is the *Skepps Handel*, at the harbour at the corner of Drottninggatan. At night, the *American Bar* is the best **drinking** haunt.

Travel details

Trains

Gothenburg to: Kalmar (1 daily; 4hr);
Karlskrona (2 daily; 4hr 20min); Karlstad
(5 daily; 2hr 50min); Luleå (1 daily; 19hr); Malmö
(hourly; 3hr); Stockholm (hourly; 3hr by X2000,
5hr InterCity); Östersund (1 daily; 12hr); Umeå
(1 daily; 14hr 30min).

Buses

Gothenburg to: Falun (1–2 daily; 8–10hr 30min);
Halmstad (5 daily; 3hr 40min); Jönköping (8 daily;
2hr 10min); Karlstad (3 daily; 4hr); Mariestad
(3 daily; 2hr 40min); Marstrand (hourly; 1hr);
Norrköping (6 daily; 4hr 40min); Stockholm
(6 daily; 7hr).

Mariestad to: Jönköping (2–4 daily; 2hr); Karlstad
(3 daily; 3hr); Örebro (3 daily; 1hr 30min).

International buses

Gothenburg to: Copenhagen via Kastrup airport
(10 daily; 4hr); Oslo (10 daily; 4hr).

International trains

Gothenburg to: Copenhagen via Kastrup airport
(12 daily; 4hr); Oslo (3 daily; 4hr).

International ferries

Gothenburg to: Frederikshavn, Denmark
(4–8 daily; 2hr by catamaran, 3hr 15min by ferry);
Kiel, Germany (1 daily; 14hr).

3.3

The southwest

T here is a real historical interest to the **southwestern** provinces of Halland, Skåne and Blekinge, not least in the towns and cities that line the coast. The flatlands and fishing ports south of Gothenburg were traded almost constantly between Denmark and Sweden from the fourteenth to seventeenth centuries, and several fortresses today bear witness to the region's medieval buffer status.

Halland, facing Denmark, has a coastline of smooth sandy beaches and bare, granite outcrops, punctuated by a number of small towns. Most charismatic is the old society bathing resort of **Varberg**, dominated by its tremendous thirteenth-century

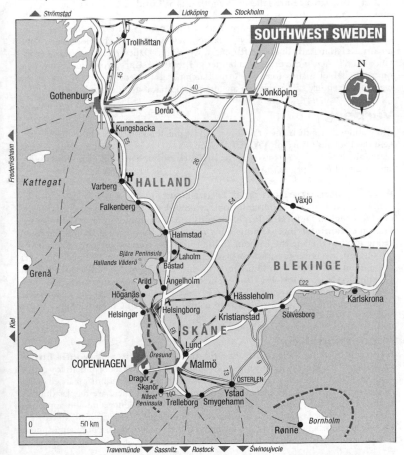

fortress. The small, beautifully intact medieval core of **Falkenberg** is also notable, while for beaches and nightlife, regional capital **Halmstad** is a popular base.

Further south, in the ancient province of **Skåne**, the coastline softens into curving beaches backed by gently undulating fields. This was one of the first parts of the country to be settled, and the scene of some of the bloodiest battles during the medieval conflict with Denmark. Although Skåne was finally ceded to Sweden in the late seventeenth century, the Danish influence died hard, and is still evident today in the thick Skåne accent, often incomprehensible to other Swedes, and in the province's architecture. The latter has also been strongly influenced by Skåne's agricultural economy, whose centuries of profitable farming have left the country-side dotted with **castles** – though the continued income from the land means that most of these palatial homes are still in private hands and not open to the public.

The popular perception of Skåne is as a fertile but largely flat and uniform landscape; however, it's worth taking a day or two to appreciate the subtle variety of the countryside – blocks of yellow rape, crimson poppy and lush-green fields interspersed with castles, charming white churches and black windmills. Skåne's glamorous tennis capital of **Båstad** is a good base from which to explore the region, while to the south, both **Helsingborg**, with its laid-back, cosmopolitan atmosphere, and Sweden's third city, bustling **Malmö**, are only a stone's throw from Denmark. Between these two centres, the university town of **Lund** has some classic architecture and a unique atmosphere.

Sweeping east towards the pretty medieval town of **Ystad**, the coastline holds some minor resorts with excellent beaches. Beyond here, in the northeast of the county, **Kristianstad**, built as a flagship town by the Danes, retains its fine Renaissance church. Across the provincial border in **Blekinge**, **Karlskrona** stands supreme on a number of islands forming a small archipelago; Sweden's second city in the eighteenth century still exudes an air of regal and naval grandeur.

Varberg

More atmospheric than any other town in Halland, the fashionable little nineteenth-century bathing resort of **VARBERG** boasts surprisingly varied sights – most obviously its imposing fortress – plus a laid-back atmosphere, opportunities to swim and plenty of good places to eat.

Arrival, information and transport

Varberg is a handy entry point into southern Sweden, linked by a year-round **ferry** (4hr) to Grenå in **Denmark**. Regular **trains** run down the coast from Gothenburg. From the **train and bus stations**, turn right down Västra Vallgatan and the town centre is off to the left, the harbour to the right. The **tourist office** at Kyrkogatan 39, just off the main square (April to mid-June & mid-Aug to Sept Mon–Fri 10am–6pm, Sat 10am–3pm; mid-June to mid-Aug Mon–Sat 9.30am–7pm, Sun 1–6pm; Oct–March Mon–Fri 10am–5pm; ☏0340/868 00, ⓦwww.turist.varberg.se) provides free maps of the town. Varberg is easy to walk around, but to explore the nearby coast, it might be worth **renting a bike** from Erlan Cykel och Sport, Västra Vallgatan 41 (☏0340/144 55; 100kr per day).

Accommodation

It's worth booking well in advance for the fortress prison ⚑ **youth hostel** (☏0340/868 28, ⓦwww.turist.varberg.se/vandrarhem; ❶), with dorm beds for 210kr. Aside from being spotlessly clean, the prison is much as it was, with original cell doors (each has its own key) complete with spy-holes. If it's full, there are regular doubles in the building next door. Alternatively, a couple of excellent-value and appealing family-run **hotels** are just a few steps away. At Norrgatan 16, *Varberg* (☏0340/161 25, ⓦwww.hotellvarberg.nu; ❹) is an excellent choice for its very friendly atmosphere, quality service and value. Built in 1899, it retains plenty of character and serves a great breakfast. *Hotel Gästis*, Borgmästaregatan 1 (℡0340/180 50, 🌐www.hotellgastis .nu; ❹/❺), includes an evening meal in its rates. There are a number of **campsites** in the area, the nearest being *Apelvikens Camping* (℡0340/64 13 00, 🌐www.apelviken .se), 2km south of the fortress along Strandpromenaden. Alternatively, you'll find plenty of places to put up a tent for free beyond the nudist beaches.

The Town

Varberg's attractions are concentrated along or near the seafront, with the thirteenth-century moated **fortress** set on a rocky promontory. It was home to the Swedish king Magnus Eriksson, and important peace treaties with Valdemar of Denmark were signed here in 1343. Standing outside, it's easy to imagine how impenetrable the fortress must have appeared to attackers in the past, as the way in is hardly more obvious today: enter on the sea-facing side by climbing the uneven stone steps to a delightful terrace café, or approach through the great archways towards the central courtyard.

Although **tours** in English (late June to mid-Aug daily 11am–4pm on the hour; 40kr) take you into the dungeons and among the impressive cocoa-coloured buildings that make up the inner courtyard, it's the **museum** that deserves most of your attention (late June to mid-Aug daily 10am–6pm; mid-Aug to late June Mon–Fri 10am–4pm, Sat & Sun noon–4pm; 50kr; 🌐www.lansmuseet.varberg.se). The most unnerving exhibit is the **Bocksten Man**, a 600-year-old murder victim who was garrotted, drowned, impaled and buried in a local bog until 1936, when a farmer dug him up. In addition to the skeleton, an unnerving Madame Tussaud-like figure with thick, ringleted blond hair now forms the centrepiece of the exhibition and provides a truly arresting idea of what the Bocksten Man really looked like. His entire outfit preserved by the bog, Bocksten Man sports the Western world's most complete medieval wardrobe, made up of a cloak, a hood, shoes and stockings. Much of the rest of the museum is missable, with sections on farming and fishing in Halland, though the room devoted to the works of the so-called **Varberg School** is worth viewing. This small colony of artists – Richard Bergh, Nils Kreuger and Karl Nordström – who joined together in the last years of the nineteenth century, developed the "national painting" style, reflecting the moods and atmosphere of Halland, and Varberg in particular. Night scenes of the fortress beneath the stars show the strong influence of Van Gogh.

Overlooking the sea, the cream-painted **fortress prison** from 1850 looks incongruously delicate in the shadow of the looming fortress. The first Swedish jail to be built with individual cells, it housed life prisoners until the last one ended his days here in 1931. Today, you can stay in a youth hostel in the fortress, which has been carefully preserved to retain most of its original features (see p.416).

A minute or so from the fortress lie a couple of fine remnants from Varberg's time as a spa resort. Facing the town just behind the fortress is the grand **Societeshuset**, a confection of cream-and-green carved wood where upper-class ladies took their meals after bathing in the splendid – and now beautifully restored – **Kallbadhuset** (cold bathhouse), just to the north of the fortress and overlooking the harbour. This dainty bathhouse has separate-sex naked-bathing areas and is topped at each corner by Moorish cupolas, lending it an imperial air.

Although the Halland coastline is still a little rocky around here, there are several excellent spots for bathing. Head down Strandpromenaden for about five minutes to get to a couple of well-known **nudist beaches**: Goda Hopp for men, and Kärringhålan for women. Alternatively, a few kilometres further north at **Getterön**, a fist of land jutting into the sea, there's a nature centre (July & Aug daily 10am–4pm; free) and an extensive bird reserve, as well as a series of secluded coves, reached by regular buses from town.

Eating and drinking

There's no problem finding a good place to **eat** in Varberg, with most of the options north of the main square along Kungsgatan. The best café in town, and great for breakfast, is *Blå Dörren* at Norrgatan 1. Nearby, *Zorba's* at Västra Vallgatan 37 serves up great Greek food (around 160kr). The fantastic ✻ *Thai La La* restaurant (☎0340/808 70), overlooking the main square at Kungsgatan 28, is an excellent place for genuine Thai fare (from 68kr). For lunch, try the grand *Societetsrestaurangen* in Societets Parken, directly behind the fortress, where the Bodegan section has burgers and other light meals, or visit on Friday evenings, when it comes alive with foxtrotting Swedes, or Saturday, when there's live bands and a disco. Finally, head to *Harry's* at Kungsgatan 18 for the town's liveliest **nightlife**.

Halmstad

The principal town in Halland, **HALMSTAD** was once a grand walled city and important Danish stronghold. Today, although most of the original buildings have disappeared, the town boasts a couple of cultural and artistic points of interest, most notably the works of the Halmstad Group, Sweden's first Surrealists, as well as extensive beaches and a wide range of good places to eat.

In 1619, Halmstad's **castle** was used by Danish king Christian IV to entertain the Swedish king Gustav II Adolf; records show that there were seven days of solid festivities. The bonhomie didn't last much longer than that, and Christian was soon building great stone and earth fortifications around the city, surrounded by a moat with four stone gateways. Shortly after, a fire all but destroyed the city; the only buildings to survive were the castle and church. Undeterred, Christian took the opportunity to create a modern Renaissance town with a grid of straight streets – the charming high street, Storgatan, still contains a number of impressive merchants' houses from that time. After the final defeat of the Danes in 1645, Halmstad lost its military significance and the walls were torn down. Today, just one of the great gateways, Norre Port, remains, while Karl XIs Vägen runs directly above the filled-in moat.

Arrival, information and accommodation

From the **train station**, follow Bredgatan to the Nissan River and cross Österbro bridge to get to the coral-red castle on the opposite bank that contains the **tourist office** (May, early June & mid-Aug to late Aug Mon–Fri 9am–6pm, Sat 10am–3pm;

▲ Beach, Halmstad

late June to mid-Aug Mon–Sat 9am–7pm, Sun 11am–6pm; Sept–April Mon–Fri 10am–5pm; ☎035/13 23 20, ⓦwww.halmstad.se/turist). Renting a **bike** is a good way to get out to the beaches on the coast hereabouts: Arvid Olsson Cykel, Norra Vägen 11 is the only outlet in the town centre, and charges 120kr per day for a five-speed bike.

The *Patricks Hills* **youth hostel** (☎035/18 66 66, mid-June to mid-Aug; ❶), with dorm beds from 175kr, is 300m southwest of the castle, at Neptunigatan 3, and has showers and toilets in all rooms.

The best of the central **hotels** is the very comfortable old *Clarion Collection Norre Park*, Norra Vägen 7 (☎035/21 85 55, ⓦwww.norrepark.se; ❺), through the Norre Port Arch north of Storgatan, overlooking the park. Convenient for the train station, the *Best Western Grand* at Stationsgatan 44 (☎035/280 81 00, ⓦwww.grandhotel .nu; ❹/❻) is full of old-world charm and dates from 1904. The nearest **campsite** is *Hagöns Camping* (☎035/12 53 63, ⓦwww.hagonscamping.se), 4km east of the centre, next to a nature reserve bordering a **nudist beach**; the site also has comfortable cabins (750kr).

The Town

At the centre of the lively market square, **Stora Torg**, is Carl Milles' *Europa and the Bull*, a fountain with mermen twisted around it, all with Milles' characteristically muscular bodies and ugly faces. Flanking one side of the square, the grand fourteenth-century **St Nikolai kyrka** (daily June–Aug 8.30am–6pm; Sept–May 8.30am–3pm) is testimony to the town's former importance, but today the only signs of its medieval origins are the splodges of bare rock beneath the plain brick columns. Leading north from the square, pedestrianized **Storgatan** holds some creaking old houses built in the years following the 1619 fire, as well as most of the town's restaurants and nightlife venues. The great stone arch of **Norre Port** marks the street's end: through here and to the right is the splendid **Norre Kattparken**, a delightful, shady place, with mature beech and horse chestnut trees sloping down to the river bank.

By the river at the northernmost edge of the park is the fine **Halmstad Museum** (Tues–Sun noon–4pm, Wed until 8pm; 40kr; ⓦwww.hallmus.se). While the archeological finds on the ground floor are unlikely to set many pulses racing, the top floor contains a decent sample of the work of the Halmstad Group. The group's six members had studied in Berlin and Paris and were strongly influenced by Magritte and Dalí, producing work that caused considerable controversy from the 1920s to the 1940s.

Eating, drinking and nightlife

There are plenty of possibilities along Storgatan, ranging from casual cafés to glamorous gourmet joints. *Gastons* at no. 31 (☎035/10 84 80), has sophisticated Mediterranean food from 200kr. Next door at no. 33, *Pio & Co* (☎035/21 06 69) is a lovely place for modern Swedish food with a massive drinks list and a speciality of steak with piles of mashed potato served on wooden planks for 185kr. For a real splurge, *Lilla Helfvetet* (☎035/21 04 20), Hamngatan 37, is the most stylishly contemporary restaurant in town, serving up lamb, halibut and beef dishes (all from 200kr) in a stunningly designed old turbine engine room overlooking the river. For **cafés**, try the old-fashioned *Skånska Hembageriet* at Bankgatan 1.

Båstad

The most northerly town in the ancient province of Skåne, **BÅSTAD** has a character markedly distinct from the other towns along the coast. Cradled by the Bjäre peninsula, which bulges westwards into the Kattegat (the water separating Sweden and Jutland), Båstad is Sweden's elite **tennis centre**, home of the annual Swedish Open (☎0431/750 75, ⓦwww.swedishopen.org; tickets 150–500kr) at the beginning of July, and boasting sixty tennis courts, five eighteen-hole golf courses

Skåne summer card

If you're spending a significant amount of time in Skåne, buying a **Skåne summer card (sommarkort)** can be an excellent way to save money. For 450kr, it allows fifty journeys (maximum 3hr each) on all buses and most trains throughout the province between June 15 and August 15; up to two children under-7 travel free. To use it, insert the card into the card reader on trains and buses before every journey. You can buy the card from the Kundcenter at Lund or Helsingborg stations or Gustav Adolfs Torg in Malmö, or online at ⓦ www.skanetrafiken.se.

and the Drivan Sports Centre. With a horizon of forested hills to the south, Båstad is pretty scenic, too; less pleasant, however, is the fact that ever since King Gustav V chose to take part in the 1930 tennis championships, wealthy retired Stockholmers and social climbers from all over Sweden have flocked here to bask in the social glow, with droves of well-heeled young men in expensive sports cars overspending and drinking to excess. The down-to-earth and friendly locals grin and bear it for the sake of their local economy.

The **harbour** makes a pretty spot for a picnic or stroll; to get there, follow Tennisvägen off Köpmansgatan through a luxury residential district until you reach Strandpromenaden; to the west, the old bathhouses have been converted into restaurants and bars.

Practicalities

From the **train station**, it's a half-hour walk east along Köpmansgatan to the main square and the **tourist office** (mid-June to mid-Aug Mon–Fri 10am–5pm, Sat 10am–3pm, Sun 11am–3pm; mid-Aug to mid-June Mon–Fri 10am–5pm, Sat 11am–2pm; ℡0431/750 45, ⓦwww.bastad.com). For a really excellent **bed and breakfast**, try *Falken*, Hamngatan 22 (℡0431/36 95 94, ⓦwww.villafalken .com; ❷), a lovingly maintained 1916-built villa set just above the harbour in delightful gardens, with lots of art on the walls and a welcoming atmosphere. The cheaper **hotels** are mostly around the station end of town; note that prices in Båstad increase dramatically during the summer due to the tennis. Try *Enehall*, Stationsterrassen 10 (℡0431/750 15, ⓦwww.enehall.se; ❹), whose rooms are in nine different houses close to the station. For a luxurious and beautifully designed alternative, try the harbourside *Hotel Skansen*, Kyrkogatan 2, (℡0431/55 81 00, ⓦwww.hotelskansen.se; ❻). **Camping** is not allowed at the waterside.

Eating and drinking is as much a pastime as tennis in Båstad, and most of the waterside restaurants and hotels both here and on the peninsula offer two-course dinners for around 150kr, with menus changing weekly. *Pepe's Bodega* (℡0431/36 91 69) is a popular pizza and TexMex place at the harbour, but for value it's hard to beat *Sveas Skafferi*, a wooden hut at the harbour's edge at Hamngatan 8 serving smoked salmon and other fish goodies on paper plates for 100kr, as well as home-baked pies and cake. 🌿 *Coffee and the Bakery*, opposite the church at Köpmansgatan 4, is a fine daytime **café** offering fresh-baked bread, soup, big salads and the best coffee and cake in town.

Helsingborg and around

Long gone are the days when the locals of **HELSINGBORG** joked that the most rewarding sight here was Helsingør, the Danish town whose castle (best known as the "Elsinore" of Shakespeare's *Hamlet*) is clearly visible just 4km away over the Öresund. With its beautifully developed harbour area, an explosion of brilliantly styled bars, cafés and restaurants both at the water's edge and among the warren of cobbled old-town streets, and an excellent museum, Helsingborg is one of the best urban bases Sweden has to offer: bright, pleasing and basking in a tremendous sense of buoyancy.

Past links between Denmark and this likeable city have been less than convivial, though – in fact, Helsingborg has a particularly bloody and tragic history. After the Danes fortified the town in the eleventh century, the Swedes conquered and lost it again on six violent occasions, finally winning out in 1710 under the leadership of Magnus Stenbock. By this time, the Danes had torn down much of the town, and on its final recapture the Swedes razed its twelfth-century castle, except for the five-metre-thick walled keep (*kärnen*) that still dominates the centre. By the early eighteenth century, war and epidemics had reduced the population to just seven hundred, and only with the onset of industrialization in the 1850s did Helsingborg wake up to a new prosperity. Shipping and the railways turned the town's fortunes around, as evidenced by the formidable

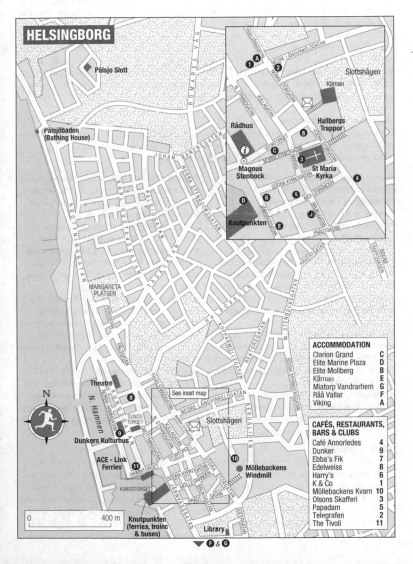

ACCOMMODATION

Clarion Grand	C
Elite Marine Plaza	D
Elite Mollberg	B
Kärnan	E
Miatorp Vandrarhem	G
Råå Vallar	F
Viking	A

CAFÉS, RESTAURANTS, BARS & CLUBS

Café Annorledes	4
Dunker	9
Ebba's Fik	7
Edelweiss	8
Harry's	6
K & Co	1
Möllebackens Kvarn	10
Olsons Skafferi	3
Papadam	5
Telegrafen	2
The Tivoli	11

late nineteenth-century commercial buildings in the centre and some splendid villas to the north overlooking the Öresund. After decades out of the limelight, Helsingborg's fortunes now seem very much on the up.

Arrival, information and city transport

Unless you approach by car on the E6, the chances are that you'll arrive at the harbourside **Knutpunkten**, the vast, glassy expanses of which incorporate the bus, train and Scandlines passenger **ferry** terminals. The **bus station** is on the ground floor behind the main hall, while the ticket and transport information offices are in the front of the complex. Below ground level is the combined **train station** for the national SJ trains and the lilac-coloured local Pågatåg trains, which run south down the coast to Lund and Malmö. One floor up are a Forex **currency exchange** office and the ferry ticket office. The ACE link passenger-only ferry to Helsingør uses the quayside at Hamntorget, 100m north.

The **tourist office** (mid-June to mid-Aug Mon–Fri 9am–8pm, Sat 9am–5pm, Sun 10am–3pm; mid-Aug to mid-June Mon–Fri 10am–6pm, Sat 10am–2pm; ☎042/10 43 50, ⓦwww.helsingborg.se) is inside the Rådhus (town hall) at the bottom of the Stortorget boulevard. It has maps, *Destination Helsingborg*, an events guide with sections in English or the very comprehensive *Helsingborg Helsingør two countries – one destination* – all free.

Accommodation

There are plenty of central **hotel** options in Helsingborg. The most glamorous are around Stortorget, while cheaper establishments are to be found opposite Knutpunkten and along the roads leading away from it.

Clarion Grand Stortorget 8–12 ☎042/38 04 00, ⓦwww.grandissimo.se. Built in 1926, this is one of Helsingborg's biggest and grandest hotels. The interior is a successful blend of modern and classic design with good-sized rooms in a superbly central location. ❹/❺

Elite Marina Plaza Kungstorget 6 ☎042/19 21 00, ⓦwww.elite.se. Right at the harbourside, next to Knutpunkten. Taking inspiration from the sun, wind and water, the newly renovated rooms at this modern and well-equipped hotel are bright, airy and contemporary in design and some have sea views. ❸/❺

Elite Mollberg Stortorget 18 ☎042/37 37 00, ⓦwww.elite.se. Every inch a premier hotel, with a grand nineteenth-century facade, though rooms are simpler, smaller and more homely than at the sister hotel, the *Marina Plaza*. ❷/❹

Kärnan Järnvägsgatan 17 ☎042/12 08 20, ⓦwww.hotelkarnan.se. Opposite Knutpunkten, this comfortable hotel prides itself on "personal touches",

including ominous English-language homilies on each room door (no. 235, for instance, has "He who seeks revenge keeps his wounds open"). There's a small library, cocktail bar and sauna. ❹/❺

Miatorp Vandrarhem Planteringsvägen 71 ☎042/13 11 30, ⓦwww.miatorp.nu. A 20min walk south of the centre along Södergatan, Västra Sandgatan and finally Planteringsvägen; all rooms at this STF hostel are modern, clean and en suite. Dorm beds 300kr, double room ❶

Råå Vallar Kustgatan in the district of Råå, 2km south of town ☎042/18 26 00, ⓦwww.nordic camping.se. Take bus #1 from the town centre. This campsite is well located for Helsingborg's nudist beach which just to the northwest of the site at the foot of Högastensgatan.

Viking Fågelsångsgatan 1 ☎042/14 44 20, ⓦwww.hotellviking.se. An appealing, quiet old hotel in a good location, close to some of the finest old buildings in town. Excellent service, cosy atmosphere and good breakfasts. ❹/❺

The Town

The most obvious place to start exploring is the waterfront, by the copper statue of Magnus Stenbock on his charger. Facing in the direction of the Öresund and Denmark, the **Rådhus** (ask about tours at the tourist office) is to your right, a heavy-handed neo-Gothic pile complete with turrets and towers designed by an architect whose admiration for medieval Italy is perhaps a little too obvious. It's worth a look inside to enjoy the extravagances of nineteenth-century provincial wealth and the fabulous stained-glass windows that tell the entire history of the town.

Crossing the road from the statue and turning right, you can't fail to notice the exceptional **Dunkers Kulturhus** cultural centre (Tues–Sun 10am–5pm, Thurs until 8pm; exhibitions 70kr; @www.dunkerskulturhus.se) at the harbour to your left. This white building, roofed in waves of aluminium and opened in 2002, holds the **city museum** on its ground floor, which explores the Helsingborg's history – via the theme of water – from Ice Age to present day with plenty of dramatic lighting and sound effects, plus a hall of artefacts. A good café-restaurant on the ground floor (see below) overlooks the harbour. The new **art museum** on the spacious upper floors has changing exhibitions. Henry Dunker, whose foundation funded the centre, was a pioneer of galoshes, and his brand, Tretorn, was a world leader till its demise in 1979.

Returning to the Stenbock statue at the bottom of **Stortorget**, you can walk up the slope to meet the steps leading to the massive castellated bulk of the medieval castle keep, **Kärnan** (April, May & Sept Tues–Fri 9am–4pm, Sat & Sun 11am–4pm; June–Aug daily 11am–7pm; Oct–March Tues–Sun 11am–3pm; 20kr). Shaped simply as a huge upturned brick, it's worth climbing more for its views than the historical exhibitions housed within. The keep and St Maria kyrka (see below) were the sole survivors of the ravages of war, but the former lost its military significance once Sweden finally won the day. In the mid-nineteenth century it was destined for demolition and only survived because seafarers found it a valuable landmark. Where cannon fire failed, neglect and the weather succeeded, and the keep fell into ruin before restoration began in 1894.

From the fine parkland around the keep, you can wander down rhododendron-edged stairs, the Hallbergs Trappor, to the **St Maria kyrka** (Mon–Fri 8am–4pm, Sat & Sun 9am–4pm), which squats in its own square by an avenue of beech trees. The church was begun in 1300 and completed a century later; its rather plain facade belies a striking interior, with a clever contrast between the early seventeenth-century Renaissance-style ornamentation of its pulpit and gilded reredos, and multi-coloured contemporary stained-glass windows. The square is surrounded by a cluster of quaint places to eat and some excellent **shops** for picnic food.

Walking back to Stortorget, **Norra Storgatan** and **Södra Storgatan** (the streets that meet at the foot of the steps to Kärnan) formed Helsingborg's main thorough-fare in medieval times, and are today lined with the town's oldest merchants' houses. Heading south along Södra Storgatan, pass through the gate to the left of the old cream painted brick building at no. 31 (opposite no. 20); from the courtyard here, a flight of steps leads up to the handsome nineteenth-century Möllebackens windmill, surrounded by a number of exquisite farm cottages. A further reward for the climb is to be found at the *Möllebackens Kvarn* restaurant (see p.424).

Eating, drinking and nightlife

Helsingborg has a range of excellent **restaurants** and some great daytime **cafés** and *konditori*. The harbour restaurants offer some stylish settings overlooking the water, though they're all pretty similar. There are also some superb food shops near St Maria kyrka, useful for picnic fare: notably Maratorgets on the south side of the square, which sells fruit; the adjacent Bengtsons Ost, a cheese shop; and to the east, for exquisite indulgence, the Peter Beier Chocalatier, a chocoholic's dream with a molten chocolate fountain in the window behind which you can consume the delicious products with a coffee.

Cafés and restaurants

Café Annorledes Södra Storgatan 15. A friendly atmosphere with jumble sale memorabilia and serving a 48kr weekday breakfast.

Dunker Kungsgatan 11. A bright and modern self-service café inside the Dunkers Kulturhus and overlooking the harbour, with light meals from 85kr, delicious cakes, and a high-tech paging system to alert you when your food is ready.

Ebba's Fik Bruksgatan 20. The most fun café in town, with authentic 1950s styling and great music to match. A must.

Edelweiss Drottninggatan 15 ☏042/21 37 37. A fun German restaurant-cum-beerhall with a tremendous selection of real German beers

as well as Wiener schnitzel, Bavarian sausages with sauerkraut and mashed potato and other German staples in the range 149–199kr. Closed Mon.
K & Co Nedre Långvinkelsgatan 9. Very friendly, with great muffins, cakes and filling ciabattas and baguettes.

🏃 **Möllebackens Kvarn** Bergaleden 11 ☎042/12 72 75. Tiny, atmospheric restaurant in a historic wooden building next to Möllebackens windmill. Dishes cost 85–190kr; specialities include fish stew with saffron and aioli, and waffles with raspberry jam and cream. It's quickest reached via the steps in the courtyard

at Södra Storgatan 31. Mon–Wed & Sun till 5pm, Thurs–Sat till 8pm; closed Jan & Feb.
Olsons Skafferi Mariagatan 6 ☎042/14 07 80. The city's best Italian restaurant, right outside St Maria kyrka. Wonderfully prepared, authentic Italian dishes with fish, meat and pasta options, and zabaglione to drool over. Mains are 129–235kr.

🏃 **Papadam** Bruksgatan 10 ☎042/12 16 00. Finally, decent Indian food has made it to Helsingborg. Balti dishes are 145kr, an excellent chicken curry with spinach is 115kr, and lunch (served until 3pm) is an exceptionally good-value 50kr.

Bars and clubs

The glamorous **bars** along Norra hamnen (the North Harbour) have provided a stylish foil to Helsingborg's traditional night-time haunts and music venues. These newer bars overlooking the Öresund are more for wine- and beer-drinking than eating, though they do serve food along new-European lines.

You might want to indulge in the **Turen**, the classic Helsingborg activity of taking the ferry to Helsingør and going back and forth all night rather than getting off in Denmark. The entertainment is the boat itself and the characters on it; hang at the bar all night to take advantage of the low prices (beer 29kr).

Harry's Järnvägsgatan 7. Very popular place for a drink at any time of evening or night. Rather more stylish than the usual *Harry's*, with soft leather armchairs and chandeliers throughout, this cavernous place is opposite Knutpunkten. There's a nightclub here on Thurs, Fri & Sat nights.
Telegrafen Norra Storgatan 14. A long-term favourite, this cosy British-style pub with stained-glass windows, wooden floors and a bar lined with

tattered old books can do no wrong – Swedes seems to love the mock-Britannia.
The Tivoli Hamntorget; ⊕www.thetivoli.nu. Lively place occupying the main part of the former train station opposite Knutpunkten, where you'll find lots of concerts and events. There's also a restaurant, *Vinyl Baren*, which is indeed filled with red vinyl bench seats and 1960s pop art.

Lund

Only 20km from Malmö and 50km south of Helsingborg is the celebrated university city of **LUND**. Like England's Oxford, with which it is often and aptly compared, there's an eccentric and bohemian atmosphere to the place – a mass of students' bikes will probably be the first image to greet you. Cultural attractions aside, it's the mix of architectural grandeur and the buzz of student life that lends Lund its unique charm, and with its justly revered twelfth-century Romanesque cathedral, its medieval streets and numerous museums, the town could easily keep you busy for a couple of days.

Arrival, information and city transport

Frequent **trains** from Malmö (12min) and Helsingborg (30min) arrive at the train station on Bangatan at the western edge of town, which is also the terminus for **buses** and within easy walking distance of everything of interest. The **tourist office** (May & Sept Mon–Fri 10am–5pm, Sat 10am–2pm; mid-June to mid-Aug Mon–Fri 10am–7pm, Sat 10am–3pm, Sun 11am–3pm; Oct–April Mon–Fri 10am–5pm; ☎046/35 50 40, ⊕www.lund.se), opposite the Domkyrkan at Kyrkogatan 11, hands out free maps and copies of *i Lund*, a monthly English- and Swedish-language diary of events with museum and exhibition listings. For internet, try 7-Eleven at Lilla Fiskaregatan 5 where there are Sidewalk Express terminals.

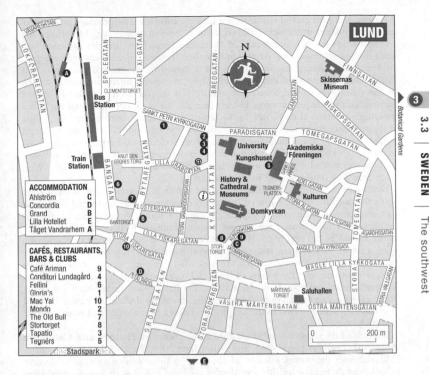

Map labels:
JÄVAREGATAN, LOKFÖRAREGATAN, SPOLEGATAN, KARL XI-GATAN, BREDGATAN, SANGGATAN, FINNGATAN, CLEMENTSTORGET, Skissernas Museum, BISKOPSGATAN, Bus Station, SANKT PETRI KYRKOGATAN, PARADISGATAN, TOMEGAPSGATAN, University, Akademiska Föreningen, Train Station, KNUT DEN STORES TORG, LILLA GRÅBRÖDERSGATAN, Kungshuset, ADELGATAN, BYTAREGATAN, GRÅBRÖDERSGATAN, History & Cathedral Museums, TEGNÉRS-PLATSEN, Kulturen, STORA ALGATAN, LILLA ALGATAN, ÅGÅRDHSGATAN, BANGATAN, KLOSTERGATAN, KYRKOGATAN, Domkyrkan, TOMEGATAN, BANTORGET, LILLA FISKAREGATAN, STORA FISKAREGATAN, STOR-TORGET, SKOMAKAREGATAN, MAGLE STORA KYRKOGATA, MAGLE LILLA KYRKOGATA, STORA VALLGATAN, STÅLBROGATAN, GRÖNEGATAN, STORA SÖDERGATAN, VÄSTRA MÅRTENSGATAN, MÅRTENS-TORGET, Saluhallen, ÖSTRA MÅRTENSGATAN, Stadspark, 0 200 m

ACCOMMODATION

Ahlström	C
Concordia	D
Grand	B
Lilla Hotellet	E
Tåget Vandrarhem	A

CAFÉS, RESTAURANTS, BARS & CLUBS

Café Ariman	9
Conditori Lundagård	4
Fellini	6
Gloria's	1
Mac Yai	10
Mondo	2
The Old Bull	7
Stortorget	8
Tapatio	3
Tegnérs	5

Accommodation

There's a decent range of **accommodation** on offer in Lund, nearly all of it in the centre.

Ahlström Skomakaregatan 3 ⓣ046/211 01 74, ⓦwww.hotellahlstrom.se. Average, very central cheapie with the option of en-suite rooms. ❷/❸
Concordia Stålbrogatan 1 ⓣ046/13 50 50, ⓦwww.concordia.se. A couple of streets southwest of Stortorget, this former student hostel has been upgraded into a very homely hotel with attentive service, though it's rather plain inside. There's a guest sauna, too. ❹/❻
Grand Bantorget 1 ⓣ046/280 61 00, ⓦwww.grandilund.se. This imposing nineteenth-century pink-sandstone edifice straddles an entire side of a small, stately and

central square. Unpretentious and comfortable, with a fantastic breakfast buffet. ❻
Lilla Hotellet Bankgatan 7 ⓣ046/32 88 88, ⓦwww.lillahotelletilund.se. Located in a typical, low-roofed Lund townhouse from the 1850s; rooms here are cosy and nicely appointed, decorated in modern Swedish style and colours. ❹/❺
Tåget Vandrarhem Vävaregatan 22 ⓣ046/14 28 20, ⓔtrainhostel@ebrevet .nu. Housed in the carriages of a 1940s train and accessed through the tunnel behind the train station with bunks exactly as they would be in a train sleeping car. Bunks 200kr, own compartment ❶

The Town

It's only a short walk east from the train station to the magnificent **Domkyrkan** (Mon–Fri 8am–6pm, Sat 9.30am–5pm, Sun 9.30am–6pm; free), whose storm-cloud charcoal and white stone gives it an unusual monochrome appearance. Before entering, head around the back, past the grotesque animal and bird gargoyles over the side entrances; at the very back is the most beautiful part of the exterior – the three-storey apse above the crypt, crowned with an exquisite gallery.

Beyond the great carved entrance, the majestic **interior** is surprisingly unadorned, an elegant mass of watery-grey, ribbed stone arches and stone-flagged flooring. One of the world's finest masterpieces of Romanesque architecture, the cathedral was built in the twelfth century when Lund became the first independent archbishopric in Scandinavia, laying the foundation for a period of wealth and eminence that lasted until the advent of Protestantism. There are several interesting features, such as the elaborately carved fourteenth-century choir stalls depicting Old Testament scenes, with grotesque carvings hidden beneath the seats, but most striking is the amazing astronomical clock just to the left of the entrance. Dating from the 1440s, it shows hours, days, weeks and the courses of the sun and moon in the zodiac; if you're here at noon or 3pm, you'll get to see an ecclesiastical Punch and Judy show, as two knights pop out and clash swords as many times as the clock strikes, followed by little mechanical doors opening to trumpet-blowing heralds and the Three Wise Men trundling slowly around the Virgin Mary.

Don't miss the dimly lit and dramatic **crypt**, which has been left almost untouched since the twelfth century. Most of the tombstones are actually memorial slabs, with just one proper tomb containing the remains of Birger Gunnarsson, Lund's last archbishop. A short man from a poor family, Gunnarsson dictated that his stone effigy should be tall and regal. Two pillars are gripped by stone figures – one of a man, another of a woman and child. Legend has it that Finn the Giant built the cathedral for St Lawrence; in return, the saint was to guess the giant's name, or failing that, give him the sun, the moon or his eyes. Preparing to end his days in blindness, Lawrence heard the giant's wife boasting to her baby, "Soon Father Finn will bring some eyes for you to play with." On hearing Lawrence declare his name, the livid giant and his family rushed to the crypt to pull down the columns and were instantly turned to stone.

Just behind the cathedral on Krafts Torg 1, the combined **History and Cathedral Museum** (Tues–Fri 11am–4pm, Sun noon–4pm; 50kr; ⓦwww.luhm.lu.se) is rather dull, although the statues from local churches in the medieval exhibition deserve a look, mainly because of the way they're arranged – a mass of Jesuses and Marys bunched together in groups, with the crowd of Jesuses on crosses looking ominously Hitchcockian.

A few minutes' walk east of nearby Tegnerplatsen is the town's best museum, the open-air **Kulturen** (mid-April to Sept daily 11am–5pm; Oct to mid-April Tues–Sun noon–4pm; 70kr; ⓦwww.kulturen.com). It's easy to spend the best part of a day just wandering around this virtual town of perfectly preserved cottages, farms, merchants' houses, gardens and even churches, brought from seven regions around Sweden and from as many centuries.

Head north from the square along Sankt Annegatan, continue up Sandgatan and then take a right on to Finngatan to reach another rather special collection, the **Skissernas Museum** (Museum of Sketches: Tues–Sun noon–4pm, Wed until 9pm; 50kr; ⓦwww.adk.lu.se), with fascinating preliminary sketches and original full-scale models of artworks from around the world. One room is full of work by all the major Swedish artists, while in the international room you'll find sketches by Chagall, Matisse, Léger, Miró and Dufy, and sculptural drawings by Picasso and Henry Moore.

As an antidote to museum fatigue, the **Botanical Gardens** (daily 6am–8pm, greenhouses noon–3pm; free), a few minutes' stroll further southwest down Finngatan (turn left at the end of the street into Pålsjövägen and right into Olshögsvägen), are as much a venue for picnicking and chilling out as a botanical experience.

Eating, drinking and nightlife

There are plenty of appealing places to eat and drink in Lund, most associated with the university. Certain **cafés** are student institutions and a number of the better **restaurants** are attached to student bodies or museums – which serves to keep prices low, especially for beer. If you want to buy your own provisions, the **Saluhallen** market at Mårtenstorget sells a range of fish, cheeses and meats, including Lund's own tasty speciality sausage, *knake*. Opposite the library on Sankt Petri Kyrkogatan, Widerbergs Charkuteri is a long-established foodie shop brimming with all the ingredients for a picnic.

Cafés, restaurants and bars

Café Ariman Kungsgatan 2. A nineteenth-century red-brick building housing a classic, deliberately shabby left-wing coffee house – goatees, ponytails and blond dreadlocks predominate. Cheap meals and coffee, and club nights at weekends.

Conditori Lundagård Kyrkogatan 17. Classic student *konditori*, with caricatures of professors adorning the walls. Justly famous for its apple meringue pie.

Fellini Bangatan 6 ☎046/13 80 20, ⊚www .fellini.se. Stylish and popular (book ahead) Italian restaurant that's stood the test of time, decked out in dull chrome and stripped wood. The lunch buffet with unlimited pizza and pasta is excellent value at 109kr; mains cost from 129kr.

Gloria's Sankt Petri Kyrkogata 9 ☎046/15 19 85. Good-value TexMex and Cajun food, from burgers to big salads, and very popular with students and tourists. Sports are shown on TV. Local bands play Fri & Sat nights when *Gloria's* is open till 3am, and there's a big, lively garden area at the back.

Mac Yai Stora Fiskaregatan 15B ☎046/13 00 93. A plain and simple Thai restaurant which is very popular with the town's student population for its decent and generous Asian stir-fries and curries: every dish is 75kr, 5kr less for takeaways.

Mondo Kyrkogatan 23. Set in a quaint, beamed house, this café serves bagels, cheesecake, brownies and the like; the large baguettes are good value.

Stortorget Stortorget 1. Housed in a National Romantic-style former bank, with walls covered in dramatic black-and-white shots of actors, this café-restaurant is a prime meeting spot and has the town's best terrace for people-watching.

Tapatio Kyrkogatan 21 ☎046/32 44 70. Trendy, popular and very reasonable Mexican place serving fajitas, burritos and enchilladas from 129kr, while the excellent hot chicken stew with potatoes and salad costs 159kr. A very good salmon steak with hot salsa and guacamole will set you back 179kr.

Tegnérs Sandgatan 2. Occupying the building next to the student union, with a main hall resplendent with gilded Ionic columns. Forget any preconceptions about student cafés being tatty, stale sandwich bars. Self-service lunch for 74kr allows you as much as you like from a choice of delicious gourmet dishes. There's seating inside or on the terrace. Daily 11.30am–2.30pm.

The Old Bull Bantorget 2. Traditional, carpeted British-style pub with solid metal tables which attracts a large student crowd during term time.

Malmö

Founded in the late thirteenth century, **MALMÖ** rose to become Denmark's most important city after Copenhagen. The high density of herring in the sea off the Malmö coast – it was said that the fish could be scooped straight out with a trowel – brought ambitious German merchants flocking to the city, an influence that can be seen in the striking fourteenth-century St Petri kyrka. Erik of Pomerania gave Malmö its most significant medieval boost when, in the fifteenth century, he built the castle and mint, and gave the city its own flag – the gold-and-red griffin of his family crest. It wasn't until the Swedish king Karl X marched his armies across the frozen belt of water to within striking distance of Copenhagen in 1658 that the Danes were forced into handing back the counties of Skåne, Blekinge and Bohuslän to the Swedes. For Malmö, this meant a period of stagnation, cut off from nearby Copenhagen and too far from its own uninterested capital. Not until the full thrust of industrialization, triggered by the tobacco merchant Frans Suell's enlargement of the harbour in 1775, did Malmö begin its dramatic commercial recovery, and the city's fortunes remained buoyant over the following two centuries. The 1990s saw a further commercial crisis after Malmö had invested heavily in the shipping industry that had been in decline since the 1970, but since the turn of the millennium there's been a heartwarming reversal of the city's fortunes, with the new university and the opening of the Øresunds Link, which links Malmö with Copenhagen, attracting an influx of investment and creating an upbeat and energetic atmosphere. The attractive medieval centre, delightful parks and sweeping beach are all major draws, while the

▲ Øresunds Link

plentiful restaurants and bars and a lively nightlife serve as another inducement to stay a while.

Arrival, information and city transport

If you've driven over from Denmark via the Øresunds Link, simply follow the signs north that take you into the centre of Malmö. All trains arrive at the **train station**, bang in the centre of town. The frequent local Pågatåg trains to and from Helsing-borg, Lund and Ystad use platforms 9–13 at the back. Catch a city bus from the square outside, Centralplan. Buses from Stockholm, Helsingborg, Gothenburg and Copenhagen/Kastrup airport arrive at the **long-distance bus terminal** at the end of Skeppsbron.

Passengers landing in Trelleborg from the TT-Line **ferry** from Travemünde or Rostock in Germany can take bus #146 to Malmö from the Trelleborg Övre stop.

Information and discount cards

The **tourist office** (June–Aug Mon–Fri 9am–7pm, Sat & Sun 10am–5pm; Sept–May Mon–Fri 9am–5pm, Sat & Sun 10am–3pm; ☏040/34 12 00, ⓦwww .malmo.se/turism) is inside the Central Station. Here you can pick up a wealth of free information, including several good maps, and the *Malmö Guide* events brochure. You can also buy the very useful **Malmökortet** (Malmö Card: available for 1, 2 or 3 days for 130kr, 160kr or 190kr respectively), which gives free museum entry, car parking and unlimited city bus journeys, plus various other discounts.

There are ATMs in the train station, and Forex **money exchanges** just opposite the tourist office, on Norra Vägen 60 and Gustav Adolfs Torg.

City transport

Although the city centre is easy to walk around, you'll need to use **buses** to reach some of the sights and some accommodation. Individual tickets cost 16kr and are valid for an hour; a 200kr magnetic card is also available and can be used by several people at the same time: all tickets are sold on the bus. If you want to use **taxis**, it's worth comparing rates. In summer, **bicycle rental** is available from Fridhems Cykelaffär at Tessins väg 13 (☏040/26 03 35). Head down Citadellsvägen past Malmöhus, take the first left, Mariedalsvägen, then right into Tessins väg. Otherwise,

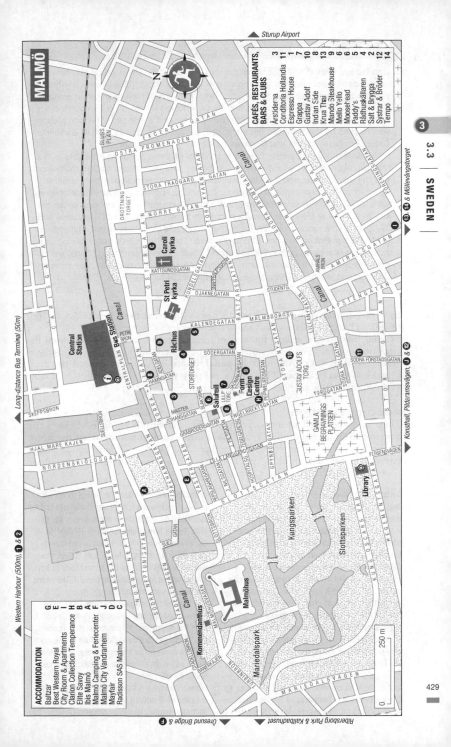

MALMÖ

ACCOMMODATION

Baltzar	G
Best Western Royal	E
City Room & Apartments	I
Clarion Collection Temperance	H
Elite Savoy	B
Ibis Malmö	A
Malmö Camping & Feriecenter	F
Malmö City Vandrarhem	J
Mayfair	D
Radisson SAS Malmö	C

CAFÉS, RESTAURANTS, BARS & CLUBS

Årstiderna	3
Conditoria Hollandia	11
Espresso House	1
Grappa	7
Gustav Adolf	10
Indian Side	8
Krua Thai	13
Mando Steakhouse	9
Mello Yello	6
Mooseland	5
Paddy's	4
Rådhuskällaren	2
Salt & Brygga	12
Systrar & Bröder	14
Tempo	14

Sturup Airport

Western Harbour (500m), 1 & 2

Long-distance Bus Terminal (50m)

Long-distance Bus Terminal (50m)

Konsthall, Pildammsvägen, J & 2

13, 14 & Möllevångstorget

Öresund Bridge & F

Ribersborg Park & Kallbadhuset

The Øresunds Link

Connecting Malmö with Copenhagen in Denmark, the **Øresunds Link** (@www .oresundsbron.se) was finally completed in the summer of 1999 after nearly half a century of debate between those who believed it would have a negative environmental impact on the Baltic Sea and those who felt it would be Sweden's most beneficial and significant construction of the twentieth century. The completion was marked by the symbolic embrace, halfway along the new bridge, of Sweden's Crown Princess Victoria and Denmark's Crown Prince Frederick.

The sixteen-kilometre-long fixed link consists of three parts; most visible is the massive eight-kilometre-long suspension bridge, with two decks for the motorway and the railway lines, and a 490m main span, raised 60m above the busy waterway by four two-hundred-metre-high pylons. The bridge ends on the four-kilometre-long artificial island of Peberholm, from where a four-kilometre-long tunnel dips under the sea to surface in Denmark, near Copenhagen airport. Around 12,000 vehicles and 17,000 train passengers per day cross the bridge, and every June a half-marathon is held between Peberholm and Malmö stadium. This is Sweden's only toll road and crossing by car costs 325kr. Taking a train between Copenhagen and Malmö will be even quicker once a new rail tunnel underneath Malmö's city centre, including an underground station at Triangeln, is completed in 2011.

try Cykelkliniken, Regementsgatan 12, across the canal from Gustav Adolfs Torg (☎040/611 66 66) where a day's rental is around 100kr.

Canal boat tours make a fun way of seeing the city; they leave daily from the canal opposite the *Elite Savoy* hotel (late April to Sept hourly 11am–7pm; @www .rundan.se; 1hr; 85kr). Alternatively, **pedal boats** let you tour around the canal network at your own pace. They're moored at Amiralsbron (late April to Sept daily 11am–7pm; @www.cityboats.se; 120kr per hr).

Accommodation

There are some excellent and surprisingly affordable **hotels** in Malmö. Being a city that attracts business travellers as well as tourists, competition between the hotels can be fierce. Prices plummet at the weekend and most hotels have good summer rate reductions, too. Booking via the tourist office website (@www.malmo.se /hotellbokning) can be cheaper than going direct to a hotel.

Baltzar Södergatan 20 ☎040/665 57 00, @www .baltzarhotel.se. Very central (between the two main squares), this is a swanky place done out in swags and flourishes that owe more to British posh-hotel design than Swedish style. ❹/❻

Best Western Royal Norra Vallgatan 94 ☎040/664 25 00, @www.bwhotelroyal.se. Exceptionally cosy rooms for a chain hotel, whose modern interiors really are a home from home. As yet, the anonymous chain-hotel feel has yet to pervade this winning little place. ❸/❺

City Room & Apartments Amiralsgatan 12 ☎040/795 94, @www.cityroom.se. Bargain-priced double rooms and small flats for rent in a newly renovated and centrally located building close to Konserthuset. All rooms have access to kitchen facilities, common rooms and balconies. ❷

Clarion Collection Temperance Engelbrektsgatan 16 ☎040/710 20, @www.choice.se. Pleasant

central hotel with modern, first-class rooms with polished dark-wood floors, cosy furnishings and top facilities including a sauna and solarium. ❹/❻

Elite Savoy Norra Vallgatan 62 ☎040/664 48 00, @www.savoy.elite.se. Nicely priced during summer, and just opposite the train station, this is where the likes of Lenin, Bardot and Dietrich have stayed, with a brass plaque to prove it. The rooms are big and very comfortable. ❹/❻

Ibis Malmö Stadiongatan 21 ☎040/672 8570, @www.ibishotel.com. Although 30–45min walk from the centre (bus #3 comes here), the prices at this simple yet functional place close to the sports stadium make up for the inconvenience. Book at least one month in advance and rooms cost just 500kr. ❷/❸

Malmö Camping & Feriecenter Strandgatan 101 in Limhamn ☎040/15 51 65, @www.camping .se/m08. Formerly known as *Sibbarps Camping*, this

pleasant campsite is not far from the Øresunds Link and can be reached by bus #34 from town. Also has a number of cottages for rent (**2**). Open all year.
Malmö City Vandrarhem Rönngatan 1 ☎040/611 62 20, © malmo.city@stfturist.se. This newly opened STF hostel has a variety of dorms sleeping up to a maximum of six people. Sixteen rooms have en-suite facilities. Check-in is 4–7pm. Dorm beds 230kr, double room. **2**

🏃 **Mayfair** Adelgatan 4 ☎040/10 16 20, ⓦ www.themayfairhotel.se. Very central

Danish-owned place, and one of the finest of Malmö's more intimate hotels. Rooms are well furnished in cherry or Gustavian pastels. Good breakfasts and weekend discounts. **3**/**5**
Radisson SAS Malmö Östergatan 10 ☎040/698 40 00, ⓦ www.radissonsas.com. Just beyond the Caroli kyrka, this hotel's unimposing facade opens into a delightful interior. The rooms are large and stylish, and breakfast is eaten inside one of Malmö's oldest houses, cunningly incorporated into the building. **5**/**6**

The City

Standing outside the nineteenth-century train station with its ornate red-brick arches and curly-topped pillars, the **canal** in front of you, dug by Russian prisoners, forms a rough rectangle encompassing the **Old Town** directly to the south and the moated castle, the **Malmöhus**, to the west, surrounded by a series of attractive interconnecting parks. First off, though, head down Hamngatan to the main square, Stortorget. On the way you'll pass the striking sculpture of a twisted revolver, a monument to non-violence, which stands outside the grand former Malmö Exchange building from the 1890s.

The Old Town

Stortorget, the proud main square, is home to a series of elaborate sixteenth- to nineteenth-century buildings, amongst which the **Rådhus** of 1546 draws the most attention. A pageant of architectural fiddling and statuary, the building's original design was destroyed during remodelling in the nineteenth century, which left the present, finicky Dutch Renaissance exterior. It's impressive, nonetheless, and to add to the pomp, the red and gold Skånian flag, of which Malmö is so proud, hangs from the eaves. There are occasional tours of the interior; check with the tourist office. The cellars, home to *Rådhuskällaren Restaurant* (see p.434), have been used as a tavern for more than four hundred years.

The step-gabled red-brick building on the opposite side of the square was once the home of sixteenth-century mayor and Master of the Danish Mint, Jörgen Kock. Danish coins were struck in Malmö on the site of the present Malmöhus, until irate local Swedes stormed the building and destroyed it in 1534. In the cellars here you'll find the *Kockska Krogan* restaurant, the only part of the building accessible to visitors. In the centre of the square, a statue of chubby King Karl X Gustav, high on his charger, presides over the city he liberated from centuries of Danish rule.

Head a block east, behind the Rådhus, to reach the Gothic **St Petri kyrka** on Göran Olsgatan (daily 10am–6pm), dark and forbidding on the outside, but light and airy within. The church has its roots in the fourteenth century and, although Baltic in inspiration, the final style owes much to German influences, for it was beneath its unusually lofty and elegantly vaulted roof that the German community came to pray – probably for the continuation of the "sea silver", the herrings that brought them to Malmö in the first place. The ecclesiastical vandalism of whitewashing over medieval roof murals started early at St Petri – almost the whole interior was turned white in 1553 – and consequently your eyes are drawn to the pulpit and four-tiered altarpiece, both of striking workmanship and elaborate embellishment. The only part of the church left with its original artwork is a side chapel, the **Krämare Chapel**. Added to the church in the late fifteenth century as a Lady Chapel, it was considered redundant at the Reformation and sealed off, thus protecting the paintings from the zealous brushes of the reformers. Best preserved are the paintings on the vaulted ceiling, mainly depicting New Testament figures surrounded by decorative foliage, while underfoot the chapel floor is a chessboard of tombs in black, white and red stone.

Södergatan, Malmö's main pedestrianized shopping street, leads south of Stortorget down towards the southern canal. At the Stortorget end there's a jaunty troupe of sculptured bronze musicians, and a collection of lively cafés and restaurants further down. On the corner of the square, take a peek inside **Apoteket Lejonet**. Gargoyled and balconied on the outside, the pharmacy interior is a busy mix of inlaid wood, carvings and etched glass.

Despite the size of Stortorget, it still proved too small to suffice as the sole city square, so in the sixteenth century **Lilla Torg**, formerly marshland, was sewn on to the southeast corner. Looking like a film set, this little square with its creaky old half-timbered houses, flowerpots and cobbles, is everyone's favourite part of the city. During the day, people congregate here to take a leisurely drink in one of the many bars, and wander around the summer jewellery stalls. At night, Lilla Torg explodes in a frenzy of activity, with people from all over the city converging on the square to visit the bars or promenade over the cobbles.

Walk through an arch on Lilla Torg and you'll reach the **Form/Design Centre** (Tues–Fri 11am–5pm, Thurs until 6pm, Sat 11am–4pm, Sun noon–4pm; free; Ⓦwww.formdesigncenter.com), housed in a seventeenth-century grain store and celebrating Swedish design in textiles, ceramics and furniture. From the beginning of the twentieth century until the 1960s, the whole of Lilla Torg was a covered market, and the sole vestige of those days, **Saluhallen**, is diagonally opposite the Design Centre. Mostly made up of specialist fine food shops and snackbars, it makes for a pleasant, cool retreat on a hot afternoon.

Malmöhus and around

Take any of the streets running west from Stortorget or Lilla Torg and you soon come up against the edge of **Kungsparken**, within striking distance of the fifteenth-century castle, **Malmöhus** (June–Aug daily 10am–4pm; Sept–May noon–4pm; 40kr includes entry to the Kommendanthus). For a more dramatic approach, walk west (away from the station) up Citadellsvägen; from here, the low castle with its grassy ramparts and two circular keeps is straight ahead over the wide moat.

Originally Denmark's mint, the building was destroyed by the Swedes in 1534. Two years later, a new fortress was built on the site by the Danish king Christian III, only to be of unforeseen benefit to his enemies who, once back in control of Skåne, used it to repel an attacking Danish army in 1677. Serving as a prison for a time (the Earl of Bothwell, Mary Queen of Scots' third husband, was its most notable inmate), the castle's importance waned once back in Swedish hands, and it was used for grain storage until opening as a **museum** in 1937.

Passing swiftly through the natural history section – a taxidermal Noah's Ark – the most rewarding part of the museum is the ambitious series of furnished rooms that takes you from the mid-sixteenth-century Renaissance through Baroque, Rococo, pastel-pale Gustavian and Neoclassical. A stylish Jugendstil (Art Nouveau) interior is equally impressive, while other rooms feature Functionalist and post-Functionalist interiors. Just as interesting are the spartan but authentic interiors of the castle itself. Finally, the modern art section has a large collection of twentieth-century Nordic art, with changing exhibitions.

Just beyond the castle to the west along Malmöhusvagen is the **Kommendanthus** (Governor's House: same hours as Malmöhus, and included in Malmöhus entry fee), containing a military museum with a fairly lifeless collection of neatly presented rifles, swords and photographs. A little further west, running off Malmöhusvagen, is a tiny walkway, **Banérskajen**, lined with higgledy-piggledy fishing shacks selling fresh and smoked fish.

Once you've had your fill of museums, the castle **grounds**, peppered with small lakes and an old windmill, are good for a stroll. The paths lead all the way down to Regementsgatan past the striking eighteen-metre-high reading room of the City Library in the southeastern corner of the park. You can continue walking through the greenery as far as Gustav Adolfs Torg by crossing Gamla Begravnings Platsen, a pretty graveyard.

South to Möllevångstorget
Tourists rarely head further south of the city than the canal banks that enclose the old town, yet with a few hours to spare, the area south along Amiralsgatan gives an interesting insight into Malmö's mix of cultures. Middle Eastern, Asian and Balkan emigré families predominate, and strolling towards **Möllevångstorget square**, you enter an area populated almost entirely by non-Swedes, with Arabic and Urdu the main languages. The large Möllevångstorget, boasting a poignant and impressive statue at its centre depicting Malmö workers straining under the weight of their toils, is a haven of cafés and exotic food shops, along with shops selling pure junk.

The Turning Torso and Malmö's beaches
Formerly home to the Kockum shipyard, the high-tech **Western Harbour** district, a ten-minute walk north of the Malmöhus, is a popular spot for sunbathing and swimming, and for gazing across to the Øresunds Link from its marina-side cafés and restaurants. Towering over it all, and visible for miles around, is the fantastic new 190m-high **Turning Torso skyscraper** (ⓦ www.turningtorso.com). This revolutionary residential tower, the highest building in Scandinavia, consists of nine stacked cubes that make a ninety-degree twist from base to top. An exhibition centre next door (daily 10am–6pm), including a film show of the building process, gives an idea of what it's like to live in the Twisting Torso with its truly fantastic views of the Øresunds Link and neighbouring Denmark.

Separated from the Turning Torso by delightful Ribersborg **park**, Malmö's long stretch of sandy **beach** extends several kilometres to the old limestone-quarrying area of Limhamn to the southwest. Fringed by dunes and grassland, the beaches are numbered according to the jetty which gives access into the water. At jetty #1, the **Ribersborgs kallbadhus** (contact for opening hours ☎040/26 03 66, ⓦ www .ribban.com) is a cold-water bathhouse offering separate-sex **nude bathing** areas and sauna; bus #32 runs here from the centre of town. The last jetty, #10, denotes Malmö's popular nudist beach.

Eating
Most of Malmö's **eating places** are concentrated in and around its central squares, with Lilla Torg attracting the biggest crowds. If you want a change of scene (and price), head south of the centre to Möllevångstorget, the heart of Malmö's immigrant community. Alternatively, to cut costs, stock up at the food shops within Saluhallen, on Lilla Torg.

Cafés and restaurants
Årstiderna Frans Suellsgatan 3 ☎040/23 09 10. This is a very fine – but rather pricey (mains around 250kr) – old cellar restaurant in the former home of Malmö's sixteenth-century mayor, Jörgen Kock. Daily lunch specials of traditional Swedish fare are much more reasonably priced.

Conditoria Hollandia Södra Förstadsgatan 8. Traditional, pricey *konditori* south of the canal, with a window full of delicious chocolate fondants.

Espresso House Sundspromenaden, Western Harbour. An outlet of the coffee-house chain, with an excellent terrace sporting bridge views, serving excellent chocolate cake, muffins and ciabattas.

🏃 **Grappa** Lilla Torg 4 ☎040/12 50 65. A designer restaurant with a pleasant terrace, serving innovative Italian dishes from 110kr.

Gustav Adolf Gustav Adolfs Torg 43. Long-established, slightly staid café-restaurant, but still a popular spot in a grand, white-stuccoed building with outside seating. As well as coffee and cakes, it serves pasta dishes, a couple of fish mains and a good brunch buffet.

🏃 **Indian Side** Lilla Torg 7 ☎040/30 77 44. Stylish Indian brasserie that is always packed: all the classics are here such as rogan josh and chicken tikka massala at quite respectable prices. Reckon on 145kr for a main course, 24–75kr for a starter.

Krua Thai Möllevångstorget 12 ☎040/12 22 87. In the big square south of the city centre, this place serves good Thai food with an informal atmosphere that's more domestic than haute cuisine.

Mando Steakhouse Skomakaregatan 4 ☎040/780 00. All the meat at this inordinately popular steakhouse with curious copper-plated interior walls comes from local farms and is grilled over lava stones to give it a special barbecue flavour. Mains cost 132–179kr.

Rådhuskällaren Stortorget 1 ☎040/790 20. Gloriously decorative setting beneath the town hall, with dishes at around 200kr, though there's also a well-cooked and beautifully served

daily economy meal at 85kr. Outside seating in summer.

Salt och Brygga Sundspromenaden 7 ☎040/611 59 40. The stylish *Salt and the Bridge* serves up acclaimed ecological food with prime views of the Øresunds Link. Lunch 89kr, dinner 135–250kr. Closed Sat & Sun in winter.

Systrar och Bröder Östra Ronneholmsvägen 26. With leatherette bench seats and 1960s ambience, this bakery is the haunt of hip Malmöites. Superb breads, cakes and sandwiches, and a great-value breakfast buffet at 65kr.

Drinking, nightlife and entertainment

The best place to head for an evening **drink** is **Lilla Torg**: the square buzzes with activity, the smell of beer wafts between the old, beamed houses, and music and chatter fill the air. However, Möllevångstorget is also worth checking out for a more alternative scene.

Mello Yello Lilla Torg 1. A popular haunt for the 25-plus age group. Gets very drunken as the night progresses.

Moosehead Lilla Torg 1. With rough brick walls and a gorgeous stucco cornice, this stylish bar is definitely one of the most fun places to drink in town and a firm favourite with the 20-something fraternity – even in winter when people huddle under gas heaters outside.

Paddy's Kalendegatan 7. Definitely more bar than pub with black-and-white pictures of Irish writers adorning the walls, this is a stylish and laid-back place for a drink right in the centre of town.

Tempo Södra Skolgatan 30. This compact little bar close to Möllevångstorget is always packed with students and would-be musicians who come here to relax and enjoy the music chosen by the resident DJ.

Music and festivals

If you know where to look, you'll find there are some decent **live music** venues in Malmö. The best places are *Palladium*, Södergatan 15 (☎040/10 30 20; ⊛www .paladium.nu), with a variety of Scandinavian R'n'B and rock bands, and Jeriko, Spånggatan 8 (☎040/10 30 20, ⊛www.jeriko.nu), which specializes in jazz and world music.

Classical music performances take place at the Malmö Konserthus, Föreningsgatan 35 (☎040/34 35 00; ⊛www.mso.se), home of the Malmö Symphony Orchestra, and at Musikhögskolan, Ystadvägen 25 (☎040/32 54 50); check with the tourist office for programme details.

The main annual **festival** in town is the week-long **Malmö Festival** (⊛www .malmofestivalen.nu) in August, which takes place throughout the city centre. Huge tables are set out and free crayfish tails served on the first night, with revellers bringing their own drinks. In Gustav Adolfs Torg, stalls are set up by the immigrant communities, with Pakistani, Somali and Bosnian goodies and dance shows.

Listings

Buses Skånetrafiken ☎0771/77 77 77.
Car rental Avis, Skeppsbron 13 ⊛www.avis.se; Europcar, Mäster Nilsgatan 22 ⊛www.europcar.se; Hertz, Jorgen Kocksgatan 1B ⊛www.hertz.se.
Doctor On call ☎1177.
Internet access Sidewalk Express has several internet points across Malmö, for example, at Central Station and at the 7-Eleven supermarkets

at Baltzargatan 22 and Södra Förstadsgatan 78A. See ⊛www.sidewalkexpress.se for complete listings. One hour costs 19kr.
Pharmacy Apoteket Gripen, Bergsgatan 48 (daily 8am–10pm).
Taxis Taxi 97 ☎040/97 97 97; Taxi Kurir ☎040/700 00; Taxi Skåne ☎040/33 03 30.
Train enquiries SJ ☎0771/75 75 75.

Southeastern Skåne: Ystad

Forty-five minutes by Pågatåg train from Malmö lies the well-preserved medieval market town of **YSTAD**, boasting a core of quaint cobbled lanes lined with hundreds of half-timbered cottages and a central square oozing rural charm. It's a splendid place to base yourself for a day or so and is a useful departure point for **ferries** to the Danish island of Bornholm and to Swinoujscie in Poland.

Arrival and information

From the harbourside **train station**, cross the tracks to St Knuts Torg, where the **tourist office** (mid-June to Aug Mon–Fri 9am–7pm, Sat 10am–6pm, Sun 11am–6pm; Sept to mid-June Mon–Fri 9am–5pm; ☎0411/57 76 81, ⌨www.ystad.se) is next door to the Art Museum. St Knuts Torg is also where SkåneExpressen **buses** from Lund (#6) and Kristianstad (#4) pull in. Regular Pågatåg trains connect Ystad to Malmö (change here for Copenhagen); to get to Kristianstad by train, you need to return to Malmö first.

Ferries to Bornholm depart from the Fyrkaden terminal right behind the train station, while those to Poland depart from the Revhusen terminal a few hundred metres to the east. **Cycling** is a great way to see the surrounding landscape, and bikes can be rented from Roslin Cykel, Jennygatan 11, just east of the bus and train terminals (☎0411/123 15).

Accommodation

There are several good and reasonably priced **hotels** in town, and one at the beach, listed below. Prices are considerably less than Malmö so if money is tight, staying here and travelling up to Malmo will save lots. Ystad also has two youth hostels, which is quite unusual for such a small place.

Anno 1793 Sekelgården Långgatan 18 ☎0411/739 00, ⌨www.sekelgarden.se. The best place to stay in town, this small family-run hotel in an eighteenth-century merchant's house is friendly and informal, with a sauna, cobbled court-yard and flower garden. There are en-suite rooms in both the main house and the old tannery at the back, and excellent breakfasts are served under the trees or in the charming dining room. ❸
Bäckagården Dammgatan 36 ☎0411/198 48, ⌨www.backagarden.nu. Small-scale guesthouse-type place in a converted home just behind the tourist office. ❷/❸
Continental Hamngatan 13 ☎0411/137 00, ⌨www.hotelcontinental-ystad.se. Classic hotel touted as Sweden's oldest, with a grand lobby of marble, Corinthian pillars and crystal chandeliers. Rooms are modern Italian-style, and the cold breakfast buffet is a treat. ❹
Kantarellen Vandrarhem Fritidsvägen 9 ☎0411/665 66, ⌨www.turistlogi.se. A great

location for this STF hostel on the beach at Sandskogen, 2km east of the town centre and reached by buses #304, 322 and 392. Dorm beds 230kr, double room ❶; Sept to mid-June advance bookings only.
Prins Carl Hamngatan 8 ☎0411/737 50, ⌨www.hotellprinscarl.com. A mid-range, non-smoking place, with rooms adapted for people with dis-abilities or allergies. ❷/❸
Vandrarhemmet Stationen Spanlenfararegatan 25 ☎0708/57 79 95, ⌨www.turistlogi.se. Independent hostel located in the train station with comfortable, high-ceilinged rooms. Dorm beds 200kr, double rooms ❶
Ystads Saltsjöbad Saltsjöbadsvägen 6 ☎0411/136 30, ⌨www.ysb.se. Renowned for its beachside position, just east of town, this large, 100-year-old hotel (though with endless modern extensions tacked on) has an excellent new spa complex and a restaurant in the original saltwater bathing house. ❹

The Town

Turning left from the station and ferry terminals then right up Hamngatan brings you to the well-proportioned **Stortorget**, a grand old square encircled by pictur-esque streets. **St Maria kyrka** is a handsome centrepiece, with additions from nearly every century since it was begun in the thirteenth. In the 1880s, changing tastes saw many of the church's rich decorative features removed, and only the most interesting ones were returned during a restoration programme forty years later. Inside, the early seventeenth-century Baroque pulpit is worth a look for the fearsome face carved beneath it and, opposite, the somewhat chilling medieval crucifix, which was placed here on the orders of Karl XII to remind the preacher of Christ's suffering.

If you stay in Ystad, you'll soon become acquainted with a tradition that harks back to the seventeenth century: from a room in the church's watchtower, a night watchman blows a haunting tune on a bugle every fifteen minutes from 9.15pm to 1am, as a safeguard against the outbreak of fire. The idea was that if one of the thatched cottages went up in flames, the bugle would sound repeatedly for all to go and help extinguish the blaze. The sounding through the night was to assure the town that the watchman was still awake; until the mid-nineteenth century, if he slept on duty he was liable to be executed.

From Stortorget, it's a short stroll up Garvaregränd, past art and craft workshops, and on up Klostergatan to the **Ystads Stadsmuseum** (June–Aug Mon–Fri 10am–5pm, Sat & Sun noon–4pm; Sept–May Tues–Fri noon–5pm, Sat & Sun noon–4pm; 30kr; Ⓦwww.klostret.ystad.se). Set in the thirteenth-century Gråbröder ("Greyfriars") Monastery, it contains the usual local history collections, given piquancy here by their preserved medieval surroundings. After the monks were driven out during the Reformation, the monastery was at various times a hospital, a poorhouse, a distillery and, finally, a dump. A decision to demolish it in 1901 was overturned, and today it's definitely worth a visit. The monastery gardens (open 24hr; tours available in summer) consist of spice, vegetable and medicinal herb gardens and a wonderful rose garden.

Not far from the St Maria kyrka on the western side of town, **Norra Promenaden**, a strip of mature horse chestnut trees and parkland, is good for a stroll. Here you'll find *Café Norra Promenaden*, a white pavilion built in the 1870s to house a genteel café and dance hall.

Eating and drinking

There's a fair selection of places to eat in Ystad, including some atmospheric **cafés** and fine **restaurants**, most of the latter around Stortorget.

Lottas Stortorget 11 ☎0411/788 00. Justifiably the most popular restaurant in town, packed each evening in summer and serving beautifully presented, scrumptious fish and meat dishes. Closed Sat & Sun. *Lottas Källare* in the cellars below is a cosy bar with several English beers including the so-called Manchester United.
Prins Charles Hamngatan 8. Next door to the *Prins Carl Hotel*, this English-style pub and restaurant serves meat and fish dishes in the evenings, with live music on Fri and Sat nights.
Steakhouse Bryggeriet Långgatan 20 ☎0411/699 99. The rough, beamed interior dominated by two copper beer casks creates a welcoming ambience at this fine restaurant.

The well-cooked fish and meat dishes, with one vegetarian option, cost between 120–185kr.
Store Thor Stortorget 1 ☎0411/185 10. Located in the cellars of the former Rådhus, and adding a breath of life to Stortorget in summer when tables are brought into the square itself. At weekends, and out of the high season, the elegant interior serves as a fitting backdrop to the less touristy Swedish menu.
The Book Café Gåsegränd. Down a tiny, cobbled street off Stora Östergatan, this precariously leaning wooden house has books – many in English – to read while you feast on the home-baked focaccia or sample one of the varieties of coffee. The gardens are delightful, too, and retain their 1778 layout.

Kristianstad

Ninety kilometres northeast of Malmö, quiet **KRISTIANSTAD** (pronounced "cri-shan-sta") is a Renaissance town created in 1614 by Christian IV, Denmark's seventeenth-century "builder-king". A good example of the king's architectural preoccupations, with proportioned central squares and broad, gridded streets, it was only to remain in Danish hands for another 44 years before being permanently ceded to Sweden during the Skåne wars.

Arrival, information and accommodation

Buses from Ystad (1hr 45min) stop at the Resecentrum bus station on Östra Boulevarden, although the quickest and most comfortable way here is by **train** from Malmö or Karlskrona.

The **tourist office** (mid-June to mid-Aug Mon–Fri 10am–7pm, Sat 10am–3pm, Sun 10am–2pm; mid-Aug to mid-June Mon–Fri 10am–5pm, Sat 11am–3pm; ☏044/13 53 35, ⓦwww.kristianstad.se/turism), with internet terminals, is located in Stora torg, a five-minute walk from the station; to get here, turn right out of the train station and then take the second left. There's a **campsite** with attached **youth hostel** at *Charlottsborg Camping* (☏044/21 07 67, ⓦwww.charlottsborgsvandrarhem .se; dorm beds 150kr), 3km west of the town centre (bus #2).

Two of Kristianstad's **hotels** are side by side, just a few steps from the train station. At Västra Storgatan 17 you'll find the appealing family-run *Anno 1937* (☏044/12 61 50, ⓦwww.hotelanno.se; ❸/❺), while at no. 15, the ironically unassuming *Quality Grand* (☏044/28 48 00, ⓦwww.choicehotels.se; ❸/❹) offers friendly service and particularly comfortable beds. The most glamorous place to spend the night is the *First Christian IV*, Västra Boulevarden 15 (☏044/20 38 50, ⓦwww.firsthotels.com; ❺) – a grand, castle-like confection in a former bank. Its beautifully renovated features include original fireplaces and parquet floors.

The Town

The obvious starting point is the **Trefaldighetskyrkan** (Holy Trinity Church: daily 9am–5pm), opposite the train station, which stands as a symbol of all that was glorious about Christian IV's Renaissance ideas. The grandiose exterior has seven magnificent spiralled gables, and the high windows allow light to flood the white interior. This being Sweden, there's a children's play area between the aisles. Diagonally across from the church, the main square, **Storatorg**, hosts the late nineteenth-century **Rådhus**, itself built in imitation of Christian's Renaissance style. Inside the entrance, a bronze copy of the king's 1643 bust is something of a revelation, with Christian sporting a goatee beard, one earring and a single dreadlock, his one exposed nipple decorated with a flower motif. Back outside in the square, Palle Pernevi's splintered *Icarus* fountain depicts the unfortunate Greek aeronaut falling from heaven into a scaffolded building site.

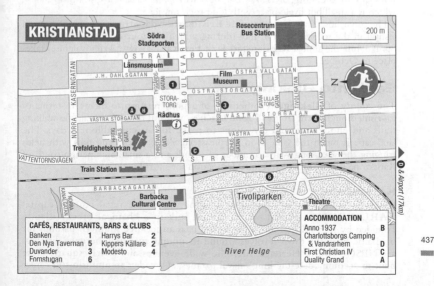

North of Storatorg, on Östra Boulevarden, is the **Regionmuseum** (Regional Museum: June–Aug daily 11am–5pm; Sept–May Tues–Sun noon–5pm; free; Ⓦwww.regionmuseet.m.se), housed in a building that was begun as a royal palace by Christian in 1616, but soon became an arsenal for Danish partisans during the bloody Skåne wars. Aside from the historical exhibits, there are some interesting textile and art collections on the top floor. If you've time on your hands, it's a pleasant stroll behind the museum to **Södra Stadsporten**, the 1790s southern town gate on Östra Boulevarden, one of the few remaining pieces of fortification.

Walking back through the town centre, a few minutes east of the Storatorg, the **Film Museum**, Östra Storgatan 53 (late June to mid-Aug Tues–Sat 1–4pm; mid-Aug to late June Sun noon–5pm; free), is heralded by a bronze early movie camera outside the door. This was Sweden's first film studio, where the country's earliest movies were recorded between 1909 and 1911; some of these flickering works can now be viewed on videotape. From here, wander down any of the roads to the south and you'll reach **Tivoliparken**, where you can stroll beneath avenues of horse chestnuts; at the park's centre is a green-painted Art Nouveau **theatre**, designed by Kristianstad-born Axel Anderberg, who also created the Stockholm Opera House.

Recently listed as a biosphere reserve, the **wetlands** around Kristianstad – the *vattenriket*, or "water kingdom" – are well worth a visit for their natural beauty and birdlife; in summer, sightseeing boats splash their way up the river to the area on two-hour trips from behind the theatre (May–Aug daily 11am, 2pm & 6pm; 100kr; Ⓦwww.flodbaten.se).

Eating, drinking and entertainment

Kristianstad has a number of good **places to eat**. Of the **cafés**, the best are *Fornstugan*, an elaborately carved Hansel-and-Gretel lodge in the middle of Tivoli-parken, and the more central *konditori*, *Duvander*, Hesslegatan 6.

Among the town's **restaurants**, *Kippers Källare*, Östra Storgatan 9 (☎044/10 62 00), is in an atmospheric cellar, and specializes in juicy steaks from 185kr. *Modesto*, Västra Storgatan 54 (☎044/12 06 30) is a modern bistro serving fantastic tapas with a Swedish edge. Greek cuisine can be sampled at *Den Nya Tavernan* (☎044/21 63 04), Nya Boulevarden 6B, with main courses from just 72kr.

For a central **drinking** place, check out the 250 or so beers at *Banken* in the old Riksbank on Storatorg, or *Harry's Bar*, next to *Kippers Källare* at Östra Storgatan 9, which is a small but lively place with loud rock music.

The town hosts two annual festivals: **Kristianstadsdagarna**, a seven-day cultural festival in the second week of July (during which the tourist office stays open till 8pm), while the annual **Kristianstad Jazz Festival** (Ⓦwww.jazzfestivalen.se) takes place in October.

East into Blekinge

The county of **Blekinge** is something of a poor relation to Skåne in terms of tourism, though there are some good beaches, plentiful fishing, several fine walking trails and enough cultural diversions to make for an enjoyable few days. The landscape is much the same as in northeastern Skåne: forests and hills with fields fringing the sea, along with a number of islands and a small archipelago south of Karlskrona that make a picturesque destination for short boat trips.

Karlskrona

Blekinge county's most appealing destination is the regal county capital **KARLSKRONA**, located on the largest link in a chain of breezy islands. Founded by Karl XI in 1680, who picked it as an ice-free southern harbour for his Baltic fleet, the town revolves around its unique maritime heritage, listed as a UNESCO World Heritage Site. The wide avenues and stately squares were built to accommodate the king's naval parades, and cadets in uniform still career

KARLSKRONA

Borgmästarefjärden

Train Station

SKEPPSBROKAJEN

JÄRNVÄGSTORGET

V. VITTUSGATAN

Stakholmen

Hoglands Park

TROSSÖ

Rådhus

STOR-TORGET

Fredriks-kyrkan

Trefaldighets-Kyrkan

Bell Tower

Rosenbom Statue

Amialiteskyrka

Marinmuseum

Båtsmankasern

Stumholmen

ACCOMMODATION

Aston	D
Clarion Collection	
Carlscrona	A
First Camp Dragsö	B
First Ja	F
First Statt	E
STF Vandrarhem	
Karlskrona	C

CAFÉS, RESTAURANTS, BARS & CLUBS

Michelangelo	2
Montmatre	1
Nivå	3
Nya Skafferiet	4
Systrarna Lindkvists Café	5

0 200 m

around streets named after Swedish admirals and battleships. However, even if you're not a naval fan, Karlskrona has plenty to offer, particularly the picturesque old quarter around the once-busy fishing port at Fisktorget and some short cruises around the islands in the archipelago; however, due to military restrictions no bathing is allowed on them (there's good swimming off the nearby island of Dragsö or at the fine bathhouse in town).

The town centre is on the former island of Trossö, connected to the mainland by the Österleden main road. Climb uphill from the train station past Hoglands Park to the main square, **Stortorget**, at the highest point and geographical centre of the island. It's a vast and beautiful space, dominated by two complementary **churches**, both designed by Tessin the Younger and stuccoed in burnt orange, with dove-grey stone colonnades. **Fredrikskyrkan** (Mon–Fri 11am–3pm, Sat 9.30am–2pm) is elegant enough, but the interior of the circular domed **Trefaldighetskyrkan** (Mon–Fri 11am–3pm, Sat 9.30am–2pm; guided tours can be requested here) holds more interest. Built for the town's German merchant community in 1709, the domed ceiling is its most remarkable feature, painted with hundreds of rosettes and brilliantly shaded to look three-dimensional. The altar is also distinctive, with golden angelic faces peering out of a gilded meringue of clouds.

Housed in the former water tower beside the square at Drottninggatan 28, the new **Museum Lionardo da Vinci Ideale** (℡0455/255 73, ⊛www.museumldv.com) is definitely worth a look. It contains a mesmorizing painting of da Vinci by van Gogh, along with other elements of the art collection of Bosnia's Kulenovic family, never before exhibited, which stretches over 500 years from the Renaissance period to the present day. Annoyingly, admission can only be arranged by telephoning or emailing in advance.

Head between the churches, down the cobbled Södra Kungsgatan, which is divided down the centre by the railway that once carried trains to the harbour. The leafy

439

square ahead is **Amiralitetstorget** and perched at its centre is the huge, apricot-and-grey wooden belltower of the **Amiralitetskyrka**. To get to the church itself, go down Vallgatan, and the beautifully proportioned wooden church is up on your right. Built in 1685, it's the largest wooden church in Sweden (visits by appointment only; ℡0455/103 56). Outside the entrance, take a look at one of the city's best-known landmarks: the wooden statue of **Rosenbom**, a local beggar who one night forgot to raise his hat to thank the wealthy German carver, Fritz Kolbe. When admonished for this, Rosenbom retorted, "If you want thanks for your crumbs to the poor, you can take my hat off yourself!" Enraged, Kolbe struck him between the eyes and sent him away, but the beggar froze stiff and died in a snowdrift by the church. Next morning, Kolbe found the beggar's body and, filled with remorse, carved a figure of Rosenbom to stand at the spot where he died, designing it so that you have to raise his hat yourself to give some money.

Karlskrona's best museums are set on the island of Stumholmen, connected to the mainland by road five minutes' walk east of Stortorget down Kyrkogatan. The excellent **Marinmuseum** (Maritime Museum: June–Aug daily 10am–6pm; Sept–May Tues–Sun 11am–5pm; free; ℗www.marinmuseum.se) has a facade like a futuristic Greek temple, while its exhibits (including several ships moored alongside the building) thoughtfully and evocatively bring seafaring ways to life.

For more of a feel of old Karlskrona, wander west past the military hardware towards the **Björkholmen** area. Here a couple of tiny wooden early eighteenth-century houses in little gardens survive, the homes built by the very first craftsmen at the naval yard. Nearby Fisktorget, originally the site of a fish market, is pleasant for a stroll, and is also the terminal for boat and river trips. A few steps inland at Borgmästaregatan 17, housed in the town's striking former cinema, the new **Konsthall** (Tues–Sun noon–5pm, Wed until 7pm; free; wwww.karlskrona.se/konsthall) is the place to look for temporary exhibitions of modern art as well as occasional dance and music productions.

Practicalities

There are **direct trains** here from Copenhagen, Gothenburg, Malmö and Kristianstad. Stena Line **ferries to Gdynia** in Poland (℡0455/36 63 00, ℗www .stenaline.se; 1–2 daily; 10hr 30min) depart from the ferry terminal to the east of the centre. Karlskrona's **tourist office** (June–Aug daily 9am–8pm; Sept–May Mon–Fri 9am–6pm, Sat 10am–4pm; ℡0455/30 34 90, ℗www.karlskrona.se/tourism) is at Stortorget 2.

The cheapest bed is to be had at the Trossö **youth hostel**, centrally located at Drottninggatan 39 (℡0455/100 20; ❶), where dorm beds cost from 190kr. The nearest **camping** is 2km away on Dragsö island (℡0455/153 54, ℗www.firstcamp .se; April–Oct); take bus #7 from the bus station to Saltö, from where it's a short walk. For **hotels**, try the pleasant, modern *Clarion Collection Carlskrona*, close to the station at Skeppsbrokajen (℡0455/36 15 00, ℗www.choice.se; ❸/❻), while the *First Hotel Ja*, Borgmästaregatan 13 (℡0455/555 60, ℗www.firsthotels.se; ❹/❻), is another good choice, with a very homely atmosphere. Within the same chain, the considerably more expensive *First Hotel Statt*, Ronnebygatan 37 (℡0455/555 50, ℗www.firsthotels.se; ❸/❻), is supposed to be its glamorous sister, but in reality it's only a smattering of Empire styling and a bit more gilt to differentiate the two. If these are out of your range, *Aston* at Landbrogatan 1 (℡0455/194 70, ℗www .hotellaston.se; ❸/❹) is plain and reasonable.

Most of the town's **konditorier** are indistinguishable, an exception being *Systrarna Lindkvists Café*, Borgmästaregatan 3, across from square from the tourist office – all fine old gilded tea cups and silver sugar tongs. Also the deli and café *Nya Skafferiet* at Rådhusgatan 9 is a really fine place for filled baguettes and luscious meats, cheeses and other picnic delights (closed Sun). The best restaurants in town are along the main Ronnebygatan, where at no. 29, ♣ *Michelangelo* (℡0455/121 95) with its rough brick walls is an elegant place for top-notch Mediterranean meat and fish dishes from 165kr; *Montmartre*, further up the hill at no. 18 (℡0455/31 18 33), is the cosiest of all the Italian places in town. The menu features all your favourite Italian dishes, plus huge pizzas from 64kr and pasta at 79kr. Another good bet is *Nivå* in Stortorget (℡0455/103 71) which is a great place for reasonably priced burgers and steaks.

Travel details

Trains

Karlskrona to: Gothenburg (2 daily; 4hr); Kristianstad (hourly; 1hr 30min); Malmö (hourly; 3hr).
Kristianstad to: Karlskrona (hourly; 1hr 30min); Malmö (hourly; 1hr 15min).
Malmö to: Ystad (hourly; 50min).
Ystad to: Malmö (hourly; 50min).

Buses

Helsingborg to: Båstad (8 daily; 1hr 15min); Halmstad (5–6 daily; 1hr).
Karlskrona to: Kalmar (1–2 daily; 1hr 15min); Lund (1–2 daily; 2hr 45min); Malmö (1–2 daily; 3hr 10min).
Kristianstad to: Kalmar (1–2 daily; 3hr); Malmö (1–2 daily; 1hr 30min).
Malmö to: Gothenburg (7–8 daily; 3hr 30min); Halmstad (4 daily; 2hr 20min); Helsingborg (5–6 daily; 1hr); Jönköping (4–5 daily; 4hr); Kalmar (1–2 daily; 4hr 25min); Karlskrona (1–2 daily; 3hr 10min); Kristianstad (1–2 daily; 1hr 30min); Lund (4 daily; 25min); Stockholm (2–3 daily; 8hr); Trelleborg (hourly; 45min).
Ystad to: Kristianstad (9 daily; 1hr 35min); Lund (hourly; 1hr 20min).

International buses

Malmö to: Copenhagen, via Copenhagen airport (6 daily; 1hr).

International trains

Karlskrona to: Copenhagen via Kastrup airport (hourly; 3hr 40min).
Kristianstad to: Copenhagen via Kastrup airport (hourly; 2hr).
Malmö to: Berlin (1 daily; 8hr 30min); Copenhagen via Kastrup airport (every 20min; 35min); Narvik (1 weekly; 28hr).

International ferries

Helsingborg to: Helsingør, Denmark (every 20min; 25min).
Karlskrona to: Gdynia, Poland (2 daily; 10hr 30min).
Trelleborg to: Rostock, Germany (3 daily; 5hr 45min); Sassnitz, Germany (5 daily; 4hr)
Varberg to: Grenå, Denmark (2 daily; 4hr).
Ystad to: Rønne, Bornholm (2–3 daily; 1hr 25min); Swinoujscie, Poland (2 daily; 6hr 30min–9hr).

3.4

The southeast

Although a less obvious target than the coastal cities and resorts of the southwest, Sweden's **southeast** certainly repays a visit. Impressive castles, lakeside sites and numerous glass-making factories hidden amongst forests are some of the mainland attractions, while off the east coast, Sweden's largest islands offer beautifully preserved medieval towns and fairytale landscapes. Train transport, especially between Stockholm and the towns close to the eastern shore of Lake Vättern, is good; you can even visit some places as day-trips from the capital.

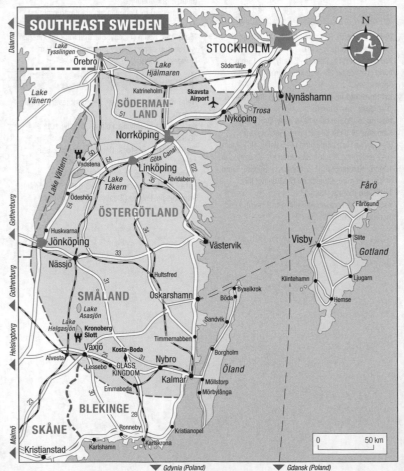

Småland province in the south encompasses a varied geography and some strikingly varied towns. The glorious historic fortress town of **Kalmar** is an essential stop, and is also the jumping-off point for the island of **Öland**. Further inland, great swathes of dense forest are rescued from monotony by the **Glass Kingdom**, a region that continues the region's famous tradition of glass production. By the mid-nineteenth century, agricultural reforms and a series of bad harvests in Småland saw mass emigration to America, and in **Växjö**, the largest town in the south, the art of glass-making and the history of Swedish emigration are the subjects of two superb museums.

The idyllic pastoral landscape of **Östergotland** stretches from the shores of the lake east to the Baltic. Popular with domestic tourists, the small lakeside town of **Vadstena** is one of the highlights, its medieval streets dwarfed by a Renaissance castle and an imposing abbey. Just to the north, bustling **Norrköping** grew up around the textile industry, a background that's preserved in a collection of handsome red-brick and stuccoed factories.

Sweden's largest islands are in the Baltic: Öland and Gotland, adjacent slithers of land with unusually temperate climates, sandy beaches and impressive historic (and prehistoric) sights. **Gotland** is one of Sweden's highlights, with its medieval Hanseatic capital, **Visby**, a stunning backdrop to the carnival atmosphere that pervades the town in summer, when ferry-loads of young Swedes come here to sunbathe and party. It's also one of the most popular places for Swedes to celebrate **Midsummer's Night**. The rest of the island, however, is little visited by tourists, and all the more worthwhile for that. **Öland** – smaller and closer to the mainland – is less celebrated, but its mix of dark forest, UNESCO-listed landscapes and flowering meadows make it a tranquil spot for a few days' exploration. Both islands are ideal for cycling, and it's easy to rent bikes.

Kalmar

Delightful, breezy **KALMAR**, set on a huddle of islands at the southeastern edge of Småland, has treasures enough to make it one of southern Sweden's most delightful towns. Surrounded by fragments of fortified walls, the seventeenth-century **town centre**, set on the Kvarnholmen islet and connected to the mainland by several bridges, is a mass of cobbled streets and lively squares, lined with some lovely old buildings. Close by is the exquisite castle, **Kalmar Slott**, scene of the Kalmar Union,

▲ Kalmar Slott

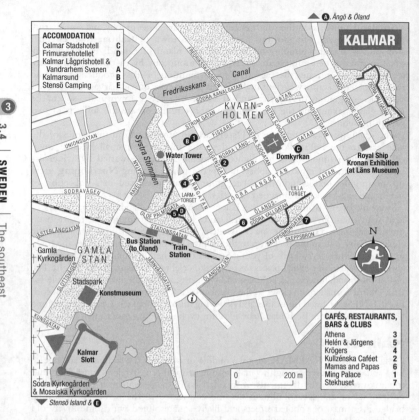

▲ Ⓐ, Ängö & Öland

KALMAR

ACCOMODATION
Calmar Stadshotell C
Frimurarehotellet D
Kalmar Lågprishotell &
  Vandrarhem Svanen A
Kalmarsund B
Stensö Camping E

CAFÉS, RESTAURANTS, BARS & CLUBS
Athena 3
Helén & Jörgens 5
Krögers 4
Kullzénska Caféet 2
Mamas and Papas 6
Ming Palace 1
Stekhuset 7

▼ Stensö Island & Ⓔ

which brought Sweden, Norway and Denmark together as a single kingdom in 1397, and now one of Scandinavia's most finely preserved Renaissance palaces. Just a short walk in the other direction, there's the fascinating exhibition on the **Kronan**, one of the world's biggest warships, which sunk off Öland over three hundred years ago. Even now, new finds are being discovered, helping to piece together the world's most complete picture of seventeenth-century maritime life.

Arrival, information and accommodation

The **bus terminal** and **train station** (from where there are several trains daily to Copenhagen, Gothenburg, Malmö and Växjö) are within spitting distance of Kalmar's **tourist office**, at Ölandskajen 9 (May, June & Sept Mon–Fri 9am–5pm, Sat 10am–1pm; July to mid-Aug Mon–Fri 9am–9pm, Sat & Sun 10am–5pm; Oct–April Mon–Fri 9am–5pm; ☎0480/41 77 00, ⓦwww.kalmar.se). Staff hand out maps and copies of the useful *Kalmar Guide*, and have information about Öland. Kalmar can be explored easily on foot, but if you want to strike out into the surrounding countryside you can rent a **bike** from Team Sportia, Södravägen 2 (☎0480/212 44; 100kr per day).

There's plenty of central accommodation to go round, though the cheapest option, the year-round *Svanen* hostel and budget hotel on Ängö island is just outside the centre, a 15min walk away at Rappegatan 1 (☎0480/129 28, ⓦwww.hotellsvanen.se; ❶), with dorm beds for 195kr. The nearest **campsite** is 3km from the centre on Stensö island (☎0480/888 03, ⓦwww.stensocamping.se), which also has cheap cabins (450kr); bus #401 drops you off near here. Kalmar boasts several very attractive central **hotels**, such as the castle-like *Frimurarehotellet*, Lärmtorget 2

(☎0480/152 30, ⌨www.frimurarehotellet.com; ④/⑤), or the well-positioned and friendly *Kalmarsund*, Fiskaregatan 5 (☎0480/48 03 80, ⌨www.kalmarsundhotel .se; ④/⑥), which has comfortable, en-suite rooms and a sauna and roof garden. If you fancy splashing out, the best-located choice is ⚹ *Calmar Stadshotell*, Stortorget 14 (☎0480/49 69 00, ⌨www.profilhotels.se; ④/⑤), a lovely old building with a stuccoed facade in Art Nouveau style exuding elegance on the main square.

Kalmar Slott

Beautifully set on its own island, a short way from the train and bus stations, the first stones of **Kalmar Slott** (May, June & Sept daily 10am–4pm; July daily 10am–6pm; Aug daily 10am–5pm; Oct Sat & Sun 11am–3.30pm; guided tours in English 11.30am, 1.30pm & 2.30pm; 80kr; ⌨www.kalmarslott.kalmar.se) were probably laid in the twelfth century. A century later, it became the most impenetrable castle in Sweden under King Magnus Ladulås when it was reinforced to defend the nearby border between Sweden and Denmark. The biggest event to take place within its walls was in 1397, when Erik of Pomerania (under the protection of his aunt, the powerful Danish queen, Margarethe) was crowned king of Denmark, Sweden and Norway, instigating the **Kalmar Union**, in which the whole of Scandinavia was united under a single monarch. Subsequently, the castle passed repeatedly between Sweden and Denmark, but despite eleven sieges, remained almost unscathed. By the time Gustav Vasa became king of Sweden in 1523, Kalmar Slott was beginning to show signs of stress and strain, and the king set about rebuilding it, while his sons Erik XIV and Johan III continued with the decoration of the interior. The fine Renaissance palace that was the eventual result of their efforts well illustrates the Vasa family's concern with maintaining Sweden's prestige in the eyes of foreign powers.

Unlike many other southern Swedish castles, this one is picture-perfect, with turrets, ramparts, moat, drawbridge, dungeon and a furnished interior that's fascinating to wander through, especially with the excellent guides who dress in period clothing. Among the many highlights is the bed – stolen from Denmark – in the **Queen's Suite**; it's decorated with carved faces, but with all the noses chopped off – it was general belief that the nose contained the soul, and so the faces were disfigured to prevent the avenging spirits of the rightful owners from taking revenge. However, it's King Erik's bedroom, the **King's Chamber**, which is the most intriguing room, with its wall frieze of vividly painted animals and a secret door to a toilet with two escape routes – Erik was convinced that his younger brother Johan wanted to kill him. This isn't as paranoid as it sounds: Erik's death in 1577 is widely believed to have been caused by eating pea soup poisoned with arsenic.

The rest of the town

On Slottsvägen, opposite the castle, Kalmar's new **Konstmuseum** (Art Museum: daily 11am–5pm, plus Thurs till 8pm; 40kr; ⌨www.kalmarkonstmuseum.se) is worth a quick look. It's a monstrous cube of a building dressed in black wooden panels and plonked unceremoniously in the middle of Slottsparken; there's an emphasis on Abstract Expressionist work inside, painted by Swedish artists in the 1940s and 1950s.

From here, head back into the elegantly laid-out Renaissance town centre, focused on the grand **Domkyrkan** (daily 9am–6pm) in Stortorget, still named so even though Kalmar has had no bishop since 1915. This vast and airy Italian Renaissance-style church was designed in 1660 by Nicodemus Tessin the Elder (as was the nearby Rådhus) after a visit to Rome. Inside, the altar, designed by Tessin the Younger, shimmers with gold, as do the sculptures of *Faith* and *Mercy* around it.

The Royal Ship Kronan Exhibition

Housed in a refurbished steam mill on Skeppsbrongatan, a few minutes' walk from the Domkyrkan, the awe-inspiring **Royal Ship Kronan Exhibition** is the main attraction of the **Läns Museum** (County Museum: mid-June to mid-Aug daily 10am–6pm; mid-Aug to mid June Mon–Fri 10am–4pm, Sat & Sun 11am–4pm;

50kr). The navy flagship *Kronan*, built by the British naval designer Francis Sheldon, was one of the world's three largest ships, twice the size of the *Vasa*, which sank near Stockholm in 1628 (see p.379). The *Kronan* went down in 1676, blown apart by an explosion in its gunpowder magazine – 800 of its 850 crew were killed, their bodies preserved for more than three hundred years on the Baltic seabed.

It wasn't until 1980 that super-sensitive scanning equipment detected the where-abouts of the ship, 26m down off the coast of Öland. A salvage operation was led by a descendant of the ship's captain, Admiral Lorentz Creutz, and the amazing finds are displayed in an imaginative walk-through reconstruction of the gun decks and admiral's cabin, accompanied by sound effects of cannon fire and screeching gulls. While the ship's treasure trove of gold coins is displayed at the end of the exhibition, it's the incredibly well-preserved clothing – hats, jackets, buckled leather shoes and even silk bows and cuff links – that brings this exceptional show to life.

Eating and drinking

There's a generous number of good places **to eat** in Kalmar. The liveliest area is **Lärmtorget**, where restaurants, cafés and pubs serve Swedish, Indonesian, Chinese, Greek, Italian and English food.

Cafés and restaurants

Athena Norra Långgatan 8 ☎0480/280 88. A bright and airy Greek restaurant with tasty traditional fare such as moussaka (95kr) or pork *souvlaki* (115kr), as well as various salads (68–95kr) and pasta dishes (70–100kr).

Helén & Jörgens Olof Palmesgatan 2 ☎0480/288 30. This popular place has a simple but tasty menu: schnitzel, steaks, chicken breast and several fish dishes all go for around 150–200kr. Three-course menus from 230kr.

Krögers Larmtorget 7 ☎0480/265 50. A popular pub-restaurant with a pleasant terrace, serving light Swedish meals from 79kr.

Kullzénska Caféet Kaggengatan 26. Kalmar's best café by far, this is an exceptional *konditori* occupying the first floor of a nineteenth-century wooden house. Its eight interconnecting rooms are awash with stoves, Indian carpets, mahogany furnishings and crumbling royal portraits – exactly as they were during the reign of the twin sisters who lived here for the best part of a century before the building was opened as a tea house. Great coffee and cakes.

Mamas and Papas Kaggensgatan 1 ☎0480/300 32. A hip tapas bar by the city walls serving Swedish and Spanish tapas such as tortilla, garlic chicken, meatballs and potato pancakes: reckon on 45–65kr per tapas.

Ming Palace Fiskaregatan 7. The premier Chinese restaurant in town, with lunch specials and main dishes from 118kr; a three-course set menu is 115kr.

Stekhuset Skeppsbron 1 ☎0480/42 38 58. This is the place to come to taste locally produced Swedish meat from the farms of Småland: steaks are 159–235kr. Fish dishes, too, from 189kr.

Öland

Linked to mainland Sweden by a six-kilometre bridge, the island of **Öland** is the kind of place a Swedish Famous Five would come on holiday: mysterious forests and flat, pretty meadows to cycle through, miles of mostly unspoilt beaches, wooden cottages with candy-striped canopies, windmills and ice-cream parlours; Swedes have been coming here in droves for over a century. This long, splinter-shaped island retains a likeably old-fashioned holiday atmosphere, with a labyrinth of walking trails and bicycle routes and some of the best bathing opportunities in Sweden.

A royal hunting ground from the mid-sixteenth century until 1801, Öland was ruled with scant regard for its native population. Peasants were forbidden to chop wood or own dogs or weapons, while Kalmar's tradesmen exploited the trade restrictions to force low prices for the islanders' produce. Danish attacks on Öland saw seven hundred farms destroyed, and following a succession of disastrous harvests in the mid-nineteenth century, a quarter of the population packed their bags for a new life in America. Today, Öland's young are just as likely to migrate to the Swedish mainland.

Getting to the island

If you're **driving**, head north of Kalmar and over the bridge to Möllstorp on Öland. **Cycling** over the bridge during the day is forbidden from mid-June to August, but there's a free hourly bike bus from Jutnabben on the mainland, which drops you off outside the island's main tourist office in Möllstorp. **Buses** #101 and #102 run almost hourly from Kalmar bus station to Borgholm (55min). If you're coming from the north, it's quicker to catch the **ferry** (T0499/449 20, Wwww.olandsfarjan .se; mid-June to mid-Aug 2 daily; 2hr 20min), which connects Oskarshamn to Byxelkrok in northern Öland; there are very few buses from there, however.

Arrival and information

Öland's most useful **tourist office** is at Sandgatan 25 in Borgholm (June & Aug Mon–Fri 9am–6pm, Sat 10am–4pm; July Mon–Fri 9am–6pm, Sat 9am–5pm, Sun 10am–4pm; Sept to May Mon–Fri 9am–5.30pm; T0485/890 00, Wwww .olandsturist.se). The only place to **rent a bike** in the town is *Hallbergs Hojjar*, Köpmangatan 19 (T0485/109 40).

Borgholm

Walking the simple grid of streets that makes up **BORGHOLM**, Öland's "capital", it's clear that tourism is its lifeblood. Although swamped well beyond its capacity each July by tens of thousands of visitors, cramming the pizzerias and bars and injecting a riotous carnival atmosphere, Borgholm is in no way the tacky resort it could be. Encircled by the flaking, turreted villas that were the pride of the town during its first period as a holiday resort in the nineteenth century, most of the centre is a friendly, if bland, network of shops and restaurants leading to a pleasant harbour.

The only real attraction here is the **Borgholm Slott ruin** (daily: May–Aug 10am–6pm; April & Sept 10am–4pm; free), just to the southwest of the centre. A colossal stone fortification with rows of huge arches and corridors open to the skies, it can be reached either through a nature reserve (a signposted 5min walk from the town centre) or from the first exit south off Route 136. Virtually destroyed by the wars of the sixteenth century, the medieval castle was rebuilt as a Renaissance palace, only to be damaged again during the 1611 Kalmar war. Plans to restore it again, this time in Baroque style, were never finalized, and the castle's deathblow was dealt by a devastating fire in 1806.

A few hundred metres south of the castle is the present royal family's summer residence, **Solliden Park**, an Italian-style villa built to a design specified by Swedish Queen Victoria (the present king's great-grandmother) in 1903. A huge, austere red-granite bust of Victoria rises out of scrubland at the entrance car park. She faces south, away from Sweden – which she was reputed to have loathed – and towards Italy – which she adored. The villa itself is closed to the public but the **gardens** (daily: mid-May to late June & mid-Aug & Sept 10am–6pm; late June to mid-Aug 11am–6pm; gates close at 5pm; 60kr) make for a pleasant stroll, or you could just head for the delightful thatch-roofed café, *Kaffetorpet*, by the car park.

Just to the north of the town centre, **Blå Rör** is Öland's largest Bronze Age cairn, a huge mound of stones excavated when a coffin was discovered here in 1849. In the 1920s, burnt bones indicating a cremation grave were also discovered, along with bronze swords and tweezers – common items in such tombs.

Practicalities

Unlike most other places in Sweden, accommodation prices on Öland rise in summer – the higher price band given, applies throughout the summer season (see p.355 for more details). *Ebbas* **youth hostel** at Storgatan 12 (T0485/990 04 06, Wwww.ebbas.se; May–Sept) in the city centre is situated above a lively garden café and has cheap double rooms (❷) as well as dorm accommodation (290kr per bed). The local **campsite**, *Kapelludden* (T0485/56 07 70, Wwww.kapelludden.se), is on a small peninsula five minutes' walk from the centre, though there's no shortage here, as on the rest of the island, of beautiful spots in which to camp rough.

The best of the **hotels** in the centre of town is *Villa Sol* at Slottsgatan 30 (☎0485/56 25 52, ⓦwww.villasol.nu; ❸). A charming old pale-yellow house set in a fruit-tree-filled garden, it's beautifully furnished, with stripped floors, old tiled fireplaces and a sun-filled veranda. Book early for July, when the place fills up. The *Borgholm*, Trädgårdsgatan 15 (☎0485/770 60, ⓦwww.hotellborgholm.com; ❹/❺), has smart en-suite rooms, while the vast *Strand Hotell*, overlooking the harbour at Villagatan 4 (☎0485/888 88, ⓦwww.strand.borgholm.se; ❹/❺), includes a nightclub, pool and sauna, though if you're not looking to be awake all night, it's best avoided.

There's a pronounced summer-holiday feel to the town's **restaurants** and bars, though standards aren't always very high. Pizza places abound around Stortorget and down to the harbour, all much the same and not cheap at 75–95kr for a pizza. *Mamma Rosa* at Södra Långgatan 2 (☎0485/129 10), serves good pizzas and meat dishes down by the harbour. Close by, *Robinson Crusoe,* Hamnvägen 1 (☎0485/777 58) is a jolly little restaurant-cum-bar serving Swedish home cooking. For the finest food on the island (with prices to match – a three-course set menu costs 565kr), head for the restaurant at the *Hotell Borgholm* (see above). For **drinking**, *Pubben*, Storgatan 18, is a cosy pub run by a friendly local who knows his malts, offering 46 varieties. Otherwise, try *Robinson Crusoe*, jutting into the water at the harbour.

Around the island

The north of the island holds Öland's most varied landscape, with some unexpected diversions to boot. Heading up Route 136, there's no shortage of idyllic villages, dark woods and flowery fields. At **FÖRA**, about 20km north of Borgholm, there's a good example of a typical Öland church, which doubled as a fortress in times of war. About 12km north of here is **KÄLLA**, 2km outside which is proud, forlorn **Källa kyrka**, empty since 1888 and now sitting in splendid isolation. Surrounded by brightly flowering meadows, this medieval church is bounded by dry-stone walls, its grounds littered with ancient, weathered tombs. Continue north and west off Route 136 across the island to the striking **Byrums Rauker**: solitary limestone pillars formed by the sea at the edge of a sandy beach. The best **beaches** in northern Öland are along the east coast; the most popular stretch is a couple of kilometres north of Böda Sand.

There are some gorgeous areas of natural beauty in the far north. The nature reserve of **Trollskogen** ("Trolls Forest") – exactly the kind of place you would imagine trolls to inhabit, with twisted, gnarled trunks of ancient oaks shrouded in ivy – offers some excellent walking. The only town in this region is **BYXELKROK**, a quiet place with an attractive harbour and a ferry to Oskarshamn in summer (see p.459).

Practicalities

There's not much in the way of proper hotels north of Borgholm, but high-standard **campsites** abound, mostly beside the beaches. The most extensive site is *Krono Camping* at Böda Sand (☎0485/222 00, ⓦwww.kronocampingoland.se; mid-May to Sept), 2km off the main road at the southern end of the beach. The STF **youth hostel**, *Vandrarhem Böda* at Mellböda (☎0485/220 38, ✉mikael.sten@telia.com; dorm beds 150kr, double rooms ❶; May–Sept), just south of *Krono Camping*, is big and well equipped and has dorm beds from 110kr. Just 6km northwest of Mellböda at **Byxelkrok**, *Solö Wärdhus* (☎0485/283 70, ⓦwww.wardshus.nu; ❷/❸) is a pleasant enough **hotel**; the town also has the only decent restaurant, *Sjöstugan* (☎0485/283 30; April–Aug), right by the shore. The food is good and varied, with fish, meat and vegetarian dishes.

Central Småland: Växjö and the Glass Kingdom

Thickly forested and studded with lakes, **Småland** makes up the southeastern wedge of Sweden – a region of appealing, if uniform, scenery. It's a part of the country that people frequently travel through – from Stockholm to the southwest, or from Gothenburg to the Baltic coast – yet beneath the canopy of greenery, there are a few spots of interest, along with opportunities for hiking, trekking, fishing and cycling.

Historically, Småland has had it tough. The simple, rustic charm of the pretty painted cottages belies the intense economic misery endured by generations of local peasants; in the nineteenth century, this led to a massive surge of emigration for America. Their plight is vividly retold at the **House of Emigrants** exhibition in **Växjö** – a town that makes an excellent base for exploring the region – but the county's most marketed tourist attraction remains the many **glass factories** hidden away in the forest.

Växjö and around

Founded by St Sigfrid in the eleventh century, **VÄXJÖ** (pronounced approximately "veck-shur") is by far the handiest place to base yourself if you are interested in touring the region's glassworks. Deep in the heart of Småland, the town itself boasts two superb museums: the extensive **Smålands Museum**, notable for being home to the **Swedish Glass Museum**, and the fascinating **House of Emigrants**, which explores the mass emigration from Sweden in the nineteenth and early twentieth centuries. While the town centre doesn't hold much else of appeal, the romantic castle ruin of **Kronoberg** is within easy reach, just 4km to the north.

The Town

Smålands Museum, behind the train station (June–Aug Mon–Fri 10am–5pm, Sat & Sun 11am–5pm; Sept–May Tues–Fri 10am–5pm, Sat & Sun 11am–5pm; 40kr; ⓦwww.smalandsmuseum.se), contains two permanent exhibitions: an intelligently displayed history of Småland's manufacturing industries and the more appealing "five hundred years of Swedish glass". The latter's exhibits range from sixteenth-century place settings to eighteenth- and nineteenth-century etched and coloured glass, along with stylish Art Nouveau-inspired pieces. Most appealing, though, are the wide-ranging displays of contemporary glass.

The plain building directly in front of the museum contains the inspired **House of Emigrants** (May–Aug Tues–Fri 9am–5pm, Sat & Sun 11am–4pm; Sept–April Tues–Fri 9am–4pm, Sat & Sun 11am–4pm; 40kr; ☎0470/201 20, ⓦwww.utvandrarnashus.se), with its moving "Dream of America" exhibition. The museum presents a living picture of the intense hardship faced by the Småland peasant population from the mid-nineteenth century onwards. Due to agricultural reforms and a series of bad harvests, a million Swedes emigrated to America between 1860 and 1930, most of them from Småland. Most boats left from Gothenburg and, until 1915, sailed to Hull in Britain, where passengers crossed by train to board the transatlantic ships. Conditions on board were usually dire: the steamer *Hero* left Gothenburg in 1866 with five hundred emigrants, nearly four hundred oxen and nine hundred pigs, calves and sheep sharing the accommodation. Today, the tables have turned and new texts in the museum detail the experiences of the many immigrants in Sweden.

The attached **research centre** charges 150kr per half-day or 200kr for a full day to help interested parties trace their family roots, using passenger lists from ten harbours, microfilmed church records from every Swedish parish and records of bodies such as the Swedish New York Society, Swedes in Australia and the Swedish Congo Veterans Association. It's worth booking ahead during the summer season.

There's not much else to see in Växjö's centre, but take a quick look at the very distinctive **Domkyrkan** (daily 9am–5pm; free), with its unusual twin green towers and apricot-coloured facade. Regular restorations, the most recent in 1995, together with a catalogue of sixteenth-century fires and a lightning strike in 1775, have left nothing of note except a unique 1775 organ and some brilliant modern glass ornaments by Göran Wärff, one of the best known of the contemporary Glass Kingdom designers. The newest addition is a striking glass altar triptych by equally celebrated Bertil Vallien.

Kronoberg Slott

Set on a tiny island in Lake Helgasjön, the ruins of **Kronoberg Slott** lie 4km north of the town centre in a beautiful and unspoilt setting – follow the signs for Evedal, or take the hourly bus #1B from the bus station. The bishops of Växjö erected a wooden fortress here in the eleventh century, but it was Gustav Vasa who built the present stone version in 1540. Entered over an old wooden bridge set at a narrow spot in the lake, it's a perfect ruin, leaning precariously and complete with rounded tower and deep-set lookouts. The grass-roofed *Café Ryttmästargården*, set in an eighteenth-century cottage overlooking the castle, serves lunch and snacks among quaint old furnishings. The old steamer *Thor* makes regular excursions from here around Lake Helgasjön, the perfect way to appreciate the lakeland scenery. Departure dates vary but Småland Museum has full details (℡0470/70 42 00 or at ✉reception@smalandsmuseum.se).

Practicalities

Växjö's **train** and **bus stations** are alongside one another in the middle of town. The **tourist office** is inside the city library at Västra Esplanaden 7 (June to mid-Sept Mon–Fri 9.30am–6pm, Sat 10am–3pm; mid-Sept to May Mon–Fri 9.30am–4.30pm; ℡0470/414 10, ✹www.turism.vaxjo.se). Free **internet** is available for free in the library.

The splendid STF **youth hostel** (℡0470/630 70, ✹www.vaxjovandrarhem .nu; ❶), with dorm beds for 210kr, is at Evedal, 6km north of the centre, in an eighteenth-century house set in parkland on tranquil Lake Helgasjön (with its own beach). To get there, take bus #1C from the bus station. Next to the hostel is a **campsite**, *Evedal Camping* (℡0470/630 34, ✹www.evedalscamping.com), with cabins (750kr).

Of the town's **hotels**, the most striking is the *Elite Stadshotell*, Kungsgatan 6 (℡0470/134 00, ✹www.vaxjo.elite.se; ❸/❺), a modern business hotel with smart rooms and lots of marble. Otherwise, try the no-frills *Esplanad*, Norra Esplanaden 21A (℡0470/225 80, ✹www.hotellesplanad.com; ❸/❹), or the good-value *Värend*, Kungsgatan 27 (℡0470/77 67 00, ✹www.hotellvarend.se; ❷/❸).

Växjö is a good place to eat traditional Småland cuisine, which features lots of berries, potatoes and game. For a **restaurant** with strong gourmet leanings, the central 🍴 *PM & Vänner* at Storgatan 24 (℡0470/70 04 44) is one of the very best **eating places** in Sweden, with an emphasis on fine modern European cuisine using lake-caught fish; main dishes in the cheaper bistro section cost from 200kr. Set in Växjö's oldest house at Sandgärdsgatan 19, *Wibrowski* (℡0470/74 04 10) serves excellent lamb, Wienerschnitzel and pepper steak, starting at 180kr. Next door, 🍴 *Kafé de Luxe* (℡0470/74 04 09), a fun 1950s-style eatery furnished with formica tables, tube-metal chairs and wooden radios, has an excellent Swedish-influenced tapas menu (from 175kr) and regular live music.

The Glass Kingdom

Between Kalmar and Växjö, in a landscape of dense birch and pine forests threaded by lakes, lie the bulk of Småland's celebrated **glassworks**. The area is dubbed Glasriket (✹www.glasriket.se), or the **"Glass Kingdom"**, with each glassworks signposted clearly from the spidery main roads. This seemingly odd and very picturesque setting for the industry is no coincidence. King Gustav Vasa pioneered glass-making in Sweden when he returned from Italy in the mid-sixteenth century and decided to set up a glassworks in Stockholm. However, it was only Småland's forests that could provide the vast amounts of fuel needed to feed the furnaces, and so a glass factory was set up here in 1742, named Kosta after its founders, Koskull and Stael von Hostein – today, under the name Kosta Boda, it's the largest glassworks in Småland.

Visiting the glassworks

All the fifteen or so glassworks still in operation in Småland put on captivating glass-blowing **demonstrations**, usually Monday to Friday between 9am and 3pm. **Bus**

Glass-making and buying glass

Demonstrations of the **glass-making process** can be mesmerizing to watch. The process involves a plug being fished out of a shimmering lake of molten glass (heated to 1200°C) and then turned and blown into a graphite or steel mould. In the case of wine glasses, a foot is then added, before the piece is annealed (heated and then slowly cooled) for several hours. It all looks deceptively simple and mistakes are rare, but it nevertheless takes years to become a servitor (glass-maker's assistant), working up through the ranks of stem-maker and bowl-gatherer. In smaller works, all these processes are carried out by the same person, but in many of Småland's glassworks, you'll see the bowl-gatherer fetching the glowing gob for the master blower, who then skilfully rolls and shapes the syrupy substance. When the blower is attaching bases to wine glasses, the would-be stem will slide off or sink right through if the glass is too hot; if too cold, it won't stick – and the right temperature lasts a matter of seconds.

If you want to **buy glassware**, which is marketed with a vengeance, don't feel compelled to snap up the first thing you see. The same batch of designs appears at most of the glassworks, a testament to the fact that the Kosta Boda and Orrefors outfits are owned by the same umbrella company, and that most of the smaller works have been swallowed up by it, too, even though they retain their own names. This makes price comparison easier, but don't expect many bargains; the best pieces go for thousands of kronor.

services to (or to within walking distance of) the glassworks are extremely limited, and without your own transport it is almost impossible to see more than a couple in a day – although you'll probably find this is enough. Glass fanatics can purchase the **Glasriket Pass** (95kr), which gives reductions on entrance fees and gift-shop sales, and free guided tours of participating factories; it's available from the glassworks, tourist offices and hotels in the area.

While each glassworks has characteristic individual designs, the Kosta Boda works give the best picture of what is available. The **Kosta Boda** and **Åfors** glassworks is also the easiest to reach from Växjö: to get there, take Route 25 to Lessebo, then follow signs to Kosta, or hop on the direct bus #218 from Växjö. The **historical exhibition** here (June to mid-Aug Mon–Fri 10am–6pm, Sat 10am–4pm, Sun noon–4pm; free) contains some of the most delicate *fin-de-siècle* glassware designed by Karl Lindeberg; for contemporary simplicity, Anna Ehrner's bowls and vases are the most elegant.

Vadstena

With its beautiful lakeside setting, a good 200km north of Växjö, **VADSTENA** is the most evocative town in the province of Östergötland, and a fine place for a day or two's stay. At one time a royal seat and an important monastic centre, the town's main attraction nowadays is its gorgeous moated castle, **Vadstena Slott**, planned in the sixteenth century by Gustav Vasa as part of his defensive ring to protect the Swedish heartland around Stockholm. Vadstena's cobbled, twisting streets, lined with cottages covered in climbing roses, also hold an impressive **abbey**, whose existence is the result of the passionate work of fourteenth-century St Birgitta, Sweden's first female saint.

The castle and abbey

Vadstena boasts a number of ancient sites and buildings, notably the Rådhus, which contains Sweden's oldest courthouse, but the town's top attraction is its castle, **Vadstena Slott** (May & Sept daily 10am–3pm; June–Aug daily 10am–6pm; Oct–April Mon–Fri 10am–2pm; May to mid-Sept 55kr, otherwise 35kr; Ⓦwww .vadstena.com). With four seven-metre-thick round towers and a grand moat (which now doubles as the local marina), it was originally built in 1545 as a fortification to defend against Danish attacks, but was then prettified into a palace to house Gustav Vasa's mentally ill third son, Magnus. His elder brother, Johan III, was responsible for its lavish decorations, but fire destroyed it all just before completion, and to save on costs the post-fire decor was merely painted on the walls, right down to the swagged curtains that can still be seen today.

From the end of the seventeenth century, the building fell into decay and was used as a grain store; the original hand-painted wooden ceilings were chopped up to make into grain boxes. As a result, there wasn't much to see inside until recently, when the acquisition of period furniture from all over Europe has created more of an atmosphere. Portraits of the Vasa family have also been crammed in, displaying some very unhappy and ugly faces that make for entertaining viewing. English-language **guided tours** of the furnished apartments and the royal chapel with its seventeen-second echo are included in the entrance fee (June & July daily 1.30pm; Aug daily 2pm; included in entry fee June).

A few minutes' walk away at the water's edge stands Vadstena's **abbey church** (daily: May 10am–5pm; June & Aug 10am–7pm; July 9am–7pm; Oct–April 11am–3.30pm), the architectural legacy of St Birgitta. Birgitta came to Vadstena as a lady-in-waiting to King Magnus Eriksson and his wife, Blanche of Namur, who lived at Bjälbo Palace. After being married at the age of 13, and having given birth to eight children, she began to experience visions and convinced her royal employers to give up their home in order to set up a convent and monastery. Birgitta's specification that the church should be "of plain construction, humble and strong" is fulfilled from the outside, but the sombre, grey exterior hides a celebrated collection of medieval artwork. More memorable than the crypts of various royals is the statue, now devoid of hands, of Birgitta "in a state of ecstasy". To the right, the rather sad "Door of Grace and Honour" was where each Birgittine nun entered the abbey after being professed – the next time she passed through the doorway would be in a coffin on her funeral day. Birgitta's bones are encased in a red velvet box, decorated with silver and gilt medallions, in a glass case down stone steps in the monks' choir stalls.

Practicalities

Reaching Vadstena by **public transport** is a bit of a hassle as there are no trains – the nearest station is 30km east at Mjölby – and the bus system is lamentably poor; see Ⓦwww.resplus.se for timetables. By **car**, it's a straight run along the E4 and Route 50. The **tourist office is** inside the castle (same hours as the castle; ℡0143/315 70, Ⓦwww.vadstena.com).

Vadstena's STF **youth hostel** is in the town centre at Skänningegatan 20 (℡0143/103 02, Ⓔvandrarhem@sevadstena.se; dorm beds 230kr, double rooms ❶). The lakeside *Vätterviksbadet* **camping** (℡0143/127 30, Ⓦwww.vadstenacamping.se) is 2km north of the centre and has two-bed cabins (450kr).

The town's **hotels**, most of them housed in converted historic buildings, are fairly expensive. The *Vadstena Klosterhotell*, in the medieval nunnery next to the abbey (℡0143/315 30, Ⓦwww.klosterhotel.se; ❸/❺), has comfortable rooms and very atmospheric public areas. A better-value option is the **B&B** *Pensionat Solgården*, Strågatan 3 (May–Sept; ℡0143/143 50, Ⓦwww.pensionatsolgarden.se; ❷), a beautifully maintained villa from 1905 in a quiet, central little street.

Vadstena has a decent selection of places to eat. The pick of the **cafés** is *Micasa Coffee & Kitchen*, Rådhustorget 9, where a young, laid-back crowd comes for the relatively cheap light meals from 75kr, while the best **restaurant** in town is *Vadstena Valven* (℡0143/123 40), in the same building, which does lunch for 89kr and fish specialities in the evening. An interesting alternative is *På Hörnet* (℡0143/131 70), next to a medieval tower at Skänningegatan 1, a neighbourhood **pub** serving well-thought-out dishes, such as marinated mushrooms and herrings. It's a great place for all-day brunch. The *Rådhuskälleren* (℡0143/121 70) in the cosy cellars of the sixteenth-century courthouse on Rådhustorget, does lunch for 89kr and dinner from 139kr and also doubles as a pub; its particularly busy on Thursday and Saturday evenings.

Örebro

One hundred and sixteen kilometres north of Vadstena and strategically located on the InterCity (though not X2000 high-speed) rail route between Gothenburg and Stockholm, the lively and youthful town of **ÖREBRO** lies near the shores of the country's fourth largest lake, Hjälmaren. At its heart is the much-fortified thirteenth-century **castle** which forms a magnificent backdrop for the water-lily-studded Svartån River. Aside from the town's attractions, **Lake Tysslingen**, a few kilometres west, makes for a good afternoon excursion by bike, while in spring the several thousand whooper swans that settle here on their way to northern Finland provide spectacular viewing.

Arrival, information and accommodation

From the train and bus stations, the knowledgeable **tourist office** is a 15-minute walk away, south along Östra Bangatan and then left into Änggatan at Olof Palmes Torg (Mon–Fri 10am–6pm, Sat 10am–2pm, Sun noon–4pm; ℡019/21 21 21, ⓦwww .visitorebro.se). The town centre is easy to see on foot, but if you want to get out into the countryside you can **rent a bike** from the city library next to the tourist office (70kr per day). Another option is take a **boat trip** around nearby Lake Hjälmaren on *M/S Gustaf Lagerbjelke* which operates from late June to mid-August (5hr cruise 295kr; lunch cruises including a buffet 195kr; ⓦwww.lagerbjelke .com); tickets can be bought at the tourist office.

The *Grenadjären* **youth hostel** (℡019/31 02 40, ⓦwww.grenadjaren se), which has double rooms (①) as well as dorm beds (210kr), is in a set of appealing old army barracks just to the north of the centre on Kaptensgatan 1. The huge *Gustavsvik* **camping site** (℡019/19 69 50, ⓦwww.gustavsvik.se; late April to Sept) is 2km south of town and features Scandinavia's biggest bathing complex.

Of Örebro's **hotels**, the best traditional option is the central ☂ *Elite Stora*, Drottninggatan 1 (℡019/15 69 00, ⓦwww.orebro.elite.se; ③/⑥), which is supposedly haunted by the ghost of a young woman and her mother. Near the castle, the

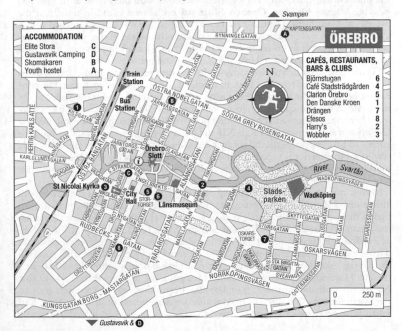

▲ Örebro Slott

superb *Clarion Örebro*, Kungsgatan 14 (☎019/670 67 00, ⓦwww.choice.se; ❸/❺)
has large and sumptuous bedrooms, while *Skomakaren*, Järnvägsgatan 20 (☎019/611
90 35, ⓦwww.hotellskomakaren.se; ❷/❹), is basic but perfectly adequate and has
good discounted rates.

The Town

A fort has defended Örebro ever since a band of German merchants settled here in
the thirteenth century, attracted by the presence of iron ore in the area. Enlarged
by King Magnus Eriksson, **Örebro Slott** sits on its own island in middle of the
Svartån, and was further fortified by Gustav Vasa, whose son Karl IX turned it into
a splendid Renaissance palace, raising the walls to the height of the medieval towers
and plastering them in cream stucco. After the town lost its importance, the castle
fell into disuse and was turned into a storehouse and prison.

The fairytale exterior you see today is the result of renovation in the 1890s, when
the castle was restored to reflect both its medieval and Renaissance grandeur. The same
cannot be said for the interior: there is no original furniture, and today many of the
rooms are used by the county governor for conferences. The few features of interest are
some finely inlaid doors and floors dating from the 1920s, depicting historical events at
Örebro, and a large portrait of Karl XII and his family, their faces painted to look the
same – all have popping eyes, the result of using arsenic to whiten their faces. The only
way to see the interior is to join the lively "Secrets of the Vasa fortress" **tour** (entry on
tours only: mid-June to mid-Aug daily in English at 2pm; 65kr), a mix of traditional
tour and play, with guides dressed as kings, servants and prisoners.

Nearby, at the top of the very oblong Stortorget, the neo-Gothic **city hall** – built
after a fire destroyed its predecessor in 1854 – features a chime with mythological
figures that pop out of the facade daily a few minutes past noon and 6pm (summer
also 9pm). The adjacent **St Nicolai kyrka** (Mon–Fri 8.30am–5pm, Sat & Sun
11am–3pm) originates from 1260, but lost most of its original medieval character
during extensive restoration in the 1860s. Recent renovations have tried to undo
the damage, but today it's the contemporary art exhibitions on show here that catch
the eye. Historically, however, the church is significant, as it was here in 1810 that
Napoleon's unknown marshal, Jean Baptiste Bernadotte, was elected successor to
the Swedish throne. The present royal family are descendants of this new king, Karl
Johan, who never spoke a word of Swedish.

From the town centre, it's a pleasant twenty-minute stroll, following the river and past the appealing Stadsparken to **Wadköping** (mid-June to mid-Aug daily 11am–5pm; mid-Aug to mid-June Tues–Sun 11am–4pm; free; ⓦwww.orebro.se /wadkoping), an entire village of centuries-old wooden cottages and shops brought to the site from the city centre to form a living open-air museum. It's all extremely pretty, but a little staged. Some of the cottages have been reoccupied, and the twee little shops sell pastel-coloured wooden knick-knacks.

Eating and drinking

Örebro boasts plenty of atmospheric **eating** places. If you're here in July, though, bear in mind that some of the smaller restaurants close for the holidays.

Björnstugan Kungsgatan 3. An inordinately fashionable place for an evening drink or two, especially in summer. DJs play the latest chart music interspersed with a few golden oldies.

Café Stadsträdgården Floragatan 1. With an unusual setting in the greenhouses at the park entrance, this is a wonderful daytime café offering fine, fresh sandwiches, home-baked cakes and superb pies, all organic.

Den Danske Kroen Kilsgatan 8. Danish bar and restaurant with a lively but relaxed and down-to-earth atmosphere, serving cheap, simple meals and open sandwiches and a wide selection of beers.

Drängen Oskarstorget 9 ☎19/32 32 96. Consistently superb locals' pub and restaurant of long standing, offering great Swedish home cooking dishes from 155kr.

Efesos Rudbecksgatan 28 ☎019/611 66 15. Renowned for generous portions of tasty Greek fare, especially kebabs and steaks (around 189kr). Be sure to reserve a table as it's always busy.

Harrys Hamnplan. A popular, bustling pub overlooking the river, with Swedish and international food.

Wobbler Kyrkogatan 2 ☎019/10 07 40. Classic Swedish cooking with a modern twist at this bright and airy place with a separate tapas lounge. Elaborate mains from 159kr.

Norrköping

It is with good reason that the dynamic, youth-oriented town of **NORRKÖPING** calls itself Sweden's Manchester. Like its British counterpart, Norrköping's wealth came from its textile industry, which thrived in the eighteenth and nineteenth centuries. The legacy from this period is the town's most appealing feature: it's one of Europe's best-preserved **industrial urban landscapes**, with handsome red-brick and stuccoed mills reflected in the waters of Motala Ström.

It was this small, rushing river that attracted the Dutch industrialist **Louis De Geer** to the town in the late seventeenth century, and his paper mill, still in operation today, became the biggest factory in the city, to be followed by numerous wool, silk and linen factories. Today, many buildings are painted a strong, tortilla-chip yellow, as are the trams – De Geer's favourite colour has become a symbol of the town. Textiles kept Norrköping booming until the 1950s, when foreign competition began to sap the market, and the last big textile mill closed its doors in 1992.

Arrival, information and accommodation

Five minutes' walk from the **train** and **bus** terminals, inside the old paper mill gate at Dalsgatan 2, is the helpful **tourist office** (late June to mid-Aug Mon–Fri 10am–6pm, Sat 10am–5pm, Sun 10am–2pm; Sept to late June Mon–Fri 10am–5pm; ☎011/15 50 00, ⓦwww.upplev.norrkoping.se), where you can get a wealth of maps and brochures. Ask at the tourist office about the 1902 **vintage tram**, which circles around the city on a sightseeing tour during summer. **Internet** connection is available at Sidewalk Express in the train station.

The central STF *Turistgården* **youth hostel** at Ingelstagatan 31 (☎011/10 11 60, ⓦwww.turistgarden.se; dorm beds 235kr, double rooms ❶) is just a few hundred metres behind the train station. The closest **campsite**, *Himmelstalund* (☎011/17 11 90, ⓦwww.norrkopingscamping.com) is 2km from the centre on Campingvägen; take tram #3. Among the town's **hotels**, *Centric* at Gamla Rådstugugatan 18–20

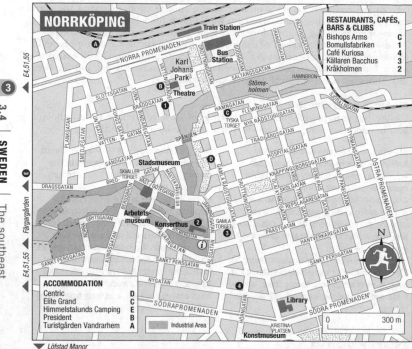

▼ Löfstad Manor

(℡011/12 90 30, ⓦwww.centrichotel.se; ❷/❸) is set in a stylish building from 1932 close to the train station. For a more upmarket experience, get a room at the grand old *Elite Grand*, bang in the centre at Tyska Torget 2 (℡011/36 41 00, ⓦwww .grandhotel.elite.se; ❸/❺), or at the *President*, also very central, at Vattengränden 11 (℡011/12 95 20, ⓦwww.profilhotels.se/hotel/president; ❸/❹).

The Town

Norrköping's main avenue, **Drottninggatan**, runs north–south from the train station through the city centre. Just a few steps down from the station, the small **Karl Johans Park** boasts (in summer) the unusual feature of 25,000 cacti, all formally arranged in thematic patterns. Continuing over the river and following the tram lines up Drottninggatan, a right turn into Repslagaregatan leads into **Gamla Torget**, overlooked by a charismatic sculpture of Louis De Geer by Carl Milles (see p.388). From here, the steely, modern riverside **Konserthus** is fronted by trees; it's worth stepping inside for a gander at its strikingly contemporary and naturally lit interior, which belies the fact that this was once one of De Geer's paper factories.

Go through the impressive, eighteenth-century paper-mill gates to the left of the concert hall and you'll find yourself in Norrköping's fabulous **industrial landscape**, with old paper and textile factories crammed around a series of waterfalls along the Motala Ström, whose waters powered the mills before steam engines took over. The area was nearly bulldozed in the 1970s but has been beautifully restored and today houses the university, offices and a conference centre.

Down the steps next to the wooden bridge there's a huge turbine pipe that has been turned into a platform from where you can watch the waterfalls; in winter, there's a colourful lightshow here every half-hour (from dusk till 9pm). Beyond the bridge stands the **Arbetets museum** (Work Museum: daily 11am–5pm, Sept–May also Tues until 8pm; free), housed in a triangular, yellow-stuccoed factory from 1917. Known as "The Iron" – though its shape and colour are more reminiscent of a wedge of cheese – the building was considered by Carl Milles to be Europe's most beautiful factory. It's a splendid place, with seven floors of exhibitions on living conditions, workers' rights and daily life in the mills. Take the stairs down, rather than the lift, to see a touching exhibition in the stairwell about the life of Alva, a woman who spent 35 years as a factory worker here.

Next door, over another little bridge, is the excellent **Stadsmuseum** (City Museum: June–Aug Tues, Wed & Fri 10am–4pm, Thurs 10am–8pm, Sat & Sun 11am–4pm; Sept–May Tues, Wed & Fri 10am–5pm, Thurs 10am–8pm, Sat & Sun 11am–4pm; free). Set in an interconnecting (and very confusing) network of old industrial properties, the permanent exhibitions include textile machines, examples of Swedish textile design, a model of the area in 1941 and a cute trade street featuring the workplaces of a milliner, confectioner and chimney sweep.

Retracing your steps back into the town centre, any interest you have in Swedish art can be satisfied at the **Konstmuseum** (Art Museum: June–Aug Tues–Sun noon–4pm, Wed until 8pm; Sept–May Tues–Sun 11am–5pm, Tues & Thurs until 8pm; free) on Kristinaplatsen, which displays some of the country's best-known Modernist works. Founded by a local snuff manufacturer around the beginning of the twentieth century, the galleries offer a fine, well-balanced progression from seventeenth-century Baroque through to contemporary paintings.

Eating and drinking

There's a fair selection of eating places in Norrköping, most of them doubling as bars.

For an old-fashioned neighbourhood **café**, try *Café Kuriosa*, in the centre of town at Horngatan 6, which serves home-baked cakes, savoury pies and ice cream in an old living-room-style environment. The *Kråkholmen* café, with a lovely setting overlooking the water next to the concert hall at Dalsgatan 15, serves lunch and drinks on weekdays in summer. The most sensational **restaurant** in town is *A Bomullsfabriken*, next door at Dalsgatan 13 (☎011/13 44 00), with an enjoyable outdoor seating area in summer and an eclectic mix of Swedish and Mediterranean flavours with mains at 139–289kr.

For **drinking**, try *Källaren Bacchus* at Gamla Torget 4, a cellar restaurant serving traditional Swedish food (from 107kr) with a long cocktail list. Alternatively, the *Bishops Arms*, Drottninggatan 2, is undoubtedly the most popular pub in Norrköping, and boasts the biggest selection of beers and whiskies in town.

Gotland

Rumours about good times on **Gotland** are rife. Wherever you are in Sweden, one mention of this ancient Baltic island will elicit a typically Swedish sigh followed by an anecdote about what a great place it is. You'll hear that the short summer season is an exciting time to visit; that it's hot, fun and lively. Largely, this is all true: the island has a distinctly youthful feel as young Stockholmers desert the capital for a boisterous summer spent on the beaches. During summer, the island (with a population of 58,000) plays host to some 750,000 tourists; bars, restaurants and campsites are packed, the streets swarm with revellers, and the sands are awash with bodies. It's not everyone's cup of tea: to avoid the hectic summer altogether, come in late May or September when, depending on your bravado, you can still swim.

Gotland itself, and in particular its capital, **Visby**, has always seen frenetic activity of some kind. A temperate climate and fortuitous geographical position attracted the Vikings as early as the sixth century, and the lucrative trade routes they opened, through to Byzantium and western Asia, guaranteed the island its prosperity. With the ending of Viking domination, a golden age followed, during which Gotland's inhabitants maintained trading posts and signed treaties with European and Asian leaders. However, by the late twelfth century the island's autonomy had been undermined by the growing power of the Hanseatic League, under whose influence Visby became one of the great cities of medieval Europe, famed for its wealth and strategic power. Prosperity persisted right into the twentieth century, when Gotlanders began relying on tourism to prop up the traditional industries of farming, forestry and fishing. Modern hype makes great play of the sun, and it's true that the flowers that give Gotland its "Island of Roses" tag have been known to bloom at Christmas. It's not all just tourist brochure fodder, however: nowhere else in Scandinavia is there such

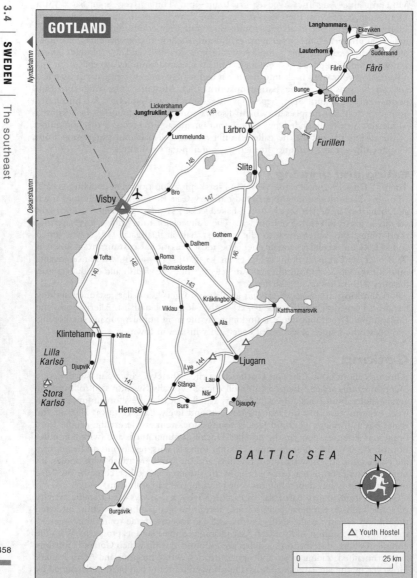

a concentration of unspoilt medieval country churches, 92 of them still in use and providing the most permanent reminder of Gotland's ancient wealth.

Getting there: ferries and planes
Ferries to Gotland are numerous and, in summer, packed, so try to plan well ahead. Two mainland ports serve the island, **Nynäshamn** and **Oskarshamn**, and crossings take about three hours. Prices depend on season, with the cheaper tickets for departures outside the summer peak: one-way tickets start at 180kr in the low season and 245kr for mid-June to mid-August sailings. Buy tickets online at Ⓦwww.destinationgotland.se.

Flights to Gotland are good value if booked early. Skyways (Ⓦwww.skyways .se) operates from both Arlanda and Bromma airports in Stockholm; Gotlandsflyg (Ⓦwww.gotlandsflyg.se) has services from Bromma and Skavsta and several provincial airports. Cheapest one-way tickets are 328kr.

Visby
Undoubtedly the finest approach to **VISBY** is by ship, when you can take in the old trading centre as it should be seen – from the sea. With its fine medieval city walls, churches and cobbled streets, Visby is a pleasure to stroll through, and is quite unlike any town in mainland Sweden.

Arrival and information
Visby **airport** is 5km from town; a ten-minute **taxi** ride into the centre will cost a maximum of 135kr.

All the **ferries** serving Visby dock at the same terminal, just outside the city walls. Just turn left and walk for ten minutes to reach the centre. The excellent main **tourist office** (May to mid-June & mid- to end Aug Mon–Fri 8am–5pm, Sat & Sun 10am–4pm; mid June to mid-Aug daily 8am–7pm; Sept Mon–Fri 8am–5pm, Sat & Sun 11am–2pm; Oct–April Mon–Fri 8am–noon & 12.30–4pm; ☎0498/20 17 00, Ⓦwww.gotland.info) overlooks the harbour at Skeppsbron 4, en route between the ferries and the old town. Here you can buy Kartförlaget's *Gotland* map with descriptions of all the island's points of interest, which is good enough for cycling. There's also a selection of **tours** available, such as the comprehensive walking tour of Visby (mid-June to mid-Aug 2–3 times a week; 85kr). There are no **internet** cafés in Visby, but the library (Mon–Fri 10am–7pm, Sat & Sun noon–4pm) at Cramergatan 5, by Almedalen, has free access.

Getting around
Visby itself is best explored on foot. Despite its warren-like appearance, it's a simple matter to find your way around the narrow, cobbled streets. The main square, **Stora Torget**, is signposted from almost everywhere. Modern Visby has spread beyond its old city walls, and today the ugly Östercentrum shopping area sprawls out past **Österport** (East Gate), a few minutes' walk up the hill from Stora Torget. From here, the **bus station** serves the rest of Gotland; the tourist office has timetables.

The best way to get around the island is to **rent a bike** outside the ferry terminal from Gotlands Cykeluthyrning, Skeppsbron 2 (from 75kr per day; Ⓦwww.gotlandscykeluthyrning.com). Rental is also possible at several outlets near Österport on Östervägen: Visby Hyrcykel at no. 1 and Team Sportia at no. 17.

Accommodation
Finding **accommodation** in Visby should seldom be a problem – there are plenty of hotels (though few are particularly cheap). Gotlandsresor (☎0498/20 12 60, Ⓦwww.gotlandsresor.se), by the ferry terminal at Färjeleden 3, and Gotlands Turist Service (Mon–Fri 9.30am–6pm; ☎0498/20 33 00, Ⓦwww.gotlandsturistservice .com), Österväg 3A near Österport, can help with **private rooms** (from 300kr

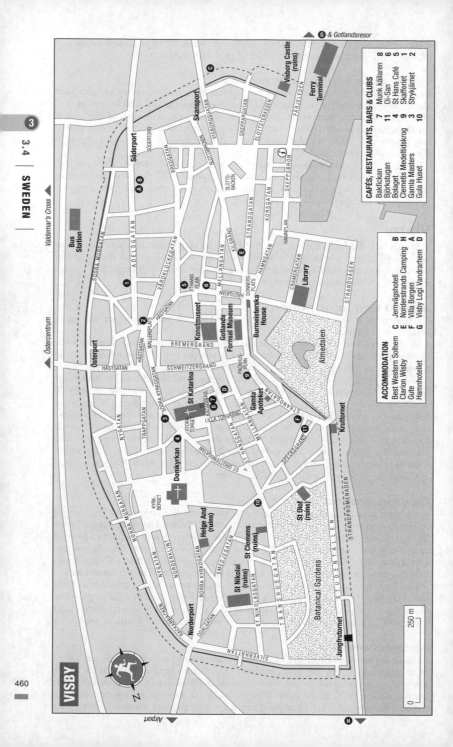

VISBY

▲ Valdemar's Cross   ▲ Östercentrum

◀ Airport

▲ G & Gotlandsresor

Visborg Castle (ruins)

Ferry Terminal

Skansport

Söderport

Bus Station

Österport

Skeppsbron

Strandgatan

Korgatan

Hamnplan

Hamngatan

Cramergatan

Library

Almedalen

Strandvägen

Burmeisterska House

Gotlands Fornsal Museum

Konstmuseet

St Katarina

Gamla Apoteket

Domkyrkan

St Hans Café

Helge And (ruins)

St Clemens (ruins)

St Nikolai (ruins)

St Olof (ruins)

Kruttornet

Botanical Gardens

Jungfrutornet

Strandpromenaden

Studentallen

Norderport

Strandgatan

Södra Murgatan

Adelsgatan

Värnklockegatan

Hästgatan

Wallersplats

S:t Hans Plan

Mellangatan

Kilgrand

Slottsbacken

Slottsterrassen

Visborgsgatan

Skeppargatan

Södertorg

Bredgatan

Nygatan

Trappgatan

Bremergränd

Schweitzergränd

Packhusgränd

Lilla Torggränd

S:t Katarinag.

Stora Torget

S:t Hansgatan

S:t Drottensgatan

Norra Murgatan

Norderklint

Nygatan

Smedjegatan

Norra Kyrkogatan

Odlgatan

S:t Nikolaigatan

Transhusgatan

Silverhättan

Bäckbacken

Kyrk-Berget

Donners Plats

Hästgatan

Spikbrogränd

ACCOMMODATION

Best Western Solhem	B	Jernvägshotell	C
Clarion Wisby	H	Norderstrands Camping	A
Gute	F	Villa Borgen	H
Hammhotellet	E	Visby Logi Vandrarhem	D

CAFÉS, RESTAURANTS, BARS & CLUBS

Bakfickan	7	Munk källaren	8
Björkstugan	11	Ol-San	6
Bolaget	4	St Hans Café	5
Clemetis Medeltidskrog	9	Skafferiet	1
Gamla Masters	3	Strykjärnet	10
Gula Huset	10		

0   250 m

N

◀ H

Visby's churches

At the height of its power, Visby maintained sixteen **churches**, and while only one, the Domkyrkan, is still in use, the ruins of eleven others can be seen. At the centre of Kyrkberget, the St Maria Cathedral or **Domkyrkan** (Mon–Wed, Fri & Sun 8am–9pm, Thurs & Sat 8am–6.30pm) was built between 1190 and 1225 and, as such, dates from just before the great age of Gothic church-building on the island. Used as both warehouse and treasury in the past, it's been heavily restored, and about the only original fixture left is the thirteenth-century sandstone font; have a look, though, beneath the pulpit, decorated with a fringe of unusually hideous angels' faces. The cathedral's most striking feature are its towers, a square one at the western front and two slimmer ones to the east; each was originally topped by a spire, but since an eighteenth-century fire they've been crowned with fancy Baroque cupolas, giving them the appearance of inverted ice-cream cones.

Seventeenth- and eighteenth-century builders and decorators found the smaller churches in the city to be an excellent source of free limestone, tiles and fittings – which accounts for the fact that most are today in ruins. Best of what's left are St Katerina on Stora Torget (visit after dark, when its fine Gothic interior is floodlit), and the great **St Nikolai** ruin, just down the road from the Domkyrkan, once the largest church in Visby. Destroyed in 1525, its part-Gothic, part-Romanesque shell hosts a week-long **chamber music festival** (ⓦwww.gotland-chamber-music -festival.info), starting at the end of July. Nearby stand the **St Clemens** ruins and, in the Botanical Gardens, the romantic **St Olof** ruins – fittingly overgrown with creepers. You can get an informative free guide with information on churches all around the island, from the tourist office.

per person, doubles ❶), as well as **cottages** both in and outside Visby. In Visby, the peak season is summer (May–Aug). Cheaper rooms are available Monday to Friday during the rest of the year (non-summer weekends are generally another 200–300kr less). See p.355 for more details.

Best Western Solhem Solhemsgatan 3 ☎0498/25 90 00, ⓦwww.hotellsolhem.se. Just outside the city walls near Skansporten, this large, comfortable hotel has a basement sauna and is quieter than the more central places. ❹/❻

Clarion Wisby Strandgatan 6 ☎0498/25 75 00, ⓦwww.wisbyhotell.se. Splendid, central hotel in a building dating back to the Middle Ages. Fine breakfasts. ❻

Gute Mellangatan 29 ☎0498/20 22 60, ⓦwww .hotellgute.se. Very central and reasonably comfortable classical-style hotel with en-suite rooms. ❹/❺

Hamnhotell Färjeleden 3 ☎0498/20 12 50, ⓦwww.gotlandsresor.se. Hotel complex centred around the yellow building visible 200m south of the ferry terminal. All rooms have TV, shower and toilet, with a good breakfast in the on-site restaurant. ❸/❹

Jernvägshotell Adelsgatan 9 ☎0498/20 33 00, ⓦwww.gotlandsturistservice.com/SVE/Boende /Wisby_Jernvagshotell. Although train services

on Gotland ceased in 1960, this former railway hotel, now a youth hostel, is still in operation with modern, comfortable rooms, though with no dorms. Double rooms ❶

Norderstrands Camping Österväg 3A ☎0498/21 21 57, ⓦwww.norderstrandscamping.se. Barely 800m outside the city walls – follow the cycle path that runs through the Botanical Gardens along the seafront, though reception is at Gotlands Turist Service (see p.459). June–Aug only. Has cabins for rent (650kr).

Villa Borgen Adelsgatan 11 ☎0498/27 99 00, ⓦwww.guteinfo.com/villaborgen. Attractive family hotel in the middle of the action, yet with lovely, peaceful gardens. En-suite rooms, sauna and solarium. ❹/❺

Visby Logi Vandrarhem St Hansgatan 31 ☎070/752 20 55. Five cosy double rooms decorated in tasteful whites and greys make up this youth hostel in an atmospheric old house dating from the 1600s. Rooms are up to 250kr cheaper outside the peak June–Aug period. ❸

Visby is much older than its medieval remnants suggest – the name derives from its status as a Stone Age sacrificial site: "the settlement" (*by*) at "the sacred place" (*vi*). The magnificent **defensive wall** that encircles Visby is the most obvious manifestation of its previous importance. It was hardly a new idea to fortify trading centres against outside attack, although this land wall, built around the end of the thirteenth century, was actually constructed to separate the city's foreign traders from the rest of the island's inhabitants. Annoyed at having all their old trade monopolized, the Gotlanders saw something sinister in the wall's erection. They didn't have to wait long to be vindicated: in 1361, during the power struggle between Denmark and Sweden, the Danish king, Valdemar III, took Gotland by force and advanced on Visby. The burghers and traders, well aware of the wealth of their city, shut the gates and sat through the slaughter outside. Excavations during the twentieth century revealed the remains of two thousand bodies, more than half of them women and children. **Valdemar's Cross**, a few hundred metres east of Söderport (South Gate), marks their mass grave. Erected by the survivors of the carnage, it reads: "In 1361 on the third day after St James, the Goths fell into the hands of the Danes. Here they lie. Pray for them."

Back inside the city walls, the merchants surrendered, and a section of the wall near Söderport was broken down to allow Valdemar to ride through as conqueror. Valdemar's Breach is recognizable by its thirteen crenellations representing, so the story goes, the thirteen knights who rode through with the Danish king. Valdemar soon left clutching booty and trade agreements, and Visby continued to prosper while the island's countryside around it stagnated, its people and wealth destroyed.

The old **Hanseatic harbour** at Almedalen is now a public park, and nothing is much more than a few minutes' walk from here. Pretty **Packhusplan**, the oldest square in the city, is bisected by curving Strandgatan, which runs southwards to the fragmentary ruins of **Visborg Castle** – blown up by the Danes in the seventeenth century – and northwest towards the sea and the lush **Botanical Gardens** (unrestricted access), just beyond which is the **Jungfrutornet** (Maiden's Tower), where a local goldsmith's daughter was walled up alive – reputedly for betraying the city to the Danes. **Strandgatan** itself is notable for the impressive, step-gabled merchants' houses looming over the narrow street, with storerooms above the living quarters and cellars below – the **Burmeisterska house** is particularly striking. One of the most picturesque buildings is the old pharmacy, **Gamla Apoteket**, a lofty place with gloriously higgledy-piggledy windows.

The fine **Gotlands Fornsal Museum** at Strandgatan 14 (June to mid-Sept daily 10am–6pm; mid-Sept to May Tues–Sun noon–4pm; 75kr; ⓦ www.lansmuseetgotland .se) provides comprehensive coverage of Visby's past. Housed in an eighteenth-century distillery and a medieval warehouse, it holds five storeys of exhibition halls covering eight thousand years of history, as well as a good courtyard café and bookshop. Among the most impressive sections are the **Hall of Picture Stones**, a collection of richly carved stones dating mostly from the fifth to eleventh centuries, and the display of the **Spillings Hoard** – the richest of Gotland's seven hundred hoards. Found in 1999, this treasure, mostly from the Arab world, England and Germany, weighs 85 kilos. The **Hall of Prehistoric Graves** is equally fascinating, its glass cases displaying skeletons dating back six thousand years. Other rooms trace the history of **medieval Visby**, with exhibits including a trading booth, where the burghers of Visby and foreign merchants dealt in commodities – furs, lime, wax, honey and tar – brought from all over northern Europe. A series of tableaux brings the exhibition up to 1900, starting with Erik of Pomerania, the first resident of Visborg Castle, and leading on through the years of Danish rule, up to the island's sixteenth-century trading boom. A couple of streets up, **Konstmuseet**, at St Hansgatan 21 (mid-June to mid-Aug daily 11am–5pm; mid-Aug to mid-June Tues–Sun noon–4pm; 50kr; ⓦ www.lansmuseetgotland .se), puts on innovative temporary exhibitions of contemporary painting, sculpture and installations that really tease the eye. The permanent work is not so exciting, but does include some twentieth-century local art.

Strolling aimlessly around the rest of the twisting streets is rewarding enough in itself, but if you need a focus, aim for **Norra Murgatan**, above the cathedral, once one of Visby's poorest areas. At the end nearest Norderport (North Gate) – the highest point in the old town – you'll be treated to the best view of the walls and city rooftops, including **Kruttornet**, the dark, atmospheric tower back on Strandgatan and the **Helge And** church ruin.

Eating, drinking and nightlife

Visby's centre is small enough to wander around and size up the eating options. Near Österport, **Wallersplats** and adjoining **Hästgatan** are both busy at lunchtime, while neighbouring **Adelsgatan** is lined with cafés and snack bars.

Daytime cafés

Björkstugan Speksgränd 6. In a fabulous, lush garden on Visby's prettiest cobbled street, this little café serves tasty pies and coffee. Open till 5pm.

Gula Huset Tranhusgatan 2. Close to the Botanical Gardens and a favourite amongst locals: cosy and serving delightful home-baked port-wine cake and concoctions of almonds, chocolate and fruit in an unspoilt garden setting outside a vine-covered cottage. Open noon–5pm.

Skafferiet Adelsgatan 38. A lovely eighteenth-century house turned into an appealing café, which boasts a lush garden at the back. Baked potatoes, great cakes and vast, generously filled baguettes that suffice for a full meal.

St Hans Café St Hansplan 2. Between May and September this café has outdoor seating in the rear garden amid a series of atmospheric medieval church ruins – for atmosphere it's hard to beat. Terrific cakes, muffins and pies as well as light lunches.

Restaurants and bars

Bakfickan Stora Torget 1 ☎0498/27 18 07. A relaxed little restaurant with a tiled interior, specializing in some of the best seafood in town (100–200kr). Also good for a drink.

Bolaget Stora Torget 6 ☎0498/21 50 80. A delightful, though extremely small, French bistro

right on the main square with classic dishes such as confit de canard and bouillebaisse.

Clematis Medeltidskrogen Strandgatan 20. No reservations. Set in the vaulted cellars of a thirteenth-century house, this is Visby's most brilliantly atmospheric and evocative restaurant by far, lit with candles only, with mead served in flagons and food in rough ceramic bowls and on wooden platters. The full medieval banquet includes nuts, rose petals, honey-fried cabbage and pear toffee. From 6pm.

Gamla Masters Stora Kyrkogatan 10 ☎0498/21 66 68. A justifiably popular bistro decked out with mosaic tiles which serves everything from solid Swedish home cooking to more upmarket, sophisticated meat and fish dishes.

Munkkällaren Lilla Torggränd, ☎0498/27 14 00. Massively fashionable, and consequently crowded. There's an extensive à la carte menu of grilled meat and fish dishes from 180kr.

Ol-San St Hansgatan 51, ☎0498/25 65 50. Fantastic, innovative European and Asian crossover cuisine with mains from 200kr and three-course menus from 350kr.

Strykjärnet Wallersplats 3 ☎0498/28 46 22. A fantastic crêperie at the corner of Adelgatan and Hästgatan with a wide range of savoury galettes (including vegetarian options) from 78kr; sweet crêpes from 39kr.

Medieval Week

For a week at the beginning of August, Visby becomes the backdrop for a boisterous re-enactment of the conquest of the island by the Danes in 1361. The visual feast that is **Medieval Week** (⊛www.medeltidsveckan.com) sees music in the streets, medieval food on sale in the restaurants (no potatoes – they hadn't been brought to Europe by then) and, on the first Sunday, a procession recreating Valdemar's triumphant entry through Söderport to Stora Torget. Here, modern-day burghers are stripped of their wealth before the procession moves on to the Jungfrutornet. Locals and visitors to Gotland really get into this festival – you'll see crowds on the boats over to Visby already dressed in home-made medieval garb, and at least half the people on the streets of the town will be dressed up in period costume.

▲ Medieval Week, Visby

The rest of the island

There's a real charm to the rest of Gotland – rolling green countryside, forest-lined roads, fine beaches and small fishing villages, and everywhere the rural skyline is dominated by churches, the remnants of medieval settlements destroyed in the Danish invasion. The **south** of the island, in particular, boasts numerous wonderful villages and beaches, and with Gotland's many Bronze-Age stone ships and remains of prehistoric farmsteads signposted off the road. **Cycling** is immensely enjoyable, since the main roads are quiet and minor roads are positively deserted. Gotland's **buses** are very few; outside Visby, they tend to run only twice daily. Plan your trip carefully with the free timetable, available from the tourist office in Visby or online at ⓦwww.gotland.se/kollektivtrafiken.

Southern Gotland

Near to Visby, **ROMAKLOSTER** has some impressive monastery ruins that are used for (Swedish-language) Shakespeare performances; the village shops here are the best on the island for local handicrafts. The so-called "capital" of the south, **HEMSE**, around 50km from Visby (buses ply the route almost hourly), is little more than a main street, but there are a couple of banks and a good local café, *Jonassons Bageri & Konditori* at Storgatan 54, and you can rent **bikes** from *Endrells*, Ronevägen 4, which is the cheapest place in town (ⓣ0498/48 03 33). Travelling northeast along Route 144, the countryside is a glorious mix of wild-flower meadows, medieval farmholdings with ancient windows and carved wooden portals and dark, mysterious forest. Tiny **BURS**, east of Hemse, has a gorgeous thirteenth-century saddle church, so-called because of its low nave and high tower and chancel. Inside there's a fabulously decorated ceiling, medieval stained-glass windows and ornately painted pews. Nearby, *Burs Café* is a friendly locals' joint serving cheap, filling meals. The next place you come to is the tranquil and pretty hamlet of **NÄR**, notable for its church, set in an immaculate churchyard. The tower originally served as a defensive fortification in the thirteenth century, but more arresting are the bizarre portraits painted on the pew ends right the way up the left side of the church. All depict women with demented expressions and bare, oddly placed breasts.

For good **beaches**, and the nearest thing Gotland has to a resort, the slow-paced and relaxing village of **LJUGARN** (ⓦwww.ljugarn.com) makes a decent base. The village, 50km from Visby and served by several buses a day, manages to retain an authentic feel. This is a place where it's easy to find a range of eating places to suit most tastes, and accommodation, unlike most of the island, is not restricted here to camping or hostels. *Rum* (**rooms**) are advertised in several appealing-looking cottages, and start at 150kr per person; some are listed on the village website and the map handed out at local shops and kiosks. There's an STF **youth hostel** overlooking the beach at Storgatan 1 (℡0498/49 31 84, ℮ljugarn @gotlandsturist.se; dorm beds 180kr, double rooms ❷; mid-May to Aug). *Café Espegards* at Storvägen 58 has excellent coffee and cakes. The best place for food though is ✈Ljugarns *Strandcafé & Restaurang*, located on the beach at Strandvägen 6 (℡0498/49 33 78; June–Aug daily 10am–midnight), serving delicious, top-notch Mediterranean-style mains.

Northern Gotland

There's an interesting natural phenomenon 23km north of Visby near Lickershamn, where you'll see the highest of Gotland's *raukar*, coastal **limestone stacks** that are the remnants of reefs formed over four hundred million years ago. This stack, 11.5m high and known as **Jungfruklint**, is said to look like the Virgin and Child – something you'll need a fair bit of faith and imagination to deduce.

On the whole, though, it's far better to press on north, where **BUNGE** is worth visiting for its bright fourteenth-century fortified church and open-air museum (mid-May to mid-Aug daily 10am–6pm; 30kr).

Beyond here, **Fårö** (Sheep Island), at the northern tip of Gotland, is mostly flat limestone heath, with shallow lakes and stunted pines much in evidence. The five-kilometre white sand arc at **Sudersandsviken** is a popular destination; swimming can also be done at **Ekeviken**. The remainder of the coastline is rocky, spectacularly so at **Lauterhorn** and, particularly, **Langhammars**, where *raukar*, are grouped together on the beach. The island can be reached by taking a bus to the town of Fårösund (where there's a café, *Fårösund Grill*, supermarket and bicycle rental) and making the ten-minute ferry crossing (daily every 15–30min; 5min) from the quay ten minutes' walk to the south, on the main road. Note that there's no public transport on Fårö.

Travel details

Trains

Kalmar to: Gothenburg (2 daily; 4hr); Malmö (8 daily; 3hr); Växjo (11 daily; 1hr).
Norrköping to: Malmö (hourly; 3hr 10min); Stockholm (hourly; 1hr 15min).
Örebro to: Luleå (1 daily; 16hr); Gothenburg (6 daily; 2hr 50min); Stockholm (10 daily; 2hr).
Växjö to: Gothenburg (6 daily; 3hr); Kalmar (11 daily; 1hr).

International trains

Kalmar to: Copenhagen via Kastrup airport (8 daily; 4hr).
Norrköping to: Copenhagen via Kastrup airport (2 daily; 4hr).

Buses

Kalmar to: Oskarshamn (2 daily; 2hr); Stockholm (2 daily; 6hr).
Norrköping to: Gothenburg (6 daily; 5hr); Kalmar (2 daily; 4hr); Stockholm (11 daily; 2hr).
Vadstena to: Stockholm (2 per week; 4hr).

Ferries

Nynäshamn to: Visby (mid-June to mid-Aug 5 daily; mid-Aug to mid-June 2 daily; 3hr).
Oskarshamn to: Visby (mid-June to mid-Aug 2 daily; mid-Aug to mid-June 1 daily: 3hr).

International ferries

Nynäshamn to: Gdansk, Poland (3–4 per week; 18hr).

The Bothnian coast

Facing Finland across the waters of the Gulf of Bothnia, Sweden's **east coast** forms a corridor of land that, with its jumble of erstwhile fishing towns and squeaky-clean modern cities, is quite unlike the rest of the north. The coast is dominated by towns and cities, the endless forest so characteristic of other parts of northern Sweden having been felled here to make room for the settlements that dot almost the entire coastline. Some, such as **Gävle**, still have their share of old wooden houses, offering evocative images of the past, though much was lost during the Russian incursions of the eighteenth century. Others, such as **Sundsvall**, **Umeå** and **Luleå**, are more typical – modern, bright and airy. Throughout the north you'll also find traces of the religious fervour that swept the region in centuries past: **Luleå** boasts an excellently preserved *kyrkstad*, or church village, clusters of wooden cottages dating from the 1700s, where villagers from outlying districts would spend the night after making the lengthy journey to church in the nearest town.

The highlight of the Bothnian Coast, however, is undoubtedly **Höga Kusten**, or the High Coast, north of Härnösand – an indented stretch of shimmering fjords, tall cliffs and a string of pine-clad islands on which it's possible to island-hop up the coast. The weather may not be as reliable as further south, but you're guaranteed clean beaches – often all to yourself – crystal-clear waters and some fine walking.

Getting around

The **train** line hugs the coast until Sundsvall, where services currently terminate. However, upon completion of Botniabanan, the new coastal railway line north of Sundsvall, trains should continue up to Umeå from late 2010. Until then you'll need to catch one of the Kustbussen coaches to reach either Umeå or Luleå, where you can connect back onto the train. Heading inland, there's a handy rail link from Sundsvall to Östersund and onwards towards Trondheim in Norway. Island-hopping by **ferry** along the High Coast is a wonderful way to take in one of northern Sweden's most beautiful regions. Ferries between the Bothnian coast and **Finland** are limited to the year-round link between Umeå and Vaasa.

Gävle and around

It's only a one-hour thirty-minute train ride north from Stockholm to **GÄVLE** (pronounced "Yerv-luh"), capital of the district of Gästrikland and the southern-most city in Norrland, the region that makes up two-thirds of Sweden and covers more or less everything north of Uppsala. Gävle is an old city – its town charter was granted in 1446 – although this is hardly obvious from the brutally modern centre, with its large squares, broad avenues and monumental buildings. Almost completely rebuilt after a devastating fire in 1869, the spacious layout of present-day Gävle reflects its industrial success in the late nineteenth century, when it was the export centre for locally produced iron and timber.

Arrival, information and accommodation

The city centre is concentrated in the grid of streets that spreads southwest from the **train station**. The **bus station**, for both local and long-distance services, is on the east side of the train station, and connected to it by a tunnel. The small

NORWAY

Mo-i-Rana

Kvikkjokk

Jokkmokk

Adolfström

Ammarnäs

Arjeplog

Tärnaby

Arvidsjaur

Älsvbyn

Boden

Gammelstad

Luleå

Kukkolaforsen

Haparanda

Tornio

FINLAND

NORRBOTTEN

Piteå

Storuman

Skellefteå

Bastuträsk

Lycksele

Burträsk

VÄSTERBOTTEN

Östersund

Åsele

Vännäs

ÅNGERMANLAND

Umeå

Mellansel

Örnsköldsvik

Långsele

Sollefteå

Ångerman River

Vaasa

Kramfors

Höga Kusten

MEDELPAD

Härnösand

Sundsvall

FINLAND

HÄLSINGLAND

Hudiksvall

Bollnäs

Söderhamn

Gulf of Bothnia

Gäyle

Furuvik

GÄSTRIKLAND

Åland Islands

Uppsala

Railway line (under construction)

Inlandsbanan

Gällivare & Kiruna

Gällivare & Kiruna

N

0   100 km

THE BOTHNIAN COAST

467

Arlanda Airport & Stockholm

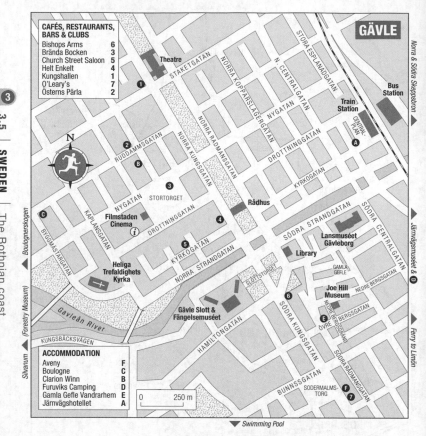

CAFÉS, RESTAURANTS, BARS & CLUBS

Bishops Arms	6
Brända Bocken	3
Church Street Saloon	5
Helt Enkelt	4
Kungshallen	1
O'Leary's	7
Österns Pärla	2

GÄVLE

ACCOMMODATION

Aveny	F
Boulogne	C
Clarion Winn	B
Furuviks Camping	D
Gamla Gefle Vandrarhem	E
Järnvägshotellet	A

▼ Swimming Pool

tourist office is a ten-minute walk away, inside the Gallerian Nian shopping mall at Drottninggatan 9, on the corner of Stortorget (Mon–Fri 9am–7pm, Sat 10am–4pm, Sun noon–4pm; ☎026/14 74 30, ⓦwww.gastrikland.com). If you need **internet** access, head for Sidewalk Express in the train station.

Gävle has a good selection of central accommodation and reservations are rarely necessary as the town is rarely overrun with visitors.

Aveny Södra Kungsgatan 31 ☎026/61 55 90, ⓦwww.aveny.nu. Small and comfortable family-run hotel south of the river. ❸/❹
Boulogne Byggmästargatan 1 ☎026/12 63 52, ⓦwww.hotellboulogne.com. Close to Boulogner-skogen park, this is a cosy, basic hotel with the feeling of staying in a private home – breakfast is presented on a tray in the room. ❷
Clarion Winn Norra Slottsgatan 9 ☎026/64 70 00, ⓦwww.clarionwinngavle.se. Another smart hotel, with its own pool, sauna and sunbeds. Rooms are tasteful if bland, with neutral colours and wooden floors. ❸/❹
Furuviks Camping Södra Kungsvägen, Furuvik

☎026/17 73 00, ⓦwww.camping.se/x12. Gävle's campsite is located off Östnäsvägen, Furuvik, a bus ride away on #838, which leaves roughly every half-hour. Also has cabins for rent (450kr).
Gamla Gefle Vandrarhem Södra Rådmansgatan 1 ☎026/62 17 45, ⓔstf.vandrarhem@telia.com. Beautifully located in the cobbled old town. It's worth timing your arrival carefully as reception is not staffed from 10am–5pm. Dorm beds 210kr, double room ❶
Järnvägshotellet Centralplan 3 ☎026/12 09 90, ⓦⓦww.jarnvagshotellet.nu. Another cheap option, located on a busy corner opposite the train station. Toilets and showers are in the corridor. ❷

The City

Central Gävle is easy to navigate, with the broad, straight streets of the modern city bisected by a stretch of park that runs roughly north–south. To the south, across the river, lies Gamla Gefle, the only part of the city that survived the fire of 1869, and the first place to head for.

Gamla Gefle

The part of the city known as **Gamla Gefle** passes itself off today as the old town, though unfortunately there's not much left of it. The few remaining narrow cobbled streets – notably Övre Bergsgatan, Bergsgränd and Nedre Bergsgatan – are lined with pastel-coloured wooden cottages complete with window boxes bursting with summer flowers. For a glimpse of social conditions a century ago, visit the **Joe Hill Museum** (June–Aug daily 10am–3pm; free; other times by arrangement on ⊙026/61 34) at Nedre Bergsgatan 28. Joe Hill, born in the house as Joel Hägglund in 1879, emigrated to the United States in 1902, where with a new name he went on to become a working-class hero whose songs and speeches served as rallying cries to comrades everywhere. Framed for murder in Salt Lake City, he was executed in 1915. The syndicalist organization to which he belonged runs the museum, a collection of standard memorabilia – pictures and belongings – given piquancy by the telegram announcing his execution.

The county museum, **Länsmuséet Gävleborg**, is at Södra Strandgatan 20 (mid-June to mid-Aug Mon–Fri 11am–5pm, Sat & Sun noon–4pm; mid-Aug to mid-June Tues–Fri 10am–4pm, Wed until 9pm, Sat & Sun noon–4pm; 50kr; Wed free; ⑩www.lansmuseetgavleborg.se). Its extensive displays of artworks by most of the great Swedish artists from the 1600s to the present day, including Nils Kreuger and Carl Larsson, make this a rarity among provincial museums, and attract visitors from across the country.

The rest of the city

The modern city lies over the Gavleån River, its wide streets and tree-lined avenues originally designed to prevent fires from spreading. A central boulevard of parks, trees and fountains runs from the sculpture-spiked **Rådhus** up to the beautiful nineteenth-century **theatre**, neatly dividing the modern city into two, while the concrete expanse of **Stortorget** has the usual open-air fruit and veg market (Mon–Sat).

Gävle's other sights – none of them major – are out of the centre but close enough to reach on foot. Back at the river by the main double bridge, **Gävle Slott**, the seventeenth-century residence of the county governor, lost its ramparts and towers years ago and now lurks behind a row of trees like some minor country house. You can't go inside, although you can visit the **Heliga Trefaldighets kyrka**, the Church of the Holy Trinity, a short walk west following the river and over the wooden bridge to Kaplansgatan. The church is a seventeenth-century masterpiece of wood-carved decoration; check out the pulpit, towering altarpiece and screen – all the superb work of a German craftsman, Ewardt Friis. Cross back over the river and take a stroll down **Kungsbäcksvägen**, a narrow street lined with old wooden houses painted yellow, green and orange, with tulips and wild roses growing outside their front doors. Continue and you'll come to the rambling **Boulognerskogen**, which opened in the mid-nineteenth century and still provides an oasis of trees, water and flowers just outside the city centre – a good place for a picnic and a spot of sunbathing.

On a rainy day, you may find yourself contemplating the **Järnvägsmuséet** (Railway Museum: June–Aug daily 10am–4pm; Sept–May Tues–Sun 10am–4pm; 40kr; ⑩www.jarnvagsmuseum.se) at Rälsgatan 1, a fifteen-minute walk south from the station following the train tracks. The old engine shed houses fifty or so locomotives, some of them over 100 years old.

Eating, drinking and entertainment

There's a fair choice of **eating places** in Gävle, but for the best options stick to the central grid of streets around Stortorget. Nearly all cafés and restaurants double up as bars.

Bishops Arms Södra Kungsgatan 7. Popular English-style pub near the youth hostel that is the place for a drink with outdoor seating in summer.

Brända Bocken Stortorget. Young and fashionable eatery, with outdoor seating in summer. Lunch for 75kr, and beef and pork dishes, hamburgers and salmon from around 100kr.

 Church Street Saloon Kyrkogatan 11 ☎026/12 62 11. Fun, loud Western-style bar and restaurant. Closed Sun.

Helt Enkelt Norra Kungsgatan 3 ☎026/12 06 04.

Excellent, stylish restaurant-bar serving Swedish fare from 130kr.

Kungshallen Norra Kungsgatan 17 ☎026/18 69 64. Mammoth-sized pizzas from 65kr and cheap beer.

O'Leary's Södra Kungsgatan 31. An incredibly busy bar catering for a young crowd: t*he* place to do your boozing and boogying. A 10min walk south from the centre. Closed Mon.

Österns Pärla Ruddammsgatan 23 ☎026/51 39 68. Chinese restaurant, serving all the usual favourites from 118kr.

Sundsvall

The capital of the tiny province of Medelpad, **SUNDSVALL**, known as "Stone City", is immediately and obviously different. Once home to a rapidly expanding nineteenth-century sawmill industry, the whole city burned to the ground in June 1888, and nine thousand people lost their homes. Rebuilding began at once, and within ten years a new centre constructed of stone had emerged. The result is a living document of late nineteenth-century neo- architecture, based around wide esplanades intended to serve as fire breaks and designed and crafted by the same architects who were involved in rebuilding Stockholm's residential areas at the same time. However, the reconstruction was achieved at a price: the workers who had laboured on the new buildings were shifted from their homes in the centre and moved south to a poorly serviced suburb, highlighting the glaring difference between the wealth of the new centre and the poverty of the surrounding districts.

Arrival and information

From the **train station**, it's a five-minute walk to the city centre. The helpful **tourist office** (June to mid-Aug Mon–Fri 10am–6pm, Sat 10am–3pm; mid-Aug to May Mon–Fri 10am–5pm; ☎060/61 04 50, ☻www.sundsvallturism.com) is in the main square, Stora Torget. The **bus station** is at the northern end of Esplanaden for Kustbussen services north towards Haparanda; for a **taxi**, call ☎060/19 90 00. For **internet** head for Pressbyrån at Esplanaden 2 where you'll find a couple of Sidewalk Express terminals.

Accommodation

There's no shortage of reasonably priced **hotels** in Sundsvall. The majority of the city's **hotels** are centrally located, and throw up some incredibly good bargains.

Cave Rådhusgatan 11 ☎060/61 33 12, ☻www .cavehotell.com/default.html. Airy, bright and charmingly decorated in shades of light grey and off-white, the nine doubles and two singles at this newly renovated, family-owned hotel are justifiably popular. All rooms have a flat-screen TV. ❸

Clarion Collection Grand Nybrogatan 13 ☎060/64 65 60, ☻www.choice.se. Rooms are on the small side, though are nicely

decorated in classic, modern Swedish style with wooden floors and smart furnishings. Tremendous value in summer when doubles go for less than 600kr. ❸/❺

Continental Rådhusgatan 13 ☎060/15 00 60, ☻www.continentalsundsvall.se. Fairly cheap hotel between the station and the main square; all rooms are en suite. Sun terrace. Cable TV in all rooms. ❷/❸

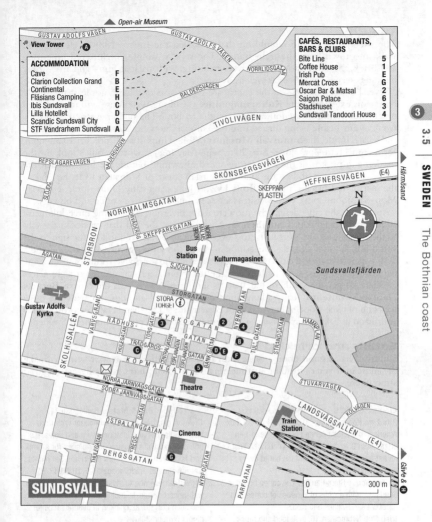

CAFÉS, RESTAURANTS, BARS & CLUBS

Bite Line	5
Coffee House	1
Irish Pub	E
Mercat Cross	G
Oscar Bar & Matsal	2
Saigon Palace	6
Stadshuset	3
Sundsvall Tandoori House	4

ACCOMMODATION

Cave	F
Clarion Collection Grand	B
Continental	E
Fläsians Camping	H
Ibis Sundsvall	C
Lilla Hotellet	D
Scandic Sundsvall City	G
STF Vandrarhem Sundsvall	A

SUNDSVALL

0   300 m

Fläsians Camping Västra långgatan 69A ☎060/55 44 75, ⓦwww.camping.se/y2. Open mid-May to Aug, Sundsvall's campsite is 4km south of town, close to the E4. Also has two-bed cabins for rent (450kr).

Ibis Trädgårdsgatan 31 ☎060/64 17 50, ⓦwww .ibishotel.com. Excellent value for such a central location, though breakfast is an extra 70kr. All rooms are en suite. ②

Lilla Hotellet Rådhusgatan 15 ☎060/61 35 87, ⓦwww.lilla-hotellet.se. One of the most reasonably priced places in town, with just eight rooms, all en suite and with cable TV. ② / ③

Scandic Sundsvall City Esplanaden 29 ☎060/785 62 00, ⓦwww.scandic-hotels.com. Top-range hotel with good views, and winter prices to match the opulence. There's a cinema complex in the same building. ④ / ⑥

STF Vandrarhem Sundsvall Gaffelbyvägen, Norra Berget ☎060/61 21 19, ⓦwww.gaffelbyn .se. The youth hostel is a half-hour walk north of town at Norra Berget, the mountain overlooking the city. Accommodation in cosy en-suite cabins. Any bus for Norra Berget from the bus station also comes here. Dorm beds 210kr, double rooms ①

The City

The sheer scale of the rebuilding that followed the fire of 1888 is clear as you walk into town from the train station. The style is simple, uncluttered limestone and brick, the dimensions often overwhelming, with palatial four- and five-storey buildings serving as offices as well as homes.

Several of the buildings in the centre are worth a second look, not least the sturdy bourgeois exterior of the **Kulturmagasinet** ("Culture Warehouse") four connected nineteenth-century warehouses down by the harbour. The buildings stood empty for twenty years before being turned into the complex now housing a museum, a library and a café. Inside, the **Sundsvall Museum** (Mon–Thurs 10am–7pm, Fri 10am–6pm, Sat & Sun 11am–4pm; June–Aug 20kr, Sept–May free) is worth a quick look for the models and photos of the city centre and the sawmills before the fire. Towards the other end of town, follow the main pedestrian street of Storgatan to its far end to the soaring red-brick **Gustav Adolfs kyrka** (June–Aug daily 11am–4pm; Sept–May Mon–Sat noon–3pm), where visitors are welcomed with free coffee and biscuits.

Apart from the city's design, the most attractive diversion is the tiring three-kilometre climb to the heights of **Gaffelbyn** on Norra Berget, the hill that overlooks the city to the north; walk up Storgatan, cross over the main bridge and follow the sign to the youth hostel. On a clear day, the panorama from the **view tower** is fantastic, giving a fresh perspective on the city's planned structure and the restrictive nature of its location, hemmed in on three sides by hills and the sea. From here you can see straight across to Södra Berget, the southern hill, with its ski slopes. Also here is the **Norra Bergets Hantverksmuseum** (daily 11am–5pm; 20kr), an open-air museum with the usual selection of twee wooden huts and assorted activities; in the handicrafts area you can try your hand at baking some *tunnbröd*, the thin bread that's typical of northern Sweden.

Eating and drinking

Sundsvall has a good choice of **restaurants** – something you may want to make the most of if you're heading further north. The town's **bars** generally have a good atmosphere.

Bars, cafés and restaurants

Bite Line Köpmangatan 20 ☎060/61 00 29. Fun American pizza joint serving genuine deep-pan pizzas from 95kr for a two-person number. There's an eat-as-much-as-you-can taco buffet every evening until 9pm.

Coffee House Storgatan 31. *The* coffee house in Sundsvall, with dozens of varieties of coffee and excellent sandwiches and cakes.

Irish Pub Nybrogatan 16. Irish food and music, darts and a broad selection of different beers, including Caffrey's and Kilkenny's.

Mercat Cross Esplanaden 29. Attached to the *Scandic* hotel at the southern end of Esplanaden, this Scottish theme pub is complete with heavy wood panelling and just about every variety of whisky you can think of.

Oscar Bar & Matsal Bankgatan 11. A good, lively Euro-loungebar with retro floral wallpaper and leather chairs and sofas. It's one of Sundsvall's most popular places for a drink and is packed to the rafters on Fri and Sat nights.

Saigon Palace Trädgårdsgatan 5 ☎060/17 30 91. Vietnamese and Chinese restaurant with some well-priced dishes, including a buffet lunch for 75kr and such delights as chicken in peanut sauce for dinner (around 80kr).

Stadshuset Rådhusgatan 22 ☎060/12 92 60. Exquisite Swedish food served inside the grand town hall; lunch is 90kr, dinner from 150kr.

Sundsvall Tandoori House Kyrkogatan 12 ☎060/17 59 59. One of Sweden's best Indian restaurants, serving up first-class Indian meals (mains 120–150kr) in a newly opened restaurant with open-air roof terrace.

The Höga Kusten (High Coast)

Between Sundsvall and Umeå lies the **Höga Kusten** or High Coast (🌐www .highcoast.net), the beautiful stretch of Bothnian coastline characterized by rolling hills and verdant valleys that plunge precipitously into the Gulf. During the Ice

The great outdoors

From vast coniferous forests, undulating hillsides of lavender and rapeseed, giant slabs of granite jutting into the sea and hushed, duned beachfronts, the four countries of mainland Scandinavia together boast easily the most diverse geography in Europe. This variety – and its often surprisingly proximate juxtaposition – makes for a marvellous array of outdoor activities: plunging into frozen waters off an Arctic icebreaker, pitching a tent for two in a quiet birch forest, riding a husky-drawn sledge or kayaking across a still, sunlit fjord. The permutations in Scandinavia for communing with Mother Nature are endless.

Husky safari ▲

Ice climbing, Briksdal glacier, Norway ▼

Ice-fishing, Norway ▼

Winter

There's no way around the cold hard fact that the Scandinavian climate can be unforgivingly frigid: in the far reaches of the Arctic, where snow can remain on the ground well into June, **winter** temperatures can plunge to -45°C/ -49°F; in most parts, though, they remain an acceptable 0°C/32°F. Even so, visiting during the cold season doesn't have to mean woolly underwear and stories in front of the fire – locals make the best of the subzero temperatures: office workers trade trainers for skis, while frozen lakes and rivers become playgrounds for skaters, snowmobilers and ice-fishermen. Visitors, too, will find unique ways to exploit the winter weather. Both Northern Sweden (Jukkasjärvi) and Finland (Kemi) are home to spectacular **ice hotels** (see p.501 & p.613), complete with requisite vodka bars; Kemi is also the departure point for **icebreaker cruises** through the Gulf of Bothnia's dense winter icefields. **Husky safaris** (see p.630) are an unusual way to explore the region's stark landscape, while throughout Scandinavia you'll find ample opportunity for solo or guided **trekking** and **hiking**, especially in Finland's national parks (see p.626, p.629 & p.631) and on Norway's Jostedalsbreen glacier (see p.272). **Cross-country skiing** is something of an institution in Norway, where you can explore the backwoods via a network of trails (some floodlit) – you'll have no trouble renting gear at ski resorts such as Geilo (see p.236). And everywhere in Finland you'll be encouraged to experience the curative national ritual of hopping from steamy **sauna** into bone-chilling lake, a great way to unwind both body and mind.

Northern winters are also the time to see the bright, fiery tapestries of the aurora borealis or northern lights, most dazzling on clear evenings between September and October and from February to March.

Summer

Though best known as a winter playground, Scandinavia does thaw out during the **summer** months. You'll want a pullover for the occasional chilly evening, but the climate is temperate in most parts from May to September. From June to August, temperatures in most places remain a comfortable 20°C/68°F (though they can reach as high as 35°C/95°F in some inland regions).

Walking is the transportation of choice when the weather's good, and the region's well-maintained **hiking trails** are peppered with campsites and huts in which to bed down for the night – Karhunkierros in northern Finland (see p.618), Kungsleden in Swedish Lapland (see p.503) and the Jotunheimen or Rondane national parks in central Norway (see p.231) offer some of the best walks. Hopping on a **bicycle** is an equally rewarding way to see the countryside, especially in Denmark, where gorgeous scenery and fairly flat land are particularly conducive to two-wheeled excursions.

Summer is also an opportune time to get acquainted with Scandinavia's diverse **fauna**, most notably deer, wolf, bear and countless bird species. Reindeer and elk prance about the northern stretches of forest and fell, as do Arctic foxes, wolverines and lemmings. In Finland, **bird-watching** is the pastime of choice for many, and Denmark and Norway are home to migratory water birds such as the godwit and dunlin. Superb reel- and

▲ Stora Sjöfallet National Park, Sweden

▼ Bird-watching, Jutland, Denmark

▼ Cycling in Swedish Lapland

Lofoten Islands, Norway ▲

Halland, Sweden ▼

fly-fishing can be found all over the region, and **whale-watching** excursions from Andenes in Norway are understandably popular (see p.312), given you've a 99 percent chance of at least one sighting.

From late May to mid-July, the extraordinary midnight sun – 24 hours of daylight – can be experienced in much of the Scandinavian Arctic. To see the full effect, where the whole sun is visible at midnight, you'll need to be above the Arctic Circle, the "line" drawn at 66° 33' latitude which stretches across Norway, Sweden and Finland.

Best beaches

▶▶ **Åland, Finland** Bake under the midnight sun, broil in a sauna, then cool off in the Baltic at the archipelago's languorous resorts. See p.569.

▶▶ **Gotland, Sweden** This Baltic island's gorgeous beaches swell in the summer with nearly a million tourists. See p.457.

▶▶ **Grenå, Denmark** Stake out your own private dune or cove along this 7km, child-friendly Jutland beach. See p.144.

▶▶ **Halland, Sweden** The so-called Swedish Riviera receives more sun-shine than anywhere else in the country. See p.415.

▶▶ **Hietaniemi, Finland** Easily accessible by bus, this Helsinki beach offers loads of amenities and the occasional nudist. See p.538.

▶▶ **Lofoten, Norway** With sprawling fjords and handsome fishing villages, the Lofoten Islands also boast Norway's most picturesque beachfronts. See p.315.

▶▶ **Sjøsanden, Norway** Norway's finest strand is the 800m stretch of golden sand at the pretty resort of Mandal. See p.215.

▶▶ **Svaneke, Denmark** Set at Bornholm's easternmost tip, this open stretch of strand regularly rates as Denmark's sunniest. See p.106.

Age, the region sank some 800m under the weight of the three-kilometre-thick sheet of ice; the rebound has caused the High Coast to rise slowly but dramatically ever since, creeping back up at a rate of 8mm per year. The resulting dynamic landscape has recently been added to the World Heritage list: the rugged shoreline is composed of sheer cliffs and craggy outcrops of rock, along with some peaceful sandy coves. Offshore are dozens of islands, some just skerries no more than a few square metres in size, others much larger and covered with dense pine forest – it was on these that the tradition of preparing the foul-smelling *surströmming* (fermented Baltic herring) is thought to have first started.

The coastline is best seen from the sea, and a trip out to one of the islands gives a perfect impression of the scale of things; however, it's also possible to walk virtually the entire length of the coast on the **Höga Kusten leden**, a long-distance hiking path that extends 130km from the Golden Gate-style suspension bridge just north of Härnösand – one of the longest in the world – to Örnsköldsvik; accommodation is in huts, farmhouses and villages along the way; the tourist office in Sundsvall can help with bookings.

The islands

A trip out to the islands off the High Coast has to rank as the highlight of any trip up the Bothnian Coast. Using a combination of buses and boats, you can make your way to two of the most beautiful islands in the chain: **Högbonden** and **Ulvön**.

Högbonden

After just ten minutes' boat ride from the mainland, the steep sides of the tiny round island of **Högbonden** (Ⓦ www.hogbonden.se) rise up in front of you. There are no shops, hotels or flush-toilets – in fact, the only building on Högbonden is a lighthouse situated at the highest point on a rocky plateau where the pine and spruce trees have been unable to get a foothold. The lighthouse has now been converted into a **youth hostel** (☎0613/230 05, Ⓦ www.hogbonden.se; May–Oct; dorm beds only 300kr; breakfast 70kr), with stunning views and just thirty beds. To make the most of it, you need to stay a couple of nights, exploring the island's gorge and thick forest by day, and relaxing in the traditional wood-burning **sauna** down by the sea in the evenings.

To **get there** from Sundsvall, head first for Härnösand then take an early bus to Ullånger, change on to the bus for Nordingrå, then change again to get to Bönhamn (2hr in total from Härnösand), from where *M/S Högbonden* (mid-June to mid-Aug daily 10am, noon, 3pm & 6pm; 150kr return) makes the trip out to the island.

Ulvön

The largest island in the chain, **Ulvön** (Ⓦ www.ulvon.com) is really two islands: Norra Ulvön and, across a narrow channel, the uninhabited Södra Ulvön. Before the last war Ulvön boasted the biggest fishing community along the High Coast, but many islanders have since moved to the mainland, leaving around forty permanent residents.

All boats to the island dock at the main village, **Ulvöhamn**, a picturesque one-street affair with red-and-white cottages and tiny boathouses on stilts. The island's only **hotel**, *Ulvö Skärgårdshotell* (☎0660/22 40 09, Ⓦ www.ulvohotell.se; ③), is at one end of the street, just to the right of where the boats from Ullånger and Docksta put in. Continue along the one and only road and you'll soon reach a seventeenth-century fishermen's chapel, decorated with flamboyant murals; the road leading uphill to the right just beyond here leads to the **youth hostel** (☎0660/22 41 90; dorm beds 175kr; late June to late Aug). At the other end of the main street is the village shop.

To **get to Ulvön**, make your way to **Docksta by bus**, from where *M/S Kusttrafik* (☎0613/105 50, Ⓦ www.hkship.se; 125kr one-way, 175kr day return) leaves daily June–August at 10.15am, arriving in Ulvöhamn at 11.30am, and returning at 3pm. From **Härnösand**, there are frequent bus services to Docksta. The year-round *M/S Ulvön* runs to Ulvön from Köpmanholmen, 25km south of Örnsköldsvik, daily at

10.40am and 7.10pm, with return trips at 6.45am and 3.45pm; out of summer, there's generally one departure daily, depending on ice – check at ⓦwww.dintur.se or any tourist office.

Umeå

UMEÅ is the biggest city in northern Sweden, with a population of around 110,000. Demographically, it's probably Sweden's most youthful city, with an average age of just 36, no doubt influenced by the presence of Norrland University and its 25,000 students. Strolling around the centre, you'll notice that those who aren't in pushchairs are pushing them, while the cafés and city parks are full of teenagers. With its fast-flowing river and wide, stylish boulevards, Umeå is a distinctly likeable city, and it's no bad idea to spend a couple of days here sampling some of the bars and restaurants – the variety of which you won't find elsewhere in Norrland.

Arrival, information and accommodation

It's a ten-minute walk from either the **train station** or long-distance **bus station** (ⓣ0771/10 01 10, ⓦwww.tabussen.nu) on Järnvägsallén to the centre, down one of the many parallel streets that lead in the general direction of the river. **Ferries** from Vaasa in Finland dock at Holmsund, 20km southeast of town.

A good first stop is the helpful **tourist office** (May to mid-June & mid-Aug to Sept Mon–Fri 10am–6pm, Sat 10am–2pm; mid-June to mid-Aug Mon–Fri 8.30am–7pm, Sat 10am–4pm, Sun noon–4pm; Oct–April Mon–Fri 10am–5pm; ⓣ090/16 16 16, ⓦwww.visitumea.se) in the ugly concrete square of Renmark-storget. The staff dish out maps and the *Summerguide* (also available online).

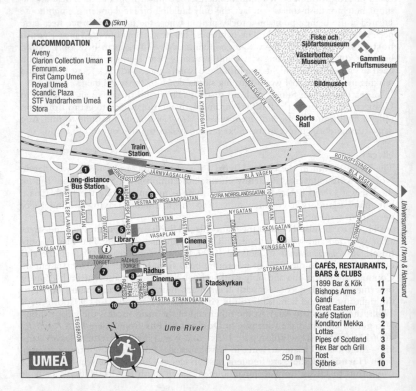

ACCOMMODATION

Aveny	B
Clarion Collection Uman	F
Femrum.se	D
First Camp Umeå	A
Royal Umeå	E
Scandic Plaza	H
STF Vandrarhem Umeå	C
Stora	G

CAFÉS, RESTAURANTS, BARS & CLUBS

1899 Bar & Kök	11
Bishops Arms	7
Gandi	4
Great Eastern	1
Kafé Station	9
Konditori Mekka	2
Lottas	5
Pipes of Scotland	3
Rex Bar och Grill	8
Rost	6
Sjöbris	10

UMEÅ

0   250 m

Umeå has a good selection of central **hotels**, the like of which you won't experience anywhere north of here; in short, splash out and treat yourself.

Accommodation

Aveny Rådhusesplanaden 14 ☎090/13 41 42, ⓦwww.profilhotels.se. Brand-new, upmarket hotel with comfortable, large rooms. ④/⑤

Clarion Collection Uman Storgatan 52 ☎090/12 72 20, ⓦwww.choice.se. Comfortable, modern rooms, with evening coffee and newspapers for all guests. ③/⑤

Femrum.se Kungsgatan 93 ☎090/10 99 10, ⓦwww.femrum.se. As the Swedish name suggests, just five rooms make up this cosy little guesthouse: each has been tastefully and individually decorated to create a real sense of home from home. ③

First Camp Umeå Nydalasjön 2, Nydala ☎090/70 26 00, ⓦwww.firstcamp.se/umea. Umeå's campsite is located 5km from town on the shore of a lake; take buses #2, #6, #7 or #9, get off at Nydala and walk for around 5min towards Nydalabadet, which is signposted. It has cabins for two people (800kr), individual double rooms in other cabins (①) and *trätält* (tiny two-bed huts; ①).

Royal Umeå Skolgatan 62 ☎090/10 07 30, ⓦwww.royalhotelumea.com. Pleasant, centrally located hotel with sauna, whirlpool and solarium. ③/⑤

Scandic Plaza Storgatan 40 ☎090/205 63 00, ⓦwww.scandic-hotels.com. Voted one of the best hotels in Sweden, this is very smart, with marble washbasins in the bathrooms and superb views from the sauna suite on the fourteenth floor – all at excellent rates. ④/⑥

STF Vandrarhem Umeå Västra Esplanaden 10 ☎090/77 16 50, ⓦwww.umeavandrarhem.com. With bright and airy en-suite rooms, this centrally located hostel, just 450m from the stations, is one of Sweden's best. Dorm beds 190kr, double room ①

Stora Hotellet Storgatan 46 ☎090/77 88 70, ⓦwww.storahotelletumea.se. One of the city's oldest hotels which opened in 1894 and is still full of many of the original features such as a grand, sweeping staircase, ornate chandeliers and period furniture. Every room is individually decorated. ④/⑥

The City

Umeå is known as the "City of Birches" for the trees that were planted along every street following a devastating fire in 1888. Most of the city was wiped out in the blaze, but rebuilding began apace, and two wide esplanades, together forming Rådhusesplanaden, were constructed to act as firebreaks should a similar disaster occur again. You'll be hard pushed to find any of the original wooden buildings, but around the little park in front of the former **Rådhus**, lingering bits of c.1900 timber architecture still look out over the river responsible for the town's name: *uma* means "roar" and refers to the sound of the rapids along the Ume River, now put to use by the hydroelectric power station further upstream.

Umeå also offers one terrific museum complex, **Gammlia** (late June to late Aug daily 10am–5pm; ⓦwww.vasterbottensmuseum.se; free), which merits a good half-day. The original attraction around which everything else developed is the **Friluftsmuseum**, a group of twenty regional buildings, the oldest being the seventeenth-century gatehouse on the way in. As usual, the complex is brought to life by people dressed in period costume – you can watch them preparing traditional unleavened *tunnbröd* in the bakery – while cows, pigs, goats, sheep and geese are kept in the yards and farm buildings. Look for the summer traditional **dance** evenings (Tues from 7pm), where the locals will be sure to whisk you off for a spin around the wooden dancefloor.

The main collection is housed in the indoor **Västerbotten Museum** (mid-June to mid-Aug daily 10am–5pm; mid-Aug to mid-June Tues–Fri 10am–4pm, Sat noon–4pm, Sun noon–5pm; free; ⓦwww.vasterbottensmuseum.se): a number of exhibitions canter through the county's development, from prehistory (including the oldest ski in the world, dated at 5200 years old) to the Industrial Revolution. It's all good stuff, well laid out and complemented by an array of videos and recordings, with a useful English leaflet available. Next door, the **Bildmuséet** (mid-June to mid-Aug Wed–Sun noon–5pm; mid-Aug to mid-June Tues–Sat noon–4pm, Sun noon–5pm; free; ⓦwww.bildmuseet.umu.se) houses interesting displays of contemporary Swedish and international art, photojournalism and visual design. Back outside, county history continues in the separate **Fiske och Sjöfartsmuseum** (Fishing and Maritime Museum; late June to late Aug daily noon–5pm; late Aug to late June Tues–Sat noon–4pm, Sun noon–5pm; free), an attempt at a maritime museum that is really no more than a small hall clogged with fishing boats.

Eating and drinking

Umeå's **eating and drinking** possibilities are the best in Norrland. Most of the restaurants can be found around the central pedestrianized Kungsgatan and Rådhusesplanaden.

Bars, cafés and restaurants

1899 Bar & Kök Stadskajen. Located on the *Vita Björn* boat moored off Västra Strandgatan, and a great place to sit on deck with a cup of coffee and enjoy a view over the river.

Bishops Arms Renmarkstorget 8. Umeå's attempt at an English-style pub and consequently one of the most popular places to see and be seen – it's always packed. There's outdoor seating in summer, and for those chilly evenings, blankets and free-standing gas heaters.

Gandhi Rådhusesplanaden 17 ☎ 090/17 50 75. Despite its dingy basement, *Gandhi* offers excellent Indian food and is good value, too, with dishes around 110kr.

Great Eastern Magasinsgatan 17 ☎ 090/13 88 38. The best Chinese restaurant north of Stockholm. With a 75kr deal, it's busy at lunchtime, while in the evening there's chicken and beef dinners from 92kr, as well as a Mongolian barbecue.

Konditori Mekka Rådhusesplanaden 15. Close to the train station, this long-established café is known for its delicious cakes, especially its mouth-watering, squidgy blueberry and carrot *kladdkaka* cakes.

Lottas Nygatan 22 ☎ 090/12 95 51. This British-style pub is a great place to go drinking. The adjoining restaurant has fish and chips or Mexican fajitas both for 159kr as well as pasta and pizzas.

Pipes of Scotland Rådhusesplanaden 14. Umeå's newly opened Scottish pub really pulls the crowds with its After Work specials on food and drink. It's a fun spot for a drink, though, at any time and a good place to meet the city's student population.

Rex Bar och Grill Rådhustorget ☎ 090/12 60 50, ⊛ www.rexbar.com. Inside the town hall, this is the most popular – and stylish – place to eat. A pricey à la carte menu in which northern Swedish specialities are supplemented with bar meals from 115kr.

Rost Rådhusesplanaden 4B ☎ 090/13 58 00. A superb and justifiably popular vegetarian restaurant decked out in mosaic tiles. There's a small outdoor seating area that fills up fast when the sun is shining. All food is freshly prepared and they even produce their own cheeses: mains cost 70–120kr.

Sjöbris Kajplats 10 ☎ 090/77 71 23. Excellent fish restaurant on board an old white fishing boat moored off Västra Strandgatan.

Luleå and around

The last city on the Bothnian Coast, **LULEÅ** lies at one end of the Malmbanan, the iron-ore railway that connects the ice-locked Gulf of Bothnia with the ice-free Norwegian port of Narvik in the Norwegian Sea. If you're heading north for the wilds of Gällivare and Kiruna, or to the sparsely populated regions inland, it's a good idea to spend a day or so here enjoying the lively atmosphere, the sights and the impressive range of bars and restaurants: Luleå is the last oasis in a frighteningly vast area of forest and wilderness spreading north and west.

Luleå was founded in 1621 around the medieval church and parish village of nearby Gammelstad (meaning Old Town; see p.478). Even in those days trade with Stockholm was important, and Gammelstad's tiny harbour soon proved inadequate to the task. In 1649, by royal command, the city was moved lock, stock and barrel to its present site – only the church and parish village remained behind. Shipping is still an important part of the local economy (in summer, you'll see a fleet of huge icebreakers resting in the harbour), but over recent years Luleå has become the high-tech centre of northern Sweden, specializing in metallurgy, research and education.

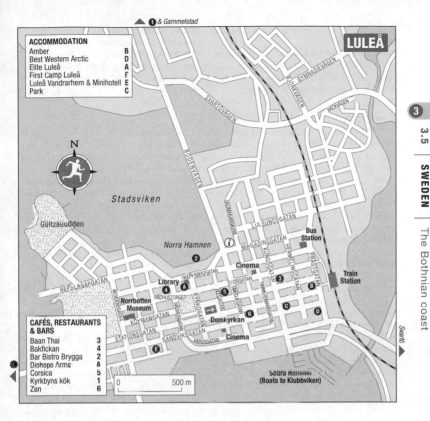

ACCOMMODATION
Amber	B
Best Western Arctic	D
Elite Luleå	A
First Camp Luleå	F
Luleå Vandrarhem & Minihotell	E
Park	C

CAFÉS, RESTAURANTS
& BARS
Baan Thai	3
Bakfickan	4
Bar Bistro Brygga	2
Diohopo Arms	0
Corsica	5
Kyrkbyns kök	1
Zan	6

LULEÅ

N

Stadsviken

Gültzauudden

Norra Hamnen

Bus Station

Train Station

Cinema

Library

Norrbotten Museum

Domkyrkan

Cinema

Södra Hamnen
(Boats to Klubbviken)

0   500 m

Arrival and information

The **train** and **bus** stations are about 500m apart at one end of the grid of parallel streets that make up the city centre. Luleå's **tourist office** is a short walk away in Kulturens Hus, Skeppsbrogatan 17 (mid-June to mid-Aug Mon–Fri 9am–7pm, Sat & Sun 10am–4pm; mid-Aug to mid-June Mon–Fri 10am–6pm; ☎0920/45 70 00, ⍵www.lulea.se). Ask here about boat trips to some of the hundreds of mostly uninhabited islands in the archipelago off the coast. For **internet** access head to Sidewalk Express at Pressbyrån, Storgatan 67.

Accommodation

Given Luleå's thriving economy and popularity as a conference centre, demand for rooms can be high; hence it's a good idea to book accommodation well in advance.

Amber Stationsgatan 67 ☎0920/102 00, ⍵www.amber-hotell.se. Small and cosy family-run place in an old wooden building near the train station. ❷/❹

Best Western Arctic Sandviksgatan 80 ☎0920/109 80, ⍵www.arctichotel.se. This smart little hotel, very handy for the train station, has cosy rooms with wooden floors and chic Nordic decor in bold reds and greens. ❸/❺

Elite Luleå Storgatan 15 ☎0920/27 40 00, ⍵www.lulea.elite.se. The oldest and smartest of the city's hotels, right in the centre of town, with tasteful, old-fashioned rooms and a huge breakfast buffet. ❸/❺

First Camp Luleå Arcusvägen 110, Karlsvik ☎0920/603 00, ⍵www.firstcamp.se/lulea. At a superb waterside location with views back towards Luleå. To get there, take bus #6 from Smedjegatan in the city centre (every 1–2hr; 20min). Also has cabins for rent (1100kr).

Luleå Vandrarhem & Minihotell Sandviksgatan 26 ☏0920/22 26 60, ⓦhttp://web.telia.com /~u92017710. Luleå's non-STF hostel is 15min walk from the centre and open all year round, though it is located beside a busy main road and can be noisy. Dorm beds 165kr, double room ❶

Park Kungsgatan 10 ☏0920/21 11 49, ⓦwww .parkhotell.se. The least expensive of Luleå's central hotels, basic but perfectly adequate, with very cheap doubles (not en suite) in summer. ❷/❸

The City

Luleå only really has one main street, the long **Storgatan**, south of which, past the main square, Rådhustorget, is the **Domkyrkan**. The medieval original disappeared centuries ago and the current edifice, built in 1893, contains a modern barrage of copper chandeliers hanging like Christmas decorations. Walking west up Köpmangatan from the Domkyrkan you'll find the **Norrbotten Museum** (Mon–Fri 10am–4pm, Sat & Sun noon–4pm; closed Mon in winter; free; ⓦwww .norrbottensmuseum.se) at Storgatan 2. Among the humdrum resumé of county history, there's an excellent film, *Herdswoman* (in Swedish with English subtitles) about three generations of Sámi woman from Nordmaling near Umeå and their ground-breaking court case in 2006 to establish traditional indigenous grazing rights for their reindeer herds. From the museum, head back into town and at **Kulturens Hus**, Skeppsbrogatan 17, Konstens Hus Arts Centre (Mon–Fri 10am– 6pm, Sat noon–4pm; free) is worth a look, with interesting displays of changing work from modern Swedish artists and sculptors.

If the weather's good, the next stop should be the **Gültzauudden** – a wooded promontory with a sandy beach that's easily reached on foot from the centre by heading west from Norra Hamnen. For more room to stretch out, you're better off taking the *M/S Stella Marina* out to the island of **Klubbviken**, the prettiest of the score of tiny islets that lie in the archipelago offshore. Here you'll find an enormous sandy beach and enough privacy to satisfy even the most solipsistic of souls. Boats leave from the southern harbour (Södra Hamnen) from late June to early August, with a reduced service running from late early to late June and from early Aug to early September; routes and times change from year to year but the latest timetable can be found at ⓦwww.lulea.se/english or by contacting the tourist office in Luleå. A one-way ticket to Klubbviken is 50kr.

Gammelstad

The original settlement of Luleå, **GAMMELSTAD** is 10km northwest of the city centre. When the town moved to the coast a handful of the more religious stayed behind to tend the church, and the attached **parish village** (see box below) remained in use. One of the most important places of historical interest north of

---

Parish villages

Consisting of rows of simple wooden houses grouped tightly around a church, **parish villages** are common throughout the provinces of Västerbotten and Norrbotten. After the break with the Catholic Church in 1527, the Swedish clergy were determined to teach their parishioners the Lutheran fundamentals. Church services became compulsory: in 1681, it was decreed that those living within 10km of the church should attend every Sunday, those between 10km and 20km every fortnight and those between 20km and 30km every three weeks. Within a decade parish villages had appeared throughout the region to provide the travelling faithful with somewhere to spend the night after attending church. The biggest and most impressive is in Gammelstad near Luleå (see p.478), while the parish village in Arvidsjaur (see p.495) is crowded with Sámi huts. They're no longer used in their traditional way, but people still live in the old houses, especially in summer, and sometimes even rent them out to tourists.

▲ Gammelstad church

Uppsala, the site now proudly boasts inclusion on the UNESCO World Heritage List. The **church** itself (June to mid-Aug daily 8am–6pm; mid-Aug to May Mon–Fri 10am–2pm; free) was completed at the end of the fifteenth century and adorned with the work of church artists from far and wide: both the decorated choir stalls and the ornate triptych are medieval originals, while the sumptuous pulpit is a splendid example of Bothnian Baroque, trimmed with gilt cherubs and red and gold bunches of grapes. Look out for the opening above the south door, through which boiling oil was generously poured over unwelcome visitors. Around 450 well-kept cottages are gathered around the church, making this the biggest parish village in Sweden, though nowadays they're mostly unoccupied except during important religious festivals.

Near the church at Kyrktorget 1 is Gammelstad's **visitor centre and tourist office** (June–Aug daily 9am–6pm; Sept–May Tues–Thurs 10am–noon & 1–4pm; ☎0920/45 70 10,ⓦwww.lulea.se-gammelstad), which has an exhibition and slide show about the village and is also the starting point for **guided walks** (June–Aug hourly 10am–4pm). Just down the hill is the **Friluftsmuséet Hägnan** (Hägnan Open-Air Museum: June to mid-Aug daily 11am–5pm; free; ⓦwww.lulea.se /hagnan), an open-air heritage park whose main exhibits are two old farmstead buildings from the eighteenth century. During the summer there are demonstrations of rural skills such as sheep husbandry, the crafting of traditional wooden roof slates and the baking of *tunnbröd*, northern Sweden's unleavened bread. **Getting to Gammelstad** from Luleå is straightforward: bus #9 runs 1–2 hourly from the main bus stop on Smedjegatan.

Eating and drinking

Storgatan is stuffed with **restaurants** and **bars**, and you'll find that during the light summer evenings many young people simply drink their way from one end of the street to the other.

Baan Thai Kungsgatan 22 ☎0920/23 18 18.
Authentic and extensive Thai menu with all meat
dishes at 109kr. Don't miss it.
Bakfickan Storgatan 11 ☎0920/22 72 72.
Mediterranean-style food including grilled tuna
with scallops (245kr) is delicious, or, alternatively,
there's a range of northern Swedish dishes such
as ptarmigan (268kr) and reindeer fillet with cep
mushrooms (242kr).

🎿 **Bar Bistro Brygga** Norra Hamnen
☎0920/22 00 00. On a boat in the northern
harbour, the *Bar Bistro Brygga* is popular with
a 30-something crowd for international food
(150–250kr) and partying.
Bishops Arms Storgatan 15. Attached to the *Elite
Stadshotellet*, this pseudo-English pub with its

bookshelves of battered old novels is undoubtedly
the most popular place for a drink in town and is
always busy with hotel guests and locals alike.
Corsica Nygatan 14 ☎0920/158 40. Dark and
dingy interior but worth seeking out for its pasta
dishes which go for just 89kr.
Kyrkbyns kök Lulevägen 1, Gammelstad
☎0920/25 40 90. One of the best restaurants
in the entire north of Sweden serving Norrbotten
delicacies like reindeer and Arctic char for around
265kr.
Zan Smedjegatan 10 ☎0920/104 41. A great
Persian restaurant with lots of skewered meats
and *meze* (85kr for a plateful). Alternatively, there's
marinated beef or chicken with rice and grilled
tomato for 195kr. Pizzas and pasta, too.

Haparanda

Hard by the Finnish border and at the very north of the Gulf of Bothnia,
HAPARANDA is not an easy place to like. The train station sets the tone of the
place – an austere and rather grand-looking building reflecting Haparanda's aspirations to be a major trading centre. That never happened, and walking up and down
the streets around the main square, Torget, can be a pretty depressing experience.

To fully understand why Haparanda is so grim, you need to know a little history:
the key is the neighbouring Finnish town of **Tornio** (Torneå in Swedish). From 1105
to 1809, Finland was part of Sweden and Tornio was an important trading centre,
serving markets across northern Scandinavia. But things began to unravel when
Russia attacked and occupied Finland in 1807; the Treaty of Hamina then forced
Sweden to cede Finland to Russia in 1809 – thereby losing Tornio. It was decided
that Tornio had to be replaced, and so in 1821 the trading centre of Haparanda was
founded, on the Swedish side of the new border along the Torne River. However, it
proved to be little more than an upstart compared to its neighbour across the water.
Nearly two hundred years on, with Sweden and Finland both now members of
the European Union, Haparanda and Tornio have declared themselves a "Eurocity"
– one city made up of two towns from different countries.

There are only a couple of sights in town: the train station building from 1918 and
the peculiar **Haparanda kyrka**, a monstrous modern construction that looks like
a cross between an aircraft hangar and a block of flats topped off in dark-coloured
copper. When the church was finished in 1963 it caused a public scandal and has
even been awarded a prize for being the ugliest church in Sweden. Then, after noting
that Haparanda has the world's only golf course that crosses an international border,
it's time to move on.

Practicalities

There are no **border formalities** and you can simply walk over the bridge to
Finland and wander back whenever you like; it's worth remembering that Finland is
an hour ahead of Sweden.

Haparanda's **tourist office** (Finnish time: June to mid-Aug Mon–Fri 7am–7pm,
Sat & Sun 10am–6pm; mid-Aug to June Mon–Fri 8am–5pm; ☎0922/120 10,
Ⓦwww.haparandatornio.com) is actually in Finland. The building is just over the
bridge to Tornio in the Green Line Welcome Center. Haparanda's STF **youth
hostel** (☎0922/611 71, Ⓦwww.haparandavandrarhem.se; dorm beds 180kr, double
room ❶) is a smart riverside place at Strandgatan 26 and has the cheapest beds in
town, with good views across to Finland. Alternatively, there's *Haparanda Stadshotel*,
at Torget 7 (☎0922/614 90, Ⓦwww.haparandastadshotell.se; ❸/❺), the only other

accommodation in town, an elegant and sumptuous place, dating from 1900, with squeaky parquet floors and chandeliers.

Tornio (see p.613) has many more **bars** and **restaurants** than its Swedish neighbour, so you may want to do what the locals do and nip over into Finland for a bit of high life, especially at the weekend. In Haparanda, however, *Hasans Pizzeria* (☎0922/104 40) at Storgatan 88, close to Torget, does pizzas for 44kr. Lunch and pizzas are also served at the Chinese restaurant *Leilani* (☎0922/107 17), Köpmangatan 15, as well as a range of Chinese and Thai dishes in the 92–128kr bracket. *Nya Konditoriet* on Storgatan does decent coffee and cakes. There are no pubs in Haparanda.

Travel details

Trains

Gävle to: Falun (2 hourly; 1hr); Kiruna (1 daily; 15hr); Luleå (2 daily; 14hr); Östersund (3 daily; 5hr); Stockholm (hourly; 1hr 20min); Sundsvall (hourly; 2hr); Umeå (1 daily; 9hr 30min); Uppsala (hourly; 45min).

Luleå to: Gällivare (3 daily; 3hr); Gävle (2 daily; 14hr); Gothenburg (1 daily; 18hr 30min); Kiruna (3 daily; 4hr); Stockholm (2 daily; 14hr); Umeå (1 daily; 4hr 45min); Uppsala (2 daily; 13hr 15min).

Sundsvall to: Gävle (hourly; 2hr); Östersund (8 daily; 2hr 30min); Stockholm (hourly; 3hr 30min).

Umeå to: Gävle (1 daily; 9hr); Luleå (1 daily; 5hr 30min); Stockholm (1 daily; 11hr); Uppsala (1 daily; 10hr).

Buses

The reliable Kustbussen services run five times daily between Sundsvall and Luleå, generally connecting with trains to and from Sundsvall; three of the five departures continue to Haparanda. From Sundsvall, the buses call at Härnösand,

Gallsäter, Ullånger, Docksta, Umeå, Skellefteå and Luleå. Other bus services run from the coast into central northern Sweden, often linking up with the Inlandsbanan.

Haparanda to: Kiruna (1–3 daily; 6hr).

Luleå to: Arvidsjaur (2–4 daily; 2hr 30min); Gällivare (4 daily; 3hr 15min); Jokkmokk (3 daily; 3hr); Kiruna (2 daily; 4hr 45min).

Skellefteå to: Arvidsjaur (3 daily; 1hr 50min).

Sundsvall to: Östersund (3 daily; 2hr 30min).

Umeå to: Östersund (2 daily; 6hr 30min); Storuman (2–4 daily; 3hr 40min); Tärnaby/Hemavan (Mon–Sat 3–4 daily, Sun 1 daily; 6hr).

International trains

Luleå to: Narvik, Norway (2 daily; 7hr).

International buses

Haparanda to: Tornio, Finland (hourly; 5min).
Umeå to: Mo-i-Rana, Norway (1 daily; 8hr).

International ferries

Umeå to: Vaasa, Finland (1 daily; 4hr).

3.6

Central and northern Sweden

n many ways, the long wedge of land that comprises **central and northern Sweden** – from the shores of **Lake Vänern** up to the Finnish border north of the Arctic Circle – encompasses all that is most typical of the country. Rural and underpopulated, it fulfils the image most people have of Sweden: lakes, pine forests, wooden cabins and reindeer – a vast area of land that is really one great forest broken only by the odd village or town.

Folklorish **Dalarna** province is the most intensely picturesque region. Even a quick tour around one or two of the more accessible places gives an impression of the whole: red cottages with white doors and window frames, sweeping green countryside and water that is bluer than blue. Dalarna's inhabitants maintain a cultural heritage (echoed in contemporary handicrafts and traditions) that goes back to the Middle Ages. And the province is *the* place to spend midsummer, particularly Midsummer's Eve, when the whole region erupts in a frenzy of celebration featuring the age-old tradition of dancing around the maypole (an ancient fertility symbol), countless impromptu musical gatherings and much beer drinking.

The privately owned **Inlandsbanan**, the great inland railway, cuts right through central and northern Sweden and links most of the towns and villages covered in this

Inlandsbanan practicalities

The **Inlandsbanan** – the inland railway that links central Sweden with Swedish Lapland – is a mere shadow of its former self today. In 1992, spiralling costs and low passenger numbers forced Swedish Railways to sell the line to the municipalities the route passes through, and a private company, Inlandsbanan AB, was launched. It now operates only as a tourist venture in summer – generally from June to August.

Every day, one train trundles each way on the **Mora–Östersund** (6hr; 395kr) and **Östersund–Gällivare** (14hr; 795kr) sections; if you want to travel the line in one go, the distances are such that it'll take two days, with an overnight stop in Östersund. However, you'll get much more out of it if you make a couple of stops on the way and take in some of the stunning scenery passing by your train window first-hand – special guides available on board contain commentaries and information about places along the route. Timetables are approximate and the train is likely to stop whenever the driver feels like it, maybe for a spot of wild strawberry picking or to watch a beaver damming a stream. It's certainly a fascinating way to reach the far north of the country, but isn't recommended if you're in a rush.

Tickets cost 123kr per 100km. Alternatively, you can buy the **Inland Railway Card** (normal price 1395kr), which gives unlimited travel during the entire period of operation. Seat reservations are best made at least 24 hours in advance and cost 50kr per seat. Two children under 15 can travel free if accompanied by an adult; otherwise they pay half-price. Bicycles can be carried on board if space allows.

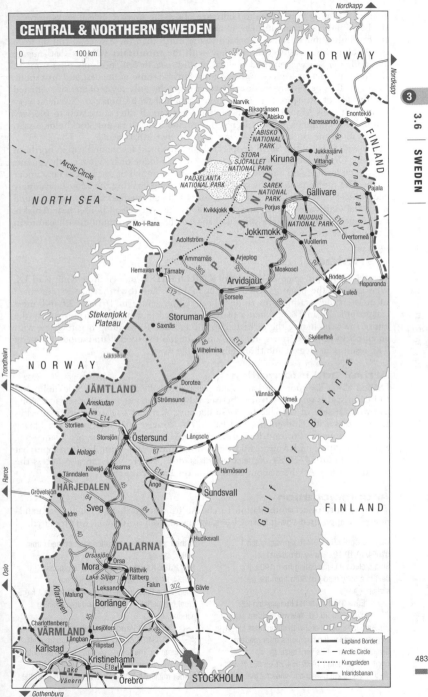

CENTRAL & NORTHERN SWEDEN

0   100 km

Nordkapp ▲

Nordkapp ►

N O R W A Y

F I N L A N D

Narvik
Riksgränsen
Abisko
Karesuando
Enontekiö

ABISKO NATIONAL PARK

STORA SJÖFALLET NATIONAL PARK

Jukkasjärvi
Vittangi

Kiruna

Arctic Circle

PADJELANTA NATIONAL PARK

N O R T H S E A

SAREK NATIONAL PARK

Gällivare

Pajala

T o r n e   V a l l e y

Kvikkjokk
Porjus

MUDDUS NATIONAL PARK

Mo-i-Rana

Adolfström

Jokkmokk

Övertorneå

Vuollerim

Ammarnäs
Arjeplog

Hemavan
Tärnaby

Moskosel

Boden
Haparanda

Arvidsjaur

Sorsele

Luleå

L A P L A N D

Stekenjokk Plateau

Storuman

Saxnäs

Skellefteå

NORWAY

Gäddede

Vilhelmina

JÄMTLAND

Dorotea

Vännäs
Umeå

Strömsund

Åreskutan
Åre

Storlien

Storsjön

Östersund

Långsele

G u l f   o f   B o t h n i a

Trondheim

Holags

87

Klövsjö
Åsarna

Härnösand

Tänndalen

Ånge

Sundvall

FINLAND

HÄRJEDALEN

Grövelsjön

84

Idre

Sveg

84

Hudiksvall

DALARNA

Orsasjön
Mora
Orsa
Rättvik
Tällberg

Lake Siljan
Leksand
Falun
302
Gävle

Malung

Borlänge

Charlottenberg
VÄRMLAND
Lesjöfors
Långban
Filipstad

206

Karlstad
Kristinehamn

Lake Vänern
Örebro

E18

STOCKHOLM

— · — · — Lapland Border
— — — Arctic Circle
· · · · · · · Kungsleden
———— Inlandsbanan

483

chapter. Running from **Mora** to **Gällivare**, above the Arctic Circle, it ranks amongst the best European train journeys, an enthralling two-day, 1100-kilometre adventure. It's certainly a much livelier approach to the north than the east-coast run up from Stockholm. Buses connect the rail line with the **mountain villages** that snuggle alongside the Norwegian border – the Swedish *fjäll*, or fells, not only offer some of the most spectacular scenery in the country but also some of the best, and least spoilt, hiking in Europe. North of Mora, **Östersund** is the only town of any size, situated by the side of Storsjön, the "Great Lake", reputed to be home to Sweden's very own Loch Ness Monster. From here, trains head in all directions: west to Norway through the country's premier ski resort, **Åre**, south to Mora and Stockholm, east to Sundsvall on the Bothnian Coast, and north to Swedish Lapland.

The wild lands of the **Sámi** people make for the most fascinating trip in northern Sweden. Omnipresent reindeer are a constant reminder of how far north you are, but the enduring Sámi culture, which once defined much of this land, is now under threat. The problems posed by tourism are escalating, making the Sámi increasingly economically dependent on selling souvenirs and handicrafts. Further north, around industrial **Gällivare** and **Kiruna**, and as far as the Norwegian border near **Abisko**, the rugged **national parks** offer a chance to hike and commune with nature in Europe's last great wilderness.

Karlstad

Capital of the province of Värmland, **KARLSTAD** is named after King Karl IX, who granted the place its town charter in 1584. The town has had its fair share of disasters: devastating fires ripped through the centre in 1616, 1729 and, most catastrophically, in 1865, when a blaze that started in a bakery burnt virtually the entire town, including the cathedral, to the ground. Rebuilding began apace, with an emphasis on wide streets and large open squares to guard against another tragedy. The result is an elegant and thoroughly likeable town.

Arrival and information

Draped along the shores of Lake Vänern roughly halfway between Stockholm and Oslo, Karlstad is served by **trains** between the two capitals as well as services along the western side of the lake from Gothenburg. Karlstad is also linked by Swebus Express **bus** with Gothenburg and Falun. The **tourist office** is inside the library at Västra Torggatan 26 (mid-June to mid-Aug Mon–Fri 9am–7pm, Sat 10am–6pm, Sun 10am–4pm; mid-Aug to mid-June Mon–Thurs 9am–6pm, Fri 9am–5pm, Sat 10am–3pm; ☏054/29 84 00, ⓦ www.karlstad.se), where you can also access the internet for free. Ask here about **boat trips on Lake Vänern**.

Accommodation

There's plenty of accommodation to choose from in Karlstad, including a brand-new, well-appointed youth hostel; booking ahead, even in summer, isn't required.

Clarion Collection Drott Järnvägsgatan 1 ☏054/10 10 10, ⓦ www.drotthotel.se. Smart, elegant place dating from 1908; it's next to a busy road just 50m from the train station. ❸/❺

Elite Stadshotellet Kungsgatan 22 ☏054/29 30 00, ⓦ www.karlstad.elite .se. Karlstad's best hotel with sumptuous old-style elegance, though the bedrooms offer modern Swedish design at its very best. ❸/❺

Freden Fredsgatan 1A ☏054/21 65 82, ⓦ www .fredenhotel.com. Cheap and cheerful place close

to the train station, also offering dorm beds from 160kr. ❶/❷

Ibis Hotel Karlstad City Västra Torggatan 20 ☏054/17 28 30, ⓦ www.ibishotel.com. Good-value hotel in the centre of town with a large breakfast buffet (70kr extra) and free evening parking. ❷/❸

Karlstad Vandrarhem Kasernhöjden 19 ☏054/56 68 40, ⓔ karlstad.vandrarhem @swipnet.se. The town's elegant, new STF youth hostel with top-quality beds is set in a grand former military building located just 1km from the centre (bus #6 also comes here). Dorm beds 245kr, double rooms **②** **Scandic Karlstad City** Drottninggatan 4 ☏054/770 55 00, ⓦwww.scandichotels.com. One of the most stylish hotels in town: its Nordic minimalist decor and warm wooden floors represent Swedish design at its best. **③**/**④**

The Town

It's best to start your wanderings around town from the airy main square, Stora Torget, one of the largest market squares in the country. The rather austere **Peace Monument** in front of the Town Hall commemorates the peaceful dissolution of the union between Sweden and Norway in 1905, which was negotiated in Karlstad. Unveiled fifty years after the event, it portrays an angry woman madly waving a broken sword whilst planting her right foot firmly atop a dismembered soldier's head: "feuds feed folk hatred, peace promotes people's understanding" reads the inscription. The Neoclassical **Rådhuset** was the cause of much local admiration upon its completion in 1867, just two years after the great fire – town worthies were particularly pleased with the two fearsome Värmland eagles that adorn the building's roof, no doubt hoping they would ward off another devastating blaze. Across Östra Torggatan, the nearby **Domkyrkan** was consecrated in 1730, although only its arches and walls survived the flames of 1865. Its most interesting features are the altar, made from Gotland limestone with an Orrefors crystal cross, and the crystal font.

Continuing east along Kungsgatan and over the narrow Pråmkanalen, the road swings left and changes its name to Nygatan ahead of the longest arched stone bridge in Sweden, **Östra Bron**. Completed in 1811, this massive construction spans 168m across the eastern branch of the Klarälven River. It's claimed that the builder, Anders Jacobsson, threw himself off the bridge and drowned, afraid his life's work would collapse – his name is engraved on a memorial stone tablet in the centre of the bridge. On sunny days (and Karlstad is statistically one of the sunniest places in Sweden) the nearby wooded island of **Gubbholmen**, reached by crossing the stone bridge and turning right, is a popular place for catching the rays; take a picnic and dip your toes in the refreshing waters of the river.

Back in town, at the junction of Norra Standgatan and Västra Torggatan, the two-storey yellow wooden building with the mansard roof dates from 1781, one of the handful of dwellings that weren't destroyed in the great fire. This building, the **Biskopsgården** (Bishop's Residence), owes its survival to the massive trees on its south side, which formed a natural firebreak, as well as to the sterling fire-fighting efforts of the bishop of the time. The only other houses that survived are located in the **Almen district**, next to the river at Älvgatan; the oldest parts of these wooden buildings date from the 1700s, but their facades are all nineteenth-century.

A half-hour walk along Jungmansgatan, Hööksgatan and then Rosenborgsgatan will bring you to **Mariebergsskogen** (June–Aug daily 7am–10pm; free; ⓦwww .mariebergsskogen.se). Originally modelled on the Skansen open-air museum in Stockholm, this contains a number of old wooden buildings from across Värmland. There's also a petting zoo, a children's train and a small nature museum (Tues–Sun 11am–5pm; free).

Eating and drinking

Eating and **drinking** in Karlstad is a joy, with a good selection of restaurants specializing in everything from Spanish to vegetarian dishes. For a Swedish provincial town, **bars** are also thick on the ground.

Bishop's Arms Kungsgatan 22. Classic British-style pub with a wide range of beers. A great location overlooking the river, with outdoor seating in summer.

Blå Kungsgatan 14 ☏054/10 18 15. One of the more upmarket bar-restaurants facing the Stora Torget, with quality Swedish dishes from 169kr and a pleasant summer terrace.

Glada Ankan Kungsgatan 12 ☎054/21 05 51. Lively first-floor restaurant and bar with a balcony overlooking Stora Torget. It serves TexMex and Swedish dishes (from 129kr) and is a nice place for coffee.
Habibi Drottninggatan 7 ☎054/18 00 05. Attractive Lebanese restaurant with a truly enormous selection of hot and cold in the range 59–89kr.

Harrys Kungsgatan 16 ☎054/10 20 20. American-style bar, café and restaurant in the main square, popular with drinkers in the evening, and with open-air seating in summer. Pub grub from 95kr.
Tom-Yam Drottninggatan 35 ☎054/18 51 00. A small and friendly Thai restaurant serving authentic dishes from 142kr.

Falun

From Karlstad, the handy Swebus Express bus will whisk you directly to **FALUN**, one of the biggest and most interesting towns in Dalarna, in just four hours (Mon–Fri 1 daily; ⓦwww.swebusexpress.se). Indeed, if you're in Dalarna for more than a couple of days, this attractive copper-mining town can be a relief after the folksiness of the lakeside and the visiting hordes that dominate the area in summer. Bizarrely, this is where a 14-year-old Osama bin Laden spent two summers with his family in the early 1970s, driving around in a Rolls Royce flown in from Saudi Arabia, and staying at a cheap hotel.

Just twenty minutes northeast of Borlänge, Dalarna's biggest – and dullest – town, Falun is essentially an industrial settlement, though a surprisingly pleasant one at that. At its peak in the seventeenth and eighteenth centuries the mine here produced two-thirds of the world's copper ore, and Falun acquired buildings and a layout commensurate with its status as Sweden's second largest town. In 1761, two devastating fires wiped out virtually all of central Falun – the few old wooden houses to survive can be found in the areas of Elsborg (south of the centre), Gamla Herrgården and Östanfors (both north of the centre), which are worth seeking out for an idea of the cramped conditions the mineworkers had to live in.

The **mine** itself, 1km west of town at the end of Gruvgatan, was said by the botanist Carl von Linné to be as dreadful as hell itself. An unnerving element of eighteenth-century mining was the omnipresence of copper vitriol gases, a strong preservative: one case is recorded of a young man known as Fat Mats whose body was found in the mines in 1719. He'd died 49 years previously in an accident, but the corpse was so well preserved that his erstwhile fiancée, by then an old woman, recognized him immediately. The famous "Falun red" paint, which is made from the copper mine's waste materials, also contains the wood-preserving vitriol, which explains why millions of Swedes paint their timber houses deep red.

The mine and the surrounding industrial landscape is a UNESCO World Heritage Site, and there's a new **visitor centre** (see tour times below; ⓦwww.kopparberget .com) highlighting the area's history. Hour-long **guided tours** of the mine (May–Sept daily 9.30am–4.30pm; Oct–April daily noon–4pm; 150kr; English commentary available) begin with a lift ride that takes you 55m down to a network of old mine roads and drifts – be warned that the temperature drops to 6°C. Make sure you also walk around the various old mining buildings and peer into the one-hundred-metre-deep "Great Pit", **Stora Stöten**, which appeared on Midsummer's Day in 1687 – the result of a huge underground collapse caused by extensive mining and the unplanned driving of galleries and shafts.

Apart from the mines, Falun's attractions boil down to **Dalarnas Museum** at Stigaregatan 2–4 (Tues–Fri 10am–5pm, Sat & Sun noon–5pm; Sept–May Wed until 9pm; free; ⓦwww.dalarnasmuseum.se), which includes sections on the province's folk art and author, Selma Lagerlöf, who once lived in Falun.

Practicalities

From the **train** and **bus stations**, east of the centre, take the underpass beneath the main road and head towards the shops in the distance and Falun's **tourist office** (mid-June to mid-Aug Mon–Fri 9am–7pm, Sat 9am–5pm, Sun 11am–4pm;

mid-Aug to mid-June Mon–Fri 10am–6pm, Sat 10am–2pm; ☎023/830 50, ⓦwww
.visitfalun.se), opposite the *First Hotel Grand* on Trotzgatan.

The nearest **youth hostel** (☎023/105 60, ⓦwww.stfvandrarhemfalun.com),
a modern affair with dorm beds from 140kr, lies 3km east of the train station,
at Vandrarvägen 3 – take bus #701 from the centre. The nearest **campsite**
(☎023/835 63) is about fifteen minutes' walk from town (or take bus #705) up on
the hill, Lugnet, where there's also *Scandic Lugnet Falun* hotel at Svärdsjögatan 51
(☎023/669 22 00, ⓦwww.scandic-hotels.com; ❸/❻). In town the smartest place
to stay is the central *First Hotel Grand* at Trotzgatan 9–11 (☎023/79 48 80, ⓦwww
.firsthotels.se; ❸/❺), whose rooms are sumptuous to say the least.

In terms of **eating and drinking**, Falun far outstrips the towns around Lake Siljan
in quality as well as choice. In town, the most popular place is *Banken* (☎023/71 19
11) at Åsgatan 41, housed in an old bank building and serving grilled meat, fish and
hamburgers from 130kr. Another popular spot is *Rådhuskällaren* (☎023/254 00), a
cellar under the town hall in the main square, Stora Torget, serving delicious, traditional Swedish dishes from 159kr. The *Bakfickan* **bar** next door is the place to hang
out among Falun's trendy young things, while the excellent *Kings Arms* at Falugatan
3 also serves bar food (from 99kr).

Around Lake Siljan

Swedes consider the area around **Lake Siljan** (ⓦwww.siljan.se) to be the heartland
of the sizeable **Dalarna** province, itself perhaps the most typically "Swedish" area
of the country. The idyllic landscape here is one of verdant cow pastures, gentle
rolling meadows sweet in summer with the smell of flowers, and tiny rural villages
nestling on the lakeshore. The lush vegetation of the Siljan region, enriched by the
waters of the lake and benefiting from the relative lack of forest, has produced what
the Swedes call *öppna landskap* (literally, "open landscapes"). Indeed, the temperate
surroundings of Lake Siljan, coupled with age-old traditions and local handicrafts, weave a subtle spell on many visitors, too, and it certainly all adds a pleasing
dimension to the small, low-profile towns and villages of this part of Dalarna. **Mora**
and **Leksand** are the best of the lakeside towns; **Orsa**, on the other hand, with its
massive bear park, is a must for all animal lovers and makes a perfect stop on any
journey north from Dalarna.

Trains call at the towns around the lake and terminate in Mora. **Inlandsbanan
trains** (see p.482) call at Orsa on their way north from Mora. Another good way to

▲ Lake Siljan

get around Lake Siljan is to rent a **bike** from one of the tourist offices, which also dole out the handy, free *Siljanskartan* cycling map of the region. Since Lake Siljan and its surrounding districts are popular Swedish holiday destinations, there's no shortage of **accommodation** – though it can be a good idea to book ahead in the peak season of mid-June to mid-August.

Leksand

Located at the southernmost point of Lake Siljan, three hours from Stockholm, **LEKSAND** is perhaps the most popular and traditional of Dalarna's lakeside villages and is certainly worth making the effort to reach at midsummer, when **festivals** recall age-old dances performed around the maypole (Sweden's maypoles, incidentally, aren't erected until June: spring comes late here, and in May there are few leaves on the trees and often some lingering snow). Celebrations culminate in the church boat races, an aquatic procession of sleek wooden longboats that the locals once rowed to church every Sunday. The race starts on Midsummer's Day in nearby Siljansnäs and continues for ten days around the lake, reaching Leksand on the first Saturday in July. Between twenty and 25 teams take part, all cheered on by villagers at the water's edge. Another event worth coming here for is **Musik vid Siljan** (Music by Lake Siljan: ⓦ www.musikvidsiljan.se) in the first week of July: nine days of nonstop classical, jazz and dance-band music performed in churches, on the lakeside and at various locations in the surrounding forest – check with the tourist office for the latest details on this and the boat races.

At other times, there's little to do in Leksand other than take it easy for a while. Stroll along the riverside down to **Leksands kyrka**, which enjoys a magnificent setting overlooking the river and the lake. One of the biggest churches in the country, it has existed in its present form since 1715, although the oldest parts date back to the thirteenth century.

All **trains** to Mora stop in Leksand; the **tourist office** (mid-June to mid-Aug Mon–Fri 10am–7pm, Sat & Sun 10am–5pm; mid-Aug to mid-June Mon–Fri 10am–5pm; ⓣ 0247/79 61 30; ⓦ www.siljan.se) is at the train station. Leksand's comfortable **youth hostel**, one of the oldest in Sweden, is over the river, around 2km from the train station in Parkgården (ⓣ 0247/152 50, ⓦ www.vandrarhemleksand .se; doubles ❷, dorm beds 190kr). Otherwise, there's the beautiful *Korstäppan* at Hjortnäsvägen 33 (ⓣ 0247/123 10, ⓦ www.korstappan.se; ❹), tastefully done out in traditional style. The nearest **campsite**, *Leksands Camping*, is a twenty-minute walk from the tourist office along Tällbergsvägen (ⓣ 0247/803 13, ⓔ kommunen@leksand .se). The best place **to eat** is at *Siljans Konditori & Bageri*, facing the main square at Sparbanksgatan 5, with excellent open sandwiches, light snacks and salads from 50kr – in summer there are a couple of tables on the front terrace. Alternatively, try *Bosporen* (ⓣ 0247/132 80), just opposite at Torget 1, a passable place serving pizzas from 60kr and meat and fish dishes and is also a good spot for a **drink**.

Mora

If you've only got time to see part of the area, then **MORA** is the place to head for, especially if you're travelling further north with the Inlandsbanan (see p.482). The largest of the lakeside settlements, Mora's main draw is the work of Sweden's best-known artist, **Anders Zorn** (1860–1920), who moved here in 1896 and whose paintings are exhibited in the excellent **Zorn Museum** at Vasagatan 36 (mid-May to mid-Sept Mon–Sat 9am–5pm, Sun 11am–5pm; mid-Sept to mid-May Mon–Sat noon–5pm, Sun 1–5pm; 35kr; ⓦ www.zorn.se) – look out for the self-portrait and the especially pleasing *Midnatt* (*Midnight*) from 1891, which depicts a woman rowing on Lake Siljan, her hands blue from the cold night air.

You might also want to wander across the lawn and take in his home, **Zorngården** (mid-May to mid-Sept Mon–Sat 10am–4pm, Sun 11am–4pm; mid-Sept to mid-May daily hourly guided tours noon–3pm; 60kr), where he lived with his wife, Emma, during the early 1900s. However, what really makes this place unusual is the cavernous

The Arctic Circle

Ten kilometres south of Jokkmokk, Route 45 and the Inlandsbanan finally cross the **Arctic Circle**, the imaginary line marking the southernmost latitude where the Midnight Sun can be seen at the summer solstice. On the train, this is occasion enough for a bout of whistle-blowing as it pulls up to allow everyone to take photos of the hoardings announcing the crossing. Due to the fluctuating inclination of Earth's axis, the line moves north and south within a 180-kilometre-wide area in a forty-thousand-year-cycle, and is currently creeping northwards at a rate of up to 15m a year. The actual place of the circle is now around 1km north, but for argument's sake this spot is as good as any (though it will be back at the marked spot in the year 22,000, if you can wait). Painted white rocks curve away over the hilly ground, a crude but popular representation of the circle: one foot on each side is the standard photographic pose.

ten-metre-high hall where the couple lived out their roles as darlings of local society, with its steeply V-shaped roof, entirely constructed from wood and decked out in traditional Dalarna designs and patterns. Also on Vasagatan, but on the other side of the church, is the **Vasaloppsmuséet** (Vasaloppet Museum: mid-June to mid-Aug daily 10am–5pm, plus Thurs till 3pm; mid-Aug to mid-June Mon–Fri 10am–5pm 10am–5pm, plus Thurs till 3pm; 30kr; ⓦ www.vasaloppet.se), with an exhibition on the history of the Vasaloppet cross-country ski race, which started 500 years ago with the attempts of two Mora men to catch up with King Gustav Vasa, who was fleeing from the Danes. Held every March, the ninety-kilometre race attracts 14,000 skiers.

Once you've covered the town's sights, you might want to take a **cruise** (mid-June to mid-Aug only) on the lake aboard the lovely old steamship *M/S Gustaf Wasa* (timetables vary; check sailing times with the tourist office or at ⓦ www.wasanet .nu), which depart between May and September; it costs 150kr for a round trip to Leksand or 100kr for a two-hour lunch cruise.

Practicalities

Mora's **tourist office** (mid-June to mid-Aug Mon–Fri 10am–7pm, Sat & Sun 10am–5pm; mid-Aug to mid-June Mon–Fri 10am–5pm; ☎0250/59 20 20, ⓦ www .siljan.se) is at Strandgatan 14, opposite Mora Strand train station (not Mora station). **Buses** (ⓦ www.dalatrafik.se) use the bus station opposite, actually on Moragatan, but just off the main Strandgatan. The cheapest place to stay is the *Kristineberg* **youth hostel**, right opposite the Mora train station at Kristinebergsgatan 1 (☎0250/150 70, ⓦ www.trehotell.nu; doubles ②, dorm beds 130kr); its reception is inside the *Hotell Kung Gösta* (see below). Mora's **campsite**, *Mora Camping* (☎0250/276 00, ⓦ www.moraparken.se), is a ten-minute walk from the centre along Hantverkar-egatan, which begins near the bus station: there's a good beach here. Among the **hotels**, the biggest and best is the *Best Western Mora* at Strandgatan 12 (☎0250/59 26 50, ⓦ www.morahotell.se; ③/④), while *Hotell Kung Gösta*, Kristinebergsgatan 1, is handy for Mora train station (☎0250/150 70, ⓦ www.trehotell.nu; ③/④).

As for **eating and drinking**, all the hotels serve up a decent *dagens rätt* for around 60kr – there's little to choose between them. *Wasastugan* (☎0250/177 92), a huge log building overlooking the lake at Tingnäsvägen 6, is particularly lively in the evenings, with TexMex dishes from 68kr. Alternatively, ⚑ *Claras* at Vasagatan 38 (☎0250/158 98 40) is a homely place for Swedish home cooking from 89kr. In summer, coffee and cakes can be enjoyed alfresco at *Helmers Konditori* at Kyrkogatan 10.

Orsa and the bear park

North of Mora, the Dalarna landscape becomes more mountainous and less populous, and the only place of any note, **ORSA**, is also the last town of any significance for miles around. Sitting astride Orsasjön, a northerly adjunct of Lake Siljan, Orsa is right in the heart of Sweden's bear country: it's reckoned that there are several hundred **brown bears** roaming the dense forests around town, though few sightings are made, except by the hunters who cull the steadily increasing numbers. Your best chance of seeing one is to visit the bear park, **Orsa Grönklitt Björnpark** (mid-June to mid-Aug daily 10am–6pm; mid-Aug to mid-June daily 10am–3pm; 160kr; ⓦwww.orsagronklitt.se), 13km outside town and reachable by twice-daily bus #118 from Mora, which stops at Orsa train station. The bears here are not tamed or caged, but wander around the 217-thousand square metres of the forested park at will; instead, it's the humans who are restricted, having to clamber up viewing towers and along covered-in walkways. Funny, gentle and vegetarian for the most part, the bears are occasionally fed the odd dead reindeer or moose that's been killed on the roads. Out of season, they hibernate in specially constructed lairs that are monitored by closed-circuit television cameras.

From the train station on Järnvägsgatan, it's a short walk to Orsa's **tourist office** at Dalagatan 1 (mid-June to mid-Aug Mon–Fri 10am–7pm, Sat & Sun 10am–5pm; mid-Aug to mid-June Mon–Fri 10am–5pm; ⓣ0250/55 25 50, ⓦwww.siljan.se). If you need to stay, try the atmospheric *Orsa Hotell* (ⓣ0250/409 40, ⓦwww.orsahotell .se; ③) in the old station building at Järnvägsgatan 4. Alternatively, the STF **youth hostel** (ⓣ0250/421 70, ⓦwww.orsaandrarhem.se), located 1km east of the centre at Gillevägen 3, has private rooms (①) and dorm beds for 280kr.

Östersund

North of Orsa, the Inlandsbanan passes through a series of pint-sized villages before reaching the shores of the enormous Storsjön lake and pulling into one of central Sweden's most agreeable towns, **ÖSTERSUND**. It's well worth spending a day or two in what is the last large town until Gällivare, some 700km to the north inside the Arctic Circle – if you're heading north this is your final chance to indulge in a bit of high life, since the small towns and villages beyond have few of the entertainment or culinary possibilities available here. Östersund is also a major **transport hub**: the E14 highway cuts through town, offering good links to Sundsvall and west to Trondheim in Norway, while as well as the summer Inlandsbanan service there are trains west to Åre and on to Trondheim in Norway, east to Sundsvall and south to Stockholm and Gothenburg, plus express buses north to Gällivare, which run all year and are a better option than the Inlandsbanan if you're in a hurry.

Arrival and information

From the **train station** on Strandgatan it's a five-minute walk north to the town centre; the **bus station**, off Rådhusgatan, is more central. A couple of blocks to the north, the excellent **tourist office** (June Mon–Fri 9am–7pm, Sat & Sun 10am–3pm; late June & July Mon–Fri 9am–8pm, Sat & Sun 9am–7pm; Aug Mon–Fri 9am–5pm, Sat & Sun 10am–3pm; Sept–May Mon–Fri 9am–5pm; ⓣ063/14 40 01, ⓦwww.turist.ostersund.se) is opposite the minaret-topped Rådhus at Rådhusgatan 44, and sells the **Östersundshäftet** (valid March–Oct; 125kr), a booklet of coupons giving free or discounted museum entry and boat trips as well as reductions in the town's shops and restaurants. Pressbyrån at the train station has internet access with Sidewalk Express.

Accommodation

Unlike many other places in central northern Sweden, Östersund has good-quality **hotels** at reasonable prices; you won't find their like north of here until Gällivare.

Älgen Storgatan 61 ⓣ063/51 75 25, ⓦwww .hotelalgen.se. Small, central and handy for the train station, with comfortable en-suite rooms. ④
Best Western Gamla Teatern Thoméegränd 20 ⓣ063/51 16 00, ⓦwww.gamlateatern.se. An

atmospheric hotel in an early twentieth-century theatre with sweeping wooden staircases, tall doorways and wide corridors, but with disappointingly plain rooms. ③/⑤

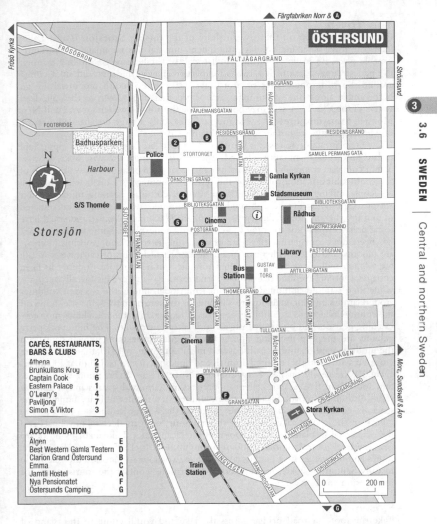

Map labels:
Färgfabriken Norr & Ⓐ
Frösö Kyrka
FRÖSÖBRON
FÄLTJÄGARGRÄND
BROGRÄND
FÄRJEMANSGATAN
RESIDENSGRÄND
RESIDENSGRÄND
SAMUEL PERMANS GATA
Strömsund
FOOTBRIDGE
Badhusparken
Police
STORTORGET
KYRKGATAN
RÅDHUSGATAN
Gamla Kyrkan
Harbour
N
TÖRNSTENS GRÄND
Stadsmuseum
S/S Thomée
BIBLIOTEKSGATAN
BIBLIOTEKSGATAN
Storsjön
Cinema
Rådhus
POSTGRÄND
MAGISTRATSGRÄND
HAMNGATAN
Library
PASTORGRÄND
SJÖTORGET
STRANDGATAN
Bus Station
GUSTAV III TORG
ARTILLERIGATAN
THOMÉEGRÄND
KO-MANGÅN
S:ORGÅN
PRÄSTGATAN
KYRKGATAN
TULLGATAN
SÖDRA GRÖNGATAN
STUGUVÄGEN
Cinema
RÅDHUSGATAN
DRUNNSGRÅND
Mora, Sundsvall & Åre
GRUNDLÄGGARGRÄND
STORSJÖSTRÅKET
GRANSGATAN
Stora Kyrkan
N HANTVÄGEN
Train Station
RINGVÄGEN
BANGÅRDSGATAN
TORGBRUNNEN
0   200 m
Ⓖ

CAFÉS, RESTAURANTS, BARS & CLUBS

Athena	2
Brunkullans Krog	5
Captain Cook	6
Eastern Palace	1
O'Leary's	4
PavILjong	7
Simon & Viktor	3

ACCOMMODATION

Älgen	E
Best Western Gamla Teatern	D
Clarion Grand Östersund	B
Emma	C
Jamtli Hostel	A
Nya Pensionatet	F
Östersunds Camping	G

Clarion Grand Östersund Prästgatan 16 ☏063/55 60 00, ⊛www.choice.se. Östersund's finest hotel whose very best rooms have their own marbled hallway, sitting room and sumptuous double beds. Book early and the discounted rates are definitely worth the splurge though the cheaper rooms are much less glamorous. ❸/❹

Emma Prästgatan 31 ☏063/51 78 40, ⊛www.hotelemma.com. Large, nicely renovated en-suite rooms in an old building on the main shopping street. ❸/❹

Jamtli Hostel Rådhusgatan, inside the Jamtli museum ☏063/12 20 60,

⊛www.jamtli.com. Housed in an old timber building within the Jamtli museum complex and is a wonderfully atmospheric choice. Dorm beds 190kr, double rooms ❶

Nya Pensionatet Prästgatan 65 ☏063/51 24 98, ⊛www.nyapensionatet.se. Near the train station, this tastefully decorated house, dating from around 1900, has just six rooms, with a shared toilet and shower in the corridor. ❷

Östersunds Camping Krondikesvägen 95C ☏063/14 46 15, ⊛www.camping.se/plats/z11. Located a couple of kilometres south of the town centre and perfect for the fantastic indoor swimming complex, Storsjöbadet.

3.6 | SWEDEN | Central and northern Sweden

491

The Town

Östersund's position on the eastern shore of the mighty **Storsjön** (Great Lake) lends the town a seaside holiday atmosphere, unusual this far inland. An instantly likeable place, it's made up of the familiar grid of parallel streets. Strolling through the pedestrianized centre is a relaxed experience; take time out and sip a coffee around the wide open space of Stortorget and watch Swedish provincial life go by, or amble along one of the many side streets that slope down to the still, deep waters of the lake. Here you may be lucky enough to spot Sweden's own Loch Ness Monster, **Storsjöodjuret** (Ⓦwww.storsjoodjuret.com), a huge dog-headed creature of which sightings are numerous if unsubstantiated.

The main attraction in town is **Jamtli** (late June to late Aug daily 11am–5pm; Sept to late June Tues 11am–5pm; 110kr late June to late Aug, otherwise 60kr; Ⓦwww .jamtli.com), an impressive open-air museum a quarter of an hour's walk north of the centre along Rådhusgatan. For the first few minutes it's a bit bewildering, full of people milling around in traditional country costume, farming much as their ancestors did. They live here throughout the summer and everyone is encouraged to join in – baking, tree-felling, grass-cutting. Kids, naturally, love it, and you'd have to be pretty cynical not to enjoy the enthusiastic atmosphere. Some intensive work has been done on getting the settings right: the restored and working interiors are gloomy and dirty, with no hint of the usual pristine historical travesty. You'll see women milking cows, and children running around barefoot in dimly lit farm cottages. Outside, even the planted crops and roaming cattle are historically accurate, while there's an old-fashioned local store, Lanthandel, among the wooden buildings around Jamtli's bustling main square. The indoor **museum** on the same site shows off the county collections: a rambling houseful of local exhibits that includes monster-catching gear devised by nineteenth-century lakeside worthies. The museum's prize exhibits are the awe-inspiring Viking **Överhogdal tapestries**, which date from the ninth or tenth centuries – discovered in an outhouse in 1910, the tapestries are crowded with brightly coloured animals and buildings. Close to Jamtli at Infanteri-gatan 30, the newly opened **Färgfabriken Norr** (Thurs & Fri noon–5pm, Sat & Sun noon–4pm; free) is an excellent modern art museum with a constantly changing series of thought-provoking exhibitions. Housed in a former military building, the spacious exhibition hall can easily be visited on the way to Jamtli.

Back in the centre, take a look at the **harbour**, with its fleet of tiny boats and the occasional seaplane bobbing about on the clean water. **Lake cruises** on board *S/S Thomée* – a creaking old wooden steamship built in 1875 – depart from here; routes and timetables vary but always include a two-hour trip around the lake (June to early Sept; from 90kr), amongst other destinations; contact the tourist office for information and bookings.

Frösön

Take the foot- or road-bridge across the lake and you'll come to the island of **Frösön**. People have lived here since prehistoric times – Frösön's name derives from the Viking settlement on the island and its association with the pagan god of fertility, Frö. There's plenty of good walking here, as well as a couple of historical stops. Just over the footbridge, look out for the eleventh-century **rune stone** that tells of a man called Östmadur (East Man), son of Gudfast, who brought Christianity to the people of Jämtland – presumably from some point to the east. From here you can clamber up the nearby hill of Öneberget, where you'll find the remains of the fourth-century settlement of Mjälleborgen – the most extensive in Norrland.

Follow the main road west and up the hill for about 5km (or take bus #3 from the centre of Östersund) to the beautiful **Frösö kyrka**, an eleventh-century church with a detached wooden belltower. In 1984, archeologists digging under the church's altar came across a bit of birch stump surrounded by the bones of bears, pigs, deer and squirrels – evidence of the cult of ancient gods, the *æsir*, and an indication that the site has been a place of worship for almost two thousand years. Today, the church is one of the most popular in Sweden for marriages – especially at midsummer, for which you have to book years in advance.

Eating, drinking and nightlife

Gastronomically, Östersund has more to offer than any town further north – make the most of it before pushing on.

Athena Stortorget 3 ☎063/51 63 44. Pompously decorated place tucked away in a corner of Stortorget, offering tasty pizzas from 70kr and dinner mains around 200kr.

Brunkullans Krog Postgränd 5 ☎063/10 14 54. This old-fashioned restaurant, with polished lanterns and a heavy wooden interior, is Östersund's premier eating place, offering traditional Swedish fare as well as more international fish and meat dishes.

Captain Cook Hamngatan 9 ☎063/12 60 90. A selection of delicious Australian-style grilled delights (around 200kr) that really draw in the crowds – also a popular place for a drink, with an extensive beer and whisky selection.

Eastern Palace Storgatan 15 ☎063/51 00 15. The best option for Chinese and Mongolian food, with all the usual dishes for around 80kr; the Mongolian buffet is great value at 129kr.

O'Leary's Storgatan 28. Popular American sports pub offering a large selection of beer and a Tex-Mex menu with mains around 125kr.

Paviljong Prästgatan 50B ☎063/13 00 99. The best Thai and Indonesian restaurant in central northern Sweden – make the most of it. Main courses go for around 129kr (try the excellent chicken with garlic chilli and Thai basil).

Simon & Viktor Prästgatan 19. An English-style watering hole at the top end of Stortorget serving upmarket pub grub from 95kr.

West to the Norwegian border

The E14 highway and the train line from Östersund follow the route trudged by medieval pilgrims on their way to Nidaros (now Trondheim) over the border in Norway, a twisting course that threads its way through sharp-edged mountains rising high above a bevy of fast-flowing streams and deep, cold lakes. Time and again the eastern Vikings assembled their armies beside the holy Storsjön lake to begin the long march west, most famously in 1030 when King Olaf of Norway collected his mercenaries for the campaign that led to his death at the Battle of Stiklestad. The Vikings always crossed the mountains as quickly as possible, and so today – although the scenery is splendid – there's nothing much to stop for en route, other than the skiing and walking centre of **Åre**.

Åre

The alpine village of **ÅRE**, just over one-hour's train ride from Östersund, is Sweden's most prestigious ski resort, with 44 lifts and snow guaranteed between December and May. During the snowbound season, rooms are like gold dust and prices sky-high: if you do come to ski, book accommodation well in advance through the tourist office or, better still, come on a package tour. Equipment rental isn't too expensive: downhill and cross-country gear starts at 290kr per day – contact the tourist office.

In summer, the village is a haven for ramblers, sandwiched as it is between Åresjön lake and a range of craggy hills overshadowed by the mighty 1420-metre-high Åreskutan mountain. A network of **walking tracks** criss-crosses the hills or, for a more energetic scramble, take the **Kabinbanan**, Sweden's only cable-car (110kr return), up to a viewing platform, from where it's a thirty-minute clamber to the summit. The view is stunning – on a clear day you can see over to the border with Norway and a good way back to Östersund. Bear in mind, though, that even the shortest walk back to Åre takes two hours and requires some stamina.

The **tourist office** (May to mid-June & early Sept to mid-Dec Mon–Fri 9am–5pm, Sat & Sun 10am–3pm; mid-June to early Sept & mid-Dec to May daily 9am–6pm; ☎0647/177 20, ⓦwww.visitare.se) is in the impressive new train station building known as Station Åre at St Olavsväg 35. It has detailed mountain maps and endless information on hiking and mountain biking in the nearby mountains and further afield – ask for the excellent *Sommarguiden* booklet.

When it comes to **hotels**, the cheapest option is the new *Åre Torg Hotell*, in the park below the square (℡0647/515 90, ⓦwww.hotellaretorg.se; dorms beds 190kr in summer, from 240kr in winter) with bright, airy dorms sleeping 4–5 people. Alternatively, for something a little more luxurious, there's the newly built Holiday Club (℡0647/120 00; ⑥), opposite the train station at Årestrand. Åre's **eating** possibilities aren't up to much, but there are several cheap places around the square: try the cheerful *Café Bubblan*, which does reasonable lunches of pies and sandwiches, or the more substantial dishes and pizzas served at nearby *Werséns* (℡0647/66 55 60). Near the cable car, *Dahlbom på Torget* (℡0647/508 20) is a smart brasserie offering porcini pasta, Asian salad with chicken and other international fare.

North to Swedish Lapland

Beyond Östersund the **Inlandsbanan** slowly snakes its way across the remote Swedish hinterland heading for **Swedish Lapland**, known in Swedish as the province of Lappland; a truly enormous region stretching from just south of the town of Vilhelmina to the Finnish and Norwegian borders in the north, and east towards (but not including) the Bothnian Coast. This is a vast and scarcely populated region where the train often has to stop for elk and reindeer – and occasionally bears – to be cleared from the tracks. On the other occasions that the train comes to a halt with no station in sight, it's usually for a reason – a spot of berry-picking, perhaps – while at the Arctic Circle everyone jumps off for photos.

Route 45, the **Inlandsvägen**, shadows the train line on its way north to Gällivare. It's easy to drive and well surfaced, though watch out for suicidal reindeer – once they spot a car hurtling towards them they'll do their utmost to throw themselves underneath it. **Bus** travellers on the Inlandsexpressen from Östersund to Gällivare will also take this route. A direct bus, the Lapplandspilen, also links Vilhelmina with Stockholm.

Vilhelmina

Four hours up the Inlandsbanan from Östersund, **VILHELMINA** is a pretty little town that was formerly an important forestry centre. The timber business moved out of town some ten years ago, however, and the main source of employment nowadays is a telephone-booking centre for Swedish Railways. Sweden's coldest temperature on record was set in a small village near here in December 1941, when it plummeted to -53°C. Despite the grandeur hinted at by the town's name (from Fredrika Dorotea Vilhelmina, the wife of King Gustav IV Adolf), Vilhelmina remains a quiet little place with just one main street. The principal attraction is the **parish village**, nestling between Storgatan and Ljusminnesgatan, whose thirty-odd wooden cottages date back to 1792 when the first church was consecrated. It has since been restored, and today the cottages can be rented out via the **tourist office** (mid-June to mid-Sept daily 8am–7pm; mid-Sept to mid-June Mon–Fri 9.30am–5pm; ℡0940/152 70, ⓦwww.sodralappland.se), a ten-minute walk from the **train and bus stations** at Storgatan 9.

Vilhelmina's **campsite**, *Saiva Camping* (℡0940/107 60, ⓦwww.saiva.se), is about ten minutes' walk from the centre and has cabins for rent from 290kr, as well as a great sandy **beach**; head down Volgsjövägen from the centre and take the left turn just before the Volvo garage. There are two central **hotels** in town: ostentatious *Wilhelmina* (℡0940/554 20, ⓦwww.hotell.vilhelmina.com; ③/⑤), at Volgsjövägen 16, and friendly *Lilla* (℡0940/150 59, ⓦwww.lillahotellet.vilhelmina.com; ③) at Granvägen 1.

There isn't exactly a multitude of **eating** and **drinking** options: try the à la carte restaurant at the *Hotell Wilhelmina* for traditional northern Swedish dishes and 75kr lunches, or *Krogen* in the main square at Torget 3 which has simple dishes such as pasta carbonara and meatballs for 59kr, and is also a popular place for a drink or two. Coffee, cakes and lunch can also be had at *Stenmans Konditori*, Volgsjövägen 21.

Arvidsjaur

Three and a half hours north of Vilhelmina on the Inlandsbanan, **ARVIDSJAUR** is by far the largest town you'll have passed since Östersund – though that's not saying much. For centuries this was where the region's Sámi gathered to trade and debate, until their agenda was hijacked by the Protestant missionaries who established their first church here in 1606. Arvidsjaur's success was secured when silver was discovered in the nearby mountains and the town flourished as a staging point and supply depot. Despite these developments, the Sámi continued to assemble here on market days and during religious festivals, building their own parish village, the **Lappstaden** (daily tours mid-June to mid-Aug at 10.30am & 6pm, 30kr; otherwise free), of simple wooden huts at the end of the eighteenth century. About eighty of these have survived at the north end of town; they're still used today for the Storstämningshelgen festival over the last weekend in August. There are still around twenty Sámi families in Arvisdjaur, making their living from reindeer husbandry.

The **tourist office** (mid-June to mid-Aug Mon–Fri 9.30am–6pm, Sat & Sun noon–4.30pm; mid-Aug to mid-June Mon–Fri 8.30am–4.30pm; ☏0960/175 00, ⓦwww.polcirkeln.nu) is at Östra Skolgatan 18c, just off Storgatan and five minutes' walk from the train station up Lundavägen. They can advise on activities in the surroundings, such as pedalling down a disused railway line on a rail inspection trolley (70kr for 5hr), or white-water rafting on the nearby Pite River (☏070/260 05 83, ⓦwww.laplandraftingcafe.se; 445kr). The best place to stay is *Lapland Lodge* at Östra Kyrkogatan 18 (☏0960/137 20, ⓦwww.laplandlodge.eu; ❸), a comfortable bed and breakfast place near the church. There's also the cosy *Lappugglan* hostel, conveniently situated at Västra Skolgatan 9 (☏0960/124 13), with dorm beds for 145kr and double rooms (❶); or you could try *Camp Gielas* (☏0960/556 00), which also has **cabins** (600kr) set beside Tvättjärn, one of the town's many lakes, a few minutes' walk along Storgatan from the tourist office. The best **hotel** in town is *Hotell Laponia* at Storgatan 45 (☏0960/555 00, ⓦwww.hotell-laponia.se; ❷/❹), with a swimming pool and comfortable, modern en-suite rooms, some of which are in a budget annex (❶). Be warned that in winter much of the town's accommodation is booked by Europe's leading car companies, who come to the area to test-drive new models on the frozen lakes hence the higher price code; book well in advance to secure a room.

For **snacks** and **coffee**, try *Greya Knut* at Stationsgatan 20, which has sandwiches and salads for around 55kr. There's a small choice of **restaurants**: for pizzas and Greek food, try *Afrodite* (☏0960/173 00) at Storgatan 10, which has a 75kr lunch deal. For finer food, head for *Hotell The Square*, Storgatan 34 (☏0960/212 50), a stylish gourmet restaurant where the delicious à la carte meals include local reindeer and other Lapland delicacies (mains around 250kr). If you're self-catering, consider visiting the Renomera shop at Larstorpsvägen 22, which sells delicious fresh reindeer products such as sausages and smoked meat.

Jokkmokk

During his journey through Lapland, the botanist Carl von Linné said, "If not for the mosquitoes, this would be earth's paradise"; his comments were made after journeying along the river valley of the Lilla Luleälven during the short summer weeks when the mosquitoes are at their most active. **JOKKMOKK**'s Sámi name comes from one particular bend (*mokk*) in the river (*jokk*), which runs through a densely forested municipality the size of Wales with a population of just 6500; needless to say, the town is a welcome oasis, though not an immediately appealing one. Once wintertime Sámi quarters, a market and church heralded a permanent

▲ Reindeer

settlement by the beginning of the seventeenth century. Today, as well as being a well-known handicrafts centre, the town functions as the Sámi capital and is home to the only further education college teaching handicrafts, reindeer husbandry and ecology in the Sámi language.

Jokkmokk's fantastic **Ájtte Museum** (*ájtte* means "storage hut" in Sámi), a brief walk east of the centre at Kyrkogatan 3, off Storgatan (May & mid-Aug to mid-Sept Mon–Fri 10am–4pm, Sat & Sun 11am–3pm; mid-June to mid-Aug daily 9am–6pm; mid-Sept to April Tues–Fri 10am–3pm; 50kr; Ⓦ www.ajtte.com), is the place to really mug up on the Sámi. Displays and exhibitions recount the tough existence of the original settlers of northern Scandinavia and show how things have slowly improved over time – today's Sámi are more dependent on snow scooters and helicopters to herd their reindeer than on the age-old methods employed by their ancestors. There are some imaginative temporary exhibitions on Sámi culture and local flora and fauna (including mosquitoes), and the museum staff can also arrange day-trips into the surrounding marshes for a spot of mushroom-picking. Close to

The Jokkmokk Winter Market

Now over 400 years old, the great **Jokkmokk Winter Market** (Jokkmokks Vintermarknad; Ⓦ www.jokkmokksmarknad.com) is held in the first week of February (Thurs–Sun), and sees 30,000 people force their way into town, increasing the population tenfold. It's the best and coldest time of the year to be in Jokkmokk – there's a Wild West feeling in the air – with lots of drunken stall-holders trying to flog reindeer hides and other unwanted knick-knacks to even more drunken passers-by – and all in, literally, Arctic temperatures. The **reindeer races** can be a real spectacle: held on the frozen Talvatissjön lake behind the *Jokkmokk* hotel, man and beast battle it out on a specially marked track on the ice; however, the reindeer often have other ideas and frequently veer off with great alacrity into the crowd, sending spectators fleeing for cover. Staying in town at this time of year means booking accommodation a good year in advance (although some private rooms become available in the autumn before the market). A smaller and less traditional autumn fair is held at the end of August (around the 25th) – an easier though poorer option.

the museum on Lappstavägen, the **alpine garden** (early June to mid-Aug Mon–Fri 11am–5pm; July to mid-Aug also Sat & Sun noon–5pm; 25kr; 50kr including Ájtte) is home to moor king, mountain avens, glacier crowfoot and other vegetation to be found on the fells around Jokkmokk.

Have a look, too, at the **Lappkyrka**, off Stortorget, a recent copy of the eighteenth-century church that stood on this site. The octagonal design and curiously shaped tower betray a Sámi influence, but the surrounding graveyard wall is all improvisation: the space in between the coarsely hewn timbers was used to store coffins during winter until the thaw in May, when the Sámi could go out and dig graves again – temperatures in this part of Sweden regularly plunge to -30°C and below in winter.

Practicalities

Arriving by **Inlandsbanan**, it's a short walk south up Stationsgatan to Stortorget, the central square where you'll find the main bus stop. If you're here for the Winter Market (when the Inlandsbanan isn't running), you'll need to take the Inlandsexpressen **bus**, or alternatively get off the coastal train at Murjek (between Boden and Gällivare), from where buses run west to Jokkmokk five times a day.

Jokkmokk's **tourist office**, at Stortorget 4 (mid-June to mid-Aug daily 9am–7pm, Sat & Sun 10am–6pm; mid-Aug to mid-June Mon–Fri 8.30am–noon & 1pm–4pm; during the Winter Market Thurs–Sat 9am–6pm, Sun noon–4pm; ☏0971/222 50, ⓦwww.turism.jokkmokk.se), is a few minutes' walk from the train station along Stationsgatan and also has internet acces. The **youth hostel** (☏0971/559 77, ⓦwww .jokkmokkhostel.com; doubles ❶, dorm beds from 175kr) is located in a wonderful old house with a garden at Åsgatan 20, behind the tourist office. The *Jokkmokk-Camping-Center* **campsite** (☏0971/123 70, ⓦwww.jokkmokkcampingcenter.com) is a three-kilometre walk southeast of town on the Lilla Lule River, off Route E97 to Luleå. Of the town's two **hotels**, ⚑ *Jokkmokk* has a convenient and attractive lakeside setting at Solgatan 45 (☏0971/777 00, ⓦwww.hoteljokkmokk.se; ❹/❺), large en-suite rooms and a big sauna area; *Hotell Gästis* at Herrevägen 1 (☏0971/100 12, ⓦwww.hotell-gastis.com; ❸/❹) is nothing to write home about, with simple, modern en-suite rooms.

Jokkmokk has a limited number of **eating** and **drinking** possibilities. The cheap and cheerful *Restaurang Kowloon* at Föreningsgatan 3 has lunch for 65kr and Chinese meals for around 99kr at other times, while pizzas from 65kr and simple fry-ups are available at *Restaurang Opera* at Storgatan 36. For traditional Sámi dishes such as reindeer, head for the restaurant at the Ájtte Museum, where lunch costs 65kr. The best place to drink is the bar inside the *Jokkmokk* hotel – if you've drunk your way round Jokkmokk this far you won't mind the inebriated late-night company here.

Gällivare

Last stop on the Inlandsbanan and by far the biggest town since Östersund, **GÄLLIVARE** is far more pleasant than you'd imagine from its industrial surroundings. Strolling around its open centre is a great antidote to the small inland villages along the train route. There's a gritty ugliness to Gällivare that gives the place a certain charm: a steely grey mesh of modern streets that has all the hallmarks of a city, although on a scale that's far too modest for the title to be applied with any justification.

Arrival, information and accommodation

Gällivare's **train station** is right next to the **tourist office** at Centralplan 3 (mid-June to mid-Aug daily 8am–10pm; mid-Aug to mid-June Mon–Fri 8am–5pm; ☏0970/166 60, ⓦwww.visit.gellivare.se). Here you can get good free maps, hiking information and tickets for the mine tours (see pp.498–499).

Dundret Per Högströmsgatan 1 ☏0970/550 40, ⓦwww.hotelldundret.se. Actually a small pension, : with just seven rooms and shared shower and toilet. ❸

Gällivare Camping Malmbergsvägen 2
ⓣ 0970/100 10, ⓦ www.gellivarecamping.com.
Open all year and close to the centre by the river,
off Porjusvägen (Route 45 to Jokkmokk). There
are also simple cabins (300kr) with no facilities
(200kr more for private facilities) and dorm beds
(180kr).
Gällivare Värdshus Hellebergsvägen 5
ⓣ 0970/162 00, ⓦ gellivarevardshus.com.
A pleasant cheapie that's an excellent central choice
and a good place to meet backpackers. ③ / ④

Grand Hotel Lapland Lasarettsgatan 1
ⓣ 0970/77 22 90, ⓦ www.grandhotellapland.com.
Opposite the station, this is the best central hotel,
with tastefully decorated rooms and a decent
sauna. ④ / ⑥

Rallarrosen youth hostel Barnhemsvägen
2A ⓣ 0970/143 80; ⓔ info@explorelapland
.com. Behind the train station (cross the tracks by
the metal bridge), this place offers a good sauna
in the main building and accommodation in small
cabins. Dorm beds 150kr, double rooms ①

The Town

Gällivare is one of the most important sources of **iron ore** in Europe, offering a
rare opportunity to see an open working mine. Bus tours, starting from the tourist
office (daily 9.30am; 250kr), visit **Malmberget underground iron-ore mine**.
Descending over one thousand metres to an ear-popping depth of 315m below sea
level (the deepest outside the Dead Sea), you'll see rock-crusher stations crunching
some of the eight million tonnes of iron ore that the mine produces each year. In
winter, it's a balmy 15°C in the mine. It's hard to imagine that before the arrival of

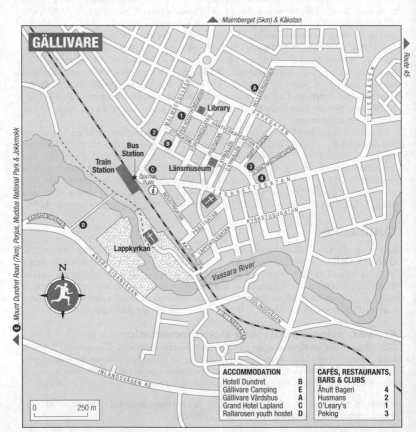

▲ Malmberget (5km) & Kåkstan

GÄLLIVARE

Route 45

Library

Bus
Station

Train
Station

Länsmuseum

CENTRAL
PLAN

Lappkyrkan

Vassara River

N

ACCOMMODATION		CAFÉS, RESTAURANTS, BARS & CLUBS	
Hotell Dundret	B	Åhult Bageri	4
Gällivare Camping	E	Husmans	2
Gällivare Värdshus	A	O'Leary's	1
Grand Hotel Lapland	C	Peking	3
Rallarosen youth hostel	D		

the railway, iron ore was dragged to Luleå on reindeer sleds, with one load of 100kg taking up to two months to get there.

The **Aitik open-cast copper mine** tour (Mon, Wed & Fri 2pm; 220kr) takes you down into the 350-metre-deep pit, the biggest in Europe, which produces nineteen million tonnes of copper ore and two tonnes of gold per year. The bus stops near the gigantic shovel machines and bulldozers (often operated by women – the mine's statistics prove they're better, more efficient drivers), and you may be allowed to climb into one.

Gällivare occupies the site of a Sámi village and one theory has it that the town's name comes from the Sámi language – *djelli* (a crack or gorge) *vare* (in the mountain). Down by the river near the train station, you'll come across the Sámi church, **Lappkyrkan** (June–Aug 10am–3pm), a mid-eighteenth-century construction. It's known as the Ettöreskyrkan (One Öre Church) after the one öre charity drive throughout Sweden that paid for it.

There's precious little else to see or do in Gällivare and you'd be wise to use your time strolling up the **Dundret** mountain, overshadowing the town, which is the target of midnight sun spotters. Alternatively, buses head up here specially for the Midnight Sun (mid-June to mid-July daily at 11pm; mid-July to end July daily at 10pm; early to mid-Aug daily 9.30pm); tickets, available from the tourist office, cost 140kr return.

Eating and drinking

If you're arriving from one of the tiny villages on the Inlandsbanan, the wealth of **eating and drinking** possibilities in Gällivare will make you quite dizzy; if you're coming from Luleå, grit your teeth and bear it. Good places for lunch are the *Åhult Bageri & Café* at Lasarettsgatan 19, serving great cakes and sandwiches, and the *Husmans* at Malmbergsvägen 1, which has a selection of burgers and home-cooking fry-ups. For more exotic food, *Peking* (☏0970/176 85) at Storgatan 21B serves pizzas and reasonable Chinese food from 110kr. As for **drinking**, the place to be seen is *O'Leary's* at Per Högströmsgatan 9.

Kiruna and around

KIRUNA was at the hub of the battle for the control of the iron ore supply during World War II. Ore was transported north from Kiruna by train to the great harbour at Narvik over the border in Norway, and much German firepower was expended in an attempt to interrupt the supply to the Allies and wrest control from the Axis. In the process, Narvik suffered grievously, whilst Kiruna – benefiting from supposed Swedish neutrality – made a packet selling to both sides. Today, the train ride to Kiruna rattles through sidings, slag heaps and ore works, a bitter contrast to the surrounding wilderness. A brooding reminder of Kiruna's prosperity, the **LKAB iron-ore mine**, which churns out 13 million tonnes of ore a year, dominates the town: despite the new central buildings and open parks, Kiruna retains a gritty industrial air.

Guided tours of the mines are arranged by the tourist office (mid-June to mid-Aug 4 daily; early June & late Aug 2 daily; 280kr). A coach takes visitors through the underground road network and then stops off at a "tourist mine", a closed-off section of a leviathan structure containing service stations, restaurants, computer centres, trains and crushing mills – an interesting, but far less authentic experience than the iron-ore mine tours in Gällivare (see opposite). Incidentally, due to severe **subsidence** from the mines over a kilometre below the town, Kiruna is sinking. Plans have been formalized to move the entire city to the northwest of its current site, near Luossavaara hill. First to relocate will be the train station and the E10 highway, followed by individual houses, which will be loaded onto trailers for transportation. Oddly, local people seem unperturbed by the enormity of the task ahead, perhaps because they are painfully aware that without the iron-ore mines on which Kiruna is totally dependent, the place would cease to exist.

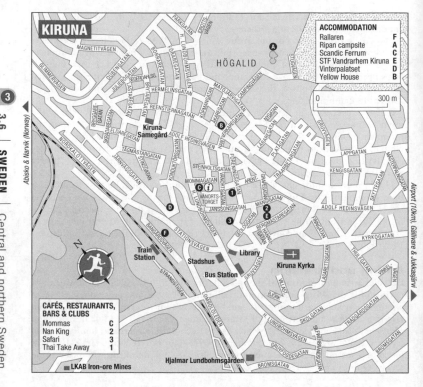

All the other sights in town are firmly wedded to the all-important metal in one way or another. The tower of the **Stadshus** on Hjalmar Lundbohmsvägen (June–Aug daily 8am–4pm; Sept–May Mon–Fri 8am–5pm) is obvious even from the train station, a strident metal pillar harbouring an intricate latticework clock-face and sundry bells that chime raucously at noon. It was designed by Bror Marklund, and the whole hall unbelievably won the 1964 award for the most beautiful Swedish public building. Inside, there's a tolerable art collection and Sámi handicraft displays in summer.

Only a few minutes up the road, **Kiruna kyrka** (daily 11am–4.45pm) raises a few eyebrows. Built in the style of a Sámi hut, it's a massive origami creation of oak beams and rafters the size of a small aircraft hangar, with an impressive 3500-pipe organ. LKAB, the mining company that to all intents and purposes *is* Kiruna, and which paid for church's construction, was also responsible for the nearby **Hjalmar Lundbohmsgården** (Tues, Thurs & Fri 8am–4pm, Wed 10am–4pm; 35kr), a country house once used by the managing director of the company and "founder" of Kiruna. Displays inside mostly consist of early twentieth-century photographs featuring the man himself and assorted Sámi in their winter gear. Visit before going down the mine and everything will take on an added perspective – without the mine, Kiruna would be a one-reindeer town instead of the thriving place it is today. The **Kiruna Samegård**, at Brytaregatan 14 (Mon–Fri 7am–noon & 1–4pm; 20kr), is the most rewarding exhibition of Sámi culture in town. The handicrafts may be familiar but what won't be is the small display of really very good Sámi art featuring scenes from everyday life.

Practicalities

Most flights to Kiruna's **airport**, 10km east of town, are met by the bus to the centre of town (June to mid-Sept only; 40kr); otherwise, you'll need a taxi (250kr). Arriving by **train**, it's a brisk five-minute walk from the station uphill to the **tourist office** mid-June to Aug Mon–Fri 8.30am–8pm, Sat & Sun 8.30am–5pm; Sept to mid-June Mon–Fri 8.30am–5pm, Sat 8.30am–3pm; ☎0980/188 80, ⓦwww .lappland.se) in Folkets Hus, on the central square off Mommagatan where there's also internet access.

Kiruna's city centre STF **youth hostel** (☎0980/171 95, ⓦwww.kirunahostel .com; doubles ❸, dorm beds for 210kr) is 900m from the train station at Bergmästaregatan 7. It fills quickly in summer, as does the other hostel in town, the *Yellow House* at Hantverkaregatan 25 (☎0980/137 50, ⓦwww.yellowhouse.nu), which has double rooms (❶) and dorm rooms from 140kr per person. The *Ripan* **campsite** (☎0980/630 00, ⓦwww.ripan.se), a twenty-minute walk north on Campingvägen, has year-round cabins (1000kr/1500kr) available. In winter, you can sleep in an **ice igloo** (Dec–April; ❻), with a window in the roof for watching the northern lights, a much better-value and more romantic option than the *Icehotel* (see below); the price includes a flask of warm lingonberry juice, breakfast and a sauna in the morning. The reception rents out skis for the nearby cross-country trails and can organize dog-sledging.

Of Kiruna's central **hotels**, the large *Scandic Ferrum Kiruna* next to the tourist office at Lars Janssonsgatan 15 (☎0980/39 86 00, ⓦwww.scandichotels.se /ferrum; ❹/❺) has superb views of the midnight Sun from its excellent sixth-floor sauna area, while the ⚑ *Hotell Vinterpalatset* at Järnvägsgatan 18 (☎0980/677 70, ⓦwww.vinterpalatset.se; ❸/❺), is a smaller upmarket option. Another good choice is *Rallaren* at Bangårdsvägen 4 (☎0980/611 26, ⓦwww.hotelrallaren .se; ❸/❺) with snug, individually decorated rooms in Sámi colours and styles. Kiruna is hardly a centre of haute cuisine, but there are several decent places to eat: the best is *Thai Take Away at* Föreningsgatan 17 with Thai specials from 125kr. *Nan King* at Mangigatan 26 is an inexpensive Chinese place while *Mommas*, inside the *Scandic Ferrum*, does its best to be an American steakhouse and is a good place for a drink. Coffee and cakes are served up at *Safari*, Geologgatan 4.

Around Kiruna: Jukkasjärvi

Just 15km east of Kiruna, the tiny village of **JUKKASJÄRVI** is a Mecca for many tourists travelling in Lapland in winter – albeit a disproportionately expensive one for the dubious pleasure of spending a night in subzero temperatures. The **Icehotel** (☎0980/668 00, ⓦwww.icehotel.com) that is built here every October is the world's biggest igloo and stands proudly by the side of the frozen Torne River until it melts in May. Thousands of tons of ice and snow are used to make the igloo, after which artists decorate the interior with elaborate carvings and lighting. Inside, there are bedrooms with compacted snow beds covered with reindeer hides, a bar, an exhibition hall, a cinema and a wedding chapel. Winter temperatures are generally around -20 to -30°C, which means that inside the igloo it's a positively balmy -5°C.

Guests are provided with special sleeping bags, warm coats, hats and gloves. There are several types of room here: a standard **double room** (known as a snowroom) containing nothing more than a reindeer-hide-swathed block of snow and ice for a bed costs 3800kr, and the more stylish **iceroom** featuring ice carvings a pricey 4900kr. Suites, with more ornamentation, cost up to 7000kr per night. If you chicken out, there are also regular (warm) double rooms and cabins for rent on the site (both 3395kr). A hotel bus picks up customers from the airport or train station (100kr per person), but undoubtedly the best way to arrive at the *Icehotel* is by **dog sledge** from the airport; for a hefty 5900kr, you and three friends can be met from your plane and pulled to your room. At the southern end of the village, there's a small wooden Sámi **church** from 1608, next to which is the *Nutti Sámi Siida* travel agency (℡0980/213 29, Ⓦwww.nutti.se), which organizes Sámi-related adventures including dog- and reindeer sledging and accommodation in Sámi tepees. In **summer**, Jukkasjärvi is a good place for river-rafting, fishing and hiking – ask the *Icehotel* for details. In the *Icehotel*'s Art Centre (open year round), you can also see ice sculptures and the massive blocks of ice cut from the river in March in readiness for the next season's construction.

The two **eating** options in the village are both run by the hotel; the *Icehotel* restaurant (winter only; ℡0980/668 84) right across the road serves pricey gourmet Lapland dishes (200–300kr) and better-value lunches; 800m away, the ⚶ *Old Homestead* restaurant (open all year) has a 85kr lunch menu and more Lappish dishes, from 150kr.

From Kiruna to the Norwegian border

Quite amazingly, it's only since 1984 that there's been a choice of ways to continue your journey towards Norway: until then, only the train covered the last leg of the long run from Stockholm or Luleå towards Narvik. Today, though, there's the **Nordkalottvägen** road, which runs parallel to the railway, threading its way across the barren plateaus (the lakes up here are still frozen in mid-June) before slicing through the mighty Norwegian mountains. It's an exhilarating run that passes the start of the **Kungsleden** trail at Abisko (see box opposite): get off the train at Abisko Turiststation (not Abisko Östra, which is the village) where the adjoining fell station and ⚶ STF lodge (℡0980/402 00, Ⓦwww.abisko.nu; doubles ❸, dorm beds from 310kr) offers advice for hikers and has a good restaurant.

Take the **chairlift** (140kr return) and walk a few kilometres to reach Nuolja peak, with fantastic views of the surrounding wilderness, including the spectacular U-shaped valley of Lapporten, the seventy-kilometre-long Torneträsk lake and the vast wooded expanses of Abisko National Park. Tucked away in one corner of

▲ Cycling, Abisko

Hiking in the national parks

It's not a good idea to go hiking in the national parks of northern Sweden on a whim. Even for experienced walkers, the going can be tough and uncomfortable in parts, downright treacherous in others. Mosquitoes are a real problem: it's difficult to imagine the utter misery of being covered in a blanket of insects, with your eyes, ears and nose full of the creatures. Yet this is one of the last wilderness areas left in Europe: the map of this part of the country shows little more than vast areas of forest and mountains, and roads and human habitation are the exception rather than the norm. Reindeer are a common sight since the parks are breeding grounds and summer pasture, and Sámi settlements are dotted throughout the region. Although there are some good short trails in the national parks, suitable for beginners, the goal for more ambitious hikers is the northern section of the Kungsleden trail (see p.503), which crosses several parks.

The best **time** to go hiking in the Swedish mountains is from late June to September. During May and early June, the ground is very wet and boggy due to the rapid snow melt. Once the snow has gone, wild flowers burst into bloom to make the most of the short summer months. The **weather** is very changeable – one moment it can be hot and sunny, the next cold and rainy – snow showers are by no means uncommon, even in summer. It goes without saying that you'll need to be **well equipped** with hiking gear, a sleeping bag, decent boots and *Lantmäteriet* (Swedish National Survey) hiking maps.

the café at the end of the chairlift, the **Aurora Sky Station** is the best place for miles around to observe the **northern lights**; Abisko lies in a rain shadow and the sky is consequently often free of cloud. Containing all kinds of equipment to measure and hear the lights (they often emit a series of hisses and clicks), it's a perfect introduction for the non-initiated into this most compliated of scientific phenomena since experts are on hand to explain what you're seeing and hearing. The Aurora Sky Station is open in connection with special organized tours to see the lights which depart from the Turiststation (early Dec to late March, Wed, Fri & Sat; 475kr).

Both train line and road continue on to **RIKSGRÄNSEN**, the last settlement in Sweden, a popular ski resort with good snow right up to late June. There's a **hotel** here, the *Hotell Riksgränsen* (☎0980/400 80, ⓦwww.riksgransen.nu; ❹/❺), opposite the train station, which has information about **hiking**, **mountain biking** and **canoeing** in the area. This is Sweden's wettest area, with the wind whips off the Atlantic rising against the mountains here – intriguingly, Abisko, just 30km away, is the country's driest spot, sitting in the rain shadow of these mountains.

The Kungsleden

The **Kungsleden** is the most famous and popular of Sweden's hiking trails, a five-hundred-kilometre route from **Abisko** in the north to **Hemavan**, near Tärnaby, in the south. From Abisko to Kvikkjokk, north of the Arctic Circle, and in the south between Ammarnäs and Hemavan there are STF cabins and fell stations. Huts are placed at intervals of 15 to 20km, a distance that can be covered in one day, while shelter from the wind is provided at various places along the route. The Kungsleden is an easy trail to walk: it's well marked; all the streams en route are crossed by bridges, and patches of marshy ground are overlaid with wooden planks; and there are also boat services or rowing boats for crossing the several large lakes on the way. If you're looking for total isolation this is not the trail for you – it's the busiest in the country. Avoid July and you'll find it easier going.

Travel details

Trains

The **Inlandsbanan** runs from Mora to Gällivare via Östersund, generally from early June to late Aug although this is subject to change from year to year. Northbound trains leave Östersund daily for Gällivare at 7.15am. Southbound trains leave Gällivare daily at 6.50am for stations to Östersund.

Abisko to: Gällivare (2 daily; 2hr 20min); Kiruna (2 daily; 1hr 20min); Riksgränsen (2 daily; 40min); Stockholm (1 daily; 18hr).

Gällivare to: Kiruna (3 daily; 1hr); Luleå (3 daily; 2hr 20min); Stockholm (1 daily; 15hr 30min).

Kiruna to: Luleå (3 daily; 3hr 20min); Stockholm (1 daily; 16hr 30min).

Riksgränsen to: Abisko (2 daily; 40min); Gällivare (2 daily; 3hr); Kiruna (2 daily; 2hr); Stockholm (1 daily; 19hr).

International trains

Abisko to: Narvik, Norway (2 daily; 1hr 30min).
Gällivare to: Narvik, Norway (2 daily; 2hr).
Kiruna to: Narvik, Norway (2 daily; 3hr).
Riksgränsen to: Narvik, Norway (2 daily; 1hr).

Buses

The **Inlandsexpressen** (#45) runs north from Östersund to Gällivare via Vilhelmina, Arvidsjaur and Jokkmokk. It operates daily all year round.

Åsarna to: Klövsjö (5 daily; 20min); Mora (2 daily; 4hr); Östersund (6 daily; 1hr 10min).

Gällivare to: Jokkmokk (5 daily; 1hr 30min); Kiruna (4 daily; 1hr 30min); Luleå (4 daily; 3hr 15min); Ritsem (2 daily; 3hr 20min).

Jokkmokk to: Gällivare (5 daily; 1hr 30min); Luleå (3 daily; 3hr); Kvikkjokk (2 daily; 1hr 50min).

Karlstad to: Stockholm (7 daily; 4hr 10min).

Kiruna to: Abisko (2 daily; 1hr 20min); Gällivare (4 daily; 1hr 30min); Jukkasjärvi (7 daily; 30min); Luleå (2 daily; 4hr 45min); Riksgränsen (daily; 2hr 10min).

Kvikkjokk to: Jokkmokk (2 daily; 1hr 50min).

Mora to: Åsarna (2 daily; 4hr); Leksand (hourly; 1hr 20min); Orsa (hourly; 20min); Östersund (2 daily; 5hr 10min); Stockholm (3 daily; 4hr 30min); Sveg (2 daily; 2hr 5min).

Östersund to: Åre (2 daily; 1hr 30min); Åsarna (6 daily; 1hr 10min); Mora (2 daily; 5hr 10min); Sveg (3 daily; 2hr 40min); Umeå (2 daily; 6hr).

Storuman to: Hemavan (4 daily; 2hr 30min); Tärnaby (5 daily; 2hr); Umeå (2–4 daily; 3hr 40min).

International buses

Arvidsjaur to: Bodö, Norway (daily; 7hr).
Karlstad to: Oslo (4–5 daily; 3hr).
Kiruna to: Narvik, Norway (daily; 2hr 30min).
Storuman to: Mo i Rana, Norway (daily; 4hr 15min).

Finland

Finland Highlights

✳ **Travel by tram, Helsinki**
The best and most leisurely
way to take in the capital's
diverse and striking
architecture – from Art
Nouveau to hyper-modern.
See p.525

✳ **Pihlajasaari island,
Helsinki** This forested isle
of bathing huts, cafés and
great beaches makes the
perfect day-trip, and is a
good spot to work on your
all-over tan. See p.540

✳ **Turku Castle, Turku** Delve
into Finland's often uneasy
relationship with neighbouring Sweden at this former
seat of power – the largest
extant medieval building in
the country. See p.563

✳ **Åland Islands** A summer
paradise of sprawling
flowery meadows, sheltered
swimmable creeks and
undulating countryside lanes
perfect for biking. See p.569

✳ **Savonlinna Opera Festival,
Savonlinna** One of Europe's
most sought-after musical
extravaganzas, with arias
performed in a spectacular
fifteenth-century fortress.
See p.592

✳ **Sauna, Kuopio** Experience
the steamy reality of the
Finnish national pastime
in the world's biggest
woodsmoke sauna, and
get tips from the locals on
technique. See p.601

✳ **Rovaniemi, Lapland** Get
face to face with some
Nordic wild reindeer and
visit Santa Claus to place
your order for Christmas – at
any time of the year. See
pp.619–623

✳ **Inari, Lapland** Pan for
gold in babbling brooks or
deepen your knowledge of
Sámi history and culture
at Inari's first-rate village
museum. See p.628

▲ Playing in the snow

Introduction and basics

Mainland Scandinavia's most culturally isolated and least understood country, Finland has been independent only since 1917, having been ruled for hundreds of years by imperial powers: first the Swedes and then the tsarist Russians. Much of its history involves a struggle simply for recognition and survival.

Today, though, the battle has been won and the Finns are the proudest of all the Nordic nations, trumpeting the fact that this little-known country on the very edge of Europe is truly one of the continent's best-kept secrets. Finland is without a doubt the most welcoming of all of the Scandinavian countries; Finns of all ages are inordinately proud of their nation's achievements (it is, after all, only by a quirk of history that Finland was not invaded by the Soviet Union and well and truly taken into Moscow's sphere of influence) and are anxious that visitors learn more about their country, where a joy in all things Finnish goes hand in hand with eager participation in the European Union. Forget any lingering perceptions that Finland is mundane, grey or even Communist – today it's a welcoming, honest and prosperous society keen to make up for years of living on the sidelines and, in the capital at least, one whose nightlife scene rivals that of any cosmopolitan European centre.

During the Swedish period, the Finnish language (one of Europe's least familiar and most difficult) was regarded as fit only for peasants – which the majority of Finns were – and attempts were later made to forcibly impose Russian. All publications were in Swedish until the *Kalevala* appeared in the early nineteenth century. A written collection of previously orally transmitted folk tales telling of a people close to nature, living by hunting and fishing, the *Kalevala* instantly became regarded as a truly Finnish history, and formed the basis of the **National Romantic** movement in the arts that flourished from the mid-nineteenth century, stimulating political initiatives towards Finnish nationalism.

It's not surprising, therefore, that modern-day Finns have a well-developed sense of their own culture, and that the legacy of the past is strongly felt in the still widely popular Golden Age paintings of Gallen-Kallela, Edelfelt and others; in the music of Sibelius; and in the National Romantic architecture which paved the way for modern, Modernist greats like Alvar Aalto. Equally in evidence, even among city-dwellers, are the deeply ingrained, down-to-earth values of rural life, along with a sense of spirituality epitomized by the **sauna**, which for Finns is as much a meaningful social ritual as it is a health and fitness activity.

Some elderly rural dwellers are prone to suspicion of anything foreign, but in general

Finland on the web

ⓦ**www.festivals.fi** Listings and descriptions of the country's biggest and most popular music and culture festivals.

ⓦ**www.visitfinland.com** The official tourist board site, with bundles of info in a functional layout.

ⓦ**www.outdoors.fi** The Finnish Forest Service's website, offering hundreds of pages of information in English on hiking and staying in and around Finland's national parks.

ⓦ**www.sauna.fi** Home of the Finnish Sauna Society, with indispensable practical advice on sauna do's and don'ts.

ⓦ**www.santaclaus.fi** Old St Nick's "official" site, with stories, interviews and even a webcam so you can keep an eye on where all that brandy really goes.

ⓦ**virtual.finland.fi** News and views, facts and figures from the Finnish Foreign Ministry.

the Finnish population is much less staid than its Nordic neighbours, and the disintegration of its once powerful neighbour, the Soviet Union, has allowed it to form closer ties with Europe through membership of the European Union. By the end of the 1990s Finland's **economy** was buoyant enough to allow it to join the first wave of countries in the European Monetary Union. It's currently the only one of the three Nordic EU members to have introduced the euro, and with the success of Finnish telecommunications giant Nokia, a flourishing IT sector and a booming economy, the country reached the millennium with an unprecedented confidence and renewed self-belief. However, unemployment remains high in some places, particularly in rural areas, and some sections of Finnish society are being left behind in Finland's drive to become a technological world leader.

Where to go

Topographically, Finland is mainly flat, and filled by huge forests and lakes – you'll need to travel around a lot to appreciate the country's wide regional variations. The **south** contains the least dramatic scenery, but the capital, **Helsinki**, more than compensates, with its brilliant architecture and superb museum collections. Stretching from the Russian border in the east to the industrial city of **Tampere**, the water systems of the **Lake Region** provide a natural means of transport for the timber industry – indeed, water here is a more common sight than land.

Ostrobothnia, the upper portion of the west coast, is characterized by near-featureless farmlands and long sandy beaches which are – to Finns at least – the region's main draw. Here, too, you'll find the clearest Swedish influence: in parts up to a third of the population are Swedish-speaking – known as "Finland-Swedes" – and there's a rich heritage from the days of Swedish trading supremacy. **Kainuu** is the thickly forested heart of the country, much of its small population spread among scattered villages. The land begins to rise as you head north from here, folding into a series of fells and gorges that are ripe for spectacular hiking and cross-country skiing. Completely devoid of large towns, **Lapland** – or Sápmi to the region's indigenous people – contains the most alluring terrain of all, its stark and haunting landscapes able to absorb any number of visitors on numerous hiking routes. This region is home to the Sámi people, sedentary reindeer herders whose traditional ways of life meld relatively smoothly with modern Finnish society.

When to go

The official **holiday season** for Finns is early July to mid-August, ignited by the midsummer celebrations of *Juhannus* in late June; during these weeks there's a nationwide exodus from the towns to the country. The best time to visit the rural regions is either side of these dates, when things will be less crowded and hectic – though no cheaper.

In **summer**, regarded as being from June to early September, Helsinki, the south and the Lake Region enjoy mild and sunny weather, while areas further north are on the whole cooler – though recent years have experienced significant variation in the length and intensity of the warm season. On average, temperatures are usually 18–24°C (65–75°F), sometimes reaching 32°C (90°F) in the daytime, but they drop swiftly in the evening, when you'll need a light jacket. The north is always a few degrees cooler and often quite cold at night, so carry a thick jumper at least. The midnight sun can be seen from Rovaniemi northwards for two months over midsummer; the rest of the country experiences a night-long twilight from mid-June to mid-July.

Winter, roughly from late October to early April in the south, plus a few weeks more on either side in the north, is painfully cold. Helsinki generally fluctuates between 0°C and -20°C (32°F and -4°F), the harshest months being January and February; in the north it's even colder, with just a few hours of daylight; and in the extreme north the sun doesn't rise at all. The snow cover generally lasts from November to March in the south, a few weeks longer in the north. On the plus side, Finland copes easily with low temperatures and transport is rarely disrupted.

Thanks to its relatively flat terrain, Finland is one of the most enjoyable countries in Scandinavia to go **hiking**, one of the Finns' favourite pastimes. The best time for hiking is from May to September in the south and from June to September in the north. You'll need a good-quality tent, a warm sleeping bag, rainwear, spare warm clothing, thick-soled waterproof boots, mosquito repellent, a compass and detailed maps, all of which can be bought in tourist centres close to the hiking routes.

Finnish and Swedish place names

On most maps and many transport timetables cities and towns are given their **Finnish names** followed by their **Swedish names** in parentheses. Both Swedes and Finland-Swedes will frequently use the Swedish rather than the Finnish names. The main places in question are listed below, with the Finnish name first.

Helsinki (Helsingfors)
Porvoo (Borgå)
Turku (Åbo)
Pori (Björneborg)
Hamina (Fredrikshamn)
Lappeenranta (Villmanstrand)
Kajaani (Kajana)

Iisalmi (Idensalmi)
Tampere (Tammerfors)
Mikkeli (St Michel)
Savonlinna (Nyslott)
Vaasa (Vasa)
Kokkola (Gamla Karleby)
Oulu (Uleåborg)

Getting there from the rest of Scandinavia

Finland's geographical position – effectively separated from the rest of Scandinavia by the Gulf of Bothnia – means that except in the extreme north of the country the easiest approaches are usually by ferry or plane. Crossing from the east coast of Sweden is easy, with regular **ferry** services from a number of points and (usually) good onward links once you've arrived. Further north, Sweden and Norway both have land borders with Finland and these are no fuss to cross by **bus**, although in a few spots you may have to wait a day between connections. From Denmark, it's impossible to get to Finland without passing through Sweden unless you **fly**, although there's a direct bus–ferry service and fairly frequent trains.

By train

There are no direct **train** connections between Finland and other Scandinavian countries. The nearest railhead is at Boden in Sweden, at the northern end of the Gulf of Bothnia, around 100km before the Finnish border at Haparanda–Tornio (InterRail and Eurail passes are valid on buses from Luleå/Boden to Haparanda). Other train connections, such as those between Helsinki and Stockholm or Copenhagen (1–2 daily; 25hr), make use of ferry crossings for much of their route.

By bus

In the Arctic North, **buses** connect the Norwegian–Finnish border towns of **Karasjok–Karigasniemi** and **Skibotn–Kilpisjärvi**, as well as the Finnish border villages of **Utsjoki**, **Polmak** and **Nuorgam**; fares and schedules, beyond what we've included under the "Travel details" at the end of the relevant chapters, can be checked at any tourist office or bus station, though on the whole these infrequent services don't change too much from year to year. There are also regular services from points in northern Sweden via the twin border towns of **Haparanda–Tornio**, at the northern end of the Gulf of Bothnia.

Long-distance bus-and-ferry connections to Finland are also fairly frequent. The service **from Copenhagen** to Finland runs four times a week to Helsinki, via **Stockholm** and **Turku**. Naturally, it's a fairly exhausting journey, taking 25 hours.

By ferry

The most frequent **ferries** from Sweden to Finland run between **Stockholm** and Helsinki and are operated by Silja Line (Ⓦ www.tallinksilja.com; 16hr; €31 obligatory cabin, €52 car) and Viking Line (Ⓦ www.vikingline.fi; 16hr; €36 deck passenger, €42 car), though frequent discounts are offered by both throughout the year, and you can occasionally land a bed in a four-person cabin for around €20. Both companies have a year-round overnight service, leaving at 5pm and arriving at 9.30am, and both also run a twice-daily service from Stockholm to **Turku**, which takes ten or eleven hours (Silja cabin €15.50, €21 day, €42 night; Viking Line foot passenger €10). Quicker still (4hr) are the daily services between Stockholm and **Mariehamn**, run by Viking (passengers €11, car €11). Prices for all the routes are usually cheapest on daylight trips outside the summer months and during the week. There are no ferries from Denmark to Finland.

As these routes are extremely popular among Finns and Swedes, it's a good idea to plan ahead, though you shouldn't have a problem getting hold of a last-minute place on the boat, assuming you don't mind foregoing a cabin. For current details on timetables and the numerous discounts available – ranging from fifty percent reductions for holders of InterRail or Eurail cards to other generous concessions for children and senior citizens – check with a travel agent or the relevant ferry office.

By plane

Finnair (Ⓦ www.finnair.com) and Scandinavian Airlines (Ⓦ www.scandinavian.net) both have daily nonstop flights to Helsinki from **Copenhagen** (hourly; 1hr 30min), **Stockholm** (hourly; 1hr) and **Oslo** (6–9 daily; 1hr 30min). Both also offer flights between Stockholm and a number of Finnish regional cities including

Tampere (6 daily; 1hr), **Oulu** (3 daily; 1hr 20min), **Vaasa** (4 daily; 1hr 15min) and **Turku** (3 daily; 1hr), though getting to these cities from Copenhagen or Oslo involves flying via Stockholm or Helsinki. Blue1 (@www .blue1.com), the budget arm of Scandinavian, operates direct flights between all the Scandinavian capitals, as well as several less-travelled, direct daily routes like Stockholm–Vaasa and Gothenburg–Helsinki; prices start at €78 return, but last-minute flights can be frighteningly expensive. Check with a travel agent or visit the airlines' websites for occasional bargain fares.

Getting around

Save for the fact that traffic tends to follow a north–south pattern, you'll have few headaches **getting around** the more populated parts of Finland. The chief form of public transport is the train, backed up, particularly on east–west journeys, by long-distance coaches. For the most part trains and buses integrate well, and you'll only need to plan with care when travelling through sparsely inhabited areas such as the far north and east. Feasible and often affordable variations come in the form of ferries, planes, bikes and even hitching – car rental is strictly for the wealthy.

The complete **timetable** (*Suomen Kulkuneuvot*) for train, bus, ferry and air travel within the country is published every four months; it's sold primarily at large bookshops for €30. This is essential for plotting complex routes; for simplified details of the major train services, pick up the *Rail Pocket Guide* booklet, available at most train stations for around €1 (or downloadable as a PDF for free from @ww.vr.fi).

Trains

The swiftest land link between Finland's major cities is invariably the reliable **train service**, operated by the state railway company, Valtan Rautatie (VR). Large, comfortable *pikajuna* ("express" trains, though often quite slow), super-smooth IC (inter-city trains) and an increasing number of state-of-the-art tilting *pendolino* trains serve the principal **north–south** routes several times a day, reaching

as far north as Rovaniemi on the Arctic Circle, although occasional services penetrate as far north as Kemijärvi. Elsewhere, especially on east–west hauls through sparsely populated regions, rail services tend to be skeletal and trains are often tiny two-carriage affairs. The Arctic North has a very limited network of services. More details on Finnish Railways can be found at @www.vr.fi.

InterRail, BIJ and Eurail Scandinavia **passes** are valid on all trains; if you don't have one of these and are planning a lot of travelling, get a **Finnrail Pass** before arriving in Finland (you can't buy it in Finland itself) from a travel agent or Finnish Tourist Office (for addresses, see p.43). This costs €129 for three days' unlimited travel within a month, €171 for five days or €232 for ten days. Another option is the summer-only **Lomapassi**, available for purchase within Finland at all train stations and many travel agencies from June to August. This allows for three days of unlimited travel within one month and costs €139.

Otherwise, train **fares** are surprisingly reasonable. As a guide, a one-way, second-class ticket from Helsinki to Turku (a trip of around 200km) costs around €27, Helsinki to Kuopio (465km) €53; and Helsinki to Rovaniemi (900km) €77. If you've brought a car with you, car sleeper services are a convenient way of covering long distances. A one-way trip from Helsinki to Rovaniemi for a car and up to three passengers (including sleeping berths) costs between €218 and €319, depending on the time of year.

Tickets are purchased for specific dates and times, though there is no fee if you want to change the date or routing. Some journeys also allow you to break your journey en route – check when you purchase. You should **buy tickets** from station ticket offices (*lippumyymälä*), although you can also pay the inspector on the train. If there are three or more of you travelling together, **group tickets**, available from a train station or travel agent, can cut the regular fares on journeys over 80km by at least fifteen percent (twenty percent for parties of eleven or more). **Senior citizens** (those) over 65 with valid identification are entitled to a fifty percent discount on regular tickets; pensioners under 65 must purchase a Finnish Senior

Citizens railcard (€9). The cost of **seat reservations** depends on the distance travelled but is generally around €5 – remember that although they are not necessary on express trains, reservations can be a good idea if you're travelling over a holiday period or on a Friday or Sunday evening.

Buses

Run by local private companies but with a common ticketing system, **buses** cover the whole country, and are often quicker and more frequent than trains over the shorter east–west hops, and essential for getting around the remoter regions; they are not necessarily cheaper than trains, however. In the Arctic North there is a very limited railway network, so almost all public transport is by road; hence it's here that you'll find buses most useful. The main operators are Gold Line (☎016/334 5500, Ⓦwww.goldline.fi) and Eskelisen Lapin Linjat (☎016/342 2160, Ⓦwww.eskelisen-lapinlinjat.com). The free bus **timetable**, *Suomen Pikavuorot*, lists all the routes in the country and can be picked up at most long-distance bus stations but is not very user-friendly, especially if you're not fluent in Finnish. Schedules and detailed information in English on travel in Finland by coach and bus can also be found at Ⓦwww.matkahuolto.fi. South of the Arctic Circle, you're more likely to use the excellent network of rail services than hassle with buses.

All **fares** are calculated according to the distance travelled: Helsinki to Lahti (100km) costs around €21; Helsinki to Kuopio (400km) around €58. Express buses charge a supplement of approximately €3 per journey and are worth it for the correspondingly faster journey times. All types of ticket can be purchased at bus stations or at most travel agents; only ordinary one-way tickets can be bought on board the bus, though on journeys of 80km or less there's no saving in buying a return anyway. On return trips of over 80km, there is a reduction of ten percent.

Ferries

As **lake travel** is aimed more at holidaying families than the budget-conscious traveller, **prices** are high considering the distances, and progress is slow as the vessels chug along the great lake chains. If you have the time, money and inclination, though, it can be worth taking one of the shorter trips simply for the experience. There are numerous routings, and details can be checked at any tourist office in the country and at Finnish Tourist Offices abroad; we've detailed some of the more scenic routes in the Guide.

Planes

With their range of discounts, domestic **flights** can be comparatively cheap as well as time-saving if you want to cover long distances, such as from Helsinki to the Arctic North. That said, travelling by air means you'll miss many interesting parts of the country. Finnair (Ⓦwww.finnair.com) and Blue1 (Ⓦwww.blue1.com) offer a variety of off-peak summer reductions which can be checked online or at travel agents and airline or tourist offices in Finland. Youth **fares** are available for 17 to 24-year-olds and offer a fifty percent discount on the normal fare, though it's usually cheaper to look for special offers or to buy a weekend ticket which is always cheaper than the standard fare. Flights operate daily between most large cities, and one-way fares start at €39, though to ensure seats this cheap you must book several weeks in advance.

Driving and hitching

Renting a car is extremely expensive in Finland (as is petrol), and with such a good public-transport network, it's only worth considering if you're travelling in a group. The big international companies (detailed in Basics, p.35) have offices in most Finnish towns and at international arrival points. If you're in Helsinki it's also worth checking the local company Transvell (☎08000/7000, Ⓦwww.transvell.fi), a subsidiary of SIXT. They all accept major credit cards; if paying by cash, you'll need to leave a substantial deposit. You'll also need a valid driving licence, at least a year's driving experience and to be a minimum of 19 to 24 years old, depending on the company you rent from.

Rates for a medium-sized car start at around €50 per day, with reductions for longer periods – you'll pay upwards of €220 for a fortnight's use. On top of this, there can be a surcharge of up to 75 cents per kilometre (which may be waived on long-term rentals) and a drop-off fee of €80–180 if you leave the car somewhere other than the place from which it was rented. For more details on car rental before arriving in Finland, visit the website of one of the international companies mentioned above, or ask at a Finnish Tourist Board office.

If you **bring your own car** to Finland, it's advisable (though not compulsory) to have a Green Card as proof that you are comprehensively insured in the event of an accident. Some insurers in EU countries will offer you a Green Card for free as part of your insurance package, while others will charge a premium. Further **information** about driving in Finland can be obtained from Autoliitto, the Automobile and Touring Club of Finland, Hämeentie 105A, 00550 Helsinki (℡09/7258 4400, ℡www.autoliitto.fi).

Once underway, you'll find the next financial drain is **fuel**, which costs around €1.50 a litre (unleaded), though bear in mind that in rural areas, especially in Lapland, fuel is considerably more expensive than in Helsinki. Except in the far north, **service stations** are plentiful and usually open from 7am to 9pm between Monday and Saturday, and are often closed on Sunday – although in busy holiday areas many stay open round the clock during the summer. Larger towns will also have automatic pumps which function round the clock and accept cash and credit cards, though many of these machines do not recognize foreign cards. Though fuel prices may well impoverish you, take some consolation in the fact that you can drive on all Finnish motorways for free, as there are no tolls. Though **roads** are generally in good condition there can be problems with melting snow, usually during April and May in the south and occasionally early June in the far north. Finnish **road signs** are similar to those throughout Europe, but be aware of bilingual place names; one useful sign to watch for is *Keskusta*, which means "town centre". **Speed limits** vary, though generally the legal limit is between 30kph and 40kph in towns, and from 80kph to 100kph on major roads – if it's not signposted, the basic limit is always 80kph. On motorways the maximum speed is 120kph in summer, 100kph in winter.

Other **rules of the road** include using headlights all the time when driving outside built-up areas, as well as in fog and in poor light, and the compulsory wearing of seatbelts by drivers and all passengers. As elsewhere in Scandinavia, penalties for drink-driving are severe – the police may stop and breathalyse you if they think you've been driving erratically. In some areas in the north of the country, reindeer and elk are liable to take a stroll across a road, especially around dusk. These are sizeable creatures and damage (to the car) is likely to be serious; all such collisions should be reported at the nearest police station and the Finnish Motor Insurers' Centre (*Liikennevakuutuskeskus*), Bulevardi 28, 00120 Helsinki (℡09/680 401, ℡www.vakes.fi/lvk), which can also help with local breakdown companies.

Hitching is generally easy, and sometimes the quickest means of transport between two spots. Finland's large student population has helped accustom drivers to the practice, and you shouldn't have to wait too long for a ride on the busy main roads between large towns. Make sure you have a decent road map and emergency provisions/shelter if you're passing through isolated regions. While many Finns speak English, it's still handy to memorize the Finnish equivalent of "let me out here" (*jään pois tässä*).

Cycling

Cycling can be an enjoyable way to see the country at close quarters, particularly because the only appreciable hills are in the far north and extreme east. Villages and towns may be separated by several hours' pedalling, however, and the scenery can get monotonous. You can take your bike along with you on an inter-city train for a €10 fee – as this isn't too common a practice you shouldn't need to reserve a spot ahead of time. Finnish **roads** are of high quality in the south and around the large towns, but are much rougher in the north and in isolated areas; beware the springtime thaw when the winter snows melt and sometimes cover roads with water and mud. All major towns have bike shops selling spares – Finland is one of the few places in the world where you can buy bicycle snow tyres with tungsten steel studs. Most youth hostels, campsites and some hotels and tourist offices offer **bike rental** from €10 per day,

€45 per week; there may also be a deposit of around €30.

Accommodation

Whether you're at the end of one of Finland's long-distance hiking trails or in the centre of a city, you'll find some kind of **accommodation** to suit your needs. You will, however, have to pay dearly for it: prices are high, and only by making use of special offers and travelling during low season will you be able to sleep well on a budget.

Hotels

Finnish **hotels** (*hotelli*) are rarely other than polished and pampering: TV, phone and private bathroom are standard fixtures; breakfast is invariably included in the price; and there's often free use of the sauna and swimming pool, too. Chain hotels dominate mid-to-upper-level accommodation in most cities, and many of the rooms follow a very strict, homogenous layout. Costs can be formidable – frequently in excess of €100 for a double – but planning ahead and taking advantage of various discount schemes and seasonal reductions can cut prices, often to as little as €50.

One trend that's catching on in Finland is that of the unmanned **concept hotel**, in which guests book over the internet or by toll phone call, receive a password to enter their room and carry out their entire stay with zero interaction with on-site hotel staff – who, incidentally – don't exist. Rooms are sleekly designed with many environmentally aware considerations, and while they might feel very Ikea furnished, they are nevertheless a welcome change from the predictable furnishings of so many large Finnish hotels. The best aspect is the price: as low as €36 per night in some cases, though to get these rates you need to book several weeks in advance. Omena Hotel was the pioneer of this idea; they have six such hotels in southern Finland (and have over a dozen more planned for the rest of the country). Other companies such as GreenStar have since added their own hotels to the mix. Note that booking a room in these hotels via the internet is free, while phone bookings incur a hefty surcharge – often as much as €9 – which explains why we only print the website for such hotels.

Room rates commonly move up and down depending on the season and whether there is a town festival being staged; on the whole, though, accommodation is much more expensive on weekdays and in winter. This is especially the case at the larger, business-oriented hotel chains (Cumulus, Scandic, Sokos and Best Western) in major cities, when winter weekday prices can frequently be double that of a weekend in the summer; there are frequent bargains at such hotels during July and August, and on Fridays, Saturdays and Sundays throughout the year. Exact details of these change frequently, but it's worth checking the current situation at a local tourist office. Reductions are also available to holders of Helsinki Cards and the similar cards issued for Tampere. Otherwise, between July and August you're unlikely to find anything under €50 by turning up on spec, except of course in a youth hostel.

Hotels in country areas are no less comfortable than those in cities, and often a touch less costly, typically €40–50. However, space is again limited during summer. Expense can be trimmed a little by using the **Finncheque** (@www.finncheque.fi) system: you buy an unlimited number of €39 or €48 vouchers, each valid for a night's accommodation for one person (double occupancy), plus breakfast, in any of the 130 participating hotels from June to September (weekends only the rest of the year). The two price categories correspond to the quality of room. You can only buy Finncheques outside Finland at a Finnish Tourist Board office (see p.43) or a specialist travel agent, who will also supply addresses of the hotels involved. Don't worry about buying more vouchers than you might need – they are refundable at the place of purchase. Another discount is offered by the Scanhotel chain's Scandic Holiday Cheque vouchers. They're valid at all Scandic hotels (@www.scandichotels.com) in Finland (as well as the group's hotels in other European countries) throughout the summer and on weekends during the rest of the year, and cost from €75 per double room including breakfast, though beware that some hotels add on a "quality surcharge". The cheques are widely available from travel agents outside Finland.

Accommodation price codes

The hotels and guesthouses listed in the Finland chapters of this Guide have been graded according to the following price bands, based on the cost of the **least expensive double room in summer**, usually mid-June to mid-August. However, winter is considered peak season in most places so many hotels offer summer and/or weekend discounts, and in these instances we've given two grades, covering both the discounted and the regular rate (eie ❸/❺).

❶ €25 and under		❹ €76–100	
❷ €26–50		❺ €101–125	
❸ €51–75		❻ €126 and over	

In many towns you'll also find **tourist hotels** (*matkustajakotit*) or **guesthouses** (*majatalot*), more basic types of family-run hotels, though the qualitative difference between these and standard hotels may only be that they're not owned by a chain. They charge €30–45 per double room and sometimes have cheaper wood cabins out back, but may well be full throughout the summer. The facilities of **summer hotels** (*kesähotelli*), too, are more basic than regular hotels, since the accommodation is in student blocks which are vacated from June to the end of August: there are universities in all the major cities and in an impressive number of the larger towns. Reservable with any Finnish travel agent, summer-hotel prices are around €35 per person. Bear in mind that identical accommodation – minus the bed linen and breakfast – comes a lot cheaper in the guise of a youth hostel.

Youth hostels

The easiest and cheapest place to rest your head is often a **youth hostel** (*retkeilymaja*). There are 88 such hostels throughout the country, in major cities (which will have at least one) and isolated country areas, and are run by the Finnish Youth Hotel Association, *Suomen Retkeilymajajärjestö* (SRM). It's always a good idea to phone ahead and reserve a place, which many hostel wardens will do for you, or book online at the address below. If you're arriving on a late bus or train, say so when booking and your bed will be kept for you; otherwise bookings are only held until 6pm and reception often closes around 8pm and you can usually make arrangements to check in later, provided you let staff know in advance. Hostels are busiest during the peak Finnish holiday period, roughly mid-June to mid-August. Things are quieter after mid-August, although a large number of hostels close soon after this date – check that the one you're aiming for doesn't. Similarly, many hostels don't open until June.

Overnight **charges** are generally around €20 per person (though can be as little as €10 and as much as €50), depending on the type of accommodation, with hostels ranging from the basic dormitory type to those with two- and four-bed rooms and at least one bathroom for every three rooms. Bed linen, if not already included, can be rented for an extra €3–7. With a Hostelling International Card (see p.36; not obligatory) you can get a €2.50 reduction per person per night. The SRM publishes a useful free guide, *Hostels in Finland*, available directly from them at Suomen Retkeilymajajärjestö, Yrjönkatu 38B, 00100 Helsinki (☎09/565 7150, ⊛www .srmnet.org), listing all Finnish hostels, and the very helpful staff there can also provide a free map showing locations.

All youth hostels have wardens to provide general assistance and arrange **meals**: most hostels offer breakfast, usually for €4–6, and some serve dinner as well (around €7.50). Hostel breakfasts, especially those in busy city hostels, can be rationed affairs and – hunger permitting – you'll generally be better off waiting until you can find a cheapish lunch somewhere else (see "Food and drink", p.516). The only hostel breakfasts really worth taking advantage of are those offered at summer hotels, where hostellers can mingle with the hotel guests and, for €5–7, partake of the help-yourself spread.

Campsites and holiday villages

There are some two hundred official **campsites** (*leirintäalue*) in Finland, and several hundred more operating on a less formal basis. Most open from May to September, although around seventy stay open all year. The approved sites, marked with a blue and white tent sign in a letter C, are classified by a star system: one-star sites are in rural areas and usually pretty basic, while on a five-star site you can expect excellent cooking and laundry facilities and sometimes a well-stocked shop. The cost for two people sharing is €10–12 per pitch, depending on the site's star rating. Campsites outside major towns are frequently very big (a two thousand-tent capacity isn't uncommon), and they're very busy at weekends during July and August. Smaller and more remote sites (except those serving popular hiking routes) are, as you'd imagine, much less crowded.

Holiday villages have been sprouting up throughout Finland in the last few years and there are now over two hundred of them. Standards vary considerably, with accommodation ranging from basic cabins to luxurious bungalows. All provide fuel, cooking facilities, bed linen and often a sauna – but you'll need to bring your own towels. Costs range from €115 to €510 per week for a cabin sleeping up to four people, though for a luxury bungalow you might well pay upwards of €1100.

To camp in Finland, you'll need a Scandinavian Camping Card, available at every site for €7 and valid for a year. The card is valid in all four Nordic countries and offers discounts on many campsites all over Finland. If you're considering **camping rough**, remember it's illegal without the landowner's permission – though in practice, provided you're out of sight of local communities, there shouldn't be any problems.

Hiking accommodation

Hiking routes invariably start and finish close to a campsite or a youth hostel, and along the way there will usually be several types of basic accommodation. Of these, a *päivätupa* is a cabin with cooking facilities which is opened during the day for free use; an *autiotupa* is an unlocked hut which can be used by hikers to sleep in for one night only – there's no fee but often no space either during the busiest months. A *varaustupa* is a locked hut for which you can obtain a key at the tourist centre at the start of the hike – there's a smallish fee and you'll almost certainly be sharing. Some routes have a few *kämppä* – cabins originally erected for forest workers but now used mainly by hikers; check their exact location with the nearest tourist centre. On most hikes there are also marked spots for pitching your own tent and building fires.

Food and drink

Finnish **food** is full of surprises and demands investigation, especially now that Nordic cuisine is in the middle of a Renaissance. Food is pricey, but you can keep a grip on the expenses by using markets and Finland's many down-to-earth dining places, saving restaurant blowouts for special occasions. Though tempered by many regulations, alcohol is more widely available here than in much of Scandinavia: there are many places to **drink** but also many people drinking, most of them indulging moderately but quite a number doing it to excess on a regular basis.

Food

Though it may at first seem a stodgy, rather unsophisticated cuisine, **Finnish food** is an interesting mix of Western and Eastern influences. Many dishes resemble those you might find elsewhere in Scandinavia – an enticing array of delicately prepared fish (herring, whitefish, salmon and crayfish), together with some unusual meats like reindeer, elk and bear – while others bear the stamp of Russian cooking: solid pastries and casseroles, strong on cabbage, pork and mutton.

All Finnish and Scando-European fusion restaurants will leave a severe dent in your budget, as will the foreign places, although the country's innumerable pizzerias are relatively cheap by comparison. The golden money-saving rule is to treat **lunch** (*lounas*, usually served 11am–2pm, sometimes until 3pm) rather than the much dearer **dinner** (*päivällinen* or *illallinen*, usually from 6pm) as your main meal. Also, eke out your funds with stand-up snacks and by selective buying in supermarkets. If you're staying in a hotel, don't forget to load up on the inclusive **breakfast** (*aamiainen*) – often an open table laden with herring, eggs, cereals, porridge, cheese, salami and bread. See our Menu reader on p.716.

Snacks, fast food and self-catering

Economical **snacks** are best found in market halls (*kauppahalli*), where you can get basic foodstuffs along with local and national specialities. Adjoining these halls are cafeterias, where you're charged by the weight of food on your plate. Look out for *karjalan piirakka* – oval-shaped Karelian pastries containing rice and mashed potato, served hot with a mixture of finely chopped hard-boiled egg and butter for around €2. Also worth trying is *kalakukko*, a chunk of bread with pork and whitefish baked inside it – legendary around Kuopio but available almost everywhere. Expect to spend around €4 for a chunk big enough for two. Slightly cheaper but just as filling, *lihapiirakka* are envelopes of pastry filled with rice and meat – ask for them with mustard (*sinappi*) and/or ketchup (*ketsuppi*). Most train stations and the larger bus stations and supermarkets also have cafeterias proffering a selection of the above and other greasier nibbles.

Less exotically, the big **burger** franchises are widely found, as are the Grilli and Nakkikioski roadside fast-food stands turning out burgers, frankfurters and hot dogs for around €3; they're always busiest when the pubs shut.

Finnish **supermarkets** – Sokos, K-Kaupat, Pukeva and Centrum are widespread names – are fairly standard affairs. In general, a substantial oval loaf of dark rye bread (*ruisleipä*) costs €2, eight *karjalan piirakkas* €2.50, a litre of milk €1 and a packet of biscuits around €2. A usually flavoursome option containing hunks of meat and vegetables, Finnish tinned **soup** (*keitto*) can be an excellent investment if you're self-catering.

Coffee (*kahvi*) is widely drunk – per capita, more than anywhere else in the world, in fact – and costs €1–1.50 per cup; in a *baari* or *kahvila* (bar or coffee shop) it's sometimes consumed with a *pulla* – a kind of doughy bun. It's normally drunk black, although milk is always available if you want it; you'll also commonly find espresso and cappuccino, although these are more expensive. **Tea** (*tee*) costs around €1, depending on where you are and whether you want to indulge in some exotic brew. In rural areas, though, drinking it is considered a bit effete. When ordering tea, it's a good idea to insist that the water is boiling before the teabag is added – and that the bag is left in for more than two seconds.

Lunch and dinner

If you're in a university town, the campus cafeteria or **student mensa** is the cheapest place to get a hot dish. Theoretically you have to be a student, but outside Helsinki you are unlikely to be asked for ID. There's a choice of three meals: *Kevytlounas* (KL), the "light menu", which usually comprises soup and bread; *lounas* (L), the "ordinary menu", which consists of a smallish fish or meat dish with dessert; and *Herkkulounas* (HL), the "delicious menu" – a substantial and usually meat-based plateful. All three come with bread and coffee, and each costs €5–6. Prices can be cut by half if you borrow a Finnish student ID card from a friendly diner. The busiest period is lunchtime (11.30am–12.30pm); later in the day (usually 4–6pm) many *mensas* offer price reductions. Most universities also have cafeterias where a small cup of coffee can cost as little as 60 cents.

If funds stretch to it, you should sample at least once a **ravintola**, or restaurant, offering a lunchtime buffet table (*voileipäpöytä* or *seisova pöytä*), which will be stacked with tasty traditional goodies that you can feast on to your heart's content for a set price of around €10. Less costly Finnish food can be found in a **baari**. These are designed for working people; they generally close at 5pm or 6pm and serve a range of Finnish dishes and snacks (and often the weaker beers; see "Drink", p.518). A good day for traditional Finnish food is Thursday, when every *baari* in the country dishes up *hernekeitto ja pannukakut*, thick pea soup with black rye bread, followed by oven-baked pancakes with strawberry jam, and buttermilk to wash it down – all for around €6. You'll get much the same fare from a *kahvila*, though a few of these, especially in the big cities, fancy themselves as being fashionable and may charge a few euro extra.

Although *ravintola* and *baaris* are plentiful, they are often outnumbered by **pizzerias**. They're as varied in quality here as they are in any other country, but especially worthwhile for their lunch specials, when a set price of around €9 buys a pizza, coffee and everything you can carry from the bread and salad bar. Many of the bigger pizza chains offer discounts for super-indulgence – such as a second pizza for half-price and a third for free if you can polish off the first two. **Vegetarians** are likely to become well acquainted with pizzerias – specific vegetarian restaurants are thin on the ground, even in major cities. Now that Finland has opened its doors to immigration, kebab restaurants are found in a number of cities. This isn't necessarily a cheap option though: most kebab plates or sandwiches will cost upwards of €8.

Drink

Finland's **alcohol** laws are as bizarre and almost as repressive as those of Norway and Sweden, although unlike those countries, boozing is tackled enthusiastically, and is even regarded by some as an integral part of the national character. Some Finns, men in particular, often drink with the sole intention of getting paralytic; younger people these days are on the whole more inclined to regard the practice simply as an enjoyable social activity, though spend a few nights in any town and you're sure to witness your share of plastered, stumbling Finnish youth – boys and girls alike.

What to drink

Finnish spirits are much the same as you'd find in any country. **Beer** (*olut*), on the other hand, falls into three categories: "light beer" (*I-Olut*) – more like a soft drink; "medium-strength beer" (*Keskiolut*, *III-Olut*) – more perceptibly alcoholic and sold in many food shops and cafés; and "strong beer" (*A-Olut* or *IV-Olut*), which, at 5.2 percent, is well on a par with the stronger international beers and can only be bought at the ALKO shops and fully licensed (Grade A) restaurants and nightclubs.

The main – and cheapest – outlet for alcohol of any kind are the state-run **ALKO**

shops (Mon–Fri 9am–8pm, Sat 9am–6pm). Even the smallest town will have one of these, and prices don't vary. In 2004, in an effort to ensure that Finns would buy their alcohol at home instead of cheaper places like Estonia, the government slashed the excise tax on hard liquor, resulting in a price decrease of up to thirty percent in ALKO shops. In these shops, strong beers like Lapin Kulta Export – an Arctic-originated mind-blower – and the equally potent Karjala, Lahden A, Olvi Export and Koff porter cost around €1.30 for a 300ml bottle. Imported beers such as Heineken, Carlsberg and Becks go for €2.20 a bottle. As for **spirits**, Finlandia vodka and Jameson's Irish Whiskey are €19 and €26.50 respectively per 75cl bottle. There's also a very popular rough vodka called Koskenkorva, ideal for assessing the strength of your stomach lining, which costs €14.70 for 75cl. The best **wine** bargains are usually Hungarian or Bulgarian, and cost around €15 per bottle in a restaurant, though you can buy bottles in ALKO for under €7. ALKO's French wines range from €6 to €60 a bottle.

Where to drink

Continental-style **brasseries** or British-influenced **pubs** are the most pleasant places to have a drink. Frequented by both men and women of all ages, you're most likely to feel more at home in these familiar environments than in the smoky, generally all-male bars which proliferate in many of the small towns away from Helsinki, especially in the north; these charmless drinking dens are nothing more than places to get seriously hammered.

Most **restaurants** have a full licence, and some are actually frequented more for drinking than eating; it's these that we've listed under "Drinking" throughout the text. They're often also called bars or pubs by Finns simply for convenience. Just to add to the confusion, some so-called "pubs" are not licensed; neither are *baari*.

Along with ordinary restaurants, there are also **dance restaurants** (*tanssiravintola*). As the name suggests, these are places to dance rather than dine, although most do serve food as well as drink. They're popular with the over-40s, and before the advent of discos were the main places for people of opposite sex to meet. Even if you're under 40, dropping into one during the (usually early) evening sessions can be quite an eye-opener. Expect to pay an €3–5 admission charge.

Once you've found somewhere to drink, there's a fairly rigid set of **customs** to contend with. Sometimes you have to queue outside the most popular bars, since entry is permitted only if a seat is free – there's no standing. Only one drink per person is allowed on the table at any one time except in the case of porter (a stout which many Finns mix with regular beer). There's always either a doorman (*portsari* or *järjestuksenvalvoja*) or a cloakroom into which you must check your coat (and bag, if you have one) upon arrival (again around €2). Bars are usually open until midnight or 1am, though a handful may stay open till 2am or, in the case of discos and clubs, 4am. Last call is announced half an hour before the place shuts by a winking of the lights – the *valomerkki*.

Some bars and clubs have **waitress/ waiter service**, whereby you order, and pay when your drinks are brought to you. A common order is *iso tuoppi* – a half-litre glass of draught beer, which costs €3–4 (up to €6 in some nightclubs). This might come slightly cheaper in **self-service** bars, where you select your tipple and queue up to pay at the till. Though saying "beer" and pointing to the tap will generally work, you might get a more friendly response by offering up *Yks pist olut, kiitos* Finnish, for "A pint, please".

Wherever you buy alcohol, you'll have to be of **legal age**: at least 18 to buy beer and wine, and 20 or over to have a go at the spirits. ID will be checked if you look too young – or if the doorman's in a bad mood.

The media

The biggest-selling **Finnish newspaper**, and the only one to be distributed all over the country, is the daily *Helsingin Sanomat* (€2), whose online edition (❷ www.helsingin sanomat.fi) also includes a small section in English. Most other papers are locally based and sponsored by a political party; however, all carry entertainment listings – only the

cinema listings (where the film titles are translated into Finnish) present problems for non-Finnish speakers. A better bet may be the Swedish-language tongue-twister, *Hufvudstadsbladet*, a quality daily that can be found in Helsinki. The best information about **what's on**, if you're in Helsinki, Tampere or Turku, is the free *City* (appearing fortnightly in Helsinki, monthly in Turku and Tampere), which carries regional news, features and entertainment details in Finnish and English; it's available at tourist offices.

Overseas newspapers, including most British and some US titles, can be found, often on the day of issue, at the Academic Bookstore, Pohjoisesplanadi 39, Helsinki. Elsewhere, foreign papers are harder to find and less up-to-date, though they often turn up at the bigger newsagents and train stations in Helsinki, Turku, Tampere and, to a lesser extent, Oulu.

Finnish **television**, despite its four channels (one of which is called MTV, but is unrelated to the music station), isn't exactly inspiring and, as it usually goes off the air at midnight, shouldn't keep you off the streets for long. Moderately more interesting is the fact that, depending on where you are, you might be able to watch Swedish, Norwegian, Estonian and Russian programmes. A few youth hostels have TV rooms, and most hotel-room TVs have the regular channels plus a feast of cable and satellite alternatives. As with films shown in the cinema, all TV programmes are broadcast in their original language with Finnish subtitles.

The only **radio station** that non-Finnish speakers are likely to find interesting and useful is YLE Mondo (❷ www.yle .fi/ylemondo), a multi-language channel which relays programmes from foreign broadcasters including the BBC, NPR and Deutsche Welle; a large part of the day's programming is given over to English material, and generally between 4pm and 8pm, and 10.30pm to 7.30am, there'll be a series of news programmes in English. Broadcast on 97.5FM in Helsinki, the channel also transmits a short English-language news summary (Mon–Fri 7.30am & 8.55am) put together by the Finnish national broadcaster YLE. This bulletin can also be heard at the same time in Lahti on 90.3FM, Jyväskylä

Sports and outdoor activities

Canoeing

With many lakes and rivers, Finland offers challenges to every type of canoe enthusiast, expert or beginner. There's plenty of easygoing paddling on the long lake systems, innumerable thrashing rapids to be shot€ and abundant sea canoeing around the archipelagos of the south and southwest coast. Canoe rental (available wherever there are suitable waters) costs around €3 per hour, €8–20 per day or €60 per week, with prices dependent on the type of canoe. Many tourist offices have plans of local canoeing routes, and you can get general information from the Finnish Canoe Federation, Olympiastadion, Eteläkaarre, 00250 Helsinki (℡09/494 965, ⊕www.kanoottiliitto.fi).

Fishing

Although angling and ice-fishing are considered public rights in Finland and require no permit, non-Scandinavians do need a General Fishing Licence if they intend to fish with a lure in Finland's waterways; this costs €6 for a seven-day period from post offices. In certain parts of the Arctic North and the Åland Archipelago you'll need an additional licence costing between €5–10 per day and obtainable locally. Throughout the country you'll also need the permission of the owner of the particular stretch of water, usually obtained by buying a permit on the spot. The nearest campsite or tourist office will have details of this, and advise on the regional variations on national fishing laws.

Nude bathing

Finns are uptight and very un-Scandinavian in their attitude to public nudity. Hence, sections of some Finnish beaches are designated nude bathing areas, more often than not sex-segregated and occasionally with an admission charge of around €1.50. The local tourist office or campsite will part with the facts – albeit rather reluctantly. However, you should encounter no problem sunbathing naked by a secluded lake or in the forest.

Saunas

These are cheapest at a public swimming pool, where you'll pay €2–3 for a session. Hotel saunas, which are sometimes better equipped than public ones, are more expensive (€5–7) but free to guests. Many Finnish people have saunas built into their homes and it's common for visitors to be invited to share one. Note that the sauna – and subsequent bathing in the nearest lake – is the one locale where nudity is commonly and publicly practised; it's fine to take along a towel or bathing suit, but bear in mind that your Finnish host will probably remain *au natural*.

Travel essentials

Costs

Though the cost of a meal or the bill for an evening's drinks can occasionally come as a shock, prices in Finland are generally comparable with those in most European capitals, and there is no shortage of places catering for those on tighter budgets, even in the more far-flung locales. Bargain lunchtime "specials" are common, and travelling costs, in particular, can come as a pleasant surprise – travel by train, for example, is cheaper (though less efficient) in Finland than in the other Scandinavian countries.

There are ways to cut **costs**, which we've detailed where relevant, but as a general rule you'll need £25–35/US$35–50 a day even to live fairly modestly – staying mostly at youth hostels or campsites, eating out every other day and supplementing your diet with food from supermarkets, visiting only a few selected museums and socializing fairly rarely. To live well and see more, you'll be spending closer to £50/US$70.

Customs

There are few, if any, border formalities when entering Finland from another Scandinavian country by land; many of the old customs booths and checkpoints are these days largely abandoned, ramshackle edifices. The same applies when crossing by sea; only by air do you usually need to show your passport. Much more a headache are crossings into Russia, still full-on bureaucratic nightmares with rubber stamps, scrupulous passport checks and askance eyes cast towards your baggage. In any event you'll need to plan well ahead to obtain the visa paperwork for a visit – the one exception being the cruises along the Saimaa canal into Karelian Russia (see box, p.557 for details).

Internet

Finland comes second only to the US in terms of per-person home **internet** use, a fact made clear by the near absence of public internet points in many towns. For web and email access, the most reliable option should be your hotel. Free wi-fi connections are offered (having to pay for an Internet connection in a Finnish hotel is very rare) which should suit if you have a laptop. Otherwise, many hotels (and even some bars) have a computer terminal or two available for guest use; these are also often free. Apart from your hotel, another source of internet access is tourist offices, where terminals are always free. Larger towns will have cafés with free wi-fi access for customers, and finally there are public-library terminals, which are always free. Most have short-use terminals, but for anything longer than ten minutes or so you will probably have to book a spot (possibly the day before). As a last resort, you could try to find an internet café, where you'll usually pay €3–5 per hour.

Mail

In general, **communications** in Finland are dependable and quick, although in the far north, and in some sections of the east, minor delays arise due simply to geographical remoteness.

Unless you're on a hiking trek through the back of beyond, you can rest assured your letter or postcard will arrive at its destination fairly speedily. The cost of mailing anything weighing under 20g internationally is 60 cents, or 70 cents with priority handling. You can buy **stamps** from **post offices** (Mon–Fri 9am–5pm; longer hours at the main post office in Helsinki), street stands or R-Kiosks, and at some hotels. **Poste restante** is available at the main post office in every large town.

Money

The Finnish **currency** is the euro (€), which comes in coins of 5 to 50 cents, €1 and €2, and notes of €5 to €500. Note that Finland no longer circulates 1- and 2-cent coins as the government considered them too low a value; as a result any such coins are now collector's items and examples in good condition can fetch well over a thousand times the face value. The **exchange rate** at the time of writing was €1.12 to £1, €0.79 to US$1, €0.61 to CA$1, €0.50 to AUS$1 and €0.40 to NZ$1. For up-to-date rates, visit the web site ⓦwww.oanda.com.

Credit cards are one of the best ways to pay for goods – in addition to being easy to carry around securely, they offer the most competitive exchange rates and few Finnish establishments will charge any over-and-above commission for you to use one. Major credit and charge cards – Amex, MasterCard, Visa, Diner's Club – are usually accepted by hotels, car rental offices, department stores, restaurants and sometimes even by taxis. However, it's still advisable to check beforehand.

For **cash**, your best bet is withdrawing money from ATMs using your home bank **debit card**. Nearly all foreign bank cards will work in a Finnish ATM/cash machine (known as a *pankkiautomaatti*), and banks usually give good exchange rates and charge 1–3 percent commission for foreign cash withdrawals. Note that there may be a minimum charge, so it could be worth taking out a larger amount when you use the machine; check with your bank for the charges they apply. Though they are much less convenient, **traveller's cheques** still remain a popular way to access cash; they also make a good backup in the event that you lose or damage your card. These can be changed at most **banks**, which open Monday to Friday from 9.15am to 4.15pm; the charge is usually €2 (though several people changing money together need only pay the commission once). You can also change money at hotels, though normally at a much worse rate than at the banks. In a country where every cent counts, it's worth looking around for a better deal: in rural areas some banks and hotels are known not to charge any commission at all. Outside normal banking hours, the best bet for changing money is the **currency-exchange desks** at transport terminals which open to meet international arrivals, where commission is likely to be €3–5, roughly the same as at banks, though airport exchange rates are often a little more generous.

There are no restrictions on the amount of money you can take into or out of Finland.

Opening hours and public holidays

On the following days, shops and banks close and most public transport operates a Sunday schedule; museum opening hours may also be affected. Holidays are: January 1, May 1, December 6, December 24, 25 and 26; variable dates are Epiphany (between Jan 6 and 12), Good Friday and Easter weekend, the Saturday before Whit Sunday, Midsummer's Eve and All Saint's Day (the Sat between Oct 31 and Nov 6).

Phones

Due to Finland's ridiculously quick adoption of mobile-phone technology, all Finnish **public telephones** are scheduled to be decommissioned by 2010. This stems from a deal between Nokia and the Finnish government – one which will install Finns as the world's foremost users of mobile technology.

Emergencies

For police, ambulance and fire service, dial ☎112.

As the bill for using a hotel phone is often unfathomably expensive, the best bet for making calls is to use your **mobile phone** (for general advice on which, see Basics, p.42). If you plan to make a lot of calls while in Finland, you'd be wise to invest in a Finnish SIM card for use in your phone. For around €20 you'll get a Finnish number plus about sixty minutes of domestic calling time or a few hundred domestic text messages.

International dialling codes for calling from and to Finland are given on p.43. Operator numbers are ☎118 for domestic calls and ☎92020 for reverse-charge international calls.

Shops and markets

Supermarkets are usually open Mon–Fri 9am–8pm, Sat 9am–6pm. Some in cities keep longer hours, for example 8am–10pm. In Helsinki the shops in Tunneli are open until 10pm. In the weeks leading up to Christmas some stores and markets are open on Sunday too.

Markets In larger towns usually take place every day except Sunday from 7am to 2pm. There'll also be a market hall (*kauppahalli*) open weekdays 8am–5pm. Smaller places have a market once or twice a week, usually including Saturday.

4.1

Helsinki and the south

The southern coast of Finland is the most populated, industrialized and richest part of the country, centred around the capital, **Helsinki**, a city of half a million people with the friendliness of a peasant village on market day. Helsinki's innovative architecture and batch of fine museums and galleries collectively expose the roots of the national character, while at night the pubs and clubs strip it bare. It may seem the perfect prelude to exploring the rest of Finland, and in the practical sense it is, being the hub of the country's road, rail and air traffic routes. However, if you can, try to arrive in Helsinki after seeing the rest of the country, as only with some prior knowledge of Finland does the significance of the city as a symbol of Finnish self-determination become clear.

A couple of towns **around Helsinki** further evince the change from ruralism to Modernism. **Porvoo** sits placidly locked in the nineteenth century, while the suburban area of **Espoo** forms a showpiece of twentieth-century design. Further away, in the country's southeastern extremity, the only community of significant size and importance between Helsinki and the Russian border is the shipping port of **Kotka** – not wildly appealing in itself, but at the heart of a historically intriguing coastal region.

Helsinki only became the capital in 1812, after Finland had been made a Russian Grand Duchy and Tsar Alexander I had deemed the previous capital, **Turku**, too close to Sweden for comfort. Today Turku, facing Stockholm across the Gulf of Bothnia, handles its demotion well. Both historically and visually it's one of Finland's most enticing cities; indeed, the snootier elements of its Swedish-speaking contingent still consider Åbo (its Swedish name) the real capital, and Helsinki just an uncouth upstart.

Between Helsinki and Turku, along the entire southern coast, only small villages and a few slightly larger towns break the continuity of the forests. Beyond Turku, though, things are more interesting, with the two most southerly of the Finland-Swedish

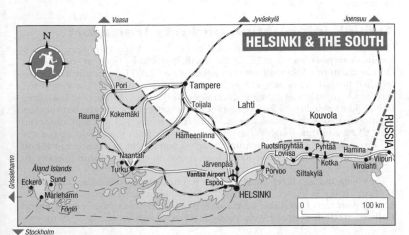

communities: **Rauma**, with its unique dialect and well-preserved town centre; and the likeably downbeat **Pori**, famous for its summer jazz festival.

Where this corner of Finland meets the sea it splinters into an enormous archipelago, which includes the curious **Åland Islands** – a grouping of thousands of fragments of land, only about half a dozen of which are inhabited, connected by small roadways skirting the sea. There's a tiny self-governing population here, Swedish-speaking but with a history that's distinct from both Sweden and Finland.

Much of the region is most easily reached from Helsinki, from where there are frequent bus and rail services to Turku. Rauma and Pori are best reached by bus from Turku, and from Pori there are easy rail connections to Tampere and the Lake Region (covered in the following chapter). Daily ferries also connect Turku to the Åland Islands.

Helsinki and around

HELSINKI has a character quite different from the other Scandinavian capitals, and in many ways is closer in mood (and certainly in looks) to the major cities of eastern Europe. For years an outpost of the Russian empire, its very shape and style was originally modelled on its powerful neighbour's former capital, St Petersburg. Yet throughout the twentieth century the city was also a showcase for independent Finland, much of its impressive **architecture** drawing inspiration from the dawning of Finnish nationalism and the rise of the republic. Equally the **museums**, especially the National Museum and the Art Museum of the Atheneum, reveal the country's growing awareness of its own folklore and culture.

Much of central Helsinki is a succession of compact granite blocks, interspersed with more characterful buildings, alongside waterways, green spaces and the glass-fronted office blocks and shopping centres you'll find in any European capital. The city is hemmed in on three sides by water, and all the things you might want to see are within walking distance of one another – and certainly no more than a few minutes apart by tram or bus. The streets have a youthful buzz, and the short summer is acknowledged by crowds strolling the boulevards, cruising the shopping arcades and mingling in the outdoor cafés and restaurants; everywhere there's prolific **street entertainment**. At night the pace picks up, with a great selection of pubs and clubs, free rock concerts in the numerous parks and an impressive quota of fringe events. It's a pleasure just to be around, merging with the multitude and witnessing the activity.

Arrival, information and city transport

However you arrive you'll be deposited somewhere close to the heart of town. Helsinki's **airport**, Vantaa, 20km to the north, is served by frequent airport buses (35min; €5.90 or €3.80 with a tourist ticket, see p.525). These stop at the Finnair terminal behind the *Scandic Hotel Continental*, halfway between the city centre and the Olympic Stadium, before continuing to the train station; they leave from lane 30 just behind the *Vltava* restaurant at the east entrance to the train station. A cheaper, if slightly slower airport connection is city bus #615 (50min); this costs €3.80 and runs roughly every fifteen minutes from the airport to the city bus terminal beside the train station, though if you ask the driver you can get off beforehand at any number of fixed stops. A taxi to the city centre should cost about €35.

The Viking and Silja **ferry** lines have their terminals on opposite sides of the South Harbour (at docks known respectively as Katajanokka and Olympia), and disembarking passengers from either have a walk of less than 1km to the centre. **Central Railway station**, equipped with luggage lockers, is right in the heart of the city on Kaivokatu, next door to the **city bus terminal**. All trams stop immediately outside or around the corner along Mannerheimintie, across from which, between Simonkatu and Salomonkatu, is the modern Kamppi shopping centre, which houses the new **long-distance bus terminal**.

Information

The **City Tourist Office**, at Pohjoisesplanadi 19 (May–Sept Mon–Fri 9am–8pm, Sat & Sun 9am–6pm; Oct–April Mon–Fri 9am–6pm, Sat & Sun 10am–4pm; ☏09/3101 3300, ⓦwww.hel.fi/tourism), supplies free street and transport maps, along with the useful free tourist magazine *Helsinki This Week*, which contains masses of listings for forthcoming events in the capital as well as a couple of decent maps on the back pages; it also has the monthly *We Are Helsinki*, which lists hip shops, bars and restaurants. While here, try to get hold of another worthy brochure, *See Helsinki On Foot* (€2), which uses both Finnish and Swedish street names on its maps; since Finland is officially bilingual you will find this dual-naming practice in use throughout the city. If you're staying for a while and plan to see as much of the capital and its museums as possible, consider purchasing a **Helsinki Card** (available from the City Tourist Office), which gives unlimited travel on public transport, including the ferry to Suomenlinna, and entry to around fifty museums. The three-day card (€53) is the best value, although there are also two-day (€43) and one-day (€33) versions.

For information on the rest of the country, ask at the Helsinki Tourist Board, which hands out brochures and offers a wealth of information. The public office of the **Finland Tourist Board** has closed and it's uncertain whether it will reopen.

City transport

Much of Helsinki is quite easily covered on foot, though the central area and its immediate surrounding are covered by an integrated transport network of buses, trams and a small metro system. A **single journey ticket** costs €2.20, while a group ticket, valid for two adults and up to four children is €8; both are valid for unlimited transfers within one hour. A **tram** ticket entitling you to one single journey without changing costs €2 if bought from the driver, or €1.80 if bought in advance at the tram machines located at many stops. You can also buy a **tourist ticket** covering the city and surrounding areas such as Espoo and Vantaa for one (€12), three (€24) or five days (€36), which permits travel on buses and trams displaying double arrows (effectively all of them); obviously, this is only a cost-cutter if used frequently. If you don't intend to leave the city proper, you're better off with a **Helsinki-only tourist ticket**, again available in one- (€6), three- (€12) and five-day (€18) versions. All these tickets can be bought from drivers or conductors, R-kiosk stands, the long-distance bus station at Kamppi or the City Tourist Office.

On **buses** you enter at the front, where you must either buy or show your ticket. On **trams**, if you don't have a ticket enter at the front and purchase one from the driver; if you have a ticket you can enter any of the other doors by pressing the round button marked "Avaa". **Metro** tickets can be bought from the machines in the stations. If you're tempted to fare-dodge in Helsinki, note that there's an €80 on-the-spot fine plus the cost of a single ticket. **Taxis** can either be hailed in the street (a vehicle is free if the yellow "taxi" sign is illuminated) or pre-booked: call the Taxi Centre on ☏0100/0700 for immediate travel, or ☏0100/0600 for trips more than an hour or so away. There's a basic charge of €5, with a further €1.30 per kilometre, plus an €2.70 surcharge between 8pm and 6am weekdays and from 4pm Saturday to 6am Monday.

Tram **#3T** follows a figure-of-eight route around the city, and if you're pushed for time will take you past the most obvious attractions. For a more leisurely exploration, join one of the two-hour guided **bus tours** (€25) run by Helsinki Expert, Lönrotinkatu 7B (☏09/2288 1600, ⓦwww.helsinkiexpert.fi), which also offers

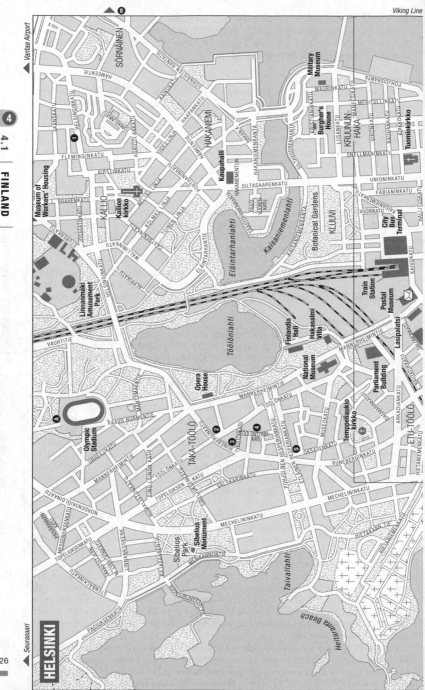

HELSINKI

Viking Line

◄ Vantaa Airport

◄ Seurasaari

B ▲▲

A

1
2
3
4
5

SÖRNÄINEN

HÄMEENTIE

HELSINGINKATU

VAASANKATU

FLEMINGINKATU

AGRICOLANKATU

KAARLENKATU

HAAPANIEMENKATU

SÖRNÄISTEN RANTATIE

HAKANIEMI

PORTHANINKATU

HÄMEENTIE

VIIDES LINJA

VIERES LINJA

Museum of
Workers' Housing

KALLIO

BRAHENKATU

KIRSTINKATU

Kallion
kirkko

KALLE RTIE

NELJÄS LINJA

KOLMAS LINJA

TOINEN LINJA

ENSI LINJA

SILTASAARENKATU

HAKANIEMENTORI

Kauppahalli

HAKANIEMENRANTA

HAKANIEM

Military
Museum

MAURINKATU

KRISTIANINKATU

Burgher's
House

LIISANKATU

MERITULLINKATU

POHJOISRANTA

MAAVESIKATU

VIRONKATU

KRUUNUN-
HAKA

SNELLMANINKATU

Tuomiokirkko

UNIONINKATU

FABIANINKATU

WALLININKATU

ALPPIKATU

HELSINGINKATU

ELÄINTARHANTIE

ELÄINTARHANTIE

Eläintarhanlahti

PÄIJÄNTEENTIE

KAISANIEMENKATU

Botanical Gardens

KAISANIEMENRANTA

Kaisaniemenlahti

KLUUVI

VUORIKATU

KAISANIEMENKATU

KAIVOKATU

City
Bus
Terminal

HALLITUSKATU

Linnanmäki
Amusement
Park

VAUHTITIE

Töölönlahti

Train
Station

Postal
Museum

Lasipalatsi

Finlandia
Hall

Hakasalmi
Villa

MANNERHEIMINTIE

Olympic
Stadium

PAAVO NURMEN TIE

Opera
House

MANNERHEIMINTIE

National
Museum

Parliament
Building

ARKADIANKATU

ETU-TÖÖLÖ

URHEILUKATU

TAKA-TÖÖLÖ

MANNERHEIMINTIE

TÖÖLÖNKATU

TÖÖLÖNTORIN-
KATU

MUSEOKATU

Temppeliaukio
kirkko

OKSASENKATU

RUNEBERGINKATU

HIETANIEMENKATU

MANNERHEIMINTIE

TOPELIUKSENTIE

EINO LEINON KATU

TÖÖLÖNKATU

HAKASALMENKATU

TÖÖLÖNKATU

POHJOINEN HESPERIANKATU

ETELÄINEN HESPERIANKATU

VÄLSKÄRINKATU

MECHELININKATU

NORDENSKIOLDINKATU

TOPELIUKSENKATU

MESSENIUKSENKATU

RUNEBERGINKATU

LINNANKOSKENK.

CYGNAEUKSENK.

Sibelius
Monument

Sibelius
Park

MERIKANNONTIE

STENBACKINKATU

PACIUKSENKATU

SAARENKATU

Taivallahti

Hietaranta Beach

HIETARANNAN

HIETARANTA TIE

526

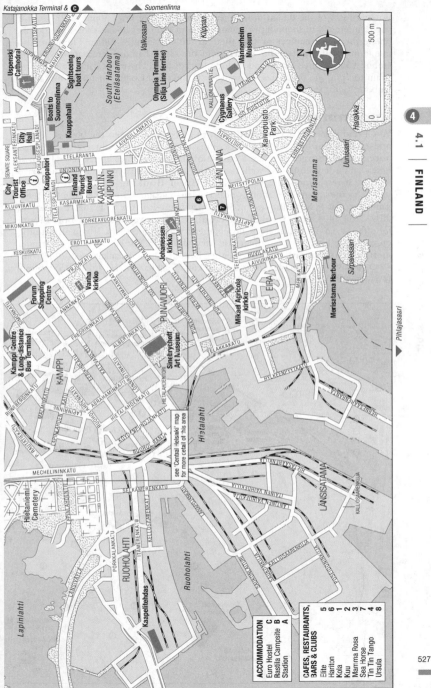

Uspenski Cathedral

Boats to Suomenlinna

Sightseeing boat tours

Kauppahalli

South Harbour (Eteläsatama)

Olympia Terminal (Silja Line ferries)

Valkosaari

Klippan

Mannerheim Museum

N

500 m

0

Cygnaeus Gallery

Kaivopuisto Park

Harakka

Merisatama

City Hall

SENATE SQUARE

City Tourist Office

i

Kauppatori

Finland Tourist Board

i

ETELÄRANTA

POHJOISESPLANADI

UNIONINKATU

KAARTIN-KAUPUNKI

ULLANLINNA

8

Uunisaari

Merisatama

6

7

Johanneksen kirkko

PUNAVUORI

Mikael Agricola kirkko

EIRA

Sirpalesaari

Merisatama Harbour

Forum Shopping Centre

Vanha kirkko

Kamppi Centre & Long-distance Bus Terminal

KAMPPI

Sinebrychoff Art Museum

Hietalahti

MECHELININKATU

see 'Central Helsinki' map for more detail of this area

Hietaniemi Cemetery

LÄNSISATAMA

RUOHOLAHTI

Ruoholahti

Lapinlahti

Kaapelitehdas

▲ *Pihlajasaari*

ACCOMMODATION
Euro Hostel   C
Rastila Campsite   B
Stadion   A

CAFES, RESTAURANTS, BARS & CLUBS
Elite   5
Hariton   6
Kola   1
Kuu   2
Mamma Rosa   3
Sea Horse   7
Tin Tin Tango   4
Ursula   8

walking tours of the design district (June–Aug Mon & Fri 1.30pm; €12), good if you're interested in shopping or seeing some of the city's design shops. For details, phone the above number or visit them at the City Tourist Office. There are also numerous **boat sightseeing tours** from the south harbour, Eteläsatama, costing around €35 for three hours, and including a bus tour. These run daily from around 11am to 7pm, and brochures are available at the tourist office, or from touts at the harbour itself.

Accommodation

You'll find plenty of **accommodation** in Helsinki, although the bulk of it is in mid-range chain hotels. Various discounts (see p.515) can reduce costs in these places, or alternatively there are a couple of cheaper summer hotels, several tourist hotels and a few hostels, as well as a string of new designer hotels. If you arrive without a reservation, the very helpful **Hotel Booking Centre** in the train station, to the left of the platforms near the left-luggage office (June–Aug Mon–Fri 9am–8pm, Sat & Sun 10am–6pm; Sept–May Mon–Fri 9am–6pm, Sat 10am–5pm; ☎09/2288 1400, ⓦwww.helsinkiexpert.fi), will book you a hotel or hostel room for a fee of €5, though there is no charge if you phone them. If you're planning on staying in town for more than just a few days, it might be worth considering a short-term **apartment rental**; try either Domin, Uudenmaankatu 4–6 (☎09/687 7940, ⓦwww.dominrental.com) or Citykoti, Telakkakatu 1C (☎050/555 0058, ⓦwww.citykoti.com).

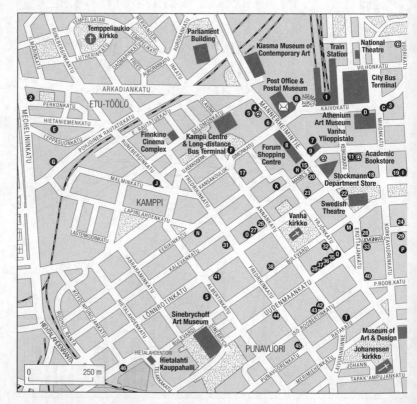

Hotels and tourist hotels

While Helsinki has long had its share of bland Scandinavian chain accommodation, there are now a cluster of boutique hotels in the capital, though staying in these comes at a cost. Less bling are the "Scandinavian modern" rooms in a number of chain hotels, most of which retain some degree of charm (in contrast to similar chain places in other Finnish cities). The city does have a small handful of moderately priced hotels, and while they lack some luxuries they can be a good-value alternative. Most have en-suite bathrooms and offer inexpensive meals.

Note that many places drop their rates dramatically in the summer tourist season, while nearly everywhere offers reductions at weekends. To take advantage of any bargains, it's essential to book as early as possible – either online, by phoning the hotel directly or by making a reservation through a travel agent or the Booking Centre (see opposite). However much you pay, it's unlikely that you'll leave any Helsinki hotel feeling ripped off: service and amenities – such as the inclusive help-yourself breakfast which is generally included in the price of the room – are usually excellent.

Of Helsinki's **campsites**, only one makes a reasonable base if you're planning to spend time in the city. This is *Rastila* (℡09/3107 8517, ℻3103 6659), 12km to the east, conveniently on the metro line (Rastila station; 18min ride) and also served by buses #90, #90A, #965 and #98 from Mannerheimintie. Open year-round with an array of cottages (❶ to ❺) as well as a beach, restaurant, saunas, internet access and bicycle and kayak rentals, it's one of the most popular camping spots in all of Finland.

CENTRAL HELSINKI

ACCOMMODATION	
Academica	E
Anna	T
Arthur	A
Carlton	C
Cumulus Seurahuone	D
Erottajanpuisto	Q
Finn	H
GLO	C
Helka	G
Hostel Suomenlinna	U
Kämp	I
Katajanokka	L
Klaus K	M
Omena Hotelli	N & O
Palace	R
Radisson SAS Royal	J
Rivoli Hotel Jardin	P
Scandic Simonkenttä	F
Sokos Hotel Aleksanteri	S
Sokos Torni	K
Sokos Vaakuna	B

BARS & CLUBS	
A21	26
Ateljeebaari	K
Baker's	20
Bar 9	36
Bar Tapasta	39
Erottaja Bar	28
Kaarle XII	34
Kosmos	15
Loose	31
Lost and Found	42
mbar	5
Meri Makasiini	46
Molly Malone's	3
Rafla	37
The Rock Bar	41
Rymy-Eetu	30
Teatteri	22
Vanha	9
We Got Beef	43
Zetor	7

CAFÉS & RESTAURANTS			
Aalto	11	Juuri	29
Bellevue	13	Kappeli	21
Chez Dominique	24	Kynsilaukka Ravintola Garlic	44
Demo	35	La Societé du Cochon	6
Ekberg	38	Lasipalatsi	4
Eliel	1	Loft	32
Engel	10	Mai Thai	17
Esplanad	18	Ravintola Perho	2
Farouge	40	Ravintola Suomi Lautasella	27
Fazer	8 & 12	Romanov	23
Golden Rax Pizzabuffet	8	Sipuli	14
Grotesk	33	Strindberg	19
Havis Amanda	16	Tori	45
		Zucchini	25

Note that unless otherwise stated, the places below are marked on the central Helsinki map (pp.528–529).

Moderate and inexpensive

Arthur Vuorikatu 19 ℡09/173 441, ⓦwww .hotelarthur.fi. You can cut the price of a room in half in this good-quality, basic hotel by taking a room with a shared bathroom – but book ahead as there are only five of them. ④/⑤

Cumulus Seurahuone Kaivokatu 12 ℡09/69 141, ⓦwww.cumulus.fi. A stylish, classic hotel opposite the train station, with the historic *Café Bellman* attached. Big, splendid rooms with original features, and it manages to feel like much less of a chain hotel than others. ④/⑥

Finn Kalevankatu 3B ℡09/684 4360, ⓦwww .hotellifinn.fi. Compact and rather down-at-heel hotel in an anonymous office building, though the slightly cramped rooms (the cheapest have shared bathrooms) are still good value considering the city-centre location. ④

Omena Hotelli Two locations: Eerikinkatu 24 and Lönnrotinkatu 13 ⓦwww.omena.com. Travellers watching their purse strings should book a room online at one of these two receptionless, postmodern concept spots, whose snazzy rooms sport fridge, microwave, coffee machine and flat-screen TV with internet. Booking far advance gets the best prices. ②

🏃 **Radisson SAS Royal** Runeberginkatu 2 ℡09/69 580, ⓦwww.radisson.com. White-tiled, glamorous hotel that calls to mind buildings like the Opera House and Finlandia Hall. Rooms are well kitted out with sleek Scandi designs and large, very comfy beds, and many on the higher floors have sprawling city views. Rates are cut by half in the summer. ④/⑥

Rivoli Hotel Jardin Kasarmikatu 40 ℡09/681 500, ⓦwww.rivoli.fi. Though mistakenly called a "boutique" hotel, this recently renovated place offers some style (as well as great showers) and is a breath of fresh air from the predictable chains. It's a 2min jaunt to the *Esplanad* (see pp.533–534), meaning you're never very far from a great shot of espresso. ④/⑥

🏃 **Sokos Hotel Aleksanteri** Albertinkatu 34 ℡020/1234 643, ⓦwww.sokoshotels.fi. This glamorous hotel features a maze of stairways and a sprawling lobby with bar and restaurant. Its location is refreshingly residential. ④/⑤

Boutique and expensive

Anna Annankatu 1 ℡09/616 621, ⓦwww .hotelanna.com. Small, central place set in a former Christian mission. Despite fairly run-of-the-mill plain rooms, the overall atmosphere is more cosy than a chain hotel. ⑤/⑥

Carlton Kaisaniemenkatu 3 ℡09/684 1320, ⓦwww.carlton.fi. Opened in 2007 in a lovely old 1930s building, this new boutique choice has rooms in shades of cream, beige and light browns that sport dim mood lighting and designer sheets. It's a minute's walk from the train station. ⑤

🏃 **GLO** Kluuvikatu 4 ℡09/675 111, ⓦwww .palacekamp.fi. This wonderful boutique hotel offers exposed pine, gorgeous black marble baths and huge plush beds. You can order anything you want to your room – gym equipment, bright-light lamps and even spa treatments – and there is a very good Basque-Catalonian restaurant. Surprisingly affordable too, with weekend rates that can rival those of the chains. The street can get noisy at weekends. ⑥

🏃 **Helka** Pohjoinen Rautatiekatu 23 ℡09/613 580, ⓦwww.helka.fi. Ignore the unassuming exterior and settle down in one of the city's newest boutique hotels, with super-comfortable beds, black-tiled bathrooms and quirky accoutrements such as life-size photographs of farming scenes on the ceiling. One of the cheaper design-minded places in the city, it's set a few paces north of the Kamppi centre. ⑤/⑥

Kämp Pohjoisesplanadi 29 ℡09/675 111, ⓦwww .hotelkamp.fi. Opened in 1887, this *belle époque* affair is one of Helsinki's most luxurious hotels – it played host to the secret meetings of the underground Kagel movement in the early 1900s, and Sibelius and Gallen-Kallela were regular guests. Today, marble bathrooms, polished stonework and lavish rooms make for decadent glamour. ⑥

🏃 **Katajanokka** Vyökatu 1 ℡09/686 450, ⓦwww.bwkatajanokka.fi. This nineteenth-century jail has been retrofitted as a sleek luxury hotel whose small-ish rooms feature comfy beds, silk cushions and striped brown and orange carpeting that make them feel less, well, imprisoning. Tram #6 lets you off right on the doorstep. ⑥

Klaus K Bulevardi 2 ℡020/770 4700, ⓦwww .klauskhotel.com. The capital's reigning house of style, with a 1970s-styled lobby, beautiful reception staff and velvet wallpapered rooms which serve as studies in ultra-modern interior design. It's pricey, but if there's a celebrity in town, they're almost guaranteed to be staying here. ⑥

Palace Eteläranta 10 ℡09/1345 6656, ⓦwww .palacehotel.fi. Sleek, luxurious property next to the *kauppahalli* overlooking the Olympic Harbour. Boxy rooms and baths are functional enough, but you're really paying for the spectacular sea views from the rooms and restaurant. A quiet day in summer

▲ Lobby, Klaus K hotel

can bring substantial reductions, although to land a discount on a panorama room you have to be pushy. ⑥

🏃 **Scandic Simonkenttä** Simonkatu 9 ☎09/68 380, ⓦwww.scandichotels.com. A steel and glass facade and efficiently designed standard rooms that are the greenest in the city: parquet floors are made from specially cultivated Nordic trees, trash bins are recycled rubber and 97 percent of the rest of the materials are recyclable. Some rooms have balconies, others a terrace and sauna. ④/⑥

Sokos Torni Yrjönkatu 26 ☎09/43 360, ⓦwww.sok.fi. Across from the classic sauna and pools on Yrjönkatu, this sophisticated hotel is a Jugend Art Nouveau-styled masterpiece. On a clear day, the thirteenth-floor bar with a patio gives views, so the locals claim, all the way to Estonia. The drinks are pricey, as are the rooms – though weekend rates can drop dramatically, especially last-minute. ⑤/⑥

Sokos Vaakuna Asema-Aukio 2 ☎09/43 370, ⓦwww.sokoshotels.fi. Flanking the train station, this smart hotel was built for the 1952 Olympic Games and retains many of its original, quintessentially Finnish architectural features. The lobby is a grand semicircular sitting room reminiscent of a Soviet legislative chamber, while the restaurant on the top floor – where breakfast is served – has grand views of city rooftops. ⑤/⑥

Hostels

There are a number of **hostels** about the city, all with excellent facilities and all but one with no evening curfew. All are open year-round unless otherwise stated.

Academica Hietaniemenkatu 14 ☎09/1311 4334, ⓦwww.hostelacademica.fi. The grim 1960s exterior gives way to a more cheery and sociable hostel scene inside. Open in the summer and offering a morning sauna and pool, this relatively central spot offers spotless doubles (②) and four-person dorms (€23) as well as wi-fi (€2 per hr) and very good cooking facilities. Open June–Aug.

Erottajanpuisto Uudenmaankatu 9 ☎09/642 169, ⓦwww.erottajanpuisto.com. Small and homely place on the second floor of a residential office building offering simply furnished dorms (€23.50)

and some doubles (②), as well as friendly staff and a large salon with worn leather couches, often abuzz with travellers trading war stories. Perfect for party types as it's near some great bars (though there is a strict policy of no noise inside after 11pm).

Euro Linnankatu 9 (see Helsinki map, pp.526–527) ☎09/622 0470, ⓦwww.eurohostel.fi. Comfortable place in a clean modern building with free morning sauna and a restaurant. It's in the quiet Katajanokka area, close to the Viking Line arrival point; take tram #4. Dorm beds (€4.10) are set in double rooms, and there are private doubles as well; those with shared bath are the cheapest. ❸

🏃 **Hostel Suomenlinna** Suomenlinna ☎09/684 7471, ⓦwww.leirikoulut.com. While hardly central, this year-round hostel with dorms (€25) and doubles (❸) boasts what is perhaps the most idyllic location of a hostel in Europe: the island of Suomenlinna. Located 15min by ferry from the market square, it gets eerily quiet here – even in the summer – and if you arrive in the winter you can bank on having the place to yourself. The last ferry is at 2am, the first at 6am.

Stadion Olympic Stadium (see Helsinki map, pp.526–527) ☎09/477 8480, ⓦwww .stadionhostel.com. An efficient if dated setup 2km from the city centre up Mannerheimintie, with private doubles (❷) and dormitories (€19) sleeping up to twelve and offering large shower rooms. Trams #3T, #4, #7A and #10 from Mannerheimintie stop outside, as does the Finnair bus from the airport (ask for "Opera").

The City

Following a devastating fire in 1808, and the city's elevation to capital in 1812, Helsinki was totally rebuilt in a style commensurate with its status: a grid of wide streets and Neoclassical, Empire-style brick buildings, modelled on the then Russian capital, St Petersburg. This grid forms the basis of the modern city, and it's a tribute to the vision of planner Johan Ehrenström and architect Carl Engel that in and around **Senate Square** the grandeur has endured, often quite dramatically. The square itself, overlooked by the gleaming Lutheran cathedral, is still the city's single most eye-catching feature, while just a few blocks away, past the South Harbour and the waterside market, the twin thoroughfares of Pohjoisesplanadi and Eteläesplanadi, known collectively as **Esplanadi**, form a handsome tree-lined avenue with a narrow strip of greenery along the centre. Meeting the western end of Esplanadi, the great artery of **Mannerheimintie** – the main route into the centre from the suburbs – carries traffic and trams past Finlandia Hall and the Olympic Stadium on one side, and the National Museum and the streets leading to Sibelius Park and the vast Hietaniemi Cemetery on the other. The bulge of land that extends **south of Esplanadi** has long been one of the most affluent sections of town. Dotted by palatial embassies and wealthy dwellings, it rises into the rocky **Kaivopuisto** park, where the peace is disturbed only by the rumble of the trams and a handful of summer rock concerts.

West of Kaivopuisto are the narrow streets of the equally exclusive **Eira** quarter, while to the north of the city centre and divided by the waters of Kaisaniemenlahti, the districts of **Kruununhaka** and **Hakaniemi** contain what little is left of pre-seventeenth-century Helsinki, in the small area up the hill behind the cathedral, compressed between the botanical gardens and the bay; over the bridge is a large marketplace and the hill leading past the formidable **Kallion kirkko** towards the modern housing districts further north. Helsinki also has innumerable offshore islands, the biggest of which are **Suomenlinna** and **Seurasaari**. Both of these, despite their location close to the city centre, offer untrammelled nature and a rewarding crop of museums.

Senate Square and Esplanadi

The heart of Helsinki lies in and around **Senate Square**, a compact area of broad bustling streets, grand buildings, famous (to Finns) shops, and, in Esplanadi, the most popular promenading spot in the entire country. Most of the streets leading into Senate Square are fairly narrow and unremarkable, however, a fact that serves to increase the impact as the square comes into view and you're struck by the sudden burst of space, the graceful symmetry of the buildings and most of all by the exquisite form of the **Tuomiokirkko** (Lutheran Cathedral: June–Aug daily 9am–midnight; Sept–May Mon–Sat 9am–6pm, Sun noon–6pm), raised on granite steps that support it like a pedestal. Designed, like most of the other buildings on the square, by Engel, its construction was overseen by him until his death in 1840, before being finally completed, with a few variations, in 1852. Among the post-Engel additions are the statues of the twelve apostles that line the roof, which may seem familiar if you've visited Copenhagen: they're copies of Thorvaldsen's sculptures for Vor Frue Kirke. After the Neoclassical extravagances of the exterior, the spartan Lutheran interior comes as a disappointment; better is the gloomily atmospheric **crypt**, which is now used as a café (June–Aug Mon–Sat 11am–5pm, Sun 1–5pm; entrance on Kirkkokatu). On the eastern side of the cathedral's pedestal at Snellmaninkatu 2 is the entrance to the **Museum of the Bank of Finland** (Tues–Fri 11am–5pm, Sat & Sun 11am–4pm; free; ⓦwww.rahamuseo.fi), which features examples of the pre-euro Finnish currency, the *markkaa*, as well as an interesting exhibition on shortlisted designs for euro notes.

The buildings around the square contribute to the pervading sense of harmony, and although none is open to the public, some are of great historical significance. The **Valtioneuvosto** (Government Palace), known as the Senate House until independence and seating the Senate from 1822, consumes the entire eastern side. It was here that an angry Finnish civil servant, Eugen Schauman, became a national hero by assassinating the much-hated Russian governor-general Bobrikov in 1904. Opposite are the Ionic columns of **Helsingin Yliopisto** (Helsinki University), next door to which is the **Yliopiston Kirjasto** (University Library), considered by many to be Engel's finest single building, although only students and bona fide researchers are allowed in.

Just north of the square between Kirkkokatu and Rauhankatu is **Säätytalo** (The House of Scientific Estates), the seat of the Diet that governed the country until 1906, when it was abolished in favour of a single-chamber parliament elected by universal suffrage (at the time, Europe's most radical parliamentary reform). In the small park behind the Government Palace is the **Ritarihuone** (House of Nobility), where the upper crust of Helsinki society rubbed shoulders a hundred years ago.

Directly opposite the cathedral at Aleksanterinkatu 18 is Helsinki's oldest stone building, **Sederholm House** (Wed & Fri–Sun 11am–5pm, Thurs 11am–7pm; free), dating from 1757. It now houses a small museum concentrating on aspects of eighteenth-century life in the city, with particular reference to industrialist Johan Sederholm. There are exhibitions on trade, education and construction, but what makes it perhaps most enjoyable is the eighteenth-century music collection – you can ask to hear a range of classical CDs while you wander around. A more high-tech record of Helsinki life can be found one block south from Sederholm House at the **City Museum**, Sofankatu 4 (Mon–Fri 9am–5pm, Sat & Sun 11am–5pm; free; ⓦwww.helsinkicitymuseum.fi), where a permanent exhibition entitled "Time" gives glimpses of Helsinki from its origins as a country village right up to the present day. It's an impressive show, beautifully lit with fibre optics and halogen lamps, though the chronology jumps around disconcertingly.

The square at the eastern end of Aleksanterinkatu is overlooked by the red-and-green onion-shaped domes of the Russian Orthodox **Uspenski Cathedral** (Mon–Fri 9.30am–4pm, Sat 9.30am–2pm, Sun noon–3pm; closed Mon Oct–April, Tues till 6pm May–Sept; ⓦwww.ort.fi/helsinki; tram #4) on Katajanokka, a wedge of land extending out to sea between the North and South harbours and currently the scene of a dockland development programme, converting the area's old warehouses into pricey new restaurants and apartments. In contrast to its Lutheran counterpart, the cathedral is drab outside, but as the largest Orthodox church in western Europe, it houses a rich display of icons and other sumptuous adornments, including an impressive array of chandeliers dangling from the vaulted ceiling.

Esplanadi and around

Walking from the Uspenski Cathedral towards the South Harbour along Aleksanterinkatu takes you past the **Presidential Palace**, noticeable only for its conspicuous uniformed guard, and the equally bland **City Hall**, used solely for administrative purposes. There's more colour and liveliness along the waterfront among the stalls of the **kauppatori**, or market square (Mon–Thurs 8am–5.30pm, Fri 8am–6pm, Sat 8am–3pm), laden with fresh fruit and vegetables; you can buy fresh fish directly from the boats moored around the edge of the harbour and, if your principles allow it, the market is also the best place to buy fur – mink and fox hats and coats are cheaper here than in the city's many fur salons. Owners of classic American cars – Finland has thousands of them – gather to show their cars off on the square the first Friday of each month. A bit further along, the **Wanha Kauppahalli** (Old Market Hall: Mon–Fri 8am–6pm, Sat 8am–4pm; ⓦwww .wanhakauppahalli.com), with its interior of original carved mahogany and carved pediments, is a good place for snacks such as reindeer kebab and Russian caviar.

Across a mishmash of tram lines from here lie the twin thoroughfares of Pohjoisesplanadi and Eteläesplanadi, together known as **Esplanadi**. At the height of the Swedish/Finnish language conflict that divided the nation during the mid-nineteenth century, this neat boulevard was where opposing factions demonstrated their allegiance – the Finns walking on the south side and the Swedes on the north. Nowadays it's dominated at lunchtime by office workers, later in the afternoon by buskers, and at night by strolling couples and imbibing, skateboarding teens. Musical accompaniment is provided free on summer evenings from the hut in the middle of the walk – expect anything from a Salvation Army band to rock groups. Entertainment of a more costly type lies at the far end of Esplanadi in the dreary off-white horseshoe of the **Swedish Theatre** building – its main entrance is on Mannerheimintie.

Around the Stockmann Department Store

If you think Esplanadi is crowded, wait until you step inside the brick Constructivist **Stockmann Department Store**, at the junction of Mannerheimintie and Aleksanterinkatu. Europe's largest department store, this is the place to buy everything from bubble gum to a Persian rug. Also part of Stockmann's (though it has its own entrance on Aleksanterinkatu), the **Academic Bookshop** (complete with internet café) claims to hold more titles than any other bookstore in Europe, including many English-language paperbacks and a sizeable stock of foreign newspapers, magazines and stationery supplies. Directly across Mannerheimintie is the massive **Forum shopping mall** which, along with Kamppi, is helping to put a dent in Stockmann's profits.

Opposite Stockmann's main entrance is the eye-catching *Three Smiths* statue by Felix Nylund; a trio of naked men swinging hammers in unison around a centrally positioned anvil, it commemorates the workers of Finland who raised money to erect a building for the country's students. This building is the **Vanha Ylioppistalo** (the Old Students' House) – its main doors facing the statue. The Finnish Students' Union is based here, owning what is now some of the most expensive square metres of land in Finland and renting them out at considerable profit. In the Vanha, as it's usually known, is the **Vanhan Galleria** (during exhibitions usually 10am–6pm; free), a small gallery with frequent displays of modern art. It's worth becoming acquainted with the building's layout, as it contains a couple of lively bars which are worthy of an evening visit. Taking a few strides further along Mannerheimintie brings you to the Bio cinema; beside it, steps lead down into a little modern courtyard framed by burger joints and pizzerias, off which runs the entrance to **Tunneli**, an underground complex containing shops, the central metro station and a pedestrian subway to one of the city's most striking structures – the train station.

The train station and National Theatre

Erected in 1914, **Central Railway Station** ranks among architect Eliel Saarinen's greatest achievements. In response to criticism of his initial design, Saarinen jettisoned the original National Romantic features and opted for a style more akin to late Art Nouveau. Standing in front of the huge doors (so sturdy they always give the impression of being locked), it's hard to deny the sense of strength and solidity the building exudes. Yet this power is tempered by gentleness, a feeling symbolized by four muscular figures on the facade, each clasping a spherical glass lamp above the heads of passers-by. The interior details can be admired at leisure from either one of the station's two restaurants. Later, Saarinen was to emigrate to America; his son Eeros, in turn, became one of the best-known postwar American architects, whose most famous creation is the TWA terminal building in New York.

Just northeast of the station is the imposing granite form of the **National Theatre**, home of Finnish drama since 1872. Under the country's then governing Swedish-speaking elite, "Finnish culture" was considered simply a contradiction in terms, while later under the tsars it was felt (quite rightly) to pose a nationalist, anti-Russian threat – Finnish theatre during the Russification process became so politically charged that it had to be staged away from the capital in the southwest coastal town of Pori. At the forefront of Finnish drama during its early years was Aleksis Kivi, who died insane and impoverished before being acknowledged as Finland's greatest playwright. He's remembered here by Wäinö Aaltonen's bronze sculpture. Interestingly, nobody knows for sure what Kivi actually looked like, and this imagined likeness, finished in 1939, has come to be regarded as a true one. Just across from the train station inside the city's main post office is the surprisingly enjoyable and newly renovated **Posti Museo** (Postal Museum: Mon–Fri 9am–6pm, Sat & Sun 11am–4pm; €6; ⓦwww.posti.fi/english/postmuseum), a remarkably innovative collection displaying the unlikely-looking implements connected with more than 350 years of Finnish postal history, along with interactive computer games, multi-screen displays and a special crayoning area for toddlers.

The Atheneum Art Museum

Just southeast of the train station is the **Atheneum Art Museum** (Tues & Fri 9am–6pm, Wed & Thurs 9am–8pm, Sat & Sun 11am–5pm; €6, €8 for special exhibitions). Chief among the large collection of Finnish paintings here is the stirring selection of works from the late nineteenth century, the so-called Golden Age of Finnish painting, when the spirit of nationalism was surging through the country and the movement towards independence gaining strength; indeed, the art of the period was a contributing factor in the growing awareness of Finnish culture,

▲ Helsinki Central Railway Station

both inside and outside the country. Among the prime names of this era were **Akseli Gallen-Kallela** and **Albert Edelfelt**, particularly the former, who translated many of the mythic scenes of the *Kalevala* onto canvas – about a half-dozen of them are on display here, the rest spread around at museums all over Finland and abroad. Slightly later came **Juho Rissanen** with his moody and evocative studies of peasant life, and **Hugo Simberg**, responsible for the eerie *Death and the Peasant* and the powerful triptych *Boy Carrying a Garland*. Cast an eye, too, over the works of **Helene Schjerfbeck**, for a long time one of the country's most underrated artists but now enjoying an upsurge in popularity – and collectability. Among the best examples of pure Finnish landscape are the works of **Pekka Halonen**: *Pioneers in Karelia* is typical, with soft curves expressively denoting natural scenes.

The first floor holds a series of installations by innovative contemporary local artists, but the best of the Finnish art is assembled on the floors above: the second floor contains the bulk of the museum's Golden Age works, while the third floor houses the provocative expressionism of **Tyko Sallinen** and the November Group, most active around 1917, as well as some token **foreign** masters – a couple of large Munchs, a Van Gogh, a Chagall and a few Cézannes. Before you leave, check out the excellent art bookshop on the ground floor.

North along Mannerheimintie

The logical route for exploring north of the city centre, the wide thoroughfare of **Mannerheimintie** is named after the military commander and statesman C.G.E. Mannerheim, who wielded considerable influence on Finnish affairs in the first half of the twentieth century. He's commemorated by a statue near the busy junction with Arkadiankatu, a structure on which the city's bird population has left its mark.

The Lasipalatsi

Opposite the Postal Museum is the recently renovated **Lasipalatsi** (ⓦwww .lasipalatsi.fi), built for the 1940 Olympics as the main transit and entertainment building. Reopened in 1998, the functional two-storey building is typical of late 1930s Finnish Art Nouveau design, and contains some 25 shops, galleries, exhibition sites and cafés, as well as a media centre embodying the Finns' faith in publicly accessible new technology – enough to feed mind and body for a few hours at least. On the glass-fronted lower level check out the **mbar** (Mon & Tues 9am–midnight, Wed & Thurs 9am–2am, Fri & Sat 9am–3am, Sun noon–midnight), with internet terminals inset into glass-topped tables, and the glass-fronted studio of **YLE**, the main Finnish TV company. It overlooks the street and is periodically surrounded by hordes of teenagers anxious to catch a glimpse of the stars at work inside. Also on the ground floor is **Bio Rex** (ⓣ09/611 300, ⓦwww.biorex.fi), a cinema that specializes in screening independent films that you probably won't find anywhere else in the city, though it also has mainstream Hollywood movies. Upstairs, the **Cable Book Library** (Mon–Thurs 10am–10pm, Sat & Sun noon–6pm) has magazines and two dozen free internet terminals, as well as wi-fi access.

Behind the Lasipalatsi stands the sleek, aluminum-and-glass-framed **Kamppi** shopping and apartment complex; built in 2005, its basement also houses the long-distance bus terminal.

Museum of Contemporary Art: Kiasma

Just beyond the Lasipalatsi at Mannerheiminaukio 2 is the **Kiasma Museum of Contemporary Art** (Tues 10am–5pm, Wed–Sun 10am–8.30pm; €7, evenings free first Wed of every month; ⓦwww.kiasma.fi), a highly forbidding, steel-clad and tube-like structure that looks from the side like a mix of the Sydney Opera House and the Guggenheim in Bilbao – a vaguely pretentious building for the usually functionalist Finns. Inside the catacomb-like interior are sweeping curves and well-lit hallways; on the ground floor natural light pours in from a variety of angles onto a brilliant-white interior that looks like it gets a new coat of paint on a weekly basis. Entry to this floor is free, and there's a decent café, internet access, one of the best art bookshops in Finland and an interactive children's playroom.

The Kiasma draws its **exhibition** material from an archive of thousands of pieces of contemporary art, as well as works by visiting artists. Nothing is permanently on display, although as you explore you begin to feel that it's the building itself – with its play on space, light and technology – that is the principal exhibit. Some rooms are blacked out completely; others have high overhanging arches through which the light spills into the display area, giving the place an almost religious feel. Various touchscreen terminals built into the walls at strategic points tell you all you need to know about the works on display. Exhibitions change every two to three months – check the museum's website for details, and keep an eye out, too for performances, lectures and film screenings staged at the museum's small **theatre**.

The Parliament Building and National Museum

The section of Mannerheimintie north from the Kiasma passes a number of outstanding buildings, the first of which is the **Parliament Building** on the left (guided tours July & Aug Mon–Fri 11am & 1pm, Sat 11am & 12.30pm, Sun noon & 1.30pm; Sept–June Sat & Sun only, same times; when in session, access is to the public galleries only; free; ◉www.eduskunta.fi). The work of J.S. Sirén, the porridge-coloured building, with its fourteen pompous Corinthian columns and choking air of solemnity, was completed in 1931. Intended to celebrate the new republic, its style was drawn from the revolutionary Neoclassicism that dominated public buildings from Fascist Italy to Nazi Germany, and its authoritarian features can appear wildly out of place in Helsinki, though it's worth a look nonetheless.

North of here things improve with the **National Museum** (Tues & Wed 11am–8pm, Thurs–Sun 11am–6pm; €7; ◉www.nba.fi), whose design was the result of an early twentieth-century competition won by the three Young Turks of Finnish architecture – Armas Lindgren, Herman Gesellius and Eliel Saarinen. With National Romanticism at its zenith, they steeped their plan in Finnish history, drawing on the country's legacy of medieval churches and granite castles (even though many of these were built under Swedish domination), culminating in a weighty but slender tower that gives the place a cathedral-like profile. The entrance is guarded by Emil Wikström's sculptured bear and the interior ceilings are decorated by Gallen-Kallela with scenes from the *Kalevala*.

The museum may seem the obvious place to discover what Finland is all about but, especially if you've spent hours exploring the copiously stocked national museums of Denmark and Sweden, you might well find the **collections** disappointing. Being dominated by other nations for many centuries, Finland had little more than the prerequisites of peasant life to call its own up until the mid-1800s (when moves towards Finnish nationalism got off the ground), and the rows of farming and hunting tools alongside endless displays of bowls and spoons from the early times do little to fire the imagination. The most interesting section is an exhibition entitled The Past Century, which relates to the rise of Finnish self-determination and the early years of the republic. Large photographs show the enormous crowds that massed in Helsinki's streets to sing the Finnish anthem in defiance of their (then) Russian rulers, and cabinets packed with small but intriguing objects outline the left–right struggles that marked the early decades of independence and the immediate postwar years – periods when Finland's political future teetered precariously in the balance, a long way from the stability and prosperity enjoyed in more recent times.

Finlandia Hall to the Olympic Stadium

Stylistically a far cry from the National Museum building but equally affecting, **Finlandia Hall** (guided tours at 1pm when not in use, though dates vary; €6; ring ☎09/40 241 or check at the City Tourist Office; ◉www.finlandiatalo .fi) stands directly across Mannerheimintie, partially hidden by the roadside foliage.

Designed by the country's premier architect, **Alvar Aalto**, a few years before his death in 1976, Finlandia Hall was conceived as part of a grand plan to rearrange the entire centre of Helsinki. Previously, Eliel Saarinen had planned a traffic route from the northern suburbs into a new square in the city centre, to be called Vapaudenkatu ("Freedom Street") in celebration of Finnish independence. Aalto plotted a continuation of this scheme, envisaging the removal of the rail-freight yards, which would enable arrivals to be greeted with a fan-like terrace of new buildings reflected in the waters of Töölönlahti. Finlandia was to be the first of these, and only by looking across from the other side of Töölönlahti do you perceive the building's soft sensuality and the potential beauty of the greater concept. Inside the hall, Aalto's characteristic wave pattern (the architect's surname, as it happens, means "wave" in Finnish) and asymmetry are in evidence. From the walls and ceilings through to the lamps and vases, the place has a quiet and graceful air – but the view from the foyer is still of the rail-freight yards, and the great plan for a future Helsinki remains under discussion.

Next door is **Hakasalmi Villa** (Wed–Sun 11am–5pm, closed mid-June to mid-Sept; free), an Italian Neoclassical construction built in the 1840s by a councillor and patron of the arts whose collection inspired the founding of the museum. It houses engaging, long-term temporary exhibitions, often strikingly designed – a recent show looked at the life of Roma (Gypsies) in Finland. Finland's **Opera House** (Mon–Fri 9am–6pm, Sat 3–6pm, Sun open 2hr before performances; guided tours early May to Aug Wed 3pm, €8; ⊛www.operafin.fi), a little way beyond Finlandia, is, like so many contemporary Finnish buildings, a Lego-like expanse of white-tiled facade. Its light-flooded interior is enlivened by displays of colourful costumes though, and its grounds and entrance spiked with minimalist black-granite sculptures.

From this point on, the decisive outline of the **Olympic Stadium** becomes visible. Originally intended for the 1940 Olympic Games, the stadium eventually staged the second postwar games in 1952. From the **Stadium Tower** (Mon–Fri 9am–8pm, Sat & Sun 9am–6pm; €2) there's an unsurpassed view over the city and a chunk of the southern coast. If you're a stopwatch-and-spikes freak, ask at the tower's ticket office for directions to the **Sports Museum** (Mon–Fri 11am–5pm, Sat & Sun noon–4pm; €3.50; ⊛www.urheilumuseo.org), whose mind-numbing collection of track officials' shoes and swimming caps overshadows a worthy attempt to present sport as an integral part of Finnish culture. The nation's heroes, among them Keke Rosberg and Lasse Virén, are lauded to the skies. Outside, Wäinö Aaltonen's sculpture of Paavo Nurmi captures the champion runner of the 1920s in full stride, and fully naked – this atypically Finnish expression of public nudity caused quite a stir when the sculpture was unveiled in 1952.

West of Mannerheimintie

As there's little of note north of the stadium, it's best to cross Mannerheimintie and follow the streets off it leading to **Sibelius Park** and Eila Hiltunen's monument to the composer, made from 24 tons of steel tubes, like a big silver surrealist organ; next to it, there's an irrefutably horrid sculpture of Sibelius's dismembered head. The shady and pleasant park is rudely cut by a main road, Mechelininkatu; following this back towards the city centre brings you first to the small Islamic and Jewish cemeteries, and then to the expanse of tombs comprising **Hietaniemi Cemetery** (usually open until 10pm). A prowl among these is like a stroll through a "Who was Who" of Finland's last 150 years: Engel, Snellman, Waltari, Tove Jansson and a host of former presidents (including Mannerheim and Kekkonen) are buried here, while just inside the main entrance lies Alvar Aalto, his witty little tombstone consisting partly of a chopped Neoclassical column; behind it is the larger marker of Gallen-Kallela, his initials woven around a painter's palette. Local schoolkids head to the cemetery when skipping off lessons during warm weather, not for a smoke behind the gravestones but to reach the **beaches** that line the bay just beyond its western walls. From these you can enjoy the best sunset view in the city.

On the way back towards Mannerheimintie, at Lutherinkatu 3, just off Runeber-ginkatu, is the breathtaking **Temppeliaukio kirkko** (mid-May to mid-Sept Mon, Tues, Thurs & Fri 10am–8pm, Wed 10am–6.45pm, Sat 10am–6pm, Sun 11.45–1.45pm & 3.30–6pm; closed Tues 1–3.30pm in winter and during services). Brilliantly conceived by Timo and Tuomo Suomalainen and finished in 1969, the underground church is built inside a massive block of natural granite in the middle of an otherwise ordinary residential square. While here, try to see it from above if you can (even if you have to shin up a drainpipe), when the copper dome that pokes through the rock makes the thing look like a ditched flying saucer. The odd combination of man-made and natural materials has made it a fixture on the tourist circuit, but even when crowded it's a thrill to be inside. Classical concerts frequently take place here, the raw rock walls making for excellent acoustics – check the noticeboard at the entrance for details.

South of Esplanadi: Kaivopuisto, Eira and Pihlajasaari island

From the South Harbour it's a straightforward walk past the Silja terminal to Kaivopuisto, but it's more interesting to leave Esplanadi along Kasarmikatu and take in some small, offbeat museums along the way. First of these is the **Museum of Finnish Architecture** (Tues & Thurs–Fri 10am–4pm, Wed 10am–8pm, Sat–Sun 11am–4pm; €3.50–5, depending upon exhibitions, free on Fri; ✆www .mfa.fi) at no. 24, which is aimed at the serious fan: architectural tours of less accessible buildings both in Helsinki and around the country can be arranged here. Combined with an extensive archive, it's a useful resource for a nation with an important architectural heritage.

A block from Kasarmikatu is Korkeavuorenkatu, with the excellent **Design Museum** at no. 23 (June–Aug daily 11am–6pm; Sept–May Tues–Sun 11am–6pm, Tues until 8pm; ✆www.designmuseum.fi; €7), which traces the relationship between art and industry in Finnish history. There are full explanatory texts and period exhibits, from Karelianism – the representations of nature and peasant life from the Karelia region in eastern Finland that dominated Finnish art and design in the years just before and after independence – to the modern movements, along with the postwar shift towards the more familiar, and less interesting, pan-Scandinavian styles.

Kaivopuisto park

Kasarmikatu ends close to the base of a hill, from where footpaths lead up to the Engel-designed **Astronomical Observatory**. Down on the other side and a few streets on is the large and rocky **Kaivopuisto** park. In the 1830s this was developed as a health resort, with a spa house that drew Russian nobility from St Peters-burg to sample its waters. The building, another of Engel's works (although greatly modified), can be found in the middle of the park's central avenue, today pulling in the crowds as a restaurant.

Off a smaller avenue, Itäinen Puistotie, runs the circular Kallionlinnantie, which contains the house where Gustaf Mannerheim spent the later years of his life, now maintained as the **Mannerheim Museum** (Fri–Sun 11am–4pm, other times by appointment, call ✆09/635 443; €8 including guided tour; ✆www.mannerheim -museo.fi). A Finnish-born, Russian-trained military commander, Mannerheim was pro-Finnish but had a middle-class suspicion of the working classes: he led the right-wing Whites during the Civil War of 1918 and two decades later the Finnish campaigns in the Winter and Continuation wars (for more on which, see the "Military Museum", p.541). His influence in the political sphere was also consider-able, and included a brief spell as president. While acknowledging his importance, the regard that Finns have for him these days, naturally enough, depends on their own political viewpoint.

Ideology aside, the house is intriguing. The interior is left much as it was when the man died in 1951, and the clutter is astounding. During his travels Mannerheim raided flea markets at every opportunity, collecting a remarkable array of plunder – assorted furniture, antiques, ornaments and books from all over the globe. Upstairs is the camp-bed which Mannerheim found too comfortable ever to change, and in the wall is the vent inserted to keep the bedroom as airy as a field-tent.

If he had lived a few decades earlier, one of Mannerheim's Kallionlinnantie neighbours would have been Frederik Cygnaeus, art patron and professor of aesthetics at Helsinki University. In 1860, Cygnaeus built a summer house at no. 8, a lovely yellow-turreted affair, and filled it with an outstanding collection of art. Later he donated the lot to the nation and today it's displayed as the **Cygnaeus Gallery** (Wed 11am–7pm, Thurs–Sun 11am–4pm; €4; ⓦwww.nba.fi). Everything is beautifully laid out in the tiny rooms of the house, with whole walls of work by the most influential of his contemporaries. The von Wright brothers (Ferdinand, Magnus and Wilhelm) are responsible for the most touching pieces – the bird and nature studies. Look out, too, for a strange portrait of Cygnaeus by Ekman, showing the man sprouting sinister wings from under his chin.

The edge of Kaivopuisto looks out across a sprinkling of little islands and the Suomenlinna fortress. You can follow one of the pathways down into **Merikatu**, along which lie several of the Art Nouveau villas lived in by the big cheeses of Finnish industry during the early part of the twentieth century. Easily the most extreme is no. 25, the Enso-Gutzeit villa, now portioned off into offices and with a lingering air of decay hanging over its decorative facade.

Eira

Inland from Merikatu, the curving alleys and tall, elegant buildings of the **Eira** district are landmarked by the needle-like spire rising from the roof of **Mikael Agricola kirkko**, named after the translator of the first Finnish Bible but making no demands on your time. A few blocks northeast, the twin-towered Johanessen kirkko is again not worth a call in itself but functions as a handy navigation aid. Following Yrjönkatu northwards from here takes you past the partly pedestrianized Iso Roobertinkatu, before reaching Bulevardi and the square containing **Vanha kirkko** (Old Church). A humble wooden structure, and another example of Engel's work, this was the first Lutheran church to be erected after Helsinki became the Finnish capital, predating that in Senate Square by some years but occupying a far less glamorous plot – a plague victim's burial ground dating from 1710.

Heading left along Bulevardi for a couple of hundred metres brings you to the Sinebrychoff brewery which, besides bestowing a distinctive aroma of hops to the locality, also finances the **Sinebrychoff Foreign Art Museum** at no. 40 (Tues & Fri 10am–6pm, Wed–Thurs 10am–8pm, Sat & Sun 11am–5pm; €7.50, higher for special exhibitions; ⓦwww.fng.fi). This rather precious museum houses mostly seventeenth-century Flemish and Dutch paintings, along with some excellent miniatures, delicately illustrated porcelain and refined period furniture. Continuing east along Bulevardi to the waterfront brings you to the wide **Hietalahdentori**, a concrete square that perks up with a daily morning flea market and, in summer, an evening market (3.30–8pm).

Pihlajasaari island

One of Helsinki's most enjoyable islands, ideal for a day-trip from the capital, **Pihlajasaari island** (ⓦwww.pihlajasaari.net) is barely a fifteen-minute boat ride from the Merisatama small-boat harbour on Merisatamanranta, opposite the junction of Merikatu and Laivurinkatu. Creaking 30-year-old wooden pleasure boats leave once or twice hourly from here (mid-May to Aug; €5 return) for the short trip across to the island, which also goes by its Swedish name of Rönnskär. The last trip back leaves the island at 7pm. Actually two small islands linked by a narrow isthmus and footbridge, Pihlajasaari is a summer haven of wild flowers, long grasses and swaying pine and rowan trees vying for space between the outcrops of smooth bare rock that are perfect for catching a few rays. In fact, on the smaller of the two islands, reached by turning left from the boat jetty and crossing the small footbridge, is Helsinki's best **nudist beach** – follow the signs for the *naturistiranta* and note that the outer limits of the area are obsessively marked by signposts so as not to offend the Finns' very un-Scandinavian unease with public nudity. Back on the main island, itself no more than one or two kilometres in length, a network of paths leads through the forest to a series of rocky beaches and a **café** near the southwestern tip, a pleasant place to sit and watch the enormous superferries glide towards their destination in Helsinki en route from Sweden.

Kruununhaka and Hakaniemi

North of Senate Square is the little district of **Kruununhaka**. Away from the city hubbub, its closely built blocks shield the narrow streets from the sunlight, evoking a forlorn and forgotten mood. At Kristianinkatu 12, the single-storey wooden **Burgher's House** (June–Aug & Dec Sun–Thurs 11am–4pm; ⓦwww.hel.fi/kaumuseo) stands in vivid contrast to the tall granite dwellings around it – and gives an indication of how Helsinki looked when wood was still the predominant building material. The house is the oldest original standing wooden structure in the city, and its interior has been kitted out with mid-nineteenth-century furnishings, the period when a city burgher did indeed reside here.

Kristianinkatu meets at right-angles with Maurinkatu, a short way along which is the **Military Museum** (Tues–Thurs 11am–5pm & Fri–Sun 11am–4pm; €4), a rather formless selection of weapons, medals and glorifications of armed-forces life, but with some excellent documentary photos of the Winter and Continuation wars of 1939–44. Finland was drawn into World War II through necessity rather than choice. When Soviet troops invaded eastern Finnish territories in November 1939, under the guise of protecting Leningrad, they were repelled by technically inferior but far more committed Finns. The legends of the "heroes in white" were born then, alluding to the Finnish soldiers and the camouflage used in the winter snows. Soon after, however, faced with possible starvation and a fresh Soviet advance, Finland joined the war on the Nazi side, mainly in order to continue resisting the threat from the east. For this reason, it's rare to find World War II spoken of as such in Finland: much more commonly it's divided into these separate conflicts.

Hakaniemi

The western edge of Kruununhaka is defined by the busy Unioninkatu (if it's a sunny day, take a stroll around the neat **botanical gardens**, just off Unioninkatu), which continues northwards across a slender body of water into **Hakaniemi**, a district chiefly visited for its **kauppahalli** (indoor market; Mon–Fri 8am–5pm, Sat 8am–2pm) in the Hakaniementori square, where you'll find an excellent array of fresh fruit, vegetables, meats and fish. Although the square is surrounded by drab storefronts and office blocks, the *kauppahalli* here is about the liveliest in the city – mainly due to its position near a major junction for city buses and trams, as well as a metro station. From the square you can see right up the hill to the impressive Art Deco brickwork of the **Kallion kirkko**, beyond which is the busy Sturenkatu and the open green area partly consumed by **Linnanmäki amusement park**. After crossing Sturenkatu, head for the nearby **Museum of Workers' Housing** at Kirstinkuja 4 (June–Aug Mon–Thurs & Sun 11am–4pm; €3; ⓦwww.hel.fi/kaumuseo), for some fascinating social history. The series of just-renovated wooden buildings that now hold the museum were constructed during the early 1900s to provide housing for the impoverished country folk who moved to the growing, increasingly industrialized city to work as street cleaners and refuse collectors. Six of the one-room homes where the new arrivals settled have been re-created with period furnishings, and a biography on the door describes each flat's occupants – woeful tales of overcrowding, overwork and sons who left for America and never returned.

Suomenlinna

Located in the southeast of the Kaivopuisto district and built by the Swedes in 1748 to protect Helsinki from seaborne attack, the fortress of **Suomenlinna** stands on five interconnected islands, reached by half-hourly ferry from the South Harbour, which make a rewarding break from the city centre – even if you only want to laze around on the dunes. (These were created by the Russians with sand shipped in from Estonia to strengthen the new capital's defences after they'd wrested control of Finland.) For information, head just west of the ferry terminal to the **Inventory Chambers Visitors Centre** (March, April & Oct Mon–Fri 11am–4pm, Sat & Sun 11am–5pm; May–Aug daily 10am–6pm; Sept Mon–Fri 11am–5pm, Sat & Sun 10am–5pm; Nov–Feb Tues–Sun 11am–4pm), housed in a former naval stores.

Here you'll also find the **Suomenlinna Museum and Experience** (daily: Jan–April & Oct–Dec 10am–4pm; May–Sept 10am–6pm; €5; @www.suomenlinna .fi), which charts the history of the fortress. Suomenlinna has half a dozen museums, none particularly riveting, although the **Ehrensvärd Museum** (Jan–April Sat & Sun 11am–4pm; May–Aug daily 10am–5pm; Sept daily 11am–4pm; €3) is worth a look, occupying the residence used by the first commander of the fortress, Augustin Ehrensvärd. He oversaw the building of Suomenlinna and now lies in the elaborate tomb in the grounds; his personal effects remain inside the house alongside displays on the fort's construction. You'll also find a **Toy Museum** (April Sat & Sun noon–5pm; May Mon–Fri 11am–4pm, Sat & Sun noon–5pm; June–Aug daily 11–5/6pm; Sept noon–5pm; €5; @www.viapori.fi/lelumuseo), which has several gorgeous examples of dolls and dolls' house miniatures dating back to 1800. Finally, the **Coastal Artillery Museum** (mid-May to Aug daily 11am–6pm; €4) records Suomenlinna's defensive actions and – for an extra €3.50 – allows you the opportunity to clamber around the darkly claustrophobic World War II submarine *Vesikko*.

Seurasaari and around

A fifteen-minute tram (#4) or bus (#24) ride northwest of the city centre (get off one stop after the big hospital on the left, from where it's a one-kilometre walk) lies **Seurasaari**, a small wooded island delightfully set in a sheltered bay. The three contrasting museums on or close by Seurasaari make for a well-spent day. Access to the island proper is by a bridge at the southern end of Tamminiementie, conveniently close to the **Helsinki City Art Museum** (Tues–Sun 11am–8.30pm; €7; @www.taidemuseo.fi). Though one of the best collections of modern Finnish art, with some eerily striking work, the museum is hardly a triumph of layout, with great clumps of stuff of differing styles scattered about the walls. But the good pieces shine through. Be warned, though, that during temporary exhibitions the permanent stock is locked away.

A few minutes' walk from the art museum, towards the Seurasaari bridge, is the long driveway leading to the **Urho Kekkonen Museum** (mid-May to mid-Aug daily 11am–5pm; mid-Aug to mid-May Wed–Sun 11am–5pm; €5, includes guided tour; @www.nba.fi) at Tamminiemi, the villa where the esteemed president lived until his death in 1986. Whether they love him or loathe him, few Finns would deny the vital role Kekkonen played in Finnish history, most significantly by continuing the work of his predecessor, Paasikivi, in the establishment of Finnish neutrality. He accomplished this largely through delicate negotiations with Soviet leaders – whose favour he would gain, so legend has it, by taking them to his sauna (open for viewing in summer only) – narrowly averting major crises and seeing off the threat of a Soviet invasion on two separate occasions. Kekkonen often conducted official business here rather than at the Presidential Palace in the city, yet the feel of the place is far from institutional, with a light and very Finnish character, filled with birchwood furniture, its large windows giving peaceful views of surrounding trees, water and wildlife.

Close by, in another calm setting across the bridge on Seurasaari itself, is the **Open-Air Museum** (June–Aug daily 11am–5pm; early Sept & late May Mon–Fri 9am–3pm, Sat & Sun 11am–5pm; €6), a collection of vernacular buildings assembled from all over Finland, connected by the various pathways that extend around the island. There are better examples of traditional Finnish life elsewhere in the country, but if you're only visiting Helsinki this will give a good insight into how the country folk lived until surprisingly recently. The old-style church is a popular spot for city couples' weddings.

Aside from the museums and the scenery, people also come to Seurasaari to strip off. Sex-segregated **nudist beaches** line part of the western edge – also a popular offshore stop for the city's weekend yachtsmen, armed with binoculars; however, Pihlajasaari island (see p.540) is an altogether more pleasing location for nude sunbathing – it's also more gay-friendly.

Outlying museums

Helsinki has a few other **museums** outside the centre that don't fit into any walking tour. All are within fairly easy reach with public transport, and sometimes a little legwork. A few kilometres northwest of the centre on the Tarvaspää peninsula, the **Gallen-Kallela Museum**, Gallen-Kallelantie 27 (mid-May to Aug daily 10am–6pm; Sept to mid-May Tues–Sat 10am–4pm, Sun 10am–5pm; €8; @www.gallen-kallela .fi), is housed inside the Art Nouveau studio of the influential painter Akseli Gallen-Kallela (1865–1931), who lived and worked here from 1913. Sadly, it's a bit of an anticlimax, lacking either atmosphere or a decent display of the artist's work. There are a few old paints and brushes under dirty glass coverings in the studio, while in an upstairs room are the pickled remains of reptiles and frog like animals collected by Gallen-Kallela's family. Inscribed into the floor is a declaration by Gallen-Kallela: "I Shall Return". Unless you're a huge fan, it's probably not worth the bother. To get there, take tram #4 from the city centre to the end of its route (on Saunalahdentie), then walk 2km along Munkkiniemi on the bay's edge to a footbridge which leads over the water and towards the poorly signposted museum. Alternatively, bus #33 runs from the tram stop to the footbridge about every twenty minutes.

To the west of the city centre, the former cable factory at Tallberginkatu 1F is now a cultural centre, the Kaapelitehdas (@www.kaapelitehdas.fi) home to dance and theatre companies and a clutch of museums, accessible on tram #8. The **Hotel and Restaurant Museum** (Tues–Sun 11am–6pm; €2; @www.hotellijaravintolamusco .fi) is specifically designed for aficionados of the catering trade, although the photos on the walls of its two rooms reveal a fascinating social history of Helsinki, showing hotel and restaurant life from both sides of the table, alongside a staggering selection of matchboxes, beer mats emblazoned with the emblems of their establishments and menus signed by the rich and infamous.

Despite its grand title, the **Finnish Museum of Photography** (Tues–Sun 11am–6pm; €6; @www.fmp.fi) comprises a shabby herd of old cameras that suggest Finnish photography never really progressed beyond the watch-the-birdie stage. Amends are made by the innovative temporary collections of photos that regularly adorn the walls. The third museum in the complex is the city's **Theatre Museum** (Tues–Sun 11am–6pm; €6; @www.teatterimuseo.fi), displaying a permanent collection of costumes, stage sets and lights. Frequent temporary exhibitions focus on different aspects behind the scenes in Finnish theatre.

Eating

As in the rest of the country, **eating** in Helsinki isn't cheap, but there is plenty of choice – both for top-notch dining and, with careful planning, places much more easy on your pursestrings. Other than all-you-can-eat **breakfast** tables in hotels (hostel breakfasts in the city tend to be rationed), it's best to hold out until **lunch**, when many restaurants offer a reduced fixed-price menu or a help-yourself buffet table, while in almost every pizzeria you'll get a pizza, coffee and all you can manage from the bread and salad bar for under €10. With all of the quiet green spots in the city, **picnic food**, too, is a viable option; visit the markets and market halls at the South Harbour or Hakaniementori for fresh vegetables, meat and fish. Several supermarkets in Tunneli, by the train station, stay open until 10pm. The central and popular **Kamppi and Forum** shopping centres both offer a number of popular, inexpensive eating places on two floors, while all-night party streets such as Iso Roobertinkatu or the area right around the train station contains a range of mid-standard, filling options open till late.

Throughout the day, up until 5pm or 6pm, you can also get a coffee and pastry or a fuller snack for around €5 at one of the numerous local **cafés**. The best cafés are stylish, atmospheric affairs dating from the beginning of the twentieth century; alternatives include myriad multinational hamburger joints and the slightly more unusual *grilli* roadside stands, which sell hot dogs and the like. If you're hungry and impoverished (and are, in theory at least, a student), you can get a full meal for €5.90 from one of the **student mensas**, the largest of which are centrally located in the main university buildings at Fabianinkatu 33, and at Mannerheimintie 3/Kaivopiha, the triangular, cobbled plaza to the side of the Vanha Ylioppilastalo. Both are open during the summer, and a dozen more are open during term time. The *mensas* can be cheaper still in the late afternoon, from 4pm to 6pm, and are also usually open on Saturdays from 9am to 1pm.

Unless otherwise stated, the cafés and restaurants listed here appear on the central Helsinki map, pp.528–529.

Cafés

Aalto Academic Bookstore, Pohjoisesplanadi 39. Designed by the world-famous Finnish architect whose name it bears, and well worth a visit after a morning's book-browsing. Sandwich prices hover around the €10 mark, but you can always soak up the atmosphere over a coffee.

Ekberg Bulevardi 9 ⓦ www.cafeekberg.fi. Opened in 1852, this landmark café retains nineteenth-century fixtures and a *fin-de-siècle* atmosphere, with starched waitresses bringing the most delicate of open sandwiches and pastries to green-marble tables.

Eliel Central Railway Station. On the station's ground floor, this has an airy, vaulted Art Nouveau interior, good-value self-service breakfasts (Mon–Sat 7am–midnight, Sun 8am–midnight) – and a roulette table.

Engel Aleksanterinkatu 26 ⓦ www.cafeengel.fi. Named after the Berlin-born designer of all the buildings you can see from its window, this is a haven of gourmet coffee, pastries, cakes and intellectual chitchat, just across from Senate Square. Try the smoked-fish salad, or the French breakfast for €11.

Esplanad Pohjoisesplanadi 37. This classic establishment may have a bit of the walnut-grain Starbucks feel, but it's still the best place in town for inexpensive eating. Filled baguettes, a choice of fresh soups daily and always a queue. Outdoor seating catches the morning sun.

Fazer Kluuvikatu 3 ⓦ www.fazercafe .fi. Helsinki's best-known bakery, justly celebrated for its lighter-than-air pastries; there's another branch in the Forum Shopping Centre. At either, try the speciality, "Bebe", a praline cream-filled pastry for €3.

Kappeli Esplanadi Park, Esplanadi. An elegant, classic-meets-Modernist glasshouse with massive wrought-iron decorated windows overlooking Esplanadi and the harbour, with lots of live entertainment outside and in during the summer.

Strindberg Pohjoisesplanadi 33. Stylish outdoor coffee sipping – though it's a good deal more pricey if you want to eat, with a large menu from the restaurant upstairs listing such items as smoked reindeer with Lapland cheese followed by slow-fried grayling and arctic cloudberry. More familiar items like roast-beef sandwiches are sizable and cost under €10.

Tin Tin Tango Töölöntorinkatu 7 (see Helsinki map, pp.526–527) ⓣ 09/2709 0972. It could only exist in Finland: a retro café that lets you wait for a load of laundry to dry as you sweat it up in a sauna and sip on a pint of Arctic lager. Set a bit north of the city centre, the stereo at this hip spot pumps out classic Argentine tango and the walls are adorned with Tintin artworks. Breakfasts, sandwiches and Beamish bitter on tap. Sauna costs €22 per hour and on-site self-service laundry €4 for a wash, €2 dry; both require reservations.

Ursula Ehrenströmintie 3 (see Helsinki map, pp.526–527) ⓦ www.ursula.fi. On the beach at the edge of the Kaivopuisto park, with a wonderful sea view from the outdoor terrace. Decent cakes, sandwiches and light lunches (around €10). All profits from here go to charity.

Restaurants

Though Finland was long been the odd man out when it came to interesting Nordic cooking, a wave of edgy, East-meets-West restaurants have sprouted up all over Helsinki recently, turning it into an outstanding place to experience new and exciting fusion cooking. Indeed, many restaurants serve such eclectic menus that it's hard to tell whether the cuisine is Finnish, French, Asian or "continental". At any of these, prepare to spend anywhere from €20 to €60 per person. There are also a few Michelin-starred places where prices are easily double that. It's still possible to find an inexpensive dinner for under €15: **pizzerias** and kebab spots are a good bet if you're looking to save cash. There are a number of **vegetarian** restaurants, which tend to be fairly high up on the price scale, as well as old **Finnish** and Russian standbys that have been around for decades – if not longer – with prices that have well exceeded the rate of inflation (mains often start at around €25). Many restaurants are open daily until around 1am, though the majority of kitchens close by 11pm (often 9pm on Sun). Monday is the most common day for closing.

Note that we've given phone numbers only for restaurants where you need to book. Hyvää ruokahaluaa (bon appetit)!

Bellevue Rahapajankatu 3, behind the Uspenski Cathedral ☏09/179 560, ⓦwww.restaurantbellevue.com. A superb Russian restaurant opened, ironically, in 1917, the year Finland won independence from Russia. Polished samovars create a period ambience for the expensive, gourmet Russian food that is considered some of Europe's best: try Marshal Mannerheim's favourite starter of minced lamb flavoured with herring for €13.15; for the more adventurous, there's also bear steak (€69). Closed Sat & Sun lunchtime.

Chez Dominique Rikhardinkatu 4 ☏09/612 7393, ⓦwww.chezdominique.fi. Finland's first and foremost Michelin-starred restaurant, this white-hued, minimalist place serves Scandinavian cuisine with a distinctive French touch. The menu changes weekly, but perennial mains (€40 and up) include pigeon filled with duck foie gras, roasted pike perch and boiled lobster. Closed Sat lunch, and Sun & Mon.

Demo Uudenmaankatu 11 ☏09/2289 0840, ⓦwww.restaurantdemo.fi. Though it has the facade of a fairly casual eating place, the extremely innovative dishes here served in part to help pull Helsinki restaurants out of the dark ages. Try roasted breast of goose, goose gizzards and kumquat sauce, or prawn bisque flavoured with fennel, apple and aioli crab salad. Open since 2003, *Demo* won Finnish restaurant of the year in 2006 and was awarded a Michelin star in 2007. Four-course menu €54.

Farouge Yrjönkatu 6 ☏09/612 3455 ⓦwww.farouge.fi. Run by two Lebanese sisters, this has become Helsinki's most desirable Middle Eastern restaurant, thankfully upping the ante from the run of ubiquitous kebab shops. Decor is sleek Scandinavian accented by the odd Arabesque flourish.

The chef is well known for her innovative use of herbs and spices; try the inexpensive *mezze* plate for four to get a good sample of her great cooking. Mains cost €17–38.

Golden Rax Pizzabuffet Mannerheimintie 18, 2nd floor of the Forum Shopping Centre. Bargain-basement unlimited pizza and pasta "megabuffet" for €8.99.

Grotesk Ludviginkatu 10 ☏010/470 2001, ⓦwww.grotesk.fi. A fusion spot with black-and-red Gothic decor. Each dish – from appetizer through to dessert – is perfectly matched to a vintage from their extensive wine list. Very good salmon and roast duck. Run by the chefs from *Demo*.

Hariton Kasarmikatu 4 (see Helsinki map, pp.526–527) ☏09/642 394, ⓦwww.hariton.fi. One of Finland's most respected Russian restaurants, and better priced than the city's other high-brow Russian places. The menu, following the Orthodox calendar, changes several times a year, but the expensive blinis – vendace or whitefish roe – always make an appearance, as do any number of wild mushroom dishes.

Havis Amanda Unioninkatu 23. The oldest and best seafood restaurant in the city, albeit pricey and somewhat staid. The atmosphere is heavily nautical: brass fittings, ship-in-a-bottle scale models and lithographs of marine life. Superb service, and most mains around €25. Try the Baltic herring, gratinated in a tasty tartar sauce.

Juuri Korkeavuorenkatu 27 ⓦwww.juuri.fi. This newish, central place serves a range of *sapas*, their self-styled Finnish tapas, succulent bite-sized dishes such as crispy mustard crayfish and cottage-cheese filled cabbage leaves. Great wine list.

Kuu Töölönkatu 27 (see Helsinki map, pp.526–527) ⓦwww.ravintolakuu.info. Between the Opera

House and Sibelius Park, this is an unpretentious place to consume filling, down-to-earth Finnish food. Mains from €17.

Kynsilaukka Ravintola Garlic Fredrikinkatu 22 ☎ 09/651 939 ⓦ www.kynsilaukka.com. The ultimate pleasure if you like garlic, as its name suggests. Most mains hover around €20; the snails in garlic sauce are a huge hit.

Lasipalatsi Mannerheimintie 22–24 ⓦ www .ravintola.lasipalatsi.fi. This massive, central restaurant seats 250 and attracts Finns of all shapes and sizes. The upscale Finnish dishes – most around €22 – are tasty enough, though the casual atmosphere and views up and down Mannerheimintie are what draw the crowds. The chef's specialities of lamb Vorschmack and pike perch á la Mannerheim are both excellent.

⚞ **La Societé du Cochon** Mannerheimintie 14 ☎ 020/761 9888, ⓦ www.cochon.fi. Excellent new chic brasserie-like spot that looks onto Mannerheimintie with a casual but upscale setting. Good burgers, roast chicken dishes and great (if small-portioned) salads. Still, you'll be lucky to get out spending under €50, with a starter, main dish and glass of wine.

⚞ **Loft** Yrjönkatu 18 ⓦ www.ravintolaloft.fi. Done up in a minimalist decor of muslin curtains and dark woods, the moody lounge music here aims in part to draw your attention away from the equally minimalist servings of food. Still, the Scandinavian dishes are outstanding, and the generous wine list provides dozens of 75cl-sized excuses for extended afternoon or evening dining.

Mai Thai Annankatu 32 ☎ 09/685 6850. The least expensive and quite possibly the best of the city's crop of Thai restaurants, though it only has seating for about fifteen. Mains from €12, full lunches for under €10. Soups and appetizers are very, very spicy so watch out. Reservations not required, but not a bad idea.

Mamma Rosa Runeberginkatu 55 (see Helsinki map, pp.526–527) ⓦ www.mammarosa.fi. One of the best mid-priced restaurants in the city; unsurprisingly, it's generally full. You're best off with the amply sized pizzas, though there's fish, steaks and pasta, too. Most items cost €9.50.

⚞ **Ravintola Perho** Mechelininkatu 7 (near corner of Hietaniemenkatu) ⓦ www.perho .fi/ravintola. This restaurant of the Finnish Culinary College is one of the last remaining bargains in the city and an excellent choice for lunch. The fish-and-potatoes-style offerings at the tasty all-you-can-eat buffet are superbly prepared and include coffee (from €8.70). Free wi-fi.

Ravintola Suomi Lautasella Lönnrotinkatu 13 ☎ 09/680 3780, ⓦ www.suomiravintola.fi. If your wallet can handle the prices, this is a must while in Helsinki, specializing in real Finnish foods like pea soup and oven pancakes, as well as Sámi specialities of smoked reindeer and warm cloudberries. Count on at least €40 for a three-course meal not including drinks.

Romanov Yrjönkatu 15 ⓦ www.romanov.fi. Old-style Russian restaurant with a deliciously over-the-top spirit-of-the-tsars atmosphere: red velvet carpeting and lavish chairs accentuated by portraits of Russian military victors and noblemen. Lunchtime is popular among office workers, while evenings see more of a tourist crowd. Try the sumptuous grilled spiced steak Romanov (€22). Closed Sat lunch & Sun. If it's too lavish for you here, try their more Soviet-styled *Kasakka*, Meritullinkatu 13 ⓦ www.kasakka.fi.

⚞ **Sea Horse** Kapteeninkatu 11 (see Helsinki map, pp.526–527) ⓦ www.seahorse.fi. Style writer Tyler Brûlé called his meal at this cavernous Helsinki classic one of his best ten ever. It's been around for nearly a century and it feels like it: dim lighting, plain walls and Finnish dishes. It's refreshingly one of the few restaurants left in the capital that doesn't feel like a design museum, and is good for people-watching. Especially renowned for its various fish dishes, which start at €10.

Sipuli Kanavaranta 7 ⓦ www.royalravintolat.com. Set in an old brick warehouse just west of the Uspenski Cathedral, and offering a tastebud-thrilling, formal and glamorous – though financially ruinous – choice of Franco–Finnish gourmet dishes, several based on traditional Sámi fare. Closed weekends.

⚞ **Tori** Punavuorenkatu 2 ⓦ www.ravintolatori .fi. Inexpensive Nordic dishes wolfed down by boho-chic 20-somethings chatting loudly in a space of lounge music. They serve simple Euro-Finnish standbys (mains from €10), but the atmosphere is one of the liveliest you'll find in the city. The terrace facing Frederikintori square makes a great spot to enjoy your breakfast eggs (€3) or a glass of wine in the evening.

Zucchini Fabianinkatu 4. A friendly and stylish lunch-only vegetarian restaurant big on aubergines, courgettes and salads (the veggie lasagne is superb). A filling meal here won't run you more than €10. Closed weekends.

Drinking

Although never cheap, alcohol is far from a dirty word in Finland. In fact, spend a few days in Helsinki and you'll see that getting blotto is a weekly rite of passage for everyone from boppy teen girls to investment bankers. Still, it need not be a binge affair for everyone, and **drinking**, especially beer, can be enjoyed in the city's many café-like pubs, which are where most Helsinki folk go to socialize. You'll find one on virtually every corner, but the pick of the bunch are listed below. The neighbourhood of Punavuori, southwest of the train station, has the highest concentration of places – have a wander along Uudenmaankatu or Iso Roobertinkatu to get a sense for what's on – while some students opt for the cheaper, decadent dives in the Kallio district. Only the really swanky places have a dress code, and they are usually too elitist – and expensive – to be worth bothering with anyway. Most bars are open from the afternoon until 2am, though a few of the more popular ones will keep the juices flowing until 3am or 4am, especially on the weekends. On the whole, Sundays to Thursdays are normally quiet, though Wednesday, known to many locals as *pikkulauantai* ("little Saturday"), can be a popular clubbing night; on Fridays and Saturdays on the other hand, it's best to arrive as early as possible to get a seat without having to queue. Most drinking dives also serve food, although the grub is seldom at its best in the evening (where places are good earlier in the day, we've included them under "Restaurants").

If you want a drink but are feeling antisocial, or just very hard-up, the cheapest method, as ever, is to buy from the appropriately named ALKO shop: there are self-service ones at Fabiankatu 7 and Vuorikatu 7.

Unless otherwise stated, the places listed below appear on the central Helsinki map, pp.528–529.

A21 Annankatu 21. Rather pretentious new cocktail bar with designer seating, lacquered tables and clientele who spend way too much time in front of the mirror. Press the doorbell just outside, and if the bartendress likes the way you look you might actually be let in.

Ateljeebaari *Sokos Torni* hotel, Yrjönkatu 26. On the thirteenth floor of a plush hotel: great views, great posing and pricey drinks – be warned that the women's toilet has bizarre ceiling-to-floor windows.

Baker's Mannerheimintie 12 ⓦ www.ravintola bakers.com. A good place to initiate yourself into drinking Helsinki-style, this central corner restaurant-bar-café-sauna complex has a reputation as a last-chance pick-up spot.

Bar 9 Uudenmaankatu 9 ⓦ www.bar9 .net. This unpretentious neighbourhood bar has been a standby for local artists and hipsters for years, and shows little sign of losing its edge. Good food, too, including massive grilled ham and cheese sandwiches, and occasional live music.

Bar Tapasta Uudenmaankatu 13 ⓦ www .marcante.fi. Small and intimate, with strikingly striped walls, this Parisian-style café-bar is often full and is a regular stop for night owls, with cheap tapas and sangria served until 11.30pm (12.30pm on weekends).

Elite Etläinen Hesperiankatu 22 (see Helsinki map, pp.526–527) ⓦ www.royalravintolat.com.

Northwest of the National Museum, this Art Deco bar-restaurant was once the haunt of the city's artists, many of whom would settle the bill not with money but with paintings – a selection of which line the walls. Especially good in summer, when you can drink on the terrace.

Erottaja Bar Erotajankatu 15–17. Central, aqua-blue bar just up from the Swedish theatre with a bit of an underground feel to it. Tables outside, but great benches and dim lighting inside. Popular with students from Helsinki's art and design school.

Kaarle XII Kasarmikatu 40 ⓦ www.kaarle .com. Friday-night queuing to get into this very casual bar and dance space (known familiarly as "Kaali") is a Helsinki institution for hundreds of people under the age of 40. Inside are six separate battered, old-wood bars, including two inside a large Art Nouveau dance hall with red-granite walls. Show up by 10pm or you might well be waiting for hours.

Kola Helsinginkatu 13 (see Helsinki map, pp.526–527). Manhattan's East Village transplanted to Kallio. Young and hip loungesters sprawl out in this carpeted 1960s-style bar reading design magazines and sipping €3.75 pints or espressos.

Kosmos Kalevankatu 3. This is where the big media cats – TV producers, PR people, the glitzier authors – hang out and engage in loud arguments as the night wears on. The wonderful interior is unchanged since the 1920s, but you'll only see it if you get past the officious doorman.

Loose Fredrikinkatu 34 Ⓦwww.barloose.com. Down-home rock 'n' roll pub done up with Stones photos and paisley wallpaper, and offering pints of beer for €4.

Lost and Found Annankatu 6 Ⓦwww .lostandfound.fi. Known to locals as *lostari*, this one-time straight-friendly gay bar is now a gay-friendly straight bar. Downstairs is a very popular dance club, *Hideaway*, that doesn't feel too Euro-trashy. On weekends around 1am, there's nearly guaranteed to be a queue out front.

mbar Lasipalatsi, Mannerheimintie 22–24 Ⓦwww .mbar.fi. A hip designer place with internet terminals, electronica DJs and the occasional live band. The terrace is very popular in summer.

Meri Makasiini Hietalahdenranta 4 (see Helsinki map, pp.526–527). Slightly out-of-the-way, on a street running off Hietalahdentori towards the waterfront, but worth a visit on a Fri or Sat night when the restaurant customers spill onto the terrace to drink while gazing at the cranes of the city's cargo harbour. Closes at midnight.

Molly Malone's Kaisaniemenkatu 1C Ⓦwww .mollymalones.fi. One of Europe's best Irish bars – and certainly Finland's – is just a few steps from the train station. There's great live Irish music most nights, and it doesn't feel too much like a hackneyed, expat bar.

Rafla Uudenmaankatu 9 Ⓦwww.ravintolarafla .fi. One of the city's newest café-resto-bars is also its least pretentious. After work 30-somethings come here to kick back and watch the world go by.

Rymy-Eetu Erottaja 15 Ⓦwww.rymy-eetu.fi. A new and very un-Finnish bar that requires you sit next to (and maybe speak to!) people you actually don't know. Almost pulls off the Bavarian *bierhalle* look and feel it's going for. Also offers a "retro lunch" weekdays between 11am and 2pm. Regular live music groups, for which there is generally a €2–4 cover.

Teatteri Pohjoisesplanadi 2. Spend a few hours in this indoor and outdoor complex – at first casual and relaxed, later rowdy and inebriated – and you'll encounter a cross-section of Helsinki characters, some of whom you may have to help get up off the ground.

The Rock Bar Bulevardi 28 Ⓦwww.therockbar.fi. True grunge ambience with Anthrax and Megadeth on the tubes, but not so loud that you can't hear yourself ordering. Your fellow drinkers may well be dressed head-to-toe in black grunge clothing, with piercings and tattoos.

Vanha Mannerheimintie 3 Ⓦwww.juhlaravintolat .fi. A self-service and hence comparatively cheap bar. It fills quickly, so try to arrive early for a seat on the balcony overlooking the bustle of the streets below. Downstairs has a more underground feel, with bench seating and a cosy – if smoky – atmosphere. Great people-watching at the busy intersection below.

We Got Beef Iso Roobertinkatu 21. Known in local argot as "Beeffi", this modish bar resembles a well-lit diner, popular with students, artsy types, schmoozers and their arm-candy. DJs spin slamming beats in a back room.

Zetor Kaivopiha, Mannerheimintie 3 Ⓦwww.zetor .net. A loud, country-themed bar designed by the people behind the irreverent Leningrad Cowboys rock group, with a rusty tractor in the middle. An older crowd gets down to hard rock and 1980s tunes, and after midnight the kitchen serves a limited menu of basic grub – think meatballs and potatoes – until 3.30am.

Live music, clubs and entertainment

Helsinki probably has a greater number of ways to spend the evening than any other Scandinavian city; there is, for example, a steady diet of **live music**. Finnish rock bands, not helped by the awkward metre of their native language, often sound absurd on first hearing, but at least seeing them is relatively cheap at €10–15 – around half the price of seeing a British or American band – and sometimes even free. The best gigs tend to be during term-time, but in summer there are dozens of free events in the city parks, the biggest of which take place almost every Sunday in Kaivopuisto. Many bands also play on selected nights in one of the growing number of surprisingly hip **clubs and discos**, in which you can gyrate, pose or just drink into the small hours – admission is usually around €5–10.

For up-to-the-minute details of **what's on**, read the entertainment page of *Helsingin Sanomat* or the free fortnightly paper *City* (found in record shops, bookshops and department stores), which has listings in English covering rock and classical music, clubs, cinema, theatre and opera. The Lasipalatsi (see p.546) has a youth service centre with information on festivals, concerts and events, or else simply watch out for posters on the streets. **Tickets** for most events can be bought at the venue or, for a small commission, at Tiketti, Yrjönkatu 29C on the third floor of Forum shopping centre, Mannerheimintie 18 (Mon–Fri 10am–7pm, Sat 10am–4pm; ☎0600/11 616, toll call, ✆www.tiketti.fi).

In terms of **cinema**, both the latest blockbusters and a good selection of fringe **films** are normally showing somewhere in Helsinki. A seat is usually €9–11, although some places offer a €6.50 matinee show. Check the listings in *City* (see p.548) or pick up a copy of *Elokuva-Viikko*, a free weekly leaflet that lists the cinemas and their programmes; it's available at the cinemas themselves. English-language films are shown with Finnish subtitles – there's no overdubbing. The Finnish Film Archive's theatre Orion, Eerikinkatu 15 (☎09/685 2546, ✆www.kava.fi/esitykset), screens art-house films three to four times daily. For Hollywood blockbusters and Finnish films, the megaplexes to head for are Tennispalatsi, Salomonkatu 15, and Kinopalatsi, just east of the train station at Kaisaniemenkatu 2 (☎0600/007 007, ✆www.finnkino.fi).

Clubs and music venues

Clubs in Helsinki change ownership, style and format with baffling rapidity, and the listings below are only a pointer to what may be on offer. For up-to-the-moment information, check out the city's listings magazines, or head for the club-heavy streets Iso Roobertinkatu and Frederikinkatu in Punavuori. Most clubs operate Wednesday to Saturday from 10pm until 4am, though some occasionally will open a bit earlier; when there is a cover charge, it shouldn't ever be more than €10, quite possibly half that. Another venue to check out is the *Kaapelitehdas*, which regularly organizes mammoth, deafening raves. If you're lucky enough to be in town to catch it, *Unity* (✆www.clubunity.org) is a dance extravaganza put on several times a summer on the nearby island of Uunisaari, offering spectacular DJs, gorgeous people and nonstop dancing till dawn. Tickets sell out almost before they go on sale, so plan well ahead.

Helmi Eerikinkatu 14 ✆www.helmi.net. Very crowded and loud resto-bar with padded beige sitting spaces and a well-stocked bar. A favourite among investment bankers, ad execs and lawyers.

Kaivohuone Kaivopuisto Park. One of the city's longest established late-night party spots and still an excellent choice for a Fri or Sat night, when those in the know come to Kaivopuisto's leafy environs to dance, drink and join the very long taxi queues for home.

Lux Urho Kekkosenkatu 1A ✆www.luxnightclub.fi. This extremely popular sprawling nightclub consists of several levels, multiple black-marble dancefloors, large terrace lounges and a couple of VIP rooms you won't ever set foot in. Set in the penthouse of the Kamppi shopping centre.

Redrum Kluuvikatu 3. This downstairs dance club has a group of DJs who hypnotize the crowd from their central throne. Younger clientele often able to slip their way in despite the over-21 stipulation.

Rose Garden Iso Roobertinkatu 10 ✆www.clubrosegarden.com. Large, labyrinthine lounge bar-cum-club with DJs playing in various themed rooms. It can get pretty hot in here when it packs in the weekend crowds after midnight; enter below the neon "Swengi" sign and head towards the silver door in the back.

Storyville Museokatu 8 ✆www.storyville.fi. Buzzing jazz joint, with live Dixieland, swing or bebop on stage every night. In the summer there's music outside on the idyllic garden terrace until 9pm. Cover is always under €10, and you can eat a pricey and filling Finnish dinner at your table. Kitchen open until 3.30am.

Studio 51 Frederikinkatu 51–53 ✆www.studio51.fi. Built in the image of New York's Studio 54 and with a deliberately decadent 1970s decor of sequined walls, red mood lighting and large disco balls, this is Helsinki's largest club, and it's recently been through a comprehensive renovation. A good place to visit after you've exhausted yourself everywhere else and are on the hunt for a second wind.

Tavastia Urho Kekkosenkatu 4–6 ✆www.tavastiaklubi.fi. The country's premier rock club, and a major showcase for Finnish and Swedish bands. Downstairs holds the stage and self-service bar; the balcony is waitress service. Next door, *Semifinal* is much smaller but similar in clientele.

Vanha Ylioppilastalo Mannerheimintie 3 ✆www.vanha.fi. The main venue for leading indie bands from around the world, just next to Stockmann's department store.

Gay Helsinki

Always the slowest of the Scandinavian countries to reform sexuality laws, Finland finally decriminalized homosexuality in 1971 and passed partnership laws in 2002. These days, public displays of affection are accepted, while the **gay scene** in Helsinki has flourished in recent years: today there's a gay choir, an annual pride parade in late June, an LBT culture festival in mid September and an impressive number of exclusively gay and gay-friendly establishments, the latter clustered around **Eerikinkatu** and the southern end of **Mannerheimintie**. For the latest details, pick up a copy of the monthly *Voltti* **magazine** – in Finnish only but with a useful listings section (ⓦwww.voltti-lehti.fi); it's widely available in larger newsagents, or from the state-supported gay and lesbian organization SETA, Mannerheimintie 170A (ⓣ09/681 2580, ⓦwww.seta.fi).

DTM (Don't Tell Mamma) Iso Roobertinkatu 28 ⓦwww.dtm.fi. Known to regulars as *mama* or *mummola*, this legendary gay and lesbian nightclub is among the best known in Europe. The disco was completely renovated in 2007, and it is still *the* place to go, with great house music most nights and regular drag shows and special events. During the day, the downstairs café offers breakfasts, pastries, snacks, coffee and free wi-fi.

Fairy Tale Helsinginkatu 7 ⓦwww.fairytale.fi. Dark and intimate little place primarily frequented by older men. Pints €2.90 until 8pm. Ring the doorbell to get in.

Hercules Lönnrotinkatu 4b ⓦwww.hercules gayclub.com. Not quite as trendy as *DTM*, this club

is quite popular with young, leather-clad men and plays a variety of music.

Mann's Street Mannerheimintie 12 (upstairs) ⓦwww.mannsstreet.com. If you're looking for karaoke, Finnish music and older gay men, you'll find generous helpings here.

Nalle Pub Kaarlenkatu 3–5 (upstairs) ⓦwww .nallepub.fi. A relaxing place that feels like some- what of a living room, this Kallio spot is a lesbian favourite. While you're sipping on bottle of Bud you can watch TV, pop a euro in for a song on the jukebox or read a paper. Happy hour daily 3–6pm.

Room Albert Kalevankatu 36 ⓦwww.roombar.fi. Recently relocated, this is one of Helsinki's better neighbourhood bars; a laid-back place that attracts the young, beautiful and leather-clad.

Listings

Airlines British Airways, Vantaa airport ⓣ09/6937 9538; Finnair, Finnair City Terminal, Elielin Aukio (next to the train station) ⓣ09/818 800; SAS, Vantaa airport ⓣ06/0002/5831; Blue1 same info as SAS. **Airport Enquiries** ⓣ09/8277 3103.
American Express Arkadiankatu 2 (Mon–Fri 9am–4pm; ⓣ09/6132 0400). After hours and for lost cards call ⓣ0800/114 646.
Banks and exchange As well as the banks dotted all around the city (Mon–Fri 9.15am–4.15pm), the bank at the airport opens long hours (daily 6am–10pm), and there's an exchange counter at Katajanokka harbour, where Viking and Finnjet ferries dock (Mon–Sat 10–11.30am, 4–5.30pm & 7.30–9.15pm, Sun 10–11.30am, 4–5.30pm & 6.30–8pm). The Forex desk in the Central Railway Station (daily 8am–9pm) and Otto, opposite the station (Mon–Fri 8am–8pm, Sat 10am–6pm), handle cash advances on all major cards.
Bike rental GreenBike Mannerheimintie 13, just under the bridge opposite the parliament building (daily 10am–6pm, sometimes until 8pm; €15 per day; ⓣ05/0404/0400, ⓦwww.greenbike.fi).

Bookshops Akateeminen Kirjakauppa, Pohjoisesplanadi 39 (ⓦwww.akateeminen.com), has the city's largest selection of books (many in English), magazines and newspapers. Suomalainen Kirjakauppa, Aleksanterinkatu 23, sells fewer titles but offers regular discounts, especially on phrase- books and dictionaries (ⓦwww.suomalainen.com).
Bus enquiries Long-distance buses ⓣ09/682 701 or 0200/4000; city buses ⓣ09/310 1071.
Car rental Avis, Pohjoinen Hiehtaniemenkatu 6 ⓣ09/441 155; Budget, Malminkatu 24 ⓣ020/746 6600; Europcar, Elielinaukio ⓣ09/4780 2220.
Dentist Dentarium (Mon–Fri 8am–5pm), Mikonkatu 8A, 7th floor ⓣ09/622 1533 or 05/0552 7295. Hammassairaala Oral (Mon–Fri 8am–8pm, occasionally later and on weekends), Erottajankatu 5A ⓣ010/400 3000 or 0600/97070, ⓦwww .hammassairaalaoral.fi). Expect to pay €30–50 for a consultation.
Doctor ⓣ09/3106 3231.
Embassies Canada, Pohjoisesplanadi 25B ⓣ09/228 530; UK, Itäinen Puistotie 17

Ferries from Helsinki to Estonia

Following Estonia's regaining of its independence and membership in the EU, a growing number of passenger vessels are plying the 85-kilometre route across the Baltic between Helsinki and the Estonian capital, Tallinn. EU citizens as well as Americans, Canadians, Australians and New Zealanders no longer need a visa but other nationalities should check the latest situation at the tourist office in Helsinki.

Estonia and Finland have similar languages, a common ancestry, and histories which had largely run parallel up until the Soviet Union's annexation of Estonia in 1940. Despite the decades of Soviet occupation, **Tallinn**, within its medieval walls, is a beautifully maintained Hanseatic city with many museums and some fine old churches, all just a few minutes' walk from the harbour – its entire old town is a UNESCO World Heritage Site. If you have time, take a look, too, at the enormous Song Festival Grounds just outside the old centre, scene of the much-publicized pro-independence rallies of the late 1980s.

While independence and EU citizenship has brought Estonia's culturally rich population many new freedoms and opportunities, it hasn't yet brought them any money. The introduction of the kroon (rhymes with "prawn", not "prune"), a new version of the pre-Soviet currency, ultimately did rather little to ease the uphill struggle faced by the country's economy and although development was slow after independence, many believe that EU membership will solidify Estonia's role as a northern European transport hub.

Crossings (1hr 30min–3hr 15min) are offered by Tallink (tickets from South Harbour booking office; ℡09/228 311, ⓦwww.tallink.fi); Linda Line, Makasiini Terminal (℡09/668 97060, ⓦwww.lindaline.fi); Nordic Jet Line, Kanavaterminaali, Katajanokan-laituri (℡09/681 770, ⓦwww.njl.fi); Silja Line, Olympiaterminaali (℡09/180 4422, ⓦwww.silja.fi); SuperSeaCat (T0600/11 112, ⓦwww.superseacat.com); Eckerö Line (℡09/2288 544, ⓦwww.eckeroline.fi); and Viking Line (09/123 5300, ⓦwww.vikingline.fi). Expect to pay €10 72 for a one way ticket; cars cost €19–67. You can find day returns for under €40. Note that the ferry terminal in Tallinn has left-luggage facilities. Buying in advance gets you the cheapest tickets, but look out for last-minute bargains in travel agency windows and on the front page of *Helsingin Sanomat*. If you're really pressed for time, Copterline (℡0200/18 181, ⓦwww.copterline.com) offers eighteen-minute helicopter shuttles between the two cities from €89 each way.

℡09/2286 5100; US, Itäinen Puistotie 14A ℡09/616 250. Citizens of Australia and New Zealand should contact the Australian embassy in Stockholm (see p.387).

Emergencies Ambulance and police ℡112. For non-urgent ambulance, ring ℡09 394 600; non-urgent police matters ring ℡09/1891.

Ferries Reservations and information: Tallink Silja Line ℡09/18 041, ⓦwww.tallinksilja.fi; Viking Line ℡09/123 51, ⓦwww.vikingline.fi.

Hospital Marian Hospital, Lapinlahdenkatu 16 ℡4711 or 09/4716 3339.

Internet access *Café Aalto*, Akateeminen kirjapauppa, Keskuskatu 1, 2nd floor; Telecenter, Vuorikatu 8; *Netcup*, Aleksanterinkatu 52. In the Lasipalatsi, Mannerheimintie 22–24, there's *mbar*. Helsinki's tourist office and main post office each have several free terminals.

Late shopping Stockmann is open Mon–Fri until 10pm, Sat & Sun until 6pm. The shops in Tunneli,

the underground complex by the train station, are open Mon–Sat 10am–10pm, Sun noon–10pm.

Laundry Rööperin pesulapalvelut, Punavuorenkatu 3 (Mon–Thurs 8am–8pm, Fri 8am–6pm, Sat 10am–3pm, Sun noon–4pm); *Café Tin Tin Tango*, Töölöntorinkatu 7 (Mon–Thurs 7am–midnight, Fri & Sat 9am–2am, Sun 10am–midnight; ring ℡09/2709 0972 to reserve).

Left luggage There are lockers (around €4) in the long-distance bus station (Mon–Thurs & Sat 9am–6pm, Fri 8am–6pm), or in the train station (Mon–Fri 7am–10pm).

Libraries (*kirjasto*) Central branches at Topeliuksenkatu 6 in Töölö, at Rikhardinkatu 3 near Esplanadi (both Mon–Thurs 10am–8pm, Fri 10am–6pm Sat 10am–4pm, Sun noon–4pm) and Elielinaukio 2G (Mon–Thurs 10am–10pm, Fri 10am–6pm Sat & Sun noon–6pm).

Lost property (*löytötavaratoimisto*) Päijänteentie 12A, 3rd floor (Mon–Fri 10am–2pm; ℡09/189 3180).

Maps Karttakeskus, Vuorikatu 14 (Mon–Fri 9am–6pm, Sat 10am–4pm; ⓦ www.karttakeskus.fi).

Newspapers Almost every central Helsinki newsstand stocks some UK or US papers. Try at the train station, the airport or inside Stockmann department store.

Pharmacy Yliopiston Apteekki (☎ 0300 20 200, toll call), Mannerheimintie 96 is open 24hr; its branch at Mannerheimintie 5/Kaivopiha is open daily 7am–midnight.

Police Pieni Roobertinkatu 1–3 ☎ 112 (emergencies) ☎ 09/1891 (non-emergencies).

Post office The main office is at Elielinaukio1A (Mon–Fri 8am–8pm, Sat & Sun 9am–2pm); poste restante at the rear door (Mon–Sat 8am–10pm, Sun 11am–10pm). Stamps are available from post offices or the yellow machines in shops.

Telephone enquiries ☎ 118 or ☎ 020202.

Train enquiries ☎ 0600 41 902 (toll call) or 09 2319 2902.

Travel agents Kilroy Travels, Kaivokatu 10D/Kaivopiha (☎ 02 0354 5769, ⓦ www.kilroytravels .fi), is the Scandinavian youth travel agent, specializing in discounted tickets for students and young people. Suomen Matkatoimisto (SMT), the Finland Travel Bureau, Kaivokatu 10A (☎ 09/18 261, ⓦ www.smt.fi), organizes trips to Russia and the necessary visas.

Around Helsinki

There's not a whole lot in Helsinki's outlying area that's worth venturing out for, but if you have a bit of time there are three places – all done in one easy day-trip from the city – that merit a visit: the visionary suburbs of **Espoo**; the home of the composer Sibelius at **Järvenpää**; and the evocative old town of **Porvoo**, which also serves as an obvious access point to the underrated southeastern corner of the country.

The Espoo area

Lying west of Helsinki, the suburban area of **Espoo** (Esbo in Swedish) comprises several separate districts. The one nearest to Helsinki, directly across the bay, is the "garden city" of **TAPIOLA**. In the 1950s, Finnish urban planners attempted to blend new housing schemes with the surrounding forests and hills, frequently only to be left with a compromise that turned ugly as expansion occurred. Tapiola was the exception to this rule, built as a self-contained living area rather than a dormitory town, with alternating high and low buildings, abundant open areas, parks, fountains and swimming pools. Much praised on its completion by the architectural world, it's still refreshing to wander through and admire the idea and its execution. The **tourist office** at Tapiontori 3A (daily 9am–5pm; ☎ 09/8164 7230, ⓦ www.espootravel.com) handles enquiries about the whole Espoo area.

About 3km north of Tapiola, the traffic-filled Hagalundintie brings you to the little peninsula of **Otaniemi** and a couple more notable architectural sites. One of these is the Alvar Aalto–designed campus of Helsinki University's technology faculty; the other – far more dramatic – is the Dipoli student union building on the same campus. Ever keen to harmonize the artificial with the natural, architects Reimi and Raili Pietilä here created a building that appears to be fused to the rocky crags above, the front of the structure daringly edging forward from the cliff face.

Though the town of Espoo itself has little to delay you, just beyond lies the hugely absorbing **Hvitträsk** (daily: May–Sept 11am–6pm; Oct–April 11am–5pm; €5), the studio-home built and shared by architects Eliel Saarinen, Armas Lindgren and Herman Gesellius until 1904, when their partnership dissolved amid the acrimony caused by Saarinen's independent (and winning) design for Helsinki's train station. Externally, this is an extended and romanticized version of the traditional Finnish log cabin, the leafy branches that creep around making the structure look like a mutant growth emerging from the forest. Inside are frescoes by Gallen-Kallela and changing exhibitions of Finnish art and handicrafts. Saarinen and his wife are buried in the grounds.

Frequent buses run throughout the day from Helsinki's long-distance bus station **to Tapiola**, but you usually need to request them to stop there; check details and times at the bus station or the City Tourist Office. To get from central Helsinki **to Hvitträsk**, take the local (line L) train to Louma (37min) and follow the signs for 3km, or take bus #166 from Helsinki (55min). To get to **Otaniemi** from central Helsinki, take bus #102 or #103 (20min); from Tapiola, take bus #2, #4 or #195 (5min).

Järvenpää: Ainola

Around 40km north of Helsinki in **JÄRVENPÄÄ**, easily reached by either bus or train, is **Ainola** (May–Sept Tues–Sun 10am–5pm; €5.50) – the house where Jean Sibelius lived from 1904 with his wife, Aino (sister of the artist Eero Järnefelt), after whom the place is named.

Though now regarded as one of the twentieth century's greatest composers, **Jean Sibelius**, born in Hämeenlinna in 1865, had no musical background, and by the age of 19 was enrolled on a law course at Helsinki University. He had, however, developed a youthful passion for the violin and took a class at the capital's Institute of Music. Law was soon forgotten as Sibelius's real talents were recognized, and his musical studies took him to the cultural hotbeds of the day, Berlin and Vienna. Returning to Finland to teach at the Institute, Sibelius soon gained a government grant, which enabled him to begin composing full time, the first concert of his works taking place in 1892. His early pieces were inspired by the Finnish folk epic, the *Kalevala*, and by the nationalist movement of the times; in 1899 the country's Russian rulers banned performances of Sibelius's rousing *Finlandia* under any name that suggested its patriotic sentiment – it was instead published simply as "Opus 26 No. 7".

While the overtly nationalistic elements in Sibelius's work mellowed in later years, his music continued to reflect a very Finnish obsession with nature: "Other composers offer their public a cocktail," he said, "I offer mine pure spring water." He is still revered in his own land, although he was also notorious for his bouts of heavy drinking, and a destructive quest for perfection which fuelled suspicion that he had completed, and destroyed, two symphonies during his final thirty years. This was an angst-ridden period when no new work appeared, which became known as "the silence from Järvenpää". Sibelius died in 1957, his best-known symphonies setting a standard that younger Finnish composers have only just begun to approach.

The house is just the kind of home you'd expect for a man who included representations of flapping swans' wings in his music: a tranquil place, close to lakes and forests. The wood-filled grounds are as atmospheric as the building, which is a place of pilgrimage for devotees, although books, furnishings and a few paintings are all there is to see. His grave is in the grounds, marked by a marble stone inscribed simply with his name. For more tangible Sibelius memories, and more of his music, visit the Sibelius Museum in Turku (see p.562).

While in Järvenpää, it would be a pity to miss out on a visit to the **Halosenniemi Museum** (Tues–Sun: May–Aug 10am–6pm; Sept–April noon–5pm; €5.50). On the Tuusula Lakeside road, just a few minutes' walk from Ainola, this is the rustic home of Pekka Halonen, one of Finland's most renowned artists. A beautifully serene place, its National Romantic decor has been painstakingly restored and now houses some of Halonen's pictures and painting materials in their original setting.

Porvoo

Some 50km northeast of Helsinki, **PORVOO** (Borgå in Swedish) is one of the oldest towns on the south coast. Lined by small wooden buildings, its narrow cobbled streets give a sense of the Finnish life that predated the capital's bold squares and Neoclassical geometry. This, coupled with its elegant riverside setting and unhurried mood, means you're unlikely to be alone – word of Porvoo's peaceful time-locked qualities has spread.

First stop should be the **tourist office** at Rihkamakatu 4 (July & Aug Mon–Fri 9am–6pm, Sat & Sun 10am–4pm; Sept–June Mon–Fri 9.30am–4.30pm, Sat 10am–2pm; ⓣ019/520 2316, ⓦwww.porvoo.fi), for a free map of the town. For something more historic, look in at the preserved **Johan Ludwig Runeberg House**, Aleksanterinkatu 3 (May–Aug daily 10am–4pm, Sun 11am–5pm; Sept–April Wed–Sat 10am–4pm, Sun 11am–5pm; €5), where the man regarded as Finland's national poet lived from 1852 while a teacher at the town school. Despite writing in Swedish, Runeberg greatly aided the nation's sense of self-esteem, especially with *Tales of Vänrikki Ståhl*, which told of the people's struggles with Russia in the 1808–09 conflict. The first poem in his collection, *Our Land*, later provided the lyrics for the national anthem. Across the road, the **Walter Runeberg Gallery** (same hours Runeberg House; ticket valid for both) displays a collection of works by Runeberg's third son, one of Finland's more celebrated sculptors. Among many acclaimed pieces, he's responsible for the statue of his father that stands in the centre of Helsinki's Esplanadi.

The old town (follow the signs for "Vanha Porvoo") is built around the hill on the other side of Mannerheimkatu. Near the top, its outline partially obscured by vegetation, is the fifteenth-century **Tuomiokirkko**. It was here in 1809 that Alexander I proclaimed Finland a Russian Grand Duchy, himself Grand Duke, and convened the first Finnish Diet. Tragically, the church was partially destroyed in a fire in 2006 started by three local teens. The gabled roof was ruined, windows were broken, chandeliers fell and the structure was charred, but a two-year renovation project has brought it up to scratch again in 2009. Check with the tourist office for the latest visiting hours. Along with other aspects of the town's past, the church can be further explored in the **Porvoo Museum** (May–Aug Mon–Sat 10am–4pm, Sun 11am–4pm; Sept–April Wed–Sun noon–4pm; €5) at the foot of the hill in the old town's main square. There are no singularly outstanding exhibits here, just a diverting selection of furnishings, musical instruments and general oddities, largely dating from the years of Russian rule.

Practicalities

Buses run all day from Helsinki to Porvoo from the long-distance bus station; the thirty-minute trip costs around €8–12, depending on type of bus and time of departure. Idling around the town is especially pleasant late in the day as the evening stillness descends; the last bus back to the city conveniently departs around midnight. There are also a couple of **boats** from Helsinki in summer: the *J.L. Runeberg* (May, June & Aug Tues & Wed, Sat & Sun, also Fri in May; July daily; €33 return) departs at 10am, arrives at 1.20pm, and departs for Helsinki at 4pm; and the quicker *M.S. RoyalCat* or *M.S. Katarina* (late June to mid-Aug Tues–Sun 10am; €39 one-way), which arrives at 1pm and leaves Porvoo at 3.30pm. The outbound trip includes a meal of salmon soup. Tickets for both boats can be bought from their respective ticket offices in the *kauppatori* in Helsinki.

If you've exhausted Helsinki, **spending a night** in Porvoo leaves you well placed to continue into Finland's southeastern corner. If possible, try to arrange accommodation while in Helsinki, particularly if you're after hotel bargains – rates in Porvoo can be rather steep. There is, however, a **youth hostel**, open all year, at Linnankoskenkatu 1 (ⓣ019/523 0012, ⓦwww.porvoohostel.cjb.net; dorms €16; double rooms ❺). *Hotel Porvoon Mitta*, Jokikatu 43, is a gorgeous family-run guesthouse with classically designed rooms (ⓣ019/580 131, ⓦwww.hotelporvoonmitta.fi; ❻). There's a summer **campsite** (ⓣ019/581 967; June to late Aug) 2km from the town centre. For **eating**, *Sevilla*, Mannerheiminkatu 9, has good Spanish food, and there's decent café fare at the charming *Helmi*, Välikatu 7. In summertime, riverside Wilhelm Å, Jokiranta, is a superb place to come for a filling meal and a drink at sunset. Or have a drink at friendly *Glory Days*, on Raukanhatu by the market square.

The Southeast

As it's some way from the major centres, foreign tourists tend to neglect the extreme **southeastern corner** of Finland; Finns, however, rate it highly, flocking here to make boat trips around the islands and to explore the many small communities, which combine a genuine rustic flavour with sufficient places of minor interest to keep boredom at bay. For Finns, the region also stirs memories: its position on the Soviet border means it saw many battles during the Winter and Continuation wars, and throughout medieval times it was variously under the control of Sweden and Russia. It's an intriguing area, worth two or three days of travel – most of it will be by bus, since rail lines are almost nonexistent.

East toward Kotka

If Porvoo seems too tourist-infested, make the 40km journey east to **LOVIISA**, an eighteenth-century fishing village pleasantly free from Helsinki day-trippers. The village, whose 7500-strong population divides into equal numbers of Finnish and Swedish speakers, is overlooked by the two old **fortresses** of Rosen and Ungern, both worth exploring. The **tourist office** Tullisilta 5 (June–Aug Mon–Fri 9am–4pm, Sat 10am–3pm; Sept–May Mon–Fri 9am 4pm; ℡019/555 234, ⓦwww.loviisa.fi), can supply details of how to get to them; off the square, a row of prettily preserved houses points the way to the **Municipal Museum** (June to early Sept Tues–Sun 11am 4pm; Sept–May Tues–Fri & Sun noon–4pm; €4), containing, besides the usual local hotchpotch of bits and pieces, a fine stock of romantic postcards. Later on, if you have the cash, spend it on a slap-up meal at *Degerby Gille*, Sepänkuja 4 (℡019/50 561, ⓦwww .degerby.com; ❹/❺), a restaurant set in a seventeenth-century house that's one of the town's most important historical sights; the menu offers tasty dishes such as smoked salmon or reindeer filet for €21. If you don't eat here, poke your head around the door anyway to marvel at the wonderfully maintained interior; the fifty hotel rooms, though well proportioned, are in an uninspiring annexe round the corner.

In the bay off Loviisa, some 13km distant, there's a less welcome modern sight – the oldest of the country's **nuclear power plants**. Finland's Cold War balancing act between East and West led to the country buying its nuclear hardware from both power blocs; this one spent the last few decades producing plutonium for (allegedly) Soviet nuclear weapons, and its run-off nuclear waste was exported to Russia for disposal – though this practice has now been made illegal. The other, Western-backed, plants are housed at Olkiluoti (near Rauma), but at the centre of the power debate these days is the construction of a fifth nuclear reactor – to be the world's most powerful – which is meant to be up and running by 2011. Parliament approved the project to help Finland meet its greenhouse gas emission targets, but the nation is somewhat divided over the merits of nuclear power in general: the country takes just under thirty percent of its energy from nuclear sources, but a growing anti-nuclear movement is calling for a switch to hydroelectric power. Whatever the outcome of the debate, mindful of the design flaws in Soviet-built reactors, the view from Louviisa is an unnerving one.

If you have the time, a couple of smaller settlements between Loviisa and Kotka can comfortably consume half a day. In 1809, the Swedish–Russian border was drawn up in this area, splitting the region of Pyhää in two. Some 20km from Loviisa is **RUOTSINPYHTÄÄ** (Strömfors in Swedish), whose local **information centre** (June–Aug daily 8am–4pm; 044/363 6616 ⓦwww .ruotsinpyhtaa.fi) is diplomatically positioned within a café on the bridge over the inlet that once divided the two feuding empires; in the winter, you'll need to contact the municipality (℡019/557 700). Historical quirks aside, the main attraction here is the seventeenth-century **ironworks**, now turned into craft studios, with demonstrations of carpet-weaving, jewellery-making and painting – all quite enjoyable to stroll around on a sunny day. You might also want to visit the oddly octagonal-shaped **wooden church** (mid-June to mid-Aug daily 11am–6pm) to admire Helene Schjerfbeck's beautiful altarpiece of the Resurrection. It was here, incidentally, that a Finnish TV company filmed a very popular soap opera, *Vihreän Kullanmaa* ("The Land of the Green Gold"), making good use of the contrast between the spacious mill-owners' houses and the cramped workers' cottages. There is also a simple, inexpensive **hostel** here, the *Krouvimäki Hostel* (book with information centre), with rooms for €50 in summer, €40 in winter.

The village of **PYHTÄÄ** is a twenty-minute bus ride further east. The municipality office at Siltakyläntie 175 can provide limited tourist information (Mon–Fri 8am–3.45pm; ☎020/721 1600, ⓦwww.pyhtaa.fi) on the town's **stone church** (June–Aug daily 11am–4pm; mid-Aug to May Sun 10–noon, at other times ring church office 05/343 1921); dated at around 1300, it's one of the oldest in the country. The interior frescoes are primitive and strangely moving, and were discovered only recently when the Reformation-era whitewash was removed. From the quay on the other side of the village's sole street there's a ferry service to the nearby islands, including Kaunissaari ("Beautiful Island"), where you can connect with an evening motorboat straight on to Kotka (see below).

The land route to Kotka takes you through **SILTAKYLÄ**, a small town significant only for the hills around it (for tourist information contact Pyhtää town hall; number above). Walks through this lovely landscape afford great views over a dramatic legacy of the Ice Age: spooky Tolkienesque forests and many miles of a red-granite stone known as *rapakivi* that's unique to southeast Finland, covered by a white moss. A number of waymarked hiking trails lead through the landscape, which is strewn with giant boulders – some are as big as four-storey buildings and support their own little ecosystems of plant life. After a day's trek, you can reward yourself with food and drink – or even a swim – at the reasonably priced *Merihotelli Mäntyniemi* (☎05/353 3084, ⓦwww.merihotellimantyniemi.com; ❸/❹), 15km east on Munapirtti island, with simple balconied doubles and a sauna.

Kotka to the Russian border

After the scattering of little communities east of Porvoo, **KOTKA**, a few kilometres on from Siltakylä, seems immense. Built on an island in the Gulf of Finland, Kotka's past reflects its proximity to the sea. Numerous battles have been fought off its shores, among them the Sweden–Russia confrontation of 1790, the largest battle ever seen in Nordic waters: almost 10,000 people lost their lives. Sixty-odd years later during the Crimean War, the British fleet reduced Kotka virtually to rubble. In modern times, though, the sea has been the basis of the town's prosperity: sitting at the end of the Kymi River and boasting a deep-water harbour, the town makes a perfect cargo transit point – causing most locals to live in fear of a major accident occurring in the industrial section, or in the freight yards. Only two roads link Kotka to the mainland and a speedy evacuation of its inhabitants would be almost impossible.

The town itself doesn't have a huge amount to offer to visitors, though there a few ways to while away an afternoon. Kotka's newest claim to fame is the **Maretime Center Vellamo** (Tues–Sun 11am–6pm, Wed until 8pm; €8; ⓦwww.merikeskus vellamo.fi), Tornatorintie 99A, at the port, Finland's new national maritime museum relocated from Helsinki in summer 2008. This engaging exhibition space – held in a gorgeous ultra-modern triangular building worth a look alone – displays thousands of maps, drawings and marine paraphernalia that together illustrate the nation's profound historical dependence on the sea.

If the life aquatic isn't your thing, spend some time touring the eighteenth-century Orthodox **St Nicolai kirkko** (June–Aug Tues–Fri noon–3pm, Sat & Sun noon–6pm), a sizeable structure which has been kept in pristine condition

Trips to Russia

Overland from Helsinki

Two trains – one Finnish and one Russian – leave Helsinki every morning (Finnish train; 7.23am) and afternoon (Russian train; 3.23pm) for the six- or seven-hour trip to St Petersburg; there's also an overnight 14hr Russian train to Moscow, which stops briefly in St Petersburg and which departs Helsinki at 6.23pm. All border formalities are carried out on the train, but you must have a Russian visa before you leave – the tourist office has a list of travel agencies that can arrange these, though be warned that they take a week to process. A one-way second-class ticket to St Petersburg on both the Finnish and Russian trains costs €54.80 including seat reservation; a sleeping compartment to Moscow costs €85.

Day cruises

If sailing to St Petersburg for a short visit sounds more attractive, Stella Lines operates overnight trips every other day throughout the year. The ferry departs Helsinki's Olympia Terminal, off Laivasillankatu, at 6pm or 7pm, arriving in St Petersburg at 8.30am (or 9.30am) the following morning and returning at 8pm the next day, arriving Helsinki 8.30am; all-inclusive return packages with cabin start at €115 (one-way without a cabin is €50, so it makes sense to get a cabin if you're coming back). If you're a Scandinavian or EU citizen, you can get a Russian group visa through a group such as Russian Tours (Ⓦwww.lahialuematkat.fi) for €55, but you must apply a week in advance. Irregular overnight cruises also leave from Lappeenranta for the Russian city of Vyborg (Viipuri), allowing several hours ashore before returning to Finland (see p.589).

after surviving the British bombardment, and houses a number of well-preserved icons, including the exquisite St Nicholas on Kotka Island, gilded and brooding in the afternoon *ruska* light. Another option is a visit to the **Langinkoski Imperial Fishing Lodge** (May daily 10am–4pm; June–Aug daily 10am–6pm; Sept & Oct Sat & Sun 10am–4pm; €5), off the main island, about 5km north of the town centre (bus #12). It was here that Tsar Alexander III would relax in transit between Helsinki and St Petersburg; the wooden building, a gift to him from the Finnish government, is most striking for its simplicity and the attractive setting in the woods near the fast-flowing Kymi River. Opportunities for salmon and sea trout fly fishing abound here, and the lodge can organize permits and equipment rental.

Practicalities

Rail and road connections bring you right into the compact centre, where the **tourist office** at Kirkkokatu 3 (late June to early Aug Mon–Fri 9am–6pm, Sun 10am–2pm; early Aug to late June Mon–Fri 9am–5pm; Ⓣ05/234 4424, Ⓦwww .kotka.fi) will fill you in on local bus details – essential for continuing around the southeast.

Grumbling stomachs can be quietened in *Canttiini*, Kaivokatu 15, an excellent Tex-Mex **restaurant** that also serves up Finnish dishes, pastas and steaks. Alternatively, try *Kotkan Klubi* (Ⓦwww.kotkanklubi.fi; closed Sun), Korkkokatu 2, which has an excellent buffet lunch for €9.90. Although Kotka is no longer popular with Eastern European sailors due to shorter onshore times, there is still a lively bar scene – the best pub in town is *Jaakko* at Kirkkokatu 10, although the Irish bar *Karoliina*, Puutarhakatu 1, puts up strong competition. A good-value **hotel** is the pleasant *Merikotka*, Satamakatu 9 (Ⓣ05/215 222, Ⓦwww.hotellimerikotka.fi; ❹/❺), offering bright, well-decorated rooms, or there's the more upmarket *Seurahuone*, Keskuskatu 21 (Ⓣ05/35 035, Ⓦwww.sokoshotels.fi; ❹/❺). The nearest guesthouse, *Kärkisaari*, is 6km north of Kotka in Mussalo (bus #13 and #27), overlooking a spectacular bay (Ⓣ05/260 4804, Ⓦwww.villakarkisaari.com; mid-May to mid-Sept; ❸), where there's also a beachside holiday village (☎05/260 5055, ⓦwww.santalahti.fi) with **camping** spaces and cabins (€65); it's open late April to early October only.

Hamina and east to the Russian border

Twenty-six kilometres east of Kotka lies **HAMINA**, founded in 1653 and sporting a magnificently bizarre town plan, the main streets branching out of and forming concentric circles around the central plaza. It was built this way to allow the incumbent Swedish forces to withstand attack – the town being the site of many Swedish–Russian battles. You can still amble around the base of the original defending wall, preserved and restored in various parts; follow the signs to the "bastoni" from the centre. Besides this, however, there's not an awful lot to amuse, although you can pick up suggestions and local information from the **tourist office** at Raatihuonetori 16 (Mon–Fri 9am–4pm; ☎05/749 2641, ⓦwww.hamina .fi), which can assist with accommodation.

The tourist office can also give you the latest schedule of the bus that runs to the densely wooded environs of **VIROLAHTI** (ⓦwww.virolahti.fi), 31km east, and within a few kilometres of the **Salpalinjan Bunkkerit** (Salpa Line Bunkers: daily June–Aug 10am–6pm; €4), massive hunks of granite stretching from here to Lapland, which acted as fortifications and were intended to protect Finland from Soviet attack during the run-up to the Winter War of 1939. These days Finnish war veterans are eager to show off the bunker's details and lead visitors to the seats (and controls) of ageing anti-tank guns. Buses from Helsinki to Viipuri, the formerly Finnish town now on the Russian side of the border (see p.589), pass through Hamina; again, details are best checked at the tourist office. If you have a burning desire for a sojourn here, you'd do well to stay out at the end of the road in Virolahti in the creaky but familial cabins at *Hurpun Tila* (☎040/701 8056, ⓦwww .hurpuntila.fi; €35), where you can rent rowing boats for a comradely paddle out to Russo–Finnish No Man's Land.

The Southwest

The area between Helsinki and Finland's **southwestern** extremity is probably the blandest section of the whole country. By road or rail the view is much the same, endless forests interrupted only by modest-sized patches of water and virtually identical villages and small towns. Once at the southwestern corner, however, things change considerably, with islands and inlets around a jagged shoreline, distinctive Finnish–Swedish coastal communities and a spectacular archipelago stretching halfway to Sweden.

Turku and around

There is very little in Åbo which has entertained me in the survey, or can amuse you by the description. It is a wretched capital of a barbarous province. The houses are almost all of wood; and the archiepiscopal palace, which has not even a single storey, but may be called a sort of barrack, is composed of no better materials, except that it is painted red. I inquired if there was not any object in the university, meriting attention; but they assured me that it would be regarded as a piece of ridicule, to visit it on such an errand, there being nothing within its walls except a very small library, and a few philosophical instruments.

Sir N.W. Wraxall, *A Tour Round The Baltic*, 1775

TURKU (or **Åbo** as it's known in Swedish) was the principal town in Finland when the country was a province of Sweden, losing its status in 1812, along with most of its buildings in a ferocious fire soon after – occurrences that clearly improved the place, if the above quotation is to be believed. These days Turku is small and highly sociable – and thanks to the boom years under Swedish rule and the students from its two universities, it's bristling with history and culture, with a sparkling nightlife to boot.

Arrival and information

The River Aura splits the city, its tree-lined banks forming a natural promenade as well as a useful landmark. The cathedral and castle stand at opposite ends of the riverside promenade, while the main museums are found along its edge. There are gleaming department stores, banks and offices on the northern side of the river in Turku's central grid, where you'll also find the **tourist office** at Aurakatu 4 (April–Sept Mon–Fri 8.30am–6pm, Sat & Sun 9am–4pm; Oct–March Mon–Fri 8.30am–6pm Sat & Sun 10am–3pm; ℡02/262 7444, ⊛www.turkutouring.fi), which has plenty of maps and leaflets, and also rents bicycles (€10 per day) and scooters (€40 per day). Outside banking hours you can **change money** at Forex, Eerikinkatu 12 (Mon–Fri 8am–7pm, Sat 8am–5pm). Both the **train station** and **bus station** are within easy walking distance of the river, just north of the centre.

Accommodation

Finding **accommodation** in Turku is rarely a problem – even in the height of summer. In addition to two solid hostel choices and an inexpensive bed and breakfast, the city has a good array of comfortable hotels, though they tend towards the pricier side of things.

Hesehotelli Läntinen Pitkäkatu 1 ☎045/634 3443, ⓦwww.hesburger.fi/hesehotelli. Close to the bus station, this hotel is run by the Heseburger fast-food chain and features modern rooms with satellite TV and free internet access. Annoyingly, "reception" is the tills at the burger joint downstairs, but the rates are some of the lowest you'll find. ❷

🏃 **Hostel Turku** Linnankatu 39 ☎02/262 7680, ⓦwww.turku.fi/hostelturku. This excellent year-round official youth hostel is one of the best in the country. Situated between the harbour and city centre, it offers good-sized doubles (❷) and dorms (€16), plus ample cooking and laundry facilities and bicycle hire. To get there, take bus #30 from the train station or #1 from the airport and bus station.

Interpoint YWCA Vähä-Hämeenkatu 12A ☎02/231 4011, ⓕ02/231 2584. Set across the river a few blocks south of the cathedral, this bare-bones hostel is the destination of choice for those on a tight budget, offering the cheapest dorm beds in town (€10). Open mid-July to mid-Aug.

Omena Hotelli Humalistonkatu 7 ⓦwww.omena .com. Simple, central automated hotel that offers high design at low prices. There is no reception and no staff and you must book online, by toll call or at the automated kiosk in the lobby. ❷

Park Rauhankatu 1 ☎02/273 2555, ⓦwww .parkhotelturku.fi. A 5min walk from the train station, this hotel was built in 1902 and oozes turn-of-the-century Art Nouveau charm. It's the best choice in Turku though the stylish rooms don't come cheap. ❺/❻

Ruissalo Camping Ruissalo Island ☎02/262 5100. Turku's most accessible campsite is located on the small island of Ruissalo overlooking the harbour, reachable from the city centre by bus #8 (15min). The campsite offers basic rooms (❷), and the island's sandy beaches, lush botanical garden and superb archipelago panoramas are just paces away. Open June–Aug.

🏃 **Sokos Hotel Hamburger Börs** **Kauppiaskatu 6** ☎02/337 381, ⓦwww .sokoshotels.fi. Smart, elegant and full of Scandinavian design features such as sleek fabrics and recessed lighting, this super central spot has everything from gorgeous suites to inviting smaller rooms that look out onto the *tori* and get great sunsets. Summer and weekend bargains make it an especially good choice out of season. ❹/❻

Tuure Tuureporinkatu 17C ☎02/233 0230, ⓦwww.tuure.fi. Near to the bus and train stations, this bed-and-breakfast sports teeny double rooms with a bit more character than those in the local hostels. ❸

The City

Arriving in Turku by train, you'll quickly make the pleasing discovery that the major places of interest unintentionally arrange themselves into a very logical pattern. By beginning at the **Art Museum**, a few strides from the station, and from there moving south through the city centre and heading westwards along the river's edge, you'll be able to take in everything worth seeing in a day – although allowing two days is more sensible if you want to have energy left for Turku's surprisingly active **nightlife**. During the 1970s and 1980s parts of Turku were subjected to some thoughtless redevelopment, resulting in a number of really hideous buildings, and a new national byword, the "Turku Disease". However, streets of intricately carved wooden houses still survive around the Port Arthur area, a lovely part of the city for simply strolling around, as is either bank of the placid River Aura.

The Art Museum

Though it's not much of a taster for the actual city, the newly renovated **Turku Art Museum** (Tues–Fri 11am–7pm, Sat & Sun 11am–5pm; €6, or €7.50 for special exhibitions; ⓦwww.turuntaidemuseo.fi), housed in a purpose-built Art Nouveau granite structure close to the train station on Torninkatu, is one of the better collections of Finnish art, with works by all the great names of the country's Golden Age – Gallen-Kallela, Edelfelt, Pekka Halonen, Simberg and others – plus a commendable stock of moderns. Not least among these are the wood sculptures of Kain Tapper and Mauno Hartman, which stirred up heated debate on the merits of carefully shaped bits of wood being presented as art when they were first shown during the 1970s.

▲ Work by Edelfelt, Turku Art Museum

The Cathedral and around

To get to grips with Turku itself, and its pivotal place in Finnish history, cut through the centre to the river, and the tree-framed space that, before the great fire of 1879, was the bustling heart of the community, and which is still overlooked by the **Tuomiokirkko** (daily: mid-April to mid-Sept 9am–8pm; rest of the year until 7pm). The cathedral, erected in the thirteenth century on the "Knoll of Sheep", a pre-Christian place of worship, was at the centre of the Christianization process inflicted by the crusading Swedes on the pagan Finns, and grew larger over the centuries as the new religion became stronger and Swedish involvement in Finland escalated. The building, still the heart and soul of the Finnish Church, has been repeatedly ravaged by fire, although the thickness of the walls enabled many of its medieval features to survive. Of these, it's the tombs that catch the eye: Torsten Stålhandske, commander of the Finnish cavalry during the seventeenth-century Thirty Years War, in which Sweden sought to protect its domination of the Baltic and the Finns confirmed their reputation as wild and fearless fighters, lies in a deliriously ornate coffin (to the right as you enter) opposite Samuel Cockburn and Patrick Ogilvie, a couple of Scots who fought alongside him. Entombed on the left-hand side is Catharine Månsdotter, commoner wife of the Swedish king Erik XIV, with whom, in the mid-sixteenth century, she was imprisoned in Turku Castle. As the only queen Finland every produced, Catharine is as popular in death as she reputedly was in life, judging by the numbers who file past her simple black-marble sarcophagus. The window behind it carries her stained-glass image – and if you crane your neck to the left, you can see a wall plaque bearing the only known true likeness of her. You can also visit the **cathedral museum** upstairs (same times as cathedral; €2), which gives a stronger insight into the building's past. There's an assortment of ancient jugs, goblets, plates and spoons, though more absorbing are the collections of church textiles.

Immediately outside the cathedral is a statue to **Per Brahe**, governor-general of Finland from 1637 and the first Swedish officer to devote much attention to the welfare of the Finns, encouraging a literacy programme and founding the country's first university. The site of this is within the nearby yellow Empire-style buildings, although the actual seat of learning was moved to Helsinki during the era of Russian rule. Next to these are the oldest portions of the **Åbo Akademi** – one of only three Swedish-language universities in Finland – while the modern, Finnish-language **Turku University** is at the other end of Henrikinkatu: these days both are more notable as places for eating, at their student *mensas*, rather than sightseeing.

Turku's most splendid museum is the combined **Aboa Vetus** and **Ars Nova** (April to mid-Sept daily 11am–7pm; rest of the year closed Mon; €8; ℗www .aboavetusarsnova.fi) on the bank of the Aurajoki River just a few steps from the university. With a name that translates in Latin as "Old Turku, New Art", the place was intended to be simply a modern art gallery, but when the building's foundations were dug in 1995 a warren of medieval lanes and cellars came to light. It was an unmissable opportunity to present the history and archeology of the city, and glass flooring allows a near-perfect view of the remains. The New Art part comprises a striking collection of five hundred works, alongside frequent temporary exhibitions. Guided tours in English are offered during July and August daily at 11.30am. There's a great café too.

Back past the cathedral and across Piispankatu is the sleek low form of the **Sibelius Museum** (Tues–Sun 11am–4pm, Wed also 6–8pm; €3; ℗www.sibeliusmuseum .abo.fi). Although Sibelius had no direct connection with Turku, this museum is a fitting tribute to him and his contribution to the emergence of an independent Finland. Chances are that the recorded strains of *Finlandia* will greet you as you enter: when not the venue for live concerts (which take place Wednesday evenings between June and August, and on various days throughout the winter), the small but acoustically perfect concert area pumps out recorded requests from the great man's oeuvre; take your place beside dewy-eyed Finns for a lunch hour of Scandinavia's finest composer. Elsewhere, the Sibelius collection gathers family photo albums and original manuscripts along with the great man's hat, walking stick and even a final half-smoked cigar. Other exhibits cover the musical history of the country, from intricate musical boxes and the frail wooden *kantele* – the instrument strummed by peasants in the *Kalevala* – to the weighty keyboard instruments downstairs.

The Luostarinmäki, Aaltonen and pharmacy museums

On the other side of the cathedral from the Sibelius museum, you'll see the small Vartiovuori hill, topped by the wooden dome of the **Observatory**, designed – rather poorly – by Carl Engel, who had arrived in Turku seeking work in the days before his great plan for Helsinki made him famous. Originally the building was intended to serve the first Turku University as an observatory, but disputes between Engel and his assistants and a misunderstanding of scientific requirements rendered the place useless for its intended purpose. To make things worse, the university moved to Helsinki, and the building was then turned into a navigational school. From the observatory, head directly down the side of the hill to the far more engrossing **Luostarinmäki Handicrafts Museum** on Luostarinkatu (mid-April to mid-Sept daily 10am–6pm; mid-Sept to late Sept & Dec Tues–Sun 10am–3pm; closed mid-Jan to mid-April, Oct & Nov; €5), one of the best – and certainly the most authentic – open-air museums in Finland. Following a severe fire in 1775, rigorous restrictions were imposed on the city's new buildings, but due to a legal technicality they didn't apply in this district. The wooden houses here were built by local working people in traditional style and evolved naturally into a museum as descendants of the original owners died and bequeathed their inherited homes to the municipality. Unpaved streets run between tiny wooden houses, which once had goats tethered to their chimneys to keep the turfed roofs cropped. The chief inhabitants now are the museum volunteers who dress up in period attire and demonstrate the old handicrafts.

A short walk from the handicrafts museum, on the southern bank of the river, is another worthwhile indoor collection: the **Wäinö Aaltonen Museum** (Tues–Sun 11am–7pm; €6, or €7 depending on exhibition; ℗www.wam.fi). Unquestionably the best-known modern Finnish sculptor, Wäinö Aaltonen was born in 1894, grew up close to Turku and studied for a time at the local art school. His first public show, in 1916, marked a turning point in the development of Finnish sculpture, introducing a freer, more individual style to a genre struggling to break from the restraints of the Neoclassical tradition and French realism. Aaltonen went on to dominate his field throughout the 1920s and 1930s and his influence is still felt today; the man's work turns up in every major town throughout the country, and even the parliament building in Helsinki was designed with special niches to hold some of his pieces. Much of his output celebrates the individuals who contributed to the growth of the Finnish republic, typically remembering them with enormous heads, or as immense statues that resemble massive Social-Realist chunks. But Aaltonen, who died in 1966, really was an original, imaginative and sensitive sculptor, as the exhibits here demonstrate. There's also a roomful of his paintings, some of which show perhaps why he concentrated on sculpture.

Across the river from the Aaltonen museum, there's a sign in the grass which spells out TURKU:ÅBO; immediately behind this is a wooden staircase running up to the front door of the **Museum of Pharmacy and Qwensel House** (mid-April to mid-Sept daily 10am–6pm; Dec Tues–Sun 10am–3pm; €4). Qwensel was a court judge who moved to the house in 1694, and it later became the home of Professor Josef Gustaf Pipping – the "father of Finnish medicine" – in 1785. Period furnishings remain, proving just how wealthy and stylish the life of the eighteenth-century bourgeoisie actually was. Many chemists' implements from around the country are on show, among them some memorable devices for drawing blood.

Turku Castle

The city's museums, and its cathedral and universities, are all symbols of Turku's elevated position in Finnish life, though by far the major marker of its many years of importance stands at the western end of Linnankatu. Follow the signs for "Turun Linna", or take bus #1 from the harbour, and you'll eventually see, oddly set among the present day ferry terminals, the relatively featureless, piebald exterior of **Turku Castle** (mid-Jan to mid-April & late Sept to Nov Tues & Thurs–Fri 10am–3pm, Wed and Sat & Sun 10am–6pm; mid-April to late Sept daily 10am–6pm; Dec Tues–Fri 10am–3pm & Sat 10am–5pm; €7; ☻www.nba.fi/en/turku_castle). Fight any dismay, though, since the compact cobbled courtyards, maze-like corridors and darkened staircases of the interior provide a good place to wander – and to dwell on the fact that this was the seat of the government of the country for centuries, as well as that much of Finland's (and a significant portion of Sweden's) medieval history took shape within these walls. Unless you're an expert on the period, you'll get a migraine trying to figure out the importance of everything that's here, and it's a sensible idea to buy one of the guide leaflets on sale at the entrance – you can safely give the guided tour a miss.

The castle probably went up sometime around 1280, when the first bishop arrived from Sweden; gradual expansion through the following years accounts for the patchwork effect of its architecture – and the bewildering array of finds, rooms and displays. The majority of the fortification took place during the turbulent sixteenth century, instigated by Swedish ruler Gustavus Vasa for the protection of his son, whom he made Duke Johan, the first Duke of Finland. Johan pursued a lavish court life but exceeded his powers in attacking Livonia and was sentenced to death by the Stockholm Diet. Swedish efforts to seize Johan were successful only after a three-week siege, and he was removed to Stockholm. The subsequent decision by the unbalanced Erik XIV to release Johan resulted not only in Johan becoming king himself, but also in poor Erik being imprisoned here – albeit with a full quota of servants and the best food and wine. The bare cell he occupied for a few weeks contrasts strongly with the splendour from Johan's time, offering a cool reminder of shifting fortunes. There's a gloomy nineteenth-century painting here, by Erik Johan Löfgren, of Erik with his head on the lap of his queen (Catharine Månsdotter), while the lady's eyes look askance to heaven.

Moominworld

Some 16km northwest of Turku, **Naantali** is famous as the home of **Moominworld** (early June to late Aug daily 10am–6pm; adults and children from €19; ⓦ www.muumimaailma.fi), a theme park set on an island and based on Tove Jansson's famous creations. Ranked as one of the world's top ten theme parks, it's a must-see if you have kids in tow, and many tour operators run buses to the park from Turku. Naantali itself is pleasant enough, with its wooden buildings and slight passageways, but hardly worth hanging around for more than a few hours, and with regular buses there's no need to stay, though there's a tourist office at Kaivotori 2 should you need further information (early June to mid-Aug Mon–Fri 9am–6pm, Sat & Sun 10am–3pm; mid-Aug to early June 9am–4.30pm; ☎02/435 9800, ⓦ www.naantalinmatkailu.fi). For a quick, tasty bite, *Merisali*, Nunnakatu 1, has a fresh fish, affordable salads and a good *smorgasbord* for around €11.80.

Eating, drinking and nightlife

You'd need to be very fussy not to find somewhere to **eat** in Turku that's to your liking. Many places offer complete lunchtime meals for under €10 – try the handful of restaurants in the new complex by the market square – and while traditional Finnish restaurants make up most of the city's offerings, there are a small number of fusion and ethnic places here as well. A dozen or so summer floating restaurants – *Papa Joe*, *Svarte Rudolf* and *Cindy*, to name a few – are popular among tourists, if not with too many locals. All serve reliably good continental-style meals and occasionally put on live music; *Cindy* even sticks around in the winter months.

Cafés and restaurants

Assarin Ulakko Rehtorinpellonkatu 4A. You'll find rockbottom-priced meals and a lively atmosphere at this student *mensa* just of Hämeentie. It's easily the cheapest option in town (€5.20 for lunch). Closed Sun. Half a dozen other student cafeteria are spread about the Åbo Akademi grounds.
Bossa Kauppiaskatu 12 ⓦ www.restaurantebossa .fi. Animated Brazilian place with weekly live music. Most of the rich meat and fish main dishes – give the *picanha* beef a try – are under €20.
Café Qwensel Läntinen Rantakatu 13. Fabulous cakes in the eighteenth-century surroundings of a courtyard behind the Museum of Pharmacy.
Enkeliravintola Kauppiaskatu 16 ⓦ www .enkeliravintola.fi. A stylishly old-fashioned café serving up wonderful cakes and coffee, although a little out of the centre up a steep hill.
Foija Aurakatu 10 ⓦ www.foija.fi. Busy cellar restaurant with vaulted ceilings and great service opposite the *kauppatori*, with good-value and delicious pastas, salads and pizzas from €7.50. They've been around for over 150 years and are still popular with the city's younger set.
Herman Läntinen Rantakatu 37 ☎02/230 3333, ⓦ www.ravintolaherman.com. Set in a bright and airy 1850s-era storehouse right on the Aura (ask for the table for two overlooking the river). The fantastic traditional meals here are fairly priced, too, with main courses that start at €20. Lunch is tremendous value at €8.60.

Koulu Eerikinkatu 18 ⓦ www .panimoravintolakoulu.fi. Set in a grand old late-1880s school building, this is the largest restaurant-brewery in Finland, with a large selection of beers and wines. Bar-food mains such as bratwurst, fried liver and beer-braised lamb start at €10.80. The great bargain lunch platter is €8.40. Dinner served until 11.30pm.
Pizzeria Dennis Linnankatu 17. Although this pizza joint might look a bit tatty on the outside, don't be put off. It's renowned for its range of decent, well-priced pizzas, priced from €9.
Ravintola Linnankatu 3 Linnankatu 3 ⓦ www.linnankatu3.fi. Set just across the River Aura, this new restaurant has a great casual interior done in adobe tile. Mains such as pan-broiled white fish and veal chops are around €20. Try the Bloody Mary soup, made with Finlandia vodka.

🎿 **Viikinkiravintola Harald** Aurakatu 3 ⓦ www.ravintolaharald.com. Cashing in on the little Finland actually has to do with the Vikings, this old-world spot effectively employs whittled wooden furnishings, earthenware plates and game trophies on the walls to win most atmospheric restaurant in town. Hearty dishes inlude the Innkeepers Shield (€24.80), massive cuts of beef breast, red deer carré, deep fried potatoes and root vegetables skewered on a sword. The €8 fish and vegetable buffet lunch, served until 3pm, is a great bargain. And try the sweet and smoky tar ice cream.

Bars and entertainment

Thanks to a thriving cultural scene, a lively student population and a good number of tourists and visitors, nights out in Turku have something for everyone. A **drink** at one of the many boats moored along Itäinen Rantakatu is a popular summer tradition, and if you want to fill your nights with something more energetic than boozing, there are several **discos**. During August, the **Turku Music Festival** (☎02/251 1162, ⊕www.turkumusicfestival.fi) packs thousands into a number of venues for performances in a wide range of musical genres. If your tastes are for classical music, try and get a ticket for a performance by one of the oldest symphony orchestras in Europe, the **Turku Philharmonic**, founded in 1790 and currently based in the Concert Hall at Aninkaistenkatu 9. The box office telephone line (☎02/262 0800) opens in mid-August, one month before concerts begin. Alternatively, check with the tourist office for a rundown of the week's films: Turku has a number of **cinemas**, the largest of which, Kinopalatsi, Kauppiaskatu 11, has nine screens. Finnkino Julia, Eerikinkatu 4, has five. Visit ⊕www.finnkino.fi for listings.

Baari Kärpänen Kauppiakatu 8 ⊕www .baarikarpanen.fi. Excellent, unconventional spot: a hard-rock bar with lovely embroidered red velvet seating inside and a cobblestone terrace in front. The scene might look rough, but the locals who come here regularly to talk music and politics as they guard their pint are some of the most sociable, chatty and friendly you'll meet in town.

Blanko Aurakatu 1. Voted trendiest bar in Scandinavia several years ago, the down-to-earth bartenders at this chilled-out lounge will still deign to serve you even if you don't look like Paris Hilton. Funky interior with pillowed couches in the back, DJs spinning electronica at weekends and tasty, well-priced fusion lunches and dinners (give the salami feta pasta a go).

Dynamo Linnankatu 7 ⊕www.dynamoklubi .com. A rocking bar set across two floors (there's dancing upstairs) with a chic-meets-alternative interior of red velour designy chairs and olive leather couches. Doesn't really get going until after around 1am. Thurs night is the very popular YouTube night, when everyone picks a favourite internet clip to screen on wall.

Edison Kauppiaskatu 4 ⊕www.bar-edison.fi. Fairly standard bistro-styled bar that's extremely popular with young locals as well as Erasmus students on exchange who come to let their hair down a bit. Two free internet terminals by the door. Best before 10pm.

El Gringo Kauppiaskatu 6. Grungy Spanish decor and inexpensive beers (€2.50 Lapin Kulta pints) draw a diverse crowd, with music that ranges from reggae to gangsta rap and R'n'B.

Kuka Linnankatu 17. One of Turku's newest nightspots, this irreverent Shoreditch-styled bar has eclectic fixtures such as a barber's chair, pod-like seats, popcorn machines as tables and a dilapidated Vespa hanging over the door. Tuesday night is Bingo night, when the tragically hip turn out in droves. Several tables out front if you can't stand the heat.

Uusi Apteekki Kaskenkatu 1 ⊕www.uuslapteekki .fi. Allegedly predating Damien Hirst's famous *Pharmacy* London bar-restaurant, this smoky, laid-back drinking hole is housed in an old chemist's shop, with drug and pill bottles scattered about the place. Popular with bikers, cigar aficionados and multiply pierced locals.

Vaakahuone Linnankatu 38 ⊕www.vaakahuone .fi. A very lively place, buzzing with Finns of all ages. An established house band plays Dixieland and bebop jazz every night during the summer, and there are reasonably priced salads, soups and pizzas on offer too.

Vessa Puutori ⊕www.puutorinvessa.fi. Quirky circular bar housed in a former public toilet. Locals can often be found with pint in hand shouting comments at Finnish television serials. Definitely worth a peek in, if not *yks pistä* (a pint).

Moving on from Turku

Continuing from Turku **north along the coast**, there are direct bus services to the nearest main towns, Rauma and Pori. It's also possible to reach Pori by train, although this takes virtually a whole day and involves going via Tampere and changing at least once, possibly three times. From **Turku harbour**, ferries sail through the vast archipelago to the Åland Islands, and on to Sweden. The harbour is 3km from the city centre and bus #1 covers the route frequently.

Rauma

RAUMA, 90km north of Turku, is one of the few places in Finland where you can't help but stop at every street corner to admire the elegance and understated charm of a town whose appearance has barely changed since the Middle Ages. Although Finns know Rauma as the most complete and best-preserved wooden town in Scandinavia, with its historic importance reflected by its designation as a UNESCO World Heritage Site, relatively few foreigners have yet realized that a couple of days spent exploring the cobbled eighteenth- and nineteenth-century streets are likely to be some of the most enjoyable spent in Finland. True, Rauma is becoming increasingly touristy, but the town still retains plenty of quiet lanes and alleyways where you can explore undisturbed.

Until the early 1900s, **Old Rauma** was entirely contained within a narrow triangle of land (bordered on two sides by the small Raumanjoki River), which had been established as a toll-free zone three hundred years before. Although modern Rauma completely and gracelessly encircles this medieval core today, it's this undisturbed medieval centre that makes the town so appealing – the layout of the narrow, winding streets, alleys and curiously shaped gardens and allotments has barely changed since the last great fire in 1682, a remarkable achievement for a wooden town. Rauma's architectural delights are best explored by simply strolling along the two main streets, **Kauppakatu** and **Kuninkaankatu**, and heading off down whichever lane takes your fancy. Although most houses are now clad in the decorative neo-Renaissance style and painted in a riot of pastel shades, you can still see a few dressed with the vertical boarding of the 1700s, or the wider Empire cladding of the 1820s. The town's rich past is expertly documented via the **Rauma Museum**, in the eighteenth-century town hall at Kauppakatu 13 (mid-May to Aug daily 10am–5pm; Sept to mid-May Tues–Fri & Sun 10am–5pm, Sat 11am–2pm; summer €6, winter €5), where you'll find a couple of scale models of the sailing ships that once brought vast wealth into the town.

Further evidence is on show at **Marela**, Kauppakatu 24 (same times as Rauma Museum; €4), a house preserved in the style of a rich shipowner's residence from the beginning of the twentieth century. Combined entry to Marela and the History Museum costs €4 (€2 Sept to mid-May) with a day pass available from either museum. If you want to plunge even further into local history, the **Old Rauma Renovation Centre** at Vähäkirkkokatu 8 (June–Aug Mon–Sat 10am–6pm, Sun noon–6pm; free) runs evening classes (unfortunately, all in Finnish) covering activities such as Rauma-style community singing, lessons in how to tie seafarers' knots and instruction in the local dialect – strangely for the west coast, this is a mainly Finnish-speaking community, although with an archaic dialect that many other Finns find hard to understand. The **Rauma Maritime Museum**, Kalliokatu 34 (early June to early Aug daily 11am–5pm; May and mid-Aug to late Aug Tues–Fri & Sun noon–4pm; €7), offers extensive displays on local maritime history, but the real draw is the navigation simulator, a fascinating contraption that allows would-be mariners the chance to man their own open-sea voyage. The system offers a choice of over a hundred sailing routes, including New York harbour and the English Channel, and the computer-generated visuals are projected onto a huge screen in front of the ship's bridge, allowing you to plot a course, navigate obstacles and bring your ship safely into port.

Practicalities

Unfortunately there are no longer train services to Rauma, and coming from Turku, the easiest solution is to take one of the frequent buses (#372 or #810) which run along the west coast. From the bus station it's a two-minute walk to the **tourist office** at Valtakatu 2 (June–Aug Mon–Fri 8am–4pm, Sat & Sun 10am–6pm; Sept–May Mon–Fri 8am–4pm; ☎02/8378 7730, ⊛www.rauma.fi), where you can pick up leaflets on local history and walking tours. If you want to stay, it's just 1km along

Poroholmantie from the old town centre to *Poroholma*, the combined **youth hostel** and **campsite** (℡02/8388 2500, ✆poroholma@kalliohovi.fi; mid-May to Aug), which offers €10 dorms and standard rooms (❷) and allows free use of its morning sauna. In terms of **hotels,** try the *Cumulus*, Aittakarinkatu 9 (℡02/837 821, ⓦwww .cumulus.fi; ❹/❻), which boasts two saunas, a pool and summer terrace.

Rauma doesn't throw up a multitude of **eating** options, but filling lunches (around €10) are served at *Villa Tallbo*, in a shipowner's restored *fin-de-siècle* summer villa near the sea at Petäjäksentie 178 (℡02/822 0733); *Wähä Tallbo*, Vanhankirkonkatu 3, is a similar option in the town itself. Best option for dinner is *La Bamba*, at Posellinkatu 6, with an extensive choice of pizzas, burgers and pasta dishes from around €10. *Wanhan Rauman Kellari*, Anundilankatu 8, has quality, well-priced Finnish food.

Pori

Due to its yearly jazz **festival** – increasingly rock- and pop-oriented in recent years – **PORI** has become one of the best-known towns in Finland. For one week each July, its streets are full of music and the 160,000 people who come to hear it – for more on the event, see box, p.569. Throughout the rest of the year Pori reverts to normality as a small, quiet industrial town with a worthy regional museum and a handful of architectural and historical oddities. The central section, despite its spacious grid-style streets, can be crossed on foot in about fifteen minutes.

Arrival, information and accommodation

It's a short walk from either the **bus station** – into Isolinnankatu and straight on – or the **train station** – follow Rautatienpuistokatu – into the centre of town, where the **tourist office** sits in the Promenadi Centre shopping mall, Yrjönkatu 17 (June to mid-Aug Mon–Fri 9am–6pm, Sat 10am–3pm; mid-Aug to May Mon–Fri 9am–4.30pm; ℡02/621 7900, ⓦwww.pori.fi). There's free internet access both here and at the library, Gallen-Kallelankatu 12 (Mon–Fri 10–7pm, Sat 10am–3pm).

The city's **campsite**, *Isomäki* (call the Pori Jazz festival office for details; ℡02 626 2200), is 2km from the centre in the Isomäki Sports Centre, next to the outdoor swimming pool, but it's only open during the jazz festival; buses #7 and #8 run from

▲ Pori Jazz Festival

the centre to the hospital (*sairaala*) close by. During the festival the Porin Linjojen Jazzliikenne bus links the main festival sites, the town square and campsite (10–4am, every 20min). At other times of year, the nearest campsite is *Yyteri*, amid sandy beaches 20km distant (☎02/634 5700, ⓦwww.pori.fi/yyteri), though it does have a shop, café, sauna and many cabins (€45); the #32 bus stops just by the campsite. Among the **hotels**, you could try the *Cumulus*, Itsenäisyydenkatu 37 (☎02/550 900, ⓦwww.cumulus.fi; ❹/❺), one of the larger places and with its own restaurant. A smarter option is the *Vaakuna*, Gallen-Kallelankatu 7 (☎02/528 100, ⓦwww .sokoshotels.fi; ❹/❻), a business-oriented place with good weekend discounts. Around the corner from the *kauppatori* at Itäpuisto 13, *Buisto* (☎02/633 0647 or 044/333 0646, ⓦwww.hostelbuisto.net; ❷) has tidy, colourful rooms.

The Town

In the centre of Pori at Hallituskatu 14, just across the road from the tourist office, stands the recently renovated **Pori Theatre** (Mon–Fri 11am–6pm; free), the temporary home of Finnish-language theatre during the period of Russification when Finnish drama was considered too provocative to appear in a larger centre like Turku or Helsinki. Built in 1884, it boasts a striking Renaissance facade, and the tiny interior – seating just three hundred – is heavy with opulent frescoes and sculptured chandeliers. To see inside, ask at the tourist office. A few steps away, at Hallituskatu 11, the **Satakunta Museum** (Tues–Sun 11am–5pm, Wed eves until 8pm; €4) has three well-stocked floors which trace the life of both Pori and the surrounding Satakunta region through medieval findings, late nineteenth-century photos and shop signs and typical house interiors, alongside interesting memorabilia from the powerful labour movement of the 1930s.

Pori's strangest sight, however, is in the big **Käppärä cemetery**, a twenty-minute walk along Maantiekatu. In the cemetery's centre is the Gothic-arched **Juselius Mausoleum** (May–Aug daily noon–3pm; Sept–April Sun noon–2pm; free), erected in 1898 by local businessman F.A. Juselius as a memorial to his daughter, Sigrid, who died aged 11. The leading Finnish church architect of the time, Josef Steinbäck, was called on to design the thing, while Gallen-Kallela decorated the interior with some of his best large-scale paintings. The artwork was adversely affected by both fire and the local sea air, but has been restored by Gallen-Kallela's son from the original sketches, enabling the structure to fulfil its purpose as powerfully, and as solemnly, as ever.

Eating and drinking

In the **evening** most people gravitate to the town centre and watch a procession of highly polished cars heading aimlessly up and down the main streets. Cafés and bars fall in and out of favour quite rapidly, although one of the most consistently popular is *Café Anton* at Antinkatu 11, where a €2 cup of coffee comes with a cloudberry liqueur chocolate. *Café Anton* also offers a decent lunch, though in the evening it's primarily a place to drink beer.

Otherwise, for **eating** try the recently opened *La Braza*, Siltapuistokatu 1, which serves Spanish specialities at around €20 for a main, or the excellent *Raatihuoneen Kellari* in the cellar of the Promenadi Centre, Yrjönkatu 17, where lunchtime spreads of various Finnish-style meat and fish dishes cost €14–28, and there's an all-you-can-eat lunch buffet for €13. Check out also the all-year spin-off from the jazz festival, the *Jazz-Café*, at Eteläranta 6 on the banks of the Kokemäenjoki; just a few doors down, there's Finnish food at the excellent, reasonably priced *Suomalainen Klubbi* at no. 10. The town also boasts an alarmingly high number of fast-food outlets; most numerous are the *grillis*, which serve a local speciality called **porilainen**, a large, thick slice of grilled onion sausage served hamburger-style in a roll with pickles, ketchup and chopped onion. For pizza, there's *Mestarit Pizza*, Länsipuisto 16, where pizzas and pasta dishes go for around €12, and *Rax* at Itäpuisto 3, with an €8 all-you-can-eat buffet.

Pori's Jazz Festival

If you're planning to come here for the **jazz festival**, it's best to have accommodation fixed up at least six months in advance – hotels, hostel and campsite fill very quickly, although the tourist office endeavours to house as much of the overspill as possible in private homes (€50 per person in a double room) or on mattresses in local schools (€10–20 per person). There are even more unconventional places to stay – such as in a disused train car in the station – though such spots are never advertised.

It's easiest to purchase festival tickets online at Ⓦwww.porijazz.com, the main festival website; alternatively, contact the Pori tourist office (see p.567). A third of the festival's 110-odd concerts are free, in any case. If you plan to stay the whole week it's best to buy a pass (costing from €200; on sale from mid-April). Individual tickets range from €30 to €70 for the bigger acts (in the past these have included Lauryn Hill, Steely Dan, Gilberto Gill, Elvis Costello and everyone's European festival favourite, Herbie Hancock). During the festival there's a Festival Centre at Pohjoisranta 11, in an old cotton mill on the left-hand side just after you cross the main Pori bridge heading away from the town centre. Here you can buy any tickets that haven't already been sold and pick up festival programmes and information.

Pori has a good selection of smaller **bars**, as well: *Bar Kino*, set in an old cinema at Itäpuisto 10A, attracts students and young professionals with regular live music, while *Punainen Kukko*, just across the road, sees a more mature crowd. For dancing, head for the town's most popular disco, *Ilon Talo*, at Yrjönkatu 9.

The Åland Islands

The flat and thickly forested **Åland Islands**, all six-thousand-plus of them, lie scattered between Finland's southwest coast and Sweden. Politically Finnish but culturally Swedish, the islands cling to a unique form of independence, with their own parliament and flag (a red and yellow cross on a blue background). The currency is the euro but the language is Swedish – which explains why the main and only sizeable town is more commonly known by its Swedish name of **MARIEHAMN** than by the Finnish **Maarianhamina** – and as Swedish is mercifully closer to English, a visit here can make a welcome break from the perpetual battle with the Finnish language. Although Mariehamn – known locally as the "town of a thousand linden trees" after the elegant specimens that line virtually every street – is a peacefully uneventful seaside resort and a pleasant place to rest up for a couple of days, the real appeal here is sea, sun and beckoning terrain in unlimited quantities. There are plenty of secluded spots perfect for nude bathing, and you can hire a boat and sail out to your very own island.

Arrival, information and transport

Ferries from Finland and Sweden (see "Travel details", p.572) stop in Mariehamn's West Harbour, and there's a **tourist office** fifteen minutes' walk away at Storagatan 8 (April, May & Sept 9am–4pm, Sat 10am–3pm; early to mid-June & mid- to late Aug Mon–Fri 9am–5pm, Sat & Sun 9am–4pm; mid-June to mid-Aug daily 9am–6pm; Oct–March Mon–Fri 9am–4pm, ☏018/24 0000, Ⓦwww.visitaland .com), which can provide the latest details regarding travel and accommodation, and also has an internet terminal (€1 for 10min). The library at Strandgatan 29 has several **internet** terminals for use free of charge, though you may have to book a slot if you need to do more than check your mail.

There's a fairly thorough **bus service** covering the main islands, but **cycling** is a sound alternative, offering not only more freedom but also slightly cheaper rental rates than on the mainland; reckon on €10 per day for a bike with gears. In Mariehamn, RO NO Rent is the best bet, with outlets at Hamngatan (☏018/12821,

@www.visitaland.com/rono) right opposite the ferry terminal, and on the waterside at Österhamn (☎018/12820) in the town proper; both open 9am to 6pm daily from June to mid-August. The latter branch also rents out Vespa-like 50cc **scooters** (€65 per day) and **boats** with outboard motors (€100 for 8hr), and will provide advice and tips on some of the best islands to visit in the archipelago, just outside Mariehamn harbour. Note that bikes can also be carried on island buses for a nominal fee.

Accommodation

Mariehamn holds several enticing **accommodation** options, though if you turn up in summer on spec you'll have a tough time finding something there are no official youth hostels on the islands and, although there are a number of cheapish guesthouses, some of which offer hostel-type facilities, these fill quickly.

A good solid central option in Mariehamn is the *Scandic Savoy*, Nygatan 12 (☎018/15 400, @www.scandichotels.com; ⑤/⑥), with well-appointed if small rooms. Elsewhere, *Kaptensgårdarna* (☎018 15400, @www.alandhotels.fi), on Stavamostersvägen just by the ferry terminals, has comfy basic rooms, and *Pensionat Solhem* (☎018 163 22, @www.visitaland.com/solhem; May–Oct), Lökskärsvägen, is set on sprawling lawns right on the water. If you're at a loss for a bed in Mariehamn, try *Kronan* at Neptunigatan 52 (☎018/12 617; ❸; breakfast included in summer only), or *Neptun* (same phone number; ❸), Neptunigatan 41; reception for both is at the *Kronan*. Other villages around Åland offer more rustic options: in Eckerö, *Villa Kuckeliku*, Sandmovägen 80 (☎018/38 659, @www.villakuckeliku.tk; ❸; July–Aug week-long rentals only, €410) has several rooms in a charming cottage with spectacular sea views, while in Degerby on Föglö, the *Föglö Wärdshus* (☎018/50 002, @www.wardshus.com; ❸) is a cosy, idyllic inn with home cooking, sauna and internet access. The great choice, though, is to **camp**: there are plentiful sites (in isolated areas you should be able to camp rough with no problems).

Exploring the islands

The Åland Islands (**Ahvenanmaa** in Finnish) were in Swedish hands through the Middle Ages, but, coveted by the Russians on account of their strategic location on the Baltic, they became part of the Russian Grand Duchy of Finland in 1807. When Finland gained independence, the future of the Ålands was referred to the League of Nations (though not before several Åland leaders had been imprisoned in Helsinki on a charge of high treason). As a result, Finnish sovereignty was established, in return for autonomy and complete demilitarization: the Ålanders now regard themselves as a shining example of Nordic cooperation, and living proof that a small state can run its own affairs while being part of a larger one.

The islands' ancient history is as interesting as the modern: many Roman coins have been found and there are scores of Viking burial mounds, plus the remains of some of the oldest Finnish churches. The excellent **Ålands Museum** (June–Aug daily 10am–5pm, open until 7pm throughout July; Sept–May Tues & Thurs 10am–8pm, Wed & Fri 10am–4pm, Sat & Sun noon–4pm; May–Sept €4, Oct–April free) in Mariehamn's Stadshusparken tells the full story, spicing it up with exhibits on modern Swedish and Finnish artists and designers. It's complemented by the ship-shaped, two-floor **Åland Maritime Museum** on Hamngatan (May Mon–Fri 9am–5pm, Sat & Sun noon–4pm; June & Aug daily 9am–5pm; July daily 9am–7pm; Sept–April Mon–Fri 10am–4pm, Sat & Sun noon–4pm; €5; @www.sjofartsmuseum.aland.fi), 1km away at the other end of Storagatan, which celebrates the fact that, despite their insignificant size, the Åland islands once had the world's largest fleet of wooden sailing ships.

Smaller local history museums in the Ålands' other communities reflect the surprisingly strong regional differences among the islands; it seems the only thing that's shared is the ubiquitous Åland maypoles – which stand most of the year round – and the fact that specific sights generally take a back seat to the various forms of nature. There are, however, several things worth making for. Toward the northeast of Mariehamn, in Tosarby Sund, are the remains of **Kastelholm** (May to mid-Sept daily 10am–5pm; July until 6pm; €5) a fourteenth-century fortress built to consolidate Swedish domination of the Baltic. Strutted through by numerous Swedish monarchs, it was mostly destroyed by fire in the mid-nineteenth century and is now being restored. In summer there are English-language guided tours (mid-June to Aug Sat & Sun 2pm; €5) of the castle, which also take in the nearby open-air **Jan Karlsgärden Museum**. The Russians also set about building a fortress, **Bomarsund**, but before it could be completed the Crimean War broke out and an Anglo-French force stormed the infant castle, reducing it to rubble; just the scattered ramparts remain. Both would-be castles are on the same bus route from Mariehamn.

Elsewhere, you can trace the route of the old **post road**, the only mail link from Stockholm to what was then tsarist St Petersburg. To their long-lasting chagrin, the Åland people were charged with seeing the safe passage of the mail, including taking it across the frozen winter sea – and quite a few died in the process. The major remnant of these times is the nineteenth-century Carl Engel-designed **Post House** in **ECKERÖ**, at the islands' western extremity. Standing on the coast facing Sweden, the building was intended to instil fresh arrivals with awe at their first sight of the mighty Russian Empire. Despite retaining its grandeur, it now looks highly incongruous amid the tiny local community.

Eating and drinking

Eating in the Ålands is not cheap, and many restaurants hike up their prices during the summer months to make a killing from the Swedish tourist traffic, but there are a few places in Mariehamn where you can try some fresh local seafood. A Mariehamn meal is best had on a terrace at sunset; after a day's hard cycling or archipelago exploration, any one of the town's outdoor spots is ideal for sipping a beer and watching the sun sink slowly towards the horizon.

For **nightlife**, the upstairs bar at *Indigo* is Åland's trendiest bar, replete with mood lighting, white leather couches and can't-be-bothered bar staff. *Dino's*, just next door and equally popular, is a small, tidy rock bar with some good live music. Weekends are busy at both these places, and most locals usually make them a requisite stop before heading to dance the night away at *Arken*, in the *Hotel Archipelago*, Strandgaten 31 – people tend to head here after midnight.

F.P. von Knorring Österhamn ⓦwww .fpvonknorring.com. Åland's most atmospheric place to eat is moored in the Österhamn near RO NO. The *F.P. von Knorring* serves fish and steak dishes starting at €20 and sandwiches for half that. In the summer, pull up a table on the aft deck at sunset and order an inexpensive burger, salad or kebab plate.

Indigo Nygatan 1 ⓦwww.indigo.aland.com. Casual spot with stone house interior offering standard Scandinavian dishes for around €20, and bottles of Stallhagen, Åland's own slightly bitter microbrew. Terrace café in the summer.

Pub Niska Strandpromenaden. Just in front of the *ÅSS Paviljongen* restarant, this casual new pub-restaurant is named after a well-known smuggler. It serves unique, tasty *plåtbröd* pizzas, with toppings that include smoked salmon, red onions and horseradish cream. One of the best places for lunch on the islands.

Restaurang Nautical Hamngatan 2. Regally outfitted island spot above the Maritime Museum with views to the water. They serve their Brändö Archipelago Board, an excellent introduction to local cuisine with lightly salted herring, roe and other seafood, plus *svartbröd*; there's also a €14 set-lunch menu.

Sollans Café Havsgatan 29. Small terrace café at the West Harbour offering coffee, cakes and loaves of tasty local *svartbröd*, a dark and chewy syrup-based bread.

Umbra Krog & Bar Norra Esplanadgatan 2 ⓦwww.umbra.ax. Run by the guys who own *Indigo*, this new and modern European restaurant serves excellent traditional Italian dishes prepared with all-local ingredients. They do a weekday buffet lunch from 11am–3pm for €9.90.

Travel details

Trains

Helsinki to: Espoo (half-hourly; 30min); Järvenpää (half-hourly; 30min); Jyväskylä (hourly; 3hr 10min–4hr 20min); Kajaani (4 daily; 5hr 40min–6hr 40min); Kuopio (9 daily; 4hr); Lahti (hourly; 1hr 20min); Mikkeli (7 daily; 2hr 20min–2hr 55min); Oulu (8–10 daily; 6hr 15min–9hr 45min); Rovaniemi (5 daily; 9hr 45min–12hr 30min); Tampere (hourly; 1hr 40min); Turku (hourly; 2hr).
Pori to: Tampere (4–6 daily; 1hr 30min).
Turku to: Helsinki (hourly; 2hr); Tampere (7–9 daily; 1hr 55min).

Buses

Helsinki to: Joensuu (3–10 daily; 6hr 35min–8hr 45min); Jyväskylä (hourly; 4hr–5hr 40min); Kotka (hourly; 2hr 10min–2hr 50min); Mikkeli (hourly; 3hr 20min–4hr 10min); Porvoo (every 20min; 1hr); Tampere (hourly; 2hr 15min–4hr 10min); Turku (every 30min; 2hr 10min–2hr 45min).
Kotka to: Hamina (hourly; 35min); Kouvola (3–10 daily; 1hr 10min).
Mariehamn to: Bomarsund (5 daily; 30min); Eckerö (5 daily; 45min); Kastelholm (5 daily; 30min).
Pori to: Rauma (hourly; 45min–1hr 5min); Turku (13–18 daily; 2hr 10min–2hr 55min).
Porvoo to: Helsinki (every 20min; 1hr); Kotka (hourly; 1hr 30min); Loviisa (hourly; 40min); Pyhtää (Mon–Fri hourly, Sat & Sun 4–8 daily; 50min–1hr 25min).

Rauma to: Pori (hourly; 45min–1hr 5min); Turku (hourly; 1hr 30min).
Turku to: Helsinki (every 30min; 2hr 10min–2hr 45min); Pori (13–18 daily; 2hr 10min–2hr 55min); Rauma (hourly; 1hr 30min).

Ferries

Helsinki to: Mariehamn (2 daily; 10–13hr).
Mariehamn to: Helsinki (2 daily; 10–13hr); Turku (4 daily; 5hr–5hr 20min).
Turku to: Mariehamn (4 daily; 5hr 30min).

International trains

Helsinki to: Moscow (1 daily; 13hr 40min); St Petersburg (2 daily; 6hr 40min).

International buses

Helsinki to: St Petersburg (2 daily; 9hr–9hr 30min); Viipuri/Vyborg, Russian (2 daily; 5hr 45min).

International ferries

Helsinki to: Stockholm (3 daily; 16hr); St Petersburg (1–3 weekly; 14hr 30min); Tallinn, Estonia (every two hours; 1hr 30min–3hr 30min).
Mariehamn to: Kappelskär (4–6 daily; 2hr); Stockholm (6 daily; 6hr).
Turku to: Stockholm (4 daily; 10–11hr).

4.2

The Lake Region

Known unofficially as *tuhansien järvien maa*, which loosely translates as "the land of a thousand lakes", Finland boasts more than 40,000 waterways and lake chains, the majority of them – chiefly the Päijanne and Saimaa systems – located in the **Lake Region**. Unique in Finland, and indeed in Scandinavia and western Europe, a third of the area here is taken up by water. Each of the lake chains features countless bays, inlets and islands interspersed with dense forests, while the settlements have grown up around paper mills which used natural waterways and purpose-built canals to transport timber to pulping factories powered by gushing rapids.

Wherever you go in the Lake Region, water is never far away, further pacifying an already tranquil and verdant landscape. Even **Tampere**, Finland's major industrial city, is likeable as much for its lakeside setting as for its cosmopolitan cultural delights. It's also the most accessible of the region's centres, being on the railway line between Helsinki and the north. Also reachable by train from Helsinki, **Lahti** comes into its own as a winter-sports resort; during summer the town is comparatively lifeless. Diminutive **Mikkeli** has more character, and makes a good stopover en route to the atmospheric eastern part of the Lake Region, where slender ridges furred with

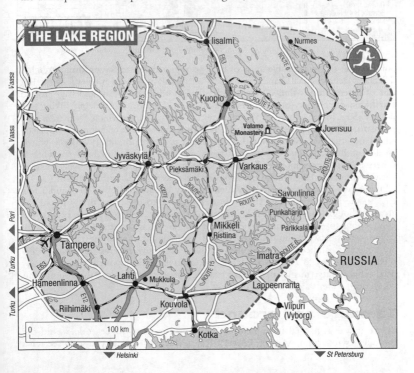

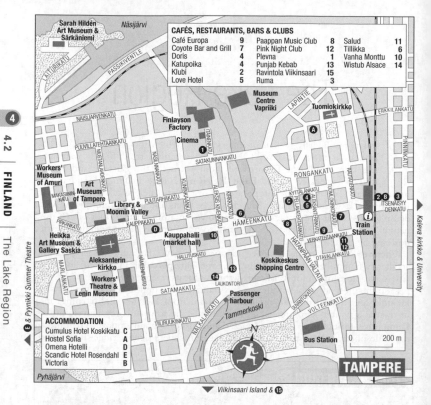

CAFÉS, RESTAURANTS, BARS & CLUBS

Café Europa	9	Paappan Music Club	8	Salud	11
Coyote Bar and Grill	7	Pink Night Club	12	Tillikka	6
Doris	4	Plevna	1	Vanha Monttu	10
Katupoika	4	Punjab Kebab	13	Wistub Alsace	14
Klubi	2	Ravintola Viikinsaari	15		
Love Hotel	5	Ruma	3		

ACCOMMODATION

Cumulus Hotel Koskikatu	C
Hostel Sofia	A
Omena Hotelli	D
Scandic Hotel Rosendahl	E
Victoria	B

TAMPERE

conifers link the few sizeable areas of land. Its regional centre, **Savonlinna**, stretches delectably across several islands, and boasts a superbly preserved medieval castle. Just east of here, a stone's throw from the Russian border, the forests and bays around **Parikkala** offer plenty of outdoors enjoyment in the form of canoeing, hiking and horse riding. To get a sense of Karelian culture (for more on which, see p.672) visit **Joensuu**, **Lappeenranta** or the city of **Kuopio**, three towns where many displaced Karelians settled after World War II. In the heart of the region lies **Jyväskylä**, whose wealth of buildings by Alvar Aalto draws modern architecture buffs to what is otherwise a sleepy, quaint student town. Down-to-earth **Iisalmi** is effectively a bridge between the Lake Region and the rougher, less watery terrain further north.

Unless you want total solitude (which is easily attained), it's best to spend a few days in the larger towns and make shorter forays into the more thinly populated areas. Although the western Lake Region is mostly well served by **trains**, rail connections to – and within – the eastern part are awkward and infrequent. With daily services between the main towns and less frequent ones to the villages, **buses** are generally handier for getting around. Slow, expensive **ferries** (including a few offering day-trips to Russia) also link the main lakeside towns, while practically every community runs short pleasure cruises, but to really explore the countryside, you'll need to rent a **car** or **bicycle**.

Tampere and around

"Here it was as natural to approve of the factories as in Mecca one would the mosques," wrote John Sykes of **TAMPERE** in the 1960s – and you soon see what he meant. But although Tampere has long been Finland's biggest manufacturing centre and is currently Scandinavia's largest inland city, it's a highly scenic place, with leafy cobbled avenues, sculpture-filled parks and two sizeable lakes. The factories that line the Tammerkoski rapids in the heart of the city actually accentuate its appeal, their chimneys standing as bold monuments to Tampere's past – it's no coincidence that the town is known colloquially as the Manchester of Finland's north. Its rapid growth began almost two centuries ago, when Tsar Alexander I abolished taxes on local trade, encouraging the Scotsman James Finlayson to open a textile factory here, drawing labour from rural areas where traditional crafts were in decline. Metalwork and clothing factories soon followed (mobile phone giant Nokia was founded here in 1865 as a wood-pulp manufacturer), their owners paternalistically supplying culture to the workforce by promoting a vigorous local arts scene. Free outdoor rock and jazz concerts, lavish theatrical productions and one of the best modern art collections in Finland maintain such traditions to this day.

Arrival, orientation and information

Tampere's **airport**, Pirkkala, lies 15km south of the city centre. Buses (35–40min; €4.10–6) meet flights at either terminal and drop passengers at the central train station. For Ryanair flights, there is a return trip departing the train station approximately two hours before scheduled departure; bus #61 from the town centre also goes there roughly once an hour.

Almost everything of consequence is within the central section of the city, bordered on two sides by the lakes Näsijärvi and Pyhäjärvi. The main streets run off either side of Hämeenkatu, which leads directly from the **train station** across Hämeensilta, the bridge over the Tammerkoski River, notable for its weighty bronze sculptures by Wäino Aaltonen, which represent four characters from local folklore. Although there's little call to use local **buses**, most routes begin from the terminal on Hämeenkatu.

Tampere's friendly and helpful **tourist office**, Go Tampere, at the train station (June–Aug Mon–Fri 9am–8pm, Sat & Sun 9.30am–5pm; Sept Mon–Fri 9am–5pm, Sat & Sun 9.30am–5pm; Oct–Dec Mon–Fri 9am–5pm, Sat & Sun 11am–3pm; Jan–May Mon–Fri 9am–5pm; ☎03/5656 6800, ⓦwww.gotampere.fi), hands out maps, hiking itineraries and copies of the excellent free *Tampere* guide; there are also two free **internet** terminals. Be sure to ask staff whether the Tampere Card, which will offer discounts on many city museums and attractions, has been implemented yet. From June to August the office also organizes daily ninety-minute sightseeing tours of the town; enquire for specifics.

Accommodation

Being one of Finland's most popular destinations, Tampere has plenty of central accommodation options for all types of budget. Still, many of these get booked up early so you'll want to book ahead if possible, lest you be left foraging for the more expensive leftovers. If you're **camping**, there are lakeside facilities at Härmälä (☎03/265 1355 or 09/6138 3210, ⓦwww.lomaliitto.fi/harmala; mid-May to Aug only), 5km south, which also rents out small cabins (€38) and several that sleep up to five (€66); take bus #1.

🏃 **Cumulus Hotel Koskikatu** Koskikatu 5 ☎03/242 4111, ⓦwww.cumulus.fi. Excellent location for this chain favourite, set right on the rapids (request a room with a view). Staff are very friendly and there is a great lounge bar and restaurant attached to the lobby. ❹/❺
Hostel Sofia Tuomiokirkonkatu 12A ☎03/254 4020, ⓦwww.hostelsofia.fi. These newly reno-vated dorm rooms breathe a bit of colour

into Finland's institutional hostel look and feel, and they're the cheapest beds in town (€20), though the doubles (❸) are also a comparatively good bargain.
🏃 **Omena Hotelli** Hämeenkatu 28 ☎200/39 000, ⓦwww.omena.com. Central, post-modern concept establishment that eschews human interaction: there is no receptionist, and bookings must be made via the internet or at the

kiosk in the downstairs "lobby" (note that booking by phone will incur an extra €6 charge); an electronic code then grants you access to the very sleek, very mod rooms. ❷

Scandic Hotel Rosendahl Pyynikintie 13 ☎03/244 1111, ⓦwww.scandichotels.com. Lakeside luxury a couple of kilometres west of the city centre, right inside Pyynikki park and next to the observation tower. The hundred or so rooms are comfortable and tidy; many have views to the lake, as well as access to the pool and several saunas. Bus #21. ❻

Victoria Itsenäisyydenkatu 1 ☎03/242 5111, ⓦwww.hotellivictoria.fi. Directly opposite the train station, the *Victoria*'s rooms are simple but spacious and well appointed, though lacking any real character. ❹/❻

The City

Short, broad streets make central Tampere very easy to explore. From the train station, **Hämeenkatu** runs across the Tammerkoski into the heart of the city, and almost everything of interest lies within a few minutes' walk of this busy thoroughfare. You'll need to cross back over the river (most easily done by following Satakunnankatu) to reach Tampere's historic **cathedral**, as well as a couple of worthwhile museums, the cinema and several upmarket restaurants – and to get the best view of the superbly maintained Finlayson Factory, on which the city's fortunes were founded; it's now home to the editorial offices of the region's main newspaper.

Hämeenkatu and around

Walking the length of Hämeenkatu from the train station leaves you in front of the upwardly thrusting neo-Gothic **Aleksanterin kirkko** (daily: May–Aug 10am–5pm; Sept–April 11am–3pm). With a riot of knobbly ceiling decorations, the effect inside is something like an ecclesiastical train station, with an unusually unpleasant artexed altar. To the left, following the line of greenery south down Hämeenpuisto, is the Tampere Workers' Theatre and, in the same building, the excellent **Lenin Museum** (Mon–Fri 9am–6pm, Sat & Sun 11am–4pm; €4; ⓦwww.lenin.fi; €3), which, oddly, is the only permanent museum dedicated to Lenin anywhere in the world. After the abortive 1905 revolution in Russia, Lenin lived in Finland for two years and attended the Tampere conferences, held in what is now the museum. It was here that he first encountered Stalin, although this is barely mentioned in the displays, one of which concentrates on Lenin himself, the other on his relationship with

▲ Tampere

Finland and on his visits to numerous Finnish cities. For a detailed explanation, borrow one of the English-language mini-books from reception.

If you want more Lenin, head to Kyttälänkatu, one block north of the train station off Rautatienkatu, where a plaque marks the otherwise undistinguished house (no. 11) where he lived during his stint in Tampere. Several blocks north of Hämeenkatu, the Amuri district was built during the 1880s to house Finlayson's workers. Lenin would have been first in line to visit the **Amurin Työläismuseokortteli** at Makasiininkatu 12 (Amuri Museum of Workers' Housing: May to mid-Sept Tues–Sun 10am–6pm; €5; during the rest of the year only the museum shop is open, same times; ⓦwww.tampere.fi/amuri), a simple but affecting collection of thirty-odd homes that together record the family life of working people over a hundred-year period. In each home is a description of the inhabitants and their jobs, and authentic articles from the relevant periods – from beds and tables to family photos, newspapers and biscuit packets.

Just around the corner at Puutarhakatu 34 is the **Art Museum of Tampere** (Tues–Sun 10am–6pm; €5; guided tours by arrangement on ☏03/3146 6580; ⓦwww.tampere.fi/taidemuseo), whose first floor holds powerful if staid temporary exhibitions featuring Finnish and international artists; the large basement galleries are filled with contemporary local work. If you're looking for older Finnish art, head instead for the far superior **Hiekka Art Museum**, a few minutes' walk away at Pirkankatu 6 (Tues–Thurs 3–6pm, Wed 3–7pm, Sun noon–3pm; other times by arrangement ☏03/212 3973; €5; ⓦwww.hiekantaidemuseo.fi). Kustaa Hiekka was a gold- and silver-smith whose professional skills and business acumen made him a local bigshot around 1900. The art collection he bequeathed to Tampere reflects his interest in traditional lifestyles; borrow a catalogue from reception, since most pieces are identified only by numbers. Amongst the most notable work (including sketches by Gallen-Kallela and Helene Schjerfbeck) are two of Hiekka's own creations: a delicately wrought brooch marking the completion of his apprenticeship, and a finely detailed bracelet with which he celebrated becoming a master craftsman. Well worth the diversion is the next-door **Gallery Saskia** (daily noon–6pm, free, ⓦwww.tampereensaskiat.com), showing intriguing and unusual new work.

Nearby, at Pirkankatu 2, stands the **Tampere library** (June–Aug Mon–Sat 9.30am–7pm; Sept–May Mon–Fri 9.30am–8pm, Sat 9.30am–3pm), an astounding feat of user-friendly modern architecture. The work of Reimi and Raili Pietilä (who also designed the epic Kaleva kirkko – see p.579), and finished in 1986, the library's curving walls give it a warm, cosy feel; believe it or not, the building's shape was inspired by a certain type of grouse (a stuffed specimen of which sits in the reception area). Strolling around is the best way to take in the many small, intriguing features, and will eventually lead you up to the top-floor café, which gives a good view of the cupola, deliberately set eleven degrees off the vertical to match the off-centre pivot of the earth. In the basement of the library, with its own entrance at Hämeenpuisto 20, **Moomin Valley** (Mon–Fri 9am–5pm, Sat & Sun 10am–6pm; €4; ⓦwww.tampere.fi/muumi) uses some two thousand dolls, models, dioramas, sets and interactive displays to re-create scenes from the incredibly popular children's books by Tove Jansson.

A few blocks south of Hämeenkatu, the passenger harbour is the departure point for summer **lake cruises** around the Pyhä (Mon 12.30pm & Wed 5.30pm; 90min; €20–27 including buffet lunch or dinner). For something simpler, take a quick trip over to nearby **Viikinsaari** (hourly Tues–Sun; 20min; €8). First known as Jomasaari ("Island of God"), this small wooded island served as a popular weekend destination for nineteenth-century Finnish nobility, but fell into some disrepute after local ne'er-do-wells claimed it as their private watering hole. Today, it houses a small chapel and a nature reserve, making it popular with many locals looking for some fresh air. At midsummer, Viikinsaari hosts evening fetes, tango dancing and a traditional *kakko*, a large bonfire lit right on the banks of lake Pyhäjärvi. The island also holds the *Ravintola Viikinsaari* restaurant (see p 579).

The Näsijärvi lakeside

Just north of Tampere's central grid-plan streets, the tremendous **Sara Hildén Art Museum** (Mon noon–7pm, Tues–Sun 11am–6pm; closed Mon Oct–May; closed mid-Jan to mid-Feb, early May & Sept; €4–7 depending upon exhibitions; ⊛ www .tampere.fi/sarahilden), built on the shores of Näsijärvi, displays Tampere's premier modern art collection by means of changing exhibitions. On display here are a number of works from 1960s Informalist painters, as well as modern masters such as Klee, Delvaux, Bacon, Lèger – there's even a Picasso. The museum is on the other side of the northern arterial road, Paasikiventie, from Amuri (take bus #16, or the summer-only #4 bus from the town centre or train station).

Occupying the same waterside strip as the Hildén collection is **Särkänniemi** (⊛ www.sarkanniemi.fi; €5), Tampere's most popular tourist destination. A sizeable complex incorporating an adventure park, dolphinarium, aquarium, planetarium and an observation tower with rotating restaurant, the site is open year-round (daily 11am–9pm, often closes later during summer), though the zoo and theme park rides operate between May and August only. Seen from the **tower** (April–Sept daily 11am–11.30pm; Oct–March Tues–Sat 11am–11.30pm, Sun & Mon 11am–9.30pm; €8), itself an unmistakable element of Tampere's skyline, the city seems insignificant compared to the trees and lakes that stretch to the horizon. The rapids that cut through them can be identified from afar by the factory chimneys alongside. The tower's admission charge is waived if you're eating at its restaurant; the other diversions cost €6 apiece and are usually crowded with families. To make a day of it, buy the €30 Adventure Key, valid for all parts of the complex except parasailing. Särkänniemi's café serves half-decent, inexpensive pizza, salads and the like.

The Tuomiokirkko and around

Cross to the eastern side of the Tammerkoski River along Satakunnankatu and you'll not only see – foaming below the bridge – the rapids that powered the **Finlayson Factory**, but also the factory building itself, still standing to the north and well worth a wander for its crafts shops. Also within the Finlayson complex is an absorbing addition to Tampere's museums, the **Vakoilumuseo** (Spy Museum: June–Aug Mon–Sat 10am–6pm, Sun 11am–5pm; Sept–May Mon–Sun 11am–5pm, Sat & Sun 10am–4pm, opens daily in summer; ⊛ www.vakoilumuseo.fi; €7). The range of gadgets, clothing, machines and documents – including a set of now-declassified KGB maps – attest to the rampant espionage on both sides of the Finnish and Russian border during the last century. Don't underestimate the kitsch value of all the gizmos on display here, which include night-vision goggles, eaves-dropping transmitters and intelligence decoders.

Immediately ahead of the Finlayson complex in a grassy square, the **Tuomio-kirkko** (daily: May–Aug 9am–6pm; Sept–April 11am–3pm) is a picturesque cathedral in the National Romantic style, designed by Lars Sonck and finished in 1907. It's most remarkable for the gorily symbolic frescoes by Hugo Simberg – particularly the *Garden of Death*, where skeletons happily water plants, and *The Wounded Angel*, showing two boys carrying a bleeding angel through a Tampere landscape – which caused an ecclesiastical outcry when unveiled. So did the viper (a totem of evil) which Sonck placed amongst the angel wings on the ceiling; Simberg retorted that evil could lurk anywhere – including a church.

Out from the centre

To learn more about Tampere's origins, visit the **Museum Centre Vapriikki** (Tues & Thurs–Sun 10am–6pm, Wed 11am–8pm; €5, special exhibitions €7; ⊛ www.tampere.fi/vapriikki), housed in a former mill just across the river from the Finlayson Factory. Though the museum covers everything from archeology to handicrafts, its most interesting section deals with the impact of the early twentieth century – a turbulent time for both Tampere and Finland. As an industrial town with militant workers, Tampere instigated a general strike against the Russification of

Finland, filling the streets with demonstrators and painting over the Cyrillic names on trilingual street signs. After independence the city became a Social Democratic stronghold, and one ruthlessly dealt with by the right-wing government following the civil war of 1918 – yet the municipal administration remains amongst the most left-leaning in Finland. Vapriiki also contains the slightly less engaging **Finnish Ice Hockey Museum** (same times and entrance fee), which accords due honour to local teams Ilves and Tappara.

Away to the east of the centre, Itsenäisyydenkatu runs uphill behind the train station to meet the vast concrete folds of the **Kaleva kirkko** (daily: May–Aug 10am–5pm; Sept–April 11am–3pm). Built in 1966, it was a belated addition to the neighbouring **Kaleva estate**, which was heralded in the 1950s as an outstanding example of high-density housing. Though initially stunning, the church's interior lacks the subtlety of the city library, despite being designed by the same team of Reima and Raili Pietilä, who this time based their plan on a fish.

Eating

Tampere boasts an eclectic range of **restaurants** and **cafés** to suit all pockets. Several places in the *Koskikeskus* shopping mall, Hatanpään valtatie 1, offer cheap lunchtime specials, but, as usual, the cheapest places to eat are the student **mensas** – in the university at the end of Yliopistonkatu, just over the railway line from the city centre – where full meals can cost as little as €5.

There are numerous **supermarkets** at which to stock up on provisions. Three central options are the big Sokos store at Hämeenkatu 21, or the two significantly cheaper Lidl shops, at Rautatienkatu 21 and Hallituskatu 14–16. There's also a large **kauppahalli** (market hall) at Hämeenkatu 19 (Mon–Fri 8am–6pm, Sat 8am–4pm), and open-air markets at Laukontori (Mon–Fri 6am–2pm, Sat 6am–1pm), Keskustori (first Mon of month 6am–6pm) and Tammelantori (Mon–Fri 6am–2pm, Sat 6am–1pm).

Coyote Bar and Grill Hämeenkatu 3 ⓦ www .coyote.fi. A full-on retro dining affair with loads of young locals chowing down on burgers and finger food, and sipping on bottles of imported beers against murals of Castro.

Katupoika Aleksanterinkatu 20 ⓦ www .aleksinravintolat.fi. A local institution, this fairly priced eatery is popular with locals and visiting families. It's known for its tasty Finnish vegetarian dishes, but is also a great place to try the local speciality *mustamakkara*, a rich blood sausage, or *lehtipihvi*, a succulent goat cheese-stuffed leaf steak (€20.70).

Plevna Itäinenkatu 4. Down-at-heel gastropub that also brews its own beer.

Punjab Kebab Kirkkokatu 10. One block from the passenger harbour, serving the city's favourite kebabs (€5–6).

Ravintola Viikinsaari Viikinsaari island ⓦ www .hopealinja.fi. Under new management, this grand old place has been in operation since 1900 and is a wonderful venue for upscale dinners at downtown

prices. Most of the traditional Finnish dishes, such as the Tallqvist onion steak, cost around €15. Take the boat to get there (see p.577).

Salud Tuomiokirkonkatu 19 ⓦ www.salud.fi. A lively Spanish restaurant serving mixed tapas plates (€8.40) and sizeable Iberian meat dishes such as *costillas de cerdo* (pork ribs; €16.70). The sprawling weekday lunch buffet (€9.50) is one of the best deals in town.

🍴 **Tillikka** Hämeenkatu 14 ⓦ www.tillikka.fi. The name translates as "inn", and this very classy place is appropriately dressed up in early twentieth-century flair, with terraces overlooking the Tammerkoski rapids. The continental fare includes interesting dishes like wild boar (€19.50) and a lamb bratwurst, barley sausage and spicy chorizo sausage platter (€12.90).

🍴 **Wistub Alsace** Laukontori 6B ⓦ www .wistubalsace.com. Excellent harbourside spot serving great southeastern French food in a charming, familial interior, with mains starting at €21.

Drinking and entertainment

Tampere is very much alive and buzzing after dark, with numerous late-night bars, cafés and clubs, though many of these places won't feel quite as active or as young as in similarly sized Turku or Jyväskylä on account of the city lacking a real student population. Still, you won't want for something to do come evenings – provided you like to drink – and many spots host **live music** acts, especially in the summer, often with little or no cover charge.

On warm nights the crowds head out to the Pyynikki area, a natural ridge on the edge of Tampere, beside Pyhäjärvi. Tickets for the **Pyynikki Summer Theatre** (☎03/216 0300, ⊛www.pyynikinkesateatteri.com) cost €27, but it's worth trekking out just to look at the revolving auditorium which slowly rotates the audience around during performances, blending the surrounding woods, rocks and water into the show's scenery. All theatre performances here are in Finnish only, but there are a number of orchestral concerts as well.

Plevna, Itäinenkatu 4 (⊛www.finnkino.fi), is the city's largest **cinema**, with ten screens and frequent runs of English-language pictures.

Café Europa Aleksanterinkatu 29. More a bar and restaurant than a café, this is one of the best places to meet Tampere's trendy young things. One of the more international places in town in terms of clientele.

Doris Kauppakatu 16. Tues is the best night to show up to mingle with Tampere's bohos and hipsters at this happening underground bar; DJs spin until 4am every day of the week.

Klubi Tullikamarin Aukio 2. An extremely popular nightclub set in an old customs house just east of the train station off Itsenäisyydenkatu. Regular DJs spin and locals party until the sun rises. Also serves inexpensive lunches. Closed Sun.

Love Hotel Hämeenkatu 10A. While there are no rooms at this large, tauntingly named nightclub, many couples here often behave like they need to get one. Tricked-out lighting displays, a maze of corridors, a lone blackjack table do their best to draw your attention away from pricey cocktails, an empty dancefloor and flirting *à la Finnois*.

Paapan Kapakka Koskikatu 9. With Guinness, Kilkenny, Carlsberg and Hoegarden on tap, this pub-styled jazz bar attracts a good range of mature drinkers. You don't even need to know the address: just follow your ears to the squealing sax, simmering snare and piano soloing of the swing-style groups that regularly hold session on the bar's intimate stage.

Pink Night Club Otavalankatu 9 ⊛www.pinkclub .fi. One of the few gay bars in the country outside Helsinki, this friendly and laid-back spot sports large mirrors and red sofas. Open Fri & Sat only; gets going after 12.30am.

Ruma Murtokatu 1 ⊛www.ruma.fi. Popular dance bar set a block away from the train station. The minimum age limit of 18 does little to deter teenagers who show up with fake IDs aplenty.

Vanha Monttu Hämeenkatu 17 ⊛www .vanhamonttu.net. Cellar bar frequented by the pierced, the bedraggled and the hard-rocking. No live music, but karaoke evenings on Tues & Wed more than make up for it. Serves €3.50 pints of Koff.

Around Tampere

Half an hour from Tampere on the busy rail line to Helsinki, **HÄMEENLINNA** (Tavastehus in Swedish) is revered both as the birthplace of Sibelius and as Finland's oldest inland town. The major attraction is **Häme Castle** (June to mid-Aug daily 10am–6pm; mid-Aug to April Mon–Fri 10am–4pm, Sat 11am–4pm; closed Jan; €5), the sturdy thirteenth-century fortress from which the town takes its name; free guided tours are available in English by appointment – call ☎03/675 6820. Next comes the **Sibelius Childhood Home** (daily: May–Aug 10am–4pm; Sept–April noon–4pm; €4) at Hallituskatu 11, where the great composer was born; it has been now reverentially restored to how it was during the first years of his life. A few blocks away at Viipurintie 2, the **Art Museum** (Tues–Thurs 11am–6pm, Fri–Sun 11am–7pm; €6) musters a mundane collection of minor works by major Finnish names, among them Järnefelt, Gallen-Kalella and Halonen.

Seeing all this won't take long, and any spare hours are better spent in the outlying town of **Hattula**, roughly 5km from the centre of Hämeenlinna. The local **Hattulan kirkko** (daily mid-May to mid-Aug 11am–5pm; other times by appointment on ☎03/631 1540) is probably the finest medieval church in Finland – outwardly plain, with an interior totally covered by 180 sixteenth-century frescoes of biblical scenes. En route to the church and 4km south of Hämeenlina, just across the river, is *Katajistan Kartana* (☎03/682 8560, ⊛www.aulanko.com;

May to mid-Aug; dorms €14, doubles ⑤), a youth hostel, **campsite** (June–Aug) and restaurant.

Moving on from Tampere

Tampere has excellent **train links** to the rest of Finland. To reach the rest of the Lake Region, however, there are two main choices. Aiming for Jyväskylä also puts you within comparatively easy reach of Varkaus, Joensuu and Kuopio. Alternatively, heading for Lahti (change at Riihimäki) makes more sense if you want to press on to Mikkeli or Lappeenranta, or see more of the eastern Lake Region. For Savonlinna, there are two alternative routes: either take a train to Pieksämäki, from where there are direct buses (which accept train passes and tickets) to the town, or head east through Riihimäki and Lappeenranta to Parikkala for the branch line to Savonlinna.

Jyväskylä

JYVÄSKYLÄ (pronounced "EWE-vah-skoo-lah") is the most low-key and provincial of the main Lake Region towns, despite an industrial section that takes up one end and a big university which consumes the other – though the latter does provide something of a youthful feel. The town also has more than its fair share of buildings by **Alvar Aalto**. The legendary architect grew up here and opened his first office in the town in 1923, and his handiwork – a collection of buildings spanning his entire career – litters the place.

After some minor projects, Aalto left Jyväskylä in 1927 for fame, fortune and Helsinki, but returned in the 1950s to work on the teacher-training college. By the 1970s this had grown into the **Jyväskylä University**, whose large campus halts traffic where the main road gives way to a series of public footpaths, leading to a park and sports ground. Although Aalto died before his ambitious plan for an Administration and Cultural Centre was complete, the scheme is still under construction along Vapaudenkatu. Across the road from the (perhaps intentionally) uninspiring police station – unveiled in 1970 – stands the **City Theatre** resembling a scaled-down version of Helsinki's Finlandia Hall.

Arrival, information and accommodation

From the train and bus stations, right in the centre, it's a short walk to the **tourist office**, in a beautiful wooden building at Asemakatu 6 (June to mid-Aug Mon–Fri

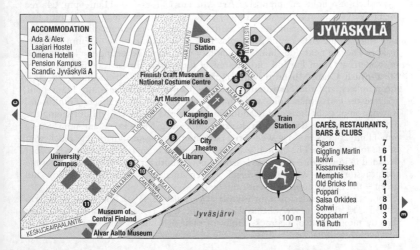

9am–6pm, Sat 10am–3pm; mid-Aug to May Mon–Fri 9am–5pm, Sat 10am–3pm; ℡014/624 903, 🖥www.jyvaskylanseutu.fi), which can supply a useful free leaflet on the local buildings designed by Aalto and has **internet** access. There's paid access available at Avatar, Puistokatu 1 (€4 per hour).

For **accommodation**, the modern, spartan, reception-less *Omena Hotelli* (🖥www.omena.com), Vapaudenkatu 57, can be one of the cheapest and best stays in the city if you book in advance. Elsewhere, both *Pension Kampus*, Kauppakatu 11A (℡014/338 1400, 🖥www.kolumbus.fi/pensionkampus; ❸), and the central, family-run *Hotel Milton*, Hannikaisenkatu 27–29 (℡014/337 7900, 🖥www.hotellimilton.com; ❹), right by the train station, are good choices. A bit higher up in standard is *Ada & Alex* (℡400 597 072, 🖥www.ada-alex.fi; ❺), Samulinranta 5, though the price can drop the more nights you stay. For more pampering, try the *Scandic Jyväskylä* at Vapaudenkatu 73 (℡014/330 3000, 🖥www.scandichotels .com; ❹/❻) – some rooms have their own private saunas. The local **youth hostel**, *Laajari* (℡014/624 885, 🖥www.laajavuori.com; dorms €19.50, doubles ❷), is a state-of-the-art affair, 4km from the centre at Laajavuorentie 15 – take bus #25 from Vapaudenkatu. The local **campsite** is closed indefinitely and the nearest option is roughly 30km away; check with the tourist office for the latest details on pitching tents or parking campers in the area.

The Town

Two of the town's most important **museums** are situated close together on the hill running down from the university towards the edge of the lake, Jyväsjärvi. At the request of the town authorities rather than through vanity, Aalto built the **Alvar Aalto Museum** at Alvar Aallon Katu 7 (Tues–Sun 11am–6pm; €6, free on Fri; 🖥www.alvaraalto.fi). The architect's best works are obviously out on the streets, making this collection of plans, photos and models seem rather superfluous, but the Aalto-designed furniture makes partial amends. The first floor hosts temporary art exhibitions and the ground floor has a pleasant if unexciting café. Aalto also contributed to the exterior of the nearby Keski-Suomen Museo (Museum of Central Finland: Tues–Sun 11am–6pm; €5, free on Fri; 🖥www.jkl .fi/ksmuseo), which contains two separate exhibitions: one devoted to Middle Finland – well designed but with no English translations – and the other representing each decade of the twentieth century through the car number-plates, music and kitchen gadgetry of the day. The collection of room interiors is worth the visit alone.

Jyväskylä also holds an impressive **Art Museum** (Tues–Sun 11am–6pm; €4, free on Fri; 🖥www.jyvaskyla.fi/taidemuseo) at Kauppakatu 25, which is split into two exhibition sites. The main site houses the permanent collection of the Ester and Jalo Sihtola Fine Arts Foundation, plus that of the Association of Finnish Printmakers. The site next door houses temporary exhibitions reflecting the latest trends in modern art from Finland and the rest of the world. Also at Kauppakatu 25 are the **Finnish Craft Museum**, with displays ranging from bell-making to spectrolite jewellery, and the **National Costume Centre** (both Tues–Sun 11am–6pm; €5, free on Fri) which holds a definitive collection of 26 complete Finnish and Karelian smocks, bodices and headdresses. Don't leave Jyväskylä without seeing the nineteenth-century **Kaupungin kirkko** (June–Aug Mon–Fri 11am–6pm, Sat & Sun 11am–2pm; Sept–May Wed–Fri 11am–2pm), in the small park one block west of the tourist office. The church was the centrepiece of town life a century ago, but declined in importance as Jyväskylä gained new suburbs and other churches. Despite recent restoration – when the interior was repainted in its original pale yellow and green – the church looks authentically dingy.

About 20km outside town, in Nyrölä at Vertaalantie 419, is the Kallioplanetario (℡050 313 3658, 🖥www.kallioplanetaario.fi; €7), a massive planetarium built directly into a vault of bedrock. Times of their 3-D shows vary, so ring them in advance to see what's on.

Eating

Jyväskylä's **eating** options range from the quotidian pizza establishments along the main streets to a few worthy upscale places. For real budget lunches during the school year, try the student *mensa* at Ilokivi, Keskussairaalantie; if you get tired of Finnish cuisine, you may want to explore the town's fetish for Tex Mex restaurants – or, rather "Mix-Tex" as one of them advertises.

Figaro Asemakatu 14 ☎014 212 255, ⊛www .figarorestaurant.com. This central, comfy family-style restaurant matches fair-priced salads, pastas, steaks and fish dishes with a well-endowed wine list and is justifiably busy. A three-course meal won't run over €30, but they also offer a great lunch buffet for €8.90. Reservations recommended on weekends.

Kissanviikset Puistokatu 3. "The Cat's Whiskers" serves sizeable Finnish fish and meat dishes (most under €20) in an elegant, old-world setting.

Salsa Orkidea Kauppakatu 6. One of the towns better Tex Mex restaurants, with tacos, tortillas, quesadillas, burritos and chimichangas, all for under €10.

Sohwi Vaasankatu 21. A popular, light and airy place serving inexpensive burgers, ribs, steaks and a number of tapas dishes. Evenings frequently feature live music, and the bar stays hopping until well after midnight.

Soppabarri Väinönkatu 26 ⊛www.soppabaari.fi. "The Soup Bar" dishes out inexpensive, innovative soups, pastas and vegetarian mains.

Drinking and entertainment

Jyväskylä's student population ensures a good crop of bars, though things are somewhat sedate in the summer out of term-time. The neighbourhood around the university is the focal point for the town's **nightlife**, and as the university hosts events in and out of term, it's always worth looking out for posters advertising parties and live music events. There is quite a strong **gay** scene in town; for information on local gay events, call in at SETA, Kilpisinkatu 8 (☎045/638 9540; ⊛www .jklseta.fi), which organizes regular parties at Ilokivi and other venues.

Giggling Marlin Kauppakatu 32. The local branch of the ubiquitous Finnish chain disco is currently *the* place to be for local ravers.

Ilokivi Keskussairaalantie 2 ⊛www.jyy.fi/ilokivi. Located in the university grounds, this lively cultural space is a hot student destination on account of its live bands, art exhibitions, theatre and stand-up "comedy" performances.

Poppari Puistokatu 2–4 ⊛www.jazz-bar.com. Live music (mostly jazz) several days a week, and open jam sessions on Tues nights.

Memphis Kauppakatu 30 ⊛www.mphis.fi. This central restaurant-cum-bar has massive front windows and attracts younger Finns, especially on

Thurs nights, when live rock bands take the stage. Less expensive beer is on offer downstairs at the *Ale Pub*.

Old Bricks Inn Kauppakatu 41 ⊛www .oldbricksinn.fi. On sunny evenings, the outdoor seating at this popular pub really pulls the crowds. There's a good selection of imported beers, great coffee and several scrumptious dinner dishes to boot.

Ylä Ruth Seminaarinkatu 19 ⊛www.yla-ruth .fi. Often smoky and filled with lively characters, generally members of the university's philosophy and politics departments here for a game of chess and/or some hard drinking.

Lahti

LAHTI doesn't know if it's a Lake Region town or a Helsinki suburb, and it's perhaps this confusion that conspires to make the place so dull. Its entire growth took place in the twentieth century (mostly since Alvar Aalto opened several furniture factories, which kept him going between architectural commissions), and although it's now the major transport junction between the Lake Region and the south, it lacks any lake-area atmosphere, while local cultural life is diminished by the relative proximity of Helsinki. Lahti's one compensation is its status as a **winter-sports** centre of international renown: three enormous ski jumps hang over the town, and there's a feeling of biding time when summer grass, rather than winter snow, covers their slopes.

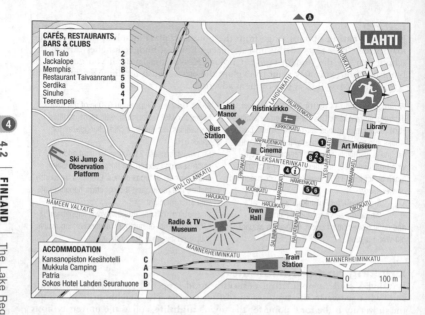

CAFÉS, RESTAURANTS,
BARS & CLUBS

Ilon Talo	2
Jackalope	3
Memphis	B
Restaurant Taivaanranta	5
Serdika	6
Sinuhe	4
Teerenpeli	1

ACCOMMODATION

Kansanopiston Kesähotelli	C
Mukkula Camping	A
Patria	D
Sokos Hotel Lahden Seurahuone	B

Unless you're here to ski, Lahti isn't a place you'll need or want to linger in – the town can easily be covered in half a day. Head first for the **observation platform** on the highest ski jump (June–Aug Mon–Fri 10am–5pm; Sat & Sun 11am–5pm; other times of the year by reservation only at ☎03/816 8223; €5 including the chairlift to the top), whose location is unmistakable. From such a dizzying altitude the lakes and forests around Lahti stretch dreamily into the distance, and the large swimming pool below the jump resembles a puddle (when frozen in winter it's used as a landing zone).

The only structures matching the ski jumps for height are the twin radio masts atop Radiomäki hill, between the train station (a 15min walk away) and the town centre. Steep pathways wind uphill towards the **Radio Ja TV Museo** (Radio and Television Museum: Mon–Fri 10am–5pm, Sat & Sun 11am–5pm; €5), inside the original transmitting station at the base of one of the masts. Here, two big rooms are packed with bulky Marconi valves, crystal sets, antiquated sound-effect discs, room-sized amplifiers and intriguing curios. Look out for the Pikku Hitler – the German-made "little Hitler", a wartime portable radio that forms an uncanny facsimile of the dictator's face.

At Radiomäki's foot, the distinctive red brickwork of Eliel Saarinen's **town hall** injects some style into the concrete blocks that make central Lahti so dull and uniform. Built in 1912, many of its Art Nouveau features were considered immensely daring at the time, and although most of the originals were destroyed in World War II, careful refurbishment has re-created much of Saarinen's design. Viewable during office hours, the modish interior is definitely worth seeing. Lahti's other notable building is at the far end of Mariankatu, which cuts through the town centre from the town hall: the **Ristinkirkko** (daily 10am–6pm), whose white roof slopes down from the belltower in imaginative imitation of the local ski jumps. Interestingly, this was the last church to be designed by Alvar Aalto: he died during its construction and the final work was overseen by his wife. Outside, Wäinö Aaltonen's discreetly emotive sculpture marks the war graves in the cemetery.

By now you've more or less exhausted Lahti, although Hämeenkatu, running parallel to the far more hectic Aleksanterinkatu, contains a number of little galleries owned by local artists, and a few secondhand bookshops. The **Art Museum** (Mon–Fri 10am–5pm, Sat & Sun 11am–5pm; €5), just around the corner at Vesijär-venkatu 11, exhibits nineteenth- and twentieth-century works, most notably by Gallen-Kallela and Edelfelt.

Finally, near a hazardous web-like junction by the bus station and hidden behind a line of trees, is the wooden nineteenth-century **Lahti Manor**. Now a historical museum (Mon–Fri 10am–5pm, Sat & Sun 11am–5pm; €5), it contains regional paraphernalia, numerous Finnish medals and coins, plus an unexpected hoard of French and Italian paintings and furniture.

Practicalities

The **tourist office** is at Aleksanterinkatu 13 (Mon–Thurs 9am–5pm, Fri 9am–4pm June–Aug also Sat 10am–2pm; ☏0207/281 750, ⓦwww.lahtitravel.fi). Both the tourist office and the library at Kirkkokatu 31 (Mon–Fri 10am–6pm, Sat 10am–3pm) provide free internet access. There are some good budget **accom-modation** options in Lahti. A decent choice is the *Patria* hostel at Vesijärvenkatu 3 (☏03/782 3783, ⓦwww.matkakotipatria.com), near the train station, which has double rooms (**2**) only in strikingly putrid colours. In summer, try the excellent *Kansanopiston Kesähotelli* (☏03/878 1181, ⓦwww.lahdenkansanopisto.fi; June to mid-Aug) also with doubles (**2**) and dorms (€22) in a very central position in the town's vocational school at Harjukatu 46. For more luxury, the *Sokos Hotel Lahden Seurahuone*, Aleksanterinkatu 14, boasts a sauna and pool, and TV and video in all rooms (☏03/851 11, ⓦwww.sokoshotels.fi; **4**/**6**). About 4km to the north of Lahti at **Mukkula**, reached directly by bus #30 from the bus station at the end of Aleksanterinkatu, is a lakeside **campsite** (☏03/753 5380, ⓦwww.mukkulacamping .fi; June–Aug) with a range of brand new cottages (**3**).

A great **eating** choice is *Restaurant Taivaanranta*, Rautatienkatu 13, which serves good continental meals and also makes its own beer, blueberry cider and whisky. *Serdika*, Hämeenkatu 21, serves rich Bulgarian dishes, while the best place for cakes and pastries is the central *Sinuhe*, Mariankatu 21. You'll find the larger **super-markets** clustered along Savonkatu. Though hardly remarkable for its nightlife, Lahti can certainly hold its own compared to smaller towns in the Lake Region. For an evening **drink**, the best two places are just around the corner from each other: *Teerenpeli* (ⓦwww.teerenpeli.com), Vapaudenkatu 20, and *Jackalope* (ⓦwww .ravintolajackalope.com), Vesijärvenkatu 22, both lively pub-like bars, the latter with slightly more atmosphere. Later on, the younger set springs for *Ilon Talo* (ⓦwww .ilontalo.fi), Vapaudenkatu 13, while their parents retire to the lively *Memphis* in the *Sokos Hotel Lahden Seurahuone* (see above).

As it's so close to Helsinki, **train and bus connections** onwards from Lahti are good. Mikkeli, to the north, is the sensible target if you're ultimately making for Kuopio, while Lappeenranta is a better destination if you're keen to discover the small towns and glorious scenery of the eastern Lake Region, and makes an enjoyable stop en route to Savonlinna.

Mikkeli

In 1986, a Helsinki bank robber chose the market square in **MIKKELI** as the place in which to blow up himself, his car and his hostage. This, the most violent event seen in Finland for decades, was perhaps an echo of Mikkeli's blood-spattered past. In prehistoric times the surrounding plains were battlegrounds for feuding tribes from east and west, while the Finnish infantry has a long association with the town, and it was from Mikkeli that General Mannerheim conducted the campaign against the Soviet Union in the Winter War.

Military matters are a strong local feature, but you don't need to be a bloodthirsty warmonger to find interest in the town's military collections – the insights they provide into Finland's recent history can be fascinating. More generally, Mikkeli

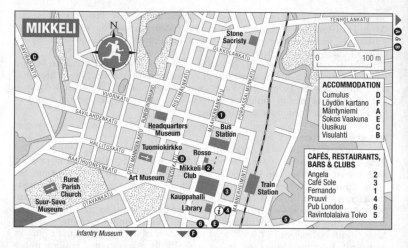

lacks the heavy industry you'll find in some Lake Region communities, functioning instead as a district market town (the daily crowds and activity within its market hall – *kauppahalli* – seem out of all proportion to its size), while sporting a handsome cathedral and a noteworthy art collection.

The military museums

Older Finns visiting Mikkeli tend to make a beeline for Ristimäenkatu, where the office used by Mannerheim is preserved as the **Headquarters Museum** (May–Aug daily 10am–5pm; Sept–April Fri–Sun 10am–5pm; €5). It's not so much the exhibits that give the museum its significance – the centrepiece is Mannerheim's desk, holding his spectacles and favourite cigars – but the fact that the Winter War, which effectively prevented a Soviet invasion of Finland in 1939 (see p.679), was waged and won from this very room. An adjoining room on the ground floor has photo displays and a not-to-be-missed English-language video which offers a first-class account of the predicament Finland found itself in during the Winter War. For more Mannerheim, peek through the windows of his **saloon car** at the train station, which clocked up an impressive 78,000km during the war years when the general used it to travel around Finland – sadly, the carriage interior is only open for viewing on Mannerheim's birthday (June 4).

When not travelling, Mannerheim spent much of his time at the **Mikkeli Club**, a cross between a speakeasy and a Masonic lodge, which still exists, occupying what is now part of the Sokos department store on Hallituskatu, facing the *kauppahalli*. The club's walls are lined with photos of Mannerheim and his staff, although less prominence is given to the snaps of him riding with Hitler during the Führer's birthday visit (these are in an unmarked folder usually lying on a side table). The club is not strictly open to the public, but the restaurant at the *Sokos Hotel Vaakuna* may be able to arrange for interested individuals to be shown around, especially if you're a paying customer. Ring ☎015 206 2602 for enquiries.

A few minutes' walk south from the town centre is the **Jalkaväkimuseo**, Jääkärinkatu 6–8 (Infantry Museum: May–Sept daily 10am–5pm; Oct–April Fri–Sun 11am–4pm; €6), which records the key armed struggles that marked Finland's formative years as an independent nation. Assorted rifles, artillery pieces and maps of troops' movements provide the factual context, but it's the scores of frontline photos and display cases of troops' letters and lucky charms that reveal the human story. A second, substantially less interesting section of the museum concentrates chiefly on the Finnish role in the United Nations Peace-Keeping Force.

The rest of the town

Raised in 1897, Mikkeli's Gothic Revival **Tuomiokirkko** (daily: June–Aug 10am–6pm; Sept–May 10–11am) sits primly on a small hill in the middle of Hallituskatu. Inside, Pekka Halonen's 1899 altarpiece attracts the eye, a radiant Christ against a dark, brooding background. Take a close look, too, at Antti Salmenlinna's stained-glass windows and you'll spot depictions of three Finnish towns (Viipuri, Sortavala and Käkisalmi) ceded to Russia after World War II.

Opposite the cathedral, the excellent **Art Museum**, at Ristimäenkatu 5A (Tues–Sun 10am–5pm, Wed noon–7pm, Sat 10am–1pm; €4), stages some engaging temporary exhibitions of the latest Finnish art, and has two permanent displays of artworks bequeathed to the town. The Martti Airio Collection is a forceful selection of early twentieth-century Finnish Impressionism and Expressionism – Tyko Saalinen's *Young American Woman* and *On the Visit* are particularly striking. The museum's other benefactor was the Mikkeli-born sculptor Johannes Haapasalo, who bequeathed nearly three hundred finished works and over a thousand sketches. One of Haapasalo's better works can be seen beside the cathedral: called *Despair*, it marks the graves of Mikkeli's Civil War dead.

If you've ever wondered how vergers in eighteenth-century Finland kept their church congregations awake, the answer (a big stick) can be seen at the tiny **Stone Sacristy**, to the north at Porrassalmenkatu 32A (late June to early Aug daily 10am–4pm; other times by appointment on ☎015/194 2424; free); the church which the sacristy served was demolished in 1776. Several other historic items from the Mikkeli diocese sit in the room, a wooden pulpit, a "shame bench" (for women deemed unvirtuous) and a wood-framed Bible among them.

A fifteen-minute walk from the town centre along Otavankatu (easily combined with a visit to the Infantry Museum) leads to the **Rural Parish Church** (mid-June to mid-Aug daily 11am–5pm), believably claimed to be one of the largest wooden churches in Finland. Size aside, the church is a modest sight, but is a more satisfying time-filler than the small stone building in its grounds which houses the **Suur-Savo Museum** (May–Aug Tues–Fri 10am–5pm, Sat 2–5pm; Sept–April Wed 10am–5pm, Sat 2–5pm; €2.50), a hotchpotch of broken clocks, cracked crockery, and even a bent-wheeled penny-farthing bicycle, which purports to be a record of regional life.

Practicalities

The **train and bus stations** are each a block away from the *kauppatori*, the southern corner of which is opposite the **tourist office** at Porrassalmenkatu 23 (Mon–Fri 9am–5pm, Sat 10am–3pm; ☎010/826 0246, ⊛www.travel.mikkeli.fi). On Sundays the office moves to the red cottage by the market square (10am–3pm). Free **internet** access is available at the library (Mon–Fri 10am–8pm, Sat 9am–2pm), opposite the tourist office at Raatihuoneenkatu 6.

Of Mikkeli's **hotels**, the best deal is the recently overhauled *Uusikuu*, 1km west of the centre at Raviradantie 13 (☎015/221 5420, ⊛www.uusikuu.fi; ❸) – any of the 49 spacious, simply-furnished rooms must be booked online or by phone between 9am and 3pm (a €6 fee is added to phone reservations); guests access all doors with a code. For more money you'll find the more central, standard chain hotels *Cumulus* (⊛www.cumulus.fi, ☎015/20 511; ❸/❹), Mikonkatu 9, and *Sokos Vaakuna* (⊛www.sokoshotels.fi, ☎015/20 201; ❹/❺), Porrassalmenkatu 9. The nearest official **youth hostel**, one of the most beautiful in the country, ⚐ *Löydön Kartano* (☎015/664 101, ⊛personal.inet.fi/yritys/kartano), lies 20km to the south, at Kartanontie 151 just outside **Ristiina** (5 or 6 Kouvola-bound buses a day stop there). This family-run hostel-in-a-mansion occupies a large, atmospheric wooden house, for two hundred years home to an aristocratic Russian general and his descendants, who bought it in 1752. Beds are €16.50 (they also have pricier, stand-alone cottages) and a generous breakfast costs €5. Mikkeli also has a couple of nearby **campsites** outfitted with cabins and bungalows: *Visulahti* (☎015/18 281, ⊛www.visulahti.com; mid-May to mid-Aug; €66), 5km from the centre (a convoluted bus ride – get details of services at the bus station or tourist office); and *Mäntyniemi*, Ihastjärventie 40B (☎015/174 220 or 0440/174 220, ⓦwww.gasthausmantyniemi.com), 7km north of the centre (no public transport).

The newest addition to Mikkeli's **eating** options is *Ravintolalaiva Toivo*, a traditional Finnish restaurant set within an 1870s-built ship moored right in the harbour. Elsewhere, there is good continental cuisine at the well-priced *Pruuvi*, Raatihuoneenkatu 4, while *Café Sole* on Porrassalmenkatu, opposite the *kauppatori*, serves filling, cheap lunches. If you want excellent pizza (€8) try *Angela*, a Turkish-run place between the bus station and the *kauppatori*. Excellent Mexican food (tacos €10.20, fajitas €15.90) can be found at *Fernando*, Maaherrankatu 17. On the other end of town at Porrassalmenkatu 10 just across from the *Vaakuna*, Mikkeli's youth drink the night away at *Pub London*. The main square hosts a particularly good daily market selling fresh breads, fish, fruit and snacks.

Lappeenranta and around

Likeable **LAPPEENRANTA** (Villmanstrand in Swedish) provides an excellent first taste of the eastern Lake Region, conveniently sited on the main rail line between Helsinki and Joensuu and along all the eastern bus routes. It's a small, slow-paced town where summer evenings find most of the population strolling around the linden tree-lined harbour. Once holding a key position on the Russian border, Lappeenranta boasts historical features that its neighbouring towns don't share, and provides an eye-opening introduction to political conflicts that not only affected medieval Finland but also had an impact on recent generations.

It's a twenty-minute walk from the train station, and ten minutes from the bus station, through the town centre to the harbour, where the main activity is strolling and snacking from the numerous stands selling the **local specialities** – spicy meat pastries called *vetyjä* and *atomeja*. If you're feeling more energetic, climb the steep path on the harbour's western side, which brings you to the top of the town's old earthen ramparts and into the Russian-built fortress area, where Lappeenranta's past soon becomes apparent. Its origins as a trading centre reach back to the mid-seventeenth century, but it was with the westward shift of the Russian border in 1721 that the town found itself at the front line of Russian–Swedish conflicts. After the

▲ Lappeenranta Fortress

Viipuri

Before it was ceded to the Soviet Union in 1944, **VIIPURI** (Vyborg in Russian and Swedish) was one of Finland's most prosperous and cosmopolitan towns. Once a major port, being the Saimaa waterway's main link to the Baltic Sea, with a mixed population of Finns, Swedes, Russians and Germans, the town's fortunes declined under Soviet administration. Lack of investment (Viipuri was never allowed to challenge Leningrad's place as the USSR's major western seaport) resulted in a dearth of new construction, and allowed many of the town's once elegant structures to reach advanced states of dilapidation.

Viipuri today has a strange, time-locked quality – a crumbling reminder both of the conflicts that have enveloped the region and of the fading power of the Soviet Union. There's still a host of medieval buildings, the magnificent Alvar Aalto public library and an enthralling covered market, while Lenin's statue continues to stand in the town's Red Square. But the depths to which the great Russian Bear has fallen are self-evident, with the town's entire infrastructure seemingly in danger of imminent collapse and aggressive-looking moneychangers clutching wads of hard currency on street corners.

From Lappeenranta, there are one or two daily bus departures to Viipuri (€24 return), which continue to St Petersburg (€62 return). Russian visas, which can take up to ten days to acquire, are needed for this journey. Contact Savon Linja (℗020 141 5670, ⓦwww.savonlinja.fi), Ajurinkatu 10. An alternative is a **visa-free day-trip by boat** (€78) from Lappeenranta, though Americans, Canadians and other non-EU or non-Scandinavian citizens must apply for a separate visa at least a week beforehand (€70). There is usually one daily sailing between mid-May and mid-September, and it's best to reserve as far in advance as possible (at least one week) as these trips get booked up early; if you do call with the hope of a last-minute booking, try asking if there have been any cancellations, but remember all bookings must be finalized the night before the cruise. Boats depart the main harbour at 8am. Contact Saimaa Matkaverkko (℗05/541 0100, ⓦwww.saimaatravel.fi) for tickets and more details.

Peace of Turku in 1743, the border was again moved, this time leaving Lappeenranta inside Russian territory. Subsequently, a garrison of the tsar's army arrived and, by 1775, had erected most of the stone buildings of the **fortress**, which sits on the short headland that forms the western wall of the harbour.

Several of these structures still line the cobblestoned Kristiinankatu, which leads across the headland before descending to the shores of the lake, three of them housing museums. Unless you've a particular interest in the military role of horses and the uniforms worn by their riders, however, the collections of the **Cavalry Museum** (June to mid-Aug Mon–Fri 10am–6pm, Sat & Sun 11am–5pm; rest of the year by appointment on ℗05/616 2261; €3) can safely be ignored. A better quick stop is the **Orthodox Church** (June to mid-Aug Tues–Sun 10am–6pm; rest of the year by appointment on ℗05/451 5511), just opposite, where the glow of beeswax candles helps illuminate the icons of what is Finland's oldest Orthodox church, founded in 1785.

Step back across Kristiinankatu and you're outside the **South Karelian Art Museum** (June to mid-Aug Mon–Fri 10am–6pm, Sat & Sun 11am–5pm; mid-Aug to May Tues–Sun 11am–5pm; €4 joint ticket with South Karelian Museum), which rotates its permanent stock of paintings with south Karelian connections – mostly a mundane bunch of landscapes and portraits, although some important Finnish artists are represented – and stages exhibitions of emerging regional artists in an adjoining building. Much more rewarding, however, is the **South Karelian Museum** (same hours; €4 joint ticket with South Karelian Art Museum) towards the end of Kristiinankatu. Surprisingly, it isn't collections from Lappeenranta that form the main displays here, but ceramics, souvenirs and sporting trophies from Viipuri, the major Finnish town 60km from Lappeenranta that was ceded to the Soviet Union after World War II (see box, p.589). Many of those who left Viipuri to stay on the Finnish side of the border began their new lives in Lappeenranta, and it's mostly they who shed a tear when looking at these reminders (including a large-scale model of their home town). Elsewhere in the museum are numerous Karelian costumes, subtle differences in which revealed the wearer's religion and (for women) marital status, and worthy displays on hunting, farming and traditional handicrafts.

Practicalities

The **tourist office** is at Kauppakatu 40 (℡05/667 788, ⓦwww.lappeenranta.fi; Mon–Fri 9am–4.30pm). There's also a small tourist booth open by the harbour in summer (℡05/411 8853, daily June to mid-Aug 9am–8/9pm). The main tourist office has two free internet terminals, and there's also gratis internet at the town library, Valtakatu 47 (June to mid-Aug Mon–Fri 10am–6pm; mid-Aug to May Mon–Fri 10am–8pm).

Lappeenranta is easily covered in a day, though you may need to stay overnight between transport links. The pick of several high-standard **hotels** is *Sokos Lappee*, Brahenkatu 1 (℡05/678 61, ⓦwww.sokoshotels.fi; ❹/❻), and the *Cumulus*, Valtakatu 31 (℡05/677 811, ⓦwww.cumulus.fi; ❹/❻). There are also some cheaper **guesthouses**, such as the year-round *Citi Motel Lappee*, Kauppakatu 52 (℡05/415 0800, Ⓔabcitimotel@gmail.com; ❸). The town's two **youth hostels** are 2km west of the centre: *Karelia Park*, Korpraalinkuja 1 (℡05/453 0405, ⓦwww.karelia-park .fi; June–Aug; dorms €20, doubles ❸); and *Huhtiniemi*, Kuusimäenkatu 18 (℡05/451 5555, ⓦwww.huhtiniemi.com; dorms €10, June–Aug only; apartments ❸, year round), which is also where you'll find the local **campsite** (same phone number).

Reward yourself after a tour of the fortress area with coffee and a home-baked pie or cake at the colourfully decorated ✝ *Café Majurska*, close to the Orthodox church on Linnoitus. Sour rye bread and the softer *rieska* bread are easily found in Lappeenranta's marketplace or by the harbour, where you'll also find stuffed waffles as well as *atomeja* and *vetyjä* pastries. For more substantial **eating**, try *Olé* (ⓦwww .ravintolaole.fi), Raatimiehenkatu 18, a new and very popular brick-and-arcade style Spanish restaurant that serves a solid range of paellas, pescados and pechugas (mains begin at €16.80). Also popular are the inexpensive pizzas at *Suzan Kebab Pizzeria*, Puhakankatu 1 (next to the Euromarket, a good place to pick up cheap provisions), or the tasty fish dishes at *Serra*, Satamatie 4, facing the harbour. A good choice for affordable meat, fish and vegetarian dishes is *Huviretki* at the *Cumulus* hotel, Valtakatu 31.

For **drinking**, the most atmospheric spot you'll find is the deck of the *Prinsessa Armaada*, where locals gather during the late summer evenings to catch the last rays and sip on a pint (or six). Elsewhere, *Totem*, Raatimiehenkatu 17, has something of an eclectic Wild West atmosphere, while the Irish-style *Old Park*, Valtakatu 36, is nearly guaranteed to be full.

Around Lappeenranta

Northeast of Lappeenranta, the forests grow denser whilst the road straddles the tranquil Saimaa lake to the west and the increasingly proximate Russian border to the east. If you're looking for outdoor adventure, there won't be much for you in the moderately sized industrial town of **IMATRA**, which offers little more of interest than the summer Rapids Shows (mid-June to mid-Aug daily 7pm), sound-and-light affairs in the evenings above the fierce, gushing Vuoksi River.

Instead, push on through for another 57km to the small town of **PARIKKALA**. Heavily wooded with oak and maple trees, the surrounding forested area offers ample opportunities for hiking, boating and goggling at the numerous species of birds – over 280 at last count – that call this part of Finland home. Solo exploration is possible, though you might be better off with a local who knows the area; try

contacting the knowledgeable birder Hanna Aalto (☎050 524 6597, ⊛www.ornio
.net), who runs personal tours for €175 per day per person, or ask at either of the
accommodation options listed below. Arriving without a car can be problematic, as
the town centre, wherein lie the train and bus stations, is several kilometres from any
decent places to stay. Tourist information is a ten-minute walk from the station at
Harjukuja 6 (☎05/686 11; ⊛www.parinet.fi). Your best choices for **accommodation** are two small places just outside town: *Laatokan Portti* (☎05/449 282, ⊛www
.laatokanportti.com), 6km south of the centre, offers a range of double rooms (❷).
Run by a Finnish-born American, it's a wonderfully idyllic setting, with a large
wooden deck at the lake's edge; you can also rent boats and fishing gear for around
€15 per day. There are slightly more comfortable rooms, as well as a lakeside sauna
and indoor swimming pool, a few kilometres north from *Laatokan Portti* at the rustic
Karjalan Lomahovi (☎05 657 7700, ⊛www.karjalanlomahovi.com; ❷). The friendly
staff here can also arrange winter **horse-and-carriage** trips along the Russian
border from the nearby thoroughbred farm in Kolmekanta. Both of these guesthouses offer hearty, well-portioned meals to both guests and non-guests; bank on
around €15. In terms of other **eating** options in the area, you're pretty much limited
to €12 lunchtime dishes like lasagna and potato gratin at *Kaakonranta*, Parikkalantie
19, also a **bar** hangout for local old-timers.

Mother Nature aside, there ain't a whole lot going on in Parikkala – the town's
church is mostly modernized inside and holds little of real interest – though you
might fancy a **lake tour** aboard the M/S *Princess of Saimaa*. The old passenger junk
occasionally plies Lake Simpele in the summertime, departing from the tiny dock
behind the *Kaakonranta* restaurant, though technical problems have beseiged the boat
in recent years, so best to check with the tourist office for latest details.

Savonlinna and around

Draped across a series of tightly connected islands, **SAVONLINNA** is one of the
most relaxed towns in Finland. Formerly sustained by its woodworking industries
and position at a major junction on the Saimaa route, the town nowadays prospers
on the income generated from tourism, and the cultural kudos derived from its
annual international Opera Festival. It's packed to the gills throughout July (when
the opera festival takes place) and early August, but on either side of the peak season
the town's streets and numerous small beaches are uncluttered. The easygoing mood,
enhanced by the slow glide of pleasure craft in and out of the harbour, makes
Savonlinna a superb base for a two- or three-day stay, giving ample time to soak up

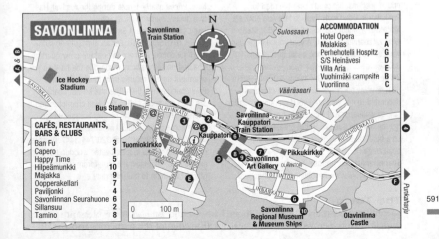

The Savonlinna Opera Festival

Begun in 1912, and an annual event since 1967, Savonlinna's **Opera Festival** lasts for the whole of July. The major performances take place in the courtyard of the castle, and there are numerous spin-off events all over the town. **Tickets**, priced €31–190, go on sale the preceding November and sell out rapidly, although the tourist office keeps some back to sell during the festival. For further details contact the **Opera Office**, Olavinkatu 27 (℡015/476 750, ⊛www.operafestival.fi).

the mellow atmosphere, discover the local sights and curiosities – such as a remarkable modern art centre and a huge nineteenth-century church – that lie within the town's idyllic surrounding.

Arrival and information

While there are very few trains to Savonlinna, there is a choice of **train stations**: Savonlinna-Kauppatori is by far the most central, although if you're making straight for the *Malakias* hotel (see below), get off at Savonlinna, 1km to the west. The **bus station**, served by six buses a day from Mikkeli and Helsinki, is also a short distance west of the centre, just off Olavinkatu. The **tourist office**, Puistokatu 1 (June & Aug daily 9am–5pm; July daily 8am–8pm; Sept–May Mon–Fri 9am–5pm; ℡015/517 510, ⊛www.savonlinnatravel.com), faces the passenger harbour. Staff can point you in the right direction to rent bicycles and also supply useful route maps for cycling in the area; there are also two internet terminals here. For longer usage, try *Herkku Pekka,* an internet café at Olavinkatu 53

Accommodation

Savonlinna has several budget accommodation possibilities and some good **hotels**, but don't expect the big discounts you might find elsewhere, as there's no shortage of summer business, and prices soar during the Opera Festival in July. The listings below give the standard rate followed by the higher, festival-time price, where applicable. There's a marked absence of **campsites** in Savonlinna: the nearest is *Vuohimäki* (℡015/537 353; June–Aug), 7km west of the centre and served by bus #3.

Hotel Opera Kyrönniemenkuja 9 ℡015/521 116, ⊛www.savocenter.fi; advance bookings when closed on ℡015/476 7515, ℻476 7540. Decent option, just past the castle near the road to Punkaharju. Open early June to late Aug only. **④**

Malakias Pihlajavedenkuja 6 ℡015/533 283, ⊛www.spahotelcasino.fi. A year-round hotel 2km west of the centre, offering basic but reliable doubles. **④**

Perhehotelli Hospitz Linnankatu 20 ℡015/515 661, ⊛www.hospitz.com. Excellent, classically decorated rooms with hardwood oak floors, classy striped wallpaper and views of either an apple garden or Lake Saimaa. Buffet breakfast is served on a boat. Be sure to book ahead as it's very popular. **④**

Savonlinnan Seurahuone Kauppatori 4–6 ℡015/5731, ⊛www.savonlinnanseurahuone.fi.

Completely renovated in 2007, this 1950s hotel is set smack on the *kauppatori*, while many of its 84 modern (ie blandly decorated) rooms look onto the lake. Prices nearly double during the festival. Has two decent restaurants. **④/⑤**

S/S Heinävesi Savonlinna Harbour ℡015/517 510. For an atmospheric summertime option, it's hard to beat the crew quarters of a working steamboat, moored in the harbour overnight once it returns from its day-trips to Punkaharju (see p.594). The shared-bath cabins are a bit cramped, but loaded with character, and evenings here during the festival are known for being some of the liveliest in town. **①**

Villa Aria Puistokatu 15 ℡020/744 3447. A score of very nice rooms in a renovated wooden building on the lake, just down the street from the tourist office. Mid-June to mid-Aug only. **⑥**

The Town

Savonlinna's centrally placed passenger harbour and *kauppatori* are pleasant spots to mingle with the crowds and enjoy a snack from one of the numerous **food stalls** –

ask for a *lörtsy*, a local pie which comes in two varieties: savoury with meat and rice, or sweet with apple jam and sugar. Within a few strides, you might poke your head inside the de facto summer art gallery at Olavinkatu 40 (Mon–Fri 11am–5pm; entry fee depends on exhibition), which provides a spacious home for temporary shows usually mounted in tandem with those at the Savonlinna Provinciàl Museum (see below); or the smartly restored **Pikkukirkko** (June to mid-Aug daily 11am–5pm), a Lutheran church which began life serving the Russian Orthodox faithful.

Fine as these places may be, however, none of them holds a candle to Savonlinna's greatest possession: the engrossing **Olavinlinna Castle** (daily: June to mid-Aug 10am–6pm; mid-Aug to May Mon–Fri 10am–4pm, Sat & Sun 11am–4pm; @www .olavinlinna.fi; €5), a fifteen-minute walk from the harbour at the end of Linnankatu. Perched on a small island and looking like some great grey sea monster surfacing from the deep, the castle was founded in 1475 to guard this important lake-transport junction at the eastern extremity of what was then the Swedish empire – a region being eyed by an expansionist Russia. The Swedes built walls five metres thick to resist attack on the eastern side, but the castle was to switch hands fairly frequently in later years; the last change saw the Russians moving in after the westward shift of the border that followed the 1743 Peace of Turku. They added the incongruous Adjutant's Apartment which, with its bright yellow walls and curved windows, resembles a large piece of Emmenthal cheese. With military importance lost when Finland became a Russian Grand Duchy in 1809, the castle ended its pre-restoration days rather ignominiously as the town jail.

The castle can only be visited on guided **tours** (in English), included in the admission fee and offered hourly during the summer, less frequently in other months. The guides' commentary is a vital aid to comprehending the complex historical twists and turns that the castle endured, and for pointing out the numerous oddities, such as the sole original indoor toilet in the maiden's chamber, through which there's a sheer drop to the lake below.

Occupying an 1852 granary a stone's throw from the castle, the **Savonlinna Provinciàl Museum** (July to early Aug daily 11am–5pm; early Aug to June Tues–Sun 11am–5pm; €4, ticket also covers the art gallery – see above) presents one of the Lake Region's better accounts of the evolution of local life, beginning with an intriguing display on the prehistoric rock paintings found near Savonlinna. The bulk of the museum's collection charts hunting and farming techniques, and the birth of the area's tar and logging industries, although the upper level holds temporary art exhibitions, often culled from the country's most interesting private collections.

Outside, docked at the end of a jetty, are three c.1900 steamers known as the **Museum Ships** (June–Aug only, same times as Provinciàl Museum; admission with same ticket), which earned their keep plying the Saimaa waterways, sometimes travelling as far as St Petersburg and Lübeck.

Eating and drinking

When it comes to **eating**, things get busiest during the festival, during which the best place to chow down is *Hilpeämunkki*, 100m or so to the left as you exit the castle, which good traditional medieval meals (€13 and up) in the whittled environs of cow pelts, antler horns and other assorted medieval accoutrements. At other times you can find good Italian food at *Capero*, Olavinkatu 51, good Chinese at *Ban Fu*, Olavinkatu no. 46, and solid Finnish meals at the large *Majakka*, Satamakatu 11 (@www.ravintolamajakka.fi). The most adventurous place to dine is *Paviljonki*, Rajalahendenkatu 4 (@www.ravintolapaviljonki.fi), where Finland's top trainee chefs serve up their latest creations. The service is excellent, and the food imaginative and well prepared; lunch here costs around €13, which includes dessert and coffee. If you're in town for an opera performance, top the night off with a meal at the cream-of-the-crop ⚞ *Oopperakellari*, Kalmarinkatu 10 (☎020 744 3445). Pre- and post-performance set menus of excellent Finnish cuisine start at around

€60, but the excitement really begins when the waiters – many of them local opera students – start bellowing out arias as they prance about the restaurant.

For **drinking** during the festival, all you need do is follow the crowds to see what's on; Olavinkatu is strewn with bars that fill to the brim during the festival. Outside the opera season, nightlife in diminutive Savonlinna is fairly tranquil, though sooner or later you'll probably end up at *Sillansuu*, Verkkosaarenkatu 1, close to the *kauppatori* and train station, known for its wide selection of beers and good earlier in the evening. *Happy Time*, nearby at Olavinkatu 36, is the most popular place to imbibe towards midnight. After everything else starts to close, anyone who's out for the night heads towards the *kauppatori* to the hotel *Savonlinnan Seurahuone*, whose nightclub *Tamino* is about as rocking a dance hall as you're going to find in off-season Savo.

East of Savonlinna: Punkaharju Ridge and beyond

According to local belief, the **Punkaharju Ridge** is the healthiest place to breathe in the world, thanks to an abundance of conifers that super-oxygenate the air. This narrow, seven-kilometre-long thread of land between lakes Puruvesi and Pihlalavesi begins 27km east of Savonlinna, and three roads and a railway line are squeezed onto it. With the water never more than a few metres away on either side, this is the Lake Region at its most beautiful, and it is easily reached on any train heading this way from Savonlinna. However, it's also heavily over-hyped in Finnish tourist literature, and, although you should make an effort to see the ridge, don't rule out other places further north.

Along the ridge, at the centre of things, you'll find **Lusto**, the national forest museum (May & Sept daily 10am–5pm; June–Aug daily 10am–7pm; Oct–April Tues–Sun 10am–5pm; €10; ⓦwww.lusto.fi). Designed, predictably, from wood, its permanent exhibits examine how forests function and survive; there's also a shop stocked with wooden items, though perhaps the best part is the restaurant-café, where you can fill up on sautéed reindeer, fillet of elk and *kuusenkerkkä*, a gloriously rich cake of *smetana*, pine kernels and Lappish berries. For exploring the area further, you can rent bikes here for €8.50 a day. It's a better idea to spend the night in Savonlinna than to be stuck out on the ridge, dependent on skeletal public transport to continue your journey. Should you want to stay, the most atmospheric **hotel** is *Punkaharjun Valtionhotelli*, Punkaharju 2 (☎015/739 611, ⓦwww.lomaliitto.fi /punkaharju; ❹/❺), an ornate wooden house on the ridge that still summons up the tsarist era, despite an insipid restoration. Their simple summer cabins (€49) are much more affordable. Another, much less attractive option is the dingy cabins at *Gasthaus Punkaharju*, Palomäentie 18 (☎015/473 123, ⓦwww.naaranlahti.com; €100).

About 25km southeast from Savonlinna, just before reaching the village of Punkaharju, the main road passes the extraordinary **Retretti Arts Centre** (daily: June & Aug 10am–5pm; July 10am–6pm; €15; ⓦwww.retretti.fi), a place devoted to the visual and performing arts. The unique element is the setting – man-made caves gouged thirty metres into three-billion-year-old rock by the same machines which dug the Helsinki metro – it cost so much to build that the project bankrupted the original owner. Outside, in the large sculpture park, fibreglass human figures by Finnish artist Olavi Lanu entwine cunningly with the forms of nature; tree branches become human limbs, and plain-looking boulders change slowly under your gaze into a pile of male and female torsos. Inside the caves, the exhibitions are changed every year, with artists developing site-specific projects to complement the dramatic setting. The interior also features underground streams, whose gushings and bubblings underpin the music piped into the air. There are also several above-ground sites that show work from well-known European masters – the last years have seen major displays by Cézanne, Monet, Repin and Munch, and Finnish Golden Age artist Ellen Thesleff.

The few daily **trains** between Savonlinna and Parikkala call at Retretti train station; their timings can be very inconvenient, however, and buses provide a more reliable alternative. Another option, though an expensive one (€29 return), is to travel by **boat** from Savonlinna's passenger harbour on the *S/S Heinävesi*, which departs at 11am, and returns from Punkaharju at 3.30pm (mid-June to mid-Aug only; ✆www.savonlinnanlaivat.fi). One way to enjoy the art without keeping an eye on your watch is to stay virtually next door at *Punkaharjun Lomakeskus* (☎020 752 9800), an extensive camping area with simple cabins (€95) and larger, fully equipped cottages (€115) as well.

Kerimäki kirkko

Though, like Retretti, it lies to the east of Savonlinna (23km distant), the village of **Kerimäki** is nearly impossible to reach by public transport without first returning to Savonlinna, from where there are several daily buses (check the latest details at the tourist office). The reason to come to this otherwise unremarkable village on the shores of Lake Puruvesi is to see the **Kerimäki kirkko** (daily May 10am–4pm; June 10am–6pm; July 10am–7pm; early Aug 10am–6pm, mid-Aug to late Aug 10am–4pm), an immense wooden construction built in 1848 to hold three thousand people, and claimed to be the largest wooden church in the world. It's a truly astonishing sight, complete with double-tiered balconies, and a yellow- and white-painted exterior which shines through the surrounding greenery. Kerimäki can be a pleasant place to spend a quiet couple of days: there's a nice little place to swim and a decent central guesthouse, the *Kerihovi* (☎015/541 225, ✆www.kerihovi.com; ❸), which has a traditional *ravintola* with home cooking and alcoholic beverages.

Valamo Monastery and Joensuu

Due to the preponderance of water in the vicinity, **train connections** around Savonlinna are extremely limited, only running east to Parikkala to link with Helsinki and Joensuu-bound express trains. However, **buses** (accepting train tickets and passes) operate from Savonlinna to **Pieksämäki**, the major rail junction in central Finland from where there are good connections north to Kuopio, Kajaani and Oulu, west to Jyväskylä, Vaasa, Tampere and Turku and east to the industrial town of **Varkaus**, which lies on the Turku–Joensuu line. In all cases, the latest timetables should be carefully checked before making plans. **Valamo Monastery**, situated off the railway line between Varkaus and Joensuu, makes for an intriguing stop, but one fraught with difficulties unless you have your own transport.

Valamo Monastery

The original **Valamo Monastery**, on an island in Lake Ladoga, was the spiritual headquarters of Orthodox Karelia from the thirteenth century onwards. In 1940, however, with Soviet attack imminent, the place was abandoned and rebuilt well inside the Finnish border, roughly halfway between Varkaus and Joensuu. One of only two Eastern Orthodox cloisters in Finland, today's Valamo Monastery (☎017/570 111, ✆www.valamo.fi) is located halfway between Joensuu and Varkaus, and is one of the most popular destinations in this part of the country. Volunteer workers arrive each summer to assist the monks in their daily tasks, and shorter-term visitors are welcome to imbibe the spiritual atmosphere and enjoy the tranquillity of the setting, though the somewhat austere regime won't suit everyone.

Informative daily English-language guided tours (€4) are given on request during the summer, and take in the grounds as well as several churches and chapels housing original accoutrements from the earlier monastery. Without transport of your own, however, **getting to the monastery** is not easy. Two daily buses leave from Varkaus for the hour-long journey, one at 1.45pm and another at 7pm (the evening bus does not operate on Sat). The return journey departs the monastery daily at 12.15pm, as well as weekdays at 8.30am. Both these services operate from Helsinki to Joensuu, calling at Lahti, Mikkeli, Varkaus and the monastery. To get there from other destinations, try contacting the monastery directly. There are both dormitories (€25) and private rooms (❷) if you want to **stay** overnight; reservations are highly recommended.

▲ Valamo Monastery

Joensuu

The capital of what remained of Finnish Karelia after the eastern half was ceded to the Soviet Union in 1944, **JOENSUU** was central to the immigration debate in the 1990s following a spate of racist violence against Somali refugees. The closure of several large industrial plants had plunged the local economy into depression, and as unemployment soared, the sizeable neo-fascist skinhead movement that grew up in Joensuu made the immigrant community a scapegoat for the social problems that accompanied the decline. While the city's economy isn't exactly booming these days, anti-immigrant violence is a thing of the past and Joensuu – with a fairly cosmopolitan population and a large student presence that makes up nearly half the city's residents – appears to be making a considered effort to welcome all visitors.

Arrival and information

Whether you arrive by bus or train (the terminals are adjacent to one another), the kilometre-long walk into the centre of Joensuu is one of the most enjoyable introductions to any Lake Region town: the route crosses the broad Pielisjoki River and bridges Ilosaari island and the narrow Joensuu Canal before reaching Eliel Saarinen's epic Art Nouveau town hall and the wide *kauppatori*. Pleasing first impressions apart, compact and modestly sized Joensuu doesn't have too much beyond the usual round of local museums and churches to fill your time – you can cover it in a day with ease.

The culture and tourist centre, **Carelicum**, in the centre of town at Koskikatu 5, houses the **tourist office** (Mon–Fri 9am–5pm plus Sat May–Sept 11am–4pm; ☎013/267 5319, ⊛www.jns.fi); staff hand out maps and useful city guides. There's also free internet access, a **box office** (☎013/267 5222) selling tickets for all the town's theatrical and musical performances and a decent café and gift shop.

Accommodation

For staying overnight, try the city's newest hotel, *GreenStar* (☎010/423 9390, ⊛www.greenstar.fi; ❸) a simple and efficient environmentally friendly concept hotel that functions without a reception; you book on the internet or at the kiosk downstairs (breakfast €5). The predictable chain option is just next door, the *Sokos Hotel Vaakuna*, Torikatu 20 (☎013/277 511, ⊛www.sokoshotels.fi; ❺/❻). A few blocks away sits *Elli*, Länsikatu 18 (☎013/225 927, ⓦwww.summerhotelelli.fi), with prices similar to the *GreenStar*. For rock-bottom prices, try the Scouts-run **hostel**, *Partiotalo* (☎013/123 381, ⓦwww.youthhostel-joensuu.net; June–Aug; dorms €12, doubles ❷; no credit cards), located 1km north of the town centre at Vanamokatu 25; the town **campsite** is beside the Pyhäselkä lake at Linnunlah-dentie 1 (☎013/126 272, ⓦwww.linnunlahticamping.fi; June–Aug), and also has small **cottages** from €35.

The City

Also housed in the tourist centre (see opposite) is the well-organized **North Karelian Museum** (same hours as Carelicum; €4); displays upstairs (many of which have interpretive information in English) trace Karelia's historical position in the middle of an East–West power struggle, with plenty of space given to the ever-changing borders between Russia and Finland. There's also a detailed scale model of early Sortavala (see p.599), now a decaying Russian town but once of great import on account of its seminary and teachers' college, which served as early training grounds for Karelian intellectuals; diverting ethnographic pieces include a seventh-century Sámi wooden ski and a number of original Karelian women's costumes. Downstairs there are rotating exhibitions about the region, as well as a permanent display on the lives of Finnish artists like Sibelius and Järnefelt who came to Karelia in search of romantic inspiration.

Considering the devastation caused by World War II, Joensuu has a surprising number of intact nineteenth-century buildings. These include the wood-framed structure that used to house the tourist office at Koskikatu, and the red-brick former schoolhouse at Kirkkokatu 23 which holds the **Art Museum** (Tues & Thurs–Sun 11am–4pm, Wed 11am–8pm; €4.50). Edelfelt's finely realized portrait, *The Parisienne*, is worth the admission fee alone. Some of Finland's more radical new artists get a showing just next door at **Ahjo** (Tues–Fri noon–6pm, Sat & Sun noon–3pm; free). Leaving the art museum and glancing either way up the aptly named Kirkkokatu, you'll spot Joensuu's major churches standing at opposite ends. To the right, the neo-Gothic **Lutheran Church** (June to mid-Aug Mon 11am–4pm, other times by arrangement through the tourist office) can seat a thousand worshippers but, aside from Antti Salmenlinna's impressive stained-glass windows, it's not wildly different from its counterparts in other towns. At the northern end of Kirkkokatu, the **Orthodox Church of St Nikolaos** (mid-June to mid-Aug Mon–Fri 10am–4pm; other times by arrangement on ☎013/266 000 or 050/587 5066) is a few years older and much more deserving of a swift peek, with some excellent examples of gilded relief iconography.

If you find yourself with time to spare, take a trip through the cactus-filled green-houses of Joensuu University's **Botanical Gardens**, Heinäpurontie 70 (April–Aug Mon & Wed–Fri 10am–5pm, Sat & Sun 11am–4pm; Sept–March Mon & Wed–Fri 10am–4pm, Sat & Sun 11am–4pm; €4). In summer the greenhouses are also home to flocks of tropical butterflies which are flown in weekly from Malaysia. Afterwards, you could explore the gardens themselves, which are claimed to hold a specimen of every plant native to northern Karelia – there are many more of these than you might expect. You might also want to cross the bridge from the town centre to Ilosaari, the island which sits between the train station and town centre. The sandy **beach** here is fairly tranquil during the week, but is busy on summer weekends with locals soaking up some much-needed sun.

If you're looking for more water-based entertainment, LuonnonKaipuu (☎050/538 2040, ⓦwww.luonnonkaipuu.com), at the southern edge of town at Länsivitta, rents out canoes, kayaks and row-boats (from €20) for paddling along the Jokaisema.

Eating, drinking and entertainment

Besides the tasty morsels which can be picked up for a few euro inside the *kauppahalli* (beside the *kauppatori*), Joensuu has a few good places to try out,

Crossing the Russian border: Sortavala and Ladoga

If you've visited the Carelicum in Joensuu, you'll have seen a scale model of **Sortavala**, one of the many Finnish towns to come under Soviet control following the postwar realignment of the border. After the collapse of the Soviet Union, it was possible for Finns (and indeed any other Westerners equipped with Russian visas) to visit the area with comparative ease, but a Russian law in 2007 required special permission to stop in areas that lie within 100km of the Russian border, making tourist excursions to this area sometimes difficult to organize. The day-long return bus-and-boat **journey from Joensuu to Ladoga** bypasses Sortavala, which occupies a scenic position on the shores of Lake Ladoga, and continues to the town of Ladoga itself. The tour departs on a handful of days between June and August at 6am, returning at 8pm. It costs €115, and includes a concert, lunch and Russian visa invitation, though non-Finns must apply for the actual visa on their own. Get the most up-to-date details from the Joensuu tourist office. For longer trips, and to visit other destinations in Russia, visit ⓦwww.monasterytours.com.

including newly opened *Kielo*, Suvantukau 12, which serves traditional Finnish dishes such as roast duck with cherry vinegar sauce (€22.50) and overnight-marinated beef with chanterelle sauce (€21), as well as *Golden China*, a solid Chinese restaurant in the new Iso Myy shopping centre just opposite the market place. For something more extravagant, try the French and Finnish cuisine and subdued atmosphere provided by an old-fashioned live orchestra at the *Hotel Kimmel* restaurant, Itäranta 1, or the central *Teatteri*, in the city theatre building just east of the market square, which serves hearty continental meat dishes such as *coq au vin*. For good Hungarian food, head for the *Astoria*, overlooking the river at Rantakatu 32, where you can eat outside in warm weather; this is the most enjoyable restaurant in town by a long chalk.

Two major festivals enliven Joensuu's entertainment calendar. The last weekend of July sees the **Gospel Festival** (ⓦwww.suomengospel.org), when thousands of singers turn up from all around Europe. Even bigger, however, is the annual **Ilosaari Rock Festival** (middle weekend of July; ⓦwww.ilosaarirock.fi), attracting top Finnish and international acts along with upwards of twenty thousand of thrill-seeking Finnish youths. If you're in any doubt as to the sheer scale of these events, take a look at the huge **Song Bowl**, which sits beside the Pyhäselkä lake, just southwest of Joensuu's centre. Tickets to both festivals can be booked via the box office in the Carelicum.

North from Joensuu: Nurmes

Should Joensuu be as rural as you want to get, swing inland (change trains at Pieksämäki) to more metropolitan Kuopio (see p.599). Otherwise, continue north from Joensuu into some of the eastern Lake Region's least populated but most scenically spectacular sections, with hilltop views stretching out above the tips of fir trees across watery expanses that stretch far into Russia. The small town of **NURMES**, 120km from Joensuu and linked to it by twice-daily train, is the obvious base for exploration, though you'll need private transport – or a lot of careful juggling with local bus timetables – to find the best of the forested and lake-studded landscape. Superbly quiet and with an appealing location between forest and saturated marshland, Nurmes offers pleasant relief from the comparative bustle of Karelian cities as well as being a well-placed point of departure for destinations further north.

There's a useful **tourist office** in the town centre at Kauppatori 3 (June–July daily 8am–10pm; Aug–May Mon–Fri 9am–5pm; ☏050/336 0707, ⓦwww.nurmes .fi); staff can book tickets for local events. You can see the town on your own by hiring a cycle (€5 per day) at Kesport Konesola, Kirkkokatu 16A (☎013/480 180). Budget **accommodation** in Nurmes can be found at the *Hyvärilä* (☎013/687 2500, Ⓦwww.hyvarila.com; dorms €10.50, doubles ❸; breakfast €8), Lomatie 12, which is also the location of the town's summer-only **campsite**. There's both modern and traditional-style accommodation at the *Bomba House* (☎013/687 2501; Ⓦwww.bomba.fi; ❺), Suojärvenkatu 1, whose stout lodge building was rebuilt in the image of an 1855 construction. The price includes use of the pool as well as sauna. There's also an exceedingly ordinary, central **hotel**, *Nurmeshovi*, Kirkkokatu 21 (☎013/256 2600, Ⓦwww.nurmeshovi.com; ❸). **Moving on** from Nurmes is surprisingly easy for such a relatively remote location – **buses** (accepting train tickets and passes) run to **Kajaani** or Kontiomäki (one stop further north), both of which are on the Kuopio–Oulu train line.

Kuopio

Located on a major inland north–south rail route and the hub of local long-distance bus services, **KUOPIO** has the feel – and, by day, much of the hustle and bustle – of a large city, although it is in fact only marginally bigger than most of the other Lake Region communities. Nonetheless, it's an important Finnish town and, especially if you're speeding north to Lapland, provides both a break in the journey and an enjoyable taste of the region. One of the best times to visit is mid-June, when the long-established Kuopio Tanssi ja Soi **dance festival** (Ⓦwww.kuopiodancefestival.fi) inundates the streets with a week of performances, workshops, classes and the like, turning Kuopio into a veritable mecca of artistic activity. Early July also sees the slightly more bacchanalian **wine festival** (Ⓦwww .kuopiowinefestival.com), where a world wine region is selected and feted in restaurants, bars and other venues all over the city.

Arrival, information and accommodation

Adjacent to one another at the northern end of Puijonkatu, Kuopio's **train and long-distance bus stations** are an easy walk from the town centre. There are good bus and train connections north from Kuopio to Iisalmi (see p.602) and on to Kajaani and Oulu (p.615 & p.608), as well as with Helsinki and all the main southern towns. The **tourist office** faces the *kauppatori* at Haapaniemenkatu 17 (June to Aug Mon–Fri 9.30am–5pm, plus Sat 10am–3pm in July; Sept–May Mon–Fri 9.30am–4.30pm; ☏017/182 585, ⓦwww.kuopioinfo.fi).

Though Kuopio has no official HI youth hostel, there are a couple of rock-bottom budget accommodation options around the train station, while most of the pricier places are closer to the town centre. The **campsite**, *Rauhalahti* (☏017/473 000; May–Aug), is 500m further south from *Hostelli Rauhalahti*; to get there take bus #7.

Best Western Atlas Hotel Happaniemenkatu 22 ☏017/211 2111, ⓦwww.hotelliatlas.com. Standard, predictable functional rooms look right onto the central market square. At least you know what you're getting. ④/⑤

Guesthouse Rautatie Vuorikatu 35 ☏017/580 0569. Decent place with no-frills double rooms (and a few singles); reception is at the train station restaurant. ③

Hostelli Rauhalahti Katiskaniementie 8 ☏030/608 30, ⓦwww.rauhalahti.com. Within a spa complex 5km south of the town centre, the doubles here are quite spacious and all have access to numerous pools, jacuzzis and saunas. Take bus #7 from the *kauppatori*. ⑤

Retkeilymaja Virkkula Asemakatu 3 ☏040/418 2178, ⓦwww.kuopionsteinerkoulu.fi/retkeilymaja _virkkula. Centrally located a block from the train station, with 30 dorm beds at €17 per night. Early June to early Aug only.

Scandic Hotel Kuopio Satamakatu 1 ☏017/195 111, ⓦwww.scandichotels.com. Unsurpassed views of the Kallavesi lake as well as a superb ground-floor sauna and pool offset the standard chain-style rooms here. ④/⑤

Sokos Hotel Puijonsarvi Minna Canthinkatu 16 ☏017/170 111, ⓦwww .sokoshotels.fi. Stellar, luxurious rooms with lake views and private saunas make this the most luxurious place to stay in town. ④/⑥

The Town

Kuopio's broad *kauppatori*, overlooked by the nineteenth-century city hall, is very much the heart of the town, with live jazz and rock music issuing from its large stage in summer. Walk the kilometre eastwards from here along Kauppakatu, towards the busy passenger harbour on the Kallavesi lake, and you'll pass most things worth seeing in town, with the exception of the extraordinary Orthodox Church Museum (see opposite). Summer lake **cruises** are a great way to take in Kuopio's environs. Leaving from the passenger harbour, the M/S *Osmo* makes daily trips from mid-June to early August (noon, 2pm, 4pm & 6pm; €11); call ☏0400 207 245 for more information.

At Kauppakatu 35, the **Kuopio Art Museum** (Tues–Fri 10am–5pm, Wed until 7pm, Sat & Sun 11am–5pm; €3; guided tours Thurs 2pm from mid-July to early Sept) fills a sturdy granite building with an enterprising assortment of contemporary exhibitions and, on the upper floor, keeps a less stimulating stock of twentieth-century Finnish painting with local connections. Further along the same street at no. 23, first glances might suggest that the **Kuopio Museum** (Tues–Fri 10am–5pm, Wed until 7pm, Sat & Sun 11am–5pm; €5), with its turreted battlements, aged stucco exterior and red-hatted towers originally functioned as a neo-medieval castle; in fact, it was purpose-built as a museum in 1807. The collection charts the evolution of local settlements, from motley Stone Age findings to the thousand-and-one uses that tree bark was put to in pre-industrial Finland. The switch from rural to urban life caused great changes in Finnish society, but one thing that remained constant was a dependency on that Nordic speciality, coffee. Using the original fittings, the museum re-creates the Kuopio institution of *Alli Karvonen's* coffee shop, which dispensed the beverage from 1933 to 1969 in cups etched with Finnish landscapes. Unless stuffed reindeer munching plastic lichen and a bleak collection of painted wooden insects set your pulse racing, the rest of the museum can be ignored, though keep an eye out for Juho Rissanen's *The Builders* on the staircase, a massive study of eleven naked Nordic men that still turns many a conservative head. Also within the Kuopio Museum, and included in the entrance fee, the **Museum of Natural History** houses a spectacular, full-size reconstruction of a woolly mammoth, one of only four in the world. Musk oxen hides have been used to simulate the beast's shaggy appearance, based on a real mammoth found in Siberia two hundred years ago. Satisfy yourself instead, however, with the knowledge that there once were mammoths in this part of Finland and that an upper molar of one was discovered near Kuopio in 1873 – hence all the museum excitement.

Turn right out of the museum and cross the road to the **Lutheran Cathedral** (Mon–Thurs 10am–3pm, Fri 10am–midnight), a handsome creation erected in 1815 using local stone. Although spacious, the cathedral's interior could hardly be described as opulent, but years ago it did contrast dramatically with the cramped living quarters of most Kuopio folk. South of here, at Kuninkaankatu 14, the **VB Photographic Centre** (June–Aug Mon–Fri 10am–7pm, Sat & Sun 11am–4pm; Sept–May Tues–Fri 11am–5pm, Wed until 7pm, Sat & Sun 11am–3pm; €5 summer, €3 winter) is a small museum of local and international photography, some of it quite inspiring. A few buildings further south on Kunniankatu is the **Old Kuopio Museum** (mid-May to Aug Tues–Sun 10am–5pm; Sept to mid-May Tues–Fri 10am–3pm, Sat & Sun 10am–4pm; €3; ⓦwww.korttelimuseo.kuopio .fi), an open-air museum where the stock of mostly wooden dwellings reveals the nineteenth-century domestic conditions that prevailed for both Kuopio's poor as well as the region's nobler-than-thou.

Another old house, interesting for a quite different reason, stands at Snellmaninkatu 19, preserved as **J.V. Snellman's Home** (mid-May to Aug daily 10am–5pm, Wed until 7pm; rest of the year by appointment on Ⓣ017/182 625; €2). From 1844, when the 39-year-old Snellman (for more on whom, see p.675) married his 17-year-old bride, the couple spent several years in this large but far from grand home. At the time, Snellman was earning a living as head of Kuopio's elementary school after the country's Swedish-speaking ruling class had booted him out of his university post, angry at his efforts to have Finnish made an official language. Aided by a few original furnishings in perfect condition and a pastel colour scheme devised by Snellman, the house is an excellent testament to the modest, pre-Modernist style of Scandinavian design that informed later minimalist artistic and architectural styles in Finland, Sweden and beyond.

Set on the brow of the hill at Kuopio's northwest corner, the enormously impressive **Orthodox Church Museum**, Karjalankatu 1 (May–Aug Tues–Sun 10am–4pm plus Wed until 6pm; Sept–April Tues–Fri noon–3pm, Sat & Sun noon–4pm; €5), draws the Orthodox faithful from many parts of the world. Even if the workings of the Orthodox religion are a complete mystery to you, there's much to be enjoyed, from elaborate Russian-made icons to gold-embossed Bibles, gowns and prayer books. The placing of the museum in Kuopio is no accident. This part of Finland has a large Orthodox congregation, many of them (or their parents) from the parts of eastern Finland that became Soviet territory after World War II. Many objects from the original Valamo Monastery (see p.595), likewise caught on the wrong side of the border, are also on display here.

One of Kuopio's highlights is an evening at the world's biggest **woodsmoke sauna** (€11), an enormous unisex affair out at the *Rauhalahti* hostel (see opposite) which can hold well over a hundred people. Its size is such that it takes 24 hours just to heat up – consequently, it's only open on Thursdays (summer only) and Tuesdays (year-round). For €29 you can avail yourself of an inclusive deal combining sauna and a traditional Finnish feast – these amazingly tame evenings also feature "lumberjack shows," replete with accordions, flannel shirts and hordes of tangoing and waltzing Finns. Visit the tourist office or call the hostel for more details.

Situated about 2km behind the train station on a ridge is the 75-metre-high **Puijo Tower** (May–Sept daily 9am–10pm, July until 11pm; Oct–April Mon–Sat

11am–10pm, Sun noon–5pm; €4), with fantastic views over the surrounding countryside, an upscale revolving restaurant (closed during winter) and access to some of the good ski trails that wend through the pines.

Eating, drinking and nightlife

While you're in Kuopio, look out for **kalakukko** – a kind of bread pie, baked with fish and pork inside it. While it's found all around the country, Kuopio is *kalakukko*'s traditional home and the town's bakeries generally sell it warm and wrapped in silver foil; a fist-sized piece costs about €2.50. You can also buy *kalakukko* hot from the oven at the *Hanna Partanen*, in a backyard at Kasarmikatu 15 (daily 5am–9pm); it's reckoned to be the best place in town, if not the whole of Finland, to sample it. A kilo loaf costs about €12.

In addition to Kuopio's expertise in pies, the city offers a number of solid options for more substantial eating, while several of the pubs serve offer good-value lunches, too. Kuopio's options for evening **drinks** are central and mostly located on the same block of Kauppakatu just east of the *kauppatori*. *Gloria* at no. 16 makes the most out of its real estate to offer bar, garden café, restaurant and disco all in one complex, though the disco here only gets hopping weekends after midnight. For midweek drinking and dancing you're probably better off next door at *Intro*, a large bar done up in red leather, with DJs playing a mixed bag of Latin, soul and disco music. The basement *Pannuhuone*, three blocks down at no. 25–27, claims to offer over 200 varieties of whisky, though most of its youthful clientele go for the draught pints of Lapin Kulta. Kuopio has a reputation for being the stamping ground of some of Finland's best rock musicians, and the town has a number of pubs where you can hear live music, several of which are packed together on Kauppakatu; *Apteekkari*, at no. 18, sees jam sessions and a number of live bands. Away from central Kuopio (but close to the campsite), the *Yölintu* bar at the *Rauhalahti* hostel stages some wild bashes on Friday nights. Find out what's happening there by asking at the tourist office, or try phoning the hotel itself on ☎017/473 473.

Cafés and restaurants

Isä Camillo Kauppakatu 25–27 ☎017/581 0450. Set in a lovely terraced ex-depository, this popular, casual restaurant serves a range of Mediterranean dishes starting at €10.

Musta Lammas Satamakatu 4 ☎017/581 0458. This cellar restaurant has been in business since 1862 and is still Kuopio's finest. Try the excellent filet of red deer with juniper berry sauce and fried mushrooms (€34). Book ahead during the summer.

Ravintola Wanha Satama At the harbour. Set in a former customs house, this modern Finnish restaurant is very popular on sunny summer evenings. The standard local-style mains are good, but the sandwich meals are less expensive and just as filling: try the Harbour Master's Sandwich, a delicious steak club (€14.90)

Restaurant Kreeta Tulliportinkatu 46–48 ⓦ www.ravintolakreeta.fi. Excellent new Greek restaurant with mains starting at a very reasonable €8.40.

Rosso Haapaniemenkatu 24–26. Just at the *kauppatori*, this is the best bet for inexpensive if predictable pizza dishes.

Iisalmi and around

The farmland around **IISALMI**, an hour north of Kuopio by bus, makes a welcome break from pine forests and marks the centre of northern Savolax, a district that, in public opinion polls, is regularly voted the least desirable place to live in Finland. The reason for this is slightly mysterious – the modestly sized town looks nice enough – but might be due to the locals' reputation for geniality mixed with a dash of laziness. Whether this is innate, or a defensive reaction by country folk who've been pitchforked into urban life, is debatable.

Whatever the stereotype, Iisalmi's two museums give a very good insight into local life. The **District Museum** (June to mid-Aug Mon–Fri 9am–6pm; rest of the year Mon–Fri 9am–5pm; free), at Kivirannantie 5 on the shores of the Paloisvirta river – cross the river from the centre of town and turn right – reveals the down-at-heel life of the peasantry via a number of wooden farmhouses once occupied by local farmers and fishermen; while the **Juhani Aho Museum** (May–Aug daily 10am–6pm; €2) in Mansikkaniemi, 5km along the main road, Pohjolankatu, by local bus, shows how the other half lived. Juhani Aho was a major influence on Finnish literature as it emerged around the beginning of the twentieth century, and the simple buildings filled with the author's possessions manage to convey the commitment of the artists who came together in the last years of Russian rule. However, it's the **Brewery Museum**, Luuniemenkatu 4 (Mon–Fri 10am–5pm; free) which is Iisalmi's greatest draw – from the tourist office, head west one block on Satama-katu before turning left into Riistakatu and walking another block; Luuniemenkatu begins at the junction with Veikonkatu. Finns flock here to see the brewing process that has created one of the nation's favourite tipples, *Olvi*, and although there's no tasting as part of the tour, there is a beer hall, *Holvi Oluthalli*, attached to the site, where it's possible to lay your hands – against hard cash – on some of the hard stuff. Don't think of coming here in the evening for a drink – it's closed.

Practicalities

Aside from the yellow, vaguely church-like *Artos* **hotel** at Kyllikinkatu 8 (☎017/812 244, ⓦwww.hotelliartos.fi; ❹), and the restaurant-outfitted and slightly more attractive *Iisalmi Seurahuone*, Savonkatu 24 (☎017/838 31, ⓦwww.iisalmenseurahuone .fi; ❹), budget accommodation in the town is limited. The **tourist office** (June to mid-Aug Mon–Fri 9am–6pm; Sept–May Mon–Fri 9am–5pm; ☎017/8303 391, ⓦwww.iisalmijatienoot.fi), at Kauppakatu 14, can point you towards summertime budget options on the outskirts, and to **campsites** with cabins, such as *Koljonvirta Camping*, Ylemmaisentie (☎017/825 252, ⓦwww.campingkoljonvirta.fi; mid-May to Sept; cabins €26). **Eating and drinking** in Iisalmi won't set your heart racing, though there is one unique option: you can wine and dine with exactly one other person at *Kuappi* (☎017/192 6430), which claims to be the smallest restaurant in the world, with seating for just two, book ahead. Otherwise, *Olutmestari* (May–Aug only), down at the harbour, has hearty Finnish dishes and *Rosso*, Savonkatu 18, offers the expected standards. Afterwards, for an evening drink, head for the slightly larger *Nelly's*, Savonkatu 20.

Around Iisalmi: Sonkajärvi

The reputation that the village of **Sonkajärvi** (ⓦwww.sonkajarvi.fi), 20km east of Iisalmi, has gained over recent years is quite out of proportion with its tiny size. Throughout Finland, and increasingly abroad, too, this otherwise undistinguished forest village is becoming known for that quintessentially northern Finnish event: the **world championships in wife carrying**. During the first Saturday in July (occasionally the second; check with the tourist office in Iisalmi for the latest details) hundreds of people from across the world crowd into Sonkajärvi to gawp at dozens of burly men negotiating obstacles as they stagger round the 250m course bearing a wife in their arms or on their backs. Confusingly, the borne female need not be the man's wife; however, she must be over 17 years of age, weigh at least 49kg and must not touch the ground during the race (otherwise penalty seconds are incurred). The winner, clearly, is the first man to cross the finishing line. Although cheesy in the extreme, it's actually quite a fun time to be in this part of Finland, and once the event is over the entire village degenerates into one mass drunken party.

About your only option for accommodation in Sonkajärvi are the **cabins** or **camping site** at Lohirannan Lomakylä (☎017/712 125, ⓦwww.saunalahti .fi/~ieva1; €50), from where you can also rent out canoes and pedal boats. They arrange gorgeously atmospheric dances on Saturday nights from May to November. Getting to Sonkajärvi isn't too much of a hassle, as a daily **bus** makes the journey out here from the bus station in Iisalmi. Other than a few snack bars on the day of the event, there are no **eating** opportunities in the village either.

Travel details

Trains

Iisalmi to: Kajaani (6 daily; 1hr); Oulu (6 daily; 3–4hr).
Joensuu to: Helsinki (10 daily; 4hr 50min–6hr).
Jyväskylä to: Tampere (11 daily; 1hr 20min).
Kuopio to: Iisalmi (7 daily; 1hr–1hr 20min); Jyväskylä (7 daily; 1hr 30min–1hr 45min); Kajaani (6 daily; 1hr 50min); Mikkeli (9 daily; 1hr 45min), Tampere (7 daily; 2hr 50min–3hr 30min).
Lahti to: Helsinki (hourly; 1hr–1hr 30min); Mikkeli (7 daily; 1hr 45min).
Lappeenranta to: Helsinki (7 daily; 2hr 30min); Lahti (7 daily; 1hr 30min); Parikkala (5 daily; 1hr 5min).
Mikkeli to: Kuopio (8 daily; 1hr 30min); Lahti (7 daily; 1hr 45min).
Savonlinna to: Parikkala (6 daily; 55min–1hr 25min).
Tampere to: Hämeenlinna (hourly; 40min–1hr); Helsinki (hourly; 1hr 45min–2hr 5min); Jyväskylä (12 daily; 1hr 20min); Kuopio (8 daily; 3hr 20min); Oulu (11 daily; 4hr 50min–7hr); Pori (6 daily; 1hr 30min); Turku (10 daily; 1hr 45min).
Varkaus to: Joensuu (4 daily; 1hr 30min).

Buses

Joensuu to: Kuopio (6–13 daily; 1hr 50min–2hr 40min); Valamo Monastery (1–2 daily; 55min–1hr 30min).

Kuopio to: Jyväskylä (4–7 daily; 2hr 15min–3hr 40min).
Lahti to: Mikkeli (11–12 daily; 1hr 45min–2hr); Savonlinna (7–10 daily; 3hr 30min–5hr 5min).
Lappeenranta to: Helsinki (8–9 daily; 3hr 10min–4hr 15min); Parikkala (1–5 daily; 1hr 45min–2hr 30min).
Mikkeli to: Savonlinna (5–12 daily; 1hr 20min–2hr 15min).
Savonlinna to: Kuopio (3–7 daily; 2hr 45min–4hr 20min); Parikkala (1–5 daily; 1hr 15min–1hr 30min); Punkaharju (1–9 daily; 45min–1hr 15min); Varkaus (4–9 daily; 1hr 30min–2hr 55min).
Tampere to: Helsinki (hourly; 2hr 15min–3hr 50min); Pori (7–14 daily; 1hr 45min–3hr 5min); Turku (frequent; 2hr 10min–4hr 5min).
Varkaus to: Joensuu (2–4 daily; 2hr); Kuopio (18 daily; 1hr 15min).

International buses

Joensuu to: Ladoga, Russia (1 daily in summer; 4hr).
Lappeenranta to: St Petersburg (1–2 daily; 5hr 30min); Viipuri/Vybourg, Russia (1–2 daily; 2hr 45min–3hr 40min).

4.3

Ostrobothnia, Kainuu and Lapland

etween them, these three regions take up nearly two-thirds of Finland, but unlike the populous south or the more industrialized sections of the Lake Region, they're predominantly rural, with small and widely separated communities. Despite this – or perhaps because of it – each region has a very individual flavour. Living along the coast of **Ostrobothnia** are most of the country's Swedish-speaking Finland-Swedes, a small subsection of the national population whose culture differs from that of both Swedes and Finns. Towns hereabouts are known as often by their Swedish names as by their Finnish, while their distance from the ravages of World War II enabled them to retain some of their old wooden architecture. Much of the region's affluence stems from its flat and fertile farmlands, although the coastal area's fortunes are changing as the once-numerous ferry connections from Sweden – the "booze cruises" – have all but gone now that European law has done away with duty-free alcohol, the main reason for the ferries' existence; today, **Vaasa** is the area's only maritime entry point. Overall, though, given the lack of exciting scenery – save for a few fishing settlements scattered along the jagged shoreline – and the region's social insularity, you'd be generous to devote more than a couple of days to it. Even busy and expanding **Oulu**, the major city, has a surprisingly anodyne quality, although you could always join the Swedes drinking their way into oblivion slightly further north at the border town of **Tornio**.

Kainuu is the thickly forested, thinly populated heart of Finland. It's traditionally peasant land – something perhaps felt more strongly here than anywhere else in the country – and over recent decades has suffered a severe economic decline as wealth has become concentrated in the south. There's still a surprising level of poverty in some parts, although tourism is beginning to help alleviate this. The only sizeable town, **Kajaani**, is a good base for wider explorations by foot, bike or canoe, and, since no railways serve the area, it's also the hub of a bus network which connects the region's far-flung settlements. **Kuhmo**, east of Kajaani, is at the centre of a notable web of nature trails and hiking routes, while heading north past **Kuusamo**, the landscapes become wilder, with great gorges, river rapids and fells on which reindeer are as common as people. Hikers here are well catered for by a number of marked trails, and there are also totally uninhabited regions traversable only with map, compass and self-confidence. The villages have little to offer beyond accommodation and transport to and from the end-points of the hikes, so stay away if you're not the rambling type.

Much the same applies to **Lapland**, one of the most thrilling places to hike in the world. **Rovaniemi**, the main stopover en route, is useful mainly for its transport connections and information on the area beyond. Beyond Rovaniemi, two roads lead into the **Arctic North**. Here you'll find wide open spaces that are great for guided and solo treks through gold-panning country and along the edges of mountain chains which continue far into Sweden and Norway. Elsewhere you can be totally isolated, gazing from barren fell-tops into Russia.

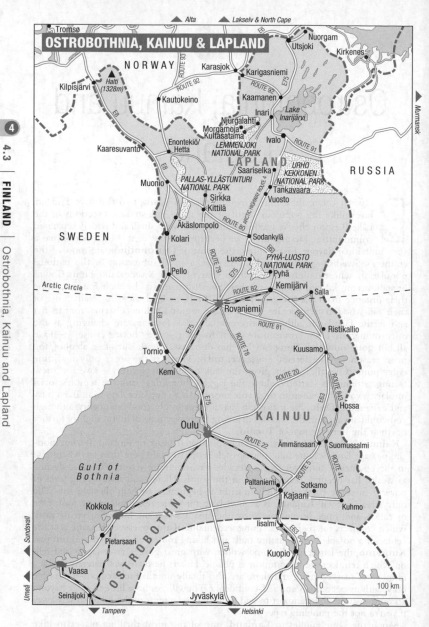

OSTROBOTHNIA, KAINUU & LAPLAND

But while the Arctic settlements are small, and few and far between, the whole region is home to several thousand **Sámi** (for more on whom, see p.338), who've lived in harmony with this special, often harsh environment for millennia. Discovering their culture and way of life can be as exciting as experiencing the Arctic North itself.

Vaasa and around

There's little reason to visit **VAASA**, although it's a useful stopover if you're travelling along the coast and has good travel connections with Oulu to the north and Pori to the south; there's also a little-advertised but very useful cross-country rail line connecting Vaasa directly with Jyväskylä. The lifeblood of the town is its harbour, through which the produce of southern Ostrobothnia's wheat fields is exported and the lucrative tourist traffic from Sweden arrives. Years of steady income have given the town a staid, commercial countenance, and its wide avenues (the old centre was obliterated by fire a century ago) are lined with shipping offices, consulates and a plethora of boozing venues aimed at Swedes from Umeå, who come here to get smashed.

Eighty-odd years ago, Vaasa was briefly the seat of the provisional government after the Reds (an alliance of Communists and Social Democrats who had taken up arms against Finland's repressive Civil Guard) had taken control of Helsinki and much of the south at the start of the Civil War in 1918; it was among Ostrobothnia's right-wing farmers that the bourgeois-dominated government drew most of its support. This barely endearing fact is recalled by the reliefs of the then president, Svinhufvud, and Mannerheim, who commanded the Civil Guard, on the front of the town hall and by the monument outside it.

Since then, it seems, little besides drunkenness has broken the peace. The pinnacle of local cultural activity is represented by the **Ostrobothnia Museum** (daily 10am–5pm, Wed until 8pm, Sat & Sun opens at noon; €5) at Museokatu 3, which recounts the history of the town and boasts an enjoyable collection of sixteenth- and seventeenth-century Dutch, Italian and Flemish art.

Practicalities

The **bus** and **train** stations are at the northern end of the town centre, within walking distance of the **tourist office**, which is located in part of the town hall at Raastuvankatu (Mon–Fri 9am–4pm; ☎06/325 1145, ⓦwww.vaasa.fi). There's free **internet** access close by at the town library, Kirjastonkatu 13 (Mon–Thurs 11am–8pm, Fri 10am–6pm, Sat 10am–3pm).

If you have to stay overnight before moving on, there are a few central **hotels**, and rates are quite reasonable, but **eating** and drinking establishments are thin on the ground in Vaasa. The best deals are to be found at the *Golden Rax Pizzabuffet*, at the top end of the main square at Kauppapuistikko 13, where the all-you-can-eat buffet is just €9. For more pleasant surrounding, head for *Fondis*, Hovioikeudenpuistikko 15, which specializes in Mediterranean food – the beef casserole with garlic, and red pepper stuffed with vegetable couscous are especially good value. A night's **drinking** in a multi-lingual town like Vaasa (one in four people here speak Swedish as their mother tongue), is divided on linguistic lines: Finnish speakers tend to be

Ostrobothnia, Österbotten and Pohjanmaa

The curious and little-encountered Latin word, **Ostrobothnia**, is allied to the Swedish name *Österbotten*, meaning "east of the Gulf of Bothnia", and confusingly refers to the western Finnish coast. To understand this apparent contradiction, it's necessary to go back to the centuries of Swedish rule when this Finnish province, on the east of the Gulf as seen from Sweden, was administered from Stockholm. *Österbotten* looked out across the sea towards the Swedish province of *Västerbotten*, "west of the Gulf of Bothnia", two Swedish provinces separated by a physical divide. Today the name *Österbotten* is still in use by the many Swedish-speaking communities in this part of Finland and stretches roughly from Vaasa to Oulu. Thankfully in Finnish there is no such confusion, since *Pohjanmaa*, the Finnish name for Ostrobothnia, simply means "northern land".

found at *Hullu Pullo*, Kauppapuitikko 15, while *Oliver's Inn* at no. 8 is preferred by Swedish-speaking Finns. For dancing, *Royal*, Hovioikeudenpuistikko 18 inside the *Radisson SAS Hotel*, is one of the more popular discos in town, regardless of mother tongue.

Accommodation

Astor Asemakatu 4 ☎06/326 9111, ⓦwww
.astorvaasa.com. Small, central hotel with classy
and charming doubles and suites. For €20 extra,
you can get a room with private sauna. Breakfast is
served in the attached Gustavian restaurant. ④/⑥

Best Western Hotel Silveria Ruutikellarintie 4
☎06/326 7611, ⓦwww.hotelsilveria.com. The
most aesthetically enticing of the city's hotels,
with use of the pool, morning sauna and breakfast
included in the room rate. It's set about 2km from
the town centre next to a sprawling park. ⑤

EFÖ Rantakatu 21–22 ☎06/317 4913, ⓦwww
.efo.fi. Located within a vocational school, this affordable summer hotel is simply furnished and decorated
in pale wood furnishings against white and off-white
panelled walls. Open mid-June to mid-Aug. ③

Kenraali Wasa Hostel Korsholmanpuistikko 6–8
☎040/066 8521, ⓦwww.kenraaliwasahostel
.com. Situated in an old army barracks, this is the
best option amongst Vaasa's budget accommodation, with a dozen homely and warm doubles with
shared bathroom. ②

Omena Hotelli Hoivokeudenpuistikko 23
ⓦwww.omena.com. The newest hotel in town,
with tidy, modern rooms but no reception – you
must book via the phone or internet or in the kiosk
downstairs. ③

Top Camping Vaasa ☎06/211 1255, ⓦwww
.wasalandia.fi. Adequate camping facilities are 2km
from the town centre right on the Vaskiluoto island
waterfront near the ferry harbour; take bus #5.
Open late May to mid-Aug. Cabins €65.

Onward from Vaasa

Ferries currently run from Vaasa to **Umeå** (RG Line; ☎0207/716 810, ⓦwww
.rgline.com; €60, car €65), generally once daily in June and July, less frequently
during the rest of the year; remember that Umeå is Uumaja in Finnish.

Heading **south from Vaasa** usually involves changing trains at Seinäjoki, from
where there are direct services to Tampere, Turku and Helsinki. There's also a direct rail
service **east** to Jyväskylä where connections can be made for Kuopio and Joensuu, as
well as numerous buses running to Pori and Turku. About 70km south of Vaasa, these
pass through Kaskinen (in Swedish, Kaskö) and neighbouring Kristiinankaupunki
(Kristinestad), notable for its surviving seventeenth-century layout.

Travelling **north from Vaasa** by bus to the major coastal city of Oulu
involves a mildly scenic journey passing fishing hamlets along the archipelago,
and the small and still largely wooden towns of Uusikaarlepyy (Nykarleby) and
Pietarsaari (Jakobstad). Northbound **trains** (once again changing in Seinäjoki)
swing inland before meeting up with the coastal road north in the uninspiring
port of **KOKKOLA**. If you feel like hanging around, the **tourist office** on
Kauppatori (June–Aug Mon–Fri 8am–5pm, Wed 8am–8pm, Sat 9am–1pm;
Sept–May Mon–Fri 8am–4pm; ☎06/828 9402, ⓦwww.kokkola.fi) can help sort
out accommodation and point you towards the only remotely interesting local
sight: the **English Park**, at one end of Isokatu, which contains a boat captured
when the British fleet tried to land here during the Crimean campaign in 1854.
A much more welcome sight, though, is the **train station** at Isokatu's other end.
Travelling on from Kokkola is straightforward since the town is on the main
rail line between Oulu and Helsinki.

Oulu

Despite **OULU**'s role as national leader in the computing and microchip industries,
the city still has sufficient remnants from the past to remind visitors of its nineteenth-
century status as a world centre for tar. The black stuff was brought by river from the
forests of Kainuu, and the international demand for its use in ship- and road-building

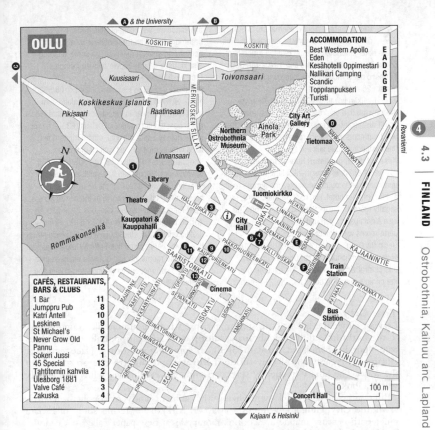

OULU

A & the University

B

KOSKITIE

KOSKITIE

C

Kuusisaari

Toivonsaari

MERIKOSKEN SILLAT

Koskikeskus Islands

Pikisaari   Raatinsaari

Northern
Ostrobothnia
Museum

Ainola
Park

City Art
Gallery

D

Tietomaa

Rovaniemi

NAHKATEHTAANKATU

MÄKELININKATU

Linnansaari

N

Library

Theatre

Rommakonselkä

Tuomiokirkko

HALLITUSKATU

City
Hall

i

Kauppatori &
Kauppahalli

ISOKATU

LINNANKATU

HEIKINKATU

ASEMAKATU

KAJAANINKATU

UUDENMAANKATU

PAKKAHUONEENKATU

HALLITUSKATU

8 11

KAUPPURIENKATU

SAARISTONKATU

9

6

7

E

12

10

KAJAANINTIE

RAUTATIENKATU

G

13

Cinema

Train
Station

RATAKATU

TEHTAANKATU

SEPÄNKATU

RANTAKATU

ALEKSANTERINKATU

TORIKATU

KIRKKOKATU

ISOKATU

UUSIKATU

KANSANKATU

Bus
Station

PL TAKATU

MANONK

HEINÄTORINKATU

LIMINGANKATU

KAINUUNTIE

PELTOKATU

JÄRVIKATU

PIRKKOKATU

OLLISKATU

Concert Hall

0   100 m

Kajaani & Helsinki

ACCOMMODATION
Best Western Apollo   E
Eden   A
Kesähotelli Oppimestari D
Nallikari Camping   C
Scandic   G
Toppilanpukseri   B
Turisti   F

**CAFÉS, RESTAURANTS,
BARS & CLUBS**
1 Bar   11
Jumppru Pub   8
Katri Antell   10
Leskinen   9
St Michael's   6
Never Grow Old   7
Pannu   12
Sokeri Jussi   1
45 Special   13
Tähtitornin kahvila 2
Uleåborg 1881   b
Valve Café   3
Zakuska   4

helped line the pockets of Oulu's merchants. Their affluence and quest for cultural refinement made the town a vibrant centre, not only for business, but also for education and the arts. Today, a handsome series of islands, a couple of highly conspicuous old buildings and a nightlife fuelled by the university's fun-hungry students bring colour into an otherwise pallid city. Though it has its share of faceless office blocks, there's an ancient feel to Oulu, too, as seen in tumbledown wooden shacks around the intricately carved *kauppahalli*.

Arrival and accommodation

Oulu is handy for **trains** in various directions, most usefully the direct services to and from Helsinki, Kajaani in the east (see p.615) and Rovaniemi in the north (see p.619). Arriving here, you'll find the platforms of the **train station** feed conveniently into an underground walkway with two exits: one runs to the nearby **bus station** (with regular services to and from Kuusamo), while the other leads towards the compact city centre, where the **tourist office** (mid-June to mid-Aug Mon–Fri 9am–6pm, Sat 10am–3pm; mid-Aug to mid-June Mon–Fri 9am–4pm; ☎08/5584 1330, ⓦwww.oulutourism.fi) is close to the city hall at Torikatu 10. It arranges free English-language tours of the city departing Kirkkokatu 11 from late June to mid-August on Wednesdays at 6pm and Saturdays at 1pm.

Low-cost **accommodation** is, unfortunately, limited, though a number of respectable mid-range options offer quite acceptable places to stay.

Best Western Apollo Asemakatu 31–33 ☎ 08/374 344, ⓦ www.bestwestern.fi. This chain hotel fortunately doesn't feel too much like one, with spectacular rooms and 1970s-meets-futuristic decor. Rooms with their own sauna cost about €20 more. ④/⑤

Eden Nallikari island ☎ 08/884 2000, ⓦ www .holidayclub.fi. If you're after luxury, this paradise won't disappoint – it's got a superb pool and offers spa treatments and steam rooms, and there's a fine restaurant. Take bus #5. ⑤

Kesähotelli Oppimestari Nahkatehtaankatu 3 ☎ 08/884 8527, ⓦ www.merikoski.fi. Having just undergone a thorough renovation, the simple rooms at this summer hotel, just north of the centre, feel slightly more livable in. Set just across from the lush Ainola park. Open mid-June to early Aug. ③, dorm rooms with hotels card only €20.

Scandic Oulu Saaristonkatu 4 ☎ 08/543 1000, ⓦ www.scandichotels.com. Opened in 2007, this central *Scandic* has quickly become one of the chain's favourite outposts. The 214 rooms

are spacious, with comfortable beds, heated bathroom floors and free access to a fitness centre and several saunas. The same building also houses a large movie theatre complex. Free wi-fi. ④/⑥

Nallikari Camping Hietasaari island ☎ 08/5586 1350, ⓦ www.nallikari.fi. Set on an island 4km from town and near to the sliver of sand that locals call a beach, with a range of cabins (€35) – some some rickety and traditional, others modern and filled with amenities – as well as pitches.

Toppilanpukseri Satamatie 13 ☎ 08/554 3335 ⓦ www.toppilanpukseeri.fi. A small and cheery guesthouse, with a few simple beds in an old house a few kilometres north of the centre across from Toppilansaari island; take bus #1 or #30. ①

Turisti Rautatienkatu 9 ☎ 08/563 6100, ⓦ www .hotellituristi.fi. Located above a convenience store, this lovely, very central hotel offers Oulu's cheapest year-round rooms, decked out with exposed pine flooring, crisp modern furnishings and florals and pastels. ③/④

The City

Leaving either the bus or train station, it's just a few minutes' walk straight ahead to the **harbour** and the neighbouring **kauppatori** and **kauppahalli** (Mon–Thurs 8am–4pm, Fri 8am–5pm, Sat 8am–3pm), an appealing and ornate place, good for cheap eats. Nearby, the sleekly modern **library** and **theatre** rise on stilts from the water. The library frequently stages art and craft exhibitions, which are usually worth a look.

Built as a luxury hotel symbolizing the affluent and cosmopolitan tar-rich town, the **City Hall**, a few minutes away on Kirkkokatu, retains some of its late nineteenth-century grandeur. A contemporary local newspaper called it "a model for the whole world. A Russian is building the floor, an Austrian is doing the painting, a German is making the bricks, an Englishman is preparing the electric lighting, the Swede is doing the masonry, the Norwegian is carving the relief and the Finn is doing all the drudgery." Nowadays, the drudgery is performed by local government officials, who've become accustomed to visitors stepping in to gawp at the wall paintings and enclosed gardens that remain from the old days. While inside, venture up to the second floor, where the Great Hall still has its intricate Viennese ceiling paintings and voluminous chandeliers.

Further along Kirkkokatu, the copper-domed, yellow-stuccoed **Tuomiokirkko** (May–Aug daily 11am–8pm; Sept–April Mon–Fri noon–1pm; free) was built in the 1770s following a great fire that more or less destroyed the city, and underwent a full and successful restoration in 1996. Within the cathedral is a portrait of Swedish historian Johannes Messinius, supposedly painted by **Cornelius Arenditz** in 1612. Restored and slightly faded, it's believed to be the oldest surviving oil painting in Finland, despite the efforts of the Russian Cossacks, who lacerated the canvas with their sabres in 1714.

Cross the small canal just north of the cathedral to reach **Ainola Park**, a pleasantly wooded space which makes a nice spot for a picnic or a late evening stroll. In the park, the **Northern Ostrobothnia Museum** (June–Aug Tues–Sun 10am–6pm; Sept–May Tues–Sun 10am–5pm; €3 free on Fri) has numerous tar-stained remnants from Oulu's past and an interesting Sámi section. There's no English labelling, but the displays are mostly self-explanatory.

If the future does more to excite your imagination than the past, or if you've got kids in tow, head for **Tietomaa** (the Science Museum), a few minutes' walk away at Nahkatehtaankatu 6 (May, June & Aug daily 10am–6pm; July daily 10am–8pm; Sept–April Mon–Fri 10am–4pm, Sat & Sun 10am–6pm; €13; ⓦ www.tietomaa .fi). Housed in an old power station, this is a great place to explore the bounds of technological possibility, with several floors of gadgets to test mental and physical abilities as well as video games, holograms, a ski-jump simulator, a giant-screen IMAX cinema and a glass elevator that takes you to the top of a tower from which you can get unparalleled views of Oulu.

Just around the corner, the **City Art Gallery** (late June to early Aug Mon–Fri 10am–8pm, Sat noon–8pm; early Aug to late June daily 10am–8pm; €3, free on Fri; ⓦ www.ouka.fi/taidemuseo), Kasarmintie 7, is located in a renovated glue factory. One of the largest galleries in Finland, it houses permanent and visiting international and Finnish contemporary art collections, plus a pleasant café – a good place to kill a few hours on a cold day.

Koskikeskus, the University and Botanical Gardens

A pleasant way to pass an afternoon is to set off for the four small islands across the mouth of Rommakonselkä, collectively known as **Koskikeskus**. The first island, Linnansaari, has the inconsequential remains of Oulu's sixteenth century castle, most of which was destroyed in an eighteenth-century thunderstorm when lightning struck its cellar gunpowder stores. Next comes Raatinsaari, followed by Toivonsaari, beyond which lie the rapids that drive a power station designed by Alvar Aalto, with twelve fountains added by the architect to prettify the plant. Pikisaari, the fourth island, is much the best to visit, reached by a short road bridge from Raatinsaari. A number of tiny seventeenth-century wooden houses here have survived Oulu's many fires, and Pikisaari has become the stamping ground of local artists and trendies, with several **art galleries** and **craft shops**.

The islands can also be glimpsed through the windows of buses #4, 6, 7 and 19, which pass them during the twenty-minute ride to the **University**, itself not a bad destination if you're at a loose end, if only for the opportunity to gorge in the student *mensa*. To work up an appetite, try finding the **Geological Museum** (Mon–Fri & Sun 11am–3pm; free) or the **Zoological Museum** (Mon–Fri 8.30am–3.45pm, Sun 11am–3pm; free), both secreted within the university's miles of corridors. The former is much as you'd expect, with a large collection of rare gems; the latter's best feature is the painstakingly hand-painted habitats created for each of the numerous specimens of stuffed Finnish wildlife.

Once you've ventured onto the campus you may as well take a look at the tropical and Mediterranean flora inside the two glass pyramidal structures that make up the **Botanical Gardens** (Tues–Fri 8am–3pm, Sun noon–3pm; €2).

Eating, drinking and nightlife

Oulu and its outlying islands boast some delightful **cafés** for lunch or a snack, and you shouldn't have a problem finding a good place for a sit-down meal, as the city's **restaurants** run the full gamut from basic to upscale. We've given phone numbers only for places where you need to book a table.

With an active Finnish and international student population, Oulu's lively nightlife revolves around its numerous **pubs** and **bars**, most within a block or two of the centre; after hours, several **clubs** provide all-night entertainment.

Cafés and restaurants

Concert Hall Lintulammentie 1–3. Sip a coffee in classy surroundings – though snacks don't come cheap, this is a great vantage point from which to admire the concert hall's gleaming Italian marble interior.

Katri Antell Kirkkokatu 17, entrance on Rotuaari. This small patisserie on the pedestrian walkway smack in the centre of town makes the best cakes in Oulu.

Pannu Kauppurienkatu 12 ⓦwww.ravintolapannu .com. Oulu's most popular pizzeria, with a family restaurant feel. The menu serves standard Finnish dishes like fillet of wild boar (€19.50) but the deep-pan pizzas (€10–15) are the best in town. Usually full, even at lunchtime, but they don't take reservations.

Sokeri Jussi Kasarmintie 13, Pikisaari island. Set in an old salt warehouse just over the bridge from the mainland, and great for a traditional Finnish lunch or just a drink outside on the huge terrace.

Tahtitornin kahvila Linnansaari island. Set high up in a century-old observation tower just across the Linnansaari bridge, this is one of Oulu's most picturesque options for a coffee or tea.

Uleåborg 1881 Aittatori 4–5 ☎08/881 1188, ⓦwww.uleaborg.fi. The pick of Oulu's restaurants. Set at the waterside in an nineteenth-century granary, and offering mains such as scallops au gratin salsa verde and breast of guinea fowl with sagenut butter and serrano ham; it also has a sizeable wine menu. The terrace waterfront out back makes for excellent sunset/moonlight meals.

Valve Café Hallituskatu 7. Cultural centre for the town's youth, with a laid-back courtyard café that's a great place to lounge about on a Sun. Movies are shown every evening at the Oulu Film Centre in the same building.

Zakuska Hallituskatu 20, This authentic mid-priced Russian restaurant was Oulu's first "ethnic" restaurant, and it's very popular for its spot-on period eighteenth-century tsarist decor. The extensive menu features scrumptious selections like the "Vladimir in Sheep's Clothing", tasty chops of garlic pork with creamy, gratin potatoes and beetroot (€17). Closed Sun.

Bars and clubs

1 Bar Kauppurienkatu 5. Sleek new place with irreverent bartenders and relaxed clientele. Oulu's current it bar.

45 Special Saarisonkatu 12 ⓦwww.45special .com. A legendary rock club whose three floors each has a different atmosphere and clientele. Frequent live bands, and the Sun jams are very popular.

Jumppru Pub Kauppurienkatu 6. Popular bar and nightclub chock full of early-twentieth-century charm, sporting opulent leather armchairs, dark wood detailing and heavy velvet drapery; pub food is available.

Leskinen Isokatu 30. With a wide selection of European beers, this is Oulu's bar of choice for international students and expat workers.

Never Grow Old Hallituskatu 13–17. Oulu's boho, dreadlocked crowd has finally found its home. Swinging wicker bungalow chairs, a painted Caribbean beachscape and reggae music all night long bring in Finns by the camperload. Gets smoky at night.

St Michael's Uusikatu 23. Oulu's best Irish pub, with 240 types of whiskey, plus Guinness, Murphy's Stout and Kilkenny on draught.

▲ Diving off the Sampo arctic icebreaker, Kemi

Towards Tornio: Kemi icebreaker tours

If you want to cross overland into Sweden, the place to make for is Tornio, 130km northwest of Oulu – reached by bus from **KEMI**, a small town on the Oulu–Rovaniemi train route around 110km northwest of Oulu. Although undistinguished during the summer months, bar the stench of wood pulp issuing from the nearby sawmills, it's during the dark winter months that Kemi really comes to life. From mid-December to late April, hundreds of people pour through this small town to experience one of Finland's most alluring winter attractions: a tour on the only private **icebreaker** in the world.

The *Sampo* departs once daily for a four-hour "cruise" through the icefields at the very top of the Gulf of Bothnia, breaking ice several metres thick (the ice is at its thickest in February and March). During the tour there's also an unmissable opportunity to don a bright orange rubber survival suit and float in the icy waters off the ship's stern – all this costs well over €200, but is undoubtedly worth the expense. The icing on the cake, however, is to depart by snowmobile from the centre of Kemi, travelling out over the ice to join the ship at its parking position out in the icefield. This seven-hour tour doesn't come cheap – upwards of €350 per person – but, if you can afford it, is a once-in-a-lifetime experience; for more information, contact Sampo Tours at Torikatu 2 in Kemi (☎016/256 548, ⓦwww.sampotours.com). Prices come down if these tours are booked via a travel agent (see p.33).

If you want to **stay** in Kemi, there's the *Snow Castle* (☎016/259 502, ⓦwww .snowcastle.net; open late Dec to March; ❻) at the harbour, a hotel and restaurant carved entirely out of snow and ice – guests are guaranteed warmth inside sub-thermal sleeping bags. For more a traditional night's stay, *Merihovi*, Keskuspuistokatu 6–8 (☎016/458 0999, ⓦwww.merihovi.fi, ❹/❺), has a drab exterior but fairly smart rooms with plush and stylish furniture, and a solid downstairs **restaurant**. Given its size, Kemi offers loads of places to eat and drink: *Hullu Pohjola* (ⓦwww .hullupohjola.fi, ☎016/458 0251), Meripuistokatu 9, serves extremely good Tex-Mex food while, down at the harbour, *Hullun Mylly*, Urheilukatu 1, a massive villa that was once the town hall, cooks great traditional Finnish food. Later on in the evening, both places become lively **bars** and **dance clubs popular with the town's younger set**. Anyone past puberty might well prefer the more sedate scene at any of the four bars within *Corner Inn*, back in town at Kauppakatu 10.

Tornio

Situated on the extreme northern tip of the Gulf of Bothnia and on the border with Sweden, **TORNIO** formerly made its living by selling booze to fugitives from Sweden's once-harsh alcohol laws. Today, Finnish alcohol prices are only slightly cheaper than those in Sweden, and the border customs house that formerly fought cross-border spirits smuggling is long gone. Nonetheless, the bulk of Tornio's nightlife remains on the Finnish side of the border rather than in Swedish Haparanda, and Tornio also sees a good number of Finnish visitors, who come here to enjoy the fishing, shoot the Tornionjoki rapids or take to the golf course, which has holes in both Sweden and Finland.

Tornio today is as low-key as any other town in the region, the loose border controls between Finland and Sweden meaning that liver-damaged Swedes still cross the border for a bit of boozing. If you find the drink-fuelled atmosphere unappealing, try visiting the seventeenth-century **Tornionkirkko** (late May to Aug Mon–Fri 9am–5pm, Sat & Sun 9.30–6pm) on the edge of the town park, or taking the rickety lift up the **observation tower** (June to mid-Aug Mon–Fri 10am–4pm; €1) for impressive views all around. There's also the **Tornio River Valley Historical Museum** (Tues–Fri 11am–5pm, Sat & Sun 11am–3pm; €4), near the corner of Torikatu and Keskikatu, a small but well-organized collection of information on the region's past, with an interesting section on the role played by western Finnish Lapland in World War II. Elsewhere, the **Aine Art Museum**

(Tues–Thurs 11am–6pm, Fri–Sun 11am–3pm; €24), Torikatu 2, has a few small exhibitions on Finnish and international artists of mild renown. The **Lapin Kulta brewery**, Finland's largest, runs interesting free one-hour tours of its premises at Lapinkullankatu 1, which includes sample tastings of the brew (☏020/717 151; June & July Tues & Thurs 1pm). After exhausting Tornio's few attractions, you might do well to hop across the border to Haparanda, which has several interesting sights and a gargantuan Ikea (see p.480).

Practicalities

If you're **arriving by bus**, the journey will terminate in Suensaari. The friendly, helpful **tourist office** is located in the Green Line Centre at the Swedish border (June–Aug Mon–Fri 8am–8pm, Sat & Sun 10am–6pm; Sept–May Mon–Fri 9am–6pm; ☏016/432 733, ⓦwww.haparandatornio.com).

The best **accommodation** remains just across the border in Haparanda (see p.480), but if you really can't bear to part with Finland, one option is the *Kaupungin-hotelli*, Itäranta 4 (☏016/433 11, ⓦwww.tornionkaupunginhotelli.fi; ❹/❻), boasting a restaurant, a bar, a nightclub, a dance club and three saunas. Much cheaper is the *Ammatti-Insititutti*, Kauppakatu 35A (☏010/192 049; June to early Aug only; ❶), a vocational school which has sparkling doubles with private bath; you must ring ahead during the week to reserve. The **campsite** on Matkailijantie (☏016/445 945, ⓦwww.campingtornio.com; mid-May to Aug) also has fifteen two-bed cottages

Tornio's dominant features are its **restaurants** and **bars**. For coffee and fresh bread and cakes, it's hard to beat *Karkiaisen Leipomo*, Länsiranta 9. *Tiramisu*, Kauppakatu 12, is a popular stop for cakes, wraps and salads, while *Umpitunneli* (ⓦwww.umpitunneli.fi), by the second road bridge over the Tornionjoki River, is a large restaurant-cum-disco serving dependable bar food like fried chicken or arctic char (€14). *Golden Flower*, Eliaksenkatu 8, cooks up great Chinese seafood dishes – try the spicy and filling curried jumbo shrimp (€12.75). Alternatively, you can buy a bag of salted and smoked whitefish along the banks of the rapids (roughly €2 for a meal's worth). For drinks, *Wanha Mestari*, Hallituskatu 5, gets quite crowded in the evenings, while at Satamakatu 3, *Wiini Huone* is a friendly wine bar and, next door,

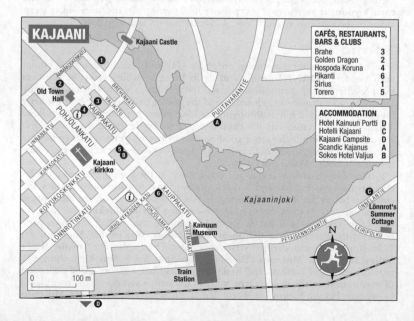

Jetset is a small rock bar, attracting the few jetsetters who haven't yet boarded the fast boat out of town.

Into Kainuu: Kajaani and around

KAJAANI, 178km southeast of Oulu by bus, could hardly be more of a contrast to the communities of the Bothnian coast. Though small and pastoral, the town is by far the biggest settlement that Kainuu province, a very rural part of Finland, has to offer; trains and buses are rare here and the pleasures of nature take precedence over everything else. Obviously there's little bustle or nightlife, but Kajaani offers some insight into Finnish life in one of the country's less prosperous regions. Fittingly, it was here that Elias Lönnrot completed his version of the *Kalevala*, the nineteenth-century collection of Finnish folk tales that extolled the virtues of traditional peasant life. During the first week of July Kajaani also hosts Finland's biggest annual **poetry festival** (Ⓦwww.runoviikko.fi), during which the main street, Kauppakatu, turns into a bustling market; in late May, meanwhile, the Kainuun Jazzkevät (Ⓦwww.jazzkevat.fi) sees performances from a number of big-name **jazz** groups.

From the gloriously Art Nouveau **train station**, Kauppakatu leads directly into Kajaani's minuscule centre, but first turn left into Asemakatu and you'll spot the decorative exterior of the **Kainuun Museum** at no. 4 (Mon, Tues, Fri & Sun noon–4pm, Wed & Thurs noon–7pm €2; Ⓦwww.kajaani.fi/kainuunmuseo). Inside, the engrossingly ramshackle collection of local art and history says a lot about the down-to-earth qualities of the area. Pressing for the centre along Pohjolankatu, you'll pass the dramatic **Kajaani kirkko** (April–Sept daily 10am–6pm; Sept–Oct Mon–Sat 5–7pm), whose wooden frame, weird turrets and angular arches were heralded as the epitome of the neo-Gothic style when completed in 1896. Resembling a leftover from a *Munsters* set, its spectral qualities are most intense by moonlight. At the far end of Kauppakatu, at the junction with Linnankatu, is the **Old Town Hall**, designed by Carl Engel.

More historically significant, perhaps, but far less thrilling, is the ruined **Kajaani Castle**. Built in the seventeenth century to forestall a Russian attack, it later served as a prison where, among others, Johannes Messenius, the troublesome Swede, was incarcerated. Although there's constant talk of schemes to rebuild it, the castle was ruined so long ago that nobody's sure what it actually looked like, and the present heap of stones is only worth seeing if you're already idling along the riverbank beside it.

Given the lack of other evening activities, idling is what you're likely to be doing if you stay here overnight. The problem of complete boredom is no less severe for the local youth, who've taken to lining the pavements of Kauppakatu in their hundreds, waiting for something to happen. About the only other way to pass the sunset hours is to take a quiet walk along the riverside footpath, from the corner of Ämmäkoskenkatu and Brehenkatu. Heading west, the path passes the **open-air theatre**, and also provides a chance to gaze at logs sliding blissfully towards destruction at the pulp mill ahead. Following the river eastwards leads to **Lönnrot's summer cottage**. Built by Elias Lönnrot, of *Kalevala* fame, for his wife, the small wooden structure now stands totally empty, isolated and seemingly insignificant; the only acknowledgement of its existence is in the name of the neighbouring *Elias Restaurant* inside the neighbouring *Hotelli Kajaani* – an odd neglect of a man whose life's work was so influential, and revered.

Practicalities

The **tourist office** (June–Aug Mon–Fri 9am–5.30pm, Sat 9am–2pm; Sept–May Mon–Fri 9am–4.30pm; ☏08/6152 5555, Ⓦwww.kajaani.fi), Pohjolankatu 16, can offer assistance with finding **accommodation**. One inexpensive option is *Kainuun Portti*, 4km south of town on Route 5 (☏08/613 3000, ℻613 3010; ❸) with regular singles and doubles; to get there, take bus #7 from the bus station – Kajaani's tent-only **campsite** is also located here (same contact details; open May–Aug). Closer to town is the quiet *Hotelli Kajaani* (T030/608 6100, www.solaris-lomat.fi/kajaani; ❹), in a handsome setting on the river. For a bit more money, the town centre holds several adequate choices, and rates drop during the summer and at weekends. Of these, *Sokos Hotel Valjus*, Kauppakatu 20 (T08/615 0200, www.sokoshotels.fi; ❹/❺) is one of the better options, though the best is the *Scandic Kajanus* (T08/616 41, www.scandic-hotels.com; ❹) across the main bridge in pleasant riverside surroundings at Koskikatu 3 (entrance on Puutavarantie).

There's not a huge number of decent places to **eat** in Kajaani, the most reliable option being the *Golden Dragon* at Kauppakatu 38. Other options lined up along Kauppakatu include the *Pikanti*, at nos. 10–12, where an all-you-can-eat lunch costs €8.90; and the classy Spanish restaurant *Torero*, Kauppakatu 20. The most atmospheric place to dine is *Sirius* (www.ravintolasirius.fi), just off the main drag by the river at Brahenkatu 5, in a building originally constructed as a residence for the Kajaani paper company and later used to accommodate visiting dignitaries including Soviet and Finnish presidents Leonid Brezhnev and Urho Kekkonen. The Finnish food here is not cheap but is certainly tasty, and they do a really good Kainuu *lounas* lunch for €38. *Hospoda Koruna* at Kauppakatu 30 and *Brahe*, immediately opposite at no. 21, are the only decent places to **drink**.

Around Kajaani: Paltaniemi

The hourly #4 bus from Kajaani winds its way to the well-preserved village of **PALTANIEMI**, 9km away on the shores of Oulujärvi – an attractive place but, since the closure of its campsite, one without anywhere to stay. In contrast to down-at-heel Kajaani, eighteenth-century Paltaniemi was home to Swedish-speaking aesthetes lured here by the importance of Kajaani Castle during the halcyon days of the Swedish empire. Their transformation of Paltaniemi into something of a cultural hotbed seems incredible given the place's tiny size and placid setting, but evidence of a refined pedigree isn't hard to find. Most obviously there's the **Paltaniemi kirkko** (May–Aug daily 10am–6pm; Sept–April guided tours only, bookable in the tourist office in Kajaani), built in 1726, a large church whose interior is deliberately chilled in order to preserve **frescoes** painted by Emmanuel Granberg between 1778 and 1781, which include a steamy vision of hell in a gruesome *Last Judgement*.

It's also fun to ferret around behind the pews, trying to decipher centuries-old graffiti. Even Tsar Alexander I paid a visit to Paltaniemi after Finland had become a Russian Grand Duchy, and his impromptu meal in a stable is reverentially commemorated in the **Tsar's Stable** by the church. **Hövelö**, the reconstructed cottage across the road, was the birthplace of **Eino Leino**, whose poems captured the increasingly assertive mood of Finland at the beginning of the twentieth century: his life and the history of Kajaani Castle form the subject of an eminently missable exhibition within (June–Aug Sun–Fri 10am–8pm; €6). Elias Lönnrot scripted a good portion of his epic *Kalevala* when he stayed here in the early 1830s and worked as the town doctor.

Moving on from Kajaani

Buses provide the easiest way of **moving on** from Kajaani. The only rail links are west to Oulu (5–6 daily), plus the six daily connections for Iisalmi, Kuopio and beyond, including a useful sleeper service direct to both Helsinki and Turku. The best direction to head for more rural delights is east towards Kuhmo, where the scenery becomes increasingly spectacular, especially around the town of Sotkamo (39km from Kajaani) and the acclaimed beauty spot of **Vuokatti** – a high, pine-clad ridge commanding views all the way to Russia. The rolling hills make this Finland's premier ski-training area.

Hiking routes around Kuhmo

The local section of the several hundred kilometres of trail that make up the **UKK hiking route** starts from the Kuhmo Sports Centre and winds 70km through forests and the Hiidenportti canyon. Several other hikes begin further out from Kuhmo and can be reached by bus from the town. **Elimyssalo**, to the east, is a fifteen-kilometre trail through a conservation area, and also to the east is **Kilpelän-kankaan**, where a cycle path runs 3.5km across heathland, passing a number of Winter War memorials. To the north, **Sininenpolku** is a hike of more than 20km over a ridge, past small lakes and rivers. In the northwest, **Iso-Palosenpolku** has two paths through a thickly forested area, where there are overnight shelters. Additionally, several **canoeing routes** trace the course of the old tar-shipping routes between Kuhmo and Oulu.

Kuhmo

With belts of forests, hills and lakes, and numerous nature walks and hikes within easy reach, **KUHMO** makes a fine base for exploring the countryside. The terrain is in some ways less dramatic than that further north, but then again it's also far less crowded.

You can get details of hiking routes, maps and other practical information from the **tourist office**, Kainuuntie 126 (June–Aug daily 8am–6pm; Sept–May Mon–Fri 8am–6pm, Sat 10am–4pm; ☎0440/755 500, ⓦwww.kuhmo.fi). The tourist office can also explain how best to reach the **Kalevala Village** on the outskirts of the town. This re-creation of a wooden Karelian village provides an illuminating account of traditional building methods, plus it's a good excuse to indulge in some pricey souvenirs – and interesting handicrafts – which are sold to the many genuine Karelians who visit. It's also the only thing close to Kuhmo of appeal to non-hikers.

Budget **accommodation** options in Kuhmo include several boarding houses, the best-established of which is the *Matkustajakoti Uljaska*, Koulukatu 38 (☎08/655 0545; ❸). Near the tourist office, *Hotelli Kainuu*, Kainuutie 84, (☎08/655 1711, ⓦwww.hotellikainuu.com; ❸/❹), is the only hotel option in town, but *Hotel Kalevala*, 3km from the centre (☎08/655 4100, ⓦwww.hotelkalevala.fi; ❺), is a better bet, with clean, modern room set on a lake with great views; it also rents out **canoes** and **bikes**. The town **campsite** (☎04/4075 5500; June–Aug) is 4km from the centre along Koulukatu.

Continuing northwards from Kuhmo leads only to more hiking lands, and if you need urbanity, nightlife and easy living, now's the time to own up and duck out. If not, and your feet are itching to be tested over hundreds of kilometres of untamed land, simply clamber on the bus for Kuusamo.

Kuusamo and around

KUUSAMO, 211km northeast of Oulu, is reached by daily express buses from Oulu, plus regular services from Rovaniemi. For full details of local hiking and accommodation, and the many summer events that bring some life to the town, call in at the **Karhuntassu Tourist & Nature Centre**, Torangintaival 2 (early May to early Aug daily 9am–5pm; early Aug to mid-Sept Mon–Fri 9am–5pm; ☎03/0650 2540 or 08/860 0200, ⓦwww.kuusamo.fi) and pick up both *Summer Info* and *Ruka News*, small handbooks which offer useful information about things to do in and around Kuusamo. For accommodation, try the well-kept, independently run **youth hostel**, across the street from the bus station at Kitkantie 35 (☎04/08 608 715, ⓦedu.kuusamo.fi/kansanopisto; doubles ❶, dorms €11), though you must book in advance and arrive between 8am and 3.45pm Monday to Friday, as there's no reception at other times. Alternatively, the soulless *Sokos Hotel Kuusamo*, Kirkkotie 23 (☎08/859 20, ⓦwww.sokoshotels.fi; ❹/❺), is a ten-minute walk from the centre of town at the junction with Ouluntie; it overlooks the Toranki lake, and has an exceptionally large indoor swimming pool. Before setting out hiking, the best places in town to **eat and drink** are *Martina's* and the adjoining *Parnell's Irish Bar* at Ouluntie 3 – fried chicken, chips, salad and a beer will cost around €15. Later in the evening, anyone still standing heads to *Fiona*, Ouluntie 7.

Kuusamo is the starting point for the **Karhunkierros Trail** (also known as the Kuusamo Bear Circuit); one of the most popular hiking routes in Finland, it's a seventy-kilometre trek weaving over the summit of Rukatunturi, dipping into canyons and across slender log suspension bridges over thrashing rapids. Herds of hikers are a far more common sight than bears, but the hike is still a good one and there are several interesting shorter routes off the main track. From Kuusamo, take the bus to **Ristikallio** for the start of the hike. Wilderness huts are placed roughly at ten-kilometre intervals along the route, though during peak months these are certain to be full. Fortunately there's no shortage of places to pitch your own tent, and about halfway along the route are three **campsites**, *Juuma* (☎08/863 212; late May to Sept), *Jyrävä* (☎050/361 4631; June to early Sept) and *Retki-Etappi* (☎08/863 218; June–Sept).

Heading north again, the tougher and little-known **Six Fells Hiking Route** (more commonly known by its tongue-twisting Finnish name Kuudentunturinkevelyreitti) starts at **Salla** (ⓦwww.salla.fi). Buses run here from Kuusamo several times a day, pulling up at *Hotel Revontuli* (☎016/879 711, ⓔrevontuli@salli .fi; ⑤) a great place to stay that gets lit up beautifully at night; nearby, there are also some **cabins** (☎016/837 766, ⓦwww.tunturimokit.com; €85), for which showers cost extra. The thirty-five-kilometre hike, actually part of the UKK trail, begins a couple of kilometres north of Salla at the *Sallan Maja* roadside café, and includes some stiff climbs up the sides of spruce-covered fells, with spectacular views from their bare summits. **Niemelä**, close to the road between Kuusamo and Salla, marks the other end of the trail. From Salla you can continue by bus into the Arctic North (see p.623), to Kemijärvi to meet the train for Rovaniemi and all points south or, provided you have sorted a visa, across the Russian border to

▲ Sámi woman, Rovaniemi

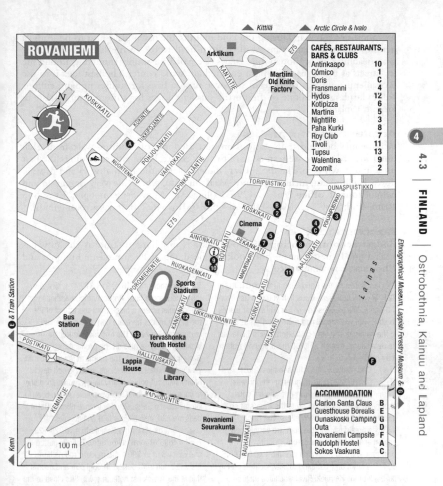

ROVANIEMI

▲ Kittilä   ▲ Arctic Circle & Ivalo

Arktikum

Martiini Old Knife Factory

CAFÉS, RESTAURANTS, BARS & CLUBS

Antinkaapo	10
Cómico	1
Doris	C
Fransmanni	4
Hydos	12
Kotipizza	6
Martina	5
Nightlife	3
Paha Kurki	8
Roy Club	7
Tivoli	11
Tupsu	13
Walentina	9
Zoomit	2

Cinema

Sports Stadium

Bus Station

Tervashonka Youth Hostel

Lappia House

Library

Rovaniemi Seurakunta

0   100 m

ACCOMMODATION

Clarion Santa Claus	B
Guesthouse Borealis	E
Ounaskoski Camping	G
Outa	D
Rovaniemi Campsite	F
Rudolph Hostel	A
Sokos Vaakuna	C

Vanha Salla (Old Salla) to see a handful of dilapidated towns that were Finnish property before World War II.

Rovaniemi and around

Easily accessible by train or bus, **ROVANIEMI** is touted as the capital of Lapland. Just south of the Arctic Circle it may be, but anyone arriving with an expectation of sleighs and tents will be disappointed by a place whose administrative buildings, busy shopping streets and *McDonald's* (the most northerly in the world) make it a far cry from the surrounding rural hinterland. Like many places in Finnish Lapland, the elegant wooden houses of old Rovaniemi were razed to the ground by departing Germans at the close of World War II, and the town was completely rebuilt during the late 1940s. Alvar Aalto's bold but impractical design has the roads forming the shape of reindeer antlers, though the centre of town is based on a familiar grid pattern. Although Rovaniemi can be quite dismal in summer, with its uniform greyish-white buildings and an unnerving newness to everything – even the smattering of antique shops contains nothing older than 1970s junk – during the **winter** the city really comes into its own, with the neutral colour of the buildings working in perfect harmony with the snow and ice that covers the streets for almost

619

six months of the year. During the cold months, the town plays host to busloads of nervous southern Europeans swathed from head to toe in the latest cold-weather gear, heading out on snowmobile safaris (see p.623) or simply stumbling around the icy streets as proof that they have endured an Arctic winter. The best idea is to use Rovaniemi only as a short-term stopover, or as a base for studies in Sámi culture, before heading off to one of the north's smaller villages for a more genuine taste of Finnish Lapland.

Arrival and information

Rovaniemi's bus and train stations are just a couple of minutes' walk from each other, located on the western edge of the city centre. From either terminus, the best route into town is to take the subway under Valtatie (the E4 highway) and to walk down Hallituskatu, turning left into Maakuntakatu, where the very organized and helpful **tourist office** is at nos. 29–31 (June–Aug Mon–Fri 8am–6pm, Sat & Sun 10am–4pm; Sept–May Mon–Fri 6am–6pm; ☎016/346 270, ⊛www.rovaniemi.fi).

Accommodation

Budget **accommodation** in Rovaniemi is not hard to find as the city has several good guesthouses – but booking ahead, especially around midsummer and Christmas, is recommended.

Clarion Santa Claus Korkalonkatu 49 ☎016/321 321, ⊛www.hotelsantaclaus.fi. If you can get over the name, this place is one of the city's best places to stay, with well-appointed rooms and great deals in the summer. The very chic Santa Claus Suite has its own sauna, though at €490 the bragging rights may not be worth it. ❹

Guesthouse Borealis Asemieskatu 1 ☎016/342 0130, ⊛guesthouseborealis .com. Great-value, family-run guesthouse with cheery en-suite rooms; close to the train station and very popular with InterRailers. The price includes breakfast, and the staff are very knowledgeable about local goings-on. ❷

Ounaskoski Camping Jäämerentie 1 ☎016/345 304. The city's only camping facility, located on the far bank of the Kemijoki River; facilities include a kiosk, café and sauna. Open late May to Aug.

Outa Ukkoherrantie 16 ☎016/312 474, ⊛www .guesthouseouta.com. An eccentric guesthouse on a very quiet street a block from the tourist office: the seven rooms here are comfy and cosy and feature microwaves, TVs and electric kettles. Washing machine also on the premises. ❸

Rudolph Koskikatu 41. The rooms at Rovaniemi's all-year youth hostel are spacious, spotless and devoid of any soul, but you're nearly always guaranteed one to yourself. There is no reception here so you book via the *Clarion Santa Claus* hotel (see above). Dorm beds are €30; also singles (❷) and doubles (❸).

Sokos Vaakuna Koskikatu 4 ☎020/123 4695 ⊛www.sokoshotels.fi. Fully gutted and renovated in 2003, the modern rooms here are saturated with design throughout, and overall this is the swankiest hotel in town. Sits close to the Ounaskoski River. ❹/❺

The City

If you have any interest in Sámi culture, make a beeline for the fascinating **Arktikum**, in the northern part of town at Kantatie 74 (mid-June to mid-Aug daily 9am–7pm; mid-Aug to Sept Tues–Sun 10am–6pm plus Mon in Aug; Oct–Nov Tues–Sun 10am–5pm; Dec to mid-Jan daily 10am–6pm; mid-Jan to mid-June Tues–Sun 10am–6pm; €12; ⊛www.arktikum.fi). Its great arched atrium emerges from the ground like a U-boat, with almost all the exhibition areas submerged beneath banks of stone. The complex contains both the **Provincial Museum of Lapland** and the recently overhauled **Arctic Centre**, which together provide a varied insight into the history and present-day lives of the peoples of the Arctic North. Taking an intelligent, unsentimental approach, the museum superbly evokes the remarkable Sámi culture and is well worth a couple of hours.

Displays range from raincoats made of seal intestine and trousers fashioned from polar bear hides to superb photographic displays on reindeer husbandry – modern technology has made its mark with cellular phones, snowmobiles and four-wheel-drive buggies now the norm. There are also pictures of the horrific devastation caused by German soldiers in 1944, when they were forced to retreat, burning every building in sight – look out for the two scale models showing the city before and after the retreat, and be sure to take in the poignant video footage that compares the heady life in Rovaniemi before the war, when loggers and lumberjacks would pour into the city's hotels and bars at weekends, with the sharply contrasting scenes of total devastation just a couple of years later – the people of Lapland have clearly still not forgiven the Germans for what happened.

Adjacent to the Arktikum is the **Marttiini Old Knife Factory** (Mon–Fri 10am–6pm, Sat 10am–2pm, also Sun noon–4pm in summer; ⓦwww.marttiini.fi), Vartiokatu 32. In the kingdom of the sharp edge, the Marttiini multipurpose knife reigns supreme, and the prices in the factory shop are the cheapest you'll find – plus you can have your name inscribed on the blade. Prices range from a few euro up to €100 for the latest model.

Back in the town centre, **Lappia House**, an Aalto-designed building a short distance from the bus and train stations at Hallituskatu 11, contains a theatre and concert hall, plus an excellent **library** (Mon–Thurs 11am–8pm, Fri 11am–5pm, Sat 11am–4pm) with several free internet terminals. There's also a **Lapland Department** (turn immediately left as you enter the building), housing a staggering hoard of books, magazines and newspaper articles in many languages covering every conceivable Sámi-related subject. This constantly growing collection is already the largest of its kind in the world, and probably the best place anywhere for undertaking Lapland-related research.

Other points of interest in Rovaniemi are few. At Rauhankatu 70, **Rovaniemi Seurakunta** (daily 9am–4pm), the parish church, repays a peek on account of its jumbo-sized altar fresco, *Fountain of Life* by Lennart Segerstråle, an odd work that pitches the struggle between good and evil into a Lapland setting. If you're here in winter, ask about the concerts that are staged here.

Moving on from Rovaniemi – cross-border bus routes in northern Scandinavia

With the exception of the train from Rovaniemi to Kemijärvi, all public transport north of the Arctic Circle is by **bus**. From Rovaniemi, services follow two main routes: northeast to Sodankylä, Ivalo, Inari and Utsjoki or northwest to Kittilä, Muonio, Karesuvanto and Kilpisjärvi – it's not possible to travel between these two routes without first backtracking to Rovaniemi. However, from the far north, cross-border services operate into Norway. Throughout the year, a daily bus leaves Rovaniemi around 11.45am for the North Cape via Inari (5pm), crossing into Norway at **Karasjok** – a total journey of eleven hours. The bus waits at the North Cape for two and a half hours before returning overnight via the same route to Rovaniemi. Connections can be made in Karasjok east towards Kirkenes and west ultimately for Tromsø. During the rest of the year this service terminates in Karasjok.

It's also possible to reach Norway and the Nord-Norgeekpressen services from **Utsjoki**: from June to September there is a direct bus from Rovaniemi departing at 5.20pm via Inari and Utsjoki to Vadsø (June to late Sept daily; Oct–May Wed–Fri & Sun). Alternatively, you can reach Norway by simply walking across the bridge in Utsjoki yourself (remember the hour's time difference between Finland and Norway); Norwegian buses do not drive over the bridge into Finland.

From June to mid-September a daily service leaves Rovaniemi at 11.30am for **Tromsø** (where it arrives at 7.30pm Norwegian time) via Muonio, Kaaresuvanto (walk on foot over the bridge here to connect with Swedish bus services in Karesuando for Kiruna) and Kilpisjärvi. Be sure to check timetables carefully and plan several days ahead: either visit ⓦwww.matkahuolto.fi or get the *Pikavuorot*, available at the bigger bus stations and at most tourist offices, where they should be able to help decipher the Finnish key.

If you have more time to kill and the weather isn't too cold (Rovaniemi is prone to chilly snaps even in summer), visit one of the two outdoor museums that lie near each other just outside town, accessible by bus #6. The **Ethnographical Museum** in Pöykkölä, 3km southeast of town (June–Aug Tues–Sun noon–6pm; €3), is a collection of farm buildings that belonged to the Pöykkölä family between 1640 and 1910, and forms part of a potpourri of objects pertaining to reindeer husbandry, salmon fishing and rural life in general. About 500m up the road is the **Lappish Forestry Museum** (June–Aug Tues–Sun noon–6pm; €3), where the reality of unglamorous forestry life is remembered by a reconstructed lumber camp. Rovaniemi also boasts a decent public **sauna** and **swimming pool**, Vesihiisi, at Nuortenkatu 11, a fifteen-minute walk from the town centre west along Koskikatu and then left into Kokintie.

Around Rovaniemi: the Arctic Circle and Santa Claus Village

Most people are lured to Rovaniemi solely for the dubious thrill of crossing the **Arctic Circle**. While the "circle" itself doesn't remain constant (it's defined as the area where the midnight sun can be seen, which shifts a few hundred metres every year), its man-made markers do – 8km north of town along Route 4 – generally heralded by a crowd of visitors taking photographs of each other with one foot either side of the line. Bus #8 goes to the circle from the train station around every hour (€5.20 return; more frequent in summer), and also calls at several stops in town.

Near the circle and served by the same bus is the **Santa Claus Village** (daily: June & Aug 9am–6pm; July & Dec 9am–7pm; rest of the year 10am–5pm; free; @ www.santaclausvillage.info). Considering its tourist pitch, the place – inside a very large log cabin – is quite within the bounds of decency: you can meet Father Christmas all year round, contemplate the reindeer grazing in the adjoining farm and leave your name for a Christmas letter from Santa (€6). Within the village is the ticket office for **Santa Park** (mid-June to mid-Aug Tues–Sat 10am–4pm; late Nov to early Jan daily 10am–7pm; €20; @ www.santapark.fi) from which a train connects to the park itself. A collection of themed fairground rides within a cavern inside a granite hill, Santa Park is predominantly aimed at those who believe the big guy with the white beard is real. For those without children, it's most definitely worth missing, unless you want to pretend you're 4 again.

Eating

While Rovaniemi has a few pleasant **cafés**, its opportunities for fine or exotic dining leave a lot to be desired – though dishes featuring reindeer are very easy to find. Most numerous are the standard kebab and pizza joints around Koskikatu, nearly all of which offer late-night snacks to bar-hoppers.

Antinkaapo Rovakatu 13 @ www.antinkaapo .com. Rovaniemi's best café, serving a lavish range of delicious pastries and butter cookies. Opens at 7.30am during the week. Closed Sun.

Cómico Koskikatu 25 @ www.comicobar.fi. Jumping on Finland's Tex Mex bandwagon, this place is a big hit with younger locals, and the burritos (€9.90), fajitas (€14.80) and greasy *gambas cajun aiollo* (€7.90) are all quite tasty. In the evenings it turns into a popular drinks place, with student bands occasionally taking to the stage.

Fransmanni *Sokos Vaakuna* hotel, Koskikatu 4. If you haven't yet tried reindeer or any other Lappish

specialities, this is a great place to take the plunge. Prices are a tad high but the food is excellent, and you're likely to find everything from reindeer heart to cloudberry liqueur on the menu.

Hydos Kansankatu 10 @ www.hydos .com. The interior to this Turkish restaurant is done up in 1980s Ottoman kitsch and chintz, making it one of the more eccentric local finds. The €7 lunch specials are popular with local workers, and dinners are well priced, too. Don't confuse the entrance with that of the erotic showbar immediately next door.

Kotipizza Koskikatu 5 ☎ 016/310 303 and Pohjolankatu 4 ☎ 016/345 666. Tasty takeaway pizzas, starting at €6.70, and busiest when the surrounding bars close.

Martina Koskikatu 11. Pizza and pasta dishes are €9 and steaks around €17 at this predictable chain restaurant, though the decor here is a bit warmer than most places in town. Just upstairs,

Rax has an all-you-can-eat pizza buffet for €8.70.

Walentina Rovakatu 21 ⓦ www.walentina.fi. Very good coffee, great sticky buns and a full collection of deliciously tooth-rotting pastries and sweets. Closed Sun.

Nightlife

With a sizeable university population during term-time and thousands of tourists visiting throughout the year, Rovaniemi offers a lively **nightlife** for every school of libation. The most popular places for a drink are just off the pedestrian walkway of Koskikatu, and there are several places for a dance, some set within the hotels. Though winter offers the most excitement, the town does wake up a bit in the summer when ROPS, the Rovaniemi football team – one of the best in the country – are playing at home. You'll hear the cheering all over town, and can even see the game for free through gaps in the fencing of the stadium (or, alternatively, shell out the €10 for a ticket), on Pohjolankatu; after the matches, the partying continues all over town, when Rovaniemi's bars are ablaze with first-rate displays of Finnish drunkenness.

Doris *Sokos Vaakuna*, Koskikatu 4. Set in the hotel basement, this is the most popular club in town and as such gets away with charging a €5–10 cover. The young and beautiful of Lapland come to dance, drink and play the €1 minimum casino tables at the back.

Nightlife *Hotel Rantasipi Pohjanhovi*, Pohjanpuistikko 2. Three bars in one, aimed at a mature crowd. Upstairs is a meat-and-potatoes Finnish bar that at times has the vague sense of a 40-something pick-up joint; at the back, there's a relaxed tango and *humppa* dancefloor, and downstairs an ever-popular karaoke bar.

Paha Kurki Koskikatu 5. Small, dark, dingy and extremely popular rock club that fills up with hardcore hipsters from all over the Arctic.

Roy Club Maakuntakatu 24 ⓦ www.royclub.fi. A somewhat relaxed atmosphere pervades upstairs, while downstairs the floor is beer-sticky

and the DJs have a thing for the dry-ice button. Usually less drunken than most other places.

Tivoli Valtakatu 19 ⓦ www.cafetivoli.fi. Great, unpretentious bar popular with students and other locals not into the disco scene. Closed Sun–Tues.

Tupsu Hallituskatu 24. Renovated in 2007, this favourite local hangout is as authentic a Finnish bar as you'll probably find. Because it's a bit out of the way near the bus station, the atmosphere is somewhat tranquil, and it's known as one of Rovaniemi's more gay-friendly bars. Sometimes puts on impromptu theatre performances, but be especially wary of the all-weekend karaoke fetes.

Zoomlt Koskikatu 10, at the corner of Korkolankatu. Popular chrome- and glass-fronted place often stuffed with trendy young things from the Lapland University. Upstairs is *ZoomUp*, a trendy new bar and grill.

Listings

Airport ⓣ 016/363 6710.
Bus information ⓣ 0200/4000 (toll call).
Car hire Avis, Valtakatu 26 ⓣ 016/310 524; Budget, Koskikatu 9 ⓣ 020/746 6620; Europcar, Pohjanpuistikko 2 ⓣ 016/332 332; Hertz, Koskikatu 23 ⓣ 020/556 2500; Scandia Rent, Valtakatu 18 ⓣ 016/342 0506.
Cinema Maxim, inside the Sampokeskus shopping centre on Pekankatu.

Hospital Lapin Keskussairaala, Ounasrinteentie 22 ⓣ 016/328 2100.
Safari companies Arctic Safaris, Koskikatu 6 ⓣ 020/786 8700, ⓦ www.arcticsafaris.com; Lapland Safaris, Koskikatu 1 ⓣ 016/331 1200, ⓦ www.laplandsafaris.com.
Train information VR ⓣ 030/710.
Train station ⓣ 0307/47 643.

The Arctic North

Squeezed inland by the northern tip of Norway, Finland's **Arctic North** mixes undulating forests, lakes and rivers with tracts of desolate upland that rise high

The best way to experience the Arctic North is to get off the bus and explore slowly, which means on foot. The rewards for making the physical effort are manifold. There's a tremendous feeling of space here, and the wild and inhospitable terrain acquires a near-magical quality when illuminated by the constant daylight of the summer months (the only time of year when hiking is feasible).

Many graded **hiking routes** cover the more interesting areas; most of the more exhilarating are distributed among the region's four national parks: **Pyhä-Luosto**, southeast of Sodankylä; **Urho Kekkonen** and **Lemmenjoki**, further north off the Arctic Highway; and **Pallas-Yllästunturi**, near Muonio in the northwest. There are challenges aplenty for experienced hikers, though novices need have nothing to fear provided basic common sense is employed. The more popular hikes can become very busy and many people find this an intrusion into their contemplation of the natural spectacle – others enjoy the camaraderie. If you're seeking solitude you'll find it, but you'll need at least the company of a reliable compass, a good-quality tent and emergency supplies.

We've included broad introductions to the major hikes throughout this chapter, and described the type of terrain that you'll find on them. Bear in mind that, though, that these aren't definitive accounts, as conditions and details often change at short notice; always gather the latest information from the nearest tourist centre or park information office. Most tourist offices hand out free trail descriptions in English and also sell excellent 1:10000 hiking maps. For copious information on hiking in Finland, visit the Finnish Forest Service's comprehensive, expertly written English-language website, Ⓦwww.outdoors.fi.

Hiking rules and tips

Obviously you should observe the **basic rules** of hiking, and be aware of the delicate ecology of the region: never leave litter, don't start fires in any old place (most hikes have marked spots for this) and don't pitch your tent out of specified areas on marked routes. You should always check that you have maps and adequate supplies before setting out, and never aim to cover more ground than is comfortable. Bathe your feet daily to prevent blisters, and carry some form of mosquito repellent – the pesky creatures infest the region and will descend en masse anytime after noon.

Hiking accommodation

To be on the safe side, you shouldn't go anywhere without a good-quality **tent**, although the majority of marked hikes have some form of basic shelter, and most have a **youth hostel** and **campsite** (and at times even comfy hotels) at some point on the trail. These fill quickly, however, and few things are worse than having nowhere to relax after a long day's trek – so make advance reservations whenever possible.

above the treeline. In these uncompromising latitudes, a fair number of the indigenous Sámi population still herd their reindeer and maintain their traditions despite serious threats from a number of sources, including modernization, tourism and – most dramatically – the fallout from Chernobyl. With the exception of attractions like reindeer farms and appearances at a few annual festivals, the Sámi tend to remain far from the prying eyes of visitors, though their angular *lávvus*, *kotas* and *tipis* (tents), wreathed in reindeer antlers, skins and all sorts of Arctic ornaments, are to be found along the region's main roads during the summer, in what can seem a rather crass and commercially inspired conformity. This is intended to appeal to the wallets of the thousands of motorists who use the **Arctic Highway**, the E75/4, the fastest approach to the Nordkapp (see p.342). But don't let this put you off: the Arctic wilderness is a ready escape, its stark and often haunting landscapes easily accessible.

Two main roads lead north from Rovaniemi: the Arctic Highway, which services the **northeast**, linking the communities of Sodankylä, Ivalo, Inari and Utsjoki; and Route 79/E8, which crosses the **northwest**, connecting Muonio and Kilpisjärvi. Inari and Sodankylä are the only settlements worth a second look, but the landscape which surrounds the Arctic North's minuscule communities will hold your gaze for much longer – provided you take the trouble to do at least some **hiking**. There's also plenty of outdoor adventure here for those who seek it – **dog-sledging**, **skiing** and **snowmobiling** are the most popular diversions – though none of it comes cheap. If you're planning to travel north from Rovaniemi on one route then back on the other, be warned that there are no roads in between, only rough tracks – with no facilities – traversing some desolate landscape. For safety, you need either to retrace your steps to Rovaniemi before taking the other route, or travel in an arc into Norway and over the other side, a journey by car of around four hours. Bus connections up in these parts are few and far between so if you're without your own vehicle, try to plan ahead to avoid finding yourself stuck in the middle of nowhere.

The northeast: Sodankylä and the national parks

North of Rovaniemi, it's an uneventful 130-kilometre drive along the Arctic Highway to **SODANKYLÄ**, a modest, comfortable town whose modern appearance belies its ancient foundation. From the late seventeenth century, Finnish settlers and Christian Sámi gathered here on high days and holidays to trade and to celebrate religious festivals. Unusually, their wooden **church** (June–Aug daily 10am–6pm) of 1689 has survived intact, its rough-hewn timbers crowding in upon the narrowest of naves and with the pulpit pressing intrusively into the pews. The old church nestles beside the Kitinen River, in the shadow of its uninspiring nineteenth-century replacement and a stone's throw from the **Alariesto Art Gallery** (Mon–Fri 10am–4pm, Sat 10am–4pm; €3), which features the work of Andreas Alariesto, a twentieth-century Sámi artist of some renown. Each canvas is an invigorating representation of traditional native life and custom, notably a crystalline *View from the Arctic Ocean* embellished with chaotic boulders, predatory fish jaws and busy Sámi. A useful catalogue available at reception explains the background to the exhibits. Other nearby activities include the **horseback rides** at Laphorse, Mantovaarantie 17 (℡0400/683 417, ⊛www.laphorse.com; €25) and outdoor activities like paintball with Nature X-Ventures (℡040/867 1786, ⊛www.naturex-ventures.fi; €25 per person).

Sodankylä is little more than an elongated main street: Jäämerentie. The bus station, post office and petrol stations are within a few metres of each other, while the **tourist office** (June–Aug Mon–Fri 9am–5pm, Sat 9am–5pm; Sept–May Mon–Fri 9am–5pm; ℡040/746 9776, ⊛www.sodankyla.fi) is in the centre of the village at Jäämerentie 3, a ten-minute walk from the bus station. In winter it's a good idea to book accommodation in advance, since Sodankylä is used by test drivers from Peugeot who come here for several months to test new models in Arctic conditions.

There are just two **hotels** in the village, the bear-themed *Karhu* (℡0201/620 610, ⊛www.hotel-bearinn.com; ❹), a five-minute walk from the bus station at Sodankyläntie 10, and offering rooms with either sauna or hydromassage shower and extremely gregarious and helpful reception staff; and the less inspiring *Hotelli Sodankylä*, Lapintie 21 (℡016/617 121, ℻613 545; ❹/❺) – both are open

---

Sodankylä's Midnight Sun Film Festival

Accommodation is especially hard to come by in Sodankylä during the **Midnight Sun Film Festival**, which draws film-loving Finns – and a re markable number of top directors and their latest cinematic offerings – to the tiny town for a week each June. For more information about the event, visit ⊛www.msfilmfestival.fi.

year-round. The *Kolme Veljestä* guesthouse, north of the bus station at Ivalontie 1 (☎0400/ 539 075, ⊛www.majatalokolmeveljesta.fi; ❸), has comfortable rooms – breakfast and use of the kitchen and sauna are included. There's also a **campsite** right on the river (☎016/612 181, ⊛www.naturex-ventures.fi; cabins €36; rooms ❸ June–Sept), which rents cheap canoes and expensive jetskis.

As for **meals**, *Annabella*, Jäämerentie 13, is a new Turkish pizza and kebab place in the centre of town that's popular with everyone. Elsewhere is *Pizza Paikka à la Riesto*, Jäämerentie 25, and *Ravintola Revontuli*, Jäämerentie 9, which offers Finnish meat and fish dishes for around €10 and is also a popular place for a drink. Just up the road at Jäämerentie 20, *Seita-baari* serves up the best local food, earning its reputation from its excellent reindeer stew, but the tacky decor may make the idea of a meal here somewhat off-putting. *Disco Paradise*, in the same building as *Revontuli*, is the choice of places to dance the night away.

Around Sodankylä: Pyhä-Luosto National Park

Off the Arctic Highway some 65km southeast of Sodankylä lies **Pyhä–Luosto National Park**, established in 2005, and the steep slopes and deep ravines of the most southerly Finnish fells. Here, the 45-kilometre **Pyhätunturi hiking trail** rises from marshlands and pine woods and round five fell summits, connecting the holiday resorts of Pyhä and Luosto. Five kilometres from the start is the impressive waterfall of the Uhrikuru gorge, after which the track circles back for a short stretch, eventually continuing to Karhunjuomalampi ("The Bear's Pool"). There's a *päivätupa* (cabin) here, but the only other hut on the route is by the pool at Pyhälampi.

Near the hike's starting point at Pyhä are a **nature centre** (June–Sept daily 9am–5pm; Oct–May Mon–Fri 10am–4pm; ☎020/564 7302, ⊛www.outdoors.fi), a **campsite** (☎016/852 103, ⊛www.lapinorava.fi; cabins €55), and two reasonably priced **hotels**: the *Pyhätunturi* (☎016/856 111, ⊛www.pyha.fi; ❸) and *Pyhän Asteli* (☎016/852 141, ⊛www.asteli.fi; ❷), both of which are incidentally well placed for skiing in the winter. The hike ends at Luostotunturi, where accommodation includes the *Scandic Hotel Luosto* (☎016/624 400, ⊛www.scandichotels.com; ❹/❺), and the more basic *Luostonhovi* (☎020/1620 660, ⊛www.luostonhovi.fi; ❷). The daily **bus** between Sodankylä and Kemijärvi (on the rail line from Rovaniemi) stops close to both ends of the trail.

Continuing north: Urho Kekkonen National Park

Travel north by car from Sodankylä on the Arctic Highway for 110km and just after the village of **Vuotso** you'll arrive at **Koilliskaira Visitor Centre** (June to mid-Aug daily 9am–6pm; mid-Aug to Sept daily 9am–5pm; Oct–May Mon–Fri 10am–6pm; ☎020/564 7251, ⊛www.tankavaara.fi), where you can reserve cabin beds, get information on dozens of hikes and watch a film about the local terrain. Just 100m from the centre lurks a gaggle of tourist establishments: the **Tankavaara Gold Museum and Panning Centre** (same hours; €8), the *Nugget* restaurant, serving Lapland specialities for around €15, and a guesthouse, the *Korundi* (☎016/626 158; ❸), with **cabins** (€40). Over the first weekend in August the town puts on the **Goldpanning Finnish Open**, where burly lumberjack types from all over the world compete to slosh out the most gold bits from piles of dirt and rock.

Twenty kilometres further north (130km from Sodankylä), at the hamlet of Kakslauttanen, is the turning for **Fell Centre Kiilopää** (daily 8am–10pm, closed May & Oct; ☎016/670 0700, ⊛www.kilopaa.fi), a popular and well-equipped fell-walking centre on the edge of the **Urho Kekkonen National Park**. The park is one of the country's largest, incorporating the uninhabited wilderness that extends to the Russian border – pine moors and innumerable fells scored by gleaming streams and rivers. With regular bus connections to north and south, the Fell Centre (also known by its Finnish name, Tunturikeskus) is easily the most convenient base for exploring the park. It's at the head of several walking trails, from the simplest of excursions to exhausting expeditions using the park's chain of wilderness cabins.

▲ Igloo saunas, Inari

As well as providing park information, selling detailed trail maps, renting mountain bikes and organizing guided walks, staff can arrange accommodation in the adjoining year-round **youth hostel** *Hotel Niilanpää* (same phone number; dorms €22, breakfast not included); the Centre also has some en-suite rooms (**②**/**③**), a good restaurant and a smoke sauna.

Ivalo, Inari and around

Try not to get stuck in **IVALO**, a town offering little charm on the side of the Arctic Highway 40km north of the Fell Centre Kiilopää. If you do need a reason to stay, however, the *Pankkila* guesthouse (℡040 070 6209, ℗www.pankkila.fi; **④**) is it. Centrally located at Ivalontie 2 opposite the S-Market, it offers several sleekish apartment-style rooms and a great fish and burger restaurant downstairs. Elsewhere is the riverside *Hotelli Ivalo* (℡016/688 111, ℗www.hotelivalo.fi; **④**), with breakfast and sauna included in the price, while the much cheaper *Näverniemen Lomakylä* (℡016/677 601), just south of town, has **camping** spots and a few simple summer **cabins** (€25). Ivalo's **tourist office**, Ivalontie 7 in the Inarilainen newspaper building (℡03/0624 4120, ℗www.readytogo.fi; June–Sept Mon–Fri 9am–6.30pm, Sat & Sun 9am–3pm; Oct–May Mon–Fri 9am–5pm), offers friendly smiles along with helpful information about the region; they also house a tourist agent which can organize a range of husky, reindeer, snowmobile and skiing excursions. Ivalo's uninspiring **eating** options amount to the hotel restaurants, of which *Pankkila's* is the best, and a few pizza places: *Anjan Pizza* on the main road near the Shell filling station and the *Lauran Grilli*, opposite, which also has kebabs. While Ivalo lacks any obvious charm, it does offer a rare direct **bus to Russia**: a once-daily

(Mon–Fri) service leaves the village at 8.30am for the three-hundred-kilometre trip to **Murmansk** via the border at Raja-Jooseppi – however, you'll need advance planning if you want to use the service, as you'll need to be equipped with a Russian visa to get on, which can be obtained in Helsinki (and, for several hundred euro more, in Kirkenes). For more information and help with visas, contact the tourist office in Inari, which also organizes trips across the border.

The road heading north to Inari winds around numerous lakes dotted with islands – it's a spectacular route if you can time your trip with the glorious Lapland **Ruska**, a season that takes in late summer and autumn, when the trees take on brilliant citrus colours that reflect in the still waters. **INARI** itself, 40km away, is quite a bit more amenable than Ivalo, straggling along the bony banks of the Juutuanjoki River as it tumbles into the freezing-cold, islet-studded waters of Lake Inarijärvi. There's nothing remarkable about the village itself, but it's a pretty little place with several appealing diversions and it buzzes in the summer season with transitory visitors taking a break from the Rovaniemi–Nordkapp beaten path. The bus stops outside the **tourist office** (daily June–Aug 9am–6pm; early to mid-Sept daily 10am–5pm; mid-Sept to May Mon–Fri 9am–5pm; ☎016/661 666, ⊛www.inarilapland.org) on the one and only main road, where helpful staff can advise on accommodation, trips to Russia and organize a fishing licence (from €10 for one week) and daily excursions to Kirkenes in northern Norway. Across the road is the Sámi handicraft store, **Sámi Duodji** (daily: July–Aug 10am–6pm; Sept–June 10am–5pm), whose exhibits are of markedly higher quality than the tourist souvenirs that pop up everywhere else in Lapland. Close by lies the Sámi museum and nature centre, **Siida** (June–Sept daily 9am–8pm; Oct–May Tues–Sun 10am–5pm; €8), the best museum in Lapland. An excellent outdoor section features a re-sited nineteenth-century village and various reconstructions illustrating aspects of Sámi life – principally handicrafts and hunting or fishing techniques – while the indoor section has a comprehensive and well-curated ethnographic exhibition on Arctic life, including a timeline tracing the Sámi from pre-history to the present day, detailing all the social, cultural and political changes which have affected them. Beginning about 2.5km from the museum, the four-kilometre **Pielpajärvi Wilderness Church hiking trail** leads to the isolated remains of a 1752 church – the trail can be very slippery when wet. If you don't fancy expending any energy to see some scenery, head for the bridge over the Juutuanjoki, from where, in summer, you can take a two-hour **lake cruise** (June to mid-Sept daily 2pm; ☎040/029 5731; €15), as well as fishing trips (all year); for the latter, a twelve-seater boat and a guide for three hours costs €300, so the per-person price depends on total number in the group. In the winter, popular snowmobile trips set out over the frozen lake, while cross-country skiing is the transport of choice for most locals.

Many travellers pass through Inari during the summer, so it's best to reserve **accommodation** during this period. One of the most enjoyable places is to stay is ⚘ *Villa Lanca* (☎040/748 0984, ⊛www.villalanca.com; ❹), run by an effusive Finnish-Sámi couple who rent out charming apartments across several floors just opposite the tourist office, as well as a nearby cottage on a secluded peninsula; they also run their own fishing, hiking, sauna and snowmobile excursions starting at €80 per person per day. Elsewhere in the village, the *Inarin Kultahovi* **hotel** (☎016/671 221, ⊛www.hotelkultahovi.fi; ❸), Saarikoskentie 2, offers 29 comfortable rooms with river views and an excellent, reasonably priced restaurant; the *Lomakylä Inari* (☎016/671 108, ⊛www.lomakyla-inari.fi), Inarintie 26, has well-kept wooden cabins (€50); while the **campsite**, *Uruniemi Camping* (☎016/671 331, ⊛www .uruniemi.com; June–Sept), 3km away on the southern outskirts of the town, has smaller cottages (€25). The ⚘ *Siida Ravintola* **restaurant** at the Siida museum (see above) is very good – go for the scrumptious hollandaise Lake Inari trout and whitefish platter with boiled potatoes (€18). If money's tight, stick to the popular *Ranta-Mari* restaurant and café, beside the bus stop, though be prepared to share the place with drunken locals at weekends.

A vast tract of birch and pinewood forest interrupted by austere, craggy fells, marshland and a handful of bubbling rivers, **Lemmenjoki National Park**, about 40km southwest of Inari, witnessed a short-lived gold rush in the 1940s. A few panners remain, eking out a meagre living.

The park's most breathtaking scenery is to be found on its southeastern side along the Lemmenjoki river valley. To get there, take the daily bus from Inari to **Njurgalahti**, a tiny settlement on the edge of the park about 12km off Route E75 to Kittilä (the district's main road), which is where the 55-kilometre, two-day hike down the river valley begins; taking the twice-daily boat (June–Aug; €15 one-way) from Njurgalahti to Kultasatama cuts 20km off the hike's full distance.

At **Härkäkoski**, hikers cross the river by a small boat, pulled by rope from bank to bank; the track then ascends through a pine forest to **Morgamoja Kultala**, the old gold-panning centre, where there's a big unlocked hut. There are a couple of other huts set aside for those walking the trail, but the nearest **campsite** (☎&🅵016/673 001), with cottages, is back on the main road at **Menesjärvi**. For organized goldpanning and camping trips – and interesting day-long Sámi felt-making workshops – plump for those offered by Kaija and Heikki Paltto (☎016/673 542, 🌐www.lemmenjoki.org), a very welcoming Sámi family in the hamlet of **Lemmenjoki** who also rent out several comfortable **cabins** (€46) with free use of a rowing boat and sauna. Just across the river, *Ahkun Tupa* (☎&🅵016/673 435, 🌐www.ahkuntupa.fi; €40), has similar-priced but less intimate accommodation in smaller cottages. For more information on the park, ask at the Lemmenjoki nature hut (June–Sept daily 9am–5pm, ☎020/564 7793) at the park entrance, which is well signposted from Inari.

North from Inari: crossing into Norway

Travelling north from Inari is rather pointless unless you're aiming for Norway. The Finnish section of the Arctic Highway continues to dreary **KAAMANEN**, though on the way, 2km past the *Kaamasen Kievari* year-round campsite (☎016/672 713, 🌐www.kaamasenkievari.fi), is a bold, stark and deeply evocative memorial in rusty red metal to World War II in Finland. In simple words, it states: "the battles of these light infantrymen in the wilds of Lapland were brought to an end in Kaamanen, Inari towards the end of October 1944. 774 killed, 262 missing, 2904 wounded."

The route then swings westwards on its way to Nordkapp, exiting Finland at **KARIGASNIEMI**, an unprepossessing hamlet that has a restaurant, *Soarve Stohpu*, which serves a yummy smoked reindeer-and-cheese soup for around €10, and pleasant rooms in the small and basic *Kalastajan Majatalo* hotel next door (☎016/676 171, 🌐www.kalastajanmajatalo.cim; ❸). You might also be tempted by the excellent **youth hostel** facilities at the *Engholm Husky Vandrerhjem*, 18km further on in Karasjok, Norway (see p.339). Karigasniemi does have two **campsites**, both with **cabin accommodation**: *Lomakylä Reisti* (☎016/676 401 or 040/087 1550; 🌐www.lomakylareisti.fi; cabins €65), and the *Tenorinne* (☎016/676 113 or 040/832 8487; 🌐www.tenorinne.com; early June to mid-Sept; cabins €35); the former rents out snowmobiles and boats (both €30 per hr), while the latter is better situated on a small beach with picnic tables looking right onto the river that divides Finland from Norway. Incidentally, **petrol** is generally quite a bit cheaper here than across the border, so you'd be wise to fill up before venturing on.

From Kaamanen, a minor road branches due north to **UTSJOKI**, a small border village beside the Tenojoki River. The nearest **campsite** (☎016/678 803; mid-June to late Aug) is a few kilometres away, by the river's edge in Vetsikko. The road on from Utsjoki runs parallel to the Norwegian border, then crosses it just beyond the hamlet of **Nuorgam**, where there's a guesthouse, the *Nuorgamin Lomakeskus* (☎016/678 312, 🌐www.nuorgaminlomakeskus.fi; ❷), which maintains a year-round **campsite** and operates motorboat (€45 per day) and snowmobile (€125 per day) tours. Once across the border, it's a 160-kilometre journey to Kirkenes (see p.344).

The northwest

Heading northwest from Rovaniemi, Route 79 sticks close to the banks of the Ounasjoki River before it reaches the straggling settlement of **KITTILÄ**, a distance of 150km. There's little to detain you here – the departing German army burnt the place to the ground in 1944, and the rebuilding has been uninspired – though both the **youth hostel**, *Retkeilymaja Majari*, Valtatie 5 (☎040/041 0592; ❷), and neighbouring **campsite** are conveniently located beside the main road, while the small, family-run *Hotel Kittilä*, Valtatie 49 (☎016/643 201, ⓦwww.hotellikittila.fi; ❸) has standard rooms, a pool and an inexpensive restaurant.

It's a further 20km to the town of **SIRKKA**, where the posh ski resort of **Levi** attracts thousands of wintering Finns with its numerous downhill trails, several dozen lifts and gondola and ample après-ski attractions. Outside winter, there is relatively little going on here, though the surrounding hills boast seven hiking (or, in winter, cross-country skiing) routes, including the enjoyable river and fell walking of the eighteen-kilometre Levi Fell trail. All the routes begin in or near the centre of Sirkka, where you should find a whole range of places to stay – during summer expect to pay around €70 for a room, double that in winter – ask at the tourist board for information. From May to November, the cheapest place to stay is the *Hullu Poro* **hostel** (☎016/651 0100), Rakkavarantie, which offers dorms for €20 and private rooms (❷). For more information on outdoor activities around Sirkka, visit the **tourist office** (June–Aug Mon–Fri 9am–7pm, Sat & Sun 11am–5.30pm; Sept–May Mon–Fri 9am–4.30, Sat & Sun 11am–4pm; ☎016/639 3300, ⓦwww.levi.fi) in the centre of town, which can also assist with finding accommodation.

Muonio and around

Sleepy **MUONIO** lies 60km northwest of Sirkka beside the murky river that separates Finland from Sweden. What passes for the town centre falls beside the junction of the E8, the main north–south highway, and Route 79 from Kittilä; the Esso filling station at the crossroads here functions as the bus station. The **tourist office** (daily 10am–6pm except Sun Oct and Nov; ☎016/532 141, ⓦwww.muonio .fi) lies beside this junction inside the *Kiela Naturium* nature centre (same hours), though sadly its star attraction, the **northern lights planetarium**, has been indefinitely taken out of service due to lack of funds to repair it. While the planetarium show can't be seen any more, there is still a fairly good chance of viewing the northern lights themselves in Muonio; there's a 55 percent chance of seeing them in the winter here, though it must be a clear night. For accommodation, head for the superbly located year-round **hostel** ⚒ *Lomamaja Pekonen* (☎016/532 237, ⓦwww .lomamajapekonen.fi; ❷), on a small hilly site overlooking a lake at Lahenrannantie 10. They also have simple, well-equipped **cabins** (€60); the ones at the top of the hill have their own saunas (€65). **Canoes** can also be hired here for €21 per day. For **snacks**, the woodsy *Naapuro*, Kosotuskeino 1, has fresh cakes, coffee and beer, while solid meals can be found next door at ⚒ *Uncle Laban*, run by a friendly Palestinian family who dish up pizza and reindeer dishes for around €10.

South of Muonio: the Harriniva Holiday Centre

Some 3km south of Muonio along the road to Kolari lies the well-organized and well-equipped *Harriniva Holiday Centre* (☎016/530 0300, ⓦwww.harriniva .fi), where you can pitch a tent, hook up your campervan or stay in a range of accommodation that runs from basic cabins (€90) to fully equipped apartments (€140). However, what makes this place special is the range of summer and winter **activities** on offer. A haven for dog lovers, Harriniva has around four hundred huskies – making it the biggest husky centre in Finland – and if you're here in winter and thinking of a **husky safari**, this is the place to do it. Although safaris are quite pricey – a week-long round-trip safari from Muonio up towards Enontekiö, covering a daily distance of around 40km, costs upwards of €1240 – you may be able to cut costs slightly by booking via a travel agent such as

Norvista rather than at the centre itself. The final price will include all food, your huskies and sledge plus overnight accommodation in log cabins – and, of course, the experience of riding across frozen lakes, winding through Lapland's silent snow-covered forests and ending the day with a roll in the snow after a genuine smoke sauna. The centre's other winter activities include a week-long **snowmobile safari** (€2370), a four-hour **reindeer safari** (€150), and a **dog-sledge day-trip** (€260). In summer, the centre offers such things as **whitewater rafting** (€28; 1hr 30min), **salmon fishing**, **quad bike excursions to a reindeer farm** (€165) and **canoe trips** (€60). There are several other adventure groups in town – ask for a list at the Muonio tourist office – though you may be gambling on level of professionalism, quality of equipment and knowledge of English.

Pallas-Yllästunturi National Park

From Muonio, buses leave for Kilpisjärvi (see p.632) and (once daily) for Enontekiö/Hetta, skirting the **Pallas-Yllästunturi National Park**, a rectangular slab of mountain plateau whose bare peaks and coniferous forests begin about 30km northeast of Muonio. A bus leaves Muonio at 9.30am Monday to Friday for the National Park, stopping outside the **visitor centre**, Pallastunturi (Jan to mid-Feb, May, Oct & Nov Mon–Fri 9am–4pm; rest of the year daily 9am–5pm; ☎020/564 7930). Pallastunturi marks the start of the **Pallas-Hetta hiking route**, an arduous 55-kilometre trail that crosses a line of fell summits, with several *varaustupa* and *autiotupa* (locked and unlocked huts) and camping areas en route, as well as a sauna about halfway along in the hut at **Hannukuru**. The highest point is the summit of Taivaskero, near the start. The track ends at Lake Ounasjärvi, which you'll need to cross by **ferry** (daily 7am–11pm); if the boat isn't there, raise the flag to indicate that you want to cross.

Hikes in the Pallas-Yllästunturi park: the Pallas-Olos-Ylläs trail

The Pallas-Yllästunturi National Park was created in 2005 when the Pallas-Ounastunturi park was merged with the Ylläs-Aakenustunturi nature reserve, adding around 500 square kilometres and making the park Finland's third largest. Although the Pallas-Hetta trail is the park's most impressive walk, and the one with the best transport links, there are several other options. Of these, the most notable is the 87-kilometre **Pallas-Olos-Ylläs trail**, which also begins from Pallastunturi visitor centre. With several unlocked huts en route, this track twists south past fells and lakes until it leaves the park and reaches the Muonio–Sirkka road close to the swanky *Lapland Hotel Olos* (☎016/536 111, ⊛www.laplandhotels.com; ◐). The hotel is primarily geared towards skiers – and package-tour ones at that – and is open only between September and April, but the hills that surround it are crisscrossed by a number of shorter walking trails that make for very pleasant hikes in the summer months.

From the hotel, the Pallas-Olos-Ylläs trail continues south, soon reaching the dam on the Särkijoki River before proceeding down to Lake Äkäsjärvi, where there's a café in a former grain mill. From here, the track heads onto the eastern slopes of Äkäskero, passing the remarkably good-value *Äkäskero Wilderness Lodge* (☎016/533 077, ⊛www.akaskero.com; ◐), set in the middle of the park and offering a total of 45 beds across cabins and rooms, as well as a half-decent restaurant (€25 for four courses) and continuing for 20km to the tiny settlement of **ÄKÄSLOMPOLO**, where there are a few places to stay, on the upper slopes of Yllästunturi. There is no transport from the lodge to Äkäslompolo so you will need to take a taxi (€45).

The **bus service** on from Äkäslompolo has been improved in recent years: there's now a daily service to Kolari weekdays at 12.25pm and 3.10pm (and 7.40am when school is in session), as well as 17.10pm (Sat) and 9.45am (Sun), eventually reaching Tornio, Kemi and Oulu. There is also a sporadic bus service to Muonio; check with the *Äkäskero Wilderness Lodge* for up-to-date information.

On the other side of the lake is the unremarkable village of **HETTA** (known administratively as **ENONTEKIÖ**). Outside the Christmas rush, when daily charter flights flood the town with thousands of Santa-seeking Brits, there isn't a whole lot going on, but it's a good jumping-off point for exploring the Finnish (and Norwegian) outdoors, and if you're here in early March, the festive celebrations of **Marianpäivä** are well attended by people from all over the region and make a great introduction to the traditions and pastimes of the Sámi. There's also the **Fell Lapland Nature Centre** (mid-June to Sept daily 9am–5pm; Oct to mid-June Mon–Fri 9am–4pm; ☎020/564 7959, ⓦwww.outdoors.fi), which functions as a tourist office of sorts, selling maps and making reservations for a host of cottages in the Pallas-Yllästunturi National Park. For accommodation in Enontekiö, try the well-appointed, modern **cabins, cottages and rooms** at the *Hetan Lomakylä* (☎016/521 521, ⓦwww.hetanlomakyla.fi; ❶/❸) or the rustic-chic fireplace-outfitted cabins at *Ounasloma* (all year, but call ahead on ☎016/521 055, ⓦwww.ounasloma.fi; €60), both of which also have **camping** facilities. Among the settlement's **hotels**, a good choice is the *Hetan Majatalo* (☎016/554 0400, ⓦwww .hetan-majatalo.fi; ❹), which offers excellent, rustic-style en-suite rooms as well as cheaper and more basic options. In winter it organizes a host of activities – ice-fishing, reindeer safaris, dog-sledge tours – and in summer fishing trips, as well as offering boat and bike rental, the latter year-round, while the hotel restaurant cooks up highly recommended traditional Lappish dinners. The *Hotelli Hetta* (☎016/521 361, ⓦwww.hetta-hotel.com; ❸/❹) offers a plush alternative, with several rooms overlooking the lake.

If you're driving north through Hetta towards Norway, 6km before you get to the border on the Alta road is **PALOJÄRVI**, where the ten log cabins of *Galdotieva* (☎016/528 630 ⓦwww.harriniva.fi; €60), some with their own sauna, offer a reasonable, if somewhat isolated, overnight spot. Camping available in summer.

North from Muonio: Kilpisjärvi and around

The thumb-shaped chunk of Finland that sticks out above the northern edge of Sweden is almost entirely uninhabited, a hostile Arctic wilderness whose tiny settlements are strung along the only road, the E8. For the most part this seems a gloomy route of desolate landscapes and untidy villages, comparing poorly with the splendour of the parallel road to the south that connects Sweden's Kiruna and Norway's Narvik. However, the E8 does have its moments as it approaches the Norwegian frontier, with the bumpy uplands left behind for dramatic snow-covered peaks.

From the E8, you might cross into Sweden via **KAARESUVANTO**, a dreary village 95km north of Muonio, to reach the Kiruna–Narvik road. Otherwise there's little reason to cross the border here or stay longer than you need to in Kaaresuvanto – if you do, use the all-year **campsite** (☎040/029 1681), which has some smart cabins (€45). Otherwise, try the *Hotelli Davvi* (☎016/522 101, ⓦwww.davvihotel .com; ❹ including breakfast), which has fully equipped cabins (€60) as well as regular rooms, and a good restaurant.

There's more to be said for continuing for 110km on the E8 to the hamlet of **KILPISJÄRVI**, on the Norwegian frontier. On the way, about 25km south of Kilpisjärvi, you'll pass the welcoming *Peeran Retkeilykeskus* **youth hostel** (☎016/532 659, ⓦwww.peera.fi; dorms €25; open March–Sept), which also serves good food. At Kilpisjärvi itself, perched beside the coldest of lakes in the shadow of a string of stark tundra summits, the *Hotelli Kilpis* (☎016/537 761, ⓦwww.pallas -hotel.com; ❸) has a gorgeous location which means it gets booked up months ahead for the March to mid-June period. For year-round accommodation, try the excellent new cabins at *Kilpisjärven Lomakeskus* (☎016/537 801, ⓦwww.kilpisjarvi .net; €110). They also offer a full range of winter adventure activities. The **Kilpisjärvi Visitor Centre** (March–Sept daily 9am–5pm; ☎020/564 7990, ⓦwww.kilpisjarvi.fi) sells maps and offers helpful information on the Käsivarsi region, and on a number of **local hikes**, the most popular of which are the brace of ten-kilometre trails running to the top of the neighbouring Saanatunturi, 1029m high. The main way up (and down) is the track on the steep north side, although another route runs behind the fell to the northern shore of Saanijärvi, where there's a *päivätupa* (cabin). For more expensive adventure, Heliflite (☎016/532 100, ⊛www .heliflite.fi), in the harbour 1.5km south of town, offers helicopter tours of the region – though at €250 for a ten-minute flight, you might be more content with an aerial-view postcard from the visitor centre.

Another hiking option is the 24-kilometre loop trail, beginning and ending at Kilpisjärvi, that runs north through the **Malla Nature Reserve** to the **Three Countries Frontier** where Finland, Norway and Sweden meet. The track crosses the rapids of Siilajärvi by footbridge, after which a secondary track ascends to the summit of Pikku Malla. The main route continues to Iso Malla. There's a steep and stony section immediately before the waterfalls of Kihtsekordsi, and then a reindeer fence marking the way down to an *autiotupa* cabin beside the Kuokimajärvi lake. From the tourist office, a stone path leads to the cairn marking the three national borders. You'll find a **campsite** at the tourist centre (June–Sept) and, nearby, a **guesthouse**, *Saananmajat* (☎016/537 746; ❷).

Travel details

Trains

Kemi to: Kemijärvi (1 daily; 3hr 5min); Kolari (1–2 daily; 3hr).
Kolari to: Kemi (1 daily; 2hr 50min).
Oulu to: Helsinki (5 daily; 6–9hr); Kajaani (5 daily; 2hr 10min), Kemi (6 daily; 1hr); Rovaniemi (6 daily; 2hr 20min).
Rovaniemi to: Helsinki (5 daily; 8hr 45min); Kemi (6 daily; 1hr 15min); Kemijärvi (1–4 daily; 1hr 15min); Oulu (6 daily; 2hr 20min).
Vaasa to: Helsinki (10 daily via Seinajöki; 4hr–4hr 30min); Oulu (5–7 daily via Seinajöki; 4hr 55min–6hr 10min); Tampere (9–10 daily; 2hr 30min).

Buses

Äkäslompolo to: Kolari (1–3 daily; 45min).
Inari to: Ivalo (3–6 daily; 40min); Kaamanen (3–5 daily; 30min); Kargasneimi (2 daily; 1hr 45min); Utsjoki (2–3 daily; 1hr 30min); Rovaniemi (3–6 daily; 4hr 45min–7hr 50min).
Ivalo to: Murmansk, Russia (5 weekly; 7hr 30min).
Kajaani to: Kuhmo (Mon–Fri 8 daily, Sat 5 daily; 1hr 40min); Kuusamo (3–5 daily; 3hr 35min–4hr 15min).
Kemi to: Tornio (hourly; 30min).
Kolari to: Äkäslompolo (1–3 daily; 45min).
Kuhmo to: Kajaani (4–7 daily; 1hr 40min).

Kuusamo to: Kajaani (1–3 daily, 3hr 35min); Ristikallio (2–3 daily (except Sat & Sun); 55min–1hr 15min Salla (1–2 daily; 2hr).
Muonio to: Kilpisjärvi (2 daily; 2hr 40min–3hr 15min).
Oulu to: Kuusamo (5–8 daily; 3hr); Rovaniemi (3–8 daily; 3hr 10min–4hr 15min).
Pallastunturi to: Enontekiö (1 daily; 2hr 30min); Muonio (1 daily; 40min).
Pietarsaari to: Kokkola (5–13 daily; 35min–55min).
Rovaniemi to: Enontekiö/Hetta (2 daily; 4hr 45min–5hr 15min); Inari (3–6 daily; 4hr 45min–7hr 50min); Ivalo (4–6 daily; 4hr 15min–4hr 55min); Kiilopää (1–2 daily; 3hr 30min–4hr 10min); Kilpisjärvi (2 daily; 6hr 15min–8hr 15min); Kittilä (4 daily; 2hr–2hr 30min); Muonio (3 daily; 3hr 20min–4hr); Pallastunturi (1 daily; 4hr 45min); Sodankylä (3–10 daily; 4hr 30min–3hr 10min).
Sodankylä to: Kemijärvi (Mon–Fri 2 daily, Sat 1 daily; 1hr 40min–2hr 10min).
Tornio to: Äkäslompolo (1 weekly; 3hr 45min).
Utsjoki to: Nuorgam (2 daily; 40min).
Vaasa to: Pori (7–8 daily; 2hr 45min–5hr 15min); Turku (10–13 daily; 5hr–8hr).

International ferries

Vaasa to: Umeå, Sweden (June & July 1 daily; Aug–May 5–6 weekly; 4hr).

Contexts

Contexts

History: Denmark

S pending much time in Denmark soon makes you realize that its history is
entirely disproportionate to its size. Nowadays a small – and often overlooked – nation, Denmark has nonetheless played an important role in key
periods of European history, firstly as home-base of the Vikings, and later
as a medieval superpower. Markers from the past, from prehistory to the wartime
Resistance movement, are never hard to find. Equally easy to spot are the benefits
stemming from one of the earliest welfare state systems and some of Western
Europe's most liberal social policies.

Early settlements

Traces of human habitation, such as deer bones prized open for marrow, have
been found in central Jutland and dated at 50,000 BC, but it's unlikely that any
settlements of this time were permanent, as much of the land was still covered by
ice. From 14,000 BC, tribes from more southerly parts of Europe arrived during
the summer to hunt reindeer for their meat and antlers, the latter providing raw
material for axes and other tools. The melting ice caused the shape of the land
to change and the warmer climate enabled vast forests to grow in Jutland. From
about 4000 BC, settlers with agricultural knowledge arrived: they lived in villages,
grew wheat and barley and kept animals, and buried their dead in **dolmens** or
megalithic graves.

The earliest metal and bronze finds are from 1800 BC, the result of trade with
southern Europe. (The richness of some pieces indicates an awareness of the cultures
of Crete and Mycenae.) By this time the country was widely cultivated and densely
populated. Battles for control over individual areas saw the emergence of a ruling
warrior class, and, around 500 AD, a tribe from Sweden calling themselves **Danes**
migrated southwards and took control of what became known as **Danmark**.

The Viking era

Around 800 AD, the Danish boundaries were marked out. However, following
Charlemagne's conquest of the Saxons in Germany, the Franks began to threaten
the Danes' territory, and they had to prepare an opposing force. The Danes built fast,
seaworthy vessels and defeated Charlemagne easily. Then, with the Norwegians, they
attacked Spanish ports and eventually invaded Britain. By 1033, the Danes controlled the whole of England and Normandy and dominated trade in the Baltic.

In Denmark itself, which then included much of what is now southern Sweden,
the majority of people were farmers: the less wealthy paid taxes to the king and those
who owned large tracts of land provided the monarch with military forces. In time,
a **noble class** emerged, expecting and receiving privileges from the king in return
for their support. Law-making was the responsibility of the *ting*, a type of council
consisting of district noblemen. Above the district *ting* there was a provincial *ting*,
charged with the election of the king. The successful candidate could be any member of the royal family, which led to a high level of feuding and bloodshed.

In 960, with the baptism of King **Harald** ("**Bluetooth**"), Denmark became
officially Christian – principally, it's thought, to stave off imminent invasion by
the German emperor. Nonetheless, Harald gave permission to a Frankish monk,

Ansgar, to build the **first Danish church**, and Ansgar went on to take control of missionary activity throughout Scandinavia. Harald was succeeded by his son **Sweyn I** ("**Forkbeard**"). Though he was a pagan, Sweyn tolerated Christianity, despite suspecting the missionaries of bringing a German influence to bear in Danish affairs. In 990, he joined with the Norwegians in attacking Britain, whose king was the well-named Ethelred "the Unready". Sweyn's son, **Knud I** ("**the Great**", also spelt Knut) – King Canute of England – married Ethelred's widow, took the British throne and soon controlled a sizeable empire around the North Sea – the zenith of Viking power.

The rise of the Church

During the eleventh and twelfth centuries, Denmark was weakened by violent **internal struggles**, not only between different would-be rulers but also among the Church, nobility and monarchy. Following the death of Sweyn II in 1074, two of his four sons, Knud and Harald, fought for the throne, with Harald (supported by the peasantry and the Church) emerging victorious. A mild and introspective individual, Harald was nonetheless a competent monarch, and introduced the first real Danish currency. He was constantly derided by Knud and his allies, however, and after his death in 1080 his brother became Knud II. He made generous donations to the Church, but his introduction of higher taxes and the absorption of all unclaimed land into the realm enraged the nobility. The farmers of north Jutland revolted in 1086, forcing Knud to flee to Odense, where he was slain on the high altar of Skt Alban's Kirke. The ten-year period of poor harvests that ensued was taken by many to be divine wrath, and there were reports of miracles occurring at Knud's tomb, leading to the murdered king's canonization in 1101.

The Valdemar era

After a series of power battles, **Valdemar I** ("**the Great**") assumed the throne in 1157, strengthening the crown by ending the elective function of the *ting*, and shifting the right to choose the monarch to the Church. Technically the *ting* still influenced the choice of king, but in practice hereditary succession became the rule.

After Bishop Eskil's retirement, **Absalon** became archbishop of Denmark, erecting a fortress at the fishing village of **Havn** (later to become København – Copenhagen). Besides being a zealous churchman, Absalon possessed a sharp military mind and came to dominate Valdemar I and his successor, Knud IV. During this period, Denmark saw some of its best years, expanding to the south and east, and taking advantage of internal strife within Germany. In time, after Absalon's death and the succession of **Valdemar II**, Denmark controlled all trade along the south coast of the Baltic and in the North Sea east of the Ejder. Valdemar II was also responsible for subjugating Norway, and in 1219 he set out to conquer Estonia and take charge of Russian trade routes through the Gulf of Finland. According to Danish legend, the national flag, the Dannebrog, fell down from heaven during a battle in Estonia in 1219.

However, in 1223 Valdemar II was kidnapped by Count Henry of Schwerin (a Danish vassal) and forced to give up many Danish possessions. There was also a redrawing of the southern boundary of Jutland, which caused the Danish population of the region to be joined by a large number of Saxons from Holstein.

Within Denmark, the years of expansion had brought great prosperity. The rules of the *ting* were written down as the **Jutlandic Code**, thus unifying laws all over the country – an act which had the effect of concentrating powers of justice in the person of the monarch, rather than the *ting*. The increasingly affluent nobles, however, demanded greater rights if they were to be counted on to support the new king. The Church was envious of their growing power and much bickering ensued in the following years, resulting in the eventual installation of Valdemar II's son, Christoffer I, as monarch.

Christoffer died suddenly in Ribe when his only son, Erik, was 2 years old; Queen Margrethe took the role of regent until **Erik V** came of age. Erik's overbearing manner and penchant for German bodyguards annoyed the nobles, and they forced him to a meeting at Nyborg in 1282 where his powers were limited by a *håndfæstning*, or charter, that included an undertaking for annual consultation with a Danehof, or forum of nobles. In 1319, Christoffer II became king, after agreeing to an even sterner charter, which allowed for daily consultations with a *råd* – a council of nobles. In 1326, in lieu of a debt which Christoffer had no hope of repaying, **Count Gerd of Holstein** occupied a large portion of Jutland. Christoffer fled to Mecklenburg and Gerd installed the 12-year-old Valdemar, Duke of Schleswig, as a puppet king.

As they proceeded to divide the country among themselves, the Danish nobles became increasingly unpopular with both the Church and the peasantry, and, after Gerd's murder in 1340 and Christoffer's death in 1332, the throne was given to **Valdemar IV** and the monarchy strengthened by the taking back of former crown lands that had been given to nobles. Within twenty years Denmark had regained its former territory, with German forces driven back across the Ejder. The only loss was Estonia, a Danish possession since 1219, which was sold to the Order of Teutonic Knights.

The Kalmar Union

Valdemar's daughter Margrethe forced the election of her 5-year-old son, Olav, as king in 1300, installing herself as regent. Following his untimely death after only a seven-year reign, Margrethe became Queen of Denmark and Norway, and later of Sweden as well – the first ruler of a united Scandinavia. In 1397, a formal document, the **Kalmar Union**, set out the rules of the union of the countries, which allowed for a Scandinavian federation sharing the same monarch and foreign policy, whilst each country had its own internal legislation. It became evident that Denmark was to be the dominant partner within the union when Margrethe placed Danish nobles in civic positions in Norway and Sweden but failed to reciprocate with Swedes and Norwegians in Denmark.

Erik VII ("**of Pomerania**") became king in 1396, and was determined to remove the counts of Holstein who had taken possession of Schleswig in northern Germany. In 1413, he persuaded a meeting of the Danehof to declare the whole of Schleswig to be crown property, and three years later war broke out with the German-influenced nobility of the region.

The conflicts with the Holsteiners and the Hanseatic League had badly drained financial resources. Denmark still relied on hired armies to do its fighting, and the burden of taxation had caused widespread dissatisfaction, particularly in Sweden. With the Holstein forces gaining ground in Jutland, Erik fled to Gotland, and in 1439 Swedish and Danish nobles elected in his place **Christoffer III** –succeeded by Christoffer I, then II – the result of which was a strong move to re-establish the power of the Kalmar Union and reduce the trading dominance of the Hanseatic League. Christoffer II invaded Sweden in 1520 under the guise of protecting the Church, but soon crowned himself king of Sweden at a ceremony attended by the cream of the Swedish nobility, clergy and the merchant class – an amnesty being granted to those who had opposed him. It was, however, a trick. Once inside the castle, 82 of the "guests" were arrested on charges of heresy, sentenced to death and executed – an event that became known as the **Stockholm Bloodbath**. This was supposed to subdue Swedish hostility to the Danish monarch but in fact had the opposite effect. Gustavus Vasa, previously one of six Swedish hostages held by Christian in Denmark, became the leader of a revolt that ended Christian's reign in Sweden and finished the Kalmar Union.

Internally, too, Christian faced a revolt, to which he responded with more brutality. At the end of 1522, a group of Jutish nobles banded together with the intention of overthrowing him, joining up with Duke Frederik of Holstein-Gottorp (heir to half of Schleswig-Holstein), who also regarded the Danish king with disfavour. The following January, the nobles renounced their royal oaths and, with the support of forces from Holstein, gained control of all of Jutland and Funen. As they prepared to invade Zealand, Christian fled to Holland, hoping to assemble an army and return. In his absence, Frederik of Holstein-Gottorp became **Frederik I**.

The Reformation

At the time of Frederik's acquisition of the crown there was a growing unease with the role of the Church in Denmark, especially with the power – and wealth – of the bishops. Frederik was a Catholic but refused to take sides in religious disputes and did nothing to prevent the destruction of churches, being well aware of the groundswell of peasant support for Lutheranism. Frederik I died in 1533 and the fate of the Reformation hinged on which of his two sons would succeed him. The elder and more obvious choice was Christian, but his open support for Lutheranism set the bishops and nobles against him. The younger son, Hans, was just 12 years old, but was favoured by the Church and the nobility. The civil war that ensued became known as the **Counts' War**, and ended in 1536 with Christian III on the throne and the establishment of the new Danish Lutheran Church, with a constitution placing the king at its head.

Danish–Swedish conflicts

New trading routes across the Atlantic had reduced the power of the Hanseatic League, and Christian's young and ambitious successor, **Frederik II**, saw this as a chance for expansion. Sweden, however, had its own expansionist designs, and the resulting Northern **Seven Years War** (1563–70) between the two countries caused widespread devastation and plunged the Danish economy into crisis.

The crisis turned out to be short-lived: price rises in the south of Europe led to increasing Danish affluence, reflected in the building of the elaborate castle of Kronborg in Helsingør. By the time **Christian IV** assumed the throne in 1596, Denmark was a solvent and powerful nation, with Copenhagen a major European capital, but a disastrous entrance to the **Thirty Years War** in 1625 – intended to combat Sweden's power in the Baltic – led to increased taxes, rampant inflation and strong opposition by merchants to the tax exemptions and other privileges enjoyed by nobles. After a Swedish occupation of Jutland in 1657 and the subsequent **Treaty of Roskilde**, Denmark was forced to surrender all its Swedish provinces.

Absolute monarchy

In Denmark, the financial power of the nobles was fading as towns became established and the new merchant class grew. The advent of firearms caused the king to become less dependent on the foot soldiers provided by the nobles, and there was a general unease about the privileges – such as exemption from taxes – that the nobles continued to enjoy. Equally, few monarchs were content with their powers being limited by *håndfæstning*.

During the Swedish siege of Copenhagen, the king had promised special concessions to the city and its people, including the right to determine their own rate of tax and – after strategic lobbying on the part of the city's burghers – the end the *håndfæstning* system and removal of hereditary rule in Denmark. Shrewdly, as he was penning the 'new' constitution himself in 1665, Frederik III changed the fine print to crown himself absolute monarch.

Christian V, king from 1670, instigated a broad system of royal honours, creating a new class of landowners who enjoyed exemptions from tax and whose lack of concern for their tenants led Danish peasants into virtual serfdom. In 1699, **Frederik IV** set about creating a Danish militia to make the country less dependent on foreign mercenaries. While Sweden turned its allegiances towards Britain and Holland, Denmark re-established relations with the French, a situation which culminated in the **Great Northern War** (1709–20). One result of this was the emergence of Russia as a dominant force in the region, while Denmark emerged with a strong position in Schleswig, and Sweden's exemption from the Sound Toll (on shipping passing through the narrow strip of sea off the coast of Helsingør) was ended.

The two decades of peace that followed saw the arrival of **Pietism**, a form of Lutheranism which strove to renew the devotional ideal. Frederik embraced the doctrine towards the end of his life, and it was adopted in full by his son, **Christian VI**, who took the throne in 1730. He prohibited entertainment on Sunday, closed down the Royal Theatre and made court life a sombre affair: attendance at church on Sundays became compulsory and confirmation obligatory.

The Enlightenment

Despite the beliefs of the monarch, Pietism was never widely popular, and by the 1740s its influence had waned considerably. The reign of **Frederik V**, from 1746, saw a great cultural awakening: grand buildings such as Amalienborg and Frederikskirke were erected in Copenhagen (though the latter's completion was delayed for twenty years), and there was a new flourishing of the arts. The king, perhaps as a reaction to the puritanism of his father, devoted himself to a life of pleasure and allowed control of the nation effectively to pass to the civil service. **Neutrality** was maintained and the economy benefited as a consequence.

In 1766, **Christian VII** took the crown. His mental state was unstable, his moods ranging from deep lethargy to rage and drunkenness. By 1771 he had become incapable of carrying out even the minimum of official duties. The king's council, filled by a fresh generation of ambitious young men, insisted that the king effect his own will – under guidance from them – and disregard the suggestions of his older advisers.

The Age of Liberalism

The Napoleonic Wars during the 1790s destroyed Denmark's international prestige and left the country bankrupt, and the period up until 1830 was spent in recovery. Meanwhile, in the arts, a **National Romantic movement** was gaining pace. The sculptor Thorvaldsen and the writer-philosopher Kierkegaard are perhaps the best-known figures to emerge from the era, but the most influential domestically was a theologian called **N.F.S. Grundtvig**, who, in 1810, developed a new form of

Christianity – one that was free of dogma and drew on the virtues espoused by the heroes of Norse mythology. In 1825, he left the intellectual circles of Copenhagen and travelled the rural areas to guide a religious revival, eventually modifying his earlier ideas in favour of a new faith in the wisdom of "the people" – something that was to colour the future liberal movement.

In 1839, **Christian VIII** came to the throne. As Crown Prince of Norway, Christian had approved a liberal constitution in that country, but surprised Danish liberals by not agreeing to a similar constitution at home. In 1848, he was succeeded by his son **Frederik VII**. Meanwhile, the liberals had organized themselves into the **National Liberal Party**, and the king signed a **new constitution** that made Denmark the most democratic country in Europe, guaranteeing freedom of speech, freedom of religious worship and many civil liberties. Legislation was to be put in the hands of a Rigsdag (parliament), elected by popular vote and consisting of two chambers: the lower Folketing and upper Landsting. The king gave up the powers of an absolute monarch, but his signature was still required before bills approved by the Rigsdag could become law.

Following the passing of a new conservative constitution in 1866, a number of opposing interests, encompassing everything from leftist radicals to followers of Grundtvig, were shortly combined into the **United Left**, which put forward the first political manifesto seen in Denmark. It called for equal taxation, universal suffrage in local elections and more freedom for the farmers, and contained a vague demand for closer links with the other Scandinavian countries. The United Left became the majority within the Folketing in 1872, the intellectual left became more active and workers began forming trade unions and workers' associations, setting the stage for the growth of **revolutionary socialism** in Denmark.

The left did its best to obstruct the government but gradually lost influence, while the strength of the right grew. The trade unions, whose membership escalated in proportion to the numbers employed in the new industries, grew in stature and were united as the Association of Trade Unions in 1898. The Social Democratic Party grew stronger with the support of the industrial workers, although it had no direct connection with the trade unions.

Parliamentary democracy and World War I

By the end of the nineteenth century the power of the right was in severe decline. The elections of 1901, under the new conditions of a secret ballot, saw it reduced to the smallest group within the Folketing and heralded the beginning of **parliamentary democracy**.

The government of 1901 was the first real democratic administration, assembled with the intention of balancing differing political tendencies – and it brought in a number of reforms. Income tax was introduced on a sliding scale and free schooling beyond the primary level began. As years went by, Social Democrat support increased, while the left, such as it was, became increasingly conservative. In 1905, a breakaway group formed the **Radical Left** (*Det Radikale Venstre*), politically similar to the English Liberals, calling for the reduction of the armed forces to the status of coastal and border guards, greater social equality and votes for women.

An alliance between the Radicals and Social Democrats enabled the two parties to gain a large majority in the Folketing in the election of 1913, and a year later conservative control of the Landsting was ended. Social advances were made, but further domestic progress was halted by international events as Europe prepared for war.

Denmark had enjoyed good trading relations with both Germany and Britain in the year preceding **World War I**, and was keen not to be seen to favour either side in the hostilities. On the announcement of the German mobilization, the now Radical-led cabinet, with the support of all the other parties, issued a **statement of neutrality** and was able to remain clear of direct involvement in the conflict.

At the conclusion of the war, attention was turned again towards Schleswig-Holstein, and under the **Treaty of Versailles** it was decided that Schleswig should be divided into two zones for a referendum. In the northern zone a return to unification with Denmark was favoured by a large percentage, while the southern zone elected to remain part of Germany. A new German–Danish border was drawn up just north of Flensburg.

The Nazi occupation

While Denmark had little military significance for the Nazis, the sea off Norway was being used to transport iron ore from Sweden to Britain, and the fjords offered good shelter for a fleet engaged in a naval war in the Atlantic. To get to Norway, the Nazis planned an invasion of Denmark. At 4am on April 9, 1940, the German ambassador in Copenhagen informed Prime Minister Stauning that German troops were preparing to cross the Danish border and issued the ultimatum that unless Denmark agreed that the country could be used as a German military base – keeping control of its own affairs – Copenhagen would be bombed. To reject the demand was considered a postponement of the inevitable, and to save Danish bloodshed the government acquiesced at 6am. "They took us by telephone," said a Danish minister.

After censorship of the press and a ban on demonstrations – intended to prevent the Nazis spreading propaganda – elections were called in 1943 in an attempt to show that freedom of political expression could exist under German occupation. The government asked the public to demonstrate faith in national unity by voting for any one of the four parties in the coalition, and received overwhelming support in the largest-ever turnout for a Danish election.

Awareness that German defeat was becoming inevitable stimulated a wave of strikes throughout the country. Berlin declared a state of emergency in Denmark and demanded that the Danish government comply – which it refused to do. Germany took over administration of the country, interning many politicians. The king was asked to appoint a cabinet from outside the Folketing, and Germans were free for the first time to round up Danish Jews. Resistance was organized under the leadership of the **Danish Freedom Council**. Sabotage was carefully co-ordinated, and an underground army, soon comprising over 43,000, prepared to assist in the Allied invasion. In June 1944, rising anti-Nazi violence led to a curfew being imposed in Copenhagen and assemblies of more than five people being banned, to which workers responded with a spontaneous general strike. German plans to starve the city had to be abandoned after five days.

The postwar period to the 1980s

After the German surrender in May 1945, a **liberation government** was created, composed equally of prewar politicians and members of the Danish Freedom Council, with Vilhelm Buhl as prime minister. Its internal differences earned the administration the nickname "the debating club".

While the country had been spared the devastation seen elsewhere in Europe, it still found itself with massive economic problems, and it soon became apparent that the liberation government could not function. In the ensuing election there was a swing to the Communists, and a minority Venstre government was formed. The immediate concern was to strengthen the economy, although the resurfacing of the southern Schleswig issue began to dominate the Rigsdag.

Domestic issues soon came to be overshadowed by the **international situation** as the Cold War began. Denmark had unreservedly joined the United Nations in 1945, and had joined the IMF and World Bank to gain financial help in restoring its economy. In 1947, Marshall Plan aid brought further assistance. As world power became polarized between East and West, the Danish government at first tried to remain impartial, but in 1947 agreed to join NATO – a total break with the established concept of Danish neutrality (though to this day, the Danes remain opposed to nuclear weapons).

The years after the war were marked by much political manoeuvring among the Radicals, Social Democrats and Conservatives, resulting in many hastily called elections and a number of ineffectual compromise coalitions distinguished mainly by the level of their infighting. Working-class support for the Social Democrats steadily eroded, and support for the Communists was largely transferred to the new, more revisionist, **Socialist People's Party**.

Social reforms, however, continued apace, not least in the 1960s, with the abandoning of all forms of censorship and the institution of free abortion on demand. Such measures are typical of more recent social policy, though Denmark's odd position between Scandinavia and the rest of mainland Europe still remains a niggling concern. A referendum held in 1972 to determine whether Denmark should join the EC resulted in a substantial majority in favour, making Denmark the first Scandinavian member of the community – Sweden, the second, didn't join until 1995 – though public enthusiasm remained lukewarm.

Perhaps the biggest change in the 1970s was the foundation – and subsequent influence – of the new **Progress Party** (*Fremskridtspartiet*), headed by Mogens Glistrup, who claimed to have an income of over a million kroner but to be paying no income tax through manipulation of the tax laws. The Progress Party stood on a ticket of immigration curbs and drastic tax cuts, and Glistrup went on to compare tax avoidance with the sabotaging of Nazi rail lines during the war. He also announced that if elected he would replace the Danish defence force with an answering machine saying "we surrender" in Russian. He was eventually imprisoned after an investigation by the Danish tax office; released in 1985, he set himself up as a tax consultant.

The success of the Progress Party pointed to dissatisfaction with both the economy and the established parties' strategies for dealing with its problems. In September 1982, Denmark elected its first Conservative prime minister of the twentieth century in **Poul Schlüter**, whose rule was characterized by spending cuts and an expansion of taxation into areas such as pension funds.

Into the new millennium

In January 1993, Schlüter's government was forced to resign over a political scandal (it was revealed that asylum had been denied to Sri Lankan Tamil refugees in the late 1980s and early 1990s, in contravention of Danish law). The Social Democrats, led by **Poul Nyrup Rasmussen**, took power and formed a four-party coalition. For the first time in ten years Denmark was ruled by a majority government – a centre-left majority coalition which came under attack for its weak policies on tax reform, the welfare state and the thorny issue of **European union**.

Though traditionally a reluctant member of the EC, Denmark had been carried into the European **Exchange Rate Mechanism** (or ERM, then viewed as the first step towards a single European currency) by Schlüter at the start of the 1990s, a move that transformed the Danish economy into one of the strongest in Europe and made its inflation rate the lowest of any EC member. The price for this, however, was soaring unemployment and further cuts in public spending.

The outcome of the **referendum on the Maastricht Treaty** (the blueprint for European political and monetary union) in June 1992, however, provided an unexpected upset to the Schlüter applecart. Despite calls for a "Yes" vote not only from the government but also from the opposition Social Democrats, over fifty percent of Danes rejected the treaty – severely embarrassing the prime minister and sending shivers down the spine of every Western European government. The government and other pro-Europe parties didn't give up, however, but set to work on a revised version of the Maastricht Treaty, with the emphasis on protecting national interests – it included a pledge allowing the Danish people to reject citizenship of a united Europe.

A **second referendum** in May 1993 was a triumph for the government, with almost 57 percent of the Danish population voting in favour of the new treaty. Anti-European feelings, already intense, reached boiling point, and the night after the referendum young left-wingers and anarchists came together in central Copenhagen to declare the area an "EU-free zone". The police moved in to break up the demonstration, battles with the demonstrators ensued, and for the first time ever the Danish police opened fire against a crowd of civilians. Fortunately nobody died, but the incident sparked off a major investigation into the actions of the police, and while Denmark avoided the risk of economic isolation in an increasingly integrated European community, doubts among the Danish people remain, along with a continuing dissatisfaction at the way the "Yes" vote was achieved.

Rasmussen and the Social Democrats retained the largest share of the vote in subsequent elections in 1998 and, as the new millennium dawned, the country was well placed for life in a new Europe. Danes were ranked at the top of the newly created "European Future Readiness Index", which measures social costs and problems such as environmental quality, healthcare costs, poverty and unemployment, while the organization Transparency International revealed that Denmark had been chosen as the world's **least corrupt nation**: of 99 countries surveyed, only Denmark received a perfect score on its "Anti-Corruption Index". All was not absolutely well, however. In 1999, crime and poverty in Copenhagen were becoming a serious worry for the first time in many years. Things came to a head during a November **riot** in the city when police used tear gas to quell more than one hundred protesters – the first such disturbance since the 1993 anti-Maastricht demonstrations. This time vandals wielded crowbars, bricks and bombs as they broke shop windows and set fires to protest about the extradition of a Danish hoodlum from Turkey. City officials were hoping dearly that it would not be the precursor of further violence.

Denmark today

In September 2000, the Danish people returned an unexpected "No" vote in the referendum held to decide if Denmark should finally enter the **Eurozone**. In spite of strong governmental support and many sound economic arguments for membership, 47 percent of the population voted against adopting the euro, leaving Denmark and the UK as the only two EU countries retaining a national currency. Support for the rejection came from the two political extremes, with the nationalist right wanting to retain "Danishness" in all its forms, and the extreme left seeking a less centralized government away from Brussels. Although financial doom was predicted as a consequence of the No vote, no major negative implications materialized and the Danish economy stayed solid.

In November 2001, the political tide changed again: Poul Nyrup Rasmussen and the centre-left coalition lost the election to a right-wing coalition led by **Anders Fogh Rasmussen**. This radical shift was widely regarded to have been a response to the global move to the political right which followed the September 11 attack in the US; a feeling of growing resentment against refugees and second-generation Danes (mainly from Turkey) had already been nurtured by the right-wing Pia Kærsgård, and after the World Trade Center tragedy, people started listening. As well as taking a hostile position toward "foreigners", the new government marked itself as anti-environment (by way of massive scaling down of energy-saving initiatives), anti-development (through cuts in overseas aid) and anti-culture (via the slashing of financial support to alternative types of entertainment). Fogh Rasmussen also upped the military budget and supported the invasion of Iraq, sending troops (and a much-ridiculed submarine) to the Gulf. Though significant anti-war demonstrations ensued, his later re-election gave a second term to his conservative coalition, though the victory was seen more as a reaction against Social Democrat leader **Mogens Lykketoft**'s lack of charisma than a mark of support for Rasmussen's political platform. This failure to engage the electorate has left the average Dane feeling increasingly disconnected from politics.

Abroad, Denmark has repeatedly found itself in the international headlines, a testament to its ability still to wield a disproportionately large amount of influence. The modicum of national joy that came from the birth of the new crown prince to Crown Prince Frederik and his Australian-born wife Mary in October 2005 was quickly tempered by the global uproar over what many saw to be anti-Muslim cartoons printed in Danish newspapers shortly thereafter, a dark episode in modern Danish history that tested political allegiances, challenged tenets of freedom of speech and heightened tensions over Denmark's treatment of its immigrant population – approximately 150,000 of which are Muslim.

To make matters worse, one of the social experiments that had prove emblematic of Danish liberalism and tolerance began to go sour. In 2002, as part of a crackdown on drug dealers, 53 arrests were made in Christiania, home to over a thousand artists, activists, hippies and misfits – two-thirds of whom either live on social welfare or have no reported income – and a locale that once attracted up to half a million tourists annually (although admittedly many of them came to buy cheap marijuana). Residents who had previously been granted free use of the land were now required to negotiate with the state and to pay a fixed monthly fee upwards of 1000kr for utilities and services. Once Christiania lost its special status, many prgnosticated that it's only a matter of time before the city kicks out the current residents and begins to develop on the land – eighty acres of prime waterfront real estate.

In another crackdown on liberalism, the Danish government enacted legislation in 2002 discouraging mixed marriages – what it termed "marriages of convenience" – between Danes and foreign-born citizens, with strict financial and housing requirements and an age stipulation that requires both partners to be at least 24 years old. While the new laws swiftly reduced the number of family reunification permits by more than 75 percent, many such couples outmanoeuvred Danish laws via passage to more liberal Sweden, which grants citizenship to Danes after only two years of residence. With a Swedish passport, a Dane can then safely return to Denmark with his or her foreign spouse under the protection of European Union regulations. Since 2002, thousands of mixed-marriage couples have crossed the Øresund – nicknamed by some as "the bridge of love" – to settle in Sweden, but many have still adamantly refused to return permanently to Denmark until the right-wing party leaves the coalition.

In many senses, then, Denmark has evolved as a tenuous, modern-day dichotomy: a socially progressive liberal democracy with cradle-to-grave care whose government's policies are often perceived as xenophobic, and who observes a liberal outlook towards gay matrimony – it was the first country in the world to legalize gay and lesbian partnerships – and yet imposes draconian regulations on marriages between Danes and foreigners. The Folkeparti has made its intentions clear with a manifesto proclaiming that "Denmark belongs to the Danes and its citizens must be able to live in a secure community ... developing only along the lines of Danish culture"

– and though these somewhat brazen statements only reflect the views of a small percentage of the population, support is growing.

One should not ignore that Denmark's economy is faring better than it has in many years, with close to zero unemployment in most regions. However, effects of the current global financial crises have yet to be realized: house prices are plummeting, banks are receiving financial help from the government and there is, as is the case in much of the world, a general state of insecurity all around. This is compounded by an unease about the consequences of European expansion for the average Dane, the ramifications of the state's increasingly conservative leanings and a falling investment in the public sector. While the situation in Denmark on the surface appears better than in many neighbouring nations, numerous underlying factors suggest that the country's prosperity will remain increasingly fragile, at least in the short term.

History: Norway

D
espite its low contemporary profile, **Norway** has a fascinating history.
As early as the tenth century its people had explored – and conquered
– much of northern Europe, and roamed the Atlantic as far as the North
American mainland. Norway's salad days were as an independent state, but
from the fourteenth century the country came under the sway of first Denmark
and then Sweden. Independent again from 1905, Norway was propelled into World
War II by the German invasion of 1940, an act of aggression that transformed
the Norwegians' attitude to the outside world. Gone was the old insular neutrality, replaced by a liberal internationalism typified by Norway's leading role in the
environmental movement.

Early civilizations

The earliest signs of human habitation in Norway date from the end of the last Ice
Age, around 10,000 BC. In the Finnmark region of north Norway, the **Komsa**
culture was reliant upon sealing, whereas the peoples of the **Fosna** culture, further
south near present-day Kristiansund, hunted both seals and reindeer. Both these
societies were essentially static, dependent upon flint and bone implements.

As the edges of the icecap retreated from the western coastline, so new migrants
slowly filtered north. These new peoples, of the **Nøstvet-økser** culture, were also
hunters and fishers, but they were able to manufacture stone axes, examples of which
were first unearthed at Nøstvet, near Oslo. Beginning around 2700 BC, immigrants
from the east, principally the semi-nomadic **Boat-Axe** and **Battle-Axe peoples**
– so-called because of the distinctive shape of their stone weapons/tools – introduced
animal husbandry and agriculture. The new arrivals did not, however, overwhelm
their predecessors; the two groups coexisted, each learning from the other how to
survive in a land of harsh infertility. These late Stone Age cultures flourished at a time
when other, more southerly cultures were already using metal. Norway was poor and
had little to trade, but the Danes and Swedes exchanged amber for copper and tin
from the bronze-making centres of the Mediterranean. A fraction of the imported
bronze subsequently passed into Norway, mostly to the Battle-Axe people, who
appear to have had a comparatively prosperous aristocracy. This was the beginning of
the Norwegian **Bronze Age** (1500–500 BC).

The Iron Age

At around 500 BC Norway was affected by two adverse changes: the climate dete-
riorated, and trade relations with the Mediterranean were disrupted by the westward
movement of the Celts across central Europe. The former encouraged the development of settled, communal farming in order to improve winter shelter and storage; the
latter cut the supply of tin and copper and subsequently isolated the country from the
early **Iron Age**. Norway's isolation continued through much of the **classical period**,
though the expansion of the Roman Empire in the first and second centuries AD did
revive Norway's (indirect) trading links with the Mediterranean. Evidence of these
renewed contacts is provided across Scandinavia by **runes**, carved inscriptions dating
from around 200 AD whose 24-letter alphabet – the *futhark* – was clearly influenced
by Greek and Latin capitals. Initially, runes were seen as having magical powers, but

gradually their usage became more prosaic. Of the eight hundred or so runic inscriptions extant across southern Norway, most commemorate events and individuals: mothers and fathers, sons and slain comrades.

The renewal of trade with the Mediterranean also spread the use of **iron**. Norway's agriculture was transformed by the use of iron tools, and the pace of change accelerated in the fifth century AD, when the Norwegians learnt how to smelt the brown iron ore, limonite, that lay in their bogs and lakes – hence its common name, **bog-iron**. Clearing the forests with iron axes was relatively easy and, with more land available, the pattern of settlement became less concentrated. Family homesteads leapfrogged up the valleys, and a class of wealthy farmers emerged, their prosperity based on fields and flocks. Above them in the pecking order were local **chieftains**, the nature of whose authority varied considerably. Inland, the chieftains' power was based upon landed wealth and constrained by feudal responsibilities, whereas the coastal lords, who had often accumulated influence from trade, piracy and military prowess, were less encumbered. Like the farmers, these seafarers had also benefited from the iron axe, which made boat-building much easier.

By the middle of the eighth century, Norway had become a country of **small, independent kingships**, its geography impeding the development of any central authority.

The Vikings

Overpopulation, clan discord and the lure of commerce all contributed to the sudden explosion that launched the **Vikings** (from the Norse word *vik*, meaning "creek", and *-ing*, "frequenter of") upon an unsuspecting Europe in the ninth century. The patterns of attack and eventual settlement were dictated by the geographical position of the various Scandinavian countries: the Swedish Vikings turned eastwards, the Danes headed south and southwest, while the Norwegians sailed west to fall upon Scotland, Ireland and England.

The whole of Norway felt the stimulating effects of the Viking expeditions. The standard of living rose and the economy was boosted by the spoils of war. Farmland was no longer in such short supply; slaves assisted labour-intensive land clearance schemes; cereal and dairy farming extended into new areas in eastern Norway; new vegetables, such as cabbages and turnips, were introduced from Britain; and farming methods were improved by overseas contact – the Celts, for instance, taught the Norwegians how to thresh grain with flails.

The Vikings' brand of **paganism**, with its wayward, unscrupulous deities, underpinned their inclination to vendetta and clan warfare. Nevertheless, institutions slowly developed which helped regulate the bloodletting. Western Norway adopted the Germanic *wergeld* system of cash for-injury compensation; every free man was entitled to attend the local **Thing** (a broadly democratic body which administered local law), while a regional *Lagthing* made laws and settled disputes. Justice was class-based, however, with society divided into three main categories: the lord, the freeman and the thrall or slave – the latter worth about eight cows. Viking **decorative art** was pan-Scandinavian, with the most distinguished work being the elaborate and often grotesque animal motifs that adorned their ships, sledges, buildings and furniture.

Norway's first widely recognized chieftain was **Harald Hårfagri** (Fair-Hair), who gained control of the coastal region as far north as Trøndelag around 900. This sparked an exodus of minor rulers, most of whom left to settle in Iceland. Harald's long rule was based on personal pledges of fealty and when he died his kingdom broke up into its component parts. Harald did, however, leave an extremely important legacy: from now on every ambitious chieftain was not content to be a local lord, but strove to be ruler of Harald's whole kingdom. His sons and grandsons warred over their inheritance for the rest of the tenth century, undermining

Norway's independence by seeking military support in Denmark and Sweden. Meanwhile, Norwegian settlers were laying the foundations of independent Norse communities in the Faroes and Iceland; Erik the Red reached Greenland in about 985; and Leif Eriksson the Lucky founded a colony he called Vinland on the shore of **North America** (probably Newfoundland) around 1000 AD.

The arrival of Christianity

In 1015, a prominent Viking chieftain, **Olav Haraldsson**, sailed for Norway from England, intent upon conquering his homeland. Significantly, he arrived by merchant ship with just a hundred men, rather than an army in a fleet of long-ships, a clear sign of the passing of the Viking heyday. Pledged to him was the support of the yeoman farmers of the interior – a new force in Norway that was rapidly supplanting the old warrior aristocracy – and Haraldsson was soon recognized as king of much of the country.

For twelve years, Olav ruled in peace, founding Norway's first national government. His authority was based upon the regional parliaments, or *Things*, and on his willingness to deliver justice without fear or favour. The king's most enduring achievement, however, was to make Norway **Christian**. Olav had been converted during his days in England, and vigorously imposed his new faith on his countrymen.

It was foreign policy rather than pagan enmity, however, that brought about Olav's downfall. By scheming with the Swedish ruler against **King Knut** (Canute) of Denmark and England, Olav provoked a Danish invasion. The Norwegian chieftains who had suffered at the hands of Olav could be expected to help Knut, but even the yeomen failed to rally to his cause. In 1028, Olav was forced to flee, first to Sweden and then to Russia, while Knut's son **Svein** and his mother, the English Queen Aelfgifu, took the Norwegian crown. Two years later, Olav made a sensational return at the head of a scratch army, only to be defeated and killed by an alliance of wealthy landowners and chieftains at **Stiklestad**, the first major Norwegian land battle.

The petty chieftains and yeoman farmers who had opposed Olav soon fell out with their new king: Svein had no intention of relaxing the royal grip, and his chieftains' subsequent rebellion seems also to have had nationalistic undertones – many Norwegians had no wish to be ruled by a Dane. Svein had to hightail it out of the country, and Olav's old enemies popped over to Sweden to bring back Olav's young son, **Magnus**, who became king in 1035.

The chastening experience of Svein's short rule transformed the popular memory of Olav. With surprising speed, he came to be regarded as a heroic champion of Norway, and there was talk of miracles brought about by the dead king's body. The Norwegian Church, looking for a local saint to enhance its position, fostered the legends and had Olav canonized. The remains of **St Olav** were then reinterred ceremoniously at Nidaros, today's Trondheim, where the miracles increased in scope, hastening the conversion of what remained of heathen Norway.

On Magnus's death in 1047, **Harald Hardråda** (Olav's half-brother) became king. The last of the Viking warrior-chiefs, Hardråda dominated his kingdom by force of arms for over twenty years. Neither was Hardråda satisfied with being king of just Norway. In 1066, the death of Edward the Confessor presented Harald with an opportunity to press his claim to the English throne. The Norwegian promptly sailed to England, landing near York with a massive fleet, but just outside the city, at Stamford Bridge, his army was surprised and trounced by Harold Godwinson, the new Saxon king of England. Hardråda was killed in the battle and the threat of a Norwegian conquest of England had – though no one realized it at the time – gone forever. Not that the victory did much for Harold Godwinson, whose weakened army trudged back south to be defeated by William of Normandy at the Battle of Hastings.

Medieval success

Harald's son, **Olav Kyrre** (the Peaceful) went on to reign as king of Norway for the next 25 years. Peace engendered economic prosperity, and treaties with Denmark ensured Norwegian independence. Three native bishoprics were established, and cathedrals built at Nidaros, Bergen and Oslo. It's from this period, too, that Norway's surviving **stave churches** date: wooden structures resembling upturned keels, they were lavishly decorated with dragon heads and scenes from Norse mythology, proof that the traditions of the pagan world were slow to disappear.

The first decades of the twelfth century witnessed the further consolidation of Norway's position as an independent power, despite internal disorder as the descendants of Olav Kyrre struggled to maintain their influence. Civil war ceased only when **Håkon IV** took the throne in 1240, ushering in what is often called "The Period of Greatness". Secure at home, Håkon strengthened the Norwegian hold on the Faroe and Shetland islands, and in 1262 both Iceland and Greenland accepted Norwegian sovereignty. When his claim to the Hebrides was disputed by Alexander III of Scotland, Håkon assembled an intimidatory fleet, but died in 1263 in the Orkneys. Three years later the Hebrides and the Isle of Man (always the weakest links in the Norwegian empire) were sold to the Scottish crown by Håkon's successor, **Magnus the Lawmender** (1238–80).

Under this ruler, Norway prospered. Law and order were maintained, trade flourished and the king's courtiers even followed a code of etiquette compiled in the *King's Mirror* (*Konungs skuggsjá*), in contrast to former rough-and-ready Viking ways. Neither was the power of the monarchy threatened by feudal barons as elsewhere in thirteenth-century Europe. Norway's scattered farms were not susceptible to feudal tutelage and, as a consequence, the nobility lacked local autonomy (castles remained few and far between) and were drawn into the centralized administration of the state.

Magnus was succeeded by his sons, first the undistinguished Erik and then by **Håkon V** (1270–1319), the last of medieval Norway's talented kings. Håkon continued the policy of his predecessors, making further improvements to central government and asserting royal control of Finnmark by the construction of a fortress at Vardø. His achievements, however, were soon to be swept away, along with the independence of Norway itself.

Medieval failure

Norway's independence was threatened from two quarters. With strongholds in Bergen and Oslo, the **Hanseatic League** and its merchants had steadily increased their influence, holding a monopoly on imports and controlling inland trade to such an extent that Norway's royal household became dependent on the taxes they paid. The second threat was **dynastic**. When Håkon died in 1319 he left no male heir and was succeeded by his grandson, the 3-year-old son of a Swedish duke. The boy, **Magnus Eriksson**, was elected Swedish king two months later, marking the virtual end of Norway as an independent country until 1905.

Magnus assumed full power over both countries in 1332, but his reign was a difficult one. When the Norwegian nobility rebelled he agreed that the monarchy should again be split: his 3-year-old son, Håkon, would become Norwegian king when he came of age, while the Swedes agreed to elect his eldest son Erik to the Swedish throne. It was then, in 1349, that the **Black Death** struck, spreading quickly along the coast and up the valleys, and killing almost two-thirds of the Norwegian population. It was a catastrophe of almost unimaginable proportions, its effects compounded by the way the country's agriculture was structured. Animal husbandry was easily the most important part of Norwegian farming, and the harvesting and drying of sufficient winter fodder was labour-intensive. Without the labourers, the animals died in their hundreds and famine conditions prevailed for several generations.

Many farms were abandoned and, deprived of their rents, the petty chieftains who had once dominated rural Norway were, as a class, almost entirely swept away. The vacuum was filled by royal officials, the *syslemenn*, each of whom exercised control over a large chunk of territory on behalf of a Royal Council. The collapse of local governance was compounded by the dynastic to-ing and fro-ing at the top of the social ladder. In 1380, Håkon died and Norway passed under Danish control with Olav, the son of Håkon and the Danish princess **Margrethe**, becoming the ruler of the two kingdoms.

The Kalmar Union

Despite Olav's early death in 1387, the resourceful Margrethe persevered with the union. Proclaimed regent by both the Danish and (what remained of the) Norwegian nobility, she engineered a treaty with the Swedish nobles that not only recognized her as regent of Sweden but also agreed to accept any king she should nominate. Her chosen heir, **Erik of Pomerania**, was foisted on the Norwegians in 1389. When he reached the age of majority in 1397, Margrethe organized a grand coronation with Erik crowned king of all three countries at Kalmar in Sweden – hence the **Kalmar Union**.

After Margrethe's death in 1412, all power was concentrated in Denmark. In Norway, Danes were preferred in both state and Church, and the country became impoverished by paying for Erik's wars. Incompetent and brutal in equal measure, Erik managed to get himself deposed in all three countries at the same time. In the meantime Sweden had left the union, and eventually a Danish count, Christian of Oldenburg, was crowned king of Norway and Denmark in 1450. Thereafter, Norway ceased to take any meaningful part in Scandinavian affairs. Literature languished as Danish displaced the old Norse **language** in every official communi-cation and within the governing class – and indeed Norse soon came to be regarded as the language of the ignorant and inconsequential. Only the Norwegian Church retained any power, but this itself was to be overwhelmed by the Reformation.

Union with Denmark

In 1536 **Christian III** declared his kingdom Protestant and, although it was slow to take root among the Norwegian peasantry, **Lutheranism** soon came to be a power-ful instrument in deepening Danish influence. The Bible, catechism and hymnal were all in Danish; the bishops were all Danes; and, after 1537, so were all the most impor-tant provincial Norwegian governors. In many respects, Norway became simply a source of raw materials – fish, timber and iron ore – whose proceeds lined the royal purse. Naturally enough, the Swedes coveted these materials too, the upshot being a long and inconclusive war (1563–70), which saw much of Norway ravaged by competing bands of mercenaries. Among the Danish kings of the period, **Christian IV** (1588–1648) proved the most sympathetic to Norway. He visited the country often, improving the quality of its administration and founding new towns including Kongsberg, Kristiansand and Christiania (later Oslo).

At last, in the middle of the seventeenth century, the Norwegian economy began to pick up. The population grew, trade increased and, benefiting from the decline of the Hanseatic League, a native bourgeoisie began to take control of certain parts of the economy, most notably the herring industry. But Norwegian cultural self-esteem remained at a low ebb: the country's merchants spoke Danish, mimicked Danish manners and read Danish pot-boilers. What's more, Norway was a constant bone of contention between Sweden and Denmark, the result being a long series of wars in which Norway's more easterly provinces were regularly battered by the rival armies.

The year 1660 marked a turning point in the constitutional arrangements governing Norway. For centuries, the Danish Council of State had had the power to elect the monarch and impose limitations on his or her rule. Now, a powerful alliance of merchants and clergy swept these powers away to make **Frederik III** an absolute ruler. This was not a reactionary coup, but an attempt to limit the power of the conservative-minded Danish nobility. In addition, the development of a centralized state machine would, many calculated, provide all sorts of job opportunities to the low-born but adept. Norway was incorporated into the administrative structure of Denmark, with royal authority delegated to the *Stattholder*, who governed through what soon became a veritable army of professional bureaucrats. There were positive advantages for Norway: the country acquired better defences, simpler taxes, a separate High Court and doses of Norwegian law, but once again power was exercised almost exclusively by Danes.

The eighteenth century

The **absolute monarchy** established by Frederik III soon came to concern itself with every aspect of Norwegian life. The ranks and duties of minor officials were carefully delineated, religious observances tightly regulated and restrictions imposed on everything from begging and dress through to the food and drink that could be consumed at weddings and funerals. This extraordinary superstructure placed a leaden hand on imagination and invention. Neither was it impartial: there were some benefits for the country's farmers and fishermen, but by and large the system worked in favour of the middle class. The merchants of every small town were allocated the exclusive rights to trade in a particular area, and competition between the towns was forbidden. These local monopolies placed the peasantry at a dreadful disadvantage, nowhere more iniquitously than in the Lofotens, where the fishermen not only had to buy supplies and equipment at the price set by the merchant, but had to sell their fish at the price set by him, too.

In the meantime, there were more wars between Denmark and Sweden. In 1700, **Frederik IV** (1699–1730) made the rash decision to attack the Swedes at the time when their king, Karl XII, was generally reckoned to be one of Europe's most brilliant military strategists. Predictably, the Danes were defeated and only the intervention of the British saved Copenhagen from falling into Swedish hands. Undeterred, Frederik tried again, and this time Karl retaliated by launching a full-scale invasion of Norway. The Swedes rapidly occupied southern Norway, but after Karl was shot dead by a sniper, the two countries agreed the **Peace of Frederiksborg** (1720), which ended hostilities for the rest of the eighteenth century.

Peace favoured the growth of trade, but although Norway's economy prospered it was hampered by the trade monopolies exercised by the merchants of Copenhagen. In the 1760s, however, the Danes did a dramatic U-turn, abolishing monopolies, removing trade barriers and even permitting a free press – and the Norwegian economy boomed. Nonetheless, the bulk of the population remained impoverished and prey to famine whenever the harvest was poor. The number of landless agricultural labourers rose dramatically – partly because the more prosperous farmers were buying up large slices of land – and for the first time Norway had something akin to a lumpen proletariat.

Despite this, Norway was one of the few European countries little affected by the French Revolution. Instead of political action, there was a **religious revival**, with Hans Nielson Hauge emerging as the principal evangelical leader. The movement's characteristic hostility to officialdom caused concern, and Hauge was imprisoned, but in reality it posed little threat to the status quo. The end result was rather the foundation of a fundamentalist movement that is still a force to be reckoned with in parts of fjordland Norway.

The early nineteenth century

The period leading up to the **Napoleonic Wars** was a good time for Norway: overseas trade, especially with England, flourished, with the demand for Norwegian timber and iron heralding a period of unparalleled prosperity. Denmark and Norway had remained neutral throughout the Seven Years War (1756–63) between England and France, and renewed that neutrality in 1792. However, when Napoleon implemented a trade blockade – the Continental System – against Britain, he roped in the Danes. As a result, the British fleet bombarded Copenhagen in 1807 and forced the surrender of the entire Dano-Norwegian fleet. Denmark, in retaliation, declared war on England and Sweden. The move was grievous for the Norwegian economy, which had suffered bad harvests in 1807 and 1808, and the English blockade of its seaports dented trade.

By 1811 it was obvious that the Danes had backed the wrong side in the war, and the idea of an equal union with Sweden, which had supported Britain, became increasingly attractive to many Norwegians. By latching onto the coat-tails of the victors, they hoped to restore the commercially vital trade with England. They also thought that the new Swedish king would be able to deal with the Danes if it came to a fight – just as the Swedes had themselves calculated when they appointed him in 1810. The man concerned, **Karl XIV Johan**, was, curiously enough, none other than Jean-Baptiste Bernadotte, formerly one of Napoleon's marshals. With perfect timing, he had helped the British defeat Napoleon at Leipzig in 1813. His reward came in the **Treaty of Kiel** the following year, when the great powers instructed the Danes to cede all rights in Norway to Sweden (although Denmark did keep the dependencies of Iceland, Greenland and the Faroes). Four hundred years of union had ended.

Union with Sweden 1814–1905

The high-handed transfer of Norway from Denmark to Sweden did nothing to assuage the growing demands for greater independence. Furthermore, the Danish Crown Prince Christian Frederik roamed Norway stirring up fears of Swedish intentions. The prince and his supporters convened a Constituent Assembly, which met at Eidsvoll in April 1814 and produced a **constitution**. Issued on May 17, 1814 (still a national holiday), this declared Norway to be a "free, independent and indivisible realm" with Christian Frederik as its king. Not surprisingly, Karl XIV Johan would have none of this and, with the support of the great powers, he invaded Norway. Completely outgunned, Christian Frederik mounted barely any resistance. In exchange for Swedish promises to recognize the Norwegian constitution and the **Storting** (parliament), he abdicated as soon as he had signed a peace treaty – the so-called **Convention of Moss** – in August 1814.

The ensuing period was marred by struggles between the Storting and Karl XIV Johan over the nature of the union. Although the constitution emphasized Norway's independence, Johan had a veto over the Storting's actions; the post of *Stattholder* in Norway could only be held by a Swede; and foreign and diplomatic matters concerning Norway remained entirely in Swedish hands. Despite this, Karl XIV Johan proved popular in Norway, and during his reign the country enjoyed a fair amount of independence. From 1836 all the highest offices in Norway were filled exclusively by Norwegians, and democratic local councils were established, in part due to the rise of peasant farmers as a political force.

The gradual increase in prosperity had important **cultural implications**. The layout and buildings of modern Oslo – the Royal Palace, Karl Johans gate and the university – date from this period, while Johan Christian Dahl, the most distinguished Scandinavian landscape painter of his day, was instrumental in the establishment of the National Gallery in Oslo in 1836. Other prominent members of the bourgeoisie championed all things Norwegian, but under both Oscar I (1844–59) and Karl XV (1859–72) it was **pan-Scandinavianism** that ruled the intellectual roost. This belief in the natural solidarity of Denmark, Norway and Sweden was espoused by the leading artists of the period, including Ibsen and Bjørnstjerne Bjørnson, but died a death in 1864, when the people of Norway and Sweden refused to help Denmark when it was attacked by Austria and Prussia (some of the loudest cries of treachery came from a young Henrik Ibsen, in his poetic drama *Brand*).

Collapse of the union with Sweden

In the 1850s, **Johan Sverdrup**, the most powerful politician in Norway, started a long and ultimately successful campaign to wrest executive power from the king and transfer it to the Storting. By the mid-1880s, Sverdrup and his political allies had pretty much won the day, but a further bout of sabre-rattling between the supporters of Norwegian independence and the Swedish king, **Oscar II** (1872–1907), was necessary before both sides would accept a **plebiscite**. This took place in August 1905, when there was an overwhelming vote in favour of the **dissolution of the union**, which was duly confirmed by the Treaty of Karlstad. A second plebiscite determined that independent Norway should be a monarchy rather than a republic, and, in November 1905, Prince Karl of Denmark (Edward VII of England's son-in-law) was elected to the throne as **Håkon VII**.

The dissolving of the union came at a time of further economic advance, largely engendered by the introduction of hydroelectric power. Social reforms also saw funds being made available for unemployment relief, accident insurance schemes and a Factory Act (1909). An extension to the franchise gave the vote to all men over 25 and, in 1913, to women too. The education system was reorganized, and substantial sums were spent on new arms and defence. This prewar period also saw the emergence of a strong trade union movement and of a Labour Party committed to radical change.

Culturally, the second half of the nineteenth century was fruitful for Norway, with the rediscovery of the Norwegian language and its folklore by a number of academics. These formed the nucleus of a National Romantic movement, which did much to restore the country's cultural self-respect. Following on were well-known authors like **Alexander Kielland**, who wrote most of his works between 1880 and 1891, and **Knut Hamsun**, who published his most characteristic novel, *Hunger*, in 1890. In music, **Edvard Grieg** (1843–1907) made his debut in the first concert to consist entirely of works by Norwegian composers, and was himself inspired by old Norwegian folk melodies. The artist **Edvard Munch** was also active during this period, completing many of his major works in the 1880s and 1890s, while the internationally acclaimed dramatist **Henrik Ibsen** returned to Oslo in 1891 after a prolonged, self-imposed exile.

The early years of independence

Since 1814, Norway had had precious little to do with European affairs, and at the outbreak of **World War I** it seemed logical to renew the country's neutrality. By and large, the Norwegians were more sympathetic to the Western Allies than their enemies, but their ships transported goods for both sides, making a lot of money in the process. By 1916, however, Norway had begun to feel the pinch, as German submarine action hit both enemy and neutral shipping, and by the end of the war Norway had lost half its chartered tonnage and two thousand crew. The Norwegian economy also suffered after the US entered the war – the Americans imposed strict trade agreements in their attempt to prevent supplies getting to Germany, and rationing had to be introduced across Norway. Indeed, the price of neutrality was high: there was a rise in state expenditure, a soaring cost of living and, at the end of the war, no seat at the conference table. In spite of its losses, Norway got no share of the confiscated German shipping, although it was partly compensated by gaining sovereignty of **Spitsbergen** and its coal deposits – the first extension of the Norwegian frontiers for 500 years. In 1920, Norway also entered the new League of Nations.

Later in the 1920s, the decline in world trade led to a decreased demand for Norway's shipping. Bank failure and currency fluctuation were rife, and, as unemployment and industrial strife increased, a burgeoning Norwegian **Labour Party** took advantage. With the franchise extended to all those over 23 and the introduction of larger constituencies, it had a chance, for the first time, to win seats outside the large towns. At the 1927 election, the Labour Party, together with the Social Democrats from whom they'd split, were the biggest grouping in the Storting. Nonetheless, because they had no overall majority and because many feared their radical leftist rhetoric, they were manoeuvred out of office after only fourteen days. **Trade disputes** and lockouts continued and troops were used to enable workers to cross picket lines.

The 1930s

During the war, **Prohibition** had been introduced as a temporary measure, and a referendum of 1919 showed a clear majority in favour of its continuation. But the ban did little to quell – and maybe even exacerbated – drunkenness, and it was abandoned in 1932, to be replaced by the government sales monopoly of wines and spirits that remains in force today. The 1933 election gave the Labour Party more seats than ever. Having shed its revolutionary image, a campaigning reformist Labour Party benefited from the increasing conviction that state control and a centrally planned economy were the only answer to Norway's economic problems. In 1935, the Labour Party, in alliance with the Agrarian Party, took power – an unlikely combination since the Agrarians were profoundly nationalist in outlook, so much so that their defence spokesman had been the rabid anti-Semite **Vidkun Quisling**. Frustrated by the democratic process, Quisling had left the Agrarians in 1933 to found the **Nasjonal Samling** (National Unification), a Fascist movement which proposed, among other things, that both Hitler and Mussolini should be nominated for the Nobel Peace Prize. Quisling had good contacts with Nazi Germany but little support in Norway – local elections in 1937 reduced his local representation to a mere seven, and party membership fell to 1500.

The Labour government under **Johan Nygaardsvold** presided over an improving economy. By 1938, industrial production was 75 percent higher than it had been in 1914, and unemployment had dropped as expenditure on roads, railways and public works had increased. Social welfare reforms were implemented and trade union membership increased. Indeed, when war broke out in 1939, Norway was lacking only one thing – adequate defence – which was, as it turned out, precisely what it needed most.

World War II

In early 1940, the Norwegians would have done well to look south to the threat posed by Germany, but instead they were preoccupied with Allied mine-laying off the Norwegian coast – part of the British attempt to prevent Swedish iron ore being shipped from Narvik to Germany. Indeed, such was Norwegian naivety that they made a formal protest to Britain on the day of the **German invasion**. Caught napping, the Norwegian army offered little initial resistance to the invaders and the south and central regions of the country were quickly overrun. King Håkon and the Storting were forced into a hasty evacuation of Oslo and headed north, eventually taking refuge in Britain where they formed the Norwegian government-in-exile. Norway was rapidly brought under Nazi domination with Hitler sending **Josef Terboven** to take full charge of affairs. The Fascist Nasjonal Samling was declared the only legal party, and the media, civil servants and teachers were brought under German control. As **civil resistance** grew, a state of emergency was declared: two trade union leaders were shot, arrests increased and a concentration camp was set up outside Oslo. In February 1942, Quisling was installed as "Minister President" of Norway, but it was soon clear that his government didn't have the support of the Norwegian people. The Church refused to cooperate, schoolteachers protested and trade union members and officials resigned en masse. In response, deportations increased, death sentences were enacted and a compulsory labour scheme was introduced. **Military resistance** escalated. A military organization (MILORG) was established as a branch of the armed forces under the control of the High Command in London. By May 1941 it had enlisted 20,000 men (32,000 by 1944) in clandestine groups all over the country. Arms and instructors came from Britain, radio stations were set up and a continuous flow of intelligence about Nazi movements sent back. Sabotage operations were legion, the most notable being the destruction of the heavy-water plant at **Rjukan**, foiling a German attempt to produce an atomic bomb.

The **government in exile** in London continued to represent free Norway to the world, mobilizing support on behalf of the Allies. Most of the Norwegian merchant fleet was abroad when the Nazis invaded, and by 1943 the Norwegian navy had seventy ships helping the Allied convoys. In Sweden, Norwegian exiles assembled in "health camps" at the end of 1943 to train as police troops in readiness for liberation. In 1944, as the tide of war turned against the Germans, so the Russians crossed the border into Norway in the far north. The Germans, forced to retreat, burned everything in their path and drove the local population into hiding. To prevent the Germans reinforcing their beleaguered Finnmark battalions, the resistance – with Allied encouragement – planned a campaign of mass rail line sabotage, stopping three-quarters of troop movements. With their control of Norway crumbling, the Germans finally **surrendered** on May 7, 1945. King Håkon returned to Norway on June 7, five years to the day since he had left for exile.

Terboven committed suicide and the Nasjonal Samling collaborators were rounded up. A caretaker government took office, staffed by resistance leaders, and was replaced in October 1945 by a majority **Labour government**. The Communists won eleven seats, reflecting the efforts of Communist saboteurs in the war and the prestige that the Soviet Union enjoyed in Norway after liberation. Quisling was shot, along with 24 other high-ranking traitors, and hundreds of collaborators were punished.

Postwar reconstruction

At the end of the war, Norway was on its knees: the far north – Finnmark – had been laid waste, half the mercantile fleet had been lost, and production was at a standstill. Recovery, though, fostered by a sense of national unity, was quick and it took only three years for GNP to return to its pre-war level. Norway's part in the war had also increased its prestige in the world. The country became one of the founding members of the **United Nations** in 1945, and the first UN secretary-general, Tryggve Lie, was Norway's foreign minister. With the failure of discussions to promote a Scandinavian defence union, the Storting also voted to enter **NATO** in 1949.

Domestically, there was general agreement about the form that social reconstruction should take. In 1948, the Storting passed the laws that introduced the welfare state virtually unanimously. The 1949 election saw the government returned with a larger majority, and Labour administrations remained in power throughout the following decade, when the dominant political figure was **Einar Gerhardsen**. As national prosperity increased, society became much more egalitarian, levelling up rather than down. Subsidies were paid to the agricultural and fishing industries, wages were increased, and a comprehensive social security system helped to erode poverty. The state ran the important mining industry, was the largest shareholder in the national hydroelectric company and built an enormous steelworks at Mo-i-Rana to help develop the economy of the devastated northern counties. Rationing ended in 1952 and, as the demand for higher-level education grew, new universities were approved at Bergen, Trondheim and Tromsø.

The 1960s

The political consensus began to fragment in the early 1960s. Following changes in the constitution concerning rural constituencies, the centre had realigned itself in the 1950s, with the outmoded Agrarian Party becoming the **Centre Party**. Meanwhile, defence squabbles within the Labour Party led to the formation of the **Socialist People's Party** (the SF), which wanted Norway out of NATO and sought a renunciation of nuclear weapons. The Labour Party's 1961 declaration that no nuclear weapons would be stationed in Norway except under an immediate threat of war did not placate the SF who, unexpectedly, took two seats at the election that year. Holding the balance of power, the SF voted with the Labour Party until 1963, when it helped bring down the government over the mismanagement of state industries. A replacement coalition collapsed after only one month, but the writing was on the wall. Rising prices, dissatisfaction with high taxation and a continuing housing shortage meant that the 1965 election put a **non-socialist coalition** in power for the first time in twenty years.

The new coalition's programme, under the leadership of **Per Borten** of the Centre Party, was unambitious. Nonetheless, living standards continued to rise, and although the 1969 election saw a marked increase in Labour Party support, the coalition hung onto power. Also in 1969, **oil and gas** were discovered beneath the North Sea and, as the vast extent of the reserves became obvious, so it became clear that the Norwegians were to enjoy a magnificent bonanza – one which was destined to pay about 25 percent of the government's annual bills.

The 1970s and 1980s

Norway's politicians, who had applied twice previously for membership of the **European Economic Community** (EEC) – in 1962 and 1967 – believed that de Gaulle's fall in France presented a good opportunity for a third application, which was duly made in 1970. There was great concern, though, about the effect of membership on Norwegian agriculture and fisheries, and in 1971 Per Borten was forced to resign following his indiscreet handling of the negotiations. The Labour Party, the majority of its representatives in favour of EEC membership, formed a minority administration, but when the 1972 referendum narrowly voted "No" to joining the EEC, the government resigned.

With the 1973 election producing another minority Labour government, the uncertain pattern of the previous ten years continued. Even the postwar consensus on **Norwegian security policy** broke down on various issues – such as the question of a northern European nuclear-free zone and the stocking of Allied material in Norway – although there remained strong agreement for continued NATO membership.

In 1983, the Christian Democrats and the Centre Party joined together in a non-socialist coalition, which lasted for just two years. It was replaced in 1986 by a minority Labour administration, led by **Dr Gro Harlem Brundtland**, Norway's first woman prime minister. Brundtland made sweeping changes to the way the country was run, introducing seven women into her eighteen-member cabinet, but her government was beset by problems for the three years of its life: tumbling oil prices led to a recession, unemployment rose (though only to four percent) and there was widespread dissatisfaction with Labour's high taxation.

At the **general election** in September 1989, Labour lost eight seats and was forced out of office – the worst result that the party had suffered since 1930. More surprising was the success of the extremist parties on both political wings – the anti-NATO Left Socialist Party and the right-wing, anti-immigrant Progress Party both scored spectacular results, winning almost a quarter of the votes cast, and increasing their representation in the Storting many times over. This deprived the Conservative Party (one of whose leaders, bizarrely, was Gro Harlem Brundtland's husband) of the majority it might have expected, the result being yet another shaky minority administration – this time a **centre-right coalition** between the Conservatives, the Centre Party and the Christian Democrats, led by Jan Syse.

The 1990s

In 1990, the new government faced problems familiar to the last Labour administration. In particular, there was continuing conflict over joining the **European Community**, a policy still supported by many in the Norwegian establishment but flatly rejected by the Centre Party. It was this, in part, that signalled the end of the coalition, for after just over a year in office, the Centre Party withdrew its support and forced the downfall of Syse. In October 1990, Gro Harlem Brundtland was put back in power at the head of a **minority Labour administration**, remaining in office till her re-election for a fourth minority term in 1993. The 1993 elections saw a revival in Labour Party fortunes and, to the relief of the majority, the collapse of the Progress Party vote. However, it was also an untidy, confusing affair where the main issue, membership of the EU, cut across the traditional left versus right axis of the political parties.

Following the 1993 election, Norway tumbled into a long and fiercely conducted campaign over membership of the EU. Brundtland and her main political opponents wanted in, but despite the near unanimity among politicians, the Norwegians narrowly rejected the EU in a **referendum** on November 28, 1994. It was a close call (52.5 percent versus 47.5 percent), but in the end farmers and fishermen afraid of the economic results of joining, as well as women's groups and environmentalists, who felt that Norway's high standards of social care and "green" controls would suffer, came together to swing opinion against joining. Afterwards, and unlike the Labour government of 1972, the Brundtland administration soldiered on, wisely soothing ruffled feathers by promising to shelve the whole EU membership issue until at least 2000. Nevertheless, the **1997 election** saw a move to the right, the main beneficiaries being the Christian Democratic Party and the ultra-conservative

Progress Party, who formed a right-of-centre minority coalition. Bargaining with its rivals from a position of parliamentary weakness, the new government found it difficult to cut a clear path – or at least one very different from its predecessor – apart from managing to antagonize the women's movement by some of its reactionary social legislation during 1998 and 1999.

Norway today

In the spring of 2000, the government resigned and Labour resumed command – but not for long: in the elections of the next year, they took a drubbing and the right prospered, paving the way for another ungainly centre-right administrative coalition. The coalition battled on until October 2005 when the Labour Party, along with its allies, the Socialist Left Party and the Centre Party, won a general election with the politically experienced **Jens Stoltenberg** becoming prime minister – as he remains at time of writing. **Stoltenberg** has bolted together one of Norway's more secure coalitions and his political agenda was – and remains – standard-issue centre-left: for instance, a flexible retirement age from 62 (it's currently 67) will be introduced in 2010; a careful incomes policy is geared to the needs of both employer and employee; there's a commitment to develop and strengthen Sámi culture; and there are detailed promises on tackling climate change and global warming. As Stoltenberg put it himself at the time of his election victory: "Our gains are due to a clear political message about jobs, education, and giving people security in their old age. Our aim is to give this country a stable and predictable government."

In the summer of 2008, however, the wheels began to come off the coalition wagon with arguments about the killing of wolves, corruption and the state of the healthcare system. Stoltenberg's popularity sank, but then came the banking crisis and, with Norway's banks hit hard, Stoltenberg started to look more like a prime minister who could take care of business - and the opinion polls gave him and his Labour Party a better rating. Quite whether this revival will save the Labour Party and its allies from defeat in the next general election in September 2009 remains to be seen.

The future

In the long term, quite what Norway will make of its **isolation from the EU** is unclear, though the situation is mitigated by Norway's membership of the European Economic Agreement (EEA), a free-trade deal of January 1994 that covers both Norway and the EU. Whatever happens, and whether or not there is another EU referendum, it's hard to imagine that the Norwegians will suffer any permanent economic harm. They have, after all, a superabundance of natural resources and arguably the most educated workforce in the world. Which isn't to say the country doesn't collectively **fret**: a modest increase in the amount of drug addiction and street crime has produced much heart-searching, the theory being that an advanced and progressive social policy should be able to eliminate such barbarisms. This thoughtful approach, so typical of Norway, is very much to the country's credit, as is the refusal to accept a residual level of unemployment (of about 2–4 percent) that is the envy of many other Western governments. Neither are fretting and a sense of happiness mutually exclusive: Norway's Lutheran roots run deep and, if an old joke is to be believed, the low point of the average Norwegian's year is the summer vacation.

History: Sweden

S weden has one of Europe's longest documented histories, but for all the upheavals of the Viking times and the warring of the Middle Ages, during modern times the country has seemed to delight in taking an historical back seat. The murders of prime minister Olof Palme in 1986 and of foreign minister Anna Lindh in 2003 briefly thrust Sweden into the international limelight, but since then, the country regained its poise, even though the current situation is fraught. Political infighting and domestic disharmony are threatening the one thing that the Swedes have always been proud of and that other countries aspire to: the politics of consensus. The passing of this, arguably, is of far greater importance than even the murders of their politicians.

Early civilizations

It wasn't until around 6000 BC that the **first settlers** roamed north and east into Sweden, living as nomadic reindeer-hunters and –herders. By 3000 BC people had settled in the south of the country and were established as farmers. From around 2000 BC a development in burial practices occurred, with **dolmens** and **passage graves** being found throughout the southern Swedish provinces.

During the **Bronze Age** (1500–500 BC) trade in furs and amber for southern European copper and tin was common. Large finds of ornaments and weapons attest to a comparatively rich culture, exemplified by elaborate burial rites.

The deterioration of the Scandinavian climate in the last millennium before Christ coincided with the advance across Europe of the Celts, which halted the flourishing trade of the Swedish settlers. With the new millennium, Sweden made its first mark upon the classical world when Pliny the Elder (23–79 AD), in the *Historia Naturalis*, mentioned the "island of Scatinavia" far to the north. Tacitus was more specific: in 98 AD he referred to a powerful people, the Suinoes, who were strong in men, weapons and ships, a reference to the **Svear**, who were to form the nucleus of an emergent Swedish kingdom by the sixth century.

Rulers of the whole country except the south, the Svear settled in the rich land around Lake Mälaren. The modern Swedish name for Sweden, *Sverige*, is a derivation "Svear rike", meaning the kingdom of the Svear.

The Viking period

The Vikings – raiders and warriors who dominated the political and economic life of Europe and beyond from the ninth to the eleventh centuries – came from all parts of southern Scandinavia. But there is evidence that the **Swedish Vikings** were among the first to leave home, impelled by a rapid population growth, domestic unrest and a desire for new lands. The raiders (and, later, traders) turned their attention largely eastwards, and by the ninth century trade had developed along well-established routes, with Swedes reaching the Black and Caspian seas and making valuable contact with the **Byzantine Empire**. From 860 onwards Greek and Muslim records relate a series of raids across the Black Sea against Byzantium, and across the Caspian into northeast Iran.

But the Vikings were settlers as well as traders and exploiters, and their long-term influence was marked. Embattled Slavs to the east gave them the name **Rus**, and their creeping colonization gave the area in which the Vikings settled its modern name, Russia. Russian names today – Oleg, Igor, Vladimir – can be derived from the Swedish – Helgi, Ingvar, Valdemar.

Domestically, **paganism** was at its height. Freyr was "God of the World", a physically potent god of fertility from whom dynastic leaders would trace their descent. It was a bloody time. Nine **human sacrifices** were offered at the celebrations held every nine years at Uppsala. Viking **law** was based on the **Thing**, an assembly of free men to which the king's power was subject. Each largely autonomous province had its own assembly and its own leaders: where several provinces united, the approval of each Thing was needed for any choice of leader.

The arrival of Christianity

Christianity was slow to take root in Sweden. Whereas Denmark and Norway had accepted the faith by the beginning of the eleventh century, Swedish contact was still with the peoples to the east, who remained largely heathen. Missionaries met with limited success and no Swedish king was converted until 1008, when **Olof Skötonung** was baptized. He was the first known king of both Swedes and Goths (that is, ruler of the two major provinces of Västergötland and Östergötland) and his successors were all Christians. Nevertheless, paganism retained a grip on Swedish affairs, and as late as the 1080s the Svear banished their Christian king, Inge, when he refused to take part in the pagan celebrations at Uppsala. By the end of the eleventh century, though, the temple at Uppsala had gone and a Christian church was built on its site. In the 1130s Uppsala replaced Sigtuna – original centre of the Swedish Christian faith – as the main episcopal seat and, in 1164, Stephen (an English monk) was made the first archbishop.

The warring dynasties

The whole of the early Middle Ages in Sweden were characterized by a succession of struggles for control of a growing central power. Principally two families, the Sverkers and the Eriks, waged battle throughout the twelfth century. **King Erik the Holy** was the first notable Sverker ruler to make his mark: in 1157 he led a crusade to heathen Finland, but was killed at Uppsala in 1160 by a Danish pretender to his throne.

Erik was succeeded by his son **Knut**, whose stable reign lasted until 1196 and was marked by commercial treaties and strengthened defences. Following Knut's death, virtual civil war weakened the royal power with the result that the king's chief ministers, or **Jarls**, assumed much of the executive responsibility for running the country; so much so that when Erik Eriksson (last of the Eriks) was deposed in 1229, his administrator **Birger Jarl** assumed power. With papal support for his crusading policies, Jarl confirmed the Swedish grip on the southwest of Finland. His son Valdemar succeeded him, but proved a weak ruler and didn't survive the family feuding after Birger Jarl's death. Valdemar's brother Magnus assumed power in 1275.

Magnus Ladulås represented a peak of Swedish royal power not to be repeated for three hundred years. His enemies dissipated, he forbade the nobility to meet without his consent and began to issue his own authoritative decrees. He also began to reap the benefits of conversion: the clergy became an educated class upon whom the monarch could rely for diplomatic and administrative duties. By the thirteenth century, there were ambitious Swedish clerics in Paris and Bologna, and the first stone churches were appearing in Sweden, among them the monumental early Gothic cathedral at Uppsala.

The nobility, meanwhile, had come to form a military class, exempted from taxation on the understanding that they would defend the crown. In the country the standard of living was still low, although a burgeoning population stimulated new cultivation. The forests of Norrland were pushed back, southern heathland was turned into pasture, and crop rotation introduced. Noticeable, too, was the increasing **German influence** within Sweden as the Hanseatic League traders spread. Their first merchants settled in Visby and, by the mid-thirteenth century, in Stockholm.

The fourteenth century – towards unity

When Magnus died in 1290, power shifted to a cabal of magnates led by **Torgil Knutsson**. As marshal of Sweden, he pursued an energetic foreign policy, conquering western Karelia to gain control of the Gulf of Finland and building the fortress at Viborg, which was lost only with the collapse of the Swedish Empire in the eighteenth century.

Magnus's son Birger came of age in 1302 but soon quarrelled with his brothers Erik and Valdemar. They had Torgil Knutsson executed, then rounded on Birger, who was forced to divide Sweden among the three of them. An unhappy arrangement, it lasted until 1317, when Birger had his brothers arrested and starved to death in prison – an act that prompted a shocked nobility to rise against Birger and force his exile to Denmark. The Swedish nobles restored the principle of elective monarchy by calling on the 3-year-old **Magnus** (son of a Swedish duke and already declared Norwegian king) to take the Swedish crown. While Magnus was still a boy, a treaty was concluded with Novgorod (1323) to fix the frontiers in eastern and northern Finland. This left virtually the whole of the Scandinavian peninsula (except the Danish provinces in the south) under one ruler.

Yet Sweden was still anything but prosperous. The **Black Death** reached the country in 1350, wiping out whole parishes and killing around a third of the population. Subsequent labour shortages and troubled estates meant that the nobility found it difficult to maintain their positions. German merchants had driven the Swedes from their most lucrative trade routes and even the copper and iron-ore **mining** that began around this time in Bergslagen and Dalarna relied on German capital.

Magnus soon ran into trouble, threatened further by the accession of Valdemar Atterdag to the Danish throne in 1340. Squabbles over the sovereignty of the Danish provinces of Skåne and Blekinge led to Danish incursions into Sweden and, in 1361, Valdemar landed on Gotland and sacked **Visby**. The Gotlanders, refused refuge by the Hanseatic League, were massacred outside the city walls.

Magnus was forced to negotiate, and his son **Håkon** – now king of Norway – was married to Valdemar's daughter Margrethe. With Magnus later deposed, power fell into the hands of a group of magnates, who shared out the country. Chief of the ruling nobles was the Steward **Bo Jonsson Grip**, who controlled virtually all Finland and central and southeast Sweden. Yet on his death, the nobility turned to Håkon's wife **Margrethe**, already regent in Norway (for her son Olof) and in Denmark since the death of her father, Valdemar. In 1388 she was proclaimed "First Lady" of Sweden and, in return, confirmed all the privileges of the Swedish nobility. They were anxious for union, to safeguard those who owned frontier estates and strengthen the crown against any further German influence. Called upon to choose a male king, Margrethe nominated her nephew, **Erik of Pomerania**, who was duly elected king of Sweden in 1396. As he had already been elected to the Danish and Norwegian thrones, Scandinavian unity seemed assured.

The Kalmar Union

Erik was crowned King of Denmark, Norway and Sweden in 1397 at a ceremony in **Kalmar**. Nominally, the three kingdoms were now in union but, despite Erik, real power remained in the hands of Margrethe until her death in 1412.

Erik was at war throughout his reign with the Hanseatic League and is vilified in popular Swedish history as an evil and grasping ruler. He was deposed in 1439 and the nobility turned to Erik's nephew; **Christopher of Bavaria**, whose early death in 1448 led to the first major breach in the union.

No one candidate could fill the three kingships satisfactorily, and separate elections in Denmark and Sweden signalled a renewal of the infighting that had plagued the previous century. Within Sweden, unionists and nationalists skirmished, the powerful unionist **Oxenstierna** family opposing the claims of the nationalist **Sture** family until 1470, when **Sten Sture** (the Elder) became "Guardian of the Realm". His victory over the unionists at the **Battle of Brunkeberg** (1471) – in the middle of modern Stockholm – was complete, gaining symbolic artistic expression in the statue of St George and the Dragon that still adorns the Great Church in Stockholm.

Sten Sture's primacy fostered a new cultural flowering. The first **university** in Scandinavia was founded in Uppsala in 1477, and the first printing press appeared in Sweden six years later. Artistically, German and Dutch influences were great, traits seen in the decorative art of the great Swedish late medieval churches.

Belief in the union still existed, though, particularly outside Sweden, and successive kings had to fend off almost constant attacks and blockades emanating from Denmark. With the accession of **Christian II** to the Danish throne in 1513, the unionist movement found a leader capable of turning the tide. Under the guise of a crusade to free Sweden's imprisoned archbishop Gustav Trolle, Christian attacked Sweden and killed Sture. After Christian's coronation, Trolle urged the prosecution of his Swedish adversaries who, gathered together under an amnesty, were found guilty of heresy. Eighty-two nobles and burghers of Stockholm were executed and their bodies burned in what became known as the **Stockholm Bloodbath**. A vicious persecution of Sture's followers throughout Sweden ensued, a move that led to widespread reaction and, ultimately, the downfall of the union.

Gustav Vasa and his sons

Opposition to Christian II was vague and unorganized until the appearance of the young **Gustav Vasa**. Initially unable to stir the locals of the Dalecarlia region into open revolt, he left for exile in Norway, but was chased on skis and recalled after the people had had a change of heart. The chase is celebrated still in the **Vasalopet** race, run each year by thousands of Swedish skiers.

Gustav Vasa's army grew rapidly, and in 1521 he was elected regent, and subsequently, with the capture of Stockholm in 1523, king. Christian had been deposed in Denmark and the new Danish king, Frederik I, recognized Sweden's de facto withdrawal from the union. Short of cash, Gustav found it prudent to support the movement towards religious reform propagated by Swedish Lutherans. More of a political than a religious **Reformation**, the result was a handover of Church lands to the crown and the subordination of Church to state. Suppressing revolt at home, Gustav Vasa strengthened his hand with a centralization of trade and government. On his death in 1560 Sweden was united, prosperous and independent.

However, Gustav Vasa's heir, his eldest son **Erik**, faced a difficult time, not least because the Vasa lands and wealth had been divided among him and his brothers Johan, Magnus and Karl. The Danes, too, pressed hard, reasserting their claim to the Swedish throne in the inconclusive **Northern Seven Years War**, which began in

1563. Erik was deposed in 1569 by his brother, who became **Johan III**: his first act was to end the war at the **Peace of Stettin**. At home, Johan ruled more or less with the good will of the nobility, but upset matters with his Catholic sympathies. He introduced the liturgy and Catholic-influenced Red Book, and his son and heir Sigismund was the Catholic king of Poland. On Johan's death in 1592, Sigismund agreed to rule Sweden in accordance with Lutheran practice but failed to do so. When Sigismund returned to Poland the way was clear for Duke Karl (Johan's brother and the last of Vasa's sons) to assume the regency, a role he filled until declared King **Karl IX** in 1603.

Karl had ambitions eastwards but, routed by the Poles and staved off by the Russians, he suffered a stroke in 1610 and died the following year. His heir was his son, the 17-year-old Gustav II Adolf, better known as Gustavus Adolphus.

The rule of Vasa and his sons made Sweden a nation, culturally as well as politically. The courts were filled with men of learning and the arts flourished. The **Renaissance** style appeared for the first time in Sweden, with royal castles remodelled – Kalmar being a fine example. Economically, Sweden remained mostly self-sufficient, its few imports being luxuries like cloth, wine and spices. With around eight thousand inhabitants, Stockholm was its most important city, although **Gothenburg** was founded in 1607 to promote trade to the west.

Gustav II Adolf: the rise of the Swedish empire

During the reign of **Gustav II Adolf**, Sweden became a European power. Though still a youth, he was considered able enough to rule, and proved so by concluding peace treaties with Denmark (1613) and Russia (1617), the latter isolating Russia from the Baltic and allowing the Swedes control of the eastern trade routes into Europe.

In 1618, the **Thirty Years War** broke out in Germany. It was vital for Gustavus that Germany should not become Catholic, given the Polish king's continuing pretensions to the Swedish crown, and the possible threat it could pose to Sweden's growing influence in the Baltic. The 1629 Altmark treaty with a defeated Poland gave Gustavus control of Livonia and four Prussian sea ports, and the income this generated financed his entry into the war in 1630 on the Protestant side. After several convincing victories Gustavus pushed through Germany, delaying an assault upon undefended Vienna. It cost him his life. At the **Battle of Lützen** in 1632 Gustavus was killed, his body stripped and battered by the enemy's soldiers. The war dragged on until the **Peace of Westphalia** in 1648.

With Gustavus away at war for much of his reign, Sweden ran smoothly under the guidance of his friend and chancellor, **Axel Oxenstierna**. Together they founded a new Supreme Court in Stockholm (and the same, too, in Finland and the conquered Baltic provinces); reorganized the national assembly into four Estates of nobility, clergy, burghers and peasantry (1626); extended the university at Uppsala (and founded one at Turku); and fostered the mining and other industries that provided much of the country's wealth. Gustavus had many other accomplishments, too: he spoke five languages and designed a new light cannon, which assisted in his routs of the enemy.

The Caroleans

The Swedish empire reached its territorial peak under the **Caroleans** – yet the reign of the last of them was to see Sweden crumble.

Following Gustav II Adolf's death and the abdication of his daughter Christina in 1654, **Karl X** succeeded to the throne. War against Poland (1655) saw some early successes and, with Denmark espousing the Polish cause, gave Karl the opportunity to march into Jutland (1657). From there his armies crossed the frozen sea to threaten Copenhagen; the subsequent **Treaty of Roskilde** (1658) broke Denmark and gave the Swedish empire its widest territorial extent.

However, the long regency of his son and heir, **Karl XI**, did little to enhance Sweden's vulnerable position, so extensive were its borders. On his assumption of power in 1672, Karl was almost immediately dragged into war: beaten by a smaller Prussian army at Brandenberg in 1675, Sweden was suddenly faced with war against both the Danes and Dutch. Karl rallied, though, to drive out the Danish invaders, the war ending in 1679 with the reconquest of Skåne and the restoration of most of Sweden's German provinces.

In 1682, Karl XI became **absolute monarch** and was given full control over legislation and *reduktion* – the resumption of estates previously alienated by the crown to the nobility. The armed forces were reorganized too, and by 1700 the Swedish army had 25,000 soldiers and twelve regiments of cavalry; the naval fleet was expanded to 38 ships and a new base was built at **Karlskrona** (nearer than Stockholm to the likely trouble spots).

Culturally, Sweden began to benefit from the innovations of Gustav II Adolf. A second university was established at **Lund** in 1668 and a national literature emerged, helped by the efforts of **George Stiernhielm**, "father" of modern Swedish poetry, while the same period saw the work of **Olof Rudbeck** (1630–1702), a Nordic polymath whose scientific reputation lasted longer than his attempt to identify the ancient Goth settlement at Uppsala as Atlantis. Architecturally, this was the age of **Tessin**, both father and son. Tessin the Elder was responsible for the glorious palace at **Drottningholm**, work on which began in 1662, as well as the cathedral at **Kalmar**. His son, Tessin the Younger, succeeded him as royal architect and was to create the new palace at Stockholm.

In 1697, the 15-year-old **Karl XII** succeeded to the throne, and under him the empire collapsed. Faced with a defensive alliance of Saxony, Denmark and Russia, there was little the king could have done to avoid eventual defeat. However, he remains a revered figure for his valiant (often suicidal) efforts to prove Europe wrong. Initial victories against Peter the Great and Saxony led him to march on Russia, where he was defeated and the bulk of his army destroyed. Escaping to Turkey, where he remained as guest and then prisoner for four years, Karl watched the empire disintegrate. With Poland reconquered by Augustus of Saxony, and Finland by Peter the Great, he returned to Sweden only to have England declare war on him.

Eventually, splits in the enemy's alliance led Swedish diplomats to attempt peace talks with Russia. Karl, though, was keen to exploit these differences in a more direct fashion. In order to strike at Denmark, but lacking a fleet, he besieged Fredrikshald in Norway in 1718 and was killed by a sniper's bullet. In the power vacuum thus created, Russia became the leading Baltic force, receiving Livonia, Estonia, Ingria and most of Karelia from Sweden.

The age of freedom

The eighteenth century saw absolutism discredited in Sweden. A new constitution vested power in the Estates, who reduced the new king **Fredrik I**'s role to that of nominal head of state. The chancellor wielded the real power and under **Arvid Horn** the country found a period of stability. His party, nicknamed the "Caps", was opposed by the hawkish "Hats", who forced war with Russia in 1741, a disaster in which Sweden lost all of Finland and had its whole east coast burned and bombed. Most of Finland was returned with the agreement to elect **Adolf Fredrik** (a relation of the crown prince of Russia) to the Swedish throne on Fredrik I's death, which duly occurred in 1751. During his reign Adolf repeatedly tried to reassert royal power, but found that the constitution was only strengthened against him. The resurrected "Hats" forced entry into the **Seven Years War** in 1757 on the French side, another disastrous venture as the Prussians repelled every Swedish attack.

The aristocratic parties were in a state of constant flux. Although elections of sorts were held to provide delegates for the Riksdag (parliament), foreign sympathies, bribery and bickering were hardly conducive to a democratic administration. Cabals continued to rule Sweden, the economy was stagnant, and reform delayed. It was, however, an age of intellectual and scientific advance, surprising in a country that had lost much of its cultural impetus. **Carl von Linné** (better known by the Latinized version of his name, Linnaeus), the botanist whose classification of plants is still used, was professor at Uppsala from 1741 to 1778. **Anders Celsius** initiated the use of the centigrade temperature scale; **Carl Scheele** discovered chlorine. A royal decree of 1748 organized Europe's first full-scale census, and by 1775 the census had become a five-yearly event. Other fields flourished, too. **Emmanuel Swedenborg**, the philosopher, died in 1772, his mystical works encouraging new theological sects; and the period encapsulated the life of **Carl Michael Bellman** (1740–95), the celebrated Swedish poet, whose work did much to identify and foster a popular nationalism.

With the accession of **Gustav III** in 1771, the crown began to regain the ascendancy. A new constitution was forced upon a divided Riksdag, and proved a balance between earlier absolutism and the later aristocratic squabbles. A popular king, Gustav founded hospitals, granted freedom of worship and removed many state controls over the economy. His determination to conduct a successful foreign policy led to further conflict with Russia (1788–90) in which, to everyone's surprise, he managed to more than hold his own. But with the French Revolution polarizing opposition throughout Europe, the Swedish nobility began to entertain thoughts of conspiracy against a king whose growing powers they now saw as those of a tyrant. In 1792, at a masked ball in the Stockholm Opera House, the king was shot by an assassin hired by the disaffected aristocracy. Gustav died two weeks later and was succeeded by his son **Gustav IV**, the country led by a regency for the years of his minority.

The battles waged by revolutionary France were at first studiously avoided in Sweden but, pulled into the conflict by the British, Gustav IV entered the **Napoleonic Wars** in 1805. However, Napoleon's victory at Austerlitz two years later broke the coalition and Sweden found itself isolated. Attacked by Russia the following year, Gustav was later arrested and deposed, and his uncle elected king.

A constitution of 1809 established a liberal monarchy in Sweden, responsible to the elected Riksdag. Under this constitution **Karl XIII** was a mere caretaker, his heir a Danish prince who would bring Norway back to Sweden – some compensation for finally losing Finland and the Åland Islands to Russia (1809) after five hundred years of Swedish rule. On the prince's sudden death, however, Marshal Bernadotte (one of Napoleon's generals) was invited to become heir. Taking the name of **Karl Johan**, he took his chance in 1812 and joined Britain and Russia to fight Napoleon. Following Napoleon's first defeat at the Battle of Leipzig in 1813, Sweden compelled Denmark (France's ally) to exchange Norway for Swedish Pomerania.

By 1814 Sweden and Norway had formed an uneasy union. Norway retained its own government and certain autonomous measures. Sweden decided foreign policy, appointed a viceroy and retained a suspensive (but not absolute) veto over the Norwegian parliament's legislation.

The nineteenth century

Union under Karl Johan, or **Karl XIV** as he became in 1818, could have been disastrous. He spoke no Swedish and, until just a few years previously, had never visited either kingdom. However, under him and his successor **Oscar I**, prosperity ensued. The **Göta Canal** (1832) helped commercially, and liberal measures by both monarchs helped politically. In 1845 daughters were given an equal right of inheritance; a poverty law was introduced in 1847; restrictive craft guilds were reformed; an education act was passed.

The 1848 revolution throughout Europe cooled Oscar's reforming ardour, and his attention turned to reviving **Scandinavianism**. There was still a hope, in certain quarters, that closer cooperation between Denmark and Sweden–Norway could lead to some sort of revived Kalmar Union. With the **Crimean War** of 1854, expectations were raised that Russia – Sweden's main enemy in the eighteenth century – could be weakened for good. But peace was declared too quickly (at least for Sweden) and there was still no real guarantee that Sweden would be sufficiently protected from Russia in the future. With Oscar's death, talk of political union faded.

His son **Karl XV** presided over a reform of the Riksdag that put an end to the Swedish system of personal monarchy. The Four Estates were replaced by a representative two-house parliament along European lines. This, together with the end of political Scandinavianism (following the Prussian attack on Denmark in 1864 in which Sweden refused to offer assistance), marked Sweden's entry into modern Europe.

Industrialization was slow to take root in Sweden. No real industrial revolution occurred, and developments such as mechanization and the introduction of railways were piecemeal. One result was widespread **emigration** amongst the rural poor, who had been hard hit by famine in 1867 and 1868. Between 1860 and 1910, over one million people left for America (in 1860 the Swedish population was only four million). Given huge farms to settle, the emigrants headed for land similar to that they had left behind – to the Midwest, Kansas and Nebraska.

At home, Swedish **trade unionism** emerged to campaign for better conditions. Dealt with severely, the unions formed a confederation (1898) but largely failed to make headway – even peaceful picketing carried a two-year prison sentence. Hand in hand with the fight for workers' rights went the **temperance movement**. The level of spirit consumption was alarming and various abstinence programmes attempted to educate the drinkers and, where necessary, eradicate the stills. Some towns made the selling of spirits a municipal monopoly – not a big step away from the state monopoly that exists today.

With the accession of **Oscar II** in 1872, Sweden continued on an even, if uneventful, keel. Keeping out of further European conflict (the Austro–Prussian War, Franco–Prussian War and various Balkan crises), the country's only worry was a growing dissatisfaction in Norway with the union. Demanding a separate consular service, and objecting to the Swedish king's veto on constitutional matters, the Norwegians brought things to a head and, in 1905, declared the union invalid. The Treaty of Karlstad confirmed the break and Norway became independent for the first time since 1380.

Two world wars

Sweden declared a strict neutrality on the outbreak of **World War I**, tempered by much sympathy within the country for Germany which was fostered by long-standing language, trade and cultural links. It was a policy agreed with the other Scandinavian monarchs, but a difficult one to pursue. Faced with British demands to enforce a blockade of Germany and the blacklisting and eventual seizure of Swedish goods at sea, the economy suffered grievously; rationing was imposed and inflation mushroomed. The **Russian Revolution** in 1917 brought further problems to Sweden. The Finns immediately declared independence, waging civil war against the Bolsheviks, and Swedish volunteers enlisted in the White army. But a conflict of interest arose when the Swedish-speaking Åland Islands wanted a return to Swedish rule rather than stay with the victorious Finns. The League of Nations overturned this claim, granting the islands to Finland who remain in control of them today.

After the war, a Liberal–Socialist coalition remained in power until 1920, when **Branting** became the first socialist prime minister. Following the Depression of the late 1920s and early 1930s, conditions began to improve after a Social Democratic government took office for the fourth time in 1932. A **welfare state** was rapidly established, meaning unemployment benefit, higher old-age pensions, family allowances and paid holidays. The **Saltsjöbaden Agreement** of 1938 drew up a contract between trade unions and employers to help eliminate strikes and lockouts. With war again looming, all parties agreed that Sweden should remain neutral in any struggle and rearmament was negligible, despite Hitler's apparent intentions.

World War II was slow to affect Sweden. Unlike in 1914, there was little sympathy for Germany, but neutrality was again declared. The Russian invasion of Finland in 1939 brought Sweden into the picture, providing weapons, volunteers and refuge for the Finns. Regular Swedish troops were refused, though, fearing intervention from either the Germans (then Russia's ally) or the Allies. Economically, the country remained sound – less dependent on imports than in World War I and with no serious shortages. The position became stickier in 1940 when the Nazis marched into Denmark and Norway, isolating Sweden. Concessions were made – German troop transit allowed, iron-ore exports continued – until 1943–44 when Allied threats became more convincing than the failing German war machine. Sweden became the recipient of countless refugees from the rest of Scandinavia and the Baltic. The end of the war was to provide the country with a serious crisis of conscience. Physically unscathed, Sweden was now vulnerable to **Cold War** politics. Proximity to the Soviet Union meant that Sweden refused to follow the other Scandinavian countries into **NATO** in 1949. The country did, however, much to Conservative disquiet, return most of the Baltic and German refugees who had fought against Russia during the war into Stalin's hands – their fate is not difficult to guess.

Postwar politics

The wartime coalition quickly gave way to a purely **Social Democratic** government committed to welfare provision and increased defence expenditure – non-participation in military alliances didn't mean a throwing down of weapons.

Sweden regained much of its international moral respect (lost directly after World War II) through the election of **Dag Hammarskjöld** as secretary-general of the United Nations in 1953. His strong leadership greatly enhanced the prestige (and effectiveness) of the organization, and he participated in the solution of the Suez crisis in 1956 and the Lebanon–Jordan affair in 1958. He was killed in an air crash in 1961, towards the end of his second five-year term.

Throughout the 1950s and 1960s, domestic reform continued unabated. It was in these years that the country laid the foundations of its much-vaunted social security system. The Social Democrats stayed in power until 1976, when a **non-Socialist coalition** (Centre–Liberal–Moderate) finally unseated them. In the 44 years since 1932, the Socialists had been an integral part of government in Sweden, tempered only by periods of war and coalition. It was a remarkable record, made more so by the fact that modern politics in Sweden has never been about ideology so much as detail. Socialists and non-Socialists alike shared a broad consensus on foreign policy and defence matters, and even on the need for the social welfare system.

Olof Palme

The Social Democrats regained power in 1982, subsequently devaluing the krona, introducing a price freeze and cutting back on public expenditure, but they lost their majority in 1985, and had to rely on Communist support to get their bills through. Presiding over the party since 1969, and prime minister for nearly as long, was **Olof Palme**. He was assassinated in February 1986, his death throwing Sweden into modern European politics like no other event. Proud of their open society (Palme was returning home unguarded from the cinema), the Swedes were shocked by the gunning down of a respected politician, diplomat and pacifist. Shock turned to anger and then ridicule as the months passed without his killer being caught. Police bungling was criticized and despite the theories – Kurdish extremists, right-wing terror groups – no one was charged with the murder.

Then, finally, the police came up with **Christer Pettersson**, who – despite having no apparent motive – was identified by Palme's wife as the man who had fired the shot that night. Despite pleading his innocence, claiming he was elsewhere at the time of the murder, Pettersson was convicted of Palme's murder and jailed. There was great disquiet about the verdict, however, both at home and abroad: the three legal representatives in the original jury had voted for acquittal at the time; and it was believed that Palme's wife couldn't possibly be sure that the man who fired the shot was Pettersson, since by her own admission she had only seen him once, on the dark night in question and then only very briefly. In 1989, on appeal, Pettersson was acquitted and released. The Swedish police appear to believe that they had the right man but not enough evidence to convict; more recent evidence has pointed to South African involvement, Palme having been a vocal opponent of apartheid.

To the millennium

Nostalgia for the good old days of Social Democracy swept the country during the general election of September 1994 and Carl Bildt's minority Conservative government was pushed out, allowing a return to power by Sweden's largest party, headed by **Ingvar Carlsson**. Social Democracy was well and truly back, with Carlsson choosing a cabinet composed equally of men and women. New social reforms were implemented, most significantly the 1995 law allowing gay couples to marry, which gives them virtually equal rights with heterosexual couples.

During 1994, negotiations on Sweden's planned membership of the **European Union** were completed and put to a referendum that saw public opinion split right down the middle. While some thought that EU membership would allow Sweden a greater influence within Europe, others were concerned that the country's standards would be forced downwards, affecting the quality of life Swedes had come to expect. However, in November the vote for membership was won, albeit by the narrowest of margins – just five percent – and Sweden joined the Union as of January 1, 1995.

Meanwhile, the welfare state was further trimmed back and new taxes announced to try to rein in the spiralling debt: unemployment benefit was cut to 75 percent of previous earnings, sick-leave benefits reduced and lower state pension payments came into force, though finance minister **Göran Persson** did at least reduce taxes on food from 21 percent to 12 percent, in an attempt to retain some public support. Just when everything appeared to be under control, Carlsson resigned to be replaced by the domineering Persson.

Following elections in September 1998, Göran Persson clung onto power but with a much reduced majority. The election was a disaster for Sweden's Social Democrats, who recorded their worst result since World War II after losing support to the far left. Many voters complained that the Social Democrats had slashed the welfare state too far in an effort to revive the flagging economy.

Sweden today

Sweden's export-led **economy** has rendered the country extremely susceptible to changes in world finances. As globalization has gathered momentum since the turn of the millennium, the country has faced a number of difficult choices which would have been totally unthinkable during the heady days of Social Democracy. During recent years privatizations, mergers and general cost-cutting measures – most visibly the virtual disappearance of the post office from Swedish high streets and the much-lamented fragmentation of the national rail network – have brought Sweden more into line with countries that went through equally painful economic change decades ago. Some economists argue that it's this enforced shaking up of the business environment from outside, rather than any direct government measures, that is responsible for Sweden's improved economic fortunes since 1998 – albeit at a reduced rate due to the world economic slowdown.

In 2003, this renewed growth and prosperity was at the centre of discussions in the months leading up to the referendum on adopting the **euro** as Sweden's currency, with the no-voters eventually claiming a clear majority. The referendum went ahead despite the shocking murder of the popular foreign minister and pro-euro campaigner **Anna Lindh** in a Stockholm department store, just days before.

After the 2002 elections, the Social Democratic Party went on to form a minority government – dependent on the support of the anti-EU Left and Greens – with Göran Persson starting his third term as prime minister. However, the perceived bungling of aid to Swedes caught up in the **tsunami disaster** in December 2004 cost Persson dear in September 2006 when he lost the general election to the Conservative, **Fredrik Reinfeldt**, who has since slashed the welfare state even further in an attempt to stimulate the economy and create jobs. The bête noire of past governments, Sweden's appalling record of sick leave, was tackled head on in new legislation in 2008 which will mean that no person is allowed to claim sick leave for over a year – unthinkable in most other countries, but all too common in Sweden where many people earn more than their regular salary by claiming an array of social welfare benefits including sick pay.

History: Finland

I nextricably bound with the medieval superpowers, Sweden and Russia, and later with the Soviet Union, Finland's history is a stirring tale of a small people's survival – and eventual triumph – over what have often seemed impossible odds. It's also a story that's full of powerful contemporary resonances – the Finns' battle to regain their independence did not go unnoticed on the other side of the Baltic Sea, serving as a model for the three ex-Soviet Baltic states in their fight for sovereignty and, more recently, EU membership.

First settlements

As the ice sheets of the last Ice Age retreated, parts of the Finnish Arctic coast were settled by tribes from eastern Europe. They hunted bear and reindeer, and fished the well-stocked rivers and lakes: relics of their existence have been found and dated to around 8000 BC. Pottery skills were introduced around 3000 BC, and trade with Russia and the east flourished. At the same time, other peoples were arriving and merging with the established population. The **Boat Axe** culture (1800–1600 BC), which originated in central Europe, spread as Indo-Europeans migrated into Finland. The seafaring knowledge they possessed enabled them to begin trading with Sweden from the Finnish west coast, as indicated by **Bronze Age** findings (around 1300 BC) concentrated in a narrow strip along the seaboard. The previous settlers withdrew eastwards and the advent of severe weather brought this period of occupation to an end.

The arrival of the Finns

The antecedents of the Finns were a race from central Siberia, from where they moved outwards in two directions. One tribe went south, eventually to Hungary; and the other westwards to the Baltic, where it mixed with Latgals, Lithuanians and Germans. The latter, the "**Baltic Finns**", were migrants who crossed the Baltic around 400 AD to form an independent society in Finland. In 100 AD the Roman historian Tacitus described a wild and primitive people called "the Fenni". This is thought to have been a reference to the earliest **Sámi**, who occupied Finland before this. With their more advanced culture, the Baltic Finns absorbed this indigenous population, although some of their customs were maintained. The new Finns worked the land, utilized the vast forests and made lengthy fishing expeditions on the lakes.

The pagan era

The main Finnish settlements were built up along the west coast facing Sweden, with whom trade was established, until the Vikings' opening up of routes further to the east forced these communities into decline. Meanwhile, the Finnish south coast was exposed to seaborne raiding parties and most Finns moved inland and eastwards, a large number settling around the huge Lake Ladoga in **Karelia**. Eventually the people of Karelia were able to enjoy trade in two directions – with the Varangians to the east and the Swedes to the west. Groups from Karelia and the more northern territory of Kainuu regularly ventured into Lapland to fish and hunt. At the end of the pagan era Finland was split into three regions: Varsinais-Suomi ("Finland proper") in the southwest, Häme in the western part of the lake region and Karelia in the east. Although they often helped one another, there was no formal cooperation between the inhabitants of these areas.

The Swedish era (1155–1809)

At the start of the tenth century, pagan Finland was caught between two opposing religions: Catholicism in Sweden on one side and the Orthodox Church of Russia on the other. The Russians wielded great influence in Karelia, but the west of Finland began to gravitate towards Catholicism on account of its high level of contact with Sweden. In 1155 King Erik of Sweden launched a "crusade" into Finland – although its real purpose was to strengthen trade routes – which swept through the southwest and established Swedish control, leaving the English **Bishop Henry** at **Turku** to establish a parish. Henry was killed by a Finnish yeoman, but became the patron saint of the Turku diocese and the region became the administrative base of the whole country. Western Finland generally acquiesced to the Swedes, but Karelia didn't, becoming a territory much sought after by both the Swedes and the Russians. In 1323, under the **Treaty of Pähkinäsaari**, an official border was drawn up, giving the western part of Karelia to Sweden while the Russian principality of Novgorod retained the eastern section around Lake Ladoga. To emphasize their claim, the Russians founded the Orthodox **Valamo Monastery** on an island in the lake.

Under the Swedish crown, Finns still worked and controlled their own land, often living side by side with Swedes, who came to the west coast to safeguard sea trade. Finnish provincial leaders were given places among the nobility and in 1362 King Håkon gave Finland the right to vote in Swedish royal elections – though the 1397 Kalmar Union brought sovereignty over all of Sweden (Finland included) to Margrethe, Queen of Denmark and Norway. While most Finns were little affected by the constitution of the Union, there was a hope that it would guarantee their safety against the Russians, whose expansionist policies were an increasing threat. Throughout the fifteenth century there were repeated skirmishes between Russians and Finns in the border lands and around the important Finnish Baltic trading centre of Viipuri (now Russian Vyborg).

The election of King Charles VIII in 1438 caused a rift in the Union and serious strife between Sweden and Denmark. He was forced to abdicate in 1458 but his support in Finland was strong, and his successor, Christian I, sent an armed column to subdue Finnish unrest. While Turku castle was under siege, the Danish noble **Erik Axelsson Tott**, already known and respected in the country, called a meeting of representatives from every Finnish estate where it was agreed that Christian I would be acknowledged as king of the Union. Tott went on to take command of Viipuri castle, and he further strengthened Finland's eastern defences by erecting the fortress of **Olavinlinna** (in the present town of Savonlinna) in 1475, as a response to a revival of Russian claims on Karelia.

Strengthened by an alliance with Denmark signed in 1493, Russia attacked Viipuri on November 30, 1495. The troops were fended off by the technically inferior Finns, an achievement perceived as a miracle. After further battles it was agreed that the borders of the Treaty of Pähkinäsaari would remain. However, the Swedes drew up a bogus version of the treaty in which the border retained its fifteenth-century position, and it was this forgery which they used in negotiations with the Russians over the next hundred years.

Within Finland, a largely Swedish-born nobility became established. Church services were conducted in Finnish, although Swedish remained the language of commerce and officialdom; because the bulk of the population was illiterate, any important deed had to be read to them. In the thirteenth and fourteenth centuries, any Finn who felt oppressed simply moved into the wild lands of the interior – out of earshot of church bells.

By the time **Gustav Vasa** took the Swedish throne in 1523, many villages had been established in the disputed border regions. Almost every inhabitant spoke Finnish, but there was a roughly equal division between those communities who paid taxes to the Swedish king and those who paid them to the Russian tsar. In the winter of 1555, a Russian advance into Karelia was quashed at Joutselkä by Finns using skis to travel speedily over the icy roads, a victory that made the Finnish nobility confident of success in a full-scale war. While hesitant, Vasa finally agreed to their wishes: 12,000 troops from Sweden were dispatched to eastern Finland, and an offensive launched in the autumn of 1556. It failed, with the Russians reaching the gates of Viipuri, and Vasa retreating to the Åland Islands, asking for peace.

In 1556, Gustav Vasa made Finland a Swedish Grand Duchy and gave his son, Johan, the title Duke of Finland. Johan was pro-Finnish, and Finland was divided between loyalty towards the friendly duke and the need to keep on good terms with the Swedish crown, now held by Erik XIV. The Swedish forces sent to collect Johan – who had been sentenced to death after breaching protocol by invading Livonia, but then pardoned – laid siege to Turku castle for three weeks, executing thirty nobles before capturing the duke and imprisoning him.

The war between Sweden and Denmark over control of the Baltic took its toll on Erik. He became mentally unbalanced, slaying several prisoners who were being held for trial and, in a moment of complete madness, releasing Johan from detention. The Swedish nobles were incensed by Erik's actions and rebelled against him – with the result that Johan became king in 1568.

In 1570, Swedish resources were stretched when hostilities again erupted with Russia, now ruled by the aggressive Tsar Ivan ("the Terrible") IV. The conflict was to last 25 years, a period known in Finland as "**The Long Wrath**". It saw the introduction of a form of conscription instead of the reliance on mercenary soldiers, which had been the norm in other Swedish wars. Able-bodied men aged between 15 and 50 were rounded up by the local bailiff and about one in ten selected for military service. Russia occupied almost all of Estonia and made deep thrusts into southern Finland. Finally the Swedish–Finnish troops regained Estonia and made significant advances through Karelia, capturing an important eastern European trading route. The war was formally concluded in 1595 by the **Treaty of Täyssinä**. Under its terms, Russia recognized the lands gained by Sweden and the eastern border was altered to reach up to the Arctic coast, enabling Finns to settle in the far north.

Sweden was established as the dominant force in the Baltic, but under Gustav II, crowned king in 1611, Finland began to lose the special status it had previously enjoyed. Conditions continued to decline until 1637, when **Per Brahe** was appointed governor-general. Against the prevailing mood of the time, he insisted that all officers should study Finnish, selected Turku as the spot for a university – the country's first – and instigated a successful programme to spread literacy among the Finnish people. After concluding his second term of office in 1654 he parted with the terse but accurate summary: "I was highly satisfied with this country and the country highly satisfied with me."

A terrible harvest in 1696 caused a **famine** that killed a third of the Finnish population. The fact that no aid came from Sweden intensified feelings of neglect and stirred up a minor bout of Finnish nationalism led by **Daniel Juslenius**. His book, *Aboa Vetus Et Nova*, published in 1700, dubiously claimed Finnish to be a founding language of the world, and Finns to be descendants of the tribes of Israel.

In 1711, Viipuri fell to the Russians. Under their new tsar, Peter ("the Great"), the Russians quickly spread across the country, causing the nobility to flee to Stockholm and Swedish commanders to be more concerned with salvaging their army than saving Finland. In 1714, eight years of Russian occupation – "**The Great Wrath**" – began. Descriptions of the horrors of these times have been exaggerated, but nonetheless the events confirmed the Finns' longtime dread of their eastern neighbour. The Russians saw Finland simply as a springboard to attack Sweden, and laid waste to anything in it which the Swedes might attempt to regain.

Under the **Treaty of Uusikaupunki**, in 1721, the tsar gave back much of Finland but retained Viipuri, east Karelia, Estonia and Latvia, and thus control of the Baltic, making Finland's eastern border totally unprotected.

The aggressive policies of the Hats in the Swedish Diet led to the 1741 declaration of war on Russia. With barely an arm raised against them, Russian troops again occupied Finland – the start of "**The Lesser Wrath**" – until the **Treaty of Turku** in 1743. Under this, the Russians withdrew, ceded a section of Finland back to Sweden but moved their border west.

The Russian era (1809–1917)

In an attempt to force Sweden to join Napoleon's economic blockade, Russia, under Tsar Alexander I, attacked and occupied Finland in 1807. The **Treaty of Hamina**, signed in September of that year, legally ceded all of the country to Russia. The tsar had been in need of a friendly country close to Napoleon's territory as a reliable ally in case of future hostilities between the two leaders. To gain Finnish favour, he guaranteed beneficial terms at the Porvoo-based Swedish Diet, which at the time still exercised control (the Finns had yet to establish their own Diet and Senate), and subsequently Finland became an **autonomous Russian Grand Duchy**. There was no conscription and taxation was frozen, while realignment of the northern section of the Finnish–Russian border gave additional land to Finland. Finns could freely occupy positions in the Russian empire, although Russians were denied equal opportunities within Finland. The long period of peace that ensued saw a great improvement in Finnish wealth and well-being.

After returning Viipuri to Finland, the tsar declared Helsinki the **capital** in 1812, deeming Turku too close to Sweden for safety. The "Guards of Finland" helped crush the Polish rebellion and fought in the Russo-Turkish conflict. This, along with the French and English attacks on Finnish harbours during the Crimean War, accentuated the bond between the two countries. Many Finns came to regard the tsar as their own monarch.

There was, however, an increasingly active **Finnish-language movement**. A student leader, the future statesman **Johan Vilhelm Snellman**, had met the tsar and demanded that Finnish replace Swedish as the country's official language. Snellman's slogan "Swedes we are no longer, Russians we cannot become, we must be Finns" became the rallying cry of the **Fennomen**. The Swedish-speaking ruling class, feeling threatened, had Snellman removed from his university post and he retreated to Kuopio to publish newspapers espousing his beliefs. His opponents cited Finnish as the language of peasants, unfit for cultured use – a claim undermined by the efforts of a playwright, **Aleksis Kivi**, whose works marked the beginning of Finnish-language theatre. In 1835, the collection of Karelian folk tales published in Finnish by **Elias Lönnrot** as the **Kalevala** became the first written record of Finnish folklore, a solidifying force for standardization of the language and a focal point for Finnish nationalism.

The liberal Tsar Alexander II appointed Snellman to Turku University, from where he went on to become minister of finance. In 1858, Finnish was declared the official language of local government in areas where the majority of the population were Finnish speaking, and the **Finnish Diet**, convened in 1863 for the first time since the Russian takeover, finally gave native-tongued Finns equal status with Swedish speakers.

The increasingly powerful Pan-Slavist contingent in Russia was horrified by the growth of the Finnish timber industry and the rise of trade with the west. They were also unhappy with the special status of the Grand Duchy, considering the Finns an alien race who would contaminate the eastern empire by their links with the west. Tsar Alexander III was not swayed by these opinions but, after his assassination in 1894, Nicholas I came to power and instigated a **Russification process**. Russian was declared the official language, Finnish money was abolished and plans were laid to merge the Finnish army into the Russian army. To pass these measures the tsar drew up the unconstitutional **February Manifesto**.

Opposition came in varying forms. In 1899, a young composer called **Jean Sibelius** wrote his majestic and dynamic *Finlandia*. The Russians banned all performances of it "under any name that indicates its patriotic character", causing Sibelius to publish it as Opus 26 No. 7. The painter **Akseli Gallen-Kallela** ignored international art trends and depicted scenes from the *Kalevala*, as did the poet **Eino Leino**. Students skied to farms all over the country and collected half a million signatures against the manifesto, and over a thousand of Europe's foremost intellectuals signed a document called "Pro-Finlandia".

But these efforts had no effect, and in 1901 the **Conscription Law** was introduced, forcing Finns to serve directly under the tsar in the Russian army. A programme of civil disobedience began, the leaders of which were soon obliged to go underground in Helsinki, where they titled themselves the **Kagel** – borrowing a name used by persecuted Russian Jews. The Finnish population became divided between the "compliants" (acquiescent to the Manifesto) and the "constitutionalists" (against the Manifesto), causing the rival sides to do their shopping in different stores and even splitting families.

In 1905, the Russians suffered defeat in their war with Japan, and the general strike that broke out in their country spread to Finland, the Finnish labour movement being represented by the Social Democratic Party. The revolutionary spirit that was moving through Russia encouraged the conservative Finnish Senate to reach a compromise with the demands of the Social Democrats, and the result was a gigantic upheaval in the Finnish parliamentary system. In 1906, the country adopted a single-chamber parliament (the **Eduskunta**) elected by national suffrage – Finnish women being the first in Europe to get the vote. In the first election under the new system the Social Democrats won eighty seats out of the total of two hundred, making it the most left-wing legislature seen so far in Europe.

Any laws passed in Finland, however, still needed the ratification of the tsar, who now viewed Finland as a dangerous forum for leftist debate (the exiled Lenin met Stalin for the first time in Tampere). In 1910, Nicholas II removed the new parliament's powers and reinstated the Russification programme. Two years later the **Parity Act** gave Russians in Finland status equal to Finns, enabling them to hold seats in the Senate and posts in the civil service. The outspoken anti-tsarist parliamentary speaker **P.E. Svinhufvud** was exiled to Siberia for a second time.

As World War I commenced, Finland was obviously allied with Russia and endured a commercial blockade, food shortages and restrictions on civil liberties, but did not actually fight on the tsar's behalf. Germany promised Finland total autonomy in the event of victory for the Kaiser and provided clandestine military training to about two thousand Finnish students – the Jäger movement who reached Germany through Sweden and later fought against the Russians as a light infantry battalion on the Baltic front.

Towards independence

When the tsar was overthrown in 1917, the Russian provisional government under Kerensky declared the measures taken against Finland null and void and restored the previous level of autonomy, so making Finland an **independent nation-state**. Within Finland there was still uncertainty over the country's constitutional bonds with Russia. The conservative view was that prerogative powers should be passed from the deposed ruler to the provisional government, while socialists held that the provisional government had no right to exercise power in Finland and that supreme authority should be passed to the Eduskunta.

Under the **Power Act**, the Eduskunta vested in itself supreme authority within Finland, leaving only control of foreign and military matters residing with the Russians. Kerensky refused to recognize the Power Act and dissolved the Finnish parliament, forcing a fresh election. This time a bigger poll returned a conservative majority.

Around the country there had been widespread labour disputes and violent confrontations between strikers and strike-breaking mobs hired by landowners. The Social Democrats sanctioned the formation of an armed workers' guard, soon to be called the **Red Guard**, in response to the growing **White Guard**, a right-wing private army operating in the virtual absence of a regular police force.

After the Bolsheviks took power in Russia, the conservative Finnish government became fearful of Soviet involvement in Finnish affairs and a de facto **statement of independence** was made. The socialists, by now totally excluded from government, declared their support for independence but insisted that it should be reached through negotiation with the Soviet Union. Instead, on December 6, a draft of an independent constitution drawn up by **K.J. Ståhlberg** was approved by the Eduskunta. After a delay of three weeks it was formally recognized by the Soviet leader, Lenin.

The civil war

In asserting its new authority, the government repeatedly clashed with the labour movement. The Red Guard, which had reached an uneasy truce with the Social Democratic leadership, was involved in gun-running between Viipuri and Petrograd, and efforts by the White Guard to halt it led to full-scale fighting. A vote passed by the Eduskunta on January 12, 1918, empowered the government to create a police force to restore law and order. On January 25 the White Guard was legitimized as the Civil Guard.

In Helsinki, a special committee of the Social Democrats took the decision to resist the Civil Guard and seize power, effectively pledging themselves to **civil war**. On January 27 and 28, a series of occupations enabled leftist committees to take control of the capital and the major towns of the south. Three government ministers who evaded capture fled to Vaasa and formed a rump administration. Meanwhile, a Finnish-born aristocrat, **C.G.E. Mannerheim**, who had served as a cavalry officer in the Russian army, arrived at the request of the government in Ostrobothnia, a region dominated by right-wing farmers, to train a force to fight the Reds.

The Whites were in control of Ostrobothnia, northern Finland and parts of Karelia, and were connected by a railway from Vaasa to Käkisalmi on Lake Ladoga. Although the Reds were numerically superior they were poorly equipped and poorly trained, and failed to break the enemy's line of communication. Tampere fell to the Whites in March. At the same time, a German force landed on the south coast, their assistance requested by White Finns in Berlin (although Mannerheim opposed their involvement). Surrounded, the leftists' resistance collapsed in April.

Throughout the conflict, the Social Democratic Party maintained a high level of unity. While containing revolutionary elements, it was led mainly by socialists seeking to retain parliamentary democracy, and believing their fight was against a bourgeois force seeking to impose right-wing values on the newly independent state. Their arms, however, were supplied by the Soviet Union, causing the White taunt that the Reds were "aided by foreign bayonets". Many of the revolutionary socialists within the party fled to Russia after the civil war, where they formed the Finnish Communist Party. The harsh treatment of the Reds who were captured – 8000 were executed and 80,000 were imprisoned in camps where more than 9000 died from hunger or disease – fired a resentment that would last for generations. The Whites regarded the war as one of liberation, ridding the country of Russians and the Bolshevik influence, and setting the course for an anti-Russian Finnish nationalism. Mannerheim and the strongly pro-German Jäger contingent were keen to continue east, to gain the whole of Karelia from the Russians, but the possibility of direct Finnish assistance to the Russian White Army – who were seeking to overthrow the Bolshevik government – came to nothing thanks to the Russian Whites' refusal to guarantee recognition of Finland's independent status.

Later that year, a **provisional government of independent Karelia** was set up in Uhtua. Its formation was masterminded by Red Finns, who ensured that its claims to make Karelia a totally independent region did not accord with the desires of the Finnish government. The provisional government's congress, held the following year, also confirmed a wish for separation from the Soviet Union and requested the removal of the Soviet troops; this was agreed, with a proviso that Soviet troops retained a right to be based in eastern Karelia. The eventual collapse of the talks caused the provisional government and its supporters to flee to Finland as a Finnish battalion of the Soviet Red Army moved in and occupied the area. Subsequently the Karelian Workers' Commune, motivated by the Finnish Communists and backed by Soviet decree, was formed.

A few days later, the state of war which existed between Finland and Russia was formally ended by the **Treaty of Tartu**. The existence of the Karelian Workers' Commune gave the Soviet negotiators a pretext for refusing Finnish demands for Karelian self-determination, claiming the new set-up to be an expression of the Karelian people's wishes. The treaty was signed in an air of animosity. A bald settlement of border issues, it gave Finland the Petsamo area, a strategic shoulder of land extending to the Arctic coast, with an ice-free harbour on the Arctic coast, providing valuable access to a northern waterway.

The republic

The White success in the civil war led to a right-wing government with a pro-German majority, which wanted to establish Finland as a monarchy rather than the republic allowed for under the 1917 declaration of independence. Although twice defeated in the Eduskunta, Prime Minister **J.K. Paasikivi** evoked a clause in the Swedish Form of Government from 1772, making legal the election of a king. As a result, the Finnish crown was offered to a German, Friedrich Karl, Prince of Hessen. Immediately prior to German defeat in World War I, the prince declined the invitation. The victorious Allies insisted on a new Finnish government and a fresh general election if they were to recognize the nation's independent status. Since the country was now compelled to look to the Allies for future assistance, the request was complied with, sealing Finland's future as a republic. The first president was the liberal **Ståhlberg**.

After years of rapidly increasing prosperity and great social reform including compulsory schooling, religious freedom and improved social services, Finnish economic development halted abruptly following the world slump of the late 1920s. A series of strikes culminated in a dock workers' dispute which began in May 1928 and continued for almost a year. It was settled by the intervention of the minister for social affairs on terms perceived as a defeat for the strikers. The dispute was seen by the right as a Communist-inspired attempt to ruin the Finnish export trade at a time when the Soviet Union had re-entered the world timber trade. It was also a symbolic ideological clash – a harbinger of events to come.

Moves to outlaw Communist activity had been deemed an infringement of civil rights, but in 1929 the Suomen Lukko was formed to combat Communism legally. It was swiftly succeeded by the more extreme and violent **Lapua Movement** (the name coming from the Ostrobothnian town, where a parade of Communist youth had been brought to a bloody end by "White" farmers). The Lapuans rounded up suspected Communists and Communist sympathizers, and drove them to the Russian border, insisting that they walk across. Even the former president, Ståhlberg, was kidnapped and dumped at the eastern town of Joensuu. The Lapuans' actions were only half-heartedly condemned by the non-socialist parties, and in private they were supported. But when the Lapuans began advocating a complete overthrow of the political system, much of this tacit approval dried up.

The government obtained a two-thirds majority in the elections of October 1930 and amended the constitution to make Communist activity illegal. This was expected to placate the Lapuans but instead they issued even more extreme demands, including the abolition of the Social Democrats. In 1932, a coup d'état was attempted by a Lapuan group who prevented a socialist member of parliament from addressing a meeting in Mäntsälä, 50km north of Helsinki. They refused to disperse, despite shots being fired by police, and sent for backup assistance from Lapuan bases around the country. The Lapuan leadership took up the cause and broadcast demands for a new government. They were unsuccessful due to the loyalty of the troops who surrounded the town on the orders of the then prime minister, Svinhufvud. Following this, the Lapuans were outlawed, although their leaders received only minor punishments for their deeds. Several of them regrouped as the Nazi-style Patriotic People's Movement. But unlike the parallel movements in Europe, there was little in Finland on which Nazism could focus mass hatred and, despite winning a few parliamentary seats, the movement quickly dwindled into insignificance.

The Finnish **economy** recovered swiftly, and much international goodwill was generated when the country became the only nation to pay its war reparations to the US in full after World War I. Finland joined the League of Nations hoping for a guarantee of its eastern border, but by 1935 the League's weakness was apparent and the Finns looked to traditionally neutral **Scandinavia** for protection as Europe moved towards war.

World War II

The Nazi–Soviet Non-Aggression Pact of August 1939 put Finland firmly into the Soviet sphere. Stalin had compelled Estonia, Latvia and Lithuania to allow Russian bases on their land, and by October was demanding a chunk of the Karelian isthmus from Finland to protect Leningrad, as well as a lease the Hanko peninsula on the Finnish Baltic coast. Russian troops were heading towards the Finnish border from Murmansk, and on November 30 the Karelian isthmus was attacked – an act that triggered the **Winter War**.

Stalin had had the tsarist military commanders executed, and his troops were led by young Communists well versed in ideology but ignorant of war strategy. Informed that the Finnish people would welcome them as liberators, the Soviet soldiers anticipated little resistance to their invasion. They expected to reach the Finnish west coast within ten days and therefore carried no overcoats, had little food and camped each night in open fields. The Finns, although vastly outnumbered, were defending their homes and farms as well as their hard-won independence. Familiarity with the terrain enabled them to conceal themselves in the forests and attack through stealth – and they were prepared for the winter temperatures, which plunged to -30°C (-18°F). The Russians were slowly picked off and their camps frequently surrounded and destroyed.

While Finland gained the world's admiration, no practical help was forthcoming, and it became simply a matter of time before Stalin launched a better-supplied, unstoppable advance. It came during February 1940, and the Finnish government was forced to ask for peace. This was granted under the **Treaty of Moscow**, signed in March by President **Kyösti Kallio**, who said "let the hand wither that signs such a paper" as his hand put pen to paper. The treaty ceded 11 percent of Finnish territory to the Soviet Union – there was a mass exodus from these areas, with nearly half a million people travelling west to the new boundaries of Finland. Kyösti Kallio was later stricken by paralysis on his right side.

The period immediately following the Winter War left Finland in a difficult position. Before the war, Finland had produced all its own food but was dependent on imported fertilizers. Supplies of grain, which had been coming from Russia, were halted as part of Soviet pressure for increased transit rights and access to the important nickel-producing mines in Petsamo. Finland became reliant on grain from Germany and British shipments to the Petsamo coast, which were interupted when Germany invaded Norway. In return for providing arms, Germany was given transit rights through Finland. Legally, this required the troops to be constantly moving, but a permanent force became stationed at Rovaniemi.

The Finnish leadership knew that Germany was secretly preparing to attack the Soviet Union, and a broadcast from Berlin had spoken of a "united front" from Norway to Poland at a time when Finland was officially outside the Nazi sphere. Within Finland there was little support for the Nazis, but there was a fear of Soviet occupation. While Finland clung to its neutrality, refusing to fight unless attacked, it was drawn closer and closer to Germany. Soviet air raids on several Finnish towns in June 1941 finally led Finland into the war on the side of the Nazis. The ensuing conflict with the Russians, fought with the primary purpose of regaining territory lost in the Winter War, became known as the **Continuation War**. The bulk of the land ceded under the Treaty of Moscow was recovered by the end of August. After this, Mannerheim, who commanded the Finnish troops, ignored Nazi encouragement to assist in their attack on Leningrad. A request from the British prime minister, Winston Churchill, that the Finns cease their advance, was also refused, although Mannerheim didn't cut the Murmansk rail line which was moving Allied supplies. Even so, Britain was forced to acknowledge the predicament of its ally, the Soviet Union, and declared war on Finland in December 1941.

In 1943, the German defeat at Stalingrad, which made Allied victory almost inevitable, had a profound impact in Finland. Mannerheim called a meeting of inner-cabinet ministers and decided to seek a truce with the Soviet Union. The US stepped forward as mediator but announced that the peace terms set by Moscow were too severe to be worthy of negotiation. Germany, meanwhile, had learned of the Finnish initiative and demanded an undertaking that Finland would not seek peace with Russia, threatening to withdraw supplies if it was not given. (The Germans were also unhappy with Finnish sympathy for Jews – several hundred who had escaped from central Europe were saved from the concentration camps by being granted Finnish citizenship.) Simultaneously, a Russian advance into Karelia made Finland dependent on German arms to launch a counterattack. An agreement with the Germans was signed by President **Risto Ryti** in June 1944 without the consent of the Eduskunta, thereby making the deed invalid when he ceased to be president.

Ryti resigned the presidency at the beginning of August and Mannerheim informed Germany that the agreement was no longer binding. A peace treaty with the Soviet Union was signed in Moscow two weeks later. Under its terms, Finland was forced to give up the Pestamo region and the border was restored to its 1940 position. The Hanko peninsula was returned, but instead the Porkkala peninsula, nearer to Helsinki, was to be leased to the Soviet Union for fifty years. There were stinging reparations, and the Finns had to drive the remaining Germans out of the country within two weeks. This was easily done in the south, but the bitter fighting that took place in Lapland caused the total destruction of many towns. It was further agreed that organizations disseminating anti-Soviet views within Finland would be dissolved, and that Finland would accept an Allied Control Commission to oversee war trials.

The postwar period

After the war, the Communist Party was legalized and, along with militant socialists expelled from the Social Democratic Party, formed a broad leftist umbrella organization – the **Finnish People's Democratic League**. Their efforts to absorb the Social Democrats were resisted by that party's moderate leadership, who regarded Communism as "poison to the Finnish people". In the first peace-time poll, the Democratic League went to the electorate with a populist rather than revolutionary manifesto – something that was to characterize future Finnish Communism. Both they and the Social Democrats attained approximately a quarter of the vote. Bolstered by two Social Democratic defections, the Democratic League narrowly became the largest party in the Eduskunta. The two of them, along with the Agrarian Party, formed an alliance ("The Big Three Agreement") that held the balance of power in a coalition government under the premiership of Paasikivi.

Strikes instigated by Communist-controlled trade unions allowed the Social Democrats to accuse the Democratic League of seeking to undermine the production of machinery and other goods destined for the Soviet Union under the terms of the war reparation agreement, thereby creating a scenario for Soviet invasion. Charges of Communist vote-rigging in trade union ballots helped the Social Democrats to gain control of the unions. The Democratic League won only 38 seats in the general election of 1948, and rejected the token offer of four posts in the new government, opting instead to stay in opposition. Its electoral campaign wasn't helped by the rumour – almost certainly groundless – that it was planning a Soviet-backed coup.

To ensure that the terms of the peace agreement were adhered to, the Soviet-dominated Allied Control Commission stayed in Finland until 1947. Its presence engendered a tense atmosphere both on the streets of Helsinki – there were several incidents of violence against Soviet officers – and in the numerous clashes with the Finnish government over the war trials. Unlike the eastern European countries under full Soviet occupation, Finland was able to carry out its own trials, but had to satisfy the Commission that they were conducted properly. Delicate manoeuvring by the Chief of Justice, **Urho Kekkonen**, resulted in comparatively short prison sentences for the accused, the longest being ten years for Risto Ryti.

The uncertain relationship between Finland and the Soviet Union was resolved, to some extent, by the signing of the **Treaty of Friendship, Cooperation and Mutual Assistance** (FCMA) in 1948. It affirmed Finnish responsibility for its own defence and pledged the country not to join any alliance hostile to the Soviet Union. In the suspicious atmosphere of the Cold War, the treaty was perceived by the Western powers to place Finland firmly under Soviet influence. The Soviets' insistence that the treaty was a guarantee of neutrality was viewed as hypocritical, given that they were still leasing the Porkkala peninsula. When it became clear that Finland was not becoming a Soviet satellite and had full control over its internal affairs, the US reinstated credit facilities – carefully structured to avoid financing anything that would be of help to the Soviets – and Finland was admitted to Western financial institutions such as the IMF and World Bank.

The postwar **economy** was dominated by the reparations demand. Much of the bill was paid off in ships and machinery, which established engineering as a major industry. The escalating world demand for timber products boosted exports, but inflation soared and led to frequent wage disputes. In 1949, an attempt to enforce a piece-work rate in a pulp factory in Kemi culminated in two workers being shot by police, a state of emergency being declared in the town and the arrest of Communist leaders. Economic conflicts reached a climax in 1956 after right-wingers in the Eduskunta had blocked an annual extension of government controls on wages and prices. This caused a sharp rise in the cost of living and the trade unions demanded appropriate pay increases. A general strike followed, lasting for three weeks until the strikers' demands were met. Any benefit, however, was quickly nullified by further price rises.

In 1957, a split occurred in the Social Democrats between urban and rural factions, the former seeking increased industrialization and the streamlining of unprofitable farms, the latter pursuing high agricultural subsidies. By 1959 a group of breakaway ruralists had set up the Small Farmers' Social Democratic Union, causing a rift within the country's internal politics that was to have important repercussions in Finland's dealings with the Soviet Union. Although the government had no intention of changing its foreign policy, the Social Democrat's chairman, **Väinö Tanner**, had a well-known antipathy to the Soviet Union. Coupled with a growing number of anti-Soviet newspaper editorials, this precipitated the **"night frost"** of 1958. The Soviet leader, Khrushchev, suspended imports and deliveries of machinery, causing a rise in Finnish unemployment. **Kekkonen**, elected president in 1956, personally intervened in the crisis by meeting with Khrushchev, so angering the Social Democrats, who accused Kekkonen of behaving undemocratically; meanwhile, the Agrarians were lambasted for failing to stand up to Soviet pressure.

Throughout the early 1960s there was mounting dissatisfaction within the People's Democratic League towards the old pro-Moscow leadership. In 1965, a moderate non-Communist was elected as the League's general secretary, and two years later he became chairman; a similar change took place in the Communist leadership of the trade unions. The new-look Communists pledged their desire for a share in government. The election of May 1966 resulted in a "popular front" government dominated by the Social Democrats and the People's Democratic League, under the prime ministership of **Rafael Paasio**.

This brought to an end a twenty-year spell of centre-right governments in which the crucial pivot had been the Agrarian Party. In 1965, the Agrarians changed their name to the Centre Party, aiming to modernize their image and become more attractive to the urban electorate. A challenge to this new direction was mounted by the **Finnish Rural Party**, founded by a breakaway group of Agrarians in the late 1950s, who mounted an increasingly influential campaign on behalf of "the forgotten people" – farmers and smallholders in declining rural areas. In the election of 1970 they gained ten percent of the vote, but in subsequent years lost support through internal divisions.

The Communists retained governmental posts until 1971, when they too were split – between the young "reformists" who advocated continued participation in government, and the older, hard-line "purists" who were frustrated by the failure to implement socialist economic policies and preferred to stay in opposition.

Modern Finland

Throughout the postwar years Finland promoted itself vigorously as a **neutral country**. It joined the United Nations in 1955 and Finnish soldiers became an integral part of the UN Peace-Keeping Force. In 1969, preparations were started for the European Security Conference in Helsinki, and in 1972 the city was the venue for the **Strategic Arms Limitation Talks** (SALT), underlining a Finnish role in mediation between the superpowers. But an attempt to have a clause stating Finland's neutrality inserted into the 1970 extension-signing of the FCMA Treaty was opposed by the Soviet Union, whose foreign secretary, Andrei Gromyko, had a year earlier defined Finland not as neutral but as a "peace-loving neighbour of the Soviet Union".

In 1971, the revelations of a Czech defector, General Sejna, suggesting that the Soviet army was equipped to take over Finland within 24 hours should Soviet defences be compromised, brought a fresh wave of uncertainty to relations with its eastern neighbour, as did the sudden withdrawal of the Soviet ambassador, allegedly for illicit scheming with the People's Democratic League.

The stature of Kekkonen as a world leader guaranteed continued support for his presidency. But his commitment to the Paasikivi-Kekkonen line ensured that nothing potentially upsetting to the Soviet Union was allowed to surface in Finnish politics, giving – as some thought – the Soviet Union a covert influence on Finland's internal affairs. Opposition to Kekkonen was simply perceived as an attempt to undermine the Paasikivi-Kekkonen line. Equally, the unchallengeable nature of Kekkonen's presidency was considered to be beyond his proper constitutional powers. A move in 1974 by an alliance of right-wingers and Social Democrats within the Eduskunta to transfer some of the presidential powers to parliament received a very hostile reaction, emphasizing the almost inviolate position that Kekkonen enjoyed. Kekkonen was re-elected in 1978, although forced to stand down due to illness in 1981.

Because Finland is heavily dependent on foreign trade, its well-being has closely mirrored world trends. The international financial boom of the 1960s enabled a range of social legislation to be passed and created a comparatively high standard of living for most Finns – albeit not on the same scale as the rest of Scandinavia. The global **recession** of the 1970s and early 1980s was most dramatically felt when a fall in the world market for wood pulp coincided with a steep increase in the price of oil. Although the country tackled the immediate problems of the recession, industry remained heavily concentrated in the south, causing rural areas further north to experience high rates of unemployment and few prospects for economic growth – save through rising levels of tourism.

The election of 1987 saw a break with the pattern of previous decades. Non-socialist parties made large gains, mainly at the expense of the Rural Party and Communists. The new government of **Harri Holkeri**, however, appeared inept – particularly in its hesitant reaction to events in the Soviet Union and continued deference to Moscow, whether real or apparent. Public disillusionment resulted in large gains for the Centre Party in the election of March 1991. The Centre Party chairman, 47-year-old **Esko Aho**, subsequently became prime minister, leading a new coalition in which many of the members reflected the comparative youth and fresh ideas of its leader.

In 1992, celebrations to mark 75 years of Finnish independence were muted by the realization that the country was entering a highly critical period, facing more problems (few of its own making) than it had for many decades. The end of the Cold War had diminished the value of Finland's hard-won neutrality and the economic and ethnic difficulties in Russia were being watched with trepidation, while another global **recession** hit Finland just as the nation lost its major trading partner – the Soviet Union – of the last fifty years.

Throughout the early 1990s Finland's economic depression was among the worst in the industrial west. Its banking system was in crisis and unemployment figures were almost the highest in Europe, while the country's growing number of asylum seekers became scapegoats for the resultant social problems, culminating in a spate of anti-immigrant violence during the mid-1990s. Such economic and societal strife forced Finland to pin its hopes on closer links with western Europe. On January 1, 1995, Finland became a full member of the **European Union** and, in the same year, the Social Democratic Party's **Martti Ahtisaari** was elected as president, with the general election resulting in a coalition win for the Social Democrats, their Chairman Paavo Lipponen forming a majority government that included conservatives, socialists, the Swedish Folk Party and the Green Party.

By the millennium, as Russia descended into farce, Finland had become more firmly linked to the EU and its economy had recovered sufficiently for it to be accepted into the first wave of countries to join European Monetary Union. In 1999, for the first time, Finland assumed the presidency of the European Union, while President Ahtisaari established himself as an important international statesman through his interventions in the war in Kosovo. When Ahtisaari decided not to seek re-election in 2000, long-standing member of parliament and then foreign minister **Tarja Halonen** ran a victorious campaign and became Finland's first female president. The independent-minded Halonen has since taken an active role in leading the country, while maintaining a 95 percent approval rating in opinion polls; in 2004, she was nominated one of ten *suuret Suomalaiset* "greatest Finns" – the only living person on the list.

The 2006 presidential campaign sparked a nationwide discussion over limiting the president's powers – an issue which brought to light Finnish concern over the degree of "democratic" decision-making effected by current heads of government – as well as talk over the age-old issue of NATO membership and its link to threats of terrorism. Most Finns are concerned that joining NATO would increase Finland's risk of terrorist attacks – by all accounts relatively low compared to its more politically vocal continental neighbours. On January 29, 2006, Halonen was re-elected by tiny margin for a second six-year presidential term. The future of Finland's long-standing neutrality in Europe was the campaign's focal issue, and Halonen's second win suggests that Finland will remain outside NATO until at least 2012.

Economically, Finland's highly educated populace and technological expertise have made it a powerful player in the world IT market, and it consistently ranks among the top three countries in the world for **technological innovation**. Finland's other industrialized sectors have helped it to maintain a per-capita output on par with that of the UK and Germany, and while the country boasts the highest prices in the EU – a whopping 23 percent above the average for EU member states – Finns have been earning money at an unprecedented rate since the turn of the millennium. The Finnish economy has been growing at a steady rate to become one of the wealthiest, heathiest and most competitive in the world, with an estimated 2008 GDP of €192 billion – despite the general global economic downturn and a slowdown in GDP growth from 4.9 percent in 2006 to 2.5 percent in 2008.

The adoption of the **euro** as Finland's currency in 2002 brought a new pride to the Finnish nation after years of living in the shadow of the Soviet Union; political and economic freedom had finally – and, most importantly, tangibly – been won. And with neighbouring Estonia now a full member of the EU, a former foe has emerged from behind the Iron Curtain to establish itself as a trade and tourism ally on equitable, if not entirely equal, footing.

But while EU membership has provided a new sense of security and confidence, the contemporary picture is not entirely rosy: the age-old issue of alcoholism and the chaos of Russia's gangster economy on the doorstep provide major worries, as do continuing debates around the role of the welfare state. The hot potato of Karelia has also crept steadily into public debate as Halonen has endeavoured to strengthen cultural and economic ties with Putin's Russia. Other pressing issues include the need to diversify an economy that is over-reliant on the Nokia phone company, and the means by which to continue development in rural areas without the support of big government subsidies. Thankfully, **unemployment** has been on the decline for nearly a decade, with the 2008 rate of 6.2 percent, about half what it had been just ten years previously. But as the baby-boomers of the early postwar period near retirement age, the labour force will need to be further empowered if Finland hopes to continue to provide adequate levels of care for its elderly and poor.

How these issues are addressed remains Finland's major concern heading into the second decade of the new millennium. However, general economic concerns notwithstanding, it's the role of the **environment** that's likely to grab the headlines in the coming years. After numerous delays, construction of Finland's fifth nuclear power station is slated to finish in late 2011 (at which point it will be more than fifty percent over budget). Once that's completed, nuclear energy will provide well over thirty percent of the country's total energy needs – Finland is one of the highest energy consumers in the world per capita due to frigid winters and the needs of the paper and wood industries, and at the moment, the country is totally dependent on Russia for natural gas, as well as for eighty percent of its oil. All this development comes at a time when most of the rest of Europe – and neighbouring Sweden – is scaling down nuclear power because of excessive cost, increasing fears of pollution and the possibility of terrorist attacks. While Finland does currently spend close to €1 billion annually on environmental protection, and is considered the most successful of all EU members in its efforts to achieve sustainable development, questions are being raised about the security and efficacy of the government's energy projects, not least by the vocal Green Party, which bailed out of the government coalition in 2002 when approval for construction of the new nuclear plant, Okiluoto 3, was approved. Groups such as Greenpeace are regularly lobbying Finnish ministers for increased energy efficiency, reduced power consumption and the introduction of eco-friendly measures such as improved public transport and the use of bicycles. Meanwhile, there are already talks in government of plans for proposing an additional three nuclear reactor plants. A heated public debate on these very sensitive issues is looking to put further pressure on the tradition of Finnish consensus politics.

Books

Precious few travellers have written in English about the joys of journeying around Scandinavia, though you might always dig out a copy of an old Baedeker's Norway and Sweden, if only for the phrasebook, from which you can learn how to pronounce "We must rope ourselves together to cross this glacier." Neither has Scandinavian history been a major preoccupation – with the notable exception of the Vikings, who have attracted the attention of a veritable raft of historians and translators whose works have focused on the surviving sagas, a rich body of work mostly written in Iceland in the ninth and tenth centuries. Scandinavian fiction is, however, an entirely different matter, with a flood of translations appearing on the market, a charge that has been led by the immaculate crime novels of the Swede Henning Mankell.

Of the **publishers**, Peter Owen (ⓌWww.peterowen.com) produces fine new translations of modern Scandinavian novels, as does Norvik Press (ⓌWww.llt .uea.ac.uk/norvik_press), which also maintains an excellent back catalogue of classic Scandinavian novels and plays and some Scandinavian literary criticism. Finally, *The Babel Guide to Scandinavian Fiction in Translation* by Paul Binding reviews books available in English by leading Scandinavian writers – both classic and modern – though it could do with being updated (it was published in 1999).

Most of the books listed below should be readily available, though some are currently **out of print** (denoted o/p) – even these, though, are often available via websites such as Amazon. Titles marked with the 🎿 symbol are particularly recommended.

Travel and general

Jeremy Cherfas *The Hunting of Whale*. Subtitled "A tragedy that must end", this is a convincing condemnation of whaling and all those – like Norway – involved in it.

Christer Elfving & Petra de Hamer *New Scandinavian Cooking*. A cook's tour through Scandinavia's capital cities mixing history, culinary trends and tips on the hottest chefs and restaurants with delicious modern recipes.

Tony Griffiths *Scandinavia*. A wide-ranging look at the cultural, artistic and political developments and exchanges of the last two centuries that have helped shape the Scandinavian psyche.

Sven Lindqvist *Bench Press*. Delightful little book delving into the nature of weight training – and the Swedish/Scandinavian attitude to it. Wry and perceptive cultural commentary.

Christopher Moseley (ed.) *From Baltic Shores*. Anthology of contemporary short stories from Denmark, Finland, Sweden, Estonia, Latvia and Lithuania. Winter and the harshness of the climate are a recurring theme.

Ben Nimmo *In Forkbeard's Wake: Coasting Around Scandinavia*. Light and lively account of the author's sailing trip around Scandinavia, brimming with sailing mishaps and encounters with Nordic types – divers, fishermen, archeologists and a drunk Swedish dentist. An all too rare modern travel book on the area.

🎿 **Christoph Ransmayr** *The Terrors of Ice and Darkness*. Clever mingling of fact and fiction as the book's main character follows the route of the 1873 Austro–Hungarian expedition to the Arctic. A story of obsession and, ultimately, madness.

Roger Took *Running with Reindeer*. A thoughtful account of Took's extended visit to – and explorations of – Russia's Kola Peninsula in the 1990s, with much to say about the Sámi and their current predicaments.

Mary Wollstonecraft *A Short Residence in Sweden, Norway and Denmark*. A curiously self-indulgent account of Wollstonecraft's three-month solo sojourn through southern Scandinavia in 1795.

General history

T.K. Derry *A History of Scandinavia*. Authoritative history from the Stone Age to the 1990s. Rather dense and scholarly, but one of the few recent works on the topic in paperback.

P.V. Glob *The Bog People*. A fascinating study of the various Iron Age bodies discovered fully preserved in north-western European peat bogs, most of them in Denmark. Excellent, if ghoulish, photographs.

Tony Griffiths *Scandinavia: At War with Trolls – A Modern History from the Napoleonic Era to the Third Millennium*. Engaging title for an engaging, well-written and well-researched book covering its subject in a very manage-able 320 pages. First published in 2004.

Knut Helle et al. *The Cambridge History of Scandinavia*. Comprehensive history, from the Stone Age onwards in three whopping (and expensive) volumes. No stone is left unturned.

John van der Kiste *Northern Crowns: Kings of Modern Scandinavia*. All you

ever wanted to know about the Scandinavian monarchies, from the nineteenth century to the present day.

Chris Mann *Hitler's Arctic War*. A new account of one of the most critical – yet often overlooked – campaigns of World War II, chronicling the German campaigns in the inhospitable environment of the Arctic, both on sea and land.

Geoffrey Parker *The Thirty Years' War*. First published in the 1980s, and subsequently reprinted on several occasions, this book provides the authoritative account of the pan-European war that so deeply affected Scandinavia in general and Sweden in particular. Superbly written and researched.

Alexander Rumble (ed.) *The Reign of Cnut*. The king of much of Scandinavia and England, Cnut was the dominant figure in northern Europe in the early eleventh century. This scholarly study examines the man and his milieu.

The Vikings and Norse mythology

Johannes Brøndsted *The Vikings* (o/p). Classic and immensely readable account of the Viking period, with valuable sections on social and cultural life, art, religious beliefs and customs. Out of print, but still easy to get hold of.

H.R. Ellis Davidson *The Gods and Myths of Northern Europe*. A handy, first-rate companion to the sagas, this "who's who" of Norse mythology includes some useful reviews of the more obscure gods.

John Haywood *Encyclopaedia of the Viking Age*. Well-selected and well-written accounts of everything to do with the Vikings and their era – from Adam of Bremen to York.

Gwyn Jones *A History of the Vikings*. Superbly crafted, erudite account of the Vikings, with sections on every aspect of their history and culture. The same author also wrote *Scandinavian Legends and Folk Tales* (o/p), an excellent and enjoyable analysis of its subject.

🏃 **F. Donald Logan** *The Vikings in History*. Scholarly – and radical – re-examination of the Vikings' impact on medieval Europe, indispensable for the Vikingophile.

Andrew Orchard *Cassell's Dictionary of Norse Myth and Legend*. Thorough guide to the complete cast of Scandinavian gods, trolls, heroes and monsters, complete with the social and historical background to the myths and coverage of topics such as burial rites, sacrificial practices and runes.

Jane Smiley et al. *The Sagas of the Icelanders*. Easy to read translations of all the main sagas – galloping tales from medieval Iceland. The index makes it an excellent reference book too.

Snorri Sturluson *Egil's Saga, Laxdaela Saga, Njal's Saga* and *King Harald's Saga*. Icelandic sagas, written in the early years of the thirteenth century, but relating tales of ninth- and tenth-century derring-do. There's clan warfare in the Laxdaela and Njal sagas, more bloodthirstiness in Egil's and a bit more biography in King Harald's, penned to celebrate one of the last and most ferocious Viking chieftains – Harald Hardråda.

Denmark

Though the amount of English-language books on Denmark is nowhere near that of many other European countries, there are a few very good finds, many of which we've listed below. For literary fiction, the most recent information on who's been published where in English translation can be found at ⓦ www .literaturenet.dk.

History, philosophy and culture

🏃 **W.H. Auden** (ed.) *The Living Thoughts of Kierkegaard*. In this bold anthology of the Danish philosopher's work, the celebrated poet Auden selected his favourite Kierkegaard essays and wrote a sparkling introductory essay contextualizing his writings and ideas.

Mette Hjort *Small Nation, Global Cinema*. A must for anyone interested in modern Danish cinema, this book looks at the emerging success of the New Danish Cinema, focusing on themes of nationalism, cultural diffusion and representation of ethnic minorities, with emphasis on the Dogme 95 movement. Though it's a decidedly academic publication, the language still makes it very accessible to most readers.

Knud Jespersen *A History of Denmark*. The only modern history of Denmark available in English, this short book provides a wealth of information on royalty, the Church, economics and politics, as well as some interesting insights into what has created a specific Danish cultural identity. The clipped style makes it a very quick read.

🏃 **Søren Kierkegaard** *Either/Or*. Kierkegaard's most important work (and his most approachable), a monumental philosophical tract packed with wry and wise musings on love, life and death in nineteenth-century Danish society. The collection includes the (in)famous "Seducer's Diary", the disturbing narrative of a man who explores his sense of detachment by deliberately arousing the passion of a young society girl.

Literature and biography

Hans Christian Andersen *Hans Andersen's Fairy Tales*. Still the most internationally prominent figure of Danish literature, Andersen's fairy tales are so widely translated and read that the full clout of their allegorical content is often overlooked: interestingly, his first collection of such tales (published in 1835) was condemned by many critics for its "violence and questionable morals". *Travels* is a small collection of accounts written while travelling in Europe and the Mediterranean, stories that offer a unique insight into Andersen's powers of observation and social critique. His autobiography, *The Fairy Tale of My Life* is an interesting perspective on the author's life. It makes a fine alternative to the half-dozen or so modern biographical portraits now available – though don't expect too much exploration of the author's darker sides.

Steen Steensen Blicher *Diary of a Parish Clerk; Twelve Stories*. Blicher was a keen observer of Jutish life, writing stark, realistic tales in local dialect and gathering a seminal collection of Jutish folk tales – published as *E. Bindstouw* in 1842.

Karen Blixen (Isak Dinesen) *Out of Africa*. This account of Blixen's attempts to run a coffee farm in Kenya after divorce from her husband is a lyrical and moving tale, and was turned into an Oscar winner by Sydney Pollack. But it's in *Seven Gothic Tales* that Blixen's fiction was at its zenith: a flawlessly executed, weird, emotive work, full of twists in plot and strange, ambiguous characterization.

Tove Ditlevsen *Early Spring*. An autobiographical novel of growing up in the working-class Vesterbro district of Copenhagen during the 1930s. As an evocation of childhood and early adulthood, it's totally captivating.

Per Olov Enquist *The Visit of the Royal Physician*. Fascinating, witty and intriguing novel set in the Danish court in the 1760s: the king is a half-wit, the queen has a lover and the forces of the Enlightenment are ranged against the reactionaries. Great stuff.

Jens Christian Grøndahl *Silence in October*. One of Europe's most widely read contemporary authors, Grøndahl already has over a dozen novels under his belt, several of which have recently been made available in English translation. *Silence* is his ninth, a stream-of-consciousness tale in which an art critic tries to come to terms with the unexpected death of his wife. The author delicately weaves the relationships between time, space and form as a metaphor for comprehending human emotion.

Martin A. Hansen *The Liar*. An engaging novel, showing why Hansen was one of Denmark's most perceptive – and popular – authors during the postwar period. Set in the 1950s, the story examines the inner thoughts of a lonely schoolteacher living on a small Danish island.

Peter Høeg *Miss Smilla's Feeling for Snow*. Høeg is easily Denmark's most famous modern author. A worldwide bestseller and Høeg's best-known work, this compelling thriller deals with Danish colonialism in Greenland and the issue of cultural identity. Other acclaimed books include *Borderliners* and his most recent novel, *The Silent Girl*, about a world-famous circus artist whose former pupil, a 10-year-old girl, is kidnapped.

Judith Thurman *Isak Dinesen: The Life of Karen Blixen*. The most penetrating biography of Blixen, elucidating details of the farm period not found in Blixen's two "Africa" books.

Rose Tremain *Music and Silence*. Captivating historical novel that follows the lives of Christian IV, his consort, his English lutenist and their lovers. Life in the many castles around Denmark is brilliantly described, and the novel provides a fascinating insight into Danish aspirations and superstitions during the period.

Jackie Wullschlager *Hans Christian Andersen: The Life of a Storyteller*. Published in 2002, this finely documented work examines the misery of Andersen's childhood, his subsequent rapid success and his troubled sexuality, arguing that it was the shock and power of these experiences that fuelled many of his mournful tales.

Norway

The Vikings have attracted the attention of dozens of English-speaking historians, though otherwise books on Norway are thin on the ground. There is however, something of a mini-boom in contemporary Norwegian crime fiction, with Karin Fossum leading the literary charge.

Travel and general

Thor Heyerdahl *The Kon-Tiki Expedition*. You may want to read this after visiting Oslo's Kon-Tiki Museum. Heyerdahl's account of the Kon-Tiki expedition aroused huge interest when it was first published, and it remains a ripping yarn – though surprisingly few people care to read it today. Heyerdahl's further exploits are related in *The Ra Expeditions* and *The Tigris Expedition* as is his long research trip to Easter Island in *Aku-Aku: The Secret of Easter Island*.

Mark Kurlansky *Cod: A Biography of the Fish that Changed the World*. This wonderful book tracks the life and times of the cod and the generations of fishermen who have lived off it. There are sections on overfishing and the fish's breeding habits, and recipes are provided too. Norwegians figure frequently – after all, cod was the staple diet of much of the country for centuries.

Bernhard Pollmann *Norway – South, A Rother Walking Guide*. Fifty suggested hikes dotted across southern Norway. The descriptions are clear and concise, the photos helpful and the maps useful for preparation. The walks themselves range from the short and easy to the long and very strenuous. Probably the best of its type on the market.

General history and mythology

Peter Christen Asbjørnsen and Jørgen Moe *Norvegian Folk Tales*. Of all the many books on Norwegian folk tales, this is the edition you want – the illustrations by Erik Werenskiold and Theodor Kittelsen are superb.

Fredrik Dahl *Quisling: A Study in Treachery*. A comprehensive biography of the world's most famous traitor, Vidkun Quisling, who got his just deserts at the end of World War II. Well-written and incisive exploration of Quisling's complex character – and one that also sheds a grim light on the nature and extent of Norwegian collaboration. Published by Cambridge University Press.

Rolf Danielsen et al. *Norway: A History from the Vikings to Our Own Times* (o/p). Thoughtful and well-presented account investigating the social and economic development of Norway – a modern and well-judged book that avoids the "kings and queens" approach to its subject.

🏃 **David Howarth** *Shetland Bus*. Entertaining and fascinating in equal measure, this excellent book, written by one of the British naval officers involved, details the clandestine wartime missions which shuttled between the Shetlands and occupied Norway.

Kathleen Stokker *Folklore Fights the Nazis: Humor in Occupied Norway 1940–1945* (o/p). A book that can't help but make you laugh – and one that also provides a real insight into Norwegian society and its subtle mores. The only problem is that Stokker adopts an encyclopedic approach, which means you have to plough through the poor jokes to get to the good ones. Stokker adopted a similar approach to her more recent *Remedies and Rituals: Folk Medicine in Norway and the New Land*.

Literature

🏃 **Kjell Askildsen** *A Sudden Liberating Thought* (o/p). Short stories, in the Kafkaesque tradition, from one of Norway's most uncompromisingly modernist writers.

🏃 **Karin Fossum** *Calling Out for You; Don't Look Back; Black Seconds*. Norway's finest crime writer, Fossum has written a string of superb thrillers in the Inspector Sejer series – and each gives the real flavour of contemporary Norway. These three novels are the best place to get started – but avoid *When the Devil holds the Candle*, which is a bit of a dud.

Jostein Gaarder *Sophie's World*. Hugely popular novel that deserves all the critical praise it has received. Beautifully and gently written, with puffs of whimsy all the way through, it bears comparison with Hawking's *A Brief History of Time*, though the subject matter here is philosophy, and there's an engaging mystery story tucked in too. Also try Gaarder's comparable *Through A Glass Darkly*.

Janet Garton (ed.) *Contemporary Norwegian Women's Writing*. Wide-ranging anthology, beginning with the directly political works of the 1970s and culminating in the more fantastical tales typical of the 2000s. Fiction, drama and poetry all make an appearance and there are lots of issues, too

– from prostitution and abuse through to women's empowerment. Also *New Norwegian Plays*, comprising four plays written between 1979 and 1983, including work by the feminist writer Bjørg Vik and a Brechtian analysis of Europe in the nuclear age by Edvard Hoem.

Knut Hamsun *Hunger*. Norway's leading literary light in the 1920s and early 1930s, Knut Hamsun (1859–1952) was a writer of international acclaim until he disgraced himself by supporting Hitler – for which many Norwegians never forgave him. Of Hamsun's many novels, it was *Hunger* (1890) that made his name, a trip into the psyche of an alienated and angst-ridden young writer, which shocked contemporary readers. In the latter part of his career, Hamsun advocated a return to the soil and basic rural values. He won the Nobel Prize for Literature for a work from this period, *Growth of the Soil*, but you have to be pretty determined to plough through its metaphysical claptrap. In recent years, Hamsun has been tentatively accepted back into the Norwegian literary fold; there's also been a biographical film, *Hamsun*, starring Max von Sydow.

🏃 **Henrik Ibsen** *Four Major Plays*. The key figure of Norwegian literature, Ibsen (see p.192) was a social dramatist with a keen eye for hypocrisy, repression and alienation. Ibsen's most popular plays – primarily *A Doll's House* and *Hedda Gabler* – pop up in all sorts of editions, but this particular collection, in the Oxford World Classics series, contains both these favourites as well as *Ghosts* and *The Master Builder*. What's more, it's inexpensive and translated by one of the leading Ibsen experts, James McFarlane. In print also are several editions of Ibsen's whole oeuvre – the Kessinger Publishing Company's version is currently the least expensive.

Jan Kjærstad et al (eds.) *Leopard VI: The Norwegian Feeling for Real*. Promoted by the queen of Norway no less, this first-rate anthology of modern Norwegian writers hits all the literary buttons – from boozy nights out in Oslo to the loneliness of rural Norway and small-town envy. Contains 28 short stories plus potted biographies of all the writers that appear.

Herbjørg Wassmo *Dina's Book: A Novel*. Set in rural northern Norway in the middle of the nineteenth century, this strange and engaging tale has a plot centred on a powerful but tormented heroine. Also *Dina's Son*, again with a nineteenth-century setting, but with intriguing sections focused on the protagonist's move from rural Norway to the city.

Sweden

There's a surprisingly small number of books available in English on all matters Swedish. Although Swedish publishing houses are producing quality titles – particularly fiction – that are translated into most European languages, remarkably few fin their way into English. What follows is a summary of some of the more readily available publications.

History and politics

Sheri Berman *The Social Democrat Movement*. A comparison of the Swedish and German social democratic system between the First and Second World Wars.

Eric Elstob *Sweden: A Traveller's History* (o/p). An introduction to Swedish history from the year dot, with useful chapters on art, architecture and cultural life.

Lee Miles *Sweden and European Integration*. A political history of Sweden focusing on the period 1950–66, and the accession to the European Union in 1995.

Vilhem Moberg *The Emigrants*. A series of emotionally poignant historical novels, centred on a husband and wife, that tell the story of the one million Swedes who emigrated to the US in the late nineteenth and early twentieth centuries. Moberg himself chose to stay in Sweden, and is recognized as a major social chronicler of his time.

Alan Palmer *Bernadotte* (o/p). First English biography for over fifty years of Napoleon's marshal, later Sweden's King Karl Johan XIV. It's lively and comprehensive, though probably for enthusiasts only.

Michael Roberts *The Early Vasas: A History of Sweden 1523–1611* (o/p). This general account of the period is complemented by Roberts' more recent *Gustavus Adolphus and the Rise of Sweden* which, more briefly and enthusiastically, covers the period from 1612 to the king's death in 1632.

Franklin Daniel Scott *Sweden: The Nation's History*. A good all-round account of Sweden's history from a poor, backward warrior nation to the prosperous modern one of today.

Literature

Stig Dagerman *The Games of Night*. Intense short stories by a prolific young writer who had written four novels, four plays, numerous short stories and travel sketches by the time he was 26. He committed suicide in 1954 at the age of 31. This is some of the best of his work.

Kerstin Ekman *Under the snow*. In a remote Lapland village, a police constable investigates the death of a teacher following a drunken brawl – the dark deeds of winter finally come to light under the relentless summer sun. An excellent means of getting to grips with the mentality of northern Swedes.

Robert Fulton (trans.) *Preparations for Flight*. Eight Swedish short stories from the last 25 years, including two rare prose outings from the poet Niklas Rådström.

P.C. Jersild *A Living Soul*. Social satire based around the "experiences" of an artificially produced, bodiless human brain floating in liquid. Entertaining, provocative reading from one of Sweden's best novelists.

Sara Lidman *Naboth's Stone*. A novel set in 1880s Västerbotten, in Sweden's far north, charting the lives of settlers and farmers as the industrial age – and the rail line – approaches.

Astrid Lindgren *Pippi Longstocking; The Brothers Lionheart*. Delightful and essentially Swedish children's books featuring independent, unconventional and, in the case of Pippi, slightly anarchist children.

Henning Mankell *Faceless Killers; Sidetracked*. Cracking yarns from Scandinavia's leading crime writer featuring Inspector Kurt Wallander, a shambolic and melancholic middle-aged police officer in Ystad struggling to make sense of it all in small-town southern Sweden.

Agneta Pleijel *The Dog Star*. Powerful tale of a young girl's approach to puberty. One of Pleijel's finest novels, full of fantasy and emotion.

Clive Sinclair *Augustus Rex* (o/p). August Strindberg dies in 1912 – and is then brought back to life by the Devil in 1960s Stockholm. Bawdy, imaginative and very funny treatment of Strindberg's well-documented neuroses.

Hjalmar Söderberg *Short Stories*. Twenty-six short stories from the stylish pen of Söderberg (1869–1941). Brief, ironic and eminently ripe for dipping into.

August Strindberg *Strindberg Plays: Two; Strindberg Plays: Three; Three Plays; Inferno/From an Occult Diary; By the Open Sea*. Strindberg is now seen as a pioneer in both his subject matter and style. His early plays were realistic in a manner not then expected of drama, and confronted themes that weren't considered suitable viewing at all, with psychological examinations of the roles of the sexes both in and out of marriage. A fantastically prolific writer, only a fraction of his sixty plays, twelve historical dramas, five novels, short stories, numerous autobiographical volumes and poetry has ever been translated into English.

Criticism and biography

Peter Cowie *Ingmar Bergman*. New edition of a well-written and sympathetic account of the director's life and career.

Michael Meyer *Strindberg on File* (o/p). A useful brief account of

Strindberg's life and work, though for a more stirring biography the same author's *Strindberg* (o/p) is the best and most approachable source.

Art and architecture

Henrik O. Andersson and Frederic Bedoure *Svensk Arkitektur* (o/p). Seminal book on Swedish architectural history from 1640 to 1970, with text in English and Swedish. Colour plates illustrate the works of each architect. One to borrow from the library.

Barbro Klein and Mats Widbom (eds) *Swedish Folk Art – All Tradition Is Change* (o/p). Lavishly produced

volume on the folk art movement, illustrating the influences of local culture on art and design up to and including Ikea.

Roger Tanner (trans.) *A History of Swedish Art* (o/p). Covers architecture, design, painting and sculpture, ranging from prehistoric rock carvings to Postmodernism. Well illustrated.

Finland

D ue to Finland's relative obscurity in terms of English-language audiences, there's a real dearth of decent publications about anything Finnish. As for traditional literature itself, many Finnish authors have found a wider audience in French, German, Italian and Swedish readers than amongst English-speaking ones, so coming to grips with who's who in the contemporary Finnish literary scene might prove problematic without a knowledge of one of these languages. It's a testament to the superiority of technology in Finland that you will always find much more written information about Finland on the internet than in any reasonably priced book.

History and society

Eloise Engel and Lauri Paananen *The Winter War: The Soviet Attack on Finland 1939–1940*. An excellent and popular account of the Finns' resistance and final defeat by overwhelming numbers of Soviet troops during the Winter War.

D.G. Kirby *Finland in the Twentieth Century – A History and Interpretation*. By far the best insight into contemporary Finland and the reshaping of the nation after independence.

Veli-Pekka Lehtola *The Sámi People: Traditions in Transition*. A well-written, fully illustrated contemporary history of the Sámi across Scandinavia, which details the social changes experienced by these once entirely nomadic reindeer herders and explains how they are currently forging for themselves a delicate path between the traditional and the modern.

Nikki Rajala *Some Like It Hot: The Sauna, Its Lore and Stories*. History of the most famous social institution in Finland, plus lots of interesting factoids about the ritual and its role in the nation's development over the years.

Fred Singleton *A Short History of Finland*. A very readable and informative account of Finland's past. It lacks the detail of most academic accounts, but is an excellent starting point for general readers.

Literature

Tove Jansson The *Moomin* books. Enduring children's tales, with evocative descriptions of Finnish nature.

Matti Joensuu *Harjunpää and the Stone Murders* (o/p). The only one of the Harjunpää series, involving the Helsinki detective Timo Harjunpää, to have been translated into English. It's set in contemporary Helsinki during a bout of teenage gang warfare.

Väinö Linna *The Unknown Soldier* (o/p). Based on his experiences fighting in the Winter War, and for the first time depicting Finnish soldiers not as "heroes in white" but as drunks and womanizers, Linna's novel triggered immense controversy. Less well known but equally poignant, *The North Star*, his first tome in the trilogy, describes a late nineteenth-century rural Finnish community, highlighting the seminal historical events which helped to mould the Finnish national character.

Elias Lönnrot *Kalevala*. The classic tome of Finnish literature, this collection of folk tales was transcribed over twenty years by Lönnrot, a rural doctor. Set in an unspecified point in the past, the plot centres on a state of war between the mythical region of Kalevala (probably northern Karelia) and Pohjola (possibly Lapland) over possession of a talisman called the Sampo. The story is regarded as quintessentially Finnish, but it's not an easy read, due mainly to its length (some 22,750 lines), and the non-linear course

of the plot. Its influence on Finnish literature is huge, though, and it was a linchpin of the Finnish nationalist and language movements.

Arto Paasilinna *The Year of the Hare*. Finland's best-known author, Paasilinna has had forty-odd books translated into dozens of languages. He has a keen eye for the Finnish character and sense of humour, and this 1977 novel, his best-known, is inventive, satirical and mythical, offering profound insight into late twentieth-century Western society. The story concerns a Finnish journalist who, after running over a rabbit and then nursing it back to health, pursues his own rebellion against social mores, politics and relationships.

Oscar Parland *The Year of the Bull*. Absorbing look at the civil-war-torn Finland of 1918 through the eyes of a young boy.

Runar Schildt *The Meat-Grinder and Other Stories*. Intriguing tales, set mostly in Helsinki before and during the Finnish civil war. Schildt (1888–1925) is probably Finland's finest short-story writer.

Kirsti Simonsuuri (ed.) *Enchanting Beasts*. A slender but captivating tome, and one of the few English translations of Finland's best modern poets.

Johanna Sinisalao *Troll: A Love Story*. Sodankylä native Sinisalao wrote her debut novel to critical acclaim in Finland and abroad, capturing the prestigious Finlandia prize. In this account, a young gay photographer is viscerally influenced by a curious find from his courtyard: a small troll which comes to awaken dark desires within him.

Merging folklore with psychology, the book fuses an engaging mythological love story with subtly astute insight into modern human relationships.

Miscellaneous

Beatrice Ojakangas *Finnish Cookbook*. Originally published in 1964, these timeless, all-round recipes shed light on one of Scandinavia's least known cuisines – everything from fish stew to prune tarts, as well as short stories about the Finnish way of life.

Micha Ramakers *Dirty Pictures: Tom of Finland, Masculinity, and Homosexuality*. An excellent account of the social and cultural issues touched upon by the work of gay-themed comic-strip artist Touko Laaksonen (aka Tom of Finland), who once memorably stated "If I don't have an erection when I'm doing a drawing, I know it's no good." Offers ample examples of the often graphically sexual penmanship of Finland's best-known pictorial artist, alongside enlightening prose.

Linus Torvalds & David Diamond *Just for Fun: The Story of an Accidental Revolutionary*. The autobiography of the 20-something Finn who revolutionized modern computer technology with his Linux operating system, all the while remaining true to his deeply religious belief in open-source computing. Reads a little choppily, with irreverent banter and off-the-cuff, email-like entries, but an enjoyable read all the same.

Richard Weston *Alvar Aalto*. Excellent overview of Aalto's life and work, with beautiful photographs and unpretentious language. Not a historical monograph, but a solid introduction to one of Finland's most beloved artistic geniuses.

Language

Language

Danish

I n some ways, Danish is similar to German, but there are significant differences in pronunciation, Danes tending to swallow the ending of many words and leave certain letters silent. English is widely understood, as is German; young people, especially, often speak both fluently. And if you can speak Swedish or Norwegian then you should have little problem making yourself understood – all three languages share the same root.

In **pronunciation**, unfamiliar **vowels** include:
æ when long between **air** and **tai**lor. When short like g**e**t. When next to r sounds more like h**a**t.
å when long like s**aw**, when short like **o**n.

ø like f**ur** but with the lips rounded.
e when long, is similar to pl**a**te, when short somewhere between pl**a**te and h**i**t; when unstressed it's as in **a**bove.

Consonants are pronounced as in English, except:

d at the end of a word after a vowel, or between a vowel and an unstressed e or i, like **th**is. Sometimes silent at the end of a word.
g at the beginning of a word or syllable as in **go**. At the end of a word or long vowel, or before an unstressed e, usually like **y**et but sometimes like the Scottish lo**ch**. Sometimes mute after an a, e, or o.
hv like **v**iew.
hj like **y**et.

k as English except between vowels, when it's as in **go**.
p as English except between vowels, when it's as in **b**it.
r pronounced as in French from the back of the throat but often silent.
sj as in **sh**eet.
t as English except between vowels, when it'o ao in **do**. Often mute when at the end of a word.
y between b**ee** and p**oo**l.

Words and phrases

Basics

do you speak English?	taler de engelsk?
yes	ja
no	nej
I don't understand	jeg forstår det ikke
I understand	jeg forstår
please	værså venlig
thank you	tak
excuse me	undskyld
good morning	godmorgen
good afternoon	goddag
goodnight	godnat
goodbye	farvel
yesterday	i går
today	i dag
tomorrow	i morgen
day after tomorrow	i overmorgen
in the morning	om morgenen

in the afternoon	om eftermiddagen
in the evening	om aftenen

Some signs

entrance	indgang
exit	udgang
push/pull	skub/træk
danger	fare
gentlemen	herrer
ladies	damer
open	åben
closed	lukket
arrival	ankomst
departure	afgang
police	politi
no smoking	rygning forbudt/Ikke rygere
no entry	ingen adgang
no camping	campering forbudt

no trespassing	adgang forbudt for uvedkommende

Questions and directions

where is?	hvor er?
when?	hvornår?
what?	hvad?
why?	hvorfor?
who?	hvem?
how much?	hvor meget?
how much does it cost?	hvad koster det?
here	her
there	der
good/bad	god/dårlig
cheap/expensive	billig/dyr
hot/cold	varm/kold
better/bigger/ cheaper	bedre/større/billigere
near/far	nær/fjern
left/right	venstre/højre
straight ahead	ligeud
I'd like ...	Jeg vil gerne ha ...
where is the youth hostel?	hvor er vandrerhjemmet?
can we camp here?	må vi campere her?
it's too expensive	det er for dyrt
where are the toilets?	hvor er toiletterne?
how far is it to ...?	hvor langt er der til ...?
where can I get a – train/bus/ferry to ...?	hvor kan jeg tage toget/bussen/ færgen til ...?
at what time does ...?	hvornår går ...?
ticket	billet

Numbers

0	nul
1	en
2	to
3	tre
4	fire
5	fem
6	seks
7	syv
8	otte
9	ni
10	ti

11	elleve
12	tolv
13	tretten
14	fjorten
15	femten
16	seksten
17	sytten
18	atten
19	nitten
20	tyve
21	enogtyve
30	tredive
40	fyrre
50	halvtreds
60	tres
70	halvfjerds
80	firs
90	halvfems
100	hundrede
101	hundrede og et
151	hundrede og enoghalvtreds
200	to hundrede
1000	tusind

Days and months

Monday	mandag
Tuesday	tirsdag
Wednesday	onsdag
Thursday	torsdag
Friday	fredag
Saturday	lørdag
Sunday	søndag

January	januar
February	februar
March	marts
April	april
May	maj
June	juni
July	juli
August	august
September	september
October	oktober
November	november
December	december

(Days and months are never capitalized).

Menu reader

Basics and snacks

bøfsandwich	hamburger
brød	bread

chokolade (varm)	chocolate (hot)
det kolde bord	help-yourself cold buffet
is	ice cream
kaffe (med fløde)	coffee (with cream)

kiks	biscuits
letmælk	semi-skimmed milk
mælk	milk
nudler	noodles
ostebord	cheese board
pølser	frankfurters/sausages
sildebord	a selection of spiced and pickled herring
skummetmælk	skimmed milk
smør	butter
smørrebrød	open sandwiches
sødmælk	full-fat milk
sukker	sugar
te	tea
wienerbrød	"Danish" pastry

Egg (æg) dishes

kogt æg	boiled egg
omelet	omelette
røræg	scrambled eggs
spejlæg	fried eggs

Fish (fisk)

ål	eel
forel	trout
gedde	pike
helleflynder	halibut
hummer	lobster
karpe	carp
klipfisk	salt cod
krabbe	crab
krebs	crayfish
laks	salmon
makrel	mackerel
rejer	shrimp
rogn	roe
rødspætte	plaice
røget sild	kipper
sardiner	sardines
sild	herring
søtunge	sole
stør	sturgeon
store rejer	prawns
torsk	cod

Meat (kød)

and(ung)	duck(ling)
dyresteg	venison
fasan	pheasant
gås	goose
hare	hare
kalkun	turkey
kanin	rabbit
kylling	chicken
lam	lamb
lever	liver

oksekød	beef
rensdyr	reindeer
skinke	ham
svinekød	pork

Vegetables (grøntsager)

artiskokker	artichokes
asparges	asparagus
blomkål	cauliflower
brune bønner	kidney beans
champignoner	mushrooms
grønne bønner	runner beans
gulerødder	carrots
hvidløg	garlic
julesalat	chicory
kartofler	potatoes
linser	lentils
løg	onions
majs	sweetcorn
majskolbe	corn on the cob
peberfrugt	peppers
persille	parsley
porrer	leeks
ris	rice
rødbeder	beetroot
rødkål	red cabbage
rosenkål	brussels sprouts
salat	lettuce, salad
salatagurk	cucumber
selleri	celery
spinat	spinach
turnips	turnips

Fruit (frugt)

æbler	apples
abrikoser	apricots
ananas	pineapple
appelsiner	oranges
bananer	bananas
blommer	plums
blåbær	blueberries
brombær	blackberries
citron	lemon
ferskner	peaches
grapefrugt	grapefruit
hindbær	raspberries
jordbær	strawberries
kirsebær	cherries
mandariner	tangerines
melon	melon
pærer	pears
rabarber	rhubarb
rosiner	raisins
solbær	blackcurrants

Danish specialities

æbleflæsk – smoked bacon with onions and sautéed apple rings.

æggekage – scrambled eggs with onions, chives, potatoes and bacon pieces.

boller i karry – meatballs in curry sauce served with rice.

flæskesteg – a hunk of pork with crispy skin, served with red cabbage, potatoes and brown sauce.

frikadeller – pork and beef meatballs.

grillstegt kylling – grilled chicken.

hakkebøf – thick minced-beef burgers fried with onions.

kalvebryst i frikasseé – veal boiled with vegetables and served in a white sauce with peas and carrots.

kogt torsk – poached cod in mustard sauce with boiled potatoes.

medisterpølse – a spiced pork sausage, usually served with boiled potatoes or stewed vegetables.

røget sild – smoked herring on rye bread garnished with a raw egg yolk, radishes and chives.

sild i karry – herring in curry sauce.

skidne æg – poached or hard-boiled eggs in a cream sauce, spiced with fish mustard, served with rye bread and garnished with sliced bacon and chives.

skipper labskovs – danish stew: small squares of beef boiled with potatoes, peppercorns and bay leaves.

stegt ål med stuvede – fried eel with diced potatoes and white sauce *kartofler*.

stikkelsbær	gooseberries	fadøl	draught beer
svesker	prunes	guldøl	strong beer
vindruer	grapes	husets vin	house wine
		hvidvin	white wine
Drink (Drikke)		kærnemælk	buttermilk
		mineralvand	soda water
æblemost	apple juice	øl	beer
appelsinvand	orangeade	rødvin	red wine
citronvand	lemonade	tomatjuice	tomato juice
eksport-øl	export beer (very strong lager)	vin	wine

Glossary of Danish words and phrases

bakke	hill or ridge	kro	inn
banegård	train station	plads	square
domkirke	cathedral	rådhus	town hall
gammel or gamle	old	rutebilstation	coach station
hav	sea	skov	wood, forest
havn	harbour	stue	room
herregård	manor house	sø	lake
jernebane	rail line	torv	market square
kirke	church	tårn	tower
klint	cliff	vand	water
kloster	monastery		

Norwegian

There are two official Norwegian languages: **Riksmål** or **Bokmål** (book language), a modification of the old Dano-Norwegian tongue left over from the days of Danish dominance; and **Landsmål** or **Nynorsk**, which was codified during the nineteenth-century upsurge of Norwegian nationalism and is based on rural dialects of Old Norse provenance. Roughly ninety percent of schoolchildren have *Bokmål* as their primary language, and the remaining ten percent are *Nynorsk* speakers, concentrated in the fjord country of the west coast and the mountain districts of central Norway. Despite the best efforts of the government, *Nynorsk* is in decline – in 1944 fully one-third of the population used it. As the more common of the two languages, *Bokmål* is what we use here in this Guide.

You don't really need to know any Norwegian to get by in Norway. Almost everyone speaks some English, and in any case many words are not too far removed from their English equivalents; there's also plenty of English (or American) on billboards, the TV and at the cinema. Mastering "hello" or "thank you" will, however, be greatly appreciated, while if you speak either Danish or Swedish you should have few problems being understood. Incidentally, Norwegians find Danish easier to read than Swedish, but orally it's the other way round.

Phrasebooks are fairly thin on the ground, but Berlitz's *Norwegian Phrasebook with Dictionary* has – as you would expect from the title – a mini-dictionary, not to mention a useful grammar section and a menu reader; Dorling Kindersley's *Norwegian Phrasebook* is comparable. There are several **dictionaries** to choose from, all of which include pronunciation tips and so forth. The best is generally considered to be the Collins *English–Norwegian Dictionary*, though this is currently out of print and you might decide to opt for the Berlitz *Norwegian Pocket Dictionary* instead.

Pronunciation

Pronunciation can be tricky. A **vowel** is usually long when it's the final syllable or followed by only one consonant; followed by two it's generally short. Unfamiliar ones are:

ae before an i, as in bad, otherwise as in say.
ø as in **fur** but without pronouncing the r.
å usually as in **saw**.

øy between the ø sound and boy.
ei as in say.

Consonants are pronounced as in English except:

c, q, w, z found only in foreign words and
  pronounced as in the original language.
g before i, y or ei, as in yet; otherwise hard.
hv as in view.
j, gj, hj, lj as in yet.

rs almost always as in **sh**ut.
k before i, y or j, like the Scottish lo**ch**;
  otherwise hard.
sj, sk before i, y, ø or øy, as in **sh**ut.

Words and phrases

Basic phrases

do you speak English?	snakker du engelsk?
yes	ja
no	nei
do you understand?	forstår du?
I don't understand	jeg forstår ikke
I understand	jeg forstår
please (is near enough,though there's no direct equivalent)	vær så god
thank you (very much)	takk (tusen takk)
you're welcome	vær så god
excuse me	unnskyld
good morning	god morgen
good afternoon	god dag
good night	god natt
goodbye	adjø
today	i dag
tomorrow	i morgen
day after tomorrow	i overmorgen
in the morning	om morgenen
in the afternoon	om ettermiddagen
in the evening	om kvelden

Some signs

entrance	inngang
exit	utgang
gentlemen	herrer/menn
ladies	damer/kvinner
open	åpen
closed	stengt
arrival	ankomst
police	politi
hospital	sykehus
cycle path	sykkelsti
no smoking	røyking forbudt
no camping	camping forbudt
no trespassing	uvedkommende forbudt
no entry	ingen adgang
pull/push	trekk/trykk
departure	avgang
parking fees	avgift

Questions and directions

where? (where is/are?)	hvor? (hvor er?)
when?	når?
what?	hva?
how much/many?	hvor mye/hvor mange?
why?	hvorfor?
which?	hvilket?
what's that called in Norwegian?	hva kaller man det på norsk?
can you direct me to ...?	kan de vise meg veien til ...?
it is/there is (is it/ is there)	det er (er det?)
what time is it?	hvor mange er klokken?
big/small	stor/liten
cheap/expensive	billig/dyrt
early/late	tidlig/sent
hot/cold	varm/kald
near/far	i nærheten/langt borte
good/bad	god/dårlig
vacant/occupied	ledig/opptatt
a little/a lot	litt/mye
more/less	mer/mindre
can we camp here?	kan vi campe her?
is there a youth hostel near here?	er det et vandrerhjem i nærheten?
how do I get to ...?	hvordan kommer jeg til ...?
how far is it to ...?	hvor langt er det til ...?
ticket	billett
single/return	en vei/tur-retur
can you give me a lift to ...?	kan jeg få sitte på til ...?
left/right	venstre/høyre
go straight ahead	kjør rett frem

Numbers

0	null
1	en
2	to
3	tre
4	fire
5	fem
6	seks
7	sju
8	åtte
9	ni
10	ti
11	elleve
12	tolv
13	tretten
14	fjorten
15	femten
16	seksten

17	sytten
18	atten
19	nitten
20	tjue
21	tjueen
22	tjueto
30	tretti
40	førti
50	femti
60	seksti
70	sytti
80	åtti
90	nitti
100	hundre
101	hundreogen
200	to hundre
1000	tusen

Days and months

Sunday	søndag
Monday	mandag
Tuesday	tirsdag
Wednesday	onsdag
Thursday	torsdag
Friday	fredag
Saturday	lørdag
January	januar
February	februar
March	mars
April	april
May	mai
June	juni
July	juli
August	august
September	september
October	oktober
November	november
December	desember

(Days and months are never capitalized).

Menu reader

Basics and snacks

appelsin, marmelade	marmalade
brød	bread
eddik	vinegar
egg	egg
eggerøre	scrambled eggs
flatbrød	crispbread
fløte	cream
grønsaker	vegetables
grøt	porridge
iskrem	ice cream
kaffefløte	single cream for coffee
kake	cake
kaviar	caviar
kjeks	biscuits
krem	whipped cream
melk	milk
mineralvann	mineral water
nøtter	nuts
olje	oil
omelett	omelette
ost	cheese
pannekake	pancakes
pepper	pepper
potetchips	crisps (potato chips)
pommes-frites	chips (French fries)

ris	rice
rundstykker	bread roll
salat	salad
salt	salt
sennep	mustard
smør	butter
smørbrød	open sandwich
sukker	sugar
suppe	soup
syltetøy	jam
varm pølse	hot dog
yoghurt	yoghurt

Meat (kjøtt) and game (vilt)

dyrestek	venison
elg	elk
kalkun	turkey
kjøttboller	meatballs
kjøttkaker	rissoles
kylling	chicken
lammekjøtt	lamb
lever	liver
oksekjøtt	beef
postei	pâté
pølser	sausages
reinsdyr	reindeer
ribbe	pork rib
skinke	ham

brun saus – gravy served with most meats, rissoles, fishcakes and sausages.

fenalår – marinated mutton that is smoked, sliced, salted, dried and served with crispbread, scrambled egg and beer.

fiskeboller – fish balls, served under a white sauce or on open sandwiches.

fiskekabaret – shrimps, fish and vegetables in aspic.

fiskesuppe – fish soup.

flatbrød – a flat unleavened cracker, half barley, half wheat.

gammelost – a hard, strong smelling, yellow-brown cheese with veins.

geitost/gjetost – goat's cheese, slightly sweet and fudge-coloured. Similar cheeses have different ratios of goat's milk to cow's milk.

gravetlaks – salmon marinated in salt, sugar, dill and brandy.

juleskinke – marinated boiled ham, served at Christmas.

kjøttkaker med surkål – home-made burgers with cabbage and a sweet and sour sauce.

koldtbord – a midday buffet with cold meats, herrings, salads, bread and perhaps soup, eggs or hot meats.

lapskaus – pork, venison (or other meats) and vegetable stew, common in the south and east, using salted or fresh meat, or leftovers, in a thick brown gravy.

lutefisk – fish (usually cod) preserved in an alkali solution and seasoned; an acquired taste.

multer – cloudberries – wild berries mostly found north of the Arctic Circle and served with cream (*med krem*).

mysost – brown whey cheese, made from cow's milk.

nedlagtsild – marinated herring.

pinnekjøtt – western Norwegian Christmas dish of smoked mutton steamed over shredded birch bark, served with cabbage; or accompanied by boiled potatoes and mashed swedes (kålrabistappe).

reinsdyrstek – reindeer steak, usually served with boiled potatoes and cranberry sauce.

rekesalat – shrimp salad in mayonnaise.

ribbe julepølse medisterkake – eastern Norwegian Christmas dish of pork ribs, sausage and dumplings.

spekemat – various types of smoked, dried meat.

trondhjemsuppea – kind of milk broth with raisins, rice, cinnamon and sugar.

spekemat	dried meat	krabbe	crab
stek	steak	kreps	crayfish
svinekjøtt	pork	laks	salmon
varm pølse	frankfurter/hot dog	makrell	mackerel

		ørret	trout
		piggvar	turbot
ål	eel	reker	shrimps
ansjos	anchovies (brisling)	rødspette	plaice
blåskjell	mussels	røkelaks	smoked salmon
brisling	sprats	sardiner	sardines (brisling)
hummer	lobster	sei	coalfish
hvitting	whiting	sild	herring
kaviar	caviar	sjøtunge	sole

småfisk	whitebait
steinbit	catfish
torsk	cod
tunfisk	tuna

Vegetables (grønsaker)

agurk	cucumber/gherkin/ pickle
blomkål	cauliflower
bønner	beans
erter	peas
gulrøtter	carrots
hodesalat	lettuce
hvitløk	garlic
kål	cabbage
linser	lentils
løk	onion
mals	sweetcorn
nepe	turnip
paprika	peppers
poteter	potatoes
rosenkål	Brussels sprouts
selleri	celery
sopp	mushrooms
spinat	spinach
tomater	tomatoes

Fruit (frukt)

ananas	pineapple
appelsin	orange
aprikos	apricot
banan	banana
blåbær	blueberries
druer	grapes
eple	apple
fersken	peach
fruktsalat	fruit salad
grapefrukt	grapefruit
jordbær	strawberries
multer	cloudberries
plommer	plums
pærer	pears
sitron	lemon
solbær	blackcurrants
tyttbær	cranberries

Cooking terms

blodig	rare, underdone
godt stekt	well done
grillet	grilled
grytestekt	braised

kokt	boiled
marinert	marinated
ovnstekt	baked/roasted
røkt	smoked
saltet	cured
stekt	fried
stuet	stewed
sur	sour, pickled
syltet	pickled

Bread, cake and desserts

bløtkake cream cake with fruit
fløtelapper pancakes made with cream, served with sugar and jam
havrekjeks oatmeal biscuits, eaten with goat's cheese
knekkebrød crispbread
kransekake cake made from almonds, sugar and eggs, served at celebrations
lomper potato scones-cum-tortillas
riskrem rice pudding with whipped cream and sugar, usually served with *frukt saus*, a slightly thickened fruit sauce
tilslørtbondepiker stewed apples and breadcrumbs, served with cream
trollkrem beaten egg whites (or whipped cream) and sugar, mixed with cloudberries (or cranberries)
vafle waffles

Drinks

akevitt	aquavit
appelsin saft/juice	orange squash or juice
brus	fizzy soft drink
eplesider	cider
fruktsaft	sweetened fruit juice
hvit	white
kaffe	coffee
melk	milk
mineralvann	mineral water
øl	beer
rød	red
rosé	rosé
skål	cheers
sitronbrus	lemonade
søt	sweet
te med melk/sitron	tea with milk/lemon
tørr	dry
vann	water
varm sjokolade	hot chocolate
vin	wine

L

LANGUAGE | Norwegian

Glossary of Norwegian words and phrases

apotek chemist
bakke hill
bokhandel bookshop
bre glacier
bro/bru bridge
brygge quay/wharf
dal valley/dale
DNT (Den Norske Turistforening) Nationwide
  hiking organization whose local affiliates
  maintain hiking paths across almost all the
  country.
domkirke cathedral
drosje taxi
E.kr AD
elv/bekk river/stream
ferje/ferge ferry
fjell/berg mountain
Flybussen Airport bus (literally "plane bus")
F.kr BC
foss waterfall
gågate urban pedestrianized area
gate (gt.) street
gamle byen Literally "Old Town"; used
  wherever the old part of town has remained
  distinct from the rest. Also spelt as one
  word.
hav ocean
havn harbour
Hurtigbåt Passenger express boat; usually a
  catamaran
Hurtigrute Literally "quick route", but familiar
  as the name of the boat service along the
  west coast from Bergen to Kirkenes.
hytte cottage, cabin
innsjø lake
jernbanestasjon train station
kirke/kjerke church

KFUM/KFUK Norwegian YMCA/YWCA
klokken/kl. o'clock
klippfisk salted whitefish, usually cod
moderasjon discount or price reduction
Moms or mva Sales tax – applied to almost
  all consumables
museet museum
NAF Nationwide Norwegian automobile
  association. Membership covers rescue and
  repair.
rabatt discount or price reduction
rådhus town hall
rorbu Originally a simple wooden cabin built
  near the fishing grounds for incoming (ie
  non-local) fishermen. Many cabins are now
  used as tourist accommodation, especially
  in the Lofoten (see p.317).
Sámi Formerly called Lapps, the Sámi inhabit
  the northern reaches of Norway, Finland and
  Sweden – Lapland.
sentrum city or town centre
sjø sea
sjøhus harbourside building where the catch
  was sorted, salted, filleted and iced. Many
  are now redundant and some have been
  turned into tourist accommodation.
skog forest
slott castle/palace
stavkirke stave church
Storting Parliament
tilbud special offer
torget main town square, often home to an
  outdoor market; sometimes spelt Torvet
vandrerhjem youth hostel
vann/vatn water/lake
vei/veg/vn. road
øy/øya islet

Swedish

N early everyone, everywhere in Sweden speaks English, and the tourist offices are often staffed with what appear to be native English speakers. Still, knowing the essentials of Swedish is useful, and making an effort with the language certainly impresses. If you already speak either Danish or Norwegian you should have few problems being understood; if not, then a basic knowledge of German is a help too. Of the phrasebooks, most useful is *Swedish for Travellers* (Berlitz).

Pronunciation

Pronunciation is more difficult than Danish or Norwegian. A **vowel** sound is usually long when it's the final syllable or followed by only one consonant; followed by two it's generally short. Unfamiliar combinations are:

ej as in mate.
y as in ewe.
å when short as in hot; when long as in raw.

ä when before r as in man; otherwise as In get.
ö as in fur but without the r sound.

Consonants are pronounced as in English except:

g usually as in yet; occasionally as in shut.
j, dj, gj, lj as in yet.
k before i, e, y, ä, or ö, like the Scottish loch; otherwise hard.

qu as kv.
sch, ski, sti as in shut; otherwise hard
tj like loch.
z as in so.

Words and phrases

Basics

hello	hej
good morning	god morgon
good afternoon	god middag
good night	god natt
goodbye	hejdå
do you speak english?	pratar du engelska?
yes	ja
no	nej
I don't understand	jag förstår inte
please	var så god
thank you (very much)	tack (så mycket)
you're welcome	var så god
today	i dag
tomorrow	i morgon
day after tomorrow	i övermorgon
in the morning	på morgonen
in the afternoon	på eftermiddagen
in the evening	på kvällen

Some signs

entrance	ingång
exit	utgång
men	herrar
women	damer
open	öppen, öppet
closed	stängt
push	skjut
pull	drag
arrival	ankomst
departure	avgång
no smoking	rökning förbjuden
no camping	tältning förbjuden
no trespassing	tillträde förbjudet
no entry	ingen ingång
police	polis

Questions and directions

where is ...?	var är ... ?
when?	när?
what?	vad?
can you direct me to ...	skulle du kunna visa mig vägen till
it is/there is (is it/is there?)	det är/det finns (är det/finns det?)
what time is it?	hur mycket är klockan?
big/small	stor/liten
cheap/expensive	billig/dyr
early/late	tidig/sen
hot/cold	varm/kall
near/far	nära/avlägsen
good/bad	bra/dålig
left/right	vänster/höger
vacant/occupied	ledig/upptagen
a little/a lot	lite/en mängd
I'd like	jag skulle vilja ha ...
... a single room	... ett enkelrum
... a double room	... ett dubbelrum
how much is it?	vad kostar det?
får vi tälta här?	can we camp here?
campingplats	campsite
tält	tent
finns det något vandrarhem i närheten?	is there a youth hostel near here?

Numbers

0	noll
1	ett
2	två
3	tre
4	fyra
5	fem
6	sex
7	sju
8	åtta
9	nio
10	tio
11	elva
12	tolv
13	tretton
14	fjorton
15	femton
16	sexton
17	sjutton
18	arton
19	nitton
20	tjugo
21	tjugoett
22	tjugotvå
30	trettio
40	fyrtio
50	femtio
60	sextio
70	sjuttio
80	åttio
90	nittio
100	hundra
101	hundraett
200	tvåhundra
500	femhundra
1000	tusen

Days and months

Monday	måndag
Tuesday	tisdag
Wednesday	onsdag
Thursday	torsdag
Friday	fredag
Saturday	lördag
Sunday	söndag
January	januari
February	februari
March	mars
April	april
May	maj
June	juni
July	juli
August	augusti
September	september
October	oktober
November	november
December	december

(Days and months are never capitalized).

Menu reader

Basics and snacks

ägg	egg
bröd	bread
glass	ice cream
grädde	cream
gräddfil	sour cream
gröt	porridge
jus	fruit juice
kaffe	coffee

knäckebröd	crispbread
mineralvatten	mineral water
mjölk	milk
olja	oil
omelett	omelette
ost	cheese
pastej	pâté
peppar	pepper
ris	rice
salt	salt
senap	mustard
småkakor	biscuits
smör	butter
smörgås	sandwich
socker	sugar
soppa	soup
strips	chips
sylt	jam
te	tea
våfflor	waffles
vinäger	vinegar

Meat (kött)

älg	elk
biff	beef steak
fläsk	pork
kalvkött	veal
korv	sausage
kotlett	cutlet/chop
köttbullar	meatballs
kyckling	chicken
lammkött	lamb
lever	liver
oxstek	roast beef
renstek	roast reindeer
skinka	ham

Fish (fisk)

ål	eel
ansjovis	anchovies
blåmusslor	mussels
fiskbullar	fishballs
forell	trout
hummer	lobster
kaviar	caviar
krabba	crab
kräftor	freshwater crayfish
lax	salmon
makrill	mackerel
räkor	shrimps/prawns
rödspätta	plaice
sardiner	sardines
sik	whitefish
sill	herring
strömming	Baltic herring
torsk	cod

Vegetables (grönsaker)

ärtor	peas
blomkål	cauliflower
bönor	beans
brysselkål	brussels sprouts
gurka	cucumber
lök	onion
morötter	carrots
potatis	potatoes
rödkål	red cabbage
sallad	salad
spenat	spinach
svamp	mushrooms
tomater	tomatoes
vitkål	white cabbage
vitlök	garlic

Fruit (frukt)

ananas	pineapple
apelsin	orange
äpple	apple
aprikos	apricot
banan	banana
citron	lemon
hallon	raspberry
hjortron	cloudberry
jordgrubbar	strawberries
lingon	cranberries
päron	pear
persika	peach
vindruvor	grapes

General terms

ångkokt	steamed
blodig	rare
filé	fillet
friterad	deep-fried
genomstekt	well-done
gravad	cured
grillat/halstrad	grilled
kall	cold
kokt	boiled
lagom	medium
pocherad	poached
rökt	smoked
stekt	fried
ugnstekt	roasted/baked
varm	hot

Drinks

apelsin juice	orange juice
choklad	hot chocolate
citron	lemon

Swedish specialities

ål – eel, smoked and served with creamed potatoes or scrambled eggs (*äggröra*).

ärtsoppa – yellow pea soup with pork; a winter dish traditionally served on Thursdays.

bruna bönor – baked, vinegared brown beans, usually served with bacon.

fisksoppa – fish soup.

getost – goat's cheese.

gravadlax – salmon marinated in dill, sugar and seasoning, and served with mustard sauce.

hjortron – a wild berry served with fresh cream and/or ice cream.

köttbullar – meatballs served with a brown sauce and cranberries.

kryddos – hard cheese with caraway seeds.

lövbiff – sliced, fried beef with onions.

mesost – brown, sweet cheese; a breakfast favourite.

potatissallad – potato salad.

pytt i panna – cubes of meat and fried potatoes with a fried egg.

sillbricka – various cured and marinated herring dishes; often appears as a first course at lunchtime in restaurants.

sjömansbiff – beef, onions and potato stewed in beer.

frukt juice	fruit juice	saft	squash
kaffe	coffee	te	tea
mineralvatten	mineral water	vatten	water
mjölk	milk	vin	wine
öl	beer	skål!	cheers!

Glossary of Swedish words and phrases

bastu	sauna	pressbyrå	newsagent
berg	mountain	rabatt	rebate/discount
bokhandel	bookshop	rea	sales (and vrakpriser,
bro	bridge		bargain)
cykelstig	path	riksdagshus	parliament building
dal	valley	sjö	lake
domkyrka	cathedral	skog	forest
drottning	queen (as in	slott	castle
	Drottninggatan,	spår	track/platform
	Queen Street)		(at train station)
färja	ferry	stadshus	town hall
gamla	old (as in gamla stan,	stora	great/big (as in
	old town)		storatorget, main
gata (g.)	street		square)
hamnen	harbour	strand	beach
järnvägsstation	train station	stuga	chalet, cottage
klockan (kl.)	o'clock	torg	central town square,
kyrka	church		usually the scene of
lilla	little (as in lilla		daily/weekly markets
	torget, small square)	universitet	university
muséet	museum	väg (v.)	road

Finnish

L

LANGUAGE | Finnish

" I t has been a year now since my arrival and I still have difficulty making myself understood in this most difficult Karelian language. There are fifteen different cases of nouns and twenty-seven different words for snow. I find, however, that the following are sufficient for almost all situations: 'Moi', 'Moi Moi' and 'Hei Toveri! Kupissani ei ole votkaa [Hey mate! There's no more vodka in my cup]'."

Sir Hillman Ledbelly, 1884

Finnish is going to pose a problem to anyone whose mother tongue is an Indo-European language such as English. There's very little common ground between Finnish and any other mainstream western European language, and this can frustrate basic understanding and communication – simple tasks like deciphering a menu are often fraught with overwhelming difficulty.

Finnish also has nothing in common with the other Scandinavian languages – something that has led to considerable misunderstanding of the Finns, particularly in neighbouring Sweden. A member of the Finno-Ugric group of languages, Finnish is closely related to Estonian, Sámi and much more distantly to Hungarian, and its grammatical structure is complex: with fifteen cases alone to grapple with, it isn't the easiest of languages to learn, although once a basic vocabulary is attained things become less impenetrable. Unlike Indo-European German, for example, which uses prepositions to determine the case of a noun, Finnish employs a set of complex suffixes, which, although straightforward to learn, are further complicated by a slew of vowel and consonant elision rules and, to a lesser extent, a process of obligatory vowel harmony. For instance, *autossa* means "in the car", *autohon* "to the car"; whereas *autostanikin* is "out of my car, too". Thankfully, in the large cities and main towns, English is spoken by the younger generation with amazing fluency – many have spent a school year abroad in an English-speaking country – but second-language ability drops significantly once you head to smaller, more remote areas and start conversing with older Finns. Swedish is a common second language, although many Finns are reluctant to use the language of their former colonial masters; it is, of course, the mother tongue of the Finland-Swedes, who live mainly in the western parts of the country, and the only language spoken on Åland. If the idea of learning Finnish makes you weak at the knees, at least have a go at memorizing the longest known palindrome in the world, Finnish *saippuakivikauppias* – the extremely useful "soapstone salesman".

If you're really turned on by the notion of attempting to crack Finnish, Routledge's *Colloquial Finnish: The Complete Course for Beginners* is a great start as it is sold with an accompanying audio CD. Fred Karlsson's *Finnish: An Essential Grammar* is the most accessible and comprehensive reference. Of the few available phrasebooks, *Finnish For Travellers* (Berlitz) is the most useful for practical purposes, also with CD; the best Finnish–English dictionary is *The Finnish Standard Dictionary* (Continuum International Publishing Group).

Pronunciation

In Finnish, words are pronounced exactly as they are written, with the stress always on the first syllable: in a compound word the stress is on the first syllable of each part of the word. Each letter is pronounced individually, and doubling a letter lengthens the sound: double "kk"s are pronounced with two "k" sounds and the double "aa" pronounced as long as the English "a" in "car". The letters b, c, f, q, w, x, z and å are only found in words derived from foreign languages, and are pronounced as in the language of origin.

a as in father but shorter.
d as in riding but sometimes so soft as to be barely heard.
e like the a in late.
g (only after "n") as in singer.
h as in hot.
i as in pin.
j like the y in yellow.
np like the m in mother.

o like the aw in law.
r is rolled
s as in said, but with the tongue a little further back from the teeth.
u like the oo in cool
y like the French u in "sur".
ä like the a in hat.
ö like the u in fur.

Words and phrases

Basics

do you speak english?	puhutteko englantia?
I don't speak finnish	minä en puhu suomea.
yes	kyllä/joo
no	ei
I don't understand	en ymmärrä
I understand	ymmärrän
please	olkaa hyvä/ole hyvä
thank you	kiitos
excuse me	anteeksi
hello	terve/moi
good morning	hyvää huomenta
good afternoon	hyvää päivää
good evening	hyvää iltaa
good day	hyvää päivää (usually shortened to päivä)
goodnight	hyvää yötä
goodbye	näkemiin/hei hei
yesterday	eilen
today	tänään
tomorrow	huomenna
day after tomorrow	ylihuomenna
in the morning	aamupäivällä aamulla
in the afternoon	iltapäivällä
in the evening	illalla
at night	yöllä

Some signs

entrance	sisään
exit	ulos
gentlemen	miehille/miehet/herrat
ladies	naisille/naiset/rouvat
hot	kuuma
cold	kylmä
open	avoinna
closed	suljettu
push	työnnä
pull	vedä
arrival	saapuvat
departure	lähtevät
police	poliisi
hospital	sairaala
no smoking	tupakointi kielletty
no entry	pääsy kielletty
no trespassing	läpikulku kielletty
no camping	leiriytyminen kielletty

Questions and directions

where's ... ?	missä on ... ?
when?	koska/milloin?
what?	mikä/mitä?
why?	miksi?
how do you say ... in finnish?	miten sanotaan ... suomeksi?
how far is it to ...?	kuinka pitkä matka on ... n?

where is the	missä on
train station?	rautatieasema?
train/bus/boat/ship	juna/bussi (or)
	linja auto/vene/
	laiva
where is the youth	missä on retkeilymaja?
hostel?	
can we camp here?	voimmeko leiriytyä
	tähän?
do you know anyone	tiedätkö ketään joka
who could put us	voisi maijoitaa
up for a night?	meidät yöksi?
do you have anything	onko teillä mitään
better/bigger/	parempaa/isompaa/
cheaper?	halvempaa?
it's too expensive	se on liian kallis
how much?	kuinka paljon?
how much is that?	paljonko se maksaa?
I'd like ...	haluaisin ...
cheap	halpa
expensive	kallis
good	hyvä
bad	paha/huono
here	täällä
there	siellä
left	vasemalla
right	oikealla
go straight ahead	ajakaa suoraan
	eteenpain
is it near/far?	onko se lähellä/
	kaukana?
ticket/ticket office	lipputoimisto
train/	rautatieasema/
bus station/	linjaautoasema/
bus stop	bussipysäkki

Numbers

0	nolla
1	yksi
2	kaksi
3	kolme
4	neljä
5	viisi
6	kuusi
7	seitsemän
8	kahdeksan
9	yhdeksän
10	kymmenen

11	yksitoista
12	kaksitoista
13	kolmetoista
14	neljätoista
15	viisitoista
16	kuusitoista
17	seitsemäntoista
18	kahdeksantoista
19	yhdeksäntoista
20	kaksikymmentä
21	kaksikymmentäyksi
30	kolmekymmentä
40	neljäkymmentä
50	viisikymmentä
60	kuusikymmentä
70	seitsemänkymmentä
80	kahdeksankymmentä
90	yhdeksänkymmentä
100	sata
101	satayksi
151	sataviisikymmentäyksi
200	kaksisataa
1000	tuhat
2000	kaksi tuhatta

Days and months

Monday	maanantai
Tuesday	tiistai
Wednesday	keskiviikko
Thursday	torstai
Friday	perjantai
Saturday	lauantai
Sunday	sunnuntai

January	tammikuu
February	helmikuu
March	maaliskuu
April	huhtikuu
May	toukokuu
June	kesäkuu
July	heinäkuu
August	elokuu
September	syyskuu
October	lokakuu
November	marraskuu
December	joulukuu

(Days and months are never capitalized).

Menu reader

Basics and snacks

juusto	cheese
kakku	cake
keitto	soup
keksit	biscuits
leipä	bread
maito	milk
makeiset	sweets
perunat	potatoes
piimä	buttermilk
piirakka	pie
riisi	rice
voi	butter
voileipä	sandwich

Meat (lihaa)

häränfilee	fillet of beef
hirvenliha	elk
jauheliha	minced beef
kana	chicken
kinkku	ham
lihapyörykat	meatballs
nauta	beef
paisti	steak
sianliha	pork
poro	reindeer
vasikanliha	veal

Seafood (äyriäisiä) and fish (kala)

ankerias	eel
graavilohi	salted salmon
hauki	pike
hummeri	lobster
katkaravut	shrimp
lohi	salmon
makrilli	mackerel
muikku	small whitefish
rapu	crayfish
sardiini	sardine
savustettu lohi	smoked salmon
savustettut silakat	smoked Baltic herring
siika	large, slightly oily whitefish
silakat	Baltic herring
silli	herring
suolattu	pickled herring
taimen or forelli	trout
tonnikala	tuna
turska	cod

Egg dishes (munaruoat)

hillomunakas	jam omelette
hyydytetty muna	poached egg
juustomunakas	cheese omelette
keitetty muna	boiled eggs
kinkkumunakas	ham omelette
munakas	omelette
munakokkeli	scrambled eggs
paistettu muna	fried egg
pekonimunakas	bacon omelette
perunamunakas	potato omelette
sienimunakas	mushroom omelette

Vegetables (vihannekset)

herneet	peas
kaali	cabbage
kurkku	cucumber
maissintähkät	corn on the cob
paprika	green pepper
pavut	beans
peruna	potato
pinaatti	spinach
porkkana	carrot
sieni	mushroom
sipuli	onion
tilli	dill
tomaatti	tomato

Fruit (hedelmä)

appelsiini	orange
aprikoosi	apricot
banaani	banana
greippi	grapefruit
kirsikka	cherries
luumu	plums
mansikka	strawberry
meloni	melon
omena	apple
päärynä	pear
pähkinä	nuts
persikka	peach
raparperi	rhubarb
sitruuna	lemon
viinirypäle	grapes

Sandwiches (voileipä)

kappelivoileipä	fried french bread topped with bacon and a fried egg

kaalikääryleet – cabbage rolls: cabbage leaves stuffed with minced meat and rice.

kaalipiirakka – cabbage and minced meat.

karjalanpaisti – karelian stew of beef and pork with onions.

kurpitsasalaatti – pickled pumpkin served with meat dishes.

lammaskaali – mutton and cabbage stew or soup.

lasimestarin silli – pickled herring with spices, vinegar, carrot and onion.

lihakeitto – soup made from meat, potatoes, carrots and onions.

lindströmin pihvi – beefburger made with beetroot and served with a cream sauce.

lohilaatikko – potato and salmon casserole.

lohipiirakka – salmon pie.

makaroonilaatikko – macaroni casserole with milk and egg sauce.

maksalaatikko – baked liver purée with rice and raisins.

merimiespihvi – casserole of potato slices and meat patties or minced meat.

piparjuuriliha – boiled beef with horseradish sauce.

porkkanalaatikko – casserole of mashed carrots and rice.

poronkäristys – sautéed reindeer stew.

sianlihakastike – gravy with slivers of pork.

silakkalaatikko – casserole with alternating layers of potato, onion and Baltic herring, with an egg and milk sauce.

stroganoff – beef with gherkins and onions, browned in a casserole and braised in a tomato and sour-cream stock.

suutarinlohi – marinated Baltic herring with onion and peppers.

tilliliha – boiled veal flavoured with dill sauce.

venäläinen silli – herring fillets with mayonnaise, mustard, vinegar, beetroot, gherkins and onion.

wieninleike – fried veal cutlet.

muna-anjovisleipä	dark bread with slices of hard-boiled egg, anchovy fillets and tomato	kahvi	coffee
		kivennäisvesi	mineral water
		konjakki	cognac
		limonaati	lemonade
oopperavoileipä	fried french bread with a hamburger patty and egg	olut	beer
		tee	tea
		tonic vesi	tonic water
sillivoileipä	herring on dark bread, usually with egg and tomato	vesi	water
		viini	wine
		viski	whisky

Drinks

appelsiinimehu	orange juice
gini	gin

Glossary of Finnish words and phrases

järvi	lake	pankki	bank
joki	river	poro	reindeer
katu	street	posti	post office
kauppahalli	market hall	puisto	park
kauppatori	market square	rautatieasema	train station
kaupungintalo	town hall	saari	island
keskusta	town centre	sairaala	hospital
kirkko	church	taidemuseo	art museum
kylä	village	tie	road
linja-autoasema	bus station	tori	square
linna	castle	torni	tower
lipputoimisto	ticket office	tiekirkko	roadside church
matkailutoimisto	tourist office	tunturi	Lappish mountain
mäki	hill	tuomiokirkko	cathedral
museo	museum	yliopisto	university
mökki	cabin	vastannotto	hotel/guesthouse
neuvonta	information		reception

Glossary of English art and architectural terms

ambulatory covered passage around the outer edge of the choir in the chancel of a church.

Art Deco geometrical style of art and architecture popular in the 1930s.

Art Nouveau style of art, architecture and design based on highly stylized vegetal forms. Particularly popular in the early part of the twentieth century.

Baroque The art and architecture of the Counter-Reformation, dating from around 1600 onwards, and distinguished by extreme ornateness, exuberance and the complex but harmonious spatial arrangement of interiors.

Classical architectural style incorporating Greek and Roman elements – pillars, domes, colonnades, etc – at its height in the seventeenth century and revived, as Neoclassical, in the nineteenth century.

fresco wall painting – made durable through applying paint to wet plaster.

Gothic Architectural style of the thirteenth to sixteenth centuries, characterized by pointed arches, rib vaulting, flying buttresses and a general emphasis on verticality.

misericord ledge on a choir stall on which the occupant can be supported while standing; often carved with secular subjects (bottoms were not thought worthy of religious ones).

nave main body of a church.

Neoclassical Architectural style derived from Greek and Roman elements – pillars, domes, colonnades, etc – popular in Norway throughout the nineteenth century.

Renaissance Movement in art and architecture developed in fifteenth-century Italy.

Rococo Highly florid, light and graceful eighteenth-century style of architecture, painting and interior design, forming the last phase of Baroque.

Romanesque early medieval architecture distinguished by squat forms, rounded arches and naive sculpture.

rood screen decorative screen separating the nave from the chancel.

Stucco Marble-based plaster used to embellish ceilings, etc.

transept arms of a cross-shaped church, placed at ninety degrees to nave and chancel.

triptych carved or painted work on three panels. Often used as an altarpiece.

vault an arched ceiling or roof.

InterRail

REE TO EXPLORE EUROPE

t back, relax and discover Europe with an InterRail Pass.
: the train take you from one city-centre to the next whilst you admire the ever-changing dscape. The InterRail Global Pass is perfect for Globetrotters with the appetite to explore rope's multiplicity giving you the freedom to travel in up to 30 countries.

ces start from € 159 for a 5-day youth pass and € 249 for an adult pass. To book go to: w.InterRailnet.com or contact your national railway company or a rail travel agent. r further information and a list of participating Railways see www.EurailGroup.com.

Stay In Touch!

Subscribe to Rough Guides' **FREE** newsletter

roughnews

ISBN 0149059930 SPRING 2006 - ISSUE 26 ■ Published by **Rough Guides**

Travel Survival
Picture Library
Playlists

Yucatán – p.9 | Japan – p.15 | Hunter Valley – p.16 | Las Vegas – p.23 | Baltic States – p.26

News, travel issues, music reviews, readers' letters and the latest dispatches from authors on the road. If you would like to receive roughnews, please send us your name and address:

UK and Rest of World: Rough Guides, 80 Strand, London, WC2R 0RL, UK
North America: Rough Guides, 4th Floor, 345 Hudson St,
New York NY10014, USA
or email: newslettersubs@roughguides.co.uk

BROADEN YOUR HORIZONS

Small print and

Index

A Rough Guide to Rough Guides

Published in 1982, the first Rough Guide – to Greece – was a student scheme that became a publishing phenomenon. Mark Ellingham, a recent graduate in English from Bristol University, had been travelling in Greece the previous summer and couldn't find the right guidebook. With a small group of friends he wrote his own guide, combining a highly contemporary, journalistic style with a thoroughly practical approach to travellers' needs.

The immediate success of the book spawned a series that rapidly covered dozens of destinations. And, in addition to impecunious backpackers, Rough Guides soon acquired a much broader and older readership that relished the guides' wit and inquisitiveness as much as their enthusiastic, critical approach and value-for-money ethos.

These days, Rough Guides include recommendations from shoestring to luxury and cover more than 200 destinations around the globe, including almost every country in the Americas and Europe, more than half of Africa and most of Asia and Australasia. Our ever-growing team of authors and photographers is spread all over the world, particularly in Europe, the USA and Australia.

In the early 1990s, Rough Guides branched out of travel, with the publication of Rough Guides to World Music, Classical Music and the Internet. All three have become benchmark titles in their fields, spearheading the publication of a wide range of books under the Rough Guide name.

Including the travel series, Rough Guides now number more than 350 titles, covering: phrasebooks, waterproof maps, music guides from Opera to Heavy Metal, reference works as diverse as Conspiracy Theories and Shakespeare, and popular culture books from iPods to Poker. Rough Guides also produce a series of more than 120 World Music CDs in partnership with World Music Network.

Visit www.roughguides.com to see our latest publications.

Rough Guide travel images are available for commercial licensing at www.roughguidespictures.com

Rough Guide credits

Text editors: Róisín Cameron, Tim Locke, Helena Smith, Monica Woods
Layout: Jessica Subramanian
Cartography: Swati Handoo
Picture editor: Emily Taylor
Production: Rebecca Short
Proofreader: Jennifer Speake
Cover design: Chloë Roberts
Photographers: Elina Simonen, Helena Smith
Editorial: Ruth Blackmore, Andy Turner, Keith Drew, Edward Aves, Alice Park, Lucy White, Jo Kirby, James Smart, Natasha Foges, Emma Traynor, Emma Gibbs, Kathryn Lane, Christina Valhouli, Mani Ramaswamy, Harry Wilson, Lucy Cowie, Helen Ochyra, Amanda Howard, Alison Roberts, Joe Staines, Peter Buckley, Matthew Milton, Tracy Hopkins, Ruth Tidball; **Delhi** Madhavi Singh, Karen D'Souza, Lubna Shaheen
Design & Pictures: **London** Scott Stickland, Dan May, Diana Jarvis, Mark Thomas, Chloë Roberts, Nicole Newman, Sarah Cummins;
Delhi Umesh Aggarwal, Ajay Verma, Ankur Guha, Pradeep Thapliyal, Sachin Tanwar, Anita Singh, Nikhil Agarwal
Production: Vicky Baldwin

Cartography: **London** Maxine Repath, Ed Wright, Katie Lloyd-Jones; **Delhi** Rajesh Chhibber, Ashutosh Bharti, Rajesh Mishra, Animesh Pathak, Jasbir Sandhu, Karobi Gogoi, Alakananda Bhattacharya, Deshpal Dabas
Online: **London** George Atwell, Faye Hellon, Jeanette Angell, Fergus Day, Justine Bright, Clare Bryson, Aine Fearon, Adrian Low, Ezgi Celebi, Amber Bloomfield; **Delhi** Amit Verma, Rahul Kumar, Narender Kumar, Ravi Yadav, Debojit Borah, Rakesh Kumar, Ganesh Sharma, Shisir Basumatari
Marketing & Publicity: **London** Liz Statham, Niki Hanmer, Louise Maher, Jess Carter, Vanessa Godden, Vivienne Watton, Anna Paynton, Rachel Sprackett, Libby Jellie, Laura Vipond, Vanessa McDonald; **New York** Katy Ball, Judi Powers, Nancy Lambert; **Delhi** Ragini Govind
Manager India: Punita Singh
Reference Director: Andrew Lockett
Operations Manager: Helen Phillips
PA to Publishing Director: Nicola Henderson
Publishing Director: Martin Dunford
Commercial Manager: Gino Magnotta
Managing Director: John Duhigg

Publishing information

This eighth edition published July 2009 by
Rough Guides Ltd
80 Strand, London WC2R 0RL
14 Local Shopping Centre, Panchsheel Park, New Delhi 110017, India
Distributed by the Penguin Group
Penguin Books Ltd
80 Strand, London WC2R 0RL
Penguin Group (USA)
375 Hudson Street, NY 10014, USA
Penguin Group (Australia)
250 Camberwell Road, Camberwell, Victoria 3124, Australia
Penguin Group (Canada)
195 Harry Walker Parkway N, Newmarket, ON, L3Y 7B3 Canada
Penguin Group (NZ)
67 Apollo Drive, Mairangi Bay, Auckland 1310, New Zealand
Cover concept by Peter Dyer.

Typeset in Bembo and Helvetica to an original design by Henry Iles.

Printed and bound in Singapore by SNP Security Printing Pte Ltd

© Rough Guides 2009

No part of this book may be reproduced in any form without permission from the publisher except for the quotation of brief passages in reviews.

736pp includes index

A catalogue record for this book is available from the British Library

ISBN: 978-1-84836-028-0

The publishers and authors have done their best to ensure the accuracy and currency of all the information in **The Rough Guide to Scandinavia**, however, they can accept no responsibility for any loss, injury, or inconvenience sustained by any traveller as a result of information or advice contained in the guide.

1   3   5   7   9   8   6   4   2

Help us update

We've gone to a lot of effort to ensure that the eighth edition of **The Rough Guide to Scandinavia** is accurate and up-to-date. However, things do get "discovered", opening hours are notoriously fickle, restaurants and rooms raise prices or lower standards. If you feel we've got it wrong or left something out, we'd like to know, and if you can remember the address, the price, the hours, the phone number, so much the better.

Please send your comments with the subject line **"Rough Guide Scandinavia Update"** to ⓔ mail@roughguides.com. We'll credit all contributions and send a copy of the next edition (or any other Rough Guide if you prefer) for the very best emails.

Have your questions answered and tell others about your trip at
ⓦ community.roughguides.com

Acknowledgements

Phil Lee would like to thank his editor, Tim Locke, for his good humour and attention to detail during the preparation of this new edition of the Rough Guide to Scandinavia. Special thanks also to Katie Lloyd-Jones and Maxine Repath for working so hard on the maps. Thanks also to Trine Winther of Scandic Hotels; Linda Kragseth and Anne Gjerstad of Fjord Tours AS; Paul Richards of Ulvik Fjord Hotel; Wenche Berger of NSB railways; Linn Falkenberg of the Bergen Tourist Board; and Annett Brohmann of Visit Oslo.

Lone Mouritsen would like to thank her beautiful, fabulous niece Nina Mouritsen Hansen for being probably the best assistant in the world, and her sister Mette Mouritsen for allowing us to go off on an adventure together. She would also like to thank Henrik Thierlein, international press officer at Wonderful Copenhagen for being his usual helpful, hospitable and entertaining self.

Roger Norum wishes to say *En voi kiittää teita kylliksi* to both Riitta Balza, Anne Lind and

Mari Lihr from the Finnish Tourist Board and Eija Kare from VR for being such wonderful hosts. Thanks too to Jenni, Annika, Anna, Javi, Alex and Elina for keeping Helsinki real after hours.

James Proctor would like to thank Philippa Sutton at the Sweden Travel and Tourism Council for organization of the first order. Special thanks, too, to ACC in Gothenburg and Jan Svensson at SJ in Stockholm. Also, to staff at tourist offices up and down Sweden who provided invaluable local help, including: Elisabet Corengia in Malmö, Sara Lood in Helsingborg, Susanne Gustavsson and Tomas Jönsson in Karlstad, Joakim Kihlberg in Östersund, Cecilia Enerud in Sundsvall, Erja Back in Umeå, Marie Almqvist in Uppsala, Petra Nordström and Mickan Flink in Nyköping, Gunn-Viol Kattilakoski in Örebro, Sara Ståhle in Varberg, Eva Holmgren in Växjö, Johanna Andersson in Halmstad, Marie-Louise Svensson in Stockholm, Lina Gahnström in Visby and Dan Björk in Jukkasjärvi.

Readers' letters

Thanks to all the readers who have taken the time to write in with comments and suggestions (and apologies if we've inadvertently omitted or misspelt anyone's name):

Tommy Andreasen; Nigel Barnack; Mike Beasley; Ard Beld; Gavin Bell; Natalie Birk; Stacy Braverman; Ross Brown; Mary Cable; Cathy Crofts; Torben Diklev; Christian Donatzky; Peter Eberth; E.K. Edwards; Gary Elflett; Margaret Fotheringham; Esther Geerling; Hilary & Malcolm Gledhill; Linda Gray; Tanya Gregson; Arlene Hansell; Sheila Hessey; Birgit Hintermann; William Ho; Jane Hollowday; Katja Kraskovic;

Alan Kraus; Frances Landeryou; Saila Lehtomaa; Yuri van der Linden; Jonas Ludvigsson; Raymond Maxwell; Greg Minshall; Ghislaine Morris; John Morrison; Leo Nieminen; Zoe Norgate; Vicki Ong; David Paul; Daniel Payne; Benjamin Perl; Dawn Robinson; Peter Rollason; Stacey Ross; Maryam Sherman; Ian Simpson; Katja Siberg; Lyn Smolenska; Alan Tait; Dr F.D. Trevarthen; Stephen Whittaker; Meredith Younghein.

Photo credits

All photos © Rough Guides except the following:

Introduction
Sognefjord, Oldenvatnet © Brian Lawrence Images/Pictures Colour Library
Detail of the replica of a ninth-century AD Viking ship, Oseberg, Norway © David Lomax/Jupiter Images
Detail of female kilt, Sámi People, Kautokeino, Norway © tbkmedia.de/Alamy
Sitting in an outside café, Copenhagen, Denmark © Chris Parker/Axiom
Two shags/green cormorants during mating season, Norway © Marten Dalfors/Jupiter Images
Family in sauna, Finland © Caroline Penn/Corbis
Stockholm, Sweden © Tom Mackie Images/Pictures Colour Library
People dancing around Maypole during Midsummer celebrations, Leksand, Sweden © Chad Ehlers/Jupiter Images

Opera House, Gothenburg, Sweden © Monica Wells/Pictures Colour Library
Cathedral, Helsinki, Finland © Vidler Vidler/Photolibray
ABBA © GAB Archives/Redferns

Things not to miss
01 Århus old town, Denmark © Carsten Madsen/iStock Pictures
02 Statue by Gustav Vigeland in Vigeland Park, Oslo © Jon Hicks/Alamy
04 Kalmar Slott castle, Kalmar, Småland © Walter Bibikow/Corbis
05 The Flåmsbana Railway in Flamsdalen, Aurland © David Robertson/Alamy
06 Vikingskipshuset, Norway © Johan Berge/Innovation Norway
07 Farm and fields in Skåne © Briljans/Jupiter Images

Selected images from our guidebooks are available for licensing from:

ROUGHGUIDESPICTURES.COM

08 Aurora borealis © Jorma Luhta/www
.visitfinland.com

09 Louisiana Museum of Modern Art, Zealand,
Denmark © Pep Roig/Alamy

10 Lifeguard Blokhus, Jutland, Denmark © FAN
travelstock/Alamy

11 Santa Claus drives his reindeer sled,
Rovaniemi Finland © Bryan & Cherry
Alexander Photography/Alamy

12 Finland, Åland islands, Foglo island © Hemis/
Alamy

13 Tivoli Gardens midnight fireworks © Johnny
Stockshooter/PhotoLibrary

14 The Swedish Inland Railway crossing the steel
bridge at Storstupet Orsa Dalarna © Kai-Uwe
Och/Alamy

17 Stave church © Pål Bugge/Innovation Norway

18 Typical Danish pastries © Ken Welsh/Alamy

19 Going back to sauna after swimming in an ice
hole © Kalervo Ojutkangas/PhotoLibrary

20 Bergen Harbour, Oslo, Norway © Kord.com/
Photolibrary

21 Vasamuséet in Stockholm © www.imagebank
.sweden

22 Grenen, Skagen, Denmark © Thomas Nykrog/
www.visitdenmark.com

23 Silhouette of killer whales, Norway © Stefan
Rosengren/Jupiter Images

24 Visitors walk towards the Jukkasjarvi Icehotel
in northern Sweden © Rainer Raffalski/Alamy

25 Århus nightlife, Denmark © www.visitdenmark
.com

26 Jotunheimen National Park © www.bildagentur
-online.com/Tips Images

27 Olavinlinna Castle © Roger Norum

28 Lofoten Islands, Norway © Frithjof Fure/
Innovation Norway

29 Sledge dogs running on trail, Finland © Ted
Levine/Corbis

30 Gamla Stan, Stockholm, Sweden © Chad
Ehlers/Tips Images

Black and whites

p.48 Beach in Funen, Denmark © FAN
Travelstock/Jupiter Images

p.80 The Gates of Christiania in Copenhagen
© PE Forsberg/Alamy

p.99 Roskilde Festival © Christian Petersen/www
.visitdenmark.com

p.118 Egeskov Castle © Bob Krist/www
.visitdenmark.com

p.127 Ribe Domkirke © Cees van Roeden/
www.visitdenmark.com

p.144 Glass sculpture at Ebeltoft Glass Museum
© Courtesy of Ebeltoft Glass Museum

p.160 Skiers in the snow, Jotunheimen
© Chromorange/Tips Images

p.179 Oslo Jazz Festival © Christian Melstrom/
Courtesy of Oslo Jazz Festival

p.182 Oslo Harbour scene © Frithjof Fure/
Innovation Norway

p.223 Pulpit Rock © Casper Tybjerg/Innovation
Norway

p.232 Flam Railway, Romsdalen Valley © Johan
Berge/Innovation Norway

p.245 The Bryggen, Bergen © PNS/Tips Images

p.268 Mundal, Fjaerlandsfjorden © Fsg Fsg/
Photolibrary

p.278 Geirangerfjord © C H/Innovation Norway

p.292 Trondheim Cathedral © Terje Rakke/
Innovation Norway

p.316 Lofoten © Johan Berge/Innovation Norway

p.329 Arctic Circle © Johan Wildhagen/Innovation
Norway

p.345 Hurtigrute coastal boat © Norbert Eisele-
Hein/Photolibrary

p.348 Visby walls © Peter Grant/
www.imagebank.sweden.se

p.370 Stockholm Harbour © Ken Stimpson
© Jupiter Images

p.390 Small island in Stockholm archipelago
© Chad Ehlers/Jupiter Images

p.398 The Paddan sightseeing boat riding past
the Radhuset © Richard Klune/Corbis

p.412 Bohuslän Coast © Briljans/Jupiter Images

p.418 Tylosand Beach in Halmstad Sweden
© Johan Furusjo/Alamy

p.428 Oresund Bridge between Sweden and
Denmark © Chad Ehlers/Alamy

p.443 Kalmar Castle in the winter © Briljans/
Jupiter Images

p.454 Örebro Castle © Rob Wyatt/FotoLibre

p.464 Visby Medieval Week © Peter Grant/
www.imagebank.sweden.se

p.479 Gammelstad © Kenneth Lundström/iStock
Photos

p.487 Vintersvanar Leksand Siljan Dalarna
© Nordicphotos/Alamy

p.496 Reindeer © Petra Wegner/Tips Images

p.502 Lapporten Mountain at Abisko © Johner
Images/Alamy

p.506 Boy in an icehole © Eero Kemilä/
VisitFinland.com

p.531 Klaus K Hotel Lobby © Courtesy of Design
Hotels

p.535 Helsinki Central Railway Station © www
.visitfinland.com

p.561 Turku Art Museum © Albert Edelfelt
painting © Courtesy of Turku Art Museum

p.567 Pori Jazz Festival © Sanna Heikintalo/
Courtesty of the Pori Jazz Festival

p.576 City of Tampere © Sylvain Grandadam/
Photolibray

p.588 Lappeenranta Fortress © Frank Naylor/
Alamy

p.596 Valamo Monastery © www.visitfinland.com

p.612 Diving off the Sampo arctic icebreaker,
Kemi © www.visitfinland.com

p.618 Rovaniemi, Sámi woman © www
.visitfinland.com

p.627 Saunas at Kakslauuttanen Igloo Village
© Anna Watson/Corbis

SMALL PRINT

Index

Map entries are in colour.

I

J

K

L

I

Map symbols

maps are listed in the full index using coloured text

———	Chapter division boundary	♦	Point of interest
—·—·	International boundary	🝖	Fuel station
——··	Provincial boundary	@	Internet access
▬▬▬	Motorway	ⓘ	Tourist office
═══	Major road	⊠	Post office
───	Minor road	⊞	Hospital
)════(	Tunnel	🅿	Parking
▬▬▬	Pedestrianized street	ⓒ	Telephone
▥▥▥	Steps	Å	Campsite
-----	Path	🏊	Swimming pool
—▬—	Railway	🕯	Lighthouse
●----●	Cable car	♜	Castle
———	Wall	▮	Tower
⊠—⊠	Gate	∴	Ruin
)(	Bridge	⊙	Statue/memorial
— —	Ferry route	⌂	Monastery
═══	Waterway	🏛	Stately home
┴┴┴	Canal	♀	Museum
▲	Mountain peak	⸸	Church (regional maps)
🜨	Mountain range	▭	Market
𓏲	Rock	◯	Stadium
🜉	Waterfall	▬	Building
🜊	Viewpoint	┼	Church (town maps)
✈	Airport	⊹	Cemetery
—Ⓣ—	T-Bana	▦	Park
Ⓜ	Metro	▨	Beach
Ⓢ	S-train	▧	Glacier
★	Bus stop		

We're covered. Are you?

ROUGH GUIDES Travel Insurance

Visit our website at www.roughguides.com/website/shop or call:

COLUMBUS DIRECT ™
Travel Insurance

ROUGH GUIDES

- ⓣ UK: 0800 083 9507
- ⓣ Spain: 900 997 149
- ⓣ Australia: 1300 669 999
- ⓣ New Zealand: 0800 55 99 11
- ⓣ Worldwide: +44 870 890 2843
- ⓣ USA, call toll free on: 1 800 749 4922

Please quote our ref: **Rough Guides books**

Cover for over 46 different nationalities and available in 4 different languages.